The Blackwell Companion to Philosophy

Blackwell Companions to Philosophy

This benchmark student reference series offers a comprehensive survey of philosophy as a whole. Written by many of today's leading figures, each volume provides lucid and engaging coverage of the key figures, terms, and movements of the main subdisciplines of philosophy. Each essay is fully cross-referenced and supported by a selected bibliography. Taken together, it provides the ideal basis for course use and an invaluable work of reference.

Already published:

1   A Companion to Ethics
    Edited by Peter Singer

2   A Companion to Aesthetics
    Edited by David Cooper

3   A Companion to Epistemology
    Edited by Jonathan Dancy and Ernest Sosa

4   A Companion to Contemporary Political Philosophy
    Edited by Robert E. Goodin and Philip Pettit

5   A Companion to the Philosophy of Mind
    Edited by Samuel Guttenplan

6   A Companion to Metaphysics
    Edited by Jaegwon Kim and Ernest Sosa

Forthcoming:

7   A Companion to the Philosophy of Law and Legal Theory
    Edited by Dennis Patterson

8   A Companion to the Philosophy of Religion
    Edited by Philip Quinn and Charles Taliaferro

9   A Companion to the Philosophy of Language
    Edited by Crispin Wright and Bob Hale

The Blackwell Companion
to Philosophy

edited by Nicholas Bunnin and E. P. Tsui-James

BLACKWELL
Reference

For Jessie and Carol

Copyright © Blackwell Publishers Ltd, 1996

First published 1996

Reprinted 1996

Blackwell Publishers Ltd
108 Cowley Road
Oxford OX4 1JF, UK

Blackwell Publishers Inc.
238 Main Street
Cambridge, Massachusetts 02142, USA

British Library Cataloguing in Publication Data
A CIP catalogue record for this book is available from the British Library

Library of Congress Cataloging in Publication Data
The Blackwell companion to philosophy/edited by Nicholas Bunnin and
E. P. Tsui-James.
Includes bibliographical references and index. p. cm.
ISBN 0-631-18788-X (alk paper) - ISBN 0-631-18789-8 (pbk: alk paper)
Philosophy. Bunnin, Nicholas. Tsui-James, E. P.
B21.B56 1995   95006545
100 20

Typeset in Melior on 10/12 pt
by Photoprint, Torquay, Devon
Printed and bound in Great Britain by T. J. Press Ltd, Padstow, Cornwall

This book is printed on acid-free paper

Contents ───────────────────────────

Preface   vii

Notes on Contributors   x

Contemporary Philosophy in the United States   *John R. Searle*   1

Contemporary Philosophy: A Second Look   *Bernard Williams*   25

1   Epistemology   *A. C. Grayling*   38

2   Metaphysics   *Simon Blackburn*   64

3   Philosophy of Language   *Martin Davies*   90

4   Philosophy of Logic   *A. W. Moore*   140

5   Philosophy of Mind   *William G. Lycan*   167

6   Ethics   *John Skorupski*   198

7   Aesthetics   *Sebastian Gardner*   229

8   Political and Social Philosophy   *David Archard*   257

9   Philosophy of Science   *David Papineau*   290

10   Philosophy of Mathematics   *Mary Tiles*   325

11   Philosophy of Social Science   *Martin Hollis*   358

12   Philosophy of Law   *N. E. Simmonds*   388

13   Philosophy of History   *Leon Pompa*   415

14   Philosophy of Religion   *Charles Taliaferro*   443

15   Ancient Greek Philosophy   *Robert Wardy*   482

16   Medieval Philosophy   *C. F. J. Martin*   500

17   Descartes, Spinoza and Leibniz   *George MacDonald Ross and
     Richard Francks*   509

18   Hobbes   *Tom Sorell*   530

19   Locke   *R. S. Woolhouse*   541

20   Berkeley   *Howard Robinson*   555

21   Hume   *Peter Jones*   571

22   Kant   *David Bell*   589

23   Hegel   *Michael Inwood*   607

24   Marx   *Richard Norman*   617

25   Bentham, Mill and Sidgwick   *Ross Harrison*   627

26   Pragmatism   *Susan Haack*   643

27   Frege and Russell   *R. M. Sainsbury*   662

28   Moore   *Thomas Baldwin*   678

29   Wittgenstein   *David Pears*   685

30   Modern European Philosophy   *David E. Cooper*   702

31   Applied Ethics   *John Haldane*   722

32   Feminism and Philosophy   *Jean Grimshaw*   732

Glossary   742

Index   764

Preface

This Companion complements the *Blackwell Companions to Philosophy* series by presenting a new overview of philosophy prepared by thirty-five leading British and American philosophers. Introductory essays by John Searle and Bernard Williams, which assess the changes that have shaped the subject in recent decades, are followed by chapters exploring central problems and debates in the principal subdisciplines of philosophy and in specialized fields, chapters concerning the work of great historical figures and chapters discussing newly developing fields within philosophy. Throughout the course of its chapters, the Companion examines the views of many of the most widely influential figures of contemporary philosophy.

Although wide-ranging, the Companion is not exhaustive, and emphasis is placed on developments in Anglo-American philosophy in the latter part of the twentieth century. A premise underlying the Companion is that major participants in philosophical debate can provide accounts of their own fields that are stimulating, accessible, stylish and authoritative.

In its primary use, the Companion is an innovative textbook for introductory courses in philosophy. Teachers can use the broad coverage to select chapters in a flexible way to support a variety of courses based on contemporary problems or the historical development of the subject. Specialist chapters can be used selectively to augment standard introductory topics or to prepare students individually for term papers or essays. Chapters include initial summaries, boxed features, cross-references, suggestions for further reading, references and discussion questions. In addition, there is a common glossary. These features and the problem-setting nature of the discussions encourage students to see the subject as a whole and to gain confidence that explorations within philosophy can lead to unexpected and rewarding insights. In this aspect, the Companion reflects the contributors' experience of small group teaching, in which arguments and perspectives are rigorously tested and in which no solution is imposed.

In its secondary use, the Companion will accompany students throughout their undergraduate careers and will also serve the general reader wishing to understand the central concepts and debates within philosophy or its constituent disciplines. Students are unlikely to read the whole volume in their first year of study, but those continuing with philosophy will find their appreciation of the work deepening over time as they gain insight into the topics of the more advanced chapters. The Companion will help them to formulate questions and to see connections between what they have already studied and new terrain.

In its final use, the Companion bears a special relationship to the *Blackwell Companions to Philosophy* series. Many readers will wish to read the integrated discussions of the chapters of the present Companion for orientation before turning to the detailed, alphabetically arranged, articles of the volumes in the Companion series. Although conceived as a separate volume, the Companion to Philosophy will serve as a useful guide to the other excellent Companions in what amounts to a comprehensive encyclopedia of philosophy.

The general reader might begin with the introductory essays and turn to chapters on Epistemology, Metaphysics, Ethics and Political and Social Philosophy, or to historical chapters from Ancient Greek Philosophy to Hume. Cross-references and special interests will lead readers to other chapters.

Cross-references in the text are marked in small capitals followed by a chapter number or page numbers in parentheses: ETHICS (chapter 6) or PROBABILITY (pp. 314–16). We have used our judgement in marking terms appearing many times in the text for cross-references, and hope that we have supplied guidance without distracting readers. The Companion also provides a glossary of 170 terms and a comprehensive index. Both appear at the end of the volume, and readers are advised to use them regularly for help in reading the chapters. When an author does not refer to a book by its first edition, a recent publication is cited in the text, and the original date of publication (or in some cases of composition) will appear in square brackets in the references.

As editors, we are fully aware of our good fortune in attracting superb contributors. The complexity of their insights and the clarity of their presentations are the chief attractions of the Companion. We appreciate their care in making the difficult not only accessible but delightful as well. We also wish to thank the Departments of Philosophy at the University of Essex and the University of Hong Kong for their support throughout the preparation of this volume. We are especially grateful to Laurence Goldstein, Tim Moore and Frank Cioffi for their comments and advice. A version of the Companion is published in Chinese by the Shandong Academy of Social Sciences, and we appreciate the friendly co-operation of our Chinese co-editors.

Our cover illustration, R. B. Kitaj's philosophically resonant 'IF NOT, NOT', is a work by an American artist working in London during the period that provides the main focus of our volume.

Nicholas Bunnin
E. P. Tsui-James

Acknowledgements

With two exceptions, the contributions to the Companion were specially prepared for the volume. John R. Searle's introductory essay initially appeared in a slightly different form in D. Easton and C. S. Schelling (eds), 1991: *Divided Knowledge*, New York: Sage. Susan Haack's chapter is a significantly extended version of her contribution to J. Dancy and E. Sosa (eds), 1992: *A Companion to Epistemology*, Oxford: Blackwell.

Notes on Contributors

David Archard is Reader in Moral Philosophy at the University of St Andrews. His interests lie in moral, social and political philosophy. His most recently published work was *Children, Rights and Childhood* (Routledge, 1993) and a series of articles on nationalism.

Thomas Baldwin until recently a Fellow of Clare College, Cambridge, is Professor of Philosophy at University of York. He previously taught at the University of York and Makerere University. He has published *G. E. Moore* (Routledge, 1990) in addition to many articles on issues in metaphysics and the philosophy of language.

David Bell is Professor of Philosophy at the University of Sheffield. He is the author of works on Frege, Husserl and Kant. His interests include the foundations of arithmetic, solipsism and the nature and origins of the Analytic Tradition.

Simon Blackburn is Edna J. Koury Distinguished Professor of Philosophy at the University of North Carolina, and Fellow Emeritus of Pembroke College, Oxford. A former editor of the journal *Mind*, he has written *Spreading the Word* (Clarendon Press, 1984), *Essays in Quasi Realism* (Oxford University Press, 1993) and *The Oxford Dictionary of Philosophy* (Oxford University Press, 1994). His current work concerns problems of realism and its alternatives as they have emerged in historical and contemporary work.

Nicholas Bunnin studied at Harvard College and then at Corpus Christi College, Oxford. He is a Fellow at the University of Essex and Director of the Philosophy Project at the Centre for Modern Chinese Studies at the University of Oxford. His main interests are in metaphysics, the philosophy of mind and political philosophy.

David E. Cooper is Professor of Philosophy at the University of Durham. His books include *Metaphor* (Blackwell, 1986), *Existentialism: A Reconstruction* (Blackwell, 1990) and *World Philosophies: An Historical Introduction* (Blackwell, 1995).

Martin Davies is Wilde Reader in Mental Philosophy at the University of Oxford and a Fellow of Corpus Christi College. He was formerly Reader in

Philosophy at Birkbeck College, London. He has published widely in the areas of philosophy of language, mind and psychology.

Richard Francks is Director of Undergraduate Studies in Philosophy at the University of Leeds. His main interests are in epistemology, the history of philosophy and the philosophy of history.

Sebastian Gardner is a Lecturer in Philosophy at Birkbeck College, London. His interests lie in aesthetics, psychoanalysis and the history of philosophy.

A. C. Grayling is a Lecturer in Philosophy at Birkbeck College, London, and Senior Research Fellow at St Anne's College, Oxford. Among his books are *An Introduction to Philosophical Logic* (Harvester, 1982), *The Refutation of Scepticism* (Duckworth, 1985), *Berkeley: The Central Arguments* (Duckworth, 1986) and *Wittgenstein* (*Past Masters* series, Oxford University Press, 1988). He has edited *Philosophy: A Guide Through the Subject* (Oxford University Press, 1995).

Jean Grimshaw teaches Philosophy and Women's Studies at the University of the West of England, Bristol. She is author of *Feminist Philosophers: Women's Perspectives on Philosophical Traditions* (Wheatsheaf, 1986) and of a number of articles, mainly on feminism and philosophy.

Susan Haack, formerly Professor of Philosophy at the University of Warwick, currently Professor of Philosophy at the University of Miami, is the author of *Deviant Logic* (Cambridge University Press, 1974), *Philosophy of Logic* (Cambridge University Press, 1978) and, most recently, *Evidence and Inquiry: Towards Reconstruction in Epistemology* (Blackwell, 1993). Her main areas of interest are the philosophy of logic and language, epistemology and metaphysics and pragmatism. She is a past President of the Charles Peirce Society.

John Haldane is Professor of Philosophy and Director of the Centre for Philosophy and Public Affairs at the University of St Andrews. He has published widely in the philosophy of mind, the philosophy of value and the history of philosophy. He is co-author with J. J. C. Smart of *Atheism and Theism* in the Blackwell *Great Debates in Philosophy* series (forthcoming, 1996).

Ross Harrison teaches philosophy at the University of Cambridge, where he is also a Fellow of King's College. Among his publications are *Bentham* (Routledge, 1983) and *Democracy* (Routledge, 1993).

Martin Hollis is Professor of Philosophy at the University of East Anglia, Norwich. He specializes in the philosophy of social science, especially in topics to do with rationality. Among his books are *Models of Man* (Cambridge University Press, 1977), *The Cunning of Reason* (Cambridge University Press, 1987), *The Philosophy of Social Science* (Cambridge University Press, 1994) and *Reason in Action* (Cambridge University Press, 1995).

Michael Inwood is a Tutorial Fellow in Philosophy at Trinity College, Oxford. He has published several books on Hegel. His other interests include ancient philosophy and Heidegger. He is especially interested in the interconnections between Greek and German philosophy.

Peter Jones is Professor of Philosophy and Director of the Institute for Advanced Studies in the Humanities at the University of Edinburgh. He is the author of numerous works, including *Hume's Sentiments* (Edinburgh University Press, 1982).

William G. Lycan is William Rand Kenan, Jr Professor of Philosophy at the University of North Carolina. He has published several books, including *Consciousness* (Bradford Books/MIT Press, 1987), *Judgement and Justification* (Cambridge University Press, 1988) and is editor of *Mind and Cognition* (Blackwell, 1990). His interests are in the philosophy of mind, the philosophy of language and epistemology.

C. F. J. Martin works principally on medieval philosophy and has written on Aristotle, Maimonides and Aquinas, as well as translating the *Hexaëmeron* of Robert Grosseteste. He has taught in Spain, at Oxford and in Glasgow.

A. W. Moore is a Tutorial Fellow in Philosophy at St Hugh's College, Oxford. He is the author of *The Infinite* (Routledge, 1990) and has edited two collections of essays: *Meaning and Reference* (Oxford University Press, 1993) and *Infinity* (Dartmouth, 1993).

Richard Norman is Professor of Moral Philosophy at the University of Kent. His publications include *The Moral Philosophers* (Clarendon Press, 1983) *Free and Equal* (Clarendon Press, 1987) and *Ethics, Killing and War* (Cambridge University Press, 1995).

David Papineau is Professor of Philosophy of Science at King's College, London. He has published widely in epistemology, the philosophy of mind and the philosophy of science. His books include *Reality and Representation* (Blackwell, 1987) and *Philosophical Naturalism* (Blackwell, 1993).

David Pears is Emeritus Professor of Philosophy at the University of Oxford and in 1995 was Visiting Professor at the University of California at Los Angeles. His most recent publications are *The False Prison: A Study in the Development of Wittgenstein's Philosophy* (two volumes, Clarendon Press, 1987 and 1988) and *Hume's System, An Examination of Book I of the Treatise* (Oxford University Press, 1991). His other interests include entomology and the visual arts.

Leon Pompa is Professor of Philosophy at the University of Birmingham. His research interests include the history of philosophy and the philosophy of history. He has published a number of articles on the problems of fact, value and narrative in history and on Descartes, Vico, Kant, Hegel, Marx, Collingwood and Wittgenstein. He co-edited with W. H. Dray *Substance and Form in History; Essays in Philosophy of History* (Edinburgh University Press, 1981), was editor and translator of *Vico: Selected Writings* (Cambridge

University Press, 1982) and is the author of *Vico: A Study of the 'New Science'* (2nd edn Cambridge University Press, 1990) and *Human Nature and Historical Knowledge: Hume, Hegel and Vico* (Cambridge University Press, 1990).

Howard Robinson is Soros Professor of Philosophy at the Eötvös Loránd University, Budapest and Senior Lecturer in Philosophy at the University of Liverpool. His main interests are in the philosophy of mind and in idealism. He is author of *Matter and Sense* (Cambridge University Press, 1982) and *Perception* (Routledge, 1994), and co-editor with John Foster of *Essays on Berkeley* (Clarendon Press, 1985). He edited *Objections to Physicalism* (Clarendon Press, 1991) and Berkeley's *Principles* and *Three Dialogues* (Oxford University Press, *World Classics* series, 1996).

George MacDonald Ross is Senior Lecturer in the Department of Philosophy at the University of Leeds, currently on leave of absence as Academic Dean of University College, Scarborough. He has written extensively on Leibniz and other seventeenth- and eighteenth-century philosophers, and is the author of *Leibniz* (*Past Masters* series, Oxford University Press, 1984).

R. M. Sainsbury is Stebbing Professor of Philosophy at King's College, London and is the editor of the journal *Mind*. He has published *Russell* (Routledge, 1979). His main interests are in philosophical logic and the philosophy of language.

John R. Searle is the Mills Professor of Mind and Language at the University of California where he has been a faculty member since 1959. Before that, he was a lecturer at Christ Church, Oxford, and he received all his university degrees from Oxford. Most of his work is in the philosophy of mind and the philosophy of language, and his most recently published work is in social philosophy. He is the author of several books, including *Speech Acts: An Essay in the Philosophy of Language* (Cambridge University Press, 1969) *Expression and Meaning: Studies in the Theory of Speech Acts* (Cambridge University Press, 1985), *Intentionality* (Cambridge University Press, 1983), *Minds, Brains and Science*, the 1984 Reith Lectures (Penguin, 1989), and *The Rediscovery of Mind* (MIT Press, 1992).

N. E. Simmonds is a Fellow of Corpus Christi College, Cambridge where he lectures in law. His interests include the philosophy of law and political philosophy. He has published *The Decline of Judicial Reason* (Manchester University Press, 1984), *Central Issues in Jurisprudence* (Sweet and Maxwell, 1986) and numerous articles on the philosophy of law.

John Skorupski is Professor of Moral Philosophy at the University of St Andrews. He is the author of *John Stuart Mill* (Routledge, 1989), and his most recent book is *English-language Philosophy 1750–1945* (Oxford University Press, 1993).

Tom Sorell is Professor of Philosophy at the University of Essex. He is the author of *Hobbes* (Routledge, 1986), *Descartes* (Oxford University Press, 1987), *Moral Theory and Capital Punishment* (Blackwell, 1987), *Scientism*

(Routledge, 1991), and (with John Hendry) *Business Ethics* (Butterworth Heinemann, 1994). He is the editor of *The Rise of Modern Philosophy* (Oxford University Press, 1993) and the *Cambridge Companion to Hobbes* (Cambridge University Press, 1995).

Charles Taliaferro is Associate Professor of Philosophy at St Olaf College. He is the author of *Consciousness and the Mind of God* (Cambridge University Press, 1994) and *An Introduction to Contemporary Philosophy of Religion* (Blackwell, forthcoming).

Mary Tiles is Professor of Philosophy at the University of Hawaii at Manoa. Her interests include the history and philosophy of mathematics, science and technology and their interactions with culture. She has published *Mathematics and the Image of Reason* (Routledge, 1991) and *Bachelard: Science and Objectivity* (Cambridge University Press, 1984).

E. P. Tsui-James studied as a postgraduate at Oriel College, Oxford. He lectured in philosophy at St Hilda's College, Oxford, before becoming Associate Professor in the Department of Philosophy at the University of Hong Kong. He has published work in the area of the philosophy of mathematics. His research interests now centre around the work of the classical pragmatists, especially William James.

Robert Wardy teaches philosophy and classics at St Catharine's College, Cambridge. He has published in the fields of ancient Greek philosophy and rhetoric, Latin literature, the philosophy of language and Chinese philosophy.

Bernard Williams is White's Professor of Moral Philosophy and a Fellow of Corpus Christi College, Oxford and Monroe Deutsch Professor of Philosophy, University of California, Berkeley. His works include *Morality* (Cambridge University Press, 1972), *Problems of the Self* (Cambridge University Press, 1973), *Descartes: The Project of Pure Enquiry* (Penguin, 1978), *Moral Luck* (Cambridge University Press, 1981), *Ethics and the Limits of Philosophy* (Fontana Press and Harvard University Press, 1985), *Shame and Necessity* (University of California Press, 1993) and *Making Sense of Humanity* (Cambridge University Press, 1995).

R. S. Woolhouse is Professor of Philosophy at the University of York. He is the author of *Locke's Philosophy of Science and Knowledge* (Blackwell and Mott, 1971), *Locke* (Harvester, 1983), *The Empiricists* (Oxford University Press, 1988) and *Descartes, Spinoza, Leibniz: The Concept of Substance in Seventeenth-Century Philosophy* (Routledge, 1993).

Contemporary Philosophy in the United States

John R. Searle

Philosophy as an academic discipline in America has considerably fewer practitioners than do several other subjects in the humanities and the social sciences, such as sociology, history, English, or economics; but it still shows enormous diversity. This variety is made manifest in the original research published by professional philosophers, whose differing points of view are expressed in the large number of books published each year, as well as in the many professional philosophy journals. There are over two thousand colleges and universities in the United States, of which nearly all have philosophy departments, and the number of professional philosophers is correspondingly large.

Because of this diversity, any generalizations about the discipline as a whole, which I am about to make, are bound to be misleading. The subject is too vast and complex to be describable in a single essay. Furthermore, anyone who is an active participant in the current controversies, as I am, necessarily has a perspective conditioned by his or her own interests, commitments and convictions. It would be impossible for me to give an 'objective' account. I am not therefore in what follows trying to give a neutral or disinterested account of the contemporary philosophical scene; rather I am trying to say what in the current developments seems to me important.

In spite of its enormous variety, there are certain central themes in contemporary American philosophy. The dominant mode of philosophizing in the United States is called 'analytic philosophy'. Without exception, the best philosophy departments in the United States are dominated by analytic philosophy, and among the leading philosophers in the United States, all but a tiny handful would be classified as analytic philosophers. Practitioners of types of philosophizing that are not in the analytic tradition – such as phenomenology, classical pragmatism, existentialism, or Marxism – feel it necessary to define their position in relation to analytic philosophy. Indeed, analytic philosophy is the dominant mode of philosophizing not only in the United States, but throughout the entire English-speaking world, including Great Britain, Canada, Australia and New Zealand. It is also the dominant mode of philosophizing in Scandinavia, and it is also becoming more widespread in Germany, France, Italy and throughout Latin America. I personally have found that I can go to all of these parts of the world and lecture on subjects in contemporary analytic philosophy before audiences who are both knowledgeable and well trained in the techniques of the discipline.

1 Analytic Philosophy

What, then, is analytic philosophy? The simplest way to describe it is to say that it is primarily concerned with the analysis of meaning. In order to explain this enterprise and its significance, we need first to say a little bit about its history. Though the United States now leads the world in analytic philosophy, the origins of this mode of philosophizing lie in Europe. Specifically, analytic philosophy is based on the work of Gottlob Frege, Ludwig Wittgenstein, Bertrand Russell and G. E. Moore, as well as the work done by the logical positivists of the Vienna Circle in the 1920s and 1930s. Going further back in history, one can also see analytic philosophy as a natural descendant of the empiricism of the great British philosophers Locke, Berkeley and Hume, and of the transcendental philosophy of Kant. In the works of philosophers as far back as Plato and Aristotle, one can see many of the themes and presuppositions of the methods of analytic philosophy. We can best summarize the origins of modern analytic philosophy by saying that it arose when the empiricist tradition in epistemology, together with the foundationalist enterprise of Kant, were tied to the methods of logical analysis and the philosophical theories invented by Gottlob Frege in the late nineteenth century. In the course of his work on the foundations of mathematics, Frege invented symbolic logic in its modern form and developed a comprehensive and profound philosophy of language. Though many of the details of his views on language and mathematics have been superseded, Frege's work is crucial for at least two reasons: Firstly, by inventing modern logic, specifically the predicate calculus, he gave us a primary tool of philosophical analysis; and, secondly he made the philosophy of language central to the entire philosophical enterprise. From the point of view of analytic philosophy, Frege's work is the greatest single philosophical achievement of the nineteenth century. Fregean techniques of logical analysis were later augmented by the ordinary language analysis inspired by the work of Moore and Wittgenstein and are best exemplified by the school of linguistic philosophy that flourished in Oxford in the 1950s. In short, analytic philosophy attempts to combine certain traditional philosophical themes with modern techniques.

Analytic philosophy has never been fixed or stable, because it is intrinsically self-critical and its practitioners are always challenging their own presuppositions and conclusions. However, it is possible to locate a central period in analytic philosophy – the period comprising, roughly speaking, the logical positivist phase immediately prior to the 1939–45 war and the post-war phase of linguistic analysis. Both the pre-history and the subsequent history of analytic philosophy can be defined by the main doctrines of that central period.

In the central period, analytic philosophy was defined by a belief in two linguistic distinctions, combined with a research programme. The two distinctions are, firstly, that between analytic and synthetic propositions, and, secondly, that between descriptive and evaluative utterances. The research programme is the traditional philosophical research programme of attempting to find foundations for such philosophically problematic phenomena as language, knowledge, meaning, truth, mathematics and so on. One way to see the development of analytic philosophy over the past thirty years is to regard it as the gradual rejection of these two distinctions, and a corresponding rejection of foundationalism as the crucial enterprise of philosophy. However, in the central period, these two distinctions served not only to identify the main beliefs of analytic philosophy, but, for those who accepted them and the research programme, they defined the nature of philosophy itself.

1.1 Analytic versus synthetic

The distinction between analytic and synthetic propositions was supposed to be the distinction between those propositions that are true or false as a matter of definition or of the meanings of the terms contained in them (the analytic propositions) and those that are true or false as a matter of fact in the world and not solely in virtue of the meanings of the words (the synthetic propositions). Examples of analytic truths would be such propositions as 'Triangles are three-sided plane figures', 'All bachelors are unmarried', 'Women are female', '2 + 2 = 4' and so on. In each of these, the truth of the proposition is entirely determined by its meaning; they are true by the definitions of the words that they contain. Such propositions can be known to be true or false *a priori*, and in each case they express necessary truths. Indeed, it was a characteristic feature of the analytic philosophy of this central period that terms such as 'analytic', 'necessary', '*a priori*' and 'tautological' were taken to be co-extensive. Contrasted with these were synthetic propositions, which, if they were true, were true as a matter of empirical fact and not as a matter of definition alone. Thus, propositions such as 'There are more women than men in the United States', 'Bachelors tend to die earlier than married men' and 'Bodies attract each other according to the inverse square law' are all said to be synthetic propositions, and, if they are true, they express *a posteriori* empirical truths about the real world that are independent of language. Such empirical truths according to this view, are never necessary; rather, they are contingent. For philosophers holding these views, the terms '*a posteriori*', 'synthetic', 'contingent' and 'empirical' were taken to be more or less co-extensive.

It was a basic assumption behind the logical positivist movement that all meaningful propositions were either analytic or empirical, as defined by the conceptions that I have just stated. The positivists wished to build a sharp boundary between meaningful propositions of science and everyday life on the one hand, and nonsensical propositions of metaphysics and theology on the other. They claimed that all meaningful propositions are either analytic or synthetic: disciplines such as logic and mathematics fall within the analytic camp; the empirical sciences and much of common sense fall within the synthetic camp. Propositions that were neither analytic nor empirical propositions, and which were therefore in principle not verifiable, were said to be nonsensical or meaningless. The slogan of the positivists was called the verification principle, and, in a simple form, it can be stated as follows: all meaningful propositions are either analytic or synthetic, and those which are synthetic are empirically verifiable. This slogan was sometimes shortened to an even simpler battle cry: the meaning of a proposition is just its method of verification.

1.2 The distinction between evaluative utterances and descriptive utterances

Another distinction, equally important in the positivist scheme of things, is the distinction between those utterances that express propositions that can be literally either true or false and those utterances that are used not to express truths or falsehoods, but rather, to give vent to our feelings and emotions. An example of a descriptive statement would be, 'The incidence of crimes of theft has increased in the past ten years'. An instance of the evaluative class would be 'Theft is wrong'. The positivists claimed that many utterances that had the form of meaningful propositions were used not to state propositions that were verifiable either analytically or synthetically, but to express emotions and feelings. Propositions of ethics look as if they are cognitively meaningful, but they are not; they have only 'emotive' or 'evaluative' meaning. The propositions of science, mathematics, logic and much of common sense fall in the descriptive class; the utterances of aesthetics, ethics and much of religion fall in the evaluative class. It is important to note that on this conception evaluative propositions are not, strictly speaking, either true or false, since they are not verifiable as either analytic or empirical. The two distinctions are crucially related in that all of the statements that fall on one side or the other of the analytic–synthetic distinction also fall within the descriptive class of the descriptive–evaluative distinction.

The importance that these two distinctions had for defining both the character of the philosophical enterprise and the relationships between language and reality is hard to exaggerate. One radical consequence of the distinction between descriptive and evaluative propositions was that certain traditional areas of philosophy, such as ethics, aesthetics and political philosophy, were virtually abolished as realms of cognitive meaningfulness. Propositions in these areas were, for the most part, regarded as nonsensical expressions of feelings and emotions, because they are not utterances that can be, strictly speaking, either true or false. Since the aim of philosophers is to state the truth, and since evaluative utterances cannot be either true or false, it cannot be one of the aims of philosophy to make any evaluative utterances. Philosophers might analyse the meaning of evaluative terms, and they might examine the logical relationships among these terms, but philosophers, *qua* philosophers, can make no first-order evaluations in aesthetics, ethics or politics, as these first-order evaluations are not, strictly speaking, meaningful. They may have a sort of secondary, derivative meaning, called 'emotive meaning', but they lack scientifically acceptable cognitive meaning.

If the task of philosophy is to state the truth and not to provide evaluations, what then is the subject matter of philosophy? Since the methods of philosophers are not those of empirical science – since their methods are *a priori* rather than *a posteriori* – it cannot be their aim to state empirical truths about the world. Such propositions are the propositions of the special sciences. The aim of philosophers, therefore, is to state analytic truths concerning logical relations among the concepts of our language. In this period of philosophy, the task of philosophy was taken to be the task of conceptual analysis. Indeed, for most philosophers who accepted this view, philosophy and conceptual analysis were the same. Where traditional philosophers had taken their task to be the discussion of the nature of the good, the true, the beautiful and the just, the positivist and post-positivist analytic philosophers took their task to be the analysis of the meaning of concepts such as 'goodness', 'truth', 'beauty' and 'justice'. Ideally the analysis of these and other philosophically interesting concepts, such as 'knowledge', 'certainty' and 'cause', should give necessary and sufficient conditions for the application of these concepts. They saw this as being the legitimate heir of the traditional philosophical enterprise, but an heir purged of the metaphysical nonsense and confusion that had discredited the traditional enterprise.

If we combine the assumption that philosophy is essentially a conceptual, analytic enterprise with the assumption that its task is foundational – that is, its task is to provide secure foundations for such things as knowledge – then the consequence for the positivists is that philosophical analysis tends in large part to be reductive. That is, the aim of the analysis is to show, for example, how empirical knowledge is based on, and ultimately reducible to, the data of our experience, to so-called sense data. (This view is called 'phenomenalism'.) Similarly, statements about the mind are based on, and therefore ultimately reducible to, statements about external behaviour (behaviourism). Necessary truth is similarly based on conventions of language as expressed in definitions (conventionalism); and mathematics is based on logic, especially set theory (logicism). In each case, the more philosophically puzzling phenomenon is shown to have a secure foundation in some less puzzling phenomenon, and indeed, the ideal of such analysis was to show that the puzzling phenomena could be entirely reduced to less puzzling phenomena. 'Phenomenalism' supposedly gave science a secure foundation because science could be shown to be founded on the data of our senses. Since the form of the reduction was analytic or definitional, it had the consequence that statements about empirical reality could be translated into statements about sense data. Similarly, according to behaviourism, statements about mental phenomena could be translated into statements about behaviour.

Within the camp of analytic philosophers who thought the aim of philosophy was conceptual analysis, there were two broad streams. One stream thought ordinary language was in general quite adequate, both as a tool and as

a subject matter of philosophical analysis. The other stream thought of
ordinary language as hopelessly inadequate for philosophical purposes, and
irretrievably confused. The philosophers of this latter stream thought that we
should use the tools of modern mathematical logic both for analysing
traditional philosophical problems and, more importantly, for creating a
logically perfect language, for scientific and philosophical purposes, in which
certain traditional confusions could not even arise. There was never a rigid
distinction between these two streams, but there were certainly two broad
trends: one which emphasized ordinary language philosophy and one which
emphasized symbolic logic. Both streams, however, accepted the central view
that the aim of philosophy was conceptual analysis, and that in consequence
philosophy was fundamentally different from any other discipline; they
thought that it was a second-order discipline analysing the logical structure of
language in general, but not dealing with first-order truths about the world.
Philosophy was universal in subject matter precisely because it had no special
subject matter other than the discourse of all other disciplines and the
discourse of common sense.

A further consequence of this conception was that philosophy became
essentially a linguistic or conceptual enterprise. For that reason, the philosophy of language was absolutely central to the philosophical task. In a sense,
the philosophy of language was not only 'first philosophy'; all of philosophy
became a form of philosophy of language. Philosophy was simply the logical
investigation of the structure of language as it was used in the various sciences
and in common life.

2 The Rejection of these Two Distinctions and the Rejection of Foundationalism

Work done in the 1950s and 1960s led to the overcoming of these two
distinctions; and with the rejection of these two distinctions came a new
conception of analytic philosophy – a conception that emerged in the 1970s
and 1980s and which is still being developed. The rejection of these two
distinctions and of the foundationalist research programme led to an enormous upheaval in the conception of the philosophical enterprise and in the
practice of analytic philosophers. The most obvious problem with traditional
analytic philosophy was that the reductionist enterprise failed. In every case,
the attempts to provide reductionist analyses of the sort proposed by the
phenomenalists and behaviourists were unsuccessful, and by 1960 the lack of
success was obvious. A series of important theoretical developments also took
place at this time, but for the sake of simplicity I shall concentrate on only five
of these: Quine's rejection of the analytic–synthetic distinction, Austin's
theory of speech acts, Wittgenstein's criticism of foundationalism, Rawls' work
in political philosophy and the changes in the philosophy of science due to
Kuhn and others.

2.1 Quine's attack on the analytic–synthetic distinction

Perhaps the most important criticism of the analytic–synthetic distinction was made by W. V. O. Quine in a famous article entitled 'Two dogmas of empiricism' (Quine, 1953). In this article, Quine claimed that no adequate, non-circular definition of analyticity had ever been given. Any attempt to define analyticity had always been made using notions that were in the same family as analyticity, such as synonymy and definition, and consequently, the attempts to define analyticity were invariably circular. However, an even more important objection that emerged in Quine's article was this: The notion of an analytic proposition is supposed to be a notion of a proposition that is immune to revision, that is irrefutable. Quine claimed that there were no propositions that were immune to revision, that any proposition could be revised in the face of recalcitrant evidence, and that any proposition could be held in the face of recalcitrant evidence, provided that one was willing to make adjustments in other propositions originally held to be true. Quine argued that we should think of the language of science as being like a complex network that was impinged upon by empirical verification only at the edges. Recalcitrant experiences at the edges of science can produce changes anywhere along the line, but the changes are not forced on us by purely logical considerations; rather, we make various pragmatic or practical adjustments in the network of our sentences or beliefs to accommodate the ongoing character of our experiences. Language, on this view, is not atomistic. It does not consist of a set of propositions, each of which can be assessed in isolation. Rather, it consists of a holistic network, and, in this network, propositions as groups confront experience; propositions individually are not simply assessed as true or false. (This holism of scientific discourse was influenced by the French philosopher of science, Duhem, and the view is frequently referred to as 'the Duhem–Quine thesis'.)

Most philosophers today accept some version or other of Quine's rejection of the analytic–synthetic distinction. Not everybody agrees with his actual argument (I, for one, do not), but now there is general scepticism about our ability to make a strict distinction between those propositions that are true by definition and those that are true as a matter of fact. The rejection of the analytic–synthetic distinction has profound consequences for analytic philosophy, as we shall see in more detail later.

At this point it is important to state that if there is no well-defined class of analytic propositions, then the philosopher's propositions cannot themselves be clearly identified as analytic. The results of philosophical analysis cannot be sharply distinguished from the results of scientific investigation. On the positivist picture, philosophy was not one among other sciences; rather, it stood outside the frame of scientific discourse and analysed the logical relations between, on the one hand, that discourse and its vocabulary and, on the other, experience and reality. Philosophers, so to speak, analysed the relation between language and reality, but only from the side. If we accept Quine's rejection of the analytic–synthetic distinction, then philosophy is not something that can be clearly demarcated from the special sciences. It is, rather, adjacent to, and overlaps with, other disciplines. Although philosophy is more general than other disciplines, its propositions do not have any special logical status or special logical priority with regard to the other disciplines.

2.2 Austin's theory of speech acts

The British philosopher J. L. Austin was suspicious of both the distinction between analytic and synthetic propositions, and the distinction between evaluative and descriptive utterances. During the 1950s, he developed an alternative conception of language (Austin, 1962). His first observation was that there is a class of utterances that are obviously perfectly meaningful, but which do not even set out to be either true or false. A man who says, for example, 'I promise to come and see you' or a qualified authority who says to a couple, 'I pronounce you man and wife' is neither reporting on nor describing a promise or a marriage respectively. Such utterances should be thought not as cases of *describing* or *stating*, but rather as *doing*, as *acting*. Austin baptized these utterances 'performatives' and contrasted them with 'constatives'. The distinction between constatives and performatives was supposed to contain three features: constatives, but not performatives, could be true or false; performatives, on the other hand, though they could not be true or false, could be felicitous or infelicitous, depending on whether or not they were correctly, completely, and successfully performed; and finally, performatives were supposed to be actions, doings or performances, as opposed to mere sayings or statings. But, as Austin himself saw, the distinctions so drawn did not work. Many so-called performatives turned out to be capable of being true or false; for example, warnings could be either true or false. And statements, as well as performatives, could be infelicitous. For example, if one made a statement for which one had insufficient evidence, one would have made an infelicitous statement. And finally, stating is as much performing an action as promising or ordering or apologizing. The abandonment of the performative–constative distinction led Austin to a general theory of speech acts. Communicative utterances in general are actions of a type he called 'illocutionary acts'.

One great merit of Austin's theory of speech acts is that it enabled subsequent philosophers to construe the philosophy of language as a branch of the philosophy of action. Since speech acts are as much actions as any other actions, the philosophical analysis of language is part of the general analysis of human behaviour. And since intentional human behaviour is an expression of mental phenomena, it turns out that the philosophy of language and the philosophy of action are really just different aspects of one larger area, namely, the philosophy of mind. On this view, the philosophy of language is not 'first philosophy'; it is a branch of the philosophy of mind. Though Austin did not live to carry out the research programme implicit in his initial discoveries, subsequent work, including my own, has carried this research further.

By treating speaking as a species of intentional action we can give a new sense to a lot of old questions. For example, the old question, 'How many kinds of utterances are there?' is too vague to be answered. But if we ask 'How many kinds of illocutionary acts are there?', we can give a precise answer, since the question asks, 'How many possible ways are there for speakers to relate propositional contents to reality in the performance of actions that express illocutionary intentions?' An analysis of the structure of those intentions reveals five basic types of illocutionary act: we tell people how things are (Assertives), we try to get them to do things (Directives), we commit ourselves to doing things (Commissives), we express our feelings and attitudes (Expressives) and we bring about changes in the world through our utterances, so that the world is changed to match the propositional content of the utterance (Declarations). (For details see Searle, 1979 and 1983.)

2.3 Wittgenstein's rejection of foundationalism

The single most influential analytic philosopher of the twentieth century, and indeed, the philosopher whom most analytic philosophers would regard as the greatest philosopher of the century, is Ludwig Wittgenstein.

Wittgenstein published only one short book during his lifetime, which represents his early work, but with the posthumous publication of his *Philosophical Investigations* in 1953, a series of his later writings began to become available. Now, we have a sizeable corpus of the work he did in the last twenty years of his life. Through painstaking analysis of the use of language, particularly through analysis of psychological concepts, Wittgenstein attempted to undermine the idea that philosophy is a foundational enterprise. He asserted, on the contrary, that philosophy is a purely descriptive enterprise, that the task of philosophy is neither to reform language nor to try to place the various uses of language on a secure foundation. Rather, philosophical problems are removed by having a correct understanding of how language actually functions.

A key notion in Wittgenstein's conception of language is the notion of a language game. We should think of the words in language as being like the pieces in a game. They are not to be understood by looking for some associated idea in the mind, or by following some procedure of verification, or even by looking at the object for which they stand. Rather, we should think of words in terms of their use, and referring to objects in the world is only one of many uses that words have. The meaning of a word is given by its use, and the family of uses that a group of words has constitutes a language game. Examples include the language game we play in describing our own sensations, or the language game we play in identifying the causes of events. This conception of language leads Wittgenstein to the rejection of the conception that the task of philosophical analysis is reductionist or foundationalist. That is, Wittgenstein rejects the idea that language games either have or need a foundation in something else, and he rejects the idea that certain language games can be reduced to certain other kinds of language games. The effect, Wittgenstein says, of philosophical analysis is not to alter our existing linguistic practices or to challenge their validity; it is simply to describe them. Language neither has nor needs a foundation in the traditional sense.

I said that Wittgenstein was the single most influential philosopher in the analytic tradition, but there is a sense in which it seems to me he has still not been properly understood, nor have his lessons been fully assimilated by analytic philosophers. I will have more to say about his influence later.

2.4 Rawls' theory of justice

The conception of moral philosophy in the positivist and post-positivist phases of analytic philosophy was extremely narrow. Strictly speaking, according to the positivists, moral utterances could not be either true or false, so there was nothing that the philosopher could say, *qua* philosopher, by way of making moral judgements. The task for the moral philosopher was to analyse moral discourse, to analyse the meaning and use of moral terms, such as, 'good', 'ought', 'right', 'obligation', etc. It is important to see that this conception of moral philosophy was a strict logical consequence of the acceptance of the distinction between evaluative and descriptive utterances. For if evaluative utterances cannot be either true or false, and if first-order moral discourse consists in evaluative utterances, and if the task of the philosopher is to state the truth, it follows that the philosopher, *qua* philosopher, cannot make any first-order moral judgements. As a philosopher, all he or she can do is the second-order task of analysing moral concepts.

Some philosophers of the positivist and post-positivist periods rejected this narrow conception of moral philosophy, and there were a series of attacks mounted on the distinction between evaluative and descriptive utterances, including some attacks by myself in the mid-1960s (Searle, 1964). It remained, however, for John Rawls to reopen the traditional conception of political and moral philosophy with the publication of his book *A Theory of Justice* in 1971. For the purposes of the present discussion, the important thing about Rawls' work was not that he refuted the traditional dichotomy of descriptive and evaluative utterances, but that he simply ignored it and proceeded to develop a theory of political institutions of a sort that has a long philosophical tradition and which the positivists thought they had overcome. Rawls, in effect, revived the social contract theory, which had long been assumed to be completely defunct; but he did it by an ingenious device: He did not attempt, as some traditional theorists had done, to show that there might have been an original social contract, nor did he try to show that the participation of individuals in society involved a tacit contract. Rather, he used the following thought experiment as an analytic tool: Think of the sort of society that rational beings would agree to if they did not know what sort of position they themselves would occupy in that society. If we imagine rational beings, hidden behind a veil of ignorance, who are asked to select and agree on forms of social institutions that would be fair for all, then we can develop criteria for appraising social institutions on purely rational grounds.

The importance of Rawls for our present discussion is not whether he succeeded in developing new foundations for political theory, but the fact that his work gave rise to a renewed interest in political philosophy, which was soon accompanied by a renewed interest in the traditional questions of moral philosophy. Moral and political philosophy had been confined to a very small realm by the positivist philosophers, and for that reason seemed sterile and uninteresting. Very little work was done in that area, but since the 1970s it has grown enormously, and is now a flourishing branch of analytic philosophy.

2.5 Post-positivist philosophy of science

Throughout the positivist period the model of empirical knowledge was provided by the physical sciences, and the general conception was that the empirical sciences proceeded by the gradual but cumulative growth of empirical knowledge through the systematic application of scientific method. There were different versions of scientific method, according to the philosophers of that period, but they all shared the idea that scientific, empirical propositions are essentially 'testable'. Initially a proposition was thought testable if it could be confirmed, but the most influential version of this idea is Popper's claim that empirical propositions are testable if they are falsifiable in principle. That is, in order for a proposition to tell us how the world is as opposed to how it might be or might have been, there must be some conceivable state of affairs that would render that proposition false. Propositions of science are, strictly speaking, never verifiable – they simply survive repeated attempts at falsification. Science is in this sense fallible, but it is at the same time rational and cumulative.

This picture of the history of science was very dramatically challenged in Thomas Kuhn's book *The Structure of Scientific Revolutions* (Kuhn, 1962). According to Kuhn, the history of science shows not a gradual and steady accumulation of knowledge but periodic revolutionary overthrows of previous conceptions of reality. The shift from Aristotelian physics to Newtonian physics, and the shift from Newtonian physics to relativistic physics are both illustrations of how one 'paradigm' is replaced by another. When the burden of puzzling cases within one paradigm becomes unbearable, a new paradigm emerges, which provides not just a new set of truths but a whole new way of looking at the subject matter. 'Normal sciences' always proceeds by puzzle-solving within a paradigm, but revolutionary breakthroughs, rather than puzzle-solving within a paradigm, are matters of overthrowing one paradigm and replacing it with another.

Just as Kuhn challenged the picture of science as essentially a matter of a steady accumulation of knowledge, so Paul Feyerabend challenged the conception of there being a unitary rational 'scientific method' (Feyerabend, 1975). Feyerabend tried to show that the history of science reveals not a single rational method but rather a series of opportunistic, chaotic, desperate (and sometimes even dishonest) attempts to cope with immediate problems. The lesson that Feyerabend draws from this is that we should abandon the constraining idea of there being such a thing as a single, rational method that applies everywhere in science; rather, we should adopt an 'anarchistic' view, according to which 'anything goes'. Reactions to Kuhn and Feyerabend not surprisingly, differ enormously among analytic philosophers. Kuhn sometimes seems to be arguing that there is not any such thing as the real world existing independently of our scientific theories, which it is the aim of our scientific theories to represent. Kuhn, in short, seems to be denying realism. Most philosophers do not take this denial of realism at all seriously. Even if Kuhn were right about the structure of scientific revolutions, this in no way shows that there is no independent reality that science is investigating. Again, most philosophers would accept Feyerabend's recognition of a variety of methods used in the history of science, but very few people take seriously the idea that there are no rational constraints on investigation whatever. None the less, the effect of these authors has been important in at least the following respect. The positivists' conception of science as a steady accumulation of factual knowledge, and of the task of the philosopher as the conceptual analysis of scientific method, has given way to an attitude to science that is at once more sceptical and more activist. It is· more sceptical in the sense that few philosophers are looking for the one single method that pervades every enterprise called 'science', but it is more activist in the sense that philosophy of science interacts more directly with scientific results. For example, recent philosophical discussions about quantum mechanics, or about the significance of Bell's theorem within quantum mechanics, reveal that it is now impossible to say exactly where the problem in physics ends and the problem in philosophy begins. There is a steady interaction and collaboration between philosophy and science on such philosophically puzzling questions.

3 Some Recent Developments

The results of the changes that I have just outlined are to make analytic philosophy on the one hand a more interesting discipline, but on the other hand a much less well-defined research project. In the way that the verification principle formed the core ideology of the logical positivists and in the way that the conceptual analysis formed the core research project of the post-positivistic analytic philosopher, there is now no ideological point of reference that is commonly agreed upon; nor is there a universally accepted research programme. For example, conceptual analysis thirty years ago was taken to be the heart of analytic philosophy, but now many philosophers would deny that it is the central element in the philosophical enterprise. Some philosophers, indeed, would say that the traditional enterprise of attempting to find logically necessary and sufficient conditions for the applicability of a concept is misconceived in principle. They think the possibility of such an enterprise has been refuted by Quine's refutation of the analytic–synthetic distinction, as well as Wittgenstein's observation that many philosophically puzzling concepts have not a central core or essence of meaning, but a variety of different uses united only by a 'family resemblance'. Many other philosophers would say that conceptual analysis is still an essential part of the philosophical enterprise, as indeed it has been since the time of Plato's Dialogues, but it is no longer seen to be the whole of the enterprise. Philosophy is now, I believe, a much more interesting subject than it was a generation ago because it is no longer seen as something separate from, and sealed off from, other disciplines. In particular, philosophy is now seen by most analytic philosophers as being adjacent to and overlapping with the sciences. My own view, which I feel is fairly widely shared, is that words like 'philosophy' and 'science' are in many respects misleading, if they are taken to imply the existence of mutually exclusive forms of knowledge. Rather, it seems to me that there is just knowledge and truth, and that in intellectual enterprises we are primarily aiming at knowledge and truth. These may come in a variety of forms, whether in history, mathematics, physics, psychology, literary criticism or philosophy. Philosophy tends to be more general than other subjects, more synoptic in its vision, more conceptually or logically oriented than other disciplines, but it is not a discipline that is hermetically sealed off from other subjects. The result is that many areas of investigation which were largely ignored by analytic philosophers a generation ago have now become thriving branches of philosophy, including cognitive science, the philosophy of biology and the philosophy of economics. In what follows, I will confine my discussion to five major areas of philosophical research: cognitive science, the causal theory of reference, intentionalistic theories of meaning, truth conditional theories of meaning, and Wittgenstein's conception of language and mind and his response to scepticism.

3.1 Philosophy and cognitive science

Nowhere is the new period of collaboration between philosophy and other disciplines more evident than in the new subject of cognitive science. Cognitive science from its very beginnings has been 'interdisciplinary' in character, and is in effect the joint property of psychology, linguistics, philosophy, computer science, and anthropology. There is, therefore, a great variety of different research projects within cognitive science, but the central area of cognitive science, its hardcore ideology, rests on the assumption that the mind is best viewed as analogous to a digital computer. The basic idea behind cognitive science is that recent developments in computer science and artificial intelligence have enormous importance for our conception of human beings. The basic inspiration for cognitive science went something like this: human beings do information processing. Computers are designed precisely to do information processing. Therefore one way to study human cognition – perhaps the best way to study it – is to study it as a matter of computational information processing. Some cognitive scientists think that the computer is just a metaphor for the human mind; others think that the human mind is literally a computer program. But it is fair to say that without the computational model there would not have been a cognitive science as we now understand it.

This conception of human cognition was ideally suited to the twentieth-century analytic tradition in philosophy of mind because of the analytic tradition's resolute materialism. It was anti-mentalistic and anti-dualistic. The failure of logical behaviourism led not to a revival of dualism but to more sophisticated versions of materialism. I will now briefly summarize some of the recent developments in materialistic philosophies of mind that led to the computational theory of the mind.

The logical behaviourists' thesis was subject to many objections, the most important being the objection that it ignores internal mental phenomena. In science and common sense it seems more natural to think of human behaviour as being *caused by* internal mental states rather than to think of the mental states as simply *consisting of* the behaviour. This weakness in behaviourism was corrected by the materialist identity thesis, sometimes called 'physicalism'. According to the physicalist identity theory, mental states are identical with states of the brain. We do not know in detail what these identities are, but the progress of the neurosciences makes it seem overwhelmingly probable that every mental state will be discovered to be identical with some brain state. In the early version of the identity thesis it was supposed that every type of mental state would be discovered to be identical with some type of physical state, but after some debate this began to seem more and more implausible. There is no reason to suppose that only systems with neurons like ours can have mental states; indeed, there is no reason to suppose that two human beings who have the same belief must therefore be in the same neurophysiological state. So, 'type–type identity theory' naturally gave way to 'token–token identity theory'. The token identity theorists claimed that every particular mental state is identical with some particular neurophysiological state, even if there is no type correlation between types of mental states and types of physical states. But that only leaves open the question, 'What is it that two different neurophysiological states have in common if they are both the same mental state?' To many analytic philosophers it seemed obvious that the answer to our question must be that two neurophysiological states are the same type of mental state if they serve the same *function* in the overall ecology of the organism. Mental states on this view can be defined in terms of their causal relations to input stimuli, to other mental states, and to external behaviour. This view is called 'functionalism', and it is a natural development from token–token identity theory.

However, the functionalist has to answer a further obvious question: 'What is it about the states that gives them the causal relations that they do have?' If mental states are defined in terms of their causal relations, then what is it about the structure of different neurophysiological configurations that can give them the same causal relations? It is at precisely this point that the tradition of materialism in analytic philosophy converges with the tradition of artificial intelligence. The computer provides an obvious answer to the question that I have just posed. The distinction between the software and the hardware, the program and the physical system that implements the program, provides a model for how functionally equivalent elements at a higher level can be realized in or implemented by different physical systems at a lower level. Just as one and the same program can be implemented by quite different physical hardware systems, so one and the same set of mental processes can be implemented in different neurophysiological or other forms of hardware implementations. Indeed, on the most extreme version of this view, the mind is to the brain as the program is to the hardware. This sort of functionalism came to be called 'computer functionalism', or 'Turing machine function- alism', and it coincides with the strong version of 'artificial intelligence' (Strong AI), the version that says having a mind just is having a certain sort of program.

I have refuted Strong AI in a series of articles (Searle, 1980a, 1980b). The basic idea of that refutation can be stated quite simply. Minds cannot be equivalent to programs because programs are defined purely formally or syntactically and minds have mental contents. The easiest way to see the force of the refutation is to see that a system, say oneself, could learn to manipulate the formal symbols for understanding a natural language without actually understanding that language. I might have a program that enables me to answer questions in Chinese simply by matching incoming symbols with the appropriate processing and output symbols, but none the less I still would not thereby understand Chinese. However, though the project of computer functionalism is almost certainly a failure, the results of the enterprise are in many respects quite useful. Important things can be learned about the mind by pursuing the computer metaphor, and the research effort has not necessarily been wasted. The most exciting recent development has been to think of mental processes not on the model of the conventional serial digital computer, but rather to think of brain processes on the model of parallel distributed processing computers. The most exciting recent development, in my view, in cognitive science has been the development of such 'neural net models' for human cognition.

In concluding this section, I want to point out that in my view the chief weakness of analytical philosophy of mind, a weakness it shares with the past 300 years in the philosophy of mind, has been its assumption that there is somehow an inconsistency between mentalism and materialism. Analytic philosophers, along with the rest of the Cartesian tradition, have character- istically assumed that 'mental' implies 'nonmaterial' or 'immaterial' and that 'material' or 'physical' implies 'nonmental'. But if one reflects on how the brain works, it seems that both of these assumptions are obviously false. What that shows is that our whole vocabulary, our whole terminology of the mental and physical, needs wholesale revision.

3.2 The causal theory of reference

A central question in analytic philosophy of language, since Frege (and indeed in philosophy since the time of Plato), has been: How does language relate to the world? How do words hook on to things? In answering this question, the analytic tradition had characteristically found a connection between the notion of reference and the notion of truth. An expression, such as a proper name, refers to or stands for or designates an object because associated with that name is some descriptive content, some concept of the object in question, and the object in question satisfies or fits that descriptive content. The expression refers to the object only because the description is true of the object. This is the standard reading of Frege's famous distinction between sense and reference, between *Sinn und Bedeutung*. Expressions refer to objects in virtue of their sense and the sense provides a description, a 'mode of presentation', of the object in question. Something analogously applies with general terms: general terms are true of an object because each general term has associated with it a cluster of features, and the term will be true of the object if the object in question has those features.

In the 1970s, this conception of the relation between language and reality was attacked by a number of philosophers, most prominently Donnellan (1970), Kripke (1972), and Putnam (1975). A variety of arguments were mounted against the traditional conception of meaning and reference, but the common thread running through these arguments was that the descriptive content associated with a word provided neither necessary nor sufficient conditions for its application. A speaker might refer to an object even though the associated description that he or she had was not true of that object; a speaker might have a description that was satisfied by an object even though that was not the object to which he or she was referring. The most famous version of this argument was Putnam's 'twin earth' example. Imagine a planet in a distant galaxy exactly like ours in every respect except that on this planet what they call 'water' has a different chemical composition. It is not composed of H_2O but has an extremely complicated formula that we will abbreviate as 'XYZ'. Prior to 1750, prior to the time that anyone knew the chemical composition of water, the people on twin earth had in their minds exactly the same concept of water as the people on earth. None the less our word 'water' does not refer to the stuff on twin earth. Our word 'water', whether or not we knew it in 1750, refers to H_2O; and this is a matter of objective causal relations in the world which are independent of the ideas that people have in their heads. Meanings on this view are not concepts in people's heads, but objective relations in the world. Well, if associated ideas are not sufficient for meaning, what is? The answer given by the three authors I have mentioned is that there must be some sort of causal connection between the use of the word and the object or type of entity in the world that it applies to. Thus, if I use the word 'Socrates', it refers to a certain Greek philosopher only because there is a causal chain connecting that philosopher and my current use of the word. The word 'water' is not defined by any checklist of features; rather, 'water' refers to whatever stuff in the world was causally related to certain original uses of the word 'water', and these uses subsequently came to be accepted in the community and were then passed down through a causal chain of communication.

There is a very natural way of connecting the computer functionalist conception of the mind with the causal theory of reference. If the mind were a computer program, and if meaning were a matter of causal connections to the world, then the way the mind acquires meanings is for the system that implements the computer program to be involved in causal interactions with the world.

3.3 Intentionalistic theories of meaning

Much of the best work in speech act theory done after the publication of Austin's *How to Do Things with Words* in 1962, and my *Speech Acts* in 1969, attempted to combine the insights of Paul Grice's account of meaning with the framework provided by the theory of speech acts. In a series of articles beginning in the late 1950s (Grice, 1957, 1968), Grice had argued that there is a close connection between the speaker's intentions in the performance of an utterance and the meaning of that utterance. In his original formulation of this view, Grice analysed the speaker's meaning in terms of the intention to produce an effect on the hearer by means of getting the hearer to recognize the intention to produce that very effect. Thus, for example, according to Grice, if a speaker intends to tell a hearer that it is raining, then in the speaker's utterance of the sentence, 'It is raining', the speaker's meaning will consist of his or her intention to produce in the hearer the belief that it is raining by means of getting the hearer to recognize his or her intention to produce that very belief. Subsequent work by Grice altered the details of this account, but the general principle remained the same: meaning is a matter of a self-referential intention to produce an effect on a hearer by getting the hearer to recognize the intention to produce that effect. Grice combined this analysis of meaning with an analysis of certain principles of conversational co-operation. In conversation, people accept certain tacit principles, which Grice calls 'Maxims of Conversation' – they accept the principles that the speaker's remarks will be truthful and sincere (the maxim of quality), that they will be relevant to the conversational purposes at hand (the maxim of relation), that the speaker will be clear (the maxim of manner) and that the speaker will say neither more nor less than is necessary for the purposes of the conversation (the maxim of quantity).

There has been a great deal of controversy about the details of Grice's analysis of meaning, but the basic idea that there is a close connection between meaning and intention has been accepted and has proved immensely useful in analysing the structure of certain typical speech act phenomena. My own view is that Grice confuses that part of meaning which has to do with representing certain states of affairs and certain illocutionary modes, and that part of meaning that has to do with communicating those representations to a hearer. Grice, in short, confuses communication with representation. However, the combination of an intentionalistic account of meaning, together with rational principles of co-operation, is immensely fruitful in analysing such problems as those of 'indirect speech acts' and figurative uses of language such as metaphors. So, for example, in an indirect speech act, a speaker will characteristically mean something more than what he or she actually says. To take a simple example, in a dinner table situation a speaker who says, 'Can you pass the salt?' would usually not just be asking a question about the salt-passing abilities of the hearer; he or she would be requesting the hearer to pass the salt. Now the puzzle is: How is it that speakers and hearers communicate so effortlessly when there is a big gulf between what the speaker means and what he or she actually says? In the case of metaphor, a similar question arises: How does the speaker communicate so effortlessly his or her metaphorical meaning when the literal meaning of the sentence uttered does not encode that metaphorical meaning? A great deal of progress has been made on these and other problems using the apparatus that Grice contributed to the theory of speech acts.

One of the marks of progress in philosophy is that the results of philosophical analysis tend to be appropriated by other disciplines, and this has certainly happened with speech act theory. Speech act theory is now a thriving branch of the discipline of linguistics, and the works of Austin and Grice, as well as my own, are as well known among linguists as they are among philosophers.

3.4 Truth-conditional theories of meaning

Philosophers such as Quine and his former student, Donald Davidson, have always felt that intentionalistic theories of meaning, of the sort proposed by Grice and Searle were philosophically inadequate, because the intentionalistic notions seemed as puzzling as the notion of meaning itself and because they could necessarily involve linguistic meaning in their ultimate analyses. So Quine and Davidson attempted to give accounts of meaning that did not employ the usual apparatus of intentionality. The most influential version of this attempt is Davidson's project of analysing meaning in terms of truth conditions. The basic idea is that one knows the meaning of a sentence if one knows under what conditions it is true or false. Thus, one knows the meaning of the German sentence 'Schnee ist weiss', if one knows that it is true if and only if snow is white. Now since a theory of meaning for a language should be able to state the meaning of each of the sentences of the language, and since the meanings of the sentences of the language are given by truth conditions, and since truth conditions can be specified independently of the intentionalistic apparatus, it seems to Davidson that a theory of truth (that is, a theory of the truth conditions of the sentences) of a language would provide a theory of meaning for that language.

In order to carry out the project of explaining meaning in terms of truth, Davidson employs the apparatus of Tarski's semantic definition of truth, a definition that Tarski had worked out in the 1930s. Tarski points out that it is a condition of adequacy on any account of truth that for any sentence s and any language L, the account must have the consequence that:

   s is true in L if and only if p,

where for s can be substituted the structural description of any sentence whatever, for L, the name of the language of which s is a part, and for p, the sentence itself or a translation of it. Thus, for example, in English, the sentence 'Snow is white' is true if and only if snow is white. This condition is usually called 'convention T' and the corresponding sentences are called 'T-sentences'.

Now Davidson notes that convention T employs the fact that the sentence named by *s* has the same meaning as the sentence expressed by *p*, and thus, Tarski is using the notion of meaning in order to define the notion of truth. Davidson proposes to turn this procedure around by taking the notion of truth for granted, by taking it as a primitive, and using it to explain meaning.

Here is how it works. Davidson hopes to get a theory of meaning for a speaker of a language that would be sufficient to interpret any of the speaker's utterances by getting a theory that would provide a set of axioms which would entail all true T-sentences for that speaker's language. Thus, if the speaker speaks German, and we use English as a meta-language in which to state the theory of the speaker's language, Davidson claims we would have an adequate theory of the speaker's language if we could get a set of axioms which would entail a true T-sentence stated in English for any sentence that the speaker uttered in German. Thus, for example, our theory of meaning should contain axioms which entail that the speaker's utterance 'Schnee ist weiss' is true in the speaker's language if and only if snow is white. Davidson further claims that we could make this into an empirical theory of the speaker's language by proceeding to associate the speaker's utterances with the circumstances in which we had empirical evidence for supposing that the speaker held those utterances to be true. Thus, if we hear the speaker utter the sentence 'Es regnet', we might look around and note that it was raining in the vicinity, and we might then form the hypothesis that the speaker holds true the sentence 'Es regnet' when it is raining in his or her immediate vicinity. This would provide the sort of empirical data on which we would begin to construct a theory of truth for the speaker's language.

It is important to note that we are to think of this as a thought experiment and not as an actual procedure that we have to employ when we try to learn German, for example. The idea is to cash out the notion of meaning in terms of truth conditions, and then cash out the notion of truth conditions in terms of a truth theory for a language, which is a theory that would entail all the true T-sentences of the language. The empirical basis on which the whole system rests is that of the evidence we could get concerning the conditions under which a speaker holds a sentence to be true. If the project could in principle be carried out, then we would have given an account of meaning which employed only one intentionalistic notion, the notion of 'holding true' a sentence.

Over the past twenty years, there has been quite an extensive literature on the nature of this project and how it might be applied to several difficult and puzzling sorts of sentences – for example, indexical sentences, sentence about mental states or modal sentences. Enthusiasm for this project seems to have waned somewhat in recent years.

In my view, the central weakness of Davidson's enterprise is as follows: any theory of meaning must explain not only what a speaker represents by his or her utterances, but also how he or she represents them, under what mental aspects the speaker represents truth conditions. For this reason, a theory of meaning cannot just correlate a speaker's utterance with states of affairs in the world; it must explain what is going on in the speaker's head which enables the speaker to represent those states of affairs under certain aspects with the utterances that the speaker makes. Thus, for example, suppose that snow is composed of H_2O molecules in crystalline form, and suppose the colour white consists of light wave emissions of all wavelengths, then the sentence 'Schnee ist weiss' is true if and only if H_2O molecules in crystalline form emit light of all wavelengths. Now this second T-sentence is just as empirically substantiated as the earlier example, 'Schnee ist weiss' is true if and only if snow is white. Indeed, it is a matter of scientific necessity that the state of affairs described by the former is identical with the state of affairs described by the latter. But the former example simply does not give the speaker's meaning. The speaker might hold true the sentence 'Schnee ist weiss' under these and only these conditions and not know the slightest thing about H_2O molecules and wavelengths of light. The T-sentence gives the truth conditions, but the specification of the truth conditions does not necessarily give the meaning of the sentence, because the specification does not yet tell us how the speaker represents those truth conditions. Does he or she represent them under the aspect of snow being white, or what is the same fact in the world, does he or she represent them under the aspect of frozen H_2O crystals emitting light of all wavelengths? Any theory that cannot give that information is not a theory of meaning.

There are various attempts to meet these sorts of objections, but, in my view, they are not successful. In the end, all truth definitional accounts of meaning, like the behaviourist accounts which preceded them, end up with a certain 'indeterminacy' of meaning. They cannot account in objective terms for all of the subjective details of meaning, and both Davidson and Quine have acknowledged that their views result in indeterminacy.

3.5 Wittgenstein's legacy

Wittgenstein's work covers such a vast range of topics, from aesthetics to mathematics, and covers these topics with so much depth and insight, that it continues to be a source of ideas and inspiration for analytic philosophers and is likely continue to be so for many years to come. I will mention only three areas.

3.5.1 Philosophical psychology One of Wittgenstein's main areas of research was that of psychological concepts such as belief, hope, fear, desire, want, expect and sensation concepts such as pain and seeing. Perhaps his single most controversial claim in this area is that concerning a private language. He claims that it would be logically impossible for there to be a language that was private in the sense that its words could only be understood by the speaker because they referred to the speaker's private inner sensations and had no external definition. Such a language would be absurd, he said, because for the application of such words there would be no distinction between what seemed right to the speaker and what really was right. But unless we can make a distinction between what seems right and what really is right, we cannot speak of right or wrong at all, and hence we cannot speak of using a language at all. 'An inner process,' says Wittgenstein (1953), 'stands in need of outward criteria.' Wittgenstein is here attacking the entire Cartesian tradition, according to which there is a realm of inner private objects, our inner mental phenomena, and the meanings of the words that stand for these entities are entirely defined by private ostensive definitions. No other single claim of Wittgenstein's has aroused as much controversy as the 'private language argument'. It continues to be a source of fascination to contemporary philosophers, and many volumes have been written about Wittgenstein's analysis of psychological concepts.

3.5.2 Following a rule Wittgenstein is part of a long tradition that emphasizes the distinction between the modes of explanation of the natural sciences and the modes of explanation of human behaviour and human cultural and psychological phenomena generally. His analysis of this problem chiefly deals with the phenomenon of human behaviour which is influenced or determined by mental contents, and, most importantly, by the phenomena of human beings following a rule. What is it for a human being to follow a rule? Wittgenstein's analysis of this stresses the difference between the way that rules guide human behaviour and the way that natural phenomena are results of causes. Wittgenstein throughout emphasizes the difference between causes and reasons, and he also emphasizes the roles of interpretation and rule following. On the most extreme interpretation of Wittgenstein's remarks about following a rule, he is the proponent of a certain type of scepticism. According to one view of Wittgenstein, he is arguing that rules do not determine their own application, that anything can be interpreted to accord with a rule, and consequently that anything can be interpreted to conflict with a rule. If taken to its extreme, this argument would have the consequence that, logically speaking, rules do not constrain human behaviour at all. And if that is right, then mental contents, such as knowledge of meanings of words or principles of action or even beliefs and desires, do not constrain human behaviour, because they are everywhere subject to an indefinite range of different interpretations. Wittgenstein's solution to this scepticism is to propose that interpretation comes to an end when we simply accept the cultural practices of the community in which we are imbedded. Interpretation comes to an end, and we just act on a rule. Acting on a rule is a practice, and it is one that we are brought up to perform in our culture. The sceptical implications of Wittgenstein's account of rule following are resolved by an appeal to a naturalistic solution: We are simply the sort of beings who follow culturally and biologically conditioned practices.

This interpretation of Wittgenstein is largely due to Saul Kripke (1982) and it has aroused considerable controversy. My own view is that Kripke has misinterpreted Wittgenstein in certain crucial respects, but whether or not his interpretation is correct, it has been a source of continuing discussion in contemporary philosophy.

3.5.3 Philosophical scepticism Important work on philosophical scepticism has been continued by philosophers who are inspired or provoked by Wittgenstein, notably, Thomson Clarke and Barry Stroud. These philosophers point out that a really serious analysis of our use of epistemic discourse shows that the problem of scepticism cannot be simply overcome by the usual analytic philosopher's methods of pointing out that the sceptic raises the demand for justification beyond that which is logically appropriate. Clarke and Stroud claim that the problem of scepticism goes deeper than this solution will allow. Following Wittgenstein in investigating the depth grammar of language, they find that any solution to the sceptic's predicament – that is, any justification for our claims to have knowledge about the world – rests on a much deeper understanding of the difference between ordinary or plain discourse and philosophical discourse. Work in this line of research is continuing at present.

4 Overall Assessment

I have not attempted to survey all of the main areas of activity in contemporary analytic philosophy. Most importantly, I have left out contemporary work in ethics. Perhaps of comparable importance, I have had nothing to say about purely technical work in logic. There is, furthermore, a thriving branch of analytic philosophy called 'action theory', which should be mentioned at least in passing. The general aim of analytic action theory is to analyse the structure of human actions in terms of the causal relations between such mental states as beliefs, desires and intentions, and the bodily movements which are in some sense constitutive of the actions. Finally, it is worth calling attention to the fact that among analytic philosophers there has been a great revival of interest in the history of philosophy. Traditional analytic philosophers thought of the history of philosophy as mostly the history of mistakes. Some of the history of the subject could be useful for doing real philosophy; but the overall conception was that the history of philosophy had no more special relevance to philosophy than the history of mathematics to mathematics, or the history of chemistry to chemistry. This attitude has changed recently, and there is now a feeling of the historical continuity of analytic philosophy with traditional philosophy in a way that contrasts sharply with the original view of analytic philosophers, who thought that they marked a radical, or indeed, revolutionary break with the philosophical tradition.

It is too early to provide an assessment of the contribution that will be made by work done in philosophy at the present time, or even in the past few decades. My own view is that the philosophy of mind and social philosophy will become ever more central to the entire philosophical enterprise. The idea that the study of language could replace the study of mind is itself being transformed into the idea that the study of language is really a branch of the philosophy of mind. Within the philosophy of mind, perhaps the key notion requiring analysis is that of intentionality – that property of the mind by which it is directed at or about or of objects and states of affairs in the world independent of itself. Most of the work done by analytic philosophers in the philosophy of mind has tended to cluster around the traditional mind–body problem. My own view is that we need to overthrow this problem: in its traditional version, it was based on the assumption that mental properties and physical properties were somehow different from each other, and that therefore, there was some special problem not like other problems in biology as to how they could both be characteristics of the human person. Once we see that so-called mental properties really are just higher-level physical properties of certain biological systems, I believe this problem can be dissolved. Once it is dissolved, however, we are still left with the task of analysing what is the central problem in the philosophy of language and in cognitive science, as well as the philosophy of mind, namely, the way that human representational capacities relate the human organism to the world. What are called 'language', 'mind', 'thinking', 'speaking', and 'depicting' are just different aspects of this mode of relating to reality.

I believe that the causal theory of reference will be seen to be a failure once it is recognized that all representations must occur under some aspect or other, and that the extensionality of causal relations is inadequate to capture the aspectual character of reference. The only kind of causation that could be adequate to the task of reference is intentional causation or mental causation, but the causal theory of reference cannot concede that ultimately reference is achieved by some mental device, since the whole approach behind the causal theory was to try to eliminate the traditional mentalism of theories of reference and meaning in favour of objective causal relations in the world. My prediction is that the causal theory of reference, though it is at present by far the most influential theory of reference, will prove to be a failure for these reasons.

Perhaps the single most disquieting feature of analytic philosophy in the fifty-year period that I have been discussing is that it has passed from being a revolutionary minority point of view held in the face of traditionalist objections to becoming itself the conventional, establishment point of view. Analytic philosophy has become not only dominant but intellectually respectable, and, like all successful revolutionary movements, it has lost some of its vitality in virtue of its very success. Given its constant demand for rationality, intelligence, clarity, rigour and self-criticism, it is unlikely that it can succeed indefinitely, simply because these demands are too great a cost for many people to pay. The urge to treat philosophy as a discipline that satisfies emotional rather than intellectual needs is always a threat to the insistence on rationality and intelligence. However, in the history of philosophy, I do not believe we have seen anything to equal the history of analytic philosophy for its rigour, clarity, intelligence and, above all, its intellectual content. There is a sense in which it seems to me that we have been living through one of the great eras in philosophy.

References

Austin, J. L. 1962: *How to do Things with Words.* Oxford: Clarendon Press.
Donnellan, K. 1970: Proper Names and Identifying Descriptions. *Synthèse*, 21, 335–58.

Feyerabend, P. 1975: *Against Method*. London: Humanities Press.

Grice, H. P. 1957: Meaning. *Philosophical Review*, 66.

—— 1968: Utterer's Meaning, Sentence-Meaning, and Word-Meaning. *Foundations of Language*, 4, 1–18.

Kripke, S. 1972: *Naming and Necessity*. In G. Harman and D. Davidson (eds), *Semantics of Natural Language*, Dordrecht: Reidel Publishing Company.

—— 1982: *Wittgenstein on Rules and Private Language*. Cambridge, MA: Harvard University Press.

Kuhn, T. 1962: *The Structure of Scientific Revolutions*. Chicago: University of Chicago Press.

Putnam, H. 1975: The Meaning of 'Meaning'. In his *Philosophical Papers, Vol. 2: Mind, Language and Reality*, Cambridge: Cambridge University Press.

Quine, W. V. O. 1953: Two Dogmas of Empiricism. In his *From a Logical Point of View*, Cambridge, MA: Harvard University Press.

Rawls, J. 1971: *A Theory of Justice*. Cambridge, MA: Harvard University Press.

Searle, J. R. 1964: How to Derive 'Ought' from 'Is'. *Philosophical Review*, 73.

—— 1969: *Speech Acts: An Essay in the Philosophy of Language*. Cambridge: Cambridge University Press.

—— 1979: *Expression and Meaning*. Cambridge: Cambridge University Press.

—— 1980a: Minds, Brains and Programs. *Behavioral and Brain Sciences*, 3, 417–24.

—— 1980b: Intrinsic Intentionality. *Behavioral and Brain Sciences*, 3, 450–6.

—— 1983: *Intentionality: An Essay in the Philosophy of Mind*. Cambridge: Cambridge University Press.

Wittgenstein, L. 1953: *Philosophical Investigations* (translated by G. E. M. Anscombe). Oxford: Blackwell.

Contemporary Philosophy: A Second Look

Bernard Williams

1 The Identity of Analytical Philosophy

Given the title of John Searle's essay, this second introduction might have been expected to complement the first geographically, by dealing with present philosophical developments in places other than the United States, but this is not in fact what it will try to do. Philosophy in the United States, in other English-speaking parts of the world, and in many other countries as well, is now very largely the same. In these places, there is one philosophical culture, and inasmuch as it contains different approaches, and some of the philosophy that is done within that culture is distinct from 'analytical' philosophy, that itself is not a matter of geographical region.

It is true that 'analytical' philosophy, the style of philosophy described in Searle's essay and overwhelmingly represented in this volume, is often professionally distinguished (in job advertisements, for instance) from 'continental' philosophy, and this does represent, in a clumsy way, something which until recently was true: that the ways in which philosophy was done in France, Germany and other countries of continental Europe were typically different from the 'analytical' style. To a much more limited extent, that remains so. (David Cooper describes the situation in continental Europe in chapter 30.) However, it is absurd to mark philosophical differences with these two labels. Apart from involving a strange cross-classification – rather as though one divided cars into front-wheel drive and Japanese – the labels are seriously misleading, in helping one to forget that the origins of analytical philosophy itself lay in continental Europe (notably so, when its founding father is taken to be Frege and its greatest representative Wittgenstein), and that the interests of 'continental' philosophy are not confined to the European continent.

Moreover, it is not simply a matter of labelling. It is not that the distinction in itself is unproblematical, and only needs more aptly chosen titles to represent it. The distinctions involved are obscure, and the titles serve to conceal this fact. The term 'continental' serves to discourage thought about the possible contrasts to analytical philosophy, and so about the identity of analytical philosophy itself. At the same time, the vague geographical resonance of the term does carry a message, that analytical philosophy is familiar as opposed to exotic, and perhaps – if some older stereotypes are in play – that it is responsible as opposed to frivolous. This is indeed what many analytical philosophers believe about it, and they believe it not so much in contrast to activities going on in some remote continent, but, in many cases, as opposed to work done in their local departments of literature. It is not true that work in other styles does not exist in the heartlands of analytical philosophy; it merely does not exist in departments of philosophy. The distinctions involved are not geographical but professional, and what is at issue is the identity of philosophy as a discipline.

In particular, what is at issue is the identity of philosophy as a subject that can sustain ongoing, cumulative, research. If it can do this, it can make a claim which the humanities do not always find it easy to make, except to the extent that they are branches of history: that there is something to be found out within their disciplines, that they can add to knowledge. It has been part of the attraction of analytical philosophy that, without the procedures of the experimental or theoretical sciences and with a more human subject matter, it can claim to achieve results which command, if not agreement, at least objective discussion, and which represent intellectual progress. It has achievements that are not arbitrarily personal, and they compare favourably to those of the social sciences (at least if one leaves aside the quite peculiar case of economics).

I do not think that these claims are empty. I think that the achievements of analytical philosophy are remarkable, and I agree with Searle that the subject is in various ways more interesting than it was 40 years ago. Its virtues are indeed virtues. I think it is hard to be in good faith a teacher of philosophy unless you believe that there is something worth doing that you, in virtue of your experience, can do and which you can help other people to do. I think that the virtues of good philosophy are to a considerable extent *workmanlike.* Quite certainly, no philosophy which is to be worthwhile should lose the sense that there is something to be got right, that it is answerable to argument and that it is in the business of telling the truth.

These things, I believe, are represented by the best of what is called analytical philosophy, and to that extent I am committed to it. My own work has largely been in its style. Yet, having now worked in it for a long time, and having, like Searle, seen it change, I am a great deal more puzzled about it than I once was; in particular, I am puzzled about the ways in which it must understand itself if it is to have those virtues, and also about the costs of sustaining those virtues. There is one understanding of these virtues which is certainly widespread among analytical philosophers, and which directly serves the promise of on-going research: that these are indeed the virtues of a science. Some philosophers who are impressed by this conception of what they are doing ritualize it into the forms of presentation familiar from the sciences. Sometimes this is mere scientism, but in other cases it signals the fact that their branch of philosophy is near neighbour to some science, such as quantum mechanics or cognitive science.

But the virtues of workmanlike truthfulness which analytical philosophy typically cultivates are much more important than any attempt to make philosophy look like a science. With many other branches of philosophy there is no plausible version of sharing a party wall with science, and yet these virtues are still regarded as virtues. In fact, even in the case of the more scientific areas of philosophy, it is obvious enough that these virtues are not recommended only because they are possessed by its scientific neighbours: they are taken to be intellectual virtues, good in the same way for philosophy and for science.

But how far can philosophy cultivate just these virtues and remain true to other aspects of the legacy of the subject, to aims that it has pursued in the past? The sciences aim to make claims that can and should be conveyed in ways that are minimally expressive; they are not meant to convey feeling, or to display much literary imagination, or to speak (at least overtly) in a persuasive mode. But if we think in particular of moral or political philosophy, is this ambition actually true to the traditions of the subject, even as those are embodied in the historical canon of analytical philosophy itself? Is it true to a tradition that contains Plato, Hobbes, Hume, Kant and (come to that) John Stuart Mill? Is it in fact true to any great figure of that tradition, except perhaps Aristotle? And if we are to take him as our model, we are left with many questions to consider – whether, for instance, the affectless treatises that we possess do represent his voice; if so, whether the tone does not represent a quite special view of ethical life; and whether we should not weigh rather soberly the fact that the closest previous imitation of Aristotle was to be found in a movement called scholasticism.

Particularly in moral and political philosophy, but not only there, there is a question of what the procedures typical of analytical philosophy mean. There are many virtuous and valuable things that they make possible, and at the same time there are resources of philosophy in the past that they seemingly exclude, and it is important not to assume that this balance is simply given to us, above all by an unquestionable and transparent interpretation of the ideals of intellectual responsibility. I do not want to suggest that the adoption of the analytical style is a mere abdication, a cowardly refusal to adopt a more imaginative and committed manner which (critics sometimes suggest) is obviously to hand. Still less is it simply a matter of scientistic camouflage. It is a feature of our time that the resources of philosophical writing typically available to analytical philosophy should present themselves so strongly as the responsible way of going on, the most convincing expression of a philosopher's claim on people's attention. But that is an historical fact, and we should try to understand it as such. I do not think that I adequately understand it, and, for that reason, I would not like to predict what other possibilities there may prove to be for a philosophy that preserves the merits of analytical philosophy.

In the rest of this essay, I shall try to give an outline of some principal concerns of analytical moral and political philosophy. This will supplement the account that John Searle has given of the state of the art in other areas, but I hope also that in describing some of what analytical philosophy has recently done for these subjects, it may encourage readers to ask what new things it might be able to do.

2 Meta-ethics

Philosophical studies have often been understood, in the analytical tradition but not only there, as being *higher-order*, in the sense that natural science, for instance, will study natural phenomena, while the philosophy of science will study, from some particular points of view, the operations of science. Some of moral philosophy (or, as I shall also call it, ethics) is certainly a higher-order study. It discusses such things as the nature of moral judgements, and asks whether they express genuine beliefs, whether they can be objectively true, and so forth. Such higher-order questions are the concern of *meta-ethics*. At one time (30 to 50 years ago) it was widely thought in analytical philosophy that ethics consisted only of meta-ethics. A powerful source of this conception was the belief in a firm distinction between fact and value, to which Searle has referred. However, the idea of ethics as simply meta-ethics does not follow directly from the distinction between fact and value, and those who used the distinction to support that idea needed two further assumptions.

One was that philosophy itself should be in the business of 'fact' (which, for the purposes of the distinction, included theory), and not of value. This was connected with a certain conception of philosophy, important to the identity of analytical philosophy, in which it is taken to derive its authority from its theoretical stance as an abstract intellectual enquiry. Some earlier philosophers, such as G. E. Moore, had indeed believed in the distinction between fact and value, but had supposed that philosophers, in one way or another, could have quite a lot to say substantively about values. The journey from the fact–value distinction to a view of ethics as only meta-ethics involved the assumption that this was impossible or inappropriate.

The second assumption involved in the journey was that meta-ethics itself could be value-neutral, that the study of the nature of ethical thought did not commit one to any substantive moral conclusions. A yet further assumption, which was not necessary to the journey but did often accompany it, was that meta-ethics should be linguistic in style, and its subject should be 'the language of morals'. This latter idea has now almost entirely disappeared, as the purely linguistic conception of philosophical study has more generally retreated. Beyond that, however, there are now more doubts about the extent to which meta-ethics can be value-neutral, and, in addition, philosophers simply feel freer in making their own ethical commitments clear. Meta-ethics remains a part of ethics, but most writings in philosophical ethics now will declare substantive moral positions, either in close association with some meta-ethical outlook or in a more free-standing manner.

Recent meta-ethical discussions have carried on the traditional interest in the *objectivity* of ethics. In this connection, 'moral judgements' are often grouped together and compared with everyday statements of fact or with scientific statements. Some theories claim that moral judgements lack some desirable property that factual statements can attain, such as objectivity or truth, while other theories claim that they can have this property. These debates, particularly those conducted under the influence of positivism, have tended to assimilate two different issues. One concerns the prospects of *rational agreement* in ethical matters. The other concerns the *semantic status* of moral judgements: whether they are, typically, statements at all (as opposed, for instance, to prescriptions), and whether they aim at truth.

Objectivity is best understood in terms of the first kind of question. There clearly are substantive and systematic disagreements about ethical questions, both between different societies or cultures, and within one society (particularly when, as now, the culture of one society may be highly pluralist). Some of these disagreements may turn out to be due to misunderstanding or bad interpretation and dissolve when local practices are better understood, but this is not true of all of them. Since ancient times it has been suggested that these disagreements have a status different from disagreements about facts or about the explanation of natural phenomena. With the latter, if the parties understand the question at issue, they see how after further enquiry they may end up in one of several positions: they may come to rational agreement on one answer or another, they may recognize that such evidence as they can obtain underdetermines the answer and leaves them with intelligible room for continued disagreement, or they may advance in understanding to a point at which they see that the question in its original form cannot be answered, for instance because it was based on a false presupposition.

By contrast, it is suggested that we can understand an ethical dispute perfectly well, and yet it be clear that it need not come out in any of these ways. Disagreeing about an ethical matter, the parties may radically disagree about the kinds of considerations that would settle the question, and the suggestion is that at the end of the line there may be no rational way of arriving at agreement. This is the suggestion that ethical claims lack objectivity. Some theories have associated this position with a view about the semantic status of moral utterances. Emotivism, a theory closely associated with positivism, held that moral utterances were merely expressions of emotion, not far removed from expletives, and it took this, reasonably enough, not to be an objectivist theory. In this case, the semantic account and the denial of objectivity went closely together. However, it is a mistake to think that the two issues are in general simply related to one another.

A clear illustration of this is Kant's theory. Kant supposed that moral statements, or at any rate the most basic of them, were actually prescriptions, and he understood the fundamental principle of morality to be an imperative. However, when the issue is expressed in terms of rational agreement or disagreement, Kant is quite certainly an objectivist: the Categorical Imperative, together in some cases with empirical information, determines for any rational agent what morality requires, and all rational agents are in a position to agree on it. Another example of objectivity which is at least non-committal about the semantics involved comes from virtue theory. Aristotle believed that experienced and discriminating agents who had been properly brought up would reach rational agreement in action, feeling, judgement and interpretation. He

believed, moreover, that this possibility was grounded in the best development
and expression of human nature, and that views about what counted as the
best human development could themselves command rational agreement. This
certainly offers a kind of objectivity, but it does not particularly emphasize
agreement in belief; no doubt some agreement in belief will matter, but so
equally will agreement in feeling and in practical decision.

However, even if objectivity need not imply rational agreement in belief, it
may be argued that the converse holds: that a theory which represents moral
judgements as basically expressing beliefs must be committed to objectivity.
Beliefs, this argument goes, are true or false. If moral judgements express
beliefs, then some of them are true and there is such a thing as truth in
morality. So if people disagree about what to believe, someone must be wrong.
This certainly sounds as though there must be objectivity. The difficulty with
this argument is that it seems to be too easy to agree that moral judgements
admit of truth or falsehood. They are certainly called 'true' and 'false', as even
the emotivists had to concede, and the claim that nevertheless they are not
really true or false needs some deciphering. Emotivism itself offered a
semantic analysis in terms of which such judgements turn out not really to be
statements, which certainly gives some content to the claim that they are not
really true or false. However, such analyses run into difficulty precisely
because the air of being a statement that surrounds moral judgements is not
merely superficial – they behave syntactically just as other kinds of statements
do.

An alternative is to argue that moral judgements can indeed be true or false,
but that nothing interesting follows from this. On some theories of truth,
sometimes called 'redundancy' theories, to claim that 'P' is true is to do no
more than to assert that P. Any theory of truth must accept the equivalence
' "P" is true if and only if P'; the peculiarity of redundancy theories is to claim
that this is all there is to the nature of truth. If this is correct, then the truth or
falsehood of moral judgements will follow simply from their taking a
statemental form, which allows them to be asserted or denied. Objectivity will
then either be understood as something that necessarily goes along with truth
and falsehood, in which case, on the redundancy theory, it will be no more
interesting or substantive than truth; or it will be more interesting and
substantive – implying for instance the possibility of rational agreement – in
which case, on the redundancy view, it will not follow just from the fact that
moral judgements can be true or false.

It is widely, though not universally, agreed that an adequate theory of truth
needs to go beyond the redundancy view, but it is disputed how far it needs to
go. Some argue that if one takes seriously the claim that a given proposition is
true, then this does imply the idea that there could be convergence in belief on
the proposition under favourable circumstances. This approach brings the idea
of truth itself nearer to that of objectivity as that has been introduced here.
Others hold that a properly 'minimalist' theory of truth need not bring in such
a strong condition.

If objectivism and the mere truth of moral statements have often been
assimilated to one another, realism, equally, is often assimilated to one or both

of them. Yet we should expect realism, if it is an issue at all, to be a further issue. Elsewhere in philosophy, for instance in the philosophy of mathematics or the philosophy of science, it can be agreed that statements of a certain kind (about numbers, or about subatomic particles) are capable of truth, and also that they can command rational agreement, and yet it is thought by many philosophers that this does not answer the question whether those statements should be interpreted *realistically*, where this means (very roughly indeed) that the statements are taken to refer to objects that exist independently of our thoughts about them. Even if it is not easy to give a determinate sense to such questions, at any rate one would not expect realism to follow trivially from the claim that moral statements can be true or false.

Some philosophers, influenced by the late John Mackie and in the line of Hume, deny realism by claiming that the moral properties of people, actions, and so forth, are not 'in the world' but are 'projected' on to it from our feelings and reactions. According to the most familiar version of this view, secondary qualities such as colours are also projected on to the world, and this raises the question whether the metaphor has not mislocated the most significant issues about moral properties. The theory implies that ethical outlooks are 'perspectival' or related to human experience in ways in which physical theory (at least) is not, but this does not take us very far: it will not tell us anything very distinctive about ethical realism to know only that ethical concepts are perspectival in a sense in which colour concepts, or perhaps psychological concepts, are also perspectival. An anti-realism that gives moral properties much the same status as colours will probably satisfy many moral realists. We need to ask how far the moral concepts and outlooks of various human groups can intelligibly differ while the rest of their ways of describing the world, in particular their psychological concepts for describing people's behaviour, remain the same. Again, how far can their psychological concepts themselves intelligibly vary, and how should we understand those variations?

In considering such questions, it is helpful to abandon a very limiting assumption which has been made up to this point in the discussion, namely, that all 'moral judgements' are essentially of the same kind and stand in the same relation to such matters as truth and objectivity. In considering moral disagreement, philosophers have concentrated on cases in which the parties express themselves in terms of the 'thin' ethical concepts such as 'good', 'right' and 'ought'. The parties share the same moral and other concepts, and disagree about whether a given judgement should be asserted or denied: they disagree, for instance, about whether capital punishment is wrong. To represent disagreement in this way may seem to isolate in a helpful way its moral focus. But a lot of moral discussion – to differing degrees in different societies – is conducted in terms of 'thick' concepts, such as 'brutality' or 'betrayal' or 'sentimentality', and it is a mistake to suppose that such concepts are merely convenient devices for associating a bunch of empirical considerations with a thin ethical concept. It has been increasingly accepted in recent discussions that the application of such concepts is guided by their evaluative point, and that one cannot understand them without grasping that point. (This does not mean that anyone who understands such a concept must have adopted it as his or her own, but it does mean that he or she needs to have imaginatively identified, as an ethnographer does, with those who use it.) At the same time, however, such concepts apply to some empirical states of affairs and not to others, and there is room for truth, objectivity and knowledge to be displayed in their application.

If this is correct, then it may be more helpful to consider ethical disagreement, not at the ultimate cutting edge of the practical judgements about what ought or ought not to happen, but further back, in the network of more substantive and thicker concepts that back up such judgements. Such concepts will typically serve more purposes than expressing bare 'moral judgements'. They may play a role, for instance, in a scheme of psychological explanation. The question will then become, rather, why and to what extent different cultures differ in their ethical concepts, and, more broadly, in the frameworks of understanding that go with such concepts. Seen in this light, meta-ethical questions move further away from being questions in the philosophy of language or the theory of justification or epistemology, and become more like questions in the theory of cultural understanding. Indeed they may become directly questions of cultural understanding. The most basic question about objectivity may turn out to be the question of the extent to which different human societies share an underlying determinate framework of ethical concepts. By turning in such a direction, philosophical discussion becomes more empirical and historical, more richly related to other disciplines, and more illuminating. At the same time, it means that philosophers have to know about more things, or people in other disciplines have to take on issues in philosophy. To that extent, philosophy tends to lose a distinctive subject matter and its identity becomes blurred.

3 Ethical Theory

I have already said that analytical philosophers are happier than they once were to recognize that what they say in moral philosophy is likely to have a substantive ethical content, and that even meta-ethics is likely to have some such consequences. There is a problem, however, about how this is related to the authority of philosophy. If philosophers are going to offer moral opinions – within their subject, that is to say, and not simply as anyone offers moral opinions – they need to have some professional claim to attention. They are not, as philosophers, necessarily gifted with unusual insight or imagination, and they may not have a significantly wide experience or knowledge of the world. Their claim to attention rests on their capacity for drawing distinctions, seeing the consequences of assumptions, and so forth: in general, on their ability to develop and control a theoretical structure. If the authority of philosophy lies in its status as a theoretical subject, the philosopher's special contribution to substantive ethical issues is likely to be found in a theoretical approach to them. One of the most common enterprises in moral philosophy at present is the development of various ethical theories.

The aim of ethical theory is to cast the content of an ethical outlook into a theoretical form. An ethical theory must contain some meta-ethics, since it takes one view rather than another of what the structure and the central concepts of ethical thought must be, though it need not have an opinion on every meta-ethical issue. It is committed to putting forward in a theoretical form a substantive ethical outlook. In doing this, ethical theories are to different degrees revisionary. Some start with a supposedly undeniable basis for ethics, and reject everyday moral conclusions that conflict with it. (It is a good question why the basis should be regarded as undeniable if it has such consequences.) Others, less dogmatically, consider the moral conclusions that would be delivered by conflicting outlooks, and decide which outlook makes the most coherent systematic sense of those conclusions that we (that is to say, the author and those readers who agree with him or her) find most convincing. Unsystematized but carefully considered judgements about what we would think it right to do in a certain situation, or would be prepared to say in approval or criticism of people and their actions, are often called in the context of such a method 'moral intuitions'. (The term 'intuition' has a purely methodological force: it means only that these judgements seem to us, after consideration, pre-theoretically convincing, not that they are derived from a faculty of intuiting moral truths.) A preferred method is to seek what John Rawls has called a 'reflective equilibrium' between theory and intuitions, modifying the theory to accommodate robust intuitions, and discarding some intuitions which clash with the theory, particularly if one can see how they might be the product of prejudice or confusion.

Moral theories are standardly presented as falling into three basic types, centring respectively on *consequences*, *rights* and *virtues*. The first are unsurprisingly called 'consequentialist', and the last 'virtue theories'. The second are often called 'deontological', which means that they are centred on duty or obligation, but this is a cross-classification, since consequentialist theories also give prominence to an obligation, that of bringing about the best consequences. (In the case of the most familiar and popular consequentialist theory, utilitarianism, the value of the consequences is expressed in terms of welfare or preference-satisfaction.) In terms of obligations, the difference is rather that pure consequentialist theories present only one basic obligation, while the second type of theory has many. A more distinctive mark of difference is to be found in the idea of a *right*: the second type of theory grounds many of an agent's obligations in the rights of others to expect certain behaviour from that agent, a kind of consideration that utilitarians and other consequentialists regard as being at best derivative, and at worst totally spurious.

Another way of understanding the division into three is in terms of what each theory sees as most basically bearing ethical value. For the first type of theory, it is *good states of affairs*, and right action is understood as action tending to bring about good states of affairs. For the second type, it is *right action*; sometimes what makes an action right is a fact about its consequences, but often it is not – its rightness is determined rather by respect for others' rights, or by other obligations that the agent may have. Virtue theory, finally, puts most emphasis on the idea of a *good person*, someone who could be described also as an ethically admirable person. This is an important emphasis, and the notion of a virtue is important in ethics. However, once the types of theory are distinguished in this way, it is hard to see them as all in the same line of business. Consequentialist and rights theories aim to systematize our principles or rules of action in ways that will, supposedly, help us to see what to do or recommend in particular cases. A theory of the virtues can hardly do that: the theory itself, after all, is going to say that what you basically need in order to do and recommend the right things are virtues, not a theory about virtues. Moreover, virtuous people do not think always, or usually, about the virtues. They think about such things as good consequences or people's rights, and this makes it clear that 'virtue theory' cannot be on the same level as the other two types of theory.

4 Morality, Politics and Analytical Philosophy

Among moral concepts, that of rights is closest to law and also to politics, and philosophical discussions of them often cross those boundaries. Given these relations, it is not surprising that the kind of theory most often constructed to articulate the idea of moral rights is contractualist, invoking the idea of an agreement that might be rationally arrived at by parties in some hypothetical situation in which they were required to make rules by which they could live together. The inspiration of contractualist theories goes back, in particular, to Kant. Kant's own construction relies on some ideas that are not shared by many modern theorists, in particular that a commitment to the basic principle of morality (the so-called 'Categorical Imperative') is presupposed by the very activity of a rational agent. It also involves a very obscure doctrine of freedom. The modern theories inspired by Kantian ideas are less committed than Kant was to showing that morality is ultimate rationality, and they allow also more empirical material into the construction than Kant did.

The leading example of such a theory is that of John Rawls. His model of a set of contracting parties reaching an agreement behind 'a veil of ignorance' has had an immense influence on thinking about morality. It was designed for a purpose in political philosophy, of constructing a theory of social justice. In Rawls' theory, the veil of ignorance is introduced to disguise from each contractor his own particular advantages and disadvantages and his own eventual position in the society that is being designed. The political theory that uses this thought experiment is liberal, giving a high priority to liberty and at the same time emphasizing redistribution of resources in the interests of the disadvantaged. It is significant that when Rawls first produced his theory he saw it in universalist terms, as offering a construction of social justice which would apply to any society that met the conditions (very roughly) of being able to think about social ideals and having the resources to implement them. Now, however, he has moved in the direction of seeing the theory of justice as one that expresses the aspirations of a particular social formation, the modern pluralist state.

Much recent political philosophy has centred on this liberal project, of defining terms of just co-existence for people living in a pluralist society. One interpretation of that aim is to look for terms of co-existence that will not presuppose a common conception of the good. On such an account, citizens can understand themselves as sharing a social existence although they have as individuals, or as members of communities less extensive than the state, varying conceptions of a good life. Rawls has interpreted his own purpose in those terms; it is expressed, for instance, in the fact that the parties in the original position were supposed to make their decision on (broadly) self-interested grounds, and not in the light of any antecedent conception of what a good society would be. The values that they were taken to have were expressed only in the list of 'primary goods' in terms of which they made their choice, a list which made it clear already that they set a high value on liberty, for instance, and did not assess everything in terms of utility.

In fact, Rawls' aim of making his theory as independent as possible from substantial claims about the good does put it under some strain. At least in the first version of the theory, the basic conception of justice included a large-scale commitment to economic redistribution, and while this made it very welcome to many liberals (particularly in the American sense of that word), it laid it open to the criticism from others more inclined to libertarianism, such as Robert Nozick, that the theory incorporated not only rightful terms of co-existence but a substantial and distinctive conception of social justice as economic equality. In the later versions of Rawls' theory, this conception is less prominent, but even more weight than before is laid on the idea that co-existence in a liberal pluralist society is not 'a mere *modus vivendi*' but a condition that calls on important moral powers of toleration and respect for autonomy. This emphasis does seem to express a distinctive conception of the good, of a Kantian kind, to a point at which it looks as though the condition of pluralism is not simply a contingency of modern life, but an important vehicle of ethical self-expression.

Others, such as Ronald Dworkin, have pursued liberal theory, and in pluralist terms, while accepting a commitment to a distinctive conception of the good. Others, again, have claimed to reject liberal pluralism altogether and have turned in what is sometimes called a 'communitarian' direction. It is hard to tell in some cases where writers of this tendency stand in relation to the politics of liberalism. While a few, notably Alasdair MacIntyre, despairing of the whole enterprise, try only to diagnose our condition and store some ethical goods for a better time, others seem to share in the liberal undertaking but prefer, in opposition to Rawls' Kantianism, a more Hegelian type of discourse to express it.

It is a rather odd feature of communitarian theories, at least if they take a traditionalist turn, that they recommend a politics that does not sit very easily with the existence of such theories themselves, except perhaps as a kind of interim measure. They seek a politics in which people's relations are formed by shared understandings which to a considerable extent must be unspoken and taken for granted, and the exchange of abstract political theories plays no obvious role in this conception of social life. (Hegel, many of whose concerns are re-enacted in these debates, thought he had an answer to this, in his conception of a society that could ultimately reconcile abstract understanding and concrete practice, but few current disputants are happy to pay the price of admission to the Hegelian system.)

The liberals, on the other hand, have a conception of modern political life which at least coherently embraces the existence of their own theories, since they understand the modern state as a formation in which authority is peculiarly vested in discursive argument, rather than in traditional or charismatic leadership. It is true that many political philosophers in the analytical tradition (unlike Rawls himself, and also unlike Habermas, who comes from a sociological tradition) do not see the role of their theories in these terms, but rather as advancing trans-historical views about the demands of a just political order. But even if liberals do not always recognize the point themselves, the role of theory in liberal political philosophy can be given a special justification in terms of current political reality. Liberals coherently believe that the project of political theory makes sense, because they are committed to thinking that in our circumstances it makes sense to engage in a political activity of explaining the basic principles of democratic government in such terms.

In this respect, moral philosophy is in an altogether worse situation. It typically lacks an account of why the project of articulating moral *theories* makes any sense at all. As many writers have pointed out, it bears little relation to the psychology of people's ethical lives, and inasmuch as it claims that turning morality into a theory makes it more rational, there is a pressing question of what concept of rationality is being invoked. To a limited extent, there may be an answer to that question, inasmuch as some ethical questions, such as those raised by medical ethics, are public questions, closely tied to politics and the law. In those cases, we need a public discourse to legitimate some answers, since it is a public issue what should be permitted, and mere appeals to ethical or professional authority will no longer do. But it would be a mistake to suppose that in such cases we are presented with a pure concept of moral rationality which we then apply to our historical circumstances. Rather, what counts as a rational way of discussing such questions is influenced by the historical circumstances, and above all by the need to give a discursive justification, in something like a legal style, for procedures which increasingly are adopted in a public domain and can be challenged in it.

Moreover, many important ethical issues are not of this kind at all. Morality has always been connected not only with law and politics, but also with the meaning of an individual's life and his or her relations to other people. In these connections, the authority of theory over the moral life remains quite opaque. Certainly, it will not do to rely on the inference: philosophy must have something to say about the moral life; the most responsible form of philosophy is analytical philosophy; what analytical philosophy is best at is theory; so philosophy's contribution to the moral life is theory. In rejecting this uninviting argument, some will want to attack the second premise. However, it may be more constructive, and offer more of a challenge to thinking about what one wants of philosophy, if one reconsiders the third premise, that what analytical philosophy does best is theory. Analytical philosophy's own virtues, such as its unfanatical truthfulness, could encourage it in ethics to remind us of detail rather than bludgeon us with theory.

Truthfulness in personal life, and even in politics, is not necessarily opposed to the exercise of the imagination. It is relevant here that an imaginative truthfulness is a virtue in the arts. Writers in moral philosophy sometimes urge us to extend our ethical understanding by turning to imaginative literature, in particular the novel. To the extent that this is good advice, it is not because novels are convenient sources of psychological information, still less because some of them are morally edifying. It is because imaginative writing can powerfully evoke the strength of ethical considerations in giving sense to someone's life or to a passage of it, and, equally, present the possible complexity, ambivalence and ultimate insecurity of those considerations. Good literature stands against the isolation of moral considerations from the psychological and social forces that both empower and threaten them. But this isolation of moral considerations from the rest of experience is an illusion very much fostered by moral philosophy itself; indeed, without that illusion some forms of moral philosophy could not exist at all. So there are lessons here not just for philosophy's use of other writing, but for philosophical writing itself. The truthfulness that it properly seeks involves imaginative honesty and not just argumentative accuracy.

Analytical philosophy, or some recognizable descendant of it, should be able to make a richer contribution to ethics than has often been the case up to now. If it is to do so, it will need to hold on to two truths which it tends to forget (not only in ethics, but most damagingly there): that philosophy cannot be too pure, and must merge with other kinds of understanding; and that being soberly truthful does not exclude, but may actually demand, the imagination.

1
Epistemology ————————————————————

A. C. Grayling

For most of the modern period of philosophy, from Descartes to the present, epistemology has been the central philosophical discipline. It raises questions about the scope and limits of knowledge, its sources and justification, and it deals with sceptical arguments concerning our claims to knowledge and justified belief. This chapter firstly considers difficulties facing attempts to define knowledge and, secondly, explores influential responses to the challenge of scepticism. Epistemology is closely related to METAPHYSICS (chapter 2), which is the philosophical account of what kinds of entities there are. Epistemological questions are also crucial to most of the other areas of philosophy examined in this volume, from ETHICS (chapter 6) to PHILOSOPHY OF SCIENCE (chapter 9) and PHILOSOPHY OF MATHEMATICS (chapter 10) to PHILOSOPHY OF HISTORY (chapter 13). Chapters on individuals or groups of philosophers from DESCARTES (see chapter 17) to KANT (chapter 22) discuss classical epistemology, while several chapters about more recent philosophers also follow epistemological themes.

Introduction

Epistemology, which is also called the theory of knowledge, is the branch of philosophy concerned with enquiry into the nature, sources and validity of knowledge. Among the chief questions it attempts to answer are: What is knowledge? How do we get it? Can our means of getting it be defended against sceptical challenge? These questions are implicitly as old as philosophy, although their first explicit treatment is to be found in PLATO (c.427–347 BC) (see chapter 15), in particular in his *Theaetetus*. But it is primarily in the modern era, from the seventeenth century onwards – as a result of the work of DESCARTES (1596–1650) (chapter 17) and LOCKE (1632–1704) (chapter 19) in association with the rise of modern science – that epistemology has occupied centre-stage in philosophy.

One obvious step towards answering epistemology's first question is to attempt a definition. The standard preliminary definition has it that knowledge is *justified true belief*. This definition looks plausible because, at the very least, it seems that to know something one must believe it, that the belief must be true, and that one's reason for believing it must be satisfactory in the light of some criterion – for one could not be said to know something if one's reasons for believing it were arbitrary or haphazard. So each of the three parts of the definition appears to express a necessary condition for knowledge, and the claim is that, taken together, they are sufficient.

There are, however, serious difficulties with this idea, particularly about the nature of the justification required for true belief to amount to knowledge. Competing proposals have been offered to meet the difficulties, either by adding further conditions or by finding a better statement of the definition as it stands. The first part of the following discussion considers these proposals.

In parallel with the debate about how to define knowledge is another about how knowledge is acquired. In the history of epistemology there have been two chief schools of thought about what constitutes the chief means to knowledge. One is the 'rationalist' school (see chapter 17), which holds that reason plays this role. The other is the 'empiricist' (see chapters 19, 20 and 21), which holds that it is experience, principally the use of the senses aided when necessary by scientific instruments, which does so.

The paradigm of knowledge for rationalists is mathematics and logic, where necessary truths are arrived at by intuition and rational inference. Questions about the nature of reason, the justification of inference, and the nature of truth, especially necessary truth, accordingly press to be answered.

The empiricists' paradigm is natural science, where observation and experiment are crucial to enquiry. The history of science in the modern era lends support to empiricism's case; but precisely for that reason philosophical questions about perception, observation, evidence and experiment have acquired great importance.

But for both traditions in epistemology the central concern is whether we can trust the routes to knowledge they respectively nominate. sceptical arguments suggest that we cannot simply assume them to be trustworthy; indeed, they suggest that work is required to show that they are. The effort to respond to scepticism therefore provides a sharp way of understanding what is crucial in epistemology. Part 2 below is accordingly concerned with an analysis of scepticism and some responses to it.

There are other debates in epistemology about, among other things, memory, judgement, introspection, reasoning, the 'a priori–a posteriori' distinction, scientific method and the methodological differences, if any, between the natural and the social sciences; however, the questions considered here are basic to them all.

1. Knowledge

1.1 Defining knowledge

There are different ways in which one might be said to have knowledge. One can know people or places, in the sense of being acquainted with them. That is what is meant when one says, 'My father knew Lloyd George.' One can know how to do something, in the sense of having an ability or skill. That is what is meant when one says, 'I know how to play chess.' And one can know that something is the case, as when one says, 'I know that Everest is the highest mountain.' This last is sometimes called 'propositional knowledge', and it is the kind epistemologists most wish to understand.

The definition of knowledge already mentioned – knowledge as justified true belief – is intended to be an analysis of knowledge in the propositional sense. The definition is arrived at by asking what conditions have to be satisfied if we are correctly to describe someone as knowing something. In giving the definition we state what we hope are the necessary and sufficient conditions for the truth of the claim 'S knows that p', where 'S' is the epistemic subject – the putative knower – and 'p' a proposition.

The definition carries an air of plausibility, at least as applied to empirical knowledge, because it seems to meet the minimum we can be expected to need from so consequential a concept. It seems right to expect that if S knows that p, then p must at least be true. It seems right to expect that S must not merely wonder whether or hope that p is the case, but must have a positive epistemic attitude to it: S must believe that it is true. And if S believes some true proposition while having no grounds, or incorrect grounds, or merely arbitrary or fanciful grounds, for doing so, we would not say that S knows p; which means that S must have grounds for believing p which in some sense properly justify doing so.

Of these proposed conditions for knowledge, it is the third that gives most trouble. The reason is simply illustrated by counter-examples. These take the form of cases in which S believes a true proposition for what are in fact the wrong reasons, although they are from his or her own point of view persuasive. For instance, suppose S has two friends, T and U. The latter is travelling abroad, but S has no idea where. As for T, S saw him buying and thereafter driving about in a Rolls Royce, and therefore believes that he owns one. Now, from any proposition p one can validly infer the disjunction 'p or q'. So S has grounds for believing 'T owns a Rolls or U is in Paris', even though, *ex hypothesi*, he has no idea of U's location. But suppose T in fact does not own the Rolls – he bought it for someone else, on whose behalf he also drives it. And further suppose that U is indeed, by chance, in Paris. Then S believes, with justification, a true proposition: but we should not want to call his belief knowledge.

Examples like this are strained, but they do their work; they show that more needs to be said about justification before we can claim to have an adequate account of knowledge.

1.2 Justification

A preliminary question concerns whether having justification for believing some p entails p's truth, for, if so, counter-examples of the kind just mentioned get no purchase and we need not seek ways of blocking them. There is indeed a view, called 'infallibilism', which offers just such a resource. It states that if it is true that S knows p, then S cannot be mistaken in believing

p, and therefore his justification for believing p guarantees its truth. The claim is, in short, that one cannot be justified in believing a false proposition.

This view is rejected by 'fallibilists', who claim that one can indeed have justification for believing some p although it is false. Their counter to infallibilism turns on identifying a mistake in its supporting argument. The mistake is that whereas the truth of 'S knows that p' indeed rules out the possibility that S is in error, this is far from saying that S is so placed that he cannot possibly be wrong about p. It is right to say: (1) '*it is impossible* for S to be wrong about p if he knows p', but it is not invariably right to say (2) 'if S knows p, then *it is impossible* for him to be wrong about p'. The mistake turns on thinking that the correct wide scope reading (1) of 'it is impossible' licenses the narrow scope reading (2) which constitutes infallibilism.

An infallibilist account makes the definition of knowledge look simple: S knows p if his belief in it is infallibly justified. But this definition renders the notion of knowledge too restrictive, for it says that S can justifiably believe p only when the possibility of p's falsity is excluded. Yet it appears to be a commonplace of epistemic experience that one can have the very best evidence for believing something and yet be wrong (as the account of scepticism given below is at pains to show) which is to say that fallibilism seems the only account of justification adequate to the facts of epistemic life. We need therefore to see whether fallibilist theories of justification can give us an adequate account of knowledge.

The problem for fallibilist accounts is precisely the one illustrated by the Rolls Royce example above, and others similar to it (so-called 'Gettier examples', introduced in Gettier, 1963), namely, that one's justification for believing p does not connect with the truth of p in the right way, and perhaps not at all. What is required is an account that will suitably connect S's justification both with his belief that p and with p's truth.

What is needed is a clear picture of 'justified belief.' If one can identify what justifies a belief, one has gone all or most of the way to saying what justification is; and *en route* one will have displayed the right connection between justification, on the one hand, and belief and truth on the other. In this connection there are several standard species of theory.

Foundationalism

One class of theories of justification employs the metaphor of an edifice. Most of our ordinary beliefs require support from others; we justify a given belief by appealing to another or others on which it rests. But if the chain of justifying beliefs were to regress without terminating in a belief that is in some way independently secure, thereby providing a foundation for the others, we would seem to lack justification for any belief in the chain. It appears necessary therefore that there should be beliefs which do not need justification, or which are in some way self-justifying, to serve as an epistemic underpinning.

On this view a justified belief is one which either is, or is supported by, a foundational belief. The next steps therefore are to make clear the notion of a 'foundation' and to explain how foundational beliefs 'support' non-foundational ones. Some way of understanding foundationalism without reliance on constructional metaphors is needed.

It is not enough barely to state that a foundational belief is a belief that requires no justification, for there must be a reason why this is the case. What makes a belief independent or self-standing in the required way? It is standardly claimed that such beliefs justify themselves, or are self-evident, or are indefeasible or incorrigible. These are not the same things. A belief might be self-justifying without being self-evident (it might take hard work to see that it justifies itself). Indefeasibility means that no further evidence or other, competing, beliefs, can render a given belief insecure. Yet this is a property that the belief might have independently of whether or not it is self-justifying. And so on. But what these characterizations are intended to convey is the idea that a certain immunity from doubt, error or revision attaches to the beliefs in question.

It might even be unnecessary or mistaken to think that it is *belief* that provides the foundations for the edifice of knowledge: some other state might do so. Perceptual states have been offered as candidates, because they appear to be suitably incorrigible – if one seems to see a red patch, say, then one cannot be wrong that one seems to see a red patch. And it appears plausible to say that one's belief that p needs no further justification or foundation than that things appear to one as p describes them to be.

These suggestions bristle with difficulties. Examples of self-evident or self-justifying beliefs tend to be drawn from logic and mathematics – they are of the 'x is x' or 'one plus one equals two' variety, which critics are quick to point out give little help in grounding contingent beliefs. Perceptual states likewise turn out to be unlikely candidates for foundations, on the grounds that perception involves the application of beliefs which themselves stand in need of justification – among them beliefs about the nature of things and the laws they obey. What is most robustly contested is the 'myth of the given', the idea that there are firm, primitive and original *data* which experience supplies to our minds, antecedent to and untainted by judgement, furnishing the wherewithal to secure the rest of our beliefs.

There is a difficulty also about how justification is transmitted from foundational beliefs to dependent beliefs. It is too strong a claim to say that the latter are deducible from them. Most if not all contingent beliefs are not entailed by the beliefs that support them; the evidence I have that I am now sitting at my desk is about as strong as empirical evidence can be, yet given the standard sceptical considerations (such as, for example, the possibility that I am now dreaming) it does not entail that I am sitting here.

If the relation is not a deductive one, what is it? Other candidate relations – inductive or criterial – are by their nature defeasible, and therefore, unless somehow supplemented, insufficient to the task of transmitting justification from the foundations to other beliefs. The supplementation would have to consist of guarantees that the circumstances that defeat non-deductive justification do not in fact obtain. But if such guarantees – understood, to avoid circularity, as not being part of the putative foundations themselves – were available to protect non-deductive grounds, then appeal to a notion of foundations looks simply otiose.

1.3 Coherence

Dissatisfaction with foundationalism has led some epistemologists to prefer saying that a belief is justified if it coheres with those in an already accepted set. The immediate task is to specify what coherence is, and to find a way of dealing in a non-circular way with the problem of how the already accepted beliefs came to be so.

Hard on the heels of this task comes a number of questions. Is coherence a negative criterion (that is, a belief lacks justification if it fails to cohere with the set) or a positive one (that is, a belief is justified when it coheres with the set)? And is it to be understood strongly (by which coherence is sufficient for justification) or weakly (by which coherence is one among other justifying features)?

The concept of coherence has its theoretical basis in the notion of a system, understood as a set whose elements stand in mutual relations of both consistency and (some kind of) interdependence. Consistency is of course a minimum requirement, and goes without saying. Dependence is more difficult to specify suitably. It would be far too strong – for it would give rise to assertive redundancy – to require that dependence means mutual entailment among beliefs (this is what some have required, citing geometry as the closest example). A more diffuse notion has it that a set of beliefs is coherent if any one of them follows from all the rest, and if no subset of them is logically independent of the remainder. But this is vague, and anyway seems to require that the set be known to be complete before one can judge whether a given belief coheres with it.

A remedy might be to say that a belief coheres with an antecedent set if it can be inferred from it, or from some significant subset within it, as being the best explanation in the case. To this someone might object that not all justifications take the form of explanations. An alternative might be to say that a belief is justified if it survives comparison with competitors for acceptance among the antecedent set. But here an objector might ask how this can be sufficient, since by itself this does not show why the belief merits acceptance over equally cohering rivals. Indeed, any theory of justification has to ensure as much for candidate beliefs, so there is nothing about the proposal that distinctively supports the coherence theory. And these thoughts leave un-examined the question of the 'antecedent set' and *its* justification, which cannot be a matter of coherence, for with what is it to cohere in its turn?

1.4 Internalism and externalism

Both the foundationalist and coherence theories are sometimes described as 'internalist' because they describe justification as consisting in internal relations among beliefs, either – as in the former case – from a vertical relation of support between supposedly basic beliefs and others dependent upon them, or – as in the latter – from the mutual support of beliefs in an appropriately understood system.

Generally characterized, internalist theories assert or assume that a belief cannot be justified for an epistemic subject S unless S has access to what provides the justification, either in fact or in principle. These theories generally involve the stronger 'in fact' requirement because S's being justified in believing p is standardly cashed in terms of his having reasons for taking p to be true, where *having reasons* is to be understood in an occurrent sense.

Here an objection immediately suggests itself. Any S has only finite access to what might justify or undermine his beliefs, and that access is confined to his particular viewpoint. It seems that full justification for his beliefs would rarely be available, because his experience would be restricted to what is nearby in space and time, and he would be entitled to hold only those beliefs which his limited experience licensed.

A related objection is that internalism seems inconsistent with the fact that many people appear to have knowledge despite not being sophisticated enough to recognize that thus-and-so is a reason for believing p – that is the case, for example, with children.

A more general objection still is that relations between beliefs, whether of the foundationalist or coherence type, might obtain without the beliefs in question being true of anything beyond themselves. One could imagine a coherent fairy tale, say, which in no point corresponds to some external reality, but in which beliefs are justified nevertheless by their mutual relations.

This uneasy reflection prompts the thought that there should be a constraint on theories of justification, in the form of a demand that there should be some suitable connection between belief possession and external factors – that is, something other than the beliefs and their mutual relations – which determines their epistemic value. This accordingly prompts the idea of an alternative: externalism.

1.5 Reliability, causality and truth-tracking

Externalism is the view that what makes S justified in believing p might not be anything to which S has cognitive access. It might be that the facts in the world are as S believes them to be, and that indeed they caused S to believe them to be so by stimulating his or her sensory receptors in the right kind of way. S need not be aware that this is how his or her belief was formed. So S could be justified in believing p without it.

One main kind of externalist theory is reliabilism, the thesis – or cluster of theses – having it that a belief is justified if it is reliably connected with the truth. According to one influential variant, the connection in question is supplied by reliable belief-forming *processes*, ones which have a high success rate in producing true beliefs. An example of a reliable process might be normal perception in normal conditions.

Much apparent plausibility attaches to theories based on the notion of external linkage, especially of causal linkage, between a belief and what it is about. An example of such a theory is Alvin Goldman's account (1986) of knowledge as 'appropriately caused true belief', where 'appropriate causation' takes a number of forms, sharing the property that they are processes which are both 'globally' and 'locally' reliable – the former meaning that the process has a high success rate in producing true beliefs, the latter that the process would not have produced the belief in question in some 'relevant counterfactual situation' where the belief is false. Goldman's view is accordingly a paradigm of a reliabilist theory.

An elegant second-cousin of this view is offered by Robert Nozick (Nozick, 1981). To the conditions

(1) p is true

and

(2) S believes p

Nozick adds

(3) if p were not true, S would not believe p

and

(4) if p were true, S would believe it.

Conditions (3) and (4) are intended to block Gettier-type counter-examples to the justified true belief analysis by annexing S's belief that p firmly to p's truth. S's belief that p is connected to the world (to the situation described by p) by a relation Nozick calls 'tracking': S's belief *tracks* the truth that p. He adds refinements in an attempt to deflect the counter-examples that philosophers are always ingenious and fertile at devising.

If these theories seem plausible it is because they accord with our pre-theoretical views. But as one can readily see, there are plenty of things to object to in them, and a copious literature does so. Their most serious flaw, however, is that they are question-begging. They do not address the question of how S is to be confident that a given belief is justified; instead they help themselves to two weighty realist assumptions, one about the domain over which belief ranges and the other about how the domain and S are connected, so that they can assert that S is justified in believing a given p even if what justifies him lies outside his own epistemic competence. Whatever else one thinks of these suggestions, they do not enlighten S, and therefore do not engage the same problem that internalist theories address.

But worst of all – so an austere critic might say – the large assumptions to which these theories help themselves are precisely those that epistemology should be examining. Externalist and causal theories, in whatever guise and combination, are better done by empirical psychology where the standard assumptions about the external world and S's connections with it are premised. Philosophy, surely, is where these premises themselves come in for scrutiny.

1.6 Knowledge, belief and justification again

Consider this argument: 'If anyone knows some p, then he or she can be certain that p. But no one can be certain of anything. Therefore no one knows anything.' This argument (advanced in this form by Unger, 1975) is instructive. It repeats Descartes' mistake of thinking that the psychological state of feeling certain – which someone can be in with respect to falsehoods, such as the fact that I can feel *certain* that Arkle will win the Derby next week, and be wrong

– is what we are seeking in epistemology. But it also exemplifies the tendency in discussions of *knowledge* as such to make the definition of knowledge so highly restrictive that little or nothing passes muster. Should one care if a suggested definition of knowledge is such that, as the argument just quoted tells us, no one can know anything? Just so long as one has many well-justified beliefs which work well in practice, can one not be quite content to know nothing? For my part, I think one can.

This suggests that in so far as the points sketched in preceding paragraphs have interest, it is in connection with the *justification of beliefs* and not the *definition of knowledge* that they do so. Justification is an important matter, not least because in the areas of application in epistemology where the really serious interest should lie – in questions about the PHILOSOPHY OF SCIENCE (chapter 9), the PHILOSOPHY OF HISTORY (chapter 13) or the concepts of evidence and proof in LAW (see chapter 12) – justification is the crucial problem. That is where epistemologists should be getting down to work. By comparison, efforts to define 'knowledge' are trivial and occupy too much effort in epistemology. The disagreeable propensity of the debate generated by Gettier's counter-examples – anticipated beautifully in Russell's review of James (Russell, 1910, p. 95) – to proceed on a chessboard of '-isms', as exemplified above, is a symptom.

The general problem with justification is that the procedures we adopt, across all walks of epistemic life, appear highly permeable to difficulties posed by scepticism. The problem of justification is therefore in large part the problem of scepticism; which is precisely why discussion of scepticism is central to epistemology.

2 Scepticism

Introduction

The study and employment of sceptical arguments might in one sense be said to define epistemology. A chief epistemological aim is to determine how we can be sure that our means to knowledge (here 'knowledge' does duty for 'justified belief') are satisfactory. A sharp way to show what is required is to look carefully at sceptical challenges to our epistemic efforts, challenges which suggest ways in which they can go awry. If we are able not just to identify but to meet these challenges, a primary epistemological aim will have been realized.

Scepticism is often described as the thesis that nothing is – or, more strongly, can be – known. But this is a bad characterization, because if we know nothing, then we do not know that we know nothing, and so the claim is trivially self-defeating. It is more telling to characterize scepticism in the way just suggested. It is a challenge directed against knowledge claims, with the form and nature of the challenge varying according to the field of epistemic activity in question. In general, scepticism takes the form of a request for the justification of those knowledge claims, together with a statement of the reasons motivating that request. Standardly, the reasons are that certain considerations suggest that the proposed justification might be insufficient. To conceive of scepticism like this is to see it as being more philosophically troubling and important than if it is described as a positive thesis asserting our ignorance or incapacity for knowledge.

2.1 Early scepticism

Some among the thinkers of antiquity – Pyrrho of Elis (*c.*360–*c.*270 BC) and his school, and Plato's successors in his Academy – expressed disappointment at the fact that centuries of enquiry by their philosophical predecessors seemed to have borne little fruit either in cosmology or ethics (this latter was broadly construed to include politics). Their disappointment prompted them to sceptical views. The Pyrrhonians argued that because enquiry is arduous and interminable, one should give up trying to judge what is true and false or right and wrong; for only thus will we achieve peace of mind.

A less radical form of scepticism overtook Plato's successors in the Academy. They agreed with Pyrrho that certainty must elude us, but they tempered their view by accepting that the practical demands of life must be met. They did not think it a workable option to 'suspend judgement' as Pyrrho recommended, and therefore argued that we should accept those propositions or theories which are more PROBABLE (pp. 314–16) than their competitors. The views of these thinkers, known as Academic sceptics, are recorded in the work of Sextus Empiricus (*c.*150–*c.*225).

In the later Renaissance – or, which is the same thing, in early modern times – with religious certainties under attack and new ideas abroad, some of the sceptical arguments of the Academics and Pyrrhonians acquired a special significance, notably as a result of the use to which René Descartes put them in showing that they are powerful tools for investigating the nature and sources of knowledge.

In Descartes' day the same person could be both astronomer and astrologer, chemist and alchemist, or physician and magician. It was hard to disentangle knowledge from nonsense; it was even harder to disentangle those methods of enquiry which might yield genuine knowledge from those that could only deepen ignorance. So there was an urgent need for some sharp, clean epistemological theorizing. In his *Meditations* (1986) Descartes accordingly identified epistemology as an essential preliminary to physics and mathematics, and attempted to establish the grounds of certainty as a propaedeutic to science. Descartes' first step in that task was to adapt and apply some of the traditional arguments of scepticism. (I shall comment on his use of scepticism again later.)

The Anatomy of Scepticism

Sceptical arguments exploit certain contingent facts about our ways of acquiring, testing, remembering and reasoning about our beliefs. Any problem that infects the acquisition and employment of beliefs about a given subject matter, and in particular any problem that infects our confidence that we hold those beliefs justifiably, threatens our hold on that subject matter.

The contingent facts in question relate to the nature of perception, the normal human vulnerability to error and the existence of states of mind – for example, dreaming and delusion – which can be subjectively indistinguishable from those that we normally take to be appropriate for acquiring justified beliefs. By appealing to these considerations the sceptic aims to show that there are significant questions to be answered about the degree of confidence that we are entitled to repose in our standard epistemic practices.

Sceptical considerations pose problems for epistemologists of both the rationalist and the empiricist camps. This division into competing schools of thought about knowledge is rough but useful, giving a shorthand way of marking the difference between those who hold that reason is the chief means to knowledge, and those who accord that role to experience. Rationalists emphasize reason because in their view the objects of knowledge are propositions that are eternally, immutably and necessarily true – the examples they offer are the propositions of mathematics and logic – and these, they say, can only be acquired by reasoning. Empiricists hold that substantive and genuine knowledge of the world can only be learned through experience, by means of the senses and their extension *via* such instruments as telescopes and microscopes. The rationalist need not deny that empirical awareness is an important, even an ineliminable, aid to reason, nor need the empiricist deny that reason is an important, even an ineliminable, aid to experience; but both will insist that the chief means to knowledge is respectively one or the other.

The refinements of debate about these matters merit detailed examination for which this is not the place. For present purposes, the point to note is that scepticism is a problem for both schools of thought. For both, possibilities of error and delusion pose a challenge. For the empiricist in particular, to these must be added distinctive problems about perception.

2.2 Error, delusion and dreams

One characteristic pattern of sceptical argument is drawn from a set of considerations about error, delusions and dreams. Consider the error argument first. We are fallible creatures; we sometimes make mistakes. If, however, we are ever to be able to claim to know (that is, at least to be justified in believing) some proposition p, we must be able to exclude the possibility that at the time of claiming to know p we are in error. But since we typically, or at least frequently, are not aware of our errors as we make them, and might therefore unwittingly be in error as we claim to know p, we are not justified in making that claim.

The same applies when a person is the subject of a delusion, illusion or hallucination. Sometimes people undergoing one or other of these states do not know that they are doing so, and take themselves to be having veridical experiences. Clearly, although they think they are in a state which lends itself to their being justified in claiming to know p, they are not in such a state. Therefore they are not justified in claiming to know p. So in order for anyone to claim knowledge of some p, they must be able to exclude the possibility that they are the subject of such states.

This pattern of argument is at its most familiar in the argument from dreaming employed by Descartes. One way of setting it out is as follows. When I sleep I sometimes dream, and when I dream I sometimes – indeed, often – do not know that I am dreaming. So I can have experiences that appear to be veridical waking experiences on the basis of which I take myself to be justified in claiming to know such and such. But because I am dreaming, I do not in fact know such and such; I merely dream that I do. Might I not be dreaming now? If I cannot exclude the possibility that I am now, at this moment, dreaming, I am unable to claim knowledge of the things I at this moment take myself to know. For example, it seems to me that I am sitting at a desk next to a window admitting a view of trees and lawns. But because I might be dreaming that this is so, I cannot claim to know it.

In these arguments the possibility of error, delusion or dreaming acts as what might be called a 'defeater' to knowledge claims. The pattern is: if one knows *p*, then nothing is acting to subvert one's justification to claim knowledge of *p*. But one can seem to oneself fully entitled to claim to know some *p*, and in fact lack that entitlement, as the foregoing considerations show. So our claims to knowledge are in need of better grounds than we standardly take ourselves to have. We must find a way of defeating the defeaters.

2.3 Perception

Both rationalist and empiricist views about the sources of knowledge are threatened by the arguments just sketched. Arguments that pose particular problems for empiricism are suggested by the nature and limitations of perception, the best current account of which tells us something like the following story.

Light reflects from the surfaces of objects in the physical environment and passes into the eyes, where it irritates the cells of the retinas in such a way as to trigger impulses in the optic nerves. The optic nerves convey these impulses to the region of the cerebral cortex that processes visual data, where they stimulate certain sorts of activity. As a result, in ways still mysterious to science and philosophy, coloured 'motion pictures' arise in the subject's consciousness, representing the world outside his or her head. This remarkable transaction is repeated *mutatis mutandis* in the other sensory modalities of hearing, smell, taste and touch, giving rise to perceptions of harmonies and melodies, perfumes and piquancies, smoothness, softness, warmth – and so forth.

This model can be used to furnish another sceptical application of the defeater argument. The complex causal story thus told is one which – so the sceptic can point out – might be interrupted in problematic ways at any point along its length. The experiences which we say result from the interaction of our senses and the world might occur in us for other reasons. They might occur when, as noted above, we dream, hallucinate or suffer delusions; or, to be fanciful, they might be produced in us by a god, or by a scientist who has connected our brains to a computer. From the point of view of the experiencing subject, there might be no way of telling the difference. So, says the sceptic, unless we find means of excluding these possibilities, we are not entitled to claim knowledge of what we standardly take ourselves to know.

2.4 Perceptual relativities

These same considerations about perception can prompt sceptical challenge by a different route. A little reflection of the kind taught us by Locke, BERKELEY (1685–1753) (chapter 20) and other earlier contributors to the debate shows that some of these properties we seem to perceive in objects are not 'in the objects themselves' but are in fact creatures of the perceptual relation. The qualities of objects – their colour, taste, smell, sound and texture – vary according to the condition of the perceiver or the conditions under which they are perceived. The standard examples are legion: grass is green in daylight, black at night; tepid water feels warm to a cold hand, cool to a hot hand; objects look large from close by, small from far away; and so on.

These perceptual relativities are cited by the sceptic to raise questions not just about whether perception is a trustworthy source of information about the world, but whether the world can be said to exist independently of perception at all. For what if the properties by whose means we detect the presence of objects cannot be described apart from their being objects of perception? Consider the old conundrum whether a sound is made by the tree that falls in the forest when no sentient being is present to hear it do so. The answer, on a standard theory of perception current in contemporary science, is that the tree falls in complete silence. For if there is no ear to hear, there is no sound; there are only at best the conditions – vibrating airwaves – which would cause sound to be heard if there were normally functioning eardrums, aural nerves and the rest to be stimulated by them.

These considerations suggest a sceptical picture in which perceivers are in something like the following predicament. Imagine a man wearing a visorless helmet which so encloses his head that he cannot see, hear, taste or smell anything outside it. Imagine that a camera, a microphone and other sensors are affixed to the top of the helmet, transmitting pictures and other information to its interior. And suppose finally that it is impossible for the wearer to remove the helmet to compare this information with whatever is outside, so that he cannot check whether it faithfully represents the exterior world. Somehow the wearer has to rely on the intrinsic character of the information available inside the helmet to judge its reliability. He knows that the information sometimes comes from sources other than the exterior world, as in dreams and delusions; he has deduced that the equipment affixed to the helmet works upon the incoming data and changes it, for example adding colours, scents and sounds to its picture of what intrinsically has none of these properties (at very least, in those forms); he knows that his beliefs about what lies outside the helmet rest on the inferences he draws from the information available inside it, and that his inferences are only as good as his fallible, error-prone capacities allow them to be. Given all this, asks the sceptic, have we not a job of work to do to justify our claims to knowledge?

2.5 Methodological and problematic scepticism

Before considering these arguments and canvassing some ways of responding to them, it is important to note two things. One is that sceptical arguments are not best dealt with by attempts at piecemeal – that is, one-by-one – refutation. The second is that there is a vitally important distinction to be drawn between two ways in which scepticism can be employed in epistemology. It is important to note these matters because otherwise the *prima facie* implausibility of most sceptical arguments will mislead us into underestimating their significance. I take each point in turn.

Attempted refutation of sceptical arguments piecemeal is, arguably, futile for two good reasons. As suggested at the outset, sceptical arguments are at their strongest not when they seek to prove that we are ignorant about some subject matter but when they ask us to justify our knowledge claims. A challenge to justify is not a claim or a theory, and cannot be refuted; it can only be accepted or ignored. Since the sceptic offers reasons why justification is needed, the response might be to inspect those reasons to see whether the challenge needs to be met. This indeed is one good response to scepticism. Where the reasons are cogent, the next good response is to try to meet the challenge thus posed.

The second reason is that sceptical arguments taken together have the joint effect of showing that there is work to be done if we are to get a satisfactory account of knowledge – and scepticism indicates what is needed. If one could refute, or show to be ungrounded, one or another individual sceptical argument, others would be left in place still demanding that such an account be sought.

These points can be illustrated by considering Gilbert Ryle's (1900–76) attempt to refute the argument from error by using a 'polar concept' argument. There cannot be counterfeit coins, Ryle observed, unless there are genuine ones, nor crooked paths unless there are straight paths, nor tall men unless there are short men. Many concepts come in such polarities, a feature of which is that one cannot grasp either pole unless one grasps its opposite at the same time. Now, 'error' and 'getting it right' are conceptual polarities. If one understands the concept of error, one understands the concept of getting it right. But to understand this latter concept is to be able to apply it. So our very grasp of the concept of error implies that we sometimes get things right.

Ryle obviously assumed that the error sceptic is claiming that, for all we know, we might always be in error. Accordingly his argument – that if we understand the concept of error, we must sometimes get things right – is aimed at refuting the intelligibility of claiming that we might always be wrong. But of course the error sceptic is not claiming this. He or she is simply asking how, given that we sometimes make mistakes, we can rule out the possibility of being in error on any given occasion of judgement – say, at this present moment.

But the sceptic need not concede the more general claims that Ryle makes, namely, that for any conceptual polarity, both poles must be understood, and – further and even more tendentiously – to understand a concept is to know how to apply it, and for it to be applicable is for it actually to be applied (or to have been applied). This last move is question-begging enough, but so is the claim about conceptual polarities itself. For the sceptic can readily cite cases of conceptual polarities – 'perfect–imperfect', 'mortal–immortal', 'FINITE–INFINITE' (chapter 10) – where it is by no means clear that the more exotic poles apply to anything, or even that we really understand them. After all, taking a term and attaching a negative prefix to it does not guarantee that we have thereby grasped an intelligible concept.

These comments suggest that sceptical arguments, even if singly they appear implausible, jointly invite a serious response; which is what, in large measure, epistemology seeks to offer. But there is still the matter of the distinction between methodological and problematic scepticism to be explained, and here a brief recapitulation of Descartes' use of sceptical arguments will be helpful.

Descartes' Method of Doubt

Descartes's aim was to find a basis for knowledge, which he did by looking for a starting point about which he could be certain. To find certainty he needed to rule out anything that could be doubted, however absurd that doubt, for only in this way would we be left with what is truly indubitable. In the first *Meditation* he embarks on this task by borrowing some sceptical arguments from the ancients. First he cites the fact that we can be misled in perception. But this is not a thoroughgoing enough scepticism, for even if we misperceive there is still much that we can know. So he next considers the possibility that on any occasion of claiming to know something, one might be dreaming. This sceptical thought catches more in its net, but is still insufficient, for even in dreams we can know such things as, for example, mathematical truths. So, to get as sweeping a consideration as possible, Descartes introduces the 'evil demon' idea. Here the supposition is that with respect to everything about which one could possibly be misled, an evil demon is indeed misleading one. Famously, what such a being cannot mislead one about is *cogito ergo sum* – when one thinks 'I exist', this proposition is true.

It is essential to note that Descartes' use of these arguments is *purely methodological*. The rest of the *Meditations* is devoted to showing that we know a great deal, because the fact (as Descartes unsuccessfully tries to prove) that there is a good DEITY (see chapter 14) guarantees that, just so long as we use our faculties responsibly, whatever is perceived with clearness and distinctness* to be true will indeed be true. This is because a good deity, unlike an evil one, would not wish us to embrace ignorance. Descartes was by no means a sceptic, nor did he think that sceptical arguments, least of all the one employed as a device to set aside as many beliefs as possible, were persuasive. The 'method of doubt' is merely a tool.

Descartes' successors, however, were far more impressed by the sceptical arguments he employed than his answer to them. For the tradition of epistemological thinking after his time, these and allied sceptical arguments were not mere methodological devices, but serious problems requiring solution. Hence the distinction I draw here between *methodological* and *problematic* scepticism.

It is clear that there are sceptical considerations that have merely methodological utility, and are not genuinely problematic, because they do not represent a stable and cogent challenge to our ordinary epistemological standards. Descartes' 'evil demon' is a case in point. Since the hypothesis that there is such a thing is as arbitrary and groundless as a hypothesis can get, it does not merit being taken seriously otherwise than as a ploy to make a point. But sceptical considerations about perception, error, delusion and dreams raise more interesting and troubling general issues, and accordingly merit examination.

Among the many things worth noting about Descartes' discussion are the following two. Firstly, as hinted earlier, his quest for certainty is arguably misconceived. Certainty is a psychological state one can be in independently of whether or not one believes truly. The falsity of a belief is no bar to one's feeling certain that it is otherwise. Descartes sought to specify ways of recognizing which of our beliefs are true, but he led himself into talk of certainty because – and this is the second point – he assumed that epistemology's task is to provide one with a way of knowing, from one's own subjective viewpoint, when one possesses knowledge. Accordingly, he starts with the private data of a single consciousness and attempts to move outside it, seeking guarantees for the process en route. Nearly all of Descartes' successors in epistemology, up to and including RUSSELL (1872–1970) (chapter 27) and Ayer (1910–89), accepted this perspective on their task. In this respect at least they are all therefore Cartesians. It is largely for this reason, as we shall see hinted below, that they found it hard to meet scepticism's challenge.

2.6 Some responses to scepticism

The sceptical challenge tells us that we suffer an epistemic plight, namely, that we can have the best possible evidence for believing some p, and yet be wrong. Stated succinctly and formally, scepticism is the observation that there is nothing contradictory in the conjunction of statements s embodying our best grounds for a given belief p with the falsity of p.

An informative representation of scepticism thus summarized is as follows. sceptical arguments open a gap between, on the one hand, the grounds a putative knower has for some knowledge claim, and, on the other hand, the claim itself. Responses to scepticism generally take the form of attempts either to bridge this gap or to close it. The standard perceptual model, in which beliefs are formed by sensory interaction with the world, postulates a causal bridge across the gap; but that bridge is vulnerable to sceptical sabotage, so the causal story at least needs support. Descartes, as noted, identified the epistemological task as the need to specify a guarantee – call it X – which, added to our subjective grounds for belief, protects them against scepticism and thus elevates belief into knowledge. His candidate for X was the goodness of a deity; rejecting this candidate (while continuing to accept his view of the epistemological task) obliges us to find an alternative. If an X cannot be found to support a bridge across the sceptical gap, the option is to try closing it – or more accurately, to show that there is no gap at all. Both the quest for X and the closing of the gap have constituted major epistemological endeavours against scepticism in modern philosophy. Some of these endeavours, in brief, are as follows.

Descartes' immediate successors were, as mentioned, unpersuaded by his attempt to bridge the gap by invoking a good divinity to serve as X. LOCKE (chapter 19), without much fanfare, employed a weaker version of the Cartesian expedient by saying that we can ignore sceptical threats to the causal story because 'the light that is set up in us shines bright enough for all our purposes'. From Locke's point of view it does not matter whether the inner light is set up by God or nature; the point is that there is something – X, the inner light which could be, perhaps, reason, empirical intuition or native trust in the reliability of the senses – that gives us grounds for accepting our ordinary knowledge-acquiring means as adequate.

Others, not content with such unsatisfactory moves, look for X elsewhere, and claim to find it in some version of foundationalism, the thought – sketched above – that our epistemic system has a basis in special beliefs that are in some way self-justifying or self-evident and which, in conjunction with the evidence we ordinarily employ in making knowledge claims, secures them against scepticism. As we saw earlier, a chief ground for rejecting such theories is alleged to be that none of them identifies satisfactory candidates for 'foundations'. But one stimulating way of making something like a foundationalist case is offered by Kant, whose attempt prompted others.

2.7 Transcendental arguments

KANT (1724–1804) (chapter 22) regarded failure to refute scepticism as a 'scandal' to philosophy, and offered his *Critique of Pure Reason* (1929) as a solution. His thesis is that our minds are so constituted that they impose a framework of interpretative concepts upon our sensory input, among them those of the objectivity and causal interconnectedness of what we perceive. Application of these concepts transforms mere passive receipt of sensory data into EXPERIENCE (pp. 590–8) properly so called. Our faculties are such that when raw data comes under the interpreting activity of our concepts, they have already had spatial and temporal form conferred on them by the nature of our sensory capacities; all our experience, considered as relating to what is outside us, is experience of a spatially structured world, and all our experience, considered as relating to its received character in our minds, is of a temporally structured world. Upon the spatio–temporal data thus brought before our minds we impose the categories, that is, the concepts that make experience possible by giving it its determinate character. And here is Kant's point: if the sceptic asks us to justify our claims to knowledge, we do so by setting out these facts about how experience is constituted.

Kant claimed HUME (1711–76) (chapter 21) as his inspiration for these ideas, because Hume had argued that although we cannot refute scepticism – reason was not, he claimed, up to the task – we should not be troubled, for human nature is so constituted that we simply cannot help having the beliefs that scepticism challenges us to justify. Those beliefs include, for example, that there is an external world, that causal relations hold between events in the world, that inductive reasoning is reliable, and so forth. From this hint Kant elaborated his theory that the concepts that the sceptic asks us to justify are constitutive features of our capacity to have any experience at all.

The strategy, if not the details, of Kant's attack upon scepticism has prompted interest in more recent philosophy. The argument he employs is a transcendental argument, briefly characterizable as one which says that because A is a necessary condition for B, and, because B is the case, A must be the case also. An example of such an argument in action against scepticism is as follows.

A typical sceptical challenge concerns belief in the unperceived continued existence of objects. What justifies our holding this belief and premising so much upon it? The transcendental arguer answers that because we take ourselves to occupy a single unified world of spatio-temporal objects, and because on this view spatio-temporal objects have to exist unperceived in order to constitute the realm as single and unified, a belief in their un-perceived continued existence is a condition of our thinking both about the world and our experience of it in this way. Since we do indeed think this way, the belief that the sceptic asks us to justify is thereby justified. A contemporary thinker who makes notable use of this style of argument is P. F. Strawson (b. 1919).

2.8 Idealism and phenomenalism

There is, in parallel to these Kantian ways of responding to the sceptical challenge, another approach, which denies the existence of a scepticism-generating gap. The chief figures in this camp are Berkeley and, more recently, the phenomenalists, who – allowing for differences among them, and for the fact that the two latter held these views only for part of their careers – include MILL (1806–73) (chapter 25), Russell and Ayer.

In Berkeley's view, scepticism arises from thinking that behind or beyond our sensory experiences there lies a *material* world. The word 'material' means 'made of matter', and 'matter' is a technical philosophical term supposed to denote an empirically undetectable substance believed by Berkeley's philo-sophical predecessors to underpin the sensorily detectable properties of things, such as their colours, shapes and textures. Berkeley rejected the concept of matter thus understood – it is a common misreading of him to take it that he thereby denied the existence of physical objects; he did no such thing – arguing that because physical objects are collections of sensible qualities, and because sensible qualities are ideas, and because ideas can only exist if perceived, the existence of objects therefore consists in their being perceived; if not by finite minds such as our own, then everywhere and at all times by an infinite mind. (We may note that Berkeley thought that his refutation of scepticism was at the same time a powerful new argument for the existence of God.)

Berkeley's habit of saying that things exist 'in the mind' has led uncritical readers to suppose he means that objects exist only in one's head, which is what a subjective idealist or solipsist might try to hold. Berkeley's idealism, whether or not it is otherwise defensible, is at least not quite so unstable a view. His 'in the mind' should be read as meaning 'with essential reference to experience or thought'.

For present purposes, the point is that Berkeley sought to rebut scepticism by denying the existence of a gap between experience and reality, on the grounds that experience and reality are the same thing. (He had a theory of how, despite this, we can nevertheless imagine, dream and make mistakes.) The phenomenalists, with one very important difference, argued likewise. Their view, briefly stated, is that all our beliefs about the world are derived from what appears to us in experience. When we analyse appearances – the 'phenomena' – we see that they are built out of the basic data of sense: the smallest visible colour patches in our visual fields, the least sounds in our auditory fields. Out of these sense-data we 'logically construct' the chairs and tables, rocks and mountains constituting the familiar furniture of the everyday world.

An alternative but equivalent way of putting this point, the phenomenalists claim, is to say that statements about physical objects are merely convenient shorthand for longer and more complicated statements about how things seem to us in the usual employment of our sensory capacities. And to say that objects continue to exist unperceived is to say – in Mill's phrase – that they are 'permanent possibilities of sensation', meaning that one would experience them if certain conditions were fulfilled.

Berkeley holds that things remain in existence when not perceived by finite minds because they are perceived by a deity. The phenomenalists argue that what it means to say that things exist unperceived is to say that certain counterfactual conditionals are true, namely, those asserting that the things in question would be perceived if some perceiver were suitably placed with respect to them. These conditionals are notoriously problematic, because it is not clear how to understand them. What, in particular, makes them true when they are (or seem quite obviously to be) true? The usual answers, in terms of possible worlds, laws, ideal regularities and similar exotica, do little to help. It is not clear that much of an advance is made over Berkeley's ubiquitous deity by substituting barely true counterfactuals in its place. Berkeley's view has the modest attraction that everything in the world is actual – anything that exists *is* perceived – whereas in the phenomenalist's universe most of what exists does so as a possibility rather than an actuality, namely, as a possibility of perception.

One thing is clear, at least: that one does not get phenomenalism simply by subtracting the theology from Berkeley's theory. One has to do that and then, in the resulting metaphysical gap, substitute a commitment to the existence of barely true counterfactuals, with an accompanying commitment to the existence of possibilia. Both Berkeley's theory and phenomenalism thus exact high prices for closing the sceptical gap.

2.9 Sceptical epistemology versus anti-Cartesianism

Some epistemologists do not attempt to refute scepticism for the good reason that they think it true or at least irrefutable. Their views might be summarized as stating that scepticism is the inevitable result of epistemological reflection, so we should accept either that we are only ever going to have imperfectly justified beliefs, always subject to revision in the light of experience, or that we have to recognize that scepticism, despite being irrefutable, is not a practical option, and therefore we have to live as most people anyway do, namely, by simply ignoring it.

Some commentators on Hume interpret him as taking this latter view of the matter, and accordingly call it the 'Humean' response to scepticism. In Stroud (1984) and Strawson (1985), something like the Humean view is taken.

Others in the recent debate are more combative, among them DEWEY (1859–1952) (see chapter 26) and WITTGENSTEIN (1889–1951) (chapter 29). Despite substantial differences in other respects, these two thinkers hold an interesting view in common, which is that scepticism results from accepting the Cartesian starting-point among the private data of individual consciousness. If instead, they say, we begin with the public world – with considerations relating to facts about the essentially public character of human thought and language – a different picture emerges.

Dewey argued that the Cartesian model makes the epistemic subject a merely passive recipient of experiences, like someone sitting in the dark of a cinema watching the screen; but, he pointed out, ours is in fact a participant perspective – we are actors in the world, and our acquisition of knowledge is the result of our doings there.

Wittgenstein contested the very coherence of the Cartesian approach by arguing that PRIVATE LANGUAGE (pp. 692–4) is impossible. A private language in Wittgenstein's sense is one that is logically available only to one speaker, which is what a Cartesian subject would need in order to begin discoursing about his private inner experience. His argument is this: language is a rule-governed activity, and one only succeeds in speaking a language if one follows the rules for the use of its expressions. But a solitary would-be language-user would not be able to tell the difference between actually following the rules and merely believing that he is doing so; so the language he speaks cannot be logically private to himself; it must be shareable with others. Indeed, Wittgenstein argues that language can only be acquired in a public setting (he likens language-learning to the training of animals; to learn a language is to imitate the linguistic behaviour of one's teachers), which similarly weighs against the idea that the Cartesian project is even in principle possible.

The anti-sceptical possibilities of the private language argument seem not to have been wholly apparent to Wittgenstein himself. In draft notes on scepticism and knowledge written in the last months of his life – later published under the title *On Certainty* (1969) – he offers a response to scepticism, which marks a return to a more traditional approach, not unlike that offered by Hume and Kant. It is that there are some things we have to accept in order to get on with our ordinary ways of thinking and speaking. Such propositions as that there is an external world, or that the world came into existence a long time ago, are simply not open to doubt; it is not an option for us to question them. Nor therefore, says Wittgenstein, can we say that we *know* them, because knowledge and doubt are intimately related, in that there can only be knowledge where there can be doubt, and vice versa.

The propositions we cannot doubt constitute the 'scaffolding' of our ordinary thought and talk, or – Wittgenstein varies his metaphors – they are like the bed and banks of a river, down which the stream of ordinary discourse flows. In this sense the beliefs that scepticism attempts to challenge are not open to negotiation; which, says Wittgenstein, disposes of scepticism.

These thoughts are as suggestive as they are in the philosophies of Hume and Kant; but one of the problems with Wittgenstein's way of putting them is that he uses foundationalist concepts in describing the relation of 'grammatical' propositions to ordinary ones, but repudiates foundationalism as such, and seems to allow a version of relativism by doing so – the river's bed and banks, he says, might in time be worn away. But relativism is just scepticism in disguise – it is, indeed, arguably the most powerful and troubling form of scepticism, for it is the view that knowledge and truth are relative to a point of view, a time, a place, a cultural or cognitive setting: and knowledge and truth thus understood are not *knowledge* and *truth*.

Concluding Remarks

There is much one would like to insist upon in trying correctly to describe the work that needs to be done in epistemology, for that is the necessary preliminary to making what progress we can. Here I shall simply underline a couple of remarks already made above.

Firstly, debates over the definition of 'knowledge' seem to me to be a sideshow. The justification of claims in the natural sciences, the social sciences (not least history) and law is where the real work cries out to be done in epistemology. And this comment applies only to the empirical case: what of the epistemological questions that press in ETHICS (chapter 6) and the PHILOSOPHY OF MATHEMATICS (chapter 10)? There can be no guarantee – and indeed it is unlikely – that high generalities about justification and knowledge will apply univocally across all these fields. 'Justification' is a dummy concept that needs to be cashed out in terms particular to particular fields; so much should be obvious from the fact that unrestrictedly general accounts of justification prove hopelessly vulnerable to counter-example.

Secondly, little in current literature about scepticism makes one confident that its nature is properly understood. Scepticism defines one of the central problems in epistemology, namely, the need to show how justification of belief is possible. This is done by meeting the challenge to show that sceptical considerations do not after all defeat our best epistemic endeavours in this or that specified field. Implicit in this characterization are two important claims: firstly, that scepticism is best understood as a *challenge*, not as a *claim* that we do or can know nothing; and secondly, that the best way to respond to scepticism is not by attempting to refute it on an argument-by-argument basis, but by showing how we come by justification for what we believe. Somehow these two points, which were obvious to our predecessors, seem to have been lost to sight.

Further Reading

General

Some useful texts are R. Nozick (1981); J. Dancy and E. Sosa (1992); B. Williams (1978); K. Lehrer (1974); L. BonJour (1985); P. F. Strawson (1985); and G. Pappas and M. Swain (1978).

The classic texts in epistemology include Plato's *Meno* and *Theaetetus*, Descartes' *Meditations*, Locke's *Essay Concerning Human Understanding*, Berkeley's *Principles of Human Knowledge* and *Three Dialogues Between Hylas and Philonous*, Hume's *Treatise of Human Nature* and *Enquiry Concerning Human Understanding*, and Kant's *Critique of Pure Reason*. One of the best short elementary books remains Russell's *The Problems of Philosophy* (1912, much reprinted).

Knowledge

The debate about knowledge and justification commands a large literature, of which the following are good examples: W. Alston (1983); L. BonJour (1985); A. Brueckner (1988); R. Chisholm (1977); J. Dancy (1985); F. Dretske (1971); R. Feldman (1985); E. Gettier (1963); A. Goldman (1979, 1980 and 1986); G. Harman (1973, 1984); K. Lehrer (1974); P. Moser (1985); R. Nozick (1981); J. Pollock (1979, 1984, 1986); R. Shope (1983); E. Sosa (1981).

Scepticism

The best general introduction to sceptical arguments remains Bertrand Russell's *The Problems of Philosophy*, but it is essential to see the arguments in a classic setting, and for this one must read René Descartes' *Meditations on First Philosophy* (translated by J. Cottingham, 1986) especially the First Meditation. Useful discussions of sceptical arguments and the sense-datum theory are to be found in A. J. Ayer (1956) and J. L. Austin (1961), although one should also look at Ayer's reply (1967). For discussion of perception see J. Dancy (ed.) (1988); T. Crane (ed.) (1992); R. Swartz (ed.) (1965); F. Jackson (1977); and M. Perkins (1983).

For an attempt at being sceptical see P. Unger (1975). For responses to scepticism influenced by Kant see P. F. Strawson (1959, 1985) and A. C. Grayling (1985). Allied lines of thought occur in G. E. Moore (1959) and L. Wittgenstein (1969). More recent discussions are B. Stroud (1984) and M. Williams (1991). Scepticism, foundationalism and coherence theories of knowledge are discussed in K. Lehrer (1974) and in useful papers collected by

G. S. Pappas and M. Swain (eds) (1978) and M. Clay and K. Lehrer (eds) (1989). For a discussion of the views variously taken by Dewey and Wittgenstein see R. Rorty (1979). A textbook which surveys the field and provides a useful bibliography is J. Dancy (1985). For the history of scepticism see M. Burnyeat (ed.) (1983) and R. Popkin (1979).

References

Classical Texts

Plato 1961: *Meno* and *Theaetetus*. In *The Collected Dialogues of Plato* (edited by E. Hamilton and H.(Cairns). Princeton, NJ: Princeton University Press.
Descartes, R. 1986 [1641]: *Meditations on First Philosophy* (translated by J. Cottingham). Cambridge: Cambridge University Press.
Locke, J. 1975 [1690]: *An Essay Concerning Human Understanding* (edited by P. H. Nidditch). Oxford: Clarendon Press.
Berkeley, G. 1995 [1710]: *The Principles of Human Knowledge* (edited by H. Robinson). Published with *Three Dialogues*. Oxford: Oxford University Press.
—— 1995 [1713]: *Three Dialogues Between Hylas and Philonous* (edited by H. Robinson). Published with *The Principles of Human Knowledge*. Oxford: Oxford University Press.
Hume, D. 1978 [1739–40]: *A Treatise of Human Nature* (edited by P. H. Nidditch). Oxford: Clarendon Press.
—— 1975 [1748]: *Enquiry Concerning Human Understanding* (edited by P. H. Nidditch). Oxford: Clarendon Press.
Kant, I. 1929 [1781 and 1787]: *Critique of Pure Reason* (1st edn 1781, 2nd edn 1787) (translated by N. Kemp Smith). London: Macmillan.

Other Writings

Alston, W. 1983: What is Wrong with Immediate Knowledge? *Synthèse*, 55.
Ayer, A. J. 1956: *The Problem of Knowledge*. London: Macmillan.
—— 1967: Has Austin Refuted the Sense-Datum Theory? *Synthèse*, 17.
Austin, J. L. 1961: *Sense and Sensibilia*. Oxford: Oxford University Press.
BonJour, L. 1985: *The Structure of Empirical Knowledge*, Cambridge, MA: Harvard University Press.
Brueckner, A. 1988: Problems with Internalist Coherentism. *Philosophical Studies*, 54.
Burnyeat, M., (ed.) 1983: *The Sceptical Tradition*. Berkeley: University of California Press.
Chisholm, R. 1977: *Theory of Knowledge*. Englewood Cliffs, NJ: Prentice-Hall.
Clay, M. and Lehrer, K. (eds) 1989: *Knowledge and Scepticism*. Boulder: Westview Press.
Crane, T. (ed.) 1992: *The Contents of Experience*. Cambridge: Cambridge University Press.
Dancy, J. 1985: *Introduction to Contemporary Epistemology*. Oxford: Blackwell.
——, (ed.) 1988: *Perceptual Knowledge*. Oxford: Oxford University Press.
Dancy, J. and Sosa, E. (eds) 1992: *A Companion to Epistemology*. Oxford: Blackwell.
Dretske, F. 1971: Conclusive Reasons. *Australasian Journal of Philosophy*, 49.
Feldman, R. 1985: Reliability and Justification. *The Monist*, 68.
Gettier, E. 1963: Is Justified True Belief Knowledge? *Analysis*, 23.

Goldman, A. 1979: What is Justified Belief? In G. Pappas, (ed.) *Justification and Knowledge*. Dordrecht: Reidel.
—— 1980: The Internalist Conception of Justification. In *Midwest Studies in Philosophy* 5, eds P. A. French et al. Minneapolis: University of Minnesota Press.
—— 1986: *Epistemology and Cognition*. Cambridge, MA: Harvard University Press.
Grayling, A. C. 1985: *The Refutation of Scepticism*. London: Duckworth.
Harman, G. 1973: *Thought*. Princeton, NJ: Princeton University Press.
—— 1984: Positive versus Negative Undermining in Belief Revision. *Noûs*, 18.
Jackson, F. 1977: *Perception*. Cambridge: Cambridge University Press.
Lehrer, K. 1974: *Knowledge*. Oxford: Clarendon Press.
Moore, G. E. 1959: *Philosophical Papers*. London: Allen and Unwin.
Moser, P. 1985: *Empirical Justification*. Dordrecht: Reidel.
Nozick, R. 1981: *Philosophical Explanations*. Cambridge, MA: Harvard University Press.
Pappas, G. and Swain, M. (eds) 1978: *Knowledge and Justification*. Ithaca: Cornell University Press.
Perkins, M. 1983: *Sensing the World*. Indianapolis: Hackett Publishing Co.
Pollock, John. 1979: A Plethora of Epistemological Theories. In G. Pappas (ed.), *Justification and Knowledge*, Dordrecht: Reidel.
—— 1984: Reliability and Justified Belief. *Canadian Journal of Philosophy*, 14.
—— 1986: *Contemporary Theories of Knowledge*. Totowa: Rowman and Littlefield.
Popkin, R. 1979: *The History of Scepticism*. Berkeley: University of California Press.
Rorty, R. 1979: *Philosophy and the Mirror of Nature*. Princeton, NJ: Princeton University Press.
Russell, B. 1912: *The Problems of Philosophy*. London: Oxford University Press.
—— 1910: *Philosophical Essays*. New York: Longman, Green and Co.
Shope, R. 1983: *The Analysis of Knowing*. Princeton, NJ: Princeton University Press.
Sosa, E. 1981: The Raft and the Pyramid: Coherence versus Foundations in the Theory of Knowledge. *Midwest Studies in Philosophy*, 5.
Strawson, P. F. 1959: *Individuals*. London: Methuen.
—— 1985: *Skepticism and Naturalism: Some Varieties*. London: Methuen.
Stroud, B. 1984: *The Significance of Philosophical Scepticism*. Oxford: Clarendon Press.
Swartz, R. (ed.) 1965: *Perceiving, Sensing and Knowing*. Berkeley: University of California Press.
Unger, P. 1975: *Ignorance*. Oxford: Clarendon Press.
Williams, B. 1978: *Descartes: The Project of Pure Enquiry*. Harmondsworth: Penguin.
Williams, M. 1991: *Unnatural Doubts*. Oxford: Basil Blackwell.
Wittgenstein. L. 1969: *On Certainty*. Oxford: Basil Blackwell.

Discussion Questions

1 How important is it to have a definition of knowledge?

2 If a proposition is false, can one be justified in believing it?

3 Why do 'Gettier examples' raise difficulties for a fallibilist account of knowledge?

4 Could states other than beliefs provide the foundations of knowledge?

5 If there are foundational beliefs, how are they related to dependent beliefs?

6 Is a belief justified if it coheres with an already accepted set of beliefs? Do we have an adequate account of the notion of coherence?

7 Does justification consist in internal relations among beliefs?

8 Can a belief be justified for someone who does not have cognitive access to what justifies the belief?

9 Is knowledge 'appropriately caused true belief'?

10 Does the notion of 'tracking' help to explain how beliefs are justified?

11 If there is no certainty, can there be knowledge?

12 Should we seek a single account of justified belief or different accounts tailored to the different areas in which epistemological questions may be asked?

13 What role does scepticism play in philosophy?

14 How can we disentangle those methods of enquiry that might yield genuine knowledge from those that can only deepen our ignorance?

15 Our knowledge claims are sometimes in error without our knowing it. Does this undermine justification for any such claims?

16 Could you be dreaming now?

17 Could the experiences I take to be of the world have some other origin, without my being able to tell that this is so?

18 Can the properties by which we detect the presence of objects be described apart from their being objects of perception?

19 Are we like the man in a visorless helmet who cannot check the information transmitted to him to see whether it faithfully represents the external world?

20 Can sceptical arguments that are singly implausible jointly require a serious response?

21 What is the importance of distinguishing methodological and problematic scepticism?

22 Can epistemology provide a way of knowing from a first-person subjective viewpoint? Is there any other viewpoint available?

23 If scepticism opens a gap between the grounds for a knowledge claim and the claim itself, is it better to bridge the gap or to close it?

24 Could the possibility of our having experience be unintelligible to us unless we held a certain belief, and yet that belief be false?

25 Are experience and reality the same thing?

26 Can we accept the role of counterfactuals in a phenomenalist account of physical objects?

27 What follows from beginning our account of knowledge with the public world rather than with the private data of individual consciousness?

28 Does the 'private language argument' show that the Cartesian project is impossible?

29 If there are propositions that are simply not open to doubt, how can we identify them? How are they related to propositions that we can doubt?

2

Metaphysics ───────────────

Simon Blackburn

Metaphysics is the exploration of the most general features of the world. We conceive of the world about us in various highly general ways. It is orderly, and structured in space and time; it contains matter and minds, things and properties of things, necessity, events, causation, creation, change, values, facts and states of affairs. Metaphysics seeks to understand these features of the world better. It aims at a large-scale investigation of the way things hang together. Within this broad description there are two conceptions of the subject. Metaphysicians may think of themselves as investigating the facts, or discovering the broad structures of reality. Or, they may see the enterprise as more self-reflective, gaining an understanding of how we represent the facts to ourselves: how our 'conceptual scheme' or perhaps any possible conceptual scheme, structures our own thought about reality. Once this description is completed, it may be that everything possible has been done, for we have no alternative but to continue to think from within the conceptual scheme whose features we have mapped.

1 Metaphysics and its Doubters

An influential distinction in the self-image of metaphysics is due to Strawson (1959). Metaphysics may be a purely descriptive enterprise. Or, it may be that there is reason for revision; the ways we think about things do not hang together, and some categories are more trustworthy than others. Revisionary metaphysics then seeks to change our ways of thought in directions it finds necessary. The distinction between revisionary and descriptive metaphysics is not sharp, for it is out of the descriptions that the need for revision allegedly arises, and in fact the metaphysicians Strawson cites as revisionary – PLATO (c.427–347) (chapter 15), DESCARTES (1596–1650) (chapter 17), BERKELEY (1685–1753) (chapter 20) – believed themselves to be discovering no more than things that are implications of our necessary ways of thinking. Revisionary metaphysics is frequently associated with ambitious, and sometimes wild, philosophical speculation; descriptive metaphysics is intellectually more conservative. But metaphysics characteristically has a practical dimension; since Plato it has been concerned to promote views about the nature of human beings, their relations with nature, or GOD (chapter 14), or with the larger SOCIAL WHOLES (p. 367) of which they are a part. Here it may be that descriptive metaphysics is ethically and politically more radical, for a preferred description of human life may have far-reaching implications, and indeed it is not possible for any serious ETHICS (chapter 6) or POLITICAL PHILOSOPHY (chapter 8) to be entirely silent about metaphysics. And radical views may have conservative implications, as when postmodernist views of the relative and contingent nature of all our judgements lead to failures of conviction, and the retreat of the intellectual into social and political inertia (Rorty, 1989).

Sometimes these themes have been presented as general topics of Being, and some authors give the impression that metaphysics is the science of Being. This is, however, misleading, for there may be nothing or little to be said about Being as such, even if there is a lot to say about the kinds of things that exist, and the categories under which they fall. And in fact the study of Being rapidly turns into the study of things in these categories, and of the relationship with them that characterizes particular thinkers at particular times. But what is right in the idea that metaphysics is the science of Being is that the most abstract study in this abstract discipline concerns the broad nature of reality, and the possibility of its objective representation.

What motivates the study of metaphysics? Centrally, problems arise when we cannot see how things hang together. We suffer from disquiet with the plurality of different kinds of things that exist, or with the mixture of elements that we want to keep together. Paradigmatic metaphysical problems arise when broad areas of our commitments clash, as for instance when we think of ourselves as complex natural organisms on the one hand, or as conscious purposive or even free agents on the other, or when we think of TIME (pp. 336–8) as flowing on the one hand, but recognize that it makes no sense to ask how fast it flows, on the other. Consider the list of minds, physical things, abstract objects, values, events, processes, dispositions, necessities, states of affairs, properties, facts and other basic categories that we seem to recognize. We need a story about how they relate to each other: Are some of them equivalent to others? Are some made up of others? Are some of them redundant, or others suspicious in other ways? And just as notably, we need a story about how we relate to them. How do we know about them, and why are they important to us? Such vague disquiet is typically focused by the discovery of paradox and inconsistency, apparently showing that our conceptions are inadequate. Among the earliest examples of philosophical argument in the western tradition are the paradoxes of motion of Zeno of Elea (fifth century BC), purporting to show that everyday thought about the flow of time and motion in space involves contradiction. What we all naturally believe cannot possibly be true. The moral Zeno wanted us to draw from this discovery is not quite clear, but the paradox served until the nineteenth century as a spur to philosophers and mathematicians to find a better way of conceptualizing change in time.

It seems that such topics should permit of some disciplined, intelligent, investigation. But it is controversial how such an investigation should be conducted. If metaphysics purports to tell us what things exist, or even just how to think about what things exist, then it seems to be trespassing on the

domain of the PHYSICAL SCIENCES (chapter 9), and it is unclear how a philosophical study can have anything significant to add to their results. The question is
whether there is anything left for philosophy to do, once fundamental science
has told us what it enables us to know about these topics. The view that there
is something further, and that by some process of rational thought we can
obtain reliable views about the nature of space, time, mind, causation and the
rest is often described as belief in a 'first philosophy', or philosophy as a
discipline with its own methods and results, and the very possibility of such
a first philosophy has been a constant object of doubt. Metaphysics is thus
preoccupied with its own possibility. It is not unique amongst philosophical
topics in this. But whereas we believe in our hearts, as it were, that there must
be such a subject as ethics, or that there must be interesting things to be said
within the THEORY OF MEANING (see chapter 3) or even mind, there is no such
presumption that there could be a disciplined method for achieving results
when the topics are the abstract categories I listed.

Consider as an example the problem of relating MIND AND MATTER (see chapter
5). Among the first philosophical thoughts many people have are ones about
their own conscious lives, and the gap there seems to be between that
consciousness and the similar lives of others, and the mystery of that
consciousness arising at all in the world as we otherwise understand it to be.
The fact of consciousness seems undeniable, but it also seems mysterious how
it can exist in a physical world of the kind to which we know ourselves to
belong. We can think of this as a problem of relating a puzzling or *exotic* fact
or kind of entity to a relatively domestic or *familiar* class of facts or entities. By
this I mean that we may begin by being happy with some kinds of fact, made
to obtain by some kinds of thing, such as the facts of physical nature, or facts
about the patterns into which events fall. We feel we understand facts of this
sort. We understand what makes them obtain, and how we know them to be
true. This class is that of the familiar (homely) aspects of the world: ones that
do not puzzle us unduly. But then we realize that we have other beliefs as
well; ones which on the face of it relate to different kinds of fact, and posit
different kinds of thing. In this case minds are posited, but we shall shortly
meet other examples. We may not be able to understand how mind is even
possible in a physical universe (how minds can relate to bodies; how they can
make physical things happen). Then the main motive to metaphysical inquiry
is to put the exotic class into some sort of intelligible relation to the familiar
class. An intelligible relation will mean that we understand how both classes
of facts exist, and how the world is constituted so that each of them obtains,
how our everyday thoughts about their relationship can be true.

If we think of it this way, we can see three main points at which choice is
possible in metaphysics. First, there is the question of the authority of the
familiar class. At a particular period of time some starting points may seem
natural. We may be at home, for example, with the results and concepts of the
physical sciences (and in fact the conviction that the world is fundamentally
nothing but a physical world is certainly the most common view among
contemporary western philosophers). If so, these results and concepts give us
our class of familiar facts, and the task is that of relating more exotic subjects

to them. But to other philosophers there may be something wrong-headed or arbitrary or prejudiced about choosing just one privileged familiar class. Perhaps, for example, when we understand how complex and strange are the facts and states of affairs posited by contemporary physics, we will lose any confidence that others are more exotic by comparison. Even deciding what facts and states of affairs belong to physics occupies a great deal of PHILOSOPHY OF SCIENCE (chapter 9): does physical theory, for example, postulate real PROBABILITIES AND CHANCES (pp. 314–16), and if so how are we to think of their existence? What justifies our tendency to take science as an objective description of independent reality, as opposed to seeing it as an INSTRUMENT (pp. 298–300) for prediction and control of empirical fact (and how is this distinction to be drawn)? But even when a privileged class has been identified and doubts about its nature and the source of its privilege satisfactorily settled, there will be a second question of what counts as a satisfactory fit between the exotic and the familiar. What kinds of relationship should put worries about mind or values or abstract objects to rest, if we wish to see our world as fundamentally the world as described by physics? What accommodations should we be looking for? Thirdly, and finally there will be different attitudes to the exotic class. If it seems sufficiently exotic, so that its objects and facts seem only dimly related to those of the familiar class, a radical response will be eliminativism, or the suggestion that it is not possible that there should exist things in the exotic categories, so that the entire exotic area is best forgotten. The task is not to relate its commitments to the familiar class, but to teach people to do without them, rather as atheists do not seek to understand talk about God in some preferred terms, but want instead to abandon it altogether. In this spirit one might want to eliminate reference to abstract objects such as properties or facts, or to values or even to minds.

Put like this the enterprise of metaphysics sounds eminently reasonable, and one can imagine well-conducted dispute in all three areas: motives for selecting a familiar class, differing views about the relationship it bears to the exotics, and different attitudes to the exotics. But the problem of a method for conducting such enquiry still remains, and we should recognize that philosophy has contained nearly as many thinkers who count themselves as radically opposed to metaphysics as ones who accept the title. In the modern (post-seventeenth century) Western tradition the first philosopher resolutely hostile to metaphysics was David HUME (1711–76) (chapter 21) (Hume, 1978). Following him there were always philosophers, especially in Britain, of a more cautious empiricist bent, but few were tough-minded enough to believe with Hume that books of metaphysics should be consigned to the flames, as containing nothing but sophistry and illusion.

Whether or not it has a method, metaphysics is swayed by larger winds that blow in the prevailing culture. It is widely realized that before the Enlightenment the prevailing tone of philosophy was THEOLOGICAL (chapters 14 and 16). It was supposed that the world was the production of an intelligent, rational, caring and perfect being, who possessed a complete understanding of its nature. We imperfect beings could do something to approximate to this understanding, but the insight we obtained in such areas as mathematics and logic afforded us only glimpses of the perfect rational understanding of the whole order of nature that God would possess (Craig, 1987). The familiar class of facts with which people were relatively content included God's nature, purposes, values and relationship to creation. The abandonment of this picture of the world by Hume and other Enlightenment figures did not, however, mark the end of metaphysics. On the contrary the rise of scientific revolution of the seventeenth century replaced one kind of familiar fact with others: notably, those of physical science and those describing the course of perceptual experience. But this 'Galilean world-view', named after Galileo (1564–1642) contained the seeds of its own metaphysical thickets, namely those surrounding the issue of idealism. When mind is sharply distinguished from matter, as it became in this world-view, the uncomfortable and apparently impassable gulf between them is most naturally closed either by making the mind material, or by making the material mental. Idealism is the umbrella title for philosophies that take the latter course. For the idealist, facts about mental life form the familiar class, and ones about the physical world need some kind of certification from them. An idealist, therefore, would be receptive to the kind of instrumental interpretation of physical science mentioned above, in which scientific descriptions are taken as instruments for prediction and control of the course of perceptual experience. Whichever priority is assumed, the problem of providing this certification dominated philosophy from the time of Descartes until the present. Indeed, perhaps the high-water mark of metaphysical speculation was reached with the attempts to marry idealism with a religious world-view in the nineteenth century. According to the accepted story, under the influence of KANT (1724–1804) (chapter 22), but forgetting the tightly critical boundaries that Kant himself put upon metaphysics, it was believed that transcendent results – which go beyond the limits of experience and concern God, freedom, immortality and above all the ultimate spiritual nature of the universe – could be established by a variety of *a priori* arguments. Kant's mistrust of transcendent reasoning was brushed aside by Fichte (1762–1814) and most influentially by HEGEL (1770–1831) (chapter 23), and the metaphysician became the specialist in the nature of THE ABSOLUTE (p. 609), or underlying ground of the cosmic order, which was identified variously with God, pure Freedom, or final Self-Consciousness, and which provided some sort of goal to the cumulative historical process. An almost religious belief in progress, coupled with a genuinely religious emphasis on the nature of the SPIRIT (p. 609), and above all its elevated moral tone, gave absolute idealism its hold on the minds of Europe.

The dominant contemporary spirit reverses this direction, privileging facts about the physical and seeking to understand statements about mind and consciousness in its terms. This is known as physicalism, or less often materialism (the word physicalism is preferred because physics itself asserts that not everything that exists is material; the world includes such items as forces and fields). Physicalism and idealism share the goal of relating mind and matter in some intelligible way, but differ over what is familiar and what exotic. The need for additional tasks of the same kind may be less obvious in advance of critical reflection. The point to remember is that whatever a philosopher might put forward by way of doubts about the possibility of metaphysics, the philosophical need for a theory relating central kinds of fact may be driven by wider aspects of the world-picture characteristic of a given time.

Hume was an opponent of metaphysics even though he bequeathed to his successors the paradigm metaphysical problems of modern philosophy. His own attitude was simply that such problems were forever insoluble. The difficulty is that it is hard to believe that metaphysical questions are unanswerable until we try to answer them. Perhaps the problems seem formidable because we are prejudiced in our choice of a familiar class (Hume himself favoured facts about the successions of our own ideas or 'perceptions' as especially basic or familiar, a choice that frequently amazes contemporary thinkers); perhaps we are blind to subtle and insightful ways of relating the exotics to it; perhaps we do not realize that we ought to get rid of exotics that refuse to be accommodated. It is difficult to believe that the entire field can be seen, in advance and from the armchair, to be a no-go area. But there has been one school this century which believed exactly that.

Perhaps the one thing that is best known about the school known as the Vienna Circle, or the logical positivists, was their resolute hostility to metaphysics. It is instructive to see how this hostility flourished, but then eventually crumbled. The positivists were influenced by the empiricism of Hume, and also by the *Tractatus Logico–Philosophicus* of WITTGENSTEIN (1889–1951) (chapter 29) (1922), a work which purports to set bounds to the limits of meaningful language. Metaphysics lies outside the bounds, representing language that has gone on holiday. The positivists held that all true thought was empirical; anything straying beyond the use of scientific method also strayed beyond the boundaries of meaning. But metaphysical theses are not properly empirical; they seemed typically to be argued about from the armchair and to bear no visible relationship to scientific thought or experiment. Hence they do not admit of verification or falsification, and are not only unscientific, but also strictly meaningless (they may be allowed some kind of emotional effect, but nothing that permits of assessment as true or false). Instead of metaphysics, all that was left to philosophy was describing the correct methods and structures of empirical science.

Positivism failed in its crusade against metaphysics, largely because of its own instability. For while in one breath it was proclaiming the subject dead, in another it was itself making remarkably confident choices in all three of the areas in which metaphysics characteristically makes choices. Positivism needed a familiar class of empirically sound and basic judgements. It needed views about what counts as a satisfactory accommodation with that class, notably so that the theories of physical science were allowed to be respectable, whereas others were not. And, finally, it had severe views about the areas that were not, by these lights, respectable. Metaphysics soon revenged itself, for all three areas gave trouble, and in all three the movement found itself pulled in different directions, making different choices and indulging in classically metaphysical dispute. Aware of this, later positivist writings grudgingly allowed a place for what looked like metaphysical assertions as recommendations about which LANGUAGE GAMES (p. 9) to play. Thus, the doctrine that there exists mind as well as matter would be construed not as an important description of a fundamental fact about reality, but as a recommendation to speak in terms of minds as well as in terms of matter (to play the mental language game). The recommendation might be useful or not, but could not be regarded as true or false. A similar attitude is characteristic of the later work of Wittgenstein (1953), which is shot through with warning that statements that might seem to be certain kinds of description of reality in fact function in different ways. Wittgenstein's exact intentions are endlessly disputed. But, at least as applied to minds and matter, any pragmatism in the approach is itself acutely uncomfortable. Consider, for instance, the simple proposition that other people besides myself are conscious in the way that I am. This seems to be a metaphysical thesis, although classifying it as one may itself represent a philosophical choice. It is certainly one that we all believe. But it is extremely strange to suppose that the question whether other people are conscious could be construed as the question of whether it was useful for me to enter the language game of reacting to them as having minds (this gloss on the question had in fact been put by William JAMES (1842–1910) (chapter 26) much earlier, especially in *Pragmatism*, and has not received a generally warm welcome). We should also notice that even if we allow the idea that what sound like descriptions of fundamental reality are construed as recommendations about language, there is still argument about what to select as familiar, what is exotic, what should be eliminated and what the relationships are between all these classes. So even the pragmatist gloss may make less difference than might appear at first sight.

Absolute Presuppositions

Their own metaphysical prejudices were invisible to the positivists. The thought that this is an inevitable feature of the philosophical condition is another, different, reason for despair about the possibility of metaphysics. This reason was voiced most notably by R. G. COLLINGWOOD (1889–1943) (pp. 423–6) (especially in *Essay in Metaphysics*, 1940), and marked a point at which his thought comes surprisingly close to that of both the earlier and later philosophy of Wittgenstein. In this conception, there are commitments that we must have that are not capable of being assessed as true or false, but that nevertheless have the greatest intellectual importance. In Wittgenstein's metaphors, they function as the riverbed within which thought flows, or as the hinges on which ordinary judgement and discourse turn; Collingwood called them the absolute presuppositions of the thought of a time. Because they are presupposed in every activity of thought, they cannot themselves be assessed for truth: in another metaphor, they can be shown but not said. For Collingwood, indeed, they could only be shown *historically*. That is, at the end of an epoch it would be possible for successors to look back and to find that a particular metaphysics had structured its thought. But at the time the basic structures would themselves be invisible, because they were themselves involved in all seeing (Hegel himself may have thought something similar; the famous remark from the Preface to his *Philosophy of Right* (1991) that 'when philosophy paints its grey on grey, then has a form of life grown old. The owl of Minerva takes wing only with the coming of the dusk' can be seen as the claim that philosophical reflection can only exist with hindsight). If this is right, the trap that caught the positivists is therefore universal; however much we aspire to care and objectivity in choosing our familiar facts, and a way of relating exotics to them, we will be working within an historically contingent framework whose main structures will be beyond our own vision, and incapable of our own assessment. Collingwood was an historian, and other episodes in the history of philosophy support his view, for it is easier to see absolute presuppositions at work in the thought of particular writers (and their contemporaries) when significant time has passed, and easy to fear that our successors will marvel at similar blindness in our own appreciation of the way we think. An example I have mentioned already is Hume's choice of the sequence of perceptions as the basic familiar fact: a choice that seems extraordinarily wrong-headed to nearly all contemporary philosophers. Once more, however, many philosophers are reluctant to admit there should exist any aspects of our own thought that cannot themselves be identified and even critically assessed. While such episodes in the history of philosophy may nourish our modesty, there seems to be no alternative to continuing to 'work from within', or in other words to do the best we can from within our own best understandings. The thought that one day these may come to look local and parochial is like the similar thought, in moral philosophy, that there might one day be a people to whom our own best judgements seemed inadequate. Perhaps there might, but while we cannot see our way to this improvement, we can, and must, simply soldier on as best we can.

There surfaces here a debate that has preoccupied many recent writers. This is the dispute between realism and its opponents. For the realist it is important that there is no residual reference to *us* (our language, our sensibilities, our conceptual scheme) when we consider the world. The realist wants real objectivity – a world of facts that are frequently entirely independent of us and that would be as they are whatever our powers of detecting and exploring them. The realist is therefore fundamentally opposed to the view that what we understand and investigate is as much a function of our constitution and our ways of thought as it is of anything independent of us. In a common metaphor, the realist believes that a good conceptual scheme 'carves reality at the joints'; nature is conceived as possessing its own structure and articulation, and good theory only reflects this. This carnivorous metaphor outrages idealists of many varieties, and even philosophers who would scarcely count themselves as idealists. The central problem is that belief that we succeed in carving nature in some especially appropriate way seems to require a way of comparing our own classifications and the kinds of concept we use, with a pre-existent, naturally ordained structure of properties. But no such comparison can be made, nor is it plain what, apart from ordinary scientific utility, could justify us in supposing that some properties are intrinsically natural whereas others are not. This problem received forceful expression in Goodman (1955); for an example of industrial-strength realism, see Lewis (1983); for mistrust of the metaphor see Taylor (1993).

The choice between realism and its opponents has echoes in many areas. For example, the realist is particularly apt to privilege some familiar class, usually that of physical theory, as being especially well-adapted to nature's joints. By comparison other commitments may seem to have less to do with the real way that things are. For instance, the sizes and shapes of things around us may seem to be more objective, more independent of us, than their colours, which seem to be largely a function of the nature of our visual systems. Idealists, impressed by the mind's contribution to any scheme of thought, including that of physics, are typically less partisan. At their most tolerant, they may, as *pluralists*, become happy to countenance almost all language games or conceptual schemes as alike reflecting the particular perspective of some user; no scheme is privileged by having a unique and special relationship with the way things are, and all are justified in so far as they embody a form of life or way of reacting to the world and coping with it. Pluralism here makes contact with PRAGMATISM (chapter 26), or the view that what ultimately justifies any mode of description of the world is its utility in enabling us to cope with our problems. For the pluralist there may be no urgent task of relating anything familiar to anything exotic, for both alike are conceived of as being no more than one mode of description amongst others. Pluralism, therefore, serves as yet another avenue from which metaphysics comes to look to be a chimera – and dislike of old-fashioned metaphysics on this ground is one of the characteristics of the postmodernist mistrust of traditional philosophy. But, once more, it is not so obvious that one can be satisfied with pluralism without already having done enough metaphysics to gain the necessarily relaxed attitude to the different categories of being and their relationships.

2 Analysis and Logic

Metaphysics needs a method, but what method can there be? It is generally said that the most influential and respected Anglo-American thought this century marks a complete change of direction from the ambitious and specu-lative metaphysical system-building characteristic of the previous period. For the first half of this century in Anglo–American philosophy, and for some time afterwards in some places, the problem of method for metaphysics was governed by the ideal of analysis. Faced with a metaphysical problem such as the nature of mind, the philosopher would assemble the central terms with which we talk about mind: thought, sensation, will or whatever; careful attention to what is meant by these terms would reveal the way we conceptualize the nature of mind. The model for such a procedure would be that of the analytical chemist, discovering the nature of a substance by breaking it into components. The negative part of this aim is clear enough. When meanings are obscure and unclear, the inferences that we are permitted to make are uncertain too, and it is this uncertainty that allows for fanciful and monstrous system-building. But if meaning were correctly located, in ways first made possible by the new logical tools developed by FREGE (1848–1925) and RUSSELL (1872–1970) (chapter 27), then those inferences would be systematized and established, and correct methods finally distinguished from impostors. Analytic technique was partly important purely as a defence against wild theorizing. In this sense the method of analysis was not new, but only a new label for procedures that are as old as philosophy. In many of his dialogues, SOCRATES (chapter 15) challenges his audience to state exactly what they mean by a disputed term; MEDIEVAL PHILOSOPHY (chapter 16), as much as later empiricism, is dominated by the aim of precise clarifications of meaning. But a number of considerations changed the impact of this work of clarification on metaphysics. One was the expansion of logic, suggesting a wholly new range for analytic techniques. Far the most influential example of this expansion in action was the theory of descriptions, revealed by Russell (1905); a 'paradigm of philosophy' whereby judgements that we seem to be making about non-existent 'things' are revealed to have quite a different LOGICAL FORM (p. 662), and to make no such commitments.

Analysis also provided the principal goal for the satisfactory accommodation between the familiar and the exotic. This is the goal of REDUCTION, in which the right attention to meaning reveals that what seem to be claims about a puzzling and exotic area are in fact claims of a familiar, homely kind. Specific problems about exotic facts and things do not arise, for they are shown to be ordinary, familiar facts and things. For example, if claims about behaviour are thought to be relatively intelligible, but claims about minds seem by contrast mysterious, then the solution might be to analyse claims about minds as disguised claims about behaviour, or dispositions to behaviour. If logical truth or logical proof are felt to be intelligible, but claims about numbers mysteriously abstract and dangerously non-empirical, the solution would be to analyse claims about numbers as disguised recipes for purely logical inferences. The programmes this approach gave rise to – the two examples given are BEHAVIOURISM (pp. 168–70) and LOGICISM (pp. 662–3), but there were many more – not only dominated much philosophical thinking in the first half of this century, but go on directing a large proportion of current research effort. If it succeeds, analysis provided an extraordinarily elegant and economical answer to the problem of the relationship of the familiar to the exotic. For if by analysis we lay bare the real 'logical form' or structure of our thought, and it turns out that the facts and things we need to refer to are not what they seem to be at first glance, then the problem is solved by absorption of the exotic into the familiar – the final and simplest kind of solution to the problem of their relationship. We are shown to have no commitments beyond the familiar and the unpuzzling.

It is important to notice that analytical philosophy arose not primarily as a crusade against metaphysics, but only against the undisciplined perversions of metaphysics, which seemed to the major early analysts to surround them. It is in fact notable that the pioneering works of MOORE (1873–1958) (chapter 28) and Russell are themselves preoccupied with questions of what there really is. The familiar class, for Frege, Moore and Russell included some beliefs that others might regard with suspicion, most notably belief in abstract objects. Moore himself at one time held the distinctly metaphysical-sounding thesis that all that really exists are propositions; Frege remained wedded to but puzzled by the distinctively metaphysical belief in the existence of abstract objects. Russell's empiricism led to flirtations both with doctrines not unlike those of the idealist Berkeley, and with neutral monism (the belief that the same primitive 'stuff', ordered in different ways makes up on the one hand the mental and on the other hand the physical world). What drove analytical philosophy was not originally hostility to metaphysics, but belief that the correct method for pursuing it had finally been found.

One objection to the method used to be made by more speculative or ambitious philosophers, writing under titles like *Clarity is not Enough*. With concerns echoing those which first arose in ANCIENT GREEK PHILOSOPHY (chapter 15), they worried that the true nature of mind or other metaphysical topics might not be revealed by analysis, because what is analysed is a compendium of common-sense prejudice or folklore which is not particularly likely to enshrine the metaphysical truth. This worry has been revised in a different, scientific, tone of voice more recently. Since common-sense concepts were formed in pre-scientific days, there is no particular reason to respect them as a source of metaphysical or any other kind of truth. Indeed, some philosophers think the right reaction to such concepts is the response we mentioned above, namely eliminativism, which is the doctrine that everyday thought about some topic is sufficiently infected with errors for its categories to be wholly unreliable. Everyday opinions about the nature of mind in principle deserve no more respect than everyday opinions about the nature of mass or the flight of projectiles, and concepts within which everyday thought frames its opinions may be quite worthless, like those of Aristotelian physics. Thought couched in these terms does not need analysis, but elimination (Churchland, 1989; Stich, 1983).

This is certainly possible. But to turn the possibility into a real likelihood, we must at least correctly identify what the common-sense scheme actually requires. What is common sense committed to, and which parts of it may need eliminating? Here there is a need for work at least significantly like that of the analytical philosopher: we would need to know exactly what the commitments implicit in the common sense scheme are, and this means correctly locating what is meant by the salient terms.

Let me give a simple example. Suppose someone remarks that one doctrine of everyday common sense is that people often behave as they do because of what they think. Suppose it is then pointed out that science tells us that physics is a closed system: physical events, such as bodies moving, must have physical causes. But, goes the objection, the description of someone as thinking something is not a physical description of them. Hence, it must be an error to believe that people behave as they do because of what they think. This is a simplified version of an argument that has obvious eliminativist leanings, for once people accept that it is wrong to think of people as behaving as they do because of what they think, then the idea of people as thinkers at all is also fairly immediately threatened. For if thought does not cause behaviour, it does not seem to do anything else either. But the argument is scarcely compelling as it stands. It raises a host of questions, and they are analytic in their nature. Is the 'because' in 'people behave as they do because of what they think' actually a causal notion? If it is, does this kind of causal explanation compete with other (neurophysiological) causal explanations, or is it compatible with them? Might it make sense to suggest that mental events are identical with physical events, and are therefore in good standing as physical causes of things? To assess the argument we must first clear up such questions, but clearing up such questions is investigating the very topics that the analytical philosopher took as primary. I return below to discussing some of the moves that have attracted attention in connection with these topics.

The Flight from Analysis

Even if eliminativism cannot entirely do without analysis, in the last 40 years, and especially in the last 20, analysis has officially lost much of its lustre as an ideal. Partly the failure of positivism taught philosophers that theory can take us beyond evidence – that concepts that may not have met strict empiricist or positivist standards for meaning are nevertheless perfectly proper. To theorize properly on the basis of data is to invent new conceptual structures. But then, the kinds of thing said when we make use of those structures will not be equivalent in meaning to the things said without them. New theoretical concepts have their own meanings, and it is futile conservatism to deny this by trying to analyse their content in old terms. The flight from analysis was also propelled from other directions. One was the failure of many of the reductionist programmes, few of which gave convincing reasons for supposing that the exotic was just the familiar in disguise. Another was a gradual disenchantment with the foundational role attributed to meaning in the analytic paradigm. Quine (1951) convinced many that the equations of meaning demanded by analysis could not be self-sufficient 'semantic' facts known merely by knowing the languages concerned, but would themselves equally represent deep theoretical and scientific choices. For example, if statements about physical objects are analysed into statements about courses of experience (phenomenalism) this will not be the result of a neutral semantic equation, but will represent a theoretical (metaphysical) conviction about what there is and the way it is to be understood. In other words, semantics is driven by science or even metaphysics as much as the other way round. It was also realized that metaphysics ought to be able to proceed even where semantics is silent. For example, in the theory of value it is notorious that value terms resist analysis into terms without evaluative implications (it is, after all, their distinct meanings that define them as value terms), but this failure of analysis surely should not halt the enterprise of trying to understand the specific nature of valuing as a human activity, not by purely semantic investigation, but by reflecting on the psychological, sociological, or even biological role of valuing (Gibbard, 1990). Values would be domesticated, but not by analysis, and perhaps similar progress can be made with other areas.

Two final elements can be discerned in the move from analysis. We have seen that the analytic paradigm was good at presenting a preferred relation between the exotic and the familiar: the one is absorbed in the other. But it is not so good at telling us what to choose as familiar in the first place. And in fact just this point has engendered kinds of conflict to which the analytic paradigm provides no ready solution. Like Hume, twentieth-century PHENOMENALISTS (pp. 55–6) found the stream of perceptions familiar, and the physical world exotic. Others exactly reverse the priority. Frege and Russell found LOGIC (chapter 4) familiar, and MATHEMATICS (chapter 10) exotic; others think that logical relations are even more in need of theory than the properties of mathematical structures. Some think that categorical properties are familiar, and that we ought to analyse DISPOSITIONS AND POWERS (pp. 564) in terms of them; others again reverse the priority, believing that categorical properties are dangerously exotic, whereas science deals familiarly with powers and dispositions. In the absence of any method of settling such questions of priority, analysis is rudderless, for we do not even know in which direction to work.

Perhaps the most sustained and influential case on behalf of a fundamentally analytic method in the second half of the twentieth century is that made by Michael Dummett (b. 1925). In many writings, but most visibly in *The Logical Basis of Metaphysics* (1991) Dummett has argued that the foundation for metaphysics, and indeed its entire legitimate domain, lies in the THEORY OF MEANING (chapter 3). Citing the stagnation and deadlock that ensues when rival metaphysicians attempt direct descriptions of reality, Dummett believes instead that we must take as our subject not so much reality as the way we think about reality. However, there is no investigation of thought of this kind which is not also an investigation of language and logic. This means we must approach metaphysical problems from the 'bottom-up', recognizing that the problem is that of 'the correct model for meaning for statements of the disputed class' (1991, p. 12). A meaning-theory, as Dummett conceives of it, will give us this model. It must provide a clear view of how our words function, for as things stand we use words with various meanings, but we do not know what it is that we are doing. We have no clear overview of our own practices, and in this sense do not understand ourselves. A meaning-theory will give a representation of what a person learns when learning a language; it will provide a 'workable account of a practice that agrees with that which we in fact observe' (1991, p. 14). Such a transparent understanding of our meanings would certify the correct logic to be used, for it is meaning that confers validity or invalidity on an inference; hence it would settle disputes such as that between realists and their opponents, anti-realists in disputed areas.

One surprising thing about such a meaning-theory is that its construction can proceed, according to Dummett, entirely innocently of metaphysics. It is the neutral basis of metaphysics, and nowhere owes anything to metaphysical doctrines or choices. And another surprising aspect is that it is itself sufficiently powerful to settle metaphysical controversy: by adjudicating between rival conceptions of truth offered by realists and their opponents, 'it will resolve these controversies without residue' (1991, p. 14). Dummett is not quite promoting a purely *a priori* method for metaphysics, for the data on which a meaning-theory would be constructed would in one sense be empirical: they would concern the inferential practices of competent users of the language. Nevertheless the data are, in principle, available to any competent language user purely by reflection upon that practice. There is no appeal to general scientific facts or empirical facts lying outside the sphere of language use. Yet the reflection will deliver results that can settle outstanding metaphysical dispute.

The pattern of Dummett's thought is clearly influenced by his own favourite example of metaphysical controversy, that between CLASSICAL MATHEMATICIANS AND INTUITIONISTS (pp. 345–9). In this example it is plausible that the dispute is metaphysical in essence, with the classicists thinking of mathematics as objective, real, independent of us, or 'out there', and the intuitionists thinking of mathematical truth as extending no further than mathematical proof (constructivism). It is also plausible that the heart of the dispute is the correct logic for mathematical proof and inference. The classical mathematician believes in bivalence (the logical law that every proposition is either true or false), whereas for the intuitionist, since there is no guarantee that every proposition is provable or disprovable, bivalence cannot be assumed. And finally, Dummett believes that the issue of the correct logic hinges upon questions that would be tackled by a meaning-theory, in the sense that he conceives of it: the intuitionists believe that classical mathematicians deceive themselves into thinking that they can make sense of notions that are in fact senseless. Deciding whether they are right about that would be the function of just the kind of perspicuous representation of meaning that Dummett advocates.

Nevertheless there are grave difficulties with the programme as it is presented. The most obvious is that it is inconceivable that a meaning-theory with the powers Dummett describes should be constructed in the innocent way that he also requires. Descriptions of what our words mean are historically among the most theory-laden of philosophical claims. They are put forward, naturally, by philosophers who take themselves to inhabit a world of one kind or another, and who believe that our mental powers take one shape or another. We need only remember empiricists and positivists of all kinds, whose conception of what we could mean by a term disallows understanding of anything not given in perceptual experience. But on top of this philosophical choice, the conception of perceptual experience was in turn not purely empirical, or obtained in some neutral scientific spirit. Rather, it was the locus of fierce doctrinal dispute, for instance between perceptual atomists such as Hume and Russell, and more holistic idealists such as Bradley (1846–1924) or Neurath (1882–1945). An even more central and prolonged dispute over the best way to conceive of understanding is represented by the problem of universals, which surfaced above in the dispute between those who do and those who do not think of science as carving nature at the joints. To some realists, meanings reflect natural similarities among things which guide and constrain the application of concepts to new cases; to others of an anti-realist persuasion they do not, but the rules that govern application are a free-standing human construction. But neither side conceives themselves as riding roughshod over empirical facts about the nature of language use.

Dummett is not, of course, denying the obvious fact that persons who think of metaphysics, ontology, perception and epistemology one way will give different descriptions of meaning from those who think of it another way. His claim is that whether or not this is in fact so, it need not be so. The impact of these intruders on a meaning-theory is, somehow, capable of being avoided. But saying that this is possible is far from showing how it is possible, and Dummett's own explorations in this direction have not proved reassuring. In his famous paper, 'The Philosophical Basis of Intuitionistic Logic' (1978), for example, he explained the Wittgensteinian doctrine that meaning is use as implying that we cannot be understood to mean anything we cannot be observed to mean, thereby betraying a fondness for observation that is not at all epistemologically or metaphysically neutral – on the contrary, it is one of the principal planks of positivism (the less contentious doctrine would be that we cannot be understood to mean anything that we cannot be thought of as meaning, leaving the relationship of thought to observation to be fought over another day).

Even more remarkable is the belief that a satisfactory meaning-theory will exhaust the field of metaphysics. We can see the magnitude of this claim by a simple example. Suppose we think of the domain of THEOLOGY (chapter 14) as a part of metaphysics. Then is there really a prospect of an innocent, theologically neutral meaning-theory, not only telling us what is meant by the various terms used by religious thinkers, but *also* telling us the metaphysical truth about such matters? Surely the gap cannot be bridged: anything innocent enough to qualify on the first score must leave the truth of theological claims undecided; anything strong enough to decide them (for instance, the claim that a term like 'God' derives its meaning from God, who must therefore exist for us to think as we do) is not the innocent, neutral starting point that Dummett requires and promises. The same dilemma is visible in other areas, such as ethics. Careful attention to the nature of evaluative language is certainly a necessary part of any worthwhile philosophy of ethics, but without a wider view of the nature of human choice, desire, and action it will not itself settle disputes between one and another metaphysics of value. And semantic doctrines that bear on such disputes, such as the view that ethical language is essentially prescriptive in function, or the view that ethical predicates work in much the same way as colour predicates, are not the neutral, purely empirical outcome of a meaning-theory, but represent instead wider philosophical thought about the way ethical commitments actually function. For a final example, consider the descriptions that are offered of the language in which we talk about necessity and possibility. The best known semantics for these languages are thoroughly 'realistic', conceiving of us as referring to possible worlds, and describing the inferences we make in classical quantificational terms (if we are talking about possible worlds, necessity becomes equivalent to 'all' and possibility to 'some', and the logic is then understood classically). The semantic success of this kind of description is undoubted, but its philosophical significance is controversial in the extreme. Those, like Lewis, whose metaphysics is driven entirely by semantics embrace the real existence of different worlds to ours; others reject any such metaphysical implications, and maintain that reference to possible worlds is some kind of useful fiction. The example shows clearly how an overview of the logic of an area can leave its metaphysics almost entirely in the dark. In spite of Dummett's impassioned and weighty advocacy, the prospects, then, for a neutral semantic methodology for metaphysics are not all that bright.

The strength of Dummett's position was its insistence that if metaphysics gives us more than vaguely agreeable pictures, then its content should be reflected in our practice. That is, if a doctrine such as realism means anything, it must make a difference whether or not we adopt it, and this difference must be manifested somewhere in our thought and language. The mathematical example is one in which the classical mathematician allows different inferences from the intuitionist; the difference is therefore one of logic. It is not, however, clear to what extent this case generalizes – certainly, many people who think of themselves as anti-realists about ethics have no objection to classical logic as a systematization of correct inference in that sphere. Kant thought that it was precisely because mathematics was our own construction that we had the right to pursue it in the certainty that every mathematical proposition is true or false. A metaphysics is an overall structure determining which explanations of our practices we find acceptable: it determines what is familiar, what exotic, what counts as an acceptable accommodation and what is intolerable to us. The difference that realism or anti-realism makes is not necessarily one of logic. It comes out primarily in what we accept as explanations of our practice, including explanations of the correctness or otherwise of various patterns of inferences, and it is because of this that classical logical practice can happily co-exist with an anti-realist explanation of its appropriateness.

Dummett's conception of the subject is almost unique in the contemporary scene in its insistence on a starting-point that is uncontaminated by scientific and metaphysical doctrines and ideologies. Much more common is the view that such doctrines will themselves be historically conditioned and therefore possibly changeable. It is important to notice that in detail the nature of such changes is often controversial. For example, it has been claimed by Rorty (1979) that the philosophy of mind and its problems are historically quite local, being mainly the upshot of the rise of Cartesian philosophy in the early seventeenth century. To others this is incredible, since it is possible to point to the universal human preoccupation with such possibilities as life after death or the transmigration of souls as a sure sign that the relationship of mind to body has seldom been fully under control. Again, some see the distinction between primary qualities on the one hand – such as extension and mass, which are thought of as real qualities of objective, independent bodies – and secondary qualities on the other hand – such as colour or taste, which are thought of as inherently subjective or mind-dependent – as the local upshot of the science of the same period. But others point to the foundation of the distinction in Greek thought, and its appearance in various forms in Indian or Chinese thought, and argue that the basis is not a particular scientific ideology, but is found in relatively universal or *a priori* considerations.

3 Naturalism and Identity

The authority of logic lay behind the analytic ideal, for logical relationships are those that are laid bare by analysis. When this authority falters, as I have described it doing, the authority of science is the natural substitute, and it is in its shelter that metaphysics is currently mainly conducted. Metaphysics, on this view, is not discontinuous with science. It is theorizing as pursued by the scientist, sometimes on the basis of familiar data and sometimes in the light of new scientific results. This is the *naturalistic* self-image, most forcibly propounded by the American philosopher W. V. O. Quine (b. 1908), and dominant in the minds of many or most contemporary philosophers. In this view, it is perfectly proper to attempt, for example, a metaphysics of MIND AND BODY (chapter 5). It is to be done in the spirit of science, with an up-to-date understanding of neurophysiology, computer science, ecology, evolutionary biology, or any other subject that rings the area. The philosopher marshals the results of the sciences, and propounds a concept of the mind–body relationship that best makes the results fit together, just as the scientist marshals the results of empirical enquiry, and propounds a concept of the nature of things that best makes those results fit together. The metaphysicians' activity differs only in the level of abstraction required, and indeed any difference from the activity of theoretical science is likely to be vague and provisional. Success in philosophizing would most dramatically be shown if the results of philosophical enquiry actually played a role in driving scientific progress.

It is easy to understand why the naturalistic self-image is so popular. First of all, it answers the question of how metaphysics is possible. It is continuous with science, and, since science is possible, so is metaphysics. Secondly, it allows the philosopher some of the prestige and glory of the scientist. It is reassuring to ally philosophical reflection with the most secure and intellectually privileged elements of the contemporary culture. Perhaps philosophy is always something of a free-loader when it comes to continuity with the most prestigious activities. When theology ruled the universities, philosophy and theology were continuous; in the first part of this century, and after the spectacular successes of modern logic, philosophy was deemed continuous with logic; then a little later with linguistics, and now philosophy marches into the future hand-in-hand with science. (The process is of course not as simple as that. Philosophy has had the scientific self-image on-and-off since Aristotle. But other paradigms have also had their day.) Thirdly, the assimilation of metaphysics to science solves the problem of method. In the abstract, it is difficult to know how to conduct metaphysical enquiry. How is one to go about solving the mind–body problem, or discussing the nature of necessity? In distant times, the answer might have been by reflection on what the deity created, by reflection on the logic of mental or modal discourse, or by reflection on the language of mental ascription or modal embeddings. But the current answer is more reassuring: scientifically.

With so much to motivate contentment with this answer, it may be well to wonder whether an element of wish-fulfilment has crept in. Is it possible that the self-image of philosophy as being continuous with science is largely fantasy – that we have been captured by the most superficial resemblances between philosophical and genuinely scientific activity? Might it be that science-envy has led philosophers to see themselves through a comfortable modern haze? Of course, if approaching a subject scientifically simply means attempting to follow it through in a disciplined way, taking account of the known facts, building on our predecessor's labours, using the best ways we have of distinguishing the good from the bad or the true from the false, then philosophy as properly practised, like any other discipline, must be pursued scientifically. But in that sense a novelist or poet may also practise their craft scientifically; the obstacle remains that such activities may bear only the most superficial resemblance to the practice of natural sciences.

The reason for this is clear if we consider what we want from a satisfactory relationship between the exotic and the familiar. Suppose we are happy with scientific facts: in the case of people, let us suppose these are facts about their behaviour and their brains. The naturalist will believe that in an important sense brains and behaviour is all that there is. What then is there to say about mind? The simplest answer is that mental states or events or properties are states, events, or properties of the preferred natural kind. The equation would be presented as like that between water and H_2O, or between lightning and electrical discharge. An enormously important shift took place when these equations emerged as new paradigms of method in metaphysics, largely in the 1970s, and it was due to the work of writers such as Putnam (1975) and Kripke (1980). It became believed that we can relate an exotic area to a domestic one in a less hazardous way than by concentrating on equations of meaning. All we may need is an identity claim about the things and properties in question. We do not also need the claim that the very same thing is meant by talking in terms of one and in terms of the other. It is sufficient, for instance, to understand water in scientific terms to know that water *is* H_2O; we do not also need the requirement that the two terms mean the same. Similarly, we would bring mind and consciousness down to natural earth if we could identify mental states, processes and events, with physical states, processes and events. We do not also have to claim that it means the same to talk in either way. Identity of things and properties became the ruling relationship to search for, not identity of meaning.

However, casual acquaintance with the modern literature shows that philosophical discussion of such an equation is not very much like scientific discussion of these equations. There, one would find various kinds of empirical evidence and theory. In the philosophical case we have a general belief that mind must be thought of as fundamentally physical, and then we conduct a great deal of armchair theorizing about the nature of the sustaining equations and identities. This theorizing does not proceed with very convincing examples of actual identities to hand, nor, indeed is it even known whether convincing 'type–type' identities exist. Thus, it is always true that lightning is an electrical discharge, or water is H_2O, but it may not always be true that a mental event such as a pain coexists with a type of physical event, or whether pain might be 'variably realized' in different brains or different psychologies. It is here that philosophers discuss whether the equation is contingent or necessary, whether it relates types of mental events to types of physical events or whether it is sufficient that each mental event is identical with some – possibly different – kind of physical event, whether it matters that description of a person's mentality often invokes relations with the environment, history and culture, and so on. Without this kind of discussion the equation is of little interest, but it is this theorizing that is insufficiently like anything the scientist does that casts doubt on the Quinean paradigm.

In fact, it may be claimed that the entire discussion of such identities waits upon a piece of analysis that is, unfortunately, not yet completed. We know how to assess questions of identity when the subjects are *things*; we may know how to assess them in cases like that of water or lightning, where what is at question is the way in which a natural kind of event is constituted. But do we know how to assess cross-category identities when the subjects are facts, events, states or properties? What does it mean, for example, to say that my state when I enjoy a glass of wine is identical with the state of some part of my brain, or that the event of my enjoyment is identical with some such event, or that the property of enjoying the wine is identical with some neurophysiological property? Such identity claims do not wear their meanings on their sleeve; nor does a metaphysics centred on asserting them. We do not even know whether each of the abstract categories involved – property, state, event or fact – relates to identity in the same way, or whether very different criteria are needed in each case. To give a simple parallel, some philosophers hold that if a padlock opens by having three notches in line, then it makes sense to say that the state or property of being unlocked is, in this padlock (not others), that of having three notches in line; other philosophers doubt if the equation makes sense, or whether, if it does, it is of any metaphysical use (Lewis, 1966, Blackburn, 1993).

It does not follow that these questions will be investigated by exactly the techniques modelled on analytical chemistry, and developed by Russell, Moore, Carnap and their followers. But support for this conception of the subject comes from the following thoughts. Suppose we need to locate a way of thinking accurately, in order to gain an understanding of the categories it uses. Then the primary data are the *inferences* that structure the area. These are conveniently thought of as of three kinds. There are things that enable us to make inferences *to* doctrines in the area (sometimes called the assertibility conditions of such doctrines), there are inferences *among* such doctrines, and there are things we may infer *from* them, or their consequences. Staying with the example of mind, the statement that someone is enjoying their glass of wine may be inferred from certain aspects of their behaviour; it enables us to infer that they believe that there is nothing poisonous about the wine (and many other things of the kind), and it enables us to infer (with less confidence) that they are likely to stay put for some while, and unlikely to start doing push-ups or spit on the carpet. The analytic ideal suggests that such inferences, and many like them, give the statement its identity. Not to make them would eventually show that someone does not fully understand what is involved in enjoying a glass of wine; it would reveal incompetence with the notions involved. But identifying these inferences is, in effect, the project of analysis. A term is analysed, in the classical tradition, precisely when we understand what licenses its application, and what consequences may be drawn from it.

The problem that many authors find with this line of thought is that the inferences in question do not seem to come in statement-sized bundles. The mental world is full of surprises and caveats: behaviour that is indicative of enjoying a glass of wine in one person may not be so in another; what else a person wants or believes when they enjoy a glass of wine may be almost indefinitely variable, and for all we know there may be cultures in which doing push-ups or spitting on the carpet is exactly what we would expect by way of showing such enjoyment. The phenomenon, often called the 'holism of the mental' means that straightforward identification of the patterns of inference associated with understanding a mental ascription is not to be expected. Once more, enjoying a glass of wine is something that can be 'variably realized' in different psychologies, evidenced by different behaviour and giving rise to different expression, depending on a whole range of other factors.

Identities nevertheless remain popular instruments for relating the familiar to the exotic. But there are cases that raise more obvious difficulties than that of mind. Consider the project of giving a naturalistic theory of values. Suppose it is pursued on the water–H_2O model, by finding a property with which a value such as goodness may plausibly be identified. Let us suppose for simplicity's sake that a property is selected, such as that of creating happiness. This is thought of as a natural, empirically respectable property, it being a fairly ordinary fact about the world (however hard to assess in some cases) that some things cause happiness and others do not. So the metaphysician naturalizes values by making the equation. Admittedly, saying that something is good is not just saying that it creates happiness – Moore refuted that idea (1903). Nevertheless, the identity-inclined metaphysician insists, the properties are the same. The puzzle with such an idea is that it is quite unclear which of the problems that ethics generates it actually solves. It leaves untouched any investigation of the particular 'take' on the creation of happiness that is had by those who think that it is good, as opposed to those who are indifferent to it, or even who think that it is bad. It does not by itself tell us what kind of mistake is made by these other people. Is it an objective mistake, or a more subjective one; is their error an empirical error, or one of logic? What, indeed, does it mean to see the creation of happiness under the ethical heading? While such questions remain, the identity seems itself a poor contribution to the overall project of giving a naturalistic understanding of our engagement with values.

The Limits of Ontology

Although doing metaphysics by means of the identity of property, state, event or fact is popular, it introduces a particular attitude to its problems: one in which the primary questions are ones of what exist; ones of *ontology*. The central question becomes whether we have two things or one, whether the things are events, properties, states, facts or other more homely items. This is also a contrast with the approach of analysts like Dummett. For the analyst, the unit of significance is the entire sentence; there is no self-standing investigation into the kinds of thing that parts of sentences such as predicates stand for (however, as Taylor (1993) remarks, realists have often felt motivated to expound the existence and nature of such items as universals and properties). But many problems, such as that of value, suggest that not all metaphysical issues are well approached in these terms. Another example where ontology scarcely seems to be the issue is the problem of natural law or necessity. This problem, brought into prominence by Hume (1739–40), is that of gaining some conception of any necessity underlying the brute empirical order of events. Events, as we apprehend them, happen one after another in contingent patterns that the natural scientist discovers. Descriptions of the way they fall out may be all right; they form the familiar class. What is exotic and hard to think about is a reason why they must fall out as they do, or why the universe must be ordered as it is, or why the order that is discovered must continue to govern its evolutions in the future. The theological world-view could take refuge in the necessity thought to attach to God's existence and to God's goodness in continuing to sustain the same natural order; when such an answer no longer appeals to peoples' minds there is urgent need for something to fill its place. The problem is essentially metaphysical, for what we are looking for is some conception of the holding of a law of nature: something lying behind or above the actual pattern of events and constraining them to fall out as they do. Now will such a problem be eased by an ontological doctrine? Many suppose it can. They believe that if we can say, sufficiently seriously, that natural laws exist, then everything is fine. It would not be sufficiently serious to say this but only to mean that there are some regularities that are so central to the enterprise of science that they deserve central and privileged places in the ways we systematize our understanding of the patterns of events. The problem is to gain any conception of what it is for these real natural laws to exist, or how things of the nature they need to have are even possible. How can there exist a straightjacket, whose nature at one time governs how things must fall out at later times or at all other times (Blackburn, 1993, chs 3, 5)? More ontology just provides more things, but things and their continued good behaviour are part of the problem, and so do not seem to be any part of the solution.

A final, even clearer example in which ontology cannot be the central issue is the problem of free will. Realizing that we ourselves, physically, are determined complexes, or at best are permitted only such departures from determination as the random events of quantum mechanics allow, philosophers friendly to free-will may struggle to find a further 'part' of us, such as a Cartesian, ghostly, governing agency. But the dilemma is not escaped by these means, for it returns to plague whatever extra is added, for it remains to be explained how it is itself neither wholly determined nor wholly random. The additional ontology is no help with the solution.

Problems with identity have led many naturalists to back down a little, and stake their faith on a different, and at first sight more tractable relation: that of supervenience.

4 Supervenience

Whether or not it makes sense to identify mental and physical events, or ethical and natural properties, at least we ought to think that the mental arises out of the physical, and the ethical out of the natural. This is commonly put by saying that the mental supervenes on the physical, and the ethical on the natural. What does this mean? The fundamental idea is that once the physical aspects of the world are completely fixed, so are the mental. And once the natural facts about a world are completely fixed, so is the question of its ethics – which actions are right and wrong, or who behaved well or badly. Once the familiar is fixed, so is the exotic. If we think in terms of God creating a world, then all He has to do, according to this idea, is to create the physical world. He will thereby have done sufficient to fix the mental facts, or the ethical facts. There is no second creative task to complete.

This idea promises many of the benefits of identity claims, without involving itself in the issues of the previous section. It needs no controversial metaphysics of facts, states of affairs or properties, nor any method of resolving disputed identity claims involving these notions. But it gives the same sense that there is in reality 'nothing but' the underlying, physical or natural world. At least it removes one kind of metaphysical distance between the two categories; the distance that would be were there a second creative task to complete, so that we could imagine the physical being as it is, but without the mental overlay, or the natural being as it is, but without the ethical overlay.

It is notable that to give us this advantage, the supervenience claim must somewhere involve a necessity. There would be a second creative task to complete if, as well as creating physics, God had to shop for one amongst several possible ways in which physics is able to fix the mental (in this world). If this relationship were contingent, capable of taking different forms in different possible worlds, then clearly there would be a second creative task to complete. It would not be strictly true that physics fixed everything; only physics plus whatever it is as well as physics that links everything else to it.

It is, I believe, worthy of note that the best understood examples of supervenience do not quite give us this sort of necessity. Many examples involve a reference to perception, as when the face in the picture supervenes upon an array of dots. It is certainly true that to create the face no more is necessary than to create the array of dots. But that seems to be because the world contains perceivers such as ourselves; relative to different perceptual powers there would no longer be a face in the picture. So, strictly, God had to do more to create the face in the picture than just arrange the dots; He also had to generate the perceptual sensitivities capable of responding to just that array in just that way. Similarly, to create secondary qualities, such as those of colour, it is not only necessary to create a world in which surfaces reflect light in various ways, but also to create the kinds of perceptual systems that detect the variations in just that way. In these cases, instead of the reassuring, physicalist-sounding thesis that everything supervenes on the underlying physics, we only get that it supervenes on the underlying physics and the relations between physics and perceivers. Granted, a full-blown physicalist will promise that this relation in turn supervenes upon the physics of the surface and the physics of the perceiver, but, so far, this remains simply a promise. We do not have, in cases like this, reassuring examples of the necessity that supervenience claims require.

In the case of ethics it is quite unsatisfactory simply to cite the supervenience of values on natural facts, and then to hope that this makes the intelligible bridge required. The problem is obviously to explain the necessity in question. Granted that any two worlds that are identical in all natural features are identical in all ethical features, why should this have to be so? What, logically or metaphysically, prevents there being a dimension of freedom, the extra thing that God has to do to fix the fact–value links? Explaining supervenience here marks a constraint on satisfactory theory. Some believe that it can be met by citing the parallel with perceptual supervenience claims such as the ones discussed above; others deny this, but think that attention to the purposes for which we value things can only be met by a value system obeying the supervenience constraint. There arises a kind of pragmatic justification for this aspect of the logic of the activity (Blackburn, 1993). Once more the issue is one of explanation, and different metaphysical choices are primarily significant because of the different explanatory packages they offer.

5 Conclusion

I have structured this survey round the problem of method in metaphysics, and some of the most influential suggestions about the source of metaphysical method and of metaphysical authority. I have also sketched some of the ways in which authoritative suggestions – analysis, meaning-theory and scientific reduction – have proved at best aids, but never final arbiters of metaphysical success. My own belief is that metaphysics is better regarded as an ocean into which all intellectual rivers flow. When the problems are as abstract and the kinds of explanation required are so difficult to formulate, there is bound to be influence from many different sources. The self-conception of a given period, the scientific paradigms of that period, the most influential examples of intellectual success, even the ethical and political agenda, as well as conceptions of the role of the intellectual, all play a role in determining whose voices will prevail at any given time. This is not a cause for regret, but it may perhaps arm us with a cautious skepticism when candidates for metaphysical certainty present themselves.

Further Reading

This chapter emphasises twentieth-century metaphysics, but readers might also wish to consult the metaphysical works of historical figures discussed in other chapters, especially Hume, *A Treatise of Human Nature* and Kant, *Critique of Pure Reason*. Craig (1987) explores the great modern change from a divine to a human context of metaphysical thought.

Russell (1905) was long considered a model for analytical treatment of metaphysical questions. Wittgenstein (1922), while having a metaphysical character of his own, inspired the strenuously anti-metaphysical attitude of the Vienna Circle. The pragmatism of Peirce, James (1907), and Dewey influenced many recent American writers, including Quine (1951), Goodman (1955), Putman (1975) and Rorty (1979, 1989). The criticism of positivism in Quine and Wittgenstein (1953) led to new perspectives on the possibility of metaphysics, especially that of Strawson (1959), whose focus on describing the contours of our ordinary conceptual scheme has been rejected in the eliminativism of Churchland (1989) and Stich (1983). Kripke (1980) and Lewis

(1983) have provided different accounts of the importance of modal logic (dealing with necessity and possibility) for metaphysics. Dummett (1978, 1991) has argued that logic and the theory of meaning are the basis for metaphysics, especially for dealing with the fundamental conflict between realism and anti-realism, a question also considered in Blackburn (1993).

References

Blackburn, S. 1984: *Spreading the Word: Groundings in the Philosophy of Language.* Oxford: Oxford University Press.

—— 1993: *Essays in Quasi-Realism.* New York: Oxford University Press.

Churchland, Paul 1989: *A Neurocomputational Perspective: The Nature of Mind and the Structure of Science.* Cambridge, MA: MIT Press.

Collingwood, R. 1940: *An Essay in Metaphysics.* Oxford: Clarendon Press.

Craig, E. 1987: *The Mind of God and the Works of Man.* Oxford: Oxford University Press.

Dummett, M. 1978: The Philosophical Basis of Intuitionistic Logic. In *Truth and Other Enigmas*, London: Duckworth.

—— 1991: *The Logical Basis of Metaphysics.* Cambridge, MA: Harvard University Press.

Gibbard, A. 1990: *Wise Choices, Apt Feelings.* Cambridge MA: Harvard University Press.

Goodman, N. 1955: *Fact, Fiction and Forecast.* London: London University Press.

Hegel, G. 1991 [1821]: *The Philosophy of Right* (translated by H. B. Nisbet, edited by A. W. Wood). Cambridge: Cambridge University Press.

Hume, D. 1978 [1739–40]: *A Treatise of Human Nature* (edited by P. H. Nidditch). Oxford: Clarendon Press.

James, W. 1907: *Pragmatism: A New Name for some Old Ways of Thinking.* New York: Longmans.

Kripke, S. 1980: *Naming and Necessity.* Cambridge MA: Harvard University Press.

Lewis, D. 1966: An Argument for the Identity Theory. In *Philosophical Papers*, vol. 1. New York: Oxford University Press, 1983.

—— 1983 New Work for a Theory of Universals. *Australasian Journal of Philosophy*, 61.

Lewis, H. D. (ed.) 1963: *Clarity is not Enough.* New York: Humanities Press.

Putnam, H. 1975: The meaning of 'meaning'. In *Mind, Language and Reality: Philosophical Papers*, vol. 2. Cambridge: Cambridge University Press, 1975.

Quine, W. V. O. 1951: Two Dogmas of Empiricism. In *From a Logical Point of View*, New York: Harper, 1961.

Rorty, R. 1979: *Philosophy and the Mirror of Nature.* Princeton NJ: Princeton University Press.

—— 1989: *Contingency, Irony and Solidarity.* Cambridge: Cambridge University Press.

Russell, B. 1905: On Denoting. *Mind*, 14.

Stich, S. 1983: *From Folk Psychology to Cognitive Science.* Cambridge, MA: MIT Press.

Strawson, P. 1959: *Individuals: An Essay in Descriptive Metaphysics.* London: Methuen.

Taylor, B. 1993: On Natural Properties in Metaphysics. *Mind*, 102.

Wittgenstein, L. 1922: *Tractatus Logico–Philosophicus.* London: Routledge.

—— 1953: *Philosophical Investigations.* Oxford: Blackwell.

Discussion Questions

1   How is metaphysics possible? How do metaphysical questions arise?

2   Does metaphysics discover the broad structure of reality or describe how our conceptual scheme structures our thought about reality?

3   Must all possible conceptual schemes have certain features in common?

4   How might a programme of revisionary metaphysics be justified?

5   Can metaphysics be assessed without considering its ethical and political implications?

6   Is metaphysics the science of Being?

7   Does metaphysics have an acceptable method?

8   Why is metaphysics preoccupied with its own possibility?

9   Is metaphysics a function of what we find familiar and what we find puzzling? Can what we find familiar change?

10 Are there limits beyond which metaphysics should not go? Does the whole of metaphysics attempt to go beyond these limits?

11 If metaphysical questions are unanswerable, should metaphysics be abandoned?

12 Are metaphysical claims meaningless?

13 Are we able to determine whether the absolute presuppositions of our thought are true or false?

14 Can philosophical reflection exist only with hindsight? What does your answer tell us about the nature of metaphysics?

15 Can we eliminate all residual reference to ourselves when we consider the world?

16 Does any conceptual scheme have a unique and special relationship with the way things are?

17 What kind of justification can there be for any way of describing the world?

18 Have philosophers been right to move away from analysis as a method for metaphysics?

19 Should we accept Russell's theory of descriptions as a paradigm of philosophy?

20 In a reductionist programme, how do we determine what requires reduction and what it should be reduced to?

21 Do common-sense concepts need elimination, not analysis?

22 Can semantics be metaphysically neutral?

23 Can logic and a theory of meaning settle metaphysical controversies?

24 Is metaphysics continuous with science?

25 Should metaphysicians search for identity of things and properties rather than for identity of meaning?

26 Why do philosophers and scientists have different questions to ask about identities?

27 Are the basic questions of metaphysics questions of ontology?

28 Should metaphysics deal with supervenience rather than identity?

29 To what extent should explanatory success determine our choice of metaphysical position?

3

Philosophy of Language ——————

Martin Davies

As an initial indication of the subject matter of this chapter, we might say –
simply – that philosophy of language is that part of philosophy that is
concerned with questions about language. But, in several ways, this leaves
the domain of enquiry seriously underspecified. As a first step towards
giving a better indication of what philosophy of language is about, we need
to make a distinction. Everyone thinks about language, and makes use of an
ordinary, everyday conception of what language is and how it is used. In
addition, some people – theoretical linguists, for example – engage in the
scientific study of language, and have a more technical conception of
language and its use. Given this distinction between the everyday conception of language and the scientific conception, we can say that philosophy
of language deals with questions that arise from our ordinary, everyday
conception of language. (Philosophy of linguistics follows up questions
that arise from the scientific study of language. The distinction between
philosophy of language and philosophy of linguistics is thus analogous to
the distinction between philosophy of mind and philosophy of psychology.) However, this still does not give a very clear idea of the sorts of
questions that belong distinctively in philosophy of language. Wittgenstein
said (1953, §119), 'The results of philosophy are the uncovering of one or
another piece of plain nonsense and of bumps that the understanding
has got by running its head up against the limits of language.' From that
point of view, it can easily seem as though virtually all of philosophy is
concerned with questions about language – about the ways in which we
understand and misunderstand language, about how we come to mistake
plain nonsense for something that is intelligible, and about what cannot be
expressed in language. But, even though language does indeed loom large
in twentieth-century philosophy, there is still a specific, recognizable area
of the discipline that is philosophy of language. Perhaps the easiest way to
point to it is to say that it begins from one absolutely basic fact about
language, namely, that expressions of a language have meaning, and can be
used to talk about objects and events in the world. For philosophy of
language, the central phenomenon to be studied is linguistic meaning. This
chapter introduces some of the ways in which that study proceeds. Readers
might also like to look at the closely related chapters on PHILOSOPHY OF MIND
(chapter 5), PHILOSOPHY OF LOGIC (chapter 4), FREGE AND RUSSELL (chapter 27) and
WITTGENSTEIN (chapter 29).

1 Introduction: Questions of Meaning

Questions in the philosophy of language – particularly, questions about meaning – can be divided roughly into two classes. In one class, there are questions about the meanings of particular linguistic expressions. Some of the questions concern words, some concern phrases, and some concern whole sentences. Central examples from this first class would be provided by questions about the meanings of subject expressions – including PROPER NAMES (chapter 27) ('Theaetetus', 'Fido') and DESCRIPTIVE PHRASES (pp. 670–2) ('the man in the gabardine coat', 'the present king of France') – and of PREDICATE (chapter 4) expressions like 'is sitting', 'barks', 'is a spy', and 'is bald', as well as questions about the meanings of complete subject–predicate sentences ('Theaetetus is sitting', 'The present king of France is bald'). Further examples of linguistic expressions for which philosophical questions about meaning arise include other subject terms – pronouns ('I', 'you', 'she', 'he', 'it', 'they') and demonstratives ('this', 'that', 'this knife', 'that butter') – along with expressions that go beyond the terms in the basic combination of subject and predicate. These latter examples include adjectives ('large' as it occurs in 'large flea', 'small' as it occurs in 'small elephant', 'good' as it occurs in 'good person' and in 'good philosopher', 'false' as it occurs in 'false sentence' and in 'false nose'), modal adverbs ('possibly', 'necessarily'), manner adverbs ('slowly', 'clumsily'), and many more.

Still in the first class, and closely related to questions about the meanings of words, phrases and sentences, are questions about the ways in which the meanings of words determine, or at least constrain, the meanings of the phrases and sentences in which they occur. Even if we know what kind of thing the meaning of a sentence is (the meaning of 'Fido barks', or of 'The man in the gabardine coat is a spy'), we also need to understand how component words and phrases make their contributions to the meanings of complete sentences. All these questions belong to *semantics* (section 4).

In the other class, there are questions about the nature of language, and particularly about the nature of meaning itself. Some of these questions are ontological. Are meanings entities; and, if so, what kinds of entities are they? One putative answer might be that the meanings of complete sentences are propositions, and that answer would lead, in turn, to questions about the nature of propositions. An alternative answer might be that, if the meanings of sentences are entities, then they are *states of affairs*. Someone following up this alternative might say that in order for a sentence to be true, the state of affairs that is the sentence's meaning needs to be a state of affairs that *obtains*. *Facts* might then be identified with states of affairs that obtain, and true sentences would be said to be true in virtue of facts. In this case, the answer to the ontological question about meanings would lead to a version of the correspondence theory of truth.

Other questions in the second class concern elucidation or analysis of the concept of meaning. Can we, for example, give any kind of philosophical analysis of the concept of linguistic meaning; and, if we can, what kinds of

ideas can legitimately be used in the analysis? How, in general, is the meaning
of a linguistic expression related to its use? Does it make sense, for example, to
suppose that there might be more to the meaning of an expression than could
ever be revealed in its use? How is the concept of meaning related to the
concept of truth? In particular, for a complete sentence, what is the relation
between the meaning of the sentence and the conditions under which an
utterance of the sentence would be true? These questions – both ontological
and conceptual – which focus on the key notions used in semantics, are said
to belong to *meta-semantics* (section 5).

The everyday idea of meaning or significance is related to the idea of what
is conveyed or communicated in the use of language. In recent philosophy of
language, a standard assumption in meta-semantics has been that there is such
a thing as the *literal meaning* of linguistic expressions, and that the total
communicative significance of a linguistic act is the product jointly of the
literal meanings of the expressions used and of contextual factors. According
to that meta-semantic view, semantics is the study of the literal meanings of
expressions, and of the way that literal meanings of complex expressions –
phrases and sentences – are determined by the literal meanings of their
component words. Strictly speaking, questions about the interaction between
literal meaning and contextual factors belong, not to semantics, but to
pragmatics (section 6).

2 Theories of Meaning

Answers to semantic questions and answers to meta-semantic questions can be
given by propounding what might be called *theories of meaning*; but that
phrase has two very different senses.

Let us consider semantic questions first. These are questions about the
meanings of words and phrases, and about the ways in which these contribute
to the meanings of whole sentences. For the words, phrases and sentences of
a particular language, someone might seek to answer these questions in a very
explicit way, by providing a certain kind of formal, axiomatized theory. The
idea would be that the axioms of this theory should specify explicitly the
meanings of the words of the language under study, and that rules of inference
should then permit the derivation, from those axioms, of *theorems* specifying
the meanings of phrases, and ultimately of whole sentences. In the case of any
given sentence (say, 'Fido barks'), the derivation of a meaning-specifying
theorem would make use of the axioms of the theory that specify the meanings
of the words occurring in that sentence (in this case, the words 'Fido' and
'barks'). This derivation (or proof) of a theorem from axioms could reasonably
be said to display how the meanings of the component words contribute to the
meaning of the complete sentence.

The construction of theories of the kind envisaged here is a far from trivial
matter. We might start off by supposing that a typical theorem would say
something like:

The meaning of the sentence 'Fido barks' is the proposition that the particular dog Fido engages in the activity of barking.

or, avoiding the explicit talk about propositions:

Th1   The sentence 'Fido barks' means that the particular dog Fido engages in the activity of barking.

and that the axioms from which this theorem is to be derived would say things like:

Ax1   The word 'Fido' means a particular dog, namely, Fido.
Ax2   The word 'barks' means the activity of barking.

But, even in the context of this extremely simple example, we can see that we would immediately confront at least two important issues. The first issue concerns the difference between subject terms and predicate terms (here, between 'Fido' and 'barks'); the second issue concerns the derivational route from the axioms to the theorem (here, from Ax1 and Ax2 to Th1).

2.1 The difference between subject terms and predicate terms

The issue about the difference between subject terms and predicate terms is this. The two axioms that we proposed have the same form. In each case, the axiom says that an expression stands in the meaning relation to something in the world – in one case, a dog, in the other case, an activity. So, those axioms do not really explain why these two words – 'Fido' and 'barks' – can go together to make up a sentence, whereas other pairs of words – such as two nouns – cannot together yield a sentence, but merely constitute a list.

We can make this point more vivid if we consider, for a moment, nouns that are closely related to predicate terms. Consider, for example, the noun 'barking'. This noun can, of course, occur in sentences: 'The barking of the neighbourhood dogs kept me awake'. Indeed, it can function as the subject term in a sentence: 'Barking is fun'. But the noun 'barking' cannot be juxtaposed with the word 'Fido' to make a sentence. Similarly, consider the noun 'baldness'. If we juxtapose this noun with a subject term, then what we get – say, 'The present king of France baldness' – is not a sentence. In order to see that it is just a list, we can imagine it as an answer to a request for information about what was discussed at a meeting.

The point, in short, is that there seems to be an important difference in meaning between predicate terms, such as 'barks' and 'is bald', and other closely related expressions. The meanings of the predicate terms somehow fit them for combining with subject terms to form sentences, while the meanings of those other expressions ('barking', 'baldness') do not so fit them. Now, suppose that we were asked to offer a meaning-specifying axiom for the noun 'barking' in the style of Ax1 and Ax2. Then we would be virtually bound to say:

The noun 'barking' means the activity of barking.

But, this says just the same about the meaning of the noun 'barking' as Ax2 says about the meaning of the verb 'barks'. Similarly, the model for axioms that we have established thus far would suggest that for the verb phrase 'is bald', and for the noun 'baldness', the axioms should be:

> The phrase 'is bald' means the property of baldness.
> The noun 'baldness' means the property of baldness.

But, as we just saw, while 'barks' and 'is bald' can function as predicate terms in sentences, 'barking' and 'baldness' cannot. There must be a difference in meaning between 'barks' and 'barking', and between 'is bald' and 'baldness'; but the axioms that we have proposed do not reveal what this difference might be.

2.2 The derivational route from axioms to theorems

The issue about the route from axioms to a theorem is this. The derivation of a theorem from axioms is supposed to have the status of a logical PROOF (pp. 328–9), and it should make use of well understood, and well-behaved, logical resources. So, suppose that we apply these requirements to the theorem that we have highlighted (Th1) and the two axioms (Ax1 and Ax2).

Certainly the theorem does not follow from the axioms just by way of the logical resources of the propositional calculus or the PREDICATE CALCULUS (p. 349), for example. The inference from Ax1 and Ax2 to Th1 is not a logically valid one. In order to obtain a valid inference, we would need to add an extra premise, in the form of another axiom.

Clearly, if we were to add the hypothetical statement:

> If the word 'Fido' means a particular dog, namely, Fido, and the word 'barks' means the activity of barking, then the sentence 'Fido barks' means that the particular dog Fido engages in the activity of barking.

then we could proceed from this statement plus Ax1 and Ax2 to the conclusion Th1 by way of familiar logical rules of inference. The form of the inference would be:

> A, B, if A and B then C; therefore, C.

which is clearly valid. But there would be good reasons to aspire after something more general than this hypothetical statement about the specific words 'Fido' and 'barks'. We should seek an axiom that speaks in general terms of the effect of putting together two terms – subject and predicate – to make a simple sentence.

Provided that we can find some account of what a subject term is and what a predicate term is, something along the following lines might suggest itself:

> Ax3   If a subject term M means something, say, X, and a predicate term N means something, say, Y, then the sentence made up of M followed by N means that X engages in, or exemplifies, Y.

This is pleasingly general in the way that it talks about M and N and their meanings X and Y, and it is a generalization that we can – it seems – instantiate in order to yield the more specific hypothetical statement about the subject term 'Fido' and the predicate term 'barks'. If that is right, then the conclusion Th1 can be validly derived from Ax1, Ax2 and Ax3. So, by making explicit the generalization in Ax3, we have made some progress with the requirement that the derivation of a meaning-specifying theorem from axioms is supposed to have the status of a logical proof.

Furthermore, we could instantiate the same generalization, Ax3, to give a hypothetical statement about the subject term 'Theaetetus', the predicate term 'is sitting', and the sentence that they go together to make up. Taken in conjunction with specific axioms about the meanings of 'Theaetetus' and 'is sitting', this hypothetical statement would enable us to derive a theorem specifying the meaning of the sentence 'Theaetetus is sitting'.

But, although this looks promising (apart from the issue about subject terms and predicate terms), there are still legitimate causes for concern as to whether statements like Ax1, Ax2 and Ax3 interact with standard logical resources in a well-behaved way. In fact, most work in semantics proceeds on the assumption that, in order to be sure of the logical status of our derivations, we should not make use of axioms and theorems that talk explicitly about meaning. We shall return to this point later (section 4.1)

The Notion of Meaning and Standard Logic

In standard logical systems we have a principle – in essence, Leibniz's law – saying, amongst other things, that if Fido = Rover, then from any statement about Fido, we can infer the corresponding statement about Rover, and vice versa. If we now imagine that one and the same dog has two names, 'Fido' and 'Rover', we can ask whether from the premise:

Fido = Rover

plus:

Ax1 The word 'Fido' means a particular dog, namely, Fido.

it follows that:

Ax1' The word 'Fido' means a particular dog, namely, Rover.

Either answer – 'yes' or 'no' – is potentially problematic.

If Ax1' does follow, then we can see – by a few more steps – that everything that can be said about the meaning of the word 'Fido' can be equally truly said about the meaning of the word 'Rover'. Furthermore, the same will go for any pair of words that pick out the same object in the world, such as the pair 'Hesperus' and 'Phosphorus', which both pick out the planet Venus. But, we should want to leave it open, at this early stage of our enquiry, whether such pairs of words can be distinguished in point of their meaning. Indeed, ahead of detailed theoretical considerations, we might reasonably expect that such pairs of words would sometimes differ in meaning, despite picking out the same object.

So, perhaps we should prefer the alternative that says that Ax1' does not follow from Ax1 plus the premise that Fido = Rover. But, in that case, we shall have to admit frankly that we are departing from what is familiar, and moving to a kind of theory whose logical behaviour is not so well understood.

We have been considering theories of meaning, in the first of two possible senses of that phrase. These are theories that seek to answer semantic questions, and we have just noted two ways in which the construction of these semantic theories is a non-trivial project. Semantic theories – which are often theories in a quite formal sense (theories with axioms and rules of inference by means of which theorems can be derived) – must be distinguished from theories about the nature of linguistic meaning itself. These latter theories are offered as answers to meta-semantic questions. A theory of meaning, in this second sense of the phrase, provides an analysis, or some other kind of elucidation, of the notion of linguistic meaning – perhaps plotting connections between that notion and the notion of use, or the notion of truth.

A theory of meaning in the first sense – a semantic theory – might take the concept of meaning as an unanalysed, and unexplained, primitive notion. A theory of meaning in the second sense – a meta-semantic theory – will, in contrast, set out to analyse or explain that concept in other terms.

3 Language, Mind and Metaphysics: Questions of Priority

A semantic theory relates pieces of language to pieces of the world. We use language to talk about the world, and to express our thoughts, which are also about the world. (The aboutness of thoughts is often called *intentionality*.) Talk, thought and world form a triangle, and in philosophy of language, PHILOSOPHY OF MIND (chapter 5), and METAPHYSICS (chapter 2) we move around this triangle (figure 3.1).

Thus, for example, we might try to give a philosophical account of some distinctions in reality – say between OBJECTS AND PROPERTIES (pp. 590–1), or between particulars and universals in terms of differences amongst words, or

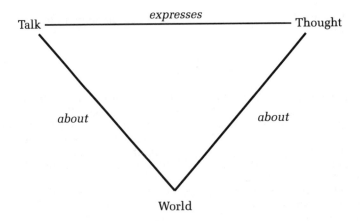

Figure 3.1   The relationship between talk, thought and the world, which is explored in the philosophy of language, the philosophy of mind and metaphysics.

in terms of differences in the realm of thought, provided that we already had some understanding of those linguistic or mental differences. Or, going the other way about, we might assume some account of those metaphysical differences, and use it in our philosophical work in the domains of talk or thought. We shall shortly consider just such a question of relative priority between philosophy of language and metaphysics.

There are also important questions of priority between philosophy of language and philosophy of mind. Indeed, any strategy for elucidating the concept of linguistic meaning will inevitably depend on our general view of the order of priority as between talk and thought. We need to be clear, first, just what notion of priority is at issue here. Then we shall consider three possible views about language and mind.

3.1 Philosophical priorities: Language and mind

The kind of priority that concerns us here is priority in the order of philosophical analysis or elucidation. To say that the notion of X is *analytically prior* to the notion of Y is to say that Y can be analysed or elucidated in terms of X, while the analysis or elucidation of X itself does not have to advert to Y. Thus to say that the notion of BELIEF (chapter 1) is analytically prior to the notion of KNOWLEDGE (chapter 1), for example, is to say that knowledge can be analysed in terms of belief, while a good analysis of belief does not need to re-introduce the notion of knowledge. (This is just to say what the claim would amount to, not whether it would be correct.)

Analytical priority should be distinguished from ontological priority and from epistemological priority. To say that X is *ontologically prior* to Y is to say that X can exist without Y, although Y cannot exist without X. For example, it might plausibly be said that individuals are ontologically prior to nations. To say that X is *epistemologically prior* to Y is to say that it is possible to find out about X without having to proceed via knowledge about Y, whereas finding out about Y has to go by way of finding out about X. So, it is plausible, for example, that the positions and trajectories of medium-sized material bodies are epistemically prior to the positions and trajectories of subatomic particles. We can find out about material bodies without investigating subatomic particles but, it might be said, our route to knowledge about subatomic particles has to go via observations of material bodies.

Having distinguished these three kinds of priority, we can make the working assumption that they are logically independent of each other. According to that assumption we can, for example, suppose that the notion of X is analytically prior to the notion of Y, without being obliged to hold that X is either ontologically or epistemologically prior to Y. Our question about the order of analytical priority as between language and mind relates, particularly, to the notion of linguistic meaning and the notion of intentionality (aboutness) for mental states. The three possible views that we need to be aware of are these.

(1)   *Mind first*: This is the view that it is possible to give a philosophical account of the intentionality of *thoughts* without essentially adverting to language,

and that the notion of linguistic meaning can then be analysed in terms of
the thoughts that language is used to express.

(2) *Language first*: This is the view that an account of linguistic meaning can be
given without bringing in the intentionality of thoughts, and that what a
person's thoughts are about can then be analysed in terms of the use of
language.

(3) *No priority (both together)*: This is the view that there is no way of
elucidating the notion of what a person's thoughts are about without
bringing in the notion of linguistic meaning, nor the other way around. The
two notions have to be explained together.

(There is in fact a fourth possible view, which involves a different kind of no
priority claim, namely that the two notions are quite unrelated. But this view,
while possible, is quite implausible.)

All three views have adherents. The no analytical priority view is characteristic of the work of Donald Davidson (b. 1917), who couples it with ontological
and epistemological no priority claims. Thus, Davidson argues that there can
be no thought without language (1975) nor language without thought, and that
there is no finding out in detail what a person believes without interpreting the
person's speech (1974). The language first view finds expression in Michael
Dummett's (b. 1925) writings (see 1973, 1991, 1993), while the mind first
approach is taken by Paul Grice (1913–88) (1989; see also Schiffer, 1972).
Given what we have assumed about the logical independence of the three
kinds of priority, we can see that one option that is available to us is to agree
with Davidson in denying the ontological or epistemological priority of mind
over language, and yet to follow Grice in trying to analyse the notion of
linguistic meaning in terms of the thoughts that language is used to express.

3.2 Philosophical priorities: Language and the world

Our example of a question of relative priority as between philosophy of
language and metaphysics comes from the work of Peter Strawson (b. 1919)
(1959, Part II; 1970a) on subject terms and predicate terms. The distinction in
language between subject and predicate terms is intuitively closely related to
the metaphysical distinction between objects or particulars, on the one hand
(corresponding to subject terms), and properties or universals, on the other
(corresponding to predicate terms). Can we use the metaphysical distinction to
help us understand the linguistic one? (As we have already seen, we certainly
need some account of the subject–predicate distinction.) Or should we,
alternatively, seek a more purely logico-linguistic account of the difference
between subject terms and predicate terms, and then try to understand the
metaphysical distinction in terms of the linguistic one?

One aspect of the subject–predicate distinction to which Strawson gives
considerable attention is what he calls the *asymmetry of subjects and
predicates regarding negation*. We can explain the basic idea like this. When a
subject–predicate sentence ('Theaetetus is sitting') is negated ('It is not the case
that Theaetetus is sitting', or 'Theaetetus is not sitting'), the negation can be
taken together with the predicate term to yield a new expression ('not sitting')
that is of the same kind – a new predicate term. But the negation cannot be

taken together with the subject to yield a new expression ('not Theaetetus') that is of the same kind – a new subject term. In short, predicate terms have negations while subject terms do not.

In order to provide (at least the beginnings of) an explanation of this fact about language, Strawson invites us to consider propositions in which – as he puts it – a general character or kind (or property or universal) is assigned to – or predicated of – a particular, or spatio–temporal individual. The important point is that these general characters come in incompatibility groups vis-à-vis such empirical particulars, while the particulars do not conversely come in incompatibility groups vis-à-vis the general characters. Thus, for example, consider the various colours (general characters) and the sundry items of furniture in the room (spatio-temporal individuals). An item of furniture cannot be more than one colour (all over); whereas more than one item of furniture can be the same colour. Or, consider the various postures that people can adopt (general characters) and the philosophers in a courtyard. Perhaps Theaetetus is sitting – and so not standing or lying – while Theodorus is also sitting and Socrates is standing. As both examples illustrate, general characters come in groups that 'compete' for spatio–temporal individuals; whereas the individuals do not come in groups that 'compete' for the general characters. There is at least the prospect, here, of an explanation of the linguistic distinction – between subject terms and predicate terms – that makes use of the metaphysical distinction between spatio–temporal individuals and the general characters that they may exemplify.

This approach exhibits an order of explanation that is the opposite of the one that is usually associated with the German mathematician and philosopher Gottlob FREGE (1848–1925) (chapter 27). On the Fregean approach, the metaphysical or ontological category of objects is to be read off from an antecedently fixed linguistic category of logical subject terms (roughly, names); so someone adopting this approach would need to be able to give a purely logico–linguistic criterion for an expression to be a name. It is not an easy matter to discharge this obligation without smuggling back in something like the distinction between objects and properties. Strawson himself, after reviewing some of the logico–linguistic marks of the subject–predicate distinction that might be drawn on in the Fregean order of explanation, remarks (1974a, pp. 13–14):

> The general relative natures of the terms combined in the fundamental combination of predication – the differences or alleged differences between subjects and predicates – have so far been discussed in almost exclusively formal terms, in terms belonging to formal logic itself or to grammar. To understand the matter fully, we must be prepared to use a richer vocabulary, a range of notions which fall outside these formal limits. We assume that the subject–predicate duality, and hence the differences so far remarked on, reflect some fundamental features of our thought about the world.

Now, it would not, in fact, be quite accurate to say that Strawson awards absolute priority to metaphysics; but we can, at least, say that he does not award a pre-eminent role to philosophy of language. In this, Strawson's position contrasts with that of Dummett. As we have already noted, when it comes to the question of priority as between language and mind, Dummett adopts the language first option. As we can now add, he also takes a Fregean view on the question about language and metaphysics. So, Dummett does regard the philosophy of language as pre-eminent. Indeed, he once wrote (1978, p. 441):

> [W]e may characterise analytical philosophy as that which follows Frege in accepting that the philosophy of language is the foundation of the rest of the subject.

This may not be an entirely happy characterization of analytical philosophy as a whole – since it would leave many analytical philosophers on the wrong side of the classification – but it does indicate one influential line of thought within analytical philosophy.

We should not, however, think that the only possible reason for interest in philosophy of language is that it might hold the key to questions in philosophy of mind and metaphysics. Questions about meaning are no less deep, and no less important, for the fact that, in order to investigate them fully, we may well need to draw on resources coming from other areas of philosophy.

4   Semantic Theories: Davidson's Programme

We have already met the idea of a formal, axiomatized theory that permits the systematic derivation of theorems specifying the meanings of complete sentences drawn from some language (section 2). The sentences might be simple or complex, and the language might be a formal language or a natural language. If we were interested in actually constructing theories of this type, then we might do well to proceed by stages.

The first and simplest stage would involve just a finite stock of sentences from a formal language, and would treat each of the sentences as an unstructured unit. Perhaps there are just three sentences, 'A', 'B' and 'C', where 'A' means that Theaetetus is sitting, 'B' means that Fido barks, and 'C' means that the man in the gabardine coat is a spy. In this case, the idea of an axiomatized semantic theory is simple to the point of triviality. For we can take just three axioms, one stating the meaning of each of the three sentences, and then the project of deriving a meaning-specifying theorem for each sentence of the language quite literally involves taking no steps at all.

The second stage would involve subject–predicate sentences from a formal language. We might have three predicate terms, 'F', 'G' and 'H' and three subject terms, 'a', 'b' and 'c', allowing us to construct nine subject–predicate sentences, amongst which, let us suppose:

'Fa'   means that Theaetetus is sitting
'Gb'   means that Fido barks

and

'Hc'   means that the man in the gabardine coat is a spy.

If we want to be able to derive a meaning-specifying theorem for each sentence in a systematic way, then we might hope to formulate a theory in which there is an axiom talking about the meaning of each subject term and an axiom talking about the meaning of each predicate term (rather along the lines of Ax1 and Ax2 in section 2 above).

At these first two stages, the total number of sentences under consideration is finite. The third stage would involve an infinite collection of sentences built from some finite stock by applying constructions over and over. We might take the three sentences, 'A', 'B' and 'C', from the first stage, and allow the application of a negation operator '¬'. This would give three more sentences, '¬A', '¬B', '¬C' (meaning that Theaetetus is not sitting, that Fido does not bark, and that the man in the gabardine coat is not a spy, respectively), and then three more, '¬¬A', '¬¬B', '¬¬C', and then three more, indefinitely. Alternatively, we could allow the application of a conjunction operator to two sentences at a time to give 'A&B', 'A&C', 'B&C', and – if we mark the order of the conjuncts – also 'B&A', 'C&A', 'C&B', and – if we allow repetition of conjuncts – 'A&A', 'B&B', 'C&C' (thus, nine new sentences to add to the original three). Then, applying the conjunction operator again, we get '(A&B)&C', '(A&C)&C', '(B&C)&C', and '(A&B)&(A&C)', and many more – in fact, 144 new sentences to add to the twelve.

We could, of course, allow the application of both the negation operator and the conjunction operator, to give us sentences like 'A&¬B'. Suppose that we do that, and then try to provide an axiomatized semantic theory for this simple, but infinite, collection of sentences. Along with axioms stating the meanings of our three building blocks, 'A', 'B' and 'C', we shall need an axiom saying something about the meaning of '¬' and one saying something about the meaning of '&'.

A first thought in this direction might be to suggest these two axioms:

'¬' means negation
&' means conjunction.

But it is quite unclear how, from this axiom about '¬', say, and the axiom stating the meaning of 'A', we could derive a theorem specifying the meaning of '¬A'. What looks more promising, for the negation operator, is something like:

> If S is any sentence at all, then the sentence made up by putting '¬' together with S means the negation of whatever S means.

This builds into the specification of the meaning of the operator an indication that it is indeed an *operator* that can be applied to any sentence to yield a new sentence. Something similar can be done for the conjunction operator; but we shall not pause any longer over these details. (In fact, this also suggests how we might make some progress with the meanings of predicate terms (see section 2.1). We could build into the axiom for a predicate term an indication that it is indeed a predicate – an expression that can go together with a subject term to make a sentence.)

A formal language with subject terms and predicate terms, plus a couple of sentence-building operators, is clearly very far indeed from the rich complexity of natural language. But, apart from the difference of scale, the step from formal languages to natural languages might seem simple in principle. If we know how to provide an axiomatized semantic theory for a formal language with subject terms and predicate terms, for example, then we also know how to provide a theory for a similarly structured fragment of natural language that uses real words and phrases instead of letters ('Theaetetus' instead of 'a', 'is sitting' instead of 'F').

However, in many cases, the relationship between sentences of a formal language and sentences of a natural language is much less clear. There is a tiny indication of this already in the case of negation, where the formal language operator attaches at the front of a complete sentence whereas natural language negation usually occurs alongside the predicate term. And, quite generally, the complexity of the relationship between formal and natural languages is shown by the difficulty of the task (familiar to most philosophy students) of regimenting into logical notation arguments that are expressed in natural language. So, one question that has to be faced is just how to regard the relationship between the superficial forms of natural language sentences, on the one hand, and the regimented forms (sometimes called *logical forms*) to which an axiomatized semantic theory could be applied, on the other hand.

Even if we ignore these differences between formal languages and natural languages, it is still the case that we have so far only envisaged a semantic theory for a simple subject–predicate language with sentence operators. Subsequent stages of the project of constructing semantic theories would involve bringing further types of expression within the scope of the enterprise.

We should, however, pause here to notice that, while it is clear that axiomatized semantic theories could be of interest to logicians, and – to the extent that they display the meanings of particular kinds of expressions such as pronouns, demonstratives, adjectives and so on – also to linguists, still it may not be evident why they should merit a philosopher's attention. In fact, the project of constructing systematic semantic theories has been a central concern in recent philosophy of language, and Davidson's work in particular reveals several reasons for focusing philosophical attention on semantic theories (Davidson, 1967a; and many other papers collected in Davidson, 1984). We shall review five of these reasons.

4.1   The format of semantic theories

The first reason for paying attention to axiomatized semantic theories concerns the proper format for the theorems that such a theory is supposed to yield. Since these theorems are supposed to be meaning-specifying, the initially obvious format would be one that relates a sentence to its meaning. If meanings are themselves regarded as entities of some kind, then we might expect a format like:

The meaning of sentence S is *m*.

If meanings are not regarded as entities, then we might expect instead:

Sentence S means *that p.*

Thus, on the first alternative, if meaning-specifying theorems are explicitly to relate sentences to propositions, say, then an example of such a theorem might be:

The meaning of the sentence 'Theaetetus is sitting' is the proposition that Theaetetus is sitting.

On the second alternative, similarly, an example might be:

The sentence 'Theaetetus is sitting' means that Theaetetus is sitting.

If, for some general reason, those formats have to be rejected – if the concept of meaning cannot, after all, figure in the theorems of a systematic semantic theory – then that would be a significant meta-semantic result.

Davidson (1967a) does indeed reject both those formats, and argues that the target theorems of a semantic theory should, instead, exhibit the format:

Sentence S is true if and only if *p*

(where 'if and only if' ('iff') expresses the *material biconditional*). Since theorems like this specify conditions under which a sentence is true, Davidson is said to favour *truth conditional semantics*. Davidson's argument for this conclusion comes in two steps.

The first step is intended to rule out the idea that, to each word, each phrase, and each sentence, there should be assigned some entity as its meaning. In this step, the so-called *Frege argument* (Frege, 1892, pp. 62–5; cf. Quine, 1960, pp. 148–9) is used to show that, under certain assumptions, all true sentences would be assigned the same entity. Clearly, no such undiscriminating assignment of entities could be an assignment of meanings, since it is certainly not correct that every true sentence has the same meaning. (Essentially the same line of argument allows Davidson (1969a) to conclude that there is no point in saying that true sentences correspond to facts. The Frege argument shows that, under certain assumptions, there is only one fact.)

The Frege Argument

The Frege argument shows that if an equivalence relation, E, on sentences meets two conditions then it classifies all true sentences as equivalent, and likewise all false sentences. The two conditions are these.

If two sentences are logically equivalent then they are equivalent according to E.

If two sentences are the same except for the fact that, where one contains a subject term *i*, the other contains another subject term, *j*, referring to the same thing, then they are equivalent according to E.

Suppose that we take any two true sentences. Let us choose, say, 'Penguins waddle' and 'The earth moves'. Then, firstly, the sentence

> (1) Penguins waddle
>
> is logically equivalent to
>
> (2) The number that is 1 if penguins waddle and is 0 if penguins do not waddle is 1.
>
> So, by the first condition, (1) and (2) are equivalent according to E. Similarly,
>
> (3) The earth moves
>
> and
>
> (4) The number that is 1 if the earth moves and is 0 if the earth does not move is 1.
>
> are equivalent according to E.
>
> But secondly, the subject term in (2), namely 'The number that is 1 if penguins waddle and is 0 if penguins do not waddle' refers to the number 1, since penguins do indeed waddle. And the subject term in (4), namely 'The number that is 1 if the earth moves and is 0 if the earth does not move', also refers to the number 1. So, sentences (2) and (4) are the same except for the fact that, where one contains a (rather lengthy) subject term, the other contains another (equally lengthy) subject term referring to the same thing. By the second condition, then, sentences (2) and (4) are equivalent according to E.
>
> Putting all this together, (1) is equivalent to (2), (2) to (4), and (4) to (3). So, (1) is equivalent to (3) according to E; and that is what we needed to show.

The second step in Davidson's argument for the truth conditional format points out that the 'means that p' construction presents logical difficulties, so that the formal derivations of meaning-specifying theorems will be highly problematic (see section 2.2). In contrast, the truth conditional format is logically well understood. The way in which theorems specifying truth conditions for complete sentences are derived from axioms assigning semantic properties to words and phrases can, to a considerable extent, be carried over from the work of Alfred Tarski (1902–83) on certain formal languages (Tarski, 1944, 1956).

This second step in the argument is technical in character, and it is a matter of dispute whether a systematic semantic theory making direct use of the 'S means that p' format is feasible. (See Schiffer, 1972, p. 162; Taylor, 1982; Davies, 1984.)

As for the status of the first step in the argument, it is now widely agreed that there are reasons for rejecting Davidson's use of the Frege argument. The Frege argument can only establish that all true sentences would be assigned the same entity as their meaning, if it is legitimate to suppose that the equivalence relation of having the same meaning would meet the two conditions that figure in the argument. But this is very far from being obvious. So, pending further argument to the contrary, we can admit that it would be possible for a systematic semantic theory to work by assigning an entity to each sentence as its meaning or semantic value. In particular, one possibility would be to assign to each sentence a certain kind of structured entity – a state of affairs with objects and properties as constituents. The situation semantics programme of Barwise and Perry (1983) constitutes one development of this possibility (see also Taylor, 1976; Forbes, 1989).

4.2 The correctness of semantic theories

The second reason for philosophical interest in systematic semantic theories relates to the conditions of adequacy or correctness for any such theory. Whatever is the right format for a semantic theory, we need some account of the conditions under which a theory in that format is the *correct* theory for the language of a particular speaker or group of speakers. We need to know, for example, what makes it correct to say that, in our language, the particular string of letters 'p'–'e'–'n'–'g'–'u'–'i'–'n'–'s' . . . and so on means that penguins waddle.

In order to be able to consider a possible reformulation of this question, we need to make use of the notion of an abstract or possible language. In the abstract, a language can be considered to be a collection of sentences together with a stipulated assignment of meanings to those sentences. So, for example, there are possible languages in which there is a sentence made up of those same letters – 'Penguins waddle' – but with the meaning that the earth moves. Given the notion of a possible language, the question whether a systematic semantic theory is correct for the language of a given group of speakers can be reformulated as the question whether the possible language for which the semantic theory is stipulated to be correct is the *actual language* of a given group (Lewis, 1975; Peacocke, 1976). What is sometimes called the *actual language relation* is thus a relation between languages (in the abstract) and groups of language users. Under the reformulation that we are envisaging, conditions of adequacy on semantic theories become constraints on the actual language relation.

Any philosophical elucidation of the key semantic concept used in semantic theories – such as meaning or truth – can be transposed into a condition of adequacy on those theories (or, equivalently, into a constraint on the actual language relation). Thus, suppose for example that an elucidation of the concept of meaning says that any sentence S has meaning m in the language of a group G if and only if some condition $C(S, m, G)$ holds. This can be transposed into a condition of adequacy as follows:

If a semantic theory for the language of a group G delivers a theorem saying that the meaning of sentence S is m then it should be the case that $C(S, m, G)$.

Similarly, it can be transposed into a constraint on the actual language relation:

A possible language in which S has the meaning m is the actual language of a group G only if $C(S, m, G)$.

This kind of transposition can be carried out in the opposite direction too. Any condition of adequacy on systematic semantic theories – or any constraint on the actual language relation – can help us elucidate the key semantic concept used in those theories. Thus, for example, consider semantic theories that adopt the truth conditional format:

Sentence S is true if and only if p.

Tarski's Convention T (1956) imposes a condition of adequacy on such theories, namely, the condition that the sentence that fills the '*p*' place should *translate* (or else be the very same sentence as) the sentence S.

This condition of adequacy on truth conditional semantic theories constitutes a partial elucidation of the semantic concept of truth in terms of the concept of translation. Intuitively, the concept of translation is very closely related to the concept of meaning; and what Convention T requires, in effect, is that the sentence that fills the '*p*' place should have the same meaning as the sentence S. If a truth conditional semantic theory meets that condition, then the truth condition specifications that it yields are guaranteed to be correct. Thus, Convention T's elucidation of the semantic concept of truth involves a connection between that concept and the concept of meaning:

> If a sentence S means that *p* then S is true iff *p*.

But Convention T provides no further help with the concept of meaning itself.

One way to shed further light on the concept of meaning – and so, via Convention T on the concept of truth – would be to spell out other conditions of adequacy on specifications of meanings (or of truth conditions). The concept for which we seek elucidation here is the concept of meaning (or truth conditions) in the language of any group. The concept of meaning is the same whether we consider a group of English speakers or a group of Chinese speakers; so we expect that a condition of adequacy should relate to groups in a very general way. One quite general thing that we can say about specifications of meaning is that they help us to describe members of a group as engaging in linguistic acts. The theorems of a semantic theory for the language of a group, G, can license the re-description of utterances of sentences by members of G, as acts of saying or assertion. For example, if the semantic theory says that a sentence S means that Theaetetus is sitting, then we might reasonably construe an utterer of S as saying or asserting that Theaetetus is sitting. Construing a person's utterances as particular linguistic acts is one aspect of *interpretation*, and what we have just seen is that we can make a link between the theorems of a semantic theory and the project of interpreting the members of a language community.

A semantic theory can play a role in facilitating an overall interpretation of the behaviour of members of a group, by offering a way of understanding their specifically linguistic behaviour. If there are legitimate constraints on ways of interpreting people, then these may yield constraints on the particular aspects of interpretation that are licensed by a semantic theory. In short, the needs of interpretation may lead us to conditions of adequacy on meaning specifications, or truth condition specifications.

In Davidson's programme, this idea of a link between semantic theories and interpretation is implemented by describing the constraints on the project of *radical interpretation*. This is the imaginary project of constructing an overall scheme of interpretation for language users about whom we know nothing at the outset. One putative constraint on radical interpretation is that speakers should be so interpreted that what they say about the world – and, presumably, what they believe about the world – turns out to be by and large correct. This is the *Principle of Charity* (see Davidson, 1967a, 1973). Thus, for example (Davidson, 1975/1984, p. 169):

> A theory of interpretation cannot be correct that makes a man assent to very many false sentences: it must be generally the case that a sentence is true when a speaker holds it to be.

The Principle of Charity has significance outside philosophy of language, since it appears to offer some prospect for ANTISKEPTICAL ARGUMENTS (pp. 53–8), in particular, for arguments to the conclusion that most of what we ourselves say and think is correct (Davidson, 1983).

But, in later work by Davidson and others (Grandy, 1973; McDowell, 1976; Wiggins, 1980), the Principle of Charity has given way to a principle that focuses on intelligibility, rather than on correctness: speakers should be so interpreted that what they say and believe about the world turns out to be by and large reasonable or intelligible. As Davidson himself says (1984, p. xvii): 'The aim of interpretation is not agreement but understanding.' Sometimes a speaker's being wrong is quite understandable, while being right would be almost miraculous. An eloquent statement of this principle – sometimes called the *Principle of Humanity* – is provided by Wiggins (1980, p. 199):

> Let us then constrain the theory ... that provides sentence by sentence interpretations of the language L by the requirement that [it] should combine with a plausible anthropology ... in such a way that *in concert*, the two theories make the best sense possible ... of the total life and conduct of L-speakers.

4.3 *Semantic theories and mental states*

Some aspects of natural languages pose particular problems for a semantic theorist working within the Davidsonian framework. One of these aspects is the use of natural language to report on people's mental states. So, a third reason for being interested in systematic semantic theories is that reflection on these theories may yield insight into the meanings of sentences about mental states, and so, also, insight into the nature of those mental states themselves.

To see how the problems arise, consider a belief report sentence like:

(BRep)   Theaetetus believes that Fido barks.

Intuitively, the meaning of this sentence depends on the meaning of the name 'Theaetetus', the meaning of the verb 'believes', and the meaning of the contained sentence 'Fido barks'. So, we might have some expectations about the way in which a meaning-specifying theorem for (BRep) would be derived in a systematic semantic theory. We might expect that the derivation would involve, firstly, proving a meaning-specifying theorem for the contained sentence 'Fido barks', and then using that, plus axioms about the meanings of 'Theaetetus' and 'believes', in order to prove the target theorem for the belief report sentence.

In the framework of truth conditional semantic theories, similarly, we might expect that the proof of a truth-condition-specifying theorem for the belief report sentence would make use of a theorem for 'Fido barks' plus axioms about 'Theaetetus' and 'believes'. But, we can see – at least, in an impressionistic kind of way – why this is liable to be problematic.

Statements about people's mental states display some of the same logical properties as statements about meaning (see the box in section 2). With statements about meaning, it is not usually thought to be the case that from:

Fido = Rover

plus:

Sentence S means that Fido barks

it follows that:

Sentence S means that Rover barks.

This logical behaviour is a departure from standard logical systems, and it raises a question about the logical resources that would be needed in a semantic theory using the 'Sentence S means that p' format. It also helps to motivate use of the alternative 'Sentence S is true iff p' format, since that is logically well behaved. Thus, for example, from:

Fido = Rover

plus:

Sentence S is true iff Fido barks

it certainly does follow that:

Sentence S is true iff Rover barks.

But, while this well-understood logical behaviour is one of the attractions of truth conditional semantic theories, it also makes it hard for truth conditional theories to give an adequate treatment of sentences that report on people's mental states.

With statements about belief, it is not usually thought to be the case that from:

Fido = Rover

plus:

Theaetetus believes that Fido barks

it follows that:

Theaetetus believes that Rover barks.

The first belief report might be true, while the second was false, for example. This is one aspect of what is called the *intensionality* of belief reports.

The problem posed for truth conditional semantics is that it is hard to see how a truth-condition-specifying theorem for the sentence:

(BRep) Theaetetus believes that Fido barks

can be derived in the way that we envisaged, without also involving the denial of the aspect of the intensionality of belief reports that we just highlighted. The derivational route that we envisaged goes via a truth-condition-specifying theorem for the contained sentence 'Fido barks', to the effect that the contained sentence is true iff Fido does indeed bark. Given the assumption that:

Fido = Rover

we can move from this theorem:

(FF) 'Fido barks' is true iff Fido barks

to:

(FR) 'Fido barks' is true iff Rover barks.

But now, consider whatever route leads from the original theorem (FF) to a truth-condition-specifying theorem for the belief report sentence (BRep), to the effect that it is true iff Theaetetus does indeed believe that Fido barks. Given the assumption that Fido = Rover, an exactly similar route will also lead via (FR) to the conclusion that the same sentence (BRep) is true iff Theaetetus believes that Rover barks. So, given the assumption that:

Fido = Rover

we are driven to the overall conclusion:

Theaetetus believes that Fido barks iff Theaetetus believes that Rover barks.

But, this goes flatly against the presumed intensionality of belief reports.

The issues here are controversial, and there have certainly been proposals for bringing within the compass of truth conditional semantics sentences that are usually reckoned to exhibit intensionality (see Davidson, 1969b). For now, however, it is enough to notice that attention to systematic semantic theories could bring questions about mental states into sharper focus.

4.4 Semantic theories and epistemology

The fourth reason for directing philosophical attention onto the construction of systematic semantic theories is epistemological. We have indicated the way in which a finite set of axioms can permit the derivation of a meaning-specifying theorem for each of infinitely many sentences. So, in the case of a given language with infinitely many sentences, someone who knew the facts stated by the finitely many axioms of a systematic semantic theory would thereby be in a position to come to know what each sentence of the language means. The existence of finitely axiomatized semantic theories thus sheds light on an epistemological problem: How is it possible for a finite being to master an infinite language?

So far as the purely formal notion of an axiomatized theory goes, the set of axioms of a theory does not have to be finite. But, Davidson (1965) uses the requirement that a language should be learnable (and learnable by a finite being) to motivate a *finite axiomatization constraint* on systematic semantic theories. Since Davidson favours truth conditional semantic theories, this yields the idea that the aim of a semantic theorist is to construct finitely axiomatized theories of truth conditions for (regimented fragments of) natural languages – building, so far as possible, on the work of Tarski. The sorts of theories envisaged are sometimes spoken of as Tarski–Davidson truth theories, and there is a very considerable body of work – much of it quite technical in character – in pursuit of this aim.

We should note, however, that there is some dispute over the finite axiomatization constraint. At least one prominent philosopher of language argues (Schiffer, 1987, ch. 7) that it may be possible for a speaker to master a language, even though no finitely axiomatized truth conditional semantic theory can be provided for it.

Even if there is a finitely axiomatized semantic theory for a language, still there is a pressing question about the explanatory relevance of the existence of such a theory. Knowledge of the facts stated by the axioms of a systematic semantic theory would suffice, in principle, for knowledge as to what each sentence of the language means. But ordinary speakers of a natural language usually lack conscious knowledge of any systematic semantic theory for their own language. So, the question that presses is how the mere existence of a finitely axiomatized semantic theory, unknown to ordinary language users, can solve the epistemological problem that they apparently face.

One approach to answering this question begins by considering a wider range of knowledge that ordinary language users have. Along with knowing what the sentences of their language mean, ordinary speakers of English also know, for example, that in the sentence:

Nigel shaved him

the word 'him' cannot refer back to Nigel, while in the sentence:

Nigel wanted Bruce to shave him

the word 'him' can refer back to Nigel. They know that the sentences:

Less than two books were on the table
More than one book was on the table

sound fine, while:

> Less than two books was on the table
> More than one book were on the table

sound somehow wrong – despite the fact that 'Less than two books' is equivalent to 'At most one book', and 'More than one book' is equivalent to 'At least two books'. And we could multiply examples of speakers' linguistic knowledge indefinitely.

Ordinary language users have conscious access to these pieces of knowledge. But they do not have conscious knowledge of any set of axioms or rules from which these particular pieces of knowledge follow. Theoretical linguists articulate sets of linguistic (especially, syntactic) rules or principles called *grammars*. But, the explanatory claims of theoretical linguistics do not end with the mere existence of grammars from which particular pieces of linguistic knowledge could be derived. In a famous passage, Noam Chomsky (b. 1928) says (1965, p. 8):

> Obviously, every speaker of a language has mastered and internalized a generative grammar that expresses his knowledge of his language. This is not to say that he is aware of the rules of the grammar or even that he can become aware of them . . . . Any interesting generative grammar will be dealing, for the most part, with mental processes that are far beyond the level of actual or even potential consciousness.

According to Chomsky (1965, 1986, 1990a, 1990b), then, ordinary language users possess a body of linguistic knowledge which is, for the most part, inaccessible to consciousness. For this reason, it is often spoken of as *tacit knowledge*. It is because they have this body of tacit knowledge of linguistic rules that they are able to know the vast host of particular things about their language.

While Chomsky is concerned primarily with knowledge of syntax, the idea that ordinary language users possess a body of tacit knowledge can also be applied in the area of semantics. Thus, one way of answering the question about the explanatory relevance of the existence of systematic semantic theories would be to credit ordinary language users with tacit knowledge of the axioms of such a theory. There is quite an extensive literature elaborating this idea of tacit knowledge of semantic theories (Evans, 1981a; Davies, 1986, 1987, 1989; Peacocke, 1986, 1989; Higginbotham, 1989), and some of these elaborations promise a close link between philosophy of language and Cognitive science (chapter 5).

However, we should also note that there are other proposals for answering the epistemological question about systematic theories and ordinary language users' semantic knowledge. For example, Dummett (1976, 1991) makes use of a notion of *implicit* knowledge that is importantly different from Chomsky's idea of tacit knowledge, and Wright (1986) sees the construction of semantic theories, not as an articulation of language users' actual knowledge, but as a matter of Rational reconstruction (p. 370).

4.5 Semantic theories and metaphysics

The fifth reason for philosophical interest in semantic theories is that the task of bringing specific linguistic constructions within the scope of a systematic semantic theory sometimes sheds light on issues in other areas of philosophy, and particularly in metaphysics. We have already discussed the relationships between philosophy of language, philosophy of mind and metaphysics, so we shall be rather brief here.

Systematic semantic theories for natural languages have to deal with pronouns ('I', 'you', 'she', 'he', 'it', 'they'), demonstratives ('this', 'that', 'this knife', 'that butter'), and other indexical expressions ('now', 'then', 'today', 'tomorrow', 'here', 'there'). Questions about the semantic contributions of these expressions (see Kaplan, 1989) inevitably highlight issues in ontology, as well as in philosophy of mind. For, when we consider the mental states that are typically expressed using these expressions, we find that they are mental states that involve thinking about persons, things, times and places in particular ways. So, an adequate account of the thoughts expressed by the use of these expressions seems to involve a commitment to talking about *ways of thinking* or, in Fregean terminology about SENSES (pp. 665–8) (see Frege, 1918; Perry, 1977, 1979; Evans, 1981b, 1982; Peacocke, 1981, 1983, 1986, 1992, ch. 4; Forbes, 1987; Davies, 1982).

Another example of a link between recent work in philosophy of language and issues in metaphysics – this time not mediated by philosophy of mind – is provided by work on the semantics of names ('Theaetetus'), definite descriptions ('the man in the gabardine coat'), and modal adverbs ('necessarily'), on the one hand, and metaphysical issues about necessity and essentialism, on the other (Kripke, 1980; Wiggins, 1976). A key claim in this area has been that names are, while definite descriptions typically are not, *rigid designators*. A subject term is said to be a rigid designator if it designates the same object with respect to all different possible situations, so long as we hold the meaning of the term constant.

To see the importance of the notion of rigid designation to questions about essentialism, consider the sentence:

Necessarily, the tallest animal in the courtyard is human.

To set the scene, suppose that Theaetetus is the tallest of a group of people talking together in the courtyard, and that there are no non-human animals in the courtyard other than a dog, Fido, and some fleas. Now, whether the sentence containing the modal adverb 'Necessarily' is true depends on whether the truth of the subject–predicate sentence:

The tallest animal in the courtyard is human

is a matter of *necessity* or *contingency*. This subject–predicate sentence is true as evaluated with respect to the described situation; but could it have been false, without any change in its meaning?

Clearly, the answer is that the sentence could easily have been false. If Theaetetus and his friends had not been in the courtyard, then Fido would have been the tallest animal, and Fido is not human. So, the question over the modal status of the subject–predicate sentence (whether it is necessarily or contingently true) does not turn on any interesting metaphysical question about whether human beings are essentially, or merely contingently, human, for example.

Consider, now, the sentence:

Necessarily, Theaetetus is human.

Whether this sentence is true depends on whether the truth of the subject–predicate sentence:

Theaetetus is human

is a matter of necessity or contingency; and this time the question of modal status does seem to turn on a question about essentialism. Might this particular human being, Theaetetus, have been other than human?

The definite description, 'The tallest animal in the courtyard', is a non-rigid designator. With respect to the situation as described, it designates Theaetetus, while with respect to an alternative possible situation, it designates Fido – and without any difference in the meanings of the words ('tallest', 'animal', and so on) that make up the definite description. In contrast, the name 'Theaetetus' is a rigid designator. With respect to the situation described, or with respect to the imagined alternative, that name designates Theaetetus – so long as it retains its meaning. What we have just seen is that, where the subject term is a rigid designator, a question about the truth of a sentence containing a modal adverb leads directly to a question about the essential properties of a particular object.

Davidson's own work provides a third example of a link between systematic semantic theories and issues in metaphysics – particularly, of the way in which the construction of a semantic theory may reveal the metaphysical commitments of the conceptual scheme that is expressed in a natural language (Bach, 1986). Sentences that contain action verbs plus adverbs, such as:

John buttered the toast slowly, in the bathroom

pose a challenge for semantic theories because, after we deal with the subject ('John') and the predicate ('buttered the toast'), it is unclear how we should cope with the adverbs. We shall not pause over the details of the challenge that adverbs pose, but simply note that Davidson (1967b, 1969c, 1985; see also Wiggins, 1986) argues that, in order to bring these sentences within the scope of a truth conditional semantic theory, we need to regiment them as involving quantification over *events*. Roughly, the idea is that an adverbially modified action sentence should be regimented in logical notation as beginning with '$(\exists e)$—' (in English: 'there is an event which —') so that, for example, the sentence about John and the toast is regimented as equivalent to:

There is an event e which is a buttering of the toast by John, is slow, and is (occurred) in the bathroom.

If this is correct, then our ordinary talk about people doing things – like buttering toast – carries metaphysical commitments, not only to material things like people and toast, but also to an ontology of events.

Adverbs and Events

Davidson's proposal leads to questions about the notion of logical form, about alternative metaphysical theories of events, and about the role of material bodies as the *basic particulars* in our conceptual scheme (Strawson, 1959, ch. 1).

Firstly, the proposal can be motivated in either of two ways, corresponding to two rather different ideas of logical form (Evans, 1976). On the one hand, there is a pattern of inference to be explained. From 'John buttered the toast slowly, in the bathroom' we can validly infer each of:

John buttered the toast slowly
John buttered the toast in the bathroom
John buttered the toast.

If the adverbially modified sentence is regimented as involving a conjunction ('*e* is a buttering of the toast by John & *e* is slow & *e* occurred in the bathroom') then these inferences can be seen as valid in virtue of the logical properties of '&' (Davidson, 1967b). On the other hand, the regimentation might be seen as being required simply in order to bring the sentences within the scope of a systematic truth conditional semantic theory (Evans, 1976). This motivation might not seem very convincing, since an alternative scheme of regimentation (involving operators that modify the predicate terms corresponding to natural language verbs) appears to be available (Strawson, 1974b). But the apparent alternative is not, in the end, formally viable (Taylor, 1985; Davies, 1991).

Secondly, the proposal leads naturally to the question whether the detailed semantic behaviour of adverbs might provide us with grounds for choosing between two conceptions of events. On the one hand, Davidson (1967b, 1969c) regards events as particulars that can be described in many different ways. One and the same event might be both a *pulling* of a trigger, a *firing* of a rifle, and a *killing* of a president, for example. On the other hand, a number of theorists (Goldman, 1971; Kim, 1976; Taylor, 1985) propose that events should be much more finely discriminated – with firings, pullings and killings distinguished from each other. There is a substantial metaphysical difference between these accounts, but it turns out that purely semantic considerations do not provide any compelling reason for favouring one over the other (Davies, 1991).

Thirdly, the proposal raises questions about an argument for Strawson's thesis that material bodies are, while events and processes are not, basic particulars in our conceptual scheme. Part of what this thesis comes to is that our ability to pick out individual events in our thought and talk depends on our ability to pick out individual material objects, but not vice versa. At one point, Strawson's argument turns crucially on the claim that our most basic understanding of the conceptually true sentence 'Every animal was born' involves possession of the concept of being born, but not possession of the concept of a birth as an individual particular. Clearly, this argument needs to be assessed in the light of Davidson's proposal for regimenting such sentences as 'This animal was born quickly, in the barn'.

5 Analysing the Concept of Meaning: Grice's Programme

We have been spending some time over five ways in which systematic semantic theories might reward philosophical attention. The philosophical significance of meta-semantic theories is much more obvious; for they are attempts at an immediately recognizable philosophical project – a project of conceptual illumination, or even conceptual analysis. Thus, for example, the programme begun by Grice (1957, 1968, 1969) aims at an analysis of the concept of literal meaning in a public language in terms of psychological concepts such as intention and belief. In this section, we shall give an outline description of Grice's programme for analysing the notion of literal meaning. (Grice's papers are collected in Grice, 1989. For further work in the same programme, see Bennett, 1973, 1976; Lewis, 1969, 1975; Schiffer, 1972, 1982; Strawson, 1964, 1970b. For a negative assessment of the prospects for the programme, see Schiffer, 1987.)

The analytical project can be regarded as having two stages. The first stage aims to characterize a concept of *speaker's meaning* that corresponds, roughly, to the idea of communicating, or attempting to communicate, a proposition. The second stage then aims to use that concept of speaker's meaning, along with the notion of a *conventional regularity*, to construct an analysis of the concept of literal linguistic meaning. The basic idea is that a sentence has as its literal meaning the proposition that it is conventionally used to communicate.

Since the project is an analytical one, it is naturally regarded as being subject to a requirement of non-circularity. The accounts of speaker's meaning and of conventional regularity – notions that are drawn on in the analysis of literal linguistic meaning – should not themselves make essential appeal to linguistic notions. Thus, Grice's programme presumes that mind is analytically prior to language. But the success of Grice's programme is not similarly conditional on any ontological or epistemological priority of mind over language (Avramides, 1989; cf. Evans and McDowell, 1976, pp. xv–xxiii). As we mentioned in section 3.1, it is logically consistent to pursue Grice's analytical programme while accepting Davidson's claims about no ontological priority, and no epistemological priority, of mind over language (though it is true that it would be surprising for someone to combine Grice's analytical views with the no-ontological-priority claim – no thought without talk).

The claim of no epistemological priority of mind over language says that it is not possible to find out about a person's mental states first, and only then to go on to investigate the meanings of the person's utterances. Rather, the assignment of both meanings and mental states – such as beliefs and intentions – is a single integrated epistemological project governed by the Principle of Charity or the Principle of Humanity (section 3.2). But Davidson goes beyond this epistemological claim. His view is that, by spelling out the constraints on interpretation, we provide all the philosophical elucidation that can be provided of the concept of linguistic meaning. The constraints on interpretation are of two kinds. On the formal side, there is, for example, the finite axiomatization constraint on the semantic theory that is used (in concert with a plausible anthropology) for interpretation. On the empirical side, there are the constraints of agreement (Charity) or intelligibility (Humanity). But the problem with these empirical constraints is that they seem to leave a lacuna.

An interpretation deploys a semantic theory – an assignment of meanings to sentences – so as to provide a description of language users as engaging in certain speech acts – saying and asserting things, for example – and as having certain propositional attitudes – believing and intending things, for example. The Principle of Humanity constrains the specifications of meaning by imposing the requirement that the resulting overall description of the language users in terms of meanings, speech acts, and propositional attitudes should make them out to be reasonable or intelligible. But the Principle of Humanity does not itself tell us which combinations of meanings, speech acts and propositional attitudes can be intelligibly attributed.

On the face of it, an account of which combinations are coherent would be provided by articulating the analytical connections between the concept of meaning, the concepts of various speech acts like saying and asserting, and the concepts of propositional attitudes like believing and intending. There might, for example, be conceptual connections that require that any one who asserts that p does so by using a sentence that literally means that p, and intends an audience to take him or her (the speaker) to believe that p. Whether there are connections like this – and if so, what exactly they are – is not a trivial question; it is something that requires detailed investigation. The bold proposal of Grice's analytical programme is that there are connections of this kind that actually permit the analysis of the concept of linguistic meaning – and the concepts of the various speech acts (Schiffer, 1972, ch. 4) – in terms of propositional attitudes.

Grice's analytical project begins from a distinction between *natural* and *non-natural* meaning (Grice, 1957 and 1989, p. 214). We are talking about natural meaning – which might also be called *indicator* meaning – when we say, for example:

> Those spots mean (indicate) measles.
> Those clouds mean (indicate) rain.

This notion of meaning – which is just a matter of causal co-variation between two kinds of states of affairs – is not the concern of Grice's programme, though it takes on considerable importance in recent work in philosophy of mind, aimed at providing an account of the contents of psychological states themselves (see Dretske 1981, 1986).

Spots indicate measles and clouds indicate rain whether or not anyone takes them in that way, and whether or not anyone intends them to be taken in that way. The various notions of meaning that Grice proposes to analyse are distinguished from natural meaning by the fact that they involve, in one way or another, the intentions of a perpetrator or utterer.

If we are aiming at an analysis of the notion:

> Sentence S means that p in the language of group G

then a first suggestion might be this:

> Members of G use the sentence S to *say* (to each other) that *p*.

There are several reasons why this would not be adequate, but the one that concerns us now is that the concept of *saying* seems already to depend on the concept of literal meaning. In order to say something (for example, to say that penguins waddle), a speaker has to use an expression that literally means that thing (here, a sentence that literally means that penguins waddle). So, any analysis along these lines would be circular.

It might be replied to this that there is something stipulative about this conception of saying – that is not obligatory to equate saying with *strictly and literally saying*. It might also be replied that perhaps, in the end, we shall have to be satisfied with an analysis that is circular – a circular analysis might be elucidatory provided that the circle of inter-defined terms is large enough. There is some justice in both these replies. But still, a second suggestion for an analysis of the concept of literal meaning might be this:

> Members of G use the sentence S to *communicate the message* that *p*.

The advantage of this second suggestion is that the concept of communicating (or getting across) a message does not seem to re-introduce the concept of literal meaning. A person can get across a message even though the sounds used have no literal meaning at all.

However, there is still a problem with this second suggestion. A sound that has no literal meaning can be used by one member of a group to communicate a message to another. The perpetrator of the sound, realizing that the sound has no literal meaning, might rely on some resemblance between the sound produced and some other sound – for example, the sound of an angry dog (see Schiffer, 1972, p. 7, for this example). But then, the same sound might be used by each member of the group when he or she wants to get across the message that he or she is angry. So, the conditions in the suggested analysis would be met. But, this still might not be a case of literal meaning; and, intuitively, the reason for this is that each person who uses a sound like an angry dog to communicate anger might take himself or herself to be making an innovative use of a resemblance between sounds.

When we have a case of literal meaning, in contrast, it seems that the reason why we use a particular sound is just that it does have the appropriate literal meaning. A little more accurately, we can say that when we make communicative use of an expression with a literal meaning, we rely upon a shared recognition on the part of speaker and hearer that the expression can be used – has been used – in just that way. Communicative use of an expression that has a literal meaning is a rationally self-perpetuating practice; and this fits in well with the idea that literal meaning is conventional meaning, since a convention is arguably a rationally self-perpetuating regularity. (The notion of convention is most famously explored by Lewis, 1969.)

5.1 Speaker's meaning

We have reached the basic idea that a sentence has as its literal meaning the proposition that it is conventionally used to communicate. Grice's programme aims to develop a detailed philosophical analysis along the lines of this basic idea. The first stage of that programme aims to characterize a concept of *speaker's meaning* roughly corresponding, we said, to the notion of communicating, or attempting to communicate, a proposition. However, we should notice that, given the overall aim of the programme, it is not essential that the concept of speaker's meaning should coincide with any antecedently given notion. It would be consistent with the overall aim that speaker's meaning should come to be regarded as a theory-internal construct.

In Grice's own exposition, the notion of speaker's meaning (utterer's occasion meaning) to be analysed is:

> Utterer U meant something by his or her utterance x directed at an audience A.

The putative analysis initially offered by Grice (1957) is as follows (Grice, 1969/1989, p. 92):

> U uttered x intending
> (1) A to produce a particular response r;
> (2) A to think (recognize) that U intends (1);
> (3) A to fulfil condition (1) on the basis of his fulfilment of condition (2).

In the case where the speaker is attempting to communicate the message that p to the audience, the primary intended response in clause (1) is that A should believe that p. If we feed this into the analysis, and also unpack clause (3) a little, then we have the proposal that:

> Utterer U meant that p by his or her utterance x directed at an audience A

should be analysed as:

> U uttered x intending
> (1) A to believe that p;
> (2) A to think (recognize) that U intends (1);
> (3) A's recognition of U's primary intention (1) to be at least part of A's reason for believing that p.

The utterance type that U uses might or might not have a literal linguistic meaning; and if it does then the communicated message might or might not coincide with that literal meaning. But, crucially, this analysis of speaker's meaning does not itself make use of the notion of literal meaning, and so is available for deployment in a non-circular analysis of that notion.

A host of revisions and extensions have been visited on Grice's initial three-clause analysis (Grice, 1969; Strawson, 1964; Schiffer, 1972). Various counter-examples seem to show that Grice's three conditions are neither sufficient nor necessary for speaker's meaning.

There are two main kinds of reason why the three conditions might not be *sufficient* for the intuitive notion of communicating a message or telling somebody something. Firstly, there is nothing in the three conditions to require that there should be some property of the utterance that the utterer should intend or expect to guide the audience towards recognition of the primary communicative intention (Grice, 1969/1989, p. 94). Secondly, the three conditions do not rule out certain kinds of convoluted plans for influencing a person's beliefs in ways that are not, intuitively, straightforwardly communicative (Grice, 1969; Strawson, 1964; Schiffer, 1972, pp. 17–18). We shall not take time over the details here, but the upshot is that – at least so far as sufficiency is concerned – a better analysis of:

Utterer *U* meant that *p* by his or her utterance *x* directed at an audience *A*

would be:

(1) *U* intended *A* to believe that *p*;

(2) there is some feature F of the utterance *x* such that *U* intended *A* to recognize *U*'s primary intention (the intention in (1)) in part by recognizing *x* to have F;

(3) *U* intended *A*'s recognition of *U*'s primary intention to be at least part of *A*'s reason for believing that *p*;

(4) *U* did not intend that *A* should be deceived about *U*'s intentions (such as those in (1), (2) and (3)).

The point of clause (4) is, specifically, to rule out cases where *U* intends *A* to be deceived about *U*'s intentions as to how *A* should arrive at the belief that *p* (Grice, 1969 and 1989, p. 99). It is not supposed to rule out the possibility that *U* might intend *A* to be deceived about other intentions that *U* has. For example, clause (4) is certainly supposed to allow that an act of speaker's meaning might also be a case of lying.

The main reason why the three or four conditions might be regarded as not *necessary* for speaker's meaning is that there are so many things that ordinary speakers do with sentences that would not be included under the three-clause or four-clause analysis. Indeed, there are many quite literal uses of sentences where the speaker does not even intend to produce in the hearer a belief corresponding to the literal meaning of the sentence (so not even clause (1) would be satisfied). Grice (1969/1989, pp. 105–9) reviews several of these cases, including examination answers, confessions, reminding, giving a review of already known facts, spelling out the conclusion of an argument, and talking to a counter-suggestible person; and Davidson also mentions (1979/1984, p. 111) 'stories, rote repetitions, illustrations, suppositions, parodies, charades, chants, and conspicuously unmeant compliments'.

There are various suggested remedies for the problems that these examples are supposed to pose. But, for present purposes, it is enough to note that the massive variety of literal uses of language is not necessarily problematic for the putative analysis of speaker's meaning, if the fundamental model for speaker's meaning is the case of telling someone something with the intention of providing new knowledge. Arguably, that notion of speaker's meaning – with straightforward telling as the central case – can be analysed roughly along the lines of Grice's four-clause definition. But, if we retain an analysis of speaker's meaning on which the majority of uses of language turn out not to be cases of speaker's meaning, then we must take that fact into account in the second stage of the analytical programme.

5.2 Conventional meaning

Given the basic idea that a sentence has as its literal meaning the proposition that it is conventionally used to communicate, the second stage of the programme should characterize the concept of convention, and most recent work in the Gricean tradition makes use of developments of Lewis' (1969) notion of a convention as a rationally self-perpetuating regularity in behaviour. According to Lewis (1975, pp. 164–6) a convention is a regularity R in action, or in action and belief, that meets the following conditions:

(1)   everyone conforms to R;
(2)   everyone believes that everyone else conforms to R;
(3)   the belief in (2) furnishes each person with a reason to conform to R;
(4)   there is a general preference for general conformity to R, rather than slightly less than general conformity;
(5)   there is at least one alternative regularity which would serve reasonably well; and
(6)   the facts listed in (1)–(5) are matters of *common knowledge*.

The most straightforward way to employ this notion and that of speaker's meaning in an analysis of literal linguistic meaning is to say:

Sentence S means that *p* in the language of group G iff there is a convention in G to use utterances of S in order to communicate that *p* (that is, in order to mean that *p*, in the sense of speaker's meaning).

In a slogan:

Speaker's meaning + Convention = Literal meaning.

This would need to be refined to allow for the ambiguity and context-dependence characteristic of natural language. But, much more importantly, the suggested analysis imposes a requirement that is far too strict to be a necessary condition for literal meaning.

We have already seen that the four-clause definition of speaker's meaning makes it a relatively rare phenomenon. So, there can certainly be literal meaning even where there is no regularity of speaker's meaning (as presently defined). If we want to give an analysis of the concept of literal meaning along the lines of the slogan, then we need to weaken the notion of speaker's meaning, or weaken the notion of convention (or weaken both). Let us first consider weakening the notion of convention.

The trouble with the notion of convention does not seem to lie in the idea of rational self-perpetuation, but rather in the commitment to there being a regularity that members of the group actually conform to. The sentence

'Penguins waddle' literally means, in our language, that penguins waddle. But there is not a regularity of using that sentence to communicate the message that penguins waddle. It is not the case, for example, that whenever anyone wants to get across the message that penguins waddle he or she uses that sentence. There are surely other ways in which that same message might be communicated. But, more important for present purposes is the fact that, although people do sometimes use the sentence 'Penguins waddle', it is not regularly used with the intentions specified in the four-clause definition of speaker's meaning. (The analyses of literal meaning suggested by recent theorists all depart in one way or another from that most straightforward way of pursuing the second stage of Grice's programme. See Bennett, 1976; Blackburn, 1984, ch. 4; Davies, 1981, ch. 1; Lewis, 1975; Peacocke, 1976; Schiffer, 1972, ch. 5.)

Grice himself (1968/1989, p. 126) suggests moving from speaker's meaning to literal meaning via the notion of 'having a certain procedure in one's repertoire'. It would not be adequate to say:

> Sentence S means that p in the language of group G iff each member of G has it in his or her repertoire to use utterances of S in order to communicate that p (that is, in order to mean that p, in the sense of speaker's meaning).

That proposed definition fails to build in the idea of rational self-perpetuation (see Schiffer, 1972, pp. 132–6). But a more plausible analysis could be built from the concept of speaker's meaning (as presently defined) plus a concept analogous to the concept of convention but with the notion of regularity replaced by the notion of having a certain procedure in one's repertoire. Thus Grice suggests that more is required than each member of the group G having the communicative procedure in his or her repertoire (1968/1989, p. 127):

> At least some (many) members of group G have in their repertoires the procedure [to use utterances of S in order to communicate that p] the retention of this procedure being for them conditional on the assumption that at least some (other) members of G have, or have had, this procedure in their repertoires.

If we do not weaken the notion of convention, then we have to introduce a concept weaker than speaker's meaning. Some literal uses of language that fall outside the scope of speaker's meaning as presently defined might well fall within the scope of a revised notion in which clause (1) is replaced by:

(1)' U intended A *actively* to believe that p.

Arguably, examples of reminding are covered by this modification. Some other literal uses are covered by a different modification:

(1)" U intended A to believe that U believed that p.

Arguably, this deals with the case of examination answers. But, in order to make it plausible that we have covered all, or at least most, literal uses of language, we need to abstract away from these details about just what attitude U intends A to take to the proposition that p.

The completely general form would be:

(1)''' There is *some* propositional attitude Ψ, such that U intends that A should Ψ that p.

We could take clause (1)''', together with clauses (2)–(4) of the four-clause definition of speaker's meaning to define a new notion of *weak speaker's meaning*. This might then be combined with the notion of convention in a putative analysis of literal meaning (Peacocke, 1976; Davies, 1981).

Whatever the details, any analysis of the concept of literal meaning along these lines will present the use of a public language as a psychologically highly complex matter. This might motivate an objection to Grice's programme; but the psychological plausibility of such accounts has been defended (Loar, 1981), and there is some agreement that Grice's analytical programme can – in the respects that we have considered so far – be carried through successfully. However, what has not been taken into account so far is the internal structure of sentences.

5.3 *Expression meaning and the structure of language*

The way in which component words and phrases make their contributions to the meanings of complete sentences is the starting point for Davidson's programme in philosophy of language (see section 3). But the analysis of the concept of literal meaning as it applies to expressions smaller than complete sentences is an extremely difficult problem within Grice's programme (Grice, 1968; Schiffer, 1972, ch. 6; Loar, 1976, 1981, pp. 253–60). Whether or not it is an absolutely insoluble problem is, at best, not clear. The issues here are very complex, and we shall only give a brief indication of the way in which the difficulty arises.

In essence, the problem is that the structure of language presents a dilemma for the general idea that literal meaning is a matter of there being conventions to use expressions with certain intentions. The primary link between meaning and convention has to be made either at the level of words and phrases, and ways of putting them together (such as subject–predicate combination), or else at the level of complete sentences. Either alternative presents problems.

Suppose that we opt for the first alternative. Then we shall credit language users with having procedures for using words, and phrases, and ways of putting them together, and also with knowledge that they and others have these procedures. We need to credit speakers with this knowledge, in order to maintain the idea of rational self-perpetuation. But it is here that the problem with this first alternative is presented. For the semantic rules that govern the use of sub-sentential components, and ways of combining components, are far from obvious. (That is why the construction of systematic semantic theories is a challenging project.) So, on the first alternative, it is practically inevitable that the analysis of meaning will commit us to attributing to ordinary language users beliefs and knowledge that they do not have: detailed beliefs and knowledge about the components and construction of their sentences (Loar, 1981, p. 256).

Suppose, instead, that we try the second alternative. The problem this time is that there are many sentences that are never used at all, and many that would never be used to communicate the proposition that is their literal meaning. An example of the latter kind is provided by the sentence: 'No head injury is too trivial to be ignored' (Bennett, 1976, p. 17). This sentence is sometimes used; but it is typically used with the intention that the hearer should believe that no head injury is *sufficiently* trivial to be ignored.

One possible response to this dilemma – perhaps the only plausible response – is to suggest that an account of literal meaning applicable to all sentences – whether used or not – should explicitly advert to the psychological mechanisms that underpin the use of some core set of sentences (Loar, 1976, p. 160). The idea here is that we should avoid the first alternative altogether, and should adopt the second alternative, but only for those sentences for which there is a practice of literal use. The notion of conventional meaning would not, then, apply directly to unused sentences. Instead, the analysis of literal meaning would be extended to those unused sentences in two steps.

Firstly, take a speaker who participates in a conventional practice of using a sentence with a certain literal meaning. Then suppose that the speaker's assignment of a meaning to the sentence is underpinned by cognitive mechanisms that correspond closely to some of the axioms of a systematic semantic theory for the language. In particular, suppose that the cognitive mechanisms subserving the assignment of a meaning to a sentence include mechanisms corresponding to the semantic theory's axioms for the words (and ways of combining words) in that sentence.

Secondly, suppose that we consider an unused sentence that is built from words that occur in used sentences (and is built in ways that are also found in used sentences). Then we allow the literal meaning for the unused sentence to be determined by the axioms that correspond to certain cognitive mechanisms; namely, the mechanisms that are implicated in the speaker's assignment of meanings to regularly used sentences built from those same resources.

One way of implementing this response would be to make use of Chomsky's notion of tacit knowledge. Instead of saying – rather vaguely – that there are cognitive mechanisms corresponding in the appropriate way to axioms of a semantic theory, we can say that those axioms are tacitly known. Indeed, Loar (1981, p. 259) suggests that 'the Chomskyan idea of the internalization of the generative procedures of a grammar has got to be invoked to . . . make sense of literal meaning'.

However, we do not have any detailed prospectus for an interdisciplinary marriage between Chomsky's and Grice's rather different projects; and we do not know how Gricean the resulting union could be (Chomsky, 1976, pp. 55–77; 1980, pp. 81–7; 1986, pp. 19–24). It is striking, for example, that the appeal to cognitive mechanisms or tacit knowledge is made at the level of individual language users, whereas Grice's programme concerns meaning in a language that is shared by a group.

In summary, we can say that there is something of a consensus that Grice's programme faces serious problems. Lycan (1991, p. 84) lists some of them:

> that most sentences of a language are never tokened at all; that since hearers instantly understand 'novel' sentences, this cannot be in virtue of pre-established conventions or expectations directed on those sentences individually; that sentences are ambiguous and have more than one standard linguistic meaning; that sentences are often (not just abnormally) used with other than their standard meanings; and that indeed some sentences are normally used with other than their standard meanings.

We have sketched one proposal for responding to some of these problems. But we should also note that one of the most authoritative exponents of Grice's programme has reached the conclusion (Schiffer, 1987) that the project of analysing literal meaning in terms of intentions and beliefs cannot be carried through. The philosophical elucidation of the concept of meaning waits on some new insights.

6 Pragmatics: Conversational Implicature and Relevance

A sentence that literally means that p can be used to communicate a message other than the proposition that p. Thus, suppose that someone asks you, 'Would you like more coffee?' and that you answer: 'Coffee keeps me awake.' In a suitable context, this answer can convey the message that you do not want any more coffee (Sperber and Wilson, 1986a, p. 34); in a different context (as when you are obliged to stay alert through a boring lecture), it might convey the message that you do want some more coffee. But neither of these possible messages is any part of the literal meaning of the sentence 'Coffee keeps me awake'. In each case, the communicated message is, rather, something implied (in some sense) in the context, by what is literally and explicitly said.

The distinction between semantics and pragmatics is, roughly, the distinction between the significance conventionally or literally attached to words, and thence to whole sentences, and the further significance that can be worked out, by more general principles, using contextual information. Grice's theory of *conversational implicature* is the seminal contribution to recent pragmatic theory. It is a theory – or the beginning of a theory – of how this further significance is generated.

6.1 Conversational implicature

The theory of conversational implicature was first developed in the context of examples such as these.

> *and*: Strawson (1952) discusses differences between the connectives of propositional logic and the corresponding words of English, and he notes that 'a statement of the form "p and q" may carry an implication of temporal order' (1952, p. 81).
>
> *or*: Strawson also notes that 'the alternative statement [statement of the form "p or q"] carries the implication of the speaker's uncertainty as to which of the two it was' (1952, p. 91).

but: The statement 'She was poor but she was honest' carries the implication that there is some kind of contrast between being poor and being honest.

looks: The statement 'That looks red to me' carries the implication that it is in some way doubtful whether the object really is red.

We can ask whether these implications are all of the same kind. Are they the products of special features of key words in the sentences – 'and', 'or', 'but', 'looks' – or are they generated by some kind of interaction between the literal meanings of the sentences that are uttered and some very general conversational principles?

In his first exposition of the idea of conversational implicature, Grice (1961) is particularly concerned with the example of 'looks'. He wants to maintain that the statement 'That looks red to me' is literally true, even when the object in question quite obviously *is* red, so that there is no question of any doubt about its colour. In that paper, Grice develops two notions – the *detachability* and the *cancellability* of an implication – that we can use to help us to identify conversational implicatures and to distinguish them from *conventional implicatures*.

In the example with 'looks', the implication is not detachable. This means that there is no form of words that can be used to state just what 'That looks red to me' can be used to state (or that has the same truth conditions as 'That looks red to me'), but without carrying the implication. The obvious candidates – 'That appears red to me', 'That seems red to me' – carry the same implication that there is some doubt about the object's colour. On the other hand, the implication is cancellable. It is quite consistent to override the implication of a doubt by saying: 'That looks red to me . . . and it really is red – there's no doubt about it'. In the examples with 'and' and 'or', the implication is likewise cancellable but not detachable; and, indeed, that is the typical profile for conversational implicature.

In the case of 'but', however, the profile is reversed. The implication is detachable, but not cancellable. The implication is detachable (as Grice uses that term) because there is another word, 'and', that makes just the same contribution to truth conditions as 'but', but does not generate the same implication: 'She was poor and she was honest' does not carry the implication of a contrast between poverty and honesty. The implication is not cancellable because it would be extremely odd – indeed, inconsistent, in some sense – to say: 'She was poor but she was honest, though of course I do not mean to imply that there is any contrast between poverty and honesty'.

In the case of the word 'but', then, the implication that is generated appears to be a feature of the literal or conventional meaning of that specific word – even though it is not a feature that helps to determine the truth conditions of sentences containing the word. In the other cases – 'and', 'or', 'looks' – the implication is generated by some more general principles governing conversation. In his early paper, Grice (1961) offers a conversational principle that at least applies to the cases of 'or' and of 'looks'. He suggests that the implications are generated, in those cases, by the assumption that there is in operation a general principle something like (1961, p. 94):

One should not make a weaker statement rather than a stronger one unless there is a good reason for so doing.

If someone makes a disjunctive statement, then the hearer can suppose – given this conversational principle – that the speaker is not in a position to make a stronger statement by using just one of the disjuncts. Similarly, 'That looks red to me' is intuitively a weaker statement than 'That is red', and a speaker's use of the weaker statement about how it looks to her (or appears to her, or seems to her) generates the implication that she is not in a position to make the stronger statement about how it is in reality. The example with 'and', however, is not dealt with by this conversational principle.

In a later paper, Grice (1975) offers a more fully worked out theory that covers the example of 'and' as well. The fundamental idea is that participants in a conversation expect each other to observe a *Cooperative Principle*:

Make your conversational contribution such as is required, at the stage at which it occurs, by the accepted purpose or direction of the talk exchange in which you are engaged.

This principle is elaborated by Grice into a series of maxims. He groups these maxims under four headings: Quantity, Quality, Relation and Manner. Examples of these maxims include (one example from each category):

Make your contribution as informative as is required (for the current purposes of the exchange).
Do not say that for which you lack adequate evidence.
Be relevant.
Be orderly.

The first of these sample maxims is one of the maxims of Quantity, and does the work of the earlier conversational principle. The last is one of the maxims of Manner, and is used to explain the implicature generated by 'and'.

The way that conversational implicatures are discerned involves the hearer in inference. Suppose that a participant in a conversation says – quite literally and explicitly – that p, and gives no indication that he is not observing the Co-operative Principle and the maxims. Then, on Grice's theory, a conversational implicature that q is generated if the supposition that the speaker believes that q is required in order to make his literally saying that p consistent with the presumption that he is operating in accordance with the Cooperative Principle and the maxims.

According to Grice, conversational implicatures can be worked out or calculated using the Cooperative Principle and the maxims together with information about the literal meaning of the sentence used, information about the context, and other background assumptions. There is no way of telling, ahead of time, what background assumptions might be helpful in working out an implicature. So, this aspect of communication involves a great deal that is not specifically to do with language. Furthermore, in Grice's view, the Co-operative Principle and the maxims themselves are not specific to language; they are simply the instantiations to the case of conversation of principles and maxims that it would be reasonable to observe in any co-operative activity – such as cooking a meal, or helping a friend to change the wheel on a car.

The mechanism of conversational implicature can be used to communicate more than is literally said – more than the literal meaning that is encoded in the words that are used. If an implicature turns out to be false, then the hearer may well be misled; but the speaker has not, strictly speaking, spoken falsely. This distinction between what is false, and what is only misleading, is of considerable general philosophical importance. If Bruce is standing squarely in front of a standard letter box in the United Kingdom in good daylight, and says, 'That looks red to me', then what he says may be misleading, to the extent that it suggests that there is some doubt about the colour of the letter box. But still, what he says is true: the letter box does look red to Bruce. (Grice (1961) uses this point to defend a version of the sense data theory of perception.)

6.2 Relevance

Although Grice's pragmatic theory is important and has been influential, there are some quite serious problems with it. One problem is that the theory is underspecified at crucial points. Consider, for example, what Grice says about irony and about metaphor (1975/1989, p. 34). In each case (irony: 'X is a fine friend'; metaphor: 'You are the cream in my coffee') what the speaker literally and explicitly says is obviously false, and obviously something that the speaker does not believe. Since this amounts – on the surface at least – to the speaker's flouting the maxims of Quality, the hearer has to find a proposition q such that, by supposing the speaker to believe that q, the hearer can see the speaker as nevertheless conforming to the Co-operative Principle and the maxims.

In the case of irony, Grice's gloss is (1975/1989, p. 34) to say:

> [U]nless A's utterance is entirely pointless, A must be trying to get across some other proposition than the one he purports to be putting forward. This must be some obviously related proposition; the most obviously related proposition is the contradictory of the one he purports to be putting forward.

In the case of metaphor, he says (1975/1989, p. 34):

> The most likely supposition is that the speaker is attributing to his audience some feature or features in respect of which the audience resembles (more or less fancifully) the mentioned substance.

But this is scarcely an account of how the implicature is calculated in either case. (Both irony and metaphor are important topics for any pragmatic theory. There is an extensive literature on metaphor, particularly. See, for example, Davidson, 1978; Searle, 1979; Sperber and Wilson, 1986b.)

A second problem is that it is unclear that Grice's theory can allow for the open-ended character of many implicatures – seen clearly in the open-ended interpretation of metaphor, for example. Grice himself says (1975/1989, pp. 39–40):

Since, to calculate a conversational implicature is to calculate what has to be supposed in order to preserve the supposition that the Co-operative Principle is being observed, and since there may be various possible specific explanations, a list of which may be open, the conversational implicatum in such cases will be disjunction of such specific explanations; and if the list of these is open, the implicatum will have just the kind of indeterminacy that many actual implicata do in fact seem to possess.

But, on Grice's general picture, what is conversationally implicated is supposed to be part of the message that is communicated: it is supposed to fall within the scope of speaker's meaning. So, what is conversationally implicated is supposed to be overtly intended. But it is far from clear that it makes sense to say that the proposition that a speaker overtly intended to communicate was an indefinitely extended disjunction. The problem here is that it is unclear exactly what belief the speaker would intend the hearer to end up with (clause (1) of the definition of speaker's meaning), and equally unclear exactly what intention the speaker would intend the hearer to recognize her as having (clause (2)).

We need to allow that, although sometimes a speaker may overtly intend the hearer to recognize a specific conversational implicature as the communicated message, this case lies at one end of a spectrum. Further along the spectrum, there are cases where the speaker intends that the hearer will recognize one or more implicatures in a more or less closely demarcated range. Further along again, there are cases where the speaker is doing little more than to invite the hearer to explore a space of possible implicatures.

What this suggests is that we might do best to focus on the ways – some specifically intended, others not – in which a hearer can *exploit* what a speaker literally and explicitly says. Conversational implicatures, meeting the standards of speaker's meaning, would then be regarded as the limiting case of a much more general phenomenon.

Dan Sperber and Deirdre Wilson (1981, 1986a, 1986b, 1986c; Wilson and Sperber, 1981) have developed a pragmatic theory that is based on a quite general account of the way in which a hearer makes use of available information. We can lead into their proposal by considering one more problem with Grice's theory.

Consider the following example from Grice:

A: Where does C live?
B: Somewhere in the south of France.

Grice's own gloss on the example is as follows (1975/1989, pp. 32–3):

There is no reason to suppose that B is opting out [from the Cooperative Principle and the maxims]; his answer is, as he well knows, less informative than is required to meet A's needs. This infringement of the first maxim of Quantity [Make your contribution as informative as is required (for the current purposes of the exchange)] can be explained only by the supposition that B is aware that to be more informative would be to say something that infringed the maxim of Quality, 'Don't say what you lack adequate evidence for', so B implicates that he does not know in which town C lives.

If we look at this gloss in the light of Grice's account of the generation of implicatures, then we see that it is implicit that measuring up to the maxim of Quality excuses violating the maxim of Quantity, when there is a clash between them. The maxim of Quality is thus implicitly ranked as more important than the maxim of Quantity. But there is nothing explicit in Grice's account about the ranking of the maxims. This is a problem with Grice's theory. The Co-operative Principle is developed in a large number of maxims, but no general account is provided of the relationships between the maxims. It would thus be tempting to look for some one over-arching aim in conversation, which would justify a single over-arching maxim.

Sperber and Wilson propose that the key to a theoretical understanding of communication – and, indeed, of cognition in general – is provided by the notion of *relevance*. Thus (Sperber and Wilson, 1986c/1991, p. 586):

> Our suggestion is that humans tend to pay attention to the most relevant phenomena available; that they tend to construct the most relevant possible representations of these phenomena, and to process them in a context that maximises their relevance. Relevance, and the maximisation of relevance, is the key to human cognition.

In order to explain the notion of relevance, we need to make clear the idea of a *context* that Sperber and Wilson use. In their theory, a context is (1986a, p. 15) 'a subset of the hearer's assumptions about the world' that provides potential premises to be used in inferences. The idea is that, at any given point in a conversational exchange, the hearer has some assumptions 'in the forefront of his attention'. When a new proposition is introduced – say, as the result of a communicative act on the part of the speaker – the newly introduced proposition and the pre-existing context interact inferentially, so as to produce *contextual effects*. An implication that depends on the new proposition and also on some of the assumptions in the context is said to be a *contextual implication* of the new proposition; and contextual implication is the simplest example of a contextual effect.

Relevance is a matter of having contextual effects (1986c/1991, p. 586):

> We claim that information is relevant if it interacts in a certain way with your existing assumptions about the world.

Roughly, the more contextual effects a proposition has, the more relevant it is. However, the cost of deriving contextual effects has to be taken into account as well. So we add a second condition – namely, that the less effort that is required in order to derive contextual effects from a proposition, the more relevant it is (1986c/1991, p. 587):

> *Relevance*
> (a) Other things being equal, the greater the contextual effects, the greater the relevance.
> (b) Other things being equal, the smaller the processing effort, the greater the relevance.

The notion of relevance then provides an account of utterance interpretation via a *Principle of Relevance* saying, roughly, that an utterance carries a guarantee that it can yield an adequate range of contextual effects without too much processing effort. (For a more detailed account, see Sperber and Wilson, 1986a, p. 158.) This principle does not merely replace Grice's maxim of relevance. It takes over the work done by all the maxims and the Cooperative Principle. Relevance theory provides persuasive accounts of many aspects of verbal communication, including metaphor and irony (Sperber and Wilson, 1986a, ch. 4; for metaphor, see 1986b; for irony, see 1981).

Implication and Implicature

While we cannot consider relevance theory in detail here, we can convey some of the basic ideas by looking at an example involving a question, along with four possible answers (based on Wilson and Sperber, 1981). We are to assume that the set of background assumptions shared between speaker and hearer already includes the assumption that Bruce is a philosopher, but does not include the assumption that Bruce is boring.

Q: Are you inviting Bruce to your party?
A: a. No, I am not inviting Bruce.
   b. Bruce is a philosopher, and I am not inviting any philosophers.
   c. I am not inviting any philosophers.
   d. I am not inviting anyone who is boring.

Each of these four replies could serve to communicate the same message – the negative answer to the question. That message is literally and explicitly expressed in (a), but is less directly conveyed in each of (b)–(d). In the case of (b), the message that the speaker is not inviting Bruce can be inferred from what is literally and explicitly said. In the case of (c), that message can be inferred from what is literally and explicitly said together with a shared background assumption. In the case of (d), the message can be inferred from what is explicitly said together with an additional premise, namely, the proposition that Bruce is boring. The idea is that, in order to maintain the presumption that the speaker's utterance is relevant in case (d), the hearer of that answer will supply the additional premise.

To give a description of even this simple example, we need at least four notions: the proposition that is *literally and explicitly expressed* in an utterance; a proposition that is *logically implied* by what is explicitly expressed; a proposition that is contextually or *pragmatically implied* – where the inference relies on both the proposition explicitly expressed and other premises drawn from the set of background assumptions (the context); and a proposition that is not already part of the context, but is supplied as an *additional premise*. These four notions can be used to describe cases of a hearer's exploiting information provided by the speaker, as well as cases – such as the example here – where the speaker overtly intends to communicate a message that is not explicitly expressed.

It may not be immediately obvious how Grice's notion of conversational implicature maps on to this relevance theory framework. In the example given, answer (b) would certainly not be a case of conversational implicature on Grice's account, since (1975/1989, p. 39) 'the truth of a conversational implicatum is not required by the truth of what is said'. Answer (c) does pass that test, but in fact the Gricean notion of conversational implicature corresponds more closely to that of an additional premise, as in answer (d).

6.3 Pragmatic contributions to explicit content

Grice's theory of conversational implicature provides an account of the way in which an implicature that q can be worked out, given that the speaker literally and explicitly advances the proposition that p. This may suggest that pragmatic principles are not involved in discerning that a speaker has explicitly advanced a certain proposition. But that idea would be incorrect. Thus, Sperber and Wilson (1986a, pp. 175–6):

> We regard verbal communication, then, as involving two types of communication process: one based on coding and decoding, the other on ostension and inference. The coded communication process is not autonomous: it is subservient to the inferential process. The inferential process is autonomous: it functions in essentially the same way whether or not combined with coded communication (though in the absence of coded communication, performances are generally poorer). The coded communication is of course linguistic: acoustic (or graphic) signals are used to communicate semantic representations. The semantic representations recovered by decoding are useful only as a source of hypotheses and evidence for the second communication process, the inferential one. Inferential communication involves the application, not of special-purpose decoding rules, but of general-purpose inference rules, which apply to any conceptually represented information.

Pragmatic principles are involved in the recognition of the proposition that is explicitly expressed. They are also involved when we discern what attitude the speaker takes towards the proposition expressed, or what kind of speech act – an assertion, a command, a question – the speaker is performing. Let us look at kinds of speech act first.

Here, it is important to avoid a confusion between *mood* and *force*. The mood of an uttered sentence – indicative, imperative, interrogative – is certainly part of its encoded literal meaning. But mood does not guarantee force. Uttering a sentence in the indicative mood, for example, is not the same thing as making an assertion. An indicative sentence can be used to express a conjecture or to make a joke; it can be used ironically or questioningly. Nor is there any further sign, over and above the mood of the uttered sentence, that guarantees that an act of assertion has been performed. Uttering a sentence in a particular tone of voice, or wearing a particular hat, for example, does not make it an assertion.

Certainly there is some conceptual connection between moods and forces, and an adequate total theory of language and its use must spell that out. Davidson (1979) makes the proposal that an utterance of a sentence in a non-indicative (for example, imperative, or interrogative) mood is rather like a pair of utterances. An utterance of 'Put on your hat' is rather like an utterance of 'My next utterance is imperatival in force' followed by an utterance of the indicative sentence 'You will put on your hat'. Whether or not this account is ultimately satisfactory, it certainly establishes a connection 'between the mood indicators and the *idea* of a certain illocutionary act' (1984, p. 275). But the crucial point for present purposes is that even though the presence of a particular mood may constitute a *prima facie* reason for taking an utterance to have a particular force, still that *prima facie* reason may be over-ridden by all manner of other considerations. There are no 'special-purpose decoding rules' for calculating the force of an utterance.

We turn now from kinds of speech act to explicit propositional content. In many respects, the literal meanings of words and the ways in which words are put together to make sentences leave us far short of determinate truth conditions. A familiar example is provided by the sentence 'I am tired'. This sentence does not, by itself, have determinate truth conditions; what the truth conditions of an utterance of the sentence are depends on who is speaking. But this kind of case can be misleading. For in this case, it is very plausible that there is a rule that specifies the way in which the truth conditions of an utterance depend on features of the context in which it is made. (Here, we use the ordinary notion of context, rather than the relevance theory notion of a set of assumptions.) However, the step from the literal meaning of a sentence to the truth conditions of an utterance in context is not, in general, governed by a neat set of rules.

The assignment of reference to pronouns, the removal of lexical ambiguity, the resolution of vagueness or indeterminacy, and the restoration of ellipsis are all sensitive to global features of the discourse situation. The fact that even explicit content – even an initial proposition from which further inferences might be drawn – depends on pragmatic, as well as semantic, factors is of the greatest importance for a theoretical understanding of the communicative use of language.

This fact has, however, been used to cast doubt on the theoretical significance of the very notion of a shared public language – the notion with which we introduced Grice's analytical programme (section 5). A hearer not only uses general contextual considerations in order to bridge the gap between literal meaning and explicit propositional content; he or she may also use the same kinds of general considerations to revise his or her assessment of a speaker's literal meanings.

A speaker and a hearer may bring to a discourse different assignments of meanings to words. A hearer may begin with one set of expectations and, finding them unfulfilled, may set about devising a new assignment of meanings to words to serve for the discourse in which he is engaged. In doing this, the hearer will operate in essentially the same way as a radical interpreter: he will try to make the best sense possible of the speaker's total life and conduct. Thus Davidson (1984, p. 278):

> agreement on what a speaker means by what he says can surely be achieved even though a speaker and hearer have different advance theories as to how to interpret the speaker. The reason this can be is that the speaker may well provide adequate clues, in what he says, and how and where he says it, to allow a hearer to arrive at a correct interpretation.

The moral that Davidson draws from this is that, although the notion of convention looms large in the analyses of literal meaning offered by those following out Grice's programme, a self-perpetuating shared assignment of meanings is not an essential feature of linguistic communication. It is, he says, of merely practical significance (1984, p. 279):

Knowledge of the conventions of language is thus a practical crutch to interpretation, a crutch we cannot in practice afford to do without – but a crutch which, under optimum conditions for communication, we can in the end throw away, and could in theory have done without from the start.

According to Davidson, then, all utterance interpretation is to be seen on the model of radical interpretation.

Future philosophy of language must address the questions as to where these considerations leave the notions of literal meaning and public language, and how we should conceive the semantics–pragmatics distinction.

Further Reading

Philosophy of language is an area where most of the reading that is recommended to students is in the form of articles. There are rather few textbooks – and fewer still at an introductory level. Simon Blackburn's *Spreading the Word* (1984) is engaging and challenging, and offers good coverage of both Davidson's and Grice's programmes. There is less on pragmatics, but the few pages on metaphor (pp. 171–9) are especially helpful. Mark Platts' *Ways of Meaning* (1979) is useful for a fairly introductory – though far from neutral – account of Davidson's programme.

Davidson's book of essays, *Inquiries into Truth and Interpretation* (1984), is essential reading, as is Grice's *Studies in the Way of Words* (1989). Amongst Davidson's papers, 'Truth and meaning' (1967a) is a good place to start – and this paper is widely reprinted in anthologies. For Grice's analytical programme, 'Utterer's meaning and intentions' (1969) covers many of the essential points. The first thirty pages or so of Stephen Schiffer's *Meaning* (1972) provide an authoritative introduction to Grice's programme, and the Introduction to the second edition (1988) sets the programme against a background of more recent concerns. Schiffer's *Remnants of Meaning* (1987) has been massively influential in persuading most philosophers of language that Grice's analytical programme cannot be carried through. It is not, however, a book for beginners in this area.

For an introduction to Chomsky's approach to the study of language, the first chapter of the seminal *Aspects of the Theory of Syntax* (1965) can be combined with one of the more recent papers, such as 'On the nature, use and acquisition of language' (1990a) or 'Language and problems of knowledge' (1990b).

Grice's 'Logic and conversation' (1975) should be the starting point for reading on conversational implicature. Sperber and Wilson's 'Pragmatics and modularity' (1986c) provides an excellent introduction to their book *Relevance: Communication and Cognition* (1986a). For readers who are particularly interested in metaphor (about which rather little has been said in this chapter), the few comments in Grice (1975) could lead on to John Searle, 'Metaphor' (1979) and Davidson's 'What metaphors mean' (1978), and then to Sperber and Wilson's excellent 'Loose talk' (1986b). Steven Davis' reader, *Pragmatics* (1991), covers the key topics thoroughly (35 papers in all) with classic papers by Grice, several papers by Sperber and Wilson, and a fine section on metaphor and irony.

The distinction between philosophy of language and philosophical logic is not sharp, and anthologies often range over both. The collection edited by A. P. Martinich, *The Philosophy of Language* (2nd edn, 1990) contains 37 papers. Many of these are about the semantics of subject terms – names, demonstratives and descriptive phrases. Adrian Moore's more compact *Meaning and Reference* (1993) has 14 papers, some of which take up questions that we have noted, but have not discussed, in this chapter. The collection, *Truth and Meaning: Essays in Semantics*, edited by Gareth Evans and John McDowell (1976) contains high-quality papers at an advanced level. Evans' own paper, 'Semantic structure and logical form' (1976) goes to the heart of questions about systematic semantic theories.

References

Avramides, A. 1989: *Meaning and Mind: An Examination of a Gricean Account of Language*. Cambridge, MA: MIT Press.

Bach, E. 1986: Natural language metaphysics. In R. Barcan Marcus, G. J. W. Dorn and P. Weingartner (eds), *Logic, Methodology, and Philosophy of Science VII*, Amsterdam: North Holland, 573–95.

Barwise, J. and Perry, J. 1983: *Situations and Attitudes*. Cambridge, MA: MIT Press.

Bennett, J. 1973: The meaning-nominalist strategy. *Foundations of Language*, 10, 141–68.

—— 1976: *Linguistic Behaviour*. Cambridge: Cambridge University Press.

Blackburn, S. 1984: *Spreading the Word*. Oxford: Oxford University Press.

Chomsky, N. 1965: *Aspects of the Theory of Syntax*. Cambridge, MA: MIT Press.

—— 1976: *Reflections on Language*. London: Fontana-Collins.

—— 1980: *Rules and Representations*. Oxford: Blackwell.

—— 1986: *Knowledge of Language: Its Nature, Origin and Use*. New York: Praeger.

—— 1990a: On the nature, use and acquisition of language. In W. G. Lycan (ed.), *Mind and Cognition: A Reader*, Oxford: Blackwell, 627–46.

—— 1990b: Language and problems of knowledge. In Martinich (ed.) (1990), 509–27

Davidson, D. 1965: Theories of meaning and learnable languages. In Y. Bar-Hillel (ed.), *Logic, Methodology and Philosophy of Science, 2*, Amsterdam: North Holland. Reprinted in Davidson (1984), 3–15.

—— 1967a: Truth and meaning. *Synthèse*, 17, 304–3. Reprinted in Davidson (1984), 17–36. Also reprinted in Martinich (ed.) (1990) and in Moore (ed.) (1993).

—— 1967b: The logical form of action sentences. In N. Rescher (ed.), *The Logic of Decision and Action*, Pittsburgh: University of Pittsburgh Press. Reprinted in Davidson (1980), 105–22.

—— 1969a: True to the facts. *Journal of Philosophy*, 66, 748–64. Reprinted in Davidson (1984), 37–54.

—— 1969b: On saying that. In D. Davidson and J. Hintikka (eds), *Words and Objections: Essays on the Work of W. V. Quine*, Dordrecht: Reidel. Reprinted in Davidson (1984), 93–108. Also reprinted in Martinich (ed.) (1990).

—— 1969c: The individuation of events. In N. Rescher (ed.), *Essays in Honor of Carl G. Hempel*, Dordrecht: Reidel. Reprinted in Davidson (1980), 163–80.

—— 1973: Radical interpretation. *Dialectica*, 27, 313–28. Reprinted in Davidson (1984), 125–39.

—— 1974: Belief and the basis of meaning. *Synthèse*, 27, 309–23. Reprinted in Davidson (1984), 141–54.

—— 1975: Thought and talk. In S. Guttenplan (ed.), *Mind and Language*, Oxford: Oxford University Press. Reprinted in Davidson (1984), 155–70.

—— 1978: What metaphors mean. *Critical Inquiry*, 5, 31–47. Reprinted in Davidson (1984), 245–64. Also reprinted in Martinich (ed.) (1990) and in Davis (ed.) (1991).

—— 1979: Moods and performances. In A. Margalit (ed.), *Meaning and Use*, Dordrecht: Reidel. Reprinted in Davidson (1984), 109–21.

—— 1980: *Essays on Actions and Events*. Oxford: Oxford University Press.

—— 1983: A coherence theory of truth and knowledge. In E. LePore (ed.), *Truth and Interpretation: Perspectives on the Philosophy of Donald Davidson*, Oxford: Blackwell, 307–19.

—— 1984: *Inquiries into Truth and Interpretation*. Oxford: Oxford University Press.

—— 1985: Adverbs of action. In B. Vermazen and M. B. Hintikka (eds), *Essays on Davidson: Actions and Events*, Oxford: Oxford University Press, 230–41.

Davies, M. 1981: *Meaning, Quantification, Necessity: Themes in Philosophical Logic*. London: Routledge and Kegan Paul.

—— 1982: Individuation and the semantics of demonstratives. *Journal of Philosophical Logic*, 11, 287–310.

—— 1984: Taylor on meaning-theories and theories of meaning. *Mind*, 93, 85–90.

—— 1986: Tacit knowledge, and the structure of thought and language. In C. Travis (ed.), *Meaning and Interpretation*, Oxford: Blackwell, 127–58.

—— 1987: Tacit knowledge and semantic theory: Can a five per cent difference matter? *Mind*, 96, 441–62.

—— 1989: Tacit knowledge and subdoxastic states. In A. George (ed.), *Reflections on Chomsky*, Oxford: Blackwell, 131–52. Reprinted in C. Macdonald and G. Macdonald (eds), *Philosophy of Psychology: Debates on Psychological Explanation*, Oxford: Blackwell, 1995, 309–30.

—— 1991: Acts and scenes. In N. Cooper and P. Engel (eds), *New Inquiries into Meaning and Truth*, Hemel Hempstead: Simon and Schuster, 41–82.

Davis, S. (ed.) 1991: *Pragmatics: A Reader*. Oxford: Oxford University Press.

Dretske, F. 1981: *Knowledge and the Flow of Information*. Oxford: Blackwell.

—— 1986: Misrepresentation. In R. Bogdan (ed.), *Belief: Form, Content and Function*, Oxford: Oxford University Press, 17–36. Reprinted in W. G. Lycan (ed.), *Mind and Cognition: A Reader*, Oxford: Blackwell, 129–43.

Dummett, M. 1973: *Frege: Philosophy of Language*. London: Duckworth.

—— 1976: What is a theory of meaning? (II) In Evans and McDowell, (eds) (1976), 67–137. Reprinted in Dummett (1993).

—— 1978: *Truth and Other Enigmas*. London: Duckworth.

—— 1991: *The Logical Basis of Metaphysics*. Cambridge, MA: Harvard University Press.

—— 1993: *The Seas of Language*. Oxford: Oxford University Press.

Evans, G. 1976: Semantic structure and logical form. In Evans and McDowell (eds) (1976), 199–222. Reprinted in Evans (1985), 49–75.

—— 1981a: Semantic theory and tacit knowledge. In S. Holtzman and C. Leich (eds), *Wittgenstein: To Follow a Rule*, London: Routledge and Kegan Paul, 118–37. Reprinted in Evans (1985), 322–42.

—— 1981b: Understanding demonstratives. In H. Parret and J. Bouveresse (eds), *Meaning and Understanding*, Berlin: W. de Gruyter. Reprinted in Evans (1985), 291–321.

—— 1982: *The Varieties of Reference*. Oxford: Oxford University Press.

—— 1985: *Collected Papers*. Oxford: Oxford University Press.

Evans, G. and McDowell, J. (eds) 1976: *Truth and Meaning: Essays in Semantics*. Oxford: Oxford University Press.

Forbes, G. 1987: Indexicals and intensionality: A Fregean perspective. *Philosophical Review*, 96, 3–31.

Forbes, G. 1989: *Languages of Possibility: An Essay in Philosophical Logic*. Oxford: Blackwell.

Frege, G. 1892: On sense and reference. In P. Geach and M. Black (eds), *Translations from the Philosophical Writings of Gottlob Frege*, Oxford: Blackwell, 1970, 56–78. Also reprinted in Martinich (ed.) (1990) and in Moore (ed.) (1993).

—— 1918: The thought: A logical inquiry. In P. F. Strawson (ed.), *Philosophical Logic*, Oxford: Oxford University Press, 1967, 17–38.

Goldman, A. I. 1971: The individuation of action. *Journal of Philosophy*, 68, 761–74.

Grandy, R. 1973: Reference, meaning and belief. *Journal of Philosophy*, 70, 439–52.

Grice, H. P. 1957: Meaning. *Philosophical Review*, 66, 377–88. Reprinted in Grice (1989), 213–23. Also reprinted in P. F. Strawson (ed.), *Philosophical Logic*, Oxford: Oxford University Press, 1967, 39–48; and in Martinich (ed.) (1990).

—— 1961: The causal theory of perception. *Proceedings of the Aristotelian Society, Supplementary Volume, 35*, 121–52. Reprinted in Grice (1989), 224–47. Also reprinted in G. Warnock (ed.), *The Philosophy of Perception*, Oxford: Oxford University Press, 1967.

—— 1968: Utterer's meaning, sentence-meaning, and word-meaning. *Foundations of Language*, 4, 1–18. Reprinted in Grice (1989), 117–37. Also reprinted in J. Searle (ed.), *Philosophy of Language*, Oxford: Oxford University Press, 1971.

—— 1969: Utterer's meaning and intentions. *Philosophical Review*, 78, 147–77. Reprinted in Grice (1989), 86–116.

—— 1975: Logic and Conversation. In P. Cole and J. Morgan (eds), *Syntax and Semantics, Volume 3: Speech Acts*, London: Academic Press, 41–58. Reprinted in Grice (1989), 22–40. Also reprinted in Martinich (ed.) (1990).

—— 1989: *Studies in the Way of Words*. Cambridge MA.: Harvard University Press.

Higginbotham, J. 1989: Knowledge of reference. In A. George (ed.), *Reflections on Chomsky*, Oxford: Blackwell, 153–74.

Kaplan, D. 1989: Demonstratives. In J. Almog, J. Perry and H. Wettstein (eds), *Themes from Kaplan*, Oxford: Oxford University Press, 481–566.

Kim, J. 1976: Events as property-exemplifications. In M. Brand and D. Walton (eds), *Action Theory*, Dordrecht: Reidel, 159–78.

Kripke, S. 1980: *Naming and Necessity*, Oxford: Blackwell. Excerpts reprinted in Martinich (ed.) (1990).

Lewis, D. 1969: *Convention*. Cambridge, MA: Harvard University Press.

—— 1975: Languages and Language. In K. Gunderson (ed.), *Language, Mind and Knowledge*, Minneapolis: University of Minnesota Press. Reprinted in Lewis (1983), 163–88. Also reprinted in Martinich (ed.) (1990).

—— 1983: *Philosophical Papers: Volume 1*. Oxford: Oxford University Press.

Loar, B. 1976: Two theories of meaning. In Evans and McDowell (eds) (1976), 138–61.

—— 1981: *Mind and Meaning*. Cambridge: Cambridge University Press.

Lycan, W. G. 1991: Review of Avramides, *Meaning and Mind: An Examination of a Gricean Account of Language*. *Mind and Language*, 6, 83–6.

McDowell, J. 1976: Truth conditions, bivalence, and verificationism. In Evans and McDowell (eds) (1976), 42–66.

Martinich, A. P. (ed.) 1990: *The Philosophy of Language* (2nd edn). Oxford: Oxford University Press.

Moore, A. W. (ed.), 1993: *Meaning and Reference*. Oxford: Oxford University Press.

Peacocke, C. 1976: Truth definitions and actual languages. In Evans and McDowell (eds) (1976), 162–88.

—— 1981: Demonstrative thought and psychological explanation. *Synthèse*, 49, 187–217.

—— 1983: *Sense and Content*. Oxford: Oxford University Press.

—— 1986: *Thoughts: An Essay on Content*. Oxford: Blackwell.

—— 1989: When is a grammar psychologically real? In A. George (ed.), *Reflections on Chomsky*, Oxford: Blackwell, 111–30.

—— 1992: *A Study of Concepts*. Cambridge, MA: MIT Press.

Perry, J. 1977: Frege on demonstratives. *Philosophical Review*, 86, 474–97.

—— 1979: The problem of the essential indexical. *Noûs*, 13, 3–21.

Platts, M. 1979: *Ways of Meaning: An Introduction to a Philosophy of Language*. London: Routledge and Kegan Paul.

Quine, W. V. O. 1960: *Word and Object*. Cambridge, MA: MIT Press.

Schiffer, S. 1972: *Meaning*. Oxford: Oxford University Press.

—— 1982: Intention-based semantics. *Notre Dame Journal of Formal Logic*, 119–56.

—— 1987: *Remnants of Meaning*. Cambridge, MA: MIT Press.

Searle, J. R. 1979: Metaphor. In A. Ortony (ed.), *Metaphor and Thought*, Cambridge: Cambridge University Press, 92–123. Reprinted in Martinich (ed.) (1990), 408–29; and in Davis (ed.) (1991), 519–39.

Sperber, D. and Wilson, D. 1981: Irony and the use-mention distinction. In P. Cole (ed.), *Radical Pragmatics*, London: Academic Press, 295–318. Reprinted in Davis (ed.) (1991), 550–63.

—— 1986a: *Relevance: Communication and Cognition*. Oxford: Blackwell.

—— 1986b: Loose talk. *Proceedings of the Aristotelian Society*, 86, 153–71. Reprinted in Davis (ed.) (1991), 540–9.

—— 1986c: Pragmatics and modularity. In A. M. Farley, P. T. Farley and K.-E. McCullough (eds), *The Chicago Linguistic Society Parasession on Pragmatics and Grammatical Theory*. Reprinted in Davis (ed.) (1991), 583–94.

Strawson, P. F. 1952: *Introduction to Logical Theory*. London: Methuen.

—— 1959: *Individuals*. London: Methuen.

—— 1964: Intention and convention in speech acts. *Philosophical Review*, 73, 439–60. Reprinted in Strawson (1971), 149–69; and in Davis (ed.) (1991), 209–301.

—— 1970a: The asymmetry of subjects and predicates. In H. E. Kiefer and M. K. Munitz (eds), *Language, Belief and Metaphysics*, New York: State University of New York Press. Reprinted in Strawson, 1971, 96–115.

—— 1970b: Meaning and truth. Inaugural Lecture at the University of Oxford. Reprinted in Strawson 1971, 170–89, and in Martinich (ed.) (1990).

—— 1971: *Logico–Linguistic Papers*, London: Methuen.

—— 1974a: *Subject and Predicate in Logic and Grammar*. London: Methuen.

—— 1974b: On understanding the structure of one's language. In *Freedom and Resentment and Other Essays*, London: Methuen. Reprinted in Evans and McDowell (eds) (1976), 189–98.

Tarski, A. 1944: The semantic conception of truth and the foundations of semantics. *Philosophy and Phenomenological Research*, 4, 341–75. Reprinted in Martinich (ed.) (1990), 48–71.

—— 1956: The concept of truth in formalized languages. In A. Tarski, *Logic, Semantics, Metamathematics*, Oxford: Oxford University Press, 152–278.

Taylor, B. 1976: States of affairs. In Evans and McDowell (eds) (1976) 263–84.

—— 1982: On the need for a meaning-theory in a theory of meaning. *Mind*, 91, 183–200.

—— 1985: *Modes of Occurrence: Verbs, Adverbs and Events*. Oxford: Blackwell.

Wiggins, D. 1976: The *de re* 'must': A note on the logical form of essentialist claims. In Evans and McDowell (eds) (1976), 285–312.

—— 1980: What would be a substantial theory of truth? In Z. van Straaten (ed.), *Philosophical Subjects*, Oxford: Oxford University Press, 189–221.

—— 1986: Verbs and adverbs, and some other modes of grammatical combination. *Proceedings of the Aristotelian Society*, 86, 273–304.

Wilson, D. and Sperber, D. 1981: On Grice's theory of conversation. In P. Werth (ed.), *Conversation and Discourse*, London: Croom Helm, 155–78.

Wittgenstein, L. 1953: *Philosophical Investigations*. Oxford: Blackwell.

Wright, C. 1986: Theories of Meaning and Speakers' Knowledge. In C. Wright, *Realism, Meaning and Truth*, Oxford: Blackwell, 204–38.

Discussion Questions

1   Is the meaning of a sentence a kind of thing?

2   How is the notion of meaning related to the notion of truth?

3   Is there such a thing as the literal meaning of linguistic expressions?

4   What relations exist between semantic and meta-semantic theories of meaning?

5   Are there good reasons to develop an axiomatized theory of meaning?

6   How does the difference between subject terms and predicate terms help us to understand the nature of sentences?

7   If two terms pick out the same object, can everything that is said about the meaning of one term be equally said about the meaning of the other?

8   Is there an order of priority among philosophy of language, philosophy of mind and metaphysics? If so, what sort of priority is involved?

9   Does the metaphysical distinction between objects and properties help us to understand the linguistic distinction between subjects and predicates?

10   Why do predicate expressions have negations, while subject expressions do not?

11   Does understanding sentences of a formal language help us to understand sentences of a natural language?

12   Should the proper format for theorems of axiomatized semantic theories say what sentences mean or give the conditions under which they are true?

13   Is it possible to avoid the conclusion that for a semantic theory specifying meanings, all true sentences are equivalent?

14   Does the notion of a possible language help to determine whether a semantic theory is correct for the actual language of a given group?

15   How does the condition of adequacy imposed by Tarski's *Convention T* help to elucidate the semantic concept of truth and its connection with the concept of meaning?

16   How might the needs of interpretation lead us to specify conditions of adequacy on specifications of meanings or of truth conditions?

17   Does 'radical interpretation' help to establish a link between semantic theories and interpretation?

18   Can truth conditional semantic theories give an adequate treatment of sentences about our mental states?

19   Does the notion of 'tacit knowledge' help to establish the explanatory relevance of systematic semantic theories?

20 How valuable is the notion of a rigid designator for dealing with questions about essentialism?

21 Does ordinary talk about people doing things carry a metaphysical commitment to an ontology of events?

22 Can we satisfactorily analyse the concept of literal meaning in terms of speaker's meaning and conventional regularity?

23 Do propositional attitudes like believing and intending have a role in the analysis of the concept of linguistic meaning?

24 How important is the distinction between semantics and pragmatics for an account of meaning?

25 How can we communicate more than we literally say?

26 Does a theory of conversational implicature need one overarching maxim? Can a principle of relevance satisfy this need?

27 Are pragmatic, as well as semantic, factors involved in determining the explicit content of what we say?

28 Is a shared assignment of meanings an essential feature of linguistic communication?

29 Is there any significant difference between ordinary and radical interpretation?

4

Philosophy of Logic ─────────────

A. W. Moore

Logic is concerned with reasoning. In particular, it is concerned with the distinction between good and bad reasoning. One of its aims is to formulate completely general criteria for this distinction. This is largely a mattter of making precise the conditions under which an argument is valid. It is also a matter of saying what validity is. The latter is the prerogative of the philosophy of logic. The philosophy of logic is the philosophical core of logic, in which the essence of the rest of the discipline comes under scrutiny. Since much of our reasoning, if not all of it, is ineliminably verbal, a large part of the philosophy of logic is concerned with questions about language. This chapter traces a route through such questions, amongst others, taking as its starting point a characterization of logic proferred by P. F. Strawson. Because of the nature of Strawson's characterization, two ideas serve to structure the entire discussion: the idea of a proposition, that is, the idea of that which is true or false; and the idea of possibility.

1 Introduction

P. F. Strawson once characterized logic as 'the general theory of the proposition' (Strawson, 1967, p. 1). At this level of abstraction we can do no better. But what is a proposition? And what is such a theory?

An initial answer might be:

A proposition is the sort of thing that is **true** or **false**. Logic deals primarily with certain relations that hold between propositions, namely those which depend on which combinations of truth and falsity are **possible**. These relations are called logical relations. Two which are of central concern are consistency and consequence. A proposition is *consistent* with others when it is possible for them all collectively to be true. (The truth of the others *allows for* the truth of it.) A proposition is a *consequence* of others when it is not possible for all of the others to be true yet it to be false. (The truth of the others *demands* the truth of it: if they are all true, then it must be true too.) Consequence is the relation that holds between the premises and the conclusion of a *valid* argument.

Each part of this answer requires clarification. In particular, attention settles on the three key terms 'true', 'false' and 'possible'. The interesting thing is that, because logic also has a philosophical component, the very process of providing such clarification is itself part of logic. More precisely, it is part of philosophical logic. Logic subdivides into two: *formal logic* and *philosophical logic*. Formal logic is concerned with the codification of these logical relations. Philosophical logic, or *the philosophy of logic* – unlike other writers, I intend no distinction between these terms – is concerned more generally with what makes these relations the relations that they are. Thus philosophical logic stands to formal logic in something like the relation in which the PHILOSOPHY OF SCIENCE (chapter 9) stands to science. One is engaged in the former when one enquires into the character, scope and preconditions of the latter.

Very well, then; let us set about clarifying the rough account of logic proffered above, beginning with the idea of a proposition.

2 Propositions

'A proposition is the sort of thing that is true or false.' Does this mean that propositions are bits of language? More specifically, does it mean that they are declarative sentences? Suppose we say yes. Still, it behoves us to say considerably more. Quite apart from the many grammatical and philosophical issues that arise from distinguishing declarative sentences from other bits of language, there are (for want of a better word) metaphysical issues that arise concerning what status 'bits of language' are supposed to have in this context. Consider: how many sentences are there in the box below?

> THE CAT IS ON THE MAT
> THERE IS AN APPLE ON THE TABLE
> THE CAT IS ON THE MAT

One could as well answer two as three. There is no special mystery about this, nor one correct answer. It is clear that the question can be taken in two ways, and it is reasonably clear also what the two ways are. Philosophers have introduced some technical terms to mark the distinction. In this case they would say that there are three sentence-*tokens* and two sentence-*types*: two of the tokens are of the same type. Philosophers speak similarly of word-tokens, letter-tokens and so forth, and of their corresponding types. If the province of logic is declarative sentences, then the question arises: declarative sentence-tokens or declarative sentence-types?

The more attractive answer, in many ways, is: declarative sentence-types. It seems alien to the very spirit of the discipline to suppose that the subject matter of logic is nothing but certain inscriptions or noises that happen to have been made. Surely, when logicians consider propositions of the form 'No *As* are *Bs*', say, what they mean to be considering are the indefinitely many propositions of that form that *could* be produced, even though most of them have never come within the ambit of anyone's consciousness and probably never will. Types are better suited to this role than tokens. For, once the type–token distinction has been drawn, there is no obstacle to admitting types that lack tokens. A sentence-type can be thought of as a particular sequence of word-types. It is true that each of the word-types will have tokens. (This is something of a palliative for those who are concerned that sentence-types are unduly abstract.) But it may well be that no one has ever actually concatenated those words in that order to produce that sentence.

The problem with types, in fact, is more basic. They are not the sort of things that are true or false. Consider the type 'I am hungry'. In itself, this is neither true nor false. At most it is true *relative* to certain people and certain times, or *as* (potentially) uttered by certain people at certain times. Of course, we could surrender the idea that propositions are, 'in themselves', either true or false, and we could dismiss the contrary suggestion as one of the many infelicities of the rough account of logic with which we started. But that would mean paying a price: there would be a considerable loss of simplicity. An alternative would perhaps be to focus on sentences that did not contain any of the troublesome words or constructions, such as 'I', which occasion this kind of context-dependence. Whether there are any such sentences in natural language is dubious. Perhaps they exist in the language of MATHEMATICS (chapter 10). Perhaps '2 + 2 = 4' is an example. But our hope, if we took this approach, would be that such sentences could at least be artificially constructed. A further hope would be that such sentences could be used to say anything that could be said by means of any other declarative sentences. (We should have to hope this if we did not want logic to be restricted in its application. And it is an important point that it would *be* a further hope. Someone might well agree that such sentences could be constructed and yet be sceptical about how much could be achieved by their means.) An example of such a sentence might be something of the form '*S* is hungry at *t*', where the 'is' was to be understood tenselessly, and where the terms replacing '*S*' and '*t*' picked out a person and a time respectively. It might be protested that there would still be a dimension of relativity, in that a sentence could mean different things in different languages, and so be true in one language and false in another. But we could stipulate that by a 'sentence' we meant something considered *as* belonging to a particular language. No, the real problem with this approach is that it would represent logic as being concerned with entities whose nature and very existence were a matter of genuine controversy. Some of this controversy will come to the fore later (see 3.1 below).

The original objection to construing propositions as declarative sentence-types was that declarative sentence-types are not in themselves the sort of things that are true or false. Before we try circumventing our current difficulties by reverting to declarative sentence-tokens, let it be noted that neither are *they*, in themselves, the sort of things that are true or false. Consider the three tokens in the box on page 141, for example. None of these is either true or false. This is because they appear there for purely illustrative purposes. They are not being used to assert anything. (In fact it would be impossible for tokens of those types to be used to assert anything without a good deal of stage-setting which I, writing this chapter, lack. Which cat? Which mat? What table?) Even when a token is used to assert something we should be wary of classifying it as true or false without qualification. Suppose that Smith, as he sets off to a meeting, pins a note to his door saying 'I am out'. And suppose that the following day, because he does not want to be disturbed, he pins the very same note to his door. Then the token-sentence on his note exhibits a disconcerting inconstancy: first true, then false. (Or are there two distinct sentence-tokens here? Is something a sentence-token only as used in a certain way?)

These difficulties combine to suggest that we do best to stop thinking of propositions as bits of language at all. The difficulties also suggest a more satisfactory construal. Propositions are what are actually asserted, or, more generally, what could be asserted, *by means of* bits of language. Smith pins his note to his door one day and thereby asserts, or perhaps conveys, a true proposition. He does the same thing the following day and asserts, or conveys, a quite different proposition, this time false. When I say, 'I am hungry,' I assert a particular proposition. You, using a quite different sentence, say of me a little while later, 'He was hungry,' and assert the very same proposition. Propositions are the message carried by the linguistic medium. But they do not depend for their existence on the contingencies and vicissitudes of actual communication. There are countless propositions that are never asserted. Logic is thus able to retain that aura of abstraction which first inclined us against construing propositions as sentence-tokens. On the other hand, propositions are entities with which we can have direct commerce, as they had better be if logic is to impinge on our ordinary thinking and reasoning in the way that it certainly does. Indeed, they enjoy a further advantage here over sentences (whether types or tokens). For our commerce with propositions can take a variety of forms. They can be thought, or entertained, or hoped, even where no sentence is directly involved, and certainly where no sentence is being used to assert anything. There is therefore no puzzle about how logic can have application in such cases, again as it certainly can. (My unexpressed hopes can be inconsistent.) Above all, propositions, on this construal, are true or false. What better then than to think in these terms? Strawson himself certainly seemed to be doing that when, in the context already referred to, he characterized propositions as what we specify by 'that'-clauses when we say things of the form 'I hope that p', 'Suppose that p', 'It follows that p', 'It is possible that p' and suchlike.

But we must be cautious. This account, for all its attractions, and partly, no doubt, because of them, glides over some of the deepest problems in the philosophy of logic. That which language is used to convey – MEANING (chapter 3) – would be regarded by many as the very stuff of logic. To take it for granted, as has just effectively been done, is to take for granted a good deal of what we, as philosophers of logic, ought precisely to be questioning. How exactly, for example, does your utterance of 'He was hungry' relate to my utterance of 'I am hungry'? In what way can two utterances share a meaning when the sentence-types concerned do not? Is it merely captious to point out that your utterance, unlike mine, conveys (affirms? presupposes?) my sex? Are propositions completely extra-linguistic? Can the same proposition be asserted by saying 'There is an apple on the table' as by saying 'Il y a une pomme sur la table'? If so, could that proposition have existed even if there had been no language? Some philosophers, notably W. V. O. Quine, are sceptical about whether there is any way through this morass of questions; and they turn their scepticism on the questions themselves. Quine gives an account of logic which is not in terms of meaning and which eschews propositions, on this construal, altogether (Quine, 1970, ch. 1).

One elegant way to cut through the entire debate would be to stop trying to identify propositions with anything extra-logical. That is, we could think of logic as having *its own distinctive subject-matter*, a kind of idealization of anything that we might normally think of as true or false. This subject matter could then serve as a model for various aspects of our ordinary thinking and reasoning. Propositions would be rather like the rational agents studied by economists, or the frictionless planes studied by physicists.

One advantage of taking this approach is that it would vindicate bringing to bear a simple true–false dichotomy on the vagueness, indeterminacy, ambiguity, inexactitude, hyperbole, figurativeness and vivid colouring of so much of what we ordinarily say and think; and on the countless uses to which we put declarative sentences where it is unclear whether an assessment in terms of truth and falsity is even appropriate, still less what principles should govern it if it is: we tell jokes, we write fiction, we define words, we praise, blame, approve and disapprove. For there is no doubt, again, that logic can have application when we do these things. A joke can be internally inconsistent. One expression of approval can be a consequence of others. On this approach we could see these facts as being no more puzzling than the fact that a car can move along a road in accordance with principles about frictionless planes. Another advantage of this approach is that it would take any *mystique* out of the fact, which was perhaps beginning to assume a spurious significance, that propositions are the sort of things that are true or false. That, now, could be viewed as nothing more than a defining characteristic (cf. Wittgenstein, 1967, §136 and 1961, 6.111). There would still be much that needed to be said about what propositions are like. But there would be some prospect now that it could be said, indirectly, through work in *formal* logic, rather than as part of some philosophical propaedeutic.

Let us turn now to the other key term that occurred in the original rough account of logic: 'possible'.

3 Possibility

It is a fundamental feature of logical appraisal that it relates to possible combinations of truth and falsity, and not, directly, to truth and falsity themselves. In particular, a valid argument can have a false conclusion, and an invalid argument can have a true one. Consider the two following (somewhat regimented) arguments.

> Mothers are always shorter than their fully grown sons
> George is fully grown
> Elizabeth is George's mother
> Therefore Elizabeth is shorter than George

If he is guilty, then his alibi is flawed
His alibi is flawed
Therefore he is guilty

The first of these arguments is valid. It is immaterial if Elizabeth is in fact taller than George. The second argument is invalid. Again, it is immaterial if the person concerned is in fact guilty. In assessing an argument as valid or invalid, we are interested only in whether the conclusion is a consequence of the premises. It does not matter how the conclusion and the premises stand in relation to reality. What matters is how they stand in relation to one another. (It is impossible for mothers always to be shorter than their fully grown sons if this does not include Elizabeth and her fully grown son, George. It is not impossible for a man's alibi, which is flawed if he is guilty, to be flawed anyway.) There is nothing more to this, really, than linguistic stipulation. It is simply a question of how we are going to use the word 'valid'.

Such linguistic stipulation does, however, point to a problem. Since our chief interest with respect to the truth or falsity of propositions is to know which are actually true and which are actually false, the question arises: why is logical appraisal of any interest?

The answer, in a nutshell, is that although logical appraisal does not bear directly on which propositions are true and which are false, it does do so indirectly. If an argument is valid, and its premises are true, then its conclusion is true. If an argument is valid and its conclusion is false, then at least one of its premises is false. If one proposition is inconsistent with others, then it, or one of the others, is false. Logical appraisal thus has a vital normative role to play. Given various things that we already know, it can determine which other things, beyond those, we ought to think or are entitled to think. It can similarly guide us whenever we are exploring different options for what to think, which is itself often an indispensable precursor to choosing the right one. We shall make singularly little progress in our efforts to discriminate between the true and the false without some articulated awareness of what the possibilities are, and in particular, without the kind of awareness that enables us to tell, by dint of reasoning, how the things that we already know and things that we do not yet know are capable of fitting together.

To see further what kind of possibility is involved here, and how it is involved, let us look at some examples of reasoning. As the examples will serve to remind us, reasoning rarely takes the rather stilted form exemplified above: rarely is one involved in assessing an argument whose premises and conclusion are all stated explicitly, in that order. Consider the following three problems.

(1)   Seven cards are laid out in front of you and you see the following array.

| A | C | C | B | G | A | C |

You are told that each card also has a single letter on the reverse.
Question: Which cards, if any, do you *not* need to turn over to test the hypothesis that every card with an 'A' on one side has a 'C' on the other?

(2)   A man needs to transport a lion, a goat and a cabbage across a river. He can
      only transport one at a time. If the lion is left unattended with the goat, it
      will eat it. If the goat is left unattended with the cabbage, it will eat it.
      Question: What should he do?

(3)   A man walks from A to B, setting off at 2 p.m. and arriving an hour later at
      3 p.m. The following day he takes the same route back from B to A. Again he
      sets off at 2 p.m. and again he arrives at 3 p.m. You are not told whether his
      rate of progress is uniform on either day.
      Question: Is there guaranteed to be some point, on the route from A to B,
      such that the man reaches that point at precisely the same time on both
      days?

Here are the three solutions.

(1)   You do not need to turn over the three cards showing a 'C'. In every other
      case it would be possible for a letter on the reverse to upset the hypothesis
      – in the case of the two cards showing an 'A', by being anything other than
      a 'C', and in the case of the cards showing a 'B' or a 'G', by being an 'A'. In
      the case of the three cards showing a 'C', however, the hypothesis would
      remain intact whatever was on the reverse.

(2)   The man should first transport the goat over. Then he should return to pick
      up either the lion or the cabbage and transport it over. Then he should
      return, with the goat, to pick up whichever of the lion and the cabbage he
      has not yet transported over and do so, leaving the goat behind. Finally, he
      should return to pick up the goat and transport it over. Each move is
      effectively dictated. This is because, for the purposes of this problem, two
      positions, which differ only in that the lion and the cabbage are inter-
      changed, are equivalent. So the man effectively has, at each stage, only one
      option which will not lead directly back to a position that he has already
      been in.

(3)   Yes, there is guaranteed to be such a point. The easiest way to see why is to
      think, not of one man undertaking these two journeys on successive days,
      but of two men undertaking equivalent journeys on the same day. One of
      them takes an hour to walk from A to B. The other, during that same period,
      walks from B to A. The question posed is equivalent to the question of
      whether the two men are guaranteed to pass each other. And of course, they
      are.

There is a fundamental three-step process which occurs at different points
in all three solutions. The first step of this process is to identify some relevant
range of possibilities; the second step is to eliminate some of these possibilities
using the parameters of the question; and the third step is to reach a verdict on
some specified question concerning the possibilities that remain. Application
of the process may well involve some special trick or method: there is no
single mechanical procedure that governs all our reasoning. (We can go
further. There is no single mechanical procedure for determining whether or
not an arbitrary argument is valid. This is something that can actually be
proved: it is called Church's theorem (see Boolos and Jeffrey, 1989, ch. 15).) Let
us identify applications of the process within each of the three solutions.

Problem (1):   Here the process is applied to each individual card. The first step,
               in this case, is to identify, as the relevant range of possibilities, the
               different things that can appear on each side of the card. The
               second step is to eliminate all those possibilities that conflict with

the information given and the stated hypothesis. The third step is to determine, of the possibilities that remain, whether they exclude any letter's appearing on the reverse of the card: if so, this is one of the cards that needs to be turned over.

Problem (2): Here the process is applied at each individual crossing. The first step is to identify as the relevant range of possibilities the different combinations of man, lion, goat and cabbage which can undertake that crossing. The second step is to eliminate all the possibilities that violate the constraints of the problem. The third step is to determine, of the possibilities that remain, which constitute progress relative to the desired overall outcome. The key here is to recognize the equivalence, for the purposes of the problem, of some of the positions.

Problem (3): Here the process is applied globally. The first step is to identify as the possibilities the different ways in which the man can walk from A to B and back again. The second step is to eliminate all except the possibilities that respect the constraints of the problem. But here the third step is already relevant. The trick is to allow the second step to be informed by the third. Exact times, we can see, are irrelevant to the eventual solution to the problem. So the uneliminated possibilities can be thought of *simply* as those in which each journey lasts an hour. Then further abstraction shows that even the fact that the journeys occur sequentially is irrelevant: one of them can be thought of as being superimposed on the other. (It is an obvious heuristic aid to think of two men undertaking such journeys at the same time.) The third step, having done this work, is now a formality. It is to determine, of the possibilities that remain, whether there is any that does not involve a cross-over point.

All of this may seem a far cry from 'the general theory of the proposition'. In fact, however, these techniques of identifying, eliminating and investigating possibilities, differently highlighted in each of the three cases, are but different means of ascertaining possible combinations of truth and falsity for a given range of propositions. The identification of possibilities is a matter of specifying some relevant feature to which the truth or falsity of the propositions is sensitive. The elimination of possibilities is a matter of supposing some of those propositions to be true or false. And the investigation of the remaining possiblities is a matter of ascertaining what follows concerning the truth or falsity of other propositions. Thus if it is true that every card with an 'A' on one side has a 'C' on the other, and it is true that a specified card has an 'A' on one side, then certain other propositions concerning that card must be false – for example, that the letter on the other side is a 'W'. The three propositions that every card with an 'A' on one side has a 'C' on the other, that a particular card has an 'A' on one side and that the letter on the other side of that same card is a 'W' are *inconsistent*: it is not possible for them all collectively to be true. In fact the initial possibilities are themselves (in the last analysis) propositions. It is their truth or falsity, ultimately, which determines the truth or falsity of all the other propositions under consideration, in accordance with which combinations of truth and falsity are possible.

But what kind of possibility *is* this? Is there one particular kind of possibility that is the special concern of logic? Is there, for that matter, one particular kind of possibility that is involved in all three of these problems?

The first thing we should be clear about here is that there are indeed different kinds of possibility. These are of varying degrees of stringency. For example, it is *scientifically* possible, though not *technologically* possible, for me to travel round the world in a minute. It is *mathematically* possible, though not scientifically possible, for me to travel round the world in a microsecond. (It is scientifically impossible because it would mean violating the physical law that nothing can travel faster than the speed of light.) On the other hand, it is not even mathematically possible for me to travel round the world infinitely many times in an hour, provided that my speed is constant. It *is* mathematically possible for me to travel round the world infinitely many times in an hour by doing so the first time in half an hour and then doubling my speed after each circuit. In other ways this is not possible. Exactly which these other ways are is a matter of deep philosophical controversy. However that may be, it is natural to suppose that there does eventually come some one, minimally stringent, kind of possibility which covers all the others and which is the special concern of logic. Thus, for example, it is *absolutely* impossible – we might say, *logically* impossible – for me to travel round the world and not do so at the same time. (Actually, we had better beware of describing this or any other sense as 'minimally stringent'. Imperfections in our own mental faculties mean that there will always be an epistemic kind of possibility which cuts right across all the others. There is always a chance, given an impossibility of some other kind, that it will be an *epistemic* possibility because whatever it is about it which makes it not a possibility is too complex or subtle for us to grasp. But putting to one side that complication, the idea that there is an ultimate, absolute kind of possibility seems right. And so does the idea that logic is concerned with it (see Wittgenstein, 1961, 6.3–6.3751).)

It is extraordinarily difficult, however, to give an adequate account of this kind of possibility, or even to agree on whether various problematic cases are instances of it. Is it, for example, absolutely impossible for today to be Thursday if tomorrow is Saturday? Or for 2 + 2 to be equal to 5? Or for a water molecule to be composed of hydrogen and carbon? Or for a surface to be both white and transparent? Or, indeed, for the man involved in problem (3) to avoid reaching some point at the same time on both days? Could he not do so if, say, space and time were each quantized (in some suitably chunky way)?

Attempts to explicate absolute possibility – or logical possibility, as we might as well call it – fall into four broad categories. Some cast it as a METAPHYSICAL (chapter 2) notion; some as an idealized EPISTEMIC (chapter 1) notion; some as a SEMANTIC (chapter 3) notion; and some as a syntactic notion. On the metaphysical approach, logical possibility is a matter of the broad and ultimate structure of reality. On each of the other three approaches, the logically possible is what cannot be ruled out in a certain way; or rather, to put it in its more convenient inverted form, the logically impossible is what can be ruled out in a certain way. On the epistemic approach, something is logically impossible if it can be ruled out *a priori*, that is, roughly, without direct appeal to experience. On the semantic approach, something is logically impossible if it can be ruled out purely by virtue of the meaning of its linguistic expression. And on the syntactic approach, something is logically impossible if it can be ruled out purely by virtue of the (grammatical) structure of its linguistic expression. Each of these approaches faces innumerable difficulties. To assess them one must grapple with problems that lie at the very heart of philosophical logic. I shall confine myself to discussion of the third and fourth approaches.

3.1 The semantic approach

On the semantic approach, it is logically impossible for an aunt to be a man, say, because it is part of the very meaning of the word 'aunt' that aunts are female. Nothing similar precludes an aunt being 150 years old. To understand the sentence 'Some aunts are male' is already to be in a position to see that it is an incorrect thing to say. To understand the sentence 'Some aunts are 150 years old', however, is not yet to be in such a position, even though it too is an incorrect thing to say (since, as it happens, no aunt is as old as that). The former sentence is said to be *analytic*, the latter *synthetic*.

So long as one limits one's attention to simple examples of this kind, one might be forgiven for thinking that nothing more needs to be said to establish a reasonably firm account of logical possibility. But in fact much more needs to be said. We have been given no real guidance when it comes to assessing the problematic cases cited earlier. Can one tell that it is incorrect to say '2 + 2 = 5' just by understanding the sentence? If we were told more about 'understanding' – indeed, if we were told more about what it is to do one thing 'just by' doing another – we might be able to make a stab at that question. As it is, the question is impenetrable.

We should anyway be suspicious about whether the meaning of a sentence like '2 + 2 = 5' can, by itself, impose constraints of this kind. Recall Quine's hostility to the view that propositions are the message carried by the linguistic medium (see section 2 above). That hostility was to the very idea of a clearly delineated and determinate meaning attaching to each of our sentences. Unsurprisingly, it carries over into hostility to the semantic conception of logical possibility. On Quine's view, if, at some point in the future, English-speakers are prepared to describe certain people as 'male aunts', in spite of their earlier insistence that such a thing is impossible, then there will be nothing to rule out their having changed their mind rather than their language or their having come to a different view about what aunts, or some of them at least, are like (Quine, 1961c).

Once the distinction between difference in language and difference in view has been blurred in the way it has been here, it may seem a small step to the conclusion that *nothing* is impossible in any 'absolute' way. For there is nothing we deny which it might not have been correct to say. Suppose, for example, that we had counted differently. Suppose we had counted: '1, 2, 3, 5, 4, . . .'. In that case it would have been correct to say '2 + 2 = 5'. And on the

current reckoning, there is no principled way of resisting the move from here
to the conclusion that 2 + 2 would have been equal to 5.

But this line of thought is confused. What is blurred, on the current
reckoning, is the distinction between a situation in which we come to say
different things because of changes in our language and a situation in which
we come to say different things because of changes in our thinking. This is
enough to cast doubt on the determinacy of meaning, and in particular on
whether meaning is sufficiently determinate to sustain the semantic conception of logical possibility. But there may still be some perfectly clear and
pertinent distinctions to be drawn between its being correct to say '2 + 2 = 5'
and 2 + 2's being equal to 5. In particular, if some *other* conception of logical
possibility can be sustained, then the first of these may count as a logical
possiblity and the second not.

In general, it is important to distinguish between talk about bits of language
and talk, by means of those bits of language, about other things: the former is
often signalled by the use of inverted commas. This distinction is nicely
illustrated by the fact that, whereas cats have four legs, 'cats' – note the
singular verb coming up – has four letters. I myself doubt whether this
distinction is always clear in its application. For example, when it is said that
Albert, who knows precious little physics, has picked up that $e = mc^2$, I doubt
that it is clear whether what has been said concerns the *sentence* '$e = mc^2$' or
the physical law itself. But I do not doubt that the distinction is an important
one. And I see nothing in Quine's views about meaning to prevent him from
acknowledging it.

Where Quine's views *may* be problematic for him, incidentally, is alongside
his insistence that there are certain privileged sentence-types that can be
classified as true or false without relativization. This is an apt point at which
to pick up on that difficulty.

The existence of such sentence-types was mooted earlier (see section 2
above), during our initial discussion of propositions. Putative examples were
'2 + 2 = 4' and a specially constructed sentence of the form 'S is hungry at t'.
It was suggested that these sentence-types might be suitable candidates for the
title of 'proposition'. Part of Quine's interest in them is that this is a suggestion
he favours. Certainly it is a suggestion that seems to go well with his general
scepticism about meaning, which prevents him from construing propositions
as the message carried by the linguistic medium (Quine, 1960, p. 208 – where,
it should be noted, he reserves the term 'proposition' for what he takes to be
the objectionable construal). In fact, however, there is tension. The tension
surfaces when it comes to saying which the privileged sentence-types are. It
will not do to say that they are those declarative sentence-types whose tokens
are either all true or all false. Some tokens of declarative sentence-types are not
used to assert anything, as we saw in section 2 above. Nor will it do to say,
coining a suitable phrase, that they are those declarative sentence-types whose
assertoric tokens are either all true or all false. Some declarative sentence-
types do not have any assertoric tokens: indeed, some (most) do not have any
tokens at all. Nor will it do to say that they are those declarative sentence-types
whose *potential* assertoric tokens are either all true or all false. That includes

the sentence 'I am a 150-year-old aunt', which ought, intuitively, to be excluded. (Being false relative to *all* people and *all* times is not the same as being false without relativization.) Nor indeed will it do to say that they are those declarative sentence-types whose potential assertoric tokens are *guaranteed* to be either all true or all false. That includes the sentence 'I do not exist'. What we have to say, intuitively, is that they are those declarative sentence-types whose potential assertoric tokens are guaranteed to be either all true or all false by the fact – and this is where the tension surfaces – that they all carry the same message, or, if you like, that they all have the same content. Quine's only recourse, given this tension, seems to be to draw up a list of words, phrases and other linguistic devices, such as 'I', 'ten years ago' and the use of the present tense, and to identify the privileged declarative sentence-types as those which are free of these devices. However, this would scarcely be illuminating.

3.2 *The syntactic approach*

Let us turn now to the fourth approach to logical possibility, the syntactic approach. On this approach, it is logically impossible for a green apple not to be an apple, say, because it is part of the very structure of the expression 'green apple' that it applies only to what 'apple' applies to. Not that this is as straightforward as it seems. It is not part of the very structure of the expression 'artificial apple' that it applies only to what 'apple' applies to. Anyone who took this approach would have to insist that 'green apple' and 'artificial apple' had different structures, despite appearances. Structure would sometimes show up only after analysis. Such analysis might involve additional words. For example, the structure of 'green apple' might incorporate the word 'and'. (Something is a green apple if it is green *and* an apple.) This in turn would fit with the most popular version of this approach, according to which there are certain designated words such as 'and', 'not', 'every' and 'is' (or perhaps formalized counterparts of these) whose role in an expression, or in an expression's analysans, determines the structure of that expression. By way of clarification: suppose one starts with an expression, or its analysans. And suppose that one keeps these designated words fixed and replaces every other subsidiary expression by a schematic symbol (traditionally just a letter) which serves to indicate which grammatical category it belongs to. Then what results will represent the structure of the expression. For example, the structure of 'Not every apple is green' is something like 'Not every A is B', where 'A' indicates a sortal noun and 'B' an adjective. 'Not every carrot is pink' presumably has the same structure. So do 'Not every number is prime', 'Not every count is bloodthirsty' and many more. The logically impossible is then what can be ruled out purely by virtue of the structure, in this sense, of its linguistic expression. If we allow ourselves to talk about declarative sentences as being true or false, we can put it like this: the logically impossible is what can be expressed by a declarative sentence that is not only false but such that any other declarative sentence with the same structure is also false. It is logically impossible for a green apple not to be an apple, then, because there are *no* true sentences with the structure 'There is something which is *B* and an *A* and not an *A*'.

As before, there is a good deal here that calls out for clarification. But the most obvious and the most pressing question is this: what is so special about the designated words? Why does 'and' count, and not 'carrot'? Why does 'not' count, and not 'count'? One intuition is that the designated words are words that are not allied to any specific subject-matter: they can be used to talk about anything whatsoever. Interesting attempts have been made to lend some precision to this intuition. Notoriously, however, no generally accepted account of the designated words has emerged, either from this direction or from any other. There is a generally accepted *label*. Such words are standardly referred to as 'logical constants'. And most people who have worked in this area have agreed about which words are clearly logical constants, which words are clearly not and which are problematic cases. But it remains an open question what, if anything, this consensus is a response to. Quine, characteristically, is inclined to play down the distinction between logical constants and other expressions. The clearest possible way of demarcating the former, in his view, would be by compiling a list (Quine, 1970, especially ch. 2). But again, that would scarcely be illuminating.

Let us, however, grant the distinction, for the sake of argument. On the syntactic approach to logical possibility, the most straightforward way of defining consistency, inconsistency, consequence and other logical relations is by first transposing talk of the structure of sentences into talk of the structure of propositions. We can then say, for example, that one proposition is inconsistent with others when any set of propositions with the same structure as these contains at least one proposition that is false. Similarly for the other relations. Thus, take the following argument:

No fish are mammals
All whales are mammals
Therefore no whales are fish

We can say that this argument is valid (in other words, that the conclusion is a consequence of the two premises) on the following grounds. No matter what triple of propositions you consider with the following structure

No *A*s are *B*s
All *C*s are *B*s
No *C*s are *A*s

if the first two are true, then so is the third; or, equivalently, there is no triple of propositions with this structure such that the first two are true and the third is false.

But this engenders the following worry. How can we be sure that we are not at the mercy of limited linguistic resources? Perhaps the reason why there is no such triple of propositions is that we do not have the linguistic wherewithal to construct them. It is true that on some views of what propositions are, propositions do not depend for their existence on any particular linguistic resources. But that serves only to redirect our anxiety:

how can we be sure that our talk about the structure of sentences is an adequate base for our talk about the structure of propositions?

One natural reply, reined to the example above, is that it is not just that there *are* no triples of the specified kind, it is that there could not possibly be. That is of little avail, however, when our aim is precisely to elucidate the relevant sense of 'possibly'.

A quite different and more sophisticated reply would involve allaying the worry directly by showing that our linguistic resources are indeed adequate for these purposes. This *can* be shown, at least on most standard conceptions of the matter: it is enough, in fact, that we can do elementary arithmetic (Quine, 1970, ch. 4). However, it can be shown only thanks to the fact that we are able to provide an independent account of what it is that is being shown.

The more one thinks about this problem, the more likely it is that one's attention will be drawn away from language to reality itself. (This shift of attention reflects one important shift in the evolution from a traditional ARISTOTELIAN (chapter 15) conception of logic to its modern descendant.) Reconsider the schematic symbols 'A', 'B' and 'C' in the example above. What ultimately matters is not how these symbols might be replaced by sortal nouns, but how they might be assigned items *of the kind that sortal nouns 'stand for'*, to use a deliberately loose phrase. It is immaterial if, in some cases, no sortal nouns actually fit the bill. (Thus the example concerning fish, mammals and whales would have been pertinent even if there had never been any such words as 'fish', 'mammal' or 'whale', nor any other words equivalent in meaning to these.) For this reason, when logicians circumscribe all the possible 'interpretations' of a symbol, what they usually do is to bypass language and go straight to the items themselves.

Here we arrive at a set of ideas, in particular, the idea of 'standing for', which are fundamental to philosophical logic, whether or not the syntactic approach to logical possibility is correct. They are ideas about the very relationship between language and reality. To elucidate them is a basic task for any philosophy of logic. This is therefore an apt point at which to turn to some of the issues associated with that task.

3.3 *Issues of sense and reference*

There are various more or less crude intuitions entangled here, and they need to be disentangled. They also need to be refined. The crudest intuition is that each bit of language acts as a label for some bit of reality: the name 'Jupiter', for example, acts as a label for one of the planets in the solar system. (This is clearly much less plausible in the case of a word like 'and'.) A much more sophisticated intuition is that each expression of some grammatically basic kind has a feature, determined by that kind, which is directly relevant to the truth or falsity of any proposition in which the expression occurs (or which it can be used to express – how one puts it will depend on one's view of propositions). This intuition, of course, is directly informed by the ideas being canvassed above.

Now it was part of the genius of arguably the greatest logician of all time, Gottlob FREGE (chapter 27), to extricate from these intuitions a deep and precisely worked out conception of 'standing for'. Frege invented logic in its modern guise. And, in the course of doing so, he first distinguished certain basic grammatical categories, then gave, for each one, an account of what any expression in that category stands for. He called this the *reference* of the expression ('*Bedeutung*' in the original German: '*Bedeutung*' is usually translated as 'meaning', but for Frege it was serving as a technical term).

At the basis of Frege's grammar, alongside declarative sentences themselves, are what he called *names*. (Eventually he reckoned declarative sentences themselves as names (Frege, 1964, §2).) These are the singular noun phrases that stand for particular things. (The term 'things' is to be understood in the most generous way possible. Examples of names are 'Jupiter', 'the positive square root of 16', 'the number of symphonies written by Schumann' and 'joy'. The second and third of these have the same reference, namely the number 4.) One of Frege's chief concerns, once he had introduced the idea of a name and its reference, was to show that there is a crucial difference between understanding a name and knowing what its reference is. For instance, someone who has it on good authority that the reference of a name in Urdu is the number 4 does not thereby understand the name. Again, someone who understands perfectly well the two names 'the positive square root of 16' and 'the number of symphonies written by Schumann' cannot tell, without further knowledge, that they have the same reference. Frege accordingly introduced what he called *senses*. A name's sense, he said, is what we *grasp* when we understand it. Two names with the same reference can have different senses. But two names with the same sense (synonyms) cannot have different references. The name's sense therefore *determines* its reference. Indeed, as Frege also said, the name's sense contains the *mode of presentation* of its reference. In grasping the sense, we think of the reference in a certain way. The whole apparatus, including the sense–reference distinction itself, is then extended to expressions in each of the other basic grammatical categories (Frege, 1993a and 1993b).

It is a little ironical that the notion of sense should emerge so directly from the syntactic approach to logical possibility. For if the notion could be given suitable philosophical grounding, then it would be perfectly suited to ground, in turn, the semantic approach to logical possibility. Senses are precisely the determinate meanings that Quine rejects.

Grice on Meaning

There have been many and varied attempts to supplement Frege's work in this area in an effort to rescue senses from Quine's sceptical attacks, or at least in an effort to explicate meaning in a way that could, if successful, be pitted against Quine. For example, H. P. Grice famously analysed meaning in a way that made it look, perhaps not completely determinate, but determinate enough (Grice, 1967). His analysis was in terms of certain complex psychological states. The first thing Grice did was to delimit what kind of meaning is at stake. He called this *non-natural meaning*, in contrast to the kind of meaning that is involved when an apple's brown skin 'means' that it is rotten. He then distinguished between what an expression means and what someone means by uttering it (on a given occasion). He took the latter to be the more appropriate point of entry for analysis: for an *expression* to mean what it does is for *people* to mean what they do by uttering it. Finally, he argued that for someone to mean what he does by uttering an expression is for him to intend his utterance to produce some particular effect in an audience by means of the recognition of this very intention.

This analysis has no influence over Quine himself, however. Quine's scepticism about senses simply gets trained on the psychological states themselves. This may look like unreasonable recalcitrance on Quine's part. But consider. How much would Grice's analysis show even if it were correct? There would still be a question about whether the psychological was in any way more basic than the semantic. It would be just as inviting to say that Grice had demonstrated certain intimate interconnections between the psychological and the semantic. After all, it is very implausible that we could divine what a person intends in uttering an expression without first finding out what the expression means. It may even be that the person could not so much as have that intention without the expression first having that meaning. So anyone such as Quine, reflecting on all of this and sceptical about the very idea of meaning involved, is bound to be sceptical about the psychology involved too.

A more immediate worry about Frege's ideas was given celebrated expression by Bertrand RUSSELL (chapter 27). Russell shared Frege's interest in what the latter had called names. He insisted, however, that they form a very heterogeneous class. On Russell's view, it is only by ignoring the crucial distinction between apparent structure and real structure – a distinction which Frege himself, ironically, had done so much to draw to our attention – that we are led to assimilate all these Fregean names in the first place. If we use Frege's own techniques of analysis, we can separate such names into funda-, mentally different kinds. Many of Frege's conclusions then begin to look unwarranted.

Russell argued as follows (Russell, 1956 and 1993). Some Fregean names, the ones that Russell himself was prepared to call names, are simple indefinable words whose meanings do not depend on the meanings of any constituent expressions. (It is hard to give examples because Russell thought that proper nouns, such as 'Plato', could be defined – in this case, presumably as something like: 'the author of *The Republic*'. Russell's own views about what would count as examples underwent various changes. At one point he held that the only two examples were 'I' and 'this' (Russell, 1988, p. 26).) To understand one of these names – a Russellian name – is to know what its reference is. The Fregean names to which this does not apply are definite descriptions – singular noun phrases of the form 'the *A*'. But these function very differently. To see why, consider a definite description that is not in fact satisfied by anything, say 'the planet between Mercury and the Sun'. In Fregean terms, this is a name with a sense but no reference. Now suppose we understand it as *purporting* to have a reference in the same way in which a Russellian name does. What then are we to say about a sentence such as 'The planet between Mercury and the Sun is green'? We are forced to say that, since it is not about anything in the way in which it purports to be, there cannot be any question of truth or falsity: no genuine proposition is in play. But surely a genuine proposition *is* in play. After all, it would be perfectly possible for someone to think, mistakenly, that the planet between Mercury and the Sun is green. We must therefore understand the description differently. We must disregard the sentence's apparent structure, and stop thinking of the description as a proper constituent of it.

This leads to Russell's alternative analysis. On that analysis, 'The planet between Mercury and the Sun is green' is equivalent to the conjunction of the following three propositions.

(1) There is at least one planet between Mercury and the Sun
(2) There is at most one planet between Mercury and the Sun
(3) Any planet between Mercury and the Sun is green

It is clear from this analysis that a genuine proposition is indeed in play. Moreover, given that there are no planets between Mercury and the Sun, we can see from (1) that the proposition is false.

Russell believed that once these ideas had been generalized, and once a suitably deep level of analysis had been reached, there would be no need to invoke senses. Senses are just a Fregean gloss on hidden structural complexity. The only semantic relation between language and reality, ultimately, is that which holds between expressions and their references.

This account is obviously very congenial to Quine. One of its bonuses, which Quine himself has pursued, is a no-nonsense view of what reality must be like in order for any proposition to be true – or false (Quine, 1961b). In particular, we are spared the drastic expedient which many have felt it necessary to adopt, of positing references for the offending descriptions (for instance, in the case of 'the planet between Mercury and the Sun', an 'unreal' planet between Mercury and the Sun): this expedient flirts with incoherence in the case of sentences which are used, or seem to be used, precisely to deny that such references exist (for instance, 'There is no such thing as the planet between Mercury and the Sun'). All that reality contains, on Quine's view, is what it is truly and clearly said to contain at the end of Russellian analysis: the things of which it is said that at least one is thus and so, or at most one is such and such, or each which is thus is also so, and so forth.

Strawson, meanwhile, recoiling from what he sees as Russell's over-zealous efforts to burrow beneath the linguistic surface, has tried to rescue part of Frege's original conception of names, though with less concern to respect the demands of formal logic (Strawson, 1993). Much of Russell's zeal, Strawson thinks, reflects insufficient sensitivity to how words are actually handled, and to the role that attendant circumstances play in this. Such insensitivity is in turn due to a failure to take into account distinctions blurred when we left behind our initial discussion of propositions in section 2. In particular, talk of whether or not there is a proposition 'in play' – this is my way of putting it, not Russell's or Strawson's – obscures the distinction between sentence-types and sentence-tokens. Meaning, says Strawson, attaches to the types, truth and falsity to the tokens, or at least to assertions made by means of those tokens. The two things are quite separate. It is perfectly possible for a meaningful sentence-type, which can be uttered in suitable circumstances in making an assertion that is true or false, to be uttered in *un*suitable circumstances in failing to make an assertion that is true or false. The latter is what happens when someone says, 'That is green', without succeeding in indicating anything, or when someone says, 'The thing on the table is green', when nothing is on the table. The same thing happens, presumably, when someone says, 'The planet between Mercury and the Sun is green' (though in this case there appears to be no such thing as a suitable context). There now seems to be no reason why we should not assimilate definite descriptions to other Fregean names, in the way in which Frege did. The fact that definite descriptions can sometimes be used without reference, in such a way that there is no question of truth or falsity, is quite compatible with their being meaningful, with the sentence-types in which they occur being meaningful, and with whoever uses such a sentence-type in unsuitable circumstances having a genuine but mistaken thought that he or she has said something true.

This dispute between Russell and Strawson means that if someone were to utter the sentence 'The planet between Mercury and the Sun is green', Russell would say that they had asserted something false, whereas Strawson would say that the question of truth or falsity did not arise. Again, Russell would say that it was part of what had been asserted that there is a planet between Mercury and the Sun, whereas Strawson would say that this was something 'implied' by the utterance about the suitability of the circumstances. Russell's account seems the more barbarous of the two. It certainly involves some butchering of our pre-theoretical intuitions. But is this such a bad thing? Such butchering often occurs in logic, for a gain in simplicity. There is a useful analogy here which it is worth digressing to consider. Recall the definition of consequence with which we have been operating: one proposition is a consequence of others when it is not possible for all of the others to be true yet it false. Very few people flinch at this definition when first presented with it. Yet it already involves considerable butchering. Take a set of propositions such that it is not possible for them all to be true, still less for them all to be true and some other proposition false. A simple example would be the pair of propositions that God exists and that God does not exist. The definition above forces us to recognize any arbitrary proposition – the proposition that grass is pink, say – as a consequence of these. Hardly the verdict of pre-theoretical intuition! But this is the price we pay for a simple, workable definition. Similarly, perhaps, with Russell's account.

One thing that must certainly be said in favour of Russell's account is that it is especially helpful when it comes to highlighting the ambiguity in certain sentences, for example 'This time yesterday the thing on the table was green'. There are two ways of subjecting this sentence to Russellian analysis. Either 'this time yesterday' governs all three of the conjuncts, and the sentence is concerned with what was then on the table, or 'this time yesterday' is part of the inner structure of the third conjunct, and the sentence is concerned with how the thing on the table then was.

However this dispute is to be resolved, one thing of fundamental importance that emerges from the work of Frege, Russell, Quine and Strawson – an importance they would all acknowledge – is a certain basic structural feature of propositions which allows us to recognize on the one hand names, used to refer to particular things, and on the other hand their predicative comple-ments, true or false *of* these things and thereby able to combine with the names to produce propositions which are true or false, full stop. The question of what underlies and explains this structure is one of the deepest in philosophical logic. It is well beyond the scope of the current chapter to make a proper attempt at answering it. But here is the sketch of a possible answer. If any expressions are to have meaning, then some of them must sometimes be used as single-expression sentences, like 'Green', which – to make the point yet one more time – are neither true nor false in themselves, but only as (potentially) uttered in certain circumstances, in the expressing of different propositions. Such variation is of the essence of the meaning of these expressions. Precisely their function is to draw attention to recurring yet transitory features of reality. But if their use as single-expression sentences is to be emulated in any other than the relevant circumstances (say, because an episode from the past is under discussion), then language itself had better be able to simulate the relativization. The expressions must count as true or false *of* certain things to which reference is made by means of other expressions.

4 Marginalia

Let us take stock. Logic, I suggested at the outset, is the general theory of the proposition. A proposition is the sort of thing that is true or false; and logic is concerned primarily with which combinations of truth and falsity are possible. Since then I have been concerned with clarifying these ideas. But it is important to see also how they might be challenged and/or supplemented.

4.1 Beyond truth and falsity

Some people have thought that logic extends beyond the realm of the true and the false. For instance, there is talk of erotetic logic and of imperatival logic: these are concerned, respectively, with questions and commands. (In some cases the issue is not whether logic extends to the given territory. The issue is whether the given territory is outside the realm of the true and the false. For instance, no one doubts that there can be inconsistency in ethics. But there is fierce debate about whether there can be truth and falsity there.) To say that logic extends beyond the realm of the true and the false is to say that logical relations apply in certain cases in which the concepts of truth and falsity (strictly speaking) do not. To the extent that this is so, I think the best explanation is of the kind I sketched in section 2: though logic is the theory of that which is true or false, that which is true or false can sometimes serve as a model for that which is not.

A more urgent worry concerns the innocuousness of the true–false dicho-tomy itself. The dichotomy certainly harbours paradoxes. The most familiar of these can be illustrated as follows.

> THE PROPOSITION EXPRESSED
> INSIDE THIS BOX IS FALSE

If the proposition expressed inside the box is true, then it is false. If it is false, then it is true.

Much work has gone into trying to solve such paradoxes (see Sainsbury, 1988, ch. 5). I shall not rehearse any of that work now. But what seems clear is that a satisfactory solution will teach us to be more circumspect in our application of the concepts of truth and falsity. Fewer things will seem apt for assessment as true or false.

Philosophers of the anti-realist school think that there is, over and above this, a much more radical circumspection waiting to be learned. Anti-realism is a revisionary philosophy of logic whose investigation has been pioneered by Michael Dummett, though he has never himself gone as far as endorsing it (Dummett, 1976, 1978b, 1978c and 1991). The main target of anti-realist circumspection is an inveterate assumption that informs all orthodox work on formal logic, namely that if something *is* apt for assessment as true or false, then it must be one or the other. This assumption comes so naturally that it seems by turns the merest tautology, then just a rule of the game, then the deepest metaphysical principle about reality which is more ultimate than logic itself.

The anti-realist challenge to this assumption concerns propositions whose truth or falsity we cannot determine. An example might be the proposition that Aristotle sneezed at least once on his first birthday. What is the harm in our assuming that such a proposition is either true or false, even if we cannot tell which? The harm, according to anti-realists, is that it blocks a satisfactory account of our grasp of the proposition. Their argument is as follows. Our grasp of a proposition is a matter of knowing what would make it true and, derivatively, what would make it false. On any view of propositions, such a grasp is a kind of linguistic understanding. As such, it must admit of public ratification. For if there were an expression whose understanding did not admit of public ratification, then nobody could ever *show* that they had understood it, which means that it could not be used for purposes of communication, which means that it would not have a meaning, which means that there would be no such *thing* as understanding it. But in order for our grasp of a proposition to admit of public ratification, the proposition had better not be true without our being able to tell that it is, or false without our being able to tell that it is false.

There are two objections to this argument on grounds of self-stultification. The first runs as follows. By insisting that our understanding of expressions must admit of public ratification, anti-realists are in effect locating the meaning of expressions in how we actually use them. So they are endorsing our standard linguistic practices. But one of our standard linguistic practices is to regulate what we say by the assumption that any proposition is either true or false.

The anti-realist reply to this objection is that anti-realists are endorsing our standard linguistic practices only to the extent that those practices allow of endorsement. It is perfectly proper to reject some of those practices for not harmonizing with others, or for being otherwise internally incoherent.

The second objection is more complex. Consider the following proposition.

(P) There is at least one proposition whose truth or falsity we cannot determine.

Now as far as the anti-realist argument goes, it is only if (P) is true that there is any harm in our assuming that every proposition is either true or false. But *is* (P) true? Well, on an anti-realist conception, only if we can tell that it is – in other words, only if there is at least one proposition such that we can tell that we cannot determine its truth or falsity. But if there is such a proposition, then we can tell, in particular, that we cannot determine its truth. The only way of telling *that*, however, again on an anti-realist conception, is by determining its falsity. So we arrive at a contradiction. It follows that (P) cannot be true. Hence, as far as the anti-realist argument goes, there cannot be any harm in assuming that every proposition is either true or false.

Anti-realists have a number of ways of responding to this objection. Most straightforward, and most heroic, is to *concede* that there cannot be any harm in making the assumption, but still not to make it. This is itself an instance of anti-realist circumspection. It is to concede that the assumption cannot be false, but still not to accept it as true. Whatever the merits of taking this stance, both the original objection and the stance itself are in my view of the utmost philosophical significance.

4.2 Beyond possibility

Let us now reconsider possibility. We can proceed here *via* the distinction between an argument's being valid and its being good. An argument is *good* if it provides good reasons for accepting its conclusion. This is not of course a definition. The word 'good' has been relocated rather than eliminated. Moreover, there may be deep reasons of principle why a definition is not available. However that may be, what I have said will suffice for current purposes.

Now there are all sorts of ways in which a valid argument may not be a good one. It may beg the question. Or we may know one of its premises to be false. Or, differently, we may know that not all of its premises can be true. An extreme example of the last of these would be the bizarre case alluded to in section 3.3:

God exists
God does not exist
Therefore grass is pink

Conversely, there are all sorts of ways in which a good argument may not be a valid one. Its premises may all be known to be true, and they may lend the conclusion a degree of support that is very high – but still inconclusive. Take the following example.

> This die has been rolled fifty times
> It has come up six every time
> Therefore it is not fair

Suppose that both the premises are true. Still it is not impossible for the conclusion to be false. The argument is not valid. But it is compelling.

Good invalid arguments of this kind differ from their valid counterparts in resting not on which combinations of truth and falsity are *possible*, but on which are *probable*, or perhaps (in some sense) *reasonable*. There are correspondingly weaker versions of the logical relations. We can call these 'confirmation relations'. We encounter them most frequently, and most interestingly, when we are drawing conclusions about the unobserved from premises about the observed (as, for instance, when someone concludes that the stranger speaking to her on the telephone has only one head), something that we do constantly, unexceptionably, but again, for the most part, invalidly.

I have said more than once that logic is concerned 'primarily' with logical relations, that is with which combinations of truth and falsity are possible. I have not ruled out the possibility that logic extends to these confirmation relations as well. I think it does. They come under the auspices of *inductive* logic, or INDUCTION (chapter 9), as opposed to the *deductive* logic that has been our sole concern so far. (It is not uncontroversial that there is such a thing as inductive logic (Popper, 1972).) It is a further question, however, whether *formal* logic extends to these confirmation relations, or rather, whether there is some codification of these confirmation relations which is of a piece with the codification that formal logic supplies of logical relations. I agree with Nelson Goodman that this is the most urgent question facing the inductive logician (Goodman, 1979, especially ch. III). Goodman is famous for having pointed inductive logic in a new direction. In the past it has been concerned with the problem of justifying our reliance on confirmation relations. This is what Goodman calls the old problem of induction. He thinks that that problem can be dissolved. The new problem is to *define* confirmation relations by taking a cue from formal logic and setting up appropriate rules. This is a problem of description rather than of justification.

The problem may well be intractable. But one thing that Goodman has demonstrated quite clearly is that, whatever role structure plays in logical relations – a defining role, if the syntactic approach to logical possibility is correct – it has no prospect of playing an analogous role here. This is because, given any good inductive argument, its structure, under any reasonable construal of structure, will always be shared by some other argument that is crazy. It will always be possible artificially to construct an expression, or a cluster of expressions, which can be used to illustrate precisely this fact. To see how, consider the following argument.

All emeralds observed before now have been green
Therefore, all emeralds are green

This argument is a good one. The fact that all emeralds observed before now have been green is a good reason for thinking that all emeralds are green. But now we can invoke Goodman's celebrated term 'grue', which applies to things observed before a certain future time if they are green and to other things if they are blue. Suppose that 'grue' is put in place of 'green' in the above argument. The resultant argument is clearly a bad one. The fact that all emeralds observed before now have been grue (hence green) is no reason for thinking that all emeralds are grue (hence, in some cases, blue). The confirmation relation that held in the original case has been lost.

In giving his own solution to this problem, Goodman defines confirmation relations in terms of those arguments that we do in fact endorse, or have endorsed in the past. He therefore tries to find a grounding in our actual practices for what is essentially normative – to distinguish between what is crazy and what is not crazy by appeal to the commitments that we are ourselves prepared to make. This brings with it a shift of philosophical interest from the more formal questions about meaning which concern the deductive logician to substantive questions about how we actually classify things together. Self-consciousness about *that* forces us into a notoriously delicate position. For how we actually classify things together can seem on the one hand completely natural and on the other hand completely arbitrary. Several of the deepest problems in philosophy (and not just in the philosophy of logic) are involved in working towards a proper resolution of this dissonance.

Anyone familiar with the work of Ludwig WITTGENSTEIN (chapter 29) will recognize hints of some of his preoccupations in that last paragraph. It is apt for me to finish in Wittgensteinian territory, if only because it gives me a chance to explain, half-apologetically, why I have made no mention of him before now – except in a couple of references.

Wittgenstein's work, as is well known, was divided into two phases. (The *locus classicus* of the earlier phase was Wittgenstein, 1961, that of the later phase, Wittgenstein, 1967.) In the earlier phase, his aim was to draw the limits of what can be thought and expressed. In his efforts to realize this aim, he assigned the most fundamental of roles to logical relations (relying heavily on the work of Frege and Russell). For he believed that the limits of what can be thought and expressed were set by logic itself. It would not be an exaggeration to describe his early work as an attempt at a 'general theory of the proposition'. Later he repudiated much of this attempt. He shrugged off his earlier aspirations to generality, and began to look more intently at less formal and less abstract issues concerning the different ways in which normativity and meaning reside in our different practices – issues of the very kind that have just come to light. He remained convinced, however, that a proper grasp of logical relations was crucial to a proper understanding of the problems of philosophy. And, in both the earlier phase and the later phase, he made contributions to the philosophy of logic of unrivalled depth and significance. Yet I have so far left him completely out of account. Why?

Part of the explanation lies in Wittgenstein's own ambivalent and idiosyncratic attitude to the philosophy of logic. In his early work, the philosophy of logic subserved and contributed to a unified network of concerns that were so intimately bound up with one another that it is actually somewhat misleading to describe him as practising the philosophy of logic at all, in so far as this suggests one separable activity among others. Later, in aiming for something more piecemeal and more exploratory, he came to deplore the kind of systematic theorizing about logic and its foundations that I have been attempting to survey in this chapter. To have reckoned with all of that in the context of such a survey would have taken us too far afield. The fact remains that there can be no satisfactory progress in the philosophy of logic that does not take Wittgenstein's insights and strictures fully into account. This indicates perhaps just one respect among many in which my survey has had to be selective to the point of travesty.

Further Reading

Blackburn, Simon 1984: *Spreading the Word: Groundings in the Philosophy of Language.* Oxford: Oxford University Press.

Carnap, Rudolf 1956: *Meaning and Necessity: A Study in Semantics and Modal Logic* (2nd edn). Chicago: University of Chicago Press.

Davidson, Donald 1984: *Inquiries into Truth and Interpretation.* Oxford: Oxford University Press.

Dummett, Michael 1978: *Truth and Other Enigmas.* London: Duckworth.

—— 1981: *Frege: Philosophy of Language.* London: Duckworth.

Evans, Gareth 1985: *Collected Papers.* Oxford: Oxford University Press.

Frege, Gottlob 1952: *Translations from the Philosophical Writings of Gottlob Frege* (translated and edited by Peter Geach and Max Black). Oxford: Blackwell.

Geach, P. T. 1962: *Reference and Generality.* Ithaca, N. Y.: Cornell University Press.

Haack, Susan 1978: *Philosophy of Logics.* Cambridge: Cambridge University Press.

Hodges, Wilfrid 1977: *Logic: An Introduction to Elementary Logic.* Harmondsworth: Penguin.

Kripke, S. A. 1980: *Naming and Necessity.* Oxford: Blackwell.

Moore, A. W. (ed.) (1993: *Meaning and Reference.* Oxford: Oxford University Press.

Putnam, Hilary 1971: *Philosophy of Logic.* New York: Harper and Row.

Quine, W. V. O. 1960: *Word and Object.* Cambridge, Mass: The MIT Press.

—— 1961: *From a Logical Point of View: Logico–philosophical Essays.* New York: Harper and Row.

—— 1970: *Philosophy of Logic.* Englewood Cliffs, N. J.: Prentice–Hall.

Russell, Bertrand 1940: *An Inquiry into Meaning and Truth.* London: Allen and Unwin.

Russell, Bertrand 1956: *Logic and Knowledge*. London: Allen and Unwin.

Sainsbury, Mark 1991: *Logical Forms: An Introduction to Philosophical Logic*. Oxford: Blackwell.

Strawson, P. F. 1952: *Introduction to Logical Theory*. London: Methuen.

—— (ed.) 1967: *Philosophical Logic*. Oxford: Oxford University Press.

Wittgenstein, Ludwig 1961: *Tractatus Logico–Philosophicus* (translated by D. F. Pears and B. F. McGuinness). London: Routledge and Kegan Paul.

—— 1967: *Philosophical Investigations* (translated by G. E. M. Anscombe) (3rd edn). Oxford: Blackwell.

References

Boolos, George S. and Jeffrey, Richard C. 1989: *Computability and Logic* (3rd edn). Cambridge: Cambridge University Press.

Dummett, Michael 1976: What is a Theory of Meaning? (II). In Gareth Evans and John McDowell (eds), *Truth and Meaning: Essays in Semantics*, Oxford: Oxford University Press, 67–137.

—— 1978a: *Truth and Other Enigmas*. London: Duckworth.

—— 1978b: Truth. In Michael Dummett (1978a), (1–24).

—— 1978c: The Philosophical Basis of Intuitionistic Logic. In Michael Dummett (1978a), 215–47.

—— 1981: *Frege: Philosophy of Language* (2nd edn). London: Duckworth.

—— 1991: *The Logical Basis of Metaphysics*. London: Duckworth.

Frege, Gottlob 1964: *The Basic Laws of Arithmetic: Exposition of the System* (translated by Montgomery Furth). Berkeley and Los Angeles: University of California Press.

—— 1993a: On Sense and Reference (translated by Max Black). In A. W. Moore (ed.) (1993), 23–42.

—— 1993b: Letter to Jourdain (translated by Hans Kaal). In A. W. Moore (ed.) (1993), (43–5).

Goodman, Nelson 1979: *Fact, Fiction, and Forecast* (3rd edn). Sussex: Harvester Press.

Grice. H. P. 1967: Meaning. In P. F. Strawson (ed.) (1967), 39–48.

Moore, A. W. (ed.) 1993: *Meaning and Reference*. Oxford: Oxford University Press.

Popper, Karl 1972: Conjectural Knowledge: My Solution to the Problem of Induction. In Karl Popper, *Objective Knowledge: An Evolutionary Approach*, Oxford: Oxford University Press, 1–31.

Quine, W. V. O. 1960: *Word and Object*. Cambridge, MA: MIT Press.

—— 1961a: *From a Logical Point of View: Logico–Philosophical Essays* (2nd edn). New York: Harper and Row.

—— 1961b: On What There Is. In W. V. O. Quine (1961a), 1–19.

—— 1961c: Two Dogmas of Empiricism. In W. V. O. Quine (1961a), (20–46).

—— 1970: *Philosophy of Logic*. Englewood Cliffs, N. J.: Prentice–Hall.

Russell, Bertrand 1956: On denoting. In Bertrand Russell, *Logic and Knowledge* (edited by R. C. Marsh), London: Allen and Unwin, 41–56.

—— 1988: Knowledge by acquaintance and knowledge by description. In Nathan Salmon and Scott Soames (eds), *Propositions and Attitudes*, Oxford: Oxford University Press.

—— 1993: Descriptions. In A. W. Moore (ed.) (1993), 46–55.

Sainsbury, R. M. 1988: *Paradoxes*. Cambridge: Cambridge University Press.

Strawson, P. F. (ed.) 1967: *Philosophical Logic*. Oxford: Oxford University Press.

—— 1993: On referring. In A. W. Moore (ed.) (1993), 56–79.

Wittgenstein, Ludwig 1961: *Tractatus Logico–Philosophicus* (translated by D. F. Pears and B. F. McGuinness). London: Routledge and Kegan Paul.
—— 1967: *Philosophical Investigations* (translated by G. E. M. Anscombe, 3rd edn). Oxford: Blackwell.

Discussion Questions

1   What kind of theory is a theory of propositions?

2   What makes logical relations the relations that they are?

3   How useful is the distinction between sentence-tokens and sentence-types for understanding the nature of propositions?

4   How does the requirement that propositions be true or false constrain our account of what propositions are?

5   Are propositions bits of language?

6   How are propositions related to assertions?

7   Is it helpful to say that propositions are what we specify by 'that'-clauses?

8   Can our account of logic do without meaning and propositions?

9   Does logic have its own distinctive subject matter?

10   What kinds of possibility are there? Is there one particular kind of possibility which is of concern to logic?

11   What is the role of consistency in logic?

12   Is there a difference between our knowledge that it is incorrect to say 'Some aunts are male' and our knowledge that it is incorrect to say 'Some aunts are 150 years old'?

13   Can the logical impossibility of a claim be determined just by understanding the meaning of the sentence expressing it?

14   How determinate does meaning have to be in order to sustain the *semantic* conception of logical possibility?

15   Can we distinguish sentence-types that can be classified as true or false without relativization, from other sentence-types?

16   What kind of analysis and what kind of structure of expressions can help us to understand logical impossibility?

17   Can we do anything more than compile a list of logical constants to shed light on their special role in determining logic?

18   How can we be sure that our talk about the structure of sentences is an adequate base for our talk about the structure of propositions?

19   Could inadequate linguistic resources mislead us about what is logically impossible?

20   Do expressions of different grammatical kinds contribute differently to the truth or falsity of propositions?

21   Can meaning be analysed in terms of psychological states?

22   How can we determine whether there is one kind of name or many logically heterogenous kinds of names?

23   Is the only semantic relation between language and reality, ultimately, that which holds between expressions and their references?

24   In our account of propositions, to what should we assign meaning and to what should we assign truth and falsity?

25   What explains the basic structure of propositions, according to which names and predicates combine to produce propositions which are true or false? Why is this a deep question?

26   Can there be propositions that are neither true nor false?

27   If confirmation relations are defined in terms of our actual practice concerning confirmation, are they defined in terms of something completely arbitrary?

5

Philosophy of Mind ——————————

William G. Lycan

The philosophy of mind abounds in arresting questions: issues of consciousness, personal identity, survival of one's physical death, freedom of the will, mental illness, the role of mind in behaviour, the nature of emotion, the comparison between human and animal psychologies, and many more. But each of these issues ultimately depends on a single, fundamental question, called simply 'the mind–body problem': what is a mind, *per se*, and what is its relation to body, or to the physical in general? Accordingly, this chapter will focus on that question and some proposed answers.

1 Mind–Body Dualism

The first answer to the mind–body problem proposed in the Modern period was that of DESCARTES (chapter 17), who held that minds are wholly distinct from bodies and from physical objects of any sort. According to *Cartesian dualism*, minds are purely spiritual and radically non-spatial, having neither size nor location. On this view, a normal living human being or person is a duality, a mind and a body paired (though there can be bodies without minds, and minds can survive the destruction of their corresponding bodies). Mysteriously, despite the drastic distinctness of minds from bodies, they interact causally: bodily happenings cause sensations and experiences and thoughts in one's mind; conversely, mental activity leads to action and speech, causing the physical motion of limbs or lips.

Cartesian dualism has strong intuitive appeal, since from the inside, our minds do not *feel* physical at all; and we can easily imagine their existing disembodied or, indeed, their existing in the absence of any physical world whatever. And until very recently, in fact, the philosophy of mind has been dominated by Descartes' 'first-person' or from-the-inside perspective. With few exceptions, philosophers have accepted the following claims: (1) that one's own mind is better known than one's body, (2) that the mind is metaphysically in the body's driver's seat, and (3) that there is at least a theoretical *problem* of how we human intelligences can know that 'external', everyday physical objects exist at all, even if there are tenable solutions to that problem. We subjects are immured within a movie theatre of the mind, though we may have some defensible ways of inferring what goes on outside the theatre.

Midway through the present century, all this suddenly changed, for two reasons. The first reason was the accumulated impact of logical positivism and the verification theory of meaning. Intersubjective verifiability or testability became the criterion both of scientific probity and of linguistic meaning itself. If the mind, in particular, was to be respected either scientifically, or even as meaningfully describable in the first place, mental ascriptions would have to be pegged to publicly, physically testable verification-conditions. Science takes an intersubjective, 'third-person' perspective on everything; the traditional first-person perspective had to be abandoned for scientific purposes and, it was felt, for serious METAPHYSICAL (chapter 2) purposes also.

The second reason was the emergence of a number of pressing philosophical objections to Cartesian dualism. Here are a few:

(1) Immaterial Cartesian minds and ghostly non-physical events were increasingly seen to fit ill with our otherwise physical and scientific picture of the world, uncomfortably like spooks or ectoplasm themselves. They are not needed for the explanation of any publicly observable fact, for neurophysiology promises to explain the motions of our bodies in particular and to explain them completely. Indeed, ghost-minds could not very well help in such an explanation, since nothing is known of any properties of spookstuff that would bear on public physical occurrences.

(2) Since human beings evolved over aeons, by purely physical processes of mutation and natural selection, from primitive creatures such as one-celled organisms which did not have minds, it is anomalous to suppose that at some point Mother Nature (in the form of population genetics) somehow created immaterial Cartesian minds in addition to cells and physical organs. The same point can be put in terms of the development of a single human zygote into an embryo, then a foetus, a baby and finally a child.

(3) If minds really are immaterial and utterly non-spatial, how can they possibly interact causally with physical objects in space? (Descartes himself was very uncomfortable about this. At one point he suggested *gravity* as a model for the action of something immaterial on a physical body; but gravity is spatial in nature even though it is not tangible in the way that bodies are.)

(4) In any case it does not seem that immaterial entities could cause physical motion consistently with the conservation laws of physics, such as that regarding matter–energy; physical energy would have to vanish and reappear inside human brains.

2 Behaviourism

What is an alternative to dualism? Carnap (1932–3) and Ryle (1949) noted that the obvious verification-conditions or tests for mental ascriptions are behavioural. How can the rest of us tell that you *are in pain*, save by your wincing-and-groaning behaviour in circumstances of presumable disorder, or that you *believe that broccoli will kill you* save by your verbal avowals and your avoidance of broccoli? If the tests are behavioural, then (it was argued) the very meanings of the ascriptions, or at least the only facts genuinely described, are not ghostly or ineffable but behavioural. Thus *behaviourism* as a theory of mind and a paradigm for psychology.

In academic psychology, behaviourism took primarily a methodological form. Psychological behaviourists claimed (1) that psychology itself is a science for the prediction and control of behaviour, (2) that the only proper data or observational input for psychology are behavioural, specifically patterns of physical responses to physical stimuli, and (3) that *inner* states and events, either neurophysiological or mental, are not proper objects of psychological investigation – neurophysiological states and events are the business of biologists, and mental states and events, so far as they exist at all, are not seriously to be mentioned. Officially, the psychological behaviourists made no metaphysical claims; minds and mental entities might exist for all they knew, but this was not to be presumed in psychological experiment or theorizing. Psychological theorizing was to consist, *à la* logical positivism, of the subsuming of empirically established stimulus–response generalizations under broader stimulus–response generalizations.

In philosophy, behaviourism did (naturally) take a metaphysical form: chiefly that of *analytical behaviourism*, the claim that mental ascriptions simply *mean* things about behavioural responses to environmental impingements. Thus, 'Edmund is in pain' means, not anything about Edmund's putative ghostly ego, or even about any episode taking place within Edmund, but that either Edmund is actually behaving in a wincing-and-groaning way or he is disposed so to behave (in that he would so behave were something not keeping him from doing so). 'Edmund believes that broccoli will kill him' means just that, if asked, Edmund would assent to that proposition, and, if confronted by broccoli, Edmund would shun it, and so forth.

But it should be noted that a behaviourist metaphysician need make no claim about the meanings of mental expressions. One might be a merely *reductive behaviourist*, and hold that although mental ascriptions do not *simply mean* things about behavioural responses to stimuli, they are ultimately (in reality) made true just by things about actual and hypothetical responses to stimuli. (On the difference between *analytic* reduction by linguistic meaning and *synthetic* reduction by *a posteriori* identification, see section 3 below.) Or one might be an *eliminative behaviourist*, and hold that there are no mental states or events at all, but only behavioural responses to stimuli, mental ascriptions being uniformly false or meaningless.

Any behaviourist will subscribe to what has come to be called the *Turing Test*. In response to the perennially popular question 'Can machines think?', Alan Turing (1964) replied that a better question is that of whether a sophisticated computer could ever pass a battery of verbal tests, to the extent of fooling a limited observer (say, a human being corresponding with it by mail) into thinking it is human and sentient. If a machine did pass such tests, then the putatively further question of whether the machine really *thought* would be idle at best, whatever metaphysical analysis one might attach to it. Barring Turing's tendentious limitation of the machine's behaviour to verbal as opposed to non-verbal responses, any behaviourist, psychological or philosophical, would agree that psychological differences cannot out-run behavioural tests; organisms (including machines) whose actual and hypothetical behaviour is just the same are psychologically just alike.

Besides solving the methodological problem of intersubjective verification, philosophical behaviourism also adroitly avoided a number of the objections to Cartesian dualism, including (1)–(4) above. It dispensed with immaterial Cartesian egos and ghostly non-physical events, writing them off as metaphysical excrescences. It disposed of Descartes' admitted problem of mind–body interaction, since it posited no immaterial, non-spatial causes of behaviour. It raised no scientific mysteries concerning the intervention of Cartesian substances in physics or biology, since it countenanced no such intervention. Thus it is a *materialist* view, as against Descartes' immaterialism.

Yet some theorists were uneasy; they felt that in its total repudiation of the inner, the private and the subjective, behaviourism was leaving out something real and important. When this worry was voiced, the behaviourists often replied with mockery, assimilating the doubters to old-fashioned dualists who believed in ghosts, ectoplasm or the Easter Bunny; behaviourism was the only (even halfway sensible) game in town. None the less, the doubters made several lasting points against it. Firstly, people who are honest and not anaesthetized know perfectly well that they experience, and can introspect, actual inner mental episodes or occurrences, that are neither actually accompanied by characteristic behaviour nor merely static hypothetical facts of how they would behave if subjected to such-and-such a stimulation. Place (1956) spoke of an 'intractable residue' of conscious mental states that bear no clear relations to behaviour of any particular sort; see also Armstrong (1968, ch. 5) and Campbell (1984). Secondly, contrary to the Turing Test, it seems perfectly possible for two people to differ psychologically despite total similarity of their actual and hypothetical behaviour, as in a LOCKEAN (chapter 19) case of 'inverted spectrum': it might be that when you see a red object, you have the sort of colour experience that I have when I see a green object, and vice versa. For that matter, a creature *might* exhibit all the appropriate stimulus–response relations and lack a mental life entirely; we can imagine building a 'zombie' or stupid robot that behaves in the right ways but does not really feel or think anything at all (Block and Fodor, 1972; Kirk, 1974; Block, 1981; Campbell, 1984). Thirdly, the analytical behaviourist's behavioural analyses of mental ascriptions seem adequate only so long as one makes substantive assumptions about the rest of the subject's *mentality* (Chisholm, 1957, ch. 11; Geach, 1957, p. 8; Block, 1981); for example, if Edmund believes that broccoli will kill him and he is offered some broccoli, he would shun it only if he does not *want* to die. Therefore, the behaviourist analyses are either circular or radically incomplete, so far as they are supposed to exhaust the mental generally.

So matters stood in stalemate between dualists, behaviourists and doubters, until the mid-1950s, when U. T. Place (1956) and J. J. C. Smart (1959) proposed a middle way, a conciliatory compromise solution.

3 The Identity Theory

According to Place and Smart, contrary to the behaviourists, at least some mental states and events are genuinely inner and genuinely episodic after all. They are not to be identified with outward behaviour or even with hypothetical dispositions to behave. But, contrary to the dualists, the episodic mental items are neither ghostly nor non-physical. Rather, they are neurophysiological. They are identical with states and events occurring in their owners' central nervous systems; more precisely, every mental state or event is numerically identical with some such neurophysiological state or event. To be in pain is, for example, to have one's c-fibres, or more likely a-fibres, firing in the central nervous system; to believe that broccoli will kill you is to have one's B_{bk}-fibres firing, and so on.

By making the mental entirely physical, this *identity theory of the mind* shared the behaviourist advantage of avoiding the objections to dualism. But it also brilliantly accommodated the inner and the episodic as behaviourism did not. For, according to the identity theory, mental states and events actually occur in their owners' central nervous systems. (Hence they are *inner* in an even more literal sense than could be granted by Descartes.) The identity theory also thoroughly vindicated the idea that organisms can differ mentally despite total outward behavioural similarity, since clearly organisms can differ neurophysiologically in mediating their outward stimulus–response regularities; that would afford the possibility of inverted spectrum. And of course the connection between a belief or a desire and the usually accompanying behaviour is defeasible by other current mental states, since the connection between a B- or D-neural state and its normal behavioural effect is defeasible by other psychologically characterizable interacting neural states. The identity theory was the ideal resolution of the dualist–behaviourist impasse.

Moreover, there was a direct deductive argument for the identity theory, hit upon independently by David Lewis (1966, 1972) and D. M. Armstrong (1968). Lewis and Armstrong maintained that mental terms were *defined* causally, in terms of mental items' typical causes and effects. For instance, the word 'pain' *means* a state that is typically brought about by physical damage and that typically causes withdrawal, favouring, complaint, desire for cessation, and so on. (Armstrong claimed to establish this by straightforward 'conceptual analysis'. More elaborately, Lewis held that mental terms are the theoretical terms of a common-sensical 'folk theory', and with the Positivists that all theoretical terms are implicitly defined by the theories in which they occur. That common sense theory has since come to be called '*folk psychology*'; see sections 12 and 13 below.) Now if by definition, pain is whatever state occupies a certain causal niche, and if as is overwhelmingly likely, scientific research will reveal that that particular niche is in fact occupied by such-and-such a neurophysiological state, it follows straightway that pain is that neurophysiological state; QED. Pain retains its conceptual connection to behaviour, but also undergoes an empirical identification with an inner state of its owner. (An advanced if convoluted elaboration of this already hybrid view is developed by Lewis, 1980; for meticulous discussion, see Block, 1978, Shoemaker, 1981, Tye, 1983 and Owens 1986.)

Notice that although Armstrong and Lewis began their arguments with a claim about the meanings of mental terms, their 'common sense causal' version of the identity theory was itself no such claim, any more than was the original identity theory of Place and Smart. Rather, all four philosophers relied on the idea that things or properties can sometimes be identified with 'other' things or properties even when there is no synonymy of terms; there is such a thing as synthetic and *a posteriori* identity that is none the less genuine identity. While the identity of triangles with trilaterals holds simply in virtue of the meanings of the two terms and can be established by reason alone, without empirical investigation, the following identities are standard examples of the synthetic *a posteriori*, and were discovered empirically: clouds with masses of water droplets; water with H_2O; lightning with electrical discharge; the Morning Star with Venus; Mendelian genes with segments of DNA molecules; and temperature with mean molecular kinetic energy. The identity theory was offered similarly, in a spirit of scientific speculation; one could not properly object that mental expressions do not mean anything about brains or neural firings.

So the dualists were wrong in thinking that mental items are non-physical but right in thinking them inner and episodic; the behaviourists were right in their materialism but wrong to repudiate inner mental episodes. But alas, this happy synthesis was too good to be true.

4 Machine Functionalism

Quite soon, Hilary Putnam (1960, 1967a, 1967b) and Jerry Fodor (1968b) pointed out a presumptuous implication of the identity theory understood as a theory of 'types' or *kinds* of mental items: that a mental state such as pain has *always and everywhere* the neurophysiological characterization initially assigned to it. For example, if the identity theorist identified pain itself with the firings of c-fibres, it followed that a creature of any species (earthly or science-fiction) could be in pain only if that creature *had* c-fibres and they were firing. But such a constraint on the biology of any being capable of feeling pain is both gratuitous and indefensible; why should we suppose that any organism must be made of the same chemical materials as we are in order to have what can be accurately recognized as pain? The identity theorist had over-reacted to the behaviourists' difficulties and focused too narrowly on the specifics of biological humans' actual inner states, and in so doing they had fallen into species chauvinism.

Putnam and Fodor advocated the obvious correction: What was important was not its being c-fibres (*per se*) that were firing, but what the c-fibre firings were doing, what their firing contributed to the operation of the organism as a whole. The *role* of the c-fibres could have been performed by any mechanically suitable component; so long as that role was performed, the psychology of the containing organism would have been unaffected. Thus, to be in pain is not *per se* to have c-fibres that are firing, but merely to be in some state or other, of whatever biochemical description, that plays the same causal role as did the firings of c–fibres in the human beings we have investigated. We may continue to maintain that pain 'tokens' – individual instances of pain occurring in particular subjects at particular times – are strictly identical with particular neurophysiological states of those subjects at those times – in other words, with the states that happen to be playing the appropriate roles; this is the thesis of 'token identity' or 'token' materialism or physicalism. But pain itself, the kind, universal or 'type', can be identified only with something more abstract: the causal or functional role that c-fibre firings share with their potential replacements or surrogates. Mental state-types are identified not with neurophysiological types but with more abstract functional roles, as specified by state-tokens' causal relations to the organism's sensory inputs, behavioural responses, and other intervening psychological states. *Functionalism*, then, is the doctrine that what makes a mental state the type of state it is – a pain, a smell of violets, a belief that koalas are dangerous – is its distinctive set of functional relations, its role in its subject's behavioural economy.

Putnam compared mental states to the functional or 'logical' states of a computer: just as a computer program can be realized or instantiated by any of a number of physically different hardware configurations, so can a psychological 'program' be realized by different organisms of various physiochemical composition, and that is why different physiological states of organisms of different species can realize one and the same mental state-type. Where an identity theorist's type-identification would take the form, 'To be in mental state of type M is to be in the neurophysiological state of type N', Putnam's *machine functionalism* (as I shall call it) has it that to be in M is to be merely in some physiological state or other that plays role R in the relevant computer program (that is, the program that at a suitable level of abstraction mediates the creature's total outputs given total inputs and so serves as the creature's global psychology). The physiological state 'plays role R' in that it stands in a set of relations to physical inputs, outputs and other inner states that matches one-to-one the abstract input–output–logical-state relations codified in the computer program.

Functionalist Levels of Description

The functionalist, then, mobilizes three distinct levels of description but applies them all to the same fundamental reality. A physical state-token in someone's brain at a particular time has a neurophysiological description, but it may also have a functional description relative to a machine program that the brain happens to be realizing, and it may further have a mental description if some mental state is correctly type-identified with the functional category it exemplifies. And so there is after all a sense in which 'the mental' is distinct from 'the physical'. Though presumably, there are no non-physical substances or stuffs, and every mental token is itself entirely physical, mental characterization is not physical characterization, and the property of being a pain is not simply the property of being such-and-such a neural firing. Moreover, unlike behaviourism and the identity theory, functionalism does not strictly entail that minds are physical; it might be true of non-physical minds, so long as those minds realized the relevant programmes.

5 Cognitive Psychology

In a not accidentally similar vein, behaviourism has almost entirely given way to 'cognitivism' in psychology. Cognitivism is roughly the view that (1) psychologists may and must advert to inner states and episodes in explaining behaviour, so long as the states and episodes are construed throughout as physical; (2) human beings and other psychological organisms are best viewed as in some sense *information-processing* systems; and (3) the vehicle of information processing is internal *representation*, a repertoire of brain states that represent features of the external world. As cognitive psychology sets the agenda, its questions take the form, 'How does this organism receive information through its sense-organs, represent the information, process it, store the result, and then mobilize its total information in such a way as to result in intelligent behaviour?' The working language of cognitive psychology is highly congenial to the functionalist, for cognitivism thinks of human beings as systems of interconnected functional components, interacting with each other in an efficient and productive way. This was nowhere better exemplified, in the early days of the cognitivist revolution, than in Chomsky's (1959) review of Skinner (1957), which argued for a functionalist information-processing account of language use, against the best behaviorist model.

6 Artificial Intelligence and the Computer Model of the Mind

Meanwhile, researchers in computer science have pursued fruitful research programmes based on the idea of intelligent behaviour as, for given input, the output of skilful information-processing. *Artificial Intelligence* (AI) is, roughly, the project of getting computing machines to perform tasks that would usually be taken to demand human intelligence and judgement. Computers have achieved some modest success in proving theorems, guiding missiles, sorting mail, driving assembly-line robots, diagnosing illnesses, predicting weather and economic events, and the like. A computer *just is* a machine that receives, interprets, processes, stores, manipulates and uses information, and AI researchers think of it in just that way as they try to program intelligent behaviour. An AI problem takes the form, 'Given that the machine sees this as input, what must it already know and what must it accordingly do with that input in order to be able to . . . [recognize, identify, sort, put together, predict, tell us, and so on]? And how, then, can we start it off knowing that and get it to do those things?' So we may reasonably attribute such success as AI has had to self-conscious reliance on the information-processing paradigm.

This encourages the idea that *human* intelligence and cognition generally are matters of computational information-processing. Indeed, that idea has already filtered well down into the everyday speech of ordinary people, as anyone can verify by talking with children for a while. This tentative and crude coalescing of the notions *cognition, computation, information*, and *intelligence* raises two general questions, one in each of two directions: (1) to what extent might computers approximate to minds? (2) to what extent do minds approximate to computers?

The first question breaks down into three more, which differ sharply and importantly from each other. (1a) What intelligent tasks will any computer ever be able to perform? (1b) Given that a computer performs interesting tasks X, Y and Z, does it do so *in the same way* that human beings do? (1c) Given that a computer performs X, Y and Z and that it does so in the same way humans do, does that show that it has psychological and mental properties, such as (real) intelligence, thought, consciousness, feeling, sensation, emotion, and the like? Sub-question (1a) is one of engineering, (1b) is one of cognitive psychology, and (1c) is philosophical; theorists' answers will depend accordingly on their commitments in these respective areas. But for the record let us distinguish three different senses or grades of 'AI': AI in the weakest sense is cautiously optimistic as regards (1a); it says these engineering efforts are promising and should be funded, for their own sake. AI in a stronger sense says that the engineering efforts can well serve as modelling of human cognition, and that their successes can be taken as pointers toward the truth about human functional and representational organization. AI in the strongest sense favours an affirmative answer to (1c) and some qualified respect for the Turing Test: it says that if a machine performs intelligently *and* does so on the basis of a sufficiently human-like information-processing aetiology, then there is little reason to doubt that the machine has the relevant human qualities of mind and sensation. On this view, any system or organism that (genuinely) realizes such-and-such a program or flow chart would have mental states like ours. Thus, if we could build a machine to certain functional specifications, we could artificially create a thinking, feeling machine. Some theorists welcome this consequence warmly, and look forward to the day. Others find the prospect grotesque and preposterous, a reduction of functionalism to absurdity. (AI in the strongest sense is very strong, but notice carefully that it does not presuppose affirmative answers to either (1a) or (1b).) The opposite issue, that of assimilating minds to computers, is very close to the philosophical matter of functionalism. But here too there are importantly distinct sub-questions, this time two: (2a) Do human minds work in very like the way computers do as computers are currently designed and construed – for instance, using flipflops grouped into banks and registers, with an assembly language collecting individual machine-code operations into subroutines and these subroutines being called by higher-level manipulations of real-world information according to programmed rules? (2b) Regardless of architecture, can human psychological capacities be entirely captured by a third-person, hardware-realizable design of *some* sort that could in principle be built in a laboratory? Subquestion (2a) is currently much discussed (see section 12 below), but is not particularly philosophical. (2b) is tantamount to the fate of functionalism strictly so-called.

The computer model of the mind has opponents of several sorts; of these, perhaps the best known are Dreyfus (1979) and Searle (1980). Dreyfus is thoroughly pessimistic in regard to (1a) and gives an emphatically negative answer to (2a). Drawing on the PHENOMENOLOGICAL tradition of HUSSERL and HEIDEGGER (chapter 30), Dreyfus challenges several of the assumptions underlying classical AI, and diagnoses some of AI's known failures as stemming from those assumptions. In particular, Dreyfus argues that, in real life as opposed to the toy 'micro-worlds' constructed by AI researchers, such standard AI tasks as problem solving and language understanding presuppose unpredictably relevant and nearly endless knowledge of the world (consider just the general problem of understanding ambiguous sentences in context); but no human being's knowledge of the world could ever be made explicit, or even completely formalized in a set of representations and rules. Rather, human knowledge and understanding inhere non-discursively in our biology, our bodily embedding in our environment, our interests and our cultural surround – of which digital computers have at best distant analogues. (See also Haugeland, 1979.)

More recently, however, Dreyfus has granted that *connectionist* AI (see section 12 below) evades his main criticisms of classical AI (see especially Dreyfus and Dreyfus, 1986).

Searle offers a hypothetical case in which a human program is executed, not by a mechanical or biological computer in the normal way, but by a simple human being who is given 'inputs', say on index cards, and following some rules written in a manual, writes some 'outputs' on new index cards and drops those in an 'output' bin. Suppose the 'inputs' are sequences of Chinese characters, the program is that which a functionalist would say constitutes a human Chinese speaker's understanding of the Chinese language, and consequently the 'outputs' are grammatical utterances of Chinese also; but the functionary who does the simple rule-following operation is a monoglot English-speaker and only just bright enough to follow the program's very simple instructions. There is here no actual understanding of Chinese, Searle claims, but only a computational imitation of a real Chinese speaker and understander. Thus, sub-questions (1c) and (2b) are answered firmly in the negative.

A number of differing rejoinders are available to partisans of AI in its strong and strongest senses (they are made by various commentators in the *Behavioral and Brain Sciences* symposium – see Searle, 1980). The hypothetical example is not really possible, even if we seem to be able to imagine it; or, though it is possible, its protagonist would (*contra* Searle) really understand Chinese; or, though Searle is right about the example as described, it can be accommodated by an only slightly modified functionalist theory (in particular, see section 10 below).

And Morality?

It may be wondered whether materialist theories of the mind and/or functionalist theories have any interesting implications for morality and ethics. Three materialists take this up explicitly: Smart (1963, ch. VIII), tries to exhibit a materialist basis for morals; Michael Levin (1979, ch. VII) addresses the specific charge that materialists cannot allow freedom of the will or whatever else may be necessary to make room for moral responsibility; Lycan (1985) explores some moral consequences of the computational view of the mind. A main purpose of Dennett's (1978) is also to show why moral responsibility and the mental vernacular that supports it are possible despite Dennett's instrumentalist – sometimes fictionalist – treatment of the mental (see section 11 below).

---

7 Homuncular Functionalism and Other Teleological Theories

As we saw, machine functionalism supposed that human brains may be described at each of three levels, the first two scientific and the third familiar and common-sensical. At the first level, biologists would map out human neurobiology and provide neurophysiological descriptions of brain states. At the second level, psychologists would (eventually) work out the machine program that was being realized by the lower-level neuroanatomy and would describe the same brain states in more abstract, computational terms. At the third level, psychologists would also explain behaviour, characterized in everyday terms, by reference to stimuli and to intervening mental states such as beliefs and desires, type-identifying the mental states with functional or computational states as they went. Such explanations would themselves presuppose nothing about neuroanatomy, since the relevant psychological– computational generalizations would hold regardless of what particular biochemistry might happen to be realizing the abstract programme in question.

Machine functionalism has more recently been challenged on a number of points, that together motivate a specifically teleological notion of 'function' (Sober, 1985, speaks aptly of 'putting the function back into functionalism'): we are to think of a thing's function as what the thing is *for*, what its job is, what it is supposed to do. There are five challenges.

Firstly, the machine functionalist still conceived psychological explanation in the logical positivists' terms of subsuming observed data under wider and wider universal laws. But Fodor (1968a), Dennett (1978) and Cummins (1983) have defended a competing picture of psychological explanation, according to which behavioural data are to be seen as manifestations of subjects' psychological capacities, and those capacities are to be explained by understanding the subjects as systems of interconnected components. Each component is a 'homunculus', in that it is thought of as a little agent or bureaucrat operating within its containing subject; it is identified by reference to the function it performs. And the various homuncular components co-operate with each other in such a way as to produce overall behavioural responses to stimuli.

The 'homunculi' are themselves broken down into sub-components whose functions and interactions are similarly used to explain the capacities of the subsystems they compose, and so again and again until the sub-sub- ... components are seen to be neurophysiological structures. Thus biological and mechanical systems alike are hierarchically organized, on the principle of what computer scientists call 'hierarchical control'. (An automobile works – locomotes – by having a fuel reservoir, a fuel line, a carburettor, a combustion chamber, an ignition system, a transmission and wheels that turn. If one wants to know how the carburettor works, one will be told what its parts are and how they work together to infuse oxygen into fuel; and so on.) But nothing in this pattern of explanation corresponds to the subsumption of data under wider and wider universal generalizations.

The second challenge is that the machine functionalist treated functional 'realization', the relation between an individual physical organism and the abstract program it was said to instantiate, as a simple matter of one-to-one correspondence between the organism's repertoire of physical stimuli, structural states and behaviour, on the one hand, and the program's defining input–state–output function on the other. But this criterion of realization was seen to be too liberal; since virtually anything bears a one–one correlation of some sort to virtually anything else, 'realization' in the sense of mere one–one correspondence is far too easily come by (Block, 1978; Lycan, 1987, ch. 3). For example, the profusion of microscopic events occurring in a sunlit pond (convection currents, biotic activity, or just molecular motion) *undoubtedly* yield some one–one correspondence or other to any psychology you like, but this should not establish that the pond is, or has, a mind. Some theorists have proposed to remedy this defect by imposing a teleological requirement on realization: a physical state of an organism will count as realizing such-and-such a functional description only if the organism has genuine organic integrity and the state plays its functional role properly *for* the organism, in the teleological sense of 'for' and in the teleological sense of 'function'. The state must do what it does as a matter of, so to speak, its biological purpose. This rules out our pond, since the pond is not a single organism having convection currents or molecular motions as organs. (Machine functionalism took 'function' in its spare mathematical sense rather than in a genuinely *functional* sense. One should note that, as used here, the term 'machine functionalism' is tied to the original liberal conception of 'realizing'; so to impose a teleological restriction is to abandon machine functionalism.)

Thirdly, of the machine functionalist's three levels of description, one is common-sensical and two are scientific, so we are offered a starkly two-levelled picture of human psychobiology. But that picture is unbiological in the extreme. Neither living things nor even computers themselves are split into a purely 'structural' level of biological–physiochemical description and any one 'abstract' computational level of machine–psychological description. Rather, they are all hierarchically organized at many levels, each level 'functional' with respect to those beneath it but 'structural' or concrete as it realizes those levels above it. This relativity of the 'functional'–'structural' or 'software'–'hardware' distinction to any specified level of organization has repercussions for functionalist solutions to problems in the philosophy of mind (Lycan, 1987, ch. 5), and for current controversies surrounding *Connectionism* and neural modelling in AI.

Fourthly, the teleologizing of functional realization has helped functionalists to rebut various objections based on the 'qualia' or 'feels' or experienced phenomenal characters of mental states (Lycan, 1981; Sober, 1985; and see section 8 below).

Finally, Van Gulick (1980), Millikan (1984), Dretske (1988), Fodor (1990a) and others have argued powerfully that teleology must enter into any adequate analysis of the *intentionality* or aboutness or referential character of mental states such as beliefs and desires, by reference to the states' psychobiological functions (see sections 9 and 10 below). Beliefs, desires and other *propositional attitudes* such as suspecting, intending and wishing are directed upon states of affairs which may or may not actually obtain (for instance, that the Republican candidate will win), and are *about* individuals who may or may not exist (such as King Arthur). Franz Brentano (1838–1917) (1973) drew a distinction between psychological phenomena, which are directed upon objects and states of affairs, even non-existing ones, and physical objects, which are not so directed. If mental items are physical, however, the question arises how any purely physical entity or state could have the property of being 'directed upon' or about a non-existent state of affairs or object; that is not the sort of feature that ordinary, purely physical objects (such as bricks) can have. According to the teleological theorists, a neurophysiological state should count as *a belief that broccoli will kill you*, and in particular as *about broccoli*, only if that state has the representing of broccoli as in some sense one of its psychobiological functions. If teleology is needed to explicate intentionality, and machine functionalism affords no teleology, then machine functionalism is not adequate to explicate intentionality.

All this talk of teleology and biological function seems to presuppose that biological and other 'structural' states of physical systems really do have functions in the teleological sense. The latter claim is, to say the least, controversial. Some philosophers dismiss it as hilariously false, as a superstitious relic of primitive animism, Panglossian theism or at best the vitalism of the nineteenth century; others tolerate it but only as a useful metaphor; still others take teleological characterizations to be literally true but only relative to a convenient classificatory or interpretive scheme (Cummins, 1975). Only a few fairly recent writers (Wimsatt, 1972, Wright, 1973, Millikan, 1984 and a few others) have taken teleological characterizations to be literally and categorically true. This may seem to embarrass teleologized functionalist theories of mind.

Yes and no. Yes, because if a homuncular and/or teleological functionalist type-identifies mental items with teleologically characterized items, and teleological characterizations are not literally true, then mental ascriptions cannot be literally true either. Equivalently, if people really do have mental states and events, on their own and not merely in virtue of anyone's superstitious or subjective interpretation of them, but their physical states do not have objectively teleological functions, then mental states cannot be type-identified with teleological states.

Fortunately for the teleological functionalist there is now a vigorous industry whose purpose is to explicate biological teleology in naturalistic terms, typically in terms of aetiology. For example, a trait may be said to have the function of doing F in virtue of its having been selected for because it did F; a heart's function is to pump blood because hearts' pumping blood in the past has given them a selection advantage and so led to the survival or more animals with hearts. Actually, no simple aetiological explication will do (Cummins, 1975, Boorse, 1976, Bigelow and Pargetter, 1987), but philosophers of biology have continued to refine the earlier accounts and seek to make them into adequate naturalistic analyses of genuine function.

It should be noted that the correctness of type-identifying mental items with teleological items does not strictly depend on the objectivity or even the truth of teleological descriptions. For, corresponding to each metaphysical view of teleology, including deflationary and flatly derisive ones, there is a tenable view of mind. Just as teleology may be a matter of interest-relative inter-pretation, so, after all, may mental ascriptions be (see section 11 below). For that matter, just as teleology may be only metaphorical, fictional or illusory, so may mental ascriptions be; some philosophers now hold that mental ascrip-tions are in the end false (see section 12 below). But we shall consider those possibilities in due course.

Functionalism, and cognitive psychology considered as a complete theory of human thought, inherit some of the same difficulties that earlier beset behaviourism and the identity theory. These remaining obstacles fall into two main categories: qualia problems and intentionality problems.

8 Problems with Qualia and Consciousness

The *quale* of a mental state or event (particularly a *sensation*) is that state or event's *feel*, its introspectible 'phenomenal character', its nature as it presents itself to *consciousness*. Many philosophers have objected that neither func-tionalist metaphysics nor any of the allied doctrines aforementioned can 'explain consciousness', or illuminate or even tolerate the notion of *what it feels like* to be in a mental state of such-and-such a sort. Yet, say these philosophers, the feels are quintessentially mental – it is the feels that make the mental states the mental states they are. Something, therefore, must be drastically wrong with functionalism.

'The' problem of consciousness or qualia is familiar. Indeed, it is so familiar that we tend to overlook the most important thing about it: that its name is Legion, for it is many. There is no *single* problem of qualia; there are at least nine quite distinct objections that have been brought against functionalism (some of them apply to materialism generally).

(1)   Early critics of the identity theory argued that our immediate mental access to qualia militates against their being features of any purely neurophysiological item.

(2)   Saul Kripke (1972) made ingenious use of modal distinctions against type or even token identity, arguing that unless mental items are *necessarily* identical with neurophysiological ones, which they are not, they cannot be identical with them at all. Kripke's close reasoning has attracted considerable critical attention.

(3)   Block (1978) and others have urged various counter-example cases against functionalism – examples in which some entity seems to realize the right program but which lacks one of mentality's crucial qualitative aspects. (Typically the 'entity' is a group of human beings, such as the entire population of China acting according to an elaborate set of instructions, but our pond would also serve. Neither, it seems, would be *feeling* anything on its own.) Predictably, functionalists have rejoined by arguing, for each example, either that the proposed entity does not in fact succeed in realizing the right programme (for example, because the requisite teleology is lacking) or that there is no good reason for denying that the entity does have the relevant qualitative states.

(4)   Farrell (1950), Gunderson (1970, 1974) and Nagel (1974) have worried over first-person–third-person asymmetries and the perspectivalness or subjective-point-of-view-ness of consciousness. Science is designed to *abstract away from* perspective and subjectivity; materialism seems to deny the reality of the first-person experience.

(5)   Nagel (1974) and Jackson (1982) have appealed to a disparity in knowledge, as a general anti-materialist argument: I can know *what it is like to have* such-and-such a sensation only if I have had that sensation myself; no amount of objective, third-person scientific information would suffice. In reply, functionalists have offered analyses of 'perspectivalness', complete with accounts of 'what it is like' to have a sensation, that make those things compatible with functionalism. Nagel and Jackson have argued, further, for the existence of a special, intrinsically perspectival kind of *fact*, the fact of 'what it is like', which intractably and in principle cannot be captured or explained by physical science. Functionalists have responded that the arguments commit a logical fallacy (specifically, that of applying Leibniz's law in an intensional context; some have added that in any case, to 'know what it is like' is merely to have an ability, and involves no fact of any sort, while, contrariwise, some other theorists have granted that there are facts of 'what it is like' but insisted that such facts can after all be explained and predicted by natural science.

(6)   Jackson (1977) and others have defended the claim that in consciousness we are presented with mental individuals that themselves bear phenomenal, qualitative properties. For instance, when a red flash bulb goes off in your face, your visual field exhibits a green blotch, an 'after-image', a *thing* that is really green and has a fairly definite shape and exists for a few seconds before disappearing. If there are such things, they are entirely different from anything physical to be found in the brain of a (healthy) human subject. Belief in such 'phenomenal individuals' as genuinely green after-images has been unpopular among philosophers for some years, but it can be powerfully motivated (see Lycan, 1987, pp. 83–93).

(7)   A number of philosophers, most notably Sellars (1963), have stressed the ultra-smoothness, homogeneity or grainlessness of phenomenal feels, and contended for this reason that those feels cannot peacefully be dissolved into a metaphysic of little brute particles and their erratic motion through the void.

(8)   If human beings are functionally (even teleologically) organized systems of physical components and nothing more, then their 'behaviour' is only the mechanical, physically determined outcome of physical inputs and internal energy transformations. The inputs are themselves only the physical impacts of environmental causes, which causes are themselves the results of events completely external to us. We are merely automata. (It is no accident that Putnam's original inspiration was the Turing Machine.) But we know from the inside that this is false. Our conscious choices and our deliberate actions are entirely up to us; they feel entirely free. If I simply wish to raise my hand, then nothing can stop me from doing so unless quite externally and by making news (such as a madman suddenly pinning me to the floor or a Phantom Jet hurtling through the wall of the building).

(9)   Levine (1983) has complained of an 'explanatory gap': that no functionalist theory can *explain why* such-and-such a sensation feels to its subject in just the way it does. The question, 'But why do such-and-such functional goings-on constitute or produce a sensation like *this*?' seems always open. Some functionalists contend that a functionalist psychology could indeed explain such facts; others try to show why it need not, consistently with the truth of functionalism.

This is a formidable array of objections, and, on the face of it, each is plausible. Materialists and particularly functionalists must respond in turn and in detail. Needless to say, materialists have responded at length; some of the most powerful rejoinders are formulated in Lycan (1987).

9 Problems with Intentionality

The problem arising from our discussion of Brentano was to explain how any purely physical entity or state could have the property of being about or 'directed upon' a non-existent state of affairs. The standard functionalist reply is that propositional attitudes have Brentano's feature because the internal physical states and events that realize them *represent* actual or possible states of affairs. What they represent (their *content*) is determined at least in part by their functional roles.

There are two main difficulties. One is that of saying exactly *how* a physical item's representational content is determined; in virtue of what does a neurophysiological state represent precisely *that the Republican candidate will win*? An answer to that general question is what Fodor has called a *psychosemantics*, and several attempts have been made.

The second difficulty is that ordinary propositional attitude contents do not supervene on the states of their subjects' nervous systems, but are underdetermined by even the total state of that subject's head. Putnam's (1975) *Twin Earth* and *indexical* examples show that, surprising as it may seem, two human beings could be molecule-for-molecule alike and still differ in their beliefs and desires, depending on various factors in their spatial and historical environments. Thus we can distinguish between 'narrow' properties, those that are determined by a subject's intrinsic physical composition, and 'wide' properties, those that are not so determined. Representational contents are wide, yet functional roles are, ostensibly, narrow. How, then, can propositional attitudes be type-identified with functional roles, or for that matter with states of the brain under any narrow description?

Functionalists have responded in one of two ways. The former is to understand 'function' widely as well, specifying functional roles historically and/or by reference to features of the subject's actual environment. The latter is simply to abandon functionalism as an account of content in particular, giving some alternative psychosemantics for propositional attitudes, but preserving functionalism in regard to attitude types. (Thus what makes a state *a desire* that P is its functional role, even if something else makes the state a desire *that P*). These options will be explored briefly in section 10; and the rest of this chapter will be devoted to problems raised by the propositional attitudes. In section 13 we shall note the impact of the 'narrow'–'wide' distinction on the ontological status of folk psychology itself.

Emotions

In alluding to sensory states and to mental states with intentional content, we have said nothing specifically about the emotions. Since the rejection of behaviourism, theories of mind have tended not to be applied directly to the emotions; rather, the emotions have been generally thought to be conceptually analysable as complexes of more central or 'core' mental states, typically propositional attitudes such as belief and desire (and the intentionality of emotions has accordingly been traced back to that of attitudes). Armstrong (1968, ch. 8, section III) took essentially this line, as do Solomon (1977) and Gordon (1987). Recently, however, there is a nascent literature on Functionalism and the emotions; see Rey (1980) and some of the other papers collected in Rorty (1980). Some psychological literature on the topic is collected in Clark and Fiske (1982) and Scherer and Ekman (1984).

---

10 The 'Language of Thought' Hypothesis

Our basic problem about intentionality is to explain how a purely physical system or organism can be in states having such features.

A key point to note is that intentional or representational features are semantical features: beliefs are true, or false; they *entail* or imply other beliefs; they are (it seems) composed of concepts and depend for their truth on a match between their internal structures and the way the world is; in particular their 'aboutness' is very naturally regarded as a matter of mental *referring*. Some philosophers, most notably Sellars (1963), Fodor (1975, 1981, 1987) and Field (1978), have taken the semantic nature of beliefs as a strong clue to the nature of intentionality itself, suggesting that beliefs and thoughts have their intentionality in virtue of properties they share with other semantically characterized items, the sentences of public natural languages such as English and Chinese.

Sellars argued (against the behaviourists) that people's intentional states are indeed inner and are indeed representations. They are physical states of the central nervous system. None the less (*contra* Brentano) they are physical states *that have semantical properties*. They have those properties in virtue of the functional roles they play in their owners' behavioural economies, closely analogous to the inferential roles that corresponding linguistic tokens play in public, entirely physical language-games. To put the thesis slightly more formally: For a subject S to think or 'occurrently believe' that P is for there to be a state of S's central nervous system that bears the semantic content that P; the state bears that content in much the same sense and in much the same way that a sentence of English or another natural language means that P. Let us call this the *representational theory of thinking*.

It is tempting to gloss the representational theory by speaking of a *language of thought*, and its leading proponents have given in to that temptation. Fodor argues that representation and the inferential manipulation of representations require a medium of representation, no less in human subjects than in computers. Computers employ machine languages of various kinds; it is reasonable to posit one or more human 'machine languages' in which human thought and cognition take place. On the other hand, there are obvious disanalogies between private thought and public speech, so if we are to take representationalism seriously we must specify, in at least a preliminary way, what similarities are being claimed.

On the representationalist's behalf, let us say that physically realized thoughts and mental representations are 'linguistic' in the following sense: (1) They are composed of parts and are syntactically structured; (2) their simplest parts refer to or denote things and properties in the world; (3) their meanings as wholes are determined by the semantical properties of their basic parts together with the grammatical rules that have generated their overall syntactic structures; (4) they have truth-conditions (that is, putative states of affairs in the world that would make them true), and accordingly they are true or false depending on the way the world happens actually to be; (5) they bear logical relations of entailment or implication to each other. Thus, according to the representational theory: Human beings have systems of physical states that serve as the elements of a lexicon or vocabulary, and human beings (somehow) physically realize rules that combine strings of those elements into configurations having the complex representational contents that common sense associates with the propositional attitudes. And that is why thoughts and beliefs are true or false just as English sentences are, though a 'language of thought' (Mentalese, or Brainese) may differ sharply in its grammar from any natural language.

The arguments for the representational theory take a number of impressively different forms (most recently, Fodor 1981, 1987; Devitt and Sterelny, 1987; Lycan, 1988). Though they are formidable, the theory has also come in for a good deal of criticism in recent years, and there too the arguments take a number of impressively different forms. Some leading objections are these:

(1) Chisholm (1972) and others have pointed out that the meanings of natural-language sentences are conventional, and so depend on the beliefs and intentions of human speakers. Beliefs and intentions are propositional

attitudes. How, then, without circularity or regress, can attitude content be explicated in terms of meaning in the public-linguistic sense?

(2) Dennett (1978) argues on several grounds that the idea of 'sentences in the head', implemented as inscriptions scrawled in brain chalk upon a brain blackboard, is fanciful, not to say grotesque. (Though his target seems to be a stronger and more outlandish version of representationalism than the one sketched above.)

(3) Churchland and Churchland (1983) (cf. Churchland, 1989) contend that the 'language of thought' idea is distinctly *unbiological*. When one recalls that human beings are card-carrying members of the animal kingdom and that we have evolved in the usual way by natural selection, our linguistic abilities, and our cognitive functions on any highly linguisticized account of them, seem to be an evolutionary afterthought at best, and a tiny fragment of the psychology that actually gets us around in the world. P. S. Churchland (1986) and P. M. Churchland (1986, 1989) compellingly depict a brain that works by connectionist networking (see section 12 below) and by physically hard-wired co-ordinate transformation, not by digital-computer-like inferential computation over syntactically structured sentences or logical formulas (see also the complaints raised by Dreyfus (1979) against classical AI).

(4) While public language is (again) conventional in each of several ways, there is obviously nothing social or conventional about the workings of the brain. The 'reference' of the alleged language-of-thought's vocabulary items must be natural. The English word 'dog' is an arbitrary vocable, which is socially attached by the English-speaking community to dogs, but the Mentalese word for 'dog' must somehow be naturally connected to dogs, without human intervention. That is hard to swallow.

(5) Fodor himself (1975) argues, with reservations but without shame, that if the 'language of thought' story is correct so far, then Mentalese concepts must also be *innate* in a very strong sense: Every normal child must naturally and at a very early age develop every concept to which he or she can ever afterward attach a public word of a natural language. (But Devitt and Sterelny (1987) safely block this outrageous implication.)

(6) The search for an adequate psychosemantics is debilitating at best. If thoughts and beliefs can be about Margaret Thatcher or about Santa Claus because the neurophysiological states that realize them somehow semantically refer to Margaret Thatcher or Santa Claus, and if the neurophysiological states do their referring in virtue of some physical, functional or otherwise naturalistic property they have, what is that property? We may imagine that our thoughts of Thatcher stand in some historical relation to Thatcher herself, but our thoughts of Santa Claus do not stand in any historical relation to Santa Claus himself, for he does not exist. Nor, in trying to say what it is in virtue of which some neurophysiological state 'refers to' anything, may we invoke unexplicated propositional attitudes or representational content, and that proves to be a biting constraint.

Psychosemantics admits of (so far) two basic lines of approach, which are reconcilable though entirely distinct in origin.

The first is the causal–historical approach, in the spirit of Kripke (1972) and Putnam (1975), according to which a mental–brain item M refers to a thing X just in case X figures appropriately in M's causal history or aetiology. Practitioners of this approach cash the important qualifier 'appropriately' in any number of hopeful ways; any successful way will have to account for reference to *non-existent* things, which is no small task in itself and multiply hard given that one may not, on pain of circularity, invoke unexplicated propositional-attitude contents.

The second approach to psychosemantics is the teleological, as mentioned in section 7. The teleological approach began life as 'indicator semantics', the idea that M represents X just in case M is a reliable indicator of X (see Dretske, 1981; Stalnaker, 1984); but in order to account for *false* representations, that idea was soon teleologized. The main hurdle for teleosemantics is to secure full generality: human mental states can be about anything, but so far as the external world is concerned, no individual brain state can have more than a few psychobiological functions at a time; how can neurophysiological states be about anything but food, shelter, predators and sexual partners? Fodor (1990a, although written earlier) was the first teleological theorist to solve that problem – however quickly and however inadequately. (He has since vigorously repudiated his original solution in a book that, sardonically, has the identical title (Fodor, 1987, and in 1990b).

11 Instrumentalism

The identity theorists and the functionalists (machine or teleological) joined common sense and current cognitive psychology in understanding mental states and events both as *internal to human subjects* and as *causes*. Beliefs and desires in particular are thought to be caused by perceptual or other cognitive events and as in turn conspiring from within to cause behaviour. If Armstrong's or Lewis' theory of mind is correct, this idea is not only commonsensical but a conceptual truth; if functionalism is correct, it is at least a metaphysical fact.

In rallying to the inner-causal story, as we saw in section 3, the identity theorists and functionalists broke with the behaviourists, for behaviourists did not think of mental items as entities, as inner, or as causes in any stronger sense than the bare hypothetical. Behaviourists either dispensed with the mentalistic idiom altogether, or paraphrased mental ascriptions in terms of putative responses to hypothetical stimuli. More recently, other philosophers have followed them in rejecting the idea of beliefs and desires as inner causes and in construing them in a more purely operational or instrumental fashion. D. C. Dennett (1978, 1987) has been particularly concerned to deny that beliefs and desires are causally active inner states of people, and maintains instead that belief-ascriptions and desire-ascriptions are merely calculational devices, that happen to have predictive usefulness for a reason that he goes on to explain. Such ascriptions are often objectively true, he grants, but not in virtue of describing inner mechanisms.

Thus Dennett is an INSTRUMENTALIST (pp. 298–300) about propositional attitudes such as belief and desire. (According to a contemporary interpretation, an 'instrumentalist' about Xs is a theorist who claims that although sentences about 'Xs' are often true, they do not really describe entities of a special kind, but only serve to systematize more familiar phenomena. For instance, we are all instrumentalists about 'the average American homeowner', who is white, male, and the father of exactly 1.9 children.) To ascribe a 'belief' or a 'desire' is not to describe some segment of physical reality, Dennett says, but is more like moving a group of beads in an abacus. (It should be noted that Dennett has recently moderated his line: see 1991.)

Dennett offers basically five grounds for his rejection of the common-sensical inner-cause thesis: (1) He thinks it quite unlikely that any science will ever turn up any distinctive inner-causal mechanism that would be shared by all the possible subjects that had a particular belief. (2) He offers numerous objections to 'language of thought psychology', which is the most popular inner-cause theory. (3) He compares the belief–desire interpretation of human beings to that of lower animals, chess-playing computers and even lightning-rods, arguing that (3a) in their case we have no reason to think of belief-ascriptions and desire-ascriptions as other than mere calculational–predictive devices and (3b) we have no *more* reason for the case of humans to think of belief-ascriptions and desire-ascriptions as other than that. (4) Dennett argues from the verification conditions of belief-ascriptions and desire-ascriptions – basically a matter of extrapolating rationally from what a subject *ought* to believe and want in his or her circumstances – and then he boldly just identifies the truth-makers of those ascriptions with their verification-conditions, challenging inner-cause theorists to show why instrumentalism does not accommodate all the actual evidence. (5) He argues that in any case if a purely normative assumption (the 'rationality assumption', which is that people will generally believe what they ought to believe and desire what they should desire) is required for the licensing of an ascription, then the ascription cannot itself be a purely factual description of a plain state of affairs.

Stich (1981) explores and criticizes Dennett's instrumentalism at length (perhaps oddly, Stich (1983) goes on to defend a view nearly as deprecating as Dennett's, though clearly distinct from it). Dennett (1981) responds to Stich, bringing out more clearly the force of the 'rationality assumption' assumption. (Other criticisms are levelled against Dennett by commentators in the *Behavioral and Brain Sciences* symposium that is headed by Dennett, 1988.)

A close cousin of Dennett's view, in that it focuses on the rationality assumption, is Donald Davidson's (1970) *anomalous monism*. Unlike Dennett's instrumentalism, it endorses token physicalism and insists that individual mental tokens are causes, but it rejects on similarly epistemological grounds the possibility of any interesting materialistic type-reduction of the propositional attitudes.

12 Eliminativism and Neurophilosophy

Dennett's instrumentalism breaks fairly radically with common sense and with philosophical tradition in denying that propositional attitudes such as belief and desire are real inner causal states of people. But Dennett concedes – indeed, he urgently insists – that belief-ascriptions and desire-ascriptions are true, and objectively true, none the less. Other philosophers have taken a less conciliatory, still more radically uncommon-sensical view: that mental ascriptions are not true after all, but are simply *false*. Common sense is just mistaken in supposing that people believe and desire things, and perhaps in supposing that people have sensations and feelings, disconcerting as that nihilistic claim may seem.

Following standard usage, let us call the nihilistic claim 'eliminative materialism', or 'eliminativism' for short. It is important to note a customary if unexpected alliance between the eliminativist and the token physicalist: the eliminativist, the identity theorist and the functionalist all agree that mental items are, *if anything*, real inner causal states of people. They disagree only on the empirical question of whether any real neurophysiological states of people do in fact answer to the common-sensical mental categories of 'folk psychology'. Eliminativists praise identity theorists and functionalists for their forthright willingness to step up and take their empirical shot. Both eliminativists and token physicalists scorn the instrumentalist's sleazy evasion. (But eliminativists agree with instrumentalists that functionalism is a pipe-dream, and functionalists agree with instrumentalists that mental ascriptions are often true and obviously so. The three views form an Eternal Triangle of a not uncommon sort.)

Paul Feyerabend (1963a, 1963b) was the first to argue openly that the mental categories of folk psychology simply fail to capture anything in physical reality and that everyday mental ascriptions were therefore false. (Rorty, 1965 took a notoriously eliminativist line also, but, following Sellars, 1963, tried to soften its nihilism; Lycan and Pappas, 1972, argued that the softening served only to collapse Rorty's position into incoherence.) Feyerabend attracted no great following, presumably because of his view's outrageous flouting of common sense. But eliminativism was resurrected by Paul Churchland (1981) and others, and defended in more detail.

Churchland argues mainly from the poverty of 'folk psychology'; he claims that historically, when other primitive theories such as alchemy have done as badly on scientific grounds as folk psychology has, they have been abandoned and rightly so. P. S. Churchland (1986) and Churchland and Sejnowski (1990) emphasize the comparative scientific reality and causal efficacy of neurobiological mechanisms: given the scientific excellence of neurophysiological explanation and the contrasting diffuseness and type-irreducibility of folk psychology, why should we suppose – even for a minute, much less automatically – that the platitudes of folk psychology express truths?

P. S. Churchland's intense interest in neuroscience and her distrust of the categories of folk psychology are matched within a recent sector of the AI community, in an equally intense upsurge of 'neural modelling'. In particular, what is called 'connectionism' or Parallel Distributed Processing ('PDP' for short; McClelland et al., 1986) has aroused much current interest as an AI research programme that diverges from the standard deployment of 'rules and representations' (as outlined in section 10 above) and from the idea of linear or monotonic theorem-proving from a pre-loaded data-base. PDP employs (although in practice it only simulates) an array of 'units', each being connected by ligatures to other units and each having an 'activation potential' that is directly affected by the potentials of adjoining units; the obvious, and intended, allusion is to the brain's neural nets. Some units are designated as inputs, others as outputs; the rest are 'hidden', and mysteriously regulate output when they are given input according to various algorithms. A major focus of PDP research is on *learning over time*; connectionist networks are good at learning pattern recognition tasks.

Connectionism is an engineering approach within AI. But the term has caught on among both psychologists and philosophers, and is now often used neologistically, as naming either: (1) a psychological theory, roughly that such-and-such behavioural capacities are explained by connectionist architecture actually realized in organisms' brains; or (2) a philosophical contention reminiscent of Ryle (1949), roughly that intelligent human capacities, including thinking and rationality, are somehow holistically emergent from connectionist architecture in the brain rather than being a matter of the manipulation of internal beliefs or other representations according to rules.

Some philosophers take connectionism in one or another of its several senses to refute – or at least embarrass – the idea that human cognition is a matter of hosting internal representational states such as beliefs and desires; see particularly Churchland (1989) and Ramsey, Stich and Garon (1991). But, logically speaking, connectionism seems entirely compatible with representationalism (Smolensky, 1988; Bechtel 1987), and arguably it is *an instance of* representationalism (Fodor and Pylyshyn, 1988; Lycan, 1991). The matter needs considerable further examination.

13 The Status of 'Folk Psychology'

In the previous section we were introduced to the somewhat strange idea that mental terms and mental entities themselves are at risk. The idea that mental terms are the theoretical terms of a folk science – the *'theory' theory*, as Morton (1980) calls it – was first urged by Sellars, Feyerabend and Quine in the 1960s. After an understandable period of incredulity, the 'theory' theory became widely accepted. But as we have seen, the 'theory' theory leads in a disconcerting direction. If the only reason we have for accepting the existence of mental entities is the utility and presumed truth of folk psychology, and if folk psychology should turn out to be largely *false* or seriously infirm in some other way (as scientific theories and especially folk theories often do), then presumably some version of eliminativism is correct.

We have already looked at some eliminativist arguments. In this section we shall turn to a special issue regarding propositional attitude content – the issue of *methodological solipsism* in Putnam's (1975) phrase – and examine its consequences for the cogency of folk psychology.

Suppose, for the sake of argument, that we attribute representational content to the internal states of computers – as in real life we do, however anthropomorphically. A computer sometimes thinks this or wants that; at the very least, it computes this or computes that, such as the GNP of Monaco, the outcome of a Presidential election or the balance of our bank account.

Now, to take a key example of Fodor's (1980), it is quite possible that two computers, programmed by entirely different users for entirely different purposes, should happen to run physically in parallel. They might go through precisely the same sequence of electrical currents and flipflop settings and yet have their outputs interpreted differently by their respective users, especially if what they write to their screens is all in numerical form. One of them would naturally and correctly be described as figuring out the GNP of Monaco, while the other would just as naturally and correctly be described as figuring out the batting averages of the New York Yankees. The point, plain enough when we think about it, is simply that *what* a machine is computing is not fully determined by the physical or even the abstract-functional operations that are going on entirely inside the machine. What the machine is computing depends to some extent on something outside the machine itself – users' intentions, causal-historical chains (see sections 9 and 10 above), teleology, interpretation by observers or just the convenience of the beholder.

The point is not particularly surprising. But Putnam (1975) drew a broader conclusion, that was developed to startling effect by Fodor (1978) and by Stich (1983): as it is with computers, so it is with humans. The representational content of a human subject's propositional attitudes is underdetermined by even the total state inside that subject's head. As we noted in section 9 above, intentional properties are not determined by their subject's intrinsic molecular constitution.

The fact that attitude contents are 'wide' rather than 'narrow' raises serious problems about the vaunted role of propositional attitudes in the explaining of behaviour, and attendant methodological questions for psychology (Fodor, 1980; Stich, 1983). But for our purposes in this section, the main question is this: If the representational content of a propositional attitude depends on factors outside the physical boundary of its owner's skin, what are those factors, and more importantly, can we still suppose that the attitude contents are genuine properties of the owner-subject? The spectre of elimination reappears; perhaps it is not really, objectively true of people that they believe this or desire that.

The question of what the environmental factors are is just the question of psychosemantics again. But what about the ontological status of people's beliefs and desires themselves? There are several different possible positions:

(1) The external semantical interpretation of an organism's internal physical–functional states is entirely up for grabs: any interpretation that suits anyone's convenience is good enough, and if two interpreters' interpretations conflict, neither is correct to the exclusion of the other. (Schiffer (1981) discusses this possibility sympathetically, and construes Quine's (1960) famous doctrine of the 'indeterminacy of translation' as getting at this position.) If we fall in with this view, we can hardly call it a hard fact that a subject believes one thing rather than another.

(2) The semantical interpretation of beliefs is not up for grabs; it is at least loosely determined by various contextual factors, and some interpretations are correct while others are just wrong. But the contextual factors in question are intolerably vague and messy, and social and interest-infested, making

them quite unsuitable for incorporation into any genuine science. To ascribe the belief that P to someone is no more scientific, explanatory or useful than is calling something 'nice'. (2) is the position of Stich (1983).

(3)   The semantical interpretation of beliefs is loosely determined by various contextual factors, and some interpretations are correct while others are just wrong, and this is what it is for the subject to believe one thing rather than another. Some complex causal-historical and/or teleological feature of the subject's environment makes it objectively true that the subject believes so-and-so rather than such-and-such, whether or not the feature is scientifically interesting or well-behaved. (Lycan (1988) defends this view.)

(4)   There is nothing messy, interest-relative or whatever, about the contextual factors in question, even though they extend outside the boundary of the skin. They are a matter of *simple* nomological or teleological fact. This position was endorsed by 'indicator' semanticists, among others.

(1) is essentially an eliminative view, and certainly flouts the folk-psychological thesis that propositional attitudes *qua* propositional attitudes are real causal constituents of the world. (2) allows that attitude ascriptions may be true (however interest-infested), so that people do believe one thing rather than another, but still rejects the folk-psychological view that the attitudes genuinely cause behaviour. (3) and (4) are entirely compatible with folk psychology. (2) and (3) differ from each other, it seems, only in degree, so the real issue so far is that of whether (2) or (3) is more plausible.

There is a further and deeper issue. Even if we grant that (2) is true or even that (1) is true, why should we care about wide properties at all? What explanatory need do they fulfil? Surely it is only narrow properties that figure in the causal explanation of behaviour. Among others, Horgan and Woodward (1985), Burge (1986) and Fodor (1987) try to answer that deeper question; Devitt (1990) investigates further.

One may of course dispute the 'theory' theory itself as a thesis about mental concepts. Ryle (1949) and Wittgenstein (1953) staunchly opposed it before it had explicitly been formulated. More recent critics include Morton (1980), Malcolm (1984), Baker (1988), McDonough (1991) and Wilkes (1993).

Further Reading

Beakley and Ludlow (eds) (1992) offer classical and contemporary readings on the philosophy of mind. Block (1980) contains classic works on the mind–body problem in vol. 1, while vol. 2 takes up special topics, including the imagery debate, the philosophy of linguistics and innate ideas. Campbell (1984) provides a fine introduction to the mind–body problem. Churchland (1984) introduces the mind–body problem from the neurophilosophical point of view. Fodor (1968b) is a founding document of functionalism. Haugeland (1981) contains important papers from the 1970s on Artificial Intelligence. Lycan (1990) is the successor to Block (1980) and offers some general writings on the mind–body problem and some more specialized readings in the philosophy of cognitive science. Rosenthal (1991) contains classical and contemporary readings on mind and cognitive science.

References

Armstrong, D. M. 1968: *A Materialist Theory of the Mind*. London: Routledge and Kegan Paul.

Baker, L. R. 1988: *Saving Belief*. Princeton, NJ: Princeton University Press.

Beakley, B. and Ludlow, P. (eds) 1992: *The Philosophy of Mind*. Cambridge, MA: Bradford Books/MIT Press.

Bechtel, W. 1987: Connectionism and the philosophy of mind: An overview. *Southern Journal of Philosophy*, 26 (Supplement), 17–41. Reprinted in Lycan (1990).

Bigelow, J. and Pargetter, R. 1987: Functions. *Journal of Philosophy*, 84, 181–96.

Block, N. J. 1978: Troubles with functionalism. In W. Savage (ed.), *Minnesota Studies in the Philosophy of Science, Vol. IX: Perception and Cognition*, Minneapolis: University of Minnesota Press, 261–325. Excerpts reprinted in Lycan (1990).

—— (ed.) 1980: *Readings in Philosophy of Psychology*, 2 vols. Cambridge, MA: Harvard University Press.

—— 1981: Psychologism and behaviorism. *Philosophical Review*, 90, 5–43.

Block, N. J. and Fodor, J. A. 1972: What psychological states are not. *Philosophical Review*, 81, 159–81. Reprinted in Block (1980).

Boorse, C. 1976: Wright on functions. *Philosophical Review*, 85, 70–86.

Brentano, F. 1973 [1874]: *Philosophy from an Empirical Standpoint*. London: Routledge and Kegan Paul.

Burge, T. 1986: Individualism and psychology. *Philosophical Review*, 95, 3–45.

Campbell, K. 1984: *Body and Mind*. (2nd edn) Notre Dame, IN: University of Notre Dame Press.

Carnap, R. 1932–3: Psychology in physical language. *Erkenntnis*, 3, 107–42. Excerpt reprinted in Lycan (1990).

Chisholm, R. M. 1957: *Perceiving*. Ithaca, NY: Cornell University Press.

—— 1972: Contributions to 'The Chisholm–Sellars correspondence on intentionality'. In A. Marras (ed.) *Intentionality, Mind, and Language*, Urbana, IL: University of Illinois Press, 214–48.

Chomsky, N. 1959: Review of B. F. Skinner. See Skinner, 1957. *Language*, 35, 26–57.

Churchland, P. M. 1981: Eliminative materialism and the propositional attitudes. *Journal of Philosophy*, 78, 67–90. Reprinted in Churchland (1989) and in Lycan (1990).

—— 1984: *Matter and Consciousness*. Cambridge, MA: Bradford Books/MIT Press.

—— 1986: Some reductive strategies in cognitive neurobiology. *Mind*, 95, 279–309.

—— 1989: *A Neurocomputational Perspective*. Cambridge, MA: Bradford Books/MIT Press.

Churchland, P. S. 1986: *Neurophilosophy*. Cambridge, MA: Bradford Books/MIT Press.

Churchland, P. S., and Churchland, P. M. 1983: Stalking the Wild Epistemic Engine. *Noûs*, 17, 5–18.

Churchland, P. S. and Sejnowski, T. 1990: Neural representation and neural computation. In Lycan (1990), pp. 224–52.

Clark, M. S. and Fiske, S. T. 1982: *Affect and Cognition*. Hillsdale, NJ: Lawrence Erlbaum Associates.

Cummins, R. 1975: Functional analysis. *Journal of Philosophy*, 72, 741–64. Reprinted in Block (1980).

—— 1983: *The Nature of Psychological Explanation*. Cambridge, MA: MIT Press/Bradford Books.

Davidson, D. 1970: Mental events. In L. Foster and J. W. Swanson (eds) *Experience and Theory*, Amherst, MA: University of Massachusetts Press, 79–101. Reprinted in Block (1980).

Dennett, D. C. 1978: *Brainstorms*. Montgomery, VT: Bradford Books.

—— 1981: Making sense of ourselves. *Philosophical Topics*, 12, 63–81. Reprinted in Lycan (1990).

—— 1987: *The Intentional Stance*. Cambridge, MA: Bradford Books/MIT Press.

—— 1988: *Précis* of The Intentional Stance. *Behavioral and Brain Sciences*, 11, 495–505.

—— 1991: Real patterns. *Journal of Philosophy*, 88, 27–51.

Devitt, M. 1990: A narrow representational theory of the mind. In Lycan (1990), 371–98.

Devitt, M. and Sterelny, K. 1987: *Language and Reality*. Cambridge, MA: Bradford Books/MIT Press.

Dretske, F. 1981: *Knowledge and the Flow of Information*. Cambridge, MA: Bradford Books/MIT Press.

—— 1988: *Explaining Behavior*. Cambridge, MA: Bradford Books/MIT Press.

Dreyfus, H. L. 1979: *What Computers Can't Do* (2nd edn). New York, NY: Harper and Row.

Dreyfus, H. and Dreyfus, S. 1986: *Mind over Machine*. New York, NY: Free Press, Macmillan.

Farrell, B. A. 1950: Experience. *Mind*, 50, 170–98.

Feyerabend, P. 1963a: Materialism and the mind–body problem. *Review of Metaphysics*, 17, 49–66.

—— 1963b: Mental events and the brain. *Journal of Philosophy*, 60, 295–6.

Field, H. 1978: Mental representation. *Erkenntnis*, 13, 9–61.

Fodor, J. A. 1968a: The appeal to tacit knowledge in psychological explanation. *Journal of Philosophy*, 65, 627–40.

—— 1968b: *Psychological Explanation*. New York, NY: Random House.

—— 1975: *The Language of Thought*. New York, NY: Thomas Y. Crowell.

—— 1980: Methodological solipsism considered as a research strategy cognitive psychology. *Behavioral and Brain Sciences*, 3, 63–73.

—— 1981: *RePresentations*. Cambridge, MA: Bradford Books/MIT Press.

—— 1987: *Psychosemantics*. Cambridge, MA: Bradford Books/MIT Press.

—— 1990a: Psychosemantics. In Lycan (1990), 312–37.

—— 1990b: *A Theory of Content*. Cambridge, MA: Bradford Books/MIT Press.

Fodor, J. A. and Pylyshyn, Z. W. 1988: Connectionism and cognitive architecture: A critical analysis. *Cognition*, 28, 3–71.

Geach, P. 1957: *Mental Acts*. London: Routledge and Kegan Paul.

Gordon, R. M. 1987: *The Structure of Emotions*. Cambridge: Cambridge University Press.

Gunderson, K. 1970: Asymmetries and mind–body perplexities. In M. Radner and S. Winokur (eds) *Minnesota Studies in the Philosophy of Science, Vol. IV: Analyses of Theories and Methods of Physics and Psychology*, Minneapolis, MN: University of Minnesota Press, 273–309.

—— 1974: The texture of mentality. In R. Bambrough (ed.) *Wisdom – twelve essays*, Oxford: Oxford University Press, 177–93.

Haugeland, J. 1979: Understanding natural language. *Journal of Philosophy*, 76, 619–32. Reprinted in Lycan (1990).

—— (ed.) 1981: *Mind Design*. Cambridge, MA: Bradford Books/MIT Press.

Horgan, T. and Woodward, J. 1985: Folk psychology is here to stay. *Philosophical Review*, 94, 197–226. Reprinted in Lycan (1990).

Jackson, F. 1977: *Perception*. Cambridge: Cambridge University Press.

—— 1982: Epiphenomenal qualia. *Philosophical Quarterly*, 32, 127–36. Reprinted in Lycan (1990).

Kirk, R. 1974: Zombies *vs.* materialists. *Aristotelian Society Supplementary Volume* 48, 135–52.

Kripke, S. 1972: Naming and necessity. In D. Davidson and G. Harman (eds), *Semantics of Natural Language*, Dordrecht: D. Reidel, 253–355.

Levin, M. 1979: *Metaphysics and the Mind–Body Problem*. Oxford: Oxford University Press.

Levine, J. 1983: Materialism and qualia: The explanatory gap. *Pacific Philosophical Quarterly*, 64, 354–61.

Lewis, D. 1966: An argument for the identity theory. *Journal of Philosophy*, 63, 17–25.

—— 1972: Psychophysical and theoretical identifications. *Australasian Journal of Philosophy*, 50, 249–58. Reprinted in Block (1980).

—— 1980: Mad pain and Martian pain. In N. J. Block (ed.) *Readings in Philosophy of Psychology, Vol. One*, Cambridge, MA: Harvard University Press, 216–22.

Lycan, W. 1981: Form, function, and feel. *Journal of Philosophy*, 78, 24–50.

—— 1985: Abortion and the civil rights of machines. In N. Potter and M. Timmons (eds) *Morality and Universality*, Dordrecht: D. Reidel, 139–56.

—— 1987: *Consciousness*. Cambridge, MA: MIT Press/Bradford Books.

—— 1988: *Judgement and Justification*. Cambridge: Cambridge University Press.

—— (ed.), 1990: *Mind and Cognition: A Reader*. Oxford: Blackwell.

—— 1991: Homuncular Functionalism meets PDP. In Ramsey, Stich and Rumelhart (1991), 259–86.

Lycan, W. and Pappas, G. 1972: What is Eliminative Materialism? *Australasian Journal of Philosophy*, 50, 149–59.

Malcolm, N. 1984: Consciousness and causality. In D. Armstrong and N. Malcolm, *Consciousness and Causality: A debate on the nature of mind*. Oxford: Blackwell.

McClelland, J. L., Rumelhart, D. E. and the PDP Research Group 1986: *Parallel Distributed Processing: Explorations in the Microstructure of Cognition*. Cambridge, MA: Bradford Books/MIT Press.

McDonough, R. 1991: A culturalist account of folk psychology. In J. Greenwood (ed.) *the Future of Folk Psychology*, Cambridge: Cambridge University Press, 263–88.

Millikan, R. G. 1984: *Language, Thought, and Other Biological Categories*. Cambridge, MA: Bradford Books/MIT Press.

Morton, A. 1980: *Frames of Mind*. Oxford: Oxford University Press.

Nagel, T. 1974: What is it like to be a bat? *Philosophical Review*, 83, 435–50. Reprinted in Block (1980).

Owens, J. 1986: The failure of Lewis' functionalism. *Philosophical Quarterly*, 36, 159–73.

Place U. T. 1956: Is consciousness a brain process? *British Journal of Psychology*, 47, 44–50. Reprinted in Lycan (1990).

Putnam, H. 1960: Minds and machines. In S. Hook (ed.) *Dimensions of Mind*, New York, NY: Collier Books, 136–64.

—— 1967a: The mental life of some machines. In H.-N. Castañeda (ed.) *Intentionality, Minds, and Perception*, Detroit, MI: Wayne State University Press, 177–200.

—— 1967b: Psychological predicates. In W. H. Capitan and D. Merrill (eds) *Art, Mind, and Religion*, Pittsburgh, PA: University of Pittsburgh Press, 37–48. Reprinted in Block (1980) under the title 'The Nature of Mental States'.

—— 1975: The meaning of 'meaning'. In K. Gunderson (ed.) *Minnesota Studies in the Philosophy of Science, Vol. VII: Language, Mind and Knowledge*, Minneapolis: University of Minnesota Press, 131–93.

Quine, W. V. O. 1960: *Word and Object*. Cambridge, MA: MIT Press.

Ramsey, W., Stich, S. P., and Garon, J. 1991: Connectionism, eliminativism, and the future of folk psychology. In Ramsey, Stich and Rumelhart (1991), 199–228.

Ramsey, W., Stich, S. P., and Rumelhart, D. (eds) 1991: *Philosophy and Connectionist Theory*. Hillsdale, NJ: Lawrence Erlbaum Associates.

Rey, G. 1980: Functionalism and the emotions. In Rorty (1980), 163–95.

Rorty, A. O. (ed.) 1980: *Explaining Emotions*. Berkeley and Los Angeles, CA: University of California Press.

Rorty, R. 1965: Mind–body identity, privacy, and categories. *Review of Metaphysics*, 19.

Rosenthal, D. (ed.) 1991: *The Nature of Mind.* Oxford: Oxford University Press.

Ryle, G. 1949: *The Concept of Mind.* New York, NY: Barnes and Noble.

Scherer, K. R. and Ekman, P. 1984: *Approaches to Emotion.* Hillsdale, NJ: Lawrence Erlbaum Associates.

Schiffer, S. 1981: Truth and the theory of content. In H. Parret and J. Bouveresse (eds) *Meaning and Understanding*, Berlin: Walter de Gruyter, 204–22.

Searle, J. 1980: Minds, brains and programs. *Behavioral and Brain Sciences*, 3, 417–24.

Sellars, W. 1963: *Science, Perception and Reality.* London: Routledge and Kegan Paul.

Shoemaker, S. 1981: Some varieties of functionalism. *Philosophical Topics*, 12, 93–119.

Skinner, B. F. 1957: *Verbal Behavior.* New York, NY: Appleton–Century–Crofts.

Smart, J. J. C. 1959: Sensations and brain processes. *Philosophical Review*, 68, 141–56.

—— 1963: *Philosophy and Scientific Realism.* London: Routledge and Kegan Paul.

Smolensky, P. 1988: On the proper treatment of Connectionism. *Behavioral and Brain Sciences*, 11, 1–23.

Sober, E. 1985: Panglossian Functionalism and the philosophy of mind. *Synthèse*, 64, 165–93. Revised excerpt reprinted in Lycan (1990) under the title 'Putting the Function Back Into Functionalism'.

Solomon, R. 1977: *The Passions.* New York, NY: Doubleday.

Stalnaker, R. 1984: *Inquiry.* Cambridge, MA: Bradford Books/MIT Press.

Stich, S. 1978: Autonomous psychology and the belief–desire thesis. *Monist*, 61, 573–91. Reprinted in Lycan (1990).

—— 1981: Dennett on intentional systems. *Philosophical Topics*, 12, 39–62. Reprinted in Lycan (1990).

—— 1983: *From Folk Psychology to Cognitive Science.* Cambridge, MA: Bradford Books/MIT Press.

Turing, A. 1964: Computing machinery and intelligence. In A. R. Anderson (ed.) *Minds and Machines*, Englewood Cliffs, NJ: Prentice–Hall, 4–30.

Tye, M. 1983: Functionalism and type physicalism. *Philosophical Studies*, 44, 161–74.

Van Gulick, R. 1980: Functionalism, information, and content. *Nature and System*, 2, 139–62.

Wilkes, K. 1993: The relationship between scientific and common sense psychology. In S. Christensen and D. Turner (eds) *Folk Psychology and the Philosophy of Mind*, Hillsdale, NJ: Lawrence Erlbaum Associates, 144–87.

Wimsatt, W. 1972: Teleology and the logical structure of function statements. *Studies in History and Philosophy of Science*, 3, 1–80.

Wittgenstein, L. 1953: *Philosophical Investigations* (translated by G. E. M. Anscombe). New York, NY: Macmillan.

Wright, L. 1973: Functions. *Philosophical Review*, 82, 139–68.

Discussion Questions

1 If minds are immaterial and non-spatial, how can they interact with bodies?

2 Could the success of neurophysiology eliminate the mind from explanations of what we do?

3 To what extent should the philosophy of mind be constrained by our current view of science?

4   If a machine could pass the Turing Test, what would be the consequences for the philosophy of mind?

5   When you see a red object, could you have the sort of colour experience I have when I see a green object, and vice versa?

6   Are mental states and events identical with states and events in our central nervous systems? What notion of identity is involved in this claim?

7   Are mental terms defined causally?

8   Does an adequate account of the mind require distinct levels of description, all applied to the same fundamental reality?

9   How should cognitive psychology and philosophy of mind be related?

10 Does work in artifical intelligence help to answer philosophical questions about human intelligence?

11 Can human psychological capacities be entirely captured by a third-person, hardware-realizable design that could be built in a laboratory?

12 Could a human being's knowledge ever be completely formalized in a set of representations or rules?

13 Do we need a teleological notion of function for our account of the realization of psychological states and psychological explanation?

14 How can a mental state be *about* something? How can a mental state be about something *which does not exist*?

15 Can there be an adequate naturalistic analysis of teleological function?

16 Does functionalist metaphysics leave out the most important feature of the mental: *what it feels like* to be in a mental state of any certain sort?

17 If mental items are not *necessarily* identical with neurophysiological ones, can they be identical with them at all?

18 Can we explain consciousness?

19 If you have an after-image, does it show that functionalism is mistaken?

20 Do we know from the inside that we are not merely automata?

21 How is the representational content of a state of the brain determined?

22 If functional roles are 'narrow' and representational contexts are 'wide', can propositional attitudes be identified with functional roles?

23 Are intentional features *semantic* features?

24 What is a 'language of thought'? Can there be an adequate theory of thinking which denies that there is a language of thought?

25 Does the causal history of a mental item determine what that item refers to?

26 Can the ascription of beliefs and desires be objectively true, but not in virtue of describing causally active inner states of people?

27 To what extent does our ascription of beliefs and desires to people depend upon the assumption that people will generally believe and desire what they ought to believe and desire?

28 Does connectionism offer greater insight into philosophical problems than the standard 'rules and representations' model of artificial intelligence?

29 Are mental terms theoretical terms of a folk science? Should we be prepared to give them up in favour of the terms of a superior theory?

30 If the representational contents of a propositional attitude depend on external factors, are the contents genuine properties of the subject? What are the consequences of your answer for the ontological status of beliefs and desires?

6

Ethics ———————————————————————

John Skorupski

In radically different ways, philosophers from Socrates to Wittgenstein have found in ethics a source of deep philosophical perplexity. Virtues, principles and consequences for human well-being have all been proposed as the most important focus of ethical understanding. Intertwined with these are concerns about rationality, impartiality and moral freedom. Philosophers have also asked questions about ethics: for example, if there are special moral facts, how could we know them; without such facts, what else could make ethical judgements true or false? This chapter considers general theories of ethical value as general theories of reasons for action, focusing on the powerful and illuminating utilitarian and Kantian contractarian theories. Readers will want to consult chapters on POLITICAL AND SOCIAL PHILOSOPHY (chapter 8); HUME (chapter 21); KANT (chapter 22); BENTHAM, MILL, AND SIDGWICK (chapter 25) and on APPLIED ETHICS (chapter 31). Chapters about several other historical figures contain discussions of their moral philosophy, and chapters on EPISTEMOLOGY (chapter 1), METAPHYSICS (chapter 2), PHILOSOPHY OF MIND (chapter 5), AESTHETICS (chapter 7), and PHILOSOPHY OF RELIGION (chapter 14) can help to understand issues raised here.

1 The Scope of Ethics

Reflection about ethics has been a vital component of all the traditions of philosophising that we know. China, Greece, India and medieval and modern Europe all asked basic ethical questions. What is the good? What makes a life a good life? What are the virtues of a human being? Is there one good, or one unified scheme of virtues? What duties do we have to each other or to ourselves? So far as we have records of non-literate cultures and their oral traditions, we find the same questions being asked there too.

They are philosophical questions if they examine moral habits and teachings in a reflective way. CLASSICAL GREECE (chapter 15) also moved to a second level of philosophical reflection – it asked questions about such questions. Can they have objective answers? If so, what kind of knowledge of these answers can we have? Are they matters of reason or feeling? These higher-order issues are often called *meta-ethical*. A striking feature of the Western tradition in philosophy is the urgency with which it has recurrently worried about them, from its Greek beginnings. And in this century meta-ethical questions have been pursued with an urgency and a perseverance never known before. We shall have to say something about meta-ethics as well as about ethical questions themselves.

But first, what is the scope of ethics as such? It does not deal with the whole domain of value. If I enquire into the beautiful or the sublime I am more likely to be doing AESTHETICS (chapter 7) than ethics – though my interest might certainly be ethical as well, in one way or another. Ethics, one may suggest, is concerned with *morality*, rather than with art. True – but it does not stand to morality quite as aesthetics stands to art. It has wider scope, since questions about the relations between morality and art belong to it, as do questions about the relations between morality and prudence or between morality and reason. So if I ask what makes a piece of music beautiful, or what makes a good tennis technique, I am not asking an ethical question, on even the widest sense of 'ethical'; but if I ask what place in my life, or in other people's lives, music or tennis, together with the skills and excellences proper to them, should have, then I am asking an ethical question. I can ask an ethical question about morality itself – what role in life should morality play? Ethical questions have a certain detachment and comprehensiveness which give them a governing role in the philosophy of value. Questions of PROFESSIONAL ETHICS (chapter 31) in business, medicine or journalism have a similar governing role, bearing on the nature of the profession, its place in social life and the consequent application of general ethical principles to it.

Ethical questions have this governing role because ethical enquiry is concerned quite generally with reasons for ACTION (pp. 599–600). Not all reasons are reasons to act. There are reasons to believe and reasons to feel: indeed, we deal in reasons at every turn. To be alive and awake is to be alive to reasons for believing, doing, feeling. You, for example, have reason to believe that I did not change the oil in your car; you have reason to feel irritated; your have reason to take action – to deduct something from my bill. Our evaluations of a person regularly turn on how that person responds or fails to respond to reasons in one or other of the three domains of belief, feeling and action. Personality is the manner of one's sensitivity to reasons in all three of them. An irritable person is more irritated than he or she has reason to be. A credulous person believes when there is insufficient reason to believe. A precipitate person acts when there is no reason to act.

Even at its widest, though, ethics does not deal with this whole normative domain of reasons. It does not deal with whether a conclusion is rightly or wrongly drawn from premises, with whether evidence is good or bad, or with what hypothesis we ought to adopt. Such questions are the province of LOGIC (chapter 4). Ethics in its widest sense stands to questions about what there is reason to do, as logic in its widest sense stands to questions about what there is reason to believe. It is the normative theory of conduct, as logic is the normative theory of belief. Through its concern with action and reasons for action ethics also becomes concerned with character, as it bears on action and reasons for action. (The word 'ethics' derives from the Greek *ethos*, which means 'character', or, in plural, 'manners'.) And, through that concern with character, it becomes concerned with questions about what there is reason to feel, and how reasons to feel connect with reasons to act. But the best way to make this clearer is to turn directly to some of the feelings with which ethics is concerned. Of these, three at least are fundamental – blame, admiration and desire.

2 Blame, Admiration and Desire

Blame is a central category of morality. So much so that one may characterize morality by reference to it. For we have many ways of disapproving actions – holding an action morally wrong is only one. An action may be idiotic or tasteless, but not morally wrong. To call it morally wrong is a more serious matter. 'It was worse than immoral, it was tasteless,' would be a quip, like Boulay de la Meurthe's comment (on the execution of the Duc d'Enghien) – 'It was worse than a crime, it was a mistake.' The quip could make a point, say in the spirit of Oscar Wilde, but it would do so precisely by paradox.

What is it then that marks the special disapproval or hostility conveyed in calling something morally wrong? To call the action morally wrong is to blame the agent. Blame is an act or attitude whose notional core is a feeling, in the way that feeling sorry is the notional core of apology – I mean that, even when the feeling is not actually present, it is nevertheless invoked in every act of apology or blame. Call this emotional core of blame 'the blame-feeling' – it disposes to punish, as feeling sorry disposes to make amends. Moreover, just as apologizing *is* already making amends to some degree, so public blame (and also self-blame in the form of guilt) already is a degree of punishment. This often makes people reluctant to 'apportion blame'. There is, it should be noted, a wider sense of the word 'blame', in which we may, for example, blame the car's faulty brakes for the accident – in other words – identify them as its relevant cause. But we certainly feel no similar reluctance to blame in that sense.

The relation between this wider and the narrower, moral, sense of blame is a fascinating and deep issue in ethics, but we must pass it by. Characterizing the morally wrong as the blameworthy in the narrow sense, we can say that the morally right is that which it would be morally wrong not to do. Similarly, we can say 'X is morally obligatory', or 'X morally ought to be done' will hold just if the non-performance of X is blameworthy. Of course it is true and important that we admire people for going beyond the morally obligatory – 'beyond the call of duty' – even though we do not blame them for not doing so. We can say that admiration of such actions is moral admiration, because we admire them for the reasons that impelled them, and those reasons are moral reasons. For example, lack of consideration for others' feelings, when it reaches a certain point, becomes blameworthy thoughtlessness. But there are degrees of care for others' feelings that go well beyond what we would expect, on pain of blame, from people in general, but which we still admire when we meet with them. (There are also excesses of solicitousness of course.) The outstandingly and the ordinarily thoughtful person are impelled by the same reasons – consideration for others' feelings. And we can say that those reasons are moral reasons – as against, say, prudential or aesthetic reasons, since their absence from a person's mind beyond a certain point becomes blameworthy.

Now for another important point: 'blameworthy' means 'ought to be blamed'. Is this 'ought' itself a moral 'ought'? No such circularity is involved – for as we have noticed 'ought' in general can be defined in terms of reasons – in this case reasons to adopt a feeling, or feeling-based attitude. To say that an action is blameworthy is to say that there is adequate reason, taking everything into account, to blame the agent for doing it.

This is a special case of a general pattern, in which we assess reasons for feeling an emotion. So with many other terms of appraisal – 'irritating', 'despicable', 'frightening', 'moving', 'tasteless' and so on. Two things seem to be involved in such appraisals: firstly, the appraiser, in typical cases, spontaneously feels the emotion and, secondly, he expects others to feel it. But a certain normativity is built in: he feels the emotion to be *appropriate*, and believes that other good judges will share it. 'I must say I was rather bored – but I was feeling tired and distracted, and I probably didn't understand what the point of it was.' So in this case I do *not* judge that it really was boring. I am disqualifying myself as a good judge. The internal criteria of appropriateness for such feelings can be debated with great exactness and subtlety, and the 'common pursuit of true judgement' in aesthetic or moral appraisal turns on such debate. Not that commitment to the thought that other judges, who suffer from no disqualifying defect or limitation, would confirm my judgement is special to the moral and the aesthetic: it is a general logical feature of judgement as such.

Judgements about the blameworthy or the admirable, then, are judgements about when it is reasonable to respond with blame or admiration. If the emotional core of *morality* is the blame-feeling, admiration is the feeling fundamental to systems of *ideals*. I have in mind the ideals of character and excellence which play so large a part in shaping the way we live our lives. It is all too easy for ethics to ignore them, for example by making an over-simple contrast between morality and prudence. Admiration for, and debate about, physical courage, style, 'cool', imagination, presence of mind, skill, wit, resourcefulness, sensitivity, fitness, good looks and many other such things drives a great part of life – and of criticism of ways of living. These are not moral valuations, though in some cases they shade into them. Whatever one feels about, for example, obtuseness, cravenness, leaden lack of style or clumsiness – perhaps contempt, derision, embarrassment or pity – it need not be the blame-feeling.

They are not prudential valuations either. Prudential valuations build on the notion of one's well-being, of what one should pursue as an end when one's own best INTERESTS (p. 629) are exclusively in question. In this case the relevant affective core is neither admiration nor the blame-feeling, but desire. The well-being of an individual comprises whatever is found in itself desirable to that individual. And 'desirable' stands to what there is reason to desire as 'admirable' and 'blameworthy' stand to what there is reason to admire and blame.

Questions about what is desirable, for people in general or for a particular person, are questions about the ends of life. They are as much a matter of deliberation and debate as questions about what is admirable and blameworthy. When John Stuart MILL (chapter 25) argued that happiness is desirable because it is what people desire as an end 'in theory and in practice', he was not wasting his time. It is still less trivial that happiness, as he attempted to show, is the only thing desirable. Whether he was right or wrong about this, his method was sound. To reach a conclusion about what ends are intrinsically desirable I must try to reflect, without self-delusion, on what I desire and why – and if I find that I differ from others in my conclusions, I must ask whether my desires might yield to greater experience or knowledge and, indeed, whether my ideas about what those desires really are might not be distorted by personal ideals, conventional proprieties or just sheer wishful thinking.

Here too, then: there is a 'common pursuit of true judgement' – a reflective examination of one's own spontaneous feelings, carried out in dialogue with others who similarly examine theirs. But there is a difference. Though the pursuit may be common, the conclusion need not be, and is not likely to be, that what is desirable for me is just the same as what is desirable for you. Not only will different people differ on what makes them happy; they are also, despite Mill's suggestion to the contrary, quite likely to differ on how desirable happiness is to them, as against, say, knowledge, freedom or achievement. In contrast, suppose I find that many people are moved by a piece of music that I find cacophonous or dull, and that discussion and further listening does not lead me to find anything moving in it. I am unlikely (philosophical preconceptions aside) to conclude that it is 'moving to them' but not 'moving to me'. I may conclude, no doubt silently, that their appreciation is shallow – or with greater humility, that my own is. What is desirable for me may not be desirable for you – but aesthetic valuations do not naturally relativize in this way; moral valuations still less.

This difference certainly deserves further examination. (Distinctions are needed: for example, between particular objects that we desire – this oyster, a weekend in Vienna – and the categorial ends in virtue of which we desire them; or again, between wanting a thing and liking it when you get it.) Overall, however, it remains true that examination of one's own spontaneous responses, together with discussion with others, is the criterion of all valuation – including the aesthetic and the moral, and also the prudential. That is not to say that one can *define* an evaluative predicate – 'tedious', 'tasteless', 'desirable', 'delightful', 'kind' – in terms of the responses of good judges. However informed and sensitive such judges may be it is logically possible that they are wrong – that what strikes them as tasteless is not tasteless but innovative, and so on. Of course if 'good judges' are simply *defined* as 'judges who get it right', then it will be a logical truth that a thing is tedious just if good judges would find it so. But it will then be circular to define the tedious as that which good judges find tedious. Reflective agreement is, it is true, *ultimate*, in the sense that the only way of appealing against it is by forging a new reflective agreement – but it is never guaranteed to be *incorrigible*. Nor, when I judge that something is tasteless, am I judging that others will or would find it tasteless. My eye is on the object, not on what other people might think about the object.

3 Character, the Virtues and Freedom

How do virtues and vices fit into the picture that we have drawn? How, in particular, are they connected with blame, which we have made central to the notion of morality? They are connected in this way: they are traits of character which we could be *blamed* for not attempting to attain or lose. They are also connected in this way: they directly dispose to actions which are *morally* right or wrong. The various virtues involve spontaneous sensitivity to various types of reasons for acting, and the various vices similarly involve insensitivity to various types of reasons for acting.

This is not to say that we are blamed for our vices as such, as against our avoidable failures to resist them or to try to mend them. It is a basic principle that 'ought implies can' – that what I ought to do I can do. And it is also true that blame makes sense only in respect of that which ought not to have been done. So if I am in fact unable to mend my character then I cannot be blamed for failing to do so – though I can be blamed for not striving hard enough to resist its characteristic impulses on particular occasions.

This distinction, between changing my character and resisting its impulses, is a vital one to ordinary moral thought. I may be cruel, and I may not be able to do much to make myself less cruel; that is, to rid myself of those characteristic impulses to cruel acts. But I can still try to refrain from acting cruelly when I am tempted to. A person who has no control over his cruel actions is not just cruel but pathologically cruel. He does not, on this point at least, have the important kind of moral freedom that we attribute to anyone who we think of as a moral agent, and which we presuppose when we blame. Thus if I blame you for a cruel joke, for example, I assume you could have resisted the impulse to make it. If I become convinced that you are utterly unable to resist such impulses (even, say, when it is greatly to your personal advantage to do so) I am more likely to see you as mad, or at any rate as obsessed, than as bad.

This is the way in which moral freedom is presupposed in attributions of moral responsibility. It is rightly pointed out, for example, that the fact that I was free to do what I wanted to do does not suffice to show that I was morally free, because the want itself may have been so obsessive as to undermine my moral freedom. Drug addicts are not morally free even when they do what their craving compels them to do. They are the slaves of their addiction. Two kinds of thing may be happening here. Firstly, their craving may be so strong as to cloud their judgement – though there are good reasons for them to resist it, the craving itself stops them from seeing them. Secondly, the craving may not cloud their judgement, but it may impair their ability to act on it – they see clearly enough that they have good reason not to do what they crave to do, but they are unable to stop themselves.

In both these cases their moral freedom is attenuated, and their moral responsibility diminished. Thus if we suppose craving to have driven a person to some crime, then both cases, if established on the evidence, could reasonably be recognized by a judge as being, to some degree, extenuating. In general, moral freedom is a function of the total economy of one's character – the degree to which one's feelings are under the control of one's capacity to recognize reasons, instead of outrunning its control or even reducing or controlling the capacity itself. Moral freedom, so conceived, is one of the virtues, which a human being can have in greater or lesser degree. But it also has a special role in the economy of character: it is a precondition of moral agency as such, and it is facilitated by all the other virtues, since these are affective dispositions to act on particular kinds of good reasons. One can envisage, as a logical possibility, the person who sees the right clearly and, by great effort, is able to act on it, despite ever-present vicious impulses. But it is easier for one who has virtuous rather than vicious impulses in the first place to be morally free.

Moral freedom is rationality, understood as the capacity of rational self-government. This doctrine appears in PLATO's (chapter 15) conception of justice in the soul and has been continually reasserted in the Western ethical tradition. But if we are natural objects, whose behaviour is governed by causal laws, can we be in this sense morally free? This is the philosophical problem of 'free will and determinism'.

Free Will and Moral Freedom

Many philosophers have denied that, if our behaviour is governed by causal laws, we can be morally free. But others have seen no inconsistency. The issue is important for ethics, because blame, and thus morality, presuppose moral freedom. In particular, blame presupposes that the responsible agent could have refrained from acting on the motives which in fact he *did* act on – had there been reason to do so. In blaming, then, we judge that a person had the capacity to refrain – and the distinctions we make (is that person just a casual smoker or an addict?) seem not to turn at all on the truth or otherwise of any global thesis about causal determination of human behaviour. Before we blame an agent, we want to know, among other things, whether he could have refrained from doing what he did. In particular, we want to know whether he could have recognized the reasons for refraining, and refrained, given that his desires stood as they did. This is a question about his capacity of rational self-control. We are not asking whether a world is possible in which all the causes of his action stood as they did, and the action did not occur. If determinism is true, there is indeed no such world; but how does this bear on rational self-control, and thus on the issue of moral freedom?

Certainly a closer examination might yet show some connection. It is up to the philosopher who thinks that the truth of determinism would undermine moral freedom – the power of acting or not acting, according to the determinations of reason – to show what the connection is. There have been plenty of attempts to establish a connection. The resilience of the dispute bears witness to its intractability.

4 An Ethical Theory – the Case of Utilitarianism

We have spoken of how judgements about what is desirable, blameworthy and admirable are based on examination of one's feelings and discussion with others, and of how they ground the interacting value-spheres of prudence, morality and excellence in activity and character. But we have said nothing about how such judgements give us reason to act. Since ethics, on our account, is the general study of reasons for action, this important question is ethical.

One could say that ethical 'theory' simply consists of considered, thoughtful answers to it. Then it would hardly be controversial that there is such a thing. But it is controversial – because 'theory' suggests something more than a set of piecemeal and personal answers, however thoughtful. It promises system and objectivity, and many people doubt that answers to ethical questions can achieve those aims. Their doubts are not factious. By now in the history of ethics – in our world of ethical cultures which seem invincibly fragmented and disparate – they must be taken seriously. There is no point, however, in abstract claims and counterclaims about how ambitious ethical theory should be. We will make more progress by taking something which everyone agrees to be an ambitious ethical theory – UTILITARIANISM (chapter 25) – considering its structure and various objections to it, and asking, finally, when and in what way these become objections to 'ethical theory' as such. In this way we will see what difficulties face the idea of *system*; difficulties facing the idea of *objectivity* will be considered in section 11.

Utilitarianism is the thesis that the well-being of each and every individual has intrinsic ethical value, that the greater the well-being the greater its value, and that nothing else has intrinsic ethical value.

The phrase 'intrinsic ethical value' calls for explanation. Let us say that a property has ethical value if there is reason to do whatever is likely to produce or preserve it, increase its degree and so on. It has intrinsic ethical value if that reason consists just in the fact that the property *is* that property, and does not derive from any further facts about its connections with other properties. Why talk about 'properties'? The ethical value of objects and states of affairs, the reasons for acting that they give rise to, whether intrinsic or extrinsic, always seems to reside in something *about* them – they have value in virtue of features or properties that they have. Indeed this seems true for value of any kind: the value of a thing always stems from some feature or property that it has. A currently common way of putting it is to say that the value of a thing always supervenes on some properties that it has. If a certain value supervenes on some properties then anything which has just those properties will have just that value – a difference in value entails a difference in those properties.

For the utilitarian, the only thing that has intrinsic ethical value is a property of individuals, a property they can have to greater or lesser degree: that of being or faring well. The greater the well-being the greater the ethical value; that is, the greater the reason to produce or preserve it. Utilitarians will wish to spell out what well-being consists in. They will then have to consider what ends are desirable, by the method of self-examination and discussion considered in section 2. But our interest now is in the structure of the utilitarian view rather than its doctrine of what well-being, or 'utility', comprises.

The utilitarian holds that the ethical value of well-being is not affected by whose well-being it is – or at least that is true if the only individuals under consideration are human beings. But utilitarians have always freely granted that the well-being of all individuals which can be said to be sentient, or perhaps (if this is different) to have desires, should be taken into account. Now this is still a smaller class than that of individuals which can be said to have well-being at all. Living things in general can fare well or badly, and a green ethicist might hold that all such varieties of well-being have intrinsic ethical value. But utilitarians have not held that view, nor have they held that the well-being of all sentient individuals has equal ethical value. The well-being of non-human animals has an intrinsic ethical value, but it is not as great as that of human beings. Deep issues lurk here, not only for utilitarians, about what these differences of ethical value, as between the well-being of different types of individual, supervene upon.

At any rate, whatever the class of individuals whose well-being is to be taken into account, the utilitarian takes general well-being to be a positive function of the well-being of all of them, and of nothing else – a function in which the utility of every individual is taken impartially into account. Ethical value then consists in general well-being and in nothing else. But note that 'general well-being' is an abstraction constructed out of the well-being of concrete individuals. No 'general being' enjoys 'general well-being'. Only in the well-being of concrete individuals does ethical value, according to the utilitarian, really reside.

Classical utilitarianism is usually taken to hold that general well-being is fixed by the sum of the well-being of all individuals. Henry SIDGWICK (chapter 25), the third of the great trio of British utilitarians suggested that it might also be taken as the average: that is, that the greatest ethical value is realized when average, rather than aggregate, well-being is at its highest. Either of these views assumes that one can add up the levels of well-being of different individuals – it assumes that that project makes *sense*, not that it can actually be done. The practical question of measurement becomes important if one wants to apply utilitarianism, for example in welfare economics. But even as a pure ethical theory classical utilitarianism does require that comparative questions like these are intelligible: would the increase in X's well-being offset the decrease in Y's? Would X's increase be greater than the loss of Y's and Z's?

They certainly sometimes make sense. I can ask myself whether a book will give greater pleasure to Kate or Julia. I can even ask myself whether Kate would get more pleasure out of this book than Julia and Anna would from two other books at half the price. Some very rough comparing and summing is going on there. The notion of a sum of well-being may be sufficiently well-defined in some areas, for some purposes, to be meaningful, even if it is not in all. We do seem to use it. But do such questions always – even in principle –

make sense? And how important to utilitarianism is it that they always should?

John Stuart Mill would have conceded that they do not always make sense, for he thought that one can distinguish between quality and quantity of happiness. Happiness, he thought, was what well-being consists in, but some forms of happiness are 'higher' – or perhaps, deeper, truer or more valuable – in some way other than that in which having two chocolate ices is more valuable than having one. So perhaps there can be discontinuity here, in the sense that, in some contexts at least, a person may reasonably be unwilling to trade off a higher pleasure for any quantity of a lower one. He prefers the former to the latter but it will not make sense to say that he finds it *n* times as good. For if it did, he ought to be willing to sacrifice a particular higher experience for *n* or more of the lower ones. This at least gestures towards complications which are genuinely present in our thinking about what makes for a good life. We should certainly bear in mind that it may be intelligible to order possible states (perhaps only partially) by the level of well-being they produce, even if it is not generally possible to say what fraction the well-being in state X is of the well-being in state Y.

The utilitarian's basic idea was that considerations of well-being provide the only intrinsic reasons for action, and that in assessing the strength of such reasons one should consider impartially the well-being of all individuals affected. The only thing that this requires is that we should be able in principle to *order* distributions of well-being by their ethical value. Utilitarianism then holds that ethical value is a function of such distributions and of nothing else. It holds further that the function is positive: if the well-being of one or more individuals goes up, without any other change, then ethical value goes up. And finally it requires that the function be impartial. But what is involved in this notion of impartiality?

5 Impartiality

Maximizing the *sum* of individuals' well-being, if it makes sense to talk in this way at all, certainly looks impartial. No individual's well-being is given greater weight in the addition than that of any other. No one has his or her well-being multiplied by two or divided by three. This is one way of implementing the principle 'Everybody to count for one, nobody for more than one' – which in *Utilitarianism* Mill attributed to Bentham and which he took to express the principle of impartiality (Mill, 1963– , vol. X, p. 257). He was, it should be noted, talking only of the well-being of humans – if non-humans are considered as well, as we noted in the previous section, it ceases to be so plausible that impartiality forbids weighting some individuals' well-being more heavily than others. That is a point about the connection between weighting and impartiality. But another point is that adding up – with or without weighting – is only one way of being impartial. Not only is Sidgwick's idea of maximizing the average of well-being equally impartial, so is a wide variety of other distributive principles.

Consider the DIFFERENCE PRINCIPLE (p. 261) proposed by John Rawls. According to one version of this (Rawls, 1972, p. 83), resources should be so distributed as to make the worst-off group of individuals as well-off as it is possible for them to be; after that, the next worst-off group should be made as well-off as possible, and so on up the scale. Rawls himself does not propose this principle as a comprehensive ethical theory. He presents it as an account of 'justice as fairness' in the POLITICAL realm (chapter 8), an account with which he hopes people with a variety of comprehensive ethical views will be able to agree. But we could also treat it as a proposal about how impartiality should be understood in a comprehensive ethical theory, a proposal which would share with classical utilitarianism the feature that it takes ethical value to be a positive impartial function of individual well-being and of nothing else. Nor is it the only possible proposal which shares this feature with classical utilitarianism; there are many others.

The difference principle favours the worst off, in that it attaches an ethical priority to improvements in their well-being. But it can also be said to count everybody for one, nobody for more than one in this sense: it is indifferent to which concrete individual is under consideration. It takes account of no property of the individual other than his or her comparative well-being.

A distinctive feature of classical utilitarianism is that it takes an equal amount of well-being to be of equal ethical value, however it is distributed across individuals. This is not true of the difference principle, because a benefit to worse-off people will have greater ethical value than a benefit to the better-off. Note, however, that this contrast assumes that it *makes sense* to think of a given amount of well-being being distributed in various ways across individuals. Where it does not make sense to talk about moving about an equal amount of well-being it will not make sense to talk of summing or averaging either. The difference principle does not require that such talk should make sense, though it does require that we should be able to compare the *levels* of different individuals' well-being. Not that this is an ethical argument in its favour; it simply shows that as we get more sophisticated about what it makes sense to say, we will have to find subtler ways of implementing these competing distributive principles in competing welfare functions. But all of them are impartial.

How then should we understand the term 'utilitarianism' today? Critics have done their worst with it, and a case can certainly be made for burying it. But any other term, such as 'welfarism', is at least as misleading and open to distortion. And 'utilitarianism' has the merit of invoking a historically definite tradition. I suggest that we should interpret it *generically* – as naming a class of ethical theories, all of which hold that overall ethical value is some positive impartial function of individual well-being. On this weak definition, what I have called classical utilitarianism becomes a particular – and particularly simple – species of utilitarian ethical theory. 'Generic utilitarianism' generalizes it by allowing (1) distributive principles other than the aggregative principle of the classical utilitarians; and (2) different interpretations of well-being to the classical view of it as consisting exclusively of happiness. It generalizes in the way that is done when one shifts from the Euclidian paradigm of GEOMETRY (p. 328) to a class of geometries of which Euclid's is only one: by allowing certain axioms of the original theory to be varied. What distributive principle, and what account of human ends, to adopt remains open to debate among generic utilitarians.

6 What Can an Ethical Theory be Expected to Do?

Utilitarianism is a fully general theory of ethical value and so a fully general theory of reasons for acting. But two further elucidations are required.

The first is simply a reminder that there are non-ethical forms of value. Utilitarianism is a general theory of *ethical* value, not a general theory of value, so it does not have anything directly to say about those other forms. For example, what makes a piece of archaeological evidence valuable is its bearing on archaeological questions about the past not its effect on general well-being. The value of the evidence lies in the reasons it gives for believing one thing rather than another: a general account of what makes evidence valuable is a task for the epistemologist, not the ethicist. Similarly, when we judge a piano recital to be superb – or dreary – we appeal to the internal standards of that activity, the aesthetics of piano-playing.

However, we can also ask, in one or another larger context, whether it is worth pursuing an admittedly valuable piece of evidence, or putting on a brilliant piano performance. The question might be, for example, whether we should fund the piano recital or the archaeological dig. Consider a pianist who plays only for himself, or a desert-islander who pursues evidence about the history of the island that will never be known to others. The aesthetic value of the performance, like the archaeological value of the evidence, is quite unrelated to how many people derive well-being from it. But if the utilitarian is right, how many people derive well-being from it is very relevant to its *ethical* value. If the pianist enjoys his piano-playing, that gives it ethical value. If others do too, that gives it even greater ethical value. Forms of non-ethical value are translated into reasons for action via their ethical value. The utilitarians do not reduce other forms of value to ethical value; they propound a substantive doctrine of what connection there is between the two. To say that great piano-playing should be pursued or funded for its own sake, irrespective of its contribution to well-being, is to adopt another doctrine, incompatible with utilitarianism.

The second elucidation can be made by distinguishing between a theory of ethical value and a theory of decision. Utilitarianism is a fully *general* theory of ethical value but that is not the same as saying that it is a fully developed one. It is concerned with intrinsic reasons for action and in that sense offers, as the classical utilitarians said, a 'test', or 'standard' or 'criterion' of conduct. But it is another question whether it can be developed into rules or procedures for deciding what to do. It does not follow directly from the utilitarian theory of ethical value that we should all, at every moment, follow the decision-rule: 'do that action which produces greatest ethical value'. We may not know what action has greatest ethical value. It may be that attempts to follow such a decision rule would be highly counter-productive. And so on. A limiting possibility is that ethical value is greatest in a world in which no individual even believes that utilitarianism is true. In this case utilitarianism would be 'self-effacing'. It would itself imply that the best world is one in which it is not believed. These are not objections to utilitarianism. To say that utilitarianism is self-effacing is not to say that it's self-undermining.

Utilitarianism is not committed to the view that the morally right action is the optimal action – that is, the action that produces the greatest well-being, or even that 'optimal action' is in every situation even in principle well-defined. Not only is it consistent with utilitarianism to adopt the account of morality which I gave earlier – it is in fact the account that Mill himself gave. Our everyday moral thinking is by no means wholly impartial in the way the utilitarian theory of ethical value is. We believe that we have special obligations to some people because of the relation in which we stand to them – of kinship, neighbourliness, fellow-citizenship, contract. We believe that we have duties arising from our 'station in life'. We have very specific moral responses to our and others' actions in their context, responses which are certainly not pulled down from an ethical theory, utilitarian or any other.

But ethical theory need not claim that those responses are pulled down. We can recognize that they stem from spontaneous moral feelings, as discussed in section 2. Certainly utilitarianism is committed to this: where it can be shown that general well-being would be improved if a given way of doing things was changed, then it should be. That is what is meant by calling general well-being a test of conduct. Another ethical theory, such as contractualism (see section 9 below) would have the same commitment for the test of conduct which *it* favoured.

If we could never plausibly show, of any practice, that general well-being would be increased by changing it, then utilitarianism would have no cutting edge – though it could still be true. Similarly, if versions of generic utilitarianism differ in their distributive structure or their view of the ends of life but do not differ in what changes they recommend, then the distinction between them makes no practical difference.

Introducing a utilitarian standard in fact makes subtle but very important differences, as introducing standards of SCIENTIFIC METHOD (chapter 9) made to our beliefs about the world. In neither case, however, does the effect come through a 'linear' derivation, of moral rules from a welfare function, or of specific scientific hypotheses from canons of scientific method. In both cases the new or newly refined standards operate on an *existing* cosmological or moral tradition, changing it but doing so in a holistic and conserving way. 'Where it doesn't itch, don't scratch' is Quine's formula for this method of conservative holism. It applies to ethical method too.

Certainly the classical utilitarians sometimes talked in a 'linear' way, but they also had their conservative-holist moments. Mill particularly emphasized this element of conservative holism because he was responding to criticisms of Bentham and other early utilitarian radicals on precisely this point. Sidgwick then systematized the strategy at length. All this must be remembered if we are to avoid setting up over-simple contrasts between utilitarian and other views of morality.

The attraction of generic utilitarianism is two-fold. In the first place it seems perfectly possible to ask why one should obey a particular set of moral rules, say the Ten Commandments. If such responses as that they are self-evident or that they are laid down by a god seem unsatisfying, one reason at least is that we want to know the point or purpose of the rules. And once the question, What purpose does this rule serve? is accepted as proper, the generic utilitarian's answer, referring us to the standard of general well-being, is very compelling. To be told that adultery is wrong because of the hurt it causes, directly and through breakages of trust, is a bit more satisfying, though undoubtedly also a good deal more debateable, than to be told that its wrongness is self-evident or that it is forbidden in the Bible.

7 The Plurality of Value

One may ask, about utilitarianism, or any ethical theory, what its credentials are. What sort of thing could show it to be correct? Where does it fit on the intellectual map?

Spontaneous impressions of when an emotion is in place, stabilized by self-examination and discussion, generate internal criteria governing its reasonableness – norms of right feeling. The same goes for epistemic norms, which consist in judgements about what there is reason to believe – norms of right belief.

These appraisals are entwined into our ends. Finding out about ancient cultures, for example – if that is your objective you should pay attention to valuable pieces of evidence. Even more obviously, if you want to play the piano well, you should be interested in what makes a performance musical, perceptive, moving.

But though they are in this way entwined in our ends, they do not tell us what our ends should be. Logic or archaeological method tells you what evidence is important for getting at the truth about the ancient past but neither method tells you that that ought to be your objective or that you ought to pursue the truth. Internal criteria tell you what performance is not merely technically accurate, but beautiful, insightful or profound. But they cannot tell you how much time to spend on it, or what resources to put to it.

Exactly the same, it would seem, must apply to the blameworthy – at least if we think of that as determined solely by the internal criteria of the blame-feeling. Such criteria will tell us what is 'morally right' or 'morally wrong', but not what reason we have to pursue the former and avoid the latter. Just as one could write a book about the The Art of the Pianist, or about Good Method in Archaeology, without saying anything about how important these activities are compared to others, so one could write a book about The Art of Moral Goodness, without saying anything about how important it is to pursue moral goodness.

Some philosophers have argued as though these internal criteria proper to various types of activity and experience are the only ones we need. They would say that there is no space for what I have called the ethical question to arise. Is there really a question to be asked about why I should avoid doing what is morally wrong, shun boring or frightening situations, seek to achieve the qualities in myself that I find admirable in others?

Emotion can shape one's action through the links between emotion and desire, and desire and action. Guilt, boredom and fear are emotions that give rise to a desire to eliminate or avoid their object. Others, such as aesthetic delight, give rise to the opposite desire. But what are the connections at the level of reasons? Why should I avoid doing what is boring or blameworthy? Consider this: If a thing is boring (blameworthy) then there is reason not to do it. Is this a truth of logic? It does not seem so. The truth of logic is rather this: If a thing is boring (blameworthy) then boredom (blaming the person who does it) is an appropriate, justified, reasonable response. The logical connection is with norms of feeling rather than norms of action.

Doing things that are boring or blameworthy is likely to make one bored or guilty – states that most of us find unpleasant. And surely one has reason to avoid doing what is unpleasant. This last proposition is obvious enough, and makes the logical link with reasons for action. But it also gets us into the territory of ethical theory. For it is a normative proposition about reasons for action, and we can ask what its source is. But first there is an important point about the status of the moral to be considered.

A Special Status for Morality?

Morality is surely not on all fours with other norms of feeling. One can bring out the asymmetry, for example, in this way. If I honestly find a movie very boring I am quite likely to judge a person who does not find it boring rather unfavourably – perhaps as a pretty uncritical enthusiast. Or I may be led to question my own taste instead. But even if I remain convinced that the movie is boring, I can hardly argue that the *uncritical enthusiast* has reason to avoid it. He after all, uncritical fellow that he is, will enjoy it.

Can we take the same line about immoral, as against uncritical, people? If we did, we could still form an unfavourable assessment of someone who felt no guilt about doing something blameworthy – finding him shameless or blameworthy. But we could not claim that he had a reason to refrain from the immoral act.

There is no symmetry here. I should avoid doing something morally wrong because it is morally wrong, not because it will make me feel guilty, which is unpleasant. Even if it does not make me feel guilty, I still have reason not to do it. Consider a connoisseur of singing who sees that a particular piece of singing is beautiful but no longer gets anything out of it – the uninvolved connoisseur. He has no reason to attend the performance. Compare the uninvolved moral connoisseur – who sees what is right and wrong but no longer feels committed to it. He still has reason to do the right and avoid the wrong. It does not depend on how interested he feels. We want to maintain this ethical principle:

If X is morally wrong then there is reason not to do X.

And we do not think its truth depends on the holding of some further condition which may or may not obtain. For example, whether there is reason for me not to do the morally wrong does not depend on what my objectives are, or whether it will be unpleasant, or even on whether it will degrade my character. One may put this by saying that moral reasons are categorical, so the ethical principle may be called *the principle of moral categoricity.*

It is by no means uncontroversial. It has been influentially denied by, among others, Phillipa Foot and Bernard Williams (Foot, 1978, chs VII–XIV, Williams, 1981, ch. 8). One could deny it on the grounds that *moral* reasons are not categorical, or more strongly, on the grounds that no reasons are. But if we endorse it we must conclude that moral norms cannot be grounded solely in spontaneous blame-feelings. They must also be responsive to ethical considerations.

Both sides in the dispute about moral categoricity must give some ethical account of when it is that one has reason to act. Two ideas can be put forward by those who deny moral categoricity:

(1)   you have reason to pursue what is good for you and avoid what is bad for you
(2)   you have reason to do whatever will promote the objectives you have.

Reasons for acting morally will then depend on what is good for you or on what your objectives are. But where do these ideas come from? They seem to be products of rational reflection alone, just as much as is any other ethical doctrine about reasons for action. So, as well as the whole diverse range of emotion-based values that are *data* for ethical reflection, there seems to be something else, from which it stems – practical reason.

8 Practical Reason

Practical reason concerns reasons to act, as theoretical reason concerns reasons to believe. Since we have repeatedly distinguished between reasons to act, to believe and to *feel*, should we not expect a third division of reason, dealing with reasons to feel? It might be called, 'aesthetic reason'.

If 'practical' and 'theoretical' reason were simply labels for the disposition to make judgements about reasons to act and reasons to believe, a tripartite division like that would be right. But no such term as 'aesthetic reason' is in common use. The reason is that 'practical' and 'theoretical reason' do not just label dispositions; they invoke a view about the source of those dispositions, the view that judgements about reasons to act and reasons to believe are exercises of *reason*. So the notion of 'aesthetic reason' limps. For though we constantly make judgements about what there is reason to feel, these judgements are not deliverances of *reason*. To say that they were would be to say that there are rationally evident principles specifically concerned with reasons to feel. Similarly, practical reason exists if there are rationally evident principles yielding reasons for action. And theoretical reason exists if there are rationally evident principles yielding reasons for belief. But, surely, in the case of feeling there are no such principles. We may be reasonable in our feelings, or unreasonable, but it is not rational insight into principles of right feeling that tells us so. In so far as reason comes in, it does so in its theoretical guise, through rational assessment of the beliefs which our feelings presuppose. Pascal said that the heart has its reasons which reason knows nothing of. ('Le coeur a ses raisons que la raison ne connaît point' *Pensées*, sect.iv. no. 277.) He was speaking in a different context but his aphorism aptly fits the present point.

But is there such a thing as practical reason? We distinguish between reasonable and unreasonable feelings, even though there are no *a priori* principles of justified feeling. So does the distinction between reasonable and unreasonable action require that there be *a priori* principles of justified action? Come to that, does the distinction between reasonable and unreasonable beliefs require *a priori* principles of justified belief? We shall touch on this again in section 11. For the moment we simply note the contemporary tendency to group reasons to act with reasons to feel, rather than, as was traditional, with reasons to believe. It assumes, rightly or wrongly, that whereas rational belief does presuppose rationally evident principles of reasoning, rational action does not.

Idea (2) in the previous section is closely related to this, or a version of it. It says that a person has reasons for action only in relation to his objectives. The only concept of a reason for acting that we have is one that makes a reason a relation between an objective, an actor and an action, thus: there is reason for a person P whose objective is O to do X. That will hold when P's doing X is a way of bringing about O. How strong the reason is will depend on how effective doing X is – how probable it makes the achievement of O, and how much it impedes the achievement of P's other objectives. This may be called 'instrumentalism' (because it says that reason's only practical function is to select appropriate instruments for achieving objectives). Instrumentalism deflates practical reason into instrumental reason, but it does not deny that there are true reason-statements – only that there are true *categorical* ones. To hold that there are true categorical reason-statements is to take a more ambitious view of practical reason.

Among those who affirm the more ambitious view the most influential by far has been KANT (chapter 22). He held that some reasons for acting are categorical – in his terminology, categorical and not merely hypothetical imperatives. He also, very influentially, held that the only categorical reasons are moral reasons. But before considering Kant let us note some other ethical theories that must also accept the categorical nature of practical reason.

A reason for an actor to do something is categorical if it holds irrespective of that actor's objectives. This cuts a line between (1) and (2). For according to (1) you have reason to pursue what is good for you, irrespective of whether that is your objective. The person who holds that this is the *only* categorical reason for acting is the *rational egoist*. Because acting selfishly might be bad for you, rational egoists need not recommend selfishness in the usual sense. Their position is also distinct from the instrumentalist's. For what is meant by a person's objectives? The strictly instrumentalist view is that a person's objectives are those that a person in fact has, and which are basic rather than derived from more basic ones that that person in fact has. We are not talking about basic objectives that people would have if they had full rational insight, or wanted what reason tells them to want, and so on. These notions are not available to the instrumentalist. One might argue that instrumentalism itself must endorse at least one categorical principle – on pain of collapsing into pure scepticism about practical reason: 'You ought to do whatever will promote your objectives, irrespective of what they are'. It must indeed endorse that principle, but it is another question whether it has to see it as a substantial deliverance of reason (see section 11). If it can deny that it is, then it can in that sense be said to reject all categorical principles of practical reason.

Utilitarians, like rational egoists, must accept a categorical principle of practical reason. They cannot be instrumentalists, for they are not just saying that *if* one's objective is to promote general good then one has reason to promote general good. Theirs is a fundamental thesis about ethical value. It says that one has reason to promote general good whether or not one wishes to. The well-being of every individual is a source of categorical reasons for every individual.

The contrast between categorical and instrumental conceptions of practical reason is a major watershed in ethics, and since utilitarianism is so often crudely lumped with instrumentalist notions of reason it is worth stressing that cogent utilitarianism, on the contrary, like Kantianism, falls on the categorical and not the instrumental side. That was clearer to Mill than Bentham, and clearer to Sidgwick than Mill. But let us now turn to Kant's ethical doctrine.

Kant thought the complete set of moral principles could be established by means of a test whose soundness is itself derived from pure reason. This test is the categorical imperative proper:

> Act as if the maxim of your action were to become through your will a universal law of nature.

When it is applied to any maxim of action it is supposed to determine in a clearcut way – and supposedly without appeal to any empirical data – whether that maxim is or is not a categorically binding moral principle. For Kant, the moral simply *is* the rational.

So much in Kant's ethics is momentous and deep that it is easy to forget, or to allow oneself to obscure, the quite incredible ambitiousness of this central doctrine, which is the backbone of the theory. It remains incredible, even when we notice the various ways in which Kant thinks 'anthropological' facts about humans and their circumstances shape the details of morality. One should not gloss over this incredibility, because Kant's greatness as a philosopher, when combined with it, has been ruinous for more defensible doctrines of practical reason, which have suffered collateral damage from the collapse of Kant's over-ambitious project. Because reason cannot have the monopoly in determining right and wrong which Kant, the great defender of reason, sought to give it, it is thought that it can play no part at all. An extreme

form of ethical rationalism rebounds into extreme forms of ethical irrationalism. Hence it remains important to draw up an account of what in Kant's
ethics must be jettisoned and what can be retained.

9 The Categorical Imperative and Contractualism

Critics on all sides in the nineteenth century (among others, Hegel, Mill,
Schopenhauer and Nietzsche) pointed out that though Kant's substantive
moral teaching has a very definite and distinctive content, his categorical
imperative is too formal to yield any such substantive results. Consider the
maxim, 'Break your promise when it is to your advantage to do so'. Kant
suggests that it would be self-contradictory to suppose it a universal law,
because if everyone complied with it there would be no such thing as
'promising'. As it stands, this is wrong: to get a contradiction one must add
contingent non-formal assumptions, such as that it is generally known that
everyone breaks their promise when it is to their advantage to do so. But this
assumption is contingent.

Reason and Autonomy

Kant also requires that we should be able to *will* that the maxim be a universal
LAW OF NATURE (pp. 510–11), and this has seemed a more promising line of thought.
Can I really will that everyone should break their promise when it is to their
advantage to do so? It is easy to be misled here. For Kant, the will in question
must be a *purely* rational will: it is simply the moving force of pure reason. It
cannot appeal to ends that we happen, contingently, to have. Kant certainly talks
as though the will is determined by the mere idea of universal law, and this part
of his doctrine does fall to his nineteenth-century critics. But he also, less
explicitly, takes it that there are ends that pure reason requires us to have:
persons, that is rational beings, are the only ends certifiable as intrinsic ends by
pure reason alone. This leads him to another, for many people deeply resonant,
version of the categorical imperative:

> Act in such a way that you always treat humanity, whether in your own
> person or in the person of another, never simply as a means, but always at
> the same time as an end.

Resonant as this is, it is not wholly clear. What is it to treat a person, a rational
being, as an end? One view, which seems to be Kant's, is that it is to refrain from
actions which impede others or oneself from the exercise of rationality. Now for
Kant rationality is moral freedom (the notion we discussed in section 3) or, in his
word, autonomy. This is one of the most impressive, as well as one of the most
central, elements of Kant's moral philosophy. His view is that reason itself
requires that we should respect, not infringe upon, the autonomy of beings which
can *be* autonomous.

Kant's link between reason and autonomy is a substantial claim, but attempts
to extract it from conjuring tricks on statements like 'reason itself requires that
reason be respected' should be resisted. We do have a notion of rational

autonomy (as emerged in section 3) and we do, I believe, think that rationally autonomous beings have special moral claims in virtue of their rationality. But we do not think, as Kantian doctrine would require, that only rational beings have moral claims, and we do not think that their only claim on us is respect for their rationality – in other words, abstention from anything that would impede or diminish their moral freedom. In any case, Kant's formalism prevents him from giving definite content to the notion of practical rationality. On his account, rationality consists in seeing what the universal law of reason requires, and this universal law says only that one should respect rationality: nothing in this tells us what respect for rationality, and hence rationality, requires. So in the end the charge of emptiness laid against Kant's categorical imperative stands.

The missing ingredient is the notion of an individual's good. It seems that Kant thought this notion inappropriately 'anthropological' for a purely rational end. However, the notion of an individual's good is not itself anthropological – only when we give an account of what the good *consists in for a human being* do we descend to anthropology. If we equip pure reason with the abstract notion of individual good, we can see various ways of combining it with the doctrine of rational will. For example, if rationality itself tells rational agents to pursue their good, they cannot rationally will that a maxim should be a universal law of nature, where such a law of nature would be to their disadvantage. Or, we could take respect for persons to mean concern for their good, reading the categorical imperative as the injunction to treat the good of all persons as something to be promoted impartially. The good of individuals, conceived impartially, becomes the object of rational will, so that a maxim could be willed to be a universal law of nature, and thus adopted as a moral law, only if universal compliance with it would promote the general good.

Either way, we drop the Kantian idea that rationality itself is the only rational end, and substitute the non-Kantian idea that the good of individuals is the only rational end. So either of these developments, towards rational egoism or (if good is identified with well-being) towards utilitarianism, is a decisive break with Kant.

Let us consider a little further the first idea, which places the categorical imperative against a background of rational egoism. Can a rational egoist 'will' that 'Break your promises whenever it is to your advantage' should be a universal law?

Well, a rational egoist thinks it *is* a universal law of reason. But perhaps he or she cannot will it to be a universal 'law of nature', or something with which everyone always complies. It is not that such universal compliance would be inherently self-contradictory, as Kant thought; rather, it is that it looks likely to be to his disadvantage. And if it is likely to disadvantage him, he cannot will it, or do anything to bring it about. But suppose we modify Kant's test, as follows:

Accept as a moral principle only that maxim which you can will to be a universal law of nature.

A rational egoist who endorses this test of *moral* principles will not accept the principle of breaking promises when it is advantageous to do so as a moral principle. On the contrary, since he can will that people should universally comply with their promises – it would be to his advantage if they did – he accepts 'Keep your promises' as a moral principle.

This modification of Kant's test for moral principles puts us on the road to contractualism. A form of contractualism which is quite close to it is the simple view that moral rules are those which rational egoists could 'agree' to – promote as public rules of conduct. Another modification replaces rational egoism by instrumentalism – moral rules are those to which instrumentally rational agents could agree. This moves another step away from Kant, since it appears to drop the idea that there are any categorically rational principles, egoistic or other – but, by the same token, it appears to some as attractively hard-headed.

Though these forms of contractualism have been influential in recent moral and political philosophy, they have a straightforward and pretty unappetizing corollary: one has reason to obey a moral principle only if it is to one's advantage to do so, or if it promotes one's objectives to do so. The egoist or instrumentalist construction of morality can give me reason to seek, in whatever way I can, to influence people into accepting various 'moral' precepts – but it does not give me reason (even in cases like the PRISONER'S DILEMMA (pp. 377–9)) to act in accordance with those moral precepts myself when it is to my advantage, or promotes my objectives, not to do so. If one accepts the principle of moral categoricity considered in section 7 such a conclusion must be rejected, and with it the theory that gives rise to it.

Another recent form of contractualism is closer in spirit to Kant. The Kantian idea of treating persons as ends can be read as requiring that we do not take unfair advantage of them, and a contractualist view of morality based on this reading can treat moral rules as those which could be willed by a *reasonable* person – one who pursues his or her well-being or objectives while accepting that all must have an equally fair chance to do so. The rules of morality are rules which no reasonable person would reject. Thomas Scanlon (1982) provides an influential defence of this view. I will call it Kantian contractualism, though its affinity to Kant's ethics is a matter for scholarly debate which will not be pursued here.

A Comparison

Since Kantian contractualism is often presented as an alternative to utilitarianism, it is worth considering the similarities and differences between the two ethical theories. And here the proper basis for comparison is with generic utilitarianism, rather than classical aggregative utilitarianism in particular.

Both recognize impartiality, or 'fairness', as a categorical ethical principle located outside morality – so they both diverge from pure instrumentalism and pure egoism. Moral principles, for the Kantian contractualist, are those compliance with which would advantage all in a fair manner, a manner which respects their dignity as persons. In particular, they would be the sub-group of such principles which we could agree to sanction by penalties of blame for non-compliance. Now should these principles simply establish constraints of fairness, rather minimally conceived – a level playing-field for competition among individuals who pursue their own ends? Or does Kantian contractualism lead us to something stronger – a maximizing principle of justice such as Rawls' difference principle?

The upshot of this stronger option would be a test of conduct co-extensive with one or another version of generic utilitarianism. Kantian contractualists would say that their way of setting up the test, by reference to a hypothetical agreement, is likely to lead away from the classical utilitarians' views of impartiality, which allow some individuals to be disadvantaged 'unreasonably' for the sake of offsetting advantages to others. They may be right in this. But it remains debateable whether the right objection to classical utilitarianism's aggregative principle is that it is unfair. It may be unreasonable, in the way that applying similar aggregative principles of distribution within one's own life (allowing some period of one's life to fall to limitlessly increasing depths of misery for the sake of compensating advantages in other periods) may seem unreasonable. But in the latter case the unreasonableness is not connected with unfairness.

On the whole Kantian contractualism looks much closer to generic utilitarianism than to the egoistic or instrumentalist forms of contractualism with which we started. The utilitarian principle is strictly agent-neutral, in that it assigns value to the well-being of an individual irrespective of that individual's relation to the agent who is deliberating. Kantian contractualism, likewise, appeals to an agent-neutral principle of fairness. The reason I should do what is morally right is that it would be unfair not to do so. Whether or not the notion of fairness can ultimately carry this weight, it is at least clear that there is no pretence here of founding morality or justice on pure egoism or instrumentalism. Nor is there any attempt to get a substantive theory of the right from purely formal considerations, as Kant sometimes gives the impression of trying to do. Both generic utilitarianism and Kantian contractualism are committed to the view that there are principles of practical reason that are categorical but *not* merely formal.

10 Reason, Morality and Religion

Some people feel that to distinguish between reason and morality, as utilitarianism and contractualism do, is to draw an invidious line. Moral judgements, they feel, are rationally evident in their own right. Moral life has its own internal rationality. The idea that criteria of practical reason stand outside it alienates us from it.

If the utilitarian or the contractualist view alienate us from morality, that is a lamentable consequence but not an objection to their truth. The philosophical question has to centre on whether moral judgements are indeed, contrary to utilitarians and contractualists, evident in their own right. That they are so is the view of the moral intuitionist. I use this term here simply to name the view that certain moral judgements are rationally evident in their own right, without assuming any particular epistemological account of what it is for something to be rationally evident.

We have already seen that judgements about what is admirable or blameworthy, like other judgements about what it is reasonable to feel, have an internal discipline based on reflection about one's spontaneous feelings and discussion with others. But this internal discipline does not itself connect them with reasons for action; still less could it underwrite the principle of moral categoricity (see sections 2 and 7).

For the moral intuitionist, the truth or otherwise of moral judgements is known directly by purely rational reflection. This in itself still does not show why the fact that something is morally wrong – which, by the intuitionist's hypothesis, I know through pure rational reflection – gives me reason not to do it. But if the intuitionist gives pure rational reflection as big a role as this, he is hardly upping the stakes very much if he adds that I also know that I have reason not to do what is morally wrong by pure rational reflection.

Utilitarians or contractualists who grant the principle of moral categoricity cannot be as direct about it as that. They must, rather, derive the categoricity of moral reasons from the ethical principles that they hold to be primitively categorical – the general good, or fairness. Moral reasons, they can say, are those reasons for action that, given human circumstance, people should observe and should incur blame for failing to observe. If they are conservative holists (section 6) they will not claim to derive them in a linear way from their ethical criteria, but will feel free to ground them in our spontaneous dispositions to blame. In other words, they will accept that the guidance for action and evaluation given by these dispositions is legitimate in the absence of a well-made case against it; but they will insist that it *is* corrigible by a well-made case based on their preferred ethical criterion.

Their criticism of the intuitionist will be that the latter confuses spontaneous judgements about what is admirable and blameworthy with purely rational intuitions. That is a purely philosophical criticism and to my mind a very powerful one. If I examine my responses I find emotions that give rise to judgements about the admirable and the blameworthy, but I find no detailed purely rational intuitions. It is not reason that directly tells me, in concrete circumstances, whether to tell a lie to save a friend. And the utilitarian or contractual theorist can go on to draw a social consequence. When a spontaneous response of admiration and blame get transmuted in this way into a supposed rational intuition, he or she may say – with no appeal allowed to a higher court of ethical judgement, no standard of rational criticism independent of our feelings of admiration and blame – then an important source for regenerating morality is lost. Where those feelings strongly cluster around something, for example feelings of blame around homosexuality, or feelings of admiration around certain kinds of male domineering, we cannot detach from those feelings, stand back, and ask what is wrong with homosexuality or how much we really want that kind of leadership of the pack to be admired. I am not saying that this is a compelling criticism, since intuitionists can reply: firstly, that the question against them has been begged when what they claim to be rational moral intuitions are treated as feelings of admiration and blame; and, secondly, that these intuitions can be criticized from within, when they come into conflict with each other, without any appeal to an 'external' ethical criterion.

Certainly the question whether there are such rational intuitions is philosophically the basic one. The case against is simply that reason does not give us detailed moral responses. Of course the detaching language of the utilitarian or the contractualist has its own dangers, of estrangement from our moral legacy and manipulative social engineering. Ideally we would have a standard of rational criticism which yet somehow lay within morality, and did not treat it as an object. That is one of the most powerful attractions of Kant's ethics. The categorical imperative promised to give a standard of rational criticism which fulfilled this ideal. But it turned out to be empty unless it smuggled in ethical principles of fairness or general well-being, or covertly converted moral feelings into deliverances of pure reason.

Human reason and human moral feelings could be fully integrated if both flowed from some source wiser than the human. Here is a route from morality to religion which has real power for many people. If both reason and moral feeling are implanted in us as responses to the moral law laid down by GOD (chapter 14), then we could safely stay within the circle of morality without being forced into a chilly external standpoint in which reason could come into conflict with sentiments transmitted by tradition.

But two great difficulties stand in the way of this thought. The first is that any argument of this shape – something which is ethically or otherwise desirable can be guaranteed to exist only if God does, so God exists – is invalid. We have no reason to suppose that the world is as it is desirable that it should be. Some independent argument is needed to establish the existence of a wise and benevolent divinity.

The second difficulty has to do with the autonomy of good. In Plato's *Euthyphro* (1961, 10a), Socrates asks 'whether the pious or holy is beloved by the gods because it is holy, or holy because it is beloved of the gods'. One can similarly ask whether the morally good is so because it is commanded by God, or commanded by God because it is morally good. Not a few religious believers cleave to the first answer. So do some atheists: it is implicitly assumed in Nietzsche's assertion that 'God is dead' (*The Gay Science*, 1974, section 125), though Nietzsche played with the fantasy that, after the death of God, new values, beyond moral good and evil, could be created by the imposition of sufficiently forceful human will.

But this voluntarism, theological or Nietzschean, is incompatible with the categoricity of morality. If morality is the command of God, it makes perfectly good sense to ask what reason I have to obey it. Punishment and reward in the after-life, it may be said, give me a self-interested reason. To offer that as the only answer is to propose a pretty shabby philosophy of life; but setting aside its shabbiness consider its logic. I have that reason because my well-being gives me reason to act. But that locates categorical reason outside morality. We must still accept a categorical reason, independent of the command of God, and on this approach we have simply succeeded in locating it in egoism rather than morality. This is the God-assisted transition from rational egoism to morality. And note that we have attached no meaning to 'God is good' other than (perhaps) 'God obeys God's commands'. The same logical points also apply to motives for obeying God's law that are not shabby – love of God, as well as fear of hell.

The other response, in which God's goodness consists in his *recognition* of the good, seems much sounder. It recognizes the autonomy of good and in general the autonomy of reasons. The theist can argue that a benevolent God has implanted our MORAL SENTIMENTS (pp. 579–80) in us as reliable guides to the good, and that gives the theist a way of being reconciled with them. It is consistent with this to hold that the good is something autonomous, independent of God's will, and independently recognizable by us.

This was the view of Kant, one of the great proponents of the autonomy of reason:

> Even the Holy One of the gospel must first be compared to our ideal of moral perfection before we can recognise him as such . . . where do we get our concept of God as the highest good? Solely from the Idea of moral perfection which reason traces *a priori* (Kant, 1964, p. 29).

If the good is categorical it is autonomous, and if it is autonomous then it is transparent to rational beings. God's power and knowledge may allow him to implant reliable rules of conduct in us, but it does not give him greater insight into its *a priori* structure.

Once reason has been isolated in this way, a question remains about its power to inspire. One can love God, but can one love impartial practical reason? Does it make one love virtue? Can one rise above self-interest and limited sympathy without becoming desiccated, if one has no emotional medium in which to do it?

Virtue is naturally loveable, because it is based on what we spontaneously admire. Moral example can make us love the good of others. But is it not likely that only a religious or spiritual perspective can solidly and reliably make us see others' well-being as of no more or less account than our own? Well, even if the thought that there is nothing special about me is given to me by reason, it can still be a moving and liberating experience. If one wishes to call it a spiritual experience, so be it. But it need involve no theistic framework.

We must turn finally to the promised meta-ethical discussion: if judgements about reasons are autonomous, what justifies us in making them and what makes them right or wrong?

11 Meta-ethics

The judgements we make about our reasons to act, believe or feel, may be called 'normative' judgements. It is illuminating to keep them all in mind, even though our concern is meta-ethical. For questions which are often asked about the status of ethical judgements in particular can usually be raised in general, about all of them. One can ask about all normative judgements, not just the ethical ones, whether they can be assessed as true or false, correct or incorrect; and if they can be, what makes them so, and how we know them to be so.

Framed in this way, the questions go to the heartland of philosophy. Only the roughest sketch map of its geography can be provided here. Consider to begin with, then, this very common question: Are normative judgements, or can they be, 'objective'?

The word is virtually irresistible – and virtually guaranteed to sow confusion. It sounds as though its opposite ought to be 'subjective'; but as soon as we are pressed on the matter we find that we really have no notion of what a 'subjective judgement' might be.

What causes our embarrassment here? A judgement must have a CONTENT – one judges that something is so; one can also suppose it to be so, wonder whether it is, hope that it is, and so on. To *judge* that it *is* so is to judge the proposition that it is so correct. In other words, if there is no proposition – no content of judgement to be judged correct or incorrect – there is no scope for judgement. The very notion of judgement requires a distinction between the act of judging and its content, the proposition which is judged correct or incorrect. But that distinction is available only if we are also able to separate in principle between what seems to the judger to be so, or to be correct, and what is so, or what is correct. It must be *possible* that what seems to the judger to be so is not so. And this possibility supplies objectivity: an objective discourse is one for which it can be maintained. If it cannot be maintained, there is no scope for objectivity – but neither is there scope for judgement. What we should really be asking, when we ask whether normative judgements are objective, is simply whether they are genuine judgements at all. It was just this question that David HUME (chapter 21) answered in the negative, for the moral case, when he said that 'Morality . . . is more properly felt than judg'd of' (Hume, 1978, p. 470).

Hume allowed for propositions, and hence judgements, such as 'All fathers are parents', which in his terminology merely express 'relations of ideas'. We may say that they are true by definition. These cases apart, however, he took propositions to be *factual* – their truth depended on whether or not they corresponded to facts. (The notion of truth by definition certainly requires very careful examination, but we need not delve into it here: if there are no such truths Hume's thesis would simply be that *all* propositions are factual.)

It is not easy to fit normative propositions in general into either of Hume's categories. A normative proposition looks like this:

If *p* then there is reason to believe, do or feel so-and-so.

For example:

(1) If the available data are deducible from hypothesis H and no other hypothesis available to us is simpler than H then there is some reason for us to believe H.
(2) If action A promotes someone's well-being then there is reason for me to do A.

It is not plausible that propositions of this kind are true by definition. (What definition? Of what word or words?) So if propositions are either true by definition or factual, they must be factual – or not genuine propositions, despite appearances.

Hume himself thought they could not be regarded as factual and he was clear that this conclusion applied to *all* supposed normative 'propositions', not just ethical ones. There are a number of routes to this conclusion. The simplest is the sheer implausibility of fitting the correspondence theory of truth to such purported propositions as (1) and (2). To what fact, in what domain of reality, would the truth of (1) correspond? Is it some fact of meta- or ultra-physics, beyond the facts of physics? The same question applies to (2). The fact that doing A would promote someone's well-being gives me reason to do A: are we to regard that as a *further* fact? A somewhat expanded version of this line of thought, which we may call (with a sideways glance in Kant's direction) the thesis of the autonomy of norms, stresses that cognition is of facts and reasons, so that the dualism of fact and norm is inherent to it. Facts 'in the world' give reasons; but *this* cannot itself be a fact in the world. No fact can correspond to a normative proposition, about what there is reason to believe, do or feel.

The point can also be developed EPISTEMOLOGICALLY (see chapter 1) – by appeal to the empiricist thesis that a factual proposition can only be known *a posteriori*, by empirical enquiry. How else could I establish the existence of a fact independent of my judgement, yet corresponding to its content? But normative propositions are not known by empirical enquiry. Indeed, they are – in the particular case of propositions about what gives me reason to believe what – *presupposed* by empirical enquiry.

If we follow Hume we must accept that normative 'propositions' are not genuine propositions, and that normative 'judgements' are not properly speaking judgements but rather expressions of an affective attitude or a decision or volition. Responses of this broadly Humean kind have been popular this century, and have been developed to high levels of sophistication by logical positivists in the 1930s and more recently by others. They remain strikingly influential in contemporary cultures, not least among many who consider themselves opposed to logical positivism. But it is an equally interesting point that in philosophy at least they seem for the moment to be losing ground.

What are the alternatives? One may deny Hume's claim that all propositions are either 'true by definition' or factual. Or one may deny his empiricism, holding that there are, for example, 'moral facts', or 'logical facts', that can be known but that our knowledge of them is not empirical. Or finally one may take the sceptical option: holding that while normative propositions are genuine propositions, purporting to correspond to a special domain of facts, we can have no knowledge of any such domain, or there can *be* no such domain. But this kind of extreme posture tends to be attractive only so long as one refuses to think it through fully.

My own preference is for the first response, that of denying Hume's claim that all propositions are either true by definition or factual. This response is broadly Kantian in respecting the autonomy of the normative, but it does not force us into Kant's rationalism. It can recognize that 'the heart has its reasons which reason knows nothing of'. But unlike Hume, it fully acknowledges the cognitive or propositional status of normative claims. It is a false dichotomy to say that morality is *more* properly felt than judged of. It is judged of on a basis that includes feeling.

This view distinguishes between normative and factual statements – the former obeying an epistemology of self-examination and discussion and the latter an epistemology of correspondence. Unlike the realist view that there are normative facts, to which true normative propositions correspond, it does not hold that there is something that makes normative propositions true or false, or correct or incorrect – in the realist's correspondence sense. In particular, the correctness of a normative proposition does not *correspond* to the fact that verdicts on it are ideally convergent. That is not its 'truth condition': it has no non-trivial one. So it is not made true by a fact about what people would agree to in an ideal contract, either.

The shift back towards 'objectivity' – towards recognizing normative judgements generally, and moral judgements in particular, as genuine *judgements*, has been a notable feature of moral philosophy in the last 30 years. It is striking that this shift has been happening even as rejection of normative objectivity has widened and deepened in the general culture of the western world. Will the general culture respond to this objectivist turn in a generation or two, as it responded to the anti-objective turn of philosophers in the 1920s and 1930s? We can only wait and see.

Further Reading

For each section, a few readings are suggested which discuss its topics, lead on to additional reading and often take a quite different view from that adopted here.

1   The Scope of Ethics: ch. 5, 'The Object of Morality', in Mackie (1977); ch. I, 'Introduction' in Sidgwick (1922); Parts I and II of Singer (1991); and ch. 1, 'Socrates' Question', and ch. 2, 'The Archimedean Point', in Williams (1985).

2   Blame, Admiration and Desire: Part One of Griffin (1986); Hurka (1983); Skorupski 'The Definition of Morality' in Phillips Griffiths (1993); and ch. 10, 'Morality, the Peculiar Institution', in Williams (1985).

3   Character, the Virtues and Freedom: Aristotle (1954); chs VII–XIV in Foot (1978); Glover (1970); and 'Freedom and Resentment ' in Strawson (1974).

4   An Ethical Theory – the Case of Utilitarianism: Part Two of Griffin (1986); 'Utilitarianism' in vol. X of Mill (1963–); and Smart and Williams (1973).

5   Impartiality: Rawls (1972); Darwall (1983); and Nagel (1991).

6   What can an Ethical Theory be Expected to Do?: Daniels (1979); ch. VI, 'Ethical Principles and Methods' and ch. XIII, 'Philosophical Intuitionism' in Sidgwick (1922); and Part One, 'Self-Defeating Theories' in Parfit (1984).

7   The Plurality of Value: MacIntyre (1981); ch. 11, 'Morality as a System of Hypothetical Imperatives' in Foot (1978); ch. 8, 'Internal and External Reasons', in Williams (1981).

8   Practical Reason: 'Of the Influencing Motives of the Will' (II, III, i) and 'Of Virtue and Vice in General' (III, II) in Hume (1978); Kant (1964); Book II, ch. I, 'The Principle and Method of Egoism' and concluding chapter, 'The Mutual Relations of the Three Methods', in Sidgwick (1922); and Schneewind 'Autonomy, Obligation, and Virtue: An Overview of Kant's Moral Philosophy' (1992).

9   The Categorical Imperative and Contractualism: Gauthier (1986); Hare (1993) 'Could Kant Have Been a Utilitarian?'; Scanlon 'Contractualism and Utilitarianism' in Sen and Williams (1982); and O'Neill (1989).

10   Reason, Morality and Religion: Chapter VIII, 'Intuitionism' in Sidgwick (1922); McDowell 'Values and Secondary Qualities' (1985); Dancy (1993); and Berg 'How Could Ethics Depend on Religion?', ch. 46 in Singer (1991).

11   Meta-ethics: Smith (1995); and McNaughton (1988).

References

Aristotle, 1954: *The Nichomachean Ethics*. London: Oxford University Press.
Berg, J. 1991: How Could Ethics Depend on Religion? In P. Singer (ed.) (1991).
Dancy, J. 1993: *Moral Reasons*. Oxford: Blackwell.
Daniels, N. 1979: Wide Reflective Equilibrium and Theory Acceptance in Ethics. *Journal of Philosophy*, 76.
Darwall, S. 1983: *Impartial Reason*. Ithaca and London: Cornell University Press.
Foot, P. 1978: *Virtues and Vices and Other Essays in Moral Philosophy*. Oxford: Blackwell.
Gauthier, D. 1986: *Morals by Agreement*. Oxford: Oxford University Press.
Glover, J. 1970: *Responsibility*. London: Routledge and Kegan Paul.
Griffin, J. 1986: *Well-Being, Its Meaning, Measurement, and Moral Importance*. Oxford: Clarendon Press.
Hare, R. M. 1993: Could Kant Have Been a Utilitarian?, *Utilitas*, 5.
Harman, G. 1977: *The Nature of Morality: An Introduction to Ethics*. New York: Oxford University Press.
Hume, D. 1978 [1739–40]: *A Treatise of Human Nature* (edited by L. A. Selby Bigge) (2nd edition with text revised and variant readings by P. H. Nidditch). Oxford: Clarendon Press.
Hurka, T. 1983: *Perfectionism*. Oxford: Oxford University Press.
Kant, I. 1964 [1785]: *Groundwork of the Metaphysic of Morals*. In *The Moral Law* (translated and analysed by H. J. Paton). New York: Harper and Row.
McDowell, J. 1985: Values and Secondary Qualities. In Honderich, T. (ed.) *Morality and Objectivity: A Tribute to J. L. Mackie*, London: Routledge and Kegan Paul.
MacIntyre, A. 1981: *After Virtue, A Study in Moral Theory*. London: Duckworth.
Mackie, J. L. 1977: *Ethics: Inventing Right and Wrong*. Harmondsworth: Penguin Books.
McNaughton, D. 1988: *Moral Vision: An Introduction to Ethics*, Oxford: Blackwell.
Mill, J. S. 1963– : *Utilitarianism*, in *The Collected Works of John Stuart Mill*, vol. X. London and Toronto: Routledge and University of Toronto Press.
Nagel, T. 1991: *Equality and Partiality*. London: Oxford University Press.
Nietzsche, F. 1974: *The Gay Science* (translated with commentary, by W. Kaufmann). New York: Vintage Books.
O'Neill, O. 1989: *Constructions of Reason: Explorations of Kant's Practical Philosophy*. Cambridge, Cambridge University Press.
Parfit, D. 1984: *Reasons and Persons*. Oxford: Clarendon Press.

Plato 1961: *Euthyphro* (translated by L. Cooper). In E. Hamilton and H. Cairns (eds), *The Complete Dialogues of Plato*, Princeton: Princeton University Press.

Rawls, J. 1972: *A Theory of Justice*. London: Oxford University Press.

Scanlon, T. 1982: Contractualism and Utilitarianism. In Sen, A. and Williams, B. (eds.), *Utilitarianism and Beyond*, Cambridge: Cambridge University Press.

Scheffler, S. 1992: *Human Morality*. London, Oxford University Press.

Schneewind, J. B. 1992: Autonomy, Obligation and Virtue: An Overview of Kant's Moral Philosophy. In P. Guyer (ed.) *The Cambridge Companion to Kant*, Cambridge: Cambridge University Press.

Sidgwick, H. 1922: *The Methods of Ethics*. London: Macmillan.

Singer, P. (ed.) 1991: *A Companion to Ethics*. Oxford: Blackwell.

Skorupski, J. 1993: The Definition of Morality. In A. Phillips Griffiths (ed.) *Ethics*, Cambridge: Cambridge University Press.

Smart, J. J. C. and Williams, B. 1973: *Utilitarianism For and Against*. Cambridge, Cambridge University Press.

Smith, M. (ed.) 1995: *Meta-Ethics*. Aldershot: Dartmouth Publishing Company.

Strawson, P. F. 1962: Freedom and Resentment. In *Freedom and Resentment* (1974), London: Methuen; and reprinted in G. Watson (ed.) *Free Will* (1982), Oxford: Oxford University Press.

Williams, B. 1981: *Moral Luck*. Cambridge: Cambridge University Press.

—— 1985: *Ethics and the Limits of Philosophy*. London: Fontana Paperbacks.

Discussion Questions

1   What makes a question an ethical question?

2   Could we accept moral judgements while seeing no reason to act on them? Could other reasons outweigh moral reasons?

3   Is there a special moral sense of blame? Can we understand morality without understanding blame?

4   Is morality dispensable?

5   Is every excellence of character a moral virtue? If not, what makes an excellence a moral virtue?

6   Do the ends of life stand outside morality or are they objects of moral assessment?

7   Can there be experts in morality – or in any other kind of normative judgement?

8   If moral freedom is a matter of degree, how much moral freedom is required for moral responsibility?

9   What notion of rationality is involved in the claim that moral freedom is rationality?

10   Is moral freedom compatible with our being governed by causal laws?

11   In what sense, if any, can there be ethical theory?

12   Are utilitarians right in holding that only the well-being of individuals has intrinsic ethical value? What rival views might there be?

13 If the well-being of some animals has less ethical value than the well-being of humans, does the well-being of some humans have less ethical value than the well-being of others?

14 What grounds might there be for choosing among different impartial principles for distributing well-being among individuals?

15 If standards of value are internal to different human activities, is it a mistake to seek a fully general ethical theory?

16 Is it a truth of logic that if a thing is blameworthy, we have reason not to do it?

17 How can reason be practical?

18 Does the claim that Kant's formalism cannot yield substantive results misunderstand the role of the categorical imperative in his ethical thinking?

19 What does it mean to treat a person as an end?

20 Should I do what is morally right because it is unfair not to?

21 Are moral judgements rationally evident in their own right?

22 Can morality be complete without religion?

23 What, if anything, makes ethical and other normative judgements true or false?

24 Are ethical views expressions of affective attitude, for example, rather than real judgements?

7

Aesthetics ──────────────────

Sebastian Gardner

Reflection on beauty and art gives rise to a rich and diverse field of philosophical issues. The first part of this chapter outlines the view of aesthetic experience and judgement which forms the background to contemporary discussions in aesthetics. Art is then examined in three parts, concentrating on the key concepts of representation, expression and meaning. Attention is drawn to the relation of topics in aesthetics to those in ethics, metaphysics and philosophy of mind, and to the place of aesthetics in some of the great systems in the history of philosophy.

The experiences that we have when we listen to music, read poetry and look at paintings or scenes in nature, have a distinctive immediate, emotional and contemplative character, and lead us to describe what we experience in a special vocabulary, and to use terms such as beautiful, exquisite, inspiring, moving, and so on. Philosophy employs the term 'aesthetic' to circumscribe this kind of experience. The appreciation of art provides the most complex and intense form of aesthetic experience, in which we are set apart from the real world and our powers of imagination are fully engaged, in dramatic contrast with everyday practical life. A less marked form of aesthetic awareness suffuses our perception of the world. Some degree of aesthetic receptivity is shown by the quiet influence that architecture exerts on our feelings, and the choices that we make daily in designing our environment manifest aesthetic preferences. The ability to respond aesthetically, and the opportunity to appreciate art, are important components of well-being. A world without aesthetic qualities would be an inferior, if not uninhabitable, world, and a person without any capacity for aesthetic response, if imaginable, would not qualify as a fully developed human being.

Many questions naturally occur to us in the course of thinking about and discussing works of art. What makes an object qualify as a work of art? What is the relation between form and content in a work of art? Does a work of art put us in touch with the mind of the artist? What are we to think when critics disagree about the meaning of a work? Why do we attach such importance to art? And so on. The philosophy of art aims to reflect on these largely familiar questions in a systematic way.

In addition to topics in the philosophy of art, there are a number of more abstract, less familiar questions concerning the nature of aesthetic experience in general to be considered. What explains the special character of aesthetic experience? Does a judgement that an object is beautiful report a fact about the object? Or does it express a feeling of the subject's? What is beauty? Thinkers in the eighteenth century, above all HUME (chapter 21) and KANT (chapter 22), took up these questions, and their view of aesthetic experience provides the broad framework within which most contemporary, analytical aesthetics operates. The first part of this chapter describes this framework, and the unresolved philosophical questions associated with it.

1 Aesthetic Experience and Judgement

Hume and Kant regard aesthetic judgement as exemplifying *taste*. Taste, in eighteenth-century aesthetics, refers to the special mental faculty, or special mode of employment of mental faculties, exercised in aesthetic judgement. What more this means can be grasped by attending to two absolutely central features of aesthetic judgement, insisted on by Hume (1965) and Kant (1987).

The first is that aesthetic judgement rests, fundamentally, on a felt response to an object (Kant, 1987, §1). Aesthetic judgement on an object cannot be passed secondhand: it requires personal acquaintance. The testimony of others may make me confident that I will find a newly published novel rewarding; but I cannot declare it to be so until I have read it myself. The condition of felt response is reflected in the fact that an aesthetic judgement, like an avowal of emotion, can be made sincerely or insincerely.

The second feature, closely connected to the first, is that rules or principles play no role, or only a highly diminished role, in aesthetic judgement (Kant, 1987, §8). It cannot be inferred that a piece of music is rapturous simply because it is in a particular key and orchestrated for certain instruments; or that a painting is dynamic because its composition has a certain geometric form. No laws connect the aesthetic qualities of an object with its sensory, non-aesthetic properties.

The point is not just that we are ignorant of rules for aesthetic judgement, or unable to agree on them, but that there would be little point in trying to formulate a set of rules: we could not use rules to produce in ourselves felt responses to objects; we could not, in cases of disagreement, reasonably ask another person to relinquish his or her judgement on the grounds that it conflicted with the rules; and whenever our own responses departed from the rules, we would quite rightly repudiate the rules rather than our responses. The fact that rules are otiose in determining the aesthetic qualities and value of objects reflects the fact that aesthetic interest is directed essentially towards *particular* objects, appreciated for their own sake, and not towards the formulation of general truths. To judge according to rules is to miss the uniqueness of objects, and so to fail to judge aesthetically. The place of rules, in guiding aesthetic judgement, is taken by particular, *exemplary* aesthetic objects; 'established models', as Hume calls them.

Hume and Kant agree, further, in rejecting the view (of earlier, classical and rationalist aesthetics) that aesthetic qualities are objective. Aesthetic objectivism maintains that aesthetic qualities are properties inhering in objects, and that aesthetic experience gives us knowledge of these properties. These properties may be identified with the object's formal properties, such as 'ideal proportion'; or they may be regarded as *sui generis* and irreducible to formal properties (Moore, 1984, sect. 112–21; McDowell in Schaper (ed.), 1983). (These varieties of aesthetic objectivism bear comparison with naturalism and intuitionism in ethics respectively.)

Aesthetic subjectivism denies that aesthetic qualities inhere in objects, and maintains that what it is for an object to be beautiful is for it to yield a certain response in the subject. In aesthetic experience I am *affected* by the object, and my response does not consist in knowledge of its properties. The object's formal and other non-aesthetic properties are merely what occasions the response. Aesthetic subjectivism, we will see, comes in various degrees of sophistication (which again may be compared with different forms of subjectivism in ethics).

Several very powerful considerations militate in favour of aesthetic subjectivism. Firstly, as Hume observes, and as we all recognize, the tastes and verdicts of different individuals and cultures vary enormously. (Lest this be doubted: Johnson said of Shakespeare that he has 'faults sufficient to obscure and overwhelm any other merit'; Voltaire compared Shakespeare's works to a 'dunghill'.) If aesthetic qualities are really out there, inhering in the object, why do we not all pick up on them? The point is not just that divergence is a fact of aesthetic life, but that we lack agreed methods for bringing divergent judgements into line. As was said earlier, rules cannot be appealed to. And aesthetic disagreement is unlike disagreement about colour, where conditions of physiological normality and standard lighting can be checked independently. Aesthetic qualities are deeply elusive: the 'positioning' of the observer needed to discern aesthetic qualities involves a plethora of temperamental and culturally parochial factors, all strongly indicative of subjectivity.

The second point was stressed by Kant (1987, §1). Pleasure is essential to the experience which grounds an aesthetic judgement. Pleasure, like pain, is, however, a mental state that does not represent a property of its object; as Kant says, pleasure 'designates nothing whatsoever in the object'. The necessary connection of aesthetic judgement with pleasure is readily explained by the subjectivist, but it presents aesthetic objectivism with an enormous difficulty: how can there be properties inherent in objects which *necessarily* generate pleasure simply through being apprehended – if not on the theological supposition that the world has been metaphysically tailored to delight us? Such properties would be metaphysically queer in the extreme. (This objection to aesthetic objectivism may be compared with Hume's objection to ethical objectivism, that it fails to capture the necessary connection of moral judgement with the will.)

This objection can be amplified. Objectivism, because it holds that aesthetic qualities inhere in objects, necessarily introduces a distinction between reality and appearance, between how things are and how things seem. Objectivism therefore implies that, even when an aesthetic judgement has withstood all of the toughest tests, we can still be mistaken about it: it is still possible that the object lacks the aesthetic quality attributed to it and is really aesthetically worthless. But this seems mad. It is simply not intelligible that our greatest art could 'really', appearances to the contrary, be worthless. Successful 'appearances' of aesthetic quality are as good as – indeed they are the same as! – the real thing: for aesthetic reality precisely *consists* in appearances.

Put another way, the usual motivation for objectivism in philosophy – namely, showing that our experiences and theories put us in touch with the world as it really is, independently of our means of representing it – has no relevance to the context of aesthetic experience, which has instead a strong similarity to the context of personal relationships, in which rewards other than the gaining of knowledge are sought primarily. The cognitive demand that mind should 'fit the world' does not apply to aesthetic interest, which is in this respect closer to desire than belief – what we want is for the world to fit *us*.

If, however, aesthetic subjectivism is common-sensical and philosophically plausible, it appears to carry a highly uncommon-sensical and unwelcome implication. If aesthetic qualities do not inhere in objects, what is to prevent the same object being judged beautiful by one person and ugly by another – both being equally justified in their pronouncements? If, as Hume puts it, 'All sentiment is right', there is no such thing as rightness or wrongness in aesthetic matters. In that case, an aesthetic judgement merely reports the speaker's mental state, and aesthetic preferences are on a par with gustatory preferences. It follows that aesthetic judgements cannot be contested or supported with reasons. This position, like emotivism in ethics, to which it corresponds, is inconsistent with common sense (Kant 1987, § 56).

Thus the *problem of taste*: of how to maintain the subjective felt basis of aesthetic judgement, without collapsing into unrestricted RELATIVISM (pp. 379–82). Hume and Kant respond to the problem of taste in different ways.

Hume contends that a 'standard of taste' – a basis for accepting some judgements of taste as correct and rejecting others as incorrect – is both philosophically defensible and visibly at work in the way that we actually conduct our aesthetic affairs. The standard of taste lies not in the object but in the sensibility of the subject. Aesthetic sensibility varies in its 'delicacy': 'When the organs are so fine as to allow nothing to escape them, and at the same time so exact as to perceive every ingredient in the composition, this we call delicacy of taste' (1965, p. 11). A correct aesthetic judgement is one that issues from a delicate sensibility operating under ideal conditions, which include the cultivation of taste through practice, the ability to make relevant comparisons, and freedom from prejudice. We defer to the judgement of those whose sensibilities we acknowledge to be superior, that of the 'critics'. (The concept of an IDEAL OBSERVER (p. 461) plays an analogous role in Hume's moral theory.)

It follows that for Hume, aesthetic judgements do not identify aesthetic qualities inhering in objects, but nor do they simply report the subject's experiences. An object's possession of an aesthetic quality consists in its being 'fitted' to generate a certain response in us. This distances Hume from the kind of unsophisticated subjectivism which ends up in relativism.

Hume's solution to the problem of taste depends on contingent facts of nature. Firstly, the fact that some 'particular forms or qualities [in objects] are calculated to please, and others to displease'. Secondly, the contingent uniformity of human sensibility, the sameness in 'the original structure of the internal fabric' of our minds – by which is meant, not that we are all equally competent aesthetic judges, but that our sensibilities are all *of a kind*. Where sensibilities differ, the differences are not arbitrary: aesthetic judgements diverge because of differences in delicacy, and other determinable deficiencies of taste; if the sensibilities of two subjects are equally delicate and their conditions of judgement otherwise the same, their judgements will coincide.

Kant and the Normative Aspect of Aesthetics

Kant rejects the kind of account proposed by Hume. Recall that the problem of taste is one of *justification*. The question is, on what grounds can we regard certain aesthetic judgements as being correct? For Kant, there is nothing in Hume's position which accounts for this, the normative aspect of aesthetic judgement. Hume does not validate the claim, implicit in all aesthetic judgement, that one's response is *appropriate* to the object, and that others *ought* to concur. Kant interprets this demand for agreement strongly, as applying to all other people without exception. On Kant's view, Hume offers only a causal, psychological explanation of why we do, as a matter of fact, defer to the judgements of 'critics' – he does not say why we *ought* to do so.

Kant's solution to the normative problem is, in essence, very simple, although his presentation of it is extremely intricate. Suppose that, in making an aesthetic judgement, we abstract from everything that might pertain to our contingent, natural, individually variable constitutions, and base our judgements solely on conditions that are strictly universal, in the sense of being available and common to all human beings. Suppose, that is, we base our aesthetic judgement on the bare form of the object and its interaction with our basic, universal mental powers of perception and understanding. (Kant's reasoning here recapitulates his analysis of moral judgement in terms of the categorical imperative.) Kant argues that this 'universal' standpoint can be achieved through freeing our awareness of the object from desire and practical concern (what he calls 'disinterestedness'), and from our conceptual understanding of it. When these stringent conditions are met, the judgement we make is valid for everyone. We then have what Kant calls a 'pure judgement of taste', which has 'universal validity'. Kant argues that it is indeed possible for the mere form of an object to delight us: certain perceptual forms stimulate our mental faculties optimally, by engendering in us a 'harmonious free play of imagination and understanding', awareness of which is pleasurable. Kant also gives a metaphysical interpretation of aesthetic experience: it makes us conscious of a connection that we have with the world, and with one another, which lies beyond the empirical world. Beauty therefore has a semi-religious and moral significance for Kant (he calls beauty the 'symbol of the good').

Even if we grant that Kant's theory of mental harmony accounts for the experience of beauty, a cost attaches to Kant's solution to the problem of taste. Purifying aesthetic judgement in the way that Kant requires leaves us with an austere, if not impoverished view of aesthetic experience – as consisting of nothing but an estimation of form. This limitation shows up in Kant's inability to do justice to the psychologically rich diversity of experience which art offers.

We are left, then, with a choice: between accepting Hume's account, without (Kant argues) any way of securing the normative aspect of aesthetic judgement; and accepting Kant's account, at the price of excluding from aesthetic experience our cultural identities, and everything in our psychological constitutions that is not strictly universal (which, the Humean will argue, leaves all too little). The task of providing a single account which incorporates and combines the insights of Hume and Kant remains.

A number of other issues remain unresolved within the framework of aesthetic subjectivism, including the formulation of the doctrine itself. Granted that aesthetic qualities are subjective, quite how subjective are they? Are they, for instance, on a par with colours and other secondary qualities of objects? Some theories maintain that they are. Others deny that aesthetic qualities are on a par with colours and compare them with 'looks' or 'aspects' of objects, or describe them as 'powers' to produce experiences. Another, more radical, possibility is that aesthetic judgements are not descriptive at all. WITTGENSTEIN (see chapter 29) suggests (1978) that aesthetic judgements are more like gestures and exclamations. On this view, the function of an aesthetic judgement is not to say anything about an object, but to 'put across' an experience. (These options are explored in Sibley, 1959 and 1965; Sibley and Tanner, 1968; Wollheim, 1980, Essay VI; Hungerland in Osborne (ed.), 1972; Meager, 1970; and Scruton, 1974.)

It is also necessary, as both Hume and Kant saw, to clarify the nature and role of reasons and criticism in aesthetic contexts. That aesthetic judgements can be justified distinguishes them from mere likings, and makes them, in a broad sense, rational. It is the job of the critic to identify the source's of a work's aesthetic qualities and determine what responses are appropriate (a further role for criticism, to be discussed later, is interpretation). But aesthetic reason-giving differs fundamentally from reason-giving in other contexts and has a number of peculiarities, which make it hard to understand (Beardsley, 1982, ch. 12; Scruton, 1979, ch. 5). It does not consist in inferring one proposition from another; it makes no use of rules, unlike moral reason-giving; and it makes no use of induction or generalizations, unlike reason-giving in science. Even the notion of consistency has little application to aesthetic judgements: liking Wagner does not mean that one ought to dislike Mozart. The problem, in sum, is that aesthetic reasons operate independently from all of the conditions that appear integral to the very concept of a reason.

Two further unresolved issues may be pointed out in conclusion. The first, bequeathed by Kant's notion of disinterestedness, concerns the importance of the concept of an 'aesthetic attitude'. Some theorists have claimed that aesthetic experience *consists in* the adoption of a special attitude in which objects are attended to dispassionately and 'for their own sake'. Indeed, Schopenhauer identifies the point of art with the metaphysical liberation from life that aesthetic contemplation, which does not involve the will, brings in its wake (1969, vol. 1, Third Book). The distinctive phenomenology of aesthetic experience makes this idea alluring, but what can be said about the aesthetic attitude, other than that it differs from and excludes practical and cognitive attitudes? Saying that an object is enjoyed 'for its own sake' really means that it is 'not enjoyed for any ulterior end'. Because descriptions of the aesthetic attitude tend to remain fundamentally negative, it is unclear what value the concept has, stripped of the metaphysical interpretation that makes it significant for Schopenhauer (see, however, Beardsley, 1982, ch. 16).

A second issue concerns the concept of beauty, which has undergone a dramatic reversal of fortunes in the history of aesthetics. Classical aesthetics takes it for granted that beauty is the only, or at least the fundamental, aesthetic quality. Some modern writers propose by contrast that 'beautiful' is merely a catch-all term, roughly equivalent to 'aesthetically commendable', and that there is, as ordinary language implies, a limitless plurality of aesthetic qualities, encompassing elegance, grace, poignancy and so on. There is, however, a philosophical issue here which needs to be addressed. The idea that beauty is not just one aesthetic quality among many, but is somehow pre-eminent and accounts for the unity of aesthetic experience, is compelling, and anyone who denies this in favour of the 'pluralist' view is challenged to find an alternative account of the unity of the aesthetic. A recent defence of the concept of beauty is in Mothersill (1984).

2 The Essence of Art

HEGEL (see chapter 23) asserts that art 'pervades what is sensuous with mind', and that art accordingly has 'a higher rank than anything produced by nature, which has not sustained this passage through the mind' (1993, pp. 15, 34). Whether or not Hegel's view of the superiority of art is justified, the philosophy of art, to which we now turn, shares Hegel's conception of art as a synthesis of mind with something other than itself, in which the mind 'recognises itself'; and his rejection of the view that a work of art is simply an artefact possessing aesthetic qualities of a kind also found in nature. Theories of art attempt to elucidate the nature of the connection with the mind which makes an object a work of art. Such attempts assume that the concept of art picks out more than a merely nominal, or historically accidental phenomenon – that art has, in short, an essence.

2.1 Definitions of art

Attempts have been made to capture the essence of art in a simple definitional formula. Two representative examples are the definition of art as the imitation of beautiful nature, and the definition of art as the communication of feeling.

If we consider such definitions, it is clear that they are wide open to counter-examples. Not every work of art is an imitation of beautiful nature, or communicates feeling: novels are rarely if ever beautiful, instrumental music is not imitative and much visual art does not communicate feeling. And even if these formulae provided necessary conditions for art, they could hardly provide sufficient conditions: some industrial machinery is beautiful, wax-works are imitative, racist propaganda communicates feelings.

One response to the failure of definitions of this simple kind is scepticism. It has been claimed that the difficulty of defining art is a reflection of there *not being* an essence of art. Proponents of this view (discussed in Tilghman, 1984) have often appealed to Wittgenstein's notion that family resemblances between instances of a concept may be all that there is to be found.

A recent, much-discussed attempt to define art – which is built on the Wittgensteinian denial that art has an essence, but maintains that a definition is nevertheless possible – is the *institutional theory*. The institutional theory accepts that works of art cannot be defined in terms of their intrinsic, perceptible properties, and turns instead to their extrinsic, social properties. The theory says that something is a work of art if a member of the artworld has conferred on it the status of being a candidate for appreciation, or if it has been created in order to be presented to the artworld (Dickie, 1984). The artworld is a nebulous entity that includes artists, critics, and some portion of the general public. 'Work of art' is, on this account, an 'honorific' term: being a work of art is a non-perceptible property which depends upon an object's place in a cultural context (analogous to being 'in public ownership' or 'sacred'). This approach receives an additional stimulus from the way in which some avant-garde art of this century – paradigmatically, Duchamp's ready-made *Fountain*, a mass-produced urinal entered for exhibition unaltered by the artist – appears to have repudiated all traditional criteria for art.

There is, however, something missing at the heart of the institutional theory. It tells us *that* members of the artworld bestow the status of art on some objects rather than others; but not *why* they do so. It thus leaves out of account the *reasons* for calling something a work of art – the conditions taken to justify application of the concept. This is something that ought to figure in a philosophical, as opposed to a sociological, treatment of the concept of art (Wollheim, 1980, Essay I).

Proponents of the institutional theory seek to deflect this criticism by saying that they are concerned with the 'classificatory' sense of art, not the 'evaluative' sense in which to call something a work of art is to recommend it for appreciation. But this invites the further objection, that it is simply a mistake to separate the classificatory sense of art from the evaluative. Evaluation is just as integral to the concept of art as it is to moral concepts. We do not first classify objects as art, and then discover that they happen to be aesthetically rewarding: conceptually, there is only one move here.

What moral is to be drawn from these attempts to define art? It cannot be ruled out that a complex definition, perhaps combining the concepts of imitation and communication in a complex way and adding further conditions, could be devised to encompass all and only those objects that we consider to be works of art, and at the same time respect the evaluative nature of the concept of art. But what the difficulty of reading off an adequate definition of art from the surface of our ordinary conception of art may be taken to show, more importantly, is that no definition of art can be expected, and in any case cannot hold much interest, in advance of a *theory* of art. A theory of art does not require there to be a simple, manifest property shared by each and every work of art; it allows that what unifies art – its essence – may not be visible at its surface, and probes beneath the surface to locate it.

A theory of art may take one of two forms. It may aim directly at developing a single concept capturing the essence of art. Or it may proceed by building up from an examination of the various specific dimensions of works of art. The first, more traditional approach is explored below; the second, more modest approach favoured in contemporary aesthetics, is explored in the following section.

2.2 *Theories of art*

Of the numerous and enormously varied theories of art that have appeared in the history of aesthetics, three may be singled out as having greatest importance. These are the mimetic, formalist and expression theories.

Even if the concept of imitation, as ordinarily understood, does not straightforwardly define art, it may be supposed that the concept can be *developed* beyond its ordinary scope. On this claim rests the theory that art consists in *mimesis* – a Greek term rendered approximately by imitation, copying or representation (see Plato, 1955, Aristotle, 1987, and chapter 15 of this volume). The object of mimesis is usually identified with nature, inclusive of human nature. Although, as observed earlier, some art, such as instrumental music, appears to be non-representational, it is open to the mimetic theorist to contend otherwise: in antiquity it was thought that music imitates the order and harmony of the cosmos and the soul. The mimetic theory construes the connection of art with the mind asserted by Hegel in the following way: works of art carry over the mind's fundamental function of *representing* the world.

Granted that the concept of representation is open to being extended, the mimetic theory is open to an objection (Hegel, 1993, LXI–LXVII). Even if we accept that it is natural to enjoy imitation and the skill exhibited therein, as Aristotle observes, why should we find imitation valuable in the *special* way that art is found valuable? The values connected conceptually with representation are cognitive, truth-orientated values such as accuracy and comprehensiveness. These have some role in art – verisimilitude of plot and character in literature for instance – and certainly truth is something we value. But truth does not capture the real interest of art. A work of art must come into its own in the field of our experience, and not fall away in the manner of a transparent window on to the world or vehicle for communicating truths about it. The mimetic theory thus appears to misconstrue the value of art.

The mimeticist's conception of representation accordingly needs to be tightened up. Representation which is *artistic* must be circumscribed in subject and mode: it must be of particular kinds of things, represented in a particular way. It is therefore no accident that mimetic theorists have characteristically gone on to claim that art must idealize its subject matter. But once the mimetic theory has undergone this modification, the essence of art has been been shifted away from bare representation, in the direction of whatever it is about art that *enables* it to idealize its subjects.

Artistic Form

A strong candidate for this role is artistic form. Where the mimetic theory ties art down to the real world, *formalism* allows the work of art to float free, insisting that only form, the complex arrangement of parts unique to each individual work, has artistic significance. Only what is internal to the work is relevant to its status as art; any outward references, to a real or imaginary world, are irrelevant. The concept of form can be made more or less narrow; at its narrowest, only sensory parts and their relations are intended. Formalists differ over the continuity of form in art with form in nature: Kant holds that artistic form must be recognizably of a kind with natural form; Bell (1914, ch. 1), the boldest recent exponent of formalism, holds that artistic form, labelled 'significant form', is in effect exclusive to art. Appreciation of art consists, for the formalist, not in merely recognizing form, but in responding to it: Kant's theory of mental harmony has already been mentioned; Bell posits a unique kind of 'artistic emotion' accompanying the recognition of significant form. According to formalism, what the mind recognizes of itself in works of art is its power of locating *order in perception*, exercised to a specially heightened degree.

The weakness of formalism most frequently indicated by its critics concerns the concept of form, which is argued to be too indefinite to play the role that is asked of it. Asked to specify the kind of form that matters in art, the formalist uses notions such as 'balance' or 'uniformity amidst variety'; but it proves impossible to define these in a way that prevents them from applying to any object whatsoever. The formalist is consequently pushed to declare that artistic form is *indefinable*. Bell embraces this claim, but his theory is then charged with vacuousness: he explains significant form in terms of the 'artistic emotion' that it induces, but then refers us back to 'significant form' for our understanding of artistic emotion.

Whatever the force of this point against Bell, there is another objection to be pressed. Is our interest in form really as uncontaminated with ulterior, worldly concerns as formalists suppose? Formal values may sometimes be of self-sufficient aesthetic interest, but much more commonly they serve non-formal ends: form is the vehicle through which a work articulates its non-formal meaning, apart from which form tends to become artistically uninteresting and merely decorative. In other terms, the attempt to disentangle form from content leaves, on the side of form, an insufficiently significant residue.

This objection to formalism may be pressed on behalf of the mimetic theory; but it also points in the direction of the *expression* theory. The connection of art with feeling, we said earlier, cannot consist in a straightforward equation of art with the communication of feeling. The expression theory of art seeks to offer a more sophisticated and persuasive account of the central place of emotion in art.

The rudiments of the expression theory lie in writings of the Romantics, but it was first formulated philosophically by Croce (1992), who bound it up with the tenets of German idealism. The more accessible version of the theory presented by Collingwood (1937) detaches it from METAPHYSICS (chapter 2), and understands artistic expression as a special form of self-expression. Artistic expression is a process in which the artist begins with an indefinite and inchoate emotional state, for which he or she labours to find a uniquely apt concrete articulation, and in so doing transforms his or her mental state into something definite, tangible and intelligible. What the artist creates does not describe his or her state of mind, so much as incorporate it; analogously to the way in which bodily expressions such as smiles and grimaces embody mental life.

Since the product of expression can not be known before the process is complete, expression cannot consist in exercising a technique: it must take whatever particular shape is commanded by the particular emotion which the artist's mind is impelled to clarify. Because expression is not undertaken with any further end in view, artistic creation contrasts with instrumental activities, in which means and ends are distinct; these Collingwood calls 'craft', and opposes to 'art proper'. Mistaken, 'technical' conceptions of art – which include the conception of art as mimesis or communication of feeling – arise from a failure to grasp this distinction.

On the side of artistic appreciation, the theory claims that the audience retraces in the course of appreciating a work of art the route pursued by the artist: their appreciation re-enacts the artist's creative process and thereby retrieves his or her psychological state (Elliott in Osborne (ed.), 1972). The relation of the audience to the work of art thus mirrors the artist's under-standing of his or her own mind. The capacity of a work of art to transmit the artist's psychological state is a necessary consequence of successful expres-sion. The expression theory, by giving primacy to the perspective of the artist rather than (as on the mimetic and formalist theories) that of the audience, offers a very strong interpretation of Hegel's claim that the mind 'recognises itself' in works of art: works of art do not merely exhibit mental features, they, as it were, contain mind.

The expression theory's emphasis on the psychology of the artist exposes it to criticism. The mimeticist will object that not only emotions, but also ideas, which refer to the world, are expressed by art, whose legitimate subject is not restricted to the artist's own mind. At the other extreme, the formalist will challenge the expression theory to say how a supremely self-contained and self-sustaining work such as a Ming vase, can be construed as a product of personal expression.

The first objection can be met by explaining that what the theory means by emotion is any mental state, however permeated with concepts and thought, that has some emotional charge. The condition that emotion be present is plausible, for most people would agree that mere beliefs without any psychological resonance do not provide sufficient material for art. The scope of the thoughts embedded in the artist's emotion is furthermore left open, which means that the artist's moral and spiritual view of the world and conception of life are proper material for expression, and that what a work of art expresses need not include a personal, biographical reference to the artist.

The formalist's objection cannot be met by expanding the terms of the theory, and obliges the expression theorist to adopt a semi-stipulative measure. The theory must declare that objects possessing only formal virtues do not qualify as full-blooded instances of works of art. This move is obviously acceptable only on the assumption that art's centre of gravity lies in the psychology of the artist; it will be rejected by the formalist as begging the question, and as betraying the theory's fundamentally parochial, pro-Romantic bias.

Of the three theories considered, it is fair to say that – if a monopoly is to be granted – then the expression theory has strengths that give it the edge over the mimetic theory and formalism. These strengths also account for the theory's continued hold on our thinking about art. It may also be pointed out in its favour, that the expression theory allows the understanding of art to draw on the resources of psychological theory (Wollheim, 1987); an ultimate verdict on the theory will depend in part on what value is found in such developments.

A fourth theory, which is not traditional but dominates much contemporary discourse about art, should be mentioned in conclusion. This is the *semiotic* theory of art, which proposes that works and forms of art be analysed in terms of logico–linguistic categories such as signification, reference, denotation, and syntactic and semantic rules. Goodman (1976), the principal exponent of the semiotic theory, analyses representation and expression in such terms. The semiotic theory of art is also assumed by structuralist and post-structuralist literary theory, which grafts linguistic science and philosophical theories of language onto the study of literature. On the semiotic theory, art is a symbol system much like language, and not just in the metaphorical sense in which an expression theorist might grant that art is a 'language of emotion'.

What the worth of the semiotic theory turns on can be indicated with reasonable assurance. The theory derives its motivation from, firstly, a rejection of the primacy of psychological and experiential concepts (these, it claims, are not autonomous and need to be understood in terms of language and signification); and, secondly, a belief in the radically conventional nature of art (which it grounds on a blanket rejection of philosophical realism). Both strands are explicit in the work of Goodman, and in structuralism and post-structuralism. It follows that the semiotic theory's austere perspective on art must be rejected by anyone who wishes to maintain that art is essentially connected with certain forms of experience; as it may also be, on the supposition that human psychology sets universal, non-conventional parameters to art. This last idea provides the basis for a fifth theory of art, the naturalistic, which will be described in section 4 below.

3 The Dimensions of Art

Recent work in analytical philosophy of art has adopted the second, more piecemeal and empirical, approach described earlier to the construction of a theory of art. Rather than aim directly at a general, overarching characterization of art, it has concentrated on the specific dimensions which constitute works of art, in the belief that an accurate picture of art as a whole will emerge out of a proper understanding of its parts. Representation, expression and meaning have been closely analysed, in terms of the specific forms that they take in each of the arts. This section traces the debates surrounding these concepts in terms of the form of art most strongly associated with each: representation in painting, expression in music, and meaning in literature.

(Issues concerning the ontology of works of art, the nature of fiction, emotional response to fiction, and metaphor, also belong in this context, and would be included in a fuller account of analytic philosophy of art.)

3.1 Representation

When we look at Titian's *The Rape of Europa*, we do not see, or do not just see, pigment distributed across the two-dimensional surface of a canvas: we see a woman borne across the sea aloft a white bull. Paintings represent or depict things, both real and imaginary.

We are concerned here with what paintings represent in a visual, as opposed to interpretative, sense. A painting of a man clutching a stone may represent St Jerome, and a lute with a broken string in a still-life may represent Discord. In order to make such iconographic identifications, however, a human figure and a musical instrument must first be seen in the picture, and this is a perceptual matter; it is something that art historical scholarship could not do for us. Visual representation is something we take for granted. When we cease to do so, a philosophical question arises: What makes pictorial representation possible? The mimetic theory of art, it should be noted, does not answer this question: it merely assumes that pictorial representation is possible.

The philosophical puzzle surrounding pictorial representation comes into focus when one reflects on the difficulties associated with the commonsensical view of how pictures work. Common sense says that pictorial representation consists in *resemblance*: a painting represents X by *looking like* X. This may at first seem to be not just self-evident, but the only possible answer. This common sense view of pictorial representation is reflected in the idea that deception provides the test for successful representation – as illustrated by the story of Zeuxis' painting of vines, which, according to Pliny, deceived the birds into flying down to consume the grapes he had depicted.

It is, however, simply and plainly false that canvases marked with pigments resemble the things that they represent. *The Rape of Europa* does not even begin to share the physical dimensions of the scene that it represents! In fact, each canvas resembles nothing so much as other canvases – but it does not, of course, represent them.

This objection may seem too blunt, for it may seem to have missed the obvious point that for a canvas to represent something, it must be seen, not as a mere physical object, but *as a picture*. But this just re-states the problem, which now becomes: What is it for a canvas to be seen as a picture?

It may then be ventured that what the resemblance theory really means, is that a painting of X represents X when it affords us an *experience* which is like the experience of really perceiving X. Sometimes this is put by saying that the canvas gives us an 'image' which is the same as that which we would receive from the real thing.

Relocating the resemblance at the level of an experience or image, rather than that of the canvas, does not, however, advance our understanding: for, once again, what is wanted is an account of *how* the two-dimensional, differentiated surface of Titian's painting can be made to 'have the look' − afford the visual experience or create the image − of a woman carried on the back of a bull.

Very quickly it comes to seem that resemblance does not provide the explanation of pictorial representation. In its place, theorists turn to other, less obvious notions. (However, for a recent defence of pictorial representation in terms of experienced resemblance, see Peacocke, 1987.)

The case against resemblance was first set out, at length and with sophistication, by Gombrich (1960). Gombrich attacked in particular the assumption, which accompanies the resemblance view, that there is such a thing as an 'innocent eye' − that an artist can simply 'copy what he sees' by attending to his visual experience, in advance of any interpretation of the world.

Goodman (1976, ch. 1) carries this line further by rejecting altogether the idea that pictorial representation is a matter of perception. On Goodman's account, depiction is a species of denotation: knowing what a picture represents is purely a matter of interpretation, which requires a grasp of a 'symbol system'. Realism in painting is just a function of the familiarity of a symbol system, the ease with which it imparts information.

As was said earlier, the motivation for Goodman's semiotic view is very general. There is, however, much to query in his claim that pictures are interpreted. It *seems* to us that pictures give us visual experiences, and that this is how they differ from prose descriptions, maps, company logos, road signs and other visual symbols that need to be read. Goodman's theory implies that this impression of difference is an illusion. But if so, what does the illusion of having a visual experience consist in − if not in having a visual experience?

Gombrich himself does not assimilate pictorial representation to interpretation completely. On Gombrich's account, a painting represents X by giving us an *illusion* of X. How illusions are created is explained in terms of the representational practices evolved in the history of art. Art develops through a process of 'making and matching'. Visual 'schema' are originally fabricated semi-arbitrarily in order to represent objects, without resemblance playing any kind of role. They are then modified by artists in the light of their perceptual experience, a historical process which results in increasingly life-like representations (a process which Gombrich models on POPPER's (pp. 291–4) conception of the development of scientific theories). Resemblance lies, if anywhere, at the end of the history of pictorial art, not at its beginning.

It is true that some visual representations – such as Escher's *trompe l'oeil* drawings – create illusions, but it is not true that most paintings have this effect: in looking at a painting we do not find ourselves having to correct a tendency to *mistake* its content for reality, as the concept of illusion would imply. Furthermore, the illusion theory entails that in seeing what a painting represents, we stop being aware of the material canvas, as the illusion takes hold. This, however, contradicts the fact that appreciating a painting involves simultaneous, complex awareness of its brushwork and what it represents (see Wollheim, 1974, ch. 13).

Representation and Seeing In

The weaknesses of the views considered so far suggest that we need to posit a form of visual perception which is, as it were, inherently imaginative. Wollheim's theory does this (Wollheim, 1980, Essay V; 1987, pp. 46–77). It proposes that pictorial representation engages a species of perception which Wollheim calls *seeing in*. Wollheim argues for this claim as follows. An important clue as to the underlying nature of the experience of painting lies in the fact that paintings give us experiences of something absent or non-existent. Now this is something that occurs also in dreams, daydreams and hallucination. It may be ventured that pictorial representation exploits and cultivates a power that the mind possesses innately – the power to generate visual experiences out of itself. When this capacity is exercised in the course of perceiving the external world and fused with perception of external objects – as it is in numerous contexts outside painting: things are seen in Rorschach ink blots, clouds, and damp-stained walls – we then have seeing in. Seeing in is not involved in reading maps or interpreting visual signs; here there is no experience of an absent object. On this theory, what it is for Vermeer's *View of Delft* to represent a townscape is for the canvas to be marked in a way that allows us to see a townscape in it. Seeing in does not presuppose a resemblance between the canvas and what the painting represents; according to Wollheim, no systematic account can be given of how the marking of a canvas determines what is seen in it. Wollheim (1987) proceeds to develop a general account of painting which shows how its value as an art presupposes its rootedness in seeing in and other psychological powers.

3.2 Expression

It is not long before the fugue recedes into its initial calm. Soon, a final crescendo leads us to what appears to be a triumphant conclusion. But no; at the very moment when victory seems to be in our grasp, the music loses all confidence, comes to a halt on a chord that is far from final, and then sinks despondently back into the minor key. Could disillusionment be more graphically expressed? It is the cry of despair; the hoped-for consolation has failed to materialize. (Hopkins, 1982, p. 383)

This passage describes emotions expressed in the final movement of Beethoven's *Piano Sonata Op. 110*. The expressive qualities of works of art are a sub-class of their aesthetic qualities, distinguished by the employment of terms whose primary use lies in describing people's emotions. Expressive qualities are integral to the beauty and meaning of music. Since the nineteenth century, many have believed that music's incomparable power of expression secures for it a position of supremacy among the arts (Walter Pater claimed that 'all art constantly aspires towards the condition of music').

Describing music in expressive terms exemplifies a broad tendency to talk about works of art as if they were sentient entities: they are described as having 'organic unity', 'vitality' and so on. And yet, we do not, of course, really believe or mean to imply that works of art *have* feelings. So, given that a musical work is at one level just a sequence of sound, just as a painting is nothing but a pigmented canvas, the fundamental problem of expression in art, brought out most sharply by music, is the following: How is it possible for a work of art to express emotion?

The obvious answer would seem to be that musical works have expressive qualities because they serve, as the expression theory of art says, as vehicles for expressing the emotions of the composer. This is, however, no answer. Even if the expression theory of art is accepted, nothing in it explains how it is possible for a composer to use patterns of sound to express emotion. It merely takes that fact for granted.

If it does not help to think of the emotion expressed by music as located in the mind of the composer, it is equally mistaken to attempt to locate it in the mind of the listener: that is, to analyse a musical work's expression of an emotion as its power to *arouse* that emotion in the listener. Bluntly: we are not *ourselves* made melancholic, or frozen with grief, by music that we would describe in those terms – fortunately. The listener does not *have* the emotion which the music expresses, in the same sense as she has emotions in life. In listening to music, the emotion which is expressed seems to be located 'out there' in the music, not in oneself. The heart of the problem lies in understanding how emotion can be 'objectified' in this fashion – how it can be ascribed neither to the composer nor to the listener, but rather somehow hover, suspended, between them.

Further reflection shows that being moved by music consists, typically, not in simply recognizing or sharing the emotion expressed by music, but in *reacting* to it – in the way that a person may respond to the emotional condition of another, for example, by responding to their distress with pity. The relation is one of sympathy rather than empathy. We are familiar with this structure in the context of representational art, where, in drama, literature and painting, we feel for the protagonist. Its appearance in music reinforces the difficulty of musical expression, since instrumental music precisely lacks the representational content that would make emotional response to music intelligible as a case of participating in a fiction (it has no characters or plot).

At this point, one option is to re-conceive the problem of musical expression as merely one of language: of finding an adequate logical characterization of how terms are used in the ascription of expressive qualities. An account of this sort – which appears to cut rather than untie the Gordian knot – is again advanced by Goodman (1976, pp. 85–95).

An alternative way out of the problem is musical formalism, a position defended by Hanslick (1986). Hanslick grants that music has emotional *effects* on listeners; but he denies that there is any genuine sense in which music *expresses* emotion. Hanslick has both an argument for denying that music can express emotion, and an account of why we should come to suppose falsely that it can. For music to express emotion, there would have to be an intrinsic relation between them. Hanslick argues that this is impossible, on the grounds that emotions are intentional: they have objects and involve thoughts and concepts; whereas instrumental music lacks objects and does not involve thoughts or concepts. Since music is incapable of presenting any object – what it presents is only itself – it cannot have an intrinsic relation to emotion.

What music can do, Hanslick argues, is express what he calls 'musical ideas', which are its dynamic properties: 'The content of music is tonally moving forms' (1986, p. 29). Tonality provides a sort of auditory space within which the melody, harmony and rhythm of music moves (see Scruton, 1983, ch. 8). Hanslick draws an analogy with the visual movement found in arabesque ornamentation.

Like music, episodes of emotion have dynamic properties, in addition to and independently from their conceptual content, since they involve changes in intensity and bodily feeling. Because music and episodes of emotions share dynamic properties, it is possible for us to fill in, arbitrarily, the musical idea expressed by a piece of music with some particular emotion supplied by our own emotional repertoire: giving us the illusion that the music expresses that particular emotion. For Hanslick, musical appreciation stops properly at the beauty of musical form. Anything else is merely personal emotional association.

Despite its subtlety, Hanslick's repudiation of emotion is not easy to accept: describing musical works in terms of their expressive qualities seems to be, not just natural, but indispensable for justifying our estimates of their artistic value. The thought that music is intrinsically expressive should not be given up unless absolutely necessary. Can anything be salvaged?

Although music does not speak or behave, an analogy between the recognition of emotion in music and in people can be suggested. Perhaps music derives its expressive power from its resemblance to emotionally expressive features of human bodily behaviour, physiognomy and speech (Kivy, 1989). That would explain the phenomenological similarity between hearing emotion in music, and perceiving emotion in the body or voice of another person: in both, mental life seems to have been made sensuously palpable.

This theory is in a position to deflect Hanslick's objection that music lacks the conceptual components necessary for an intrinsic connection with emotion. Bodily and vocal features can express emotional states without communicating their objects: we can recognize that a person is distressed from the way they look or sound, without knowing what they are distressed about.

The human analogy theory soon encounters difficulties, however. It shares the weakness of the resemblance theory of pictorial representation – namely, the difficulty of locating relevant resemblances. What exactly are the features shared by music and human bodies? Just as canvases are unlike the things represented in pictures, a plain description of music in terms of key, rhythm and so on reveals little that is common to music and human bodies. It is true that both tempo and bodily movement can be slow, but such properties are no more emotionally definite than Hanslick's 'musical ideas': if a sad piece of music is slow, what makes its slowness that of sadness rather than serenity? The objection then arises that significant likenesses between music and human bodies can only be identified *after* the music has been re-described in expressive terms, such as '*ponderously* slow'. Only once music has been experienced as expressive does it become possible to model it imaginatively on the human figure. Musical expression remains unexplained.

A second theory that appeals to a resemblance between music and emotion is that of Langer (1942, ch. 8). On Langer's theory, musical works are symbols of a special kind. Unlike the discursive symbolism of language, music shares the 'logical form' of emotion and, by virtue of doing so, articulates and *presents* emotion, as language cannot. Here it is the *inner* aspect of emotion, rather than its outer bodily expression, which music is said to mirror ('Music is our myth of the inner life', Langer, 1942, p. 245).

A similar problem, however, confronts Langer's theory. In what non-metaphorical sense does emotion have 'logical form'? And in any case, the notion of formal similarity is so plastic and open-ended that it can surely be found between any emotion and any piece of music. Again, the alleged isomorphism of music with emotion seems to be either non-existent, or insufficiently definite to explain musical expression.

If neither the outer nor the inner aspect of emotion has a connection with music which accounts for its expressiveness, it may seem that enquiry grinds to a halt (Budd, 1985, concludes, after intensive examination of the above theories, and others, that none succeeds). One remaining avenue, however, is to suppose that the connection of music with emotion is more direct than we have hitherto assumed it must be: that it does not take a detour via resemblance.

A clue to the explanation of expressive qualities may lie in the fact that the mind has, as Hume put it, a natural propensity to spread itself on to the world, and experience objects as emotionally coloured. Projection, as this may be called, is a well-attested psychological phenomenon. If this is joined with a second, equally Humean assumption, to the effect that certain objects in the world are fitted by nature to serve as recipients for the projection of specific emotional states, then we are on the way to a conception of artistic expression as reposing on, and cultivating, a natural tendency of ours to dye objects in the world with our emotions (Wollheim, 1980, sections 15–19; 1987, pp. 80–7). If Hanslick's repudiation of emotion is to be avoided, an assumption along these lines seems to be at least necessary.

3.3 Meaning

That works of art have meaning – over and above their representational content, and aesthetic and expressive qualities – is implied by the fact that works of art allow for, and call for, understanding. Questions of meaning in art are best approached through the concept of INTERPRETATION (pp. 268–74). Interpretation aims to identify the meanings of works of art, and is one of the functions of criticism. Questions of interpretation arise of course in all the arts – is Beethoven's *Missa Solemnis* a Christian or a Romantic work? does Titian's *The Flaying of Marsyus* celebrate the triumph of spirit over body, or that of body over spirit? – but it is literature, and literary criticism, that put the issues surrounding interpretation in sharpest focus.

Of all the arts, literature allows least scope for aesthetic response to operate independently of interpretation: a liking for a literary work not accompanied by so much as a rudimentary grasp of its meaning fails altogether to qualify as an appreciation of it. This is due to the fact that the medium of literature, natural language, is, unlike pigment, sound or stone, inherently meaningful; which, plausibly, allows literary works to bear more conceptually complex meanings than works in other media; for which reason literary works generate greater interpretative controversy.

It is hard to find a great literary work for which different interpretations have not been proposed. Is *Hamlet* correctly understood in terms of Freud's theory of the Oedipus complex? Does *Paradise Lost* represent Satan as a moral being 'far superior to his God', as Shelley claims? Do Shakespeare's Sonnets comprise a unified narrative charting the course of Shakespeare's own experience? Are Kafka's writings religious or political parables, or articulations of the personal angst evident in his diaries and letters? Does a proper appreciation of Yeats' poetry presuppose knowledge of his mythological system? To each of these questions critics have returned opposite answers.

Two questions are forced on us by differences in interpretation. Firstly, can biographical information concerning the author serve as legitimate evidence for or against a certain interpretation? Secondly, can we talk of one interpretation as being the correct interpretation of a work?

The starting point for the first question is the attack made by Wimsatt and Beardsley on what they call the 'intentional fallacy' (in Newton-de Molina, 1984). On their view, critics err in supposing that information about the author, or any kind of evidence 'external' to a poetic text (for instance, about its original cultural circumstances), can elucidate its meaning as a *literary* object; all that is pertinent to the meaning of a poem can be gleaned by careful attention to the words on the page. To suppose otherwise is to commit the fallacy of confusing a psychological fact about the author with a fact about the poem, of failing to distinguish a causal explanation of a work from a literary interpretation of it.

Two opposing views of the relation between the meaning of a literary work (textual meaning) and the intentions of the author (authorial meaning) can be staked out. *Intentionalism* identifies textual meaning with authorial meaning: what the text means is what the author meant (Wollheim, 1980, Essay IV). *Anti-intentionalism* denies that textual meaning is authorial meaning, and asserts its autonomy: textual meaning resides objectively in the work, 'embodied in the language', and has nothing to do, conceptually, with what the author may have meant (if the two happen to be the same, that is a coincidence without significance, for the anti-intentionalist). These positions have connections with traditional theories of art: the expression theory is straightforwardly committed to intentionalism, formalism to anti-intentionalism (the mimetic theory is uncommitted).

What, then, are the main considerations in the argument over intentionalism? There is much to be said, but some of the most important points are the following.

On the one hand, it seems right that a literary work, considered as a work of art, should be judged in terms of the experience of reading it; if meanings do not show up in an optimally sensitive reading of the text, then, although the author may have wished to convey them, they simply do not form part of what the text means. A poem stands or falls on its own merits. This is Wimsatt and Beardsley's strongest argument for anti-intentionalism.

It can, however, be countered by the intentionalist. Whilst it is true that the author's intentions must be realized in the text and concretely apprehended there in order for the work to be artistically successful, when a work *is* successful, intentionalism is true: what we grasp is the author's meaning. The intentionalist may add that, although 'external' evidence cannot transform an artistic failure into a success, attention to such evidence may make it easier to see what meaning is contained in the words on the page. The intentionalist can also point out that, since we rarely approach literary works without some awareness of the author's historical circumstances, other writings and so on, there is in fact no firm or deep distinction between internal and external evidence, contrary to what the anti-intentionalist supposes.

The intentionalist's case can be strengthened further by drawing attention to the fact that estimates of sincerity, maturity and perceptiveness are important for our responses to literary works. Literature is flawed if it exhibits mawkishness, self-indulgence or crudity of moral vision; the fine consciousness of life and ethical complexity of George Eliot and Henry James is valued. Literary vices and virtues are qualities of moral personality apparently ascribed in full-blooded intentionalist spirit to the author, in so far as he or she is manifest in his or her work. (Amplifying this approach, see Leavis, 1986, part IV.)

The anti-intentionalist will complain that here the intentionalist has once again converted an aesthetic into a non-aesthetic matter, and is treating the text as material for literary biography, as if it were the critic's job to pass moral judgement on the author. We do value qualities such as sincerity in literature, but these are properties of *texts*: they indicate strengths in the work itself.

We have, then, intuitions favouring each of intentionalism and anti-intentionalism. Neither set of arguments is obviously decisive. Wimsatt and

Beardsley did not, therefore, establish that intentionalism involves a fallacy. They did, however, define anti-intentionalism as a theoretical option, and indicate the methodological repercussions of the issue. If intentionalism is true, then the study of literature may cast its net wide and draw, in addition to literary biography, on other disciplines – history, psychology or anthropology – concerned with factors contributing, consciously or unconsciously, to the author's meaning. If anti-intentionalism is true, then external information ought to be bracketed out.

The second question raised by differences of interpretation, which concerns the notion of correctness, can again be formulated in terms of a sharp opposition. On the monistic view, there is for each work a uniquely correct interpretation. Whether it can be identified conclusively, and gain universal acceptance, is another matter. Monists say that where interpretations differ, and yet seem equally well-supported, their conflict can be overcome by a 'super-interpretation', which incorporates what is true in each of the inter-pretations which it supersedes.

Pluralism denies that there is, even in principle, a uniquely correct interpretation for each work; it maintains that a number of different inter-pretations can meet the condition of, not correctness, if correctness is taken to imply uniqueness, but 'legitimacy'. Pluralists differ over the criteria for legitimacy of interpretation and how restrictive these should be. The argu-ments between monism and pluralism engage closely with the issue of intentionalism versus anti-intentionalism.

The pluralist focuses in the first instance on the notion of textual meaning. Correctness of interpretation presupposes that textual meaning is determinate. Wimsatt and Beardsley help themselves to the assumption that literary works have objective, determinate meanings, but the pluralist challenges the monist to say where this determinacy comes from: for even if the meaning of each individual word composing a text is determinate – a claim which is itself vulnerable in view of the ubiquity of metaphor in literature – the meaning of the work as a whole is far from being a straightforward function of the dictionary meanings of the words composing it. As we would ordinarily put it, there is 'room for interpretation', and this, according to the pluralist, means that there is room for a *number* of interpretations. Easiest, then, is for the monist to embrace intentionalism: since, if intentionalism is true, a source of determinacy is readily supplied by the author's intention.

The pluralist's second argument draws on a tenet of aesthetic subjectivism: namely, that felt response is at the core of the aesthetic. Literary interpretation should serve the kind of interest appropriate to literary works, and literary interest, as a case of aesthetic interest, centres on response. The proper goal of interpretation is therefore to enhance our experience of the work, to offer a reading which makes it mean as much as possible to us. Since the perspectives of readers will always differ, the interpretation that is optimal for one reader will not be optimal for another. Multiple interpretations of a work are therefore to be expected, and should be welcomed. To meet this argument on its own terms, the monist would have to defend the – evidently controversial –

claim that there is for each text one interpretation which is universally optimal.

Arguments between monism and pluralism tend to converge on the following scenario. The monist says that if pluralism is true, then 'anything goes' in interpretation, an implication which the monist claims reduces pluralism to absurdity – *The Ancient Mariner* can not be interpreted as a poem about issues of power and gender in Eskimo culture. The pluralist objects that the notion of a uniquely correct interpretation fosters DOGMATISM, and disregards both the richness of texts and the diversity of human interests which may legitimately be expressed in literary interpretation.

These (unresolved) philosophical issues gain a special urgency from their relevance to the present, turbulent and logomachic climate of literary studies, where theoretical and ideological commitments are explicitly adopted and appealed to in interpreting texts. The dominant deconstructionist conception of literary meaning at work here is fundamentally a form of pluralism, adopted on wholly general philosophical grounds: the very concept of determinacy of meaning is rejected, in all, not just literary contexts. To this is added a radically idealist view of literary meaning which reverses the ordinary conception of the relation of meaning and interpretation: the meaning of a literary work is conceived as created, rather than grasped by interpretation. The point of literature, on this picture, is not aesthetic: literature exists for the sake of interpretation.

4 The Point of Art

We come finally to the question of the point of art. What value does art have? What is art for? This is not a demand for a 'justification' of art in the same sense as a justification of morality is thought to be required – that would be an inappropriate demand, since the creation and appreciation of art do not share the necessity of moral obligation. The question is rather whether we can articulate and vindicate our sense of the importance of art. The fact, observed earlier, that art is an evaluative concept, means that an account of the point of art is not a mere coda to aesthetic enquiry: it should fall out conceptually from a theory of art.

That art does have some point is not beyond all doubt (Passmore, 1991). It has already been seen how the mimetic theory encounters difficulties on this score. Positive reasons for scepticism about the value of art are not hard to unearth: they derive from art's essential connections with pleasure, play and imagination, its freedom from reason and practical purposes. The sceptic will insist that art has the same sort of value as any other form of entertainment. Plato's notorious critique of art, in Book X of the *Republic*, goes further, by suggesting that art's preoccupation with appearance entrenches our ignorance of reality, and that its effects may be psychologically and morally harmful.

The distinction of ends and means figures prominently in many discussions of the point of art, and is usually employed critically: some accounts are said to reduce art to a 'mere' means, others to recognize correctly that art is an end.

This contrast is, however, not altogether felicitous, for two reasons. Firstly, art, so long as it has *some* value, can always be re-described as a means to whatever value it realizes. Secondly, it is not clear what can be meant by describing art, or its appreciation, as an end. Certainly individual works of art have to be approached in their own terms and contemplated 'for their own sake'; but it would be a mistake to move from this fact about aesthetic attention, that it terminates in its object and does not 'think ahead', to the claim that art *is* its own point and cannot have extrinsic value. Formalists such as Bell and Hanslick, who describe works of art as ends in themselves, seem to make this mistake.

What the denial that art is 'merely a means' – and the aestheticist slogan 'art for art's sake' – may be trying to say, is that the value of art realized by art cannot be realized by anything else, or cannot be realized in the same way. Thus interpreted, the doctrine meets with our agreement: we recoil from hedonistic, moral, didactic or other instrumental attitudes to art, to the extent that these suggest that other things could be substituted for art *without loss*, or that the complexity of art is redundant. Tolstoy's (1930) theory of art as the transmission of moral feeling, for example, makes little effort to distinguish art from other, potentially more efficient, ways of achieving that end. It follows that so long as art is viewed as having a *necessary* role in relation to the kind of value in question, and the complexity of art is taken account of, there is nothing necessarily wrong with assigning a hedonistic, moral, didactic or other goal to art. Schiller (1989), for instance, argues that the goal of art, as a component of 'aesthetic education', is to overcome the metaphysical contradictions in human nature in order that we may attain full 'humanity'; this goal is 'extra-aesthetic', but Schiller regards aesthetic education as the *only way* in which it can be achieved.

What forms may accounts of the value of art then take?

They may, first, be divided according to how closely they relate the value of art to the values of life. In a perspective such as that of Leavis, art is properly and inextricably bound up with the values of life: the '*raison d'être* of the work' is to 'have its due effect and play its part in life'; the 'essential business of criticism' is to locate 'the creative centre where we have the growth towards the future of the finest life' (1986, p. 283). At the other extreme, Bell holds that art is autonomous and has value only to the extent that it distances us from life: 'to appreciate a work of art we need bring with us nothing from life, no knowledge of its ideas and affairs, no familiarity with its emotions . . . In this world the emotions of life find no place. It is a world with emotions of its own' (1914, pp. 25–7).

The deeper distinction to be made among accounts of the value of art, however, is between those that are naturalistic, and those that are metaphysical; a distinction that was foreshadowed by the contrast of Hume and Kant.

Naturalistic accounts ground art in human nature. The contingent fittedness by nature of certain objects to our minds proposed by Hume provides the starting point. To exhibit the point of art, it needs to be shown how works of art engage fundamental and important mental activities (Dewey, 1934). Psychoanalysis provides one example of this approach (Wollheim, 1987). The question of the point of art is therefore answered by saying that art is *natural*: art exists because it is natural for us to create and appreciate it. As such, art is a 'form of life' (Wollheim, 1980), as necessary a component of human existence as language, culture and politics. The naturalistic view affirms that art responds to the psychological needs of human beings, but it denies that the functions which art performs could be specified, or fulfilled, through other means. When art is pictured as a necessary part of the human order, and the appreciation of art as a natural component of human well-being, the point of art merges with that of human life itself.

The naturalistic view of art therefore qualifies as a fifth theory of art, in addition to those considered earlier (it may, but need not, be formulated so as to incorporate the expression theory). By showing how the various dimensions of art map on to psychological processes, it accounts for the unity of art in terms of the unity of the mind, and locates the essence of art with reference to human psychology.

Metaphysical accounts of the point of art are, of necessity, more speculative and less pinned down to the empirical features of art than naturalistic accounts. They will also, of course, depend explicitly on a general philosophical outlook, which naturalistic accounts do not need to do. This does not, or should not, mean that they simply squeeze art into a pre-formed metaphysical system: they may, on the contrary, allow art a role in forming the system itself. This is what we find, in different ways, in Kant, Hegel, Schopenhauer, Schiller and Nietzsche (German idealism has been notably more accommodating to art than any other philosophical tradition).

The basic demand to which metaphysical accounts of art answer – and which naturalistic accounts cannot properly satisfy – derives from what might be called the 'transfigurative' aspect of our experience of art: the sense that the transformation of reality which art effects, and which locates in it a kind of value that we find consoling, is more than a fanciful embellishment. Tragedy exhibits the transfigurative power of art most clearly. The aspiration to achieve, through art, a justification of the world 'as an aesthetic phenomenon', as Nietzsche put it (1993, p. 32), is a further part of the legacy of Romanticism, and has not disappeared from the demands that we put on art.

Further reading

As an introduction to aesthetics, there is nothing to compare with Richard Wollheim's short *Art and its Objects* (1980), which offers both an overview and a distinctive approach to the subject. Other, plainer introductions are W.

Charlton *Aesthetics* (1970) and Anne Sheppard *Aesthetics* (1987). Oswald Hanfling (ed.) *Philosophical Aesthetics* (1992) contains a series of essays specifically written as a unified introduction to aesthetics, but of sufficient length to present many arguments in detail.

It is important to have a grasp at first-hand of the classic writings in aesthetics, few of which make difficult reading. Albert Hofstadter and Richard Kuhns (eds) *Philosophies of Art and Beauty* (1964) is a first-rate, currently available anthology. E. F. Carritt (ed.) *Philosophies of Beauty* (1931) is more comprehensive but the extracts are shorter. Two other excellent anthologies that also serve this end, and intersperse selections from the classics with modern writings, are George Dickie and Richard Sclafani (eds) *Aesthetics* (1977), and Melvin Rader (ed.) *A Modern Book of Esthetics* (1979). Both are organized thematically and contain helpful bibliographies (as does Wollheim, 1980). The historical development of aesthetics is traced by Monroe C. Beardsley in *Aesthetics From Classical Greece to the Present* (1966), which is also useful as a reference book.

A number of books may be singled out as offering more complex discussions with the stress on a particular topic or perspective. Arthur Danto *The Transfiguration of the Commonplace* (1981) is stimulating and addresses many problems, but with the accent firmly on contemporary art. Malcolm Budd *Music and the Emotions* (1985) gives detailed and lucid analytical treatment of some central aesthetic theories. Wollheim *On Art and the Mind* (1974) brings issues in aesthetics in relation to philosophy of mind and psychoanalysis. Roger Scruton *Art and Imagination* (1974) also emphasizes the contribution of philosophy of mind, together with that of philosophy of language; Scruton *The Aesthetic Understanding* (1983) relates aesthetics to cultural issues. Nelson Goodman *Languages of Art* (1976) has been highly influential. Anthony Savile *The Test of Time* (1982) focuses on questions of value, in the idealist tradition. Kendall Walton *Mimesis as Make-Believe* (1990) attempts to provide a general theory of artistic representation.

Important articles are collected in Dickie and Sclafani (eds) (1977), Cyril Barrett (ed.) *Collected Papers on Aesthetics* (1965), Joseph Margolis (ed.) *Philosophy Looks at the Arts* (1978), and Harold Osborne (ed.) *Aesthetics* (1972).

With respect to particular topics in aesthetics, as broken down in this chapter: Hume needs no commentary, but Kant's *Critique of Judgement* is extremely difficult, and it is best to read Mary McCloskey *Kant's Aesthetics* (1987) alongside. Three comprehensive treatments of aesthetic experience and judgement are Monroe C. Beardsley *The Aesthetic Point of View* (1982), Scruton (1974), and Mary Mothersill *Beauty Restored* (1984). Definitions of art are explored in Stephen Davies *Definitions of Art* (1991). Theories of art, and accounts of its point, are best approached through the classic writings. For detailed treatment of the debates surrounding each of the dimensions of art, Flint Schier *Deeper Into Pictures* (1986) deals with pictorial representation, Budd (1985) with expression, and David Newton-de Molina (ed.) *On Literary Intention* (1976) with literary meaning and interpretation.

References

Aristotle 1987: *Poetics* (translated by S. Halliwell). London: Duckworth.

Barrett. C. (ed.) 1965: *Collected Papers on Aesthetics*. Oxford: Blackwell.

Beardsley, M. C. 1966: *Aesthetics From Classical Greece to the Present*. Tuscaloosa: University of Alabama Press.

—— 1982: *The Aesthetic Point of View*. Ithaca: Cornell University Press.

Bell, C. 1914: *Art*. London: Chatto and Windus.

Budd, M. 1985: *Music and the Emotions*. London: Routledge and Kegan Paul.

Carritt, E. F. 1931: *Philosophies of Beauty*. Oxford: Clarendon Press.

Charlton, W. 1970: *Aesthetics*. London: Hutchinson.

Collingwood, R. G. 1937: *The Principles of Art*. Oxford: Oxford University Press.

Croce, B. 1992 [1902]: *The Aesthetic as the Science of Expression and of the Linguistic in General* (translated by C. Lyas). Cambridge: Cambridge University Press.

Danto, A. 1981: *The Transfiguration of the Commonplace*. Cambridge, Massachusetts: Harvard University Press.

Davies, S. 1991: *Definitions of Art*. Ithaca: Cornell University Press.

Dewey, J. 1934: *Art as Experience*. New York: Putnam.

Dickie, G. 1984: *The Art Circle*. New York: Haven.

Dickie, G. and Sclafani, R. J. (eds) 1977: *Aesthetics: A Critical Anthology*. New York: St. Martin's Press.

Gombrich, E. H. 1960: *Art and Illusion* (2nd edn). New York: Pantheon.

Goodman, N. 1976: *Languages of Art*. Indianapolis: Hackett.

Hanfling, O. (ed.) 1992: *Philosophical Aesthetics*. Oxford: Blackwell in association with the Open University.

Hanslick, E. 1986 [1854]: *On the Musically Beautiful* (translated by G. Payzant). Indianapolis: Hackett.

Hegel, G. W. F. 1993 [1820–9]: *Introductory Lectures on Aesthetics* (translated by B. Bosanquet). Harmondsworth: Penguin.

Hofstadter, A. and Kuhns, R. (eds) 1964: *Philosophies of Art and Beauty*. New York: Harper and Row.

Hopkins, A. 1982: *Talking About Music*. London: Pan.

Hume, D. 1965 [1757]: Of the standard of taste. In *'Of the Standard of Taste' and Other Essays*, New York: Bobbs-Merrill.

Kant, I. 1987 [1790]: 'Critique of aesthetic judgement', Part I of *Critique of Judgement* (translated by W. S. Pluhar). Indianapolis: Hackett.

Kivy, P. 1989: *Sound Sentiment*. Philadelphia: Temple University Press.

Langer, S. 1942: *Philosophy In a New Key*. Cambridge, Massachusetts: Harvard University Press.

Leavis, F. R. 1986: *Valuation in Criticism and Other Essays*. Cambridge: Cambridge University Press.

Margolis, J. (ed.) 1978: *Philosophy Looks At the Arts*. Philadelphia: Temple University Press.

McCloskey, M. 1987: *Kant's Aesthetics*. London: Macmillan.

Meager, R. 1970: Aesthetic concepts. *British Journal of Aesthetics*, 10, 303–22.

Moore, G. E. 1984 [1903]: *Principia Ethica*. Cambridge: Cambridge University Press.

Mothersill, M. 1984: *Beauty Restored*. Oxford: Clarendon Press.

Newton-de Molina, D. (ed.) 1976: *On Literary Intention*. Edinburgh: Edinburgh University Press.

Nietzsche, F. 1993 [1871]: *The Birth of Tragedy* (translated by S. Whiteside). Harmondsworth: Penguin.

Osborne, H. (ed.) 1972: *Aesthetics*. Oxford: Oxford University Press.

Passmore, J. 1991: *Serious Art*. London: Duckworth.

Peacocke, C. 1987: Depiction. *Philosophical Review*, 96, 383–409.

Plato 1955: *Republic* (translated by H. D. P. Lee). Harmondsworth: Penguin.

Rader, M. (ed.) 1979: *A Modern Book of Esthetics* (5th edn). New York: Holt, Rinehart and Winston.

Savile, A. 1982: *The Test of Time*. Oxford: Clarendon Press.

Schaper, E. (ed.) 1983: *Pleasure, Preference and Value*. Cambridge: Cambridge University Press.

Schier, F. 1986: *Deeper Into Pictures*. Cambridge: Cambridge University Press.

Schiller, F. 1989 [1793–5]: *On the Aesthetic Education of Man* (translated by E. Wilkinson and L. A. Willoughby). Oxford: Clarendon Press.

Schopenhauer, A. 1969 [1819]: *The World as Will and Representation* (2 vols.) (translated by E. F. J. Payne). New York: Dover.

Scruton, R. 1974: *Art and Imagination*. London: Methuen.

—— 1979: *The Aesthetics of Architecture*. London: Methuen.

—— 1983: *The Aesthetic Understanding*. London: Methuen.

Sheppard, A. 1987: *Aesthetics*. Oxford: Oxford University Press.

Sibley, F. 1959: Aesthetic concepts. *Philosophical Review*, 68, 421–50.

—— 1965: Aesthetic and non-aesthetic. *Philosophical Review*, 74, 135–59.

Sibley, F. and Tanner, M. 1968: Symposium on 'Aesthetics and Objectivity'. *Proceedings of the Aristotelian Society*, supplementary volume 42, 31–72.

Tilghman, B. R. 1984: *But is it Art?* Oxford: Blackwell.

Tolstoy, L. 1930 [1898]: *What is Art?* (translated by A. Maude). Oxford: Oxford University Press.

Walton, K. 1990: *Mimesis and Make-Believe*. Cambridge, Massachusetts: Harvard University Press.

Wittgenstein, L. 1978: *Lectures and Conversations on Aesthetics, Psychology and Religious Belief*. Oxford: Blackwell.

Wollheim, R. 1974: *On Art and the Mind*. Cambridge, Massachusetts: Harvard University Press.

—— 1980: *Art and its Objects* (2nd edn). Cambridge: Cambridge University Press.

—— 1987: *Painting as an Art*. London: Thames and Hudson.

Discussion Questions

1 What makes a judgement aesthetic?

2 Are the aesthetic qualities of an object any less objective than its colour?

3 Can arguments about aesthetic value be resolved, and what does it signify if they cannot?

4 Can it be shown, or must it merely be assumed, that aesthetic judgements differ from gustatory preferences?

5 In what ways, if any, can reasons be given for aesthetic judgements?

6 Are there any limits on what can be an object of aesthetic attention?

7 In what respects are aesthetic judgements like moral judgements, and in what respects are they unlike?

8 What can criticism of art hope to contribute to our appreciation of art?

9 In what respects can one's relation to works of art be compared with one's relations to other people?

10 Does aesthetic experience presuppose an aesthetic attitude?

11 Is it plausible to claim that beauty is the fundamental concept in aesthetics?

12 Does it matter if art cannot be defined?

13 What is the relation between form and content in art, and does either have greater importance than the other?

14 To what extent is it appropriate and profitable to compare art with language?

15 Does the concept of resemblance have any role to play in elucidating pictorial representation?

16 Can it be explained how music expresses emotion?

17 What assumptions are needed to uphold the claim that literary works have objective meanings, and are those assumptions acceptable?

18 Must each literary work have one correct interpretation?

19 Does the meaning of a literary work reside in the mind of its author, in the text itself, or in neither of these?

20 Is the correct interpretation of a literary work the one that makes it mean most to us?

21 Does the study of literature need to be guided by literary theory?

22 Does psychology have importance for aesthetics?

23 Do we need art?

24 Is it ever legitimate to view art as serving moral or political ends?

25 Is a paradox involved in the enjoyment of tragedy and, if so, how should it be resolved?

26 In what sense might it be true that art is a social rather than individual phenomenon?

27 Does emotional response to fiction require what Coleridge calls a 'willing suspension of disbelief'?

28 Is it more than just a contingent truth that art has a history?

29 How can one be moved by the plight of Anna Karenina, when one knows her to be merely fictional?

30 What distinguishes metaphor from nonsense?

31 Does survival of the test of time provide a criterion for artistic achievement?

32 Is photography a form of art?

33 Can it be maintained that any one form of art is superior to the others?

34 Is architecture 'frozen music'?

35 Can anything be made of the thought that music has 'metaphysical meaning'?

36 What makes a painting artistically significant?

8

Political and Social Philosophy ——

David Archard

Social and political philosophy has experienced a dramatic revival in recent decades. This chapter considers the background of work in the years after 1945, before examining the writings of the main architects of this revival, John Rawls and Robert Nozick. Also discussed are the movements of communitarianism, feminism and analytical Marxism. In a concluding section a number of themes – the nature of political philosophy and politics, value pluralism, the liberal individual, and the ideal of equality – are reviewed in the context of a recognition of the current dominance of philosophical liberalism.

1 Introduction

In a now celebrated phrase, Peter Laslett announced that 'for the moment, anyway, political philosophy is dead'. He did so in his 1950 'Introduction' to the first collection of essays entitled *Philosophy, Politics and Society*. The sixth collection was published in 1992, and the intervening years and essays show clearly enough that the reports of death were greatly exaggerated, or at least that the moment was merely a passing one. The last 40 years, and the last 25 in particular, have witnessed a quite astonishing regeneration of social and political philosophy, understood in Laslett's own terms as the concern of philosophers with 'political and social relationships at the widest possible level of generality' (Laslett, 1950, p. vii). The work has displayed a range of views, fertility of imagination, rigour of argumentation, care in critical analysis, and concern to address contemporary problems which are ample testimony to the considerable strengths of philosophy in the English-speaking world.

In the 1950s these strengths were far more selectively deployed. The study of politics was, to simplify greatly, divided between the empirical social sciences and philosophy. Exponents of the former were optimistic that political science could offer value-free but well-founded explanatory theories of its object. For its part, philosophy disdained substantive political evaluation and restricted itself to the logical and linguistic analysis of political discourse.

The title of Daniel Bell's book, *The End of Ideology*, which was published in 1960, concisely defined an historical moment, and its subtitle, 'On the

Exhaustion of Political Ideas in the Fifties', spelled out what was intended. Bell's text was a series of sociological essays about America, but its grander claims carried further afield. The 1930s and 1940s testified to the sheer awfulness of the practical realization of ideologies like fascism and Stalinism, which made simplifying and absolute claims to truth about humanity, history and reason. These years also reconciled intellectuals to the virtues of a more moderate and modest political programme. Capitalism could be tamed by a welfarist state, the economy mixed, and fundamental freedoms adequately protected by democratic constitutionalism. There was no further need for ideologies, in the sense of millenarian visions of utopia, yet to be realized. The exhaustion of ideologies in this narrow sense seemed also to betoken a disenchantment with politics in general, a retreat from the traditional concern of political philosophy to prescribe the good society.

This was mirrored in the work of philosophers. The 1950s was the high tide of conceptual analysis, and in an emblematic text, *The Vocabulary of Politics*, T. D. Weldon (1953) characterized the enduring questions of political philosophy as misplaced, resting on false assumptions and the misuse of unanalysed fundamental terms. Correctly understood, these questions are merely 'confused formulations of purely empirical difficulties' (p. 192). It is proper for philosophers to analyse the language and foundational claims of ideologies, but the evaluation of political states of affairs and institutions is more appropriately reserved for politicians and political scientists.

However, it would be a mistake to oversimplify. From 1945 until the 1960s, serious and important work was done in political philosophy. Karl Popper (1945) sought to rebut totalizing political theories such as those of PLATO (chapter 15) and MARX (chapter 24). But he did so by defending an ideal of the 'open society', and the politics of piecemeal reform rather than wholesale social engineering. F. A. von Hayek was entering upon his lifelong defence of a position that is echoed in important current views (Gray, 1984). Hayek affirmed the ideal of justice as individual freedom under the LAW (chapter 12), and defended the idea that the economic and social world displays a spontaneous, impersonal pattern. It is simply inappropriate, and ultimately destructive of freedom, for governments to impose upon this world according to a redundant ideal of 'social' justice.

The work of Isaiah Berlin is especially noteworthy, for he anticipates some major themes in the philosophical liberalism that is now dominant. For Berlin, a plausible politics must start from a recognition of a plurality in valid yet conflicting ends of life. There is no single ideal of the good life, and the proper goal of politics is to make possible the pursuit by individuals of their several ends (Kocis, 1980). Berlin (1958) famously distinguished two senses of liberty, one characterized as the absence of obstructions, and the other characterized in terms of self-mastery. He argued for the former, 'negative' liberty, as the 'truer and more humane ideal' than the latter, which he called 'positive' liberty. At the same time Berlin urged a clear separation of the notions of liberty and equality. He conceded that the degree of social inequality may determine the conditions that make liberty worth having, but insisted that these conditions do not enter into the definition of liberty.

2 John Rawls

These various writings are important, but it is those of John Rawls that are now taken to signify the beginning of a distinctly new era. The publication of Rawls' *A Theory of Justice* (1972) has proved a landmark, radically changing the character of English-speaking political philosophy and supplying the ineliminable background against which all subsequent discussion has been conducted. 'Political philosophers now must either work within Rawls's theory or explain why not' is fitting tribute from one whose own views are at a great distance from Rawls' (Nozick, 1974, p. 183).

A Theory of Justice is much lauded but it is also now an extensively criticized text. Rawls' presuppositions, methodology, and conclusions have all been subjected to such extensive criticism that it is important to be clear how and why his text set the scene. Firstly, *A Theory of Justice* is a work of substantive political philosophy. Although Rawls engages in the analysis of concepts, this serves rather than substitutes for the evaluation of political institutions. *A Theory of Justice* is more. It defends a single, unified vision of the good society – one that is recognizably liberal. Rawls gives philosophical voice to a doctrine of democratic constitutional liberalism that can with merit be urged as the only feasible theory for contemporary Western society.

Secondly, Rawls seeks to combine a recommendation of the ideal polity with a plausible account of HUMAN NATURE (pp. 531–3). This involves not just a theory of human MOTIVATION (p. 376) taken from the SOCIAL SCIENCES (chapter 11). It also – and this point has been less noticed – comprises a view of the manner in which citizens can be brought to recognize and accept as both fair and realistic the formal terms of their co-existence.

Thirdly, Rawls has provided political philosophy with an agenda. He does not just offer a theory of justice. He supplies an account of the priority of individual liberty, the defensible limits of egalitarianism, and the rule of law.

Fourthly, Rawls' work puts contemporary political philosophy back into contact with its own history. The work and concerns of past writers, such as HOBBES (chapter 18), LOCKE (chapter 19), Rousseau, HUME (chapter 21), MILL (chapter 25) and KANT (chapter 22), are given renewed pertinence.

Fifthly, *A Theory of Justice* is nevertheless a response to the particular circumstances of modernity. It is not just a principled affirmation of the virtues of liberalism against the post-war background of disillusion with more extreme ideologies. It can be seen as an attempt to affirm these virtues in the context of a more local crisis, that is, the challenge posed to the ideal of American democratic constitutionalism by the civil rights movement and the war in Vietnam. More generally again, Rawls insists, as did Berlin, that value pluralism is an unavoidable feature of modern existence to which politics must adequately respond.

The ideas of *A Theory of Justice* can best be laid out by answering a number of broad questions. Firstly, why is a theory of justice needed? Because publicly

agreed terms of social co-operation are both necessary and possible. Individuals benefit from living and working together so long as they can be
assured that social existence is well-ordered and stable. Yet there is a
predisposition to conflict inasmuch as individuals want different and not
necessarily compatible things out of their life together. Agreed PRINCIPLES
(pp. 599–601) are needed to regulate interaction and determine the proper
division of benefits and costs amongst the members of society. Such principles
are possible to the extent that individuals can see them to be necessary, and
their particular terms can be agreed under appropriate conditions.

The Primacy of Justice

Justice has *primacy* in three senses. It is the first virtue of social institutions. This
does not mean that society cannot display other virtues. Only that without at least
the assurance of justice these would have little or no value. Secondly, truth is a
demand made of a system of thought in so far as it relates to reality. Justice is
demanded of a polity in so far as it must relate to the real world. The
circumstances of justice are those first noted by David Hume, namely limited
benevolence and moderate scarcity. Humans are not well enough disposed to
make sacrifices for others, and material resources are not available in sufficient
quantity, to make formal agreement on terms of co-operation unnecessary.

Rawls adds to this understanding of circumstances the facts of modern value
pluralism. Individuals have different but not necessarily compatible aims. My
pursuit of my life's ends will conflict with your pursuit of yours. Agreement on
how to reconcile such a conflict is necessary but possible only if no one set of
individual values is affirmed over the others.

Thirdly, any theory of justice specifies and guarantees an equality of citizenship which supplies an assurance that no individual may be sacrificed for
society's greater good. Justice has primacy in that this assurance is not to be
compromised.

What is a theory of justice? It is a theory of the publicly agreed, final principles
which define the fundamental terms of social co-operation. It is a theory of
those principles that regulate the institutions, which are the 'basic structure' of
society. It does not prescribe particular outcomes; nor does it provide a
criterion for evaluating actions or the character and dispositions of individuals. It is a theory of *social* justice, which must also coincide with our
considered and reflective MORAL JUDGEMENTS (pp. 203–4). Rawls' notion of
'reflective equilibrium' allows for, indeed encourages, the possibility of mutual
adjustment in both theory and judgements. Yet any theory of justice must
capture what is essential to and shared by different accounts of justice, namely
that 'institutions are just when no arbitrary distinctions are made between
persons in the assigning of basic rights and duties and when the rules
determine a proper balance between competing claims to the advantages of
social life' (Rawls, 1972, p. 5).

What then is *A Theory of Justice*? Rawls' theory assures citizens equal liberty, and a distribution of all other goods that maximizes the expectations of the least well off. More formally, and completely:

First Principle
Each person is to have an equal right to the most extensive total system of equal basic liberties compatible with a similar system of liberty for all.

Second Principle
Social and economic inequalities are to be arranged so that they are both:
(a) to the greatest benefit of the least advantaged, consistent with the just savings principle, and
(b) attached to offices and positions open to all under conditions of fair equality of opportunity. (p. 302)

The first part of the second principle is familiarly known as the 'difference principle', and the two principles are in lexical order. That is to say that inequalities regulated by the second principle are only permitted when equality of liberty under the first principle has been guaranteed.

Provided that these principles apply or very nearly apply to the basic institutions of society, then that society is just. And individuals have a duty to abide by the rules of a just society. Although Rawls offers a contractualist argument for the rules themselves, the duty to abide by them is not itself contractually based. In Part III of *A Theory of Justice* Rawls offers an account of the acquisition of a sense of justice. This grows out of the basic attachments and relationships that constitute any society – family, friendship and broader associations. There is in the well-ordered society a concordance of fair rules and a sense of justice. Citizens can recognize that the rules are just and acknowledge their duty to abide by them. Fairness and feasibility coincide.

Lastly, *A Theory of Justice* is a theory of the right and the good. The just society is not one that realizes the good life of its community. It is one that permits its members to pursue their own conception of the good under certain conditions. Firstly, the pursuit of the good is constrained by the right, that is, the publicly agreed principles of justice. Secondly, these principles determine the distribution of primary social goods – rights, liberties, powers and opportunities, income and wealth – which are the desired prerequisites of any particular pursuit of the good. Thirdly, people pursue different ideals of the good life. 'Human good is heterogeneous because the aims of the self are heterogeneous.' (p. 554) It would be a disastrous mistake for a polity to try to impose upon its members any one particular ideal of life. Rawls has continued to believe that, in any modern society, there will be a plurality of conscientiously sought ends, and that any state, presuming or prescribing to the contrary, would have to employ extensive coercion to secure its single vision.

The final question to be answered is, Why *A Theory of Justice*? This asks what justification Rawls offers for his own principles. He sees his theory as a systematic alternative to the prevailing dominant philosophical doctrines, Utilitarianism (chapter 25) and intuitionism. Although the latter view, understood by Rawls as proposing a plurality of first principles, with no rule of priority among them, is of great importance for Rawls, the task of combatting utilitarianism occupies him more. Rawls has recourse to a contractualist methodology: the principles of justice are those that rational, self-interested, but mutually disinterested individuals would choose in an original situation specified chiefly in terms of the parties' selective knowledge.

Each is concerned to advance his or her own ends but is not concerned with those of others. All know enough to urge adoption of some set of principles, but are excluded from knowledge of those facts that would dispose them to the selection of partial and thus conflicting principles. Thus they know that the circumstances of justice obtain and that they have conceptions of the good. A veil of ignorance denies them knowledge of what their conception of the good actually is, and of their particular circumstances – that of their society, their social position, and their endowment of 'natural assets' (skills, talents and abilities). Rawls' argument is that the two principles of justice would be unanimously agreed in that situation of CHOICE (pp. 375–9) whose specifications accord with our considered moral judgements. We would not choose as fair-minded people but, properly constrained, our choices would be fair.

Not surprisingly, given its power and originality, much critical attention has been directed to the contractarian argument, and a fundamental ambivalence has been exposed. This is whether the argument is to be taken as having an independent justificatory force, or as being only an heuristic device serving to illustrate the force of a claim whose real justification lies elsewhere. If the former is the proper interpretation then there are a number of problems.

Firstly, whilst actual contracts have a real claim upon those who make them, hypothetical contracts have not merely less of a claim upon us but none at all. We cannot be bound by agreements we have not made but that, counterfactually, we would have made in specified circumstances.

Secondly, any particular hypothetical contract is vulnerable to the charge that the choices made would not be as claimed. Critics have argued that in Rawls' own original position his two principles need not be chosen. Or, at the very least, Rawls' reasons for believing that they would can be challenged.

Thirdly, different situations of choice yield, as Rawls concedes, different principles. The claim that the choice of any one set of principles is evident and uncontroversial rests on a prior demonstration that the specification of the choice situation is obvious and uncontentious. Critics claim that Rawls has not shown this. Arguably, he both rules into and rules out of his original position more than he is strictly entitled to do.

Fourthly, even if certain principles of justice would be chosen as claimed, it has still to be shown that these would remain desirable and feasible rules after the veil of ignorance has been lifted. Can and should we abide by a contract made in the dark? Is it reasonable to expect us all to submit to terms of co-operation secured only artificially and against the grain of our better informed nature? If the contractarian argument is to be understood as an heuristic device then these four problems are largely beside the point. But then the question presses of what arguments justify what the contract serves only to illustrate. It is not simply that the grounds of justification are elsewhere. It is also that these grounds must seem less firm and settled. The contractarian method offers a determinate and foundational decision procedure yielding clear outcomes. Rawls appeals to our considered and reflective moral judgements in confirmation of the correctness of his theory. The principles of justice reflect and confirm our nature as free and equal rational agents. Yet, as critics have suggested, this KANTIAN (see chapter 22) understanding of justice lacks precision. Notwithstanding its appeal, the force of such an understanding is that of any version of moral intuitionism, a doctrine criticized by Rawls for its indeterminacy and lack of foundations. Moreover, its presumed view of human nature does not sit easily with the assumptions of the contractarian approach.

However, there is another form of argument to be discerned in the latter chapters of Part III. Here, Rawls formulates the demand that the principles of justice be those of a well-ordered society. Such a society is not just stable; it is transparently fair. Its basic structure is governed by principles that are publicly known and universally acknowledged as fair. Moreover, these principles are consistent with and supported by a sense of justice which naturally arises within the relationships and attachments made possible by such a society. In a well-ordered society there is a reciprocally assured confidence that everyone will abide by the rules and make their required contributions. Finally, these principles affirm an ideal of social union and of ourselves which reflects our true moral nature. Within a well-ordered society we not only recognize but commend the fair ways in which we together but severally pursue our own lives.

Rawls contends that his principles of justice would regulate a well-ordered society, but that other suggested principles could not. To illustrate this point, consider the grounds for preferring the 'difference principle' over one of maximum average UTILITY (chapter 25). The contractarian argument relies on individuals, in what Rawls calls the original position, adopting a maximin strategy, choosing that society in which the worst off do better than in any other society. Rawls' reasons for thinking that individuals would adopt such a strategy are generally viewed as unconvincing. However, Rawls can also appeal to the idea that the difference principle, but not that of maximum average utility, conduces to a well-ordered society. The difference principle 'represents, in effect, an agreement to regard the distribution of natural talents as a common asset and to share in the benefits of this distribution whatever it turns out to be' (p. 101). This requires a sense of fraternity, a preparedness to co-operate on terms whereby the good-fortuned benefit only if the less fortunate also do better. A basic structure regulated by the two principles is well-ordered in that it requires and facilitates the appropriate sense of justice.

On the other hand, the principle of utility requires that some individuals are used as means to others' ends, and lose out so that others may benefit. Not only would this render fellow-feeling impossible but it would fatally damage the self-esteem of those who lose out. A society governed by the principle of utility could not then be well-ordered. The reciprocal attachments that generate a sense of justice would be undercut, and the equality of self-esteem, needed for good order, would be impossible.

A recognition of the argument from good order in *A Theory of Justice* is important for the following reason. Rawls has responded to criticisms of this work in a series of articles that have culminated in his second major book, *Political Liberalism* (Rawls, 1993). Its concern is with the good order of a modern liberal democratic society. It does not defend a particular theory of distributive justice, although Rawls sees no reason to rule out his own two principles as candidates for regulating the basic structure of a well-ordered society. *A Theory of Justice* started from Humean circumstances of justice, whereas *Political Liberalism* starts from the modern condition of value pluralism, that people entertain, for good reasons, different and probably incompatible comprehensive philosophical doctrines. *Political Liberalism* also repudiates the main arguments for the two principles of *A Theory of Justice*. The contractarian argument was only a 'device of representation'; no metaphysical understanding of the self was or needs to be presupposed; and it is a mistake to think agreement to the principles of justice could rely on deep-lying acceptance of a broader moral doctrine of fairness.

Nevertheless, *Political Liberalism* argues that a *political* conception of justice could command the support of an 'overlapping consensus' of various comprehensive doctrines in the society whose basic structure it regulates. A just society of free and equal citizens could thus endure over time even though deeply divided in its basic religious, moral and philosophical outlooks.

Some critics fear that Rawls' theory now only represents a pragmatic accommodation to the possibilities of consensus within particular societies. Yet *Political Liberalism* does not simply defend the politics of compromise and *modus vivendi*. It is an attempt to specify the terms of co-operation that can withstand the test of public and rational negotiation, commanding the freely given assent of equals. The worry should rather be that Rawls can no longer show why the well-ordered society must be one regulated by certain principles of justice, and vice versa. Rawls' idea of an 'overlapping consensus' may be so indeterminate as to yield very many different outcomes. Or it may deliver a specific outcome by prescriptively stipulating what shall and shall not count as reasonable doctrines. Moreover, it may miss the real nature of negotiating political difference in its representation of views and disagreement as 'reasonable'.

The last part of *A Theory of Justice* sketched an account of the development in the citizens of the just society of the requisite sense of justice. It offered a theory of moral education through the relationships of association within that society. Rawls now foreswears this kind of account. But to that extent any theory of political justice is 'thinner' and less plausible. Indeed, there is a general problem of the basic liberal approach. Rawls' conviction remains that, short of an unacceptable coerced unanimity, a domain of public agreement can be secured and clearly separated from the sphere of the heterogeneous private good. In this he remains faithful to the liberal vision of a society in which all equally and freely pursue their different lives constrained by public terms of fair co-existence. Yet such a vision may be impaled on the horns of a dilemma.

Either the terms of public agreement are so insubstantial as to yield only an empty form of political community. Or they are made substantial only by violating the requirement that disputed understandings of the good be restricted to the private sphere. A liberal political order may demand a culture of and education in liberal values. The good of society may not be so readily separable from the good of its citizens' private lives.

3 Robert Nozick

Robert Nozick's *Anarchy, State, and Utopia* (Nozick, 1974) is rightly paired with Rawls' *A Theory of Justice* when the contemporary resurgence of political philosophy is discussed. Nozick's book offers a startlingly different theory of justice from Rawls'. Where Rawls' outlook may be characterized as left-liberal, Nozick's is right-libertarian. In fact, Nozick articulates a particular strand of right-wing thinking that is quite distinct from, and probably uncongenial to, a traditional conservatism whose inspiration is more Hegelian and whose principal defenders are the British philosophers Michael Oakeshott and Roger Scruton.

Nozick's critique of Rawls is explicit and significant because it draws attention to claims of ownership and the idea of entitlement which are absent from *A Theory of Justice*. However, *Anarchy, State, and Utopia* is a very different book from *A Theory of Justice*. It is far less systematic; its arguments are often suggestive rather than conclusive, and its admissions of gaps and possible weaknesses are disarmingly frank. These features, together with its brashness of style and unattractive conclusions, have not endeared the book to many critics. But what cannot be denied is its inventiveness, originality and the force of many of its major claims. There is much of Nozick, too, within which political philosophers must work or explain why not.

Nozick's concern is a fundamental one for political philosophy: the existence and scope of the state. Should there be one, and what are the limits to its permitted activity? In Part I of *Anarchy, State, and Utopia*, Nozick argues, against anarchists, that a minimal state is justified. In Part II he argues, against interventionists, that no more than such a minimal state is warranted.

The foundations of Nozick's arguments are rights and OWNERSHIP (p. 550). The rights possessed by individuals are fundamental, and define a moral space surrounding each person whose invasion constitutes a wrong. Following Locke, Nozick holds the basic rights to be those to life, liberty, and 'estate' or property. For Nozick these rights are 'side-constraints' upon action, and have infinite moral weight. That is, no amount of good consequences, including even an overall diminution of rights violations, can justify a single violation of one of these rights. A good indication of Nozick's argumentative style is that he concedes in a footnote (p. 30) that rights violations might be allowed to avoid 'catastrophic moral horror'; and that later he considers the permissibility of actions which transgress others' rights provided that these rights holders are fully compensated. Nozick does not offer a systematic defence of his understanding of rights. At most he claims the underlying justification to be the Kantian view of INDIVIDUALS AS ENDS (p. 601), leading separate, different, consciously and deliberatively shaped lives, which should not be sacrificed or used as means to others' ends.

Nozick is egalitarian to the extent of holding that all humans equally possess these fundamental rights. He also endorses an initial equal distribution of ownership in respect of our selves. Each owns his or her own body, and its powers, capacities and abilities. Nozick believes that through an exercise of this initial self-ownership further entitlements to bits of the world are generated. He considers only one form of argument to show how this generation of entitlements might occur. This is John Locke's famous claim that one acquires rights to that with which one has mixed one's labour. Unfortunately, Nozick devotes four incisive pages to expose seemingly unanswerable difficulties in the Lockean account (pp. 174–178). This seems to leave Nozick with his own problem of unfounded entitlements, and so some critics have charged. But Nozick is appealing to the plausible background assumption that unowned objects are there to be owned, and that some sort of fruitful exercise of one's own powers grounds an entitlement to ownership of these objects. That is, provided certain conditions upon legitimate acquisition are met.

Entitlements

What occupies Nozick is less the process of acquisition than the limits that may be set upon its scope. Nozick borrows again from Locke and urges the acceptance of one fundamental proviso: 'A process normally giving rise to a permanent bequeathable property right in a previously unowned thing will not do so if the position of others no longer at liberty to use the thing is thereby worsened' (p. 178). Nozick's concern is to show that this proviso can be met by an established distribution of property entitlements, when one considers that there may no longer be any unowned objects for individuals to acquire. His answer is that individuals unable to appropriate are nevertheless better off living under a system permitting private property than they would be if no original appropriations had been permitted.

The account of entitlements is completed by acknowledging that those who hold bits of the world are entitled freely to transfer them if and to whomsoever they choose. It follows that those who receive such freely transferred holdings are themselves now entitled to hold them. Thus everything which is not unowned is legitimately owned if acquired justly (by some process which does not violate the Lockean proviso) or freely transferred from one who justly acquired it. A just set of holdings is just that set of holdings that came about in the right way.

In Part I of *Anarchy, State, and Utopia*, Nozick justifies a minimal state. He does so by constructing a plausible tale of how a state of nature might have given way to a state, that is an organization legitimately claiming a monopoly on the use of force within a given territory, without at any stage violating rights. The tale turns on the evolving competition between private agencies formed to protect their clients, with one eventually assuming a monopolistic role and adequately compensating the others for its usurpation of their functions.

Part II of *Anarchy, State, and Utopia* is devoted to a defence of the view that such a state, restricted to preventing force, theft and fraud, and enforcing contracts, is morally sufficient. Any greater role for the state is illegitimate. Of course an obvious reason for a greater role would be that people's holdings need to be redistributed in accord with a theory of justice. Nozick's own theory of justice does not require any such action by government. His task is then to show that redistributive theories of justice are mistaken, and what they require of the state illicit.

The distinction Nozick draws is between his own entitlement theory of justice, and patterned or end-state theories. His is an historical theory since the justice of a set of holdings is given by the propriety of the history which led up to it. End-state theories are unhistorical, specifying that a distribution must conform to a prescribed structure. More particularly, patterned theories prescribe a distribution of holdings according to some natural attribute or ordered set of such attributes, such as intelligence or effort. Nozick's critique of non-historical theories is both general and specific. At a general level he insists that no patterned distribution can be maintained without persistent and serious violations of the right to liberty. His reasoning is simple. Voluntary transfers of those holdings initially assured under any patterned distribution will subvert the pattern and transgress the principle underlying the pattern. Such transfers are easy to imagine, and appear eminently unobjectionable inasmuch as they can be simple, consensual, bilateral exchanges. Nozick's own famous example is of fans willingly paying extra to see an especially talented basketball player, Wilt Chamberlain. Such transfers can only be prevented by denying individuals the right to do with their holdings as they choose. Surely no consistent theory of justice can both distribute holdings and deny the individuals to whom they come any effective control over them?

Nozick's specific criticisms are of Rawlsian and egalitarian theories of justice. The fundamental weakness of Rawls' theory is that it proceeds as if individuals did not already have claims to ownership of themselves and bits of the world. A cake spontaneously given to a group might be divided amongst its members in a way close to Rawls' principles; a cake that I have baked or whose ingredients you have provided will be divided in quite another way. Rawls is simply wrong to discount the various entitlements individuals bring to any determination of who gets what. People, not least, are entitled to their natural assets, and, consequently, to any rewards that may flow from these. Rawls is mistaken to think that these assets are a collective resource, or that the difference principle which reflects this assumption would be acceptable to the well-off who are required to make a comparatively greater sacrifice so that the worst off benefit.

Nozick finds no justification either for any egalitarian principle. A demand for equality of material condition reduces to an unsubstantiated claim that the function of society is to meet the needs of its members, and simply discounts the fact that things are already attached to particular individuals. Equality is not required for self-esteem, which in fact thrives on comparable differences. At base the demand for equality is driven by envy.

Nozick's theory of justice permits the government no interventionist role beyond the rectification of injustices by the terms of the entitlement principle. It is ironic then that, given the logistic difficulties in tracking back and forward between past wrongs and present holdings, Nozick should suggest the difference principle as a rough rule of thumb for rectifying injustices (p. 231). Otherwise holdings must be left as they have come legitimately to stand. That this may result in great disparities of wealth and life prospects is regrettable, but no injustice is involved. The rich may choose to be philanthropists but they do no wrong in not being. And it would violate their rights to require that they assist the less fortunate. This seems harsh but it is not obviously wrong-headed. Liberal critics chide Nozick for offering a 'libertarianism without foundations', but this may not be quite true.

Nozick's foundations are attractive ones. Individuals do appear to have rights in the sense that it would be fundamentally wrong to do certain things to them in the name of a greater social good. Individuals do also have a claim to ownership of their selves. That this is so can be shown by considering one's reaction to the idea that bodily parts should be redistributed equitably or to benefit the least fortunate in this respect. Do the blind have a claim upon at least one of the eyes of the sighted?

Criticism of Nozick is more appropriately directed at his rendering of these foundations and how he builds upon them. There is little warrant for construing rights in an absolute and exclusively negative manner, not least when appeal is made to Kantian underpinnings. Within a moral community, individuals in need may, on Kant's own principles, have the right to contributions from those who can help them. It is an impossibly stringent requirement of rights merely that they rule out invasions of our moral space and do nothing to sustain us in our satisfaction of basic needs.

Nozick may be right to think that we, severally, own ourselves and may, in consequence and by some form of activity, come to make legitimate claims upon what is unowned. But, arguably, the conditions he sets for legitimate acquisition are too lax and too easily met in ways that favour free-market capitalism. It may very well be possible to concede an initial equality in self-ownership, and the legitimacy of some process of acquisition of unowned objects, but then to specify sufficiently tough conditions of legitimacy to ensure that a final equality of holdings is ensured. Again, the 'Lockean proviso' need not be as easily satisfied by his favoured set of economic arrangements as Nozick assumes, especially once ambiguities in both the sense of 'better off' and the baseline against which comparisons are made can be clarified.

Nozick seems to presume throughout that ownership is full and exclusive ownership by individuals, and that anything less amounts to a violation of liberty rights. Yet Nozick forgets that, for Locke, individuals made claim through their labouring not upon what was unowned, but what was communally owned. In his Wilt Chamberlain example, he assumes that individuals within the patterned distribution have holdings with which they are free to do as they choose. All forms of redistribution, including taxation, are implausibly stigmatized as coercive interferences with freedom. Yet it is possible that individuals might choose to limit in advance departures from a favoured pattern of distribution, and to do so in the name of a liberty-preserving equality of condition.

In sum, Nozick's theory is not so much libertarianism without foundations, as libertarianism with unwarranted conclusions. His case against anarchy may be accepted. His claim that state minimalism is utopian in a positive sense remains unproven.

4 Communitarianism

The wealth and diversity of post-Rawlsian political philosophy is indicated by two features: the number of distinct but interrelated themes which now form its subject matter, and the emergence of identifiable movements of thought to complement Rawls' liberalism and Nozick's libertarianism. I propose dealing with each of these features in turn. The three movements which deserve consideration are communitarianism, feminism and Marxism.

Communitarianism is distinguishable from the other movements in two ways. The writers gathered under this title – Roberto Unger (1975), Michael Sandel (1982), Michael Walzer (1983), Charles Taylor (1985), Alasdair MacIntyre (1981, 1988), and Richard Rorty (1989, 1991) – are disparate and do not consciously subscribe to a common manifesto. It is more accurate to speak of family resemblances than a single, shared programme. Secondly, in the respects in which they are all communitarian, they offer not so much an alternative political view to liberalism as a criticism of its presuppositions.

As the name suggests, communitarianism is concerned with community, and more particularly its absence from the liberal account. In fact there are four different ways in which community figures in this criticism, which need carefully to be distinguished.

Firstly, the priority which Rawls accords the virtue of justice is alleged to derive from an impoverished understanding of political association. Rawls claims that justice is the first virtue of social institutions, that it is required to deal with limited benevolence, moderate scarcity and modern value pluralism, and that it is needed to protect individuals from being sacrificed for the society's greater good. According to communitarian critics, however, justice is only the ideal of societies that do not display community. Communities proper do not need to be just, and would not be communities if they felt such a need. Michael Sandel (1982) characterizes justice as a *remedial* virtue, binding up in the best way possible a second-best form of social co-operation.

The sense in which justice has primacy for Rawls has already been indicated, and Sandel's criticism appears misplaced. Resolution in the face of death is not less of a human virtue for being redundant in immortal creatures. Sandel does not claim, as have some Marxists for instance, that the circumstances of justice will disappear in the future. He says only that some communities do not display them. But these – most notably the family –

cannot be the models for society as a whole. The family has those character-istics that make its members benevolently disposed to one another – closeness, and affectivity rooted in natural relationships – because it is not simply a smaller kind of society but something quite different altogether. Societies cannot be *familial* communities.

The second way in which community figures in the communitarian criticism is in the claim that membership of a political community is a good that liberalism neglects, ignores, or whose sense it cannot successfully capture by its own terms. Political association is viewed by liberals and libertarians as an instrumental good. It realizes the compromises necessary for individuals to derive mutual advantage from co-operating. There is no other sense of being together as citizens than is required to bring about this end. Rawls and Nozick both talk of community, or even communities, growing up within this framework. But these seem inessential and somehow added onto the basic terms of political association.

This would not be so serious a criticism were it not for the further claim that a liberal theory of justice needs more. Sandel charges that Rawls defends a difference principle without foundations. Acceptance of this principle re-quires a willingness to see one's natural assets as communally owned, and yet Rawls' theory allows for no community that could lay such a claim to ownership. On Rawls' account I see my talents as for others to derive benefits from, yet there is no reason why I should see myself as joined to these others. Rawls' own attempt in Part III of *A Theory of Justice* to supply an account of how we acquire a sense of justice that does bind us together in subscription to publicly acknowledged rules of fair co-operation has now been abandoned. Whether a satisfactory account of how a society can be both fair and well-ordered has taken its place is open to question.

The third relevant use of community is in the communitarian claim that what is good and just for individuals is defined by the community to which they belong. Alasdair MacIntyre (1981, 1988) is associated with the view that an individual's good is inseparable from the ROLE (p. 372), office or social position that he or she fills. Michael Walzer (1985) makes the further claim that, since the goods to be distributed have particular SOCIAL MEANINGS (pp. 368–74), the justice of their distribution is relative to these meanings. As these meanings have particular social and historical location, so do the associated principles of justice.

However, the besetting danger of any appeal to the existence of distinct understandings of the good and the just is RELATIVISM (pp. 379–82). *This* society is just by its own lights; *that* society is just by its own lights. And never shall the two be compared. Further, shared understandings determine not only what is just but what is unjust. Yet these particular judgements may violate what, plausibly, ought to be UNIVERSAL MORAL STANDARDS (pp. 599–601). Imagine a society by whose understanding of the master–slave relationship 20 lashes a day are fair and sufficient. If a master administers 25 he is unjust and if only 15 he behaves generously. But surely any beating is wrong, and any 'rules' of slavery are unjust, whatever the members of the society believe.

The fourth and final communitarian appeal to community figures in a criticism of the alleged 'thinness' of the philosophical liberal's understanding of the 'self'. The facts specifying the social and historical situation of each person constrain the kinds of self-understanding that person can reach, and the choices he or she will make. The Rawlsian individual is not 'embedded' in any place or time and is so emptied of substantial, individuating features as to make it difficult to be described as choosing a life. How can a self-less person be said to have any conception of the good or make choices of ends?

This criticism may rest on a misunderstanding. Rawls' concern is not to define idealized choosers of the good so much as to specify the relevant considerations entering into a jointly agreed determination of the public rules of fair co-operation. As he now insists, his theory of justice is not metaphysical but political and assumes no particular understanding of the self.

At the same time, the criticism may be overstated. To claim that individuals are wholly defined, and their identity completely constituted by their membership of some community at some historical moment, is effectively to deny them any kind of meaningful choice over their lives. It also seriously undermines any claim they might make to be MORAL AGENTS (chapter 6). And to the extent that the communitarian claim is qualified by phrases such as 'to a large extent' it is hard to see what distinguishes the communitarian from the liberal.

The communitarian challenge to liberalism is, to repeat, represented by a very assorted collection of views that seem united more by their shared distaste for the alleged ahistorical individualism of liberal theory than any single plausible and attractive alternative. Michael Walzer (1983) does defend a very substantial and original political thesis. But his work apart, the political proposals of communitarians are, as liberals quickly point out, poorly spelt out. Or, worse, they suggest an illiberal concession to whatever happens to be the shared understandings and practices of a particular time and place (Gutman, 1985).

Nevertheless, liberalism has responded in interesting ways to the communitarian challenge. A useful re-statement of basic liberal commitments is needed to show that some communitarian criticisms are unexceptionable or evidently false. This re-statement would also show communitarianism to miss its target. Community of the sort demanded by the communitarians is impossible or will betray the great gains made by liberalism – particularly, for instance, in the equal possession by all of fundamental rights. More positively, liberals can argue that what they are able to offer is a very strong kind of community, grounded in equal freedom and the mutual toleration of disparate kinds of life.

5 Feminism

Because it is covered elsewhere, I propose to say little of FEMINISM (chapter 32). In fact feminism offers two quite distinct kinds of criticism of philosophical liberalism. The first concentrates on the silence of liberal political theory and, being consciously *ad hominem*, of its male theorists about women's place in a just society. More particularly, this silence is compounded by assumptions about what this place actually is and should remain. A formal commitment to the equality of all is gainsaid by an endorsement of *patriarchalism*, which is not always only implicit. Patriarchalism here means the doctrine of the subordination of women to male power.

The Public and the Private

The crucial assumption underpinning liberal patriarchalism is that, to the distinction between public and private spheres of activity, there corresponds a difference in nature between men and women, and the roles for which these natures best suit them. The woman is confined to the family where her biology equips her to bear, rear and care. The woman is thus doubly oppressed — excluded from the public, political sphere where the liberal principle of equality operates, and the inferior of her male provider within the private household.

In terms of oppression related to the distinction between public and private spheres, Susan Moller Okin (1989) accuses Rawls of perpetuating liberal patriarchalism. He never broaches the issue of sexual justice, yet assumes both the continued existence of the institution of the family, and, more pertinently, the traditional sexual division of labour within this institution. Okin can reasonably claim that a family whose structure is deeply unjust cannot, as Rawls expects, be the appropriate institution for acquiring a sense of justice. Okin's critique of the family is nevertheless not a radical one. She merely insists that Rawlsian principles of justice be universal in scope and extend to all institutions, including the family.

The second line of feminist criticism concerns the alleged maleness of being preoccupied with justice and rights. Appeal is made to a distinctive female ethics which emphasizes attachment, responsibility, context and particularity as opposed to independence, rights, abstraction and universality. The idea that women speak in another moral 'voice' to that of men is due principally to the work of Carol Gilligan (1982) in the psychology of moral development. But the contrast between an ethics of care and one of justice now enjoys wide currency in moral and political philosophy. Gilligan herself does not see these moral outlooks as mutually exclusive; nor does she see each of them as necessarily associated with one particular gender. Indeed, she seems to favour an account of moral development which emphasizes the socializing role of parents, whatever their gender.

From the standpoint of social and political philosophy, this particular line of criticism bites only if the prevailing liberal accounts of the good society may be judged defective for omitting mention of care. It begs too many questions to suggest that justice applies in the public sphere, and care in the private. It would also grossly oversimplify to suggest that social co-operation could be governed exclusively either by rules of justice or by an ethos of care. Indeed there are reasons to agree with the Rawlsian view that justice has primacy. Care alone cannot determine who should be in receipt of what goods. And where care fails or falls short of what is desired, justice specifies what can be legitimately expected of others. Nevertheless, the opposition between care and justice highlights – as does the communitarian critique – the extent to which a society governed solely by respect for rights and a 'sense of justice' may not generate any real sense of relatedness and interdependence amongst its members.

6 Analytical Marxism

Marxism is the subject of chapter 24, but a particular form of Marxism is appropriately discussed as part of post-Rawlsian political philosophy. This is what has been termed ANALYTICAL or RATIONAL CHOICE MARXISM (pp. 619–22). As the first term implies, its protagonists have displayed the virtues of anglophone philosophy in general, namely, argumentative rigour, scrupulous attention to the text, and careful conceptual analysis. As the second term implies, most of its writers have employed assumptions common to much of current English-speaking political philosophy, chiefly that social arrangements, both actual and desired, are best understood as the outcome of the actions of rational, but differentially endowed individuals.

Whether such work is Marxist is debateable. It certainly eschews wholesale subscription to every aspect of Marx's work, and prefers instead separately to appraise the distinct claims that may be said to constitute this theory. It has rejected a certain understanding of history, teleological and HEGELIAN (chapter 23) in origin, and, in the case of Jon Elster (1985) at least, embraced a robust methodological individualism that is very unfamiliar amongst Marxists. It has been willing to jettison what many would see as central Marxist claims, for instance the labour theory of value, and has increasingly conceded the attractiveness of non-Marxian theories in political philosophy.

In what sense then is analytical Marxism Marxist? In one of its earliest and most influential texts, G. A. Cohen (1978) defended an 'orthodox' interpretation of historical materialism, whereby changes in the relations of production may be attributed to the development of the productive forces, that development tend to be historically continuous. Analytical Marxism has also insisted upon the specific character of capitalism, and sought to explicate the manner both in which such a society is fundamentally flawed, and in which socialism represents a feasible and desirable alternative. And there is the rub. To the extent that one is faithful to Marx, a plausible and coherent account is difficult to find; and to the extent that the resources of contemporary political philosophy are employed to remedy these defects such an account ceases to be distinctively Marxist.

In the first instance it needs to be shown that Marx had a theory of justice by which capitalism can be judged to be unjust. This task confronts a familiar paradox. Marx employs a language with apparent moral import, yet explicitly disdains moral criticism and theory (Lukes, 1985). The paradox is not easy to resolve, and any resolution may simply have to accommodate the fact that Marx was not consistent in his outlook (Geras, 1985).

If capitalism *is* unjust, then for Marxists that injustice must inhere in some significant feature of the relationship between capitalist and proletarian. Two candidates suggest themselves. The first is that the capitalist *exploits* the proletarian. An understanding of exploitation as the extraction of surplus value is not available to those who reject the labour theory of value. However, there is a common sense understanding of exploitation as one side taking unfair advantage of another. Does this apply? The situation may be such that one side does better, and the other worse, than both would do in some alternative set of circumstances. Further, the difference between actuality and an imagined alternative can be specified in terms of differential access to some set of resources, for instance the means of production. This approach is due to the work of John Roemer (1982). But, as it has been developed, it may not necessarily have the normative weight that would seem to be needed. Some form of exploitation may characterize every society, including socialism. Moreover, the difference in ownership of resources which defines the capitalist relation need not be unfair. It may have arisen in a perfectly legitimate fashion, for instance through the superior efforts, talents and assiduity of the capitalist or, on the other hand, the capitalist's prodigality. The idea of a 'cleanly generated capitalism' conforms to Robert Nozick's prescription of a just distribution that has arisen by just steps from an originally just situation. Marxists who accept Nozick's premises of self-ownership and entitlement to the fruits of one's labour may have to embrace this uncongenial conclusion.

The second candidate for explaining the injustice of the capitalist relation is *coercion*. Workers may be unfairly forced to work for their employers. The difficulty is that for any one worker the alternatives to employment are not so stark and restrictive as would be required to establish coercion. This is especially true in a modern welfare society where it must also be acknowledged that avenues of escape from one's class do exist for the talented and hard working. In response it may be insisted that what is possibly true of a few individuals cannot be true of the class as a whole (G. A. Cohen, 1983). Nevertheless, it remains to be shown that the whole class has a reason to abolish its 'collective unfreedom'.

Difficulties in appreciating the specific inequity of capitalism are compounded by imprecision in the recommendations of socialist justice. Notoriously Marx said little about the lineaments of the future society, and what he did say suggests utopianism in the pejorative sense of this word. Talk of a society 'beyond justice' might imply the view that the circumstances of justice will be transcended. This is unrealistic. Or it might imply the irrelevance of any evaluative criteria to such a society. This is dangerously naive. Marxists can engage with other contemporary political philosophers on the grounds of equality, emphasizing the deep, structured inequalities of present capitalist society and the manner in which these inequalities corrupt any formal equality of civic rights. But if they are to be radical egalitarians they may differ little from some liberals, or be beset by difficulties which derive from their commitment to principles, such as that of self-ownership, which liberals do not share (G. A. Cohen, 1990).

There is a final important point. Any theory that indicts the present society of fundamental injustice and recommends a future perfect society needs an account of the means of transforming the first into the second. Traditionally, Marxism relied on some combination of the historical guarantee of revolutionary change and the uniquely important role of the proletariat. Analytical Marxism is not teleologically optimistic and has tended to reticence about proletarian activism. This is partly due to its individualist presuppositions, which make it hard to appreciate the factors disposing to and inhibiting collective agency. At the same time a rational choice Marxism retaining an orthodox understanding of the proletariat's mission would need to show that what is in the interests of the majority of society's members coincided with the morally desired emancipation of all. This is increasingly difficult for there is no longer a group of individuals who satisfy the various requirements of that orthodoxy – being the exploited bulk of capitalist society with nothing to lose and everything to gain by overthrowing that society and its injustices.

Analytical Marxism has performed a signal service by bringing Marxism within the fold of contemporary political philosophy. But it may have done so at the price of exposing serious, if not fatal, shortcomings in Marxism. And to the extent that analytical Marxists have become political philosophers they have arguably ceased to be Marxists.

7 Themes

In the final section of this chapter, I want to explore some general questions about the nature and content of contemporary social and political philosophy. My discussion will illuminate more clearly differences between the various movements already examined. But it will also reveal differences of emphasis and stance within these movements, and will expose views that do not neatly fit within any of the movements. Finally, I hope to display the sorts of issues that political philosophy needs to confront, both those on which it has had a great deal to say and those about which it has been comparatively silent.

7.1 Political philosophy

Firstly, then, we should discuss the question of what political philosophy is taken to be, and what it is thought a political theory should do. I do not mean by this whether a theory should be about justice, the state, the class struggle or whatever. I mean what a theory is taken to be doing when it answers a self-chosen question such as 'What is justice?' There are four broad sorts of answer.

The first is that a theory should be built upon foundations that are universally recognized and evident truths; its procedure of argumentation and reasoning should similarly be unexceptionable and acceptable to any rational person. It is likely that these foundations will comprise some understanding of the individual human being.

Both Rawls' *A Theory of Justice* and Nozick's *Anarchy, State, and Utopia* may be represented as political theory in this foundational sense. The problem with this approach is that it risks being empty or contentious. Either the foundational understanding of the human being commands universal agreement in virtue of being emptied of real substantive content, or is a recognizably interesting view but thereby partial and controversial. A familiar criticism of Rawls is that his contracting individuals are not those of any time and place, but historically and culturally located agents – western, liberal men.

A response to these problems is self-consciously to adopt a stance that is rooted in one's own culture and history. Borrowing Plato's famous metaphor, Michael Walzer contrasts a philosophical attitude that walks out of the cave and seeks the high ground of universal objectivity with one that takes its stand in the cave and with its inhabitants. This 'way of doing philosophy is to interpret to one's fellow citizens the world of meanings that we share.' (Walzer, 1983, p. xiv) The problems with this approach are threefold. Firstly, as has already been noted, it courts relativism: the good society is each and every society that judges itself to be good by its own lights. Secondly, a society's practices, however unjust they may seem to the reasonable outsider, are not open to criticism if, on the inside, that society lacks the shared meanings which could inform such a critique. Thirdly, the approach tends to conservatism. It implies that a society's meanings are defined by its existing practices. But there is no space from which to judge these practices. Or, put another way, the meanings by which the practices could be judged appear to float outside the society (J. Cohen, 1986).

Rawls appears to have moved from his original foundationalism towards this second understanding of political theory. In *Political Liberalism* (Rawls, 1993) he views the liberal conception of justice as expressing ideas that are implicit within the institutions and public culture of constitutional democratic regimes. Yet this is not a simple shift from universal to particular, from transcendental rules of justice to the particular virtues of American constitutionalism. 'Kantianism in one country' is a fine and witty definition of Rawls' political philosophy. It is possible, and plausible, to believe that modern democracy is an historical achievement which institutes general moral principles – equality of respect for individual choices of life, and the public justifiability of agreed rules of social co-operation. Actually existent institutions may approximate to these ideals, but they nevertheless aspire to them.

At the same time Rawls would now insist that political philosophy is turned to when a society's shared understandings break down and come into conflict. Philosophy resolves these conflicts by ascending to abstractions which are nevertheless also somehow uncovered through fundamental ideas deep and implicit within the society's culture (Rawls, 1993, pp. 44–6). This is somewhat mysterious. It may also betray a false optimism that the plurality of fundamental beliefs that characterizes modern society is, at some level, eliminable. On the other hand, if the implication is that we can reach outside the terms of our present, public culture for values that validate it, then too many crucial questions have been begged. This at least is the charge of Richard RORTY (pp. 653–4) (Rorty, 1989, 1991). Whether or not democratic liberalism stands at the end of ideological history is a question that anglophone philosophy is on the whole ill-equipped to acknowledge or to answer, not least because it lacks the means to theorize ideas of modernity and historical progress. Philosophy in the English-speaking world is notoriously incapable of ·'reflexive social understanding', which would involve its being in a position to interrogate itself about its relation to the society and history in which it is situated (Williams, 1980).

One way to open a space between presently shared meanings and preferred alternatives is given by the third approach to political philosophy, which may be termed critique. Marx famously remarked that science would be unnecessary if reality and appearance coincided. His scientific concern was to disclose the real workings of capitalism, which could not be apparent to those who lived and worked under it.

Analogously, the task of political philosophy may be to reveal what our shared meanings do not and cannot say about our political world. The function of critique is to display these gaps and thus the distance between actuality and the moral pretensions generated by that actuality. To the extent that analytical Marxism shares many of the premises and concepts of contemporary philosophical liberalism it may be said to have eschewed critique in favour of criticism. However, feminist political theory does aspire to critique when it seeks to show how unspoken assumptions – about women's nature, the public–private divide, the family – explain why liberalism is both silent about, but eloquent in its implicit endorsement of, women's continued subordination.

The fourth, and final approach to political philosophy is hostile to any misjudged rationalist ambitions that theory might have. It repudiates the idea that political association must self-consciously realize any desired ends or purposes. Instead it sees the tasks of political theory as being more modest and restricted. It is the articulation of the commonly acknowledged rules of conduct that inform our actual practices. It salutes the historical achievements of modern liberalism, not least the emergence of 'individuality' and 'civility', that is, law and civic order. Yet it refuses to see these eminently practical achievements as conforming to universal, objective principles that may be laid bare. Political theorizing should be faithful to the knowledge that is already presupposed in our practice; it should 'pursue the intimations' of established traditions.

The author of this approach is Michael Oakeshott (1962, 1975). His sceptical and nuanced conservatism does not figure large in most surveys of contemporary political philosophy, perhaps because he speaks at a tangent to its main concerns. Yet his work has been influential in a British conservatism, ably represented by Roger Scruton (Scruton, 1984), which keeps its distance from both American philosophical liberalism and the free market, anti-statism that often passes for contemporary right-wing thinking. At the same time, there is in such work a Hegelian sensitivity to history and practice which importantly distinguishes it from the simple appeal to shared meanings that characterizes the second approach.

7.2 Politics

Our second important question is, What is politics? In other words, what is the scope of political activity, what distinguishes it from other forms of human activity, and what is its importance? Here it is best to consider a number of oppositions. Firstly, there is that between what we could call *instrumental* and *expressivist* understandings of politics. According to the instrumental understanding, politics is a means used by essentially independent individuals to secure the agreements that are necessary if they are to obtain the benefits of co-operation and to avoid the costs of non-agreement. It is the politics of bargaining, compromise, accommodation, and achieving a *modus vivendi*. The political sphere is like a market-place in which individuals come to make their separate deals and then return to live their lives. Politics has no further function than is necessary to facilitate and protect the agreements made.

On the expressivist understanding, political activity is itself valuable. It is an important way in which human beings express themselves as social, co-operative creatures enjoying an interdependent existence. This is the politics of participation, community and republican citizenship. The political sphere is a forum in which people come together as citizens, and it is a vital constituent of the full life led by all. Politics is impoverished to the extent that it falls short of exhibiting this character.

On the whole, liberals, and certainly libertarians, have favoured the former understanding. Their preference derives from according a primary importance to liberty and believing that individual purposes will be various. Political activism, of the sort envisaged by expressivists, is unlikely to be spontaneously universal, and will be unacceptable if it is coerced. Perhaps in part for this reason, liberals, despite a clear preference for it as a regime, have had little to say about how democracy should actually work and what particular form it should take. Democracy tends to be seen as merely the formalized process by which SOCIAL CHOICES (pp. 375–9) are generated from the rational preferences of individuals. Famous paradoxes and difficulties characterize the translation of many individual choices into a single public choice.

Socialists and feminists, on the other hand, have been much concerned with democratic theory and practice. Some of this concern is attributable to the expressivist ideal of political participation as a good (Pateman, 1970); some is also due to a worry about reconciling the formal equality of political citizenship with the various inequalities, of race, class and gender, which characterize civil society.

Related to, but distinct from, the instrumental–expressivist distinction is that between *public* and *private*, which was introduced in section 5. As this distinction is now understood, the public comprises the political, legal and economic, or the world in which individuals work, vote and are accountable to the rest of society for their actions. The private is the personal and familial, the sphere of the household in which individuals love, play and generally retreat from the public world.

To this distinction corresponds differences of motivation, relatedness and loyalty. The public world is cold, impersonal, governed by abstract rules, in which independent and mutually disinterested individuals meet. The private is the emotionally warm haven in which individuals are bound by particular relationships of affection, loyalty and mutual interdependence.

Liberals have, on the whole, refused to see the private as political. Indeed the private sphere is that with which the state has no business and into which it should not intrude. This is plausible in so far as liberals have characterized private activity as being self-regarding in J. S. Mill's sense, which means that its harmful effects, if any, are confined to the agent. Consensual sexual behaviour and procreative decisions, according to liberals, are paradigmatically private in this regard.

It is to feminism that we owe a critique of the public–private divide. This insists, firstly, that the scope and character of the private is determined publicly by law and policy. It is not that the private domain pre-exists and limits that of the public. Rather the terms of privacy are set within the public sphere. Indeed, the very inauguration of the private, and civil society, may be due to an unnoticed but deeply illegitimate 'sexual contract' in which the male subordinated the female to serve his sexual purposes (Pateman, 1988).

Secondly, the private is political if 'political' extends to describe any structure or relationship in which some individuals exercise significant power over others. The family is the object of interest here. The traditional institution is marked by a familiar sexual division of labour with the husband being dominant over the wife. Any characterization of familial relations as being private amounts to a public endorsement of their continuing inequity.

Even on their own principles, liberals should be interested in the family, for it can support or undermine broader social justice. This is not only in so far as the family is, as noted earlier, a site of moral education, or a place where a sense of justice is learned; it is also that the family is the major means by which assets – property as well as natural endowments – are transferred across generations. Differences between familial situations remain a crucial obstacle to securing equality of opportunity (Fishkin, 1983).

The final opposition sets the *political* against the *economic*. Although the economic is included within the public sphere, there is a tendency amongst liberals to be relatively indifferent towards various economic arrangements. These, to simplify their view, are to be preferred on grounds of efficiency not morality. In *A Theory of Justice*, Rawls leaves open the choice between a private property economy and socialism (1972, p. 258). In *Political Liberalism*, he maintains that the question is 'not settled at the level of first principles of justice', but depends on the contingencies of a country's particular institutions and historical circumstances (Rawls, 1993, p. 338). But the economic is political in three important regards.

Firstly, liberal principles of justice apply to the distributive sphere, which means that they determine who gets which goods once they are produced. But principles restricted to distribution leave out of account the productive sphere, which concerns what is produced by whom. Decisions may be taken as to what goods are produced and in what quantities. It can sometimes seem as if the goods to be distributed, according to liberal theories of justice, have just dropped from heaven; that is quite explicit in Bruce Ackerman's account (1980) where he speaks of manna.

Secondly, there is stronger claim, associated with Marx, that production determines distribution, which means that a distribution of goods to be consumed is a consequence of how production itself is organized. If this determinist thesis is true then principles of distributive justice are in an important sense beside the point.

Thirdly, the economic sphere is one to which political considerations directly apply. Work constitutes a significant part of an individual's life. In itself it can be rewarding or frustrating, self-realizing or alienating. It can be self-directed or performed under conditions of subordination to another. Work is also instrumentally valuable in so far as payment for employment determines one's level of subsistence and the character of one's work affects one's social status and self-esteem.

It is important then to recognize that employment – an individual's right to it, and the determination of its conditions – are proper subjects for political inquiry. Socialists have attended to these issues. They have defended an extension of democracy to the work place, and have been more generally concerned about the proper balance between market and state control, private and public ownership.

7.3 Value pluralism

I want now to turn to the currently dominant political theory, philosophical liberalism, and to interrogate it on a number of points. The first point is about value pluralism. Rawls has explicitly located the historical origins of the modern liberal democratic state in the post-Reformation tolerance of religious difference, and defines the starting point of political liberalism as the ineliminability of a diversity of reasonable, comprehensive doctrines (Rawls, 1993).

For many liberals, what follows from a recognition of value pluralism, together with the principle of equal respect for all choices of the good and the unacceptability of coerced conformity to some ideal of the good, is official *neutrality* on the question of the good (Dworkin, 1978; Ackerman, 1980, pp. 10–12). That is, a government must not in its laws or policies be guided by any particular preconception of the good life. Value pluralism is said to be consistent with the full rational autonomy of each chooser, and not to be the same as moral scepticism or relativism. Value pluralism stands opposed to *perfectionism*, the doctrine that there are specifiable human excellences such that some forms of human life are superior in themselves to others.

Rawls rejects perfectionism, but some liberals have insisted that, nevertheless, his own account of human good is too thin, and that we can make judgements about the relative worth of different forms of existence. This need not be inconsistent with a commitment to egalitarianism and tolerance

(Haskar, 1979; Galston, 1980). Moreover, there is a suspicion that Rawlsian liberalism is, at base, inconsistent. If it is strictly neutral then it cannot subscribe to any normative understanding of individuals – for example, that they should strive to be purposive, autonomous creatures. But such a view seems to be presupposed by Rawls. If, on the other hand, liberalism does include some foundational moral judgements about human beings, then it cannot reasonably claim objectivity for these judgements and refuse it for judgements about the good life.

It also seems clear that a liberal democratic culture will flourish to the extent that its citizens acquire and practice certain virtues – for example, those of tolerance, civility, respect for others and a willingness to make sacrifices for the common good. Now whether such virtues are learnt in childhood, or got through good habits, a liberal society must surely take the decision to encourage those social forms that facilitate the acquisition of such virtues.

Autonomy and Liberalism

In this context, Jo Raz (1986) is a revisionist liberal. He doubts whether liberty should be the central value, and defends instead the primacy of autonomy. His understanding of autonomy is that only a life chosen from among several moral options is autonomous. Further, Raz believes that, whilst not all forms of life are valuable, there may be several incompatible ones that are. Autonomy requires a plurality of moral life choices, and this in turn requires the creation and maintenance of social forms that are conducive to autonomy. The government has a duty to preserve these forms but, crucially, may do so in non-coercive ways. Subsidies and taxation can effectively render certain choices attractive or unattractive relative to others. Thus, Raz bites the bullet, holding that a liberal political culture should sustain its own core values, and not aspire to an implausible ideal of neutrality. Liberalism can be tolerant of diversity, interventionist and anti-perfectionist.

7.4 The liberal individual

A standard charge against liberalism is that it is individualistic. Methodological individualism is discussed elsewhere, and the various senses in which liberalism might be said to neglect community were considered in the section on communitarianism. What I wish briefly to investigate is, firstly, the moral status of the individual within liberalism and, secondly, the plausibility of its understanding of the individual.

The most notable way in which a liberal political theory can emphasize the inviolability of individuals is by according them fundamental rights. The possession of rights stipulates what cannot legitimately be done to persons by others without their consent (Nozick, 1974, p. xiv). Rights are the 'trumps' with which individuals can override considerations of the greater social good (Dworkin, 1977). Much contemporary liberalism is rights-based.

Yet should a liberal politics not also recognize the rights of groups: the right of a nation to self-determination, of a culture to self-expression, and of a religion to collective worship? These would appear not to decompose straightforwardly into the rights of the individual members of the group in question. And yet, according to some, there is a palpable inconsistency in according rights to both groups and individuals.

Philosophical liberalism has not devoted much attention to this question. But where it has done so, it has tried to argue that group rights, if they exist, can be defended in so far as such rights protect and advance the interests of individuals as members of groups (Raz, 1986, 207–9). The value of a culture is said to be that of cultural membership, and its value to the individuals who are members (Buchanan, 1991). In an original and arresting argument Kymlicka (1989) rejects the idea of group rights but commends a policy of actively seeking to preserve cultures. He does so by arguing that our cultural membership is a good in so far as it provides the necessary context from within which we are able to make and evaluate meaningful, rational autonomous choices of life. Charles Taylor has tried to defend a liberalism that might permit the state to nourish and protect a particular culture, so long as it was also able to secure the rights of those who do not share the dominant culture (Taylor, 1992).

The problem is that liberalism may be left with no other criterion for appraising different cultures than the extent to which they nurture the kind of individuals who are favoured by liberals. Should a liberal society tolerate a minority culture that does not respect autonomy, even if it supplies its members with an otherwise worthwhile life? Is cultural pluralism a good thing only if the various cultures are all consistent with liberal ideals of individuality?

These considerations lead back to the question of how liberalism understands the individual. Every political theory both presupposes and commends a particular view of human nature. That is, it must rest its claims upon a plausible conception of what human beings are like and what they can do. Equally, it recommends its political society for nurturing and sustaining a certain kind of human life. Philosophical liberalism is no different. It presupposes a capacity for rational and autonomous choice, an ability to stand back from and appraise one's circumstances, influences and projects. The rationality in question may be seen in straightforwardly 'economic' terms as the maximization of personal utility. It may extend to encompass a recognition of the obligations of justice. Liberal society is ideal in so far as it tolerates and indeed encourages individuality, which is expressed in a diversity of life choices.

Liberalism is open to challenge regarding both rationality and individual diversity. It may be urged that human beings are not rational in the stipulated sense, or that in significant ways they fall short of what the ideal of rationality prescribes. As suggested by research in psychology, human beings make decisions on grounds of which they are not conscious and which could not be acknowledged as rational. Again, human beings may be conformist, unconsciously influenced to choose in ways that do not set them apart from their peers. Even if these claims are true they may still be objectionable: individuals should *not* choose as they presently happen to choose.

But perhaps the argument can run the other way. The ideals of independence and autonomy are vulnerable to the criticism that our identity as members of groups is an ineliminable and valuable human trait. We are social creatures, belonging to particular tribes, cultures, religions, races and nations, and denying this belonging may be both impossible and damaging. Liberalism, it can be claimed, offers a deracinated politics, ignoring deep-rooted, particularized, local human identities and loyalties. Not only do some theorists believe that these facts make nonsense of liberalism's abstract individualism, they also suggest that its polity is bloodless and could not survive. With no sense of community beyond a shared commitment to the moral legitimacy of its foundations, liberalism is claimed to lack that *prior* sense of community that is necessary to sustain the mutual acceptance of the sacrifices that are demanded by membership of any political society. For a realistic sense of political community we must look to what already exists – ethnicity, tradition, cultural identity and a sense of nationhood – and work with, not against, the grain of people's rootedness. In the last analysis, this outlook may represent the best sense of communitarian and feminist criticisms of liberalism. It may also explain the comparative neglect by liberal political philosophy of issues of national, racial and ethnic identity.

7.5 Equality

The final theme arises out of a recognition of liberalism's greatest historical achievement, its institution of a principle of equality between all human beings. Political philosophy starts from a recognition that everybody is equal. But this is an ambiguous and problematic starting point. Difficulties arise both in specifying what equality requires and how it is to be combined with other ideals, most notably that of individual liberty. Rather than try to summarize all the very rich and varied arguments that are relevant, I shall briefly indicate the areas of debate.

If we are all equal in being free citizens, should this freedom be understood as the absence of constraints and obstacles, or the presence of meaningful and realizable options? Is our freedom best construed as a unity, or as a set of liberties with varying degrees of importance for us? Is a principle of equality no more than a prescription that all people are to be treated as moral equals, or does it require more substantive political, social and economic equality?

Rawls regards his first principle of justice as instituting a formal guarantee of equal citizenship, yet the difference principle tolerates social and economic inequality. Rawls sees no inconsistency here, though he concedes – as did Berlin – that differential access to resources will qualify the worth of equal liberty. The more you have the more you can make of a freedom that is shared equally with others in society. Socialist critics of liberalism have always insisted that this is unsatisfactory, arguing that real equality of freedom demands an equalization of resources. Some feminists have also argued that the public or legal equality of the genders is undermined by, and yet serves to disguise, a fundamental inequality of social power. This characterizes all male–female relationships within patriarchal society, and its elimination will require more far-reaching reform of society than simply instituting a principle of equal citizenship.

Walzer's argument (1983) is important in this context. He suggests that there are different spheres of justice, each being specified by a set of goods to be distributed and a consequent principle of their fair distribution. The unequal distribution of some goods need not in itself be unjust, but if this distribution determines the distribution of some other goods then that is unfair. It is not necessarily wrong that some people have more money than others; but it is unfair if their greater wealth buys them political power, office or greater personal health.

Walzer's approach highlights the fact that our favoured account of equality depends on what it is that we wish to see equally distributed. Is it simply some set of goods, one good, or what these goods may secure for us? Do we wish, for instance, to equalize resources or the satisfactions of consuming resources? It needs to be recognized that fairness may not require simple equality in distribution of goods; indeed, such an equality may well be unfair.

But what considerations should an egalitarian recognize as proper grounds for permitting departures from simple equality? Difference in *needs* suggests itself as an eminently plausible candidate, though the category of need is notoriously controversial. What of *desert*? We saw that Rawls refuses to acknowledge that individuals deserve their talents and anything that flows from these. Perhaps, to follow Dworkin's influential argument (1981), a principle of liberal equality should be 'endowment-insensitive' but 'ambition-sensitive'. That is, it should permit individuals' lives to flourish or founder as a result of the choices they make, but not as a consequence of their natural or social endowments. On such accounts, an individual should be recompensed for suffering disadvantages due to a handicap, but not for being less well-off through indulging an acquired expensive taste.

Any egalitarianism must also answer criticisms of both practice and principle. Egalitarianism may simply be inconsistent with certain immutable features of human motivation. It may not be possible to combine, within the individual, the attitude of universal impartiality and personal partiality (Nagel, 1991). Again, a society in which equality is guaranteed may lack the incentives necessary for maximizing the total social product and thereby improving the well-being of all. Egalitarianism must also meet Nozick's challenge that the case for equality is unproven, and anyway trumped by more fundamental ideals, such as freedom or self-ownership: a prior commitment to liberty undermines any guarantee of equality, and, correlatively, equality can only be maintained by the denial of individual freedom. The disputed relationship between equality and liberty may prove to be the most enduring and pressing issue of political philosophy. The fact that we have come full circle to the work of Berlin and Hayek certainly suggests an underlying continuity of concern in the subject.

8 Conclusion

Political philosophy is alive and well. It was not quite moribund in 1950 but the post-1970 revival now makes it appear so. The current dominance of philosophical liberalism may irk those who feel that its· approach pre-emptively biases consideration of important matters and ignores crucial facts. But those who feel that way must recognize that it is to liberals we owe the revival of political philosophy and our present ability to discuss the problems of our social and political existence. We may not wish to speak in the language of liberalism. But then philosophers can no longer, as Weldon once argued, be silent, and the onus is on those who dissent to perfect and practice the alternative languages of political criticism.

Further Reading

Of the general surveys of social and political philosophical work, Will Kymlicka's *Contemporary Political Philosophy* (1990) is the best. It is comprehensive, incisive and judicious. Raymond Plant's *Modern Political Thought* (1991) is well-informed and successfully brings out many of the main concerns of contemporary political theory (though he unaccountably ignores feminism). Philip Pettit's *Judging Justice* (1980) and Alan Brown's *Modern Political Philosophy* (1986) are also useful if more narrowly concerned with the main theories of distributive justice. *Philosophy and Public Affairs* remains the flagship journal of political philosophy in the present era. Robert E. Goodin and Philip Pettit (eds) *A Companion to Contemporary Political Philosophy* is a volume in the Blackwell Companion series. It contains extended essays on various disciplinary contributions to the subject, shorter entries on major ideologies, and short notes on special topics. The contributors are distinguished practitioners of the subject, the writing is almost uniformly excellent, and the whole text supplies an illuminating picture of post-Rawlsian political philosophy.

On Rawls the literature is voluminous. Norman Daniels (ed.) *Reading Rawls* (1975) collects the best of the earlier critical essays, and other standard commentaries are Brian Barry's *The Liberal Theory of Justice* (1973) and Robert Wolff's *Understanding Rawls* (1977). C. Kukathas and P. Pettit *Rawls. A Theory of Justice and its Critics* (1990) compares 'early' and 'late' Rawls, but before the publication of *Political Liberalism*.

Jeffrey Paul (ed.) *Reading Nozick* (1981) does for Nozick what Daniels does for Rawls, and Jonathan Wolff's *Robert Nozick* (1991) offers an unprejudiced but critical account of Nozick's theory. Stephen Mulhall and Adam Swift *Liberals and Communitarians* (1992) provides a fine, clearly written review of the debate between liberals and their communitarian critics, even if it struggles somewhat to find the common themes in communitarianism. In addition to Gutman (1985), useful evaluations of communitarianism are also in

Kymlicka (1988) and in Buchanan (1989). Buchanan (1991) also examines moral questions surrounding the issue of political secession.

G. A. Cohen has worried at and about the legacy of Marx and its relationship to current political philosophy with more acuity and assiduity than anyone. *History, Labour, and Freedom, Themes from Marx* (1988) collects together some of his best pieces. Eric Olin Wright's *Classes* (1985) is a good example of what analytical Marxism, informed by sociological research, has to say about a key Marxist concept. Andrew Levine's *Arguing for Socialism* (1988), is an open-minded and systematic defence of socialist ideals in the context of post-Rawlsian political philosophy.

Eva Feder Kittay and Dian T. Meyers (ed.) *Women and Moral Theory* (1987) gives a good sense of Gilligan's impact upon moral and political thinking. Alison M. Jaggar's *Feminist Politics and Human Nature* (1983) is a standard introduction to feminist political theory, whilst Jean Grimshaw's *Feminist Philosophers* (1986) is also clearly written and relevant.

An introduction to British conservatism is provided by Charles Covell *The Redefinition of Conservatism* (1986), and Paul Franco's *The Political Philosophy of Michael Oakeshott* (1990) offers a comprehensive, if cautious, account of his subject.

References

Ackerman, B. 1980: *Social Justice in the Liberal State*. New Haven: Yale University Press.

Barry, B. 1973: *The Liberal Theory of Justice*, Oxford: Clarendon Press.

Berlin, I. 1958: Two Concepts of Liberty. In his *Four Essays on Liberty*, Oxford: Clarendon Press, 6–19.

Brown, A. 1988: *Modern Political Philosophy*. Harmondsworth: Penguin.

Buchanan, A. 1989: Assessing the Communitarian Critique of Liberalism. In *Ethics*, 99, pp. 852–82.

—— 1991: *Secession. The Morality of Political Divorce from Fort Sumter to Lithuania and Quebec*. Boulder: Westview Press.

Cohen, G. A. 1978: *Karl Marx's Theory of History: A Defence*. Oxford: Oxford University Press.

—— 1983: The Structure of Proletarian Freedom. In *Philosophy and Public Affairs*, 12:1, 3–33.

—— 1988: *History, Labour, and Freedom*. Oxford: Clarendon Press.

—— 1990: Marxism and Contemporary Political Philosophy, or: Why Nozick Exercises some Marxists more than he does any Egalitarian Liberals. In *Canadian Journal of Philosophy*, supplementary volume 16, 363–87.

Cohen, J. 1986: Review of Walzer, *Spheres of Justice*. In *The Journal of Philosophy*, 83:8, pp. 457–68.

Covell, C. 1986: *The Redefinition of Conservatism*. Basingstoke: Macmillan.

Daniels, N. (ed.) 1975: *Reading Rawls*. Oxford: Blackwell.

Dworkin, R. 1977: *Taking Rights Seriously*. London: Duckworth.

—— 1978: Liberalism. In S. Hampshire (ed.) *Public and Private Morality*, Cambridge: Cambridge University Press, 113–43.

—— 1981: What is Equality? Part 1: Equality of Welfare and What is Equality? Part 2: Equality of Resources. In *Philosophy and Public Affairs*, 10:3, 185–246, and 10:4, 283–345.

Elster, J. 1985: *Making Sense of Marx*. Cambridge: Cambridge University Press.

Fishkin, J. S. 1983: *Justice, Equal Opportunity, and the Family*, New Haven: Yale University Press.

Franco, P. 1990: *The Political Philosophy of Michael Oakeshott*. New Haven: Yale University Press.

Galston, W. A. 1980: *Justice and the Human Good*. Chicago: University of Chicago Press.

Geras, N. 1985: The Controversy about Marx and Justice. In *New Left Review*, 150, 47–85.

Gilligan, C. 1982: *In a Different Voice*. Cambridge, Mass: Harvard University Press.

Goodin, B. and Pettit, P. (eds) 1993: *A Companion to Contemporary Political Philosophy*, Oxford: Blackwell.

Gray, J. 1984: *Hayek on Liberty*. Oxford: Blackwell.

Grimshaw, J. 1986: *Feminist Philosophers*. Brighton: Wheatsheaf.

Gutman, A. 1985: Communitarian Critics of Liberalism. In *Philosophy and Public Affairs*, 14:3, 308–22.

Haksar, V. 1979: *Equality, Liberty and Perfectionism*. Oxford: Oxford University Press.

Jaggar, A. 1983: *Feminist Politics and Human Nature*. Totowa, NJ: Rowman and Littlefield.

Kittay, E. F. and Meyers, D. T. (eds), 1987: *Women and Moral Theory*. Totowa, NJ: Rowman and Littlefield.

Kocis, R. A. 1980: Reason, Development, and the Conflict of Human Ends. Sir Isaiah Berlin's Vision of Politics. In *The American Political Science Review*, 74:1, 38–52.

Kukathas, C. and Pettit, P. 1990: *Rawls. A Theory of Justice and its Critics*. Cambridge: Polity.

Kymlicka, W. 1988: Liberalism and Communitarianism. In *Canadian Journal of Philosophy*, 18:2, 181–204.

—— 1989: *Liberalism, Community, and Culture*. Oxford: Clarendon Press.

—— 1990: *Contemporary Political Philosophy*. Oxford: Clarendon Press.

Laslett, P. 1950: Introduction. In P. Laslett (ed.) *Philosophy, Politics and Society*, Oxford: Blackwell, vii–xv.

Levine, A. 1988: *Arguing for Socialism*, revised edition. Boston: Routledge and Kegan Paul.

Lukes, S. 1985: *Marxism and Morality*. Oxford: Clarendon Press.

MacIntyre, A. 1981: *After Virtue*. London: Duckworth.

—— 1988: *Whose Justice? Whose Rationality?* London: Duckworth.

Mulhall, S. and Swift, A. 1992: *Liberals and Communitarians*. Oxford: Blackwell.

Nagel, T. 1991: *Equality and Partiality*. Oxford: Oxford University Press.

Nozick, R. 1974: *Anarchy, State and Utopia*. Oxford: Blackwell.

Oakeshott, M. 1962: *Rationalism in Politics*. London: Methuen.

—— 1975: *On Human Conduct*. Oxford: Clarendon Press.

Okin, S. M. 1989: *Justice, Gender, and the Family*. New York: Basic Books.

Pateman, C. 1970: *Participation and Democratic Theory*. Cambridge: Cambridge University Press.

—— 1988: *The Sexual Contract*. Cambridge: Polity.

Paul, J. (ed.) 1981: *Reading Nozick*. Oxford: Blackwell.

Pettit, P. 1980: *Judging Justice*. London: Routledge and Kegan Paul.

Plant, R. 1991: *Modern Political Thought*. Oxford: Blackwell.

Popper, K. 1945: *The Open Society and its Enemies*, in two volumes: I. *Plato* II. *Hegel and Marx*, London: Routledge and Kegan Paul.

Rawls, J. 1972: *A Theory of Justice*. Oxford: Oxford University Press.

—— 1993 *Political Liberalism*. New York: Columbia University Press.

Raz, J. 1986: *The Morality of Freedom*. Oxford: Clarendon Press.

Roemer, J. 1982: *A General Explanation of Exploitation and Class*. Cambridge, MA: Harvard University Press.

Rorty, R. 1989: *Contingency, Irony and Solidarity.* Cambridge: Cambridge University Press.
—— 1991: *Objectivity, Relativism and Truth.* Cambridge: Cambridge University Press.
Sandel, M. 1982: *Liberalism and the Limits of Justice.* Cambridge: Cambridge University Press.
Scruton, R. 1984: *The Meaning of Conservatism*, 2nd edn. Basingstoke: Macmillan.
Taylor, C. 1985: *Philosophy and the Human Sciences. Philosophical Papers 2.* Cambridge: Cambridge University Press.
—— 1992: *Multiculturalism and the Politics of Recognition*, commentary by A. Gutman; eds S. C. Rockefeller, M. Walzer and S. Wolf. Princeton: Princeton University Press.
Unger, R. M. 1975: *Knowledge and Politics.* New York: Free Press.
Walzer, M. 1983: *Spheres of Justice.* New York: Basic Books.
Weldon, T. D. 1953: *The Vocabulary of Politics.* Harmondsworth: Penguin.
Williams, B. 1980: Political Philosophy and the Analytical Tradition. In M. Richter (ed.) *Political Theory and Political Education.* Princeton, NJ: Princeton University Press.
Wolff, J. 1991: *Robert Nozick.* Cambridge: Polity.
Wolff, R. 1977: *Understanding Rawls.* Princeton, NJ: Princeton University Press.
Wright, E. O. 1985: *Classes.* London: Verso.

Discussion Questions

1   Are equality and liberty incompatible ideals?

2   Is value pluralism an ineliminable feature of modern society?

3   Are there any feasible ways in which the circumstances of justice could be transcended?

4   How egalitarian is the 'difference principle'?

5   Should a theory of justice be 'metaphysical' or 'political'?

6   Is the distribution of natural assets morally arbitrary?

7   Are rights 'side constraints' on actions?

8   Can we be said to own ourselves?

9   Is justice a matter of legitimate acquistion of goods, whatever the pattern of their distribution?

10   What arguments are there for equality?

11   Should autonomy rather than liberty be the central value of liberalism?

12   Is the idea of a 'liberal community' a contradiction in terms?

13   Does liberalism depend on an unacceptable conception of the individual?

14   Is a caring society morally preferable to a just one?

15   Can the family ever be a force for justice?

16 What for Marxists is wrong with capitalism?

17 Is 'analytical Marxism' Marxism at all?

18 Can political philosophy go beyond what we happen here and now to believe and value?

19 Is the human being a *political animal*?

20 Is anything really private in the sense of being beyond the public gaze and public concern?

21 Is the ideal of official neutrality on the question of the good life either feasible or desirable?

22 Why should minority cultures be protected or preserved?

23 Does justice lie beyond, between or within nations?

24 What inequalities in our material circumstances are permissible?

9

Philosophy of Science ─────────

David Papineau

The philosophy of science can usefully be divided into two broad areas. On the one hand is the epistemology of science, which deals with issues relating to the justification of claims to scientific knowledge. Philosophers working in this area investigate such questions as whether science ever uncovers permanent truths, whether objective decisions between competing theories are possible and whether the results of experiment are clouded by prior theoretical expectations. On the other hand are topics in the metaphysics of science, topics relating to philosophically puzzling features of the natural world described by science. Here philosophers ask such questions as whether all events are determined by prior causes, whether everything can be reduced to physics and whether there are purposes in nature. You can think of the difference between the epistemologists and the metaphysicians of science in this way. The epistemologists wonder whether we should believe what the scientists tell us. The metaphysicians worry about what the world is like, if the scientists are right. Readers will wish to consult chapters on EPISTEMOLOGY (chapter 1), METAPHYSICS (chapter 2), PHILOSOPHY of MATHEMATICS (chapter 10), PHILOSOPHY OF SOCIAL SCIENCE (chapter 11) and PRAGMATISM (chapter 26).

1 The Epistemology of Science

1.1 The Problem of Induction

Much recent work in the epistemology of science is a response to the problem of induction. Induction is the process whereby scientists decide, on the basis of various observations or experiments, that some theory is true. At its simplest, chemists may note, say, that on a number of occasions samples of sodium heated on a Bunsen burner have glowed bright orange, and on this basis conclude that in general *all* heated sodium will glow bright orange. In more complicated cases, scientists may move from the results of a series of complex experiments to the conclusion that some fundamental physical principle is true. What all such inductive inferences have in common, however, is that they start with particular premises about a *finite* number of past observations, yet end up with a general conclusion about how nature will *always* behave. And this is where the problem lies. For it is unclear how any finite amount of information about what has happened in the *past* can guarantee that a natural pattern will *continue* for all time.

After all, what rules out the possibility that the course of nature may change, and that the patterns we have observed so far turn out to be a poor guide to the future? Even if all heated sodium has glowed orange up till now, who is to say it will not start glowing blue sometime in the next century?

In this respect induction contrasts with deduction. In deductive inferences the premises guarantee the conclusion. For example, if you know that *Either this substance is sodium or it is potassium*, and then learn further that *It is not sodium*, you can conclude with certainty that *It is potassium*. The truth of the premises leaves no room for the conclusion to be anything but true. But in an inductive inference this does not hold. To take the simplest case, if you are told, for properties A and B, that *Each of the As observed so far has been B*, this does not guarantee that *All As, including future ones, are Bs*. It is perfectly possible that the former claim may be true, but the latter false.

The problem of induction seems to pose a threat to all scientific knowledge. All scientific discoveries worth their name are in the form of *general* principles. Galileo's law of free fall says that '*All* bodies fall with constant acceleration'; Newton's law of gravitation says that '*All* bodies attract each other in proportion to their masses and in inverse proportion to the square of the distance between them'; Avogadro's law says that '*All* gases at the same temperature and pressure contain the same number of molecules per unit volume'; and so on. The problem of induction calls the authority of all these laws in question. For if our evidence is simply that these laws have worked so far, then how can we be sure that they will not be disproved by future occurrences?

1.2 *Popper's falsificationism*

One influential response to the problem of induction is due to Sir Karl Popper (1902–94). In Popper's view (1959a, 1963, 1972), science does not rest on induction in the first place. Popper denies that scientists start with observations, and then infer a general theory. Rather, they first put forward a theory, as an initially uncorroborated conjecture, and then compare its predictions with observations to see whether it stands up to test. If such tests prove negative, then the theory is experimentally falsified, and the scientists will seek some new alternative. If, on the other hand, the tests fit the theory, then scientists will continue to uphold it – not as proven truth, admittedly, but nevertheless as an undefeated conjecture.

If we look at science in this way, argues Popper, then we see that it does not need induction. According to Popper, the inferences which matter to science are refutations, which take some failed prediction as the premise, and conclude that the theory behind that prediction is false. These inferences are not inductive, but deductive. We see that some A is not-B, and conclude that it is not the case that All As are Bs. There is no room here for the premise to be true and the conclusion false. If we discover that some body falls with *increasing* acceleration (say because it falls from a great height, and so is subject to a greater gravitational force as it nears the earth), then we know for sure that all bodies do not fall with constant acceleration. The point here is that it is much easier to disprove theories than to prove them. A single contrary example suffices for a conclusive disproof, but no number of supporting examples will constitute a conclusive proof.

So, according to Popper, science is a sequence of conjectures and refutations. Scientific theories are put forward as hypotheses, and they are replaced by new hypotheses when they are falsified. However, if scientific theories are always conjectural in this way, then what makes science better than astrology, or spirit worship, or any other form of unwarranted superstition? A non-Popperian would answer this question by saying that real science *proves* its claims on the basis of observational evidence, whereas superstition is nothing but guesswork. But on Popper's account, even scientific theories are guesswork – for they cannot be proved by the observations, but are themselves merely undefeated conjectures.

Popper calls this the 'problem of demarcation' – what is the difference between science and other forms of belief? His answer is that science, unlike superstition, is at least *falsifiable*, even if it is not provable (1959a, ch. 2). Scientific theories are framed in precise terms, and so issue in definite predictions. For example, Newton's laws tell us exactly where certain planets will appear at certain times. And this means that if such predictions fail, we can be sure that the theory behind them is false. By contrast, belief systems like astrology are irredeemably vague, in a way which prevents their ever being shown definitely wrong. Astrology may predict that Scorpios will prosper in their personal relationships on Thursdays, but when faced with a Scorpio whose spouse walks out on a Thursday, defenders of astrology are likely to respond that the end of the marriage was probably for the best, all things considered. Because of this, nothing will ever force astrologists to admit their theory is wrong. The theory is phrased in such imprecise terms that no actual observations can possibly falsify it.

Popper himself uses the criterion of *falsifiability* to distinguish genuine science, not just from traditional belief systems like astrology and spirit worship, but also from Marxism, psychoanalysis and various other modern disciplines that he denigrates as 'pseudo-sciences'. According to Popper, the central claims of these theories are as unfalsifiable as those of astrology. Marxists predict that proletarian revolutions will be successful whenever capitalist regimes have been sufficiently weakened by their internal contradictions. But when faced with unsuccessful proletarian revolutions, they simply respond that the contradictions in those particular capitalist regimes have not yet weakened them sufficiently. Similary, psychoanalytic theorists will claim that all adult neuroses are due to childhood traumas, but when faced by troubled adults with apparently undisturbed childhoods, they will say that those adults must nevertheless have undergone private psychological traumas when young. For Popper, such ploys are the antithesis of scientific seriousness. Genuine scientists will say beforehand what observational discoveries would make them change their minds, and will abandon their theories if these discoveries are made. But Marxists and psychoanalytic theorists frame their theories in such a way, argues Popper, that no possible observations need ever make them adjust their thinking.

1.3 The failings of falsificationism

At first sight Popper seems to offer an extremely attractive account of science. He explains its superiority over other forms of belief, while at the same time apparently freeing it from any problematic dependence on induction. Certainly his writings have struck a chord within the scientific community. Popper is one of the few philosophers ever to have become a Fellow of the Royal Society, an honour usually reserved for eminent scientists.

In the philosophical world, however, Popper's views are more controversial. This is because many philosophers feel that his account of science signally fails to solve the problem with which he begins, namely, the problem of induction (for example, see Ayer, 1956, pp. 71–5; Worrall, 1989). The central objection to his position is that it only accounts for *negative* scientific knowledge, as opposed to *positive* knowledge. Popper points out that a single counter-example can show us that a scientific theory is wrong. But he says nothing about what can show us that a scientific theory is right. Yet it is positive knowledge of this latter kind that makes science important. We can cure diseases and send people to the moon because we know that certain causes *do* always have certain results, not because we know that they *do not*. Useful scientific knowledge comes in the form 'All As are Bs', not 'It's false that all As are Bs'. Since Popper only accounts for the latter kind of knowledge, he seems leave out what is most interesting and important about science.

Popper's usual answer to this objection is that he is concerned with the logic of pure scientific research, not with practical questions about technological applications. Scientific research requires only that we formulate falsifiable conjectures, and reject them if we discover counter-examples. The further question of whether technologists should *believe* those conjectures, and *rely* on their predictions when, say, they administer some drug or build a dam, Popper regards as an essentially practical issue, and as such not part of the analysis of rational scientific practice.

But this will not do. After all, Popper claims to have solved the problem of induction. But the problem of induction is essentially the problem of how we can base judgements about the future on evidence about the past. In insisting that scientific theories are just conjectures, and that therefore we have no rational basis for *believing* their predictions, Popper is simply denying that we can make rational judgements about the future.

Consider these two predictions: (1) when I jump from this tenth floor window I shall crash painfully into the ground; (2) when I jump from the window I will float like a feather to a gentle landing. Intuitively, it is more rational to believe (1), which assumes that the future will be like the past, than (2), which does not. But Popper, since he rejects induction, is committed to the view that past evidence does not make any beliefs about the future more rational than any others, and therefore that believing (2) is no less rational than believing (1).

Something has gone wrong. *Of course* believing (1) is more rational than believing (2). In saying this, I do not want to deny that there is a *problem* of induction. Indeed it is precisely *because* believing (1) is more rational than believing (2) that induction is problematic. Everybody, Popper aside, can see that believing (1) is more rational than believing (2). The problem is then to explain *why* believing (1) is more rational than believing (2), in the face of the apparent invalidity of induction. So Popper's denial of the rational superiority of (1) over (2) is not so much a *solution* to the problem of induction, but simply a refusal to recognize the problem in the first place.

Even if it fails to deal with induction, Popper's philosophy of science does have some strengths as a description of pure scientific research. For it is certainly true that many scientific theories start life as conjectures, in just the way Popper describes. When Einstein's general theory of relativity was first proposed, for example, very few scientists actually *believed* it. Instead they regarded it as an interesting hypothesis, and were *curious* to see whether it was true. At this initial stage of a theory's life, Popper's recommendations make eminent sense. Obviously, if you are curious to see whether a theory is true, the next step is to put it to the observational test. And for this purpose it is important that the theory is framed in precise enough terms for scientists to work out what it implies about the observable world – that is, in precise enough terms for it to be falsifiable. And of course if the new theory does get falsified, then scientists will reject it and seek some alternative, whereas if its predictions are borne out, then scientists will continue to investigate it.

Where Popper's philosophy of science goes wrong, however, is in holding that scientific theories never progress beyond the level of conjecture. As I have just suggested, theories are often mere conjectures when they are first put forward, and they may remain conjectures as the intitial evidence first comes in. But in many cases the accumulation of evidence in favour of a theory will move it beyond the status of conjecture to that of established truth. The general theory of relativity started life as a conjecture, and many scientists still regarded it as hypothetical even after Sir Arthur Eddington's famous initial observations in 1919 of light apparently bending near the sun. But by now this initial evidence has been supplemented with evidence in the form of gravitational red-shifts, time-dilation and black holes, and it would be an eccentric scientist who nowadays regarded the general theory as less than firmly established.

Such examples can be multiplied. The heliocentric theory of the solar system, the theory of evolution by natural selection and the theory of continental drift all started life as intriguing conjectures, with little evidence to favour them over their competitors. But in the period since they were first proposed these theories have all accumulated a great wealth of supporting evidence. It is only those philosophers who have been bemused by the problem of induction who view these theories as being no better than initial hypotheses. Everybody else who is acquainted with the evidence has no doubt that these theories are proven truths.

1.4 Bayesianism

If we insist, against Popper, that we are fully entitled to believe at least some scientific theories on the basis of past evidence, then we are committed to finding some solution to the problem of induction. One currently popular account of the legitimacy of induction is found within Bayesianism, named after Thomas Bayes (c.1701–61) (Horwich, 1982, Howson and Urbach, 1989).

Bayesians are philosophers who hold that our beliefs, including our beliefs in scientific theories, come in degrees. Thus, for example, I can believe to degree 0.5 that it will rain today, in the sense that I think there is a 50 per cent likelihood of rain today. Similarly, I might attach a 0.1 degree of belief to the theory that the strong nuclear and electro-weak forces are the same force – I think it unlikely, but allow that there is a one-in-ten possibility it may turn out true.

As these examples indicate, Bayesians think of degrees of belief as the extent to which you subjectively take something to be PROBABLE (pp. 161–2). Accordingly, they argue that your degrees of belief ought to satisfy the axioms of the probability calculus. (See the box below for the 'Dutch Book Argument' for this thesis.) It is important to realize, however, that while Bayesians think of degrees of belief as probabilities in this mathematical sense, they still think of them as *subjective* probabilities. In particular, they allow that it can be perfectly rational for different people to attach *different* subjective probabilities to the same proposition – you can believe that it will rain today to degree 0.2, while I believe this to degree 0.5. What rationality does require, according to the Bayesians, is only that if you have a subjective probability of 0.2 for rain, then you must have one of 0.8 for its not raining, while if I have 0.5 for rain, then I must have 0.5 for its not raining. That is, both of us must accord, in our different ways, with the theorem of the probability calculus that $\text{Prob}(p) = 1 - \text{Prob}(\text{not-}p)$.

At first sight, this element of subjectivity might seem to disqualify Bayesianism as a possible basis for scientific rationality. If we are all free to attach whatever degrees of belief we like to scientific theories, provided only that we are faithful to the structure of the probability calculus, then what is to stop each of us from supporting different theories, depending only on individual fads or prejudices? But Bayesians have an answer, namely, that it does not matter what prejudices you start with, as long as you *revise* your degrees of belief in a rational way.

Bayesians derive their account of how to revise degrees of belief, as well as their name, from Bayes' theorem, originally proved by Thomas Bayes in a paper published in 1763. Bayes' theorem states:

$$\text{Prob}(H/E) = \text{Prob}(H) \times \text{Prob}(E/H)/\text{Prob}(E).$$

The simple proof of this theorem is given in the box. But the philosophical significance of the theorem is that it suggests a certain procedure for revising your degrees of belief in response to new evidence. Suppose that H is some hypothesis, and E is some newly discovered evidence. Then Bayesians argue that, when you discover E, you should adjust your degree of belief in H in line with the right-hand side of the above equation: that is, you should increase it to the extent that you think E is likely given H, but unlikely otherwise. In other words, if E is in itself very surprising (like light bending in the vicinity of the sun) but at the same time just what you would expect given your theory H (the general theory of relativity), then E should make you increase your degree of belief in H a great deal. On the other hand, if E is no more likely given H than it would be on any other theory, then observing E provides no extra support for H. The movement of the tides, for example, is no great argument for general relativity, even though it is predicted by it, since it is also predicted by the alternative Newtonian theory of gravitation.

Note in particular that this strategy for updating degrees of belief in response to evidence can be applied to inductive inferences. Consider the special case where H is some universal generalization – all bodies fall with constant acceleration, say – and the evidence E is that some particular falling body has been observed to accelerate constantly. If this observation was something you did not expect at all, then Bayesianism tells you that you should increase your degree of belief in Galileo's law significantly, for it is just what Galileo's law predicts. Of course, once you have seen a number of such observations, and become reasonably convinced of Galileo's law, then you will cease to find new instances surprising, and to that extent will cease to increase your degree of belief in the law. But that is as it should be. Once you are reasonably convinced of a law, then there is indeed little point in gathering further supporting instances, and so it is to the credit of Bayesianism that it explains this.

The Bayesian account of how to revise degrees of belief seems to make good sense. In addition, it promises a solution to the problem of induction, since it implies that positive instances give us reason to believe scientific generalizations.

There are, however, problems facing this account. For a start, a number of philosophers have queried whether Bayes' theorem, which after all is little more than an arithmetical truth, can constrain what degrees of belief we adopt in the future (see the box below). And even if we put this relatively technical issue to one side, it is unclear how far the Bayesian account really answers the worry raised above, that the subjectivity of degrees of belief will allow different scientists to commit themselves arbitrarily to different theories. The Bayesian answer to this worry was that Bayes' theorem will at least constrain these different scientists to revise their degrees of belief in response to the evidence in similar ways. But, even so, it still seems possible that the scientists will remain on different tracks, if they start at different places. If two scientists are free to attach different prior degrees of belief in Galileo's law, and both update those degrees of belief according to Bayes' theorem when they learn the evidence, will they not still end up with different *posterior* degrees of beliefs?

The standard answer to the objection is to appeal to *convergence* of opinion. The idea is that, given enough evidence, everybody will *eventually* end up in the same place, even if they have different starting points. There are a number of theorems of probability theory showing that, within limits, differences in initial probabilities will be 'washed out', in the sense that sufficient evidence and Bayesian updating will lead to effectively identical final degrees of belief. So in the end, argue Bayesians, it does not matter if you start with a high or low degree of belief in Galileo's law – for after 1,000 observations of constantly falling bodies you will end up believing it to a degree close to one anyway.

However, interesting as these results are, they do not satisfactorily answer the fundamental philosophical questions about inductive reasoning. For they do not work for all possible initial degrees of belief. Rather, they assume that the scientists at issue, while differing among themselves, all draw their initial degrees of belief from a certain range. While this range includes all the initial degrees of belief that seem at all intuitively plausible, there are nevertheless other possible initial degrees of belief that are consistent with the axioms of probability, but which will not lead to eventual convergence. So, for example, the Bayesians do not in fact explain what is wrong with people who never end up believing Galileo's law because they are always convinced that the course of nature is going to change tomorrow. Of course Bayesians are right to regard such people are irrational. But they do not explain why they are irrational. So they fail to show why all thinkers must end up with the same attitude to scientific theories. And in particular they fail to solve the problem of induction, since they do not show why all rational thinkers must expect the future to be like the past.

Bayesianism

The Dutch Book Argument

The axioms of probability require that

(1) $0 \leq \text{Prob}(P) \leq 1$, for any proposition P

(2) $\text{Prob}(P) = 1$, if P is a necessary truth

(3) $\text{Prob}(P) = 0$, if P is impossible

(4) $\text{Prob}(P \text{ or } Q) = \text{Prob}(P) + \text{Prob}(Q)$, if P and Q are mutually exclusive.

Bayesians appeal to the 'Dutch book argument' to show why subjective degrees of belief should conform to these axioms. Imagine that your degrees of belief did not so conform. You believe proposition P to degree y, say, and yet do *not* believe not-P to degree $1 - y$. (You thus violate the conjunction of axioms (2) and (4), because P or not-P is a necessary truth.) Then it will be possible for somebody to induce you to make bets on P and not-P in such a way that you will lose whatever happens. A set of bets that guarantee that you will lose whatever happens is called a 'Dutch book'. The undesirability of such a set of bets thus provides an argument that any rational person's subjective degrees of belief should satisfy the axioms of the probability calculus.

Bayes' Theorem

The conditional probability of P given Q – Prob(P/Q) – is defined as Prob(P and Q)/Prob(Q). Intuitively, Prob(P/Q) signifies the probability of P on the assumption that Q is true. It immediately follows from this definition that

Prob(H/E) = Prob(H) × Prob(E/H)/Prob(E)

This is Bayes' theorem. As you can see, it says that the conditional probability Prob(H/E) of some hypothesis H given evidence E is greater than Prob(H) to the extent that E is improbable in itself, but probable given H.

Bayesian Updating

Bayesians recommend that if you observe some evidence E, then you should *revise* your degree of belief in H, and set your new $Prob_{t'}(H)$ equal to your *previous* conditional degree of belief in H given E, $Prob_t(H/E)$, where *t* is the time before you learn E, and *t'* after. Bayes' theorem, applied to your subjective probabilities at *t*, then indicates that this will *increase* your degree of belief in H to the extent that you previously thought E to be subjectively improbable in itself, but subjectively probable given H.

   This Bayesian *recommendation*, that you revise your degree of belief in H by setting it equal to your old conditional degree of belief in H given E, should be distinguished from Bayes' *theorem*. Bayes' theorem is a trivial consequence of the definition of conditional probability, and constrains your degrees of belief at *a given time*. The Bayesian recommendation, by contrast, specifies how your degrees of belief should change *over time*. Bayes' theorem is uncontentious, but it is a matter of active controversy whether there is any satisfactory way of defending the Bayesian recommendation (Hacking, 1967, Teller, 1973).

1.5 *Instrumentalism versus realism*

At this stage let us leave the problem of induction for a while and turn to a different difficulty facing scientific knowledge. Much of science consists of claims about *unobservable* entities like viruses, radio waves, electrons and quarks. But if these entities are unobservable, how are scientists supposed to have found out about them? If they cannot see or touch them, does it not follow that their claims about them are at best speculative guesses, rather than firm knowledge?

   It is worth distinguishing this problem of unobservability from the problem of induction. Both problems can be viewed as difficulties facing *theoretical* knowledge in science. But where the problem of induction arises because scientific theories make *general* claims, the problem of unobservability is due to our *lack of sensory access* to the subject matter of many scientific theories. (So the problem of induction arises for general claims even if they are not about unobservables, such as 'All sodium burns bright orange'. Conversely, the problem of unobservability arises for claims about unobservables even if they are not general, such as, 'One free electron is attached to this oil drop'. In this section and the next, however, it will be convenient to use the term 'theory' specifically for claims about unobservables, rather than for general claims of any kind.)

   There are two general lines of response to the problem of unobservability. On the one hand are *realists*, who think that the problem can be solved. Realists argue that the observable facts provide good indirect evidence for the existence of unobservable entities, and so conclude that scientific theories can be regarded as accurate descriptions of the unobservable world. On the other hand are *instrumentalists*, who hold that we are in no position to make firm judgements about imperceptible mechanisms. Instrumentalists allow that theories about such mechanisms may be useful 'instruments' for simplifying our calculations and generating predictions. But they argue that these theories are no more true descriptions of the world than the 'theory' that all the matter in a stone is concentrated at its centre of mass (which is also an extremely useful assumption for doing certain calculations, but clearly false).

Earlier this century instrumentalists used to argue that we should not even *interpret* theoretical claims literally, on the grounds that we cannot so much as meaningfully talk about entities we have never directly experienced. But nowadays this kind of semantic instrumentalism is out of favour. Contemporary instrumentalists allow that scientists can meaningfully *postulate*, say, that matter is made of tiny atoms containing nuclei orbited by electrons. But they then take a SKEPTICAL (pp. 46–58) attitude to such postulates, saying that we have no entitlement to *believe* them (as opposed to using them as an instrument for calculations).

An initial line of argument open to realism is to identify some feature of scientific practice and then argue that instrumentalism is unable to account for it. One aspect of scientific practice invoked in this connection has been the *unification* of different kinds of theories in pursuit of a single 'theory of everything' (Friedman, 1984); other features of science appealed to by realists have included the use of theories to *explain* observable phenomena (Boyd, 1980), and the reliance on theories to make novel *predictions* (Smart, 1963). For, so the realist argues, these aspects of scientific practice only make sense on the assumption that scientific theories are *true* descriptions of reality. After all, says the realist, if theories are simply convenient calculating devices, then why expect different theories to be unifiable into one consistent story? Unification is clearly desirable if our theories all aim to contribute to the overall truth, but there seems no parallel reason why a bunch of instruments should be unifiable into one big 'instrument of everything'. And similarly, the realist will argue, there seems no reason to expect a mere calculating instrument, as opposed to a true description of an underlying reality, to yield a genuine explanation of some past occurrence, or a reliable prediction of a future one.

However, this form of argument tends to be inconclusive. There are two possible lines of response open to instrumentalists. They can offer an instrumentalist account of the relevant feature of scientific practice. Alternatively, they can deny that this feature really is part of scientific practice in the first place. As an example of the first response, they could argue that the unification of science is motivated, not by the pursuit of one underlying truth, but simply by the desirability of having a single all-purpose calculating instrument rather than a rag-bag of different instruments for different problems. The second kind of response would be to deny that unification is essential to science to start with. Thus Nancy Cartwright argues that science really *is* a rag-bag of different instruments. She maintains that scientists faced with a given kind of problem will standardly deploy simplifying techniques and rules of thumb which owe nothing to general theory, but which have shown themselves to deliver the right answer to the kind of problem at hand (Cartwright, 1983).

Similar responses can be made by instrumentalists to the arguments from explanation and prediction. Instrumentalists can either retort that there is no reason why the status of theories as calculating instruments should preclude them from giving rise to predictions and explanations; or they can query whether scientific theories really do add to our ability to predict and explain to start with. Not all these lines of response are equally convincing. But between them they give instrumentalism plenty of room to counter the initial realist challenge.

1.6 Theory, observation and incommensurability

A different line of argument against instrumentalism focuses on the distinction between what is observable and what is not. This distinction is crucial to instrumentalism, in that instrumentalists argue that claims about observable phenomena are unproblematic, but claims about unobservables are not. However, a number of writers have queried this distinction, arguing that observation reports are not essentially different from claims about unobservables, since they too depend on theoretical assumptions about the underlying structure of reality. Norwood Hanson (1958) has argued, for example, that scientists before and after Copernicus *saw* different things when they looked at the Sun: whereas pre-Copernicans regarded the Earth as stationary and so saw the Sun revolving round it, post-Copernican scientists saw the Sun as stationary and the Earth as rotating. Similarly, Hanson (1963) argues that the photographic plate which looks like a squiggly mess to a lay observer is *seen* as displaying a well-defined electron–positron pair by an experienced particle physicist. Examples like these undermine the distinction between what is observable and what is not, since they show that even judgements made in immediate response to sensory stimulation are influenced by fallible theories about reality.

Nor is the point restricted to recherché observations of astronomical bodies or subatomic particles. Even immediate perceptual judgements about the colour, shape and size of medium-sized physical objects can be shown to depend on theoretical assumptions implicit in our visual systems. Perhaps the best-known illustration is the Müller–Lyer illusion (see figure 9.1 opposite), which shows how our visual system uses complex assumptions about the normal causes of certain kinds of retinal patterns to draw conclusions about the geometry of physical figures. And analogous illusions can be used to demonstrate the presence of other theoretical presuppositions in our visual and other sensory systems.

As I said, in the first instance the unclarity of the observable–unobservable distinction counts against instrumentalism rather than realism. After all, it is instrumentalism, not realism, which *needs* the distinction, since instrumentalism says that we should be sceptical about unobservable claims, but not observable ones, whereas realism is happy to regard both kinds of claims as belief-worthy, so does not mind if they cannot be sharply distinguished.

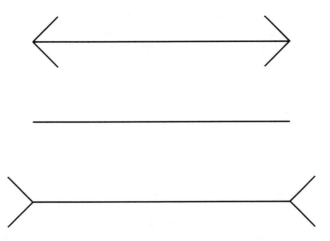

Figure 9.1 The Müller–Lyer illusion. Although all three lines are the same length, the top line, with inward-pointing arrowheads, appears to be shorter, and the bottom line, with outward-pointing arrowheads, appears to be longer, than the 'neutral' middle line.

However, there is another way of responding to doubts about the theory–observation distinction. For note that the arguments against the observable–unobservable distinction do not in fact vindicate the realist belief-worthiness of claims about *unobservables*; rather, they attack realism from the bottom up, and undermine the belief-worthiness of claims about *observables*, by showing that even observational claims depend on fallible theoretical assumptions. Obviously, if there is no observable–unobservable distinction, then all scientific claims are in the same boat. But on reflection it seems that the boat they all end up in is the instrumentalist boat of sceptical disbelief, not the realist one of general faith in science.

A number of influential recent philosophers of science, most prominently T. S. Kuhn (1962) and Paul Feyerabend (1976), have embraced this conclusion wholeheartedly, and maintained that no judgements made within science, not even observational judgements, can claim the authority of established truth. Rather, they argue, once scientists have embraced a theory about the essential nature of their subject matter, such as geocentrism, or Newtonian dynamics, or the wave theory of light, they will interpret all observational judgements in the light of that theory, and so will never be forced to recognize the kind of negative observational evidence that might show them that their theory is mistaken. Kuhn and Feyerabend independently lit on the term *incommensurable* to express the view that there is no common yardstick, in the form of theory-independent observation judgements, which can be used to decide objectively on the worth of scientific theories. Instead, they argue, decisions on scientific theories are never due to objective observational evidence, but are always relative to the presuppositions, interests and social milieu of the scientists involved.

Kuhn's and Feyerabend's blanket relativism has provoked much discussion among philosophers of science, but won few whole-hearted converts. Much of the discussion has focused on the status of observations. Most philosophers of science are prepared to accept that all observational judgements in some sense presuppose some element of theory. But many balk at the conclusion that observations therefore never have any independent authority to decide scientific questions. After all, they point out, most simple observations, such as that a pointer is adjacent to a mark on a dial, presuppose at most a minimal amount of theory, about rigid bodies, say, and about basic local geometry. Since such minimal theories are themselves rarely at issue in serious scientific debates, this minimal amount of theory-dependence provides no reason why observations of pointer readings should not be used to settle scientific disputes. If a scientific theory about the behaviour of gases, say, predicts that a pointer will be at a certain place on a dial, and it is observed not to be, then this decides against the theory about gases. It is not to the point to respond that, in taking the pointer reading at face value, we are making assumptions about rigid bodies and local geometry. For nothing in the debate about gases provides any reason to doubt these assumptions. And this of course is why scientists take such pains to work out what their theories imply about things like pointer readings – since observations of pointer readings do not depend on anything *contentious*, they will weigh with all sides in the scientific debate.

So, despite the arguments of Kuhn and Feyerabend, nearly all philosophers are realists about pointer readings and similar observable phenomena. But this still leaves us with the original disagreement between realism and instrumentalism about less directly observable entities. For, even if claims about pointer readings are uncontroversially belief-worthy, instrumentalists can still argue that theories about viruses, atoms and gravitational waves are nothing more than useful fictions for making calculations.

The realist response, as I said, is that the observable facts provide good indirect evidence for these theoretical entities, even if we cannot observe them directly. However, there are two strong lines of argument that instrumentalists can use to cast doubt on this suggestion. In the next two sections I shall discuss 'the underdetermination of theory by data' and 'the pessimistic meta-induction from past falsity'.

1.7 The underdetermination of theory by evidence

The argument from underdetermination asserts that, given any theory about unobservables that fits the observable facts, there will be other incompatible theories that fit the same facts. And so, the argument concludes, we are never in a position to know that any one of these theories is the truth.

Why should we accept that there is always more than one theory that fits any set of observable facts? One popular argument for this conclusion stems from the 'Duhem–Quine thesis'. According to this thesis, any particular scientific theory can always be defended in the face of contrary observations by adjusting auxiliary hypotheses. For example, when the Newtonian theory of gravitation was threatened by observations of anomalous movements by the planet Mercury, it could always be defended by postulating a hitherto unobserved planet, say, or an inhomogeneous mass distribution in the Sun. This general strategy for defending theories against contrary evidence seems to imply that the adherents of competing theories will always be able to maintain their respective positions in the face of any actual observational data.

Another argument for underdetermination starts, not with competing theories, but with some given theory. Suppose that all the predictions of some particular theory are accurate. We can construct a 'de-Ockhamized' version of this theory (reversing William of Ockham's 'razor' which prescribes that 'entities are not to be multiplied beyond necessity'), by postulating some unnecessarily complicated unobservable mechanism which nevertheless yields a new theory with precisely the same observational consequences as the original one.

Both of these lines of reasoning can be used to argue that more than one theory about unobservables will always fit any given set of observational data. Does this make realism about unobservables untenable? Many philosophers conclude that it does. But this is too quick. For we should recognize that there is nothing in the arguments for alternative underdetermined theories to show that these alternative theories will always be *equally well-supported by the data*. What the arguments show is that different theories will always be *consistent* with the data. But they do not rule out the possibility that, among these alternative theories, one is vastly more plausible than the others, and for that reason should be believed to be true. After all, 'flat earthers' can make their view consistent with the evidence from geography, astronomy, and satellite photographs, by constructing far-fetched stories about conspiracies to hide the truth, the effects of empty space on cameras, and so on. But this does not show that we need take their flat-earthism seriously. Similarly, even though Newtonian gravitational theory can in principle be made consistent with all the contrary evidence, this is no reason not to believe general relativity. Nor is our ability to 'cook up' a de-Ockhamized version of general relativity a reason to stop believing the standard version unencumbered with unnecessary entities.

Nevertheless, as I said, many contemporary philosophers of science do move directly from the premise that different theories are consistent with the observational evidence to the conclusion that none of them can be regarded as the truth. This is because many of them address this issue from an essentially Popperian perspective. For if you follow Popper in rejecting induction, then you will not believe that evidence ever provides positive support for any theory, except in the back-handed sense that the evidence can fail to falsify it. Accordingly you will think that all theories that have not been falsified are on a par, and in particular that any two theories that are both consistent with the evidence are equally well-supported by it.

So the arguments for underdetermination do present a problem to Popperians, since Popperians have no obvious basis for discriminating among different theories consistent with the data. But, as I pointed out above, these need not worry those of us who diverge from Popper in thinking unfalsified theories can be better or worse supported by evidence, for we can simply respond to the underdetermination arguments by observing that some underdetermined theories are better supported by the evidence than others.

Now that we have returned to Popper, it is worth noting that the Duhem–Quine argument also raises a more specific problem for Popperians. Recall that Popper's overall philosophy raised the 'problem of demarcation', the problem of how to distinguish science from other kinds of conjecture. Popper's answer was that science, unlike astrology, or Marxism and psychoanalytic theory, is falsifiable. But the Duhem–Quine argument shows that even such eminently scientific theories as Newtonian physics are not falsifiable in any straightforward sense, since they can always save themselves in the face of failed predictions by adjusting auxiliary hypotheses.

Not only does this cast doubt on Popper's dismissal of Marxism and psychoanalysis as unscientific, but it seems to undermine his whole solution to the demarcation problem. If such paradigmatic scientific theories as Newtonian physics are not falsifiable, then it can scarcely be falsifiability that distinguishes science from non-science. Still, this is Popper's problem, not ours (see Harding, 1975). If we do not reject induction, then we do not have a problem of demarcation. For we can simply say that what distinguishes successful scientific theories from non-science is that the observational evidence gives us inductive reason to regard scientific theories as true.

The arguments in the latter part of this section have presupposed that a certain kind of inductive argument is legitimate. The kind of inductive argument relevant to underdetermination is not simple 'enumerative' induction, from observed As being Bs to 'All As are Bs', but rather inferences from any collection of observational data to the most plausible theory about unobservables that is consistent with that data. But these are species of the same genus; indeed, enumerative inductions can themselves be interpreted as treating 'All As are Bs' as the most plausible extrapolation consistent with the observed As being Bs. My attitude to this more general category of inductive inferences remains the same as my attitude to enumerative induction, which I outlined earlier. We do not yet have an explanation of *why* inductive inferences are legitimate, and to that extent we still face a problem of induction. But it is silly to try to solve that problem by denying that inductive inferences are ever legitimate. And that is why the underdetermination of theory by data does not constitute a good argument for instrumentalism. For to assume that we are never entitled to believe a theory, if there are others consistent with the same data, is simply to assume the illegitimacy of induction.

The Underdetermination of Theory by Observational Data (UTD)

There are two arguments for the UTD. The first is based on the 'Duhem–Quine thesis', originally formulated by the French philosopher and historian Pierre Duhem (1861–1916) and later revived by the American logician W. V. O. Quine (b. 1908). Duhem (1951) and Quine (1951) point out that a scientific theory T does not normally imply predictions P on its own, but only in conjunction with auxiliary hypotheses H.

$$T \& H \Rightarrow P$$

So when P is falsified by observation, this does not refute T, but only the conjunction of T & H.

$$not\text{-}P \Rightarrow not\text{-}(T \& H)$$

So T can be retained, and indeed still explain P, provided we replace H by some alternative, H', such that

$$T \& H' \Rightarrow not\text{-}P.$$

This yields the Duhem–Quine thesis: any theoretical claim T can consistently be retained in the face of contrary evidence, by making adjustments elsewhere in our system of beliefs. The UTD follows quickly. Imagine two competing theories T_1 and T_2. Whatever evidence accumulates, versions of T_1 and T_2, conjoined with greatly revised auxiliary hypotheses if necessary, will both survive, consistent with that evidence, but incompatible with each other.

The other argument, first put forward by physicists like Henri Poincaré (1854–1912) and Ernst Mach (1838–1916) at the turn of the century, has a different starting point. Imagine that T_1 is the complete truth about physical reality, and that it implies observational facts O. Then we can always construct some 'de-Ockhamized' T_2 which postulates more complicated unobservable mechanisms but makes just the same observational predictions O. (Glymour 1980, ch. 5.)

For example, suppose we start with standard assumptions about the location of bodies in space–time and about the forces acting on them. A de-Ockhamized theory might then postulate that all bodies, including all measuring instruments, are accelerating by 1ft/sec.^{2} in a given direction, and then add just the extra forces required to explain this. This theory would clearly have exactly the same observational consequences as the original one, even though it contradicted it at the unobservable level.

To bring out the difference between the two arguments for UTD, note that the Duhem–Quine argument does not specify exactly which overall theories we will end up with, since it leaves open how T_1's and T_2's auxiliary hypotheses may need to be revised; the de-Ockhamization argument, by contrast, actually specifies T_1 and T_2 in full detail, including auxiliary hypotheses. In compensation, the Duhem–Quine argument promises us alternative theories *whatever* observational evidence may turn up in the future; whereas the de-Ockhamization argument assumes that all future observations are as T_1 predicts.

1.8 The pessimistic meta-induction

I turn now to the other argument against realism. This argument takes as its premise the fact that past scientific theories have generally turned out to be false, and then moves inductively to the pessimistic conclusion that our current theories are no doubt false too. (This is called a 'meta-induction' because its subject matter is not the natural world, but scientific theories about the natural world.)

There are plenty of familiar examples to support this argument. Newton's theory of space and time, the phlogiston theory of combustion, and the theory that atoms are indivisible were all at one time widely accepted scientific theories, but have since been recognized to be false. So does it not seem likely, the pessimistic induction concludes, that all our current theories are false, and that we should therefore take an instrumentalist rather than a realist attitude to them? (See Laudan, 1981.)

This is an important and powerful argument, but it would be too quick to conclude that it discredits realism completely. It is important that the tendency to falsity is much more common in some areas of science than others. Thus it is relatively normal for theories to be overturned in cosmology, say, or fundamental particle physics, or the study of primate evolution. By contrast, theories of the molecular composition of different chemical compounds (such as that water is made of hydrogen and oxygen), or the causes of infectious diseases (chickenpox is due to a herpes virus), or the nature of everyday physical phenomena (heat is molecular motion), are characteristically retained once they are accepted.

Nor need we regard this differential success-rate of different kinds of theories as some kind of accident. Rather, it is the result of the necessary evidence being more easily available in some areas of science than others. Paleoanthropologists want to know how many hominid species were present on earth 3 million years ago. But their evidence consists of a few pieces of teeth and bone. So it is scarcely surprising that discoveries of new fossil sites will often lead them to change their views. The same point applies on a larger scale in cosmology and particle physics. Scientists in these areas want to answer very general questions about the very small and the very distant. But their evidence derives from the limited range of technological instruments they have devised to probe these realms. So, once more, it is scarcely surprising that their theories should remain at the level of tentative hypotheses. By contrast, in those areas where adequate evidence is available, such as chemistry and medicine, there is no corresponding barrier to science moving beyond tentative hypotheses to firm conclusions.

The moral is that realism is more defensible for some areas of science than others. In some scientific subjects firm evidence is available, and entitles us to view certain theories, like the theory that water is composed of H_2O molecules, as the literal truth about reality. In other areas the evidence is fragmentary and inconclusive, and then we do better to regard the best-supported theories, such as the theory that quarks and leptons are the ultimate building blocks of matter, as useful instruments which accommodate the existing data, make interesting predictions, and suggest further lines for research.

At first sight this might look like a victory for instrumentalism over realism. For did not instrumentalists always accept that we should be realists about *observable* things, and only urge instrumentalism for uncertain theories about unobservable phenomena? But our current position draws the line in a different place. Instrumentalism, as originally defined, takes it for granted that everything *unobservable* is inaccessible, and that all theories about unobservables are therefore uncertain. By contrast, the position we have arrived at places no special weight on the distinction between what is observable and what is not. In particular, it argues that the pessimistic meta-induction fails to show that falsity is the natural fate of all theories about unobservables, but only that there is a line *within* the category of theories about unobservables, between those theories that can be expected to turn out false and those whose claims to truth are secure. So our current position is not a dogmatic instrumentalism about all unobservables, but merely the uncontentious view that we should be instrumentalists about that sub-class of theories which are not supported by adequate evidence.

1.9 Naturalized epistemology of science

In the last decade a number of philosophers of science have turned to a *naturalized* approach to scientific knowledge (Kitcher 1992). In place of traditional attempts to establish criteria for scientific theory-choice by *a priori* philosophical investigation, the naturalized approach regards science itself as a subject for *a posteriori* empirical investigation. Accordingly, naturalized epistemologists look to the history, sociology, and psychology of science, rather than to first principles, to identify criteria for the acceptability of scientific theories.

One apparent difficulty facing this kind of naturalized epistemology of science is that it is unclear how empirical investigation can ever yield anything more than *descriptive* information about how scientists actually operate. Yet any epistemology of science worth its name ought also to have a *normative* content – it ought to *prescribe* how scientists should reason, as well as describe how they do reason. David HUME (chapter 21) first pointed out that there is a logical gap between 'is' and 'ought'. A naturalized epistemology based on the empirical study of science seems fated to remain on the wrong side of this gap.

However, there is room for naturalized epistemologists to reply to this charge. They can agree that the empirical study of science cannot by itself yield prescriptions about how science ought to be done. But empirical study can still be *relevant* to such prescriptions. Suppose it is agreed that *technological fertility*, in the sense of generating technological advances, is a virtue in a scientific theory. Then the history, sociology and psychology of science might be able to show us that certain kinds of research strategies are effective at developing technologically fertile theories. More generally, given any agreed theoretical end Y, empirical study can show that research strategy X is an effective *means* to that end. The empirical study of science can thus yield the *hypothetical prescription* that, if you want Y, then you *ought* to adopt means X. It is this kind of hypothetical prescription that naturalized philosophers of science seek to establish: they look to the history, sociology and psychology of science to show us that scientists who *choose* theories on grounds X will in general *achieve* theories with characteristic Y.

Can the naturalized study of science tell us which research strategies are an effective means to theoretical *truth*? Different naturalized philosophers of science give different answers to this question. Many are suspicious of the idea of theoretical truth, and instead prefer to stick to the study of how to achieve more practical ends like technological fertility, simplicity, and predictive accuracy. However, there seems no good reason for this restriction. There is nothing obviously incoherent in the idea of looking to the empirical study of science to tell us which research strategies have proved a good way of developing true theories. Indeed, the discussion of the 'pessimistic meta-induction' in the previous section amounted to the sketch of just such an investigation, in that it appealed to the history of science to decide whether or not the standard procedures of scientific theory-choice succeed in identifying true theories. It is not difficult to imagine more detailed and specific studies of this kind of issue.

Let me now return briefly to the issue with which I began, namely, the problem of induction. It is possible that the naturalized study of how to get at the scientific truth will enable us to make headway with this problem. For an empirical investigation into science might be able to show us that a certain kind of *inductive* inference is in general a reliable guide to scientific truth. And this would then provide a kind of vindication of that inductive method (see Papineau, 1993, ch. 5).

It is true that this kind of defence of induction will inevitably involve an element of circularity. For when we infer that certain kinds of induction are *in general* a reliable guide to truth, on the basis of evidence from the history of science, this will itself be an inductive inference. It is a matter of some delicacy, however, whether this circularity is vicious.

Defenders of this naturalized defence of induction will point out that, from their point of view, a legitimate criterion of theory-choice need not be an *a priori* guide to truth, but only an empirically certifiable one. Given this, the original argument against induction, that it is not logically valid, will not worry naturalized philosophers of science. Induction may not provide any *a priori* guarantee for its conclusions; but from the naturalized point of view, this does not show that induction is in any way illegitimate, since it leaves it open that induction may be an empirically reliable guide to the truth. And if there is nothing to show that induction is illegitimate, naturalized philosophers of science can then argue, why should we not use it to investigate the worth of inductive inferences? Maybe this is less satisfying a defence of induction than we might originally have hoped for. But perhaps it is defence enough.

2 The Metaphysics of Science

2.1 Causation

Many issues in the metaphysics of science hinge on the notion of *causation*. This notion is as important in science as it is in everyday thinking, and much scientific theorizing is concerned specifically to identify the *causes* of various phenomena. However, there is little philosophical agreement on what it means to say that one event is the cause of another.

Modern discussion of causation starts with David Hume, who argued that causation is simply a matter of CONSTANT CONJUNCTION (p. 583). According to Hume (1978), one event causes another if and only if events of the type to which the first event belongs regularly occur in conjunction with events of the type to which the second event belongs. This formulation, however, leaves a number of questions open. Firstly, there is the problem of distinguishing genuine *causal laws* from *accidental regularities*. Not all regularities are sufficiently lawlike to underpin causal relationships. Being a screw in my desk could well be constantly conjoined with being made of copper, without its being true that these screws are made of copper because they are in my desk. Secondly, the idea of constant conjunction does not give a *direction* to causation. Causes need to be distinguished from effects. But knowing that A-type events are constantly conjoined with B-type events does not tell us which of A and B is the cause and which the effect, since constant conjunction is itself a symmetric relation. Thirdly, there is a problem about *probabilistic causation*. When we say that causes and effects are constantly conjoined, do we mean that the effects are always found with the causes, or is it enough that the causes make the effects probable?

Many philosophers of science this century have preferred to talk about *explanation* rather than causation. According to the covering-law model of explanation, something is explained if it can be deduced from premises which include one or more laws. As applied to the explanation of particular events, this implies that one particular event can be explained if it is linked by a law to some other particular event. However, while they are often treated as separate theories, the covering-law account of explanation is at bottom little more than a variant of Hume's constant conjunction account of causation. This affinity shows up in the fact that the covering-law account faces essentially the same difficulties as Hume: (1) in appealing to deductions from 'laws', it needs to explain the difference between genuine laws and accidentally true regularities; (2) it omits the requisite directionality, in that it does not tell us why we should not 'explain' causes by effects, as well as effects by causes; after all, it is as easy to deduce the height of a flagpole from the length of its shadow and the laws of optics, as to deduce the length of the shadow from the height of the pole and the same laws; (3) are the laws invoked in explanation required to be exceptionless and deterministic, or is it acceptable, say, to appeal to the merely probabilistic fact that smoking makes cancer more likely, in explaining why some particular person developed cancer?

In what follows I shall discuss these three problems in order (treating them as problems that arise equally both for the analysis of causation and the analysis of explanation). After that I shall consider some further issues in the metaphysics of science.

The Covering-Law Model of Explanation

According to this model (originally proposed by Hempel and Oppenheim, 1948, and further elaborated in Hempel, 1965) one statement (the *explanandum*) is explained by other statements (the *explanans*) if and only if the explanans contains one or more *laws*, and the explanandum can be *deduced* from the explanans. In the simplest case, where the explanandum is some particular statement to the effect that some individual *a* has property E, we might therefore have:

a has C

For all x, if x has C, then x has E

---

a has E

For example, we might deduce that a piece of litmus paper turned red, from the law that all litmus paper placed in acid turns red, together with prior condition that this piece of litmus paper was in fact placed in acid. The model can accommodate more complicated explanations of particular events, and can also allow explanations of laws themselves, as when we deduce Kepler's law that all planets move in ellipses, say, from Newton's law of universal gravitation and his laws of motion.

As applied to the explanation of particular events, the covering-law model implies a symmetry between *explanation* and *prediction.* For the information that, according to the model, suffices for the explanation of some known event should also enable us to predict that event if we did not yet know of it. Many critics have fastened on this implication of the model, however, and pointed out that we can often predict when we do not have enough information to explain (as when we predict the height of the flagpole from its shadow) and can often explain when we could not have predicted (as when we explain X's cancer on the basis of X's smoking).

These examples suggest that genuine explanations of particular events need to cite genuine causes, and that the reason the covering-law model runs into counter-examples is that it adds nothing to the inadequate constant conjunction analysis of causation, except that it substitutes the term 'law' for 'constant conjunction'. To get a satisfactory account of explanation we need, firstly, to recognize that explanations of particular events must mention causes, and, secondly, to improve on the constant conjunction analysis of causation.

There is a variant of the covering-law model which allows non-deterministic explanation as well as deterministic ones. This is termed the 'inductive–statistical (I–S)' model, by contrast with the original 'deductive–nomological (D–N)' model. An example would be:

a drinks 10 units of alcohol per diem

For p per cent of xs, if x drinks 10 units of alcohol per diem, x has a damaged liver

---

a has a damaged liver

Here the explanandum cannot be *deduced* from the explanans, but only follows with an *inductive* probability of p; and the inference appeals to a *statistical* regularity, rather than an exceptionless *nomological* generalization. In Hempel's original version of this model, it was required that the probability of the explanandum be *high.* A better requirement, however, as explained in the section on probabilistic causation below, is that the particular facts in the explanans need only make the probability of the explanandum *higher* than it would otherwise have been.

2.2 Laws and accidents

There are two general strategies for distinguishing laws from accidentally true generalizations. The first stands by Hume's idea that causal connections are mere constant conjunctions, and then seeks to explain why some constant conjunctions are better than others. That is, this first strategy accepts the principle that causation involves nothing more than certain events always happening together with certain others, and then seeks to explain why some such patterns – the 'laws' – matter more than others – the 'accidents'. The second strategy, by contrast, rejects the Humean presupposition that causation involves nothing more than happenstantial co-occurrence, and instead postulates a relationship of 'necessitation', a kind of 'cement', which links events that are connected by law, but not those events (like being a screw in my desk and being made of copper) that are only accidentally conjoined.

There are a number of versions of the first Humean strategy. The most successful, originally proposed by F. P. Ramsey (1903–30), and later revived by David Lewis (1973), holds that laws are those true generalizations that can be fitted into an ideal system of knowledge. The thought here is that the laws are those patterns that are somehow explicable in terms of basic science, either as fundamental principles themselves, or as consequences of those principles, while accidents, although true, have no such explanation. Thus, 'All water at standard pressure boils at 100° C' is a consequence of the laws governing molecular bonding; but the fact that 'All the screws in my desk are copper' is not part of the deductive structure of any satisfactory science. Ramsey neatly encapsulated this idea by saying that laws are 'consequences of those propositions which we should take as axioms if we knew everything and organized it as simply as possible in a deductive system' (1978, p. 130).

Advocates of the alternative non-Humean strategy object that the difference between laws and accidents is not a *linguistic* matter of deductive systematization, but rather a *metaphysical* contrast between the kind of links they report. They argue that there is a link in nature between *being at 100° C* and *boiling*, but not between *being in my desk* and *being made of copper*, and that this is nothing to do with how the description of this link may fit into theories. According to D. M. Armstrong (1983), the most prominent defender of this view, the real difference between laws and accidents is simply that laws report relationships of natural *necessitation*, while accidents only report that two types of events *happen* to occur together.

Armstrong's view may seem intuitively plausible, but it is arguable that the notion of necessitation simply re-states the problem, rather than solving it. Armstrong says that necessitation involves something more than constant conjunction: if two events are related by necessitation, then it follows that they are constantly conjoined; but two events can be constantly conjoined without being related by necessitation, as when the constant conjunction is just a matter of accident. So necessitation is a stronger relationship than constant conjunction. However, Armstrong and other defenders of this view say very little about what this extra strength amounts to, except that it distinguishes laws from accidents. Armstrong's critics argue that a satisfactory account of laws ought to cast more light than this on the nature of laws.

2.3 The direction of causation

Hume said that the *earlier* of two causally related events is always the cause, and the *later* the effect. However, there are a number of objections to using the earlier–later 'arrow of time' to analyse the directional 'arrow of causation'. For a start, it seems in principle possible that some causes and effects could be simultaneous. More seriously, the idea that time is directed from 'earlier' to 'later' itself stands in need of philosophical explanation – and one of the most popular explanations is that the idea of 'movement' from earlier to later depends on the fact that cause–effect pairs always have a given orientation in time. However, if we adopt such a 'causal theory of the arrow of time', and explain 'earlier' as the direction in which causes lie, and 'later' as the direction of effects, then we will clearly need to find some account of the direction of causation which does not itself assume the direction of time.

A number of such accounts have been proposed. David Lewis (1979) has argued that the asymmetry of causation derives from an 'asymmetry of overdetermination'. The overdetermination of present events by past events – consider a person who dies after simultaneously being shot and struck by lightning – is a very rare occurrence. By contrast, the multiple 'over-determination' of present events by future events is absolutely normal. This is because the future, unlike the past, will always contain multiple traces of any present event. To use Lewis' example, when the President presses the red button in the White House, the future effects do not only include the dispatch of nuclear missiles, but also his fingerprint on the button, his trembling, the further depletion of his gin bottle, the recording of the button's click on tape, the emission of light waves bearing the image of his action through the window, the warming of the wire from the passage of the signal current, and so on, and on, and on.

Lewis relates this asymmetry of overdetermination to the asymmetry of causation as follows. If we suppose the cause of a given effect to have been absent, then this implies the effect would have been absent too, since (apart from freaks like the lightning–shooting case) there will not be any other causes left to 'fix' the effect. By contrast, if we suppose a given effect of some cause to have been absent, this does not imply the cause would have been absent, for there are still all the other traces left to 'fix' the cause. Lewis argues that these counterfactual considerations suffice to show why causes are different from effects.

Other philosophers appeal to a probabilistic variant of Lewis' asymmetry. Following Reichenbach (1956), they note that the different causes of any given type of effect are normally probabilistically independent of each other; by contrast, the different effects of any given type of cause are normally probabilistically correlated. For example, both obesity and high excitement can cause heart attacks, but this does not imply that fat people are more likely to get excited than thin ones; on the other hand, the fact that both lung cancer and nicotine-stained fingers can result from smoking *does* imply that lung cancer is more likely among people with nicotine-stained fingers. So this account distinguishes effects from causes by the fact that the former, but not the latter, are probabilistically dependent on each other.

2.4 *Probabilistic causation*

The just-mentioned probabilistic account of the *direction* of causation is normally formulated as part of a more general *theory of probabilistic causation*. Until relatively recently philosophers assumed that the world fundamentally conforms to deterministic laws, and that probabilistic dependencies between types of events, such as that between smoking and lung cancer, merely reflected our ignorance of the full causes. The rise of quantum mechanics, however, has persuaded most philosophers that determinism is false, and that some events, like the decay of a radium atom, happen purely as a matter of chance. A particular radium atom may decay, but on another occasion an identical atom in identical circumstances might well not decay.

Accordingly, a number of philosophers of science have put forward models of causation which require only that causes probabilify, rather than determine, their effects. The earliest such model was the 'inductive–statistical' version of the covering-law model of explanation (Hempel, 1965). Unlike deterministic 'deductive–nomological' explanations, such inductive–statistical explanations required only that prior conditions and laws imply a *high* probability for the event to be explained, not that this event will certainly happen. However, even this seems too strong a requirement for probabilistic causation. After all, smoking unequivocally causes lung cancer, but even heavy smokers do not have a *high* probability of lung cancer, in the sense of a probability close to one. Rather, their smoking increases their probability of lung cancer, not to a high figure, but merely from a low to a less low figure, but still well below 50 per cent. So more recent models of probabilistic causation simply require that causes should *increase* the probability of their effects, not that they should give them a high probability (Salmon, 1971).

This kind of model needs to guard against the possibility that the probabilistic association between putative cause and putative effect may be *spurious*, like the probabilistic association between barometers falling and subsequent rain. Such associations are not due to a causal connection between barometer movements and rain, but rather to both of these being joint effects of a *common cause*, namely, in our example, falls in atmospheric pressure. The obvious response to this difficulty is to say that we have a cause–effect relationship between A and B if and only if A increases the probability of B, and this association is *not* due to some common cause C. However, this is obviously incomplete as an analysis of causation, since it uses the notion of (common) *cause* in explaining causation.

It would solve this problem if we could analyse the notion of common cause in probabilistic terms. It seems to be a mark of common causes that they probabilistically '*screen off*' the associations between their joint effects, in the sense that, if we consider cases where the common cause is present and where it is absent separately, then the probabilistic association between the joint effects will disappear. For example, if it is given that the atmospheric pressure *has* fallen, then a falling barometer does not make it any more likely that it will rain; and similarly, if the atmospheric pressure *has not* fallen, a faulty falling reading on a barometer is no probable indicator of impending rain. (Numerically, if C is a common cause, and A and B its joint effects, we will find that A and B are associated – Prob (B/A) > Prob(B) – but that C and its absence render A irrelevant to B – Prob(B/A & C) = Prob(B/C) and Prob(B/A & not-C) = Prob(B/not-C).) It remains a matter of some debate, however, whether this characteristic probabilistic structure of common causes is enough to allow a complete explanation of causation in probabilistic terms, or whether further non-probabilistic considerations need to be introduced.

2.5 Probability

Philosophical interest in probabilistic causation has led to a resurgence of interest in the philosophy of probability itself. Probability raises philosophical puzzles in its own right, quite apart from its connection with causation. What exactly is the 'probability' of a given event? The only part of the answer that is uncontroversial is that probabilities are quantities that satisfy the axioms of the probability calculus I specified earlier when discussing Bayesianism. But this leaves plenty of room for alternative philosophical views, for there are a number of different ways of interpreting these axioms.

One interpretation is the *subjective* theory of probability, which equates probabilities with subjective degrees of belief. This is the interpretation assumed by Bayesian confirmation theory. Most philosophers are happy to agree that subjective degrees of belief exist, and that the Dutch Book Argument (see the above box on Bayesianism) shows why they ought to conform to the axioms of probability. But many, if not all, philosophers argue that we need a theory of *objective* probability in addition to this subjective account.

One possible objective interpretation is the *frequency* theory, originally put forward by Richard von Mises (1957). According to this theory, the probability of a given kind of result is the number of times this result occurs, divided by the total number of occasions on which it might have occurred. So, for example, the probability of heads on a coin toss is the proportion of heads in some wider class of coin tosses.

This theory, however, faces a number of difficulties. For a start, it has problems in dealing with 'single-case probabilities'. Consider a particular coin toss. We can consider it as a member of the class of all coin tosses, or of all tosses of coins with that particular shape, or of all tosses made in just that way, or so on. However, these different 'reference classes' may well display different frequencies of heads. Yet intuitively it seems that there ought to be a unique value for the probability of heads on a particular toss of a particular coin. Perhaps this difficulty can be dealt with by specifying that the single-case probability should equal the relative frequency in the reference class of all tosses that are *similar in all relevant respects* to the particular toss in question. But there remain difficulties about which respects should count as 'relevant' in this sense.

In addition, there is the problem that many of these more specific reference classes will only be finite in extent. Coins with a certain distinctive shape may only be tossed in some given way ten times in the whole history of the universe. Yet the probability of heads on these tosses is unlikely to be equal to the relative frequency in the ten tosses, for luck may well yield a disproportionately high, or low, number of heads in ten tosses. Because of this, frequency theorists standardly appeal, not to actual reference classes, but to hypothetical infinite sequences, and equate the probability with the *limit* that the relative frequency *would* tend to *if* the relevant kind of trial were repeated an infinite number of times. Critics of the frequency theory object that this reliance on hypothetical infinite reference sequences makes probabilities inadmissibly abstract.

Because of these difficulties, many contemporary philosophers of probability have adopted the *'propensity'* theory of probability in place of the frequency theory. The earliest version of this theory, proposed by Popper (1959b), simply modified the frequency theory by specifying that only those relative frequencies generated by repeated trails on a given *'experimental set-up'* should count as genuine probabilities. This arguably deals with the problem of single-case probabilities, but it still leaves us with hypothetical reference classes. To avoid this, later versions of the propensity theory do not define probabilities in terms of frequencies at all, but simply take probabilities to be primitive propensities of particular situations to produce given results.

This kind of propensity theory does not seek to define objective probabilities in terms of frequencies, but in effect simply takes single-case probabilities as primitive (see Mellor 1971). But it can still recognize a connection between probabilities and frequencies. For, as long as propensities are assumed to obey the axioms of the probability calculus (though this assumption itself merits some debate), it will follow that, in a sufficiently long sequence of independent trials in each of which the propensity to produce B is p, the overall *propensity* for the observed frequency of B to differ by more than a given amount from p can be made arbitrarily small, in accord with the Law of Large Numbers. (Note how the italicized second use of 'propensity' in this claim prevents it serving as a definition of propensities in terms of frequencies.)

Both the frequency theory and the propensity theory have their strengths. The frequency theory has the virtue of offering an explicit definition of probability, where the propensity theory takes probabilities as primitive. On the other hand, the propensity theory has no need to assume hypothetical reference sequences, whereas these are essential to the frequency theory.

It may seem that the frequency theory, because it offers an explicit definition, is better able than the propensity theory to explain how we find out about probabilities. But this is an illusion. The trouble is that the frequency theory's explicit definition is in terms of frequencies in INFINITE SEQUENCES. But our evidence is always in the form of frequencies in *finite* samples. So the problem of explaining how we can move from frequencies in finite samples to knowledge of probabilities is as much a problem for the frequency theory as for the propensity theory. (There are various suggestions about how to solve this 'problem of statistical inference', none of them universally agreed. My present point is merely that this problem of statistical inference arises in just the same way for both frequency and propensity theorists.)

In the face of continued debate about the interpretation of objective probability, some philosophers have turned to physics, and in particular to the notion of probability used in quantum mechanics, to resolve the issue. Unfortunately quantum mechanics is no less philosophically controversial

than the notion of probability. There are different philosophical interpretations of the formal theory of quantum mechanics, each of which involves
different understandings of probability. Because of this it seems likely that
philosophical disputes about probability will continue until there is an agreed
interpretation of quantum mechanics.

The Interpretation of Quantum Mechanics

Modern quantum mechanics says that the state of any given system of microscopic particles is fully characterized by its 'wave function'. However, instead of
specifying the exact positions and velocities of the particles, as is done in
classical mechanics, this 'wave function' only specifies *probabilities* of the
particles displaying certain values of position, and velocity, *if* appropriate
measurements are made. *Schrödinger's equation* then specifies how this wave
function evolves smoothly and deterministically over time, analogously to the
way that Newton's laws of motion specify how the positions and velocities of
macroscopic objects evolve over time – except that Schrödinger's equation again
only decribes changes in probabilities, not exact values.

On the orthodox interpretation of quantum mechanics, quantum probabilities
change into actualities only when '*measurements*' are made. If you measure the
position of a particle, say, *then* its position assumes a definite value, even though
nothing before the measurement determined exactly what this value would be.

There is something puzzling about this, however, since any overall system of
measured particle and measuring instrument is itself just another system of
microscopic particles, which might therefore be expected to evolve smoothly
according to Schrödinger's equation, rather than to jump suddenly to some
definite value for position. To account for this, the orthodox interpretation says
that in addition to the normal Schrödinger evolution, there is a special kind of
change which occurs in 'measurements', when the wave function suddenly
'*collapses*' to yield a definite value for the measured quantity.

The '*measurement problem*' is the problem of explaining exactly when, and
why, these collapses occur. The story of 'Schrödinger's cat' makes the difficulty
graphic. Suppose that some unfortunate cat is sitting next to a poison dispenser
which is wired up to emit cyanide gas if an electron emitted from some source
turns up on the right half of some position-registering plate, but not if the electron
turns up on the left half. The basic quantum mechanical description of this
situation says that it is both possible that the electron will turn up on the right
half of the plate and that it will turn up on the left half, and therefore both
possible that the poison is emitted and that it is not, and therefore both possible
that the cat is alive and that it is dead. One of these possibilities only becomes
actual when the wave function of the whole system collapses. But when does that
happen? When the electron is emitted? When it reaches the plate? When the cat
dies or not? Or only when a human being looks at the cat to see how it is
faring?

There seems no principled way to decide between these answers. Because of
this, many philosophers reject the orthodox view that physical systems are
completely characterized by their wave functions, and conjecture that, in
addition to the variables quantum mechanics recognizes, there are various
'hidden variables' which always specify exact positions and velocities for all
physical particles. It is difficult, however, for such *hidden variable theories* to
reproduce the surprising phenomena predicted by quantum mechanics, without
postulating mysterious mechanisms that seem inconsistent with other parts of
physics.

A more radical response to the measurement problem is to deny that the wave function ever does collapse, and somehow to make sense of the idea that reality contains both a live cat and a dead cat. This 'many-worlds' interpretation of quantum mechanics flies in the face of common sense, but its theoretical attractions are leading an increasing number of philosophers to take it seriously.

2.6 Teleology

We normally explain some particular fact by citing its *cause*: for example, we explain why some water freezes by noting that its temperature fell below 0° C. There are cases, however, where we seem to explain items by citing their *effects* instead. In particular, this kind of explanation is common in biology. We often explain some biological trait by showing how it is useful to the organism in question: for instance, the explanation of the polar bear's white fur is that it camouflages it; the explanation of human sweating is that it lowers body temperature, and so on. Similar explanations are also sometimes offered in anthropology and sociology.

Until fairly recently most philosophers of science took such functional or teleological explanations at face value, as an alternative to causal explanation, in which items are explained, not by their causal antecedents, but by showing how they contribute to the well-being of some larger system. Carl Hempel's covering-law model of explanation embodied an influential version of this attitude. According to Hempel, causal explanations and functional explanations are simply two different ways of exemplifying the covering-law model: the only difference is that in causal explanations the *explaining* fact (lower temperature) temporally precedes the explained fact (freezing), whereas in functional explanations it is *explained* fact (white fur) that comes temporally before the consequence (camouflage) which explains it.

Most contemporary philosophers of science, however, take a different view, and argue that all explanations of particular facts are really causal, and that functional explanations, despite appearances, are really a *subspecies* of causal explanations. On this view, the reference to future facts in functional explanations is merely apparent, and such explanations really refer to past causes. In the biological case, these past causes will be the evolutionary histories that led to the natural selection of the biological trait in question. Thus the functional explanation of the polar bear's colour should be understood as referring us to the fact that their *past* camouflaging led to the natural selection of their whiteness, and not to the fact that they may be camouflaged in the *future*. Similarly, any acceptable functional explanations in anthropology or sociology should be understood as referring us *back* in time to the conscious intentions or unconscious selection processes which caused the facts to be explained (see Wright, 1973, Neander, 1991). (There remains the terminological matter of whether functional explanations understood in this way ought still to be called 'teleological'. Traditional usage reserves the term 'teleology' for distinctively non-causal explanations in terms of future results.

But most contemporary philosophers are happy to describe disguised causal explanations that make implicit reference to selection mechanisms as 'teleological'.)

2.7 *The logic of natural selection*

The Darwinian theory of evolution by natural selection is not just important to functional explanation, but to biological thinking in general (see Sober 1993). This raises a number of further philosophical issues. An initial question is whether Darwin's theory has any predictive content. Darwin's theory explains the evolution of species in terms of the differential survival of the '*fittest*' animals. But if 'fittest' simply means 'those animals that in fact survive', then the theory will collapse into a definitional truth, and will be unable to predict how species will evolve in the future. However, we do not have to understand 'fitness' in this entirely empty way. At a minimum, we can read 'fit' as signifying those kinds of characteristics that have proved helpful to survival in the *past*; it is then no longer a matter of definition, but predictively informative, to say that animals with these characteristics will outcompete others in the future.

A related charge is that Darwinian theory is guilty of 'adaptationism'. According to this criticism, Darwinian biologists mistakenly presuppose that all biological traits must serve some purpose, and in consequence invent 'just so stories', like Rudyard Kipling's children's tales, to provide fictional histories in which each biological trait has provided some benefit to its owners. In reality, however, the anti-Darwinians continue, many biological features serve no purposes at all, but are simply side-effects of other traits, or results of random genetic drift. So, for example, it would be a mistake to suppose that any useful purpose is served by the small size of insects; rather the smallness of insects is simply an automatic upshot of their lack of internal skeletons.

In response to this criticism, most Darwinians admit that *some* biological traits serve no function, but point out that it certainly does not follow that *all* traits serve no function. What is more, they argue, there is plenty of genuine evidence to show that specific biological traits have been historically favoured because of specific functions, and that this process has been important to the evolution of species.

Another question raised by Darwin's theory is what *kinds of entities* are selected in the competition to survive? Is it biological *species*, or *groups* of individuals within species, or single *individuals*, or the *genes* inside individuals? In recent years there has been a heated controversy about which of these entities are the central '*units of selection*'. Biologists influenced by mathematical population genetics have argued that we should view genes as the units of selection, since evolution always involves changes in the frequencies of alternative genes within a larger population. Other biologists, however, have argued that this is just a matter of 'bookkeeping', and that the causal processes responsible for evolution always involve the survival of individuals and even groups. Some progress in unravelling this knotty issue has been made by distinguishing 'replicators', namely, the genes that carry the instructions for building bodies from generation to generation, from 'vehicles', such as individuals and groups, whose survival is normally, but not always, the prerequisite for gene survival.

Work on the logic of natural selection has been associated with the development of *sociobiology*, which seeks to identify the evolutionary purpose of the characteristic *social behaviour* of animals, including humans. An obvious and often-made objection to this programme is that much social behaviour, especially in higher mammals, is due to individual learning and culture, and so not a product of evolutionarily determined genes. More extreme defenders of sociobiology, especially in its popularized versions, respond that most human behaviour really does depend on nature rather than nurture, despite widespread liberal opinion to the contrary, including even such apparently cultural behaviour as style of dress, or choice of marriage partner. A better defence of sociobiology, however, is to admit that environment is often as important for behaviour as genes, but to point out that it is still important to understand the evolutionary advantages provided by the genes that do influence behaviour.

2.8 Theoretical reduction

Another philosophical question about biology is whether it can be *reduced* to such lower level (in the sense of ontologically more basic) sciences as chemistry and physics. Obviously, this is an issue that arises not just for biology, but also for such other 'special' natural sciences as geology and meteorology, and also for such human sciences as psychology and sociology.

One science is said to 'reduce' to another if its categories can be defined in terms of the categories of the latter, and its laws explained by the laws of the latter. *Reductionists* argue that all sciences form a hierarchy in which the higher can always be reduced to the lower. Thus, for example, biology might be reduced to physiology, physiology to chemistry, and eventually chemistry to physics.

Reductionism can be viewed either historically or metaphysically. The historical question is whether science characteristically progresses by later theories reducing earlier ones. The metaphysical question is whether the different areas of science describe different realities, or just the one physical reality described at different levels of detail. Though often run together, these are different questions.

Taken as a general thesis, historical reductionism is false. Recall the earlier discussion of the 'pessimistic meta-induction from past falsity'. This involved the claim that new theories characteristically show their predecessors to be false. To the extent that this claim is true, historical reductionism is false: for a new theory can scarcely explain why an earlier theory was true, if it shows it is false.

In the earlier discussion I argued that there are some areas of science, like molecular biology and medical science, to which the pessimistic meta-induction does not apply. If this is right, then we can expect that in these areas new theories will indeed normally reduce old ones. But I did not dispute that there are other areas of science, like cosmology and fundamental particle physics, in which the normal fate of old theories is to be thrown out. It follows that we must reject historical reductionism, understood as the thesis that *all* science proceeds by new theories reducing old ones.

This does not mean, however, that metaphysical reductionism is false. Even if science proceeds towards the overall truth by fits and starts, there may be general reasons for expecting that this overall truth, when eventually reached, will reduce to physical truth.

One possible such argument stems from the *causal interaction* between the phenomena discussed in the special sciences and physical phenomena. Biological, geological and meteorological events all unquestionably have physical effects. It is difficult to see how they could do this unless they are made of physical components.

It is doubtful, however, whether this suffices to establish full-scale reductionism, as opposed to the weaker thesis (sometimes called 'token-identity') according to which each *particular* higher-level event is identical with some *particular* physical event. Thus, for example, it might be true that one animal's aggressive behaviour can be equated with a given sequence of physical movements, and another animal's aggressive behaviour can be equated with another sequence of physical movements, without there being any uniform way of defining 'aggressive behaviour', for all animals, in terms of physical movements. The case-by-case token-identity will explain how each instance of aggressive behaviour can have physical effects, like causing intruding animals to move away. But without any uniform definition of 'aggressive behaviour' in terms of physical movements there is no question of reducing ethology (the science of behaviour) to physics, and so no question of explaining ethological laws by physical laws. Instead, the laws of ethology and other special sciences will be *sui generis*, identifying patterns whose instances vary in their physical make-up, and which therefore cannot possibly be explained in terms of physical laws alone (see Fodor 1974).

Acknowledgements

I would like to thank Stathis Psillos for helping me with this chapter.

Further Reading

For an introduction to the problem of induction, and Popper's solution, see Popper, *The Logic of Scientific Discovery* (1959a) especially ch. 1. The problem and Popper's solution are further discussed in O'Hear, *An Introduction to the Philosophy of Science* (1989). There are two excellent introductions to

Bayesian philosophy of science: Horwich, *Probability and Evidence* (1982) and Howson and Urbach, *Scientific Reasoning* (1989).

The best modern defence of instrumentalism is Van Fraassen, *The Scientific Image* (1980). Churchland and Hooker (eds), *Images of Science* (1985) offers a good collection of essays on the realism–instrumentalism debate. Kitcher, *The Advancement of Science* (1993) contains a strong defence of realism.

The classic works on the theory-dependence of observation and the incommensurability of theories are Hanson, *Patterns of Discovery* (1958), Kuhn, *The Structure of Scientific Revolutions* (1962) and Feyerabend, *Against Method* (1976). A good collection of essays on these issues is Hacking (ed.), *Scientific Revolutions* (1981). The best sources for the underdetemination of theories by evidence and the pessimistic meta-induction are respectively Quine, 'Two Dogmas of Empiricism' (1951) and Laudan, 'A Confutation of Convergent Realism' (1981). For a survey of recent work on naturalized epistemology, see Kitcher's 'The Naturalists Return' (1992).

Most modern discussions of explanation begin with the title essay in Hempel, *Aspects of Scientific Explanation* (1965). Explanation and its relation to causation are further explored by the essays in Ruben (ed.), *Explanation* (1993). Armstrong, *What is a Law of Nature?* (1983) provides an excellent account of the general problem of distinguishing laws from accidents, as well as his own solution. Chapter 7 of O'Hear, *An Introduction to the Philosophy of Science* (1989) contains a good introduction to both probability and probabilistic causation. The best contemporary non-specialist discussion of the problems of quantum mechanics is to be found in chapters 11–13 of Lockwood, *Mind, Brain and the Quantum* (1989).

Sober, *Philosophy of Biology* (1993) explains the ways in which Darwinian thinking is important to the philosophy of biology. The view that events discussed in the special sciences are token-identical, but not reducible, to physical events is defended in Fodor's 'Special Sciences' (1974).

References

Armstrong, D. 1983: *What is a Law of Nature?* Cambridge: Cambridge University Press.

Ayer, A. J. 1956: *The Problem of Knowledge*. London: Macmillan.

Boyd, R. 1980: Scientific Realism and Naturalistic Epistemology. In P. Asquith and R. Giere (eds), *PSA 1980* vol. 2, East Lansing, Mi: Philosophy of Science Association, 613–62.

Cartwright, N. 1983: *How the Laws of Physics Lie*. Oxford: Oxford University Press.

Churchland, P. and Hooker, C. (eds), 1985: *Images of Science*. Chicago: University of Chicago Press.

Duhem, P. 1951 [1906]: *The Aim and Structure of Physical Theory* (translated by P. Wiener). Princeton, NJ: Princeton University Press.

Feyerabend, P. 1976: *Against Method*. London: New Left Books.

Fodor, J. 1974: Special Sciences. *Synthèse*, 28, 97–115.

Friedman, M. 1984: *Foundations of Spacetime Theories*. Princeton, NJ: Princeton University Press.

Glymour, C. 1980: *Theory and Evidence*. Princeton, NJ: Princeton University Press.

Hacking, I. 1967: Slightly More Realistic Personal Probability. *Philosophy of Science*, 34, 311–25.

—— (ed.) 1981: *Scientific Revolutions*. Oxford: Oxford University Press.

Hanson, N. R. 1958: *Patterns of Discovery*. Cambridge: Cambridge University Press.

—— 1963: *The Concept of the Positron*. Cambridge: Cambridge University Press.

Harding, S. (ed.), 1975: *Can Theories be Refuted?* Dordrecht: Reidel.

Hempel, C. 1965: *Aspects of Scientific Explanation*. New York: Free Press.

Hempel, C. and Oppenheim, P. 1948: Studies in the Logic of Explanation. *Philosophy of Science*, 15, 135–75.

Horwich, P. 1982: *Probability and Evidence*. Cambridge: Cambridge University Press.

Howson, C. and Urbach, P. 1989: *Scientific Reasoning*. La Salle: Open Court.

Hume, D. 1978 [1739]: *A Treatise of Human Nature* (edited by P. H. Nidditch). Oxford: Clarendon Press.

Kitcher, P. 1992: The Naturalists Return. *Philosophical Review*, 101, 53–114.

—— 1993: *The Advancement of Science*. New York: Oxford University Press.

Kuhn, T. S. 1962: *The Structure of Scientific Revolutions*. Chicago: Chicago University Press.

Laudan, L. 1981: A Confutation of Convergent Realism. *Philosophy of Science*, 48.

Lewis, D. 1973: *Counterfactuals*. Oxford: Blackwell.

—— 1979: Counterfactual Dependence and Time's Arrow. *Noûs*, 13, 455–76.

Lockwood, M. 1989: *Mind, Brain and the Quantum*. Oxford: Blackwell.

Mellor, D. 1971: *The Matter of Chance*. Cambridge: Cambridge University Press.

Mises, R. von 1957: *Probability, Statistics and Truth*. London: Allen and Unwin.

Neander, K. 1991: The Teleological Notion of Function. *Australasian Journal of Philosophy*, 69, 454–68.

O'Hear, A. 1989: *An Introduction to the Philosophy of Science*. Oxford: Clarendon Press.

Papineau, D. 1993: *Philosophical Naturalism*. Oxford: Blackwell.

Popper, K. 1959a: *The Logic of Scientific Discovery*. London: Hutchison.

—— 1959b: The Propensity Interpretation of Probability. *British Journal for the Philosophy of Science*, 10, 25–42.

—— 1963: *Conjectures and Refutations*. London: Routledge and Kegan Paul.

—— 1972: *Objective Knowledge*. Oxford: Clarendon Press.

Quine, W. V. O. 1951: Two Dogmas of Empiricism. In his *From a Logical Point of View*, New York: Harper, 20–46.

Reichenbach, H. 1956: *The Direction of Time*. Berkeley, CA: University of California Press.

Ramsey, F. 1978 [1929]: General Propositions and Causality. In his *Foundations*, D. H. Mellor (ed.), London: Routledge and Kegan Paul.

Ruben, D.-H. (ed.) 1993: *Explanation*. Oxford: Oxford University Press.

Salmon, W. 1971: *Statistical Explanation and Statistical Relevance*. Pittsburgh, PA: University of Pittsburgh Press.

Smart, J. 1963: *Philosophy and Scientific Realism*. London: Routledge and Kegan Paul.

Sober, E. 1993: *Philosophy of Biology*. Oxford: Oxford University Press.

Teller, P. 1973: Conditionalization and Observation. *Synthèse*, 28, 218–58.

Van Fraassen, B. 1980: *The Scientific Image*. Oxford: Clarendon Press.

Worrall, J. 1989: Why Both Popper and Watkins Fail to Solve the Problem of Induction. In F. D'Agostino and I. Jarvie (eds), *Freedom and Rationality*, Dordrecht: Kluwer, 257–96.

Wright, L. 1973: Functions. *Philosophical Review*, 82, 139–68.

Discussion Questions

1 Is it any less rational to accept induction than it is to accept deduction?

2 Is it always a mistake to save a theory when it has been falsified?

3 How can we show that it is more rational to believe some hypotheses than to believe others?

4 How do scientific theories move beyond the stage of conjecture?

5 Is belief a matter of degree?

6 Does Bayes' theorem help us to deal rationally with evidence?

7 Do scientific claims about unobservable entities differ in status from scientific claims about observable entities?

8 Is instrumentalism mistaken if it cannot account for some features of scientific practice? How can we determine what features are really a part of scientific practice?

9 Are general theories or piecemeal procedures more important to our basic characterization of science?

10 Does all observation depend on theoretical assumptions? What are the implications of your answer for an account of unobservables?

11 'Given any theory about unobservables which fits the observed facts, there will always be other incompatible theories which fit the same facts.' Does this make realism about unobservables untenable?

12 Can we be realists in some areas of science and instrumentalists in others?

13 Should we look to the history, sociology, and psychology of science, rather than to first principles, to identify criteria for the acceptability of scientific theories?

14 Can a naturalized study of science tell us which research strategies are an effective means to theoretical *truth*?

15 Is there any good reason for a philosopher to prefer to talk about explanation rather than causation?

16 How can we distinguish laws from accidentally true generalizations?

17 Must we posit an ideal system of knowledge in order to understand the notion of 'law'? What if there cannot be such a system?

18 Do scientific laws involve necessity? In what sense?

19 How can we explain the direction of causation?

20 Can we accept a model of causation according to which causes probabilify, rather than determine, their effects?

21   What problem poses greater difficulties for frequency theories of probability: 'single-case probabilities' or a reliance on hypothetical infinite reference sequences?

22   If 'propensities' are primitive, can a propensity theory give us any insight into the nature of probability?

23   How are interpretations of quantum mechanics relevant to philosophical disputes about probability?

24   Can we give up common sense in favour of a 'many-worlds' reality containing both Schrödinger's cat alive and Schrödinger's cat dead?

25   Are teleological explanations an alternative to causal explanations or a kind of causal explanation?

26   Does 'survival of the fittest' help to explain which species survive?

27   How do we determine which biological traits serve a function and which do not? What explains those traits which do not serve a function?

28   How can we settle whether species, groups, individuals or genes are the appropriate units of selection in a theory of natural selection?

29   How can we determine whether all sciences form a hierarchy in which the higher can always be reduced to the lower?

30   Do different areas of science describe different realities, or just one physical reality at different levels of detail?

10

Philosophy of Mathematics ——————

Mary Tiles

Since the time of ancient Greece, mathematics has been intimately tied to philosophy, both as a model of knowledge and as an object of philosophical reflection. Are numbers real? What is a proof? Is mathematics more certain than other knowledge? Can finite minds have knowledge of infinity? How can mathematics apply to the world? In this chapter, changing philosophical conceptions of mathematics, changes in the historical context of mathematical thought and changes in mathematics itself are explored in relation to a basic question: How can theoretical reasoning about non-concrete mathematical objects be both secure and so useful? Platonic, Aristotelian and Kantian approaches to mathematics are examined in their own right and to place in context the problems and proposed solutions of the major modern schools of logicism, formalism and intuitionism. Recent developments which do not seek foundations for mathematics are also considered. Many of the discussions of great historical figures in this volume, especially Frege and Russell (see chapter 27), are relevant to the present chapter. Readers will also wish to consult chapters on EPISTEMOLOGY (chapter 1), METAPHYSICS (chapter 2), PHILOSOPHY OF LANGUAGE (chapter 3), PHILOSOPHY OF LOGIC (chapter 4), and PHILOSOPHY OF SCIENCE (chapter 9).

Introductions to the philosophy of mathematics often begin where Körner's influential introduction (Körner, 1960) began, outlining three positions: logicism, formalism and intuitionism. These were the three contending schools to emerge from nineteenth-century mathematical moves to provide rigorous foundations for mathematical analysis (including infinitesimal calculus). The problem for the philosophy of mathematics has been that (1) these seemed to represent all the reasonable positions available and (2) in the light of Gödel's incompleteness theorems and other results proved by Turing, Church, Skolem and Tarski in the 1930s, neither logicism nor formalism seemed a philosophically viable position. Intuitionism, whilst having its philosophical credentials intact, was unacceptable to most mathematicians because it involved discarding parts of classically accepted mathematics. This apparent impasse partly explains the decline of interest in the philosophy of mathematics since the first part of this century, when for a while, with the work of Russell and Whitehead, and the Vienna Circle logical positivists, it seemed to occupy centre stage.

Hao Wang, in his perceptive retrospective analysis of the philosophy of mathematics of this period (Wang, 1988), explains this trajectory in terms of the wider movements of analytic philosophy, which were initially strongly empiricist and which consequently inherited a hostility toward abstract objects. Mathematics presents a significant challenge to empiricism, as was made painfully evident by the prominence of mathematics in Einstein's relativity theories and in the development of quantum mechanics. How is empiricism to give an adequate explanation of the certainty, clarity, universality and applicability of mathematics? Wang's answer is that the above mentioned developments in logic and the foundations of mathematics show that analytic empiricism cannot meet this challenge. It is therefore only as philosophy in general begins to move beyond analytic empiricism that more fruitful approaches to philosophy of mathematics can begin to be explored.

But how exactly is such a move to be made? Because the three foundational schools originated in the work of philosophically minded mathematicians who were seeking to resolve sophisticated conceptual problems that had arisen in the context of ongoing mathematical research, much of the work in foundations is itself technical and mathematical in character. There is no sharp line where mathematics ends and philosophy begins. Indeed, one of the striking features of the development of mathematics in the twentieth century has been the way in which attempts to solve philosophical and conceptual problems have generated new mathematics. Thus from the standpoint of the late twentieth century, work in the foundations of mathematics can by no means be ignored, but it may need to be re-evaluated. What is its status? What exactly does it tell us about contemporary mathematics? These questions must now be added to the philosophical agenda. So one of the ways of moving beyond the presuppositions built into philosophy of mathematics by analytic empiricists is to re-contextualize their work on logic and foundations in the hope of understanding its motivations, achievements and shortcomings. A first step is to sketch, using broad strokes, major features in the landscape of western philosophical reflection on mathematics, many of which were already put in place by the ancient Greeks.

1 Basic Tasks for a Philosophy of Mathematics

The basic puzzle, of which the challenge to empiricism is but a specialized variant, is to explain how theoretical reasoning about highly abstract objects can be so useful. The features of mathematics which seemed to mark it off from other disciplines are that its objects are not encountered in the world of sense experience, and yet, perhaps as a consequence, mathematical claims can be provided with proofs which seem to establish them with an exactness and certainty unparalleled in other branches of knowledge. But how is it that people shut away from the outside world, thinking, calculating and proving theorems about things which we can never hope to see or touch (numbers such as 2, 1 million, π, or structures such as circles, rings and vector spaces) produce results which other, very practical people find so useful in their dealings both with the everyday world and with the esoteric worlds of high-tech science? What right have we to be so confident of the correctness of these results?

The straightforward answer to this last question is that mathematicians are able to offer proofs of their results. For example, as geometers before the time of Aristotle realized, measurements of the internal angles of plane triangles do not yield one exact result, but results that cluster round two right angles, and, because measuring gives no insight into why this clustering should occur, it affords no assurance that a 'rogue' triangle might not some day be found whose internal angles had a markedly different sum. A proof, on the other hand, that shows why, given what it is to be a triangle, its internal angles must add up to two right angles, assures us that no rogue triangle exists. One such proof is shown in figure 10.1.

Such a proof is possible only if it can be assumed that all the lines involved are perfectly straight and have no thickness (something which is not true of the lines in the diagram). Lines which have thickness do not meet in points and if they have wriggles in them there is no sense to be given to an exact measurement of the angle between them. So even to have internal angles whose sum is exactly equal to two right angles is possible only for a perfect plane triangle, which we could not encounter in experience. The theorem proved below will hold more or less exactly for those triangles we encounter to the extent that they are more or less perfectly triangular.

There is an important assumption made here about the applicability of results proved about idealizations: a result proved about an idealization will hold for situations which approximate to that ideal in direct proportion to the closeness with which they approximate to the ideal. This assumption has traditionally underwritten applications of mathematics, but, with recent work in chaos theory, it has been shown not to be valid for systems exhibiting sensitive dependence on initial conditions (Stewart, 1989, chs 7, 14). This

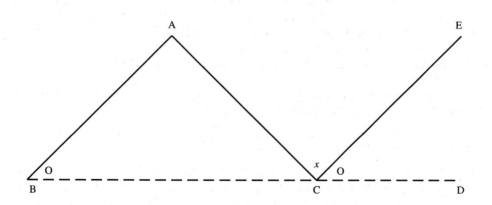

Figure 10.1 Proof that the internal angles of a triangle add up to the sum of two right angles.

work opens up new questions about the connection between proofs and the use of results proved.

But how can we tell that a purported proof really is a proof? All proofs have to start from some assumptions (we assumed above some properties of parallel lines and of addition of angles). How can we be certain that these are correct? Furthermore, how can we be sure that all inferences are made correctly? To ask for a proof for every assumption will lead to an infinite regress. So if there are to be any proofs there must be some self-evident starting points, which can be known to be necessarily true and which are neither capable of, nor stand in need of, further justification.

This means that if mathematics is a discipline in which proofs are required then it must be one which exhibits a systematic hierarchical order. Some propositions concerning mathematical entities will appear as first principles, accepted without proof: these are the foundations upon which subsequent knowledge must be built. Basic theorems are proved from first principles: these theorems are in turn used to prove further results, and so on. This is the sense in which, so long as mathematicians demand and provide proofs, their discipline must necessarily be organized along lines approximating the pattern already to be found in the *Elements of Geometry* of Euclid (which dates from around 300 BC) – a work which for centuries served as an exemplar.

The question of what principles of inference are generally valid (rationally compelling, or truth-preserving) is traditionally assigned to LOGIC (chapter 4). But one may wonder whether there are not some specifically mathematical principles of inference. Take for example, Euclid's principle that if A = B and C = D, then A+C = B+D. Is this a logical principle (a specific application of the SUBSTITUTIVITY OF IDENTICALS (p. 673))? Is it a basic principle of the theory of part and whole? If so, does this belong to logic or to mathematics? Or is it a specifically mathematical principle governing extensive magnitudes?

At this point it is already possible to see how concern for principles of valid deductive inference and for the nature and status of first principles becomes a natural part of any philosophy of mathematics that takes proof to be that on the basis of which mathematical propositions gain their aura of privileged certainty, or necessary truth. However, to equate the philosophy of mathematics with studies in logic and foundations would seem to ignore one half of the combination of features that make mathematics so philosophically puzzling and intriguing. It leaves out questions concerning the utility of mathematics.

So far we have the following schema of questions structuring the problematic of philosophical reflections on mathematics.

> *Basic Problem*: How can theoretical reasoning about non-concrete mathematical objects be both so secure and so useful?

If the question of security is presumed to be answered by the fact that theoretical reasoning produces proofs of mathematical propositions, then we have to distinguish between first principles and results proved from them, to get something like the following subsidiary problems.

(1) What is the nature and status of the first principles of mathematics?

(1.1) Can its first principles be identified?

(1.2) How can these first principles be known with certainty?

(2) How is mathematical knowledge acquired?

(2.1) *Discovery*: How are discoveries made? How are results established or proofs found?

(2.2) *Justification*: What constitutes a proof? What principles of inference are available? What is their nature and what grounds have we for thinking them reliable?

(3) Given the answers under (1) and (2), how is the applicability of proved mathematical results to be explained? Do the answers under (1) and (2) assure us that we have a right to expect mathematical results to have applications and that in their application established results will be reliable?

2 Basic Responses

Mathematics since the sixteenth century has been a highly dynamic discipline. Over this period, methods of problem-solving and of proof have undergone many changes. Philosophers have tended to take the ability to provide proofs to be the distinguishing characteristic of mathematics. But if proof methods change and are likely to continue to change, philosophic analyses of proof methods, and opinions about the foundations of mathematical claims derived from these analyses, will be historically conditioned. Similarly, the kinds of applications made of mathematics are continually changing. Any account of the applicability of mathematics will thus also have different problems to address depending on the period in which it is being offered. This means that a response to the basic problem which may be adequate at one period of history may be inadequate at a later period and so require considerable modification. This can be illustrated by seeing how the configuration of the basic problem, and hence of viable solutions to it, changed in the seventeenth and then again in the nineteenth century. In this way we can indicate, albeit very sketchily, the historical context of analytic empiricist responses.

For the purposes of a schematic overview of the philosophical terrain, it is possible to view philosophies up to the late seventeenth century as proposing variations on what we may call Platonic realist or Aristotelian conceptualist responses to the basic question. (These labels indicate the classical ancestry of these responses but should not be read literally as Plato's realism or Aristotle's conceptualism.)

2.1 *Platonic Realism*

For the Platonic realist the problem dissolves once it is realized that the cosmos has an eternal and unchanging underlying order, or harmony, and that the principles of this order are essentially mathematical. This kind of view can be traced back to the Pythagoreans who based a vision of a harmoniously ordered universe on their discovery of the association between musical harmonies and numerical ratios. It found one of its most explicit expressions in the work of Kepler (1571–1630), the famous astronomer. In his *Harmonice Mundi* (1940) he supposes the universe to be the work of a God who is not only a geometer but also a musician. The planets therefore make heavenly music as they orbit the Sun.

The same conception surfaces in many other authors of various periods. For Newton (1642–1727) in his *Opticks* (1931), the division of the spectrum into seven colours is numerically correlated with the harmonic division of a single string which yields the notes of the octave. Einstein's (1879–1955) often-quoted rejection of the claims of quantum mechanics to be a fundamental physical theory – 'God does not play dice' – reveals a similar attitude. It also found expression in the drive to mathematical elegance and unity which resulted in his theory of general relativity and in his unsuccessful quest for a grand unified field theory, a quest continued by those working on the theory of superstrings (Davies and Brown, 1988).

If the universe is mathematically ordered, this would explain the utility of mathematics but not how we can come to mathematical knowledge or the specially secure status of that knowledge. For the realist who was either Christian, or a NEO-PLATONIST (p. 500) (or someone who was both), this was readily explicable. The Christian God created not only the universe, but also human beings; we were created with an intellect that is a finite image of God's infinite intellect. This faculty was given to us precisely so that we might come to a secure knowledge of the existence of the God who created us and to a limited knowledge of God's nature. Thus God created human beings with an intellect that is innately equipped to grasp mathematical principles and to recognize them as true beyond all doubt. This requires that the intellect be exercised in the right way, namely, by turning away from sensual distractions to focus on things intellectual and the realm of pure abstractions (see for example Descartes, 1985–91b, Augustine, 1990, Bk VI, 1955, Bk II). For the neo-Platonist, the human soul (microcosm) was an integral part of the universe (macrocosm) and capable of resonating in sympathy with the world soul. The microcosm and macrocosm thus mirror each other in such a way that the harmonies of one will be recognized by and affect the other. On either account mathematical knowledge is a matter of insight, of intellectual intuition, or a seeing in the light of reason which is analogous to a religious revelation. When the mind is properly focused the first principles of mathematics will be revealed with irresistible clarity and distinctness, for they are integral to the intellect's own nature.

But because the human intellect is limited and finite it does not comprehend all things immediately in its intellectual vision, it only comprehends those things that are simple and basic. (In the mind of God all things are immediately intuited; God never needs to engage in reasoning or to make inferences. Neither does the world soul; its structures are integral to itself and immediately known to it.) Human minds have to approach progressively more complex and complete knowledge in stages. Reasoning and deductive proof do not in themselves confer the intellectual intuition that is true knowledge, but reason and intuition are, for finite minds, the necessary route to it (see Spinoza, 1992, Descartes, 1985–91a). It is hardly surprising then to find that such philosophers give priority to methods of discovery and routes to insight, over methods of justification. Proofs are less justifications than records of the real interconnections of things, the interconnections which explain, for example, why triangles must have internal angles equalling the sum of two right angles. These interconnections can be grasped in a single act of intellectual vision, by one who truly understands, but can only be recorded sequentially.

Thus for the Platonic realist the cosmos is an ordered whole. Mathematics expresses the principles of this order and gives insight into it. The route to mathematical knowledge is supernaturally linked to its utility, through the idea that the senses reveal to us only the changing phenomenal world of sense experience. To acquire knowledge of the eternal principles underlying the order of that world it is necessary to turn away from the senses and to (re-)unite the human intellect (or soul) with the intellect which orders the world (or with the world soul).

2.2 Aristotelian Conceptualism

By contrast the Aristotelian conceptualist's cosmos, although structured, is in the first instance a collection of individual things that undergo change, and whose order is partly contingent and partly a product of the natures of the things making up the universe. To comprehend the universe is thus to know the natures of individual (kinds of) things. Logic gives us some insight into the principles of the ordering of individual things into species and genera based on their specific qualities (differentia). But, in addition, it is necessary, by observation and reflection, to discover the causal principles, the forces, the powers and potentialities of the things that govern their behaviour.

Mathematics deals with things that do not change. Moreover, it can only ever yield principles that concern relations between things, because numbers are assigned only after selection of a unit of measure and geometry deals only with shapes, which in turn are characterized by the relations between their parts, and with spatial relations between shapes. This means that mathematics can never yield insight into the natures, or the principles of change, of individual things or, hence, into the causal principles that govern the universe. Arithmetic is the science of discrete magnitudes and geometry is the science of continuous magnitudes. Magnitudes themselves are a product of measurement and hence of human measuring activities. It is in experience that we encounter the various kinds of magnitudes and invent measurement systems that are appropriate to them and to our purposes.

When we invent measures, discriminate between shapes and become, for practical purposes, interested in spatial relations, for example, or the relative motions of the planets, mathematics can help us describe in systematic ways the various kinds of orders that we are interested in and to co-ordinate our various measuring units. Thus astronomy uses geometry and arithmetic to help connect the various temporal units – such as day, lunar month and solar year – in ways that make construction of a calendar possible. Geometry applied to measurements made on the ground makes building plans and maps possible. Mathematics is useful because measurement is useful and this utility arises out of the practical contexts in which measures were devised. We can have more complete knowledge here than of the natural world because it is a human invention and just as we do not have to examine the natural world to find out how to use the words of a language or to determine whether an action is or is not legal according to the legal system of a specific city or country, so we would not expect to look to the world to resolve questions about magnitudes and their relations.

But in this case would there not be as many different mathematical systems as there are legal systems? Yet one of the experiences which gives support to claims about the universal necessity of mathematics is that although different cultures have developed different numeral systems, units of measurement, methods of calculation and mathematical problem-solving, there is remarkable agreement at the level of results. Merchants speaking different languages can nevertheless bargain their way to agreed prices, adapting to different currency and measurement systems. Two plus two does not make five or three in the arithmetic of any culture.

Aristotelian conceptualists accommodate this in a way not wholly dissimilar from Platonic realists. This is not surprising since both believed in a universal human nature and emphasized intellect as an important distinguishing mark of humanity; a human is a rational animal. Thus for ARISTOTLE (chapter 15), LOCKE (chapter 19), BERKELEY (chapter 20) and even HUME (chapter 21), the human mind comes into the world disposed to impose certain kinds of structures on it. Humans are born able to start making certain basic discriminations on the basis of qualitative similarity and difference and to learn to make many more. In fact, if it is assumed that all experience is of particulars, then all relating one thing to another, whether with respect to colour, taste and smell, or with respect to size, shape, place and time, must be a function of the human mind. To be able to do this the human mind must have, in addition to innate capacities for sense perception, innate relation-imposing capacities. Reflection on these yields the basic concepts for more abstract disciplines, including mathematics; concepts such as unity, number, size, shape and indefinitely continued repetition. These abstract concepts, presupposed in ordering experience, can be said to be first in the order of understanding, or simple with respect to the intellect, because, although they may be explicitly acquired, if at all, only after intellectual reflection, they are none the less presupposed in all experiential knowledge.

Where the realist sees in these simple, innate intellectual concepts indications of a supernatural order, the conceptualist sees only structures of the human mind in terms of which it orders the natural world of particulars. Mathematical first principles thus involve concepts derived from reflection on innate human intellectual capacities to distinguish between, and to relate, particulars. In this sense they are simple innate ideas, ideas which are first in the order of understanding although not in the order of human experience, because they can only come to be known by turning away from the world and reflecting on the way in which the intellect functions. They are potentially self-evident to all human beings because they are explicit expressions of principles that are implicit in the innate, natural operation of the human intellect.

More complex concepts, however, must be built up from these simples by explicit processes of definition. Not all cultures will necessarily develop the same complex concepts, although all start from the same simples and all are measuring aspects of things in the same physical world; the definition of any complex concept should therefore be explicable to anyone, irrespective of cultural location. Results concerning more complex concepts must be proved by appeal to their definitions and to first principles, and they must proceed by deductive syllogistic reasoning. Proofs, in other words, are demonstrations in the sense outlined by Aristotle in his *Posterior Analytics* (1941a, 93a16–96a19). Since complex mathematical concepts are the work of humans, there is no ground of proof beyond the definition of complex concepts in terms of simple concepts. It can sometimes appear that more is involved because it does take work to arrive at good definitions. This is because many measurement-related concepts arise first in practical contexts where computation or diagrammatic reasoning is involved. It is only when the question of the reliability of such reasoning arises that it becomes necessary to think about explicitly defining concepts, such as a circle, a straight line, subtraction, multiplication or division. A good definition will be required to justify core components of successful computational and measurement practices, but may not preserve (or justify) every component. From this way of looking at things, justification in the form of proof receives more emphasis than discovery, for there does not appear to be much to discovery beyond giving useful definitions and deducing their consequences.

3 New Procedures, New Problems – Analytic Geometry and the Infinite

So we have two approaches to resolving the basic problem. Do we then sort out our metaphysics and on that basis take our pick? If we see the world as consisting of changeable particulars should we accept a version of Aristotelian conceptualism, whereas if we see the world as an interrelated whole governed by unchanging mathematical principles of harmony should we accept some form of Platonic realism? That would surely be too simple, yet up to the seventeenth century the choice could have looked very much like this. This was in part because mathematics itself did not constitute a large or complex domain. It came in the form of arithmetic and geometry, which dealt with discrete and continuous magnitudes respectively. However, with the Renaissance revival of neo-Platonism and of mathematics came new ambitions, which began with the extension of the domain of arithmetic by algebra and continued via the use of algebraic techniques in geometry to the development of infinitesimal calculus and its use in Newtonian mechanics.

By the late seventeenth century, the mathematical, scientific and political background had shifted in such a way that neither of the old options could seem unproblematic. In the context of the increasing religious intolerance generated by the Thirty Years War in Europe, neo-Platonism became simply too dangerous a position to hold openly because of its obvious heretical implications. To survive, the new mathematical natural philosophy needed to distance itself from that position. Descartes' attempt to underwrite the security of his rational powers (and hence the mathematics to which reasoning led him) with a proof of the existence of a benevolent God who created him, was ingenious, but it failed to convince many people and also trespassed dangerously over the border from philosophy to theology, or from the domain of reason to that of FAITH (pp. 502–3). The strategy of philosophically securing an elevated status for mathematics by supernatural means looked increasingly unattractive, as demarcations were drawn between philosophy and theology, or between what is within the legitimate scope of human reason and what must, if believed, be a matter or faith or revelation.

Aristotelian conceptualism was thus initially the more attractive route, and it certainly attracted empiricist philosophers such as Locke and Hume. But there were factors in both the new developments in mathematics and those in natural philosophy that seemed strongly to favour some form of realism – the view that mathematics deals with a subject matter which exists independently of the human mind.

The development of analytic geometry brought algebraic methods into geometry and saw the gradual emergence of the mathematical concept of a function. This took place in the context of developing a mathematics that was capable of representing change and of expressing principles of change. The equation of a parabola $(y = ax - bx^2)$, for example, could be read both as a mathematical definition of that particular conic section and as the principle according to which a projectile moves under the influence of gravity in the absence of air resistance $(s = v_0 t - gt^2)$.

Geometrical attention shifted to curves that were defined not in words but by algebraic equations, many of which were curves previously excluded from geometry because they are generated mechanically but cannot be defined in terms of ruler and compass constructions. These developments were problematic because they make the tacit supposition that any point on a plane can be assigned a pair of numbers as co-ordinates, once co-ordinate axes have been fixed.

The ancient Greeks already had proof that the hypotenuse of a right-angled isosceles triangle with unit sides must have a length $\sqrt{2}$, but that this length could not be expressed as any ratio. The discovery of the existence of such incommensurable magnitudes was one of the reasons why arithmetic and geometry had been regarded as distinct mathematical disciplines. One studied discrete magnitudes, the other continuous magnitudes and it was not thought possible to reduce the study of continuous magnitudes to that of discrete magnitudes. This ·attitude was reinforced by paradoxes, such as Zeno's paradox of Achilles and the tortoise, which were taken to show that a continuous magnitude cannot be made up of discrete parts. The history of much of the work in pure mathematics in the eighteenth and nineteenth centuries is the history of how, in spite of such paradoxes, ways were found to effect a reduction of the study of the continuous to a study of the discrete. This reduction is not without cost. The price is having to develop a mathematics of the infinite and admitting the infinite as a foundational concept. The difficulties encountered in this process make it hard to believe that continuous magnitudes are human inventions and thus transparent to the human intellect.

The invention of infinitesimal calculus and its use in mechanics gave added urgency to philosophical questions about whether, and how, it is possible to reason reliably about what is infinitely large or infinitely small. An additional feature of Newtonian mechanics is that its associated view of the physical world is of a world of small material particles moving around in, but not densely populating, space. The forces acting on particles and causing their motions are intimately connected to space and time in two ways. Firstly, they are connected by Newton's second law of motion, which states: force = mass × acceleration. This seemed to Newton to require that space and time form an absolute frame of reference, relative to which absolute motion is distinguished from relative motion (changes in absolute motion being those that result from forces acting on the moving object). For relative motions the second law can be false. A person standing on a railway platform accelerates away from a person in a train, from whose point of view the train is stationary. But there is no force acting on the person or the platform causing them to accelerate away from the train. Secondly, Newton's gravitational theory proposes that there is a gravitational attraction between any two material particles and that this force is directly proportional to the product of the masses of the two particles and inversely proportional to the square of the distance between them. In other words, spatial separation is itself a causal factor as it determines the magnitude of a fundamental force. The mathematics of space as the paradigm continuous magnitude must, it seems, be regarded as dealing with an aspect of the same physical world that is studied by the natural philosophers. If one subscribed to the vision of the world proposed by Newtonian mechanics, it would be hard not to be some form of realist about mathematics. Only by being instrumentalist about Newtonian physics – by regarding it as a mere calculatory device for better predicting and controlling events in the world of everyday human experience – would one be more likely to be attracted to some kind of conceptualism about mathematics.

But note how the ground has shifted in such a way that neither form of position is entirely stable. The new form of realism requires mathematics to relate to an independently existing, natural world of material particles in motion, not to an eternal and unchanging supernatural or spiritual world. It therefore faces serious problems about its ability to say how it can be possible for us to get certain knowledge of this world by mathematical (as distinct from experimental) methods, for this material world is explicitly described as having no affinity with the human intellect. Appeal to the benevolent Christian God certainly remained a possibility for believers, but it would be in a climate where this must be regarded as an act of faith, and thus not as something for which any rational, philosophic justification can be given. The philosophical form of the basic problem would thus have to be dismissed as insoluble and an inappropriate topic of investigation.

The new form of conceptualism also faced serious problems. The first problem area is the notion of the infinite. If the human intellect is finite how can it – either innately, or when prompted by its necessarily limited experience – be the source of a concept of the infinite? Only such a concept would be adequate to a detailed mathematical comprehension of the infinite complexity hidden within continuous magnitudes. Secondly, the problems posed by the new algebraic mathematics, and the methods of inference being used to provide solutions, made it quite clear that these forms of inference could in no way be construed as conforming to the pattern of inference from explicit definitions of concepts via deductive logical moves (or syllogisms) to conclusions. Because definitions, even in geometry, frequently came to take the form of algebraic equations, inferences from these involved computation and the handling of equations and inequalities in a central way. All of this is explicitly relational reasoning – it is not assimilable within the framework of Aristotelian syllogistic, which is basically a logic of predication.

Two new variant strategies emerged in response to the changed configuration of mathematics and its uses. One, accompanying an INSTRUMENTALIST ATTITUDE TO SCIENCE (pp. 298–300), was conventionalist or formalist. Since instrumentalism about science was not prominent in the eighteenth and nineteenth centuries, this was not a widely pursued option. The other, proposed by KANT (chapter 22), is a form of constructivism which represents a creative synthesis of elements from both Platonic realism and Aristotelian conventionalism.

The problem of the infinite, for conceptualists, lay in their assumption that to attach any significance to a word, that word must stand for an idea. That idea had in some way to represent, or to present to the mind, something infinite and should have its origin either in human experience or in the nature of the finite, human intellect. How can there be a finite representation of something infinite which adequately expresses the infinity of what is represented? Berkeley (1995, §19–20) short-circuited this problem by arguing that a sign (or word) can acquire meaning from use; it does not have to stand for an idea. If a word does not stand for an idea it does not represent any reality; however, a sign can be of use even if it has no representative function, or if it forms part of a system that we have developed for classifying, ordering and anticipating experience. This suggests that mathematicians are free to create signs so long as they do not claim to be able to express any superior or arcane knowledge by these means. The problem for such a position, as Berkeley's (1947–57) astute criticisms of Newton's mathematical methods illustrate, is how to ensure that when we try to make use of our new signs we will neither get absurd nor unreliable results.

Difficulties over space and time and the use made of mathematics in Newtonian mechanics formed one of the focuses of Kant's *Critique of Pure Reason*. His formulation of the basic question about mathematics is 'How is *synthetic a priori* knowledge possible?' His answer is to assume that it is possible (since Newtonian mechanics is accepted and is seen to work) and to ask what are the necessary conditions of its possibility. His answer rejects traditional relational accounts of space and time as well as Newton's absolute space and time. He argues effectively that space cannot be reduced to spatial relations but must be thought to be a unity which has its own characteristic properties. One argument he uses (repeated and strengthened by Nerlich, 1976) is to point out that the difference between a right hand and a left hand cannot be captured by characterizing the relations between the parts of the hand; rather, it has to do with the way the hand is 'inserted' into space. Nerlich uses the very simple shapes (which he calls 'knees') to illustrate the same point. It is not possible by sliding a right knee around on a flat surface to move it in such a way that it becomes a left knee. This can only be achieved if we lift the right knee up, turn it over and re-insert in the plane, when it will now be a left knee. Thus the difference between right and left is not intrinsic to the object, but to the way it is 'oriented' in space. Not all surfaces, however, have this characteristic. The surface of a Möbius strip is such that by moving a right knee once around the strip it becomes a left knee. Thus 'orientability', the capacity to produce right–left distinctions is a feature of space itself, not of things in it.

Kant on Space, Time and Mathematics

Kant's position on space and time is thus non-reductionist, but it is not realist. He does not assert that space and time have any reality independent of human perception. Rather, space and time are forms of human intuition and hence structure all human experience. We do not, and could not, gain these notions from experience because they are preconditions of and are presupposed in all experience. All human experience occurs in time and all experience of things outside our own mental life is experienced as occurring in space as well as time. The foundation of arithmetic is to be found in the temporal structure of our experience, and that of geometry in its spatial structure. These structures are of the world of experience, but they have that status only because the forms of human intuition are what constitute and give form to that world.

That mathematics is grounded back to *a priori* forms of intuition, rather than to innate ideas or structures of the intellect, is significant and indicates Kant's divergence from Aristotelian conceptualism. He distinguishes sharply between logical deduction, reasoning from concepts, and mathematical reasoning, which involves reasoning from the construction of concepts. It is our ability imaginatively to construct mathematical objects in pure intuition that grounds our insight into their properties. We imagine a mathematical point tracing out the curve whose co-ordinates at all times satisfy the equation for a circle, and thereby connect the algebraic definition with what it constructively defines. The algebraic definition of a curve in analytic geometry is thus viewed as a definition in the sense of a recipe for constructing an object, rather than as an Aristotelian definition of a term proceeding by a specification of genus and differentia. It is our ability, in our imagination, to carry out the operations that correspond to functional expressions, which forms the ground that makes mathematical knowledge possible. It is the fact that space and time, as forms of intuition, are such that all items of experience appear as magnitudes that assures us of the universal applicability of mathematics. The very notion of empirical reality and an objective order of experience is argued to require the supposition that the causal order of events is such as to impose determinate mathematical structures on space and time. Thus Kant, using a modified conceptualist strategy, sought to preserve the essentials of the Newtonian framework whilst avoiding the problems that were encountered by postulating absolute space and time.

However, the fact that human intellectual construction forms the ground for mathematical knowledge means that if the infinite is to have any place in mathematics, it can only be as the potential infinity of the unending, never-completed series of which the natural number series is the primary example. No actually infinite construction can be supposed to have been carried out. Kant argues both that human reason is so structured that it will tend, illegitimately, to form the idea of a completed infinite process, and that this is always a source of illusions. If we want to treat infinite series as objects we will not be able to regard them as things that are ever completed. Reasoning concerning them thus cannot obey all the same principles as reasoning about fully determinate objects. In particular, reasoning by reductio ad absurdum cannot be relied upon in such cases.

It was within a broadly Kantian framework that much of the work in mathematics and its foundations was pursued into the nineteenth century, particularly in Germany. Work by Weierstrass (1815–97) and Cauchy (1789–1857) seemed further to justify Kant's position on the infinite. They succeeded in providing definitions of limits and convergence for infinite series that use only the notion of a potential infinite and make no appeal to the actual completion of an infinite sequence of approximations. This work seemed to secure the foundations of analysis without invoking the actual infinite.

4 Foundations

4.1 Logic, set theory and analytic empiricism

Toward the end of the nineteenth century, developments within mathematics and physics, together with wider socio-cultural changes, meant that the Kantian position could no longer be regarded as adequate. In mathematics the discovery of pathological functions – functions such as Weierstrass' every-where-continuous-but-nowhere-differentiable function

$$f(x) = \sum_{n=0}^{\infty} b^n \cos (a^n x)$$

– clearly indicated that geometrical intuition was not an adequate foundation for producing reliable mathematics. It was felt that the theory of real numbers needed to be put on a wholly numerical, arithmetical footing, one which did not at any point appeal to spatial intuition.

As a part of attempts to do this and to characterize the order structure required of the real numbers, Cantor (1845–1918) introduced transfinite ordinal numbers, and then, having proved that there can be no one–one correspondence between the natural numbers and the real numbers, introduced distinct infinite cardinal numbers. That is, he not only supposed that there could be a mathematics of the actually infinite, but, having argued that it is necessary to distinguish different sizes of infinite totality, went on to develop an arithmetic of infinite numbers. Disputes over the legitimacy of the proposed introduction of these transfinite numbers, coming on top of those concerning the introduction of Gauss' (1777–1855) imaginary numbers and Hamilton's (1805–65) quaternions, made clarification of the concept of number and of the grounds on which one could legitimately claim to have introduced a new kind of number a pressing issue.

Einstein and the Nature of Mathematical Knowledge

Perhaps most damaging to the Kantian position was the discovery of non-Euclidean geometries and the application of these in Einstein's theories of relativity. In one sense Einstein's procedure was thoroughly Kantian. He argued from the causal structures indicated by the form of laws used in electromagnetism to the form required for those of mechanics (assuming that fundamental physical theories should conform to the same space–time forms) and read out the implications of this for the geometry of space–time. But this meant that it could no longer be plausibly argued that geometry gives *a priori* knowledge of the space–time structure of the material world.

The net effect of Einstein's use of non-Euclidean geometry in a physical theory was to disestablish the view that mathematics is a source of *a priori* knowledge about the empirical world. Euclidean geometry does not contain, and never had contained, truths about physical space that were guaranteed to be correct in application by their proofs. This appeared to vindicate empiricist claims that *synthetic a priori* knowledge is impossible. When mathematics forms part of empirical, scientific theories, then the correctness or otherwise of its results must be as much an empirical question as that of the correctness or otherwise of a scientific theory. But if proofs do not serve to justify applications, what do they prove? In other words, what exactly is the character and content of mathematical knowledge? If proofs do not establish claims about the world of experience, we seem to be left with the options either of a return to a form of Platonic realism or working toward a view that locates the importance of mathematics in its function and does not see it as making knowledge claims.

The overthrow of the Newtonian framework of classical mechanics was the combined effect of acceptance of relativity theory and of quantum mechanics. Again, one of its philosophical impacts was to give a boost to empiricism, particularly because quantum mechanics was accepted on the basis of its empirical success, despite conceptual problems over the interpretation of its mathematical formalism and conceptual resistance to its indeterminism. Now from an empiricist point of view, a return to a form of Platonic realism about mathematics would seem to be a non-starter. Yet, ironically, the logicist route to an empiricist account of mathematics (pursued by Russell, 1919 and Whitehead and Russell, 1913) involves a displaced form of the Platonic realist strategy. Two moves are crucial here: (1) invoking an IDEAL LOGICAL LANGUAGE (p. 669) (for science); and (2) the use of classes, or sets, to define numbers in terms of their potential applications.

Both of these moves had already been made by FREGE (chapter 27) (1884, 1893), who had no commitment to an empiricist epistemology. Frege was concerned to provide a philosophical defence of the claims of mathematics to be a body of objective knowledge. He was reacting on the one hand against what he saw to be the naturalistic psychologism of Kantian and other positions that treat knowledge as a matter of relating ideas, and on the other hand, he was reacting against conventionalist claims that mathematicians are free to create new numbers systems, since these are no more than formal symbol systems.

Frege's Realism

Frege appealed to the metaphor of geographic exploration when defending his claim that mathematics is a body of objective knowledge, and he resisted fiercely the suggestion that mathematicians have the right to create new mathematical objects or concepts. His conception of objective knowledge is thus strongly realist. Such knowledge is of an independently existing reality. It is expressed in language, which serves to represent that domain, using sentences which say either truly or falsely how things are. Whether such sentences are true or false depends on the state of the domain referred to and the result is independent of the state of human knowledge and of human cognitive capacities. What is said cannot, therefore, be a function of ideas in the minds of individual language speakers. The meanings of words must be publicly grounded in their linguistic function, which refers to the contribution that they make to fixing the truth conditions of sentences in which they occur. From the point of view of knowledge expression the sentence is the primary unit of meaning. These views on language and meaning turn the focus of philosophic attention away from ideas and thought processes, to language and its function in the communication and expression of knowledge; they constitute what has been labelled the 'linguistic turn', which is characteristic of analytic philosophy. This turn made available a broadly Platonic realist strategy, for language is here conceived not as any actually existing natural language, but as an ideal vehicle for the expression of objective knowledge to which all natural languages must approximate to the extent that they succeed in making knowledge-expression possible. The ideal logical language becomes the non-natural intermediary linking human beings to the structures of reality. It takes over some of the roles of the mind of God. We can come to know the structural principles governing faithful representation in this language because we are language speakers, and can reflect on the conditions of the possibility of language functioning in this way – a thought that found its classical expression in Wittgenstein's *Tractatus Logico–Philosophicus* (1922). Logic is an explicit codification of the principles of language in its representative, knowledge-expressing function. Its laws are not inherent in the structure of the human intellect; they are laws of truth, not laws of thought. The structures of such an ideal language, one able accurately to represent reality, must therefore also be reflections of the structure of reality.

Why should it be thought that mathematics, the study of magnitudes, can be reduced to logic, the study of the structure and relations of sentences in their knowledge-expressing function? The link here is the notion of a 'class' or 'set'. The theory of a classes, the extensions of a concepts, was traditionally a part of logic because Aristotelian syllogistic can, on one interpretation, be treated as a logic of classes and their relations. ('Whales are mammals' is treated as saying that the class of whales is included in that of mammals.) The natural numbers can be treated as measures of the sizes of sets, or classes, so that, for instance, the number 2 can be the measure of all 2-membered sets. It can be shown that negative numbers and rational numbers can be defined as sets (or ordered pairs) of natural numbers. Dedekind (1831–1916) proposed (1963) a definition of real numbers as infinite sets (or cuts) of rational numbers. This suggested that 'set', or 'class', may be the single primitive concept from which all other mathematical concepts could be defined, if geometry and analysis could themselves be reduced either to arithmetic or to the study of sets of points.

Cantor (1895) and others were basing their definitions of number on a conception that can already be found in Plato. The number 2, for example, consists of two abstract units; it is the ideal type (the one over many) to which all pairs conform. Cantor suggested that numbers are arrived at by a psychological process of abstraction from collections such as two pencils on a desk. We must imaginatively subtract all the distinguishing qualities of the pencils and their location. If we abstract from everything but their order (the order in which we count) we get an ordinal number (an order type) and if we abstract even this we get a cardinal number (a cardinality type). In other words, the Platonic universal becomes an idea in an individual mind. But Frege ruled out such psychologistic accounts. Instead, he adopted a definition that makes 2, the one over all pairs, simply the class of all pairs. What saves this from circularity is that he defines what it is to be a two-membered class without using any reference to the number 2. A class is by definition a two-membered class if and only if there is a one–one correspondence between it and the class whose only members are 0 and 1. So, to say that there are two pencils on my desk is to say that the class of pencils on my desk is such that there is a one–one correspondence between it and {0,1}. Thus if I can find one pencil on my desk and pair it with 0 and another and pair it with 1 and there are none left over, I will know that the claim is true; otherwise, it is false. Of course 0 and 1 have themselves to be defined. 0 is defined as the class of classes C such that there is a one–one correspondence between C and the extension of the concept $x \neq x$. 1 is then the class of those classes C such that there is a one–one correspondence between C and the class whose only member is 0.

In this way the number 2 is linked by definition to its potential applications. But, to justify the claim that all arithmetic truths can be proved by appeal only to definitions and formally expressed logical laws, the definitions given above must be expressed in the language of formal logic, and must use only concepts belonging to logic. Further, it must be shown that all the normally accepted arithmetic principles can be logically derived from these definitions.

Two things were crucial to this project: firstly, treating '=' as a primitive logical relation and, secondly, assuming, as a principle of logic, that every concept defined over individual objects has a class as its extension. It was also necessary to express in logical terms what it is for a relation to be a one–one correspondence between two classes. This idea can be defined as follows – 'R is a one–one correspondence between A and B if and only if for every x in A there is just one y in B such that x is R-related to y and for every y in B there is just one x in A such that x is R-related to y'. To express this as a logical condition requires a logic of relations capable of handling multiple quantification in a single sentence, and in which it is possible to express the numerical concept 'there is just one'. None of these was available in traditional logic. However, focus on the sentence as the unit of meaning enabled Frege to treat concept expressions and relational expressions (predicates) by analogy with mathematical functions of one, two or more variables, as sentence-forming operators. It was within this expanded logical framework that Frege claimed that arithmetic reduces to logic. What had previously been a major stumbling block to such a claim – the relational character of arithmetical reasoning – was overcome by the integration of a logic of relations with the logic of concepts.

This brilliant strategy, however, came to grief as a result of Russell's paradox, which demonstrated that Frege's system of 'logic' is inconsistent. The paradox arose because it is possible, in this system, to express the concept 'is a class which does not belong to itself'. Since classes are, for Frege, individual objects, and every concept defined over individual objects is assumed to have a class as its extension, this concept too must define a class – say R. Does R belong to itself? If it does then it must be a class which does not belong to itself; clearly a contradiction. But if it does not, then it is a class which does not belong to itself and hence belongs to R (itself).

However, RUSSELL (chapter 27) was attracted to Frege's strategy. If it were possible to show that all mathematics reduced to logic, then this would substantially strengthen the case for the empiricist denial of any autonomy to conceptual knowledge. Russell was an empirical realist: in other words, he assumed that there is a world that exists independently of our experience; it is a world of atomic events (or 'sense data'). The order of occurrence of such events is thus wholly contingent. Objective knowledge of this world, as attempted by natural science, takes the form of a description of global, structural features of the totality of events that constitutes the universe. It takes the form of knowledge of relations between sense data; sensed qualities, since they can only be known subjectively, must drop out of the scientific picture. Thus simple, atomic, sentences will all state that a certain relation holds between two or more sense data.

Because the order of events is contingent, we can never in fact be in a position to know the truth of any global description. Its truth conditions are such that only a non-finite being apprehending the whole space–time universe in a single intuition could directly verify its truth. The form that a direct description of such a world would take would be a list of all the true atomic sentences of the ideal logical language of science. If the use of mathematics in science is to lead to objectively true descriptive statements about this world, every description given using mathematical terms should be an abbreviation that is reducible without residue to some (possibly infinite) complex sentence built out of atomic sentences in such a way that the truth value of the complex is determined by those of its atomic components. In other words, the complex is constructed using (possibly infinite) truth-functions. Thus the definitions of all complex mathematical terms should indicate how, in principle, such an elimination could be effected. Such abbreviations are resorted to only because of the limited capacity of finite human minds. Mathematical truths are those that can be derived, logically, from an unpacking of the definitions of mathematical concepts. They do not say anything about the world, but they do help us make logically correct moves around the shorthand language that we have developed for describing it.

How did Russell propose to avoid the problem Frege ran into? His end solution is the so-called no-class theory which incorporates his 'ramified theory of types'. There are two key ideas here. (1) Classes are logical fictions, they are not real individual objects. (2) For this reason, the language which incorporates these fictions must have a hierarchical structure. At the base level we have the empirical world of individuals. Concepts are defined over these and for convenience we introduce names of classes as a shorthand way of talking about all the things to which a given concept applies. These 'classes' clearly cannot be treated as belonging to the original level, but once they have been introduced it is possible to define new concepts using them, and to introduce more classes on a yet higher level. This has the effect of ruling out the possibility that a class should belong to itself and also the possibility of defining the concept 'is a class'; it is only possible to define 'is a class of level n'. However, as Russell admitted, there was no hope of developing mathematics within this framework without two substantial assumptions: the Axiom of Infinity and the Axiom of Reducibility.

The Axiom of Infinity says that there are infinitely many individuals in the universe. This is necessary because Russell could not use Frege's definitions of the natural numbers in quite their original form. The basic idea is still the same — 2 is to be the class of all two-membered classes of individuals — but a different definition of what it is to be a two-membered class is required, namely, one which does not refer to 0 and 1. The solution was to define a two-membered class as the extension of any concept F for which the following is true: 'there are distinct objects x and y which satisfy F and every object which satisfies F is identical either with x or with y'. However, this means that in a universe containing only one object, 2 would be the empty class, and so would 3 and every larger number. Thus to ensure that there are infinitely many natural numbers, there must be assumed to be an infinite universe. This illustrates the impossibility of simultaneously restricting objects to those that actually exist in the empirical world, insisting that mathematical terms be defined in such a way as to build in all their legitimate applications in advance, and claiming that mathematics does not embody any knowledge of or make any substantive claims about that actual world.

The Axiom of Reducibility is required to be able to define real numbers as infinite classes of rational numbers. Basically, it claims that all possible ways of grouping individuals (into 'classes') are already available using concepts definable at the first level of the hierarchy; that is, the introduction of more complex concepts whose definitions make reference to already defined concepts and classes does not in fact make any new discriminations possible; it does not genuinely enlarge our vocabulary for describing the structure of the world. This assumption, is, however, equivalent to the claim that the reduction of mathematics to logic was supposed to help establish – the denial that concepts contribute to the content of what we say about the empirical world.

Recently Bostock (1974, 1979), Field (1980), Chihara (1990) and Wright (1983) have made interesting attempts to follow logicist courses somewhat different from Russell's. But in each case, as in Russell's, the question arises of what exactly falls within the scope of logic. A convincing claim to have reduced mathematics to logic would require a clear way of distinguishing between what is and what is not logic, and well-grounded philosophical motivations for making the distinction exactly where one does. One way of making that distinction can be found in Quine's work. From the point of view of empiricism, logic should not introduce any ontology of abstract objects. Thus Quine (1970) limits logic to first order predicate calculus – the only objects talked about are individual objects. Modal logic and higher order logic are discounted, but if mathematics is reducible to logic at all, at least some form of one or both of these kinds of logic seems to be required. The alternative, the one taken by mathematicians and by Quine (1963), is to say that mathematics does not reduce to logic, but can be reduced to axiomatic set theory. Philosophical questions about the status of mathematics then become questions about the status of set theory, since this is the foundation on which everything else can be built. Analytic empiricists tended to accept, increasingly unquestioningly, this focus on foundations where everything comes to rest on logic and set theory. Here again the options of Platonic realism or some form of conceptualism are available. There are those who defend Platonic realism (see Brown, 1991 and Maddy, 1990) by adopting the view that the best explanation for the successful application of mathematics is that it does express knowledge of principles underlying the structure of reality. This neatly turns the basic problem around but leaves one asking about the validity of this style of inference. What other explanations of success in application are there? How are we to adjudicate between competing explanations?

There is a competing explanatory strategy offered by Quine's (1969) NATURALIZED EPISTEMOLOGY (pp. 307–8). Although the Darwinian account of the descent of man has rendered implausible the idea that God created humans with intellects innately equipped to discern the mathematical principles according to which he created the universe, it can be used to underwrite the utility of our innate capacities. Our innate capacities are a product of evolution, that is, partly a matter of chance (random genetic variation) and partly a matter of natural selection, which favours those variations that have up to now proved to have adaptive value. Thus we find certain things self-evident because these things have, in the past, proved useful (they have conferred superior survival value). Adaptive value is, however, relative to the environing experience. We can have no guarantee that experience will not in the future require changes in mathematical theories, just as it may require changes in physical theories. Mathematical theories are no different in kind from other scientific theories; they are just more general and thus more resistant to change, because changing them means wholesale revisions in so many other areas. Acknowledging this, Quine adopts an instrumentalist attitude toward mathematics, by which it does postulate the existence of abstract objects and it does postulate them as real existents, but this is seen as part of the mythology that we have developed for dealing with the physical world. We are realist about such things, but it is (to use a term coined by Putnam) an 'internal realism' in which we can receive no justification that guarantees either ultimate truth or permanent utility.

4.2 Intuitionism, formalism and open questions

What logicist and set theoretic foundationalist approaches to mathematics significantly ignore is the question of how human beings actually acquire and use mathematical knowledge. They focus on questions of justification, relegating the study of methods of discovery to psychology. Wittgenstein and more recently Dummett, together with formalists and intuitionist critics of logicism, pointed out that the proposed logicist reduction, even if successful, begs central questions about the epistemological foundations of mathematics. This is because, to check that a full logical analysis of, for example, 'there are two things which are F' is correct, one must count occurrences of variables. In other words, a grasp of arithmetical concepts is presupposed in being able to read a formal logical language and understand its definitions of numbers. The analysis cannot indicate how we acquire a grasp of numerical concepts and hence cannot explain how we might manage to extend our grasp of finite, natural numbers to an understanding of terms purporting to refer to infinite sets, infinite series or transfinite numbers. These critics take it that one of the tasks of a philosophy of mathematics is to explain with what right human beings with finite capacities can introduce and claim to understand symbols purporting to represent the infinite – symbols whose use was intended to facilitate a knowledge of infinite structures.

Thus in various forms their concern is with the way in which, or the extent to which, a grasp of the infinite can be grounded in apprehension of the finite. Brouwer's (1881–1966) intuitionism was self-consciously Kantian in inspiration (Brouwer, 1975). It grounds the arithmetic of natural numbers in the pure form of temporal intuition: the bare two-oneness which is a pre-condition of being able to apprehend anything as a manifold (a unity having internal complexity), and hence of any knowledge whatsoever. This is used to provide a foundation for analysis, via a theory of the creative subject. Brouwer followed Kant in eschewing use of the actually infinite. He thus rejected set theoretic approaches to the definition of the real numbers. Potentially infinite sequences, the paradigm of which is the natural number sequence, can be objects of knowledge but cannot be treated as if they were fully determinate. Such a sequence can only be known through the principle which generates it, the principle which assures us that it is unending. This may (for a lawless sequence) be simply the ever-available free choice of the creative subject to extend it. As Kant had already argued, reasoning concerning incomplete, potentially infinite totalities cannot validly employ *reductio ad absurdum* proofs. This is because we have no warrant for asserting that one of P or not-P must be true (the Principle of the Excluded Middle) in advance of generating the sequence to a point where it can be directly determined either that P or that not-P is the case. For some claims we have no guarantee that such a position can ever be reached (for example, regarding the conjecture that there are only finitely many times in the decimal expansion of π that a digit in an odd-numbered place is equal to the digit in the following even-numbered place). Because intuitionists reject the Principle of the Excluded Middle, and proofs based on it, there are many proofs which classical mathematicians accept but which are rejected by intuitionists.

Having rejected the Frege–Russell framework for logic, intuitionists developed a logic that does not take the principle of the excluded middle to be universally valid. Heyting (1956), Dummett (1973) and others taking the linguistic turn, have used this alternative logic as a means of providing a framework for intuitionism which does not appeal to Kantian intuition. An account of the meaning of a mathematical claim is not to be given by stating its truth conditions, but by a specification of the conditions under which one would be entitled to assert it (the proof conditions). This links the understanding of mathematical questions to knowledge of what a proof constituting an answer would look like. In arithmetic, the basic, canonical proofs are computations. Effective computational procedures thus figure prominently in intuitionist and constructivist mathematics. For this reason much of what has been developed has been found to be useful, even by those who do not espouse intuitionist or constructivist views and who do not reject the mathematics that requires use of the actual infinite.

Hilbert (1882–1943) (1926) adopted a position very similar to that of intuitionism with respect to the arithmetic of natural numbers. In his case, however, the founding intuitions were not those of pure imagination, but are derived from the use of tally systems and the progression to written numerals. He thus focuses on mathematics as a tool, or an instrument for solving problems, rather than as an elaboration of innate human intellectual structures. This means that when it comes to the use of infinite numbers and symbols purporting to represent infinitistic operations, Hilbert's response is conventionalist and instrumentalist, rather than conceptualist. While insisting that such signs can have for us no direct representational content, he allows that they may form a legitimate part of mathematics. Symbols have meaning which is derived from their use in formal mathematical systems, and their introduction is justified if it makes possible the solution of pre-existing problems and if the total system, consisting of the new symbols together with the old system which they extend, can be shown to be consistent.

But how can consistency be proved? One way to show that a theory is consistent is to show that it has a model. Thus non-Euclidean geometries were proved consistent relative to Euclidean geometry by showing that they had models in Euclidean geometry. Riemannian plane geometry can be interpreted as geometry on the surface of a Euclidean sphere, for example. But this still leaves open the question of what assures us of the consistency of Euclidean geometry. Hilbert (1899) had provided an axiomatization of Euclidean geometry where the axioms take the form of conditions on relations between points which must be satisfied if a totality of points is to be considered a Euclidean space. He further showed that the real numbers could be used to provide a model for these axioms. This reduces the consistency question to how to ensure the consistency of the theory of real numbers. For both Hilbert and intuitionists the consistency of the arithmetic of natural numbers and of effective computational procedures (finitary arithmetic) is guaranteed by the fact that models can actually be constructed (whether in intuition or on paper). The theory of real numbers, quantification over the totality of natural numbers – when treated as obeying the law of excluded middle – and the use of symbols for infinite sets and transfinite numbers all face the problem that, *ex hypothesis*, it is not possible to find effective methods for constructing models of the infinite totalities that they presuppose. The consistency question thus reduces to how to ground the use of symbols for infinitary objects, or infinitary operations, in the finite. What came to be called Hilbert's Programme was the suggestion that one should try to treat consistency as a formal property of symbol systems. Symbol systems are themselves finite, even if they contain symbols intended to refer to infinite objects or to infinitary operations. They are governed by rules whose correct application can be checked by appeal merely to a capacity to recognize the symbolic forms of formulae, which is something that does not require a grasp of their content. Proofs in such systems are finite symbol structures constructed according to formal rules. For inconsistency to arise it would have to be possible to prove some sentence and its negation; for example, to prove a sentence with a formal structure analogous to 'P and not-P'. If it were possible to show, by reference to the formal, finitary properties of the symbol system that no such formula could be the last line of a proof, then one would have a demonstration of consistency, one which uses only finitary, constructive methods.

Gödel and Consistency

Gödel (1906–78) (1931) proved (in his First Incompleteness Theorem) that it is impossible to complete Hilbert's programme. He proved, using finitary methods, that if a formal system S capable of expressing arithmetic is consistent, then there is a sentence G expressible in the formal language of S which is such that neither it nor its negation can be proved in S. (G is so constructed that it can be interpreted as saying of itself that it is not provable.) He further showed (in his Second Incompleteness Theorem) that, as a result, an inconsistency arises if it is supposed that S can be proved consistent by finitary methods, for this would make it possible to prove in S that G is not provable in S. Since G is a formal expression of the claim that G is not provable in S, this would also be a proof of G. Hence (by the First Incompleteness Theorem) S would be inconsistent. The key idea behind this proof was to code all symbols of the formal language by numbers. Formulae and proofs, being finite symbol structures, can then also be coded by numbers, in such a way that their symbolic properties correspond to arithmetical properties of their numerical counterparts. Since the formal language was intended to be one that talks about numbers, this device allows the symbol system to have a double interpretation – in talking about numbers, it also talks about its own formulae.

This idea revealed the enormous potential of numbers as devices for coding symbolic and other structures. It is this power that was subsequently exploited to develop digital electronic computers. In this way, mathematics concerned with

> formal systems and effective computational procedures, which was developed in response to Hilbert's programme and to the emphasis placed on effective procedures by intuitionism, not only found immense practical application but also led to the development of whole new areas of mathematics, including proof theory, model theory and recursive function theory.

But where does this leave the issue of justifying the use of infinitary mathematics? The exact interpretation of the philosophical import of Gödel's theorem has been much discussed (Detlefsen, 1986) and there is no general consensus. What does seem to be agreed is that there is no hope of a complete justificational bootstrapping, using only finitary methods, to provide an unchallengeable legitimation of infinitary methods. Formal systems are themselves potentially infinite. So to prove results about a whole system S, such as C, which states, 'There is no proof in S of any formula of the form "P and not-P"', requires a proof about a potentially infinite totality. But without the assumption that it is legitimate to regard infinite totalities as completed objects (which is the assumption that a finitary consistency proof is trying to justify), there is no justification for asserting that either C or not-C must be true.

Similarly, set theory's ability to deliver definitive answers on foundational questions has been shown to be limited. What have come to be regarded as the core axioms of set theory – namely, the Zermelo–Fraenkel axiom and the Axiom of Choice which, together, we shall call ZFC – do not make possible a resolution of the question that Cantor sought to answer by introducing transfinite numbers, namely, the question of the structure of the continuum. Cantor proved that there can be no one–one correspondence between the real numbers and the natural numbers. He interpreted this result as proof that the cardinal number of the set of real numbers ($2^{\aleph_0}$) is greater than that of the set of natural numbers ($\aleph_0$). He also proved that the cardinal number ($\aleph_1$) of the set of all well-orderings of the natural numbers must be greater than that of the natural numbers, and that there could be no infinite set whose cardinality was greater than $\aleph_0$ but less than $\aleph_1$. That is, $\aleph_1$ is the next infinite cardinal number after $\aleph_0$. Cantor thought it was the case that $2^{\aleph_0}$ must be the same number as $\aleph_1$ (Cantor's Continuum Hypothesis, or CH), but he was unable to prove it. Gödel (1940) produced a model of ZFC (the constructible sets) in which this is the case, but Cohen (1966) produced one in which it is not. Together the results show that ZFC leaves the question undecided. The question remains, if we accept ZFC and use infinite sets, on what ground should we accepted or reject CH? What difference, if any, does it make in other areas of mathematics?

These foundational questions require detailed technical work from mathematicians. The larger philosophical questions, however, concern evaluation of the whole foundational trend, a trend which has not, as had been hoped, provided once and for all solutions to questions about the status of mathematics and our justification for relying on it. It has produced lots of new and interesting mathematics and this in itself must surely tell us something about contemporary mathematics. The question is, what exactly does it tell us?

5 Beyond Foundationalism and Analytic Philosophy

Foundationalism is reductionist; it seeks to determine a hierarchical ordering of a given area of knowledge by pushing back to the starting points from which all the rest deductively follows and hence can be rationally justified. Questions of the status of that whole area of knowledge thus come to focus on the status of these first principles. This presumes that there is some absolute, timeless, universal sense of rational order, or of what constitutes a rational justification. Yet as the historical outline presented here already shows, ideas about standards of rigour in mathematical proofs and about what constitutes logic have changed. The fact that mathematical reasoning was relational was enough at one time to suggest that it did not proceed solely according to principles of deductive logic. Now that relational reasoning has been incorporated into logic in the form of first order predicate calculus, that particular ground for thinking that mathematical reasoning does not reduce to logical deduction has been removed. But what are the grounds for thinking that first order predicate calculus is the ultimate, canonical form of logic? There are many potential challengers. Mathematicians have studied any number of formal 'logics', including modal logics, and many-valued logics and relevant logics. Information technology in its pursuit of the development of expert systems has in the past few years spurred a growth of interest in non-monotonic logics. Should we be monist or pluralist about logic? So long as foundationalism was the prevailing philosophic attitude toward accounts of knowledge in mathematics or any other area, it had to be presumed that there is just one system of logic, that which reveals the absolute, timeless, universal, rational order of knowledge and which provides an account of what constitutes a rational justification for belief. But foundationalism in other areas of epistemology has in the last half of this century increasingly been challenged. These assumptions about rationality no longer appear self-evident. Yet, as Bloor (1973) was aware when launching the strong programme in the sociology of knowledge, mathematics would be a test case for that programme, as it was for the analytic empiricists. It might be a bastion of a fixed, eternal rational order around which defenders of claims to universal rationality can rally. But the standards of rationality could prove less than fixed and the order presupposed by foundationalists could prove unnecessary to explain the development of actual mathematics or its applications. If this were true, then the claims of foundationalism and of access to universal standards of rationality would look shaky indeed. Bloor takes many of his cues from the anti-foundationalist later philosophy of WITTGENSTEIN (chapter 29) (1963, 1967) which emphasizes the way in which forms of life – social practices of which mathematics and language are integral parts – inform our sense of what is or is not rational. Wittgenstein's view of mathematics is non-reductionist. Moreover, he repeatedly emphasises what he calls the 'motley of mathematics' – the variety to be found in its various branches and in their applications. He raises the question that other philosophers did not at that time dream of raising – questions of how it is determined what a proof proves and of how the logical 'must' acquires its force. He regarded mathematics as an integral part of the framework of linguistic conventions, which we develop in the context of trying to live with others in a material world. These conventions are learnt by training, that is, in repetitive, corrected practice in certain kinds of contexts. The meaning (or content) of a linguistic sign thus derives wholly from its customary uses. These uses themselves derive from forms of life in which they are embedded; for example, calculating as part of exchanging money for goods of various kinds. In normal circumstances the question of justification will not arise and can receive no answer beyond, 'That is the way we do it.' This is because use is the bedrock of understanding. But as we know from the occurrences of ethical and practical dilemmas, elements of human practices can come into conflict with one another. It is in such circumstances that reflective conceptual analysis is required to make explicit what has been implicitly presumed in the practices that conflict (for instance, between reliance on both geometric intuition and on algebraic definitions in analytic geometry) and to resolve the conflict where possible by reference to values drawn from the wider framework of the form of life in which the practices are embodied.

Wittgenstein himself seems to have had a very narrow conception of the source of conceptual problems (an idea parallel to Kant's view that the human mind is prone to delude itself with illusions based on mistaking ideas of reason for real things). He thought that our everyday language tends to mislead us into belief in abstract objects. We tend to believe that wherever we have an expression that functions grammatically as a name, there must be something that it names. Analysis proceeds by revealing the logical grammar of problematic nouns – the grammar implicit in the practices of use which determine their content – and shows that the apparent names do not function as names. In this way Wittgenstein argues that neither numbers nor expressions for private sensations serve to stand for objects. But sociologists of knowledge, even when taking cues from Wittgenstein, do not necessarily limit themselves, in advance, concerning the possible sources of conceptual problems. Wittgenstein thought that the role of the philosopher in mathematics should be that of conceptual analyst, not reviser of practice. However, his own analyses led him to be highly critical of set theory and of the use of infinitistic methods. Indeed, it is hard to see how analyses intended to reveal how language misleads us could fail to be critical in their intent, by aiming to revise aspects of practice. Only if philosophers could work from a vantage point wholly outside the practices they analyse could their activity avoid being potentially revisionary. But, since participation in practice is, for Wittgenstein, the ground of understanding linguistic expressions employed in them, philosophers cannot begin their work from a stance of distanced non-engagement. Wittgenstein likened the role of philosopher to that of anthropologist; and, indeed, the philosopher faces the same problems of reflexivity as the anthropologist – the philosopher, and his or her studies become part of the object he or she is studying and so modify it.

This reflexivity is strikingly illustrated by the work of the mathematician–philosophers, such as Frege, Russell, Hilbert and Brouwer, whose foundational studies profoundly changed the way mathematics is done. In an effort to resolve conceptual problems encountered within existing mathematical practices, they sought to clarify and codify the assumptions built into those practices. But to do so they had to forge new mathematical instruments and invent new terminology to provide explicit expression for principles and structures that had previously had only practical embodiments. Even as they examined the bases of existing mathematics they were in the process of changing it, and they left a subsequent generation to examine these bases of the mathematics so produced; that pattern of development is discussed by Bachelard (1928).

If we stand back from the foundational enterprise and its tendency to focus on limited segments of pure mathematics, it is evident that there are also forces for change in mathematics that derive from its applications. Once mathematics is examined in the context of the world in which it is employed, questions about its authoritative status may be treated as questions of social or political authority. Such authority will be linked to its utility and the power that it confers, and the fact that it reflects values of twentieth-century culture, but not those of Plato's Athens (Latour, 1987, ch. 6). Some research conducted from this point of view suggests that it may indeed be fruitful to explore the relations between changing standards of proof, the demands placed on a proof, and changing patterns of application; such changes may alter the kinds of reliability about which assurance is sought. For example, the increased use of computers in science (for computer modelling) and in technology (particularly the military technology of smart weapons) has already renewed the question of what constitutes a proof and has led to the quasi-empirical exploration of fractal geometry via computer graphics. In what circumstances, if any, might hundreds of pages of computer printout constitute a proof? MacKenzie (1993) reports on the case, which nearly came to court, of the VIPER computer chip. Its manufacturers claimed to have a proof of its reliability. A prospective purchaser challenged this claim, saying that what was touted as a proof was not. Computer chips are physical embodiments of complex mathematical structures. Assuming that the physical transcription is correct, there still remains the question of whether a chip made to that design will actually perform the function for which it was designed. It would be desirable to have a proof answering this question in advance of the chip's deployment in, for example, a weapons system. Moreover, since claims made in this context are part of commercial transactions, they also come under legal jurisdiction. This means that the question of what does or does not constitute a proof needs to be agreed in such a way that a legal ruling is possible. Here are two social demands on the notion of proof. They are demands that are not guaranteed to be compatible or realizable, and they are demands that arise because of the kind of application given to a particular sub-branch of mathematics. That branch itself owes much of its development to its intended military applications. Whether, how, or the extent to which these demands can be met is a matter of reflective mathematical and conceptual analysis, combined with technical research.

Such demands push pure mathematical work in directions that it might not otherwise have taken, and they force changes in the concept of proof. What are the constraints within which such change can occur? Are there any objective constraints? If so, what is their origin? These are the kind of questions that come to the fore if foundationalism is discarded. They go back to the basic problem of the philosophy of mathematics and lead us to look afresh at the nexus of proof, discovery and application. This nexus has by now become very diverse and very complex because of the prominence of mathematics in our science and technology. This in turn means that to have any understanding of that science and technology, we must also understand the sources of the power of contemporary mathematics.

Further Reading

In many ways Frege's *Grundlagen* remains one of the best introductions to the philosophy of mathematics of the early part of this century. This could be coupled with the commentary by Dummett (1991). The selection of readings in Benacerraf and Putnam (1983) is excellent and provides a broad-based introduction to foundational approaches to the subject. Crucial papers from the period 1879–1931 are to be found in van Heijenoort (1967). Shanker (1988) is a useful collection of papers assessing the significance of Gödel's theorem. Hofstadter (1979) provides an excellent introduction to the concept of a formal system and a sense of both its power and its wider conceptual connections. Tiles (1989) provides an historical introduction to philosophical aspects of set theory in relation to the continuum hypothesis.

An historical overview of developments in mathematics and their impact on views about its status is provided by Kline (1980). Another way into the subject is through explanations of the conceptual challenges posed by and faced in mathematics that are written for non-mathematicians. Of these Dantzig (1930) remains a useful introduction to the intriguing aspects of numbers. The more recent Reid (1992) covers some of the same ground. Davis and Hersch (1983) gives a broader sampling of the kinds of issues raised by mathematics and of their history, as does Stewart (1987). Stewart (1989) is an excellent, eminently readable historical treatment of the relation between chaos and order, and it keeps mathematics in the context of its relation to physical theory. It begins with a discussion of the Newtonian vision of a clockwork universe and is mainly concerned with the origins of chaos theory. Somewhat different in character, but an interesting challenge to foundationalist approaches is Lakatos (1976).

Readers might be interested in the early history of philosophical reflections on mathematics. Most of Aristotle's remarks are to be found in *Metaphysics*

(1941b, I, M, N). Much of Plato's position we get from Aristotle's reports, the originals having been lost. But there are some remarks in *Republic* (1961a, Books 6 and 7). The *Timeaus* (1961b) was, however, the work which inspired many of the neo-Platonists, via Plotinus. Yates (1964) and French (1972) give some idea of the character of renaissance Neo-Platonism. Caspar's (1959) biography of Kepler gives insight into the way in which his vision of the place of mathematics in the world was integrated with his astronomical work.

References

Aristotle, 1941a: *Posterior Analytics.* In McKeon (ed.), *The Basic Works of Aristotle*, New York: Random House.
—— 1941b: *Metaphysics.* In McKeon (ed.), *The Basic Works of Aristotle*, New York: Random House.
Augustine, Saint, Bishop of Hippo 1955: *The Problem of Free Choice* (translated by M. Pontifex). Westminster, MD: Newman Press.
—— 1990: *De Musica* (commentary by Pizzani and Melanese). Palermo: Edizioni Augustinus. Translation in L. Schopp et al., *the Fathers of the Church*, vol. 4, Washington DC: Catholic University of America, 1947– .
Bachelard, Gaston 1928: *Essai sur la connaissance approchée.* Paris: J. Vrin.
Benacerraf, Paul and Putnam, Hilary (eds) 1964: *Philosophy of Mathematics: Selected Readings*, Englewood Cliffs, NJ: Prentice Hall. Revised edn, Cambridge: Cambridge University Press.
Berkeley, George 1995 [1710, 1713]: *Principles of Human Knowledge and Three Dialogues* (edited and introduced by Howard Robinson). Oxford: World Classics, Oxford University Press.
—— 1947–57 [1734]: *The Analyst or A Discourse Addressed to an Infidel Mathematician.* In *The Works of George Berkeley, Bishop of Cloyne* (edited by A. A. Luce and T. E. Jessop), London: Thomas Nelson and Sons.
Bloor, David 1973: Wittgenstein and Mannheim on the Sociology of Mathematics. *Studies in the History and Philosophy of Science*, 4, no. 2, pp. 173–91.
Bostock, David 1974: *Logic and Arithmetic, Vol. 1: Natural Numbers.* Oxford: Clarendon Press.
—— 1979: *Logic and Arithmetic, Vol. 2: Rational and Irrational Numbers*, Oxford: Clarendon Press.
Brouwer, L. E. J. 1975: Consciousness Philosophy and Mathematics. Proceedings of 10th International Congress of Philosophy, Amsterdam 1940. Reprinted in *L. E. J. Brouwer Collected Works, Part 1* (edited by A. Heyting), Amsterdam: North-Holland.
Brown, James R. 1991: *The Laboratory of the Mind: Thought Experiments in the Natural Sciences*, London: Routledge.
Cantor, Georg 1895: Beiträge zur Begrundung der transfiniten Mengenlehre. Part I. *Mathematische Annalen*, 46, 481–512. Translated by P. E. B. Jourdain, *Contributions to the Founding of the Theory of Transfinite Numbers*, Chicago: Open Court, 1915, and New York: Dover, 1955.
Caspar, Max 1959: *Kepler.* London and New York: Abelard-Schuman.
Chihara, Charles 1990: *Constructibility and Mathematical Existence.* Oxford: Clarendon Press.

Cohen, P. J. 1966: *Set Theory and the Continuum Hypothesis*. New York: W. A. Benjamin.

Dantzig, Tobias 1930: *Number: The Language of Science*, London: Allen and Unwin.

Davies, P. C. W. and Brown, J. (eds) 1988: *Superstrings: A Theory of Everything*. Cambridge: Cambridge University Press.

Davis, P. J. and Hersh, R. 1983: *The Mathematical Experience*. Harmondsworth: Penguin.

Dedekind, R. 1963 [1888] *Was sind und was sollen Zahlen?* Braunschweig: Vieweg. Translated by W. W. Beman, *Essays on the Theory of Numbers*, Chicago: Open Court, 1901, and New York: Dover, 1963.

Descartes, R. 1985–91a [1629]: *Rules for the Direction of our Native Intelligence*. In J. Cottingham, R. Stoothoff and D. Murdoch (eds), *The Philosophical Writings of Descartes*, Cambridge: Cambridge University Press.

—— 1985–91b [1641]: *Meditations on First Philosophy*. In J. Cottingham, R. Stoothoff and D. Murdoch (eds), *The Philosophical Writings of Descartes*, Cambridge: Cambridge University Press.

Detlefsen, Michael 1986: *Hilbert's Program*. Dordrecht: Reidel.

Dummett, Michael 1973: The Philosophical Basis of Intuitionistic Logic. In Proceedings of the Logic Colloquium, Bristol, July 1973, H. E. Rose and J. C. Shepherdson (eds) Amsterdam: North-Holland, 1975. Reprinted in Benacerraf and Putnam (1983).

—— 1991: *Frege: Philosophy of Mathematics*. London: Duckworth.

Euclid 1956: *The Thirteen Books of Euclid's Elements* (translated by T. L. Heath), Cambridge: Cambridge University Press. 2nd edn, New York: Dover.

Field, Hartry 1980: *Science without Numbers*. Oxford: Blackwell.

Frege, Gottlob 1884: *Die Grundlagen der Arithmetik*. Breslau: Koebner. Translated by J. L. Austin, *The Foundations of Arithmetic*, Oxford: Blackwell, 1959.

—— 1893: *Grundgesetze der Arithmetik, Band. 1*. Jena: Verlag Hermann Pohle. Translated by M. Furth, *The Basic Laws of Arithmetic*, Berkeley and Los Angeles: University of California Press, 1964.

French, Peter J. 1972: *John Dee: The World of an Elizabethan Magus*, London: Routledge.

Gödel, Kurt 1931: *Uber formal unentscheidare Sätze der Principia Mathematica und verwandter Systeme*. Monatshefte für Mathematik und Physik, 38. Translated as 'On formally undecidable propositions of Principia Mathematica and related systems', in van Heijenoort (1967).

—— 1940: The Consistency of the Continuum Hypothesis. *Annals of Mathematics Studies*, 3.

Heyting, Arend 1956: *Intuitionism: an Introduction*. Amsterdam: North-Holland. Selections reprinted in Benacerraf and Putnam (1964) and (1983).

Hilbert, David 1899: *Grundlagen der Geometrie*. Stuttgart: Teubner. 7th edn translated as *Foundations of Geometry*, Lasalle, Illinois: Open Court, 1971.

—— 1926: On the Infinite. Delivered before a congress of the Westphalian Mathematical Society. Originally published in *Mathematische Annalen*, 95, 161–90. English translation in Benacerraf and Putnam (1964) and (1983).

Hofstadter, Douglas R. 1979: *Gödel, Escher, Bach: an Eternal Golden Braid*. New York: Basic Books, and Hassocks, Sussex: Harvester Press.

Kepler, Johannes, 1940 [1619]: *Harmonice Mundi*, Gesammelte Werke, Vol. VI, Munich: H. Beck. Translated as *The Harmonies of the World*, Chicago: Encyclopaedia Britannica, 1990.

Kline, Morris 1980: *Mathematics: The Loss of Certainty*. Oxford: Oxford University Press.

Körner, Stephan 1960: *The Philosophy of Mathematics: An Introductory Essay*. London: Hutchinson.

Koyré, Alexandre 1973: *The Astronomical Revolution*. Paris: Hermann, and London: Methuen.

Lakatos, Imre 1976: *Proofs and Refutations*. Cambridge: Cambridge University Press.

Latour, Bruno 1987: *Science In Action*. Cambridge, Mass: Harvard University Press.

MacKenzie, Donald 1993: Negotiating Arithmetic, Constructing Proofs. *Social Studies of Science*, 23, 1, 37–65.

Maddy, Penelope 1990: *Realism in Mathematics*. Oxford: Clarendon Press.

Nerlich, Graham 1976: *The Shape of Space*, Cambridge: Cambridge University Press.

Newton, Isaac 1931 [1730]: *Opticks or A Treatise of the Reflections, Refractions, Inflections and Colours of Light*. London: Bell and Sons, and New York: Dover, 1952.

Plato 1961a: *Republic*. In E. Hamilton and H. Cairns (eds), *The Collected Dialogues of Plato*, Princeton, NJ: Princeton University Press.

—— 1961b: *Timaeus*. In E. Hamilton and H. Cairns (eds), *The Collected Dialogues of Plato*, Princeton: Princeton University Press.

Quine, W. V. O. 1963: *Set Theory and its Logic*, Englewood Cliffs, NJ: Prentice-Hall.

—— 1969: Epistemology naturalised. In his *Ontological Relativity and other Essays*, New York and London: Columbia University Press.

—— 1970: *Philosophy of Logic*. Englewood Cliffs, NJ: Prentice-Hall.

Reid, Constance 1992: *From Zero to Infinity*. Washington, DC: The Mathematical Association of America.

Russell, Bertrand 1919: *Introduction to Mathematical Philosophy*. London: Allen and Unwin.

Shanker, S. G. (ed.) 1988: *Gödel's Theorem in Focus*. Beckenham: Croom Helm and New York: Methuen.

Spinoza, B. 1992: *Ethics with the Treatise on the Emendation of the Intellect and Selected Letters*. Indianapolis: Hackett.

Stewart, Ian 1987: *The Problems of Mathematics*. Oxford: Oxford University Press.

—— 1989: *Does God Play Dice: The Mathematics of Chaos*. Oxford: Blackwell.

Tiles, Mary 1989: *The Philosophy of Set Theory: An Historical Introduction to Cantor's Paradise*. Oxford: Blackwell.

van Heijenoort, J. (ed.) 1967: *From Frege to Gödel: A Source Book in Mathematical Logic, 1879–1931*. Cambridge, Mass: Harvard University Press.

Wang, Hao 1968: *Beyond Analytic Philosophy; Doing Justice to What We Know*. Cambridge, Mass/London: MIT Press.

Whitehead, A. N. and Russell, B. 1913: *Principia Mathematica*. Cambridge: Cambridge University Press.

Wittgenstein, Ludwig 1922: *Tractatus Logico–Philosophicus* (translated by C. K. Ogden). London: Routledge.

—— 1963: *Philosophical Investigations* Oxford: Blackwell.

—— 1967: *Remarks on the Foundations of Mathematics* Oxford: Blackwell.

Wright, Crispin 1983: *Frege's Conception of Numbers as Objects*. Aberdeen: Aberdeen University Press.

Yates, Frances A. 1964: *Giordano Bruno and the Hermetic Tradition*. London: Routledge.

Discussion Questions

1   In what sense, if any, is mathematics objectively true?

2   Does mathematics need foundations?

3   How can theoretical reasoning about mathematical objects be both so secure and so useful?

4   Is mathematical knowledge different from knowledge in other disciplines?

5   Do we have a right to expect mathematical results to have applications and to be reliable in their applications?

6   Does any account of mathematics depend upon a prior choice of metaphysical perspective? Can there be mathematics without metaphysics?

7   Is grounding mathematics in *a priori* forms of intuition an improvement over grounding it in innate ideas or innate structures of the intellect?

8   Is the infinite in mathematics potentially infinite rather than actually infinite? What difference would this make?

9   Does Einstein's use of non-Euclidean geometries show that geometry does not give *a priori* knowledge of the structure of the physical world?

10 Is the correctness of mathematics as part of a scientific theory any less an empirical question than the correctness of a scientific theory?

11 What is the importance of sets or classes in our account of mathematics?

12 How can we tell whether a realist account of mathematics is the best explanation of the success of applications of mathematics to the world? Even if it is, does this provide a good reason to accept a realist ontology?

13 How can a grasp of the infinite be grounded in apprehension of the finite?

14 Is it always the case that P is true or that not-P is true?

15 What is the place of effective computational procedures in mathematics?

16 Can extending our success at problem solving justify the introduction of new mathematical symbols, even if they do not have any direct representational content?

17 If we discard foundationalism, what are the consequences for our account of proof, discovery and application?

18 Are there any specifically mathematical principles of inference?

19 Can there be an adequate finite representation of something infinite?

20 If space and time are part of nature, is mathematics a natural science? If so, can we understand mathematical certainty?

11

Philosophy of Social Science ———

Martin Hollis

Philosophical problems arise from our attempts to gain insight into ourselves and our social institutions, to comprehend other societies, and to make sense of social change. The following chapter brings together a complex array of questions in the philosophy of social science by critically exploring two crucial distinctions: scientific explanation versus interpretative understanding and individualism versus holism. Relations are traced with other major fields of philosophy: EPISTEMOLOGY (chapter 1), METAPHYSICS (chapter 2), PHILOSOPHY OF MIND (chapter 5), ETHICS (chapter 6), POLITICAL AND SOCIAL PHILOSOPHY (chapter 8), and PHILOSOPHY OF SCIENCE (chapter 9). Discussions of recent work on rationality and social relativism lead to a final agenda of unresolved problems.

If the climate of Africa became suddenly cooler and wetter, the social effects would be enormous. Agriculture would change character as some crops became easier to grow and others harder. As the demand for both sorts shifted, some people and groups would become richer and others poorer. As some rose in social esteem and others fell, social roles and relations would change. With shifts in status and the distribution of power, political effects would start to emerge. We need not speculate further to see that whole societies could be transformed.

Such changes would not simply be dictated by the change in climate, however large. What happened would depend on how people and groups responded. Some millet farmers would fare better than other millet farmers, and some kinds of farmer better than other kinds. In different places, traders, middlemen, bureaucrats or holders of public office would play different parts. Again, without speculating further, we can see that any uniformities in the response would have to lie deep below the surface of events and that, even so, local conditions and individual initiatives would matter.

Observers trying to make sense of events would have, very broadly, two directions of approach. One would be to connect the variety of reaction with differences in social structure and organization, thereby presuming that there are social systems, whose responses to pressure are transmitted to their components in ways which vary with the system. This approach could be termed 'top down'. The other would be to treat macroscopic changes as fusions of microscopic changes by a process whose final elements were at least local and perhaps individual. This approach could be termed 'bottom up'. It is not immediately plain whether these approaches are conflicting or comple-mentary.

Meanwhile the idea of 'making sense of events' is not a clear one and we can usefully gloss it, again very broadly, in two ways. One relies on notions of *explanation* that are familiar from the natural sciences and their philosophy, where the aim is to identify the causes which produce, generate or perhaps are merely correlated with what happens next. The other appeals to ideas of *understanding* that are familiar to students of history or everyday life, who seek to identify the meaning of action (in some sense of that elusive phrase). Here too it is not obvious in advance whether explanation and understanding can finally be combined, however sharply we may want to contrast them at the start.

The last two paragraphs might suggest that 'top down' goes with explanation and 'bottom up' with understanding. That is not the intended message, however. This chapter sets off from a presumption that analysis can proceed in either direction by either method. Abstractly speaking, we start with the two-by-two matrix shown in figure 11.1, which provides the framework for the chapter. Ignoring what is written in the four boxes for the moment, let us take note of the columns and rows.

Our leading question will concern the columns – the claims of Explanation and Understanding to hold the key to social scientific knowledge. Are the phenomena of the social world to be explained after the manner of the natural sciences or understood in some manner special to the study of social life? That is a complex question with three aspects. One aspect is *methodological*, inviting philosophical discussion of scientific method and of whether there is a single, universal method for natural and social sciences alike. One aspect is *epistemological*, posing the Problem of Knowledge in general and the Problem of Other Minds in particular. The third aspect is *ontological*, to do with what there is (or 'the study of being', to translate the ancient Greek terms involved literally). We shall be asking what general kinds or categories of phenomena there are in the social world, what sort of method is best able to reveal how it works and what warrants claims to knowledge of these matters.

The rows pose questions of analytical priority. They bid us think whether the social world is to be analysed finally into particulars, especially agents and actions ('individualism'), or into structures ('holism') or whether both have an irreducible claim to feature in the final account. In deciding

	Explanation	Understanding
Holism	Systems	Cultures
Individualism	Rational choices	Subjective meanings

Figure 11.1 The four keys to analysing social action

whether analysis can best proceed 'top down' or 'bottom up' we shall again be engaged in methodology, EPISTEMOLOGY (chapter 1) and ONTOLOGY (chapter 2).

But, as I have just said, the chapter is chiefly organized round the distinction between Explanation and Understanding. Section 1 will explore the case for naturalistic explanation in the social sciences, the theme being that, since human beings belong to the natural order, the social world presents no final obstacle to the methods that serve the natural sciences so well. Section 2 will mount a rival case for interpretative understanding, the theme here being that, since social actors view social life from the inside, the social sciences must make sense of it by doing likewise. Section 3 will examine the scope for collaboration between explaining and understanding, thereby identifying some fertile philosophical questions that remain unsettled, as the short concluding section will point out by way of summary.

1 Explanation

> The sole foundation for belief in the natural sciences is this idea, that the general laws dictating the phenomena of the universe are necessary and constant. Why should this principle be any the less true for the development of the intellectual and moral faculties of man than for the other operations of nature?

This beguiling question comes from a book written in 1794 amid the European ferment of ideas known as the Enlightenment. The author is the Marquis de Condorcet (1743–94), mathematician, philosopher and social scientist and the book offers what its title calls a *Sketch for a Historical Picture of the Progress of the Human Mind* (1955). Condorcet traces the historical development of human society and rejoices in the amazingly rapid progress made in the two centuries since the scientific revolution. He looks forward to an enlightened future where 'the sun will one day shine only on free men who own no other light than their reason.' His theme, and the key to this progress, is recognition that 'Truth, happiness and virtue are bound together by an indissoluble chain.'

Such optimism may ring hollow two centuries later; and Condorcet himself died in prison shortly after finishing the book, a victim of the French Revolution in which be fervently believed. But his linking of truth, happiness and virtue stems from a vision of humanity and social order which still influences the social sciences and their philosophy. If nature includes HUMAN NATURE (pp. 531–3), the progress of knowledge will find no radical obstacle in 'the intellectual and moral faculties of man'. A new science of human beings will bring us knowledge of human nature and hence the power to school and satisfy our desires. Virtue comes into the story in so far as we use this power for the benefit of humanity, thus creating a free and enlightened social order.

The quotation serves to introduce naturalism, to give it its current name, under the three aspects mentioned above. The ontology is naturalistic. Nature, as pictured by Condorcet, is an ordered realm of objects governed by natural laws. It includes 'man' and 'the intellectual and moral faculties of man', whose development has been among 'the other operations of nature'. Although this stops short of saying that human beings are solely physical creatures, it does imply that the human mind is not the sort of non-physical thinking substance (*res cogitans*) claimed by Descartes (1596–1650) (chapter 17) and Cartesian dualists. As a contemporary put it, 'Man is not fashioned out of a more precious clay; Nature has used only one and the same dough, in which she has merely varied the leaven.' This exactly captures the moving spirit of naturalism in the human sciences.

The claim that the laws of nature are general, dictate the phenomena of the universe and are 'necessary and constant' ushers in a naturalistic idea of scientific knowledge and how to acquire it. The method which Condorcet took to be the foundation of the scientific revolution was one of identifying the hidden laws of nature and using them to explain phenomena. By reason we can discern the laws and thus detect the underlying causal order of the universe.

If this broad sketch were enough to work with, we could proceed at once to questions about the intellectual and moral faculties of human beings. But, as the chapters on Epistemology (chapter 1) and the Philosophy of science (chapter 9) make clear, the sketch can be filled in several ways. So objections to one naturalistic account of the social realm may not be objections to all. Although readers will need to refer to those other chapters to make full sense of this one, we can usefully pick out some key issues which are especially relevant to the philosophy of social science.

Condorcet's remark that the laws of nature are 'necessary and constant' gestures to an old dispute, which has affected the social sciences from the start. On the one hand there is the Rationalist (chapter 17) contention that nature is constant because its laws hold of necessity; on the other, there is the empiricist retort, still novel at the end of the eighteenth century, that there is nothing necessary about nature itself and that any 'necessity' is therefore only a matter of how our minds work. We attribute necessity to what, if we reflect carefully, we know only to be constant in its workings. Although today's philosophers usually deem this contrast too stark and simple, as we shall note in a moment, it remains a useful pointer to some radical differences of approach to social theory.

The rationalist contention goes with a strongly determinist vision of nature as a system driven by hidden forces. This vision had inspired Descartes and Newton (1642–1727), the leading seventeenth-century philosophers of the scientific revolution. In a popular image of the time, the world is like a perfect watch, with 'Wheels and Springs so out of sight that we have been long a-guessing at the movement of the Universe' (de Fontenelle, 1929). In the mechanical universe, whatever happens *must* happen, given the previous state and the laws of nature, and science advances by demonstrating these necessities. Scientific knowledge, therefore, cannot depend on Sense experience (chapter 17), since, in the words of an old adage, 'the senses reveal no necessities'. It depends instead on our intellectual faculty of 'intuition', aided by mathematical models which allow demonstrative reasoning. Newtonian mechanics and Cartesian geometrical physics are classic examples.

Applied to the social world, this ambitious scheme has striking implications. Its firm distinction between 'phenomena' and 'laws' suggests some kind of social or psychological physics, of whose explanatory elements we, as actors, may be unaware. Moreover, if we too are like watches driven by hidden wheels and springs, our cherished free will may turn out to be an illusion. Many social scientists have accepted these implications, starting with Thomas HOBBES (1588–1679) (chapter 18) whose influence on social and political philosophy has been pervasive. In *Leviathan* (1990) Hobbes presents human beings as mechanical individuals for whom the will is merely 'the last appetite in deliberating' (ch. V). We are driven by an urge for self-preservation and 'a perpetual and restless desire for power after power, that ceaseth only in death' (ch. XI). We know this, he maintains, by discerning 'laws of reason' which account for human behaviour. Yet, by harnessing this knowledge, we can learn to make and maintain the social order without which human beings will destroy one another. 'Reason is the pace, increase of science the way, and the benefit of mankind the end' (ch. V).

Leviathan remains a leading example of an individualist account, in which social arrangements emerge from the interplay of individuals rationally seeking self-preservation. For a notable example of a structural account, I recommend the Preface to *A Contribution to the Critique of Political Economy* (1971) by Karl MARX (1818–83) (chapter 24). There we are told that the economic structure of society is 'the real foundation, on which rises a legal and political superstructure and to which correspond definite forms of social consciousness . . . It is not the consciousness of men which determines their being but, on the contrary, their social being which determines their consciousness.' Here too the appeal to hidden forces goes with a denial of familiar notions of free will. Yet Marx too, at least in other works and other moods, holds that men make their own history, even though not under conditions chosen by themselves, and that science can strengthen this power by revealing what is feasible. Questions of freedom and determinism are thus far from straightforward and we shall return to them.

Meanwhile, Hobbes and Marx both belong in the left-hand column of figure 11.1 and serve nicely to illustrate the bottom and top boxes respectively. But this is not to say that it is yet clear what sense attaches to 'necessity' in these and in similar accounts. Perhaps there is indeed good reason to think that laws of nature are not merely 'constant', and that, for instance, what goes up *must*, in some sense, come down because of the laws of gravity. But it is far from plain than any 'must' involved in the power of forces or the relation of causes to effects is the kind of 'must' involved in truths of mathematics. Even in the seventeenth-century image of the world as a watch the compulsion envisaged is as much to do with mechanisms as with formulae. Two distinct ideas are involved, one of logical necessity and one, more mysteriously, of natural necessity. Although this is not the moment to explore the latter, the ambiguity helps to clear the way for the rise of empiricism and the denial that necessity of any kind is a feature of the working of nature.

Here the classic source is David HUME (1711–76) (chapter 21), especially *A Treatise of Human Nature* (1978a), which was intended to lay the foundations for 'a complete system of the sciences'. It is evident, Hume said in the introduction, that all sciences relate to human nature. 'Even *Mathematics, Natural Philosophy, and Natural Religion* are in some measure dependent on the science of MAN; since they lie under the cognizance of men, and are judged by their powers and faculties.' Hence a science of human beings, grounded in an empirical study of 'Logic, Morals, Criticism and Politics' would comprehend everything which can tend to the improvement of the human mind. The method was to be 'experience and observation', applied to 'men's behaviour in company, in affairs and in their pleasures'. The aim was 'explaining all effects from the simplest and fewest causes'.

To undermine the grand pretensions of Reason, Hume drew a sharp distinction between 'matters of fact and existence' and 'relations of ideas'. Matters of fact are always contingent and known to us by experience. Any 'necessity' to them can only be due to our mental habit of expecting established correlations to continue, since genuine necessities, like those of mathematics, lie solely in relations of ideas. Thus we have no warrant in experience for holding that causes necessitate their effects, produce them or make them happen. As far as our knowledge of objects and events goes, a cause is merely immediately prior to, contiguous with and regularly conjoined with what we label its effect. 'Real' connections only reflect our expectation that regular sequences will be repeated in like conditions.

By this account social science is concerned with 'men's behaviour in company, in affairs and in their pleasures', without any presumption that scientific determinism denies human freedom. A similarly empiricist and individualist line is taken by John Stuart MILL (1806–73) (chapter 25) in *A System of Logic* (1961), whose Book VI 'On the Logic of the Moral Sciences' remains the best worked out manifesto for empiricism in social science. Chapter 7 of Book VI opens with this challenging declaration:

> The laws of the phenomena of society are, and can be, nothing but the laws of the actions and passions of human beings united together in the social state. Men, however, in a state of society, are still men; their actions and passions are obedient to the laws of individual human nature. Men are not, when brought together, converted into another kind of substance, with different properties; as hydrogen and oxygen are different from water, or as hydrogen, oxygen, carbon, and azote, are different from nerves, muscles, and tendons. Human beings in society have no properties but those which are derived from, and may be resolved into, the laws of nature of individual man.

If that still sounds determinist, it is meant to. Mill, like Hume, takes the compatibilist line that free action is caused action whose causes lie in the desires and character of the agent, guided by beliefs about its likely success in satisfying these desires. Free action thus presupposes a regular and predictable world and is given all the more scope as science learns to chart the precise regularities. If this neat reconciliation of freedom and determinism is tenable, many awkward problems for a scientific approach to human behaviour vanish.

Here readers may wish to pause and consider whether it is indeed tenable. Hobbes (1990, ch. XXI), Hume (1978a, I, viii) and Mill (1961, VI, 2) offer a useful starting point.

Hobbes, Hume and Mill together give us a strong case for believing that the intellectual and moral faculties of man are no obstacle to the extension of science to the social world. They agree that, in Hobbes' words, 'Reason is the pace', even if Hobbes is a rationalist and Hume and Mill empiricists. They agree that science advances by discovering causal laws and that determinism is no threat to human freedom, properly conceived. All three are squarely in the main line of modern philosophy, in short, and that is a good, clear way to begin. But matters cannot be kept so straightforward, I fear, and we must next think more deeply about scientific method. As we saw, Hume's corrective to a confusion about necessity was to dispense with it altogether as a real-world component of causal laws or causal explanation. That is splendidly bold. But is it satisfactory?

Does science need some stronger distinction between laws and regularities than Hume's empiricism offers? We can best focus the question with the help of a recent example. It comes from a 1970 social science textbook on scientific method, where the authors use it to illustrate the style of explanation which they recommend (Przeworski and Teune, 1970). They introduce a typical French worker, Monsieur Rouget, and enquire, 'Why does M. Rouget, age twenty four, blond hair, brown eyes, a worker in a large factory, vote Communist?' They then remark that 'to explain the vote of M. Rouget, one must rely on probabilistic statements that are relevant for voting behaviour and have been sufficiently confirmed against various sets of evidence.' When this process of evidence gathering is complete, they suggest, an explanation will emerge in the following form:

(1) M. Rouget is a young male worker employed in a large factory in a social system where the church plays an important role.
(2) Young workers in large factories vote Left with a probability of .60 to .70, and in those systems in which the role of the church is strong, men vote Left more often then women; *therefore it is highly likely* (probability of .80) that
(3) M. Rouget votes for a party of the Left.

The guiding idea here is that to explain behaviour is to arrive at reliable generalizations from which it could have been predicted with high PROBABILITY (pp. 314–16). Whether such generalizations count as causal depends solely on how well the predictions derived from them fare. In Humean spirit, there is nothing more to it by way of causal connections or hidden mechanisms. A so-called law of nature is simply a well enough confirmed hypothesis and the only test of a hypothesis is its predictive success.

This account of explanation is usually known as the covering law model and its rule of application as the hypothetico–deductive method. Figure 11.2 presents it in diagramatic form, taken (slightly simplified) from another textbook, Richard Lipsey's *Introduction to Positive Economics* (1972):

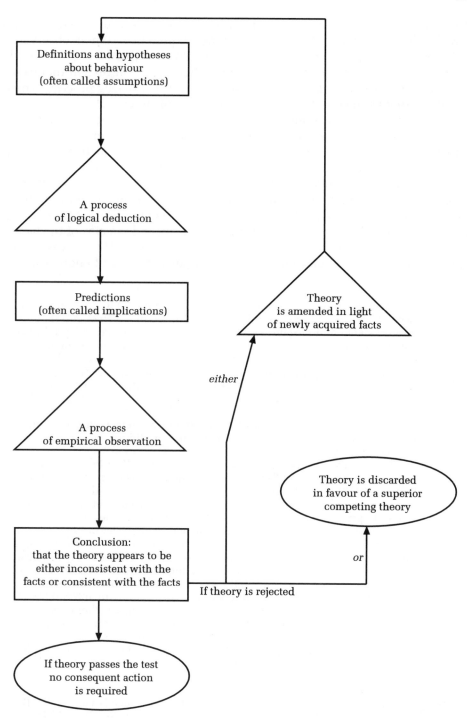

Figure 11.2 The covering law model of explanation, which uses the hypothetico-deductive method to form hypotheses, deduce implications and test them against experience

The diagram shows a process of formulating hypotheses or theories, deducing their implications and testing them against experience. When observation confirms the theory, 'no consequent action is required'; when it does not, the theory is to be amended or replaced. Again, there is no suggestion that causal laws have more to them than what is involved in this filtering process, which, in both textbooks, has to do solely with degrees of probability.

How satisfactory is this idea of explanation? On the credit side, it is as simple and elegant as one could wish, especially if one is impressed by the empiricist case for holding that only experience can justify claims to knowledge of the world. But there are several large objections.

If we focus these doubts on Monsieur Rouget, we soon wonder whether the proposed form of explanation even begins to tell us *why* he votes Communist. That he belongs to a group of which some 80 per cent votes Communist may be relevant, but is hardly revealing. *Why* do age, sex and the size of the factory and the strength of the church matter, whereas colour of hair and eyes do not? Here are three kinds of answer, each opening further lines of enquiry.

(1) *Post-empiricist*
     The explanation offered is inadequate not because it fails to unearth hidden causes but because it is too sketchy. We need more of a web of correlations, compactly stated and elegantly ordered so that they have greater predictive power for a larger set of cases. Empiricism is right to maintain that explanations stand or fall solely by the test of experience and thus rely wholly on what experience can tell us. But experience is never brute and its verdicts never unambiguous. It always involves the application of concepts, in the spirit of Kant's remark that percepts without concepts are blind. The mind is not a blank tablet on which experience writes, but an active interpreter bringing theories to bear. Hence there are no facts that are neutral between all interpretations and, in explaining anything, we are *choosing* which theory to prefer.

     This first answer has two principal sources. One is Karl Popper's idea of science as 'Conjectures and Refutations', to cite the title of the famous paper in Popper (1969). Popper argues that observation is never theory-free and can never establish or even confirm the truth of a hypothesis or conjecture. But it can in principle *refute* the genuinely empirical ones (as opposed to the 'pseudo-scientific', which, like Marxism or psychoanalysis, in his view, are so organized that they can be squared with all possible experience). But progress is possible because refutation is a moment of objective truth, even if confirmation is not. This is not radical enough for the other main source, PRAGMATISM (chapter 26), especially Quine (1953), where there are *no* moments of unvarnished truth independent of all webs of interpretation. Refutations are decisive only if we choose to regard them as such. Explanation becomes holistic, with consequences that I cannot trace in this chapter. Meanwhile the reasons for picking out M. Rouget's age and sex but not his hair and eyes are pragmatic. They instance reliable regularities which mesh well with wider patterns in our interpretation of social life.

(2) *Realist*
     No explanation has yet been offered either for M. Rouget's vote or for the leftist tendency of the groups to which he belongs. To ask, 'Why?' bids us identify *causes* – psychological or social processes, or both. Indeed it may be that processes depend in turn on causal mechanisms – powerful particulars whose powers do not somehow derive from 'laws of nature' but, in sum, are

the reality of those laws. In any case, the old idea of structures and forces external to the enquiring mind remains a necessary presupposition of science. If it is asked how we can know that there are any, and hence how we are entitled to such an ontology, the answer is that science can and should proceed by inference to the best explanation.

Whether the best explanation is psychological or social (or both) raises the 'vertical' question of individualism and holism. The individualist case has traditionally depended, as in Hobbes, Hume and Mill, on conscious or unconscious motives inherent in human nature and on an account of how these motives can generate social organizations through the interplay of individuals. In so far as the motives are conscious, there is scope for rational reconstructions of action and so for the kind of interpretative approach that is discussed below. But any such internal story is finally subordinate to a naturalistic canon of causal explanation. The leading realist analysis of causation, which is described in the chapter on the Philosophy of Science, will serve nicely.

The holist case often involves a further claim on behalf of functional explanation. Like the planetary system, which is mechanical, or a termite colony, which is organic, social systems have various equilibrium conditions. When these conditions are breached, the system tends to correct the disturbance or shift towards a fresh equilibrium. The behaviour of parts of the system can thus be explained by functional demands arising from the properties of the system as a whole. The treatment of the class struggle in a crude version of 'vulgar' Marxism, where the consciousness of humans is wholly determined by their social being is a classic example. Here M. Rouget's membership of the industrial proletariat is crucial (although the ideology purveyed by the church might mute the conflict between the economic forces and relations of production). Classic too are some of the instances of social explanation given by Emile Durkheim (1858–1917) in the course of insisting that social facts be treated as things. Like Marx, he does not belong squarely in the top left quadrant of figure 11.1, if his works are read as a whole. But the brief argument in *The Rules of Sociological Method* (1964) that there will always be crime because all societies need crimes to stigmatize for the sake of increasing social integration is a gem.

Although functional thinking is no longer as common and explicit as it was until the 1960s, it has by no means vanished. It occurs latently, for instance, even in that most individualist of social sciences, neo-Classical economics. Here the picture of individual firms pursuing their self-interest by rational calculation is tempered by a conviction that, if they falter, they will be driven out of business by the operation of market forces. These forces apparently constitute an economic system that demands efficiency and, unless subjected to political interference, achieves it, to the general benefit of the economy. Without plunging into a discussion of how seriously neo-Classicists really take the idea of market forces within an economic system, we can plausibly suggest this as an example of explanatory realism with both psychological and social components and functionalist aspects. M. Rouget's interests need not be identical with those of the firm for which he works.

(3) Interpretative

It is strange to suppose, as Przeworski and Teune seem to, that we can try to explain M. Rouget's vote without enquiring how he sees his situation. No doubt we can make sense of what termites do without interviewing any termites. But M. Rouget is not a termite and his social world is not an external structure in which he is enclosed. Or, if it is largely external to him, that does not make it external to all its inhabitants collectively. In that case explanations need to start, and perhaps even to finish, by understanding the situation from within. That promises a potentially different account of why age and sex matter but hair and eyes do not, and one which is not directly consonant with naturalism. This brings us to the idea of understanding.

2 Understanding

Meaning, according to Wilhelm DILTHEY (1833–1911), is 'the category which is peculiar to life and to the historical world.' Dilthey was one of a group of German idealists interested in the study of history. Prompted in part by the work of HEGEL (chapter 23), Dilthey came to the view that human life can be understood only by applying categories, like 'purpose' and 'value', which have no place in our knowledge of the physical world. These categories address the connectedness of life and make us realize that the meaning of its episodes must be understood by seeing it as a whole. But nothing external to humanity is involved. 'Life does not mean anything other than itself. There is nothing in it which points to a meaning beyond it' (Dilthey, 1926, vol. vii, p. 24).

This strikes a bold note on which to open our discussion of INTERPRETATIVE (pp. 247–50) understanding. It not only sets the historical world apart from the natural but also bids us to think holistically. Leaving the merits of holism until later, let us start with the idea of meaning.

Varieties of Meaning

When M. Rouget casts his vote in an election, his action has meaning in several senses, three of which are especially relevant. Firstly, we can ask what *he* means by it. What is his intention, purpose, reason or motive? How does he expect other people to interpret his action? These are questions about what we might term 'subjective meaning' – what is going on in M. Rouget's conscious mind. Secondly, we can ask what the action itself means – exactly what action is being performed, considered from a public point of view. Actions are usually taken from stock, as is clearest if we think about utterances. The words 'pandas are black and white' have a public meaning which can be found, for instance, by use of a dictionary or phrase book. They do not change their public meaning if the speaker utters them by mistake or believing that they mean something else or supposing that a panda is a kind of bird. Similarly what move one makes in a game depends on the rules of the game and commonly has no meaning outside those rules. These are matters of what we might term 'intersubjective meaning'.

Thirdly, we can ask the significance of actions, seeking perhaps to set them in a wider context or to treat them as a sign of an underlying process. There are many variants, ranging from background articles on current affairs in newspapers to ambitious attempts to probe what is hidden, as when Freudians treat slips of the tongue as clues to the unconscious or when historians seek to trace the underlying movement of history. The common element is a readiness to find meanings which the actors grasp only dimly or are not aware of at all. We might term these 'objective meanings', while noting that we shall need to enquire whether accounts of underlying significance couched in terms very remote from the actors' own belong under the heading of causal explanations.

Philosophically, the neatest way to make meaning central is to pose the problem of other minds. How does one person or group of persons know what is in the mind of another? This too is a problem of knowledge but it differs from those raised earlier in that it involves a 'double hermeneutic' (hermeneutic comes from the ancient Greek *hermeneus*, an interpreter). Section 1 gave us good reason to accept that facts do not simply obtrude but involve interpretation. Hence, we might say, there is a single hermeneutic in all our knowledge of the world, including our observation of human behaviour. But, when we interpret behaviour as action, we are interpreting twice: once in identifying the behaviour and again in ascribing its meaning as action. To know what is in other minds, we must be able to manage this double hermeneutic.

The problem, as traditionally posed, is that each of us has a kind of self-knowledge, which is denied us in our knowledge of others. We understand their thoughts, emotions and desires, the meaning (in the first sense above) of their words and actions, by inferences whose starting point is their behaviour. These inferences cross a divide which it is natural to describe as one between physical and mental or between the outward and inward aspects of a person. Yet, unlike standard inductive inferences, there is no independent way of checking conclusions in some cases, so as to have a reliable warrant for others. How, then, do we manage, epistemologically, to progress from a single to a double hermeneutic?

Let us focus the problem on the interpretation of behaviour as action. Consider, for example, blinking and winking. There is no obvious or immediate physical difference. Yet blinks belong wholly to a physiological story of response to stimulus, whereas winks are a vehicle for information – hints, reservations, conspiracy, warnings; they are, in short, speech-acts. How do we know a blink from a wink and how do we identify exactly what a wink conveys?

This is a good moment to turn to Max Weber (1864–1920) and the methodological essay at the start of *Economy and Society* (1922). Weber says there that 'the science of society attempts the interpretative understanding of social action.' In 'action' he includes 'all human action when and in so far as the acting individual attaches subjective meaning to it'. By 'social action' he means action 'which takes account of the behaviour of others and is thereby oriented in its course'. Thus cyclists entering traffic engage in social action, whereas someone putting up an umbrella does not. The former take account of other actors, the latter takes account only of the weather. There is subjective meaning in both cases, since that merely requires an intention of some kind, whereas in social action the intention relates to the intentions of others.

Weber suggests that identifying intentions is a two-step process. The first is 'direct understanding' or 'empathy', by which one knows, for instance, that a man swinging an axe is chopping wood or that a marksman is aiming a rifle. In other words, there is a process akin to perception, which lets us identify intentions, and hence actions, directly. The second step is 'explanatory understanding' by which we might come to know that the woodcutter is earning a living or the marksman taking part in a vendetta. This is done by assigning the action to 'a complex of meanings'. It can be done 'historically', where we trace the exact history and motive of a particular action, or 'sociologically', where we fill in a social context like that of revenge-killing, or 'ideal-typically', where we conduct a RATIONAL RECONSTRUCTION (p. 111) of what is going on. I shall pursue this last suggestion in a moment.

Notice that the appeal to 'empathy' effectively by-passes the other minds problem by refusing to treat the identification of some actions as the conclusion of an inference from behaviour. To revert to our first example, we do not infer that someone winked from premises about the movements of one eyelid; we *perceive* the wink, even though an ignorant alien observer might perceive nothing of the sort. This may be a shrewd move, since the problem, as traditionally posed, threatens to be insoluble. If one can get away with it, there is much to be said for simply introducing a datum level of actions as a distinctive feature of Understanding. But it clearly risks begging the question and calls for further thought about the relation between behaviour and action.

Meanwhile, the move may be vulnerable from a different direction. Weber is assuming that we can, sometimes at least, identify intentions like 'aiming a rifle' without presupposing social practices. This is an individualist assumption and, if it is wrong, holism comes swiftly into play. It need not be holism on any grand Hegelian scale. The counter-suggestion is only that to by-pass the traditional other minds problem is to go directly to the *public* meaning of action. Whereas Weber starts from what an agent means by an action (our first sense of Meaning above), a holistic account starts from our second sense — what the action means. This may seem a minor shift but it goes with a widespread recent rejection of the Cartesian *cogito* as the foundation of our knowledge of the world and of other minds. The broader theme is that subjective meanings are possible only because we share an everyday world with other people.

The key philosophical text here is perhaps *Philosophical Investigations* (1953) by Ludwig WITTGENSTEIN (1889–1951) (chapter 29). In so far as actions are typically moves in some 'game' of social life, they cannot be identified independently of the game to which they belong. This is plainest for actions that are literally moves in a game, for instance the playing of a tile in Mah-jongg, where the subjective meaning cannot be analytically prior to the intersubjective meaning. Wittgenstein bids us regard social action in general in this sort of way. Social life is made up of institutions or practices, best understood by analogy with games. Crucially, games have two sorts of rules. One sort is regulative and governs the best choice of moves at each turn. For instance, success in Mah-jongg depends on knowing some useful rules of thumb and in knowing whether the other players know them too. The other sort is constitutive and governs the very possibility of making moves at all. The constitutive rules of Mah-jongg define the procedures, pieces and purpose of the game and *must* be followed by the players, on pain of failing to take any part in the game.

Important to this fertile analogy is the fact that there is nothing (except the presence of constitutive rules) which all games have in common:

> Don't say: 'There *must* be something common, or they would not be called "games" – but *look and see* whether there is something common to all. For if you look at them you will not see something that is common to *all*, but similarities, relationships, and a whole series of them at that (Wittgenstein, 1953, §66).

There is only a complex network of similarities, overlapping and criss-crossing, or 'family resemblances'. There is no further common core to 'board games, . . . Olympic games and so on'. So we should not expect social practices to display any universal common core either. They vary within and between societies and there is nothing more global to it. 'What has to be accepted, the given, is – one could say – *forms of life*' (Wittgenstein, 1953, p. 226).

The primary understanding of action, then, is not as an expression of subjective meaning but as the following of a rule by an agent who, in a famous Wittgensteinian phrase, 'knows how to go on'. This may sound deterministic. It can seem a small step from presenting social actors as rule followers to presenting them as creatures of the rules which they follow. But that can be avoided, if the rules of the games of social life are not taken to be so complete, detailed and pervasive that they cover every possible situation in advance. On one interpretation of Wittgenstein, rules are always open-ended and are constructed to cover new cases in the course of play. (For a plausible example of this process, think how legal rules evolve through the interplay of judicial interpretations in courts of law.) In that case we have a fertile holistic approach which does not turn the actors into cultural dopes. Instead, the actors retain a positive interpretative role.

Even so, it does not leave as much room for individual initiative as an individualist might wish. It suggests not only that the 'games' of social life are analytically prior to the 'moves' made within them and that all social actions are 'moves', but also that social actors are *essentially* players. If so, it conflicts with the common belief that we are individuals who choose whether to play and what to play. Furthermore, this belief extends to the conviction that what we cannot do separately we can often do collectively. For example, many theories of political freedom and democracy presume that the institutions, rules and practices of a society can be changed by collective decision. An analysis that worked *wholly* 'top-down' in the Understanding column of figure 11.1 would thus be politically contentious, even if it left some room for players to manoeuvre within the game.

On the other hand, an analysis which worked *wholly* 'bottom up' in the Understanding column would seem wilfully blind to the point that reasons for social action are commonly bound up with the roles that people play. So let us next try embedding social actors in their social roles without thereby denying that they are individuals. If social norms are indeed as much constructed in the course of interaction as laid down in advance of it, there should be room for an individualist story about this process of construction. To tell it, we need to stress that roles enable as well as constrain action.

Roles

A 'role' is standardly defined as a set of normative expectations attached to a social position. Thus a professorship is a social position and professors are expected to do research, teach students and so on. These expectations are *normative* in that those dealing with professors are *entitled* to presume that the role will be played as required and to complain if it is not. But the requirements of the role are not expressible in a complete list of explicit rules to cover every situation. No such complete list could be specified and role players have to be left to interpret the role in some general spirit. Professors are required to be scrupulous about giving credit for ideas borrowed from others and to be conscientious and fair-minded when judging students' work; but what counts as scrupulous, conscientious and fair-minded cannot be specified in detail. That depends too much on the exact circumstances of each new case in ways that call for judgement by the actors. Roles thus take on shape as they are played and, singly and collectively, we choose much of that shape. It is a constrained choice but still a choice and, although the choices sum to define the role more closely, the shifting character of the social scene contrives to undefine it at the same time. The requirements of roles both constrain and enable the role players.

I do not wish to assert dogmatically that this is the right way to conceive of roles. But, if it is a plausible way, then it offers scope for a social individualism that is philosophically challenging on several grounds. Although there is space only for what may seem a very bald list, think of what follows as a pointer to a compromise in the Understanding column of figure 11.1 between the pure individualism of the bottom box and the thoroughgoing holism of the top one.

Firstly, we need to think further about the notion of a reason for action. There are two ideas of practical reason in common use in the social sciences. One is instrumental or what Weber, in the essay cited earlier, terms *Zweckrationalität* – the rational choice of the most effective means to the agent's ends. This, elaborated in decision theory, is basic for economics and 'economic' theories of human behaviour, as will emerge in the next section. It confines practical reason to deliberation about the likely consequences of alternative actions. The other is expressive or what Weber terms *Wertrationalität*, where the agent attaches such value to the goal or to the performance of the action that consequences do not matter. This sounds like the kind of rationality – or lack of it – that turns social actors into what I have called cultural dopes. But that need not be its implication, if we treat it as rule-following, as in the paragraphs above, and so set for a more human *homo sociologicus* the task of deliberating about what is required of him or her. Yet neither of these accounts seems to yield an analysis of practical reason that does justice to the concept of a person as someone capable of moral conduct. Nor can they be readily combined, as we shall see presently.

Secondly, mention of MORAL CONDUCT (chapter 6) invites the thought that expressive action often expresses the character of the agent, rather than the demands of a social position. Is the self not more than the sum of the roles that it plays? That leads to tangled questions of personal identity and deep into the

PHILOSOPHY OF MIND (chapter 5). Can persons be kept distinct from both personalities and *personae*? If 'personality' refers to psychological character and '*persona*' (as in *dramatis persona*, a character in a play) refers to people as manifested in social relations, is there anything further and non-physical that is special to a person? Neither 'personality' nor '*persona*' captures the elements of self-awareness and self-direction which many thinkers hold to be crucial for what it is to be a person. A promising starting point is to invoke the distinction made by William JAMES (chapter 26) between the 'I' and the 'me': 'the self as knower' and 'the self as known' (James, 1958, 1962). But there is no avoiding deeper matters than we can pursue here and, it must be said, they make the other minds problem all the harder.

Thirdly, questions about the nature of human freedom remain urgent. Those concerning moral, political and social freedom are touched on below, although chiefly dealt with elsewhere (see chapters 6 and 8). Meanwhile, we noted earlier that the problem of free will that faces anyone applying a deterministic philosophy of natural science to the social world is not indisputably settled by adopting compatibilism. One attraction of a method of Understanding that allows for self-direction on the part of social actors is that it seems less deterministic. The idea that we help to create the social order to which we belong is intriguing but does not abolish the problem either. The initial holistic suggestion that social actors are the transmitters rather than the creators of the meaning of their actions still needs very careful amendment if it is not to suck us into a residual social determinism. Nor should we forget that we have not addressed the difficulties of relating an active, autonomous self to the physical world that it inhabits.

Anyone seeking a compromise between individualism and holism to conclude this section therefore has a great deal of unfinished business. So it seems wiser to end the section with some summary remarks about Understanding. It starts by making sense of action 'from within' by disclosing both the meaning of the action and what the actor meant by it. That can demand two sorts of account, one identifying the relevant practices and forms of life, the other seeking the actors' aims and reasons. For both it is helpful to suggest that we proceed on the assumption that the action is rational. But this form of words conceals a deep division. In calling action rational we often mean that the agent has particular reasons for it, which are good reasons or at least seem to him or her to be so. That is to stress the actor's meaning. But we may also mean that the action is rational in the sense of being appropriate and in accord with the relevant rules, especially if we are seeking to understand actions that stem from the demands of roles. That is to stress the rule-governed character of social actions. It is not obvious how these two sorts of account finally relate to one another. Yet it is certainly fertile to ask.

There may also be deeper questions about the meaning of HISTORY (chapter 13) that show themselves when historians and social theorists try to identify epochs and movements. Such attempts continue to inspire many philosophers, especially those influenced by Hegel. On the other hand, they infuriate others, and Popper's fulminations in *The Poverty of Historicism* (1957) are not to be missed. There is nothing brief to say about whether the historical world is open to a dialectical interpretation that calls for a vaultingly ambitious concept of understanding. But it is worth noting that, even if Popper were right to deny it, nothing would follow about the success of naturalism. The Weberian and Wittgensteinian reflections deployed in this section stand without presupposing any hidden dialectics and we have yet to discuss the relation between understanding and explanation.

3 Explaining and Understanding

> Without adequacy on the level of meaning, our generalisations remain mere statements of *statistical* probability, either not intelligible at all or only imperfectly intelligible . . . On the other hand, from the point of view of sociological knowledge, even the most certain adequacy on the level of meaning signifies an acceptable *causal* proposition only to the extent that there is a probability . . . that the action in question *really* takes the course held to be meaningfully adequate.

This is Weber's view (1992) of how sections 1 and 2 relate. (It too comes from the opening essay in *Economy and Society*, with his italics.) It sounds entirely reasonable. On the one hand, we have statistics about people like M. Rouget; but it makes scarcely more sense to learn that 65 per cent of young workers in large factories vote Left than that 65 per cent of men with brown eyes ride bicycles. So we also need a meaningful story, which presents M. Rouget's world from the inside by means of a rational reconstruction. On the other hand, there is no inherent guarantee that a rational reconstruction yields a true story. To ensure that, we need a high empirical probability that the story is causally adequate too.

On reflection, however, this resolution is not so neat. Weber has adopted the Humean thesis that causal propositions are to be construed as statements of statistical probability. But, as we saw in section 1, there are grounds for rejecting this analysis in favour of one involving real connections or causal powers or both. In that case, statistical generalizations do not relate adequacy on the level of meaning directly to whatever '*really*' moves M. Rouget at a causal level. This in turn reveals an ambiguity in Weber's resolution. Is he saying that the social world does indeed work as a meaningfully adequate, rationally reconstructed account claims, provided only that people like M. Rouget are statistically common enough? Or is he saying that such accounts provide an essential clue to a causal level, where the elements that do the 'real' explanatory work may be of a very different sort? It is thus open to us to conclude either that the actors are usually self-propelled and know what they are doing, at least when their accounts tally, or that their social being commonly determines their consciousness; either that their social being is distinct from the fabric of meanings and causes it or that causal explanations must finally be couched in cultural terms. In other words, the tale could still end with any of the possibilities in figure 11.1.

In what follows, I shall focus on two separate centres of current debate. One concerns the right sort of way to read the 'economic' theories of behaviour mentioned earlier, thus continuing our discussion of rationality as an individualist key to social analysis. The other is the vexed question of rationality and relativism, where the dispute between Explanation and Understanding is broadly holistic on both sides. The conclusions of this chapter, given the present state of philosophy and social theory, will consist largely of an agenda.

3.1 Rationality and the theory of games

'The first principle of economics is that every agent is actuated solely by self-interest.' This much-quoted remark comes from F. Y. Edgeworth's engagingly titled book *Mathematical Psychics* (1886) and captures what is widely taken to be the key to the most forceful individualist analysis of social action, institutions and practices. As noted earlier, one of Weber's routes to explanatory understanding is by 'ideal-typical rational reconstruction' of action. This means interpreting actions as the choices made by rational agents in order to achieve their ends or to satisfy their preferences. 'Ideal-typical' refers to what is nowadays often called a 'rational choice' or 'economic' approach, which works by way of an idealized model of a world where all agents are perfectly rational. We can best begin with a brief outline of such a model.

Start by defining a perfectly rational agent as an agent with complete and consistent preferences, perfect information and perfect powers of calculation. His or her preferences range over the consequences of each action open to him or her. Information includes knowing what these consequences would be and how likely they are to occur. Calculation then identifies the rational choice in the circumstances. For example, Jack is a farmer choosing whether to breed goats or pigs. He would rather have pigs but they cost more and are more prone to disease. So he must calculate whether the greater 'utility' of pigs is more than offset by the greater costs and risks. In theory at least, he can compare the *expected utility* of goats and pigs by ranking their utility, net of costs, after discounting it for the risk that it would not materialize. A rational agent never chooses a course of action whose expected utility is less than that of another available to him.

The concept of UTILITY (chapter 25) here owes most to Jeremy BENTHAM (1748–1832) (chapter 25) and the utilitarians. Bentham held that all actions are subject to a 'principle of utility', defined as 'that property in any object, whereby it tends to produce benefit, advantage, pleasure, good or happiness . . . to the party whose interest is considered'. The principle guides each rational agent to do what, as modern economists put it, maximizes his or her expected utility. Whether an action is rational is finally a matter of the mental satisfaction which its consequences bring to the agent. (Bentham, 1970, ch. 1).

It may sound as if Bentham assumed human beings to be selfish, self-seeking creatures. The same impression is conveyed by Edgeworth's remark that 'the first principle of economics is that every agent is actuated solely by self-interest'. But, even if people are in fact all too often self-seeking, the principle of utility does not say so. It implies nothing about the specific character of preferences and tells us only that people are motivated to seek what will best satisfy whatever they happen to desire. Similarly Hume, while insisting that action is always motivated by passion, made it clear that not all passions are selfish:

> Ambition, avarice, self-love, vanity, friendship, generosity, public spirit: these passions, mixed in various degrees, and distributed through society, have been, from the beginning of the world, and still are, the source of all the actions and enterprises, which have ever been observed among mankind . . . Mankind are so much the same, in all times and places, that history informs us of nothing new or strange in this particular. (Hume, 1978b, VIII, I, 65)

Thus saints can be as rational as sinners. Whether action is rational depends solely on whether it is instrumental in furthering the agent's passions or preferences.

This becomes still more explicit in recent utility theory, where a conscious effort is made to remove all trace of psychology and to treat rationality as consistency between preferences, actions and (expected) outcomes (see especially Savage, 1954). Whereas Hume thought in terms of motivating passions, modern exponents of the pure theory of rational choice dispense with passions and require only that a rational agent has a consistent preference-order over possible outcomes. What makes rational choice theory (or decision theory) complex is not the complexity of human psychology but the problems of dealing with risk and uncertainty. We might wish to doubt Hume's claim that mankind are 'so much the same, in all times and places that history informs us of nothing new or strange in this particular.' It is at least harder to doubt the blander claim that all rational actions have a single, universal logic.

We next apply this model of individually rational action to more than one agent. Whether Jack does well to choose pigs over goats may depend on whether Jill chooses to breed goats or pigs on the neighbouring farm. If the payoff to his action depends on her strategy and vice versa, then they are playing a 'game', in a sense defined by the theory of games and far removed from Wittgenstein's. Perhaps they intend to sell their animals in a small village market which will absorb some goats and some pigs but not a glut of either. Then they may be playing a co-ordination game, as shown in figure 11.3. Here

Jill

		Pigs	Goats
	Pigs	1,1	2,2
Jack	Goats	2,2	1,1

Figure 11.3 The co-ordination game: strategies faced by Jack and Jill for breeding pigs or goats

each has a choice between the two strategies, Goats and Pigs and the game has four (2 × 2) possible outcomes. Each outcome (or cell of the matrix) yields a payoff to each player, shown as utility numbers (Jack's first and then Jill's). What exactly these numbers represent is a philosophically interesting question; but, for present purposes, let us take them to register how each player ranks the outcomes, with a higher number signifying a greater preference. Thus figure 11.3 shows both players equally well satisfied by either way of co-ordinating, where one opts for pigs and the other for goats.

This particular game has two pure 'solutions': if Jack chooses pigs, Jill's best strategy is goats, in which case Jack's best choice is indeed pigs; if Jack chooses goats, Jill's best strategy is pigs, in which case Jack's best choice is indeed goats. So there is no single best strategy for either, or none better than tossing a coin. If the game is to be played several times, however, Jack and Jill would both welcome the help of a convention to steer them towards one of the pure solutions. If it were the practice, for instance, that pigs are men's work or goats are women's work, and if each knew that the other knew this, then each would presumably opt accordingly for what game theorists term the 'salient' strategy. At any rate, as soon as a relevant convention is established, both players are well served and neither has any reason to depart from it.

The idea is simple but can be used to prompt a powerful individualist analysis of institutions. We are being invited to regard the basic rules or norms of any society as conventions that are of mutual benefit to rational individuals with separate interests. It seems very plausible to suggest that rules or norms which solve co-ordination problems exist and persist *because* they do so. More generally still, it also seems plausible to suggest that society and its basic institutions can be analysed as an association of individuals, regulated to mutual advantage.

Is it not simpler still to suppose that Jack and Jill, instead of looking round for a convention or waiting for one to emerge, will make a direct agreement? Yes it is; but that presupposes the existence of language and a practice of making agreements. In the most ambitious versions of the theory of the social contract nothing is presupposed and even language is treated as a set of conventions and practices which let individuals gain the mutual benefits of communication. Game theory therefore starts with games where initial choices are to be made without prior communication and where any emergent conventions exist without being enforced by any kind of sanctions.

Even if co-ordination is a basic game, it does not hold the key to all norms or institutions. No less crucial is the game known as the prisoner's dilemma, shown in figure 11.4. Here, let us suppose, Jack and Jill have a mutual interest in giving back any animals that stray across the boundary between their farms. (Jack has specialized in pigs and Jill in goats; so strays can be eaten but not used for the more profitable business of breeding.) But, since there is no way of proving what happens to a missing animal, each does better still to keep the other's strays and does worst of all by being the only one to return them. If each is a rational agent with the preference order given in figure 11.4, they will fail to achieve their mutual interest. Jack will reason that he does better to keep

Jill

		Keep	Return
	Keep	2,2	4,1
Jack			
	Return	1,4	3,3

Figure 11.4 The prisoner's dilemma: strategies faced by Jack and Jill for dealing with animals that stray on to their farms

Jill's strays, if she does not return his, and better to keep her strays, even if she does return his; so he does better to keep hers, *whatever she does*. Jill reasons similarly. The outcome is therefore worse for *both* than it would be if both acted co-operatively.

It might seem that they can improve on this inferior outcome by making an agreement and promising to keep it. But that will not help them, if they have the same instrumental view of agreements and promises as they so far have of other matters. Suppose that each now prefers that both keep the agreement than that neither does, but most prefers to break it (secretly, no doubt) while the other keeps it, and least prefers to keep it while the other breaks it. Then the situation is still that in figure 11.4, and each will break the agreement, thus again producing a mutually inferior outcome.

The last paragraph is contentious. It takes a line most famously put forward by Hobbes, who was cited above for his view of human beings as mechanical individuals with 'a perpetual and restless desire for power after power, that ceaseth only in death'. Hobbes goes on in *Leviathan*, chapter XIII, to argue that men can live at peace only if they can create 'a common power to keep all in awe', which can then enforce any agreements made; and in chapter XVII, he says, 'Covenants, without the Sword, are but Words, and of no strength to secure a man at all.' This argument lies at the core of his version of the social contract, which is thus strikingly different from versions grounded in the rationality of co-operating for simple mutual advantage. Here lie the origins of an enduring dispute between 'conflict' and 'consensus' models of society.

The difference might seem to turn on opposing views of human nature and whether we have enough genial passions, like Hume's 'friendship, generosity, public spirit', to make co-operation natural. But, although this may be relevant if we ask how widespread examples of the prisoner's dilemma game are, it does not affect the logic of the game. Rational choice theory implies that players with the preferences shown in figure 11.4 will choose not to co-operate, regardless of how they acquired the preferences. Reasons for action always look forward to the consequences of action and never back to how the situation came about. If the fact that a promise has been made is to serve as a reason for keeping it, the theory needs recasting.

Meanwhile enough has been said to show why 'Rational choices' belong in the bottom left quadrant of figure 11.1. In its standard form, rational choice theory slots the agent into a causal sequence between whatever gives rise to his or her preferences and the actions which his or her internal computer directs. That threatens its status as an individualist theory. But, if it is not defence enough to point out that actions result from individual preferences, there is still the case for holding that institutions are the outcome of previous interactions among individuals. On the other hand, it is at least interesting to try recasting the theory so that agents can distance themselves from their preferences and can act on other than consequentialist reasons. That would make it a candidate for the bottom right quadrant, a form of individualism which is adequate at the level of meaning along the lines indicated when we were discussing role-playing in the previous section.

3.2 Rationality and relativism

Although nothing has yet been said to prove it, it is hard to resist the idea that social action cannot be identified and described without seeing the actors' situation from within. So let us now assume for the sake of argument that the first step in the analysis of any social phenomenon belongs to Understanding. Even so, the last step may still belong to Explanation. We may need understanding to identify *what* is going on and yet also need an explanation of *how* and *why* it occurs. The implications of this thought lead us to a current dispute about rationality and RELATIVISM (pp. 300–2).

It used to be common to meet behaviourists who regarded social actors as very inferior guides to their own behaviour. Scientists, they maintained, have an access to the brain, the body, the human environment and the mechanics of interaction, which mere agents cannot aspire to. Therefore quantitative, and hence objective, evidence always trumps qualitative, and hence merely subjective, reports from the inside. Moreover, it is no objection that behavioural explanations often use concepts alien to those in which the actors think. After all, biology does not need to take a worm's eye view or worry about any subjective meaning attaching to what worms do; there is nothing inherently special about human life among the other operations of nature.

This attitude has receded and most social scientists or philosophers are now willing to start by describing social phenomena in terms which the actors would understand and assent to. This is effectively to grant that social events are significantly more historically and culturally located than those studied by physics. But naturalists do not regard this as a damaging concession, provided that an interpretative account of what happens is finally subordinate to a naturalistic account of how and why it happens. Then action can be identified from within and explained from without: a compromise favouring naturalism.

A major complication, however, is the recent growth in the sociology of science, encouraged by Thomas Kuhn's work on the structure of scientific revolutions (Kuhn, 1970). The Enlightenment view of science has always been that it is a search after truth under the guidance of reason. Kuhn put up a strong case for believing that reason cannot do everything asked of it, because all systems of thought rely on 'paradigms' which govern what counts as reasonable. A PARADIGM (pp. 11–12) has two key features. One is cognitive – a set of very general presuppositions about the nature of things, for example the Ptolemaic world view or the Copernican one which replaced it. The other is social – a set of institutional practices that entrench the presuppositions in the life of a society, for example those that maintain the professional conduct, status and influence of neo-Classical economists. Since both features regulate a canon of rational belief and action, paradigms are not subject to rational criticism from the sort of external, absolute standpoint to which the Enlightenment aspired. There can be no such standpoint.

If reason does not determine our most general beliefs, what does? One influential answer has been to extend the sociology of knowledge to include the study of whatever passes for 'knowledge' – science and epistemology no less than, say, religion and theology. In some versions, the theme is that cognitive systems are generated by the working of social systems, with these causal relations being a subject for an objective social science (Barnes and Bloor, 1982). But this seems to leave an allegedly objective social science as an exception to the claim that all cognitive systems have social determinants. Other versions are careful to include the sociology of knowledge in the sociology of knowledge. This, however, prompts a still more radical thought.

If science, natural and social, is ultimately a practice among practices, then explanation cannot finally be contrasted with understanding by opposing an external standpoint to an internal one. Explanation is a vital part of the game of science, or even the purpose of that game, but it cannot be a device for doing the impossible, namely stepping out of the game altogether in order to reveal the nature of reality. So, although it remains important to understand the claims to objectivity made in the practice of science, this can only be an exercise in seeing from within. Hence a line which set out to give understanding the first turn and explanation the second presumably ends by giving a final turn to understanding.

Meanwhile, there is something odd about this sharp contrast between cognitive systems and social systems. The former do not float in thin air and the latter do not consist of unthinking bodies. Although it is useful to draw distinctions among the many activities that comprise a social world, it is not as if we were unpicking a fabric whose threads were either social or cognitive but none of them both. Weber's distinction between the level of meaning and the causal level cannot be taken as one between separate orders of being. In relating explanation to understanding, we are trying to make sense of a single world.

The preceding paragraphs raise an urgent question about relativism, which we should next make explicit. The Enlightenment story of science relies on notions of rationality which connect reason directly with truth. The broadest idea is that there is a rational order in nature and that reason can discern the truth about it. If there is less of a rational order in the human world, that is because humans are imperfectly rational, at least when it comes to constructing social arrangements. But that simply gives reason the further task of discerning how to improve them. It will be clear by now that this story has come under heavy fire of late. In effect, critics have been trying to relativize reason by suggesting that rationality is always a matter of conforming to the rules of a particular practice. If practices, in turn, are relative to particular groups and societies, then truth too becomes unattainable or, if you prefer, a matter of conformity to local custom.

It is ironic to find Enlightenment thinkers, who set out to destroy dogma with the aid of reason, being attacked for making reason a dogma. But, if it is indeed one, then it is liberating to have it exposed as such. This, accordingly, has become a theme in recent political philosophy, especially where the target is the state as the embodiment of a domineering rational–legal order. Some LIBERTARIANS, FEMINISTS AND COMMUNITARIANS (chapter 8 and chapter 32) in particular have sought to base ideas of autonomy and respect for persons on a rejection of claims to justify centralized power by appeal to rational authority. Their case often involves a defence of relativism, apparently strengthened by insisting that, to recall the quotation from Dilthey, 'life does not mean anything other than itself. There is nothing in it which points to a meaning beyond it.'

But other libertarians, feminists and communitarians find this a dangerous line. If there is nothing beyond forms of life by which to judge forms of life, there can be no external standpoint for criticizing the state. Indeed, if life has no meaning outside existing forms of life, then we presumably need to love, honour and obey the ones we have. In that case relativism, allied with hermeneutics, is not liberating at all. Since this is not a chapter on political philosophy, I shall not try to umpire the dispute. But its existence should make us wary of relativism in epistemology too, if that were to clear the way to maintaining that a closed society is as entitled to its way of life as an open one.

Yet we should not assume that to endorse the claims of Understanding is thereby to internalize reason and truth to practices. That would be to run into deep trouble with the notorious 'hermeneutic circle'. Here lies a problem too ramified for this chapter, but there is just room for a pointer to it. Suppose that each culture or 'form of life' were self-contained in a sense which includes the possession of rules defining what is real. Thus suppose, for instance, that whether witches exist is, at heart, a question about whether there are cultures with rules for identifying and dealing with witches, so that the reference as well as the meaning of 'witch' is determined internally. Suppose, roughly speaking, that witches exist wherever belief in witches is cognitively and socially entrenched. Then generalize the idea, so that nature at large ceases to be independent of rules determining what it is rational to believe about the world. That would make it plausible to suggest that each culture determines what is real and what is rational for itself. This sounds an attractive suggestion, even if it takes a bold imagination to fancy that what holds for witches also holds for rabbits. But it poses the other minds problem in an acute form. In order to penetrate another culture, we would have to establish what it held to be rational before we could know what it held to be real; and we would have to establish what it held to be real before we could know what it held to be rational. That is the 'hermeneutic circle.'

To escape it, I think, one must either avoid internalizing reason and truth to practices or insist that some practices are universal. That is no doubt easier said than done. In mentioning it, I mean only to suggest that defenders of objective reason in hermeneutics need not give up without a struggle.

4 Conclusions

What can we conclude about the four keys to analysing social action offered in the quadrants of figure 11.5? It would make for a tidy ending if one of them were a master key. But that is unlikely. Start with the least promising claimant, 'systems' (top left), and try thinking of actions wholly as responses to changes in the actors' environment. For each actor singly, the environment includes other actors; for all collectively, it is an external structure – 'society' or perhaps 'nature'. For this to be at all plausible as an explanatory master key, it needs the backing of an ambitious functional or EVOLUTIONARY THEORY (pp. 318–19). Such theories do certainly have champions in some realms of science. For instance, bees adapt and evolve as their environment changes. Their normal behaviour, singly and collectively, can be presented as being what is required if the hive is to function in its environment. But, even so, this can hardly be the whole story. Bees are too fascinatingly particular, and humans much more so. Curiosity swiftly beckons us into the bottom left quadrant.

Individual bees are wonderfully intricate creatures, whose interactions are amazingly complex. For instance, a scout will return to the hive and perform an elaborate dance whose movements, it seems, communicate the distance, direction, quantity and quality of the nectar which it has located. But, even though we might therefore deem bees to have a language, their behaviour is always an effect of environmental events on a complex mechanism. Is this also how we want to construe the explanatory individualism of the bottom left quadrant, as applied to human beings? That is unclear. On the one hand, rational choice theory, extended to include game theory, certainly sets out to analyse collective phenomena into their individual components. Social conventions and hence enduring social institutions can be presented as the sums and deposits of individual choices. On the other hand, the 'individuals' involved are automatic translators of given preferences into expected utilities,

	Explanation	Understanding
Holism	Systems	Cultures
Individualism	Rational choices	Subjective meanings

Figure 11.5 Conclusions: the four keys to analysing social action re-visited

no more particular than different data sets fed into the same computer program. Whatever establishes the preferences could plausibly be said to dictate the choices.

Here compatibilism is philosophically crucial. If the conditions for freedom and individuality are satisfied, provided that actions are rationally consistent with particular preferences, then rational choice theory is an individualist theory of the sort wanted. While preferences remain given, and so exogenously determined, it cannot claim to provide a sole master key; but it can claim to supply an essential link between social structure and social action. Yet the individuality of human beings still seems different in kind from the particularity of individual bees. If so, we are drawn into the bottom right quadrant in search of what is special about persons.

As we cross into the Understanding column, the nature of action changes. It ceases to be independently describable behaviour caused by a mental state and becomes what the agent means by it. 'Subjective meanings' are the stuff of action, which is no doubt why Weber's method of understanding begins with empathy. Actors interpret their situation creatively and express themselves in bringing their intentions to bear on it. Intersubjective rules and meanings are proposed, negotiated and left open to renegotiation. Yet, whatever its merits as an account of social experience at first hand, this is too anarchic for even a hermeneutically inclined social science, and makes for a hopelessly one-sided analysis of roles and role-play. We cannot resist asking what the 'Cultures' of the top right quadrant have to offer.

The key idea here is that rules enable as well as constrain. Constitutive rules engender the 'games' in which social actions are 'moves'; regulative rules give rise to reliable expectations about which moves will be played. The idea conveyed by calling the rules 'cultural' is that a culture is a web of shared meanings external to each of its members, yet internal to all collectively. That is suggestive for the difference between natural facts and social facts, for instance between African weather and African politics. It recalls Wittgenstein's remark that 'What has to be accepted, the given, is – one could say – *forms of life*', apparently offering 'forms of life' as a master key. But it is hard to believe that they are so self-propelled, although I regret that there has not been room to discuss recent attempts to trace the progress of the human mind (to recall the title of Condorcet's book) in unified theories about the dynamics of cultural history. Meanwhile, my comment about African weather and African politics is double-edged. The external world of nature still constrains and enables the life of societies, providing common problems and scarce resources. We are back with the top left quadrant.

Presumably then, there is no unique master key. Human beings make some of their own history in circumstances partly of their own choosing, with greater scope if they know 'how to go on'. This knowledge mixes explanation and understanding in ways that elude social scientists and philosophers, or at least defy summary. So the chapter can best end with an agenda of questions about the borders between the quadrants. Are the reasons that prompt role-players causes of action after the manner of natural causes? Can players of the games of social life be seen consistently both as followers of rules and as makers of choices? In making sense of social facts, do we need concepts both prior to those of individual psychology and alien to those of natural science? What form of determinism, if any, shall a social science bring to bear on a world whose inhabitants claim to be its creators? How peculiar, in short, are the intellectual and moral faculties of human beings?

Nor should we forget the original Enlightenment hope that the social sciences would bring moral and political progress. A final question, then, is whether truth, happiness and virtue are indeed bound together by an indissoluble chain.

Further Reading

For a general background in the philosophy of science see the *Further Reading* for chapter 9. But I will just recommend A. F. Chalmers *What is This Thing Called Science?* (1982) as a masterly start. Among many general introductions to the philosophy of social science, Alan Ryan *The Philosophy of the Social Sciences* (1970) has proved durable. It is rich in instructive examples, although more positivist in approach than one might wish 20 years later. R. Keat and J. Urry *Social Theory as Science* (1975) is harder but casts its net wider. Three interesting, recent introductions, which give scope to Understanding, are those by Doyle and Harris (1986), Rosenberg (1988) and Braybrooke (1991). Anyone wanting to see the theme of this chapter deployed in full might try Hollis (1994).

Positivism remains important and so, therefore, does Mill (1961) Book VI, lately edited by A. J. Ayer. Milton Friedman's (1953) paper speaks volumes. But the tide has turned. Peter Winch *The Idea of a Social Science* (1958) has become classic. It makes a fertile Wittgensteinian case for the distinctness of the social sciences. A contrary view is taken by Roy Bhaskar in *The Possibility of Naturalism* (1979). Like his *Scientific Realism and Human Emancipation* (1986), it is deep but difficult reading. That goes generally for much anti-Positivist work; but Raymond Geuss *The Idea of a Critical Theory: Habermas and the Frankfurt School* (1981) is a clear initial guide. Several of the issues raised in these references lead to heated argument about relativism, as in the essays rounded up in B. Wilson (ed.) *Rationality* (1970) and M. Hollis and S. Lukes (eds) (1982).

There is clearer water for disputes between individualism and holism, at any rate on the individualist side. That owes much to Jon Elster's series of lucid and imaginative books insisting that 'the elementary unit of social life is the individual human action'. I suggest starting with *Explaining Technical Change* (1983) chs 1–3, *Logic and Society* (1978) chs 4 and 5, and *Ulysses and The Sirens* (1984), rather than the more recent (1989). There is an accessible literature on rational choice and game theory, for instance S. Hargreaves Heap et al. *Choice: A Critical Guide* (1992). Holism is harder going but D.-H. Ruben (1985) puts an exact analytical case.

References

Barnes, B. and Bloor, D. 1982: Relativism, rationalism and the sociology of knowledge. In M. Hollis and S. Lukes (eds), *Rationality and Relativism*, Oxford: Blackwell, 21–47.

Bentham, J. 1970 [1789]: *An Introduction to the Principles of Morals and Legislation*. London: Athlone Press.

Bhaskar, R. 1979: *The Possibility of Naturalism*. Hassocks: Harvester Press.

—— 1986: *Scientific Realism and Human Emancipation*. Hassocks: Harvester Press.

Braybrooke, D. 1991: *Philosophy of Social Science*. Englewood Cliffs, NJ: Prentice-Hall.

Chalmers, A. F. 1982: *What is This Thing Called Science?* 2nd. edition. Milton Keynes: Open University Press.

Condorcet, M. de 1955 [1795]: *Sketch for a Historical Picture of the Progress of the Human Mind* (translated by J. Barraclough). London: Weidenfeld and Nicolson.

Dilthey, W. 1926: *Gesammelte Werke* (edited by B. Groethuysen). Stuttgart: Teubner.

Doyle, L. and Harris, R. 1986: *Empiricism, Explanation and Rationality*. London: Routledge and Kegan Paul.

Durkheim, E. 1964 [1895]: *The Rules of Sociological Method* (translated by S. Solovay and J. Mueller). New York: Free Press.

Edgeworth, F. Y. 1886: *Mathematical Psychics*, London: Routledge and Kegan Paul.

Elster, J. 1978: *Logic and Society*. New York: Wiley.

—— 1983: *Explaining Technical Change*. Cambridge: Cambridge University Press.

—— 1984: *Ulysses and the Sirens*. Cambridge: Cambridge University Press.

—— 1989: *Nuts and Bolts*. Cambridge: Cambridge University Press.

Fontenelle, B. de 1929 [1688]: *The Plurality of Worlds* (translated by J. Glanvill). London: Nonesuch Press.

Friedman, M. 1953: Methodology of Positive Economics. In *Essays in Positive Economics*, Chicago: University of Chicago Press.

Geuss, R. 1981: *The Idea of a Critical Theory: Habermas and the Frankfurt School*. Cambridge: Cambridge University Press.

Hargreaves Heap, S., Hollis, M., Lyons, B., Sugden, R. and Weale, A. 1992: *Choice: A Critical Guide*. Oxford: Blackwell.

Hobbes, T. 1990 [1651]: *Leviathan* (edited by R. Tuck). Cambridge: Cambridge University Press.

Hollis, M. 1994: *The Philosophy of the Social Sciences*. Cambridge: Cambridge University Press.

Hollis, M. and Lukes, S. (eds) 1982: *Rationality and Relativism*. Oxford: Blackwell.

Hume, D. 1978a [1739]: *A Treatise of Human Nature*. Oxford: Oxford University Press.

—— 1978b [1748]: *An Enquiry Concerning Human Understanding*. Oxford: Oxford University Press.

James, W. 1958: *The Principles of Psychology*. New York: Dover Books.

—— 1962: *Psychology: Briefer Course*. London: Collier Books.

Keat, R. and Urry, J. 1975: *Social Theory as Science*. London: Routledge and Kegan Paul.

Kuhn. T. S. 1970: *The Structure of Scientific Revolutions* (2nd edn). Chicago: Chicago University Press.

Lipsey, R. 1972: *Introduction to Positive Economics*. New York: Harper and Row.

Marx, K. 1971 [1859]: Preface to *A Contribution to the Critique of Political Economy*. London: Lawrence and Wishart.

Mill, J. S. 1961 [1843]: *A System of Logic*. London: Longworth. Book VI, edited by A. J. Ayer, London: Duckworth, 1988.

Popper, K. 1957: *The Poverty of Historicism*. London: Routledge.

Popper, K. 1969: *Conjectures and Refutations*. London: Routledge.
Przeworski, A. and Teune, H. 1970: *The Logic of Comparative Social Enquiry*. New York: J. Wiley and Sons.
Quine, W. V. O. 1953: Two Dogmas of Empiricism. In *From a Logical Point of View*, Harvard: Harvard University Press.
Rosenberg, A. 1988: *Philosophy of Social Science*. Oxford: Clarendon Press.
Ruben, D-H. 1985: *The Metaphysics of the Social World*. London: Routledge and Kegan Paul.
Ryan, A. 1970: *The Philosophy of the Social Sciences*. London: Macmillan.
Savage, L. J. 1954: *The Foundations of Statistics*. New York: J. Wiley.
Weber, M. 1922: *Economy and Society* (edited by G. Roth and C. Wittich). Berkeley: University of California Press.
Wilson, B. (ed.), 1970: *Rationality*. Oxford: Blackwell.
Winch, P. 1958: *The Idea of a Social Science*. London: Routledge and Kegan Paul.
Wittgenstein, L. 1953: *Philosophical Investigations*. Oxford: Blackwell.

Discussion Questions

1 Does the study of society require both causal explanation and interpretative understanding?

2 Do persons and the roles they fill both have importance for social explanation?

3 Can a social science cope with human autonomy?

4 How are social facts related to facts about individuals?

5 Does any account of natural science provide a model on which social science might reasonably be based?

6 How important is the notion of a 'form of life' to the understanding of society?

7 If we are concerned about human freedom, should we be more worried by a social science which binds individuals by social laws or a social science which reduces individuals to mere carriers of culture?

8 Is it a mistake to seek a universal social science to cover all societies?

9 Do we need more than rational choice theory and game theory to analyse social institutions?

10 If social explanation is in terms of base and superstructure, how can we determine what is the base and what is the superstructure?

11 What are the implications of the claim that social understanding is essentially historical?

12 How do different conceptions of rationality affect our account of social science?

13 Is individualism or holism a better approach to understanding social institutions and practices?

14 Do moral notions like justice have a legitimate role in social explanation?

15 Can ideal types help to explain social action?

16 How is it possible to understand other societies?

17 In what sense should social science seek objectivity?

18 Are there good reasons to confine accounts of behaviour and institutions in a society to concepts available to members of that society?

19 Can an account of society based on hermeneutics explain social change?

20 Does an analysis of social action in terms of rule-following imply that social actors follow rules automatically?

21 What concept of the person is most suitable for social science?

12

Philosophy of Law ————————————

N. E. Simmonds

The philosophy of law lies at the intersection of a number of problems. These concern the relationship between law and morality; the logical status (as descriptive or prescriptive) of propositions of law; the possibility of separating adjudication from politics; and the distinction between law and organized force. Legal positivists have insisted on a morally neutral concept of law, wherein a legal system consists of posited rules ascertainable by reference to factual criteria. The natural law tradition, by contrast, draws attention to law's rootedness in notions of justice and the common good. Modern debates have often centred on the process of adjudication, in particular upon the question of the extent to which judges may properly rely upon their personal moral judgement, and how far they are limited to the application of technical legal rules.

For most of us, most of the time, law seems to be nothing more than a set of governmental arrangements whereby transactions are regulated and undesirable forms of conduct discouraged. Why should this give rise to philosophical problems? Or rather, why should it give rise to philosophical problems other than the problems of APPLIED ETHICS (chapter 31), which may arise in relation to any set of human arrangements?

A convincing answer to this question will require us to outline a number of puzzling features of the phenomenon of law. The philosophy of law lies at the intersection of these puzzles, and seeks to construct a coherent understanding of the nature of law in such a way as to resolve the puzzles. Some problems are of a kind that might occur to any thinking person, while others spring from the technical understanding and experience of lawyers. Some problems are generated by the special role that law enjoys within modern political life, while others arise only against the background of specific philosophical commitments imported from areas of enquiry such as EPISTEMOLOGY (chapter 1) or ETHICS (chapter 6). Philosophers of law hope to offer solutions that are both enlightening and integrated, in the sense that a single theory of law should provide a basis for the resolution of all the central problems.

Unsurprisingly, a diversity of theories has been offered. The debate is significantly complicated, however, by the fact that different legal philosophers and jurists conceive of the debate in quite different ways: they disagree about the nature and status of legal theory just as much as they disagree about the nature and status of law. Some theories purport to be purely 'analytical' or 'clarificatory', while others argue that an adequate solution to the philosophical problems of law requires a theory that has a prescriptive aspect and that is rooted in POLITICAL PHILOSOPHY (chapter 8); some theories defend claims about the 'necessary' constituents of the 'concept' of law, while others seek a reflective understanding of specific social practices. These disagreements will inevitably complicate our survey.

1 Problems of Jurisprudence

1.1 Law and force

Law may at times strike us as being nothing more than a set of governmental arrangements worth studying for practical purposes, but devoid of philosophical interest. We do not always, however, think of law in this mundane guise. We treat the idea of law as a moral *aspiration* that is systematically connected to a range of other values. We contrast the rule of law with political regimes that are based solely on force; we think of law as having deep connections with individual LIBERTY (pp. 258–61) and with JUSTICE (chapter 8); we speak of law as imposing obligations upon us, and as conferring rights. The law seems to be *both* mundane *and* aspirational: a mundane set of arrangements, and at the same time an embodiment of aspirations that have a central place within our political morality.

This ambivalence of law manifests itself at every turn. We might think, for example, of the relationship between law and force. We contrast forms of government based on 'the rule of law' with government based merely on organized force. Indeed the object of law might be thought to be the elimination of force from human relations, and its replacement by peaceful compliance with shared rules. The 'rule of law' seems to represent a situation where citizens and officials regulate their conduct by publicly recognized rules that are accepted as binding on all concerned. Yet are not legal systems simply very well-organized and systematic structures of violence? Is the binding force of law any more than its backing by coercive sanctions? Unlike a gang of robbers, the state authorities can deploy overwhelming force against those who defy them, and they will generally use that force in regular and predictable ways. But does that make them the embodiment of a value to be radically contrasted with rule by force?

The attempted answers to such questions are often divided into two different groups. On the one hand are theories (generally called 'natural law theories') claiming that law is in its essential nature connected with the values of justice, right, and the common good. A governing regime can truthfully claim to govern by law only if its actions and decrees are devised to serve the common good or to do justice. If a government simply exploits a subject population without even the pretence of seeking to do justice it governs by force, not by law, however many of the trappings of legitimacy it may assume.

On the other hand, so-called 'legal positivist' theories insist on a morally neutral concept of law. Such theories are inclined to analyse law in terms of purely formal features, such as the presence of organized sanctions, or the publication of black-letter rules (namely, rules which are established in a definite verbal formulation, such as the provisions of a statute or an explicitly formulated rule laid down by a judge) which are quite independent of the good or bad content of the law, and the good or bad intentions of the law-makers. Like natural law theories, positivist theories vary widely in their reasons for advocating such a neutral concept of law, as well as in their conceptions of the nature of the philosophical enquiry. The contrast between 'natural law' and 'legal positivism' is therefore a slippery one which needs to be handled with care, but it can serve as a preliminary organizing device.

1.2 Positivism and reductionism

Law tells us what we 'ought' to do; it confers rights; it imposes obligations. Do not these terms import a dimension of moral authority? How can we speak of law as imposing obligations and conferring rights unless we regard the law as morally binding? If law is simply an apparatus of rules established by those who happen to have extensive coercive force at their disposal, how could it ever alter our rights and obligations?

The mere possibility of asking such questions demonstrates that, even if the positivist could convince us that all laws are posited rules emanating from authoritative sources, this would not suffice to establish the separation of law and morals. KANT (chapter 22), for example, argued in *The Metaphysics of Morals* that, even in a system of wholly posited laws, one would still require a basic natural law that established the moral authority of the lawgiver. In the absence of some such acknowledged moral claim upon our conduct, how could we view the law as a source of obligation?

The positivist reply to this line of argument consists in the claim that a legal obligation is not a species of moral obligation, nor is a legal right a species of moral right. Law may or may not impose moral obligations on us, the positivist claims: moral obligatoriness is not a logically necessary feature of law. Law *does* impose legal obligations on us, but these are not moral obligations and they involve no commitment to the law's moral authority or moral bindingness.

Having claimed that legal rights and obligations are not a species of moral right or obligation, the positivist is faced with the task of explaining what they *are*. Earlier versions of positivism tended to respond to this challenge by adopting a REDUCTIONIST (pp. 319–20) stance. They claimed that the apparently prescriptive language of law could be analysed reductively as a disguised form of descriptive or predictive language. When I state that you have a legal obligation to pay me £100 I seem to be making a prescriptive claim about how you *ought* to behave. But in fact (it was argued) all that my assertion actually means is that if you do *not* pay me £100 you are likely to suffer a sanction. In this way, propositions of law concerning legal rights and obligations could be treated as factual statements about the issuing of certain commands, predictions of the likely reactions of courts or the likelihood of suffering sanctions.

This type of reductionist analysis appealed to positivists because it seemed to translate legal concepts into terms that were free of all moral connotations. The analysis encountered some rather obvious difficulties, however. For example, I may *not* be likely to suffer a sanction if I fail to pay you £100 (I may be out of the jurisdiction and have no intention of returning, or it may be clear that you would not dream of suing for such a small sum) but it may nevertheless be the case that I have a legal obligation to pay. Similarly, courts generally invoke the existence of certain legal obligations incumbent on the litigants as a *reason* for deciding the case one way rather than another, and as a *justification* for imposing a sanction. This would make no sense if, correctly analysed, statements about legal obligations were *predictions* of the reactions of courts or the imposition of sanctions.

More modern positivists have therefore sought to analyse propositions of law in a way that preserves their prescriptive character without equating them with moral judgements. This has proved to be a very delicate balancing act.

The legal positivist Hans Kelsen (1881–1973) sought to avoid reductionism by treating legal discourse as based on a fundamental presupposition to the effect that the regime which is in effective control within a certain territory ought to be obeyed. He called this presupposition 'the basic norm'. To invoke such a basic norm looks at first like an abandonment of positivism, since the need for some such basic assumption seems to be precisely the point that is being made by Kant in his above mentioned remark from *The Metaphysics of Morals*. Yet Kelsen argued that this basic presupposition of legal science can be deployed simply for the purpose of grounding a cognition of positive law, and without collapsing questions of legal doctrine back into moral questions about justice. He described the basic norm as the minimum element of natural law without which a (non-reductionist) cognition of law is impossible.

Other approaches have been explored by those legal theorists who have found the notion of a basic normative presupposition unattractive. H. L. A. Hart (1907–93), for example, argues in his book *The Concept of Law* (1961) that reductionist theories of law proceed from the external viewpoint of someone observing the workings of a legal system, rather than the viewpoint of a participant in that system. To avoid the errors of reductionism, legal theory needs to reproduce the viewpoint of a participant within the system. Such a participant regards the legal rules as standards that ought to be complied with. Statements about legal rights and obligations do not predict sanctions, but draw conclusions about the applicability of legal rules to particular circumstances. The 'internal' point of view from which such language is deployed need not, Hart argues, be an attitude of moral approval of the law; nor need it be expressive of a judgement as to law's moral bindingness. The internal point of view rests on a judgement that the law ought to be obeyed, but this 'ought' need not be a moral 'ought'. A great many diverse considerations might underpin the conclusion that one 'ought' to obey the law. Legal theory can be neutral, it is argued, on what those considerations might be.

The problem with this way of avoiding reductionism in legal theory is that very little middle ground seems to be left between the viewpoint of the external observer and the judgement that law is morally binding. Someone who obeys the law purely from fear of sanctions would seem to take an *external* view, since his only concern will be with identifying those forms of conduct that are in fact likely to incur sanctions. If the participant's internal point of view is not one of simple sanction-avoidance, what can it be other than a belief in law's moral bindingness? The legal theorist could simply exclude such questions as irrelevant, thereby treating the 'ought' as foundational for legal discourse, while bracketing out all questions about what reasons underpin the 'ought' judgement. This approach, however, seems to depend upon a fundamental normative presupposition in very much the same way that Kelsen's theory does. It is therefore doubtful whether Hart succeeded in offering a genuine alternative to Kelsen's approach.

1.3 Law and politics

The debate between legal positivism and natural law is commonly thought of as a debate with an ancient and continuous history. Philosophers from SOCRATES (chapter 15) to the present day have reflected on the relationship between might and right, and have asked whether law is simply a body of decrees issued by those enjoying a monopoly of coercive power, or whether it is an expression of moral right which serves to concretize the abstract requirements of justice. Yet in more recent times these fundamental issues have acquired from the circumstances of modernity a peculiar salience and a distinctive character. New questions have arisen, and old ones have acquired new resonances, as a result of the central role that conceptions of law play in modern political life.

The ancient understanding of politics placed questions about the nature of the good life at the centre of political enquiry. Political institutions were thought to exist in order to inculcate and make possible a way of life that would be worthy and excellent. Such a fully valuable life was to be attained within public life by participation in the political affairs of one's collectivity. The private realm, which consists of labour, the family, and the household economy, was considered to be a realm of necessity that was of value only in so far as it made a public political life possible. In the modern world, however, these priorities have been largely reversed. Political philosophers since HOBBES (chapter 18) have tended to search for a form of politics that would leave each individual free, so far as possible, to pursue his or her own conception of a good and excellent life. On this approach, the private realm is seen as a critically important area of autonomy within which the individual can choose and pursue wholly personal goals and projects. The existence of such private areas of autonomy necessitates the clear demarcation and enforcement of individual entitlements. Law and the state exist primarily to sustain the clear areas of entitlement that comprise the private realm.

To the extent that it emphasizes the role of individual entitlements, together with the need for PLURALISM (pp. 280–1) and autonomy, the modern conception of politics takes on a profoundly jurisprudential character. For it is law that defines and enforces entitlements, and the possibility of coherent and determinate principles of law is a necessary foundation for the modern view. Yet, if modern LIBERAL (chapter 8) political thought tends to promote individual autonomy above collective participation, the latter value nevertheless has a vital part to play, and a part that adds a further dimension to the problems of legal philosophy. For the modern world no longer regards the structures of civil society, the economy, and the family as immutable structures forming a natural horizon within the parameters of which political life must be conducted. We are deeply aware of the mutability of such structures and of their openness to transformation through politics. In valuing democracy, we value our ability to decide collectively upon the general profile that our social structures should exhibit. In this sense, we value our ability to pursue collective projects of social reform.

Liberal politics, therefore, values both collective project pursuit and (in the form of the liberal's concern for liberty or autonomy) individual project pursuit. But these two values compete. A society which allowed its overall character to be determined solely by the uncoordinated actions and transactions of individuals pursuing their own projects would forfeit any power of collective control over its general profile and structure. On the other hand, a society which sought to regulate collectively every facet of its existence would inevitably erase any scope for autonomous individual project pursuit.

It is the possibility of a stable legal system that renders the liberal scheme of values coherent. If the rule of law is possible, collective project pursuit can find its sphere of expression within political decisions concerning the general rules which are to be enacted in law, and the general entitlements which are to be conferred. Action within the scope of such rules and entitlements will then be protected whether or not it serves to advance the goals of the collectivity as a whole.

This conception of the rule of law assumes, however, that one can identify and apply the rules and principles of existing law without re-opening the political questions of collective project pursuit that may have led to the enactment of those rules and principles. It assumes that a judge can determine whether or not a citizen has acted within the scope of his or her legal rights without asking whether that citizen's actions serve to advance desirable collective goals. If these assumptions are false, then one's entitlements will extend only so far as one's actions serve collective goals. In other words, the value of individual autonomy will be wholly subordinated to the demands of collective project pursuit.

A major area of investigation in the philosophy of law concerns the attempt to sustain a viable distinction between law and politics. This debate has largely been conducted in the context of general theories of law and adjudication, but it has also involved detailed studies of particular areas of legal doctrine with a view to assessing the extent to which they can resolve disputes without collapsing all questions back into basic issues of collective goals and distributive policies.

1.4 Legal positivism and the criteria of validity

Legal positivism offers a morally neutral conception of law. It claims that valid laws may be identified by reference to criteria of a purely factual nature. H. L. A. Hart, for example, argues that every legal system contains a basic 'rule of recognition', accepted by officials, which identifies certain sources (such as decisions of courts or enactments of the legislature) as sources of law. A rule that emanates from an appropriate source is a valid rule regardless of its justice or injustice. Correspondingly, a rule that does not emanate from an appropriate source is not a valid rule, no matter how just or reasonable it may be.

Hart's legal positivism has much to recommend it. It offers pleasingly clear-cut answers to a number of questions, and seems to provide a simple way in which a distinction between legal doctrine and political dispute may be maintained. If, however, the theory is construed as an attempt to elucidate the criteria of validity actually employed by lawyers, the theory seems less convincing. Expert lawyers frequently disagree about what the existing legal rules are. For example, many lawyers believe that the English law of contract contains a doctrine of 'common mistake', holding that a contract is void if it was entered into on the basis of a fundamental mistake shared by both parties. Other lawyers deny the existence of any such doctrine. But if lawyers employ criteria of a factual kind in order to establish the content of the law, how is this type of disagreement possible?

Rather than providing a simple refutation of Hart's legal positivism, however, such examples raise the question of whether his theory aims simply to record the criteria of validity implicit in lawyers' practices, or whether it might not be seen as proposing a revised conception of law, constructed in the light of more general theoretical considerations. Hart was Professor of Jurisprudence at Oxford University during the 1950s and 1960s, and he worked in close collaboration with members of the Oxford ordinary language school of philosophy. This leads many to assume that his object in legal theory was the unearthing and articulating of deep criteria that lawyers and citizens unconsciously employ in making judgements about legal validity. Yet we shall see later that there are good grounds for rejecting this interpretation of Hart's work.

1.5 Law and adjudication

When courts come to apply legal rules, they are frequently confronted by difficult questions of interpretation. Factual situations do not come neatly packaged and labelled in legal vocabulary, and there can be ample scope for doubt about whether a particular legal rule should or should not be applied in the individual case. Can such questions be resolved by reference to formal semantic rules? Generally, the meaning of an utterance will be a function of formal linguistic rules in conjunction with the implications of the pragmatic context of the utterance. But legal rules frequently lack any obvious pragmatic context: they may have been enacted long ago with intentions that are now obscure, but they nevertheless purport to regulate the present. It may be tempting to interpret legal rules in the light of desirable policy objectives, but this threatens to collapse fundamentally the distinction between law and politics.

Different theorists have drawn different conclusions. Hart sought to sketch out a middle course between two extreme positions which he called 'formalism' and 'rule-scepticism'. By 'formalism' he meant the view that all conceivable cases can be decided by applying pre-existing rules of law, without any need to ask questions about non-legal considerations such as justice or social policy. 'Rule-skepticism', on the other hand, is the view that judges are never really bound by rules, so that the decisive factors in each case are always extra-legal considerations of social policy. Hart argued that formalism ignores the fact that language exhibits an 'open texture': while words have a 'core of settled meaning' they also possess a 'penumbra of uncertainty' where it will be unclear if the word is properly applicable or not. In so far as legal rules are linguistic entities they too will exhibit this 'open texture'. Cases of penumbral uncertainty will inevitably arise in any conceivable system of laws, and such cases can only be resolved by the court exercising its discretion. On the other hand, rule-skeptics (Hart argued) over-estimate the extent of penumbral uncertainty and ignore the fact that the great majority of cases fall within the 'core of settled meaning' of the rule.

Hart's response to the rule-sceptics is not entirely satisfactory. In the first place his argument places great reliance on the assumption that legal rules have a definite verbal formulation. This is, of course, true of statutory rules, but within the common law developed by the courts it is not true. The binding part of a precedent is called the *ratio decidendi*, a phrase which refers to that part of the court's reasoning (as published in its judgement) which was necessary to justify the conclusion reached. All other observations made in the judgements are said to be *obiter dicta*. The distinction between *ratio* and *obiter* is extremely pliable, since a later court may take a different view from the original court about what exactly was necessary to the decision. Even where a court *does* offer a definite verbal formulation of the rule that it is applying, such a rule never becomes law *simply* by virtue of having been so pronounced, for it is always possible that a later court may treat the rule as *obiter*. In this way, courts constantly modify the rules in the course of applying them.

Suppose that we, as judges, have to decide a case that is somewhat similar to an earlier precedent. The court in the earlier case laid down a principle the wording of which appears to apply exactly to the case in front of us. It will nevertheless be possible for us to avoid applying the principle as formulated in the earlier case if we can identify facts in the present case that were absent from the earlier case, and those facts appear to justify deciding the two cases differently. We will say that the principle as formulated in the earlier case was 'too wide', was not necessary for the decision in the earlier case (since a narrower principle, containing an exception for cases with facts like those of the present case would have served equally well), and was therefore *obiter*. We will then decide our case by reference to a revised version of the earlier principle, now including an exception for cases exhibiting facts of the kind found in the present case.

The apparent pliability of the distinction between *ratio* and *obiter*, combined with the resulting tendency of courts to modify rules in the course of applying them, raises a problem of rule-skepticism that is not addressed by Hart. For if courts can alter the rules whenever they think it best (on grounds of justice, for example) then they are not really bound by rules: to be bound by a rule involves having to apply it even when you think that its application is *not* for the best.

Is it possible to argue that courts may *alter* the law while still being *bound* by the law? Hart's successor at Oxford University, Ronald Dworkin (b. 1931), has developed a theory which seems to explain how that might be possible, but only by radically breaking with the assumptions of legal positivism. Dworkin argues that law does not consist solely of rules deliberately established in precedents and statutes. In his view, law also includes general principles which are implicit within the established black-letter provisions. Judges have the task of constructing a coherent moral theory that provides an appropriate abstract justification for the established rules and institutions. They may interpret and modify established rules in a way that brings them more closely into line with the overarching abstract justification. Thus, even when judges *modify* established legal rules they are doing so in the application of deeper legal principles.

On the one hand Dworkin's theory resembles rule-scepticism in its denial that black-letter rules, viewed in abstraction from considerations of justice, provide reliable guides to judicial decision in most cases. On the other hand, the theory resembles formalism, since it claims that the judge need never step outside the law to decide the case on extra-legal grounds of social policy. Every case, in Dworkin's view, can be decided by reference to the law: but law comprises much more than the black-letter rules allowed for by the positivist.

2 The Enterprise of Legal Theory

Even after we have become familiar with the range of problems outlined so far, we may remain uncertain about the type of solution that they require or invite. We need a general theoretical account of the nature of law that will, for example, explain the relationship between law and force, elucidate the criteria of legal validity and clarify the nature of adjudication. Yet what type of theory is being sought here? Would such a theory be *descriptive*, as talk of investigating the 'nature' of law seems to suggest? Descriptive of what? What facts about law are accessible only to philosophical enquiry and unknown to conventional legal or social scientific scholarship?

Or would such a theory be *prescriptive*? Would it be offering moral ideals and critical standards for the evaluation of legal systems? And, if so, is it not misleading to express the search for such a theory in the language of an investigation into law's 'nature'?

The philosophy of law is often said to be divided into two fields, known as 'analytical jurisprudence' and 'normative jurisprudence'. Analytical jurisprudence claims, not to offer prescriptions (which is the job of its normative partner), but to 'analyse' concepts, including the concept of law. Different theorists have inevitably had somewhat different conceptions of what such analysis might amount to.

The form of analysis developed by the legal positivist John Austin (1790–1859) sought to dispel problems by breaking down the concept of 'law' into simpler elements that would be more transparent. Thus Austin claimed that laws were the commands of a sovereign person or body in an independent political society. Each of these terms ('sovereign', 'command', and so on) was then defined in more basic and, Austin hoped, more transparent terms. The 'sovereign' in a society was to be identified not by any legal criterion (this would render the theory circular) nor by a moral standard (which would convert the theory into a natural law theory) but by direct reference to observable facts about patterns of behaviour. Thus the 'sovereign' was said to be that person or body that is habitually obeyed by the bulk of the population, and is not itself in the habit of obeying any other determinate person or body.

Despite the considerable influence that Austin's theory came to exert in late nineteenth-century England, it exhibited a number of serious defects. In many legal systems it is not possible to identify any person or body satisfying Austin's definition of sovereignty: power and obedience are divided according to shared constitutional rules. Moreover, Austin's theory is thoroughly reductionist in character, claiming that propositions about legal duties are statements about the likelihood of suffering sanctions in certain circumstances.

Hart endeavoured to develop a version of legal positivism that would overcome the limitations of Austin's approach while remaining faithful to the basic objectives of legal positivism. Thus Hart sought to demonstrate that valid laws could be identified by criteria of a factual, non-moral kind, without running into the difficulties encountered by Austin's account of the sovereign; and that propositions of law (about legal obligations and rights) could be distinguished from moral judgements without adopting a reductionist analysis that denied their prescriptive character.

Hart took the view that Austin's account of the sovereign was misconceived in so far as it attempted to identify a fundamental source of law by direct reference to observable behavioural patterns. What was required, in Hart's view, was not the notion of a basic 'habit of obedience' but the notion of the acceptance of a rule. An accepted rule differs from a mere habit of obedience in that, in addition to a regular pattern of conforming conduct (which Hart called the 'external aspect'), a rule involves the existence of a critical reflective attitude on the part of participants (the 'internal aspect'): the pattern of conforming conduct is thought of as a standard that ought to be complied with; those who deviate are criticized; and the criticism is thought of as justified.

> ### Hart on Primary and Secondary Rules
>
> Austin's theory also lacked another distinction developed by Hart: the distinction between primary and secondary rules. Primary rules are rules directly regulating conduct, such as rules prohibiting theft or violence. Secondary rules are rules that regulate the identification, modification and application of other rules. Hart claimed that the invention of secondary rules was as important as the invention of the wheel, and described it as representing the step from the pre-legal to the legal world. A social order containing only primary rules would exhibit various defects such as inflexibility and inefficiency. Most importantly, if such a society were of any complexity it would be likely to exhibit great uncertainty about the scope and content of its primary rules. Uncertainty of this kind could be overcome by adopting a basic 'rule of recognition' which stipulated some criterion by which the society's primary rules might be identified. A very simple rule of recognition might provide that all the rules carved on a certain stone tablet were to be obeyed. Developed legal systems will have highly complex rules of recognition, identifying sources of law such as enactments of the legislature and decisions of the courts, and regulating the relations between those various sources.
>
> As we noted earlier, Hart sought to avoid the reductionism of Austin's theory and to preserve the prescriptive character of propositions of law by reproducing the 'internal point of view' of the participants. Hart's object was to elucidate the meaning of propositions of law by exhibiting their role within a specific social context. Propositions of law (reporting the content of legal rights, duties, powers, and so forth) derive their significance from a social context characterized by the existence of a basic rule of recognition. But they are not *descriptions* of that social context. They express conclusions about the applicability of the rule of recognition and the rules derived from it. They are, as it were, prescriptive judgements made from the viewpoint of a specific system of rules. One might compare them, by analogy, with judgements about what is required by the rules of a game. Such judgements are, within the parameters of the game, prescriptive; but they bracket out all questions about whether there is good reason for playing the game in the first place.

Hart's theory does not purport to offer moral prescriptions: it represents an enterprise of conceptual clarification, which Hart conceives as being prior to substantive moral or empirical inquiries into law. But what exactly does Hart take 'conceptual clarification' in this context to be?

The central objective of Hart's positivism is a defence of what he calls the 'separation of law and morals'. This 'separation' has two main facets. One aspect involves the claim that legal validity is a matter of a rule's derivability from a basic rule of recognition in a legal system: a rule that emanates from an appropriate source is valid irrespective of its justice or injustice (and, similarly, the justice of a rule does not make it law if it does not emanate from an appropriate source). A regime exhibiting certain formal features (acceptance by officials of a basic rule of recognition, combined with general compliance with the laws flowing from that basic rule) is a legal system irrespective of whether it pursues justice or exploitation.

The other aspect of the separation of law and morals is the claim that knowledge of the content of the law does not, in itself, have any bearing on what one should do from a moral point of view. There may or may not be a moral obligation to obey the law. If there is, then knowledge of the law will give precise content to that obligation, but such an obligation is not entailed by the concept of legal validity. It is not part of the *concept* of law that it is morally binding.

Why did Hart believe that we should accept these claims about the concept of law? His long association with the Oxford ordinary language school of philosophy has led some to assume that Hart saw himself as simply unearthing and laying before us the criteria that are implicit in our ordinary usage of the word 'law'. It should be obvious, however, that ordinary usage is unlikely to provide an enlightening guide on these issues. To a large extent ordinary usage simply expresses and evinces the ambivalences articulated within theoretical debate.

Dworkin has drawn a distinction between 'borderline' disputes and 'pivotal' disputes. In a borderline dispute, we have a shared criterion but disagree about the extent of its applicability: for example, we agree on some general concept of 'art' but disagree about whether that concept is applicable to photography. In a pivotal dispute, we have no shared criterion: here our disagreement about photography is merely symptomatic of a deeper disagreement about the essential nature of art. Dworkin appears to suggest that Hart viewed legal theory as being concerned with borderline disputes, whereas (in Dworkin's view) legal theory is concerned with a pivotal dispute.

This clearly misrepresents Hart's conception of legal theory. Hart himself pointed out, in the introduction to his *Essays in Jurisprudence and Philosophy* (1983), that his analysis of the concept of 'law' was not intended as a piece of ordinary language philosophy. In Hart's view, the uncertainties surrounding the concept of law require a choice to be made between rival theoretical standpoints: they cannot be resolved simply by close attention to ordinary usage. Nor do they require a simple decision on the applicability of the concept's 'penumbra'. The 'core of settled meaning' of the concept of 'law' may reflect, not a shared criterion so much as agreement on a range of instances where diverse theoretical positions and criteria happen to overlap. Thus we may all agree that the enactments of legislatures in France, the United Kingdom and Canada are central instances of 'law', yet we may have quite different reasons for so regarding them. In your view the critical fact may be the moral authority of those legislatures, or the justice of their enactments, while in my view it may be the effective control that they exert over their territory.

Hart's reason for adopting a positivist theory of law appears to be his belief that positivism reflects the most important features of law as a social phenomenon. Such a judgement obviously requires criteria of 'importance' and, if the theory is to play a clarificatory role as a preliminary to substantive enquiry, the criteria should be drawn from values that are as weak and widely shared as possible. Reconstruction of Hart's arguments in *The Concept of Law* suggests that his point is as follows. Given the very minimal and widely shared goal of survival, and given certain very general facts about human nature and circumstances (Hart speaks here of a 'minimum content of natural law') it can be demonstrated that societies require rules of conduct. In a society of any complexity, shared rules will be sustainable only if they are publicly identifiable by means of a rule of recognition. The provision of such a set of publicly identifiable rules is a function of law.

Hart's theory develops an account of law's nature that emphasizes its central role in providing publicly ascertainable rules. Only rules identifiable by reference to the basic rule of recognition are acknowledged by Hart to be instances of 'law'. More open-ended criteria of justice or fairness, even though admitted in forensic debates and regarded by lawyers as legal doctrinal arguments, are treated by Hart as extra-legal considerations that may be looked to when the legal rules fail to yield a determinate answer. The justification for semantic regimentation of this kind is not that it reflects ordinary usage, nor that it adjudicates on penumbral uncertainties, but that it reflects the most important and distinctive features of law, judged from the viewpoint of human survival.

Once the minimal element of evaluation involved in Hart's view of law is exposed, however, it can be difficult to prevent it spreading so far as to endanger the positivism of the theory. For example, Hart claims that positivism clarifies the issue that is faced by a citizen who has to decide whether to obey an unjust law. In Hart's view it is better and more honest to say, 'This is law, but because it is unjust I should perhaps disobey it,' rather than, 'Because this rule is unjust, it is not law.' Yet why, we might ask, should one way of expressing the point be thought clearer than the other?

The most plausible answer is one that involves a *rejection* of Hart's strict separation of law and morals. If publicly ascertainable rules are necessary for survival, that seems to give us a moral reason for complying with them even when they are unjust. After all, if people were prepared to comply only when they considered the rules to be perfectly just, there would be no point in having a system of publicly ascertainable rules in the first place. These moral reasons for compliance continue to apply even when they are outweighed by conflicting considerations (the rule is, let us say, *grossly* unjust). The best reason for insisting on continuing to apply the label 'law' even to unjust rules is that this usage acknowledges the continued force and applicability of the moral considerations stemming from the need for a system of publicly ascertainable rules. To refuse to acknowledge the legal validity of an unjust rule would be to treat it as a mere non-entity lacking all moral significance, and so would be to deny the continued relevance of the need for publicly ascertainable rules.

Hart is concerned to defend two theses, which we might call 'the exclusivity of sources' and 'the moral neutrality of propositions of law'. 'The exclusivity of sources' is the idea that legal validity is a matter of derivability from the rule of recognition, and not a matter of the rule's just or unjust content. 'The moral neutrality of propositions of law' is the idea that knowledge of one's legal duties does not in itself entail any judgements about how, from a moral point of view, one should behave. Yet the most powerful reasons for advocating the exclusivity of sources require the rejection of the 'moral neutrality' thesis. This would be totally unacceptable if it forced on us the view that law is morally *conclusive* of how one should behave. No such move is required, however. The 'moral neutrality' thesis should be abandoned in favour of a much weaker claim, that can be labelled 'the moral non-conclusivity of law'. This thesis claims that propositions of law are indeed a species of moral judgement: they are judgements about the applicability of those moral reasons flowing from the need for a body of publicly ascertainable rules. Yet such judgements can never be morally *conclusive*, since they embody only one range of moral considerations which will need to be balanced against many other factors.

3 From Positivism to Natural Law

Legal positivism originated in opposition to theories of natural law. Some positivists rejected the claims to objective knowledge of morality that formed the bedrock of the natural law tradition. Kelsen, for example, adopted an ETHICAL NON-COGNITIVIST (p. 428) stance which denied the possibility of knowledge of moral norms or values. The central core of his work was the attempt to demonstrate that scientific knowledge of positive *legal* norms was in fact possible. It is in the context of this project that we should interpret his remark (mentioned earlier) about the basic norm as the minimum element of natural law without which a cognition of law is impossible.

Hart's positivism was closer to a tradition of thought initiated by Jeremy BENTHAM (1748–1832) (chapter 25). Bentham did not wish to deny that we can have knowledge of moral right and wrong. In fact, his legal positivism was in many respects the consequence of his view that the PRINCIPLE OF UTILITY (chapter 25) (requiring that we should act so as to maximize the greatest happiness of the greatest number) is the supreme principle of morality. This utilitarian stance led him to regard theories of natural law as being founded on confusion and posing a threat to ordered liberty under law.

The opening salvo of Bentham's positivist assault on natural law was directed against the work of the English judge and jurist Sir William Blackstone (1723–80). Blackstone was the author of the first systematic exposition of English law, published as the *Commentaries on the Laws of England* in 1765. Prior to Blackstone, one acquired a knowledge of English law by immersion in its chaos of details. Law books were mostly huge compendia of legal knowledge arranged on no very rational principle. Adopting models drawn from continental legal scholarship, Blackstone arranged the institutions of English law around a basic scheme of natural rights. In accordance with the view of natural law writers such as John LOCKE (chapter 19) (1632–1704), Blackstone treated English law as the concretization and enforcement of people's natural rights. The law was not simply a massive list of disorderly rules, but a systematic body of principles. It was capable of systematic study and exposition precisely because and in so far as it was based on principles of natural law. Consequently, Blackstone's account of English law was inclined to pass smoothly from exposition of the law to justification, since the very scheme of exposition was structured by natural law precepts.

In Bentham's opinion, this type of natural law theory confused questions about what the law *is* with questions about what it *ought to be*. The exposition of existing legal rules is one thing, he argued, while their critical evaluation is another. It does not follow from the *existence* of a legal rule that it is morally *right*. Nor does it follow from the immorality of a rule that it is not law. Bentham believed that confusion of these different questions was likely to induce either supine conformity without any preparedness to criticize the law (since it would be assumed that the law, being law, *must* be right) or, alternatively, irresponsible anarchism (since it could be claimed that any particular rule which is considered to be unjust is therefore not law at all).

It is doubtful if Blackstone was really guilty of the crude confusions that Bentham claimed to discover in his work. Much of Bentham's fire was directed not so much at Blackstone's view of the relationship between law and morals as at Blackstone's emphasis on natural *rights* as the basis of morality. Bentham considered all talk of natural rights to be 'nonsense' and he believed that such talk merely served to divert our attention away from the only relevant considerations: considerations of utility.

Indeed Bentham's whole theory of law was fundamentally shaped by what he took to be the requirements of utility. He developed an elaborate analytical framework for the intellectual reconstruction of positive law, by means of which he sought to explain the entire apparatus of legal concepts (including rights, duties, powers and property) in terms of a general theory that viewed law as a set of commands backed by sanctions. For Bentham, such reconstruction served an essentially practical point, by making law and legal thinking more closely fitted to its role as an instrument of utility, and by eliminating the confusions that so often (in Bentham's view) obscured the true requirements of utility and insulated the law from the demands of reform. His aim was not to *explicate* legal thinking so much as to *revise* it.

The move away from Bentham's clear UTILITARIAN (chapter 25) objectives, and towards a more purely 'analytical' jurisprudence, commenced with the work of Bentham's own disciple John Austin, whom we mentioned earlier. Austin's theory of law is in many respects a simplified version of Bentham's. But, whereas Bentham might have presented the theory as a deliberate proposal to *revise* ordinary assumptions about law, Austin seems to intend his theory as an *explication* of those assumptions. Indeed, far from mounting an assault on the vested interests of lawyers in the way that Bentham might have wished, Austin's version of legal positivism provided a powerful underpinning for the lawyer's claim to be an expert in a technical and self-contained area of knowledge distinct both from morality and from politics.

Austin and his disciples thus introduced into legal theory a basic uncertainty concerning the status of investigations into the nature of law. This uncertainty continues to dog the subject.

Superficial examination of the writings of legal positivists might lead one to believe that their theories treat law in entirely formal terms, involving no judgement about law's purpose or value. Yet, if the legal positivist is to offer an integrated solution to the various problems outlined at the start of this chapter, some features must be selected from the immensely complex social phenomena of law and given a central role within the theory, so that they may serve as a point of focus around which other features can be arranged. Thus Hart chooses to emphasise the lawyer's reliance upon rules emanating from a limited number of authoritative sources (especially legislative enactments and judicial decisions). Other features of law are either re-interpreted or marginalized. This selection of focus expresses Hart's judgement about the fundamental purpose or function of law: the provision of a body of publicly ascertainable rules as a basis for the ordering of conduct in a world characterized by disagreement. Yet the ghostly influence of Austin seems to induce in Hart a desire to leave this basic foundation of his theory understated and relatively unexplored. As the contemporary natural lawyer John Finnis (b. 1940) aptly puts it, 'Hart's method points out a land which is left to his readers and hearers to hazard to enter.'

Finnis on Natural Law

In Finnis' view, the tradition of natural law thought has been misunderstood and misrepresented by legal positivists. Positivists have tended to assume that the central thesis of natural law theory is the claim that legal validity is a matter of moral bindingness (or, perhaps, of justice) so that a rule that is not morally binding (or not just) cannot be said to be legally valid. As it is traditionally, if somewhat misleadingly, put 'lex injusta non est lex' ('an unjust law is not a law'). Positivists regard this claim as simply being confusing, and prefer to apply the label 'law' to all the rules emanating from particular formal sources within a legal system, irrespective of their moral status. Yet, as we have seen, the claim that this way of thinking is clearer, and reflects the most distinctive and important features of the social phenomena of law, itself requires some evaluative stance from which we can make the required judgement of 'importance'.

Finnis claims that natural lawyers have never really wished to deny validity in the lawyer's sense to unjust or immoral rules. Rather, their object has been to explore the land to which Hart's method points. In other words, they believe that a coherent theory of law can only be the consequence and expression of a deeper moral and political theory. In fact, Finnis claims, we understand the nature of law by grasping the way in which law is the solution to a problem of practical reason.

With this end in view, Finnis develops an account of the objective 'goods' or 'forms of human flourishing' which we will pursue if we are fully rational. These goods can be pursued only within a community, and the maintenance of a community that sustains the ability of each individual to pursue the objective goods amounts to 'the common good'. The common good is therefore not an aggregative conception, involving the 'maximization' of individual goods, but a framework of institutions and conditions making individual pursuit of a good life possible. The existence of an appropriate community requires the co-ordination of conduct around shared rules, and the provision of such a set of rules is the central task of law.

In one sense, therefore, Finnis' conception of law is not dissimilar to Hart's. They both view law as a set of publicly ascertainable rules. Finnis, however, believes that this conclusion is to be arrived at only by means of an understanding of law's relationship with the requirements of practical reason. In its 'focal' sense, law serves the common good, and this relationship to the common good inevitably shapes our thinking about law, and the vocabulary (using terms such as 'rights' and 'duties') we use to describe law. Legal institutions may at times be used for purposes of oppression or exploitation, but these are degenerate

instances of law which we can only understand by grasping the ways in which
they resemble, and yet diverge from, law in its 'focal' instances. The traditional
maxim '*lex injusta non est lex*', Finnis concludes, was intended to highlight the
degenerate nature of such uses of law.

Finnis has performed a great service in overturning hitherto prevailing
caricatures of natural law theory. Yet he seems to underestimate the significance of Hart's apparent desire to construct his theory of law from a
standpoint (of the aim of 'survival') which is both weak and widely shared.
Hart's reliance upon such a minimal evaluative starting point reflects an
understanding of his enterprise as a clarificatory one which is prior to
substantive moral enquiry or empirical investigation. Hart hopes to construct
a coherent concept of law that may be employed as a tool in moral and
empirical debate, thereby overcoming the problems which arise when different participants in debate employ different conceptions of law; or, still worse,
when controversial moral or empirical theories about law are introduced in
the guise of definitions of 'law'. Finnis appears to view Hart's minimalism as
a failure to explore fully the underpinnings of his own theory; but it is
probably better to regard it as a refusal to build the clarificatory enterprise on
a richly controversial foundation when a weak and minimal foundation will
serve equally well.

4 Theory as Interpretation

Philosophy is often thought to be characterized by a concern for the necessary
and universal. Particular, contingent facts are thought of as matters for
empirical enquiry, not philosophical reflection. Thus the philosophy of law
traditionally concerns itself with features of law that are logically *necessary*, as
defining features of a supposedly universal concept of law. The peculiar
characteristics of this or that particular legal system are matters for social
science rather than philosophy. Writers such as Hart and Finnis offer concepts
of law that purport to be universal. They do not simply describe characteristic
features of the legal systems of the United Kingdom or Australia: rather, they
offer us criteria for saying of *any* form of social ordering whether or not it
should be regarded as an instance of law.

Familiar though this conception of philosophy may be, it is not beyond
challenge. We may reflect upon the meaning and significance of practices
within our own society and culture, without any pretension to universality,
and such reflections may bear many of the hallmarks of philosophical thought.
Indeed, we may discover that it was the desire reflectively to understand our
own practices that drove us into the search for universal and necessary
features in the first place.

The theory of law developed by Dworkin adopts a focus that is culturally
specific rather than universal, and that seeks a reflective understanding of our

own practices. According to Dworkin, the philosophical debate concerning the nature of law is not, when properly understood, a search for a semantic definition of 'law', or a search for a universal concept. Rather it arises out of the adoption of an 'interpretive attitude' in relation to our own practices. The interpretive attitude raises a question about the general point or rationale of a practice, not as a theoretical but as a practical issue: the ultimate question is how best to continue the practice.

Questions such as those concerning the nature of law reflect disputes about the meaning or point of our legal practices. Such disputes cannot be resolved by reference to the intentions or understandings of the participants in the practice, because the participants will themselves be embroiled in the dispute. Thus a society might have practices of courtesy, involving raising one's hat to people in certain circumstances, or opening doors for them. Yet the participants in these practices might disagree about the underlying point of courtesy. Is the object to express a judgement of respect about the recipient of courtesy? Or, quite to the contrary, is the object to provide a neutral, non-judgemental, way of dealing with people regardless of what you think of them? The choice between rival interpretations of this kind might make a difference to what we would see as an appropriate way of continuing the practice. Should we, for example, make a special effort to raise our hats to soldiers returning from a war?

If we cannot have recourse to the intentions and understandings of the participants, how are we to choose between rival interpretations of a practice? Dworkin offers a general theory of interpretation which he calls 'constructive interpretation'. On this view, the best interpretation will satisfy two criteria, of 'fit', and of 'appeal'. Criteria of fit concern the ability of the interpretation to accommodate the uncontroversially observable features of the practice. An interpretation need not be a perfect fit, but it must come up to a certain threshold of adequacy. Within the constraints of fit, we must choose the interpretation that makes the practice into the most appealing practice it can be from a moral point of view.

We noted above that there is room for some uncertainty about whether philosophical enquiry into the nature of law is intended to be descriptive or prescriptive. Dworkin's theory of interpretation presents legal theory as having both a descriptive and a prescriptive aspect. Interpretive theories of law will be descriptive to the extent that they must satisfy the constraints of fit; they will be prescriptive in so far as one must choose the morally most appealing interpretation amongst those that satisfy the constraints of fit.

A theory of law (or any other interpretation of a practice) will, Dworkin holds, involve three stages. At the 'pre-interpretive' stage we must achieve a rough preliminary identification of the practices we are discussing. Dworkin concedes that even the pre-interpretive stage involves interpretation (every description of human conduct involves interpretation) but the interpretations involved at this stage may be wholly uncontroversial. Next comes the 'interpretive' stage, where we must arrive at a general interpretation of the meaning, point or rationale of the practice, choosing (within the constraints of fit) the interpretation that makes the practice into the best practice it can be from a moral point of view. Finally comes the 'post-interpretive' stage, where we revise our original understanding of what the practice requires in the light of the interpretation now adopted (for instance, we decide that, since courtesy is an expression of one's judgements of respect, it requires us to raise our hats to soldiers returning from a war, but not to the local squire).

This account of the nature of legal theory, and the view of interpretation on which it depends, raise a large number of questions. Some positivists feel, for example, that important questions are begged when a prescriptive, justificatory, aspect is built into one's conception of the legal theoretical enterprise. Is it not the whole object of positivism, they ask, to present law as being morally neutral? On the other hand, one can argue that Dworkin actually overestimates the contrast between his conception of legal theory and that held by Hart and others. For, as we have seen, Hart's theory also adopts an interpretation of the point of law (the provision of a set of publicly ascertainable rules) and then revises our ordinary understanding in the light of that interpretation.

Dworkin also seems oblivious to the way in which an interpretive and culturally specific view of the tasks of legal theory fundamentally erodes the distinction between philosophy and sociology (formerly policed by the distinction between the universal or the necessary and the particular or the contingent). In resisting attempts to collapse the philosophy of law into sociology, Dworkin maintains that the interpretation of a practice is necessarily prior to a study of its social or historical context. We may well wish to challenge this claim, however. When viewed in isolation, a practice may have an apparent meaning that is subverted once it is relocated in its social context. Practices of male courtesy towards women, for example, may take on a different meaning when located in the context of a male-dominated society within which women are generally subordinated. Equally, an understanding of the historical context may well be necessary if we are to grasp the genesis and character of the interpretive disputes that arise: such disputes are, after all, not free-floating, but arise out of historically produced fractures and tensions within formerly unproblematic practices. An historical and sociological enquiry may therefore be necessary if philosophy is to attain a fully transparent and self-conscious understanding of the interpretive disputes in which it hopes to engage.

Dworkin's neglect of law's social context is particularly ironic since, as we shall see, he views law as a deep expression of equality and interprets in this light the lawyer's concern for consistency and principle. Radical critics of law, such as MARXISTS (chapter 24) and FEMINISTS (chapter 32), might well agree that law involves a 'discourse' of equality; but they would point out that the apparent meaning of this discourse is subverted once we locate law in the context of a deeply hierarchical society founded on oppression and domination. The law then appears not as the expression of a deep concern for equality, but as an attempt to mystify and misrepresent social relations by presenting them as being founded on equality.

5 Law as Integrity

Having outlined Dworkin's views on the nature of legal theory, what of his substantive conclusions about the nature of law? What interpretation of our legal practices does he adopt?

Dworkin considers three rival interpretations or theories of law, which he calls 'conventionalism', 'pragmatism' and (his own preferred theory) 'law as integrity'. Each theory is evaluated against the descriptive criteria of 'fit' and the prescriptive criteria of moral 'appeal'.

Conventionalism resembles legal positivism in its emphasis on the public ascertainability of legal rules, but it proffers this view in the context of a wider interpretation of the point of law. According to the conventionalist, the point of law is to give citizens fair warning of the circumstances in which the state's coercive powers will be used, and to protect the expectations formed in reliance on this warning. In Dworkin's view, this theory fails to fit the facts of law, since it cannot explain the ability of courts to innovate by granting new remedies in cases that are not clearly covered by any existing rules. What if the conventionalist responds by saying that the value of protecting expectations must be traded off against the demands of flexibility, so that some judicial innovation in cases not covered by existing rules is permissible? In that case, Dworkin argues, conventionalism will fail *prescriptively* since it proposes an irrational way of trading off flexibility against the protection of expectations. If such a trade-off is the point of law, it is best effected case-by-case, so that the expectations engendered in each case can be identified and weighed.

Pragmatism is a theory that proposes precisely such a case-by-case approach. The pragmatist is really a species of rule-sceptic since he or she holds that judges should not view themselves as being *bound* by pre-existing legal rules. Rather, the judge's task should be to give the decision that will have the best consequences, all things considered. The expectations that have been created by the publication of legal rules must be taken account of by the pragmatist judge when he or she tries to determine which decision will be for the best. It may frequently be the case, therefore, that the pragmatist judge has very powerful reasons for applying pre-existing legal rules. Yet such reasons are never conclusive in advance of the particular facts of the case: they must always be weighed against other conflicting considerations.

Pragmatism in its turn is rejected by Dworkin, and he turns to the development of his own theory. This hinges on the value of 'integrity' in law. Dworkin claims that we expect the law to express and embody some more or less coherent moral vision. While the law may contain competing moral values we would not expect it to strike wholly arbitrary compromises between rival moral positions, even if such compromises gave expression to the prevailing balance of power (in terms of numbers of votes) between the advocates of rival positions. We value the moral coherence or integrity of the law quite independently of the value we put on the law's justice, for we expect the law to exhibit a certain deep moral coherence even when we personally subscribe to some rival moral vision.

When the state employs its coercive apparatus in accordance with a coherent moral position, it treats its citizens as equals. The point of law, Dworkin claims, is to ensure that governments treat their citizens as equals in that sense. The lawyer's concern with principles and consistency is a concern not with the public ascertainability of rules but with the moral coherence that is a deep expression of equality.

Dworkin on Adjudication

How then should a judge set about the task of adjudication? At this point Dworkin brings his theory of interpretation into play once again. A judge is to decide cases by reference to the morally best interpretation of the materials of law. Rather than thinking of the judge as confronted by a finite number of black-letter rules which, once exhausted, throw us back on to extra-legal considerations of social policy, the judge confronts an enormous array of statutes and cases which must be subjected to a process of interpretation. The judge must find interpretations of these materials that discover within them some coherent moral vision. Such interpretations must satisfy the constraints of fit, and within those constraints must make the law as good as it can be from a moral point of view. In fact, Dworkin claims, this process of interpretation is of a piece with the investigations of legal theory so that jurisprudence (or the philosophy of law) is but the first and most abstract stage of adjudication.

This theory offers an elegant solution to a number of intractable problems. For example, we noted earlier the way in which it enables us to explain how judges can modify the established rules of law while still being bound by law, a feature of adjudication which poses severe difficulties for most other theories. Some serious problems remain, however. On Dworkin's theory, judges must decide cases not by reference to what they consider to be just in the abstract, but by reference to the conception of justice that they find embodied in the existing law. Yet, in deciding what that conception is, they must rely upon their personal moral viewpoint. Since it is quite likely that the 'constraints of fit' will prove not so constraining after all, is there not ample scope here for different judges to reach dramatically diverse conclusions about what the existing law is? Indeed, Dworkin insists that it is up to each citizen to decide for himself or herself what is required by law, and it is in principle possible for a citizen to be correct when all the judges are wrong. Of course, convergence in legal judgements may be secured by pre-existing convergence in moral judgement. But is it not plausible to suggest that a major object of having law is to make it possible for us to have shared rules even in a world characterized by serious and far-reaching moral disagreements?

The perceived need for authoritative rules in a context of moral diversity makes conventionalism seem attractive. Dworkin's criticisms of conventionalism are in fact somewhat misconceived, for they assume that the conventionalist is concerned with the protection of expectations that have been formed in reliance on published rules, and this type of concern could be adequately accommodated by a pragmatist approach. But a better account of conventionalism would see it as being concerned to *encourage the formation* of stable mutual expectations about conduct, and a pragmatist approach to adjudication would be inferior to conventionalism when judged by this objective.

Some problems with Dworkin's analysis stem from the character of a modern legal order. When Blackstone systematized his exposition of English law around a handful of basic natural rights, the law was mainly concerned to enforce rights of property and to deal with obvious wrongs such as theft or assault. Also, the law had been mainly developed by judges, who were concerned to preserve the coherence of their decisions with the existing fabric of law. Once the law is largely a product of statute, and the statutes are enacted in pursuit of a host of very loosely related or even conflicting social policies, is there any good reason to expect it to exhibit a high degree of moral coherence?

The growing muddle and complexity of most modern legal orders might, in fact, provide a powerful explanation of Dworkin's own theory. Lawyers regularly construct theories as a basis for the decision of cases, in the sense that they need to generalize from certain specific instances, or to find a perspective from which to interpret specific statutory words. Yet the lawyer's theories operate at a very low level of abstraction. What is so striking about Dworkin's vision of law is the abstract philosophical plane on to which he drives legal doctrinal argument. Such abstraction, however, may itself be a response to the growing complexity and incoherence of the law. If one is determined to seek coherence, one must seek it at ever more abstract levels. Legal positivism might be seen as the opposite response to the same problem: faced by growing incoherence at the level of general principles, one focuses more and more narrowly and exclusively upon black-letter rules.

Dworkin's theory can be compared and contrasted with the work of Lon Fuller (1902–78). Fuller's work seems to have influenced Dworkin in several fundamental respects, although the influence is not acknowledged. Like Dworkin, Fuller sees the judge as being confronted by a task that cannot be reduced to the application of a basic rule of recognition. Adjudication is, in Fuller's view, a purposive enterprise guided by the complex moral aspiration of 'fidelity to law'. Whereas Dworkin connects the value of law to a left-liberal concern for equality, Fuller interprets the central value of law in terms of a more conservative concern for liberty and order under the governance of general, prospective and published rules. In many cases, fidelity to law will require adherence to posited rules; but, Fuller claimed, to imagine that this represents the ultimate guiding principle of adjudication is to confuse fidelity to law with 'subservience to authority'. Thus, a power to modify the rules in some cases may be consistent with the judge's fundamental duty. On appropriate occasions, fidelity to law may require a refusal to apply the rules established by authority (as where, for example, those rules are so vague as to defeat the idea of governing conduct by prospective rules: an idea that Fuller takes to be an integral part of the concept of 'law'). In some situations, the judge's duty may give rise to intractable moral dilemmas: enforcing a hopelessly vague statute may undermine the ideals of clarity that are inherent in the rule of law, but assuming a power to strike down such statutes may itself give rise to great uncertainty. A complex process of moral and philosophical reflection is therefore *internal* to the application of law.

6 Unger and the Critical Legal Studies Movement

We saw earlier that liberalism requires a firm distinction between law and politics. Political debate and decision results in the enactment of certain rules and the conferment of certain entitlements. Action within the scope of such rules and entitlements should be protected even when it does not serve the general welfare, or advance the political objectives of the collectivity. Yet can we apply the rules and decide upon the exact scope of the entitlements without re-opening the political questions of social policy or distributive justice that resulted in their enactment?

The suggestion that we *cannot* successfully separate legal doctrine from politics lies at the heart of the arguments put forward by the Critical Legal Studies movement (CLS), a loose association of leftist lawyers centred in the United States. Much of the work of CLS takes the form of detailed studies of particular areas of legal doctrine, with a view to demonstrating the doctrine's open-endedness, incoherence, or its tendency to collapse back into basic political issues. When CLS adherents seek to offer more general theoretical statements, they frequently exhibit a high degree of confusion and a lack of clarity which poses severe obstacles to interpretation. This provides us with a justification for focusing on the work of one leading figure who has exerted a powerful influence on CLS even if his views are not altogether typical of the movement generally. The work of Roberto Unger exhibits a much higher degree of sophistication than most other CLS writings, and merits consideration even in a very brief survey of legal philosophy.

In Unger's first book, *Knowledge and Politics* (1976) he identified two problems that are internal to liberal political theory, which he called 'the problem of legislation' and 'the problem of adjudication'. The problem of legislation concerns the question of how liberal political theory can find a basis for generating just rules for the conduct of social life given its commitment to neutrality between conceptions of the good life. This problem is a central topic within political philosophy, and we shall leave it on one side in order to focus on a problem that is specific to the philosophy of law, namely, 'the problem of adjudication'. Here Unger argued that, even given the enactment of authoritative legal rules, those rules could not be applied in specific cases without collapsing the issue back into political value judgements. He saw this claim as following from liberalism's rejection of 'essentialism', which is understood as the thesis that words have stable meanings by virtue of representing fundamental 'essences'. Liberalism's moral neutrality (as Unger characterized it) required a rejection of essentialism, and yet liberalism's faith in law could not be sustained *without* essentialism.

In effect, Unger was arguing that, once legal theory abandoned *formalism* (which is the claim that all cases can be resolved simply by applying legal rules without reference to any other considerations) it would have no way to avoid collapsing adjudication into politics. In his later work, *The Critical Legal Studies Movement* (1986) Unger employed the term 'formalism' in a wider sense to refer to all theories that assert the existence of a distinction between legal doctrine and open-ended ideological controversy: he claimed that 'formalism' in its more narrow and conventional sense is simply the extreme end point of the same general thesis. Unger argued that when we come to apply legal rules, we are forced back into deeper questions about the principles underpinning the rules: we are forced to assume that the rules represent a morally coherent and defensible scheme of human association (an assumption that Unger terms 'objectivism', and which we may find best exemplified by Dworkin's theory of law). Yet this assumption, he claims, is unsustainable. Law already represents within itself the conflict between *rival* social visions. For every principle that we discover in the legal doctrine, therefore, we will also find a counter-principle that tends to subvert it. There may be a way in which the principle and counter-principle are conventionally balanced against each other, but this balance will not itself be grounded in any deeper principle. Rather, it is an expression of the erroneous assumption that social arrangements have to take more or less the form that they presently do. Once we grasp the essentially plastic and revisable nature of our forms of association, Unger argues, we will see that there is no reason why the counter-principles should not be extended at the expense of the principles. This 'deviationist' form of doctrinal argument reveals the hollowness of legal doctrine's claim to be separable from politics, while simultaneously revealing the doctrine's potential as an instrument of revolutionary social transformation.

It is doubtful whether Unger's argument is successful. As John Finnis has pointed out, on the assumption that the law is pursuing a plurality of different 'goods' or moral values, there is no reason why the particular balance struck between those goods should itself be required by a deeper principle; there may be different, equally reasonable, ways of striking the balance. Alternatively, a more conservative view might point out that, if a part of law's object is to stabilize mutual expectations about conduct, one would expect the law to reflect those forms of human association that currently exist; the mere fact that they could be otherwise would, from this perspective, be irrelevant.

7 Philosophical Reconstruction of Legal Doctrine

The juxtaposition of Dworkin's emphasis on the internal coherence of law with Unger's assertion of its conflict-ridden incoherence has spawned an upsurge of philosophically informed studies of particular areas of legal doctrine. The aim has been to identify the general moral theories or values that appear to underpin major legal institutions such as contract, tort, liability and criminal law.

The most well-established field for this type of philosophical research has long been criminal law and the penal system. Bentham offered a sweeping justification of punishment in utilitarian terms, backed up by corresponding justifications for such features of criminal law as the mental defences (criminal responsibility generally requires either intention or foresight on the defendant's part), the defence of duress, and the exclusion of liability for the insane. Such utilitarian accounts have been relentlessly opposed by rival theories, often drawing their inspiration from Kant.

More recently, theorists have turned their attention to private law, particularly contract and tort. Here the major split has been between those theorists who see private law doctrines as being inextricably connected to wider conceptions of distributive justice or aggregate welfare, and rival theorists who seek to confine such distributive or aggregative concerns to the tax and welfare sectors of the law, and who seek to explain private law in terms of the value of 'corrective justice'. Amongst the former group, scholars of 'the economic analysis of law' have been prominent, generally seeking to explain and justify legal doctrines as instruments of efficient resource allocation or wealth maximization. Inevitably, these debates are connected both with general questions about the nature of law and with wider issues of political philosophy.

Further Reading

Cotterrell (1989), Lyons (1984) and Simmonds (1986) provide elementary introductions to the subject. After that, it is probably best to tackle Hart (1961), Fuller (1969), Finnis (1980) and Dworkin (1986). Dworkin's earlier books also repay detailed study. Hart (1983) contains a number of very important and immensely lucid essays.

Kelsen's work provides a very different form of legal positivism from that of Hart, and the best place to begin is with Kelsen (1992). The 1992 English translation contains a very valuable introduction by Stanley Paulson.

Joseph Raz is one of the most important contemporary writers on the philosophy of law, and he has developed a sophisticated defence of positivism that is strongly influenced by both Hart and Kelsen, in *The Authority of Law* (1979), and in numerous other publications. His work is also notable for the connections that it develops between philosophy of law and theories of practical reason. For various views on the relationship between law and practical reason, see Raz (1975), MacCormick (1978), Beyleveld and Brownsword (1986), and Finnis (1980).

Recent debates on the moral underpinnings of legal doctrines may be explored by reading Fried (1981), Coleman (1992) and Hart (1968).

Unger (1976) is a rather wayward book that is inclined to resort to crude caricatures. Nevertheless, it contains some arguments that are interesting, and which have exerted a powerful influence on the critical legal studies movement. Unger (1986) contains a powerful critique of Dworkin (referred to as 'the rights and principles school') in its early pages. This might be compared with the essay by Finnis in *Oxford Essays in Jurisprudence*,

Eekelaar and Bell (eds) (1987). Kelman (1987) and Altman (1990) provide useful guides to the confused debate surrounding critical legal studies.

References

Altman, A. 1990: *Critical Legal Studies: a Liberal Critique*. New Jersey: Princeton University Press.
Austin, J. 1832: *The Province of Jurisprudence Determined* (1955 edn). London: Weidenfeld and Nicolson.
Beyleveld, D. and Brownsword, R. 1986: *Law as a Moral Judgment*. London: Sweet and Maxwell.
Coleman, J. 1992: *Risks and Wrongs*. Cambridge: Cambridge University Press.
Cotterrell, R. 1989: *The Politics of Jurisprudence*. London: Butterworths.
Dworkin, R. 1978: *Taking Rights Seriously* (revised edn). London: Duckworth.
—— 1985: *A Matter of Principle*. Cambridge, MA: Harvard University Press.
—— 1986: *Law's Empire*. London: Fontana.
Eekelaar, J. and Bell, J. (eds) 1987: *Oxford Essays in Jurisprudence* (3rd series). Oxford: Clarendon Press.
Fried, C. 1981: *Contract as Promise*. Cambridge MA: Harvard University Press.
Finnis, J. 1980: *Natural Law and Natural Rights*. Oxford: Clarendon Press.
Fuller, L. 1969: *The Morality of Law* (2nd edn). New Haven: Yale University Press.
Hart, H. L. A. 1961: *The Concept of Law*. Oxford: Clarendon Press.
—— 1968: *Punishment and Responsibility*. Oxford: Oxford University Press.
—— 1983: *Essays in Jurisprudence and Philosophy*. Oxford: Oxford University Press.
Kelman, M. 1987: *A Guide to Critical Legal Studies*. Cambridge, MA: Harvard University Press.
Kelsen, H. 1992 [1934]: *Introduction to the Problems of Legal Theory* (translated by B. L. Paulson and S. L. Paulson). Oxford: Clarendon Press.
Lyons, D. 1984: *Ethics and the Rule of Law*. Cambridge: Cambridge University Press.
—— 1993: *Moral Aspects of Legal Theory*. Cambridge: Cambridge University Press.
MacCormick, N. 1978: *Legal Reasoning and Legal Theory*. Oxford: Clarendon Press.
Raz, J. 1975: *Practical Reason and Norms*. London: Hutchinson.
—— 1979: *The Authority of Law*. Oxford: Clarendon Press.
—— 1980: *The Concept of a Legal System* (2nd edn). Oxford: Clarendon Press.
Simmonds, N. E. 1986: *Central Issues in Jurisprudence*. London: Sweet and Maxwell.
Unger, R. M. 1976: *Knowledge and Politics*. New York: Free Press.
—— 1986: *The Critical Legal Studies Movement*. Cambridge, MA: Harvard University Press.

Discussion Questions

1 Can a single theory of law deal satisfactorily with all the major puzzling features of legal thought and practice?

2 Is it more important for philosophers to analyse the concept of law or the social practices of which law is a part?

3 What, if anything, distinguishes the rule of law from a regime based solely on force?

4 Are legal rights and obligations species of moral rights and obligations?

5 Can a reductionist programme deal with the apparently prescriptive language of law?

6 Does Kelsen's basic norm allow law to be prescriptive without being absorbed into moral questions about justice?

7 How minimal is the 'minimum element of natural law' required for a positivist account of law?

8 Should we accept Hart's claim that an adequate positivist account of legal obligation can be provided by taking account of the 'internal' viewpoint of a participant of a legal system?

9 What importance does the modern notion of autonomy have for the theory of law?

10 Discuss the claim that rules are laws if they emanate from an appropriate source, whether or not they are just.

11 Must we choose between the 'formalist' position that all conceivable cases can be decided by pre-existing rules of law and the 'rule-sceptical' position that all legal cases are decided by extra-legal factors?

12 Do judges have the task of constructing a coherent moral theory? Can different judges construct different theories?

13 What is the importance of a rule of recognition in the theory of law?

14 Does legal positivism provide a middle way between supine acceptance of the law and irresponsible anarchism?

15 Should philosophy of law be a matter of reflectively understanding law in a particular society rather than the determination of a universal theory?

16 Is it a fault of Dworkin's interpretive and culturally specific theory that it erodes the distinction between philosophy and sociology?

17 Should we value moral coherence or integrity in law even if we subscribe to a different moral view?

18 How does Fuller's 'fidelity to law' differ from subservience to authority?

19 What are the consequences if we cannot separate legal doctrine from open-ended ideological controversy?

20 Does the possibility of striking different balances among the plurality of moral values pursued by the law undermine the authority of the actual balance struck by the law?

13

Philosophy of History ─────────────

Leon Pompa

Historians are concerned with the human past, with what happened, and how and why it happened. But the past is a difficult object of study. It is beyond the reach of perception and requires special methods of enquiry which may lead to results that fail to satisfy the criteria of knowledge that perception satisfies. Its contents are almost limitless and can be studied in greater and lesser degrees of detail, requiring decisions of selection which may affect historians' claims to truth. It contains the deeds and practices of past individuals and communities which may be sufficiently different from our own that we cannot be sure that we can reach any true explanation or understanding of them. Finally, historians must express their results in forms that may also affect the epistemological status of their claims. Modern philosophy of history has engaged with all of these difficulties. An underlying concern has been to establish how far the capacity of historians to reach objective truth is affected by the difficulties which arise in each of these areas of enquiry. This will be the central question in this chapter, starting with what historians themselves consider the least philosophically puzzling aspects of their activity and proceeding to those that they consider more problematic.

1 Knowledge of Historical Fact

Historians normally adopt a realist view of knowledge, involving three claims: that individual events, actions and occurrences really took place in the past; that true historical statements or historical facts are statements about some of these occurrences; and that these statements are known because sufficient evidence for them is available in the present. Thus, when we know that Napoleon lost the Battle of Waterloo, we know that a certain event, Napoleon's losing the battle, took place in the past. We know this because we know that the statement that it did take place is true, and we know that the statement is true because there is sufficient evidence in the present to justify our claim to know it. But this threefold conception is deceptively simple and has been challenged at every stage. I shall consider each of these in turn.

It is clear that this whole view would be at risk if we had reason to doubt that there was a real past at all. Such a reason was first offered by Bertrand RUSSELL (chapter 27), who pointed out that it is logically possible for the world to have come into existence five minutes ago, with a population having a complete range of 'memories' of apparently prior times (Russell, 1921, pp. 159–60). But if the world came into existence five minutes ago, not only would most of our memories be false but so would almost all of our historical knowledge. It might be thought that we can avoid this conclusion by appealing, as historians normally do, to the evidence presently available to us. But this will not help for, according to the hypothesis, everything would now be as it is, including all that historians think of as evidence for the past. Hence, were there no past before five minutes ago, nothing that we take as evidence for that past could really be evidence for it.

Russell took his hypothesis seriously enough to suggest that our supposed 'knowledge' of the past should be translated into statements about the present contents of mind because he believed that, through perception, we are directly acquainted with the reality that makes statements about the present true in a way in which we cannot be with regard to the past. The hypothesis has been subject to a number of objections (Danto, 1965, pp. 83–4) but I shall concentrate upon one which depends upon important features of the nature of historical evidence. According to this objection, it does not follow from the logical possibility of the hypothesis either that the world began five minutes ago or that we cannot know whether or not it did, because 'present evidence would not be what it is if no past had existed' (Gorman, 1982, p. 72). To understand the force of this objection it is necessary to note two points. Firstly, it is an important feature of historical language that it contains what are called 'past-entailing' or 'past-referring' terms. These are terms 'whose correct application to some present object or event *logically* involves a reference to some earlier object or event'. Thus to describe somebody as having a scar entails that at some earlier time he or she suffered a wound (Danto, 1965, pp. 71–2). Secondly, the use of some artefact as a piece of historical evidence requires use of such past-entailing terms. Thus when an historian describes some document as a letter written by Gladstone, he or she is making a past-entailing assertion. For he or she is applying to a document which exists in the present a description which entails that some event happened in the past, namely that Gladstone wrote this letter (Gorman, 1982, pp. 56–8). Thus, given the past-entailing nature of the descriptions under which documents count as historical evidence, the refutation takes the form of asserting that we cannot maintain our present past-entailing conception of historical evidence and admit that the hypothesis could be true.

. It might seem, however, that this fails to refute Russell's hypothesis, since it is part of the latter that, even if the world came into existence five minutes ago, everything in it would remain the same *for us*, including therefore our present conception of historical evidence. So we would continue to describe present artefacts in past-entailing terms, even though the events 'entailed' never took place. In fact, however, the refutation is substantially correct. For Russell must allow for the reality of *some* period of time – let us say his 'five minutes' – before which the past may not have existed, in order to allow us to understand the doubt expressed in the hypothesis. This means that he must allow that some past-entailing descriptions, namely those that relate something now present to something in the past five minutes, are true. But if this is so, he must show how it is possible that some past-entailing terms really have the implications for the past that we take them to have while others, which are of precisely the same kind and satisfy precisely the same criteria, do not. But this cannot be shown. For the consistent use of criteria is necessary not only for historical thought but for any coherent thought whatsoever. Hence the sceptical challenge could be maintained not as a challenge about the reality of some *part* of the past but only as a challenge about the reality of the *whole* of the past. But this would be self-defeating since the contrast between a real past (the 'five minutes') and an unreal past, which is needed to make the hypothesis coherent, would then be lost.

So far, therefore, there is no reason to doubt that there was a real past. But realism involves the view that the past to which historians are committed is also an *independent* past, in other words, it is a past filled with events that occurred *irrespective of whether or not we shall ever come to know of them*. Historians conceive of their task as *discovering* the contents of this past but not of *creating* it. This view has, however, been challenged from an idealist point of view, via a theory now generally known as 'constructionism' (Nowell-Smith, 1977). The constructionist thesis accepts that historians come to know truths about the past. But the past to which these relate is not the real past, as we normally understand it – that is, as an independent past of real events which await discovery; it is seen as a peculiarly 'historical' past that exists as something that we construct from present evidence. Accordingly, were we to come into possession of new evidence and construct it differently, not only would our knowledge alter but so also would the historical past itself. But if this is so, the standard historical belief in realism, and the conception of knowledge which presupposes it, would be false.

The principal reason given for this claim is that since the real past no longer exists, it can have no part to play in the verification of the historian's account. Accordingly, it is claimed, the past that the historian brings into view is not the past as it might have been in itself but one that exists relative only to its capacity to explain our beliefs about the evidence. The idea that historians discover a past that existed independently of our knowledge of it is therefore rejected in favour of the idea of a past that exists only as a construction to explain present evidence (Goldstein, 1976, 1977). It should be noted, although it cannot be pursued here, that this view has affinities with some forms of scientific ANTI-REALISM (pp. 298–300).

Constructionism involves the same assumption as Russell made: that because historical statements are about a past which we can no longer perceive, there is something problematic about its ontological status. But this is a very doubtful assumption. Most kinds of knowledge, both everyday and scientific, are about what is currently unobservable. Our memories, for example, are about what we cannot now perceive. So, too, are our beliefs about the speed of light or the existence of neutrons. Were it the case, therefore, that a statement about something that is unobservable cannot be about an independent reality, the range of statements about what we take to be real entities would need to be replaced by a range of statements about constructed entities. To take a simple case, one person's reason for claiming to know the colour of Queen Elizabeth II's coronation dress may be that he remembers having seen it on Coronation Day, while another's may be that she has consulted the order books of the royal dress makers – she has, that is, undertaken some simple historical research. If the constructionist account is correct, the two claims cannot be about the same dress, for each will be about a dress that exists only in relation to the mode in which our knowledge of it is constructed. Thus there will be two dresses, one existing as part of an 'historical' past and the other as part of a 'memorial' past, rather than, as we would normally think, one dress which we can know about in either of two different ways. This conclusion, moreover, will apply to the constituents of all of our different kinds of knowledge that go beyond simple reports of what is present to perception. Thus the book in the past that I remember will differ not only from that whose history I reconstruct but from that whose past physical or chemical properties can be analysed in terms of theories proper to chemistry or physics. But in this case we shall be unable to use our knowledge, say, of the chemical properties of some past object to help us in our historical thinking about that object, perhaps by helping us to date it, since the object whose past chemical properties we construct will be a different object from that whose historical existence we construct. Thus there would be a number of different objects 'existing' in a number of different realities, each relative to a particular mode of research, rather than, as the realist believes, objects existing in one and the same reality, whose different properties can be known by different kinds of research.

This thesis certainly conflicts with our everyday view of the real world. But this is perhaps not too important since, while philosophy should not ignore everyday belief, it cannot be wholly constrained by it. More importantly, it conflicts with the requirement that we must think of all knowledge as being about one single reality because, unless we do so, we shall be unable to relate the products of our different disciplines to one another. Constructionism, and the strong verificationism upon which it depends, must be rejected because it leads to results that conflict with this requirement.

These points do not, however, rule out historical knowledge being reached by the use of argument in the way in which the constructionists suggest. They show only that there is no reason to believe that the arguments result in statements about some peculiarly 'historical' past rather than about a real past which we can know in a variety of different ways. How they do this has been shown in an account that emphasizes the need for historical evidence to be described in past-entailing terms in the way indicated above (Gorman, 1982, pp. 56–68). When the historian has carried out his research correctly and checked for authenticity, he will be in possession of an evidential statement such as 'Here, before us . . . is a letter written by Gladstone', the truth of which both entails and requires that Gladstone wrote the letter. Thus there is a relationship of mutual entailment between past-referring *evidential* statements and *historical* statements, in virtue of which we can truly assert the latter on the strength of the former.

But while this shows how evidential statements, *if true*, entail true historical statements about a real past, it leaves room for a third and final sceptical doubt. For in order to arrive at an evidential statement such as that about Gladstone's letter, we need both to employ a theory of interpretation and to be satisfied that it is the correct one. Because the example given is in English, this is a point that is often overlooked by English speakers, where we just assume that we are using the correct language. But the fact that a theory of interpretation is employed becomes evident if we consider the case where the evidential statement is in some language which we do not understand. Then we need to turn to dictionaries and grammar books to enable us to translate the language of the document. This, of course, is rarely difficult, although it can become so in practice when historians are dealing with documents in old and relatively unknown languages. But it illustrates the fact that a theory of interpretation is always in use, even if not explicitly.

The sceptical doubt that now arises, however, concerns the justification of the theory of interpretation that is employed. For recent work in the PHILOSOPHY OF LANGUAGE (chapter 3) has shown that there is always the possibility of more theories of interpretation than any which we employ. It follows that we cannot, especially when dealing with the past, simply rest content with the belief that we are employing the correct theory of interpretation, the one enabling us to justify the claim that we are in possession of *true* past-entailing statements. We require some reason to support this belief. Thus, to revert to the example of Gladstone's letter, it is a fact that we have a theory of interpretation under which the word 'Gladstone' is taken to be the name of a particular historical individual. Moreover, our use of 'Gladstone' is linked to the use of many other similarly functioning names, such as 'Disraeli' and 'Queen Victoria'. If we are wrong in our interpretation of the word 'Gladstone', we shall be wrong also about all these connected names. The doubt is not therefore simply about our right to interpret a single name in a certain way but about our right to rely upon the whole theory governing the interpretation of that and many other names.

This doubt about justifying any theory of interpretation we employ provides a threat not only to our knowledge of the past but to a considerable amount of our knowledge of the present, since our use of past-entailing terms means that much of what we take to be knowledge of the present involves truths about the past. We think of ourselves, for example, as having personal and communal histories that interlink in innumerable ways. Indeed, such beliefs comprise an important component in our conception of personal identity. Thus if it were not true, say, that there was a 1914–18 war, all that part of people's personal histories which involve reference to the war would be false. In so far, therefore, as much knowledge of the present involves claims about the past, the sceptical threat to historical knowledge also threatens much of our knowledge of the present.

One possible response to this doubt is to point to the fact that our present procedure leads to coherence in our claims about the past. Claims about Gladstone are linked to claims about Disraeli, the Irish problem and so on. But an appeal to coherence alone is inadequate to justify a theory of interpretation.

For there are many other possible theories of interpretation which could lead to equally coherent sets of claims which are incompatible with those that we now accept.

A Framework of Basic Historical Facts

Another way of countering the doubt concerning justification for our theory of interpretation would be by supporting the theory by linking it to some knowledge of the past reached by a different route. If it could be shown, for example, that, prior to examination of the evidence, the historian already knows that Gladstone existed, we could use that knowledge to justify his or her use of a theory of interpretation in which the word 'Gladstone' is the name of that historical individual. The problem then would be not how to defend the theory of interpretation that allows the historian to conclude that an individual called Gladstone existed and wrote the letter in front of him or her, but the much simpler problem of deciding whether the historian can show that the letter was written by the Gladstone of whose existence he or she already knows or whether it was written, perhaps forged, by some other person.

But how is it possible to support this refutation which, at the moment, amounts to little more than asserting what the sceptic is questioning: that we know *some* things at least about what happened in the past? What we need here is an account of how, *independently of argument from evidence under a theory of inter-pretation*, we can have some such knowledge. Since others have not written on this subject, I must here fall back upon my own suggestion that some of our knowledge of the past has actually come from the past – in other words, that it is transmitted within societies with appropriate institutional mechanisms, from the past to the present, and that, in virtue of existing in such a society, the historian is in possession of knowledge of a framework of basic facts with which to support his or her theory of interpretation (Pompa, 1993). Thus, instead of arguing from evidence under a theory of interpretation to, say, Gladstone's existence, the historian takes his or her inherited knowledge of Gladstone's existence as justification for a theory of interpretation in which that existence is presupposed. On this view, any attempt to interpret the evidence in such a way as to throw doubt upon Gladstone's existence would be disallowed and any theory of interpretation that seems to allow such doubt would be rejected as unjustified. The suggestion, therefore, is that our theory of interpretation is justified because it presupposes some historically acquired knowledge of the past. The historian is then entitled to use it to discover new facts about the past that are not part of our inherited knowledge.

It should be noted, however, that this suggestion conflicts with the widely held FALLIBILIST (pp. 40–1) theory of knowledge, according to which no belief is in principle immune from the possibility of revision, including therefore the most central of our present historical beliefs, such as that there was a Crimean War. But the reply to the fallibilist must be that although it is a LOGICAL POSSIBILITY that the Crimean War never occurred, it is not an *epistemological* possibility. For we can allow that it is an epistemological possibility only if we can envisage some way in which some future historian could try to justify the claim that the war never occurred without accepting the sort of theory just outlined. But if he is unable to do this, he will be open to sceptical doubt about his or her theory of interpretation and therefore about his or her claims to knowledge about the past.

2 Explanation and Understanding

The discussion so far lends support to the belief that historians can produce knowledge of what actually happened in the past. But a large part of their work is concerned with explaining what happened. The analysis of the proper way in which to do this has been the source of a major controversy involving two opposing viewpoints: that they should offer 'scientific' explanations or that they should focus upon a humanistic form of understanding.

The view that explanations in history either are or should be of the same form as those in the natural sciences was advanced in a particularly strong way by Carl Hempel (b. 1905) who, building upon the work of Karl Popper (1902–94) in the PHILOSOPHY OF SCIENCE (chapter 9) advanced a general thesis (Hempel, 1959) about what it is for something to be an explanation. The thesis, subsequently known as the COVERING LAW MODEL or the deductive-nomological theory, involves two points: that to explain an event is to show it to be predictable; and that to be shown to be predictable, the event must be shown to be subsumable under some set of causal laws. Thus, although historians normally explain the occurrence of particular events, such as the 1914–18 war, in terms of a combination of particular causes – such as the development of national rivalries for political supremacy in Europe in the nineteenth century or the common need for new sources of raw materials and new markets to maintain the industrialization of western Europe – this can be an explanation only if the particular causes cited are instances of a causal law or laws to the effect that whenever there is a build up of national rivalries for political supremacy and a common need for new sources of raw materials and new markets, a war breaks out. Hempel realized that the sorts of generalizations mentioned in this example were not laws in the sense that they held without exception and, indeed, that properly supported causal laws were rarely, if ever, used by historians. For this reason he referred to the explanations that historians actually give as 'explanation sketches', claiming that they offered more or less vague indications of the relevant laws and pointed the way for the further empirical research necessary to establish them as required in a fully supported explanation. On this account, therefore, historical explanations are incomplete explanations of the same form as those to be found in the physical sciences.

A strength of the covering law model is that it satisfies one feature that one would expect of any explanation, namely, that it should explain why one event occurred rather than some other (Donagan, 1966). It does this because, by subsuming an event under causal laws, it shows that the event *had* to occur. This means, however, that the kind of explanation it offers is deterministic and this, as we shall see, has been the main underlying reason for the strongest objections to it.

Objections to the theory divide into two kinds. First there are those that emphasize that historical explanations do not, as a matter of fact, conform to it. There have been many objections of this sort (White, 1965, pp. 14–104, offers a reformulation of the theory; see also Donagan, 1966, pp. 142–6), but these cannot be conclusive. If the theory claims that this is the form that any fully supported explanation *must* take, objections that historical explanations do not take this form can be met by the reply that historians are failing to offer fully supported explanations. For this reason, I shall concentrate on objections of the second kind, which claim that the subject matter of history is such that the theory is wrong in principle.

The first of these objections, which has weighed particularly strongly with historians, is that the theory fails to recognize the uniqueness of the events and individuals featuring in history (Oakeshott, 1933, p. 154). There was, and can be, only one 1914–18 war. Hence, if historians succeed in explaining what caused this unique event, it cannot be by conforming to the requirements of the covering law model since the laws in question hold between different *kinds* of events rather than unique events. But the claim to uniqueness must be treated with care, for much depends upon the sort of uniqueness in question. The covering law model does not deny, for example, that the *events* that it offers to explain, such as the occurrence of the 1914–18 war, are unique. It must insist, of course, that these events, although unique, are describable in general terms, in order to be subsumable under laws about kinds of things. But it can hardly be denied that although events are unique in being the particular events that they are, they must also be describable in general terms, for this is necessary in order for us to be able to say anything at all about them. The 1914–18 war was a unique event, but to talk about it we must bring it under the general term 'war', a term that can be applied to many other unique events. Hence the mere appeal to the uniqueness of historical events is an insufficient objection to the covering law model.

What historians sometimes mean, however, when they appeal to uniqueness, is the way in which the occurrence of events depends upon the activities of unique individuals *about whose behaviour there can be no laws*. If there can be no laws about the behaviour of individuals, the explanation of any events that their behaviour affects cannot involve subsumption under general laws. Nevertheless, while some covering law theorists have accepted that different individuals are unique, they have rejected the claim that this precludes the application of the model, on the grounds that there can be laws about unique individuals. We can explain what a particular individual does, for example, by asserting that he or she always acts like that, which involves referring to his or her dispositions (White, 1965, pp. 47–53). There is, however, an important difference between causal laws and the dispositions of individuals to act in certain ways. For causal laws *necessitate* events and hence will support deductive predictions about them. The dispositions of individuals, on the other hand, are simply patterns of behaviour that are characteristic of them; explanations and predictions based on knowledge of them lack the rigorous character that the covering law model requires. One can explain somebody's acting in a certain way by reference to his or her general tendency to do so, but that does not mean that he or she may not upon occasion act in an entirely different way in the same sort of situation: a fact that we acknowledge when we say that what he or she did was out of character. We cannot both admit this possibility and maintain that explanation in terms of dispositions carries the same implications of law-governed predictability as is required by the covering law model.

The issue of individuality is given increased importance by the fact that historians are not usually concerned with the individual as such but with the individual in particular historical roles, such as that of the King or Queen of England. We can be interested in Elizabeth Tudor as the individual she was but this is largely to understand her behaviour as Queen Elizabeth I of England, which involves her acting in a certain role or set of roles, and how, as the unique individual she was, she affected the character of the roles that she occupied. This raises the issue of ROLE THEORY (p. 372). Very roughly, we may note that the occupancy of a role involves the possession of powers and responsibilities that range from those that are fairly specific, even legally defined, to others that are relatively indeterminate – and even in areas of legal definition there is considerable flexibility in the ways in which the individual may properly behave in the role. As a result, the behaviour of the individuals who occupy the roles can have as much effect on the nature of the roles as the requirements of their role upon their behaviour. Tracing this interplay is among the most important ways in which historians seek to explain the historical development of roles. Thus, there has been ongoing discussion as to how far changes in the respective powers of Parliament and Monarchy in sixteenth-century England were due to Elizabeth's conduct in her role. This does not mean that these changes may not have been affected also by religious, social and economic changes but, since these further changes also involve reference to individuals in their roles, the relationship between individual and role still remains at the centre of the discussion. Given its flexibility, it seems that there could be no laws able to explain either this relationship or the historical development of roles to which it has contributed (Berlin, 1966, pp. 23–4). Thus the covering law model is in principle inapplicable here.

These difficulties suggest that the failure of the covering law model is due to an incorrect assimilation of explanation in history to explanation in the natural sciences. An alternative viewpoint, which stresses the primacy of understanding over explanation, has built upon the work of R. G. Collingwood (1889–1943), who distinguished between the subject matter of science, which is the physical world, and that of history, which is the world of human activity. Accordingly, he argued, historical explanations differ from scientific explanation because human activity is always an expression of thought, which it is the historian's task to understand. 'When an historian asks "Why did Brutus stab Caesar?" he means "What did Brutus think, which made him decide to stab Caesar?" ' (Collingwood, 1993, pp. 213–15). Thus we explain the agent's action by establishing his or her reason for deciding to do what he or she did. The mistake of thinking that historical explanations are the same in kind as those in the natural sciences stems from a failure to recognize this distinction in subject matter.

Rational Reconstruction

Collingwood's claims have been very influential in the development of an alternative model of historical explanation, involving what is often called a RATIONAL RECONSTRUCTION (p. 370). The central idea here is that the historian's principal task is to understand human ACTION (pp. 369–72) in a specifically human way, which he or she does by showing some event to be an INTENTIONAL ACT (p. 369) undertaken in accordance with beliefs that rendered it sensible to the agent in question (Dray, 1957, 1980, 1993; Martin, 1977). The action is explained when we understand why the agent decided to act in that way. This, however, is only a part of the explanation since, as Collingwood insisted, historians are interested not only in why people acted in certain ways but also in the success or failure of their actions. Hence, once the agent's reasons and beliefs are established, they must undergo further critical examination, since the success or failure of actions often depends upon the merits or defects of the beliefs and reasons behind them. Thus, it may be that although the agent's actions made good sense from his or her point of view, some of the relevant beliefs were false, as were the beliefs the Romans held about Hannibal's position at the Battle of Trasimeno. Once, however, the historian has established what the Romans believed and that those beliefs were false, he or she can use this knowledge to explain their defeat.

If historians attempt to understand actions in terms of rational reconstruction, the explanation will be true only if they can establish what the agent's reason for acting really was. It has been argued, however, that to do this they must establish the additional facts that the agent was rational and that, in the agent's kind of situation, rational agents invariably do the kind of thing which he or she did. The need for a covering law is thus re-introduced, this time relating the beliefs of rational agents in certain kinds of situations to certain kinds of actions (Hempel, 1974, pp. 98–105). This is a useful objection to consider, for it highlights the difference between the deterministic assumptions of the covering law model and the voluntarist assumptions of the rational reconstruction model. The objection assumes that an appeal to an agent's rationality will suffice only if his or her behaviour was an instance of some sort of *causal law* governing the behaviour of rational agents. But this is what the rational reconstruction model denies. According to the latter, when we say that an agent was rational we are saying that his or her action was caused by a decision based upon an appraisal of his or her situation undertaken in the light of, *but not caused by*, his or her knowledge of certain standards of appropriateness. When we act we must have some idea of what it is appropriate to do to achieve our ends. But standards are not laws. They are simply beliefs about the sorts of things one ought to do, either for their own sake, as in the case of moral standards, or in order to achieve certain ends, and there can be many different beliefs of both kinds. The fact that we make use of standards when considering what to do does not *necessitate* that some particular action be done on a particular occasion – hence the fact that an agent's action is a consequence of a decision taken in the light of standards does not mean that it was caused or necessitated by them.

The crucial weakness in the covering law model to which this points is thus not the assumption that the historian can explain the occurrence of something only by showing why that action occurred rather than some other action; rather, the weakness is the further assumption that he or she can do this only by showing that that action *had* to occur. But this is a requirement that neither can nor needs to be met. To show why one action occurred rather than another, it is sufficient to show why that action rather than the other *in fact* occurred and to do this the historian need only show why, from among the historically available options (the options available to a given individual in a specific historical society), one course of action seemed preferable to the others.

The importance of standards in this conception, however, gives rise to a problem which does not beset the covering law theorist. For standards vary in different historical societies. The Greeks, for example, consulted the oracles for advice in certain situations. Because we do not ourselves normally consult oracles (although some people do), we may wonder whether the Greek standard of rationality was the same as ours and, if it was not, whether we can understand rational reconstructions of Greek actions in the way in which we can understand those of our contemporaries. This difficulty has been exacerbated, moreover, by the claim that standards are peculiar to, and part of, the lived experience of specific societies. We understand the standards of our own society because they are rules which we are *taught* how to follow by living in our society. But since we cannot share the lived experience of past societies and be taught their rules of conduct, we can have no way of understanding them. Even if we manage to make statements about them, they will not come out as standards the rationality of which we can grasp. This position, sometimes called historicism, relativizes the notion of rationality to particular historical societies and in doing so challenges our right to claim to understand why people in those societies acted as they did.

One might try to counter this difficulty by pointing out that, despite it, historians do succeed in making the activities of past societies intelligible to us. But this might seem to beg the question, which concerns how far we *really* understand the kind of rationality in dispute. A more effective response is to question whether *historical* societies have the self-contained character suggested. For to talk of an historical society is often just a way of talking about earlier phases of the career of some present society. It is sometimes thought that historicism is provided some support by the difficulties that anthropologists encounter when trying to grasp the rules which can make sense of the practices of primitive societies. But this is an unhelpful parallel for, while anthropologists often start with no knowledge whatsoever of the language of the societies they study, this is not so in the historical case. As argued in the previous section, the historian is not completely alien to the past which he or she seeks to understand, for the society in which an historian finds himself or herself is a product of that past. It carries within it many social and linguistic practices, some of which are developments, and others remnants, of earlier practices. If present standards have arisen from earlier ones, there seems no reason in principle preventing the historian from working backwards to their earlier stages. If this is so, we can refute this version of an historicist argument by appealing to the fact that we do not find understanding all standards in earlier parts of history as impossible as the objection suggests. Certainly there seems to be no more difficulty in understanding the Greeks' recourse to the Delphic Oracle than a contemporary non-believer might find in understanding a believer's recourse to prayer. It could be argued, of course, that non-believers have *no understanding at all* of religious practice. But this would limit the concept of understanding to what we believe and that is far too severe a standard. We can, surely, understand early cosmological theories even if we do not believe them. Moreover, the attempt to limit what we can understand to what we believe would have sceptical implications for much shared everyday understanding that we take to be quite unproblematic. But investigation of this possibility is beyond the scope of this chapter.

The scope of rational reconstruction extends beyond action in the strict sense to include what has been made – including the different political and economic institutions, technologies and artistic creations of the past – by enabling us to understand the point of these creations and, through this, to understand why they have changed. In histories of art, for example, past influences play a very important part, as in the case of the effect which the re-discovery of classical architecture and sculpture had upon Renaissance art and architecture. But rational reconstructions are required here precisely because the influence of the re-discovery of the classical world lay in the way the Renaissance artists and architects assimilated classical thought into their own and through that saw the expanded range of possibilities which they could incorporate into their aims.

Nevertheless, rational reconstructions are not the only kind of explanations to be found in history. Collingwood claimed that all historical explanation should be in terms of the agent's thought, but this was certainly an overstatement. The political supremacy of Athens depended upon a fleet of very expensive triremes, a fleet which Athens could not have built without the discovery of new sources of silver. Even if an explanation of Athenian success involves establishing the reasons why the city took the unusual decision to invest this wealth in building the triremes, the explanation cannot omit this discovery, without which Athens could not even have considered the decision. Humans live in a natural environment and many of their practices derive from trying to cope with this environment. Reference to it can therefore never be wholly omitted. But to recognize this is not to re-admit the covering law model. It is simply to accept that while historians are primarily concerned with understanding historical actions, they often need to refer to the natural world to achieve this.

It must be mentioned, however, that many philosophers do not accept that a person's reason for doing something can be a cause of doing it. They argue that an action is an event, albeit of a special kind, and events can be brought about only by other events. This is an issue much debated in the PHILOSOPHY OF MIND (chapter 5). Here, however, we need note only that, even if this were correct, it would give no support to the covering law theory as we have been considering it. For if reasons can be causes only if they are in some sense *physical* events, they will need to be stripped of the descriptions under which they are cited as reasons, including, for example, 'ambitious for literary fame' or 'felt maltreated', whereas the covering law theory requires that there be laws about the behaviour of agents under these descriptions, including laws about would-be literati or maltreated subjects.

3 Objectivity and Value

The previous sections support the claim that historians are primarily concerned with what is of interest in the past from a human point of view. In this case, however, they must also be concerned with human values. This raises no problem for the rational reconstruction model itself, provided that the historicist difficulty can be overcome, since many actions are undertaken in the light of an agent's values. It has been argued, however, that the historian's own value judgements must affect his or her account in a number of ways and it is possible that this may affect the claim that historians can give true accounts of what really happened.

Past and Present Viewpoints

We may see one way in which the issue concerning value judgements arises by asking whose point of view the historian is interested in recapturing. If the historian were *confined* to seeing things in terms of rational reconstructions it would seem that it must be the point of view of historical agents, since it is their view of their situation that the reconstruction is concerned to elucidate. But historians do not confine their accounts in this way and often they explain things in their historical context by reference to factors unknown and even unknowable within that society.

Whether they should do this has been a source of controversy, reflecting different views about the value of studying history. One view (Lovejoy, 1959) is that its most important value lies in its capacity to enable us to grasp the possibilities of other ways of living and, hence, of other sets of values than our own. This suggests that the historian should be primarily concerned with the past in its own terms and as a contrast to the present. Others, however, have claimed that its value lies in its capacity to enable us to understand certain aspects of the present. But this means that our concern will be with those parts that link up with current interests. It has sometimes been held that these two viewpoints are incompatible although historians usually interweave them both. They frequently make claims about the truth that conflict with what was believed at the time, often because their knowledge of what subsequently occurred enables them to show that the agent's views were mistaken. More importantly, however, they often describe and give significance to things in ways which, because they require hindsight, were unavailable to past agents.

The role of hindsight can most easily be shown by attending to a particular kind of sentence which historians use, now known as a 'narrative sentence' (Danto, 1965, p. 143ff.). A narrative sentence is one in which an event or person is described in the light of a connection with something that occurred later. Its truth can therefore be known only by someone who knows the truth about the later event and not by anyone at the time of the earlier event. The earlier event is thus seen as part of a temporal whole. To use one of Danto's own examples, an historian may assert that when Petrarch climbed Mount Ventoux he opened the Renaissance, to emphasize Petrarch's significance in the set of events that constitute the Renaissance. The truth of such an assertion could not have been known by anybody who witnessed Petrarch's ascent since he or she could not know the future. Nevertheless, the description is not incompatible with something which the eye-witness could have known, namely, Petrarch's ascent of Mount Ventoux. All that is happening, therefore, is that the same event is being described from two different temporal perspectives and in the light of its connection with different events. Since the statements are compatible, however, it is not the case that if statements which reflect one reason for studying the past are true, those reflecting the other must be false. Thus these different views of the value of studying the past give rise to no problems about the objectivity of the accounts offered.

There are, however, two other ways in which it has been claimed that value judgements have a determining influence upon how the historian construes the past, and these may have consequences for the objectivity of the accounts offered. To see why this is so, it is necessary to allude briefly to the current debate about the cognitive or non-cognitive status of VALUE JUDGEMENTS (pp. 4–6). Cognitivists hold that value judgements are either true or false. If this is so, and if historical accounts presuppose such judgements, then the truth or falsity of historical accounts will depend upon that of the particular judgements made. Non-cognitivists, however, claim that value judgements are expressions of attitude or emotion and, as such, that they have no truth values. If this is so and if historical accounts presuppose them, they will turn out to be accounts expressive of certain attitudes towards the past but not accounts which can be said to be true or false. Thus, although the individual statements and explanations they contain can still be true, the account as a whole cannot be true. There remains the further possibility, however, that historical accounts do not presuppose value judgements, in which case their objectivity will not be affected by them.

The first argument to be considered concerns the question whether, since historians cannot include everything in their accounts, they must use value judgements in their selection of what to include. Many reasons have been offered to show that they must but here I can consider only one: that the historian must decide which events were more important than others and, since there are no objective criteria of importance, this requires historians to make their own value judgements about them (Dray, 1993, pp. 42–6). Whether their accounts are true will then depend, at least in part, upon whether their judgements of importance are true.

Attempts to meet this claim by arguing that there are objective criteria of importance have not been generally accepted. The most plausible suggestion is that historians should choose those events that have the widest range of causal consequences. But since not all the causal consequences of an event can be taken into account – indeed, it is not clear how they can even be calculated –

it seems that only the most important should be taken into account. In this case, however, further judgements of importance will be required. It has been noted also that this criterion has little relevance to histories which describe and interpret the main characteristics of an age, such as G. M. Young's *Victorian England: Portrait of an Age*. 'What', it has been asked, 'would we think of a volume length "portrait" of Victorian England that ignored the working class movement?' Such an omission would need justification and the only one available seems to be that what was included was more important than what was excluded (Dray, 1993, p. 42).

It is not clear, however, that this argument must lead to the conclusion that the historian cannot avoid making *his or her own* value judgement. To see this, it is worth considering two possible objectivist responses, relating to the two different reasons for studying history mentioned above. If the portrait is meant to be a portrait of a people as they saw themselves to be – and this is what Young claims in his Introduction – the historian will not get very far in his or her research without making the *empirical* discovery that the state and activities and condition of the working class were widely perceived as a matter of importance by very large parts of the population, including workers, factory owners, politicians, philanthropists and many others. It is true that the historian needs to know which sources he or she should consult to learn this, but this is precisely what a well-trained historian is taught to know. An historian starting research with the hypothesis that the working class was not a cause of concern to the Victorians would surely need to abandon this if the sources indicated that it was wrong. This implies that the sources have, in a certain sense, a capacity to speak to the historian. They were not, of course, produced to speak to historians but they were produced to speak to somebody, and it hardly requires a value judgement to hear what they were saying, what worries they were expressing or, if many are about the same thing, to conclude that that was a matter of widespread concern. The historian may, therefore, need to abandon an initial hypothesis in view of what the sources reveal and, if this is so, there is no reason to believe that doing so involves making a value judgement. It is true, of course, that there may be areas of life where there was no such consensus of importance, but if this is so, it is surely an historian's duty to report this fact.

But, as noted above, historians often write from the point of view of the bearing of the past upon present interests and for an historian of this sort the fact that the Victorians thought the development of the working class was important would not provide a criterion for including it in an account of Victorian England. But although this is true, an alternative objective criterion for the inclusion of the development of the working class in this sort of account can be found in the importance that the historian can show that development had for certain later changes. Would it, one might ask, have been so misleading for an historian of this sort to have omitted an account of the development of the working class in favour of something else had that development not come to transform almost the whole subsequent structure of British social, economic, political and constitutional life? What must be remembered here is that historical reality is a process of ongoing but continuous change and that, as the worlds in which historians find themselves differ, different aspects of the past become relevant to an understanding of the present. On this view, what determines an historian's selection of material is not what he or she personally holds important, but what that historian can find to explain the things involved in a society's perception of itself. The reason why a contemporary historian of this kind would give more prominence to an account of the working class than, say, an historian in the late nineteenth century must surely be that the working class now affects so many more aspects of the structure of our present world, and is so much a part of what we take that world to be, that a portrait of the period in which it first arose that omitted that development would no longer be acceptable.

This is a consequentialist but not a narrowly causal criterion. It could be argued, however, that, since it appeals to what we think important about the present, all that it does is make judgements of importance about the past consequent upon others about the present. But this seems implausible. For it is surely an objective fact that the working class now occupies a certain place in the economy, that it has institutions which claim to speak for it and to protect its interests, and that this is part of our shared understanding of our present world. Accordingly, historians must include in their accounts whatever they can find to explain this fact if their intention is to explain the present in terms of the past. Moreover, in removing the basis of selection from the individual historian's own judgement of importance to the self-perception of the society for which the historian writes, this criterion provides a shared basis on the strength of which individual historians can reasonably ask one another to justify their selection of some things in preference to others.

The second objection that raises questions about the relation between value and objectivity is the argument from characterization. The claim here is that before deciding that a certain item is sufficiently important to be included in an account, in the case of certain kinds of history at least, the historian must first decide whether the item should be characterized in such as way as to make it the right kind of candidate for inclusion and that such a decision again requires a value judgement by the historian. The sorts of histories which most obviously seem to raise this difficulty are histories of art and religion, where it must be decided whether a certain work is genuinely a work of art or a certain action genuinely religious before deciding whether to include it in the relevant history. But the case can, it has been argued, be extended also to political history where it can be asked whether the actions of the IRA or the PLO are acts of terrorism or acts of war. The judgements made will decide the kinds of history for which they are candidates for inclusion (Dray, 1980, p. 45, and 1993, pp. 49–51).

In considering this view it is not necessary to deny that events find their way into their relevant histories only as characterized or under certain descriptions. The question at issue is solely the basis of the characterization. The first point to be noted is that we would lose our capacity to talk about anything, past or present, were there not a widespread basis of shared characterizations. The IRA, for example, may describe its actions as executions rather than murders, but this claim cannot be taken as literally true in the absence of the institutional legal and judicial procedures that must operate before something can be an execution. In describing its acts as executions rather than murders the IRA may be expressing its rejection of the legitimacy of British rule in Ulster, but that is not sufficient to turn murders into executions unless the acts issue from alternative legal and judicial processes, the legitimacy of which is established. This example, of course, raises the question of political legitimacy, which is too large to be discussed here. Nevertheless, it remains the case that we must have a shared basis of characterization, and hence shared criteria of characterization, before we can discuss anything. This does not eliminate the existence of borderline cases, but it does mean that the majority of cases must be unarguable and, indeed, that it is by reference to them that we can identify and discuss borderline cases.

It must be noted, however, that criteria are normally implicit and often cannot be made explicit without reference to objects that exemplify them. This is evident when we turn to histories, even of those areas which seem most appropriate for the characterization argument. For here it is noticeable that the historical process itself has produced the characterization as works of art or as religions of the things that constitute the subject matter of most histories of art or religion. But these cannot simply be disregarded in favour of new characterizations which an historian might wish to propose. It would surely be very odd if an historian who was also a devout Christian, were to exclude the rituals at Delphi as a candidate for inclusion in a history of religion simply because they involved no beliefs which accorded with those of orthodox Christianity or none which he or she personally was prepared to evaluate as 'genuinely' religious. The claim that they should be excluded on these grounds cannot be correct since, by parity of argument, an historian belonging to any other faith would be entitled to write a history of religion for which Christianity is not a candidate. Indeed, on this line of reasoning, there would be nothing to block the claim that one religion was the only appropriate candidate for a history of all religion. It would be equally unacceptable, for the same reasons, if an historian of Italian art were to exclude the works of Michelangelo as candidates for his or her account. Surely such cases raise questions about the claim that a history of art or religion has been produced rather than questions about the entitlement of the works and institutions to be characterized as appropriate candidates for inclusion in these histories. Thus, there is what might be called a 'verdict of history' but this is not a verdict that historians have reached; instead it is one that has arisen through the internal historical development of their subject matter. This is not to deny that criteria may change, but, if they do, this can only be as a consequence of major new developments in their subject matter and not of historians' value judgements.

As with the argument from selection, it might be replied that this does not show that value judgements have no part to play in the characterization of historical phenomena, since it merely replaces the part played by the historian's value judgement by shared characterizations which have arisen through past value judgements. But if the argument is correct, there is a significant difference between the two positions, for it means that the historian must respect the state that the historical development of the subject matter has reached, with all the characterization of material that that involves, and cannot be thought of as being in a position to reconstruct it *ab initio*, as it were, according to his or her own values.

As noted above, borderline cases will inevitably remain, but there is no harm in this provided that they are so recognized. An historian is unlikely to command much support, however, in attempts to make these central and to re-arrange all other items of characterization accordingly. It is difficult to imagine what sort of history might be produced by an historian who accepted an IRA killing as a central case of an execution and tried to write a history of politics, with attendant revisions of the notion of political authority, on such an assumption. It is even more difficult to believe that such a history, if written, would be accepted as a true account of the past.

4 Narrative and Realism

Historians have traditionally presented the results of their research in the form of a narrative. That this is as it ought to be has been challenged by the development of new schools of historians. These include, for example, econometric historians who use quantitative economic techniques to establish 'objective' accounts of the causes of social and political change or the French *annaliste school*, which gives preference also to quantitative techniques and treats individuals and events as relatively superficial consequences of deeper underlying structures and processes, the existence of which can be discerned only over different lengths of time. Nevertheless, despite calls for further developments of these kinds of history, narratives have remained the most characteristic way of presenting historical knowledge and there has been a strong debate about their epistemological status and their ontological implications.

The basic issue arises from claims about the nature of narrative itself. Narratives must have some form in virtue of which we can follow what they say and various analyses of their typical form have been proposed (Gallie, 1964; White, 1965; Danto, 1965; White, 1973). In all of these analyses it is agreed that, although a narrative presupposes a chronological sequence of events, it goes beyond this in various ways, for instance, by connecting different events and actions through their necessary conditions (Gallie, 1964) or by explaining later aspects of the object of enquiry in terms of earlier causes (White, 1965). But, drawing upon modern literary theory, two challenging claims have been made about narratives in general: firstly, that narratives are literary artefacts and, as such, constructions of the literary imagination; secondly, that there are many different forms that a narrative might take and nothing to determine that an author, whether historian or novelist, should adopt one rather than another. Thus, there is indeterminacy at the level of narrative construction. Applying these considerations to historical narratives, it has been claimed that we cannot think of the past as a determinate reality of which a narrative *as a whole* is true for there is no one right way of composing an historical narrative about the past and, hence, of claiming that through it we have captured the meaning of the past. Rather, there are a number of different, irreconcilable ways of creating narratives about the past and, through them, of *imposing* upon it a variety of meanings that it does not possess of itself. Since meaning is not an objective feature of the past, it cannot be claimed that the historical narratives, which project meaning upon it, are expressions of objective truth (White, 1973, pp. 1–42; Mink, 1978). To mention one point in illustration of this view, it is a necessary feature of a story that it should have a beginning, middle and end. But reality has no beginnings, middles and ends. Hence, when we think about the past in terms of beginnings, middles and ends, as narratives invite us to do, we are imposing upon it a structure which it does not itself possess. One must note, however, that the claim allows that some things in the narrative can be true, such as the facts that it cites or the explanations that it offers. For were this not possible, the distinction between fact and fiction would be destroyed. But the anti-realist's intention is not to challenge this distinction. It is, rather, to preserve the historian's right to present us with a variety of different but incompatible ways of thinking about the past. It is only the way in which the narrative organizes these into a coherent whole, it is claimed, which cannot express a further truth about real connections in the past. Thus, to think, as the realist does, that the narrative *as a whole* asserts something that is true of the past, in the way in which some of its constituent parts do, is a mistake. It is the mistake, as it has been put, of thinking of the past as 'an untold story waiting to be told' (Mink, 1978).

The controversy is therefore about whether, in constructing a narrative about the past, the historian must inevitably falsify it. Although this claim has been applied only to narrative histories, it has implications for other forms of history, many of which have narrative elements in them. An interpretative history such as Young's *Victorian England* contains many passages of narrative. Indeed, it is difficult to see how any form of history which involves tracing and explaining at least some developments can fail to contain narrative elements. Moreover, although the claim has not been extended to other forms of history such as econometric history, it would seem that, in so far as all kinds of historical accounts require some form of literary expression, objections of the same kind must apply to them.

Before discussing this position, one other reason that has been advanced for it should be mentioned, namely that a narrative contains much that involves hindsight. This, as we saw earlier, is true. Thus, an historian can talk, retrospectively, of 'hopes unfulfilled, plans miscarried, battles decisive and ideas seminal'. But, it is claimed, these are aspects of stories and not of life, for in life there are only 'hopes, plans, battles and ideas' (Mink, 1970). Hence, by using hindsight, the historian falsifies the past. But this argument cannot be correct for, although it is true that we can only *know* certain things at certain times, there is no reason why we should take what we know only at certain times, for instance, while the event is occurring, as the sole way of characterizing reality. For, as we saw when discussing narrative sentences, the descriptions that historians offer retrospectively are not incompatible with those that can be given at the time of the event. There can only be a 'hope unfulfilled' if there was a 'hope' in the first place. But the fact that the former presupposes the latter is not a reason for believing that only the latter can be true. Nor can the role of retrospective descriptions be denied by confining the concept of reality to life as we experience it, for it is part of life as we experience it that we see our situation, at any particular moment, in terms of fulfilled or unfulfilled hopes, successful or unsuccessful plans and so on, and abandon or revise our further hopes and plans in the light of this knowledge. Thus, it is false that, as this objection asserts, retrospectivity is a feature of narratives but not of life.

Given the strongly anti-realist implications of these claims about narratives, it is hardly surprising that there has been a strong realist reaction against them. One of these builds upon the point just made: that, contrary to what the anti-realists assert, we both live out narratives in our own lives and understand our lives in terms of those narratives. Hence, it is appropriate to understand the lives of others in the same way (MacIntyre, 1984, p. 197ff). But while this is an adequate response to anti-realist objections to retrospectivity, it cannot be an adequate response to the more fundamental claims about the relation of narratives to reality. For a narrative history is not merely an account of the way in which individuals have lived out their lives. The focus may, as we saw earlier, be upon the human past, but the latter requires social, economic and natural contexts, many of which will impinge upon individuals in ways unknown to them. The historian will, of course, draw upon these in giving a narrative account, but in doing so he or she is going well beyond the sort of understanding which we have when we try to understand ourselves in narrative terms. Historical reality does not consist solely of human agents and there is therefore no reason why we should conclude that because lived experience has a narrative structure, the same must be true of historical reality.

A stronger and much simpler realist defence is to challenge the anti-realist's way of setting up the problem. We can do this by accepting the claim that stories need structures and authors. If, therefore, the realist is committed to the notion of past reality as 'an untold story waiting to be told', he or she is indeed committed to an incoherent conception, since past reality would then both need but not have an author. However, this can be shown to be an unacceptable way of presenting the problem by the fact that, if this is so, *all* claims about the past, including those that the anti-realist wishes to accept, would be incoherent. To see this, let us consider the case of some statement made by an historian about the past which was never made by anyone in the past. Statements are less complex than narratives but they also require a literary structure, usually a sentence, and an author. Hence, if, as the anti-realist claims, the narrative realist is committed to the conception of the past as an 'untold story waiting to be told', a statement realist would be committed to the conception that part of the past, that which the anti-realist needs to accept to preserve the distinction between fiction and history, involves the equally incoherent notion of 'unstated sentences waiting to be stated'. On this view, then, the idea of any independent historical reality whatsoever must be abandoned as incoherent. But this would produce a scepticism that applies not merely to narrative histories, but to any claims of any sort about the past. Since, however, as we saw in the first section, a scepticism of this sort would itself be incoherent, the anti-realist argument which entails it cannot be correct.

The use of narratives thus cannot have the implications that the anti-realist claims. Nevertheless, to reject the anti-realist view is not the same as to understand how narratives relate to the past. From considerations presented earlier, it might seem that they do so by telling us what happened and by showing us how to understand why it happened. But this seems to do scant justice to the role of the narrative itself which, as the anti-realists have rightly insisted, involves relating individuals, events and contexts of many different kinds and from different points of view, including those of the agents and the historian. Furthermore, neither would it explain the fact, troubling for realists, that historians disagree so much in their overall accounts nor would it identify the source of their disagreements.

One promising suggestion involves the notion of an historical narrative as providing a special form of 'configurational understanding' which is characteristic of history (Mink, 1987, Dray, 1993). There are two aspects to this idea, which may be taken separately. The first is that the narrative integrates different parts of the past as parts of a temporal whole. This can be quite easily understood if we return to the idea of a narrative sentence. Here some event or institution is described in the context of a larger-scale event or process which did not end until after the termination of the original event or institution. It is clear, however, that historians could not maintain claims to the truth of such sentences if they were to connect earlier and later events in an arbitrary way. We can describe Petrarch's ascent of Mount Ventoux as the opening of the Renaissance, but hardly as the opening of the Industrial Revolution. Nor is this just a matter of time-scale for events very distant from one another can be related in narrative sentences. What is required is what has been called a 'colligatory concept' *of an appropriate type* (Walsh, 1967). A colligatory concept is one that refers to some large-scale underlying movement or some developing idea, within which the events or individuals in whom the historian is interested will be seen in various sets of relationships and thus acquire different kinds of significance. But what determines whether such a concept is of the appropriate type? Why, for example, is the Renaissance but not the Industrial Revolution appropriate for Petrarch? There are two parts to the response to this question. The first is that the historian must be able to show that the new relationships which he or she can trace by adopting this viewpoint are empirically true. There is no reason in principle why any colligatory concept may not be used in the attempt to understand the significance of the activities of any individual. But a minimum condition of appropriateness must be that the historian can provide empirical support for the possibilities opened up. The second is that a colligatory concept must not be one which merely allows events to be re-classified in general terms – a murder as an execution, for example. It must be one that refers to specific historical items, such as the Renaissance or the French Revolution. Thus, colligating under appropriate concepts is a specifically historical form of understanding because it involves understanding specific historical phenomena in the light of their relationships to other specific phenomena, the character of which can be ascertained only with historical hindsight.

If this is one of the main characteristics of historical narratives, it might seem that it can explain what is a problem for realists, the existence of apparently irresolvable large-scale disagreement between historians. For the same events and people can be brought under different appropriate colligatory concepts. To see this, one merely needs to think of the significance of Luther's Ninety-Five Theses against the abuse of indulgence in relation, for example, to the histories of the Roman and Protestant churches, to theology, to changes of relationships between churches and states and to the development of the modern Protestant conscience. In fact, however, while the use of different colligatory concepts can explain how historians come to give different narrative accounts of the same events, it could show that these differences are irresolvable only if the colligatory concepts were contradictory. But since they are concepts of specific large-scale historical phenomena, which are known to have existed, they cannot be contradictory. When such disagreement occurs, therefore, it can be put down only to disagreement about the relative importance of the themes referred to by the colligatory concepts in question. But there is no reason why historians should think that these accounts are incompatible, unless they believe that there is one and only one way in which historical reality can truly be described. But, as we saw earlier, a realist can accept that there is only one reality, to parts of which all true statements and accounts refer, without needing to deny that there are many different ways of referring to and describing that one reality.

It is necessary to turn to the second aspect of this conception of historical narrative: the notion that it is a *configuration*. This concept has been much used in trying to characterize how narratives express their truth. It arises from a reluctance to accept either of two alternatives. The first is that narratives *state* the truth, for in this case it might seem that their truth was little more than a function of the statements and explanations that they contain. The alternative is that a narrative is simply a literary way of dressing up the results of the historian's research and, in this case, one cannot ascribe to the narrative as such any truth value at all. The main claim made in connection with the concept of configuration, however, is that historical narratives go beyond the explanatory value of their contents to a form of understanding, in which the parts are related to a whole, as described above, but in such a manner that the historian's conclusions cannot be grasped other than by the way in which they are expressed in the narrative. Thus, rather than state the truth, the narrative displays it. One analogy used here is with music, where it is often claimed that there is no way of understanding what a piece of music is about other than by listening to it. In the same way, it is suggested, it is not possible to understand the historical narrative other than by grasping the relationships between parts and whole in just the way in which, by the end, it has displayed them.

The analogy with music, however, is both helpful and unhelpful. It is helpful in the sense that one can contrast listening to a piece of music sequentially, as it were, noting how one theme is related to or develops out of another, and grasping, by the end, the piece *as a whole*. In the latter case, one can gain a much more complex understanding of the same parts of the piece by seeing, for example, how some foreshadow what comes later. Similarly, since narratives presuppose chronological sequences, they have a sequential structure – yet the historian enables us to understand the parts of a chronological sequence in many different ways, by relating them to different sets of relations and contexts through the use of colligatory concepts and through a capacity to see reality retrospectively. The analogy with music is unhelpful, however, in that it is not clear that music is about something in the same sense that an historical narrative is about something. The interrelationships that one can come to grasp in the musical example do not refer to anything that stands outside the piece of music. But those which one should come to grasp in a narrative history, even if one can do so only by the way in which they are presented in the narrative account, must be features of that which the narrative is about, that is, historical reality. Moreover, this attempt to give the narrative a unique cognitive value by presenting it as a way of displaying the character of a whole rather than stating it, runs into the difficulty that historians can and do detach their conclusions from their narratives and argue their merits in a way that is incompatible with the suggestion that conclusions are undetachable from the narrative. For we can, and do, ask whether two different narrative accounts of the same historical event are substantially in agreement or not, and, having allowed for differences that might arise because they are addressed to different readers, we can fairly easily decide. These difficulties do not refute the account we are considering of what narratives, in virtue of being narratives, relate, but they cast doubt upon the claim that narratives *exhibit* this in virtue of their own internal configuration. There seems no reason therefore to deny that narratives are implicit statements of truths about the past which are different in kind from those stated by any of their parts, but which can nevertheless be made explicit should that be required.

It remains to be asked, however, whether some historical disagreements are in principle irresolvable. The suggestion that they are has been powerfully defended upon the grounds that ultimately they may depend upon different METAPHYSICAL (chapter 2) or evaluative presuppositions (Walsh, 1967, 1986). This can be illustrated by reference to the different ways in which Marxist and Whig historians have written narrative accounts of the nineteenth century. For the Marxist, the unifying theme is the collapse of capitalism, while for the Whig it is the growth of freedom. But behind these obvious differences, there lie different metaphysical conceptions of the nature of human beings. For the Marxist, human beings are pre-eminently producers of their own means of subsistence, and all that follows is to be explained in the light of the needs of the related technological, economic and ideological systems that develop necessarily to enable this to be done (see chapter 24). For the Whig, on the other hand, humans are essentially free, and the underlying theme of human history is the creation of the set of institutions that could best satisfy their inalienable right to liberty. Hence, where the Marxist historian sees the development of so-called 'liberal' institutions in the nineteenth century as concealed expressions of the needs of capitalism in a particular phase, the liberal sees them as the collective constructions of people becoming ever more aware of their inalienable rights (Mandelbaum, 1971). These are, of course, incompatible metaphysical views and there is no way of resolving them other than by metaphysical discussion of the sort in which historians do not normally engage. It could be argued that if this is so, they ought to engage in it. But this is too optimistic, for disagreement could be removed once and for all only if the possibility exists of establishing the truth of some metaphysical system once and for all. But this seems an impossible dream. In the end, therefore, claims to the objectivity of large-scale historical accounts must be relativized to the metaphysical perspective upon which they rest. But although this imposes an ultimate limit upon the kind of objectivity to which history can aspire, it does not show that historical knowledge is any less reputable than any other kind of knowledge. For there is no branch of knowledge whose conclusions are not subject to the same qualification. The fact that there appears to be less disagreement in, say, the natural sciences than in history, is simply a consequence of the fact that the theories of natural science involve agreed assumptions about the nature of reality, but not that they involve none at all, whereas historians often do not agree about at least some of their assumptions.

5 Conclusion

Historians live within, share the interests of, and write for, specific historical societies. They seek objective truth but, if the main elements in the previous discussion are correct, the degree of objectivity that can be claimed for their final accounts must be relativized in various ways: to the self-perception of their societies, to their own implicit metaphysical assumptions and also, perhaps, to their evaluative standards. But such relativization does not mean that they are not warranted ways of thinking of the past. It could only mean this if the historian could escape the temporal and conceptual constraints of his or her situation to achieve some God's-eye viewpoint from which to see the whole. But it is not clear that the idea of such a whole and such a viewpoint is intelligible. The fact that historical knowledge must be from a perspective cannot therefore vitiate it. It does, however, put an end to the old hope of a once-and-for-all universal history, for historical knowledge is not simply aggregative in the way that such a hope requires. The present is not simply an addition to the past but a development of it; and, as new presents come into being, so must new temporal standpoints from which we can discern, if they exist, new relationships between different parts of the past or between present and past, requiring new colligatory concepts. But this alone would not mean that what can now be discerned must be false for, as we have seen, colligatory concepts cannot be contradictory. The ultimate reason, therefore, why any account as a whole must be thought revisable lies in the fact that the perspective from which it operates involves revisable metaphysical assumptions.

Further Reading

There are three excellent general introductions. Gorman (1992) is explicitly written as an introduction to analytic philosophy through philosophy of history but includes an account of econometric history which I have had to omit here. Walsh (1967) remains a clear and helpful discussion of some of the above issues. Dray (1993) is more comprehensive and more detailed, containing an excellent assessment of the varieties of causal judgement in history, which I have again had to omit, while also putting the case for the ineliminability of value judgements at its strongest. C. Behan McCullagh's *Justifying Historical Descriptions* (1984), while too difficult to be an introduction, has excellent chapters on historical generalizations, historical causes and causal significance, together with a wealth of examples.

Constructionism retains its appeal and readers should consult L. J. Goldstein's *Historical Knowing* (1976) and the essays in *History and Theory*, 1977, 4, for the start of the debate and, for later developments, Michael Krausz's 'History and its objects' in *The Monist*, 74. The problem of interpretation has received greater attention by European writers. For a comprehensive but difficult discussion, leading to results different from those outlined here, Hans-Georg Gadamer's *Truth and Method* (1975) is indispensable.

The scientific conception of causal explanation has remained important. For a devastating attack on the covering law model itself and an impressive argument for its replacement by a more comparative conception of causal explanation, which nevertheless remains naturalistic, see R. W. Miller's *Fact and Method* (1987). For a completely anti-positivist view, see H. L. A. Hart's and T. Honoré's *Causation in the Law*, 2nd edn 1985. To the writings on Understanding discussed in the chapter should be added G. H. Von Wright's *Explanation and Understanding* (1971) and P. Winch's *The Idea of a Social Science* (1958).

The ontological and epistemological implications of narrative continue to be a source of much dispute. For both sides of the debate, see the articles in *History and Theory*, 1986, 4, and 1987, 4. For a strong defence of its epistemological adequacy, and an equally strong denial of it, see D. Carr's *Time, Narrative and History* (1986), and F. R. Ankersmit's *Narrative Logic* (1983), respectively.

References

Ankersmit, F. R. 1983: *Narrative Logic*. The Hague: Nijhoff.
Berlin, I. 1966: The concept of scientific history. In W. H. Dray (ed.), *Philosophical Analysis and History*, New York and London: Harper and Row.
Carr, D. 1986: *Time, Narrative and History*. Bloomington: University of Indiana Press.
Collingwood, R. G. 1993: *The Idea of History* (revised edn). Oxford: Oxford University Press.

Danto, A. C. 1965: *Analytic Philosophy of History*. Cambridge: Cambridge University Press.

Donagan, A. 1966: The Popper–Hempel theory reconsidered. In W. H. Dray (ed.), *Philosophical Analysis and History*, New York and London: Harper and Row.

Dray, W. H. 1957: *Laws and Explanation in History*, Oxford: Oxford University Press.

—— 1980: *Perspectives on History*. London: Routledge and Kegan Paul.

—— 1993: *Philosophy of History* (2nd edn). Englewood Cliffs, NJ: Prentice-Hall.

Gadamer, H.-G. 1975: *Truth and Method*. London: Sheed and Ward.

Gallie, W. B. 1964: *Philosophy and the Historical Understanding*. London: Chatto and Windus.

Goldstein, L. J. 1976: *Historical Knowing*. Austin, Texas: University of Texas Press.

—— 1977: History and the primacy of knowing. *History and Theory*, 16, 4.

Gorman J. L. 1982: *The Expression of Historical Knowledge*. Edinburgh: Edinburgh University Press.

—— 1992: *Understanding History: An Introduction to Analytical Philosophy of History*. Canada: University of Ottawa Press.

Hart, H. L. A. and Honoré, T. 1985: *Causation and the Law* (2nd edn). Oxford: Clarendon Press.

Hempel, C. G. 1959 [1942]: The function of general laws in history. In P. Gardiner (ed.), *Theories of History*, New York: The Free Press.

—— 1974: Reasons and covering laws. In Gardiner (ed.), *The Philosophy of History*, London: Oxford University Press.

Krausz, M. 1974: History and its Objects. *The Monist*, 74, 2.

Lovejoy, A. O., 1959: Present standpoints and past history. In Hans Meyerhoff (ed.), *The Philosophy of History in Our Time*, New York: Doubleday and Company.

MacIntyre, A. 1981: *After Virtue*. Notre Dame: University of Notre Dame Press.

Mandelbaum, M. 1971: *History, Man and Reason: A Study in Nineteenth-Century Thought*. Baltimore and London: The Johns Hopkins Press.

McCullagh, C. B. 1984: *Justifying Historical Descriptions*. Cambridge: Cambridge University Press.

Miller, R. W. 1987: *Fact and Method*. Princeton, NJ: Princeton University Press.

Mink, L. O. 1970: History and fiction as modes of comprehension. *New Literary History*, I.

—— 1978: Narrative form as a cognitive instrument. In R. H. Canary and H. Kozicki (eds), *The Writing of History: Literary Form and Historical Understanding*, Madison: The University of Wisconsin Press.

—— 1987: *Historical Understanding* (edited by B. Fay, E. O. Golob and R. T. Vann). Ithaca: Cornell University Press.

Nowell-Smith, P. 1977: The constructionist theory of history. *History and Theory*, 16, 4.

Oakeshott, M. 1933: *Experience and Its Modes*. Cambridge: Cambridge University Press.

Pompa, L. 1993: The possibility of historical knowledge. *The Supplementary Proceedings of the Aristotelian Society*.

Russell, B. 1921: *The Analysis of Mind*. London: George Allen and Unwin.

Von Wright, G. H. 1971: *Explanation and Understanding*. London: Routledge and Kegan Paul.

Walsh, W. H. 1967: *An Introduction to Philosophy of History* (2nd edn). London: Hutchison and Co.

—— 1986: Fact and value in history. In M. C. Doeser and J. N. Kraay (eds), *Facts and Values*, Dordrecht: Martinus Nijhoff.

White, H. 1973: *Metahistory: The Historical Imagination in Nineteenth-Century Europe*. Baltimore and London: The Johns Hopkins Press.

—— 1978: The historical text as literary artefact. In R. H. Canary and H. Kozicki (eds), *The Writing of History: Literary Form and Historical Understanding*, Madison: The University of Wisconsin Press.

White, M. 1965: *Foundations of Historical Knowledge*. New York and London: Harper and Row.

Winch, P. 1958: *The Idea of a Social Science*. London: Routledge and Kegan Paul.

Young, G. M. 1936: *Victorian England: Portrait of an Age*. London: Oxford University Press.

Discussion Questions

1 Is it logically possible that the world came into existence five minutes ago? If it is, what implications would it have for our knowledge that there was a real past more than five minutes ago?

2 Is the past in which historians believe a past that could exist in its own right or can it exist only as a construction from present historical evidence?

3 What is a past-entailing expression? What is its function in enabling us to infer from historical evidence to historical statements?

4 Can we justify our belief that we are in possession of a theory of interpretation which gives us access to historical truths?

5 Is the covering law theory adequate as an account of the logical form of historical explanations?

6 Can there be laws about the behaviour of individuals? If there can, how would this affect the character of historical explanations?

7 Can there be laws about the development of historical roles?

8 Is historical understanding different in kind from historical explanation? If it is, what does it enable us to grasp which historical explanations do not?

9 Are historical explanations deterministic?

10 How can the transmission of influence in history be made intelligible?

11 What is historicism? Does it render the understanding of the past in its own terms impossible?

12 Is there an incompatibility between understanding the past as a contrast to the present and understanding it in relation to the present?

13 What are the logical features of narrative sentences? What is their function in historical accounts?

14 If historical accounts depend upon value judgements, how does this affect their truth?

15 Must historians make judgements of importance when deciding what to include in their accounts? If they must, on what would these judgements depend?

16 Events can be candidates for specific kinds of history only if they are characterized in certain ways. On what does their characterization depend?

17 How would a history of politics be affected by the judgement that a killing by the IRA was a central case of an execution rather than a murder?

18 Must historians appeal to their own religious beliefs when deciding what might be appropriate for inclusion in a history of religion? What would be the consequences for histories of religion if they must?

19 Must narrative histories impose on the past meanings that it cannot possess?

20 What is a colligatory concept? Does it introduce a specifically historical form of understanding into history?

21 How do historical narratives relate to what they are about?

22 Are there some disagreements in history that cannot be resolved? If so, what is the source of their irresolvability?

23 Can historical accounts reach a degree of truth such that all future histories merely add later truths to them? If not, how does the future of reality affect them?

14

Philosophy of Religion ——————————

Charles Taliaferro

Philosophy of religion explores philosophical issues that arise from reflection on the nature and truth of religious belief and the meaning of religious practices. If the field is defined broadly enough, then the historical record of the beginning of philosophy marks the beginning of the philosophy of religion. The field includes philosophical arguments for and against belief in a Creator of the cosmos, comparative treatments of the Divine, accounts of the meaning of religious language and faith, the ethical implications of religious commitments, the relation between faith, reason, experience and tradition, concepts of the miraculous, the afterlife, revelation, the mystical, prayer, salvation and other religious concerns.

This chapter reviews the current practice of the philosophy of religion, highlighting arguments on the nature of religious belief, the intelligibility of competing conceptions of God and the debate over the role of evidence in shaping religious convictions, and it examines some recent work on arguments for and against belief that there is a God. Philosophy of religion is integrally related to metaphysics, epistemology, ethics, the philosophy of mind and to other areas, not the least of which is the history of philosophy itself, as virtually all the seminal historical figures of philosophy held views that bear on religious matters.

1 Overview of the Current State of the Field

In the West today, especially in the United States, topics in the philosophy of religion (typically arguments for and against belief in God) are a mainstay in introductory philosophy texts, and they are meant to convince students of the relevance and importance of philosophical enquiry. The philosophical exploration of religious belief may be motivated by a wide range of reasons, from the purely intellectual to the personal and political, and these reasons are often taken to carry even greater weight today owing to a growing appreciation of the need to address the diversity of world religions and cultures. Religious and philosophical diversity has compelled many to re-think their particular religious beliefs (or their lack of religious belief) with reference to competing positions. Currently, the study of philosophy of religion has been undergoing tremendous growth in the English-speaking world, with the establishment of new journals and philosophical societies dedicated to the discipline, the latter including the Society for the Philosophy of Religion in Great Britain and the

Society of Christian Philosophers in the United States. In addition to religious and philosophical pluralism, another reason for this growth is a general dissatisfaction with the radical empiricism that dominated the intellectual climate of much mid-twentieth-century philosophy in Europe and America.

A strict empiricism was the hallmark of logical positivism, especially as this was fashioned in the work of the Vienna Circle in the 1920s and 1930s. This launched a wide-ranging critique of traditional philosophy by insisting that the perennial topics of philosophy be addressed along strictly empirical and conceptual lines. There were many versions of the empiricism promoted by logical positivism, but the following empiricist principle is representative: for a propositional claim to be meaningful it must either be about the bare formal relations between ideas such as those enshrined in mathematics and analytic definitions ('A is A', 'triangles are three-sided') or there must in principle be perceptual experience providing evidence of whether the claim is true or false. Ostensibly factual claims that have no implications for our experience are empty of content. Metaphysical claims like 'The Absolute is outside of time' and 'There are Platonic properties' were thereby swept away as nonsense. In line with this form of logical positivism, A. J. Ayer (1910–89) and others claimed that religious beliefs were meaningless. How might one empirically confirm that God is omnipresent or loving or that Krishna is an avatar of Vishnu? In an important debate in the 1950s, philosophical arguments about God were likened to debates about the existence and habits of an unobservable gardener. The idea of a gardener who is not just invisible but who also cannot be detected by any sensory faculty seemed nonsense. Using this garden analogy and others crafted with the same design, Antony Flew (see his essay in Mitchell, 1971) made the case that religious claims do not pass the empirical test of meaning. Due to the popularity of positivism, philosophers of religion responded either by applying empiricist demands across the board, taking in ethics too, or to fighting a rearguard action to expose inadequacies of the positivist critique.

Empirical verificationism is by no means dead. Some critics of the belief in an incorporeal God continue to advance the same critique as that of Flew and Ayer, albeit with further refinements. Michael Martin (1990) and Kai Nielsen (1982) are representatives of this approach. Further, the empiricist critique of religion can still be seen as part of a comprehensive philosophical outlook and is not just a matter of selectively attacking religion alone. Notwithstanding the continued legacy of positivism, empiricist challenges to the meaningfulness of religious belief are now deemed less impressive than they once were.

The charge that positivism is itself meaningless has been advanced on the grounds that the empiricist criterion of meaning itself does not seem to involve the formal relation between ideas as with tautologies, nor does it appear to be empirically verifiable. How might one empirically verify whether the principle is correct? At best, the principle of verification seems to be a recommendation as to how to describe those statements that logical positivists are prepared to accept as meaningful. But then, how might a dispute about which other statements are meaningful be settled in a non-arbitrary fashion? To religious believers for whom talk of 'Brahman' and 'God' is at the centre stage of meaningful discourse, the use of the principle of empirical verification will seem arbitrary and question-begging. If the principle is tightened up too far, it seems to threaten various propositions that at least appear to be highly respectable, such as scientific claims about physical processes and events that are not publicly perceptible. For example, what are we to think of states of the universe prior to all observation or physical strata of the cosmos that cannot be observed directly or indirectly but only inferred as part of an overriding SCIENTIFIC THEORY (chapter 9)? Or what about the mental states of other persons, which may ordinarily be reliably judged, but which, some argue, are under-determined by external, public observation? Also worrisome was the whole-sale rejection of ethics. Are we willing to give up a normative account of ethics and all value judgements? The latter question had some force against an empiricist like A. J. Ayer who regarded ethical claims as lacking any truth value and yet at the same time construed empirical knowledge in terms of having the right to certain beliefs. Can an ethics of belief be preserved if one dispenses with ethics altogether? The strict empiricist account of meaning was also charged as meaningless on the grounds that there is no coherent, clear basic level of experience with which to test propositional claims. The experiential 'given' is simply too malleable, often reflecting prior conceptual judgements and, once one appreciates the open-textured character of experience, it may be proposed that virtually any experience can verify or provide some evidence for anything. A mystic might well claim to experience the unity of a timeless spirit everywhere present. A. J. Ayer allowed that in principle mystical experience might give meaning to religious terms. Those who concede this appeared to be on a slippery slope leading from empirical verificationism to mystical verificationism. A growing number of philosophers were led to conclude that the empiricist challenge was not decisive. Critical assessments of positivism can be found in work by, among others, Alvin Plantinga (1967, 1974, 1993), Richard Swinburne (1977, 1979), and John Foster (1985).

Once verificationism was called into question, the floodgates seemed to open and the philosophy of religion came to include highly speculative accounts of God's nature, power, knowledge and goodness. In addition, debate got under way in the cross-cultural philosophy of religion (comparing religious conceptions of the self, the afterlife, the experience of the Divine and Nirvana) in ways that would have seemed entirely unworthy of attention earlier. The abandoning of strict empiricism cleared the way for the return of many of the projects that were at the heart of MEDIEVAL (chapter 16) or ANCIENT (chapter 15) philosophy of religion.

Another factor shaping contemporary philosophy of religion and also contributing to its growth has been the belief that philosophy need not be practised in a strictly uniform fashion, with common starting assumptions and methodology. A single model of philosophy made sense in a tight empiricist framework or in a widely upheld rationalism, but it is frequently argued that neither of these positions (nor any substitute) demands universal assent by all intellectually responsible enquirers, which means that the path is clear for a variety of philosophical projects. According to some philosophers today (though by no means all), philosophy can be specific to a particular community, something to be worked out in relation to a particular faith or tradition (see Beaty, 1990, as an example of this approach to the philosophy of religion). Dethroning a more magisterial view of philosophy as standing above all traditions has led many philosophers to work at closer range with philosophical issues that arise from within their faith traditions. There is, for example, a huge contemporary philosophical literature on different views specific to the Christian faith (topics like the Trinity, the incarnation and atonement) and interfaith dialogue (philosophical comparisons between the concepts of God across religions) that has currency among 'the believers', but does not have built into it the need to justify all its projects to a secular, external skeptic. This outlook receives some support from philosophers who repudiate any overarching treatment of truth which is independent of historical conceptual schemes.

With philosophy of religion revivified, a number of philosophers whose primary work is in other areas have been drawn to it in order to articulate their views. So, different arguments and concepts about space and time, free will and determinism, which are at home in METAPHYSICS (chapter 2), the PHILOSOPHY OF MIND (chapter 5) and the PHILOSOPHY OF MATHEMATICS (chapter 10), have been explored in reference to the idea of God – for instance, if there were a God, could God have created a first moment of time? Philosophy of religion, then, has its place today, not just in the domain of the history of philosophy but also in many other central areas of philosophical specialization.

2 Religious Beliefs and Religious Forms of Life

A natural way to begin the philosophical exploration of religion is to outline the various metaphysical claims about the cosmos and God, to check the claims with reference to standard moves in metaphysics (the way one would argue about the nature of the material world or about numbers), and then to examine the claims in terms of epistemology (why do we think the metaphysical claims are true?), and ethics (is the theory of values elaborated in the religion credible?). Adopting this approach, the following categories are important to note. *Theism*, common to traditional Judaism, Christianity, and Islam, is the view that the cosmos is created and kept in existence by an omnipresent, omniscient, omnipotent, supremely good being. It preserves some distinction between God and the creation, according to which the two are not identical however interwoven they might be. Typically, the term 'theism' is used to designate *monotheism*, though contexts may arise when it will be quite important to note explicitly the differences between monotheism (there is one God), *polytheism* (there are many gods), and *tritheism* (there are three Gods or gods – this usage comes into play in philosophical work on the Trinity in Christianity). *Henotheism* is the recognition of one God for purposes of devotion and worship without denying the existence of other Divine beings. The term 'theism' can be used today with some flexibility so that it would still be possible to call oneself a theist if one were a monotheist who believed God was omnipresent and all the rest except for being omnipotent. Some self-described 'theists' claim God is 'almighty' (very powerful) without being omnipotent. *Pantheism* is the view that all is God, while *Panentheism* occupies a position midway between theism and pantheism. For panentheists, while it is not strictly true that everything is God, everything is lodged or embedded within God, making the two interdependent.

This metaphysical approach to religion allows for the relatively neat division between various forms of belief in the Divine as distinct from atheism (from the Greek *atheos* 'without god', a term commonly used to deny theism as well as all other notions of the Divine) and agnosticism (from the Greek *agnosis* meaning 'without knowledge' and designating the thesis that the Divine is unknown or, in an extreme form, that the Divine *cannot* be known.)

Three obstacles to this way of proceeding should be noted, the first two only briefly. Firstly, the term 'religion' is not at all easy to define and so the boundaries of the philosophy of religion are likewise difficult to lay out with precision. A necessary condition for being a 'religion' cannot be the belief that there is a God (Theravada Buddhism is a religion which, in the main, is atheistic). Definitions that require the promotion of reverence or awe for what is believed to be sacred are difficult to use with much confidence because of the vagueness of the terms 'reverence' and 'awe,' and there is also the problem that some religions may not enshrine these 'religious emotions'. Consider, for example, religious practices that appear to treat the Divine only as a vehicle for ensuring healthy crops, much like Euthyphro's economic approach to God in PLATO's (chapter 15) dialogue *Euthyphro*, and note the prevalence of many today who repudiate all religion and yet seek to live with reverence for life. Debates over such matters (Is capitalism a religion? Is Marxism?) can very quickly appear philosophically sterile. What follows of philosophical interest if capitalism is defined as a religion? The way philosophers usually handle the problem of defining religion is by noting the major traditions recognized today as 'religions' and casting the field of philosophy of religion as enquiry into those specific religions and *the traditions and practices resembling them*. If it is plausibly argued that a secular, atheist humanism has many religious characteristics and should be considered as one religion among the others, this may have important political and social consequences (perhaps in terms of government protection or persecution), but settling the matter does not seem to involve very high stakes philosophically. All it means for philosophers of religion is that the primary topic of what is considered their field has widened somewhat.

A second worry is that the systematic categorizing of religions by registering their metaphysical commitments will invariably depreciate the enormous diversity within any given religious tradition. For example, there are important figures within the great traditions of Judaism, Christianity and Islam who sometimes adhere to views that seem either atheistic, agnostic, pantheist or panentheist. There is also considerable cross-referencing today in which religious practitioners will describe themselves as Buddhist Christians and the like. All one can do here is simply exercise caution, being ready heavily to qualify one's description of the different religious traditions as one works at close range on religious figures and movements.

A third obstacle to consider is more potent philosophically and emerges largely from the work of Ludwig WITTGENSTEIN (1889–1951) (chapter 29). In his early philosophical development, Wittgenstein deeply influenced the empiricism of the Vienna Circle, while his mature work took a very different turn with its open-ended approach to the many different ways in which language may be used. Following Wittgenstein's later views on truth, belief and forms of life, some philosophers of religion have gone so far as to contend that all religions are principally matters of practice and that metaphysical concerns are latent and marginal.

Wittgenstein launched an attack on what has been called the picture theory of meaning, according to which statements may be judged true or false depending upon whether reality matches the picture represented by the belief. This understanding of truth and beliefs – essentially the correspondence theory of truth in which the statement 'God exists' is true if and only if God exists – seemed to Wittgenstein to be misguided. It gives rise to insoluble philosophical problems and it misses the whole point of having beliefs, which is that their meaning is to be found in the life in which they are used. By shifting attention from the referential meaning of words to their use, Wittgenstein promoted the idea that we should attend to what he called 'forms of life'. As this move was applied to religious matters, a number of philosophers have either denied or at least played down the extent to which religious forms of life involve metaphysical claims. Norman Malcolm (1975), B. R. Tilghman (1993), and D. Z. Phillips (1970) have all promoted this approach to religion. It may be considered *non-cognitivist* in the sense that it does not treat religious beliefs as straightforward metaphysical claims that can be adjudicated in a realist manner as either true or false. By their lights, the traditional metaphysics of theism got what it deserved when it came under attack in the mid-twentieth century by radical empiricists and under the earlier philosophical attacks in the eighteenth century by David HUME (1711–76) (chapter 21), because the traditional, cognitive outlook profoundly misconstrued what it meant to be religious.

This challenge, then, appears to place in check much of the way philosophers in the West have approached religion. When, for example, LOCKE (1632–1704) (chapter 19), BERKELEY (1685–1753) (chapter 20), Hume, Butler (1692–1752) and Reid (1710–96) argued for and against the justification of belief in God, metaphysics was at the forefront. And the same is largely true of ancient or medieval philosophical reflection about the Divine. When St Thomas AQUINAS (1224–74) (chapter 16) articulated his proofs for God's existence he was engaged in fully fledged metaphysics. In terms of the history of the field, the Wittgensteinian stance is closest to Kantianism, radically recasting and yet continuing the Kantian move of locating the role of religious belief in terms of ethical practices. KANT (1724–1804) (chapter 22) opposed metaphysical arguments supporting religious traditions, claiming that none was successful, but he then went on to argue that there were practical, moral grounds for acting on the basis of a religious view of life and history.

Several points can be made on behalf of twentieth-century non-cognitivism. Firstly, it has some credibility based on the sociology of religion. In the practice of religion itself it appears that we have something more (one might well say something deeper) than 'mere' metaphysical theorizing. Religion seems pre-eminently to be focused upon how we live. Phillips has looked at different religious practices such as prayer and the belief in an afterlife, concluding that both are intelligible and that the motives behind each can be held intact without any of the metaphysical baggage traditionally linked with them. Prayer to God by parents for the recovery of a child's health may be read as an expression of their anguish and an effort to centre their hope on the child's getting better and not as an attempt to influence God's will. A second reason that might be offered (considered in greater detail in section 4) is that the classical and contemporary arguments for specific views of God have seemed unsuccessful to many philosophers (though not to all). Tilghman takes this line and argues that if the traditional arguments for God's existence are re-interpreted as part of religious life and not treated as if they were scientific truth-claims, then they have an intelligibility and force that they otherwise lack. So, if one expects to argue convincingly to the existence of a Divine designer on the basis of the appearance of design in the cosmos, one is in philosophical trouble. One is in far better shape casting religious references to God's design of the cosmos in terms of religious practices like living with respect for humanity. It might appear that this non-cognitivism would lead religious adherents into some highly paradoxical positions. Does it make sense for there to be Christian atheists, for example? But this worry might be met, at least in part. After all, if the Wittgensteinian critique holds, is not the atheist as much committed to the unacceptable picture theory as the theist? If so, then the non-cognitivist can understand religious life as neither atheist nor theist. Finally, on behalf of non-cognitivism, it may be noted how such a stance receives support from more than the Wittgensteinian movement, but also by the current revival of PRAGMATISM (chapter 26), especially in North America, and the appropriation of some of the work of HEIDEGGER (1889–1976) (chapter 30). There is currently a renewed interest in John DEWEY's (1859–1952) (chapter 26) emphasis on practice over theorizing, and with Heidegger's stress on coping and activity as opposed to conscious, detached reflection. Practice, then, rather than metaphysical theories seems predominant in these philo-sophical outlooks.

Non-cognitivist views have their critics from the vantage point both of atheists, such as Michael Martin (1990) and theists, such as Roger Trigg (1989). By way of a preliminary response it may be pointed out that even if a non-cognitivist approach is adopted this would not mean altogether jettisoning the more traditional approach to religious beliefs. If one of the reasons advanced on behalf of non-cognitivism is that the traditional project fails, then the traditional project will still need investigating and, assuming that if it has failed the failure is not overwhelmingly obvious, constant re-thinking. This is similar to a move in reply to a Kantian philosophy of religion. As Kant built his case against traditional metaphysics, in part, on the basis that theoretical, metaphysical reason leads to contradictory positions (for example, that the world has an origin and that the world does not have an origin), the ongoing assessment of the tenability of a Kantian stance requires rethinking of the metaphysical approach and checking to see if the contradictions are in fact unavoidable.

A more substantial reply to the Wittgensteinian non-cognitivism has been the charge that it undermines the very intelligibility of religious practice. Let us concede that practice is antecedent to theory, which is a concession not shared by all. If one has a religious practice, such as prayer to God or Buddhist meditation to see through the illusion of having a substantial ego, the development of some sort of theory of the cosmos to make sense of this practice seems inevitable. Once such a theory is in place, it is intelligible to raise the question of its truth. While Malcolm has proposed that it makes sense to believe *in* God without believing *that* God exists, others have submitted that lack of belief that God exists makes belief in God meaningless. *Belief that X* is prior to *belief in X*. One may *hope* that something will occur (a child recovers from illness) without the accompanying belief it will occur, but it is more puzzling to suppose one can trust in a child recovering or a Divine being, without believing there was some reality there to rely upon. Also to be recognized as high on the list of objections to non-cognitivism is the point that it seems to leave us with severe problems adjudicating between forms of life – the religious versus the Nazi way of life, for example. While non-cognitivists might seem to lay the groundwork for greater tolerance between religions (and between religions and the secular world) because it subverts the battle over which religion has a true picture of the cosmos, critics have lamented the loss of a normative way of choosing between religions, ways that seem to be used in commonplace reflection on the merits of religion. So, today it is still not at all unusual for people to claim they have changed religions (or stayed with their own or abandoned all religion), for reasons like the appeal to religious experience, answered or unanswered prayer, miracles or the lack of them, moral and cultural relativism, an overwhelming sense of the reality of good and evil, and so on.

As noted above, one of the reasons behind religious non-cognitivism is the claim that a metaphysical investigation into religion is fruitless. Let us now review some of the metaphysical moves that have been made in the philosophy of God.

3 Divine Attributes

Most philosophy of religion in the West has focused on different versions of theism. Ancient philosophy of religion wrestled with the credibility of monotheism and polytheism in opposition to skepticism and very primitive naturalistic schemes. For example, should Plato's view that God is singularly good be preferred to the portrait of the gods that was articulated in Greek poetic tradition, according to which there are many gods and they are often imperfect and subject to vice and ignorance? The emergence and development of Judaism, Christianity and Islam on a global scale secured the centrality of theism for philosophical enquiry, but the relevance of a philosophical exploration of theism is not limited to those interested in these religions and the cultures in which they flourish. One may be a theist without adopting any religion whatever, and one may find theistic elements (however piecemeal) in Confucianism, Hinduism, some versions of Mahayana Buddhism as well as in the religions of some smaller scale societies. The debate over theism also has currency for secular humanism and religious forms of atheism as in Therevada Buddhist philosophy. In addition, theism may be deemed philosophically interesting in so far as it provides an arena for studying the nature and limits of certain concepts used to describe human life such as human knowledge, power, creativity and goodness. All these are utilized in theism when God is described as all-knowing, powerful, creative and good. This generates much philosophical work, analysing how these terms function in a transcendent (or supernatural) plateau, noting in particular how our use of them may be informed or undermined by different theories of human life. As God is also described in some theistic traditions as necessarily existing, immutable (unchanging), eternal, and incorporeal, this invites philosophical study of the meaning of such notions and the justification of the ensuing idea of a being with either all or most of these supreme attributes.

It will be useful first to get a clearer idea about the general ways in which the language about God has been treated and then to consider some specific cases of philosophical reflection on the attributes of God.

Terms applied both to God and to any aspect of the world have been classified as either *univocal* (sharing the same sense), *equivocal* (used in different senses) or *analogical*. There are a range of accounts of analogous predication, but the most common – and the one assumed here – is that terms are used analogously when their use in different cases (John limps and the argument limps) is based on what is believed to be a resemblance (John's leg is impaired and the argument is weak in some respect). It seems clear that many terms used to describe God in theistic traditions are used analogously, as when God is referred to as a fountain. More difficult to classify are descriptions of God as good, personal, knowing and creative. Heated philosophical and theological disputes centre on unpacking the meaning of such descriptions, disputes that are often carried out with the use of thought experiments.

In thought experiments, hypothetical cases are described – cases that may or may not represent the way things are. In these descriptions, terms normally used in one context are employed in expanded settings. Thus, in thinking of God as omniscient, one might begin with a non-controversial case of a person knowing that a proposition is true, taking note of what it means for someone to possess that knowledge and of the ways in which the knowledge is secured. A theistic thought experiment would seek to extend our understanding of knowledge as we think of it in our own case, working toward the conception of a maximum or supreme intellectual excellence befitting the religious believers' understanding of God. Various degrees of refinement would then be in order, as one speculates not only about the extent of a maximum set of propositions known but also about how these might be known. That is, in attributing omniscience to God, would one thereby claim God knows all in a way that is analogous to the way we come to know truths about the world? Too close an analogy would produce a peculiar picture of God relying upon, for example, induction, sensory evidence or the testimony of others. One move in the philosophy of God has been to assert that the claim 'God knows something' employs the word 'knows' univocally when read as picking out the thesis that God knows something, while it uses the term in only a remotely analogical sense if read as identifying *how* God knows (Swinburne, 1977).

Here a medieval distinction comes into play between the *res significata* (what is asserted – for instance, that God knows *X*) and *modus significandi* (the mode or manner in which what is signified is realized or brought about – for instance, how God knows *X*). We might have a good grasp of what is meant by the claim that a being is omnisicient while being sceptical about grasping how a being might be so. Thought experiments aimed at giving some sense to the Divine attribute of omniscience have been advanced by drawing attention to the way we know some things immediately (bodily positions, feelings and intentions), and then by extending this, coaxing us into conceiving a being that knows all things about itself and the cosmos immediately (see Beaty, 1991 for a constructive view and Blumenfeld in Morris (ed.), 1987 for criticism).

Utilizing thought experiments and language in this way, philosophical theology has a stake in the soundness and richness of the imagination, picturing the way things might be 'in one's mind's eye', whether or not this relies on any actual imagery. Philosophers are now more cautious about drawing such inferences as we are increasingly aware of how some features of an imagined state of affairs might be misconceived or overlooked. Even so, it has been powerfully argued that if a state of affairs appears to one to be possible after careful reflection, checking it against one's background knowledge in other areas, then there is at least some warrant in judging the state of affairs to be a *bona fide* possibility (Sorensen, 1992). Understanding the current debate over the limits of our thinking about God and the Divine attributes can be sharpened by distinguishing between three important cases: a case of claiming to conceive of *a possible state of affairs*, a case in which one conceives of *the impossibility of a state of affairs*, and a case in which one simply *fails to conceive of a state of affairs*, perhaps accompanied by an argument to the effect that the state of affairs cannot be conceived regardless of whether it is possible or impossible. A strong atheist strategy is to argue that even the best candidates for conceiving of God represent something impossible; the idea of God is as incoherent as the idea that one equals three. Not all atheists take this tack, however; some allow that while it is possible that God exists, God does not exist. Some theists have been fairly agnostic when it comes to conceiving of God's very being, assuming that virtually all language about God is highly analogical at best and that univocal language is appropriate chiefly when making claims about what God is not (for instance, that God is not a material object, not wicked or contingent). The idea of God can be approached through the use of imagination (the *via imaginativa*) and varies to the extent that it employs positive attributions (the *via positiva*) or negative (the *via negativa*). While Brian Davies (1993) adopts a more qualified, *via negativa* philosophy of God, Swinburne (1977) adopts a theism that is more informed by the *via positiva*.

As these strategies become more explicit it becomes easier to note the ways in which philosophy of religion intersects with other areas of philosophy. Consider this with respect to the philosophy of mind. According to certain forms of eliminative materialism, the very notion of possessing such things as beliefs, desires or love rests on confusions; only physical objects, states and entities exist. Adopting this radical eliminativism will probably lead to scepticism about the intelligibility of there being an all knowing, loving, non-physical being in line with classical treatments of God. If, on the other hand, one adopts a dualist understanding of the human person according to which we are non-physical minds, souls or persons who are materially embodied, this scepticism will be tempered. Supposing that there is a non-physical supreme mind will not seem intellectually confused from the very start. A range of philosophers attribute their reservations about theism to their scepticism about dualism (Kenny, 1979, Barnes, 1972) and for this reason a substantial number of theists have linked their defence of theism to a defence of the intelligibility of dualism (for instance, Swinburne, 1977, Taliaferro, 1994). Some theistic philosophers do not think one need go quite so far to defend the intelligibility of theism; all that is required is to defend the *possibility* that God is non-physical and possesses the divine attributes regardless of how *we* happen to be constituted. On this view, God might be non-physical and person-like even if all created persons are exclusively physical. Thus, William Alston (1991) defends the coherence of theism on the basis of a neutral, functionalist reading of human persons. Alston thinks that so long as we are not eliminativists and we recognize mental terms as intelligible as they function in human life, theism can be defended without having recourse to dualism. Such three-way debate is quite common between those claiming to have good reason to believe that a given idea of God is incoherent, those claiming equally good reason to conclude it is conceptually coherent, and those claiming that the question of God's existence is left unresolved despite all such *pro* and *contra* argument.

God and Ineffability

Before concentrating on specific attributes, consider the prospects for a religiously motivated robust agnosticism according to which God or ultimate reality is completely beyond description or conception. St Anselm (1033–1109) held that God is greater than that which can be conceived. What if all concepts must by their very nature fail in making any reference to the Divine, even in highly nuanced, analogous ways, not because there is no God, but because there is one? This proposal is sometimes put as the claim that God is ineffable (from the Latin, *ineffabilis* for 'not being capable of being expressed'). The insistence on God's ineffability has played a role in the mysticism and thought of important figures in the great monotheistic traditions, and in Buddhist and Hindu traditions as well.

Qualifications about the adequacy of our concepts to represent the Divine are common in religiously sympathetic philosophical systems. Achieving philosophical proficiency in mapping out a robust understanding of the Divine may require an order of experience far beyond what we now have or could ever have. Perhaps, as Joseph Albo (c.1380–c.1444) put it in the fifteenth century, 'To Know God's nature one would have to be God Himself.' It does not seem obviously wrong to suppose that certain conceptual schemes allow us to obtain only a very thin understanding of ultimate reality, but problems arise when it is claimed that ultimate reality or God are altogether beyond *all* conceptual descriptions no matter how tenuous and circuitous. Philosophers like Plantinga (1980) have objected that this kind of strict ineffability is incoherent, because, firstly, to be described as ineffable is itself a description, secondly, descriptions like 'if it is, it is' must be irresistible and, thirdly, we have good reason for thinking there can be no such ineffable *X* 'out there'. Even if these charges fail, it is very difficult to see what use positing an ultimately ineffable *X* would have, religiously, practically, philosophically or scientifically. Denying the existence of *X* might make as much (or as little) sense as affirming it. Fortunately, very few religions rule out in principle all conceptualizing of God, even if they are quite wary of such theorizing, and so philosophers of religion can still engage in conceptual analysis without having to admit from the outset that they are already cut off from the religions they are attempting to explore philosophically.

In proceeding to treat divine attributes some selectivity is in order. I shall cover those that have occasioned the most intense philosophical scrutiny in recent years.

3.1 Omnipotence

Some of the most vigorous philosophical debate has centred on whether it makes sense to think of God as a supreme, maximally powerful being responsible for the origin and continued conservation of the cosmos. Begin with a claim like 'God can do anything whatever' or 'All things are possible for God' and one is bound to run into obstacles that may be classified as external or internal. External difficulties would hinder any being whatever from being omnipotent, while internal problems would prevent us from recognizing as omnipotent God as conceived in the three main monotheistic traditions. Consider external problems first.

The external barrier here might be purely logical or it may take on broader metaphysical dimensions. There are problems with supposing that anything or anyone can do what is logically impossible. Can God make 2 + 2 = 6? It would appear to be nonsense to suppose that this could be done by any being. The problem has an additional metaphysical edge if one assumes that there are certain matters, such as 'time is one-directional', which are indeed necessary, but not due to bare logical relationships (its denial does not involve a contradiction). Grant that there are necessary metaphysical truths and it seems that nothing can be omnipotent, because nothing can alter such metaphysically necessary truths. These problems are often treated at one stroke by insisting that what is or *should be* meant by the claim that there is an omnipotent being is that if a being is omnipotent, it can do anything that is logically or metaphysically possible. This approach has the implication that the mathematical and time-bending tasks mentioned above are idle pseudo-tasks or absolute nonsense. This is no worse than 'conceding' that an omnipotent being cannot make the concept of justice jump around the number 7 or eat happiness.

This strategy of defining the possibility of Divine omnipotence is fairly common and has antecedents going back to medieval philosophy of religion. It is sometimes refined to take into account different levels and sequences of action. Consider the question of whether God could make something that God could not control. It would appear so, given a certain conception of freedom of the will. Arguably, a being is free only if it is not completely under the control of another being. If God creates a free creature, has God ceased to be omnipotent because now there is a being God cannot control? Presumably, these sorts of 'limits' on Divine freedom can be cast in terms of God's being limited by the limits God introduces. To expect an omnipotent being to be able to make a creature both free and not free at the same time would be akin to expecting that an omnipotent being could make something that is square while lacking four right angles.

Can we envisage a maximal power that is deeper than, or behind, the laws of logic? Perhaps there is some room to move if one adopts an anti-realist treatment of abstract objects and of LOGIC (chapter 4), according to which logical laws are merely the codification of human designs and language. Alternatively, one might follow DESCARTES (1596–1650) (chapter 17) who thought that God was responsible for the creation of necessary truths. This has not been widely accepted by theists on the grounds that theistic voluntarism would undermine the necessity of logical and metaphysical truths. If God could make $A = A$, then God would have the power to make $\neg A = A$ and thus the law of identity would be contingent and not necessary. A group of contemporary philosophers has sought to bolster Descartes' stance, however.

Plantinga (1974), Menzel and Morris (1986) and others, propose preserving the necessity of logical and metaphysical truths and yet insist that they are true in virtue of God's creative will, a creative will which could not be otherwise. The necessity of $A = A$ and other such truths is thereby affirmed and accounted for by a deeper Divine necessity. This revival of Descartes' position may be articulated using the convention of talking of possible worlds. A possible world may be said to be a way things could be. The actual world is one possible world; in a different possible world you wrote this chapter and I did not. Using this terminology, one could say that, in all possible worlds, God wills that $A = A$, and so on for all necessary truths. This revised version of Descartes' stance has been commended on the grounds that it preserves the desired necessities, that it offers some account of the truths at issue rather than leaving the necessities suspended in Platonic strata and that the explanation it offers has greater simplicity than rival accounts.

Is there an ultimate limit to what, in principle, we could credit to a maximally powerful being? Could there be a being that could take credit even for its own existence and constitution? Could God have created God? The idea that any being could create itself (*causa sui* means cause of itself) has been dismissed on the grounds that to create itself a being would have to exist already, which is an absurdity; but it has recently been suggested that if creating itself did not require a first moment of existing, the prospect for *causa sui* might improve. One proposal by Menzel and Morris is that in an important respect God could be like a machine. Imagine a machine – the Menzel–Morris machine – that creates matter from nothing. It has always existed and has continuously replaced all its parts systematically, not all at once (in which case it would have to cease to be and then create itself) but incrementally (for instance, on Mondays it would replace its right side, on Tuesdays its left). With every cycle of replacement, would it not have created itself? The standard move in the philosophy of God is to resist these possibilities (perhaps it is absurd to think of God as a machine or having parts or being in time), and to think instead that, if there is a God, God's being God is not something God could have brought about or altered. Perhaps God did not make God omnipotent, but that does not mean God is harnessed by something external to God or is somehow defective.

Consider now some internal obstacles to imagining omnipotence, especially as these are borne out in the monotheistic traditions. God is believed to be non-physical. If so, can God remain God and yet swim? God is thought of existing necessarily. If so, can God cease to be? God is thought of as necessarily good. Does this mean that God could not bring about an evil state of affairs, without there being some overriding ethical reason to do so? Would this mean that there could be something more powerful than the God of these religious traditions, namely a being that could swim, cease to be, commit evil acts and so on?

Some ways of handling these puzzles include proposing that God *can* do such things as swim (God can assume a body), bring about evil and so on. Alternatively, one can concede that God cannot do these things, but deny that omnipotence requires doing any act possible for some conceivable creature; rather an omnipotent being has maximal power, such that there can be no being more powerful. Perhaps God cannot commit suicide, but an omnipotent God would none the less possess a scope of power that cannot be surpassed by beings capable of self-annihilation. Another response to these paradoxes has been to re-examine the relation between Divine attributes and the motivation for ascribing them to God. Schlesinger (1988) and Morris (1987), among others, have contended that the rationale behind ascribing great-making qualities to God is to make explicit the idea that God is perfect. What one is after, then, is locating those properties that, together, form the greatest compossible set of properties. On this schema, two properties are compossible if they can both be instantiated simultaneously of the same being. If God's being perfectly good in any way limits God's being all-powerful, it does so only in a fashion that, overall, contributes to the excellence of God. God would be less great, less worthy of worship if God could commit evil. This shifting of attention from bare power to thinking of power in terms of values has been heralded by some feminist and social critics of religion as a healthy departure from a more male-based celebration of a power that only too quickly turns into oppressive, suffocating pictures of the Divine. The Morris–Schlesinger strategy is in the same spirit of earlier tactics, such as that of Boethius (c.480–524) in the sixth century, who concluded that the ability to commit evil was far from being a positive power or sign of greatness. In his dialogue *The Consolation of Philosophy* (1969) there is the following exchange: ' "There is nothing that an omnipotent God could not do." "No." "Then, can God do evil?" "No." "So that evil is nothing, since that is what He cannot do who can do anything." '

3.2 Omniscience

We have already considered some aspects of omniscience. Omniscience is typically defined in terms of knowing all propositions, or (with some elaboration) knowing with respect to all true propositions that they are true and with respect to all false propositions that they are false. Some of the debate on omniscience stems from philosophical debate over the nature of propositions. Some propositions contain indexical terms (terms having their reference determined according to which person is using them). If you think that some true propositions containing first-person indexical terms, like 'I am in pain now', can only be known by the individual 'I' who is entertaining them, then you would not be able to cast omniscience in terms of knowing all true propositions. On this view, indefinitely many propositions could be true but known only by particular individuals. My knowing that Smith is in pain would involve my knowing a different proposition to be true than that known by Smith. He knows, 'I am in pain', and I know, 'Smith is in pain'. This puzzle is dealt with typically by denying the existence of such hyper-private propositions (Kvanvic, 1986). More sustained debate, with less promise of resolution, has occurred over the scope of omniscience.

Omniscience and Freedom

Are omniscience and freedom compatible? Imagine there is a God who knows the future free action of human beings. If God does know you will freely do some act A, then it is true that you will indeed do A. But if you are free, would you not be free to avoid doing A? Given that it is foreknown you will do A, it appears you would not be free to refrain from the act. Initially this paradox seems easy to dispel. If God knows about your free action, then God knows that you will freely do something *and* that you could have refrained from it. God's foreknowing the act does not make it necessary. Does not the paradox only arise because we confuse two propositions: 'Necessarily, if God knows X, then X' with 'If God knows X, then necessarily X'? AUGUSTINE (354–430) (chapter 16), Boethius, Anselm, Aquinas and others sought to preserve the reality of freedom along with God's foreknowledge, and this is a stance widely represented today. The problem is retained, however, when the point is pressed concerning the grounds for foreknowledge. If God does know you will freely do X, then it appears that there must now be a fact of the matter about what you will and will not do, and thus some residual sense in which your freely doing X is not something that can be altered. If the problem is put in first-person terms and one imagines God foreknows you will freely turn the next page, then an easy resolution of the paradox seems elusive. Imagine God tells you what you will freely do. Under such conditions, is it still intelligible to believe you have the ability to do otherwise if it is known by God as well as yourself what you will indeed elect to do?

Various replies have been given, of which I note three. Some adopt what is called compatibilism, affirming the compatibility of free will and determinism, and conclude that foreknowledge is no more threatening to freedom than determinism. A second position involves adhering to the radically libertarian outlook of insisting that freedom involves a radical, indeterminist exercise of power, and concludes that God cannot know future free action. What prevents such philosophers from denying that God is omniscient is that they contend there are no truths about future free actions. Prior to someone's doing a free action, there is no fact of the matter that he or she will do a given act. This is in keeping with ARISTOTLE's (chapter 15) philosophy of time and truth. Aristotle thought it was neither true nor false prior to a given sea battle whether a given side would win it. Some theists, such as Swinburne (1977), adopt this line today, holding that the future cannot be known. If it cannot be known for metaphysical reasons, then omniscience can be read as knowing all that it is possible to know. That God cannot know future free action is no more of a mark against God's being omniscient than God's inability to make square circles is a mark against God's being omnipotent. Other parties, including Linville (1993), deny the original paradox. They insist that God's foreknowledge is compatible with libertarian freedom and seek to resolve the quandary either by claiming that God is not bound in time (God does not so much *fore*know as eternally know) or by arguing that the unique vantage point of an omniscient God prevents any impingement on freedom. God can simply know the future without this having to be grounded on the future somehow being already fixed. Some advocates of this position hold that God knows not just what will occur, but what would occur given all possible future events. God knows whether you will freely turn the page and also knows whether you would freely do so if any number of other events were to occur prior to the act (for instance, God knows what you would do if you saw an elephant just now, even though you are not seeing one). This kind of knowledge of possible free choices is referred to as *middle knowledge* as it designates knowledge mid-way, as it were, between *what will occur* and *what could occur*. Middle knowledge involves knowing *what would happen under all possible conditions*.

3.3 Eternal or everlasting?

Could there be a being that is outside time? In the great monotheistic traditions, God is thought of as without any kind of beginning or end. God will never, indeed, can never, cease to be. Some philosophical theists hold that God's temporality is very much like ours in the sense that there is a before, during and an after for God – or a past, present, and future for God. This view is sometimes referred to as the thesis that God is *everlasting* (Wolterstorff, 1982). Those adopting a more radical stance claim that God is independent of temporality, arguing either that God is not in time at all, or that God is 'simultaneously' *at* or *in* all times. This is sometimes called the view that God is *eternal* as opposed to everlasting (Leftow, 1991). Why adopt the more radical stance? One reason, already noted, is that if God is not temporally bound, there may be a resolution to the problem of reconciling freedom and foreknowledge. As Augustine put it: 'For He does not pass from this to that by transition of thought, but beholds all things with absolute unchangeableness; so that of those things which emerge in time, the future, indeed, are not yet, and the present are now, and the past no longer are; but all of these are by Him comprehended in His stable and eternal presence' (*The City of God*, 1972, XI, 21). If God is outside time, there may also be a secure foundation explaining God's immutability (changelessness), incorruptibility and immortality. Furthermore, there may be an opportunity to use God's standing outside of time to launch an argument that God is the creator of time.

Those affirming God to be unbounded by temporal sequences face several puzzles which I note without trying to settle. If God is somehow at or in all times, is God simultaneously at or in each? If so, there is the following problem. If God is simultaneous with Rome burning, and also simultaneous with your reading this book, then it seems that Rome must be burning at the same time you are reading this book. A different problem arises with respect to omniscience. If God is outside of time, can God know what time it is *now*? Arguably, there is a fact of the matter that it is now, say, midnight on 1 July 1996. A God outside of time might know that at midnight on 1 July 1996 certain things occur, but could God know when it is *now* that time? The problem is that the more emphasis we place on the claim that God's supreme existence is independent of time, the more we seem to jeopardize taking seriously time as we know it. Finally, while the great monotheistic traditions provide a portrait of the Divine as supremely different from the creation, there is also an insistence on God's proximity. For some theists, describing God as a person or person-like (God loves, acts, knows) is not to equivocate. But it is not clear that an eternal God could be personal.

3.4 *The goodness of God*

All known world religions address the nature of good and evil and commend ways of achieving human well-being, whether this be thought of in terms of salvation, liberation, deliverance, enlightenment, tranquillity or an egoless state of Nirvana. Notwithstanding important differences, there is a substantial overlap between many of these conceptions of the good as witnessed by the commending of the Golden Rule ('*Do unto others as you would have them do unto you*') in many religions. Some religions construe the Divine as in some respect beyond our human notions of good and evil. In Hinduism, for example, Brahman has been extolled as possessing a sort of moral transcendence, and some Christian theologians have likewise insisted that God is only a moral agent in a highly qualified sense. To call God good is for them very different from calling a human being good (Davies, 1993). Belief in the supreme goodness of God has, however, been a mainstay of the great monotheistic traditions, and belief in the goodness of God has also had considerable force independent of these traditions. Disputes over the goodness of God lay at the heart of the initial quarrel between philosophy and poetry. Plato was so repelled by the moral incoherence of the polytheism displayed in the poetry of Hesiod and Homer, with the complicity of the gods in infanticide, patricide, murder, rape and adultery, that he proposed banning poets from his ideal Republic.

Here I note some of the ways in which philosophers have articulated what it means to call God good. In treating the matter, there has been a tendency either to explain God's goodness in terms of standards that are not God's creation and thus, in some measure, independent of God's will, or in terms of God's will and the standards God has created. The latter view is termed *theistic voluntarism*. A common version of theistic voluntarism is the claim that for something to be good or right simply means that it is willed by God and for something to be evil or wrong means that it is forbidden by God.

Theistic voluntarists face several difficulties: moral language seems intelligible without having to be explained in terms of the Divine will. Indeed, many people make what they take to be objective moral judgements without making any reference to God. If they are using moral language intelligibly, how could it be that the very meaning of such moral language should be analysed in terms of Divine volitions? New work in the PHILOSOPHY OF LANGUAGE (chapter 3) may be of use to theistic voluntarists. According to a causal theory of reference terms like 'water' may well turn out to be necessarily identified with H_2O (it is not a contingent fact that water is H_2O), notwithstanding the fact that many can use the term 'water' without knowing its composition. Similarly, could it not be the case that what it means for something to be good is that it is God's will, even though many use 'good' without being aware that this is so? Another difficulty for voluntarism lies in accounting for the apparent meaningful content of claims like 'God is good'. It appears that in calling God good the religious believer is saying more than 'God wills what God wills'. If so, must not the very notion of goodness have some meaning independent of God's will? Also at issue is the worry that if voluntarism is accepted, the theist has threatened the normative objectivity of moral judgements. Could God make it the case that moral judgements were turned upside down? Could God make cruelty good? Arguably, the moral universe is not so malleable. In reply, some voluntarists have sought to understand the stability of the moral laws in light of God's immutably fixed, necessary nature. Recall the similar move in the Cartesian strategy of anchoring the necessity of logic and metaphysics in God's very being. For sympathetic treatments of voluntarism, see Adams (1987) and Owen (1965).

By understanding God's goodness in terms of God's being (as opposed to God's will alone), we come close to the non-voluntarist stand. Aquinas and others have held that God is essentially good in virtue of God's very being. All such positions are non-voluntarist in so far as they do not try to unpack the thesis that what it *means* for something to be good is that God wills it to be so. The goodness of God may be explained in various ways, either by arguing that God's perfection requires God being good as an agent or by arguing that God's goodness can be articulated in terms of other Divine attributes such as those outlined above. For example, because knowledge is in itself good, omniscience is a supreme good. God has also been considered good in so far as God has created and conserves in existence a good cosmos. Debates over the problem of evil (if God is indeed omnipotent and perfectly good, why is there evil?) have a poignancy precisely because they challenge this chief judgement over God's goodness. This debate is considered in the last section.

The choice between voluntarism and a more internalist picture is rarely strict. Some theists who oppose a full-scale voluntarism allow for partial voluntarist elements. According to one such moderate stance, while God cannot make cruelty good, God can make some actions morally required or morally forbidden which otherwise would be morally neutral. Arguments for this have been based on the thesis that the cosmos and all its contents are God's creation. According to some theories of property, an agent making something good gains entitlements over the property. The crucial moves in arguments that the cosmos and its contents belong to their Creator have been to guard against the idea that human parents would then 'own' their children (they do not, because parents are not radical creators like God), and the idea that Divine ownership would permit *anything*, thus construing our duties owed to God as the duties of a slave to a master (a view to which not all theists have objected). Theories spelling out why and how the cosmos belongs to God have been prominent in all three monotheistic traditions. Plato defended the notion, as did Aquinas and Locke. (See Brody, 1974 for a current defence of Locke's version of Divine ownership.)

One other effort worth noting to link judgements of good and evil with judgements about God relies upon the ideal observer theory of ethics. According to this theory, moral judgements can be analysed in terms of how an ideal observer would judge matters. To say an act is right entails a commitment to holding that if there were an ideal observer, it would approve of the act; to claim an act is wrong entails the thesis that if there were an ideal observer, it would disapprove of it. The theory can be found in work by Hume, Adam Smith (1723–90), Sidgwick (1838–1900) (chapter 25), Hare and Firth (1970). The ideal observer is variously described, but typically is thought of as impartial, omniscient regarding non-moral facts (facts that can be grasped without already knowing the moral status or implications of the fact – for instance, 'He did something bad' is a moral fact; 'He hit Smith' is not), and as omnipercipient (Firth's term for adopting a position of universal affective appreciation of the points of view of all involved parties). The theory receives some support from the fact that most moral disputes can be analysed in terms of different parties challenging each other to be impartial, to get their empirical facts straight, and to be more sensitive – for example, by realizing what it feels like to be disadvantaged. The theory has formidable critics and defenders. If true, it does not follow that there is an ideal observer, but if it is true and moral judgements are coherent, then the idea of an ideal observer is coherent. Given certain conceptions of God in the three great monotheistic traditions, God fits the ideal observer description (and more besides, of course). Should an ideal observer theory work, a theist would have some reason for claiming that atheists committed to normative, ethical judgements are also committed to *the idea of a God* or a *God-like being*.

3.5 Other aspects of the philosophy of God

I note very briefly some additional, recent work in the philosophy of God. With respect to transcendence, there is considerable debate over whether God is best thought of as an individual being or as Being itself. Some resist thinking of God as an individual because they think of individuals as being one thing among others. That is, if there is an individual, it must be thought of as part of a genus. But, by hypothesis, God is *sui generis* (one of a kind or a genus unto itself) and hence not an individual. Also high on the list of transcendent properties, some philosophers have rekindled the notion that God is ultimately simple, without parts and not possessing distinguishable attributes. It makes sense to distinguish the Divine attributes, as we have done above, but this should be seen as an artificial device, not reflecting any *real* distinction within the Godhead. The appeal of this philosophical theism will depend upon one's theory of properties, just as the earlier debate on being and individual will depends upon one's overall ontology. For a defence of God as BEING (p. 65) see Davies (1993), and for Divine simplicity see Kretzmann and Stump (in Morris (ed.), 1987).

On Divine immanence, much of the debate has turned on claims about whether God is impassible (not subject to passions). If one adopts a high, non-temporalist view of God's eternity, one will be more likely to affirm the impassibility of God as, arguably, undergoing passion requires change. One might still allow for *certain* change for God, sometimes called 'Cambridge change' (because it satisfies the criterion of change suggested by Russell and others in Cambridge without involving real change in the subject), but this will not be a substantial change on God's side. An example of Cambridge change would be the change in Jones when he becomes shorter than Smith as a result of Smith's getting taller while Jones remains the same size. A Cambridge change regarding God might be for God to be thought about by Jones on one day but not on another. The only 'real' alteration is on Jones' side, not God's. Would recognizing that God can undergo Cambridge change be enough to make philosophical sense of the idea that God suffers and feels pleasure over the different ills and goods of the cosmos? Perhaps God can suffer and feel pleasure in creation, but does so in some non-temporal fashion or possibly at each time God is in different affective states. Those who believe God *does* feel passion tend to believe God is everlasting and thus in time. How one decides such issues will have an impact on how one construes higher-order Divine properties like God's omnipresence. Thus, if one accepts that God is subject to passions, God's being everywhere present might involve a full host of Divine properties – for example, God would know what is occurring everywhere, God could exercise maximal power without limit (except, perhaps, by the limits of logic and necessary metaphysical truths), no place would exist without God's conserving, creative power, and there would be the additional Divine attribute of affective responsiveness to values. Thus, for God to be present in the cosmos would mean, in part, that God feels sorrow and pleasure in response to its ills and goods.

4 Evidence, Religious Experience and Secular Explanations

There is currently some philosophical unease about whether metaphysics or epistemology should have priority. Modern western philosophy may be seen to have followed Descartes in championing epistemology over metaphysics.

On Cartesian grounds, each individual must start from himself or herself and then work outward, eventually achieving a knowledge of God, other people and the external world. It is a hallmark of some philosophy now that it takes deliberate issue with this approach. Thus, it has been held that any starting point of an epistemological kind will already house within it certain assumptions about what exists. Are we all able to agree on a common starting point? A common criticism of Descartes is that if you begin with his *Meditations*, you will never escape an exasperating skepticism. We simply lack the self-evident axioms and the clear and evident ideas required to have any sort of constructive philosophy of the world. As the effort to build up one's understanding of the world from a Cartesian foundation is losing its appeal, there have been widespread repercussions in the philosophy of religion.

One way of carrying out philosophy of religion along non-foundationalist lines has been to build a case for the comparative rationality of a religious view of the world. It has been argued that the intellectual integrity of a religious world view can be secured if it can be shown to be no less rational than the available alternatives. It need only achieve intellectual parity. John Hick (1990) and others emphasize the integrity of religious ways of seeing the world that are holistic, internally coherent, and open to criticism along various external lines. On the latter front, if a religious way of conceiving the world is at complete odds with contemporary science, that would count as good grounds for revising the religious outlook. The case for religion need not, however, be scientific or even analogous to science. If Hick is right, religious ways of seeing the world are not incompatible with science, but complementary. Independent of Hick but in the same spirit, Plantinga (1993) has proposed that belief in God's existence may be taken as properly basic and fully warranted without having to be justified in relation to standard arguments for God from design, miracles and so on. Plantinga argues that the tendency to believe in God follows natural tendencies of the human mind. This stance comprises what is commonly referred to as *Reformed Epistemology* because of its leaning on work by the Reformed theologian John Calvin (1509–64) who maintained that we have a sense of God (*sensus divinitatus*) leading us to see God in the world around us. Plantinga has thereby couched the question of justification within the larger arena of metaphysics. By advancing an intricate, comprehensive picture of how beliefs can be warranted when they function as God designed them, he has provided what some believe to be a combined metaphysical and epistemic case for the rationality of religious convictions.

Who has the burden of proof in a debate between a theist and an atheist? Antony Flew (1984) thinks it is the theist. By his lights, the theist and atheist can agree on a whole base line of truths (such as the findings of the physical sciences). The question then becomes, Why go any further? Flew wields a version of Ockham's razor, arguing that if one has no reason to go further, one has reason not to go further. His challenge has been met on various fronts, with some critics claiming that Flew's burden of proof argument is wedded to an outmoded foundationalism, that any burden of proof is shared *equally* by atheists and theists, or that the theist has an array of arguments to help shoulder a greater burden of proof. The position of *fideism* is a further option. Fideism is the view that religious belief does not require evidence and that religious faith is self-vindicating. Karl Barth (1886–1968) advocated a fideistic philosophy. Hick and Plantinga need not be considered fideists because of the high role each gives to experience, coherence and reflection. (For a superb study of fideism, see Penelhum, 1983.)

Perhaps the justification most widely offered for religious belief concerns the occurrence of religious experience or the cumulative weight of testimony of those claiming to have had religious experiences. Putting the latter case in theistic terms, the argument appeals to the fact that many people have testified that they have felt God's presence. Does such testimony provide evidence that God exists? That it is evidence has been argued by Yandell (1993), Alston (1991), Gutting (1982), Swinburne (1979) and others. That it is not (or that its evidential force is trivial) is argued by Martin (1990), Mackie (1985), Nielson (1982) and others. In an effort to stimulate further investigation, I shall briefly sketch some of the moves and countermoves in the debate.

The Importance of Religious Experience: Objections and Replies

OBJECTION: Religious experience cannot be experience of God for experience is only sensory and if God is non-physical, God cannot be sensed.

REPLY: The thesis that experience is only sensory can be challenged. Yandell (1993) marks out some experiences (as when one has 'a feeling' someone is present but without having any accompanying sensations) that might provide grounds for questioning a narrow sensory notion of experience.

OBJECTION: Testimony to have experienced God is only testimony that one *thinks* one has experienced God; it is only testimony of a conviction, not evidence.

REPLY: The literature on religious experience testifies to the existence of experience of some Divine being on the basis of which the subject comes to think the experience is of God. If read charitably, the testimony is not testimony to a conviction, but to experiences that form the grounds for the conviction.

OBJECTION: Because religious experience is unique, how could one ever determine whether it is reliable? We simply lack the ability to examine the object of religious experience in order to test whether the reported experiences are indeed reliable.

REPLY: As we learned from Descartes, all our experiences of external objects face a problem of uniqueness. It is possible in principle that all our senses are mistaken and we do not have the public, embodied life we think we lead. We cannot step out of our own subjectivity to vindicate our ordinary perceptual beliefs any more than in the religious case.

OBJECTION: Reports of religious experience differ radically and the testimony of one religious party neutralizes the testimony of others. The testimony of Hindus cancel out the testimony of Christians. The testimony of atheists to experience God's absence cancels out the testimony of 'believers'.

REPLY Several replies might be offered here. Testimony *to experience the absence of God* might be better understood as testimony *not to experience God*. Failing to experience God might be justification for believing that there is no God only to the extent that we have reason to believe that if God exists God would be experienced by all. Theists might even appeal to the claim by many atheists that it can be virtuous to live ethically with atheist beliefs. Perhaps if there is a God, God does not think this is altogether bad, and actually desires religious belief to be fashioned under conditions of trust and faith rather than knowledge. The diversity of religious experiences has caused some defenders of the argument from religious experience to mute their conclusion. Thus, Gutting (1982) contends that the argument is not strong enough fully to vindicate a specific religious tradition, but that it is strong enough to overturn an anti-religious naturalism. Other defenders use their specific tradition to deal with ostensibly competing claims based on different sorts of religious experiences. Theists have proposed that more impersonal experiences of the Divine represent only one aspect of God. God is a person or is person-like, but God can also be experienced, for example, as sheer luminous unity. Hindus have claimed the experience of God as personal is only one stage in the overall journey of the soul to truth, the highest truth being that Brahman transcends personhood.

How one settles the argument will depend on one's overall convictions in many areas of philosophy. Currently it is popular to see the individual arguments favouring and opposing God's existence as part of cumulative, mutually supportive lines of reasoning. This view stresses the holistic character of concepts, such as the view that concepts cannot be isolated but must be seen as part of conceptual frameworks. The holistic, interwoven nature of both theistic and atheistic arguments can be readily illustrated. If you diminish the implications of religious experience and have a high standard regarding the burden of proof for any sort of religious outlook, then it is highly likely that the classical arguments for God's existence will not be persuasive. Moreover, if one thinks that theism can be shown to be intellectually confused from the start, then theistic arguments from religious experience will carry little weight. Testimony to have experienced God will have no more weight than testimony to have experienced a round square, and non-religious accounts of religious experience – like those of Freud (a result of wish-fulfilment), Marx (a reflection of the economic base) or Durkheim (a product of social forces) – will increase their appeal. If, on the other hand, you think the theistic picture is coherent and that the testimony of religious experience provides some evidence for theism, then your assessment of the classical theistic arguments might be more favourable, for they would serve to corroborate and further support what you already have some reason to believe. From such a vantage point, appeal to wish-fulfilment, economics, and social forces might have a role, but the role is to explain why some parties do *not* have experiences of God and to counter the charge that failure to have such experiences provides evidence that there is no religious reality. Some interconnections among theistic arguments and among anti-theistic arguments will be noted below.

5 Four Arguments about the Existence of God

We have already covered considerable ground that is traversed in arguments supporting and opposing theism. I will map some of the strategies that are employed in four additional areas where recent philosophical activity has been focused. I will recount what appear to be strong and lively versions of the various arguments and leave readers to explore matters further, rather than offer the dozen or so versions of each argument that are now under debate.

5.1 Ontological arguments

There is a host of arguments under this title; all of them are based principally on conceptual, *a priori* grounds which do not involve *a posteriori* empirical investigation. If a version of the argument works, then it can be deployed using only the concept of God and some modal principles of inference, that is, principles concerning possibility and necessity. The argument need not resist all empirical support, however, as I shall indicate.

The focus of the argument is the thesis that, if there is a God, then God's existence is necessary. God's existence is not contingent – God is not the sort of being that just happens to exist. That this is an accurate picture of what is meant by God may be shown by appealing to the way God is conceived in Jewish, Christian and Islamic traditions. This would involve some *a posteriori*, empirical research into the way God is thought of in these traditions. Alternatively, a defender of the ontological argument might hope to convince others that the concept of God is the concept of a being that exists necessarily by beginning with the idea of a maximally excellent being. If there were a maximally excellent being what would it be like? It has been argued that among its array of great-making qualities (omniscience and omnipotence) would be necessary existence. Once fully articulated, it can be argued that a maximally excellent being, which existed necessarily, could be called 'God'.

The ontological argument goes back to St Anselm, but I shall explore a current version relying heavily on the principle that if something is possibly necessarily the case, then it is necessarily the case (or, to put it redundantly, it is necessarily necessary). The principle can be illustrated in the case of propositions. $1 + 1 = 2$ does not seem to be the sort of thing that might just happen to be true. Rather, either it is necessarily true or necessarily false. If the latter, it is not possible, if the former, it is possible. If one has good reason to believe it is possible that $1 + 1 = 2$, then one has good reason to believe that 1 plus 1 does indeed, necessarily equal 2. Do we have reason to think it is possible God exists necessarily? In support of this, one can also appeal to *a posteriori* matters, noting the extant religious traditions that uphold such a notion. There does not appear to be anything amiss in their thinking of God as existing; if the belief that God exists is incoherent this is not obvious. Indeed, a number of atheists think God might exist, but conclude God does not. If we are successful in establishing the possibility that God necessarily exists, the conclusion follows that it is necessarily the case that God exists.

There have been hundreds of objections and replies to this argument. Perhaps the most ambitious objection is that the argument can be used with one minor alteration to argue that God cannot exist. Assume all the argument above but also that it is possible God does *not* exist. Atheists can point out that many theists who believe there is a God at least allow for the bare possibility that they could be wrong and there is no God. If it is possible that there is no God, then it would necessarily follow that there is no God. Replies to this objection emphasize the difficulty of conceiving of the non-existence of God. The battle over whether God is necessary or impossible is often fought over the coherence of the various divine attributes discussed in section 3. If you think these attributes are compossible, involve no contradictions and violate no known metaphysical truths, then you may well have good grounds for concluding that God is possible and therefore necessary. However, if you see a contradiction, say, in describing a being who is at once omniscient and omnipotent, you may well have good grounds for concluding that God's existence is impossible.

Another objection is that it makes no sense to think of a being existing necessarily; propositions may be necessarily true or false, but objects cannot be necessary or contingent. Some philosophers reply that it makes no less sense to think of an individual (God) existing necessarily than it does to think of propositions being necessarily true.

A further objection is that the ontological argument cannot get off the ground because of the question-begging nature of its premise that if there is a God, then God exists necessarily. Does admitting this premise concede that there is some individual thing such that *if it exists, it exists necessarily*? Replies have claimed that the argument only requires one to consider an ostensible state of affairs, without having to concede initially whether the state of affairs is possible or impossible. To consider what is involved in positing the existence of God is no more hazardous than considering what is involved in positing the existence of unicorns. One can entertain the existence of unicorns and their necessary features (that necessarily if there were unicorns, there would exist single-horned beasts) without believing that there are unicorns.

Finally, consider the objection that, if successful in providing reasons to believe that God exists, the ontological argument could be used to establish the existence of a whole array of other items, like perfect islands. Replies to this sort of objection have typically questioned whether it makes sense to think of an island (a physical thing) as existing necessarily or as having maximal excellence on a par with God. Does the imagined island have excellences like omniscience, omnipotence (a power which would include the power to make indefinitely many islands), and so on?

Classical, alternative versions of the ontological argument are propounded by Anselm, Spinoza and Descartes, with current versions by Plantinga (1974), Hartshorne and Malcolm (both in Hick and McGill, 1967), and Dore (1984); classical critics include Guanillo and Kant, and current critics are many, including Rowe (1993), Barnes (1972) and Mackie (1985).

5.2 Cosmological arguments

Arguments in this vein are more firmly planted in empirical, *a posteriori* reflection, but some versions employ *a priori* reasons as well. There are various versions. Some argue that the cosmos had an initial cause outside it, a First Cause in time. Others argue that the cosmos has a necessary, sustaining cause from instant to instant. The two versions are not mutually exclusive, for it is possible both that the cosmos had a First Cause and that it currently has a sustaining cause.

The cosmological argument relies on the intelligibility of the notion of something which is not itself caused to exist by anything else. This could be either the all-out necessity of supreme pre-eminence across all possible worlds used in versions of the ontological argument, or a more local, limited notion of a being that is uncaused in the actual world. If successful, the argument would provide reason for thinking there is at least one such being of extraordinary power responsible for the existence of the cosmos. At best, it may not justify a full picture of the God of religion (a First Cause would be powerful, but not necessarily omnipotent), but it would none the less challenge naturalistic alternatives and bring one closer to theism.

Both versions of the argument ask us to consider the cosmos in its present state. Is the world as we know it something that necessarily exists? At least with respect to ourselves, the planet, the solar system and the galaxy, it appears not. With respect to these items in the cosmos, it makes sense to ask why they exist rather than not. In relation to scientific accounts of the natural world, such enquiries into causes make abundant sense and are perhaps even essential presuppositions of the natural sciences. Some proponents of the argument contend that we know *a priori* that if something exists there is a reason for its existence. So, why does the cosmos exist? If we explain the contingent existence of the cosmos (or states of the cosmos) only in terms of other contingent things (earlier states of the cosmos, say), then a full cosmic explanation will never be attained. At this point the two versions of the argument divide. Arguments to a First Cause in time contend that a continuous temporal regress from one contingent existence to another would never account for the existence of the cosmos, and they conclude that it is more reasonable to accept there was a First Cause than to accept either a regress or the claim that the cosmos just came into being from nothing. Arguments to a sustaining cause of the cosmos claim that explanations of why something exists now cannot be adequate without assuming a present, contemporaneous sustaining cause. The arguments have been based on the denial of all actual infinities (Craig, 1980) or on the acceptance of some infinities (for instance, the coherence of supposing there to be infinitely many stars) combined with the rejection of an infinite regress of explanations solely involving contingent states of affairs (Taylor, 1963). The latter has been described as a vicious regress as opposed to one that is benign. There are plausible examples of vicious infinite regresses that do *not* generate explanations: for instance, imagine that I explain my possession of a book by reporting that I got it from A who got it from B, and so on to infinity. This would not explain how I got the book. Alternatively, imagine a mirror with light reflected in it. Would the presence of light be successfully explained if one claimed that the light was a reflection of light from another mirror, and the light in that mirror came from yet another mirror, and so on to infinity? Consider a final case. You come across a word you do not understand; let it be 'ongggt'. You ask its meaning and are given another word which is unintelligible to you, and so on, forming an infinite regress. Would you ever know the meaning of the first term? The force of these cases is to show how similar they are to the regress of contingent explanations. Versions of the argument that reject all actual infinities face the embarrassment of explaining what is to be made of the First Cause, especially since it might have some features that are actually infinite. In reply, Craig and others have contended that they have no objection to potential infinities (although the First Cause will never cease to be, it will never become an actual infinity). They further accept that prior to the creation, the First Cause was not in time, a position relying on the theory that time is relational rather than absolute. The current scientific popularity of the relational view may offer support to defenders of the argument.

It has been objected that both versions of the cosmological argument set out an inflated picture of what explanations are reasonable. Why should the cosmos as a whole need an explanation? If everything in the cosmos can be explained, albeit through infinite, regressive accounts, what is left to explain? One may reply, either by denying that infinite regresses actually do satisfactorily explain or by charging that the failure to seek an explanation for the whole is arbitrary. The question, 'Why is there a cosmos?' seems a perfectly intelligible one. If there are accounts for things in the cosmos, why not for the whole? The argument is not built on the fallacy of treating every whole as having all the properties of its parts. But if everything in the cosmos is contingent, it seems just as reasonable to believe that the whole cosmos is contingent as it is to believe that if everything in the cosmos is invisible, the cosmos as a whole would be invisible.

Another objection is that rather than explaining the contingent cosmos, the cosmological argument introduces a mysterious entity of which we can make very little philosophical or scientific sense. How can positing at least one First Cause provide a better account of the cosmos than simply concluding that the cosmos lacks an ultimate account? In the end, the theist seems bound to admit that why the First Cause created at all was a contingent matter. If, on the contrary, the theist has to claim that the First Cause had to do what it did, would not the cosmos be necessary rather than contingent?

Some theists come close to concluding that it was indeed an essential feature of God that creation had to occur. If God is supremely good, there had to be some overflowing of goodness in the form of a cosmos (see Kretzmann and Stump in Morris, 1987, on the ideas of Dionysius the Areopagite). But theists typically reserve some role for the freedom of God and thus seek to retain the idea that the cosmos is contingent. Defenders of the cosmological argument still contend that its account of the cosmos has a comprehensive simplicity lacking in alternative views. God's choices may be contingent, but not God's existence and the Divine choice of creating the cosmos can be understood to be profoundly simple in its supreme, overriding endeavour, namely to create something good. Swinburne (1977) has argued that accounting for natural laws in terms of God's will provides for a simple, overarching framework in terms of which to comprehend the order and purposive character of the cosmos. At this point we move from the cosmological to the teleological arguments.

Defenders of the cosmological argument include Swinburne (1979), Taylor (1963), Meynell (1982), Reichenbach (1972), and Rowe (1993); prominent opponents include Flew (1984), Martin (1990), and Mackie (1985).

5.3 Teleological arguments

These arguments focus on characteristics of the cosmos that seem to reflect the design or intentionality of God or, more modestly, of one or more powerful, intelligent God-like agents. Part of the argument may be formulated as providing evidence that the cosmos is the sort of reality that would be produced by an intelligent being, and then arguing that positing this source is more reasonable than agnosticism or denying it. As in the case of the cosmological argument, the defender of the teleological argument may want to claim only to be giving us *some* reason for thinking there is a God. Note the way the various arguments might then be brought to bear on each other. If successful, the teleological argument may provide some reason for thinking that the First Cause of the cosmological argument is purposive, while the ontological argument provides some reason for thinking that it makes sense to posit a being that has Divine attributes and necessarily exists. Behind all of them an argument from religious experience may provide some initial reasons to seek further support for a religious conception of the cosmos and to question the adequacy of naturalism.

One version of the teleological argument will depend on the intelligibility of purposive explanation. In our own human case it appears that intentional, purposive explanations are legitimate and can truly account for the nature and occurrence of events. In thinking about an explanation for the ultimate character of the cosmos, is it more likely for the cosmos to be accounted for in terms of a powerful, intelligent agent or in terms of a naturalistic scheme of final laws with no intelligence behind them? Theists employing the teleological argument will draw attention to the order and stability of the cosmos, the emergence of vegetative and animal life, the existence of consciousness, morality, rational agents and the like, in an effort to identify what might plausibly be seen as purposively explicable features of the cosmos. Naturalistic explanations, whether in biology or physics, are then cast as being comparatively local in application when held up against the broader schema of a theistic metaphysics. Darwinian accounts of biological evolution will not necessarily assist us in thinking through why there are either any such laws or any organisms to begin with. Arguments supporting and opposing the teleological argument will then resemble arguments about the cosmological argument, with the negative side contending that there is no need to move beyond a naturalistic account, and the positive side aiming to establish that failing to go beyond naturalism is unreasonable.

In assessing the teleological argument, we can begin with the objection from uniqueness. We cannot compare our cosmos with others, determining which have been designed and which have not. If we could, then we might be able to find support for the argument. If we could compare our cosmos with those we knew to be designed and if the comparison were closer than with those we knew to be undesigned, then the argument might be plausible. Without such comparisons, however, the argument fails. Replies to this line of attack have contended that were we to insist that inferences in unique cases were out of order, then we would have to rule out otherwise perfectly respectable scientific accounts of the origin of the cosmos. Besides, while it is not possible to compare the layout of different cosmic histories, it is in principle possible to envisage worlds that seem chaotic, random or based on the laws that cripple the emergence of life. Now we can envisage an intelligent being creating such worlds, but, through considering their features, we can articulate some marks of purposive design to help us judge whether the cosmos was designed rather than created at random. Some critics appeal to the possibility that the cosmos has an infinite history to bolster and re-introduce the uniqueness objection. Given infinite time and chance, it seems likely that something like our world will come into existence, with all its appearance of design. If so, why should we take it to be so shocking that our world has its apparent design and why should explaining the world require positing one or more intelligent designers? Replies repeat the earlier move of insisting that if the objection were to be decisive, then many seemingly respectable accounts would also have to fall by the wayside. It is often conceded that the teleological argument does not demonstrate that one or more designers are *required*; it seeks rather to establish that positing such purposive intelligence is reasonable and preferable to naturalism. Defenders of the argument this century include Schlesinger (1977) and Swinburne (1979). It is rejected by Mackie (1985), Martin (1990) and others.

One feature of the teleological argument currently receiving increased attention focuses on epistemology. It has been contended that if we do rely on our cognitive faculties, it is reasonable to believe that these are not brought about by naturalistic forces, forces that are entirely driven by chance or are the outcome of processes not formed by an overriding intelligence. An illustration may help to understand the argument. Imagine coming across what appears to be a sign reporting some information about your current altitude (some rocks in a configuration giving you your current location and precise height above sea-level in metres). If you had reason to believe that this 'sign' was totally the result of chance configurations, would it still be reasonable to trust it? Some theists argue that it would not be reasonable, and that trusting our cognitive faculties requires us to accept that they were formed by an overarching, good, creative agent. This rekindles Descartes' point about relying on the goodness of God to ensure that our cognitive faculties are in good working order. Objections to this argument centre on naturalistic explanations, especially those friendly to evolution. In evolutionary epistemology, one tries to account for the reliability of cognitive faculties in terms of trial and error leading to survival. A rejoinder by theists is that survival alone is not necessarily linked to true beliefs. It could, in principle, be false beliefs that enhance survival. In fact, some atheists do think that believing in God has been crucial to people's survival, though the belief is radically false. Martin (1990) and Mackie (1985), among others, objects to the epistemic teleological argument; Plantinga (1993), Creel (1995) and Taylor (1963) defend it.

A more sustained objection against virtually all versions of the teleological argument takes issue with the assumption that the cosmos is good or that it is the sort of thing that would be brought about by an intelligent, completely benevolent being.

5.4 Problems of evil

If there is a God who is omnipotent, omniscient and completely good, why is there evil? The problem of evil is the most widely considered objection to theism in both Western and Eastern philosophy. There are two general versions of the problem: the *deductive* or *logical* version, which asserts that the existence of any evil at all (regardless of its role in producing good) is incompatible with God's existence; and the *probabilistic* version, which asserts that given the quantity and severity of evil that actually exists, it is unlikely that God exists. The deductive problem is currently less commonly debated because it is widely acknowledged that a thoroughly good being might allow or inflict *some* harm under certain morally compelling conditions (such as causing a child pain when removing a splinter). More intense debate concerns the likelihood (or even possibility) that there is a completely good God given the vast amount of evil in the cosmos. Consider human and animal suffering caused by death, predation, birth defects, ravaging diseases, virtually unchecked human wickedness, torture, rape, oppression and 'natural disasters'. Consider how often those who suffer are innocent. Why should there be so much gratuitous, apparently pointless evil?

In the face of the problem of evil, some philosophers and theologians deny that God is all-powerful and all-knowing. MILL (1806–73) (chapter 25) took this line, and panentheist theologians today also question the traditional treatments of Divine power. By their lights, God is immanent in the world, suffering with the oppressed and working to bring good out of evil, although in spite of God's efforts, evil will invariably mar the created order. Another response is to think of God as being very different from a moral agent. Davies (1993) and others have contended that what it means for God to be good is different from what it means for an agent to be good. Those who think of God as *Being* as opposed to *a being* have some reason to adopt this position. A more desperate strategy is to deny the existence of evil, but it is difficult to reconcile traditional monotheism with moral skepticism. Also, in so far as we believe there to be a God worthy of worship and a fitting object of human love, the appeal to moral skepticism will carry little weight. The idea that evil is a privation of the good, a twisting of something good, may have *some* currency in thinking through the problem of evil, but it is difficult to see how it alone could go very far to vindicate belief in God's goodness. Searing pain and endless suffering seem altogether real even if they are analysed as being philosophically parasitic on something valuable. The three great monotheistic traditions, with their ample insistence on the reality of evil, offer little reason to try to defuse the problem of evil by this route. Indeed, classical Judaism, Christianity and Islam are so committed to the existence of evil that a reason to reject evil would be a reason to reject these religious traditions. What would be the point of Judaic teaching about the Exodus (God liberating the people of Israel from slavery) or Christian teaching about the incarnation (Christ revealing God as love and releasing a Divine power that will, in the end, conquer death), or the Islamic teaching of Mohammed (the holy prophet of Allah who is all-just and all-merciful) if slavery, hate, death and injustice do not exist?

In part, the magnitude of the problem of evil for theism will depend upon one's commitments in other areas of philosophy, especially ethics, epistemology and metaphysics. If in ethics you hold that there should be no preventable suffering for any reason, no matter what the cause or consequence, then the problem of evil will conflict with accepting traditional theism. Moreover, if you hold that any solution to the problem of evil should be evident to all persons, then again traditional theism is in jeopardy, for clearly the 'solution' is not evident to all. Debate has largely centred over the legitimacy of adopting some position in the middle: a theory of values that would preserve a clear assessment of the profound evil in the cosmos as well as some understanding of how this might be compatible with the existence of an all powerful, completely good Creator. Could there be reasons why God would permit cosmic ills? If we do not know what those reasons might be, are we in a position to conclude that there are none or that there could not be any? Exploring different possibilities will be shaped by one's metaphysics. For example, if you do not believe there is free will, then you will not be moved by any appeal to the positive value of free will and its role in bringing about good as offsetting its role in bringing about evil.

Theistic responses to the problem of evil distinguish between a *defence* and a *theodicy*. A defence seeks to establish that rational belief that God exists is still possible (when the defence is employed against the logical version of the problem of evil) and that the existence of evil does not make it improbable that God exists (when used against the probabilistic version). According to the defence response, no creature should expect to be able to solve the problem of evil; it is beyond our epistemic capacities to stand in judgement here. Some have adopted the defence strategy while arguing that we are in a position to have rational beliefs in the existence of evil and in a completely good God who hates this evil, even though we are unable to see how these two beliefs are compatible. A theodicy is more ambitious, and is typically part of a broader project, arguing that it is reasonable to believe that God exists in light of the good as well as the evident evil of the cosmos. In a theodicy, the project is not to account for each and every evil, but to provide an overarching framework within which to understand at least roughly how the evil that occurs is part of some overall good – for instance, the overcoming of evil is itself a great good. In practice, a defence and a theodicy often appeal to similar factors, the first and foremost being what many called the Greater Good Defence.

Evil and the Greater Good

In the Greater Good Defence, it is contended that evil can be understood as either a necessary accompaniment to bringing about greater goods or an integral part of these goods. Thus, in a version often called the *Free Will Defence*, it is proposed that free creatures who are able to care for each other and whose welfare depends on each other's freely chosen action constitute a good. For this good to be realized, it is argued, there must be the *bona fide* possibility of persons harming each other. The free will defence is sometimes used narrowly only to cover evil that occurs as a result, direct or indirect, of human action. But it has been speculatively extended by those proposing a defence rather than a theodicy to cover other evils which might be brought about by supernatural agents other than God. According to the Greater Good case, evil provides an opportunity to realize great values, such as the virtues of courage and the pursuit of justice. Reichenbach (1982), Tennant (1930) and Swinburne (1979) have also underscored the good of a stable world of natural laws in which animals and humans learn about the cosmos and develop autonomously, independent of the certainty that God exists. Some atheists accord value to the good of living in a world without God, and these views have been used by theists to back up the claim that God might have reason to create a cosmos in which Divine existence is not overwhelmingly obvious to us. If God's existence *were* overwhelmingly obvious, then motivations to virtue might be clouded by self-interest and by the bare fear of offending an omnipotent being. Further, there may even be some good to acting virtuously even if circumstances guarantee a tragic outcome. John Hick (1978) so argued and has developed what he construes to be an Irenaean approach to the problem of evil (named after St Irenaeus of the second century). On this approach, it is deemed good that humanity develops the life of virtue gradually, evolving to a life of grace, maturity and love. This contrasts with a theodicy associated with St Augustine, according to which God created us perfect and then allowed us to fall into perdition, only to be redeemed later by Christ. Hick thinks the Augustinian model fails whereas the Irenaean one is credible.

Some have based an argument from the problem of evil on the charge that this is not the best possible world. If there were a supreme, maximally excellent God, surely God would bring about the best possible creation. Because this is not the best possible creation, there is no supreme, maximally excellent God. Following Adams (1987), many now reply that the whole notion of a best possible world, like the highest possible number, is incoherent. For any world that can be imagined with such and such happiness, goodness, virtue and so on, a higher one can be imagined. If the notion of a best possible world is incoherent, would this count against belief that there could be a supreme, maximally excellent being? It has been argued on the contrary that Divine excellences admit of upper limits or maxima that are not quantifiable in a serial fashion (for example, Divine omnipotence involves being able to do anything logically or metaphysically possible, but does not require actually doing the greatest number of acts or a series of acts of which there can be no more).

Those concerned with the problem of evil clash over the question of how one assesses the likelihood of Divine existence. Someone who reports seeing no point to the existence of evil or no justification for God to allow it seems to imply that if there were a point they would see it. Note the difference between *seeing no point* and *not seeing a point*. In the cosmic case, is it clear that if there were a reason justifying the existence of evil, we would see it? Rowe (1993) thinks some plausible understanding of God's justificatory reason for allowing the evil should be detectable, but that there are cases of evil that are altogether gratuitous. Defenders like Hasker (1989) and Wykstra (1984) reply that these cases are not decisive counter-examples to the claim that there is a good God. These philosophers hold that we can recognize evil and grasp our duty to do all in our power to prevent or alleviate it. But we should not take our failure to see what reason God might have for allowing evil to count as grounds for thinking that there is no reason.

Some portraits of an afterlife seem to have little bearing on our response to the magnitude of evil here and now. Does it help to understand why God allows evil if all victims will receive happiness later? But it is difficult to treat the possibility of an afterlife as entirely irrelevant. Is death the annihilation of persons or an event involving a transfiguration to a higher state? If you do not think that it matters whether persons continue to exist after death, then such speculation is of little consequence. But suppose that the afterlife is understood as being morally intertwined with this life, with opportunity for moral and spiritual reformation, transfiguration of the wicked, rejuvenation and occasions for new life, perhaps even reconciliation and communion between oppressors seeking forgiveness and their victims. Then these considerations might help to defend against arguments based on the existence of evil. In so far as one cannot rule out the possibility of an afterlife morally tied to our life, one cannot rule out the possibility that God brings some good out of cosmic ills.

5.5 Other arguments

I have not been able to cover the many other arguments for and against the existence of God, but I shall now mention a few of these. The argument from miracles starts from specific extraordinary events, arguing that they provide reasons for believing there to be a supernatural agent or, more modestly, reasons for skepticism about the sufficiency of a naturalistic world view. The argument has attracted much philosophical attention, especially since David Hume's rejection of miracles. The debate has turned mainly on how one defines a miracle, understands the laws of nature, and specifies the principles of evidence that govern the explanation of highly unusual historical occurrences.

There are various arguments that are advanced to motivate religious belief. One of the most interesting and popular is a wager argument often associated with Pascal (1623–62). It is designed to offer practical reasons to cultivate a belief in God. Imagine that you are unsure whether there is or is not a God. You have it within your power to live on either assumption and perhaps, through various practices, to get yourself to believe one or the other. There would be good consequences of believing in God even if your belief were false, and if the belief were true you would receive even greater good. There would also be good consequences of believing that there is no God, but in this case the consequences would not alter if there were no God. If, however, you believe that there is no God and you are wrong, then you would risk losing the many goods which follow from belief that God exists and actual Divine existence. On this basis, it may seem reasonable to believe there is a God.

In different forms the argument may be given a rough edge (for example, imagine that if you do not believe in God and there is a God, hell is waiting). It may be put as an appeal to individual self-interest (you will be better off) or more generally (believers whose lives are bound together can realize some of the goods comprising a mature religious life). Objectors worry about whether one ever is able to bring choices down to just such a narrow selection – for example, to choose either theism or naturalism. Some think the argument is too thoroughly egotistic and thus offensive to religion. For a recent defence of the argument see Rescher (1985).

6 New Directions in the Field

Growth in the philosophy of religion shows no sign of abating. There are currently efforts to explore cross-cultural philosophy of religion, to articulate feminist challenges to traditional religions, to address postmodern versions of religion, and to consider a host of practical, moral and social problems from the standpoint of a philosophically articulate religious ethic, focusing on environmental, medical and political concerns. Specific issues internal to religious traditions are also receiving increased attention with philosophical speculation on the afterlife, heaven, hell, the sacraments, the meaning of revelation and the nature of religious communities.

Acknowledgements

The author gratefully acknowledges student comments on earlier versions of this chapter, especially from M. Okerlund, C. Gossett and G. Gentry.

Further Reading

Readers new to the philosophy of religion may begin with any of the introductory texts mentioned in the first section of the references, supplemented by one or more of these useful anthologies containing important papers or excerpts from books: P. Quinn and C. Taliaferro (forthcoming) includes 78 original essays spanning the history of the field in eastern and western philosophy. Mitchell (1971) contains papers on the early debates about the meaning of religious language, and includes early papers by Flew and Mitchell. T. V. Morris (1987) is an extremely useful collection on the concept of God, with papers by Kretzmann, Stump, Blumenfeld and Rowe.

Other valuable collections are edited by Pojman (1987), Rowe and Wainwright (1989), Brody (1974), Hick (1970), Geivett and Sweetman (1992), Hudson (1991), Beaty (1990), and MacDonald (1991).

Readers interested in exploring particular topics discussed in the chapter can turn to the books and articles in the second section of references.

Journals that are particularly strong in addressing the philosophy of religion are: *The International Journal for Philosophy of Religion, Religious Studies, Faith and Philosophy, Sophia, The Journal of Religion, The Journal of Religious Ethics*, and *The Heythrop Journal for Philosophy and Theology*. Papers in philosophy of religion are published in virtually all the main philosophy journals in the English-speaking world.

References

Introductory Texts

Abraham, W. 1985: *An Introduction to the Philosophy of Religion*. Englewood Cliffs, NJ: Prentice-Hall.
Davies, B. 1993: *An Introduction to the Philosophy of Religion*. Oxford: Oxford University Press.
Evans, S. C. 1985: *Philosophy of Religion*. Downers Grove, IL: Intervarsity.
Hick, J. 1990: *Philosophy of Religion* (4th edn). Englewood Cliffs, NJ: Prentice-Hall.
Peterson, M. et al. 1991: *Introduction to the Philosophy of Religion*. Oxford: Oxford University Press.
Rowe, W. 1993: *Philosophy of Religion*. Belmont: Wadsworth.
Taliaferro, C. (forthcoming): *An Introduction to Contemporary Philosophy of Religion*. Oxford: Blackwell.
Tilghman, B. R. 1993: *An Introduction to Philosophy of Religion*. Oxford: Blackwell.
Wainwright, W. 1988: *Philosophy of Religion*. Belmont: Wadsworth.

Other Books and Articles

Adams, R. M. 1987: *The Virtue of Faith*. Oxford: Oxford University Press.
Alston, W. 1991: *Perceiving God*. Ithaca: Cornell University Press.
—— 1991: The Inductive Argument from Evil. *Philosophical Perspectives*, 5, 29–68.
Augustine 1972 [426]: *The City of God* (translated by H. Bettenson). Harmondsworth: Penguin.
Barnes, J. 1972: *The Ontological Argument*. London: Macmillan.
Beaty, M. (ed.) 1990: *Christian Theism and the Problems of Philosophy*. Notre Dame: University of Notre Dame Press.
Beaty, M. and Taliaferro, C. 1990: God and Concept Empiricism. *Southwest Philosophy Review*, 6:2.
Boethius 1969 [524]: *The Consolation of Philosophy* (translated by V. E. Watts). Harmondsworth: Penguin.
Brody, B. (ed.) 1974: *Readings in the Philosophy of Religion*. Englewood Cliffs, NJ: Prentice-Hall.
Brown, D. 1987: *Continental Philosophy and Modern Theology*. Oxford: Blackwell.
Craig, W. 1979: *The Kalam Cosmological Argument*. New York: Barnes and Noble.
—— 1980: *The Cosmological Argument from Plato to Leibniz*. New York: Barnes and Noble.
Creel, R. 1995: *Divine Impassibility*. Cambridge: Cambridge University Press.
Dore, R. 1984: *Theism*. Dordrecht: D. Reidel.
Firth, R. 1970: Ethical Absolutism and the Ideal Observer. In W. Sellars and J. Hospers (eds), *Readings in Ethical Theory*. Englewood Cliffs, NJ: Prentice-Hall.
Flew, A. 1984: *God, Freedom and Immortality*. Buffalo: Prometheus Books.
Foster, J. 1985: *Ayer*. London: Routledge and Kegan Paul.
Geivett, R. and Sweetman, B. (eds) 1992: *Contemporary Perspectives on Religious Epistemology*. Oxford: Oxford University Press.

Gutting, G. 1982: *Religious Belief and Religious Skepticism*. Notre Dame: University of Notre Dame Press.

Hasker, W. 1989: *God, Time, and Knowledge*. Ithaca: Cornell University Press.

Helm, P. 1988: *Eternal God*. Oxford: Oxford University Press.

Hick, J. 1966: *Rational Theistic Belief Without Proof*. London and Basingstoke: Macmillan.

—— (ed.) 1970: *Classical and Contemporary Readings in the Philosophy of Religion*. Englewood Cliffs, NJ: Prentice-Hall.

—— 1978: *Evil and the God of Love*. New York: Harper and Row.

Hick, J. and McGill, A. (eds) 1967: *The Many Faced Argument*. New York: Macmillan.

Hudson, Y. (ed.) 1991: *The Philosophy of Religion*. London: Mayfield Publishing Co.

Hume, D. 1947 [1779]: *Dialogues Concerning Natural Religion* (edited by N. Kemp Smith). London: Nelson.

Kvanvic, J. 1986: *The Possibility of an All-Knowing God*. London: Macmillan.

Kenny, A. 1979: *The God of the Philosophers*. Oxford: Clarendon Press.

Leftow, B. 1991: *Time and Eternity*. Ithaca: Cornell University Press.

Linville, M. 1993: Divine Foreknowledge and the Libertarian Conception of Human Freedom. *Journal of the Philosophy of Religion*, 33.

MacDonald, S. 1991: *Being and Goodness*. Ithaca: Cornell University Press.

Mackie, J. 1985: *The Miracle of Theism*. Oxford: Clarendon Press.

Malcolm, N. 1975: The Groundlessness of Religious Beliefs. In S. Brown (ed.), *Reason and Religion*, Ithaca: Cornell University Press.

Martin, M. 1990: *Atheism*. Philadelphia: Temple University Press.

Menzel, C. and Morris, T. V. 1986: Absolute Creation. In *American Philosophical Quarterly*, 23, 353–62.

Meynell, H. 1982: *The Intelligible Universe*. Totowa: Barnes and Noble.

Mitchell, B. (ed.) 1971: *The Philosophy of Religion*. Oxford: Oxford University Press.

Mitchell, B. 1973: *The Justification of Religious Belief*. London: Macmillan.

Morris, T. V. 1987: *Anselmian Explorations*. Notre Dame: University of Notre Dame Press.

Morris, T. V. (ed.) 1987: *The Concept of God*. Oxford: Oxford University Press.

Nielsen, K. 1982: *An Introduction to the Philosophy of Religion*. New York: St. Martin's Press.

Owen, H. P. 1965: *The Moral Argument for Christian Theism*. London: George Allen and Unwin.

Penelhum, T. 1983: *God and Skepticism*. Dordrecht, Reidel.

Phillips, D. Z. 1970: *Concept of Prayer*. London: Routledge and Kegan Paul.

Plantinga, A. 1967: *God and Other Minds*. Ithaca: Cornell University Press.

—— 1974: *The Nature of Necessity*. Oxford: Oxford University Press.

—— 1980: *Does God Have a Nature?* Milwaukee: Marquette University Press.

—— 1993: *Warrant* (2 vols). Oxford: Oxford University Press.

Pojman, L. (ed.) 1987: *Philosophy of Religion: An Anthology*. Belmont, CA: Wadsworth.

Quinn, P. and Taliaferro, C. (eds) (forthcoming): *A Companion to Philosophy of Religion*. Oxford: Blackwell.

Reichenbach, B. 1972: *The Cosmological Argument*. Springfield, IL: Thomas Press.

—— 1982: *Evil and a Good God*. New York: Fordham University Press.

Rescher, N. 1985: *Pascal's Wager*. Notre Dame: University of Notre Dame Press.

Rhees, R. 1969: *Without Answers*. New York: Schocken Books.

Rowe, W. and Wainwright, W. J. (eds) 1989: *Philosophy of Religion: Selected Readings*. New York: Harcourt Brace Jovanovich.

Schlesinger, G. 1977: *Religion and Scientific Method*. Dordrecht: Reidel.

—— 1988: *New Perspectives on Old-Time Religion*. New York: Oxford University Press.

Sharma, Arvind 1990: *A Hindu Perspective on the Philosophy of Religion*. New York: St. Martin's Press.

Sorensen, R. A. 1992: *Thought Experiments*. Oxford: Oxford University Press.

Swinburne, R. 1977: *The Coherence of Theism*. Oxford: Clarendon Press.

—— 1979. *The Existence of God*. Oxford: Clarendon Press.

Taliaferro, C. 1994: *Consciousness and the Mind of God*. Cambridge: Cambridge University Press.

Taylor, R. 1963: *Metaphysics*. Englewood Cliffs, NJ: Prentice-Hall.

Tennant 1930: *Philosophical Theology*. Cambridge: Cambridge University Press.

Trigg, R. 1989: *Reality at Risk*. London: Harvester.

Wainwright, W. 1981: *Mysticism: A Study of Its Nature, Cognitive Value, and Moral Implications*. Madison: University of Wisconsin Press.

Wierenga, E. 1989: *The Nature of God*. Ithaca: Cornell University Press.

Wolterstorff, N. 1982: God Everlasting. In S. M. Cahn and D. Shatz (eds), *Contemporary Philosophy of Religion*, Oxford: Oxford University Press, 77–98.

Wykstra, S. 1984: The Humean Obstacle to Evidential Arguments from Suffering. *International Journal for Philosophy of Religion*, 16, 73–93.

Yandell, K. 1993: *The Epistemology of Religious Experience*. Cambridge: Cambridge University Press.

Discussion Questions

1   On the merits and problems of verificationism: How might an empiricist go about assessing the meaningfulness of the claim that God is non-physical, all-good and creative? If there is a non-physical God, does it follow that God cannot be perceived? If it is allowed that we can perceive (or somehow experience) God, can God's being omnipotent or being everywhere present be something perceivable? What about the other Divine attributes? Assuming an empiricist theory of meaning and the existence of God, how would God know about the cosmos? To be omniscient, would God have to have a massive number of (or perhaps infinitely many) sensory experiences?

2   Assess non-cognitive approaches to religious belief. Most versions of non-cognitivism assume a substantially 'all or nothing' position. Could a modified version of non-cognitivism be defended in which, say, the practice of prayer is treated cognitively, while belief in the afterlife is treated along non-cognitive lines? Is it intelligible to have faith in God without believing that God exists? Does it make any more (or less) sense to have hope that God will do something without belief that there is a God?

3   Given your understanding of the following terms, as used to describe human life, would using them as predicates to describe a supremely excellent, non-physical reality, require using them analogically or could they be used univocally? Knowledgeable, powerful, creative, good, intelligent, loving and wise. Alternatively, do you think any of them would have to be used equivocally?

4   How might one's theory of persons affect one's theory about God? Could it be that all created persons are physical while God is a person that is

non-physical? How many of the traditional, theistic Divine attributes could be preserved on the assumption that God is physical?

5   Illustrate some of the ways in which one's philosophy of religion is influenced by other areas of philosophy, including metaphysics, epistemology, ethics, the philosophy of language and the philosophy of history. Alternatively, consider a case where one's views in the philosophy of religion will have an influence on one's view of these other areas.

6   Critically analyse the following argument. If God is all-powerful, God can make a stone too heavy for anyone to lift. If God is all-powerful, God can lift any stone. God is not all-powerful, because God cannot create a stone too heavy for anyone to lift (because God can lift any stone) or God cannot lift any stone (if God succeeded in creating a stone too heavy for God to lift).

7   Is the existence of freedom compatible with foreknowledge? If not, can even God be free?

8   Analyses of omniscience typically focus on the scope of God's knowledge. Should the way in which God knows be considered as part of the meaning of what it is to be omniscient?

9   If a being is omnipotent, must it also be omniscient? To what extent, if any, can a being create itself? What is your view of the Menzel–Morris machine?

10   Do you find coherent the thesis that God is eternal? If God were eternal, could God know what time it is *now*? Could God have created time?

11   What is your assessment of the ideal observer theory and how this might articulate a God's-eye ethical point of view? Can theistic voluntarism be defended?

12   Can the failure to experience God be employed in a plausible argument providing evidence that there is no God? What is the difference between experiencing the absence of God and not experiencing God?

13   Assess the arguments for and against God's existence in this chapter, including:

arguments from religious experience, ontological arguments (consider both the traditional theistic version and the version cited above in which one argues against God's existence), cosmological arguments, teleological arguments, the problem of evil, arguments from miracles and wager arguments. How might these arguments be interconnected, so that the force of one argument depends on the others?

14 Does one need a successful theistic argument, such as the teleological, cosmological or ontological argument, in order for the belief that there is a God to be justified? Is there a burden of proof that is borne more by the religious believer than the naturalist?

15 In what way, if any, may traditional or other conceptions of an afterlife help us to deal with the problem of evil?

15

Ancient Greek Philosophy ─────────

Robert Wardy

> Western philosophy has its origins in ancient Greece, with speculation, problems and arguments stretching from the Presocratics to the major Hellenistic schools. Instead of concentrating on the rich variety of philosophical doctrines explored and defended in this brilliant formative period, the following chapter focuses on the deeply original conceptions of method developed by Socrates, Plato, Aristotle and the Hellenistic Stoics and Epicureans. This study of method provides a framework for understanding conceptions of philosophy, the goals of philosophers and the point of particular philosophical questions not only in ancient Greece, but also in subsequent philosophical periods, including our own.

Why read ancient Greek philosophy? The most obvious answer is that if the history of philosophy is a worthy object of study, then any serious philosopher must know something of the Greek contribution to the subject. This priority is not simply a matter of ancestral piety. It is not merely that Western philosophy began in ancient Greece. Because many of the defining techniques, characteristic preoccupations and perennial difficulties of philosophy arose during its brilliant first phase, anyone working in ignorance of those achievements and failures labours under a significant handicap. This large claim can be given both 'historical' and 'philosophical' specifications. Much MEDIEVAL (chapter 16) and later philosophy is unintelligible to those unacquainted with the Greek material that in large measure set the agenda for subsequent thinkers; while views of the distinctive goals and methods of philosophical investigation will be seriously impoverished if the initial Greek conceptions are left out of account.

Greek philosophy is as good as any philosophy ever done. During this century it has attracted many of the very best philosophical historians, and the explosion in scholarship within recent decades makes even a brief overview of work on a number of central issues impossible. New interpretations of Presocratic philosophy continue to appear, accompanied by renewed reflection on what factors distinguish the momentous new movement of rationalistic investigation from older, mythological patterns of thought (Lloyd, 1979, pp. 10–58). Much insight has been gained about the Greek invention of axiomatics, and about how philosophers and mathematicians might have interacted (Barnes, 1975; Lloyd, 1979, pp. 59–125). Revitalized interest in the theory of the virtues, practical reason and the naturalistic turn in ETHICS (chapter 6) has sharpened the appreciation that Aristotle (384–322 BC) is perhaps the West's most important ethical thinker (MacIntyre, 1981; Williams, 1985). Advances in the history of EPISTEMOLOGY (chapter 1) have established that Hellenistic skeptical controversy played a vital part in the evolution of theories of knowledge (Burnyeat, 1980, Annas and Barnes, 1985). Although Aristotle's LOGIC (chapter 4) continues to benefit from innovative new interpretations (Lear, 1980), there is also a steady increase in the illuminating study of hitherto neglected ancient logical systems (Frede, 1974, Brunschwig, 1980, Barnes, 1980, Denyer, 1991). A massive project of translation and exegesis is currently making generally available the vast resources of the late commentators on Aristotle, whose philosophical creativity had hitherto been neglected on the erroneous presumption that the exegetical format prohibits originality and because of the sheer difficulty of the largely untranslated, unexplored sources (Sorabji, 1987–   ).

1 Socrates and Dialectical Method

This list is only a very incomplete catalogue of ongoing research. Apart from a few passing illustrations, I shall concentrate exclusively on only one especially vigorous field, the study of dialectical method in ancient Greece. My discussion will still be heavily curtailed, but it will summarize some of ancient thought's most fruitful achievements and indicate current problems which should exercise all philosophers.

Philosophy has been provocatively described as 'footnotes to Plato'. In the contemporary scene it would be more accurate, if no less provocative, to characterize philosophy as answers to Socrates (c.470–399 BC). Why is he of such overwhelming importance? Although the argumentative exploration of reality and illusion which is philosophy was undertaken for the first time in the Greek colonies of Asia Minor roughly a century before his time, the indomitably rationalistic Socrates of the Platonic dialogues has completely dominated the western portrait of the archetypical philosopher, as can be seen during the Renaissance in Rabelais (c.1494–1553) and Montaigne (1533–92), and during the nineteenth-century intellectual upheaval in Kierkegaard (1813–55) and NIETZSCHE (1844–1900) (chapter 30).

Whether as hero or as villain, Socrates epitomizes the promise and the threat of philosophy. That these evocations of Socrates appear as often on the margins of philosophy as in its main text increases rather than diminishes his stature: the Socratic image connects philosophy with the great movements in literature, politics and religion which collectively give philosophy its place in culture. The Socrates of Plato's *Symposium* (1961) is a figure of almost grotesque physical ugliness concealing unequalled intellectual gifts, who devotes unceasing, singleminded effort to the discovery of vital ethical truths through disciplined argument. His effect on almost everyone is unsettling: he shakes their most cherished convictions, and arouses shame at failure to think rationally and live consistently by the light of reason. He inspires a passion beside which ordinary erotic feelings dwindle into insignificance.

Philosophy during the twentieth century in the English-speaking world has emerged from infatuation with an exceedingly narrow self-conception as the handmaid of the natural sciences; but it remains a self-contained, highly technical academic discipline largely inaccessible even to highly educated non-specialists. In consequence, Anglo-American philosophy has sadly almost completely lost the strength it gave to and received from the culture at large, and too easily lapses into esoteric scholasticism. Some responsibility for this isolation must rest with a longstanding feature of philosophy, its claim to transcend merely personal persuasion by conforming solely to the dictates of objective canons of argument; people outside philosophy are not readily inclined to listen to unattractively impersonal, difficult messages. The central enigma of Socrates is that whereas the standards of argument to which he adhered are a model of rigour, he worked not in an academy, but in the market-place and streets of Athens. In the Platonic image of Socrates, irresistible personality and dialectical force, subjective and objective appeal, inextricably combine. Contemporary philosophers worried about the marginalization and inaccessibility of their subject do well to ponder Socrates' universal impact; philosophers complacent about their specialism do even better if forced to awaken from their dogmatic slumbers by the Socratic gadfly (Plato, *Apology*, 1961, 30E).

In what sense was Socrates a street-philosopher? As portrayed in the earlier Platonic dialogues, he can do philosophy not by himself, but rather with and against an interlocutor. He examines anyone whomsoever with a reputation for wisdom (*Apology*, 23B), including but not limiting himself to professional thinkers, and deliberately seeks out the politicians, poets and artisans of Athens (*Apology*, 21B–22E). (Since the women of ancient Greece did not engage in public affairs, Socrates does not argue with them, but that is not on account of lack of interest; when he describes his attitude towards existence after death, if such there be, he indicates his enthusiasm at the prospect of continuing his characteristic debates with famous men *and women* in the afterlife (*Apology*, 41C).) Why did Socrates carry on in this fashion? As he famously declares, 'the unexamined life is not worth living for a human' (*Apology*, 38A). Although he abstained as much as possible from involvement in political affairs as conventionally understood, his conviction was that the only way to achieve virtue was to understand it; Socratic philosophy, so far from being an academic avoidance of the active life, was the essential means of conducting life properly, and challenged everyone without exception.

The Socratic method of doing philosophy, adversarial co-operation, sounds paradoxical; how did it work? Its Greek name, *elenchos*, occurs outside philosophical contexts and means 'testing' or 'examination'. Nowhere does Socrates formally delineate, let alone justify, his procedure, but it is possible to derive a description of his standard practice from a consideration of the Platonic dialogues where it is put to work. Socrates gets his interlocutor to offer an answer to the question 'What is X?', where the value of 'X' is usually, if not always, a virtue such as courage, justice or piety. In these dialogues *that* there is such a thing as, say, courage is taken for granted; and *what sort of thing* it might be – an item in the world, as people and colours are in their different ways, or a mental item, or a feature of the Greek language – is also never made an object of enquiry. Thus Socratic *elenchos* is a matter of definition, yet vital questions concerning the nature and import of definition are not raised.

Once his partner has offered a candidate definition, Socrates typically proceeds by eliciting his support for further propositions. Sometimes the connection between these propositions and the original definition is immediately obvious, sometimes not; but the eventual result is always an argument using the definition whose conclusion either directly contradicts it, or at least conflicts with assumptions the interlocutor is not willing to surrender. The outcome is consistently negative: Socratic 'examination' is refutation, establishing that a proposed definition of some virtue is unacceptable because it entails contradiction directly or indirectly. Socrates concludes that his partner has no better grasp on the nature of that which is being defined, the *definiendum*, than he himself, and urges that they persevere in the definitional quest, since nothing could be more important than knowledge of what they demonstrably do not know.

The logic of the Socratic *elenchos* has continuously fascinated workers on Greek philosophy, and recently provoked a series of extremely important studies from the late Gregory Vlastos (1907–91), the leading Socratic scholar of this century. Vlastos is exercised by two closely interrelated questions. The *elenchos* as described can evidently at best hope to establish the consistency, not the truth, of the interlocutor's beliefs, but it is overwhelmingly obvious that Socrates aspires to objective validity; how can he suppose that his philosophical method might get beyond merely human agreement? Then, in the so-called 'middle' dialogues, the Platonic Socrates is made to propound a collection of TRANSCENDENTAL (chapter 22), METAPHYSICAL (chapter 2) and EPISTEMOLOGICAL (chapter 1) doctrines strikingly different from anything encountered before in the corpus. It is now common ground to almost all scholars that these pronouncements represent Plato's own later philosophy, supplementing but also largely supplanting the *elenchos*, which is itself perhaps to be identified with the method of the historical Socrates. So Vlastos tries to understand how the real Socrates could justifiably have used the *elenchos* as an instrument reaching beyond consistency to truth, and why Plato ultimately rejected his hero's position.

In 'The Socratic Elenchus', Vlastos (1983) makes a proposal which has excited the greatest interest. He emphasizes that the procedure of eliciting contradiction sketched above is a significantly incomplete description of Socrates' procedure. In addition, it is essential that we recognize that Socrates demands that his interlocutor's responses be *sincere*: the *elenchos* is examination, not of neutral propositions which might be held, but rather of *asserted propositions*, these being the sincere beliefs of Socrates' dialectical partner. This feature of the method is of vital importance to Vlastos because he argues that if the *elenchos* works on commitments rather than bare, unasserted propositions, it can yield substantive results on one, admittedly remarkable, assumption: namely, that the belief-sets of all human beings always contain true propositions on the basis of which it is always possible to refute their false beliefs. Socrates can transcend mere inconsistency because inconsistency with the truth is not just inconsistency – it is falsehood. Finally, we are to understand Plato's eventual renunciation of the *elenchos* – and with it the populism characteristic of authentic Socratic street-philosophy – as the outcome of his dissatisfaction with Socrates' startling epistemological faith, a dissatisfaction issuing eventually in the philosophy transcending ordinary beliefs and experience intimately associated with his name.

Vlastos' proposal has produced intense debate rather than easy consent. His thesis is intrinsically unstable. The leading theme of his later book is that the procedures and convictions of the 'real' Socrates and the later, Platonic 'Socrates' 'contrast as sharply with one another as with any third philosophy you care to mention'. (Vlastos, 1991, p. 46.) One aspect of this near schizophrenia is the total epistemological naivety, or at least total silence on epistemological topics, of the 'real' Socrates: Vlastos' analysis of the logic of the *elenchos* is inferred from, rather than seen in, the actual text of the dialogues. Thus he must attribute to Socrates highly contentious and un-defended, if not indefensible, philosophical tenets, while maintaining that they remain wholly implicit in the practice of their original proponent and only break out in order to be rejected in Plato's subsequent reflections. This scenario strains credibility, and has not won general support; the nature and implications of Socratic questioning continue to trouble readers of Greek philosophy.

It is now easy to see why I labelled the *elenchos* 'adversarial': propositions are asserted by Socrates' partner in the course of the search for a definition, and are *refuted* on the basis of his further admissions. But how is this method also 'co-operative'? Anticipating or reacting to his interlocutors' irritation at being worsted, Socrates declares time and again that examination of his type is not a personal matter: for example, when in the *Gorgias* he is about to elicit further damaging admissions, he insists that he does this 'not for your sake, but for the argument, so that it will advance in the fashion best able to render what is under discussion clear to us' (Plato, *Gorgias*, 1961, 453C). Dialectical argument does not fall within the scope of a personal pronoun; it is neither 'yours' nor 'mine'; rather, it progresses through the phases of critical examination to the intellectual and moral benefit of questioner and answerer alike. Dialectic is ultimately for the sake of knowledge. If it appears to attack or spare the interlocutor, that is a mere appearance. The argument itself is not only our chief but our sole concern: we interact with our partner only because and in so far as he contributes to the investigation. By the same token we do not care about our own dialectical fate as such, that is, whether whatever fragment or figment of truth emerging from the discussion is 'ours'. Truth, on this Socratic conception, is not a commodity accessible at some positions within a hierarchy at the expense of the occupants of other positions; all participants in the discussion share success – arriving at the truth – communally.

Perhaps the most salient characteristic of ancient Greek society is that it was *agonistic*, or competitive: whether in politics, art or athletics, Greeks *com-peted*. Intellectual life was no exception to this generalization. The prototypes of what we now distinguish as western philosophy, science, medicine and even mathematics were invented by the Greeks not by dispassionate, disinterested investigation in a calm institutional setting, but rather in an arena of strident, often highly personal, debate. Of the many metaphorical descriptions of philosophy itself that appear in Plato's writings, those likening it to combat predominate: philosophy is a struggle in which one opponent is worsted by another with argumentative weapons. This gladiatorial conception survives to this day – witness the ease with which contemporary philosophers speak admiringly of a 'knock-down argument' – and is largely responsible for the suspicion, hardening into active dislike, in which philosophy is now often held. The view is prevalent that philosophical reason is, together with science, a mere intellectual manifestation of distinctively masculine aggression concealing its violence beneath the ideology of objectivity. This largely FEMINIST (chapter 32), occasionally non-western, critique of the arrogance of reason deserves to be treated with the utmost seriousness, and we cannot do better than to turn to Socrates not for a definitive answer, but for highly suggestive indications of where an answer might lie. The *elenchos* does not abjure aggressive argument; it does, however, insist that rational enquiry resides in a special form of disciplined competition aiming at mutual benefit rather than at victimization for its own sake. There is good reason to query the tenability, perhaps even the coherence, of Socrates' *elenchos*, but philosophers eager to confront the modern attack on their rationalistic pretensions still have everything to learn from his ideal.

I have mentioned Vlastos' insistence that under discussion in Socratic dialectic are sincere beliefs; given the importance of the *definienda*, the virtues, what are examined are a person's deepest commitments, that person's *life*, not academic opinions defended only in school. This assertion raises a final problem for us. Vlastos is emphatically interested in the historical truth; he is anything but insensitive to the fact that information about Socrates is filtered to us through the medium of Plato's writings, among others, but he still avowedly conceives of his task as the *historical* exercise of extracting factual information from documentary sources.

Thinking About Method

Vlastos champions Plato as the historical, not just the philosophical, authority on Socrates. Leaving aside the persistent controversy over the merits of this judgement, what we should recognize is that the 'sincere beliefs' underpinning interlocutors' 'lives' in Plato's writings are words given to characters in dialogues. Socrates and Plato together should encourage the student to think hard about philosophical method, not now in the sense of the *elenchos* as opposed to some other particular mode of enquiry, but in the sense of oral as opposed to written, aporetic as opposed to demonstrative, and 'scientific' as opposed to 'literary'. The real Socrates wrote nothing down; the Platonic Socrates is constantly engaged in argumentative discussion, but is not represented as going off to record his negative results in any sort of treatise. Doubtless in large measure as a consequence of the uniform failure of candidate definitions, Socratic philosophy is not a written product, but an oral process; it is something that happens between partners in dialectic, not a body of formulizable doctrine to be learnt by the passive reader. It is almost impossible to exaggerate the significance of this feature of Socratic practice, which survives with modifications throughout ancient philosophy. The core of Greek philosophy remains a live encounter between dialecticians debating a thesis according to more or less well-articulated rules of argumentation, and this undoubtedly led to an especially sophisticated sensitivity to and exploitation of the logic of self-refutation, most ably expounded by Burnyeat (Burnyeat 1976a, 1976b and 1990). The first, most difficult, and most important lesson for any aspiring student is that philosophy is properly understood not as a body of ideas, no matter how interesting, but as a living activity of argument undertaken by practitioners who, ideally at least, share standards of rational debate rather than an official set of opinions. Reading Plato's descriptions of Socrates at work is no guarantee that this lesson will be learned, but it can provide matchless insight into how philosophy, as opposed to 'the history of ideas', is actually done.

2 Plato

Platonic dialogue is written philosophy, but it, no less than the Socratic model, challenges unthinking assumptions about how a philosopher should communicate. It is a commonplace of scholarship and culture at large that Plato ranks as a uniquely gifted literary artist as well as a philosopher of genius; yet, all the best intentions notwithstanding, a disastrous tendency persists to conceive of his dialogues as hard philosophical content tricked out in attractive but disposable literary ornament. At least so far as his own writings are concerned, we have no idea of what Plato himself thought about anything. The character 'Socrates' is no more Plato than Hamlet is Shakespeare. The dialogues confront us with arguments whose construction we can observe in fictional debates between fictional characters and which should therefore force us to react to them as products of a fabricated *mise en scène*. Some 'literary' factors are potentially as influential as conventionally 'philosophical' ones, and conclusions are always *ad hominem*, rather than of universal import.

The Platonic dialogue is an invitation to argue, not a record of endorsed propositions. It offers an alternative – devastating in its seductive and irritating charm – to the model of the expository treatise, one which constitutes an outstanding *prima facie* counter-example to this century's prevalent dogma: that philosophy achieves a probative force beyond fiction by austerely sacrificing the meretricious attractions of literary artifice. To a considerable extent, the potency of Plato's challenge to philosophers' comfortable but limiting presumptions about what they should be doing and how they should be doing it, derives from the methodological *self*-reflection with which the dialogues abound. Consider this striking exchange from *Protagoras* (1982):

> SOCRATES: 'Being, as it happens, a rather forgetful sort of person, Protagoras, I tend to forget, faced with a lengthy statement, the original point of the argument. Now, suppose I happen to be hard of hearing: if you meant to hold a conversation with me, you would think it necessary to speak more loudly than normal; so now that you are faced by a man with a poor memory, please cut your answers down and make them short enough for me to follow.'

PROTAGORAS: 'What do you mean "make my answers short"? Am I to make them shorter than is necessary?'
SOCRATES: 'Certainly not.'
PROTAGORAS: 'As short as is necessary, then?'
SOCRATES: 'Yes.'
PROTAGORAS: 'Am I then to make my answers as short as I think necessary, or as short as you think necessary?' (334C–E)

Socrates' representation of his dissatisfaction with the way his interlocutor has been going on at (what he feels to be) evasive length as merely the upshot of a feeble memory is, of course, a particularly abrasive instance of his celebrated irony. Plato is indirectly inviting us to ponder the relative merits of extended, narrative exposition and sharp, argumentative dialectical interchange. But we must not jump to the conclusion that this is no more than a cryptic invitation to endorse uncritically the procedure of the Socratic 'hero', and reject that of the 'sophistical' villain, Protagoras. Protagoras – who is also a Platonic character – is given an excellent riposte by the philosophical dramatist when he is made to ask *whose* authority arbitrates, who decides just how much is enough. The last thing we attentive, perhaps even argumentative, readers of Platonic dialogues are here encouraged to do is to take anything for granted. The classic dilemma confronting enemies of complacency is how they might attack the tyranny of unthinking convention without themselves, if successful, becoming yet further figures of baleful authority. Plato has certainly become such a figure; but a careful reading of the dialogues should, on the contrary, persuade us that he expended the wealth of his philosophical and literary genius on the most ingenious efforts to frustrate our most likely expectations – that is, to make us think philosophically. Contemporary scholars more readily admit the profound consequences of the dialogue form than in the past, but continue to struggle to come to terms with its daunting implications. Hubbard and Karnofsky (1982) is a highly exceptional effort to help the student catch the repercussions of Plato's format; their 'Socratic commentary' strives to overcome the self-defeating dogmatism of traditional Platonic interpretation by restricting itself exclusively to questions.

3 Aristotle

As with Socrates and Plato, so too in Aristotelian studies it is the case that especially important recent work focuses on methodology. A major concern throughout the history of philosophy has been the discovery, analysis and evaluation of convictions deeply entrenched within a given society or, in the case of especially ambitious philosophical projects, held by humanity at large. We have already seen how Socrates' definitional project skirts the question of *what sort of thing* is being defined. Plato's development of Socratic practice was an answer with a vengeance: postulation of the existence of unqualified, perfect exemplars beyond space and time, the so-called Platonic Forms.

Aristotle, however, pursues dialectical investigation by working from what he calls the *endoxa* and the *phainomena*, which it was once standard practice to translate as 'common beliefs' and 'phenomena' respectively. But, largely under the influence of G. E. L. Owen (1922–82) (1986; and supplemented by Nussbaum, 1986), it is now generally agreed that these renderings are unacceptable for reasons central to the proper understanding of Aristotle's method. *Endoxa* are not merely common beliefs, although they might be widespread; they are *reputable* beliefs, espoused either by 'the many' or 'the wise'. Similarly, *phainomena* are not limited to, although they include, observable 'phenomena'; they are 'appearances' which embrace what people are inclined to accept without prompting across a spectrum much broader than the latter-day empiricist connotations of the word 'phenomena' might suggest.

Aristotle's characteristic method when addressing questions in the philosophy of nature as well as in ethics and politics is first of all to gather together these appearances and reputable opinions. Often when collected they seem to conflict, either superficially or in some more serious fashion. This (ostensible) conflict is what he calls an *aporia*, a puzzle. For him the role of the philosopher is to take on not any random problem but puzzles generated in this way by disharmony in suggestions which deserve a high degree of initial credence. The philosopher's job is essentially conciliatory, to explain that the conflict is a matter of mere appearance wherever this is the case, and, where the difficulty runs deeper, to adjudicate between the opposing views, effecting the minimal adjustments necessary to resolve the conflict.

In Aristotelian dialectic, Greek philosophy attained a degree of analytical subtlety and breadth of scope which has been equalled but never surpassed. Yet the method has troubling implications. The *endoxa* also include what we, at least, are inclined to view as linguistic phenomena: Aristotle draws sweeping conclusions from 'what we say' – that is, what ordinary people say in Greek. The sceptical modern reaction is to ask how his claims about Greek morphology, syntax and usage support substantial propositions valid beyond the confines of his linguistic community, even if they are correct. Furthermore, the fear that a method otherwise admirably inclined to treat untutored opinion with considerable respect might yet spill over into ideological justification for pernicious beliefs and practices finds ample justification in Aristotle's notorious theories that certain people – slaves – are 'living instrumental property' (Aristotle, 1984, *Politics*, I.2) and that the female sex is a 'natural deformation' of the male standard, defined by incapacity (Aristotle, 1984, *De Generatione Animalium*, A.20 – a devastating critique is to be found in Lear, 1988). There is no comparison between Aristotle's methodological self-consciousness and Socrates' silence about how the *elenchos* works, but precisely the same problem which impelled Vlastos to attribute to Socrates an undefended conviction that everyone's belief-set contains some true beliefs about virtue re-emerges when we reflect on Aristotle's philosophical practice: how can he be confident that his dialectic ever achieves objective truth, rather than just coherent (and perhaps coherently *false*) belief?

Irwin on Aristotle's Dialectic

Irwin proposes an evolutionary answer to the problem (Irwin, 1988). He argues that Aristotelian dialectic passes through two stages. An initial 'weak' form does indeed aspire to no more than coherence, but it is superseded by 'strong' dialectic, which tries to establish results that are 'true' by the standards of metaphysical realism and valid by reference to the world, not our attitudes. For Irwin this evolution is possible because 'strong' dialectic proceeds from a privileged subset of beliefs, those which cannot be rejected on pain of forfeiting rationality, such as the principle of non-contradiction. This principle rejects the possibility of a proposition and its negation both being true. Irwin's argument has excited much interest, but is vulnerable on two major fronts. Firstly, even if so-called 'strong' dialectic can be isolated, it is hard to see how anything beyond a very few fundamental principles could meet its forbidding standards and thus yield 'strong' results; since Aristotle's philosophy covers so much more than the foundations of metaphysics and epistemology, most of his dialectical work would remain 'weak'. Secondly, Irwin's reading of Aristotle is unashamedly KANTIAN (chapter 22): his solution attributes to him a type of transcendental argument which gained currency in the history of philosophy long after the Greek period. Furthermore, transcendental arguments themselves might face the same problem of moving beyond coherence to truth.

An alternative approach searches for an answer constructed exclusively from Aristotelian materials (Wardy, 1991). The Aristotelian natural world is teleological: that is, many, perhaps all, characteristics of the structure and behaviour of natural kinds are to be explained in terms of what is good for them. Although the import of Aristotle's arguments for teleology is a matter for debate (Sedley, 1991 and Wardy, 1993), it is perfectly clear that Aristotelian teleological explanations are irreducible. They can often be supplemented by causal accounts which cite, say, material processes, but they cannot be reduced to non-teleological explanation. A teleological explanation constitutes a perfectly legitimate reason, complete in itself, for some state of affairs to be as it is. The alternative interpretation of Aristotle's dialectic is simply an application of this global teleology to the human species. For Aristotle, we are *essentially* knowers; a human being is a rational animal endowed with innate speculative curiosity. Since Aristotle's teleological philosophy dictates that no animal kind can be radically frustrated in fulfilling its nature, it follows that the world must be accessible to human enquiry. Just as the lower animals are obliged to struggle to survive, so too we cannot uncritically accept the *phainomena* and *endoxa* without modification – but the real truth is there to be found. Aristotle's confidence in the utility of his dialectical method as an instrument for discovering absolute truth relies on his philosophical biology. Since his biology in turn is derived from an exercise in that very dialectic, the purported 'justification' seems to beg the question. But it might be that dissatisfaction with this circularity is the product of imposing post-Kantian epistemological concerns on Aristotle, with the inevitable result that his thought is either severely distorted or found seriously wanting.

The argument between these candidate solutions to the riddle of Aristotle's method remains unresolved. Quite apart from the obvious intrinsic interest of comprehending his procedure, the debate is a particularly apt illustration within Greek philosophy of an inescapable dilemma in all philosophical historiography. One might feel that the Kantian reading is anachronistic, while the teleological explanation lands Aristotle with a strange position that is totally inaccessible to contemporary philosophers. All historical study entails commitments taking the investigator far beyond mundane factual reportage. In the history of philosophy, this commitment is to doing philosophy when doing the history of philosophy. If philosophers are to learn from their past, then they must abandon hope of an easy formula dictating interpretations which succeed in engaging with old arguments while avoiding anachronistic deformation. One of the most valuable gifts the history of philosophy has to offer us can be a glimpse of how *different* philosophy was at other times. By 'different' I mean not just that earlier thinkers propounded a rich variety of doctrines now unfamiliar, although there is no doubt that historical expertise makes available a range of potential ideas easily overlooked by too narrow a concentration on contemporary views. The more challenging sense of 'difference' accessible through history is the realization that the very terms in which the apparently constant problems of philosophy are posed, the logical and heuristic considerations to which thinkers are sensitive, the standards to which they submit their arguments, might themselves be susceptible to historical change (not necessarily progress). The debate over Aristotelian method exemplifies this most fruitful dilemma, and the expansion of philosophical perspective it encourages.

4 Hellenistic Methodology

If one had to select the single most important development in work on ancient Greek philosophy in recent times, it would doubtless be the renaissance in Hellenistic studies. Until a few years ago, the prevailing attitude towards the Hellenistic period even among ancient Greek specialists was dismissive. The usual view left Plato and Aristotle in splendid isolation, the first figures in a parade of great philosophers all too often followed immediately by a contingent from the seventeenth century. Although later Greek philosophers had their able advocates, the relative inaccessibility of the scattered source materials, all too often in the form of biased indirect testimony, exacerbated the neglect into which Hellenistic philosophy had lapsed since the time of the Enlightenment. The publication of a major new study (Long and Sedley, 1987) utterly transformed the situation. Their invaluable collection of the sources both in the original languages and in translation with extensive commentary permits all philosophers to penetrate the relatively unknown territory of the Hellenistic period with assurance.

An immediate advantage from some familiarity with Hellenistic philosophy is proof that one hallowed notion, that of the 'timeless' problems of philosophy, crumbles on inspection. To name but the most obvious examples,

Hellenistic philosophers invented two issues, determinism and skepticism, which so came to dominate later preoccupations that the unwary are tempted into supposing that these topics are eternally present in philosophy. This mistake at once instils false expectations of what can be reasonably expected when evaluating earlier periods – for example, bewildered surprise at the incapacity of Aristotle's theory of voluntariness to cope with determinism, or grave misconstruals of Plato's epistemological concepts – and prohibits recognition of the sheer creativity of the Hellenistic contribution.

But, as on so many other points we have canvassed, there is a healthy lack of consensus on one particularly important question. In at least some respects, the Greek chapter in philosophical history is surprisingly unified. The period stretching from the Presocratics to the later Neoplatonists is more than a millennium, but even the very latest work falling within it demonstrates an acute appreciation of inherited insights and a largely shared problematic. The remarkable force of this coherence becomes apparent when we reflect that Aquinas (1224–74) is closer to us in time than figures at the two ends of the Greek millennium were to one another. This intellectual cohesion lends Greek philosophy much of its appeal, but readily shades into a highly questionable methodological principle: namely, that ancient philosophers react to the work of their more or less immediate predecessors in obedience to our sense of chronology and importance. Application of this principle has produced the assumption that since Aristotle is a towering figure for us, he must similarly have dominated the formation of Hellenistic philosophy – which is indeed a guiding assumption of much recent scholarship. Central Hellenistic doctrines have been regularly interpreted as products of reflection on Aristotelian insights or as efforts to circumvent some of his criticisms. But an alternative school maintains that Aristotelian philosophy went into rapid eclipse shortly after his death and did not regain prominence until long after the formative phase of Hellenistic philosophy (Sandbach, 1985). Long and Sedley themselves differ over this issue, only the former routinely explaining features of Hellenistic positions by adducing an Aristotelian forerunner.

What did the Hellenistic philosophers have to say about our major theme regarding method, the recognition, assessment and exploitation of non-philosophical belief? I stressed that translation of the cardinal term *endoxon* in Aristotle as 'common belief' is a grave error; *reputable* opinion is his dialectical material. Hellenistic method worked with a very different set of assumptions: its dialectic did indeed operate on *general* opinions, designated 'common preconceptions'. The leading schools active in this period shared the concept 'common preconception', but differed sharply over its signification and, of course, what the preconceptions actually were. The Stoics, on one side, argued that Nature, identified as a divine, providential reason informing the entire cosmos, leads us to form certain notions on which we might ultimately build a comprehensive philosophy to guide us through every aspect of life. Their arch-opponents, the Epicureans, denied the existence of any such divine rationality, while arguing that human beings naturally construct reliable preconceptions on the basis of sense perception. Although the schools disagreed about the mechanism responsible for our natural intellectual endowment, they largely agreed on the reality, reliability and philosophical significance of our preconceptions. Both camps also propounded Naturalistic ethical theories: life has a goal which is determined by nature itself, and success in living depends entirely on perceiving and conforming to the conditions which might permit us to achieve the good according to nature. For the Epicureans, this goal was pleasure and the absence of pain; for the Stoics, it was 'living according to reason'.

How do 'common preconceptions' have a bearing on the argument between Epicureans and Stoics concerning the real goal of life? Neither school asserted, implausibly, that people apprehended their favoured doctrine in all its detail as a matter of naturally-acquired knowledge: that extreme position could not even accommodate the existence of wrong-headed Stoics (or Epicureans) without embarrassment. Instead, *pre*conceptions were made to provide a fundamentally sound initial indication of the truth which is, however, vulnerable to subsequent corruption, and requires elaboration and defence from, of course, the correct philosophy. The result was a brace of fascinating developments in dialectical technique. The Hellenistic thinkers were the first philosophers to adduce the evidence of infantile behaviour in support of their doctrines: Epicureans claimed that babies *naturally* seek pleasure and shun pain, Stoics that they strive for self-preservation and avoid extinction (these arguments have received magisterial attention from Brunschwig, 1986). Secondly, the common allegiance to a form of innatist epistemology led proponents of rival philosophies to criticize hostile citation of ostensible 'preconceptions' for a variety of intriguing reasons.

It is easy to adopt a jaundiced attitude towards such Hellenistic debate. For any issue, it might seem to us that if it appeared to favour Epicureanism, then its champions would say that it is a trustworthy expression of our natural intellectual equipment, incorrigible within the limits of its only partial articulation of the truth; while the Stoics would protest that, although there certainly are reliable conceptions realizable by grace of providential reason and harmonizing with Stoicism, in this instance social contamination has in some way bastardized the opinion. If, on the other hand, the Stoics claimed the support of a common preconception, the Epicureans could readily reply that in this case spontaneous, true instinct has been adulterated by the admixture of unhealthy social conditioning. The ever-present availability of the charge of corruption-by-society ensured that the testimony of common preconceptions could never control the excesses of inter-school dialectic, which threatens to degenerate into mere polemic. It is clear from Brunschwig's study that although Hellenistic philosophers believed that human nature is manifest at a pre-cultural age, they evinced little inclination to engage in the scrupulous observation of infants evidently called for by this belief; and the search for such data was anything but systematic. Nevertheless, we should avoid too harsh a judgement. The doctrine of preconception encouraged the Stoics in particular to turn to non-philosophical witnesses, especially literary ones, which made their philosophy receptive to an enriching diversity of influences.

If Hellenistic philosophy is vulnerable to heavy criticism of the opportunities it often missed by manipulating, rather than reacting circumspectly to, formulations of common belief, we must remember that this philosophical problem does have a good claim to figure on a cautious list of 'perennial' challenges to philosophers. All but the most obstinately scientistic and increasingly old-fashioned modern thinkers would concede that philosophy cannot avoid deriving substantial impetus from sources clearly related to both Aristotelian *endoxa* and Hellenistic common preconceptions. We, of course, subscribe neither to the proto-Kantianism dubiously attributed to Aristotle, nor to the epistemic teleology to which he undoubtedly subscribed, nor again to the Hellenistic philosophers' ambitious epistemic naturalism. But whether or not we go so far as to characterize our activity as conceptual or linguistic analysis, the fact remains that we are often in the uneasy position of armchair theoreticians obliged to pronounce on what people 'really' believe. If contemporary philosophers do rather better than their pioneering Hellenistic ancestors in assimilating the discoveries of a multiplicity of empirical disciplines, they still face the uncomfortable task of distinguishing in a well-motivated, convincing fashion between innocent belief and the construction put on it by philosophy.

I warned at the outset that my treatment of ancient dialectic would be obliged to omit even the mention, let alone the sustained discussion, of crucial episodes in the history of Greek philosophical methodology. But it would be very wrong to leave the topic without encouraging the reader to connect positive Hellenistic epistemic naturalism with the period's negative epistemological invention, scepticism. The primary challenge confronting ancient sceptics was whether it was possible consistently to maintain that all the schools of dogmatic philosophy had failed to reach the truth, or at least had failed to prove that they had reached it, while nevertheless avoiding an ironically self-refuting dogmatic commitment to the truth of scepticism itself. Further, the vigorous dialectic of the Hellenistic era helped to create and feed another important development in the philosophical deployment of common beliefs, a development which has also only just begun to achieve the scholarly respect it deserves. Philosophers of the so-called sceptical schools, Academics and neo-Pyrrhonists, were not only adept in pitting ordinary beliefs against the philosophical doctrines of their 'dogmatist' rivals – the Stoic, Epicurean, Peripatetic or Platonist – and in alleging intolerable inconsistencies between what opposing schools claimed as 'natural' beliefs, tendencies or practices. They also *displayed* the ordinary beliefs and practices of different places, times, and cultures *as* different, but as equally valid – or equally invalid. All such manipulations of common conceptions were intended to contribute to the desired sceptical end: the suspension of belief in the face of as yet unresolved, and perhaps irresolvable, universal conflicts between ideas, beliefs, perceptions and arguments. One of the most interesting current debates about ancient scepticism precisely concerns the questions whether such suspension extends to all beliefs, and whether, if so, any human life, let alone a desirable one, is possible in such a state (Burnyeat, 1980; Frede, 1984).

The aim of this limited exercise has been to demonstrate how even a narrowly focused survey of some aspects of the philosophical methods of Socrates, Plato, Aristotle and the Hellenistic schools immediately reveals a provocative mixture of argument and assumption about how philosophy could and should be conducted; the exercise could easily be repeated again and again for many other essential topics. No philosopher can afford to ignore the history of Greek philosophy; but, then again, no philosopher would want to.

Further Reading

Barnes (1980) and Brunschwig (1980) make fascinating companion-pieces, while Brunschwig (1986) is a model of philosophically illuminating historical reconstruction. The works of Burnyeat (1976a, 1976b, 1980 and 1990) have all been deservedly hailed as masterpieces (the last is quite possibly the finest modern commentary on a Platonic dialogue). Frede (1974) remains the classic study of Stoic logic. Lear (1988) is the best of the many single-volume introductions to Aristotle for philosophers. No student should be unacquainted with the uniformly brilliant, unfailingly provocative essays collected in Owen (1986).

References

Plato and Aristotle

There are many valuable translations of Plato and Aristotle, but readers might find it helpful to use two standard collections:

Plato 1961: *The Collected Dialogues of Plato* (edited by E. Hamilton and H. Cairns). Princeton: Princeton University Press.
Aristotle 1984: *The Complete Works of Aristotle* (edited by J. Barnes) 2 vols. Princeton: Princeton University Press.

In addition, Oxford University Press has published two series of translations with philosophical commentary:

Plato, *Clarendon Plato* series 1973– : Oxford: Oxford University Press.
Aristotle, *Clarendon Aristotle* 1975– : Oxford: Oxford University Press.

Other Works

Annas, J. and Barnes, J. 1985: *The modes of scepticism, ancient texts and modern interpretations.* Cambridge: Cambridge University Press.
Barnes, J. 1975: *Aristotle's Posterior Analytics, translated with notes.* Oxford: Clarendon Press.

—— 1980: 'Proof destroyed'. In M. Schofield, M. F. Burnyeat and J. Barnes (eds) *Doubt and dogmatism, studies in Hellenistic epistemology*, Oxford: Clarendon Press, 161–81.

Brunschwig, J. 1980: Proof defined. In M. Schofield, M. F. Burnyeat and J. Barnes (eds), *Doubt and dogmatism, studies in Hellenistic epistemology*, Oxford: Clarendon Press, 125–60.

—— 1986: The cradle argument in Epicureanism and Stoicism..In M. Schofield and G. Striker (eds), *The norms of nature, studies in Hellenistic ethics*, Cambridge: Cambridge University Press, 113–44.

Burnyeat, M. F. 1976a: Protagoras and self-refutation in Plato's *Theaetetus*. *Philosophical Review*, 85, 172–95.

—— 1976b: Protagoras and self-refutation in later Greek philosophy. *Philosophical Review*, 85, 44–69.

—— 1980: Can the Sceptic live his scepticism? In M. Schofield, M. F. Burnyeat and J. Barnes (eds), *Doubt and dogmatism, studies in Hellenistic epistemology*, Oxford: Clarendon Press, 20–53.

—— 1990: *The Theaetetus of Plato* (with a revised translation by M. J. Levett). Cambridge: Hackett Publishing Company.

Denyer, N. C. 1991: *Language, thought and falsehood in ancient Greek philosophy*. London: Routledge.

Frede, M. 1974: *Die stoische Logik*. Göttingen: Vandenhoeck and Ruprecht.

—— (1984). The sceptic's two kinds of assent and the question of the possibility of knowledge. In R. Rorty, J. B. Schneewind and Q. Skinner (eds), *Philosophy in History. Essays on the historiography of philosophy*, Cambridge: Cambridge University Press, 255–78.

Hubbard, B. A. F. and Karnofsky, E. S. 1982: *Plato's Protagoras, a Socratic commentary*. London: Duckworth.

Irwin, T. H. 1988: *Aristotle's first principles*. Oxford: Clarendon Press.

Lear, J. 1980: *Aristotle and logical theory*. Cambridge: Cambridge University Press.

—— 1988: *Aristotle, the desire to understand*. Cambridge: Cambridge University Press.

Lloyd, G. E. R. 1979: *Magic, reason and experience, studies in the origins and development of Greek science*. Cambridge: Cambridge University Press.

Long, A. A and Sedley, D. N. 1987: *The Hellenistic philosophers, translations of the principal sources, with philosophical commentary* (vol. 1) and *Greek and Latin texts with notes and bibliography* (vol. 2). Cambridge: Cambridge University Press.

MacIntyre, A. 1981: *After virtue*. London: Duckworth.

Nussbaum, M. C. 1986: Saving Aristotle's appearances. In her *The fragility of goodness: luck and ethics in Greek tragedy and philosophy*, Cambridge: Cambridge University Press.

Owen, G. E. L. 1986: *Tithenai ta phainomena*. In his *Logic, science and dialectic, collected papers in Greek philosophy* (edited by M. C. Nussbaum). London: Duckworth.

Sandbach, F. H. 1985: *Aristotle and the Stoics*. Cambridge: The Cambridge Philological Society.

Sedley, D. N. 1991: Is Aristotle's teleology anthropocentric? *Phronesis*, 36, 179–96.

Sorabji, R. (ed.) 1987– : *The ancient commentators on Aristotle*. London: Duckworth.

Vlastos, G. 1983: The Socratic elenchus. *Oxford Studies in Ancient Philosophy*, 1, 27–58.

—— 1991: *Socrates, ironist and moral philosopher*. Cambridge: Cambridge University Press.

Wardy, R. 1991: Transcendental Dialectic. *Phronesis*, 36, 88–106.

—— 1993: Aristotelian Rainfall or the Lore of Averages. *Phronesis*, 38.

Williams, B. 1985: *Ethics and the limits of philosophy*. London: Fontana.

Discussion Questions

1 Do philosophers today have any reason to study ancient Greek philosophy?

2 How did Greek philosophy help to form the distinctive goals and methods of philosophy?

3 What is the Socratic method in philosophy and why is it important?

4 Can disciplined argument reach ethical truths?

5 How should philosophy be related to the culture at large?

6 In what sense could a philosopher be a 'gadfly'?

7 How can we decide whether philosophy is best conducted in dialogue?

8 In order to achieve virtue in our life, must we understand what virtue is?

9 Can the Socratic method reach beyond consistency to truth?

10 If Plato rejected the Socratic *elenchus*, why did he do so?

11 What is the difference between philosophy as a disciplined competition aiming at mutual benefit and philosophy as individual pursuit?

12 Should either oral philosophy or written philosophy have priority over the other?

13 In what sense should a reader of philosophy be active?

14 What distinguishes philosophy (and the history of philosophy) from the history of ideas?

15 Is there any reason for philosophy to start from reputable beliefs and from what people are inclined to accept?

16 Can Aristotle's dialectic ever achieve objective truth, rather than mere coherence?

17 Can we agree that we have knowledge because we are essentially knowers?

18 Are 'reputable opinions' or 'common preconceptions' a better starting point for philosophical argument?

19 Did the Stoics or the Epicureans provide a better basis for determining what are our common preconceptions?

20 Did the Hellenistic use of common preconceptions require an epistemic naturalism?

21 Can infantile behaviour tell us anything important about philosophical doctrines?

22 How can we know when dialectic degenerates into mere polemic?

23 How can discoveries in other disciplines have consequences for philosophy?

24 If scepticism is true, is it self-refuting?

25 Are the ordinary beliefs and practices of different places, times and cultures equally valid or equally invalid?

26 What is the scope of the suspension of belief licensed by scepticism?

16

Medieval Philosophy ——————

C. F. J. Martin

> In its concern to integrate faith and reason, or theology and philosophy, medieval philosophy had an orientation very different from that of modern philosophy. Many medieval philosophers sought to avoid the complete subordination of reason to faith, while arguing that reason was not completely autonomous. This chapter traces discussions of this major theme from Augustine and Boethius to the revival of Aristotelian learning and the development of sophisticated logical and metaphysical approaches to the question. The story ends with the proliferation of late medieval schools and the coming of modern philosophy with Descartes.

The earlier limit of the Middle Ages, as they are considered by philosophers, is St Augustine (354–430), who may be called the first of the medieval philosophers; the later limit is Descartes (1596–1650), who can be called the first of the modern philosophers. The last 100 years or so of medieval philosophy overlaps what might be called 'Renaissance philosophy', which is distinguished from contemporary medieval philosophy by its interest in rhetoric and its scorn for logic, by its interest in Plato, and its careful and scientific attitude to ancient texts. The mark of medieval philosophy as such might be said to be its close relation to THEOLOGY (chapter 14).

1 The Augustinian Basis

The close relation between medieval philosophy and theology is to be seen clearly in St Augustine himself. He found that the understanding of the world, of the place of the human being in it, and of its relation to its maker, which he had derived from careful study of the neo-Platonic philosophers of late antiquity, was completely transformed by the new understanding he felt he had gained from his conversion to Christianity. He believed that the new knowledge derived from FAITH (p. 464) included, but also transcended and illumined, all previous knowledge. All his previous beliefs could now be examined by a sure rule, that of the understanding of faith. If false, they could be shown to be false and rejected; if true, they could be taken up into the new understanding, and could both cast light on the truths of the faith and have light cast on them by faith. This notion of an integral understanding that would include both knowledge derived from God's revelation and knowledge derived from human study was, in great part, to set the programme for medieval philosophers.

Little knowledge is required to realize to what extent this conception of philosophy differs from contemporary ones. St Anselm (1033–1109) summed up the Augustinian programme in the words *'credo ut intelligam'*: I believe in order that I may understand. This is very alien to modern conceptions.

Philosophers today can fall into two opposing errors with regard to medieval philosophy: that of exaggerated historicism and that of exaggerated ahistoricism. They can see the medievals as beings wholly alien to ourselves, and their activities which they or we might wish to call philosophical as having nothing in common with the philosophy of our day except the name. Alternatively, they can insist on seeing the work of the medievals as having value only in so far as it appears to contribute to some contemporary debate.

The extreme historicist will be able give an account of the relations between the different authors of the medieval period, and between the different discussions in which they took part, but will never consider whether anyone nowadays might derive anything of benefit for his or her life or thought from reading them. The extreme ahistoricist will mine medieval texts for arguments that seem to bear on contemporary questions, and discard the rest as dross. Neither will derive from their reading of the medievals the chief benefit which is to be obtained: the grasp of a profoundly different cast of mind as it approaches fundamental questions, some versions of which arise spontaneously in the human mind.

Understanding Medieval Philosophy: Arguments from Authority

Let us take a case in point: that of the medieval attitude to arguments from authority. A typical medieval text will contain frequent appeals to authoritative statements, drawn from Scripture, from Augustine, say, or from Aristotle or Cicero. This is not a feature of contemporary philosophy: we quote philosophers chiefly to disagree with them, or because a previous author has made our point better and more concisely than we can. We do not – or, at least, we claim we do not – bring in dicta of, for example, Wittgenstein to support our views, with the implication that if Wittgenstein said so it must be so. But the medievals seem to act in just such a way.

One reaction to this is to say that therefore the medievals were not doing what we would call philosophy, and that the study of their philosophy must be principally of historical interest – 'merely' historical interest, some would say, with the implication that medieval philosophy is a suitable study for the historian of ideas, but not for the philosopher. Someone who takes this line will be able to learn from medieval philosophy, at best, what the historian of science might learn from the works of, for example, the phlogiston theorists.

An alternative reaction would be to ignore the appeals authority as irrelevant – to skip them – and to concentrate on what a contemporary philosopher would regard as the 'real' arguments. Such a philosopher would learn something of philosophical value from the medievals, but not much: he or she would learn from a medieval author solely what could have been learned from a contemporary philosopher who happened to use arguments roughly formally parallel. If such readers learn anything new from the medievals, it will only be because of the mere chance that no contemporary author happens to have hit on roughly parallel arguments.

Neither kind of reader will learn what a reading of the medievals truly can teach in this case: to rethink our current preconceptions and prejudices about the use of authority. Medieval use of authority was conscious and articulate, not blind and all-trusting. As it happens, we profess, in our day, a blind and all-doubting rejection of authority which, by contrast with the nuanced views of the medievals, can be seen as very crude. The medievals accepted the fact, which most contemporary philosophers would implicitly or explicitly deny, that most of the interesting and important things that we know, we know from authority. Since the medievals recognized this fact, they were able to examine it, what weight to give to authority, and when to give it. Since we refuse to recognize the fact, we are all at sea; we blindly accept authority, often enough, without even knowing that we are doing so; and, at moments where a conscious acceptance of authority might be of genuine use to us, we conspire to reject it. By reading the medievals intelligently, avoiding the extremes mentioned above, being aware of how different was their thought from ours, but not for that reason abandoning it as of 'merely historical interest', we can genuinely learn from them to correct the mistakes that our age is too prone to make.

2 Faith and Reason

So much for the problems that we can find in reading medieval philosophy. The principal problem that faced the medieval philosopher (who, as often as not, was at least as much a theologian as a philosopher) was one of integration: above all, that of the integration of faith with reason and of theology with philosophy. There were two extremes that the philosopher could fall into: an exaggerated subordination of reason to faith, which is often called fideism, or an exaggerated autonomy of reason from faith, which in this context we could call rationalism.

The problem of integration was one which Augustine and his heirs thought they had solved. God's wisdom was greater than human wisdom, so of course reason had to be subordinated to faith and philosophy had to be subordinated to theology. This subordination was not achieved principally in or through a curriculum or course of studies, but rather in the life and mind of the student. Subordination of faith to reason did not mean tyranny of faith over reason: since both faith and reason, when properly understood, were reflections, in different ways, of the truth of God's knowledge, they could not contradict one another. Where they appeared to contradict one another, there had to be a mistake somewhere in the student's mind: either his reasoning power or his understanding of the faith were amiss. But as the understanding of the faith developed, and more and more exact authoritative interpretations were given of its content, the odds against the understanding of the faith being amiss seemed to lengthen. Faith then came to acquire more and more authority over reason: a process which could end in FIDEISM (p. 464).

For Augustine, as for most other leading medieval thinkers, when reason was amiss it could be corrected by reason itself. The correcting reason needed to be illumined by the light of faith, of course, but it was none the less reason for all that. The danger came when a particular thinker was incapable of correcting erroneous reason by means of illumined reason: he or she was left with the stark choice of rejecting reason, and falling into fideism, or asserting the autonomy of reason and falling into rationalism. Both rationalism and fideism, then, tended to separate faith and reason, and to make impossible the achievement of the medieval aim of integration.

3 The Boethian Alternative

There were other strands in medieval thought besides the Augustinian: a major one could be called the Boethian, after the great lay philosopher and theologian Boethius (c.480–524). Boethius, though he shared the integrative aim of Augustine, tended in his work to make a methodological distinction between what could be known by reason alone and what could be known by reason illumined by faith. To such lengths did he take this distinction that at times it has been suggested that the theologian Boethius and the philosopher Boethius were two different people; or, perhaps, that after writing his theological works Boethius had apostatized from his faith and become a purely pagan philosopher. It can easily be seen that such a methodology could lead to rationalism, and be as destructive of the ideal of integration as could fideism.

These two strands continued through the Middle Ages. Augustine was not unique in his approach: similar attitudes can be found in the (mostly theological) work of the pseudonymous author, probably a sixth-century Syrian monk known as Pseudo-Dionysius the Areopagite. His Christian neo-Platonism had great influence on the seventh-century Irish monk John Scotus Erigena (c.810–c.875). Anselm, already mentioned, is clearly in the August-inian tradition: so is Hugh of St Victor (died 1141), whose *Didascalion*, a discussion of how knowledge and study should be organized, can be seen as a blueprint for the Augustinian university that was about to arise from the jumble of Paris schools. Meanwhile, on the Boethian side, there is the near-contemporary of Augustine, Chalcidius, who transmitted to the later middle ages Plato's thoughts on cosmology and theology.

4 Logic and Metaphysics: The Aristotelian Revival

The two tendencies came into conflict in the eleventh century, when schools in western Europe were well developed and the first universities were about to be established. The clash came over the re-discovery of the works of ARISTOTLE (384–322 BC) (chapter 15): first the logical works, read both in Boethius and in more complete versions, and then, bit by bit, the whole Aristotelian corpus.

There were already the seeds of dispute in the Augustinian integration. The neo-Platonist philosophers whom Augustine had taken as representatives of the highest human wisdom – people like Porphyry (*c.*232–*c.*304) – had already adopted the Aristotelian logic as a more powerful tool than anything that was provided by their master, Plato. But the LOGIC (chapter 4) of Aristotle was developed together with his METAPHYSICS (chapter 2): it thus sat ill with the more ideal metaphysics of Plato. The logic of Aristotle, and elements of his metaphysics, were also available to the West through the translations and summaries of Boethius.

Augustine had accepted the fundamental metaphysics of Platonism, according to which individual things on earth were only the reflections of Ideas or Forms: he only stipulated that these ideas were genuinely the ideas of someone, ideas in God's mind, exemplars according to which God made the world. But how did this reality relate to ordinary reality, and to the ordinary language which we use in talking about it?

Anselm is thought by some to have espoused 'extreme realism', the view that our concept-words stand not for anything in earthly reality but for the unchangeable, universal ideas in the mind of God. He was opposed by a scholar named Roscelin (*c.*1050–1120) who held the opposite view, that our words are mere conventional names for individuals. By the turn of the twelfth century the chief upholder of extreme realism was William of Champaux: he was opposed in the name of an intermediate position, that of 'moderate realism', by Abelard (1079–1142), who, like William, was a teacher in Paris.

Abelard saw the possibilities of applying his logical insights more widely, and began to work on metaphysics, ETHICS (chapter 6) and theology. His work here was seen by many as disruptive of the integration of faith and reason, and even as subversive to the faith. He was rebuked by the influential figure of St Bernard: and accepted the rebuke. But the possibilities of tension continued.

They were realized as the works of Aristotle began to filter through to the West. The works of Aristotle had had a curious history: they had been the mainstay of several schools of theology in the Eastern Empire, and had been translated into Syriac. As the Eastern Empire declined, and more and more of its territory came under the control of Islamic rulers, contact arose between Syrian Aristotelians and Muslim sages, who, like the Christians, were seeking an integration and an understanding of their faith. The Syriac translations of Aristotle were re-translated into Arabic, and formed the centre of an often heated debate between theologians and philosophers. Figures who stand out in the Islamic world are Avicenna of Baghdad (Ibn Sina, 980–1036), Maimonides, a Spanish Jew who fled from the persecutions of the Almohads to Cairo (Moishe ben Maimon (1135–1204), and Averroes of Cordoba (Ibn Rushd, 1126–1198). The problems of integration, of rationalism and fideism were to be found in these other religious traditions, too.

Aristotle's thought thus began to filter into the West, mostly through the works of the great Jewish school of translators of Toledo, bringing with him what must have seemed to many western Christians a double danger. The more obvious and less serious danger was that the texts thus transmitted contained a great deal of commentary and interpretation from Islamic scholars: and what might have helped integrate Aristotle into Islamic thinking would very often obstruct its integration into Christian thinking. This danger was met by the work of commentators such as Albert the Great (1206–80) and translators such as Robert Grosseteste (c.1170–1253) and William of Moerbeke (c.1215–86), who provided the West with a text of Aristotle, and an understanding of that text, free from Islamic accretions. The greater danger arose from Aristotle himself.

Augustine and his heirs had sought to integrate the highest human wisdom, which they thought they had found in neo-Platonism, with the divine wisdom of the Christian faith. But now there suddenly appeared a rival version of human wisdom: in many ways more complete and more attractive than the neo-Platonist, Augustinian picture. Could this be integrated, or not? Was it necessary to abandon the neo-Platonic elements in Augustinianism, or even abandon the Augustinian search for integration altogether?

Some seem to have worked in such a way as to lay themselves open to the charge of abandoning the search for integration altogether. There were many in the thirteenth century – Siger of Brabant (1235–82) is the most famous of them – who were thought by their enemies to have followed Averroes too closely, and to have reached the unorthodox conclusion with which Averroes himself was charged, of having created two incompatible truths, one philosophical and one religious. If this were so, then integration was impossible, and it would be necessary to accept either fideism or rationalism, or an unhappy and inconsistent combination of the two.

Others seemed to be more successful in their pursuit of integration. The work of St Thomas Aquinas (1224–74) is often, justly, seen both as a triumphant vindication of the Augustinian project, and a culmination of Aristotelian learning: he produced a transcendent synthesis of both Augustinianism and Aristotelianism. There is no space here to dilate on his achievement. He is undoubtedly the medieval philosopher most widely read today and the one whose work it is most difficult to ignore. But though large parts of his work achieved widespread acceptance very quickly, he seems to have left no heir who shared his overall integrative vision. While to us Aquinas very often appears to be the medieval theologian or philosopher *par excellence*, his contemporaries and successors did not see him in that light. Pure Augustinian schools continued, marked by their suspicion of Aristotelianism. Other schools developed, with other tendencies. For St Bonaventure, Aquinas' contemporary and colleague in Paris (1221–74) Aristotle was of interest only as a natural philosopher: he could not cast any light on metaphysics, knowledge or God. Duns Scotus (c.1265–1308), though he rejected the ancient Augustinian theory of human knowledge as divine illumination, had a radically new and non-Aristotelian, non-Thomist view of the relations between the human mind and the world. William of Ockham (c.1285–1349) practised, if he did not preach, a separation between the realms of logic and of theology. The philosophy of the later middle ages, despite the presence of great figures, gives the appearance of having dissolved into a set of bickering schools, a situation made worse by the re-entry on the scene of

Plato's original texts in the late fifteenth century. This gave rise to a new interest in beauty and rhetoric, and a rejection of the solid logical achievements of the Middle Ages. By the end of the sixteenth century the time was ripe for Descartes to decide that a clean sweep of the accumulated unresolved discussions of centuries had to be made, in order to be able to clear down to indubitable and indisputable bedrock truths. The medieval project can be said to have failed, in the end: unless, perhaps, there are people today who might wish to enter on it again.

Further Reading

Try Barnes (1982) or the more difficult essay 'Aristotle' in Anscombe and Geach (1961) for some background knowledge of Aristotle. Good general introductions to medieval philosophy are Copleston (1946–75) and (1972), Knowles (1988) and Marenbon (1983) and (1987). Important and fairly accessible texts are the *Confessions* of Augustine (1991), *The Consolation of Philosophy* of Boethius (1976), and the *Monologion* and *Proslogion* of Anselm (1973). For the more systematic later period it may be worth reading Kretzmann, Kenny and Pinborg (1982). For an introduction to Aquinas, read 'Aquinas' in Anscombe and Geach (1961), Copleston (1976) or Kenny (1980). A good transition to reading the text of Aquinas may be provided by Aquinas (1988) or Kenny (1993). Leff (1975) will give a helpful introduction to Ockham. There is no good introduction to Scotus at present.

References

Medieval Philosophers

Anselm, Saint 1973: *The Prayers and Meditations of St Anselm* (translated by B. Ward). Harmondsworth: Penguin.
Aquinas, Saint Thomas 1963–75: *Summa Theologiae* (edited by T. Gilby). London: Eyre and Spottiswoode.
—— 1988: *The Philosophy of Thomas Aquinas: Introductory Readings* (edited by C. F. J. Martin). London: Routledge.
Augustine, Saint 1991: *Confessions* (translated by H. Chadwick). Oxford: Oxford University Press.
Boethius 1976: *The Consolation of Philosophy* (translated by V. E. Watts). Harmondsworth: Penguin.
Duns Scotus, Blessed John 1962: *Philosophical Writings* (a selection edited and translated by A. Wolter). London: Nelson.
Ockham, William 1964: *Philosophical Writings: A Selection* (edited and translated by P. Boehner). Indianapolis: Bobbs-Merrill.

Other Writers

Adams, M. 1987: *William Ockham* (2 vols). Notre Dame: Notre Dame University Press.

Anscombe, G. E. M. and Geach, P. T. 1961: *Three Philosophers*. Oxford: Blackwell.

Barnes, J. 1982: *Aristotle*. Oxford: Oxford University Press.

Broadie, A., 1993: *Introduction to Medieval Logic* (2nd edn). Oxford: Oxford University Press.

Chadwick, H. 1986 *Augustine*. Oxford: Oxford University Press.

Copleston, F. A. 1946–75: *History of Philosophy*, vol. 2. Westminster, Md.: Newman Bookshop.

—— 1972: *History of Medieval Philosophy*. London: Methuen.

—— 1976: *Aquinas*. London: Search Press.

Gibson, M. M. T. 1981: *Boethius*. Oxford: Blackwell.

Gilson, E. 1961: *The Christian Philosophy of St Augustine* (translated by L. E. M. Lynch). London: Gollancz.

Kenny, A. J. P. 1980: *Aquinas*. Oxford: Oxford University Press.

—— 1993: *Aquinas on Mind*. London: Routledge.

Kirwan, C. 1989: *Augustine*. London: Routledge.

Knowles, D. 1988: *The Evolution of Medieval Thought* (2nd edn). London: Longman.

Kretzmann, N., Kenny, A. J. P. and Pinborg, J. 1982: *Cambridge History of Later Medieval Philosophy*. Cambridge: Cambridge University Press.

Kretzmann, N. and Stump, E. (eds) 1993: *Cambridge Companion to Aquinas*. Cambridge: Cambridge University Press.

Leff, G. 1975: *William of Ockham: The Metamorphosis of Scholastic Discourse*. Manchester: Manchester University Press.

Marenbon, J. 1983: *Early Medieval Philosophy (480–1150): An Introduction*. London: Routledge.

—— 1987: *Later Medieval Philosophy (1150–1350): An Introduction*. London: Routledge.

Discussion Questions

1 What is the nature of conversion?

2 Can we gain knowledge through revelation? How would knowledge gained through revelation be related to other human knowledge?

3 'I believe in order that I may understand.' Can belief enable us to understand? Can we have insight into medieval philosophy without accepting this claim?

4 To what extent do *historicist* and *ahistoricist* perspectives help us to understand medieval philosophy? To what extent do they hinder such understanding?

5 What can medieval philosophy teach us about the use of authority?

6 If theology had a legitimate role to play in medieval philosophical thought, how can we decide whether it has a similar role today?

7 What problems arise for the claim that reason should be subordinated to faith? What problems arise for the claim that reason should be autonomous with respect to faith?

8 If reason and faith are both reflections of the truth of God's knowledge, why should one have priority over the other?

9 What part should an account of God's knowledge play in characterizing and assessing human knowledge?

10 How could a medieval student improve his or her understanding of the faith? Need this improvement ultimately lead to fideism?

11 What explanations are possible if reason and faith appear to contradict one another?

12 Can reason correct reason? Why might it be claimed that reason needs to be illumined by faith to do so? How can we understand the notion of 'being illumined by faith'?

13 Why should adopting Aristotle's logic raise difficulties for philosophers who accepted Plato's metaphysics? What does this show about the relation between logic and metaphysics?

14 Augustine held that individual things on earth reflect Platonic Forms. Does his further view that Forms are ideas in God's mind improve upon Plato's metaphysics?

15 How might one attempt to resolve medieval disputes over what words or concepts stand for? Why were these disputes important?

16 Could philosophy and religion provide two truths, which are incompatible with one another?

17

Descartes, Spinoza and Leibniz ——

George MacDonald Ross and Richard Francks

The seventeenth century was a period of profound transformation in
philosophy, science and theology, and in the conception of human life. The
scholastic philosophy of the universities was challenged, and many themes
still at the centre of philosophical debate were initiated. This chapter is
devoted to three major figures, Descartes (1596–1650), Spinoza (1632–1677)
and Leibniz (1646–1716). All were powerful metaphysical thinkers, who
used reason to criticize both the philosophy of their medieval predecessors
and common-sense views of the world. The rival accounts of substance
offered by these authors are explored in the context of attempts to establish
modern explanatory science. These accounts include Descartes' divinely
created extended substance and thinking substances; Spinoza's single
substance, God or Nature; and Leibniz's soul-like monads, each existing in
isolation but reflecting the whole system of reality according to a divinely
created pre-established harmony. For each account, the implications for
nature, God and human beings are traced. Readers will wish to consult
several of the historical chapters in this volume, but especially those
dealing with other seventeenth-century philosophers, HOBBES (chapter 18)
and LOCKE (chapter 19). They will also wish to read chapters on METAPHYSICS
(chapter 2), EPISTEMOLOGY (chapter 1), PHILOSOPHY OF MIND (chapter 5), PHILOSO-
PHY OF SCIENCE (chapter 9) and PHILOSOPHY OF RELIGION (chapter 14).

1 Descartes

René Descartes has been referred to since the eighteenth century as 'The Father
of Modern Philosophy', but as conceptions of philosophy have altered during
that time, so too has the meaning of the title. In the nineteenth and for most of
the twentieth century, English-speaking philosophers have seen Descartes
primarily as an EPISTEMOLOGIST (chapter 1), whose work set the agenda for the
central philosophical task of showing why we are justified in believing what
we believe. At the same time in CONTINENTAL PHILOSOPHY (chapter 30) Descartes'
concentration on the individual thinking self and its relation to its surround-
ings has led to his being regarded primarily as the originator of the
Phenomenological and Existentialist traditions. No one would deny Descartes' importance in those two areas, but more recent work has given us a
rather different Descartes: by looking more closely at the historical context

within which Descartes was working, recent philosophers have offered a different perspective on his work, and in so doing have allowed him to keep his title, while changing its meaning back to something nearer to what those who originally gave it to him might have had in mind.

'Philosophy' in the seventeenth century was not the name of a specific academic discipline, but meant more generally something like 'learning' or 'knowledge', construed as any attempt to understand the world by purely natural, rational means. In that context, to say that Descartes was the father of modern philosophy is to say that he was the great champion of the self-proclaimed 'modern' movement of the seventeenth century. That movement was very diverse, very diffuse and very widespread, and was united by little more than the conviction that the traditional learning had failed, but that a secure and practically useful understanding of the world could be achieved if only we would renounce the mistaken methods and assumptions of the past and refound knowledge on a new basis. The movement was variously referred to as the 'New Philosophy', the 'Mechanical Philosophy' and the 'Experimental Philosophy', and the perceived success of its adherents in taking over or replacing the intellectual establishment of the day is a central part of the complex process which later historians came to refer to as the 'Scientific Revolution'.

Descartes did not start the modernist movement, nor was his work the cause of its success. His reputation as the father of the modern view derives from the fact that for many years both before and after his death he was considered its leading theorist and publicist. His carefully worked out and brilliantly presented philosophical vision of the world and humanity's place in it played a large part in establishing the possibility of a viable alternative to the traditional account, and in legitimizing belief in it. The life of Descartes was a classic story of a man with a message in which he passionately believes but which he knows will be unpopular with much of the intellectual, religious and political establishment of his time. He was constantly working to avoid persecution, to win influential people over to his side, and to disguise or suppress his true opinions wherever he thought it necessary, while at the same time inventing a series of superb literary and conceptual devices to propagate his message whenever it was safe to do so.

To present modernism as a viable alternative to traditional learning, Descartes essentially had to do three things: to describe in very general terms the nature of the world according to his version of modernism, to show how that world related to a Christian GOD (chapter 14), and how it related to humanity. We will set out this sketch of his work under those three headings.

1.1 Nature

Descartes saw the whole non-human natural world as a single, deterministic, mechanical system. He held that just as Kepler (1571–1630) had reduced the apparently wandering paths of the planets to simple mathematical laws, or as Galileo (1564–1642) had found similarly simple mathematical laws underlying all the diverse phenomena of falling objects on earth, so in fact *all* natural phenomena, from the shining of the sun to the biting of a flea, could, if properly understood, be seen to be governed by unchanging LAWS OF NATURE (pp. 310–11) such that, if only we knew enough about them, we would see them not as random and isolated events but as the only possible outcomes of the timeless facts of nature. And those unchanging facts, he held, were ultimately the laws of mechanics. The laws of meteorology, for example, and of zoology might appear very different; but underlying both of them are more fundamental laws governing the mechanical interaction of particles of inert matter. The laws of optics, for example, he held to be a consequence of the laws of mechanics, because he saw light as a stream of highly energetic particles which either penetrate or bounce off surfaces in the same way as arrows will either penetrate or bounce off a surface of custard or of steel. Kepler's laws of planetary motion he held to be derivable from mechanics because the planets were pushed along in their orbits by a swirl or 'vortex' of tiny material particles swinging around the sun, in just the same way that a leaf is swirled around by a current of air, or a cork by an eddy in a stream. In biology, too, mechanism ruled: the heart of a living creature beats because of a constant repetition of heating and cooling – themselves mechanical phenomena to be explained by the accelerating and decelerating of particles – which the blood undergoes in moving through the body; a seed grows because of the gradual accretion of some of the particles which are constantly pushed through it by its (mechanical) digestive processes – and so on. Thus the whole of nature comes to be seen as a giant clockwork – the seventeenth century's favourite analogy – wound up by God at creation, and ticking along until the end of the world, powered by an unending series of pushes and pulls, bumps and twists, shakings and swirlings.

At this point the modern reader may be inclined to take a rather patronizing view of Descartes' work: this purely mechanical view seems childishly naive, an obviously inadequate resource for explaining all the phenomena of nature. And indeed, Descartes' biology was a research programme that was never successfully carried out, his anatomy was rejected in favour of that of Harvey (1578–1657), within a generation his cosmology and his optics were being replaced by Newton's (1642–1727), and even his mechanics itself was increasingly abandoned. Two points, though, should be made in his defence. Firstly, Descartes was a pioneer, and however unsuccessful his physical theory may have been in detail, the philosophical vision that inspired it was enthusiastically adopted even by those who abandoned his own cherished discoveries, and in fact still forms the basis of the modern view of the world.

The second point in defence of Descartes' mechanism is more complex, and gives a better view of Descartes' relation both to his predecessors and to his successors. Descartes' world is characterized above all by its *intelligibility*. As with all those of the modernist party, his constant complaint against supporters of the debased Aristotelianism of the universities was that they left the world mysterious, by postulating incomprehensible faculties, powers, virtues and goals in nature. Instead of explaining such well-known and politically and economically important phenomena as that of the compass, for example, they merely re-described its behaviour in technical terms which had no content beyond the very phenomena they were invented to explain. Descartes' mechanism, by contrast, succeeded in reducing the unknown to the known, by showing how initially puzzling phenomena can be explained as the operation of an unperceived but perfectly well understood cause, namely the impact of invisible particles. Significantly, this emphasis on explicability was what distinguished the Cartesian world picture from those of many of his contemporaries and successors who proclaimed themselves his fellow modernists. The disagreement with Harvey, for example, over the operation of the heart derives from a rejection by Descartes of Harvey's acceptance of the living power of the heart as something not itself explained; whereas for Harvey the heart is imbued with life, as befits the central organ of the body around which the blood circulates like courtiers around a king, for Descartes it is merely a lump of matter, alternately dilated and contracted by the mechanical pressure of the blood it contains. In the same way, later Cartesians sought unsuccessfully to defend his system of vortices and ether against the Newtonian theory for precisely the same reason: Newton's view contained as a given the fact that all bodies have the power to draw other bodies towards them with no intervening medium through which such force is transmitted. As compared to Descarte's theory, this is a clear betrayal of the modernist ideal, and a re-introduction of the occult powers of the SCHOLASTICS (pp. 503–6), in that it claims to explain the fact that heavy objects fall to earth not by means of a flow of invisible particles which push them downward, but by imbuing the physical world with the pseudo-property of 'gravitas'.

Vital powers and gravitational attraction were not the only categories of things that Descartes' bare ONTOLOGY (chapter 2) of matter in motion ruled out. And here we return to an aspect of his work which subsequent generations have for the most part accepted. The bare material particles of his mechanical world are equipped only with the mechanical properties of shape, size, and motion, and *all* their other properties must be a function of those few. Thus whereas an ordinary person might say that a sword, for example, was shiny, sharp and dangerous, Descartes would say that in itself the sword is none of those things: in itself, as it really is, the sword is an extended object of a certain size and shape; all its other PROPERTIES (p. 545) are REDUCIBLE (pp. 319–20) either to those bare mechanical properties, or to the interaction of those mechanical properties with the human sensory system. Colour is a classic example, which Descartes and his contemporaries insisted again and again must be removed from the list of an object's real properties. The colour of an object is not a property it possesses, as its shape or its size is, but rather a function of the way in which the shape, size and motion of its constituent parts interact with those of particles that make up rays of light to operate on our sensory system. 'Silver-coloured' and 'shiny', therefore, are words that refer not to properties in the object, but only to experiences that humans typically have when confronted by it.

Descartes' World

The world of Descartes is a bare, mechanical place operating in accordance with timeless laws of motion, and, in itself, it is devoid of most of the properties that could make us feel at home in it. In fact, even the mechanical properties that it *does* possess turn out to be importantly different from the shàpe, size and motion with which we are familiar. Their importance for Descartes, and their suitability to explain everything that happens in the natural world, lies not in their familiarity, but in the fact that they are *measurable*, and so can be expressed and manipulated *mathematically*. Galileo had already written that the book of nature is written in the language of mathematics, and the idea is central to Descartes' more fully worked out metaphysical and epistemological position. For Descartes, what we see when two billiard-balls collide is only an appearance; the reality of the event is appreciated not by the eye of the body, but by the eye of the mind. Thus, the only really accurate account of the event – the one which most fully corresponds to what is really there in the world, purged of any reference to its effects on our sensory apparatus, is a mathematical description, in which size, shape, weight, speed and direction are all expressed (with the help of what we still refer to as Cartesian co-ordinates) as numbers. The outcome of that collision is then expressible as a new set of such numerical values, and the transformation from one set to the other is governed by laws of motion, central among which is that of the conservation of the total amount of motion in the system as a whole.

It is a testimony to the success of Descartes and his fellow modernists in propagating their views of nature that much of that story seems so familiar, indeed obvious, to us today. Our contemporary view is a direct descendant of the philosophical innovations of the seventeenth century, to such an extent that it is hard for us to see how anyone could ever have seen things otherwise. In particular, we take for granted Descartes' fundamental metaphysical claim that the world of experience, the world of the ordinary person, is not the world as it really is, but only the way that real world *appears* to us. The world as we experience it is a rich and varied succession of qualities and values; the world as it really is, is a stately transformation of number sequences in accordance with immutable laws. The view of the expert is not a fuller and more detailed version of the view of the common person, but a radically different view, which is expressible not in the language of common sense but in the language of mathematics; the real world is simply unavailable to the sensory apparatus of the ordinary person, and is discoverable only by the arcane investigations of the 'philosopher'.

This contrast between the common sense view and the view of the expert is one of the most striking features of Descartes' writing. Time and again he has to try to persuade his audience that they cannot trust the way the world appears to be to their senses; they must work out rationally what it is really like. It may appear to the casual observer as if the blood in the arteries and that in the veins is of a different kind, but the philosopher can show that in reality they are the same; it may look to the senses as if the earth stands still while the heavenly bodies move around it, but the philosopher can show that in reality the earth moves around the sun.

1.2 *God*

Descartes was acutely aware, especially after the public condemnation of Galileo in 1633, that many would regard his physical and metaphysical theories as tantamount to heresy, but he himself saw them as perfectly

compatible with, and indeed inseparable from, his version of Christianity. To
see the relation, we need to look more closely at his account of material
substance.

Descartes, for all his modernity, was not an atomist. Although he maintained
that the properties of objects were a function of the way their minute parts
were put together, he did not think that all matter was made up in the end of
impenetrable and irreducible atoms. For Descartes, remember, the reality of
the world is what can be described numerically, so it follows that just as there
is no smallest possible number, so there can be no smallest possible particle or
atom. Matter, therefore, must be infinitely divisible. For the same reason,
Descartes denied the possibility of a vacuum. If the true description of the
world is its mathematical description, and matter just *is* its dimensions
('extension'), then a space between objects, since it possesses shape, size,
duration and motion, is every bit as real a physical thing as are the objects on
either side of it. There is therefore no such thing as genuinely empty space:
just as a room which the common person would say was empty is known by
the philosopher to be full of air, so the space between the planets and that
above the column of mercury in Torricelli's famous experiment is held by
Descartes to be in reality filled with a fine, fluid, 'subtle' matter, through which
light and gravity are mechanically transmitted. The relation between objects
and the spaces around them must therefore be seen as analogous to that
between a whirlpool and the water that surrounds it. A whirlpool can be seen,
and can be touched; if it is fast enough, it can feel quite hard, even
impenetrable. And yet it is made up of the very same stuff as the water around
it: there is nothing in the whirlpool that is not in the water, and there is no
more of it in the whirlpool than there is in the rest of the sea. The only
difference between the two is relative motion: all the water that we consider as
part of the whirlpool is moving in unison, and moving at a high speed relative
to the otherwise indistinguishable water around it. That is Descartes' model
for the individuation of physical objects in the seamless continuum of
extended matter: what we call an object is what we might now describe as a
high-pressure area in the material continuum. For Descartes, the ordinary
person's pluralist view of a world made up of an indefinite number of separate
physical objects is a childish error, from which the man of science must
escape. Those separate physical 'objects' are in reality, he says, only adjectival
in nature. Just as the shape of an apple or the fall of a leaf are not separate
things over and above the apple and the leaf to which they belong, but only
'modes' or 'modifications' of their respective substances, so, according to
Descartes, the apple and the leaf themselves, like every other physical object in
existence, are not in reality separate things or substances, but only modes of
the one single extended substance: they are areas of a continuum differentiated
by us 'modally' on the basis of relative motion, but are not 'really' or
'substantially' distinct.

The relation of God to that physical continuum is a double one. On the one
hand, God created the material world *ex nihilo* and set its parts in motion, and
that original motion has been conserved through all the mechanical interactions which have taken place from that day to this. With the exception of

occasional MIRACLES (p. 575), therefore, the whole history of the natural world can be explained purely naturalistically, purely scientifically, through the laws of mechanics.

But that is only part of the story. In addition to creating the universe and setting it in motion, God also sustains it in being from moment to moment. Therefore the reason why, for example, some particular beam of light is reflected from a surface at an angle of 30 degrees is not only because it hit the surface at an angle of 30 degrees, but also because God was at that time maintaining the law of reflection whereby the angle of incidence equals the angle of reflection. In the same way, the reason why a stone lying in a field will continue to lie in that field is not only because no one comes along to move it, but also because God keeps in operation during this period the laws which determine its nature and its structure. In this way God's 'concourse' or 'concurrence' is involved at every moment of history; without the continual involvement of God, the clockwork mechanism of the universe would not tick along regardless, but would fall apart into chaos and nothingness.

In this sense, therefore, the modal relation which we have seen to exist between the properties of an object and the object itself, and also between any given object and extended substance in general, is mirrored in the relation between God and that extended substance itself. Just as to talk about the shape of an object is not to talk about a separate thing, but to talk about one aspect of the object itself, and to talk of an individual object is in reality to talk about one particular aspect of material substance, so to talk about matter at all is, when correctly understood, only a way of talking about one aspect of God. Strictly speaking, God is the only true substance, the only real thing; the material world is only an expression, or a consequence, of God's nature.

These two strands in Descartes' account of God and the world – the divine clock maker and the one true substance – obviously tend to pull in different directions, and they were developed in different directions by his successors. Their combination in his work means that Descartes had a very strong defence against those who tended to see the new SCIENCE (chapter 9) of nature as tantamount to atheism: Descartes could claim that the investigation of nature, far from being incompatible with Christian duty, was actually co-extensive with the discovery of God's true nature and intentions.

1.3 Humanity

Descartes' mechanist view of nature covers the entire physical world, including the creation of the earth itself as a consequence of the break-up of a larger vortex of matter. It extends also to the entire plant world, and the entire non-human animal kingdom. The life of an animal is not a mysterious faculty or a vital principle infused into matter, but simply a series of mechanical interactions, exactly like the working life of a machine: an animal has mechanically produced drives and appetites, and it makes its way around the world seeking by mechanical means to achieve those ends with the help of its mechanical sensory system – it is a 'beast machine', a very complex and sophisticated natural robot. The human body is another mechanism of exactly the same kind, with just the same kind of mechanical life which is responsible for all of its natural processes, and most of its desires and aversions, its actions and reactions. But there we reach the limits of mechanical explanation: there is more to a human being than those mechanical properties alone can explain. Unlike any other creature on earth, we can consider the past, the future and the distant present, far beyond the scope of our physical senses; we can sometimes stand back from our desires and choose which ones to satisfy and which to deny; and we can have knowledge of things which are no part of the physical world revealed by the physical senses, notably things such as the truths of mathematics, the minds of other people, and God. Descartes' explanation for these remarkable human capacities is that there is more to a human being than the area of the physical continuum which is his or her body; in addition, human beings also possess a soul, an immaterial substance which can understand and choose, and which is a finite imitation of the infinite immaterial substance which is God.

This, then, is the famous 'Cartesian Dualism', the suggestion that a human being is an area of the physical continuum *together with* an individual thinking mind or soul. The status of each such individual thinking substance is the same as that of the one material substance: it is dependent on God both for its initial creation and for its continued being.

Descartes holds that this theory is obvious from the facts of nature that we have surveyed, but in addition he brought forward a dramatic proof of its truth. In perhaps the most famous single moment in the whole of Western philosophy, he claimed that the existence of the individual thinking substance is indubitable for any thinker. It makes perfect sense, he claimed, for me to pretend that I have no physical body, and indeed that the entire physical worlds that my senses reveal to me is nothing but a dream, or an illusion created by some evil power. But no matter what mistakes I may make, and no matter how deceived I may be, I must still exist in order to be mistaken. The mere fact that I am able to make judgements at all, even mistaken ones, proves that I exist: *cogito ergo sum*. And the fact that I can think away the entire physical world but cannot think away my own existence surely proves that I myself, the thing that is doing this thinking, cannot be merely a part of that physical world.

The relations between that MIND AND BODY (chapter 5) have always been perceived as problematic. Descartes proposed a system whereby the hydraulic fluids which operate the muscles of the body are all routed through the pineal gland in the centre of the brain, so that by making tiny adjustments in the position of that gland, the soul is able to control the flow of those fluids and in that way to re-direct the actions of the body in accordance with its decisions. However quaint the mechanics of that story might seem, the view of human nature which it embodies is one that is very natural, and very powerful. The soul, because it is immaterial, is not subject to the effects of physical decay, and so is immortal. It is God-like in its immateriality, and thus is not part of the crude, base material world, although it is tied to it by its incarnation. The actions of the soul are human versions of the divine activities of understanding and willing, the former a perfect but finite copy of God's divine intelligence, the latter prone to misuse and corrupted by the Fall. In making judgements, the understanding presents an idea to the mind, which the will then affirms or denies.

In this way Descartes is able to show that intellectual mistakes and moral and religious deviance are alike, in that both result from the misuse of the free will. Descartes is thus able to represent his project for a re-founding of human knowledge as not only a scientific investigation with important practical benefits, but also as a religious and moral reformation of human society and of the human spirit: by coming to see the world as it really is, through the eye of reason, we are liberating our true, active immaterial thinking selves from their subjection to the deceitful physical senses, and we are allowing the pure, immaterial, divine soul to take precedence over the corrupt physical body and achieve a view of the world which is closer to that of God.

This, then, is the metaphysical, psychological and theological underpinning of Descartes' celebrated work in epistemology. His task here was to show that despite the failure of the established authorities as embodied in the universities, and despite the fashionable pessimism of philosophers who were skeptical as to the possibility of any genuine human knowledge, it is indeed possible for us to escape from the world of appearances and establish a stable and useful body of knowledge as to how the world really is, if only we can abandon traditional learning and adopt the new methods of the modernist party.

Again, the device of the *cogito* takes centre stage: because it begins from Descartes' 'hyperbolical' doubt about the ultimate deception, and shows that even in those extreme circumstances genuine knowledge would be attainable, it means that no matter how extreme the skeptical doubts may be, the possibility of certainty cannot coherently be denied, provided only that we escape from the illusory appearances of common sense to the clear understanding of the rational soul. Our common-sense views are part of our animal nature, useful for finding our way around in the world, but deeply misleading as to its true nature; the *cogito* proves that by reason and reflection we can overcome that deception and work out rationally what is really going on. What we must do is to look behind the apparent contingency of events in the world to find the underlying structures which determine them, and our aim is to work towards a unified science of nature which could be laid out like Euclid's *Elements* as a single axiomatic system of nature, in which all natural phenomena are represented as the inevitable outcome of unchanging universal laws.

2 Spinoza

If Descartes was the leading light of the modernist movement, Baruch Spinoza (Benedict de Spinoza) was its most perfect expression. By developing Descartes' vision of a new, scientific understanding of things to its ultimate conclusion, he produced an account of God, the universe and humanity's place in it which was of unparalleled breadth, consistency and beauty. As a result he was excommunicated from his Jewish community, his books were publicly burned, and his name became a byword for wickedness and atheism until 100 years after his death, when he was rediscovered, and misinterpreted, by the Romantics.

In contrast to Descartes, who was constantly trying out new ways of representing and re-expressing different aspects of his message, Spinoza worked for years to polish and perfect a single, comprehensive and definitive account of how things are. His work is therefore very brief, dense and deeply obscure. We shall use the same three headings used for Descartes to survey Spinoza's thought, covering his accounts of nature, God and humanity.

2.1 Nature

Spinoza's account of the material world was thoroughly Cartesian. He believed that all physical phenomena are determined by unchanging universal laws, and that all physical laws depend ultimately on laws of motion. He denied the possibility of a vacuum, and of atoms, and he held, like Descartes, that what common sense takes to be individual physical objects are in reality only conventionally individuated modes of an extended continuum, which Spinoza called the Attribute of Extension.

All of that is, and was, familiar. In his account of mental phenomena, though, Spinoza was much more radical. Whereas for Descartes the mental world consists of an indefinite number of individual immaterial thinking substances, some of which are temporarily linked by God to specific areas of the material continuum, Spinoza posits a second, non-material mental continuum – the Attribute of Thought – of which all mental phenomena are modes, just as all physical phenomena are modes of the Attribute of Extension. The two attributes are co-extensive, and exactly parallel: everything that exists in one has an exact counterpart in the other. In fact, Spinoza claims, those counterparts, and the attributes on which they depend, are in reality the same thing: there is only a single substance, which is expressed in those two different ways (among others).

What are we to make of such a story? It has been read in a variety of ways, as equivalent to certain varieties of Buddhist thought, as a return to some kind of primitive animism, and as a mystical poetic vision of a World Soul underlying all the phenomena of nature. It may be all or any of those things; but what it is also is an attempt to extend Descartes' modernism into the mental realm, and by so doing to create a universal explanatory framework for a complete science of nature.

Descartes' view of the mind is a surprisingly conservative one, in that the appearance–reality distinction which so dominated his account of matter is almost completely absent. Whereas the common-sense view of the material world is completely transformed when we come to see with the eye of reason, the common-sense view of the mind turns out to be surprisingly accurate. The uneducated layman's belief that the mind is some extra, immaterial thing which is united with the body and which leaves it at death is shared by the philosopher. The expert may have a more complete and a more systematic knowledge of the mind's operations than does the person in the street, but that knowledge is still expressed in terms of the categories of the ordinary person's experience, such as willing, understanding, feeling and perceiving. The mind is known, as it were, entirely from within: what it is to think just *is* to have certain kinds of experience, and there is no deeper level of understanding which explains that experience in the way in which a knowledge of Cartesian physics explains the experience of touching a solid object.

Thought

Spinoza's Attribute of Thought is an attempt to provide an objective, scientific explanation of the phenomenon of thought. Just as Descartes extends the concept of materiality from actual solid objects to universal extension, and in so doing explains away those solid objects as merely local concentrations of a universal stuff, so Spinoza tries to extend the concept of thought from individual thinking agents to a universal mentality, and by so doing seeks to explain away our individual minds as merely local concentrations of a universal characteristic of things. Everything is extended, even so-called empty space, and when extension is arranged appropriately, the result is what we experience as a solid object. Similarly, everything is mental, even so-called inert objects, and when mentality is arranged appropriately, the result is what we experience as a thinking thing.

The idea is a strange one, but perhaps no more so than the parallel move in the material world, which we find much easier to accept. It offers a non-materialist way of representing the mind as an emergent phenomenon. But in so doing, the theory pays a price which many will find unacceptable: it denies the ultimate individuality, and even identity, of the human mind, which becomes merely a local concentration of thought, conventionally individuated from lesser concentrations around it. The mind of a person is not a separate, individual thing with its own identity and independence, but merely a convenient way of talking about a constantly changing body of interrelated thought, which comes together, develops and changes over time, and eventually dissipates, like a whirlpool in the bath water.

Whether or not we find Spinoza's picture of thought acceptable, its motivation is clear: when seen through the eye of reason, *all* the phenomena of nature are seen as precisely that – mere phenomena, generated by the unchanging features of nature which a true science would reveal. The task of understanding is therefore to rise above the level of experience, at which we perceive the world as a multiplicity of objects in time and space, and to see things from the point of view of eternity (*sub specie aeternitatis*), as temporary local manifestations of the unchanging facts of nature.

2.2 God

Spinoza's theology is as radical as his psychology, and again his radicalism takes the form of extending the Cartesian system to its ultimate, and non-Cartesian, conclusion. Descartes' God was the one true substance, which underlies and supports all created substances; but God was also simultaneously a pre-existing, independent immaterial being who freely chose to bring matter and minds into existence for God's own purposes. Spinoza sees those two elements as inconsistent, and he simply eliminates the second: 'God or Nature', as he famously calls it, is the one substance that exists, and which is expressed simultaneously both as extension and as thought; God is the single unchanging reality which underlies all the phenomena of experience, and which a perfect science would reveal.

This pantheistic doctrine is, and was, startling to many people. God is not the creator of the world, but the world itself – not the world as we experience it, but the world as it really is, in itself. God or Nature therefore creates the world not as something external to itself, in the way that a potter creates a pot, but as an expression of itself, in the way that the nature of matter, as described by the fundamental laws of physics, creates the physical universe and everything in it, and as the nature of thought, described by the fundamental laws of psychology, creates the mental universe and all it contains.

Although the idea is startling, Spinoza claims that it is not new, and that in fact it is this God that all theists have believed in, though some have perceived it more clearly than others. This is the true sense in which God created the world, stripped of misleading analogies with human creativity. This is the being of which the prophets spoke, though they spoke in figurative terms for an uneducated audience. This is the omnipotent, omniscient, omnipresent being which NECESSARILY EXISTS (pp. 466–7), which it is our highest blessedness to know, and which to know is perfect freedom. In fact, the only characteristic of traditional Gods which Spinoza's lacks is personality: God or Nature is not a person, or anything like one; it does not have desires or feelings or intentions, it cannot love or be angry, or be concerned with the fate of human beings. To those who maintain that any conception of God must have these features, Spinoza pityingly replies that we naturally tend to project human qualities on to nature, no doubt in the same way that triangles, if they could speak, would claim that God is eminently triangular.

2.3 Humanity

The account of human beings which emerges from this metaphysic is a mixture of austerity and passion. As we have seen, Spinoza's overriding conviction is that humanity is part of nature, a natural phenomenon like any other, to be understood in the same dispassionate, naturalistic way. There is therefore no such thing as the Cartesian free will: human actions are natural events, like the actions of clouds or rainstorms, and to understand them is to see them as necessary, determined by the unchanging nature of God.

This means that MORALITY (chapter 6) as conventionally understood is impossible: terms like 'right' and 'good' are merely words that we apply to things we want, and we deceive ourselves if we think they are anything else. Similarly, POLITICS (chapter 8) and the LEGAL SYSTEM (chapter 12) are purely pragmatic devices for organizing and directing human action, and to seek any higher purpose or claim any higher justification for our decisions is absurd. Yet out of this austere, rational, scientific account of human existence there arises a vision of the good life for humanity which is remarkably optimistic.

We are all capable, to some extent, of understanding, of seeing things as they really are: and that understanding can be enhanced and extended. To the extent that we understand ourselves and the world around us, we act rationally, and we know why we act. In that sense, when we think clearly, we are in control of our own action, whereas when we act irrationally we are at the mercy of forces operating on us.

Those forces may be internal or external: when we gaze at the sun like a fool, and jump to the conclusion that it moves around the earth, we are passive and enslaved, with a belief foisted on us by circumstances; when we *understand* why things appear that way, we are active, free, rational AGENTS (pp. 203–4), our beliefs are the result of our own thinking processes. In exactly the same way, when we react angrily to an insult, we are at the mercy of our own emotions and are driven hither and thither by alien forces within ourselves; but when we understand why the insult was offered, and understand why we feel as we do in response, then we ourselves are able to *choose* how to react to it, and in that sense we are free, *self*-determining agents. The picture is now almost complete. To the extent that we are self-determining, rational agents, we will agree with others of the same kind; and to the extent that we understand ourselves and the world around us, we see ourselves as we really are, in our eternal dependence on almighty God.

3 Leibniz

Philosophers have always been notorious for the strength of their disagreements, and for their inability to resolve them by rational debate. Leibniz was a diplomat by profession, and he applied the techniques of diplomacy to bring about peace and harmony in the world of philosophy. Although his philosophical system had many original features, he presented it not as one new system among many, but as incorporating the common ground on which the warring factions could agree.

His approach can be summed up in his dictum that philosophers are generally right in what they assert, and wrong in what they deny. He liked to illustrate this with an analogy: different views of a town give prominence to some features and hide others, so that observers at various viewpoints will give different descriptions of it. But these descriptions are mutually compatible, as long as individual observers do not deny the existence of features they cannot themselves see. Leibniz's ambition was to achieve a God-like perspective which encompasses everything, and reveals all other perspectives as partial, but true as far as they go.

Unlike the other modern philosophers, who saw themselves as making a more or less complete break with the past, Leibniz accepted *all* philosophers as making positive contributions to philosophical truth – not merely canonical figures such as Plato (*c.*429–347 BC) and Aristotle (384–322 BC), but more exotic thinkers like Pythagoras (b. *c.*570 BC) and the Neoplatonists, the much-derided scholastic philosophers, and mystics and alchemists. Again, he was less Eurocentric than most of his contemporaries, and he learned as much as he could about Chinese philosophy, to show how it complemented the western tradition.

3.1 Nature

Descartes and Spinoza both held that the realm of nature was a unitary whole, whether distinct from, or merely an aspect of God. Two alternative views of the world which they consciously rejected were the atomist view that it derives all its reality from the discrete atoms of which it is composed, and the vitalist view that all physical objects are either living beings, or collections of living beings. Leibniz held that all three views contained part of the truth, and that they could be reconciled by reviving the Aristotelian–scholastic concept of a substantial form.

Firstly, Descartes and Spinoza were right to insist on the systematic wholeness of nature – it is more than just a chaotic jumble of atoms. But they were wrong to say that only the universe as a whole is a real substance, since it is a compound of its parts, and the parts must be at least as real as the whole. The question is, what are the ultimate parts of which the universe is a compound? Everyone agreed that everyday physical objects like sticks or stones do not qualify, since they are only temporary collections of smaller parts. The atomists held that there are very small parts of matter of various shapes and sizes, which cannot be divided into further parts, and which are the ultimate substances. For Leibniz, size was irrelevant, since whether something is big or small is relative to the observer – a grain of sand too small to be noticed by an elephant would be a mountain to a microbe. From a mathematical point of view, there is no less possibility of subdividing a spherical atom than a cannonball; and it is simply arbitrary to assert that atoms, unlike cannonballs, can never be broken down into their component parts. In short, there is no such thing as the smallest conceivable material atom.

The conclusion Leibniz drew was not (like Descartes and Spinoza) that there are no fundamental units of nature, but that these units are not material particles. In their enthusiasm for the mechanistic view of the world, the modern philosophers had overlooked the crucial distinction between things which are mere collections of parts, and things which are organic wholes. For Descartes, a clock, a cat and the live body of a human being would all be transitory manifestations of matter of the same kind. The main difference between a cat and a clock is that the mechanism is more complicated; the difference between a cat and a human body is that the human body has a temporary special relationship with an immaterial soul. For Leibniz, the clock is a mere collection of parts, whereas both the cat and the live human body are *organisms*. An organism is a being of a completely different kind. At the common-sense level, it has the capacity to initiate motion, to act purposefully, to react to stimuli and to reproduce. But of special significance to Leibniz was his belief that an organism is a unitary whole, in that its parts are peculiar to itself – every organ and every cell (indeed, every part of every cell) bears unique characteristics that link it to the body to which it belongs. So even if the parts of the body become physically separated, they are still parts of the same organism (rather as a family is a single family, even if its members do not live under the same roof). For Leibniz, then, the only fundamental units of nature are organisms, since they alone possess true unity.

In this, Leibniz sided with the vitalists, whose understanding of nature was modelled on the purposeful, vital forces of living beings, and who saw life everywhere. Even though the majority of macroscopic physical objects we see around us are not themselves living organisms, they are in fact composed of tiny organisms. Leibniz appealed to the evidence of the recently invented microscope, which revealed apparently homogeneous substances, such as chalk, blood or semen, as containing masses of tiny creatures. Indeed, since matter is infinitely divisible, he maintained that every organism is a colony of smaller organisms, and so on *ad infinitum*.

However, although Leibniz accepted the metaphysics of the vitalists, he could not go along with their rejection of the new mechanistic science. In order to achieve a reconciliation of the two world-views, he drew on the traditional Aristotelian distinction between matter and form. For Aristotle, every being has two aspects: its form (the active principle which each individual shares with other members of the same species), and its matter (the passive principle, which bears the characteristics by which one individual is distinguished from another). In the case of animate beings, the form was identified with the soul. Perhaps influenced by Spinoza's double aspect theory, Leibniz maintained that nature had two aspects: the material aspect, consisting of the bodies of all the organisms of which it is composed; and the vital aspect, consisting of all the forms or souls. The material aspect could be understood only in terms of the mathematical laws governing the interactions of pieces of matter characterized by different shapes, sizes and masses. The vital aspect could be understood only in terms of the life principle of striving for perfection. As with Spinoza, there was a perfect one-to-one correlation between what is true of matter, and what is true of forms, or 'monads' (unities), as he later called them. So, for example, a bullet fired from a gun can be seen equally as blindly obeying the laws of mechanics, and as striving for the best possible state with the greatest economy of effort.

3.2 God

If the universe consists in an infinity of individual substances, how does it form a systematic whole? Leibniz's answer was that God is needed to ensure that the components of the universe interact as harmoniously as possible – indeed, he often referred to his philosophical system as the 'system of universal harmony'. This does not mean that the universe is perfect in all its parts, otherwise it would be an absolutely perfect being, and therefore identical with God. Unlike Spinoza, Leibniz insisted that God must be distinct from the universe he created. But as a perfect being, God must have created the best universe which it is logically possible to create, so that if it were made better in some respect, it would be worse overall. The evil, pain and ugliness that we see around us are real enough; but the solution to the problem of evil is to recognize that they contribute to a greater good.

Monads and the Harmony of the Universe

What is it for the universe to be a harmonious system? Monads, being soul-like, have characteristics analogous to those of human souls. In particular, they have something akin to a perceptual state in human souls, only lacking consciousness. In effect, they represent everything that has any influence on them, with greater or less clarity, depending on the strength of the influence. For example, the motion of a particle is affected, however remotely, by all other particles in the universe; and in order to 'know' which direction to move in, it must register all these influences. This led Leibniz to describe monads as 'living mirrors of the universe', each representing all other monads from a distinct and individual point of view. God perceives everything with equal clarity, and without any point of view; whereas created monads are limited by their perspectival point. The harmony of the total system consists in the fact that the perceptions of each individual monad interlock to form a single, consistent view of the universe as perceived by God, like a jig-saw puzzle of infinitely many dimensions. Moreover, since the perceptual state of each monad is constantly changing, the harmony of the universe has to be re-established from one instant to the next.

How does God bring this about? Leibniz considered three possibilities. One was that monads evolve in harmony because they exert causal influences on each other. He rejected this on the ground that it was inconceivable how one soul-like substance could exert any physical force on another: as he put it, monads are 'windowless', and influences cannot leave or enter them. He also rejected the theory, attributed to the philosopher Malebranche (1638–1715), that God continuously adjusts things so that harmony is preserved, since this would make the natural course of events miraculous. The only alternative was that each monad had been pre-programmed with such accuracy that each would spontaneously evolve in perfect harmony with every other – anything less would imply an imperfection in God's creative act.

Leibniz sometimes used the imagery of God as the perfect clockmaker, whose clocks keep perfect time with each other to eternity, and do not need to be connected to each other or adjusted. At a deeper level, Leibniz explained God's creative act as one of endowing a concept with reality. Since God is omniscient, his mind contains all possible concepts, in all their possible permutations and combinations. Every logically consistent set of possibilities constitutes a possible world. These possible worlds can be graded as to their perfection – their fullness of being, coherence, variety, orderliness, harmony or beauty, for instance. In the competition for existence, the best of the possible worlds is the one which is actualized. One of Leibniz's projects was to devise an ideal language for every possible concept, which would make their logical relationships patent (his 'universal characteristic'). If concepts were given numbers rather than names, and the main logical operators reduced to arithmetical operators, it would then be possible to replace fallible human reasoning by purely mechanical computation – and he designed and built a prototype machine for doing just this. In his more mystical moments, he speculated that all concepts were generated out of the binary numbers 1 and 0, with 1 representing pure being, or God, and 0 representing absence of being, or the void. Individual substances are dependent on God like the light radiating from the sun; and they are distinct from God and from each other because of their varying proportions of darkness or non-being. In effect, the universe is the most perfect number, other than 1 itself.

3.3 Humanity

Leibniz's account of humankind falls somewhere between those of Descartes and of Spinoza. He agreed with Spinoza that humans are part of nature, and that there are no special soul-substances exempting them from the laws of nature. On the other hand, he held that humans differ sufficiently in degree to give them a special status in the scheme of things. Although most of our perceptions are, like those of other monads, below the threshold of conscious-ness, some of the time, some of our perceptions are sufficiently clear and distinct to give rise to consciousness – a state in which we do not merely perceive, but are aware of ourselves as perceiving. Similarly, our desires and ambitions are not mere unconscious goal-directed behaviour, but set in a context of self-improvement, rationality and moral choice. Drawing on ST AUGUSTINE's (354–430) (chapter 16) great work, *The City of God*, Leibniz held that humans shared with angels and other superior conscious and rational beings the privilege of being members of the City of God, or the 'realm of grace'.

Just as form and matter are different aspects of the same reality, so are the realms of grace and of nature. As part of nature, all human actions are explicable in purely deterministic, mechanical terms, as motions of particles of matter. But since we are also citizens of the realm of grace, our actions are also describable as the outcome of completely free, rational choices. As scientists, we investigate the causal determinants of human behaviour, but as subjects of God's kingdom we are each contributing to the fulfilment of God's plan for the moral perfection of the universe. Thanks to the gift of reason, we can and should make it our goal in life to raise ourselves above a limited and parochial view of the world, to one which is as close as possible to the divine perspective.

Further Reading

For the three philosophers featured in this chapter we first suggest a major source of their writings translated into English: Descartes (1985), Spinoza (1985) and Leibniz (1969) and then a more convenient selection of their works: Descartes (1988), Spinoza (1992) and Leibniz (1995). For Descartes, readers often concentrate on *Discourse on Method* (published 1637) and *Meditations on First Philosophy* (published 1641), but we would suggest also reading parts of *Principles of Philosophy* (published 1644), *Replies to Objections to the Meditations* (published 1641–2), and some of Descartes' correspondence. We do not discuss *Passions of the Soul* (published 1649), but that is worth reading as well. Readers might seek some understanding of Spinoza's demanding masterpiece, the *Ethics* (published 1677), before turning to his other writings. The fullest accounts of many of Leibniz's ideas appear in his letters, but an overview may be gained from such works as *Discourse on Metaphysics* (written in 1686, published 1846) and the mature accounts in *New Essays on Human Understanding* (written 1704, published 1765), *Theodicy* (published 1710) and the *Monadology* (written 1714). His *Correspondence with Arnauld* (published posthumously in 1846) and *The Leibniz–Clarke Correspondence* (published posthumously in 1717) are classic exchanges which help to explain the grounds for his system.

Readers might begin their additional reading with books comparing all three authors: Cottingham (1988) and Woolhouse (1993).

Garber (1992) shows the relationship between Descartes' philosophical and scientific aims. The articles in Cottingham (ed.) (1992) provide a comprehensive and up-to-date exploration of current philosophical responses to Descartes. Hooker (ed.) (1978) and Moyal (ed.) (1991) offer extremely useful collections of articles about Descartes.

Freeman and Mandelbaum (eds) (1975), Grene (ed.) (1979), and Grene and Nails (eds) (1986) are collections offering wide-ranging critical responses to Spinoza. Donagan (1988) explores Spinoza's doctrines with balance and sophistication, while Bennett (1984) examines the details of Spinoza's system with engaging vigour.

Leibniz's life of brilliant achievement in many fields is explored in Aiton (1985). MacDonald Ross (1984) provides a helpful introductory account. Woolhouse (1993) and Jolley (ed.) (1995) are collections offering guidance for more advanced work.

References

Descartes

Descartes, R. 1985: *The Philosophical Writings of Descartes*, 2 vols (edited and translated by J. Cottingham, J. R. Stoothoff and D. Murdoch). Cambridge: Cambridge University Press.
—— 1988: *Descartes: Selected Philosophical Writings* (edited and translated by J. Cottingham, R. Stoothoff and D. Murdoch). Cambridge: Cambridge University Press.

Writers on Descartes

Cottingham, J. (ed.) 1992: *The Cambridge Companion to Descartes*. Cambridge: Cambridge University Press.
Garber, D. 1992: *Descartes' Metaphysical Physics*. Chicago: University of Chicago Press.
Hooker, M. (ed.) 1978: *Descartes: Critical and Interpretive Essays*. Baltimore: Johns Hopkins University Press.
Moyal, G. J. D. (ed.) 1991: *René Descartes: Critical Assessments*. London: Routledge.

Spinoza

Spinoza, B. 1985: *The Collected Works of Spinoza*, vol. 1 (edited and translated by E. Curley). Princeton: Princeton University Press.
—— 1992: *Ethics with the Treatise on the Emendation of the Intellect and Selected Letters* (edited by S. Feldman, translated by S. Shirley). Indianapolis: Hackett.

Writers on Spinoza

Bennett, J. 1984: *A Study of Spinoza's Ethics*. Cambridge: Cambridge University Press.
Donagan, A. 1988: *Spinoza*. London: Harvester–Wheatsheaf.
Freeman, E. and Mandelbaum, M. (eds) 1975: *Spinoza: Essays in Interpretation*. La Salle, IL: Open Court.
Grene, M. (ed.) 1979: *Spinoza: a Collection of Critical Essays*. Notre Dame: University of Notre Dame Press.
Grene, M. and Nails, D. 1986: (eds) *Spinoza and the Sciences*. Dordrecht: Reidel.

Leibniz

Leibniz, G. W. 1969: *G. W. Leibniz: Philosophical Papers and Letters* (edited and translated by L. E. Loemker). Dordrecht: Reidel.
—— 1995: *G. W. Leibniz: Philosophical Writings* (edited by G. H. R. Parkinson and translated by M. Morris and G. H. R. Parkinson). London: Everyman.

Writers on Leibniz

Aiton, E. J. 1985: *Leibniz: A Biography*. Bristol: Adam Hilger.
Jolley, N. (ed.) 1995: *The Cambridge Companion to Leibniz*. Cambridge: Cambridge University Press.
MacDonald Ross, G. 1984: *Leibniz*. Oxford, Oxford University Press.
Woolhouse, R. S. (ed.) 1993: *G. W. Leibniz: Critical Assessments*. London: Routledge.

Writers on Descartes, Spinoza and Leibniz

Cottingham, J. 1988: *The Rationalists*. Oxford: Oxford University Press.
Woolhouse, R. S. 1993: *Descartes, Spinoza, Leibniz: The Concept of Substance in Seventeenth-Century Metaphysics*. London: Routledge.

Discussion Questions

1 What is the importance of method in philosophy?

2 Is the non-human world a single, deterministic, mechanical system?

3 What would make some laws of nature more fundamental than others?

4 Was Descartes right to demand that scientific theories be *intelligible*?

5 How can we determine when an account explains and when it merely re-describes a phenomenon?

6 Must properties be measurable if we are to use them in scientific explanation?

7 Is the book of nature written in the language of mathematics? What are the implications of your answer?

8 If what we see is only an appearance, how can we gain knowledge of what really happens in the world?

9 Should Descartes have been an atomist?

10 Can there be genuinely empty space? How are objects related to the spaces around them?

11 If God's concurrence is needed at every moment to sustain the universe, how can the laws of nature be laws?

12 If animals are explicable in purely mechanical terms, can humans be explained entirely in this way as well?

13 Does the fact that I can make judgements, even mistaken ones, prove that I exist?

14 If I can think away the entire physical world, but cannot think away my own existence, does it follow that I am a thinking thing, and not merely part of the physical world?

15 Should we follow Descartes' method of doubt?

16 Does Spinoza offer a better universal explanatory framework for a science of nature than Descartes?

17 Should the appearance–reality distinction apply to the mind?

18 Can we explain away individual minds while retaining mentality?

19 What would things be like if seen from the point of view of eternity? Could there be such viewpoint?

20 How can we decide whether Spinoza is correct in claiming that there is only one substance: God or Nature?

21 Should we accept Spinoza's account of the link between rationality and free action?

22 How valuable is Spinoza's account of the emotions?

23 Should a philosophical system seek to incorporate rather than to reject past philosophical thought?

24 What is at stake in deciding whether nature is a systematic whole?

25 Could the fundamental units of nature be organisms rather than material particles?

26 What are monads? In what sense is each monad meant to reflect all the others?

27 Would pre-established harmony or causal interaction among monads be a better explanation of the harmony of the universe?

28 What is the role of Leibniz's concept of possible worlds? How can we determine whether this is the best of all possible worlds?

29 Could Leibniz's project of devising an ideal language be realized?

30 Does the notion of substance help or hinder philosophical understanding?

31 Does Descartes, Spinoza or Leibniz have the best understanding of human freedom?

32 Does Descartes, Spinoza or Leibniz give the best insight into how the mind and the body are related?

18

Hobbes ————————————————————————————

Tom Sorell

Modern political theory had its origins with Thomas Hobbes (1588–1679).
In *Leviathan* and other works, Hobbes presented a bleak picture of violence
and disorder as the inevitable condition of humans in the state of nature.
Peace, the main concern of politics, could be realized only by a strong
sovereign established through a social contract. Subjects would have no
rational grounds to challenge the rule of the sovereign so long as peace was
maintained. Hobbes, who wrote during the turmoil of the English Civil War,
has had wide influence among subsequent political and social theorists. His
materialist method is worth examining in his discussion of many other
topics.

1 Introduction

Thomas Hobbes is best known as a philosopher of HUMAN NATURE (p. 259) and
HUMAN SOCIETY (pp. 550–1). He is famous for maintaining that the natural
condition of people is one of war, in which life is 'solitary, poor, nasty, brutish
and short', and he was an early social contract theorist: he believed that the
STATE (pp. 265–9) could be understood as the outcome of an agreement
between free human beings to submit to government. *Leviathan* (1651),
published in London, is widely regarded as his masterpiece, and it is the most
commonly quoted source of his views about humanity and about the state. It is
not, however, Hobbes' only full-length work of political philosophy – there
were two others – and it is not the work in which he thought that he had given
the best or most rigorous statement of his theory of the state.

Nor was politics Hobbes' only preoccupation as a philosopher. He was a
very forthright and thoroughgoing materialist, and, perhaps above all, a
contributor to, and systematizer of, some of the new NATURAL SCIENCE (chapter
17) of the seventeenth century. In his own opinion he deserved to go down in
the history of philosophy as the originator of a true science of natural JUSTICE
(chapter 8) or politics, and as an innovator in optics. He also claimed some
distinction as the first to boil the whole of philosophy or science down to its
'elements' – the concepts necessary to understand body or matter, man and
citizen. His *Elements of Philosophy*, comprising *De Cive* (1642), *De Corpore*
(1656a), and *De Homine* (1658), was the largest intellectual project he

undertook, occupying as it did nearly two decades of thought and writing. In so far as Hobbes had a complete system of philosophy, it is expounded in this trilogy.

2 Hobbes' Politics

There are two rather different ways in which Hobbes' political writings can be understood. On the one hand, they can be interpreted as partisan interventions in a debate between English parliamentarians and royalists between 1628 and 1650, that is, the period that climaxed in the English Civil War of the early 1640s. In this debate Hobbes' own position was determined by the royalist allegiances of his aristocratic employers. He sided with Charles I, and approved of many of his actions – to do with taxation, the forced billeting of troops in private houses and the curtailment of parliamentary powers – that were highly unpopular in England in the pre-war period. Was it these actions that Hobbes' theoretical works of politics were intended to legitimatize? The suggestion fits the early *Elements of Law* (1640) better than *Leviathan*, for the *Elements* was actually written as a sourcebook or brief for aristocrats who spoke in defence of the king in parliamentary debates in 1640, while *Leviathan* seems to justify the actions of any *de facto* sovereign power, including, explicitly, the regime that replaced the monarchy in England after the death of Charles I.

The second reading of Hobbes' politics is as a contribution, albeit a revolutionary contribution, to a lofty debate concerning questions of politics in the abstract, questions discussed in a long line of treatises going back to the Greeks and the Hebrews. This reading fits neither the *Elements of Law* nor *Leviathan* as well as it does the third of Hobbes' three political treatises, *De Cive* (1642). *De Cive* has a certain pre-eminence among Hobbes' three political treatises: it was on the strength of writing this work that Hobbes claimed to have done something original in POLITICAL PHILOSOPHY (chapter 8). *De Cive* was the first book, according to Hobbes, to deal scientifically with the recognized central questions of political philosophy. Other works, he conceded, had taken up those questions, but not by a method that had any chance of putting conclusions beyond dispute. *De Cive*, on the other hand, purported to do for its subject-matter – commonwealths or bodies politic and their main-tenance – what had only ever been done before for lines and figures. In short, *De Cive* was supposed to expound a science of politics comparable to geometry, with conclusions as compelling to an open mind as those of Euclid (fl. 300 BC).

3 Human Nature and the State of War

De Cive was published in 1642, two years after the *Elements of Law*, and nearly nine years before the appearance of *Leviathan*. It opens (ch. 1, ii) with a strong denial of one of the cardinal principles of ARISTOTLE's (chapter 15) politics, that humans are by nature cut out for life in the *polis*. According to Hobbes, human beings are *not* naturally made for the political life. They think too much of themselves, put too much value on present gratification, and they are bad at predicting the consequences of their actions. One effect of these tendencies is for people to come into conflict with one another, especially when they feel that they are undervalued in other people's eyes. The conflict can consist of the denigration of one person in the conversation of another person, or it can take the form of outright quarrelling and even violence. And if these are familiar patterns of behaviour when there is LAW (chapter 12) and custom and good manners to restrain people, how much more extreme must the hostility be when these things are absent and naked human nature is allowed to express itself without interference?

What would Life be Like without Law?

Hobbes' answer (Hobbes, 1640, Pt. I, ch. 14; 1642: ch. 1; 1651, ch. 13) is that, left to do what comes naturally, human beings would quickly find themselves in a state of war. They would have to see to their own survival and happiness guided not by a government's sense of what was conducive to survival and happiness, but only by their conflicting, fluctuating and irremediably diverse private judgements about what was best. Not being required to defer to anyone else's judgements, but not being able, either, to rely on others to seek the good co-operatively or benevolently, people would have rationally to expect the worst from one another and, if they thought that their safety demanded it, take pre-emptive action. Thus, even those who were not naturally greedy or violent might begin to see their own survival and well-being in taking as much of what they wanted as they could, or in killing anyone who might be a potential enemy – which could mean anyone. As for those who *were* naturally violent and greedy, and who were normally able to get away with it, they would fight and appropriate goods until stopped by people stronger than themselves. Whoever was a potential victim would have a reason to take action against them first. In this way life with no holds barred would quickly degenerate into fearful insecurity and a permanent struggle for survival. Or, as Hobbes puts it, life in the state of nature is war – the anti-social condition *par excellence*.

In relation to the seeds of war in human nature, the argument of *De Cive* (1642) is not very different from that of the *Elements of Law* (1640) or *Leviathan* (1651). Hobbes maintains in all three treatises that life would be extremely unpleasant if law and coercive government were to disappear; he also holds that any government that does exist is constantly in danger of being subverted, that is, forced by rebels into a state of collapse that re-introduces the war of all against all. The seeds of this war are not only the dangerous passions of individual people, who can be aroused by their circumstances or their corporeal constitutions. The seeds also include the lack of science and capacity for reasoning, for it is only in the absence of these things that the PASSIONS (pp. 579–80) succeed in determining individuals' behaviour. Again, Hobbes believed that people were easily swayed by clever politicians and put in fear of Hell by a manipulating clergy. They were thus prone to resent the restrictions of life under government, or to imagine that obedience would cost them salvation. It was a short step from these resentments and fears to civil war.

4 The Laws of Nature and the Rationale for the State

Hobbes' rules for avoiding civil war if a commonwealth exists, and for ending war in the pre-political state of nature, are called laws of nature. Though statements of other 'laws of nature' existed long before the *Elements of Law, De Cive* and *Leviathan*, Hobbes' own list (Hobbes, 1640, Pt. I, chs 16–17; 1642, chs 2–3; 1651, chs 14–15) was unusual, and he claimed he was the first to find an uncontroversial basis for laws of nature. What is more, the basis would make it irrational for anyone to ignore them. It is partly because he was able to identify a single, uncontroversial good that the laws of nature all promoted that Hobbes believed his statement of the laws of nature amounted to a moral science.

The basic good that he identified was the good of peace or the absence of war; or, as he sometimes put it, the good of safety. Because war threatened the possession of all good things, not least life itself, any action that helped to avoid war or to put an end to it, and that did not itself threaten too many goods, was a rationally compulsory thing to do. There were two laws of nature that Hobbes put before the rest, which he called fundamental: firstly, to seek peace by all means if to do so was not too unsafe; and, secondly, to adopt one particular means of seeking peace if other people agreed to do the same: namely, to lay down rights that get in the way of peace.

In the state of nature, the right that people have to give up in order to secure peace is the 'right of nature' – the right to be one's own judge of what will make one safe and happy. So long as each is his or her own judge of these things, there is no insurance against war. The right must therefore be given up. Hobbes was not thinking of a simple renunciation of this right: he had in mind a transfer of it (Hobbes, 1640, Pt. 1, ch. 15, iii; 1642, ch. 2, iv; 1651, ch. 14) by most in the state of nature to a few or to one in the state of nature, who would then decide for the many what would make each as safe and happy as possible. The one or the few would become a SOVEREIGN POWER (pp. 265–9), and the many would become subjects of that power, and be obliged to live in keeping with the sovereign's judgements about safety and well-being, as expressed in the sovereign's laws.

The transfer of the right of nature to a sovereign power is what creates a state or commonwealth. Once transferred, the right of nature cannot be taken back, except for the sake of a personal safety which a weak or incompetent sovereign is no longer able to secure. In other words, one gets back one's right of nature if obedience to the sovereign is not after all a means of avoiding war (Hobbes, 1640, Pt. 2, ch. 1, v; 1642, ch. 6, iii; 1651, ch. 17). On the other hand, if a commonwealth *is* keeping one safe, one is obliged to obey the sovereign's laws, either by the act that transferred one's right of nature, and by the duty to abide by one's agreements; or by some act of submission if one did not enter the commonwealth from the state of nature.

Drawing back from the details, one can see that Hobbes has both a secular conception of the state, and one that tries to show that the existence of the state is reasonable, not arbitrary. There is no divine right of the sovereign to rule that obliges one to obey, nor yet is it a matter of the sovereign's simply being more powerful than one is oneself. The obedience springs from a transfer of right for the sake of peace. The state is thus seen as a security or peace-keeping device whose existence is in the interest of the many, rather than as a facsimile on earth of a divine ordering of things by nobility or rank or station.

5 The Obligations of Subjects and the Rights of Sovereigns

The sovereign's subjects are obliged by a sort of agreement among themselves to obey the sovereign's laws; but the sovereign, though he is a beneficiary of the agreement, is not party to it. The many make a gift to a person or body of people of their submission; but the submission does not oblige the sovereign to please the many in return. The sovereign would perhaps be *imprudent* if he did not do his best to arrange for the peace and well-being of his subjects; for if he allows the state to descend into lawlessness, his subjects take back their right of nature, act once more as laws unto themselves and regard no one as their sovereign. In such a case a former sovereign, being only solitary or a small group, is no more secure than anyone else. So it is in the sovereign's interest not to disappoint his subjects. But he is not obliged to do so, and if his laws only bring about a peace in which everyone is safe but living austerely, that does not amount to an injustice against his subjects, even if they are hugely dissatisfied with their lot. On the contrary, the sovereign is left free by his subjects to act as he sees fit to secure peace and well-being; it is the subjects who act unjustly if they try to re-interpret the agreement as one in which *they* decide how the peace and well-being are to be got, and of what they will consist.

The sovereign, then, has very extensive freedoms or rights (Hobbes, 1640, Pt. 2, ch. 1; 1642, ch. 6; 1651, ch. 18). He decides what is legal and illegal, who owns what, who is to hold the offices of state, who is to be allowed to preach and make political speeches, how people are to be allowed to trade and associate. He has powers to legislate and to tax and of making war. Nothing less than these rights would enable the sovereign to make and keep the peace. But it is one thing for a sovereign to have these extensive rights; it is another for him to exercise them; and Hobbes lists as one of the principal causes of civil war the fact that sovereigns fail to exercise them. This failure, just as much as the failure of subjects to acknowledge the rights of sovereignty, can disturb the peace.

It is not hard to work out the consequences of Hobbes' theory in relation to the question of whether Charles I was within his rights to force a loan from his rich subjects, to billet soldiers and to circumvent parliament in the period before the civil war. He was within his rights in all of these areas; and that civil war ensued was as much traceable to a mistaken understanding of the rights of subjects, as to ineptitude in the exercise of sovereign rights.

We have come far enough to see that both readings of Hobbes' politics fit after all. There can be no doubt that, in his three major works on the commonwealth, Hobbes frames his account of the rights of sovereigns (and of the causes of civil war) with the events of England in the 1630s and 1640s in his mind. But it is also true that the theory takes up abstract questions that transcend his historical period and which go back to Plato and Aristotle. Hobbes has an answer to the question of what the state is for, of what human happiness can consist in and what goods are promoted by morality; he is not only operating through his writings as a policy adviser to a certain English king or kings and their entourage.

6 Strengths and Weaknesses of Hobbes' Politics

How successful is Hobbes' theory of subjection and sovereignty as a piece of political philosophy? One of its most distinctive ideas is that peace rather than happiness is what the institution of the state is for. Hobbes thought that the concept of peace was clearer than the concept of happiness, and also that, while people had different, and sometimes irreconcilable, conceptions of happiness, people could reach agreement about what constituted peace. He also believed that people could not rationally repudiate the demands of peace. Against this background, a theory of the state and of morality geared to peace was supposed to make a great advance on preceding theories. Unfortunately, all of the supposed advantages of the concept of peace can be questioned. Firstly, the concept of peace is *not* very clear in Hobbes' writing. It is defined as any time when there is not war. But because Hobbes thinks that war is not only open fighting but also includes the vague phenomenon we now call 'cold war', the concept of the absence of war is bound to have the vagueness that the concept of war itself has.

Secondly, Hobbes sometimes seems to identify the chief aim of the state with that of securing peace and sometimes with that of achieving public safety (Hobbes, 1651, ch. 30). The public safety, however, he defines in broad and in narrow senses. The narrow sense of safety is protection from physical attack; the broad sense is safety in the narrow sense plus as much well-being as is compatible with safety in the narrow sense. Plainly, if the advisability of obedience to the state is to be judged by the state's success in making people safe in the broad sense, then, since safety in the broad sense is open to many interpretations, there is perhaps too much scope for the conclusion that the state is *not* fulfilling its functions and that obedience is *not* due. The expectation of safety from the state starts to become as destabilizing as the expectation of happiness, which is not surprising, since safety in the broad sense overlaps with the concept of happiness.

Hobbes' problems do not disappear if the concept of safety is narrowed down to the concept of safety from physical attack, for individuals in the state never lose their right to judge when they are under threat of physical attack, and they never lose their right to do what they like to protect themselves if they really do think they are under such threat. Stuck in the middle of a riot, for example, they may take up arms and kill if they think that is how to survive. But even in what is outwardly a peaceful state someone may sincerely believe that an underground paramilitary movement is secretly working its way towards a successful takeover of the state and a future policy of genocide; it is unclear that this belief, even if paranoid, would not free an individual from the ties of the social contract. Because Hobbes insists on the inalienability of the right to be one's own interpreter of present dangers, he may leave too much room for pretexts for taking the law into one's own hands: precisely what he prides himself on having excluded.

7 The Rest of Hobbes' Philosophy

Hobbes' politics is not unrelated to the rest of his philosophy – to his materialistic metaphysics, for instance, or his theories of optics. On the contrary, Hobbes thought that his metaphysics, his politics, his optics, as well as other philosophers' findings in other branches of learning, could be arranged into one orderly body of science in general.

In his METAPHYSICS (chapter 2) Hobbes argued against a belief in immaterial things. Here he took issue with DESCARTES (chapter 17), on whose *Meditations* he was one of the first to comment. Hobbes denied that there were irreducibly immaterial substances, either finite or infinite; in his replies to Bishop Bramhall (1594–1663) in a controversy over free will, Hobbes said that even GOD (chapter 14) was a corporeal spirit; and he insisted that MENTAL ACTIVITY (chapter 5) was motion in the head and in the nervous and circulatory systems. Another kind of immaterialism he denied was the belief in abstract objects – such as the nature of a triangle. Descartes had insisted on the reality of such things in his Fifth Meditation: Hobbes, for his part, thought that everything important about triangles could be understood as flowing from linguistic conventions governing the word 'triangle', rather than from triangularity.

In optics, Hobbes advocated the theory that we see things as a result of the displacement of a medium and the agitation of the sense organs by the motion of a luminous object, like the sun.

The thread running through all of his own contributions to the sciences is a strong antagonism to the old learning of the scholastics, and especially the hero of the scholastics, Aristotle. Hobbes developed his theory of vision in opposition to the Aristotelian theory that we see things by a process of transfer of forms or species from the seen object to the intervening medium to the eye. He developed his politics, as we have seen earlier, partly in opposition to the Aristotelian theory that human beings are animals that are suited to the polity. And he arrived at his materialism partly in opposition to Aristotle's theory that the main branches of science all have discrete and distinctive subject matters which exist in their own ways. For Hobbes, to exist was to be material, and the explanation of everything in nature was to be referred to different types of motion in matter. On the surface, Hobbes followed Aristotle in dividing up sciences according as their subject matter was natural or artificial; but even here he broke the mould, for neither of the sciences he reckoned to be concerned with artifacts, namely geometry and politics, was counted as artificial by Aristotle, and to be artificial for Hobbes was still to be material and the result of motion. To be sure, the motion that gives rise to artifacts is motion initiated by the human will, but the will itself is mechanically explicable; so there was no fundamental distinction for Hobbes between the subject matters of the natural sciences and the sciences of artifacts: both were sciences of motion or mechanistic sciences.

In the case of politics, the subject matter was something made by and out of human beings, namely a commonwealth. The purpose of the science was not, however, primarily explanatory, but productive: Hobbes claimed he would teach how to construct a lasting commonwealth, much as Euclid had taught how to construct circles. Precepts dominate Hobbes' politics; statements about the possible causes of observed effects dominate his contributions to the natural sciences. So a rough way for Hobbes to distinguish between the political or moral sciences and the natural sciences is by way of the difference between ought and is; or, more precisely, between statements of what one ought to do, backed by reasons, and conjectures of causes of observed effects, backed by reasons.

Further Reading

Those working on Hobbes should begin by reading *Leviathan* (1651). Peters (1956) offers a clearly written study of the whole of Hobbes' philosophy, while Sorell (1986) provides a study of Hobbes' metaphysics and politics against the background of his philosophy of science. Gauthier (1978), Oakeshott (1975), Macpherson (1962), and Warrender (1957) are classic appraisals of Hobbes' political thought. Mintz (1970) deals with the context and early reception of *Leviathan*, and Sommerville (1992) is a very clear and comprehensive guide to the historical context of Hobbes' political writings. Johnston (1986) explores the tensions between the scientific pretensions of some of Hobbes' political writings and their persuasive purpose. A short study by Tuck (1989) argues for the importance of philosophical scepticism in Hobbes' thought. Most of the papers in Rogers and Ryan (1988) are accessible, and there is coverage of Hobbes' metaphysics, philosophy of science and politics. Sorell (1995) contains an authoritative biographical account and articles on all aspects of Hobbes' thought, including his mathematics and optics and his theories of law and religion, as well as his metaphysics, politics, and philosophy of science.

References

Hobbes

The standard edition of Hobbes' works is divided between his English and Latin
    writings:
Hobbes, T. 1966a: *The English Works of Thomas Hobbes* (edited by Sir W. Molesworth).
    11 vols, second reprint. Aalen: Scientia Verlag.
—— 1966b: *Opera Latina* (edited by Sir W. Molesworth). 5 vols, second reprint. Aalen:
    Scientia Verlag.
Individual works, unless cited otherwise, are to be found in the collected works.
    Leviathan is available in several recent editions.

Hobbes, T. 1889 [1640]: *The Elements of Law Natural and Politic* (edited by F. Tonnies).
    London: Simkin and Marshall.
—— 1976 [1641 or 1642]: *Thomas White's 'De Mundo' Examined* (translated by H. W.
    Jones). Bradford: Bradford University Press.
—— [1641]: *Third Set of Objections to Descartes's Meditations.* In E. Haldane and G.
    Ross (eds), *The Philosophical Works of Descartes*, Cambridge: Cambridge University
    Press.
—— [1642]: *De Cive*, short title for *Elementorum Philosophiae, Section Tertia, De Cive*
    (translated by Hobbes into English (1651) as *Philosophical Rudiments Concerning
    Government and Society*).
—— [1646]: *A Minute or First Draught on Optics.*
—— [1651]: *Leviathan, or the Matter, Form and Power of Commonwealth, Ecclesiastical
    and Civil.*
—— [1654]: *Of Liberty and Necessity.*
—— [1656a]: *De Corpore*, short title for *Elementorum Philosophiae, Secto Prima de
    Corpore*, 1655, translated into English as *Elements of Philosophy, the First Section
    concerning Body*, 1656.
—— [1656b]: *The Questions Concerning Liberty, Necessity and Chance, Clearly Stated
    and Debated between Dr. Bramhall, Bishop of Derry, and Thomas Hobbes of
    Malmsbury.*
—— [1656c]: *Six Lessons to the Professors of Mathematics . . . in the University of
    Oxford.*
—— [1658]: *De Homine, sive Elementorum Philosophiae Sectio Secunda* (edited by B.
    Gert, translated by C. T. Wood, T. Scott-Craig and B. Gert, as *On Man* in *Man and
    Citizen*, New York: Humanities Press, 1962.
—— [1662a]: *Seven Philosophical Problems.*
—— [1622b]: *Considerations of the Reputation, Loyalty, Manners, and Religion, of
    Thomas Hobbes of Malmsbury.*
—— [c.1666]: *Dialogue Between a Philosopher and a Student of the Common Laws of
    England.*
—— c.1668]: *Behemoth, or the Long Parliament. Dialogue of the Civil Wars of
    England.*
—— [1678]: *Decameron Physiologicum or Ten Dialogues of Natural Philosophy.*

Other writers

Brandt, F. 1928: *Hobbes' Mechanical Conception of Nature*. London: Hachette.
Brown, S. M. 1959: Hobbes: The Taylor Thesis. *Philosophical Review*, 68.
Dewey, J. 1974: The Motivation of Hobbes' Political Philosophy. In R. Ross, H.
    Schneider and T. Waldman (eds), *Thomas Hobbes in his Times*, Minneapolis:
    University of Minnesota Press.

Gauthier, D. 1978: *The Logic of Leviathan: The Moral and Political Theory of Thomas Hobbes*. Oxford: Blackwell.

Goldsmith, M. 1966: *Hobbes's Science of Politics*. New York: Columbia University Press.

Johnston, D. 1986: *The Rhetoric of Leviathan*. Princeton: Princeton University Press.

Levin, M. 1982: A Hobbesian Minimal State. *Philosophy and Public Affairs*, 11.

Macpherson, C. B. 1962: *The Political Theory of Possessive Individualism*. Oxford: Clarendon Press.

McNeilly, F. S. 1968: *The Anatomy of Leviathan*. London: Macmillan.

Mintz, S. 1970: *The Hunting of Leviathan*. Cambridge: Cambridge University Press.

Nagel, T. 1959: Hobbes's Concept of Obligation. *Philosophical Review*, 68.

Oakeshott, M. 1975: *Hobbes on Civil Association*. Oxford: Blackwell.

Peters, R. 1956: *Hobbes*. Harmondsworth: Penguin.

Raphael, D. D. 1977: *Hobbes: Morals and Politics*. London: George Allen and Unwin.

Robertson, G. C. 1886: *Hobbes*. Edinburgh: W. Blackwood.

Rogers, G. A. J. and Ryan, A. (eds) 1988: *Perspectives on Thomas Hobbes*. Oxford: Clarendon Press.

Sacksteder, W. 1982: *Hobbes Studies (1879–1979)*. Bowling Green: Philosophy Documentation Center.

Shapin, S. and Schaffer, S. 1985: *Leviathan and the Air Pump*. Princeton: Princeton University Press.

Skinner, Q. 1966: The Ideological Context of Hobbes' Political Thought. *The Historical Journal*, 9.

Sommerville, J. 1992: *Thomas Hobbes: Political Ideas in Historical Context*. London: Macmillan.

Sorell, T. 1986: *Hobbes*. London: Routledge.

—— (ed.) 1995: *The Cambridge Companion to Hobbes*. Cambridge: Cambridge University Press.

Taylor, A. E. 1938: The Ethical Doctrine of Hobbes. *Philosophy*, 13.

Thomas, K. 1965: The Social Origins of Hobbes's Political Thought. In K. C. Brown (ed.), *Hobbes Studies*, Oxford: Blackwell.

Tuck, R. 1989: *Hobbes*. Oxford: Oxford University Press.

Warrender, H. 1957: *The Political Philosophy of Hobbes*. Oxford: Clarendon Press.

Zarka, Y. 1987: *La decision metaphysique de Hobbes – Conditions de la politique*. Paris: Vrin.

Discussion Questions

1 Can we understand Hobbes' contributions to abstract political theory without grasping his role in the political controversies of his time?

2 Why did Hobbes wish to deal scientifically with the questions of political philosophy? Did he succeed?

3 What follows from Hobbes' denial that human beings are made for political life?

4 How can we decide whether people are peaceable or by nature prone to conflict and violence?

5 Is life in the state of nature war?

6 Assess Hobbes' moral psychology in a state of nature and under a coercive government.

7 Did Hobbes have good reasons for asserting that even strong governments are vulnerable to rebellion and collapse?

8   Do science and a capacity for reasoning prevent the passions from determining an individual's behaviour?

9   Did Hobbes find in peace a single, uncontroversial good on which to base laws of nature?

10 In relinquishing rights in order to secure peace, do Hobbesean actors give up too much?

11 Can we accept Hobbes' account of how one or a few might become a sovereign power? How else might a sovereign power be established?

12 What is a state or commonwealth? Would a transfer of rights from individuals be sufficient to establish a state?

13 Are there circumstances other than renewed hazards of war which would justify rejecting the sovereign's laws?

14 Can we accept that the sovereign has no obligation to maintain the peace, but does so only as a matter of prudence?

15 Would subjects have a reasonable complaint against a sovereign whose laws left them safe, but hugely dissatisfied with their lot?

16 Do subjects act unjustly if *they* try to decide what constitutes peace and well-being and how they are to be obtained?

17 Was Hobbes right to see danger in a sovereign's failure to exercise rights?

18 Does it make better sense to say that the institution of the state is for peace or for happiness?

19 Can Hobbes' theory be altered to give a greater role to well-being?

20 Is the expectation of safety from the state as destabilizing as the expectation of happiness?

21 Does Hobbes, contrary to his intention, leave too much room for taking the law into one's own hands?

22 Can we avoid any commitment to immaterial things?

23 Can everything important about triangles be understood as coming from linguistic conventions about the word 'triangle'?

24 Does Hobbes succeed in establishing a materialist theory of the mind? Consider especially his account of the will.

19

Locke ——————————————————————

R. S. Woolhouse

John Locke is one of the most important European philosophers of the 'early modern' or immediate post-Cartesian period. Born in Somerset, England, in 1632 and educated in Oxford, he died in Essex in 1704. Besides being involved in Protestant politics and public affairs through his employer, Lord Ashley, later Earl of Shaftesbury, he found time to write on a wide variety of broadly philosophical topics – religion, education, economics, political philosophy. He is known primarily for his epistemological masterpiece, *An Essay Concerning Human Understanding* (published 1690), but also for his *Two Treatises of Government* (published 1690) and *The Reasonableness of Christianity* (published 1695). Readers will find it helpful to look at chapters on EPISTEMOLOGY (chapter 1), METAPHYSICS (chapter 2), POLITICAL AND SOCIAL PHILOSOPHY (chapter 8), PHILOSOPHY OF RELIGION (chapter 14), DESCARTES, SPINOZA AND LEIBNIZ (chapter 17), HOBBES (chapter 18), BERKELEY (chapter 20) and HUME (chapter 21).

1 The *Essay Concerning Human Understanding*

Locke's *Essay* was begun some 20 years before it was published, and it went through various drafts. It embodies and draws together many of the thought-currents that were commonplace in the latter half of the seventeeth century – negative ones, such as anti-Aristotelianism, and positive ones, such as that of the mechanical philosophy and the new experimental philosophy. A hint of these themes is given in the 'Epistle to the Reader' of the *Essay*, where Locke contrasts the impediments to knowledge thrown up by SCHOLASTIC PHILOSOPHY (chapter 16), with the lasting monuments to posterity produced by contributors such as Robert Boyle (1627–91) and Isaac Newton (1642–1727), to 'the commonwealth of learning'. The chemist Robert Boyle was a founder member of the Royal Society of London for the Advancement of Experimental Knowledge, and the mathematician and theoretical physicist Isaac Newton was one of its first presidents. Locke was elected a Fellow to the Society in 1668 not long before he began work on the *Essay*.

Besides thus being a product of its century, the *Essay* had a great influence on the Enlightenment of the next century, whose RATIONALISM (chapter 17) wears the colours of the individualism which pervades both Locke's expression and his explicit doctrine. Running through the *Essay* is an insistence that opinions are carefully to be weighed, impartially considered and judged on their own merits, by individuals for themselves independently of what others say, particularly those in the majority or in authority.

Though there are METAPHYSICAL and ONTOLOGICAL (chapter 2) elements in the *Essay* its main concern is the EPISTEMOLOGICAL (chapter 1) one of the extent to which the human mind has the capacity to acquire knowledge. 'My purpose', Locke says, is 'to enquire into the original, certainty, and extent of human knowledge; together with the grounds and degrees of belief, opinion and assent' (1975, I, I, ii). It is plain, moreover, that one of Locke's concerns in setting out 'to take a survey of our own understanding, [to] examine our powers, and to see to what things they were adapted' (1975, I, I, vii) was to make a response to scepticism about the very possibility of knowledge. He speaks of the sceptical despair, and the tendency to disclaim all knowledge, which can arise when people realize that 'some things are not to be understood' (1975, I, I, vi):

> Men, extending their enquiries beyond their capacities . . . 'tis no wonder that they raise questions . . . which never coming to any clear resolution, are proper only to . . . confirm them at last in perfect scepticism. (1975, I, I, vii)

His interest in this matter was not purely theoretical. He had a practical interest in the human predicament in general, and in the question of what kind of creature GOD (chapter 14) has seen fit to make us and in the question of how, as a consequence, we should arrange and manage our lives and thoughts. He wished, therefore, 'to find out those measures, whereby a rational creature put in that state, which man is in, in this world, may, and ought to govern his opinions, actions depending thereon' (1975, I, I, vi).

Locke's general position, as outlined at the very outset of his detailed investigation, is that there is some truth in scepticism: our knowledge *does* indeed have its limits. There are things of which we are completely ignorant, and there are things about which we can merely opine and believe. But this is no cause for despair for, so Locke believed, our capacities for knowledge are suited to our needs. 'How short soever . . . [people's] knowledge may come of an universal or perfect comprehension of whatsover is, it yet secures their great concernments' (1975, I, I, v).

Yet, what *are* our needs and concernments? In Locke's view we are put here by God in this world, with some hope of a life hereafter in another. Our needs are met, therefore, if we know enough for the everyday practicalities of life in this world and, in terms of our duties and obligations to each other and to God, for our salvation in the next. And, in Locke's view, these needs *are* met, or, with some reasonable effort on our part, *can* be met. People should be 'well satisfied with what God hath thought fit for them, since he hath . . . put within the reach of their discovery the comfortable provision for this life and the way that leads to a better' (1975, I, I, v).

This is not to say that God has actually given us what knowledge is necessary and useful; the whole of book 1 of the *Essay* is devoted to rejecting roundly any suggestion that any of our knowledge or ideas is innate, and possessed from birth. It is rather that God, by equipping us with an understanding, has enabled us to acquire what is necessary; and, without striving against or complaining about its limits, we should make use of that ability. I do not, he says, 'disesteem, or dissuade the study of nature', but only 'that we should not be too forwardly possessed with the opinion, or expectation of knowledge where it is not to be had' (1975, IV, XII, xii). This ability, moreover, has been given to each one of us, and each one of us must autonomously make his own individual use of it. Locke is passionately dismissive of those who

> taking things upon trust, misimploy their power of assent, by lazily enslaving their minds to the dictates and dominion of others, in doctrines which it is their duty carefully to examine. (1975, I, IV, xxii)

Having rejected any suggestion of an innate endowment of knowledge, Locke sets out to show how its 'fountain' is experience. It is in experience that 'all our knowledge is founded; and from which it ultimately derives itself' (1975, II, I, ii). On account of statements like this, Locke has been characterized as an empiricist. (Indeed, his place in the history of philosophy has often been seen as the founder of the so-called school of British Empiricism, a school of which BERKELEY (chapter 20), HUME (chapter 21) and, later, MILL (chapter 25), are supposed to be members.)

But it is important to see that he does not hold that knowledge is immediately 'made out to us by our senses' (1990, p. 75) by themselves. What is immediately derived from experience are 'ideas', and ideas in themselves are not knowledge. They are, rather, 'the materials of knowledge' (1975, II, I, ii). Besides having SENSES (pp. 49–50) which give them ideas from experience, humans have reason and understanding too, and it is by their means that knowledge is *ultimately*, as Locke carefully says, *derived from* ideas: 'reason . . . by a right traceing of those ideas which it hath received from sense or sensation may come to . . . knowledge . . . which our senses could never have discovered' (1990, p. 75). The frequent classification of Locke as an empiricist must not be allowed to hide that he clearly holds that reason too is essentially involved in the ultimate derivation of knowledge.

What the classification as an empiricist does correctly capture is Locke's view that, prior to experience, the human mind is 'white paper, void of all characters, without any *ideas*' (1975, II, I, ii), and that 'all those sublime thoughts which tower above the clouds, and reach as high as heaven itself, take their rise and footing' (1975, II, I, xxiv) in experience. But how is our knowledge derived from this experiential material and how does our reason come to knowledge on its basis?

Locke takes knowledge to be 'the perception of the connexion and agreement, or disagreement and repugnancy of any of our ideas' (1975, IV, I, ii). His thought is that some ideas have necessary connections with others. Knowledge of the truths about these connections consists in the 'perception', the recognition by our understanding, of the connections. So, our knowledge that a triangle's three angles are equal to two right angles consists in our intellectual 'perception' of the connection between the idea of this equality and the idea of the triangle's three angles. We intellectually 'see' that 'that equality to two right ones, does necessarily agree to, and is inseparable from the three angles of a triangle' (1975, IV, I, ii).

Such connections are sometimes direct and immediate, sometimes indirect and mediated by connections with other ideas. When 'the mind perceives the agreement or disagreement of two ideas immediately by themselves, without the intervention of any other' we have *intuitive* knowledge, as when we 'perceive' directly 'that *three* are more than *two*, and equal to *one* and *two*' (1975, IV, II, i). When the connection is indirect, we have *demonstrative knowledge*, as when we cannot know that the angles of a triangle are equal to two right angles 'by an immediate view and comparing them', but need instead to 'find out some other angles, to which the three angles of a triangle have an equality; and finding those equal to two right ones, comes to know their equality to two right ones' (1975, IV, II, ii).

Besides *intuitive* and *demonstrative* knowledge Locke recognizes *sensitive* knowledge: knowledge of 'the existence of particular extended objects, by that perception and consciousness we have of the actual entrance of ideas from them' (1975, IV, II, xiv), that is, knowledge by our senses of what is now going on before our eyes. Sensitive knowledge seems not to fit Locke's official definition of knowledge: it does not pertain to some connection between two ideas, but to the present existence of something in the world corresponding to our present sensory perceptions or ideas.

These three 'degrees' of knowledge cut across a classification Locke proposes of the agreement or connection between ideas, the perception of which constitutes knowledge, into four 'sorts': '*Identity*, or *diversity*'; '*relation*'; '*co-existence*, or *necessary connection*'; and '*real existence*' (1975, IV, I, iii). These four sorts of connection give rise, respectively and roughly, to intuitively known propositions such as that '*white* is *white*' or that '*three* is more than *two*'; to intuitively or demonstratively known propositions such as those about geometrical figures; to propositions about the properties of substances such as gold; and to the propositions that make up sensitive knowledge.

It is plausible to think that our knowledge of the properties of triangles is based on our grasp, by means of our understanding, of connections between ideas. But what of our knowledge of the properties of silver (that it dissolves in nitric acid, for example), or of gold (that it does not so dissolve)? Here, as Locke freely says, there is no connection, discoverable by and intelligible to our understanding, between our ideas; here, he acknowledges, we are 'left only to observation and experiment' (1975, IV, III, xxviii). His position on this is, simply, that these are *not* cases of knowledge. They are cases of what he calls 'belief' or 'opinion' (1975, IV, XV, iii).

Knowledge and Belief

Locke's notion of KNOWLEDGE (chapter 1) as he defines it is related to the more recent one of *a priori* or 'conceptual knowledge'. His statement that 'in some of our ideas there are certain relations, habitudes, and connexions, so visibly included in the nature of the ideas themselves, that we cannot conceive them separable from them, by any power whatsoever' (1975, IV, III, xxix) parallels what has sometimes been said in this century about the *a priori* knowledge such as that which we have in mathematics. Similarly, his notion of 'belief', which is based on 'observation and experiment' because of 'a want of a discoverable connection between those ideas which we have' (1975, IV, III, xxviii), can be related to the notion of the *a posteriori* knowledge of the kind which we have, in a systematic form, in the empirical sciences. Yet just as Locke would call such empirical knowledge not 'knowledge' as such but rather 'belief', so he would not call an organized body of it, as in chemistry, 'a science'. Geometry and arithmetic are sciences for him, and (so he says) MORALITY (chapter 6) could become one, but 'natural philosophy is not capable of being made a science' (1975, IV, II, x).

Locke's view is, then, quite clearly, that there is a horizon and limit to our knowledge. Moreover, the question we might ask of him – namely, why this is so, why it is that in some cases there are intelligible and graspable connections between our ideas, and in other cases there are not – is one to which he gives a structured answer. Along the way to uncovering that structure we will review some other, but related, aspects of his philosophy too.

As a help to supporting his claim that all our ideas, all the materials of knowledge, stem from experience, Locke makes an appeal to a distinction between simple and complex ideas – an appeal which had been made earlier by Gassendi (1592–1655) and was to be made by some later philosophers including Hume. So, for example, the ideas of a centaur, of God, and of infinity (ideas of whose objects we can hardly have had experience) are *complex* ideas, whose component simples or parts must (perhaps as parts of other complexes) have come from experience. At the same time he divides complex ideas into various categories, of which *substances* and *modes* are two.

'Substances', says Locke, are ideas of 'things subsisting by themselves' (1975, II, XII, vi); they are, as is plain from his examples, ideas of naturally occurring kinds of material thing – just the kind of thing, in fact, about whose properties we form beliefs on the basis of experience and observation.

Locke distinguishes these properties that make up our idea of gold into 'primary and original', and 'secondary'. This famous distinction, which he shared with other early modern philosophers and scientists, such as Galileo (1564–1642), DESCARTES (chapter 17), and Boyle, is made against the background of corpuscularianism – a theory common in the seventeenth century, but one derived from the classical Greek atomists, Democritus (*c*.460–*c*.370 BC) and Epicurus (341–270 BC), who held that matter is composed of tiny, imperceptible particles. Primary qualities are qualities that belong not only to substances such as gold, but also to the insensible corpuscles which make them up. Thus, a piece of gold is solid, has extension and shape, and can be moved; and, according to the corpuscular theory, its corpuscles have these qualities too. Secondary qualities, such as colour and taste, belong to a piece of gold but not to its component corpuscles. It is because these secondary qualities were supposed to arise from the arrangement of the solid, shaped, and moveable corpuscles which constitute gold, that is, from the primary or 'original' (originating) qualities of the parts, that they were not to be attributed to the corpuscules themselves.

A further point to be noted, and one which has led to continuing controversy, is that Locke says about our complex ideas of substances that their main component of the complex is 'the supposed, or confused idea of substance', something which he also calls 'substratum' or 'pure substance in general' (1975, II, XXIII, ii). Locke is sometimes taken to be saying here that material things are more than 'bundles of co-existing properties' (as Bertrand RUSSELL (chapter 27) later held), but have, in addition to their properties, a propertyless 'substratum' which 'supports' their properties. According to another interpretation, however, Locke is not interested in abstract questions about the difference between 'things' and 'properties' or in the ontology underlying the distinction between SUBJECT AND PREDICATE (pp. 93–4). Rather, his talk of a 'substratum' supporting properties is a reference not to some featureless I-know-not-what, but to matter as understood by the corpuscular theory, and in terms of which the properties of a substance are to be explained.

Our complex idea of gold, which we have derived from experience, comes to be that for which the word 'gold' stands – Locke speaks of it as 'nothing but that abstract idea to which the name is annexed' (1975, III, VI, ii), and, as such, he refers to it as a 'nominal essence'. But this nominal essence of gold, composed as it is from various qualities which experience and observation have shown us go together in the material stuff we call 'gold', is different from what Locke calls its 'real essence'. This latter is that 'upon which depends this nominal essence, and all the properties of that sort' (1975, III, VI, ii); it is that 'on which all the properties of the species depend, and from which alone they all flow' (1975, III, V, xiv). In the case of substances it is, in short, that arrangement of primary-qualitied imperceptible corpuscles on which depend the primary and secondary qualities of the substance as we experience it. Different material substances have different observable qualities because there are differences in the shape, size, arrangement and motion of the 'insensible corpuscules' (1975, IV, III, xxv) which make up their real essences or real constitutions.

This account of a substance's real essence in terms of the corpuscular theory of matter is one of the anti-Aristotelian features of the *Essay* which were mentioned earlier. 'Concerning the real essences of corporeal substances', he says, 'there are ... two opinions'. His, the 'more rational', takes it that substances 'have a real, but unknown constitution of the insensible parts, from which flow those sensible qualities, which serve us to distinguish them one from another'. The other belongs to the hylomorphic theory of the Aristotelians according to which a material substance is a composite of 'form' (*morphe*) and 'matter' (*hyle*). Accordingly, it supposes 'a certain number of forms or molds, wherein all natural things, that exist, are cast, and do equally partake' (1975, III, III, xvii). Like Robert Boyle, the Royal Society chemist – who made the point in his book *The Origin of Forms and Qualities* (published 1666) – Locke and other 'modern' philosophers of the seventeenth century felt that this account of real essences had 'very much perplexed the knowledge of natural things' (1975, III, III, xvii). Material substances were better understood, they thought, in terms of another classical Greek theory, that of atomism.

Now the reason why natural philosophy, the study of substances such as gold or lead, is 'incapable of being made a science' is simply that the nominal essence of those substances, our ideas of them, are not ideas of their real essences; even supposing that the corpuscular theory is true, we do not know the actual details of the corpuscular constitution of any substance. As a consequence, our ideas or nominal essences of the various substances relate instead to some collection of the properties which are supposed to flow from and depend on their real essences. Now though, it may be supposed, gold's malleability is necessarily connected with its real, atomic constitution; because our idea of gold is not of that constitution, there is no necessary connection between gold's malleability and *our* idea of gold. Natural philosophy is not capable of being made a science because we do not have the right ideas; we do not have knowledge of the corpuscular details of the real essences of the substances which it studies.

The case with GEOMETRY (chapter 10) and the modes it studies is much the same, but different in at least one very important respect. Like substances, geometrical figures, such as the triangle, have a real essence too, a real essence on which their properties depend. Of course, since the triangle is not a material thing but rather a shape, or a way in which material things may be arranged, its real essence is not a corpuscular constitution or arrangement of atomic particles. However, just as gold *is*, in its real essence, atomic particles arranged in a certain way (the details of which are unknown to us), a triangle *is*, quite obviously, 'a figure of three lines enclosing a space'. This is, as Locke says, 'not only the abstract idea to which the general name is annexed' (1975, III, III, xviii), not only the nominal essence of triangularity and what a triangle is to us, but also the real essence, what a triangle really is: it is 'the very *essentia*, or being, of the thing it self, that foundation from which all its properties flow, and to which they are all inseparably annexed' (1975, III, III, xviii).

So the properties of a triangle, such as its having external angles equal to its internal opposites, flow from, and so are necessarily connected with, its real essence, and our idea of the triangle is an idea of its real essence. It follows that there *is* a necessary connection, in this case, between our idea of a triangle and its various properties. The following passage points up this contrast between the way our knowledge is limited in natural philosophy, due to a want of the relevant ideas, and the way it is not limited in this way in geometry.

> Substances afford matter of very little general knowledge; and the bare contemplation of their abstract ideas, will carry us but a very little way in the search of truth and certainty. . . . Experience here must teach me, what reason cannot: and it is by trying alone, that I can certainly know, what other qualities co-exist with those of my complex idea, *v.g.* whether that yellow, heavy, fusible, body, I call gold, be malleable, or no; which experience . . . makes me not certain, that it is so, in all or any other yellow, heavy, fusible bodies, but that which I have tried. . . . Because the other properties of such bodies, depending not on these, but on

that unknown real essence, on which these also depend, we cannot by them discover the rest. (1975, IV, XII, ix)

Our knowledge in natural philosophy is, therefore, severely limited by the nature of our ideas, by the fact that they are not ideas of the relevant real essences. But geometry and mathematics are not the only areas where it is not subject to similar limits. On the grounds that the ideas of morality are, like those of mathematics, modes, whose real essences we might come to know, Locke suggests the possibility of

> plac[ing] morality amongst the sciences capable of demonstration: wherein I doubt not, but from self-evident propositions, by necessary consequences, as incontestable as those in mathematics, the measures of right and wrong might be made out. (1975, IV, III, xviii)

The 'moral science' Locke envisages would have as one of its bases the idea of God, 'infinite in power, goodness, and wisdom' (1975, IV, III, xviii) whose dictates are 'the only true touchstone of moral rectitude' (1975, II, XXVII, viii). It would have as another the idea of ourselves as dependent creatures of God who have sufficient understanding and rationality to understand his will: from this we 'as certainly know that man is to honour, fear and obey God, as . . . that three, four, and seven, are less than fifteen' (1975, IV, XIII, iii). Though not supposing this systematic moral science to be more than a possibility yet to be realized, Locke nevertheless thought that we had already reasoned our way to some items of moral knowledge. He makes clear, however, particularly in the *Reasonableness of Christianity*, that what he calls reason's 'great and proper business of morality' (1873, p. 140) is not an easy one. So those who are immersed in the necessities of everyday life, and have neither the time nor ability to uncover moral truths by reason can find it in the Gospels. The 'law which God has set to the actions of men . . . [is] promulgated to them by the light of nature [reason], or the voice of Revelation [the Gospels]' (1975, II, XXVIII, viii).

But even though morality can be shown to us by REVELATION (p. 501) and without recourse to reason, the voice of revelation is still answerable to the light of nature. For one thing, we need to be assured that the voice is genuine, and reason must be the judge of this. Moreover, we cannot be as certain of this as we are of knowledge which is based directly on the use of our own reason. 'The knowledge, we have, that this revelation came at first from God, can never be so sure, as the knowledge we have from the clear and distinct perception of the agreement, or disagreement of our own ideas' (1975, IV, XVIII, iv).

As we have seen, it is a God-given duty carefully to examine any proposition before autonomously giving or witholding our individual assent: it 'would be to subvert the principles, and foundations of all knowledge . . . [if] what we certainly know, give way to what we may possibly be mistaken in' (1975, IV, XVIII, v).

Reason is superior over revelation in another way too. Though some things are discoverable only by revelation, any knowledge that is necessary for salvation can be reached by our natural faculties. God has 'given all mankind so sufficient a light of reason, that they to whom this written word [the Bible] never came, could not (whenever they set themselves to search) either doubt of the being of a God, or of the obedience due to Him' (1975, III, IX, xxiii).

Personal Identity

In the course of reaching conclusions about the origin and limits of knowledge Locke had occasion to concern himself with topics which are of philosophical interest in themselves. One of these is the question of identity, which includes, more specifically, the question of personal identity: what are the criteria by which a person at one time is numerically the *same person* as a person at another time? Here he makes the point, taken up by later writers, that there is a relativity about identity. When we point and ask whether 'this' is what was here before, it matters what kind of thing 'this' is meant to be. If 'this' is meant as a mass of matter then it is what was before so long as it consists of the same material particles; but if it meant as a living body then its consisting of the same particles does not matter and the case is different. 'A colt grown up to a horse, sometimes fat, sometimes lean, is all the while the same horse: though . . . there may be a manifest change of the parts' (1975, II, XXVII, iii). So, when we think about personal identity, we need to be clear about a distinction between two things which 'the ordinary way of speaking runs together' – the idea of 'man', and the idea of 'person'. As with any other animal, the identity of a man consists 'in nothing but a participation of the same continued life, by constantly fleeting particles of matter, in succession vitally united to the same organised body' (1975, II, XXVII, vi). But the idea of a person is not that of a living body of a certain kind. A person is a 'thinking, intelligent being, that has reason and reflection' (1975, II, XXVII, ix) and such a being 'will be the same self as far as the same consciousness can extend to actions past or to come' (1975, II, XXVII, x). Locke is at pains to argue that this continuity of self-consciousness does not necessarily involve the continuity of some immaterial substance, in the way that Descartes had held. For all we know, says Locke, consciousness and thought may be powers which can be possessed by 'systems of matter fitly disposed' (1975, IV, III, vi); and even if this is not so the question of the identity of *person* is not the same as the question of the identity of *an immaterial substance*. For just as the identity of a horse can be preserved through changes of matter, and depends not on the identity of a continued material substance but on 'the unity of one continued life' (1975, IV, XXVII, x), so the identity of a person does not depend on the continuity of an immaterial substance. The unity of one continued consciousness does not depend on its being 'annexed only to one individual substance, [and not] . . . continued in a succession of several substances' (1975, II, XXVII, x). For Locke, then, personal identity consists in an identity of consciousness, and not in the identity of some substance whose essence it is to be conscious.

---

2 Locke's Political Philosophy

Locke's anonymous *Treatises of Government*, which contain his political philosophy, were published in the same year as his *Essay*, and two years after the Glorious Revolution in which William of Orange replaced James II on the English throne. But their composition dates from some ten years earlier, and to the time of the Exclusion crisis during which Lord Shaftesbury, Locke's patron, sought, with others, to exclude James from succession to the Throne. *The Treatises* supported their arguments for government by consent, and for the right to religious dissent.

The *First Treatise* contains criticism of theories of absolute monarchy, and of the divine right of Kings, theories for which Robert Filmer (c.1588–1653) had argued in his *Patriarchia* (published 1680). Locke found quite unworkable the theory that Adam had been given absolute and total political authority by God, authority which was then passed on to his heirs. The theory cannot show of any particular ruler that he is a genuine heir to Adam's original authority, and so it is incapable of justifying any actual political authority.

In the *Second Treatise* Locke sought some other, and more workable, foundation for political authority. Subjects do have a duty to God to obey their ruler, he did not deny. But rulers themselves correspondingly have duties to their subjects. Rulers are not absolute, and if their commands do not deserve obedience then resistance to them might be justified.

Locke began with the idea of families and informal groups of people living in a STATE OF NATURE (p. 533). In such a natural state there are no political authorities and people's duties stem directly from God; they are duties not to 'harm another in his life . . . liberty . . . or goods' (1960, II, § 6). But what makes the 'goods', to which a person has a right, *his* goods in the first place? How, in the state of nature, can it come about that a person has a *right* to the land he cultivates? According to Filmer, just as absolute political authority is passed down from Adam to his heirs, so is possession of the earth and its fruits. According to Locke's labour theory of property, by contrast, just as all men were made free and equal in God's eyes, with no one directly set in power over them, so God gave the earth and its fruits to all men equally. Clearly it follows from this that Adam and his heirs could not be alone in having private property, but this is not because *no one* has private property and because there is worldwide communal ownership. The land someone cultivates, and its fruits and crops, are his, Locke explains, because each individual has a God-given right to his own life and labour, and consequently, an individual right to what he 'mixes' that labour with and produces by it. 'Whatsoever then, he removes out of the state that nature hath provided, and left it in, he hath mixed his labour with, and joined to it something that is his own, and thereby makes it his property' (1960, II, § 27).

The rights and duties, concerning life, liberty and possessions, which people have in the state of nature, may not necessarily be respected and obeyed. People may lack the power to defend their rights, or go too far in their defence. They therefore agree to come out of the state of nature and to form POLITICAL SOCIETY (chapter 8). They agree to unite, and to 'enter into society to make one people, one body politic, under one supreme government' (1960, II, § 89). They agree to empower an authority over them; they 'set up a judge on earth with authority to determine all the controversies and redress the injuries that may happen to any member of the commonwealth' (1960, II, § 89). But this authority into whose hands people put power is not, in Locke's analysis of civil society, absolute. He is answerable to 'the will and determination of the majority' (1960, II, § 96). The views and wishes of the majority are a court of appeal against the decisions of the ruling authority. Lockean political society is not only begun by 'the consent of any number of freemen capable of a majority' (1960, II, § 99), it is continued and sustained by it too. People under an absolute authority (whether divinely established as in Filmer's view, or set up, as in the equally absolutist account of HOBBES (chapter 18) by the people) are, for Locke, not in a civil society; they are effectively still in a state of nature.

Of course, unlike those who for some time have been in a state of nature, most people are simply born into an already existing civil society. It is not by any choice of theirs that they come under its laws and authority; they entered into no agreement to unite and set up the authority. But just as continuing consent is what underwrites an authority as well as what created it, so Locke distinguishes between tacit and explicit consent. A person may not choose where to be born, and so whose authority to be subject to; but by remaining there he gives his tacit consent.

From the idea that it is the 'will and determination of the majority' (1960, II, § 96) that is the ultimate basis of political authority, there follows the possibility of legitimate resistance to that authority, a possibility which does not follow from Filmer's divine right theory.

> The community perpetually retains a supreme power of saving themselves from . . . their legislators, whenever they shall be so foolish, or so wicked, as to lay and carry on designs against [their] liberties and properties. (1960, II, § 149)

Just as it is in the will of the people that power resides, so it is that 'the People shall be Judge' (1960, II, § 240) of when that power should be used.

Further Reading

James Gibson's *Locke's Theory of Knowledge* (1917) and R. I. Aaron's *John Locke* (1937) are two valuable classic accounts of Locke's epistemological thought. There are more recent general accounts by Dunn (1984), Mabbot (1973), Woolhouse (1983), and Yolton (1985). More detailed and specialized (whether historically or philosophically) treatments can be found in Ayers (1992), Bennett (1971), Mackie (1976), Woolhouse (1971) and Yolton (1970). Ashcraft (1987) and Dunn (1969) deal specifically with Locke's political philosophy, Colman (1983) with his moral philosophy, and Ashcraft (1969) and Cragg (1950) with his philosophy of religion. The last full-length biography of Locke is that of Cranston (1957). An exhaustive list of books and articles on Locke is provided by Hall and Woolhouse (1983).

References

Locke

Locke, John 1990 [1671]: *Draft A of An Essay Concerning Human Understanding* (edited by Peter H. Nidditch and G. A. J. Rogers). Oxford: Clarendon Press.
—— 1975 [1690]: *Essay concerning Human Understanding* (edited by P. H. Nidditch). Oxford: Clarendon Press.
—— 1960 [1690]: *Two Treatises of Government* (edited by Peter Laslett). Cambridge: Cambridge University Press.
—— 1873 [1695]: *The Reasonableness of Christianity*. Vol. 7 of *The Works of John Locke*. London.

Other writers

Aaron, R. I. 1937: *John Locke*. Oxford: Clarendon Press.
Alexander, P. 1985: *Ideas, Qualities and Corpuscles: Locke and Boyle on the External World*. Cambridge: Cambridge University Press.
Ashcraft, R. 1969: Faith and Knowledge in Locke's Philosophy. In J. W. Yolton (ed.), *John Locke: Problems and Perspectives*, Cambridge: Cambridge University Press, 194–223.
—— 1987: *Locke's Two Treatises of Government*. London: Allen and Unwin.
Ayers, M. 1992: *Locke* (2 vols). London: Routledge and Kegan Paul.
Bennett, J. 1971: *Locke, Berkeley, Hume: Central Themes*. Oxford: Oxford University Press.
Chappell, V. 1994: *The Cambridge Companion to Locke*. Cambridge: Cambridge University Press.
Colman, J. 1983: *John Locke's Moral Philosophy*. Edinburgh: Edinburgh University Press.
Cragg, G. R. 1950: The Religious Significance of John Locke. In G. R. Cragg, *From Puritanism to the Age of Reason*, Cambridge: Cambridge University Press, ch. 6.
Cranston, M. 1957: *John Locke: A Biography*. London: Longmans.
Dunn, J. 1969: *The Political Thought of John Locke*. Cambridge: Cambridge University Press.
—— 1984: *Locke*. Oxford: Oxford University Press.
Gibson, J. 1917: *Locke's Theory of Knowledge and its Historical Relations*. Cambridge: Cambridge University Press.
Hall, R. and Woolhouse, R. 1983: *80 Years of Locke Scholarship: A Bibliographical Guide*. Edinburgh: Edinburgh University Press.
Mabbot, J. D. 1973: *John Locke*. London: Macmillan.
Mackie, J. L. 1976: *Problems from Locke*. Oxford: Clarendon Press.
Martin, C. B. and Armstrong, D. M. (eds) 1968: *Locke and Berkeley: A Collection of Critical Essays*. London: Macmillan.
Tipton, I. (ed.) 1977: *Locke on Human Understanding: Selected Essays*. Oxford: Oxford University Press.
Woolhouse, R. S. 1971: *Locke's Philosophy of Science and Knowledge*. Oxford: Blackwell.
—— 1983: *Locke*. Brighton: Harvester.
Yolton, J. W. 1970: *Locke and the Compass of Human Understanding*. Cambridge: Cambridge University Press.
—— 1985: *Locke: An Introduction*. Oxford: Blackwell.

Discussion Questions

1 Did the mechanical philosophy and the experimental philosophy of the seventeenth century improve upon Aristotelian philosophy?

2 Was Locke's method well suited to his project of surveying our understanding?

3 If our knowledge has limits, how can we determine what they are?

4 Is our knowledge best understood as answering theoretical demands or as answering the practical needs of everyday life?

5 How is knowledge related to experience?

6 To what extent was Locke an 'empiricist'?

7 What does Locke mean by 'idea'?

8 Must senses, reason and understanding all be involved in our explanation of human knowledge?

9 Prior to experience, is the mind a 'white paper, void of all characters, without any *ideas*'?

10 How adequate is an account of knowledge in terms of perceiving the connection or disagreement of ideas?

11 Was Locke justified in thinking that empirical science cannot yield knowledge?

12 How can we tell when an idea is simple?

13 Should we accept the distinction between primary and secondary qualities?

14 Was Locke correct in claiming that our ideas of physical things are not ideas of their real essences?

15 What, for Locke, is the role of real essences in geometrical knowledge?

16 Can morality be a science?

17 Is reason superior to revelation?

18 Are questions of *identity* relative to the kinds to which the things asked about belong? What are the implications of your answer for questions of *personal identity*?

19 What problems might arise for the claim that personal identity consists in the continuity of consciousness? What other views are worth considering?

20 Would being an heir to original legitimate authority justify one in holding current political authority?

21 What role does the 'state of nature' play in Locke's political thought? Would it matter if a rival view of the state of nature turned out to be more accurate? Or if there never was a state of nature?

22   How can something be the *property* of a person?

23   What is civil society? What is the ultimate basis of authority in such a society? What limits the authority of its rulers?

24   Is 'tacit consent' consent at all?

20

Berkeley

Howard Robinson

As a critic of Locke and a precursor of Hume, Berkeley offered a profoundly original perspective on central questions in epistemology and metaphysics. This chapter, informed by recent critical discussion of Berkeley's idealism, focuses on his immaterialism: his claim that the physical world and its contents cannot be understood as existing independent of the mind. Berkeley's discussion of abstract ideas, which is intimately related to his immaterialism, is examined along with other important supporting arguments. The chapter ends with an exploration of two features completing the Berkelian system, namely his doctrine of spirits and the role he assigned God in explaining our experience.

In sections 1–4 of this chapter I consider two groups of arguments that Berkeley (1685–1753) used in his attempt to prove idealism.

With regard to the first group, after investigating Berkeley's attack on abstract ideas, I conclude that a revised version of the argument shows that we can have no positive conception of matter. This is strengthened by a proof that no sensible quality – nor, probably, anything analogous to a sensible quality – could be mind-independent. As mind-independent matter would have to be more than an empty structure, and as only something like a sensible quality could fill such a structure, the concept of mind-independent matter is defective.

With regard to the second group, Berkeley's overstrong implication that, because my thought is in my mind, so is its object, can be reformed to the weaker claim that, because all our conceiving of objects is of them as they are from viewpoints, it follows that we conceive of them, not as they are 'in themselves' but as they are to a potential perceiver. I raise doubts about whether this is correct, but augment it with Berkeley's argument that size is perception-dependent, for bodies cannot be mind-independent if their dimensions are not. In section 5 I briefly discuss Berkeley's use of his doctrine of spirit and his invocation of God to explain experience in the absence of a mind-independent world.

1 Introduction: Berkeley, Common Sense and the 'New Philosophy'

Common sense is usually thought to affirm the following two principles.

(CS1) In normal visual and tactile experience we are directly aware of physical objects.
(CS2) The existence of physical objects does not depend on, nor consist in, their being perceived: they are mind-independent.

The 'new philosophy' of the seventeenth century was taken by many philosophers and scientists as refuting the first of these principles: the objects of our awareness are not objects in the external world. This had to be so because objects in the external world do not themselves possess secondary qualities in the form in which those qualities are perceived. The external physical world is colourless, odourless and silent; secondary qualities in the form we know them are *ideas in the mind*. All we are aware of are our ideas; the physical world, which is a great machine composed of insensible atoms, lies concealed behind the veil of perception that is constituted by those ideas.

Berkeley accepted the arguments that were supposed to show that we could not be directly aware of a mind-independent physical world. Instead of concluding, like his more conventional contemporaries, that we are not directly aware of the physical world, he concluded that the physical world is not mind-independent: he chose, that is, to save CS1 rather than CS2. He had two motives for this preference. Firstly, he thought that putting the physical world behind the 'veil of perception' opened the way to SKEPTICAL DOUBT (p. 52) about its existence; secondly, he feared that the mechanistic conception of the world behind the veil favoured by the new science, smacked of a materialist and, therefore, an atheist metaphysic (Berkeley, 1713).

Berkeley's idealistic theory of the physical world is expressed in the maxim that *esse est percipi* – to be is to be perceived. This famous maxim is equivalent to the affirmation of CS1 without CS2, for it is the affirmation that the physical world is that of which we are directly aware, together with the denial that it is mind-independent. By making the physical world directly accessible to experience, this strategy seems to avoid the threat of Scepticism, and by making the world mental it avoids materialism. Of course, if CS1 and CS2 are both parts of common sense, Berkeley, in rejecting CS2, sets himself against common sense. According to Berkeley, however, the claim that the physical is mind-independent is not truly a part of common sense, for he believes that it rests on a confusion between the truth that the physical world is more than the experience of any given individual and hence independent of any given mind, and the falsehood that it transcends all the experiences that might be had of it by all minds taken together (Berkeley, 1713, III, 230–1). According to Berkeley, this latter kind of mind-independence is not merely not common sense, it is strictly unintelligible. So it is not just that when faced with an exclusive choice between accepting the direct perceivability of the physical world and accepting its mind-independence, he prefers the former; rather, he denies the intelligibility of a fully mind-independent physical existence.

Berkeley has a variety of arguments against the possibility of mind-independent or unperceived objects. My strategy in this chapter is to examine these arguments sympathetically, which involves development as well as exposition. I shall organize Berkeley's more or less independent arguments so that they form two groups, each group constituting an extended line of argument. One line of argument starts from Berkeley's attack on abstract ideas. By reforming that attack, and augmenting it with a cluster of arguments centring on the maxim that 'nothing can be like an idea but an idea', we can find in Berkeley a plausible case for believing that we can form no contentful conception of MATTER (pp. 512–13). The other group of arguments starts from the claim that we cannot conceive of unperceived objects; by buttressing this with his arguments about the sense-dependence of size, we can develop reasons for thinking that all the supposedly objective properties of the external world are really perception-relative.

attack abstract idea → immaterialism

belief in unperceived object depend on the doctrine of abstract idea

2 Abstract Ideas, Relative Ideas and Immaterialism

HUME (chapter 21) remarked that Berkeley's dismissal of abstract ideas was 'one of the greatest and most valuable discoveries that has been made of late years in the republic of letters' (Hume, 1739, Bk I, VII). Berkeley himself regarded his attack on abstract ideas as a vital component in the argument for immaterialism, for '[i]f we thoroughly examine [the belief in unperceived objects] it will, perhaps, be found at bottom to depend on the doctrine of *abstract ideas*' (Berkeley, 1710, § 5). But many philosophers have been puzzled as to the exact connection between abstraction and matter, and tend to leave it on the sidelines when expounding Berkeley's arguments for idealism. It will be helpful, therefore, to look carefully at what the attack on abstraction is about.

Berkeley's argument has an immediate target and a remote target. The immediate target is LOCKE's (chapter 19) account of the ideas of determinable or generic things, such as red, as opposed to any particular shade of red, for example, or triangle, as opposed to an isosceles triangle or a right-angled triangle. The remote target is any doctrine of concepts that allows that they are, in some sense, intrinsically universal: he is, that is, trying to carry to completion the idea that *everything*, whether outside the mind or within it, is particular, and thereby to free his philosophy of the perennial problem of universals, which, in some form or other, had been the heart of most scholastic metaphysics. According to this ambitious theory, not only are there no forms, species or universals in the world itself, but even concepts are, in themselves, purely particular. Locke, too, believed in particularism, but, according to Berkeley, he adopted an incoherent form of it. The particularist programme faces a dilemma, expressed by Locke and quoted by Berkeley: 'Since all things that exist are only particulars, how come we by general terms?' (Locke, 1689,

III, III, vi; quoted in Berkeley, 1710, § 11). How can a concept, for example, the concept of red, which by definition is something that covers many things, simply be a particular, rather than being universal? Even if one can manage to avoid realism about universals in things, surely one must be a conceptualist, that is, a realist about universality in the mind, in the concepts through which we think? Locke gives the answer 'Words become general by being made the signs of general ideas.' Locke grouped all mental contents, including concepts, together as *ideas* and treated ideas as mental images (see Yolton, 1984 and Ayers, 1991, vol. 1, pp. 60–9 for, respectively, an attack on this imagist interpretation and a defence of it). Taken in a literal way as a kind of mental picture, a mental image is pretty clearly a particular, but how can it have as its content a generic or determinable concept such as *red* or *triangle*? According to Berkeley, Locke's answer is to say that this kind of image has an indefiniteness to it.

> does it not require some pains and skill to form the general idea of a triangle . . . for it must be neither oblique nor rectangle, neither equilateral, equicrural, nor scalenon, but *all and none* of these at once. In effect, it is something imperfect that cannot exist, an idea wherein some parts of several different and *inconsistent* ideas are put together (Locke, 1689, IV, VII, ix; quoted in Berkeley, 1710, § 13).

So there is an indefiniteness which is expressed in two different ways. On the one hand the image is triangular without being scalene or equilateral; on the other hand it is all of these incompatible properties at once, because it includes them all. In this way one has a particular object – the image – which both leaves out all specific forms, and is a superimposition of the specific forms: in these ways it is deemed to encompass just the right generality of things. Berkeley's objection is that one can have neither indeterminate particulars, lacking a specific form, nor contradictory ones, containing incompatible forms. Locke's attempt to combine imagism with intrinsic generality, therefore, fails.

Many commentators have argued that Berkeley misinterprets Locke's account of abstraction, but the exegetical question is not very important. The theory of generality ascribed to Locke by those who think Berkeley misinterprets him is the theory Berkeley himself adopts; and, although some philosophers allow that images can be genuinely vague to some extent, it is generally agreed that they cannot be vague to the extent and in the way that the theory attributed to Locke requires. So everyone agrees that the view Berkeley attacks is false: they also agree that the account he wishes to replace it with is the only other one available to the imagist. The real issue, therefore, is whether Berkeley's own theory is adequate.

Berkeley's theory of generality has two parts. The central claim is that 'an idea, which considered in itself is particular, becomes general, by being made to represent or stand for all other particular ideas of the same sort' (Berkeley, 1710, § 12). So an entirely particular image of a triangle, for example, is taken as standing for triangles as a whole. This account explains the meaning of an idea in terms external to it – that is, by making it consist in the idea's relations to other ideas. But the meaning of the ideas we think is something we experience in our thinking – we know that in a certain act of thinking we mean 'triangle'. This subjective element in general ideas Berkeley explains by the second part of his account, which is the doctrine of *selective attention* or *partial consideration*:

> a man may consider a figure merely as triangular, without attending to the particular qualities of the angles or relations of the sides . . . In like manner we may consider Peter so far forth as man, or so far forth as animal, without framing the forementioned abstract idea, either of man or of animal, in as much as that all that is perceived is not considered (Berkeley, 1710, § 16).

So the significance of a particular idea consists in the way it represents other particulars and in the way a feature of it can be grasped whilst neglecting the rest.

The connection between this account of thought and idealism is quite straightforward and can be stated in a simple argument.

(1) Ideas are images. Therefore,
(2) abstract ideas would be abstract images.
(3) There are no abstract images. Therefore,
(4) there are no abstract ideas.
(5) If there were an idea of matter – or of unperceived existence or mind-independent existence – it would be an abstract idea. Therefore,
(6) there is no idea of matter – or of unperceived existence nor mind-independence.

(1) asserts Berkeley's imagism; (2) follows by simple logic; (3) is the core of the argument against Locke's supposed position; (4) follows from (2) and (3) by simple logic (namely, *modus tollens*). The crucial claim is in (5). We have seen that, for Berkeley, a non-abstract idea is one that can be identified with an image or an aspect of an image. It is difficult to see how the ideas of matter, unperceivedness or mind-independence could be actual, realized features of images. Images can occur in dreams and hallucinations, so they cannot actually possess the properties of materiality, unperceivedness or mind-independence, for such images are purely mental objects of awareness. (6) follows from (4) and (5), also by *modus tollens*.

Objections to Berkeley's Imagism

The argument is valid but unsound because Berkeley's account of generality – explained above and enshrined in (1) – is subject to two massive objections. Firstly, he presents no account of what he means by 'representing' or 'standing for'. This is not merely a gap in the argument; it suggests a complete failure to understand the problem. The problem of universals, classically referred to as the problem of the 'one over the many', is essentially about what is involved in something comprehending or standing for many instances. To invoke as an unexplained notion the idea of *standing for* is, therefore, to name the problem, not to propose a solution to it. The second feature of Berkeley's theory is open to an additional objection. What, within Berkeley's particularist ONTOLOGY (chapter

2), is it to attend to an aspect of an idea? Attending might seem to be a purely sensory thing, analogous to focusing a camera, but, because the focusing is on an *aspect* not a *region* of the image the focusing is a conceptual one. One cannot focus on the triangularity of a triangle – as opposed to its colour or size, for example – except by deploying the concept 'triangle'. Selective attention is of no help in explaining how the concept could be no more than the image, for the selection in question is no more than bringing a certain concept to bear on the image. If one is seeking an account of concepts, the notion of *selective attention* will not help, any more than will the notion of *standing for.*

Given the inadequacy of Berkeley's imagism, can anything be saved of the argument for immaterialism that rests upon it? To see that something can, we must consider the distinction between *positive* and *relative* ideas, which Berkeley adopted from Locke (Locke, 1689, II, XXIII, iii; Berkeley, 1710, § 80; and for a full contemporary discussion see Flage, 1987, pp. 134–42). To have a positive idea of something is to know what it is like in itself – to know its intrinsic nature. To have a relative idea of something is not to know its intrinsic nature, but only that it stands in some specific relation to something of which we have a positive idea. Divested of imagism and of the misconceived attempts to solve the problem of universals by giving a particularist analysis of concepts, Berkeley's arguments can be used to show that we do not have a positive idea of matter or of unperceived or mind-independent existence. This would be done by replacing the hopeless theory that ideas are images with the more plausible claim that the contents of positive ideas can be represented in images. This is not a theory about what ideas or concepts are in themselves, but a far more modest theory about the conditions under which we can know what *that of which it is a concept or idea* is like in itself. The claim is that, as far as aspects of the empirical world are concerned, we can only know what they are like in themselves if they can feature as aspects of sensory ideas. This is the complement of the claim often expressed by saying that our theoretical or purely scientific knowledge of the world is *topic neutral*, meaning that it tells us about the structural, relational and causal properties of things, but not about their intrinsic or qualitative natures: only direct sensory contact will give you the latter (Lockwood, 1989). This then generates a new argument.

(7)   Any feature of the physical world of which we can have a positive idea can be specifically represented in a sensory idea; that is, in an image. Therefore,

(8)   if we have a positive idea of matter – or unperceived existence or mind-independence – then it can be specifically represented in an image.

(9)   Matter – or unperceived existence or mind-independence – cannot be specifically represented in an image. Therefore,

(10) we do not have a positive idea of matter – or unperceived existence or mind-independence.

I have already suggested the plausibility of (7), and (8) is merely an instantiation of (7). The arguments for (9) are the same as those for (5), for there is no feature of an image which just is, or is dedicated to the representation of, materiality or unperceivedness or extra-mentality: any feature of an image must be a sensible feature of it and so must represent something more specific and sensible than materiality, unperceivedness or extra-mentality.

There are in fact two different questions in the air here. Firstly, what sort of properties is mind-independent matter supposed to possess? Secondly, what kinds of ideas (if they are real ideas at all) are the ideas of *materiality*, *unperceived existence* and *mind-independence*? I have argued that we cannot have a positive idea of these latter, because we cannot experience or image the properties in question. Berkeley considers the suggestion that we have a relative idea of materiality – that is, of that component in matter which is more than its qualities.

We may note that the question of the intelligibility of mind-independence and of unperceived existence is more complicated than the question of matter. Hume in his *tour de force* 'On scepticism with regard to the senses' (Hume, 1739, I, IV, ii) showed how we come, through a series of mistakes, to attach sense to the former two, which is consistent with deriving all our ideas from sense. This is why the Berkelian needs a separate argument against the possibility of there being external qualities.

Returning to the main argument, we can see that to have a relative idea of one related thing (*relatum*), one must have a positive idea of both the other *relatum* and the relation itself. In the case of matter we cannot form a proper conception of the relation it is supposed to stand in to that of which we have the positive idea. The example Berkeley considers is that matter is the SUBSTRATUM (p. 546) for the quality of extension, which he explains as meaning that matter supports extension. Thus we have a relation Rxy, with y being identical to the quality of which we know the nature directly (that is, some instance of extension), R being the relation of supporting, and x, matter, being known only as that which stands in the *supporting* relation to the extended quality. Berkeley challenges this by denying that we have a clear idea of the relation in question. Pillars support roofs and bridges, but it is not in that sense that matter supports qualities. It is doubtful whether a property-less substratum can be said to do anything: nor is it clear that it makes sense to say that an unextended substratum stands under and supports the quality of extension. This shows that it is hard to see how one could have a relative idea of materiality (Berkeley, 1713, I, 197ff).

There are complications here, however. Berkeley is discussing the possibility of a relative idea of matter according to which there is no more to matter than the bare property of being a support. He is discussing, that is, the idea of materiality as such. This is not the same as discussing the question of the nature of matter. Locke has usually been taken as claiming that matter consists of substratum and primary qualities. Berkeley shows that we cannot make much sense of the substratum element, but one might try to get by on the qualities alone. This brings us to another battery of famous Berkelian arguments which are intended to show that there cannot be extra-mental qualities. These can best be approached through the claim that an idea can be like nothing but an idea; which means that nothing external could be like a feature of a mental image; which means in turn that we could have no positive idea of any external quality.

3 Qualities, Ideas and Sensations

The claim that an idea could be like nothing but an idea has been given fairly short shrift on the grounds that it is simply question-begging against representationalism (Berkeley, 1710, § 8). What is more, any force that it seems to possess comes from the confusion arising from Locke's extension of the ordinary notion of 'idea'. When 'idea' means something like 'concept' or 'thought' then it does seem to be a category mistake to have replicas of them in the physical world, but once *idea* is extended to include sense-contents, the issue seems quite different. But the argument can be expanded and made quite plausibe, as follows:

(1) A sensation could be like nothing but a sensation; most especially, nothing extra-mental could be like a sensation.
(2) There is no distinction in kind between sensations and ideas. Therefore,
(3) An idea could be like nothing but an idea; most especially, nothing extra-mental could be like an idea.

The first premise is entirely intuitive: the idea of an extra-mental pain or itch seems to make no sense and, hence, the suggestion that there could be such could plausibly be regarded as a category mistake. The second premise is what Berkeley is defending when he argues that the feeling of heat and a certain kind of pain are continuous, so that the latter is nothing more than an intense version of the former (Berkeley, 1713, I, 176ff).

Two kinds of objection are made to this argument's second premise. One is to affirm that we can distinguish the perception of heat from the feeling of pain, even when they occur together, so that they are not merely differences of degree. The other accepts that Berkeley's argument is true for the senses that operate by contact, but denies that it applies to vision. Firstly, I shall provide a clarification of the argument. Berkeley does not need to deny that the painful aspect of a sensation is distinguishable from its hot aspect; he needs only to affirm that they are aspects of the same thing, such that one cannot exist in a different way from the other. The timbre and pitch of sounds, or the brightness and hue of colours would be examples of this. It is not necessary, therefore, to claim that they differ *only* in degree, and Berkeley can allow that the pain is an extra feature of the heat phenomenon it acquires through intensity. The issue then concerns whether the painfulness – or any similar sensational feature that can accompany tactile experience – is experienced as *caused by but separable from* some other feature of the experience, or as just another aspect of it. It seems to me to be highly plausible to claim that (1) the purely sensational element in tactile experience and (2) those parts of tactile experience thought to be candidates for being the direct perception of something external are not separable.

In fact, this point is best brought out by considering a visual case (Berkeley, 1709, is largely devoted to showing that vision, in itself, does not present externality). If I look at an unpleasantly dazzling light, three things are true: (1) the light, including its dazzlingness, seems to be outside me; (2) I experience the unpleasantness as a kind of sensation, that is, as something internal to me, a feature of how I am affected; (3) the unpleasantness of the experience is not separable from the dazzling quality of the light. The paradox is that the unpleasant sensational quality is both an external feature of the world and a sensational feature of my experience. It is more clear phenomenologically than in the case of heat and pain that light, brightness and unpleasant dazzle are only a matter of degree, for there is not a recognizable separate sensation of pain, distinct from the dazzle.

Someone might try arguing that there is a difference between the datum of extreme brightness and the feeling of its unpleasantness and that the latter is merely caused by the former, not an aspect of it. That this is not plausible is brought out by the following thought-experiment. Imagine that someone blind from birth were given a dazzling-light experience by direct stimulation of the cortex: do you think (1) that they would experience the light as putatively external or merely as a sensation no less internal to themselves than a bodily sensation? Assuming the answer to (1) is that they would not experience the light as external, (2) do you think that they would experience the unpleasantness as other than a feature of the brightness? The answer seems to me to be plain, and it is that they would think of them both as integral features of the sensation; this strongly suggests a Berkelian interpretation. This interpretation is that whether or not something is experienced as external is a matter *not* of its intrinsic phenomenology but of how it is interpreted into one's picture of the world. Such interpretation does, in one sense, alter the *phenomenology*, but it does not alter the *ontological standing* of the content: learning to see colours *as if* external does not make them external.

This seems to me to be a strong argument for the assimilation of ideas to sensations and, therefore, for saying that nothing extra-mental could be like them. In reply it might be argued that it only shows that the ideas of secondary qualities are assimilable to sensations, not that those of primary qualities are. But even if this is so it does not subvert the argument. One Berkelian response would be to point out that there is no idea of, say, shape independent of the secondary qualities of a given sense (Berkeley, 1710, § 10). So visual shape is inseparable from colour and tactile shape from felt sensation, hence the associated primary quality cannot be extra-mental. Even if shapes could exist independently of these secondary qualities, it is generally agreed that such primary qualities alone could not constitute a world because they are too formal – merely shapes without any filling. Something analogous to a secondary quality is necessary to give body to this conception. Although the argument has only shown that our actual secondary qualities are assimilable to sensations, it strongly suggests that any intensive quality of a kind like that of our secondary qualities *would be* of that kind *by being* a mode of experience and that, therefore, the idea of something like a secondary quality, yet extra-mental, is of dubious intelligiblity (Foster, 1982, pp. 84–107). So all ideas are essentially modes of sensation, and the argument is sound; nothing extra-mental could be like an idea. This discredits the suggestion that an external world could possess or consist of anything like, or be analogous to, the qualities we experience.

We started by looking at Berkeley's attack on abstract ideas both to understand it in itself and to see how it related to his immaterialism. We discovered that Berkeley's anti-abstractionism as he conceives of it is a tissue of confusions, but it is closely associated with arguments that are very powerful. If the imagist theory of thought is transformed into an imagist criterion for positive empirical content and combined with arguments that suggest that all monadic qualities are sensational ('an idea can be like nothing but an idea') then Berkeley's arguments show that it is doubtful whether mind-independent matter could possess any intrinsic properties at all and, hence, whether such a thing could exist.

There are standard conceptions of matter according to which it does not possess any intrinsic monadic properties, but only relational and dispositional ones. The idea that it consists solely of powers, forces or fields is such a conception. So is a Lockean view that matter is just impenetrability distributed in space. There is no room to consider this here, but readers might wish to look at recent discussions (Foster, 1982, pp. 67–72; Robinson, 1982, pp. 108–23).

4 Conceivability, Perceivability and Intrinsic Properties

Berkeley's Master Argument

In what has been called his 'master argument' Berkeley claims that we cannot conceive of unperceived things.

> But say you, surely there is nothing easier than to imagine trees, for instance, in a park, or books existing in a closet, and nobody by to perceive them. I answer, you may [say] so, there is no difficulty in it. But what is all this, I beseech you, more than framing in your mind certain ideas which you call *books* and *trees*, and at the same time omitting to frame the idea of anyone that may perceive them? But do you not yourself perceive or think of them all the while? This therefore is nothing to the purpose. It only shows that you have the power of imagining or forming ideas in your mind; but it does not show that you can conceive it possible, the objects of your thought may exist without the mind. To make out this, it is necessary that you conceive them existing unconceived or unthought of, which is a manifest repugnancy. When we do our utmost to conceive the existence of external bodies, we are all the while only contemplating our own ideas (Berkeley, 1710, § 23).

There must be something wrong with this argument because, by parity of reasoning, one could prove the impossibility of conceiving of ideas in *other people's* minds or of ideas had at other times: one could prove, that is, solipsism of the present moment. The argument moves from the premise that whatever I think of, the thought is in my mind, to the conclusion that what I think of is in my mind. By parity of reasoning, when I form the idea of an idea in someone else's mind, this thought is in my mind: and if I form the thought of an idea in my own mind at some other time, this thought is in my mind now: so these thoughts can only be about objects that are now in my mind. This pattern of argument rests on denying that ideas are intrinsically intentional – that is, on

---

denying that they make essential reference beyond themselves. This follows from treating them simply as images, for an image is only a pattern of sensible qualities and such qualities are not about anything but themselves.

Suppose that we accept the intentionality of thought, does this remove all force from the argument? It does not, if one accepts some connection between what we can CONCEIVE (pp. 590–8) and what we can imagine. Whenever we imagine an object, we imagine what it would be like perceived from a certain viewpoint: we do not imagine what it is like in itself, in abstraction from some possible perception. Any attempt to conceive of the object as it is independently of some possible perceptual perspective would have to be more abstract than a concrete imagination. As a physical object is an empirical object, with empirical properties, it might seem that there was something peculiar about the idea that it possesses a mode of existence that could not be represented imagistically, that is, in a form in which those empirical properties are actualized.

The natural reply to this is that a good perspective on an object enables one to form a conception of the object as it is in itself. This is most simply represented by a clear view of a flat surface, which enables one to see it not merely *from* a perspective but *as it is* in its own plane. Our visual perception comes to be structured in three dimensions, so its having a perspective does not force us into having a merely abstract conception of the object in its own space, as it would do if vision were two dimensional and distance was only inferred.

Another of Berkeley's arguments can be deployed here. The conception of *how the object is in itself*, independent of any perceptual perspective, includes the idea of what size it is in itself. Berkeley argues that there is no such notion of size: to a mite everything is larger than to a human, which is to say that, ultimately, size is not separable from the proportion of a sensory field that an object occupies (Berkeley, 1713, I, p. 188). It is, of course, no answer to this to say that there are objective units of measurement – the foot, the inch, the metre – for what kind of content is ultimately given to these except by their connection with perception? The obvious answer is that size is purely relative. Once one understands the *comparative* size of something an inch long when constrasted with something a foot long, and one has these set in a context relating them to the size of human beings, cats, mountains, the distance to the sun, and so on, then there is nothing more to know about size. It is, after all, generally accepted that it makes no sense to think of everything doubling in size, and this could only be because there is nothing more to size than what can be analysed relationally. This answer, though plausible, is not, I think, adequate. SPACE (p.594) is not purely relational, in the sense that it is not simply a relation of numerical magnitudes; an intuitive notion of space or extendedness is also required to give these formal relations an empirical interpretation (Foster, 1982, pp. 73–88). Things would look larger to an intelligent mite than to a human being, even though they agreed in all their relational judgements. The mite and the human disagree precisely in respect of the intuitive element that is essential for the empirical interpretation of space.

They are, therefore, disagreeing about something that is essential to the nature of experienced space.

This disagreement could be defused only if the intuitive element could be wholly projected on to and absorbed by the relational physical structure, so that the only way of characterizing the size of the intuitive, phenomenal component in spatial experience was in terms of the physical measurements that are essentially relational. That this is not so follows from the fact that objects 'look huge' to the mite. The situation is as follows. Physical size can be treated as purely relational but only at the cost of not being realist about it. Any real space must include the intuitive element as well as the relation of magnitudes, and the intuitive element is not separable from how it seems to a certain kind of subject, this not being collapsible into the relational.

It would be wrong to think that Einstein's relativity theory can be invoked against Berkeley here. Einstein is concerned with the variability of size in different frames of reference, which means frames of reference that are in motion in relation to each other. In a sense, the Berkelian point is an extension of Einstein's, for it adds a further frame of reference to the determinants of size, namely the phenomenal field of the subject; though it is not a determinant of *physical* size, which is an abstraction from the phenomenal.

5 From Phenomenalism to Theism

Rather than trying in this chapter to give a guided tour around the whole of Berkeley's system, I have concentrated on showing to their best effect his arguments for denying the existence of mind-independent matter, for it is this feature of his system that is of most fundamental interest and to which there is most natural resistance. My approach so far, therefore, emphasizes the negative thrust of his system and thereby ignores the things that mainly distinguish it from the sceptical PHENOMENALISM (pp. 55–6) of Hume. To rectify this imbalance I shall end by sketching the rationale for moving from immaterialism to theism.

This move has two elements, both of which distinguish Berkeley from Hume. Firstly, there is the notion of spirit which is essential for Berkeley's conceptions of the SELF (pp. 515–17) and of GOD (chapter 14); secondly, there are his reasons for claiming that our experience is caused by God. Although he had originally toyed with conceiving of the self as merely a collection of ideas, thus anticipating Hume, by the time of writing the *Principles* he had decided that we are aware of ourselves as active as well as being aware of the objects on to which our activities are directed. Because ideas are passive and the self is active we cannot have an idea of spirit. We can, however, understand it because we are conscious of ourselves *in* our activities, though not as an *object* of them; he calls this having a *notion*, rather than an idea, of ourselves.

> 'I say . . . that I have a notion of spirit, though I have not, strictly speaking, an idea of it. I do not perceive it as an idea or by means of an idea, but know it by reflexion' (Berkeley, 1713, III, p. 233).

In response, Hylas, a main character in Berkeley's *Three Dialogues*, immediately suggests that if spirit can be let in without a corresponding idea, so can matter. But the asymmetry with material substance is preserved; we cannot have a notion of matter because that is not directly available to consciousness, even in the form of reflection. So the association between meaningfulness and conscious acquaintance is not lost.

Having established the ontology of spirits and ideas, all that is needed is to show that God is responsible for those ideas that are not the products of our imagination – that is, for those that constitute the physical world. We can conceive of God because God is spirit in the same sense as we are, with all the limitations and imperfections thought away.

It is natural to believe – and Berkeley believes – that our experience has some kind of systematic cause. The simplest hypothesis is that it is caused by mind-independent physical objects, but this explanation has been ruled out by the arguments for immaterialism. This leaves us with a choice between postulating some kind of immaterial cause or of abandoning the natural belief that there is a cause. The latter is Hume's sceptical phenomenalism. Berkeley chooses the former. Because we do not seem to be the causes of our own experiences, either as single individuals or as a species, we are forced to postulate some other immaterial agent and Berkeley naturally casts God in this role. One could, in principle, opt for a pagan Berkelianism, as did W. B. Yeats, and postulate a whole tribe of gods and demons, but Berkeley's Irishness was of a more rationalistic kind than Yeats' and he stuck to the orthodox picture. The real rival to Berkelian theism comes, once idealism has been established, from the double Humean challenge: firstly, that experience in general requires no explanation; and, secondly, that nothing could constitute such an explanation even if it were required. For Hume, something requires an explanation only if its occurrence without an explanation is improbable, and something is improbable only if experience suggests that it would not naturally happen. Consequently, how an aeroplane can fly requires an explanation. That experience (seemingly of a physical world) continues to flow in its normal course, however, is the standard run of events and needs of no explanation: that is just the way the world is. The opinion that *the way the world is* needs explanation cannot be based on experience, for experience cannot show how things in fact usually are to be improbable. For such things to be judged improbable, one must employ a standard of *a priori* PROBABILITY (pp. 314–16), and Hume did not believe that there was any such standard for empirical matters. Furthermore, asking for an explanation in this context is asking what *brought about* the world of experience. This involves a concept of causation as real power or force, which Hume rejects. For Hume, a causal explanation of the world merely involves marshalling phenomena into constantly conjoined pairings so that one can have the satisfaction of seeing the world as an ordered structure. All this is no more than the regimenting of actual and possible experiences and has nothing of a general kind to say about what brings experience about; it is wholly internal to the world of phenomena.

Berkeley's position is more common sensical than Hume's and is expressed in §§ 25–6 of the *Principles*.

> 25 All our ideas, sensations or the things which we perceive, by whatsoever names they may be distinguished, are visibly inactive, there is nothing of power or agency included in them . . .
>
> 26 We perceive a continual succession of ideas, some are anew excited, others are changed or totally disappear. There is therefore some cause of these ideas whereon they depend, and which produces and changes them. That this cause cannot be any quality or idea or combination of ideas, is clear from the preceding section. It must therefore be a substance; but it has been shewn that there is no corporeal or material substance: it remains therefore that the cause of ideas is an incorporeal active substance or spirit. (Berkeley, 1710, §§ 25–6; see also Berkeley, 1713, III).

There is nothing in Berkeley to suggest that he was aware of the possibility of scepticism about *a priori* probabilities. He treats it as obvious that experience must come from somewhere. He had entertained Humean-style scepticism about causal efficacy and held to such a view concerning causation in the realm of ideas and, hence, the physical world as he understood it. But he believed that reflection made us aware of the real causal efficacy of the will. By such efficacy, he held, God's will produces in our minds the ideas which constitute the external world.

Further Reading

Urmson's excellent book on Berkeley in the *Past Masters* series is an elegant and brief introduction. Tipton (1974), Pitcher (1977), Dancy (1987), Grayling (1986) and Winkler (1989) are more detailed and more concerned to argue their own theses, but all can be used as general guides. Bennett (1971) relates Berkeley to Locke and Hume in a philosophically stimulating way, though rather too much to Berkeley's disadvantage and, some think, with too little regard to the historical context.

Contemporary defences of roughly Berkelian forms of idealism can be found in John Foster's contribution to Robinson (1993), which is a much simpler version of the difficult Foster (1982): there are defences also in Robinson's contribution to Foster and Robinson (1985) and in the final chapter of Robinson (1982). An idealism that owes much to Berkeley, but which finally takes a Hegelian form is defended by Sprigge (1983).

References

Berkeley

The standard edition is Berkeley, 1948–55: *Works of George Berkeley, Bishop of Cloyne*, (edited by A. A. Luce and T. E. Jessop), 7 vols. London: Nelson. Easily available one-volume paperback editions, containing at least the *Principles* and the *Three Dialogues* include: *Philosophical Works: including the works on vision* (edited and with an introduction by M. R. Ayers), Everyman, Dent, London, 1993; *Principles of Human Knowledge/Three Dialogues* (edited and with an introduction by Roger Woolhouse), Harmondsworth: Penguin Classics, 1988; *The Principles of Human Knowledge with other writings* (edited and with an introduction by G. J. Warnock), Glasgow: Fontana Press, 1962; and *Principles of Human Knowledge and Three Dialogues* (edited and with an introduction by Howard Robinson), Oxford: Worlds Classics, Oxford University Press, 1995.

With one exception, my references to Berkeley's texts are either to *The Principles of Human Knowledge* (1710) or to *Three Dialogues between Hylas and Philonous* (1713). References to the former give the section number alone, for the sections are generally shorter than a page and this facilitates the use of any edition. There is no such short-cut with the *Dialogues*, and here I cite the number of the dialogue and the page reference in volume two of Luce and Jessop's standard edition of Berkeley's works. There is one reference to *An Essay Towards a New Theory of Vision* (1709). Locke, *An Essay Concerning Human Understanding* (1689) and Hume, *A Treatise of Human Nature* (1739) are also mentioned.

Other writers

Ayers, M. 1991: *Locke* 2 vols. London: Routledge and Kegan Paul.
Bennett, J. 1971: *Locke, Berkeley, Hume: Central Themes*. Oxford: Oxford University Press.
Dancy, J. 1987: *Berkeley: An Introduction*. Oxford: Blackwell.
Flage, D. E. 1987: *Berkeley's Doctrine of Notions*. Beckenham: Croom Helm.
Foster, J. 1982: *The Case for Idealism*. London: Routledge and Kegan Paul.
Foster, J. and Robinson, H. (eds) 1985: *Essays on Berkeley*. Oxford: Oxford University Press.
Grayling, A. C. 1986: *Berkeley: The Central Arguments*. London: Duckworth.
Lockwood, M. 1989: *Mind, Brain and the Quantum: The Compound 'I'*. Oxford: Blackwell.
Martin, C. B. and Armstrong, D. M. (eds) 1968: *Locke and Berkeley*. London: Macmillan.
Pitcher, G. 1977: *Berkeley*. London: Routledge and Kegan Paul.
Robinson, H. 1982: *Matter and Sense*. Cambridge: Cambridge University Press.
—— 1993: *Objections to Physicalism*. Oxford: Oxford University Press.
Sosa, E. (ed.) 1987: *Essays on the Philosophy of George Berkeley*. Dordrecht: Reidel.
Sprigge, T. 1983: *The Vindication of Absolute Idealism*. Edinburgh: Edinburgh University Press.
Tipton, I. C. 1974: *Berkeley: The Philosophy of Immaterialism*. London: Methuen.
Turbayne, C. (ed.) 1982: *Berkeley: Critical and Interpretive Essays*. Manchester: Manchester University Press.
Urmson, J. O. 1982: *Berkeley*. Oxford: Oxford University Press.
Warnock, G. J. 1953: *Berkeley*. Harmondsworth: Pelican.
Winkler, K. P. 1989: *Berkeley: An Interpretation*. Oxford: Oxford University Press.
Yolton, J. W. 1984: *Perceptual Acquaintance from Descartes to Reid*. Oxford: Blackwell.

Discussion Questions

1 How is Berkeley's attack on abstract ideas related to his arguments for immaterialism?

2 What are the advantages and disadvantages of Berkeley's own account of the generality of ideas?

3 Does representative realism of the kind found in Locke really open the way to scepticism about the existence either of the external world or of God?

4 Is the doctrine that 'an idea can be like nothing but an idea' better than question-begging as an objection to representative realism?

5 In what sense, if any, is the physical world mind-independent?

6 Should we agree that 'to be is to be perceived'?

7 Is it true that a painful heat and a pleasant heat differ not in kind, but only in degree? How can one set about trying to answer questions of this kind?

8 Does the fact that we cannot image an instance of a primary quality without a secondary quality show that it is – or *might* be – impossible for a primary quality to exist without a secondary one?

9 Would someone who had gained sight after being blind from birth be in a position to recognize particular shapes visually on the strength of having previously felt them? If not, would it mean that visual and tactile shapes are different qualities?

10 Does the fact that whenever we imagine a physical object we imagine it as it would appear from a particular perspective mean that we cannot form a proper conception of how anything is in itself?

11 Must there be an intuitive element in any adequate account of real space?

12 How can we determine whether experience as a whole requires explanation?

13 To what extent are Berkeley's doctrines matters of common sense?

14 Is it possible to have a notion of spirit if we cannot have an idea of it? Is the case different for matter?

15 If God is directly responsible for my experience, do I have any reason to think that there are any other agents – human minds, for example – connected with the things that I experience?

16 How does an idealist account of the physical world affect natural theology?

21

Hume

Peter Jones

David Hume (1711–76) is without doubt one of the greatest philosophers to write in English. His elegant style complemented the depth and originality of his philosophical thought. The range of his work is wide, but he is best known today for his views on causation, induction, perception, personal identity and on the nature of morality. He agreed with his predecessors that understanding how and why things change is the only way to explain the past and to plan for the future, and that only a knowledge of causes can help to dispel our most natural fears. He believed, however, that many had misunderstood the precise nature of such knowledge, and had thus failed to benefit from it. He also held that it was not enough to examine the natural world; as the investigator, human beings set out to know, but often in ignorance of their own contributions to a task. Philosophy should begin, therefore, with an investigation into the nature of humanity, for this would also enable us to understand the nature and limits of our knowledge. Hume argued that we are all governed much less by reason than has often been claimed, and are motivated essentially by our passions. Moreover, in everyday life we must learn to live with probabilities rather than certainties. The public, and intensely practical, benefits which could result from such an understanding are profound.

1 Biography

David Hume was born in Edinburgh in 1711. He enrolled at the University of Edinburgh at the age of eleven, and studied there for three, or possibly four, years. As was usual at the time, he left without graduating. After a brief study of the law, he embarked on a long and private study of philosophy. From 1734 until 1737 he lived in France and wrote *A Treatise of Human Nature* (Hume, 1978a), which was published anonymously in 1739–40. In 1740, to boost disappointing sales of the book, Hume published an anonymous summary of its main theses. The document, now simply called the *Abstract* (Hume, 1978b), emphasized precisely those tenets he chose to discuss when he later re-wrote parts of the *Treatise*.

Hume was over 40 years of age before he obtained his first full-time job. He had twice failed to become a professor of philosophy, in Edinburgh in 1745, and Glasgow in 1752. In 1741 and 1742 he had published two volumes of essays, under the title *Essays, Moral, Political, and Literary* (Hume, 1985a), and thereafter re-wrote parts of the first and third books of the *Treatise*; these appeared in 1748 and 1751 and are now known as the *Enquiry Concerning Human Understanding* (Hume, 1975b), and the *Enquiry Concerning the Principles of Morals* (Hume, 1975c). In 1752 he published, under his own name, a very successful set of essays on political and economic topics, under the title *Political Discourses* (1985b). In the same year, he was appointed Keeper of the Advocates' Library in Edinburgh. Using their magnificent collection, which later became the National Library of Scotland, he published between 1754 and 1762 the six volumes of his *History of England* (1985c) which were also immensely successful.

From 1763 until 1766 Hume served in Paris, first as Secretary and then as Chargé d'affaires at the British Embassy. He became friendly with almost all the great philosophers and writers of the day, such as Diderot (1713–84), D'Alembert (1717–83) and Rousseau (1712–78), but to their mutual regret he never met Voltaire (1694–1778).

On returning to London Hume became Under Secretary of State, handling diplomacy with foreign powers to the north of France, including the Russia of Catherine the Great. He was also in charge of home affairs for Scotland, and official patron of the Scottish Church.

In 1769 Hume retired to Edinburgh, renewed old friendships, particularly with Adam Smith (1723–90), and played host to all the important visitors to the city, such as Benjamin Franklin (1706–90). In retirement Hume continually revised new editions of his *History*, and worked on his *Dialogues Concerning Natural Religion*, modelled on Cicero (106–43 BC) and published posthumously in 1779.

2 Philosophy

Great philosophers very often are not the first people to express the ideas for which they themselves become famous; their distinction lies in the routes they take in what they see as the context of their thought, in the syntheses they offer, and above all in the precise arguments they offer for their conclusions. Moreover, all philosophers write in the first place for their contemporaries, and are influenced by other thinkers whose work may be unknown to later generations. Hume himself was profoundly influenced by the Roman politician Marcus Tullius Cicero, and by the seventeenth-century French philosopher Nicholas Malebranche (1638–1715). Moreover, the historical context in which he lived was very different from our own. For example, when he was writing, nothing was known about latent heat or the composition of air and water, about any powers other than light and heat, about animal generation or evolution, about the age of the earth or the size of the universe; and such commonplace terms as 'police', 'magistrate', 'government', 'agriculture', 'art' and 'city' carried different meanings from today. If concepts like these irradiate our thought today, then we need to identify what we must unthink in order to understand Hume's thought. It must be remembered, therefore, that although many contemporary problems have a Humean ancestry, in a very obvious sense Hume was not discussing twentieth-century issues.

2.1 Causation

Hume was interested in the processes by which we acquire KNOWLEDGE (chapter 1); the processes of perceiving and thinking, of feeling and reasoning. He recognized that much of what we claim to know derives from other people secondhand, thirdhand, or worse; moreover, our perceptions and JUDGEMENTS (pp. 590–4) can be distorted by many factors – by what we are studying, as well as by the very act of study itself. The main reason, however, behind his emphasis on 'probabilities and those other measures of evidence on which life and action entirely depend' (Hume, 1978b) is this:

> it is evident that all reasonings concerning *matter of fact* are founded on the relation of cause and effect, and that we can never infer the existence of one object from another unless they are connected together, either mediately or immediately. (Hume, 1978b)

When we apparently observe a whole sequence, say of one ball hitting another, what exactly do we observe? And in the much commoner cases, when we wonder about the *unobserved* causes or effects of the events we observe, what precisely are we doing?

Questions about Causality

In considering causality Hume separated importantly different issues:

(1) Questions about the causal *relation*: what exactly is it for one event to be the *cause* of another? What is the evidence of *causal* relations between events?
(2) A question about the causal *inference*: what entitles us to *infer* from the occurrence of one event that another event is its cause or its effect?
(3) Questions about the causal *principle*: why do we insist that *every* event has a cause, and what entitles us to do so?
(4) Three extra questions about *necessity*: (4a) why do we insist that what distinguishes a genuine *causal* relation from a merely casual relation is the *necessity* of that particular pair of events occurring together? (4b) what entitles us to *infer* that if one event is the cause or effect of another, then it *must* have occurred with it, or immediately before or after it? (4c) why do we insist that *every* event *must* have a cause?

Hume recognized that a notion of 'must' or necessity is a peculiar feature of causal relations, inferences and principles, and challenges us to explain and justify the notion. He argued that there is no observable feature of events, nothing like a physical bond, which can be properly labelled the 'necessary connection' between a given cause and its effect; events simply *are*, they merely *occur*, and there is no 'must' or 'ought' about them. However, repeated experience of pairs of events sets up the habit of expectation in us, such that when one of the pair occurs we inescapably expect the other. This expectation makes us *infer* the *unobserved* cause or unobserved effect of the observed event, and we mistakenly project this mental inference on to the events themselves. There is no necessity observable in causal relations; all that can be observed is regular sequence: there is necessity in causal inferences, but because inferences are what observers do, we can say that this necessity is only in the mind. Once we realize that causation is a RELATION (p. 673) between pairs of events, we also realize that often we are not present for the whole sequence which we want to divide into 'cause' and 'effect'. Our understanding of the causal relation is thus intimately linked with the role of the causal inference, because only causal inference entitles us to 'go beyond what is immediately present to the senses' (Hume, 1978a, I, III, ii). But now two very important assumptions emerge behind the causal inference: the assumption that 'like causes, in like circumstances, will always produce like effects', and the assumption that 'the course of nature will continue uniformly the same' – or, briefly, that the future will resemble the past (Hume, 1978b). Unfortunately, this last assumption lacks either empirical or a priori proof; that is, it can be conclusively established neither by experience nor by thought alone.

Hume frequently endorsed a standard seventeenth-century view that all our ideas are ultimately traceable, by analysis, to sensory impressions of an internal or external kind. Accordingly, he claimed that all his theses are based on EXPERIENCE (p. 54), understood as sensory awareness together with memory, since only experience establishes matters of fact. But is our belief that the future will resemble the past properly construed as a belief concerning only a matter of fact? As Bertrand Russell remarked, earlier this century, the real problem that Hume raises is whether future futures will resemble future pasts, in the way that past futures really did resemble past pasts. Hume declares that 'if . . . the past may be no rule for the future, all experience becomes useless and can give rise to no inference or conclusion' (Hume, 1975b, IV). And yet, he held, the supposition cannot stem from innate ideas, since there are no innate ideas in his view, nor can it stem from any abstract formal reasoning. For one thing, the future can surprise us, and no formal reasoning seems able to embrace such contingencies; for another, even animals and unthinking people conduct their lives as if they assume the future resembles the past: dogs return for buried bones, children avoid a painful fire, and so on. Hume is not deploring the fact that we have to conduct our lives on the basis of PROBABILITIES (pp. 314–16); and he is not saying that inductive reasoning could or should be avoided or rejected. Rather, he accepted inductive reasoning but tried to show that whereas formal reasoning of the kind associated with mathematics cannot establish or prove matters of fact, factual or inductive reasoning lacks the 'necessity' and 'certainty' associated with mathematics. His position, there-fore, is clear: because 'every effect is a distinct event from its cause', only investigation can settle whether any two particular events are causally related; causal inferences cannot be drawn with the force of logical necessity familiar to us from *a priori* reasoning, but, although they lack such force, they should not be discarded. In the context of causation, inductive inferences are inescapable and invaluable. What, then, makes 'past experience' 'the standard of our future judgment'? The answer is *custom*: it is a brute psychological fact, without which even animal life of a simple kind would be more or less impossible. 'We are determined by *custom* alone to suppose the future conformable to the past' (Hume, 1978b); nevertheless, whenever we need to calculate likely events we must supplement and correct such custom by self-conscious reasoning.

2.2 Some implications: free will, history and the uniformity of nature

Hume was well aware of the potential impact of his analysis, and he began his explanation of its implications by trying to reconcile the arguments of those who hold that all our actions are determined, and those who hold that we are genuinely free to do what we choose. The determinists are right, he said, to insist that every event has a cause, but mistaken in the view they take of necessity, failing to see that it belongs only to an inference in the mind; advocates of free will, on the other hand, are right to say that responsibility makes sense only if we are truly the agents of our actions, but mistaken in holding that 'free' in this sense means 'uncaused'. Hume's view is that our ACTIONS (compare pp. 599–601), like all other events, have causes, namely, the choices and decisions that immediately precede our actions, and for which we accept responsibility. However, although these mental happenings function as the MOTIVES (p. 532) of our actions, they themselves have causes, of which we are normally unaware and for which we are not held responsible. His point in discussing the free-will issue is to show that human actions can be understood, and are properly understandable, in terms of what he has said about causation in general – we notice patterns of behaviour, we infer motives precisely in order to offer 'interpretations' of actions:

> were there no uniformity in human actions, and were every experiment which we could form of this kind irregular and anomalous, it were impossible to collect any general observations concerning mankind, and no experience, however accurately digested by reflection, would ever serve to any purpose. (Hume, 1975b, VIII)

Such thoughts were important when he came to reflect on the nature of HISTORY (chapter 13). Here, however, two features of the discussion should be noticed. Firstly, human behaviour is capable of causal explanation, and therefore also of prediction, he was saying, albeit not yet with the same degree of precision or certainty that we expect in the natural sciences. The second feature is related to this. So important is our belief that similar causes produce similar effects, that we hold to it even when we cannot find the required uniformities; and when we find something puzzling or inexplicable we neither suppose that the laws of nature have changed, nor that we have encountered a causeless event. *Absence of adequate evidence* for a cause is not taken as adequate evidence for the *absence of a cause*.

External Objects

In 'Of scepticism with regard to the senses' (1978a, I, IV, ii), Hume discussed problems that have particularly interested twentieth-century philosophers, namely, those concerning our knowledge of external objects and personal identity. Hume regarded both external objects and the self, in an important sense, as imaginative CONSTRUCTIONS (p. 56). The texts, together with their various modern commentaries, are unusually complex and reward close examination.

Everyone assumes that the world goes on around us, whether we are awake or asleep, unconscious or dead. But this view is troublesome to philosophers who held that we are only really conscious of our internal perceptions, and that ultimately sensory experience consists of unconnected atomic instants (for instance, 1978a, I, IV, vi, pp. 252, 259). Hume asked 'whether it be the *senses, reason* or the *imagination*, that produces the opinion of a continu'd or of a *distinct* existence' of objects (1978a, I, IV, ii, p. 188). He argued that immediate sense experiences cannot generate any notion of unsensed objects, and 'never give us the least intimation of any thing beyond' themselves (1978a, I, IV, ii, p. 189). The solution to such problems lies in the power of the imagination to disguise the disjointed and interrupted character of sensory experience, by uniting or bonding our ideas of it in the mind (1978a, I, IV, vi, p. 260). 'The opinion of the continu'd existence of body depends on the *coherence* and *constancy*' (1978a, I, IV, ii, p. 195) of some of our impressions, namely those which our memory assures us preserve some degree of resemblance and repetition over time; this feature of our perceptions is then projected on to the external world. When we do 'infer the continu'd existence of objects of sense from their coherence' it is 'in order to bestow on the objects a greater regularity than what is observ'd in our mere perceptions' (1978a, I, IV, ii, p. 197). Philosophers since Hume have made much of the theoretical and practical advantages of projecting on to the objects we sense a greater coherence than seems to be strictly warranted by the sensory evidence itself.

2.3 Personal identity

Hume anchored his discussion of external objects in reflections on identity, or sameness and change: he told us that his aim was 'to prove, that all objects, to which we ascribe identity, without observing their invariableness and unin-terruptedness, are such as consist of a succession of related objects' (1978a, I, IV, vi, p. 255). It is hardly surprising, then, that he stated: 'the identity, which we ascribe to the mind of man, is only a fictitious one, and of a like kind with that which we ascribe to vegetables and animal bodies' (1978a, I, IV, vi, p. 259). (Fiction, it must be noted, meant 'hypothesis' or 'invention', in Hume's day.) In fact, however, Hume asked different questions about personal identity, and consequently said different things about it. He asked: 'how far we are *ourselves* the objects of our senses'? what is 'the nature of the uniting principle, which constitutes a person' (1978a, I, IV, ii, p. 189)? what 'impression gives rise to the idea of self' (1978a, I, IV, vi, p. 251)? He held that 'what we call a *mind*, is nothing but a heap or collection of different perceptions, united together by certain relations, and suppos'd tho falsely, to be endow'd with perfect simplicity and identity' (1978a, I, IV, ii, p. 207; see also I, IV, vi, p. 261). He likened the mind to a 'republic or commonwealth' (1978a, I, IV, vi, p. 261) but

also to a 'theatre, where several perceptions successively make their appearance'; the identity 'is nothing really belonging to these different perceptions,
and uniting them together; but is merely a quality, which we attribute to them,
because of the union of their ideas in imagination' (1978a, I, IV, vi, pp. 253,
260) – and the capacity of the memory which is said to 'not so much *produce*
as *discover* [that is, reveal] personal identity' (1978a, I, IV, vi, p. 262).
Commentators have pointed out that Hume confined his mainly first-person
account to mental phenomena, and in these contexts did not consider the roles
of physical criteria or social behaviour in our idea of the self. His reflections in
other passages, however, on moral, social and political structures and
behaviour considerably enriched his formal consideration of persons. Nevertheless, his discussions of identity, especially his reflections on 'numerical and
specific identity' (1978a, I, IV, vi, p. 257), need radical revision and
supplementation.

2.4 Miracles and religion

The cases that most clearly conflict with what Hume has said about causation
are those of alleged miracles. His own discussion was eventually published in
the 1748 *Enquiry* (Hume, 1975b) but it is not primarily about whether miracles
occur – he rather brusquely defines them as impossible; rather, it is about the
nature and reliability of evidence for factual claims of any kind whatsoever.
The recurrent term in his discussion is *testimony*, that is, reports of
evidence.

Hume readily concedes that all of us have to rely on reports from other
people; knowledge is a social phenomenon in the sense that agreement about
what happened is important in defining what we count as knowledge.
Moreover, none of us has enough first-hand experience of our own to make
very extensive claims. Hume holds that, as a general rule, testimony is reliable,
and he does so for two reasons: our memories are moderately reliable, and
humans have a natural inclination, strongly re-enforced by social sanctions, to
tell the truth, and to feel shame if detected in falsehood. These general
assurances, however, cannot help us in particular cases of doubt, so Hume
suggests that in weighing the probability of evidence the content and the
context of what a witness says must both be examined. We need to consider
not only the type and quantity of evidence, but also the manner and motive in
giving it. In the end we must rely on 'experience and observation'. But surely
we must be told whose experience is to count, and why and how the tests of
evidence are to be performed. *Ex hypothesi*, we cannot appeal to our own
experience in order to test reports by others of experiences unlike our own;
and in weighing what people say we neither appeal indiscriminately to
anyone, nor require the assent of everyone. Hume relies on a notion of experts,
or qualified observers, to whom we can appeal for help. Typically we learn
who count as the experts whilst learning the procedures for making reports of
the kind in question; the learning may be quite informal, even unconscious,
and the experts range from the sublime to the ridiculous – at its lowest, anyone
might count as an expert who seems to know more than oneself. Parents and

teachers are the first experts children encounter, but their own friends also play this role for children on many occasions. Hume uses the notion of experts and agreement to secure both the social dimension of our judgements, and their objectivity – although that term was not used in the eighteenth century.

Hume takes stories of miracles to be reports of unique events, the cause of which is allegedly known by inference, not by experience, even though none of the conditions for establishing an inferred cause is satisfied. We are entitled to infer a cause, he holds, with a greater or lesser degree of probability, when the event to be explained resembles others which we have directly experienced in conjunction with their causes. Many questions arise here. How much resemblance is needed to warrant such an inference? What properties or characteristics is one entitled to assign to such an inferred cause? Hume's extended reflections on such issues were published posthumously in 1779 in his brilliant *Dialogues Concerning Natural Religion* (Hume, 1947).

Protestant theologians in Hume's day were eager to embrace what little they understood of Newtonian science and its methods, and they popularized an ancient argument known as the argument from design. This was supposed to establish the nature of God by means of inferences from the observable world around us – in Hume's words, it was 'an argument drawn from effects to causes' (Hume, 1975b, XI). Schematically it ran like this: it is impossible to describe all the diverse phenomena in the known universe without implying some overall plan behind it, which causally explains the nature of the phenomena and their interconnections; such a plan, however, would need to be of such complexity itself, that it could be attributed only to some being with capacities far exceeding human capacities – in brief, it could belong only to God. Sophisticated versions of this argument are still popular, but Hume maintained that they inherently lack a determinate base in experience, that they are untestable, unrevisable and claim a dogmatic finality and uniqueness inimical to genuine scientific enquiry. The necessary reliance on inductive arguments in such enquiry, after all, means that in any given case we could turn out to be mistaken. No event, considered by itself, points beyond itself to its causes or effects; these have to be discovered by experience, and what is more, *no* features of a cause need resemble any of the effect – they could be 'totally different' (Hume, 1975b, IV). Factual inferences rest on the assumption of similarity of cases, and can be assigned various degrees of probability. In the absence of direct experience we are allowed only to postulate what is *sufficient* to bring about the alleged effects. Hume is quick to see that this fails to satisfy his own definition of what a causal relation is, and of how we can know one, since the crucial notion of necessity is lacking. He concludes that allegedly 'unique' causes cannot legitimately be inferred from, or used to explain, allegedly 'unique' effects. When uniqueness is claimed for an event, we can never know whether we have adequately identified or circumscribed it. In addition, if we have no experience of a thing's attributes we cannot pick it out from among other things, and if we cannot do this even vaguely, we have no means to confirm that it exists. It is useless to postulate a cause whose attributes, by definition, are unknown. Finally, there is too much pain, suffering and chaos in the world as we know it, to justify any inference to a fully competent cause of it all.

2.5 Moral philosophy

Hume regarded his own moral views as those of a common-sense man, albeit with a strictly secular outlook. He held that a human being cannot be adequately defined or understood as an essentially rational animal, as ARISTOTLE (chapter 15) and so many other philosophers and theologians had proclaimed. Indeed, pure thought, or abstract reasoning of the kind associated with pure mathematics, is itself inert, and cannot motivate anyone to do anything; all that such thought can do is enable us to recognize relations between things. This recognition can somehow influence what does motivate us, namely, our sentiments, which are forms of the most basic desires to avoid pain and attain pleasure. In the *Treatise* Hume dramatically summarized his view that thought plays only a subordinate role in the moral life by declaring that 'reason is, and ought only to be, the slave of the passions' (Hume, 1978a, II, III, iii). It helps in the formulation of our goals, but not in our motivation towards them. When he came to re-write this passage in 1751, however, he toned it down: 'no doubt *reason* and *sentiment* concur in almost all moral determinations and conclusions . . . [but] it is probable . . . that this final sentence depends on some internal sense or feeling, which nature has made universal in the whole species' (Hume, 1975c, I). For such views, Hume drew inspiration from Shaftesbury and from Francis Hutcheson, Professor of Moral Philosophy in Glasgow until his death in 1746. One of the features which most distinguished the philosophers of the Scottish Enlightenment from their successors in the French and German Enlightenment, is an emphasis on the essential part played in our lives by the passions; their influence is a brute psychological fact, to be neither condemned nor condoned, but a fact nevertheless that theories of humanity and morality ignore at their peril. Very often, as it happened, the French and German writers regretted the fact, thought it to be avoidable, and proclaimed the sovereignty of reason.

In deciding what to do, we all weigh the possible consequences, but the merit of an action, Hume holds, derives from the motive behind it. It is worth recording that Hume's language is sometimes confusing: he uses the term *sentiment* to mean both feeling and thought, and this makes his claim that passions or sentiments are the sole causes of action more plausible than it might otherwise appear. He draws a distinction between 'artificial' and 'natural' virtues. 'Artificial' virtues are those which we might nowadays describe as sociologically conditioned, in the sense that they are procedures we adopt, as individuals or groups, and often unselfconsciously, to help things run smoothly and to temper our self-seeking and divisive tendencies. For example, our sense of JUSTICE (chapter 8) arises 'artificially, though necessarily, from education and human convention'; indeed, at one place, Hume states that 'public utility is the *sole* origin of justice' (Hume, 1975c, III). 'Natural' virtues, by contrast, are said to be grounded in our universal tendency to share, quite literally, the feelings of others. Such 'sympathy' (and the notion is not equivalent to the modern idea of compassion) ultimately explains even the artificial virtues. Both artificial and natural virtues, then, are understood as qualities which human beings find useful or agreeable both in their own case, as owners of those qualities, and in other people whom they observe as spectators. Hume's notion of 'sympathy' proved fruitful, and was taken up and developed by Adam Smith, as was the idea of learning to judge ourselves impartially.

2.6 Art, taste and aesthetic judgement

Hume's brief account of AESTHETIC JUDGEMENTS (chapter 7) builds on what he says about moral goodness and moral judgement. By talking about the thing that currently pleases or displeases someone, we can change that person's response to it; that is, we can change how they perceive it, think of it, or react to it, and in this way induce them to feel differently about it. Such emphasis on feeling, however, should not be taken to imply that our discussions are incurably personal or subjective. On the contrary, Hume tries to show that agreement is possible, and of a kind that is quite strong enough to satisfy our deepest yearning for so-called objectivity. Three conditions must be met: firstly, the conventions of language must be observed by all disputants and, if necessary, clarified in the particular context; secondly, it must be possible to establish publicly shareable viewpoints and referents; and finally, we must assume a shared psychological make-up among the disputants. Personal idiosyncrasies due to age or background should be recognized as idiosyncrasies and discounted. And the old saying that there can be no disputing in matters of taste should be seen as being harmlessly, because only trivially, true. If the exercise of taste involves no judgement, then, indeed, there can be no dispute or discussion; but if it does involve judgement, as most people think, then discussion is not only possible but desirable. Moreover, judgement, understood as public discourse, is always capable of reaching a pragmatic, if not a formal, resolution of difficulties.

Hume's remarks on art mostly occur when he was discussing features of our social life. That is why he considers art from the standpoint of human actions: the artist is trying to get something done, and spectators are trying to establish the why and the wherefore of what the artist does. Works of art, in this way, are pleasurable means of communication, and their acceptance depends on their making sense to spectators who can agree in their responses. Hume held that as an historical phenomenon, art occurs only when a person has time to turn aside from the brute necessities of living. Nevertheless, in the more leisurely context of Hume's own epoch, the arts could be held to refine the temper and make people more sociable, because an artist trying to please spectators had to consider their needs and interests. This point has an important consequence for criticism of the arts: because art is a human activity, one of the general criteria for understanding any human action applies to it – namely, knowledge of how the agent viewed the context and appropriateness of what he or she was doing. So we should consider works of art in terms of the audience for which they were intended, as well as in terms of their internal character, their genre, style and tradition. Hume held that one can achieve the 'proper sentiment' towards most, and certainly towards the best, works of art. There are two elements in his claim. To be causally affected by a work's properties, we must adopt the right frame of mind or viewpoint, as well as the right physical standpoint. The second element is even more important. What distinguishes a *proper response* from a merely *passive reaction*, as when we enjoy basking in the hot sun, is the active contribution of the spectator. This involves an INTERPRETATION (pp. 247–50) of the work's meaning and value, over and above identification of the aspects we find affecting; meaning, after all, cannot be detected by the five senses alone, any more than necessity. Interpretation involves the exercise of the mind.

Hume's views on art and criticism receive their most sustained treatment in a single essay, 'Of the Standard of Taste', published in 1757, and they belong to a period when the modern notion of aesthetics was receiving only its first tentative formulation. Public concerts were beginning to take place, easel painting was becoming popular, and the first novels were appearing; except for those who travelled to Europe, however, most people saw very few paintings, had access to no museums, had little knowledge of Greek – as opposed to Roman – sculpture and architecture, and knew nothing of the art of other cultures.

2.7 Views on history and politics

Hume's view of the nature of historical writing and understanding, which brings together his thoughts on evidence and human testimony, as well as on agency and motivation, rests on two fundamental tenets: firstly, agents act with certain intentions, but are necessarily ignorant, when they set out, of the outcome; secondly, observers know the outcome, but are doomed merely to conjecture the intentions necessary for understanding it. The unbridgeable gap between foresight and hindsight of the 'actor' and 'spectator', as Hume called them, can baffle the most diligent enquirer. One important point here is the tension between the agent's passions, which alone can motivate him or her, and the spectator's reason, which functions in his or her understanding: 'Mens' views of things are the result of their understanding alone: Their conduct is regulated by their understanding, their temper, and their passions' (Hume, 1985c, LIII). Spectators do have access, however, to data logically unavailable to the agent: in particular, to the longer term consequences of the agent's acts and to the varying significance ascribed to them from different perspectives, and in relation to different sets of issues. The judgements of hindsight are transient, nevertheless, because the possibility of re-interpretation is ever present in the light of succeeding events.

A central theme of Hume's historical reflections concerns the unavoidable struggle between LIBERTY (pp. 258–61) and authority. He is primarily concerned with liberty under the LAW (chapter 12) and with constraints upon it exercised by various kinds of authority; to a lesser degree he considers limits on personal liberty imposed by habit or education. For Hume, a discussion of liberty is not ultimately separable from a discussion of virtue, and thus of how to live as a social being; the real threat to society stems from faction. On one point Hume was adamant: 'violent innovations no individual is entitled to make' (Hume, 1975b, 'On the Original Contract'). And precisely because the consequences of excess cannot be foreseen, there is never a case for instigating a revolution or resisting the law. The stability and very structure of society depend on the upholding of law, and society faces its greatest peril when resistance to law is itself proclaimed as 'lawful or commendable'. Gradual change should be sought, in the recognition also, that the complexity of political questions means that 'there scarcely ever occurs, in any deliberation, a choice, which is either purely good, or purely ill. Consequences, mixed and varied, may be foreseen to flow from every measure: and many consequences, unforeseen, do always, in fact, result from every one' (Hume, 1975b, 'On the Protestant Succession', published 1752).

Throughout his writings, Hume observes that personal inclinations, political interests, religious zeal, are constant threats to society. It is 'not enough for liberty to remain on the defensive', not least because, however carefully framed, no laws could 'possibly provide against every contingency' (Hume, 1985c, XLVIII and XLVII). Hume held that TOLERATION (p. 550) developed historically not as a result of positive policy, but from a slow recognition that attempts at repression merely stiffened resistance. He did not think, however, that toleration always wins through. In this context, Hume faced a deep recurring conflict in his philosophy between upholding moderation and stabilizing the unavoidable tension between liberty and authority. Since there is no criterion of moderation in advance of a particular context with clear boundaries (for moderation is definable only by reference to limits), there can be no fully intelligible principle of moderation independent of cases: but how are such cases to be identified? Moreover, it is unclear how an attitude of moderation could, in practice, motivate anyone to displace deeply engrained habits, on the one hand, or fanaticism, on the other.

The aim of government, in Hume's view, is to establish and then to preserve just laws. But the laws must not suppose that human nature can be very much changed. The law-makers, in other words, whether in the sphere of government or morality, must first seek to understand HUMAN NATURE (pp. 531–3). They must also grasp that threats to liberty stem from various sources. On the economic front Hume saw the national debt, with its attendant taxation levies, together with the prospect of nationalization of property, as especially dangerous. He considers that low interest rates, controlled labour costs, and competitive pricing are all essential to ensure both successful foreign trade, and a buoyant home economy which motivates the labour force. He attacked all isolationism in politics or economics, and recognized that diversification would be necessary for an economy resting on a few staple products, because such an economy is always vulnerable to decreasing demand, and to lower pricing by successful competitors. It might be added that he disapproved of state ownership on the grounds that a state can always secure itself against enquiry and accountability. The Scotland of Hume's day was poor, sparsely populated, and entirely agrarian; how far his reflections are adaptable to modern, urban, industrial society, and for populations of immensely greater size, is hotly debated.

2.8 Scepticism

Hume was by no means ashamed of his sceptical stance and his sceptical arguments, although his opponents, using the same label, regarded it extremely unfavourably. As a general term of abuse *sceptic* covered all those who challenged orthodox views, asked difficult questions (even when no one else claimed to know the answer), omitted mention of God or canvassed views that left little or no room for a God, denied the existence of things for which words nevertheless existed, or merely confessed ignorance. On all these grounds Hume qualifies for the label. At different times he explicitly denies that we have innate ideas; that the causal relation is observably anything other than constant conjunction; that there are observable necessary connections anywhere; that there is either an empirical or demonstrative proof for the assumptions that the future will resemble the past, and that every event has a cause; that there is an irresolvable dispute between advocates of free will and determinism; that formal reasoning is crucially involved in everyday life; that there is a case for believing reports of miracles; that there is explanatory force to the design argument; that extreme scepticism is coherent; and that he can find the experiential source of our ideas of self, substance or God.

In spite of this list, which can easily be supplemented, Hume thought of his own position as one of only moderate scepticism. In this, he was carrying forward the scientific temperament of the seventeenth century and also following his mentor Cicero, who urged that, even if we lack a foolproof test for distinguishing truth from falsehood, in practical life probability is enough; things have to get done, and we do not need the last ounce of evidence in order to do them. Hume was frequently misunderstood, however, as denying the truth of certain claims, when he was asking how we know them to be true.

2.9 Influence and disputed questions

However much we may think that his contemporaries misunderstood Hume's views, there is no doubt that they reacted strongly to them. Adam Smith derived many of his notions in moral, economic and political philosophy from Hume, extending them where need be – as in the case of 'sympathy' and 'the impartial spectator'. Adam Ferguson (1723–1816), likewise, developed his conception of civil society against the background of Hume's reflections. In America, James Madison (1751–1836) and Alexander Hamilton (1755–1804) studied Hume's political writings and *History* with great care whilst formulating their views on the future structure and direction of their nation. In France, too, Hume's political, economic and historical writings were widely admired and discussed by the leading intellectuals before the Revolution. In Scotland, Thomas Reid (1710–96), devoted a great deal of time to rebutting Hume's views on the nature of both knowledge and morality. One of the most troublesome notions for many of Hume's contemporaries, however, was that of

causation: in Germany, Immanuel KANT (1724–1804) (chapter 22), having
credited Hume with waking him from a dogmatic slumber, devoted a
considerable portion of his philosophy to formulating a cogent alternative to
Hume's position. A great deal of western philosophy since the end of the
eighteenth century can be associated with the rival views of Hume and
Kant.

In terms of sales the most popular of Hume's works was the *History*. It went
through 150 editions within a century of publication, whereas the *Treatise* had
to wait nearly as long for a second printing. In the nineteenth century a few
philosophers claimed Hume as their mentor, such as August Comte
(1798–1857) in France, and J. S. MILL (chapter 25) and T. H. Huxley (1825–95)
in England; William JAMES (chapter 26), in America, drew much inspiration
from him. There has been an astonishing resurgence of interest in Hume's
work since the 1960s, although in the earlier part of this century his name had
been kept alive in Scotland. In the first place, dispute has centred on the
appropriate contexts for understanding Hume's work and the due weight to be
given to his various claims, which were made over a 40-year span in works of
different kinds. Hume was trying to displace many of his readers' views on the
nature of humanity and society, and his own knowledge of their beliefs
profoundly influenced the style, content and emphasis of his approach. In this
context there is dispute over Hume's conception of philosophy and its roles,
and over the nature and scope of his scepticism.

On more particular topics, there is considerable disagreement about the
need for, or the possibility of, modifying his account of causation to cope with
developments in modern science, especially at the level of very small or very
large phenomena. Do appeals to statistical frequencies avoid the sceptical
elements in Hume's position? Are his own views on inductive argument and
the weighing of probabilities fundamentally sound? If our sensory experience
is a seamless continuum, as some people maintain, does it make sense to
divide it up into events with beginnings and ends? If we cannot explain how
we identify, separate and classify events, can we talk of separate causes and
effects at all? Hume emphasized the importance of resemblance or similarity
in this theory of causation: similar causes are assumed to produce similar
effects. Things are similar, however, only in certain respects. How do we
decide on the relevance and existence of similarities?

His views on the nature of the self provoke lengthy argument in legal and
medical spheres, as well as among philosophers; and his views on freedom
and determinism, the roles of reason and sentiment, and the nature of justice,
are much debated. His economic views are now closely compared with those
of Adam Smith. Studies of seventeenth-century and eighteenth-century
Scottish legal thought, and the precise theological issues of the day, together
with attempts to establish the nature of Hume's rather slight scientific
knowledge, are likely to lead to revised interpretations of his work. One sign of
a great thinker is that later readers deem it a cultural duty to define their
position in relation to that thinker, and to treat him or her, however
anachronistically, as a contemporary. With the attention now being given to

the whole range of his works, including the *Essays* and the *History*, it is unlikely that his views will soon suffer neglect.

Further Reading

There is no standard or uniform edition of Hume's works, but most of them are available in paperback. Convenient editions of Hume's *Essays* and also of his *History* are published in the *Liberty Classics* series (1985a and 1985c respectively). There are many editions of *An Enquiry Concerning Human Understanding* and *An Enquiry Concerning the Principles of Morals*, and they are printed together in the Clarendon Press edition edited by Nidditch (1975a). Nidditch has also edited *A Treatise of Human Nature* (1978a), which is published along with the *Abstract*. The best edition of the *Dialogues Concerning Natural Religion* (1779), is edited by N. Kemp Smith, who also provided a long introduction.

Mossner (1980) has become the standard biography, with the Scottish Enlightenment and other contexts explored in Daiches, Jones and Jones (1986), Jones (ed.) (1989), Jones (1982) and Sher (1985).

Classic studies of Hume include Church (1934), Laird (1932), Passmore (1952), Price (1940) and Smith (1941). Of recent general studies of Hume's philosophy, I can mention Capaldi (1974), Norton (1982), Noxon (1973), Penelhum (1975), Stroud (1977), and Wright (1983). Bennett (1971) explores major themes in Locke, Berkeley and Hume.

Ardal (1966), Baier (1991), Fogelin (1985), Flew (1961) and Pears (1991) examine different aspects of the *Treatise*. Beauchamp and Rosenberg (1981) and Strawson (1989) consider Hume's account of causation, which is also a central concern of Mackie (1974). Stove (1973) discusses Hume on induction.

Hume's philosophy of religion is discussed by Gaskin (1978), Hurlbutt (1965), Jeffner (1966), and Tweyman (1986), and his politics is discussed by Millar (1981).

References

Hume

Hume, D. 1978a [1739–40]: *A Treatise of Human Nature* (edited by P. H. Nidditch) (2nd edn). Oxford: Clarendon Press.
—— 1978b [1740]: *An Abstract of a Treatise of Human Nature*. Reprinted in Hume (1978a).
—— 1985a [1741–2]: *Essays, Moral, Political, and Literary*. Indianapolis: Liberty Fund, Inc. Published with *Political Discourses* (Hume, 1985b).
—— 1975a [1748–51]: *Enquiries Concerning Human Understanding and Concerning the Principles of Morals* (edited by P. H. Nidditch) (3rd edn). Oxford: Clarendon Press.

—— 1975b [1748]: *Enquiry Concerning Human Understanding*. In Hume (1975a).
—— 1975c [1751]: *Enquiry Concerning the Principles of Morals*. In Hume (1975a).
—— 1985b [1752]: *Political Discourses*. Indianapolis: Liberty Fund, Inc. Published with *Essays, Moral, Political, and Literary* (Hume, 1985a).
—— 1985c [1754–62]: *History of England*. 6 vols. Indianapolis: Liberty Fund, Inc.
—— 1947 [1779]: *Dialogues Concerning Natural Religion* (edited by N. Kemp Smith). London: Nelson.

Other writers

Ardal, P. S. 1966: *Passion and Value in Hume's Treatise*. Edinburgh: Edinburgh University Press.
Baier, A. C. 1991: *A Progress of Sentiments: Reflections on Hume's Treatise*. Cambridge: Harvard University Press.
Beauchamp, T. L. and Rosenberg, A. 1981: *Hume and the Problem of Causation*. Oxford: Oxford University Press.
Bennett, J. F. 1971: *Locke, Berkeley, Hume: Central Themes*. Oxford: Oxford University Press.
Capaldi, N. 1974: *David Hume: The Newtonian Philosopher*. Boston: Twayne.
Church, R. W. 1934: *Hume's Theory of the Understanding*. London: Allen and Unwin.
Daiches, D., Jones, E. J. and Jones, P. 1986: *A Hotbed of Genius*. Edinburgh: Edinburgh University Press.
Flew, A. 1961: *Hume's Philosophy of Belief*. London: Routledge.
Fogelin, R. J. 1985: *Hume's scepticism in the Treatise of Human Nature*. London: Routledge.
Gaskin, J. C. A. 1978: *Hume's Philosophy of Religion*. London: Macmillan.
Hall, R. 1978: *Fifty Years of Hume Scholarship*. Edinburgh: Edinburgh University Press.
Hendel, C. W. 1963: *Studies in the Philosophy of David Hume*. Indianapolis: Garland.
Hurlbutt, R. H. 1965: *Hume, Newton and the Design Argument*. Lincoln: University of Nebraska Press.
Jeffner, A. 1966: *Butler and Hume on Religion*. Stockholm: Diakonistyrelsens bokforlag.
Jones, P. 1982: *Hume's Sentiments: Their Ciceronian and French Context*. Edinburgh: Edinburgh University Press.
—— (ed.) 1989: *The Science of Man in the Scottish Enlightenment: Hume, Reid and other Contemporaries*. Edinburgh: Edinburgh University Press.
Laird, J. 1932: *Hume's Philosophy of Human Nature*. London: Methuen.
Livingston, D. W. 1984: *Hume's Philosophy of Common Life*. Chicago: University of Chicago Press.
Livingston, D. W. and King, J. T. 1976: *Hume: A Re-evaluation*. New York: Fordham University Press.
Mackie, J. L. 1974: *The Cement of the Universe*. Oxford: Clarendon Press.
—— 1980: *Hume's Moral Theory*. London: Routledge.
Michaud, Y. 1983: *Hume et la fin de la philosophie*. Paris: Presses Universitaires de France.
Millar, D. 1981: *Philosophy and Ideology in Hume's Political Thought*. Oxford: Clarendon Press.
Mossner, E. C. 1980: *The Life of David Hume* (2nd edn). Oxford: Clarendon Press.
Norton, D. F. 1982: *David Hume: Common Sense Moralist, sceptical Metaphysician*. Princeton: Princeton University Press.
—— (ed.) 1993: *The Cambridge Companion to Hume*. Cambridge: Cambridge University Press.

Norton, D. F., Capaldi, N. and Robison, W. L. (eds) 1979: *McGill Hume Studies*. San Diego: Austin Hill Press.

Noxon, J. 1973: *Hume's Philosophical Development*. Oxford: Clarendon Press.

Passmore, J. 1952: *Hume's Intentions*. Cambridge: Cambridge University Press.

Pears, D. 1991: *Hume's System*. Oxford: Oxford University Press.

Penelhum, T. 1975: *Hume*. London: Macmillan.

Price, H. H. 1940: *Hume's Theory of the External World*. Oxford: Clarendon Press.

Sher, R. B. 1985: *Church and University in the Scottish Enlightenment*. Edinburgh: Edinburgh University Press.

Smith, N. K. 1941: *The Philosophy of David Hume*. London: Macmillan.

Stove, D. C. 1973: *Probability and Hume's Inductive scepticism*. Oxford: Oxford University Press.

Strawson, G. 1989: *The Secret Connexion: Causation, Realism and David Hume*. Oxford: Clarendon Press.

Stroud, B. 1977: *Hume*. London: Routledge.

Tweyman, S. 1986: *Scepticism and Belief in Hume's Dialogues Concerning Natural Religion*. The Haig: Nijhoff.

Wright, J. P. 1983: *The sceptical Realism of David Hume*. Manchester: Manchester University Press.

Discussion Questions

1 Are there causal relations between events? What grounds are there for believing so?

2 If necessity cannot be observed, how can causality involve necessity?

3 Why should we believe the claim that every event has a cause?

4 Will the future resemble the past? Can we prove it? Are we justified in believing it?

5 What are ideas? Do they all have their origin in impressions?

6 Does experience provide a sufficient basis for knowledge of matters of fact? What else might be needed?

7 Does custom *justify* inductive inference or *explain* why we make such inferences even though they are not justified?

8 Do we act freely even if all our actions are caused?

9 Could we ever be justified in supposing that the laws of nature had changed or that we have encountered an event without a cause?

10 Does each of our perceptions exist independent of any other perception?

11 Are we justified in believing that there are physical objects?

12 Why did Hume come to believe that his account of personal identity was unsatisfactory? If there is a deficiency, can it be remedied?

13 Should our account of personal identity differ from our account of the identity of physical objects?

14   What is the role of agreement in our account of knowledge? Is knowledge possible where experts disagree?

15   What philosophical problems arise from reports of miracles? How can these philosophical problems be resolved?

16   Can the complexity and order of the world tell us anything about the existence of God? Can they tell us anything about the nature of God?

17   Does Hume's naturalism answer his scepticism?

18   What role does reason have in explaining actions?

19   What makes a quality a virtue?

20   How is it possible to judge oneself impartially?

21   Can aesthetic judgements be objective? Can aesthetic disputes be resolved?

22   Must the intention of the artist or relevance to an audience enter into judging a work of art?

23   In historical knowledge, how can we combine the knowledge of the actor and that of the spectator?

24   How is there room for *re-interpretation* in historical knowledge?

25   Can liberty and authority be reconciled?

26   Is there ever a right to resist the law? Is there a right to instigate a revolution?

27   What are the main threats to liberty?

28   Is Hume's thought concerning law, government and society applicable today?

22

Kant —————————————————————————

David Bell

There is hardly an area of philosophy to which Immanuel Kant (1724–1804) did not make massive and profound contributions, including metaphysics, philosophy of mind, epistemology, philosophical logic, the foundations of mathematics, ethics, aesthetics, philosophy of science, and political philosophy. There are, however, two centres of Kant's philosophical thought, which comprise the foundation for the whole. On the one hand, there is the 'critical' or 'transcendental' metaphysics outlined in his *Critique of Pure Reason* (first published in 1781), and, on the other hand, there is the ethical theory that he published in a number of works after 1784. In the former he developed an account of the mind and its place in nature that was designed to overcome the limitations inherent in the thought of his rationalist and empiricist predecessors. In his works on ethics, he formulated a compelling vision of how moral law, autonomy, rationality, freedom, duty and virtue are related to one another in moral life. The following chapter concentrates on these two central areas of Kant's thought.

1 Life

Immanuel Kant was born in Königsberg, a flourishing Prussian port on the Baltic Sea. He went to the local grammar school, by all accounts an unwholesome place, where the pietist religious atmosphere was enforced by the 'pedantic and gloomy discipline of fanatics', but where he nevertheless succeeded in supplementing his limited means with his winnings from billiards and cards. At the age of 16 he began his studies at Königsberg University. During the next decade he studied, amongst other disciplines, mathematics, theology, physics and philosophy.

In 1755 Kant gained the qualifications necessary for him to become a *Privatdozent* (an independent teacher) at the university. As a *Privatdozent* he was entitled to no salary, but instead received a small fee from each student he taught. In order to survive financially Kant was forced to lecture for up to 36 hours per week, on subjects as diverse as logic, metaphysics, geography, ethics, physics, pedagogics, arithmetic, geometry, trigonometry, natural theology, astronomy, meteorology and anthropology; and in 1764 he was offered, but declined, the post of Professor of Poetry. In spite of this 'monstrous academic workload', Kant was anything but a recluse. One contemporary recalled that Kant 'spent almost every midday and evening outside his house in social activities, frequently taking part also in a card party, and only getting home around midnight'. During this 'pre-critical' period Kant published a number of minor works on a variety of subjects. (Though important for a full understanding of Kant's thought, these pre-critical writings (Kant, 1968) will not be examined in the present chapter.)

Kant became Professor of Logic and Metaphysics in Königsberg in 1770, but it was not until some 11 years later, at the age of 57, that he produced the first in the series of incomparably great, and massively influential works that was to embody his so-called Critical Philosophy: the first edition of the *Critique of Pure Reason* appeared in 1781. It was followed, with remarkable rapidity, by the *Prolegomena* (published in 1783), the *Foundations of the Metaphysics of Morals* (published in 1785), the *Metaphysical Foundations of Natural Science* (published in 1786), the second, substantially revised edition of the *Critique of Pure Reason* (published in 1787), the *Critique of Practical Reason* (published in 1788), and the *Critique of Judgement* (published in 1790).

Two months before his eightieth birthday Kant died in Königsberg. His funeral was attended by many thousands of mourners, and it is clear that he was universally revered as much for his humanity and moral integrity as for his philosophical genius. On his tombstone was inscribed, appropriately, a motto taken from the passage with which he had concluded the *Critique of Practical Reason*: 'Two things fill the mind with ever new and increasing admiration and awe, the oftener and more steadily we reflect on them: the starry heavens above me, and the moral law within me'.

As this last sentence hints, the two great issues to which Kant's critical philosophy is addressed are, firstly, the nature of our understanding of the universe and, secondly, the nature of our moral life. These issues are the topics, respectively, of the following two sections.

2 The Metaphysics of Experience

How *can* we understand the universe and the things it contains? How is this even possible? As this is a huge, and hugely complex problem, we might begin by breaking it down into more manageable parts. We might ask: In what ways *do* we, as a matter of fact, understand the world and the things it contains? And for an initial, very rough answer, we might say something like this. On the one hand, our understanding of *the world* is couched very largely in terms of objects – objects that possess properties, participate in events, occupy space, persist through time, interact causally with one another, are substantial and obey the laws of logic, arithmetic, geometry and physics. We might call these the *object-related* aspects of the problem. On the other hand, *our understanding* of the world is based on our observations and perceptions, our concepts, thoughts, judgements and inferences. We might call these, in contrast, the *subject-related* aspects of the problem.

The object-related aspects can be made more explicit in a number of METAPHYSICAL (chapter 2) questions. For example: What is an OBJECT (p. 576)?

What is a PROPERTY (pp. 96–7)? What is an event? What are TIME and SPACE (pp. 328–9)? What is CAUSALITY (chapter 9)? How is logic, or mathematics or natural science possible? Correspondingly, the subject-related aspects yield a number of questions that belong, broadly speaking, to EPISTEMOLOGY (chapter 1) and the PHILOSOPHY OF MIND (chapter 5): What is it to perceive something? What is a concept? What is a JUDGEMENT (p. 669)? How are concepts related to judgements? How are concepts related to perceptual experiences? How are perceptual experiences related to sensations? The questions mentioned in this paragraph are amongst the most important that Kant addresses in the *Critique of Pure Reason*, and they are questions to which, indeed, he there provides specific and often provocative answers.

There is, however, a very general, overarching philosophical problem which can itself be characterized intrinsically as neither object-related nor subject-related; for it is, precisely, the general problem of how things that are object-related can possibly fit together with those that are subject-related. Again, this problem can be spelled out in a number of more specific questions. For example: How do our concepts refer to items in reality? How do our subjective sensations and experiences give us objective knowledge of the material universe? How can our inner thoughts and judgements be objectively true of the external world?

Kant's critical philosophy makes this overarching metaphysical problem its most fundamental concern; and that philosophy as a whole is characterized, above all else, by his insistence that in any acceptable solution to the metaphysical problem, object-related and subject-related phenomena must be taken to be mutually dependent and, ultimately, inseparable. In other words, no coherent theory of either one is possible that is not, already, a theory of the other. In particular, Kant claimed, no coherent theory of (objective) properties, objects, events, causal relations, substance, time, or space can be provided that is not already also an account of our (subjective) perceptions, concepts, and judgements concerning such things. In the last analysis, that is, the nature of the reality we know is inseparable from the nature of the mind that knows it. This is how Kant famously expressed this doctrine in the Preface to the second edition of the *Critique of Pure Reason*:

> Hitherto it has been assumed that all our knowledge must conform to objects. But all attempts [for instance, to account for the possibility of objective knowledge] have, on this assumption, ended in failure. We must therefore make trial whether we may not have more success in the tasks of metaphysics, if we suppose that objects conform to our knowledge. (1929, B xvi)

Kant called this change in metaphysical perspective his 'Copernican revolution'. The resulting theory is a form of transcendental idealism.

The Copernican Revolution

Copernicus, a sixteenth-century astronomer, pointed out that the apparent motion of the sun and stars had hitherto been assumed to be real motion: it was claimed that the reason the sun appears to rise in the east, travel across the sky, and set in the west, is simply that it really is moving round a stationary earth. Copernicus, however, argued that precisely the same appearances would result if, instead, the sun were in fact stationary and the earth were spinning on its axis. Copernicus replaced the naive theory, which took the apparent motion of the sun to be real motion, with a theory according to which the apparent motion of the sun is in effect a product of the real motion of the observer: it is because we are spinning that the sun seems to move across the sky. Kant's so-called Copernican revolution is analogous. It had hitherto been assumed that there appear to be spatio-temporal objects that exist independently of us because there really are such things. Kant replaced this naive realism with a theory according to which the apparent nature and independence of the objective world is a product of our perceptions, concepts and judgements; in the last analysis, it is because we perceive and think as we do that the world seems to be as it does.

Kant's idealism is motivated by a number of considerations, one of which is as follows. There are certain very basic principles and judgements which form the foundation of our understanding of the universe. These principles and judgements include, for example, the truths of arithmetic, the truths of geometry, the principle that every event has a cause, the judgement that objects never simply go out of existence, and likewise the judgement that objects never simply come into existence, out of nowhere and out of nothing. According to Kant such claims as these have a number of interesting and problematic characteristics:

(1)   They are necessarily true, and cannot be either justified or falsified by appeal to contingent facts or perceptual experience (that is, they are *a priori*).
(2)   They are not merely logical truths, or truths by definition (that is, they are *synthetic*).
(3)   They are essential to our understanding of reality.

Kant called the knowledge we have of truths of this kind 'synthetic *a priori* knowledge', and his idealism is motivated by a combination of two beliefs: (1) that without synthetic *a priori* knowledge, no knowledge, or understanding, or meaningful experience would be possible at all; and (2) synthetic *a priori* knowledge is not knowledge we can possibly receive 'from without', as a result of our experience of the world. On the contrary, synthetic *a priori* knowledge is only possible if it encodes the judgements and principles we adopt in making sense of our experience. The Copernican revolution in philosophy is necessary, in other words, because without it we cannot make intelligible the possibility of synthetic *a priori* knowledge – and in the absence of that possibility, Kant believed, the very possibility of any knowledge or understanding whatsoever would become unintelligible.

Synthetic Knowledge *a priori*

'Analytic' is short for 'analytically true', and a judgement is analytic if its truth is solely a consequence of the concepts it contains. So, for example, the truths of logic are analytic, as are such conceptual truths as, for instance, the fact that all bachelors are unmarried, or that red is a colour. 'Synthetic' simply means 'not analytic'. The term '*a posteriori*' is short for 'acquired *a posteriori*', and something is known *a posteriori* if the knowledge is acquired on the basis of sensory experience, that is, if it is in principle falsifiable by experience. The term '*a priori*' simply means 'not *a posteriori*'. So synthetic *a priori* knowledge is knowledge that is necessarily true, which cannot be falsified by experience, but which is not merely trivially, logically, or analytically true.

In conformity with this idealist perspective, the *Critique of Pure Reason* analyses both the object-related and the subject-related elements of knowledge with the aim of showing that all *a priori* elements must ultimately be explained by appeal to our essential subjective constitution – the ways in which we necessarily perceive, conceptualize and think – and cannot be explained by appeal to the way the world is independently of any access we may have to it. It is not because reality, in and of itself, is spatial, temporal, or causal that we experience it as such. Rather, the explanation runs in the opposite direction: it is because of the essential nature and structure of our minds that our experience is, precisely, of a spatial, temporal, causal reality. Kant puts it bluntly: 'we can know *a priori* of things only what we ourselves put into them' (1929, B xviii).

The overall structure of Kant's critical philosophy – and, as we will see, the organization of the *Critique of Pure Reason* itself – depends upon Kant's distinction between three fundamental, irreducible powers of the mind. Firstly, we have the capacity to receive or register sensory items such as sensations, impressions, sense-data, percepts and the like. Kant's term for such sensory items is 'intuitions', and he calls the capacity to register them 'sensibility'. Secondly, we have capacities of an essentially intellectual kind, involving the power to conceptualize, to think and to judge. Kant assigns such abilities to what he calls 'the understanding', a faculty which is responsible for our ability to use concepts. Thirdly, we are able to infer logically, to draw valid conclusions – that is, to reason. Sensibility, according to Kant, is largely passive: sensations and intuitions are things we undergo or that happen to us. Understanding, however, and reason are essentially active: concepts are things we use, and of course thinking and reasoning are things we do.

Kant is adamant about two claims. The first is that sensibility and understanding are quite distinct. They have their own operations, principles, and functions. The second is that in all knowledge whatsoever that is available to us, both sensibility and understanding – both intuitions and concepts – must be involved. Kant categorically denies, in other words, that we can have any knowledge that is purely sensory, or, equally, that we can have any knowledge that is exclusively conceptual; for 'thoughts without content are empty, intuitions without concepts are blind' (1929, B 75).

The organization of the *Critique of Pure Reason* is complex, and can indeed be baffling. The distinction between sensibility, understanding and reason can, however, help us to make some sense of it. Figure 22.1 (which is not exhaustive) represents some of the most important divisions within the structure of Kant's text.

The following remarks may be of some help in navigating this maze. The main division of the *Critique of Pure Reason* into the Transcendental Aesthetic and the Transcendental Logic corresponds to Kant's distinction between sensibility, on the one hand, and understanding and reason on the other. The Transcendental Aesthetic is so-called – from the Greek word *aisthesis*, meaning perception or sensation – because it deals with the *a priori* elements that are to be found in sensory, perceptual experience (so this part of the text in fact has nothing to do with 'aesthetics' as that word is used now). One of Kant's main objectives in this part of the *Critique* is to demonstrate that space and time are *a priori* forms of sensory experience. In other words, as a transcendental idealist, he aims to show that it is because (1) our intuitions have *a priori* spatial and temporal forms that (2) empirical objects in the external world are spatio-temporal. He believes no attempt to explain (1) in terms of (2) can be coherent. The Transcendental Logic is so-called – from *logos*, the Greek word for proposition or meaning – because it deals with the *a priori* elements that are present in our conceptual, intellectual make up (so this section is only partially and indirectly related to 'logic' as the term is used today). Within the Transcendental Logic itself, the Transcendental Analytic concerns itself primarily with the nature of our understanding, that is, with the necessary features on which our entire ability to judge and apply concepts ultimately rests. Here Kant argues, amongst other things, that if we did not possess and apply certain fundamental, primitive, *a priori* concepts (he calls them the 'categories'), then no understanding or thought would be possible. The categories include such basic, *a priori* concepts as those which we typically express, for example, with the words *all, one, not, is, maybe, exists* and *causes*. (Kant respectively labels these categories Totality, Unity, Negation, Reality, Possibility, Existence and Causality.) In the Transcendental Dialectic, on the other hand, Kant addresses the philosophical problems associated with our capacity to use – and, more importantly, with our tendency to abuse and misuse – our powers of reason. (Kant calls reasoning 'dialectical' when it is invalid or fallacious.) The overall aim of the Transcendental Dialectic is to show that pure reason alone, when divorced from any input from, or application to, sensory experience, can provide us with no genuine knowledge whatsoever. That, in essence, is Kant's criticism or 'critique' of pure reason. Within the Transcendental Dialectic, the section entitled the Paralogisms of Pure Reason aims to show that any attempt to deduce facts about the mind or self, on purely rational grounds and independently of all reference to sensory experience, is doomed to failure. (A paralogism is a certain sort of invalid argument.) In the Antinomies of Pure Reason, Kant attempts to demonstrate the impossibility of purely conceptual, sense-independent knowledge of the material world. (An antinomy is a paradox or contradiction.) And in the Ideal of Pure Reason, he attempts to prove that pure reason alone can yield no knowledge of God.

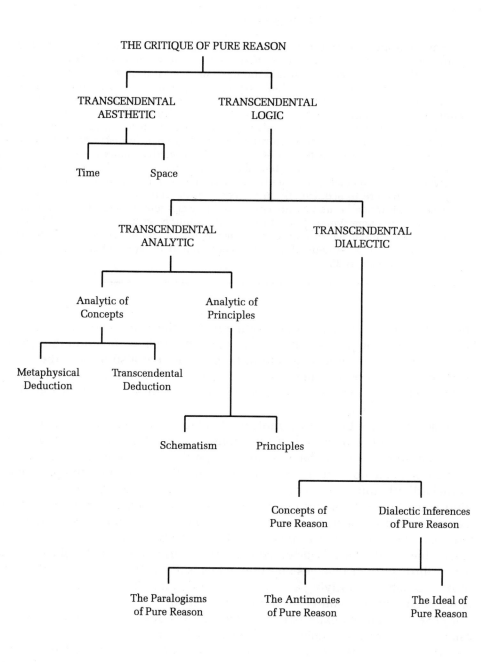

Figure 22.1   The main divisions of Kant's *Critique of Pure Reason*

A Transcendental Enquiry

As Kant typically uses it, the term 'transcendental' is intended to contrast sharply with two other terms, namely 'immanent' and 'transcendent'. Something is immanent with respect to certain bounds or limits if it lies within them. Something is 'transcendent' if it lies beyond those bounds or limits. Something is 'transcendental', however, if it lies neither within nor without those limits, but is, rather, a matter of the essential nature of those very limits themselves. Kant was concerned to establish the essential, *a priori* limits of human knowledge. Now nothing can possibly provide information about what is transcendent, that is, whatever by definition lies beyond the limits of knowledge. Science and common sense provide us with information about what lies within the limits of the knowable. But a special, non-scientific, peculiarly metaphysical investigation is required if we are to acquire any knowledge of the very limits of the knowable themselves. Kant calls such an investigation 'transcendental': 'I entitle transcendental all knowledge which is occupied, not so much with objects, as with the mode of our knowledge of objects in so far as this mode of knowledge is to be possible *a priori*. A system of such concepts might be entitled transcendental philosophy' (1929, B 25).

The heart of Kant's metaphysics is contained in the Transcendental Analytic; for it is here that he provides his analysis not only of how the mind must work if understanding or knowledge are to be possible, but also of how the world must be if it is to be capable of being known or understood. The remainder of this section is devoted to an examination of Kant's account in the Transcendental Analytic.

Our senses present us with a multiplicity of different sensations or, in Kant's terminology, with a manifold of intuitions. These intuitions are extended in time, and some of them have spatial properties, but their intrinsic nature guarantees them no permanence, stability, determinacy, objectivity, or conceptual articulation. A manifold of intuitions is what HUME (chapter 21) had in mind when he wrote of consciousness as containing sensory contents 'which succeed each other with an inconceivable rapidity, and are in a perpetual flux and movement.' Now if our awareness is ever to be, say, an awareness of an intelligible, predictable world, containing determinate, stable objects that persist through their changes and interact causally with one another, then we must be capable of unifying and interpreting this manifold of intuitions. That is, we must have the ability to find our way about within the diversity of our ever-changing sensory experience. And we do this by construing those sensory states as experiences of objects in the external world.

Kant takes it as axiomatic that 'the combination of a manifold in general can never come to us through the senses', and he concludes that 'all combination, be we conscious of it or not . . . is an act of understanding.' He then adds: 'To this act the general title of "synthesis" may be assigned' (1929, B 130). In short, if we are to be able to make any sense of the diversity of sensations we undergo, we must be able to combine or unite those sensations so that they come to represent to us aspects of objects in the world. For

instance, I may take a manifold comprising certain particular tactile sensations, sensations of shape, colour and movement, sensations of sound, smell,
and the like, as belonging together, by taking them to be various forms of
awareness of one and the same object – my motorbike, say. To take a variety of
disparate sensory intuitions as belonging together, in virtue of their being
different experiences of one and the same thing, just is to synthesize those
intuitions. To unify one's sensory states is to understand them to be
representations of objects and properties in the external world. So, in the
absence of such synthesizing activities, Kant claims, we could have no
awareness of an external world, and indeed no experience that would make
any sense to us.

Synthesis cannot, of course, be a merely random or arbitrary process, but
must proceed in conformity with rules. Moreover, the most fundamental rules
governing synthesis cannot be learned or acquired on the basis of experience,
for they are precisely the rules which must already be in place if there is to be
any knowledge or coherent experience. Kant therefore concludes that the basic
rules governing synthesis are *a priori* rules – and the most fundamental of all
are the *a priori* rules which enable a number of different sensory states to be
referred to one and the same object. Now according to Kant, concepts are
nothing but rules for synthesis, and the categories are the most basic, *a priori*
such rules. So the categories together specify the rules to which human
understanding must conform if we are to be able to take our various sensory
states as representing objects in the world. In Kant's own terminology, the
categories together comprise 'the concept of an object in general'. Kant writes
that the categories 'serve as the antecedent conditions under which alone
anything can be . . . thought as object in general' (1929, B 125).

In the Metaphysical Deduction, Kant attempts to identify just those concepts
which are categories. (There are twelve of them: Unity, Plurality, Totality,
Reality, Negation, Limitation, Substance, Causality, Community, Possibility,
Existence and Necessity.) In the section called the Transcendental Deduction
of the Categories, Kant offers a complex set of arguments aimed at proving the
claim that in the absence of synthesis in conformity to *a priori* rules (the
categories), no objective, intelligible experience would be possible at all.

One central train of thought that runs through the Transcendental Deduction
is, in briefest outline, as follows. There is an inescapable condition that must
be met by any plurality of mental states and mental contents if they are all to
belong to one, single, unified consciousness – if, for example, they are all to be
my states and contents of consciousness. The necessary condition, according
to Kant, is that the consciousness or mind in question should possess self-
consciousness: I must not merely have the capacity to be in an arbitrary mental
state, S, I must also be able to *know* that I am in that state. And this requires,
in turn, that I have the ability to ascribe state S to myself, roughly speaking by
being able to make the judgement, '*I am aware of S*'. Kant writes: 'It must be
possible for the "I think" [or "I am aware"] to accompany all my representations' (1929, B 131); 'for the manifold of representations . . . would not be one
and all *my* representations, if they did not all belong to one self-consciousness'
(1929, B 132). In other words, the unity of consciousness requires self-

consciousness, and self-consciousness in turn requires the ability to ascribe one's mental states to oneself. The principle which governs the unity of consciousness Kant calls the transcendental unity of apperception.

The Transcendental Unity of Apperception

This term does not stand for an object or entity of any sort, and in particular it is not the name of anything like an ego, self, soul or mind. Rather, it is the name of the formal principle which is responsible for the unity of consciousness. 'Apperception' is any form of consciousness that involves self-consciousness; and the unity of apperception is 'transcendental' because it is an *a priori* condition for the possibility of intelligible experience. So the transcendental unity of apperception is a condition that consciousness must meet if it is to comprise a coherent, integrated unity or whole – the condition, namely, that it be a form of self-consciousness. Kant expresses the condition thus: 'It must be possible for the "I think" to accompany all my representations.' If this condition were to fail, he claims, then self-consciousness would be impossible, in which case the unity of consciousness would be impossible, in which case one could have no intelligible experience of any kind.

In the final stage in the Transcendental Deduction Kant examines in more detail the conditions that must obtain if the ascription of different experiences to oneself is to be possible: What exactly must I be able to do, if I am to have the capacity to be self-conscious? P. F. Strawson writes: 'Kant's answer must be admitted to have a certain sublimity. What is required for a series of experiences to belong to a single consciousness is that they should possess precisely that rule-governed connectedness which is also required for them collectively to constitute [the] experience of a single objective world.' (Strawson, 1966, pp. 92–3.) In other words, the unity of my consciousness requires me to synthesize my different sensory experiences in conformity with the rules embodied in the categories. But for me to synthesize my various experiences in this way just is for me to experience a single objective world – a world made up of stable, material objects that possess properties, persist through time, and interact causally with one another.

On the basis of this argument Kant feels justified in concluding that knowledge, intelligible experience, even the unity of consciousness itself would be impossible if we did not possess and apply the *a priori* categories in ways that provide us with experience of an objective, external world. 'In other words,' as Kant himself says, 'the consciousness of my existence is at the same time an immediate consciousness of the existence of other things outside me' (1929, B 276).

3 Autonomy and the Moral Law

Kant's major contributions to ETHICS (chapter 6) are contained in two works: *The Foundations of the Metaphysics of Morals* (1785) (whose original title, *Grundlegung zur Metaphysik der Sitten*, is variously translated into English, not only as *The Grounding, The Groundwork, The Foundations* or as *The Fundamental Principles of the Metaphysics of Morals*, but also under the title *The Moral Law*), and the second Critique, entitled *The Critique of Practical Reason* (1956). The first of these works is beyond doubt one of the most profound and influential works of moral philosophy ever written. The first section opens resoundingly with the famous words: 'It is impossible to conceive of anything in the world, or indeed anything beyond the world, which can be considered good without qualification, except a *good will.*' And, as Kant himself puts it, 'the sole aim' of the book is to 'seek out and establish the *supreme principle of morality.*' Kant's aim, in other words, is to identify and defend the most basic moral principle or law which directly determines the ETHICAL VALUE (p. 199) possessed by acts of WILL (p. 216), and which, as a consequence, indirectly determines all other moral values without exception. He calls this supreme principle of morality the categorical imperative.

The underlying picture, in terms of which we can begin to make sense of Kant's moral theory, is as follows. Like all animals, human beings are governed to a great extent by their desires: much of our behaviour is intelligible when it is seen as directed towards ends that are determined by our wishes, passions, appetites, desires, and the like. In this respect, as Hume said, 'reason is and ought to be the slave of the passions.' Here the role of practical reason is merely to supply rational, efficient means for the attainment of the things we want. On the other hand, and unlike many animals, we are capable in certain circumstances of acting on principle, and of following the dictates of reason – even when this in fact goes against our appetites and desires. We do this when, for instance, we keep a promise at significant cost or inconvenience to ourselves, when we volunteer for some unpleasant task purely out of a sense of duty, or when we decide we must 'do the right thing' in spite of a strong inclination to do otherwise. When we act in this way, Kant says, the moral worth of our action does not reside 'in the purpose to be attained by it, but in the maxim in accordance with which it is decided upon.'

A maxim is a general rule or principle which a person can use as a guide to action: 'Always tell the truth'; 'If you think it will rain, carry an umbrella'; 'Don't always take the biggest piece of cake'; 'Never eat trout on a Thursday', and so on. As these examples show, however, not every maxim is a moral one; for there are maxims that express principles of prudence, say, or etiquette, or even whim and superstition. For an action to be a purely moral one, Kant demands that three conditions must be met:

(1) The maxim governing the action must be a genuinely moral maxim (and not one of mere prudence, say, or etiquette).
(2) The action itself must not merely *conform to* the maxim, but rather must be done *for the sake of* the moral principle that the maxim embodies. A purely moral action, in other words, is one motivated exclusively by a desire to implement a moral principle. It is one that is performed, as Kant says, 'exclusively from a sense of duty' and 'for the sake of duty'.
(3) The action must be performed freely, by an autonomous agent.

Autonomy

Kant believed that mature, adult human beings are autonomous, and that it is for this reason that they possess moral dignity, deserve moral respect, and ought never to be treated as mere means to an end, but always as ends in themselves. Possession of genuine autonomy depends upon the presence of three things. Firstly, an autonomous agent must be free, that is, capable of acts of will that are not causally determined, either by inner forces like inclinations, desires and passions, or by external forces in the outer world. Secondly, autonomy requires that agents can exercise rational self-control over their decisions and their actions. And, thirdly, autonomy requires that the rational principles governing such self-control are the sole responsibility of the individual agent: no genuinely autonomous agent can relinquish responsibility for the principles on which he or she acts to any external authority – whether it be the church, the state, the law, society, family, teachers or friends. On the contrary, all such principles must be chosen and imposed by the agent alone. And the supreme principle of rational, moral autonomy is the Categorical Imperative.

At this point we need to ask: When does a maxim embody an intrinsically *moral* principle? How, that is, are we to tell a genuinely moral maxim from one that has no intrinsic moral content or relevance? The answer to this question is stated below, at the beginning of the following paragraph. Before providing the answer, however, some preliminary scene-setting is required. We can predict, in advance, that the answer will be highly abstract and general – after all, we are asking for nothing less than a principle which will enable us to identify all and only those maxims that are morally good, irrespective of where, when, and by whom they are formulated, and regardless of the particular acts, or goals, or agents they are intended to govern. We can also predict that the principle will be both synthetic and *a priori*. It must be *a priori*, for in so far as it is to determine the moral value of any possible act, performed by any possible rational agent, in any possible circumstance, it must clearly be independent of all that is merely contingently the case. In particular, it must be independent of whatever contingent desires and inclinations an agent might possess, and of whatever contingent consequences an action might have in particular circumstances. The principle must also be synthetic because a merely trivial, analytic answer to our question would be incapable of providing the substantive knowledge we seek. And finally, the answer to our question will itself be a moral principle, albeit a very general, abstract one. What we require at this point is not a descriptive assertion specifying what *is* the case and the ways in which we *do* in fact act, but rather a normative rule which will specify what *should be* the case and how we *ought* to act. Moral principles, that is, have the primary function of regulating and evaluating behaviour, and as such, Kant believed, they have imperative force. So what we seek, in answer to our question, is a (second-level) moral imperative that specifies which maxims (first-level imperatives) we *ought* to adopt as reasons for action.

A maxim comprises a morally good basis for action when it conforms to the Categorical Imperative; and the Categorical Imperative is precisely a second-level, universally applicable, abstract, normative, *a priori*, synthetic rule for the evaluation of first-level maxims. In its most famous formulation the Categorical Imperative reads: 'Act only on that maxim through which you can at the same time will that it should become a universal law.'

The Categorical Imperative

An imperative is a command, instruction or rule governing how one should act. An imperative is 'categorical' when it is exceptionless, that is, when it is binding on all rational agents, in all circumstances, at all times. Kant believed that what he called 'the supreme principle of morality' was just such a categorical imperative, and he provided a number of different formulations of it. The most important are:

(1) Act only on that maxim through which you can at the same time will that it should become a universal law.
(2) So act as to use humanity, both in your own person and in the person of every other, always at the same time as an end, never simply as a means.
(3) So act as if you were always through your maxims a law-making member of a kingdom of ends.

The Categorical Imperative is, for Kant, an *a priori*, abstract law which governs the moral value of the maxims on which we act – maxims which, in turn, determine the moral value of those acts themselves. So an act is morally good if it is performed for the sake of a morally good maxim; and a maxim is morally good if it conforms to the Categorical Imperative.

The relation of Kant's moral theory to his metaphysics of experience is complex and obscure. One thing, however, is clear. In the *Critique of Pure Reason* Kant had attempted to establish the limits of genuine knowledge, that is, to discover the *a priori* conditions that must obtain if knowledge is to be possible. One of his conclusions was that, for us, there can be no knowledge of any super-sensible, non-empirical reality. In other words, a necessary condition of the possibility of human knowledge is that it involve not only intellectual concepts, but also sensory intuitions. For Kant, therefore, there could be no *knowledge* of God, the immortality of the soul, or the freedom of the will. To such matters as these, he maintained, concepts like observation, discovery, evidence, truth, science, explanation and the like must remain forever inapplicable. But about such matters we can nevertheless have *faith*. Faith in God, commitment to the moral law, respect for other persons, appreciation of the dignity that autonomy bestows – these were for Kant amongst the highest ideals that his philosophy, as a whole, was intended to protect. And in particular, his metaphysics of experience and his account of the limits of knowledge were intended to show that no empirical, naturalistic, or scientific treatment of these transcendent matters could possibly be intelligible. As he says in the Preface to the second edition of the *Critique of Pure Reason*: 'I have therefore found it necessary to limit knowledge, in order to make room for faith' (1929, B xxx).

Further Reading

For those who are new to Kant, a number of general, introductory works are available which cover all or most of the major aspects of Kantian thought. F. Copleston, *A History of Philosophy* vol. VI, parts I and II (1964) presents a conscientious, accessible and detailed, though rather unexciting, overview. Roger Scruton, *Kant* (1982) is briefer and more spirited. John Kemp, *The Philosophy of Kant* (1968) and Stefan Körner, *Kant* (1955) are both reliable introductions, though they are slightly less elementary than those mentioned above. Ralph C. S. Walker, *Kant* (1978) is another excellent, though non-elementary, introduction to Kant's thought as a whole.

Amongst introductory works that concentrate specifically on themes from *The Critique of Pure Reason*, the following are noteworthy. C. D. Broad, in *Kant: An Introduction* (1978), presents a thorough, helpful discussion of the first *Critique*. T. E. Wilkerson, *Kant's Critique of Pure Reason: A Commentary for Students* (1976) is sometimes helpful as an introduction, though it is too often unsympathetic and impatient. W. H. Walsh, in *Kant's Criticism of Metaphysics* (1975) writes with exemplary clarity and sophistication, as does Graham Bird, whose book *Kant's Theory of Knowledge* (1962) is a good introduction to Kantian epistemology. For rather more advanced readers, Jonathan Bennett's two works, *Kant's Analytic* (1966) and *Kant's Dialectic* (1974) are idiosyncratic and iconoclastic, but can assist not only in understanding Kant's thought, but also in finding it philosophically exciting. In *The Unity of the Understanding: A Study in Kantian Problems* (1990), Hubert Schwyzer provides a sympathetic and accessible treatment of some of the most central concerns of the first *Critique*. Henry Allison, *Kant's Transcendental Idealism* (1983) is clear, scholarly and insightful. Although P. F. Strawson, *The Bounds of Sense* (1966) has been hugely influential, it is perhaps most suitable for advanced readers. Paul Guyer's exhaustive study *Kant and the Claims of Knowledge* (1987), though doubtless important, is too dense and too long to be recommended to any but the most determined reader.

On individual philosophical topics, important and helpful material can often be found in collections of articles (though this material is rarely of an elementary or introductory nature). Amongst the most accessible and useful of such anthologies are: Ralph C. S. Walker (ed.), *Kant on Pure Reason* (1982); Robert P. Wolff (ed.), *Kant: A Collection of Critical Essays* (1967); Paul Guyer (ed.), *The Cambridge Companion to Kant* (1992); and Eva Schaper and Wilhelm Vossenkuhl (eds), *Reading Kant* (1989).

For those seeking help in understanding particular sections, passages, or even words and phrases in the *Critique of Pure Reason*, a number of commentaries are available which provide detailed textual clarification. Amongst the most important are Norman Kemp Smith, *A Commentary to Kant's 'Critique of Pure Reason'* (1923); H. J. Paton, *Kant's Metaphysic of Experience: A Commentary on the First Half of the Kritik der reinen Vernunft* (1936); and A. C. Ewing, *A Short Commentary on Kant's Critique of Pure Reason* (1938).

An introduction to the overall philosophical context of Kant's moral philosophy can be obtained from Marcus G. Singer, *Generalization in Ethics* (1961), and C. D. Broad, *Five Types of Ethical Theory* (1930). Sympathetic, scholarly and clear treatments of Kantian ethics are to be found in Henry E. Allison, *Kant's Theory of Freedom* (1990); in Roger J. Sullivan, *Immanuel Kant's Moral Theory* (1989); in H. J. Paton, *The Categorical Imperative: A Study in Kant's Moral Philosophy* (1947); and in H. B. Acton, *Kant's Moral Philosophy* (1970). There are, in addition, a number of excellent commentaries on Kant's ethical writings. Amongst the best are: Lewis White Beck, *A Commentary on Kant's Critique of Practical Reason* (1960); Sir David Ross, *Kant's Ethical Theory: A Commentary on the Groundwork of the Metaphysics of Morals* (1954); and Robert P. Wolff, *The Autonomy of Reason: A Commentary on Kant's Groundwork of the Metaphysics of Morals* (1973).

References

Kant

Kant, I. 1929 [1781, 1787]: *Critique of Pure Reason* (1st edn (A), 1781, 2nd edn (B), 1787) (translated by N. Kemp Smith). London: Macmillan.
—— 1783: *Prolegomena to Any Future Metaphysics.* In various translations: translated by L. W. Beck, Indianapolis: Bobbs-Merrill (1950); translated by P. G. Lucas, Manchester: Manchester University Press (1953); translated by J. Ellington, Indianapolis: Hackett (1985).
—— 1785: *The Groundwork of the Metaphysics of Morals.* In various translations: translated by H. J. Paton, London: Hutchinson (1949); translated by L. W. Beck (as *The Foundations of the Metaphysics of Morals*), Indianapolis: Bobbs-Merrill (1959).
—— 1956 [1788]: *Critique of Practical Reason* (translated by L. W. Beck). Indianapolis: Bobbs-Merrill.
—— 1790: *Critique of Judgement.* In various translations: translated by J. Meredith, Oxford: Clarendon Press (1952); translated by J. H. Bernard, New York: Haffner (1968); translated by W. S. Pluhar, Indianapolis: Hackett (1987).
—— 1968: *Selected Pre-Critical Writings and Correspondence with Beck* (translated by G. B. Kerford and D. E. Walford). Manchester: Manchester University Press.

Cambridge University Press is currently preparing new English translations of all Kant's published works, under the series title *The Cambridge Edition of the Works of Immanuel Kant.* Its general editors are Paul Guyer and Allen W. Wood.

Kant's life and historical background

Beck, L. W. 1969: *Early German Philosophy: Kant and His Predecessors.* Cambridge, MA: Harvard University Press.
Cassirer, E. 1951: *The Philosophy of The Enlightenment* (translated by F. C. A. Koelln and J. P. Pettegrove). Princeton, NJ: Princeton University Press.
—— 1981: *Kant's Life and Thought* (translated by J. Haden). New Haven and London: Yale University Press.

Gulyga, A. 1987: *Immanuel Kant: His Life and Thought* (translated by M. Despalatovic). Boston: Birkauser.

General surveys of Kant's thought

Beck, L. W. 1965: *Studies in the Philosophy of Kant.* Indianapolis: Bobbs-Merrill.
Coppleston, F. 1964: *A History of Philosophy* vol. VI, parts I and II. New York: Image Books.
Guyer, P. (ed.) 1992: *The Cambridge Companion to Kant.* Cambridge: Cambridge University Press.
Kemp, J. 1968: *The Philosophy of Kant.* Oxford: Oxford University Press.
Körner, S. 1955: *Kant.* Harmondsworth: Penguin Books.
Scruton, R. 1982: *Kant.* Oxford: Oxford University Press.
Walker, R. C. S. 1978: *Kant.* London: Routledge and Kegan Paul.
Wolff, R. P. (ed.) 1967: *Kant: a Collection of Critical Essays.* London: Macmillan.

Metaphysics and epistemology

Allison, H. E. 1983: *Kant's Transcendental Idealism.* New Haven: Yale University Press.
Ameriks, K. 1982: *Kant's Theory of Mind: an Analysis of the Paralogisms of Pure Reason.* Oxford: Clarendon Press.
Aquila, R. E. 1983: *Representational Mind: a Study of Kant's Theory of Knowledge.* Bloomington: Indiana University Press.
Bennett, J. 1966: *Kant's Analytic.* Cambridge: Cambridge University Press.
—— 1974: *Kant's Dialectic.* Cambridge: Cambridge University Press.
Broad, C. D. 1978: *Kant: an Introduction.* Cambridge: Cambridge University Press.
Bird, G. 1962: *Kant's Theory of Knowledge.* London: Routledge and Kegan Paul.
Ewing, A. C. 1938: *A Short Commentary on Kant's Critique of Pure Reason.* Chicago: University of Chicago Press.
Friedman, M. 1992: *Kant and the Exact Sciences.* Cambridge, MA: Harvard University Press.
Guyer, P. 1987: *Kant and the Claims of Knowledge.* Cambridge: Cambridge University Press.
Kemp Smith, N. 1923: *A Commentary to Kant's 'Critique of Pure Reason'.* London: Macmillan.
Kitcher, P. 1990: *Kant's Transcendental Psychology.* Oxford: Oxford University Press.
Paton, H. J. 1936: *Kant's Metaphysic of Experience: A Commentary on the First Half of the Kritik der reinen Vernunft.* London: George Allen and Unwin.
Pippin, R. B. 1982: *Kant's Theory of Form: an Essay on the Critique of Pure Reason.* New Haven: Yale University Press.
Schaper, E. and Vossenkuhl, W. (eds) 1989: *Reading Kant: New Perspectives on Transcendental Arguments and Critical Philosophy.* Oxford: Blackwell.
Schwyzer, H. 1990: *The Unity of Understanding: a Study in Kantian Problems.* Oxford: Clarendon Press.
Strawson, P. F. 1966: *The Bounds of Sense.* London: Methuen.
Walker, R. C. S. (ed.) 1982: *Kant on Pure Reason.* Oxford: Oxford University Press.
Walsh, W. H. 1975: *Kant's Criticism of Metaphysics.* Edinburgh: Edinburgh University Press.
Wilkerson, T. E. 1976: *Kant's Critique of Pure Reason: A Commentary for Students.* Oxford: Oxford University Press.
Wolff, R. P. 1963: *Kant's Theory of Mental Activity: a Commentary on the Transcendental Analytic of the Critique of Pure Reason.* Cambridge, MA: Harvard University Press.

Moral philosophy

Acton, H. B. 1970: *Kant's Moral Philosophy*. London: Macmillan.

Allison, H. E. 1990: *Kant's Theory of Freedom*. Cambridge: Cambridge University Press.

Beck, L. W. 1960: *Commentary on Kant's Critique of Practical Reason*. Chicago: University of Chicago Press.

Broad, C. D. 1930: *Five Types of Ethical Theory*. London: Routledge and Kegan Paul.

O'Neill, O. 1989: *Constructions of Reason: Explorations of Kant's Moral Philosophy*. Cambridge: Cambridge University Press.

Paton, H. J. 1947: *The Categorical Imperative: a Study in Kant's Moral Philosophy*. London: Hutchinson.

Ross, D. 1954: *Kant's Ethical Theory. A Commentary on the Groundwork of the Metaphysics of Morals*. Oxford: Clarendon Press.

Singer, M. 1961: *Generalization in Ethics*. New York: Alfred A. Knopf.

Sullivan, R. J. 1989: *Immanuel Kant's Moral Theory*. Cambridge: Cambridge University Press.

Williams, T. C. 1968: *The Concept of the Categorical Imperative*. Oxford: Clarendon Press.

Wolff, R. P. 1973: *The Autonomy of Reason. A Commentary on Kant's Groundwork of the Metaphysics of Morals*. New York: Harper and Row.

Discussion Questions

1   How, if at all, does Kant reconcile the claims (1) that all our actions are causally determined, and (2) that as moral agents we can act freely?

2   Which of Kant's various formulations of the categorical imperative is ethically the most defensible?

3   'Thoughts without content are empty, intuitions without concepts are blind.' What does this mean? Is it true?

4   How convincing are Kant's central arguments in the Transcendental Deduction?

5   Does Kant's treatment of the Transcendental Unity of Apperception comprise a solution to Hume's problems concerning the self?

6   Did Kant show that there could be no 'ontological proof' of God's existence?

7   How adequate an account of causality does Kant provide in the Second Analogy?

8   What are Kant's aims in the Schematism chapter of the second *Critique*? How successfully does he realize those aims?

9   Is time a necessary form of all sensory experience? If so, does this give us any grounds for claiming that time is transcendentally ideal?

10   How good is the case that Kant makes for the claim that we have knowledge that is both synthetic and *a priori*?

11   What is the relation, if any, between morality and rationality?

12 Are there any necessary limits to what can be known, and if so, how could we establish what they are?

13 Which is more morally significant: the motives from which a given action is performed, or the consequences that that action has?

14 Can one consistently be a transcendental idealist and at the same time an empirical realist?

15 Are there any *a priori* concepts? If so, how did we acquire them?

16 Are the truths of geometry [or arithmetic] synthetic and *a priori*?

17 Can an object simply come into existence, out of nowhere and out of nothing?

18 If we cannot perceive identity [or necessity; or substance; or causality], how can we have any empirical knowledge of it?

19 Could a moral agent lack autonomy?

20 What is metaphysics?

23

Hegel ————————————————————————————

Michael Inwood

Hegel created a great and deeply influential system of philosophy, ranging over metaphysics, epistemology and logic; ethics, political, social and legal philosophy; and aesthetics, religion and the nature of philosophy itself. He was fundamentally concerned with rationality, freedom and self-consciousness, but saw them as historical phenomena, developing through an intelligible succession of forms, moved by 'spirit' and structured by 'dialectic'. Hegel's response to Kant provides an initial basis for understanding his difficult texts. His work illuminates the thought of his contemporaries Fichte and Schelling and later idealists as well as features of Marx's writings. Many English-speaking philosophers turned away from Hegelianism after criticism by Russell and Moore at the beginning of the century, but the last 20 years has seen a strong revival of interest in many aspects of Hegel's thought.

1 Introduction

Georg Wilhelm Friedrich Hegel (1770–1831) was born in Stuttgart, Germany, in 1770. He trained as a theologian at the Tübingen theological seminary, where his room-mates were Hölderlin (1770–1843) and Schelling (1775–1854), and throughout his life he remained a devout Lutheran. After a period as a house-tutor in Bern (1793–7) and Frankfurt (1797–1800), he began to lecture, in 1801, at the university of Jena, where Schelling was already professor of philosophy; here he published his first book, on the *Difference between Fichte's and Schelling's System of Philosophy* (1977a), and co-edited with Schelling *The Critical Journal of Philosophy* (published 1802–4). Napoleon's victory at Jena in 1806 interrupted Hegel's career and in 1807 he became editor of a Napoleonic newspaper in Bamberg in Bavaria. His first major work, the *Phenomenology of Spirit* (1977b), was completed in 1806 and published in 1807. In 1808 he became rector of a high-school in Nuremberg, where he married Marie von Tucher in 1811 and published the *Science of Logic* (1969) in three parts between 1812 and 1816. In 1816, he became a professor at Heidelberg and in 1817 published his *Encyclopaedia of the Philosophical Sciences* (1991a), which was originally intended as a bare outline to accompany his lectures but was greatly expanded in further editions in 1827 and

1830. From 1818 until his death (of cholera) in 1831 he was professor of philosophy at Berlin, where he published *The Philosophy of Right* (1991b) in 1821. He was buried in Berlin next to Fichte, his predecessor as professor of philosophy at Berlin. His friends and pupils edited his works posthumously, including his lectures on aesthetics, history, the philosophy of religion and the history of philosophy.

Hegel's first significant writings, produced between 1793 and 1801 but not published until 1907, dealt with religious questions such as 'How did Christianity degenerate from a religion of love into a "positive" religion of rules and dogmas?' and 'Can the complexity and fluidity of the world as religion conceives it be adequately captured in philosophical and conceptual terms?' At this stage he tended to disfavour the methodical rigour of the conceptual understanding. The world is to be conceived in terms of 'life' and 'love', notions which, he held, cannot be captured in philosophical concepts; he preferred the natural simplicity of early Christianity, or of the Greek city-state, to the complex order of modern bourgeois society and its religion. But on moving to Jena he began to develop a philosophy adequate for the conceptualization of the world as a whole, and especially of the modern world. This task occupied him for the rest of his life.

Hegel's Response to Kant

Hegel's knowledge of the philosophy of the past, especially GREEK PHILOSOPHY (chapter 15), was both wide and deep. But the immediate context of his philosophical activity was the thought of KANT (chapter 22) and of the philosophers inspired by it, notably Fichte and Schelling. Like them, Hegel was dissatisfied with Kant's view that we cannot know 'things-in-themselves': Kant's attempt to assign limits to our knowledge is self-defeating, since to be aware of a limit is to transcend it. Hegel often spoke of Kant as a 'subjective idealist' and argued that the categories or thoughts that structure our experience are not, as Kant held, simply imposed by us on our sensory intuitions, but are embedded in the nature of things. He felt that Kant's thought was insufficiently systematic, and that this was largely due to Kant's failure to examine our categories, and their systematic interconnections, in sufficient depth. The categories are not, as Kant supposed, the same for all people at all times; they develop over HISTORY (chapter 13), not haphazardly, but in a way that broadly reflects their logical order. While Kant focused on mathematics and the natural sciences as the primary forms of our categorial knowledge, Hegel regarded every specifically human enterprise – morality, social institutions, political life, art, religion and philosophy – as a way in which we come to understand our world and ourselves; the enterprises are not all of equal status – philosophy, for example, is superior to art – but they all help to domesticate the initially alien world and to make us at home in it. In general, Kant, as Hegel viewed him, accepted the stark oppositions of the understanding: between thought and reality, concept and intuition, duty and inclination and between 'is' and 'ought'; Hegel attempts to overcome these oppositions in a higher synthesis of 'speculative reason'.

2 Phenomenology of Spirit

Hegel developed these ideas reflecting his response to Kant in his lectures at Jena, but he first gave them public, if somewhat chaotic, expression in the *Phenomenology of Spirit* (1977b). The work begins with an EPISTEMOLOGICAL (chapter 1) problem stemming from Kant: if we regard cognition as an instrument that we apply to the object, or else as a medium by which the 'ray' from the object is transmitted to us, we cannot be sure that the object is not distorted by cognition and that access to 'the absolute' (that is, things as they are in themselves) is not forever closed to us.

Hegel proposed to meet this difficulty by examining not objects directly, but the 'forms' of our consciousness of objects, since we cannot coherently suppose that our knowledge of the form of our consciousness is distorted in the same way as our knowledge of objects may be. In this way we can, he believed, survey the rise of knowledge or 'science', since a form of consciousness develops into another, higher form as a result of its internal defects. Thus we begin with 'sense certainty', which attempts to pick out individual items in its experience by means of such terms as 'this', 'here' and 'now'. It finds that it is unable to do this, since such terms are 'universal': anything whatsoever, for example, can be referred to as 'this'. Sense certainty is thus transformed into 'perception', which deals in explicitly universal terms, regarding things as bearers of universal properties. Plagued by its inability to give a coherent account of the relation between a thing and its properties, perception gives way to 'understanding', which views the surface qualities of things as the manifestation of inner forces and the laws that govern them.

The forms of consciousness considered so far are situated in no particular social or historical context. But from now on – beginning with the account of 'self-consciousness', in which two people fight to secure recognition from each other and thus to confirm or realize their self-consciousness – the work becomes a review of human cultural development, examining phases of our history (such as medieval Christianity and the French Revolution) which are nevertheless of general significance. Hegel believed that knowledge is not wholly separate from our religious, moral and political practices; he believed that it is a social, interpersonal enterprise – the work of 'spirit' or of the 'I that is a we and the we that is an I', rather than of a lone individual – and that it changes in an intelligible way from one epoch to another. Since Hegel's own system was the latest phase of this evolution, the *Phenomenology* attempted to record the historical preconditions of its emergence. At the same time it was intended as an introduction to this system. The reader is led by successive stages to the 'absolute knowledge' with which the work concludes. Absolute knowledge is what Hegel himself had; it enabled him to review, in a way that no earlier form of consciousness could, all the forms by which it was reached and to distil the logic that underlay their development.

3 Hegelian Logic

The *Phenomenology* was originally conceived as the first part of Hegel's system, to be followed by logic and the 'sciences' of nature and spirit. He did not fulfil this plan, and the logics that he eventually produced, the *Science of Logic* (1969) and the first volume of the *Encyclopaedia* (1991a), were conceived independently of the *Phenomenology*. (The *Encyclopaedia Logic* is preceded by an alternative Introduction, including a critique of previous German philosophy; a philosophical system cannot dispense with an introduction – however simple and apparently self-evident our starting-point may be, we need to explain why we are able to adopt that starting-point and what is the point of doing so, and this explanation forms an integral part of the system.) Logic is an examination of the abstract thought-determinations or categories that constitute the core of the human mind and are involved (with varying degrees of explicitness) in our ordinary experience and discourse, in our practical activities and institutions, in our systematic ways of understanding the world – such as religion, the sciences and philosophy – and in the very structure of the world itself. The first section of the Logic, the 'Doctrine of Being', examines the categories involved in the surface features of things: it begins with pure being (the obvious starting-point, since it is an all but empty concept, little more than the blank space of our thinking), which 'passes into' nothing, and thus gives rise to 'determinate being', the determinate quality that makes something 'other' than something else. From there it proceeds to 'quantity'. The quantitative features of something, such as the *size* of a field, are initially seen as independent of its quality, of the fact that it is a field, but in the third phase of this section, 'measure', quality and quantity are interdependent: if, for example, a field increases in size sufficiently it becomes a plain or prairie rather than a field, and the measurement of 'intensive' quantities, such as temperature, presupposes abrupt qualitative changes (such as that of water into ice) at certain nodal points on a continuous scale.

The second section, the 'Doctrine of Essence', considers the paired concepts in terms of which scientists and traditional METAPHYSICIANS (chapter 2) have understood the relation between the outer surface of things and their inner nature: these paired concepts include essence and appearance, thing and properties, substance and accident, cause and effect and the reciprocal interaction of substances.

The final section, the 'Doctrine of the Concept', begins with the 'concept', in part as a response to the difficulty of explaining, for example, the growth of a plant in causal terms, without reference to the concept encoded in the seed. But it expands into an account of the forms of 'subjective' logic: universal (such as 'coloured'), particular (such as 'red'), and individual concepts; the types of judgement; and the types of inference or syllogism. (Hegel tended to regard these too as forms not only of our thinking, but also of objective entities such as the solar system and the state.)

Next, Hegel turned to 'objectivity' and considered three increasingly sophisticated ways in which objects are conceived: mechanism, chemism and teleology or purposiveness. Finally he comes to the 'idea', the unification of subjectivity and objectivity. The most primitive version of such unity is 'life'. But from there he proceeds to our attempts to achieve unity on a higher plane, in cognition of 'the true' and in realization of 'the good'. The climax of the Logic is the 'absolute idea', which represents the ultimate unification of subject and object, and serves several purposes in Hegel's system: it represents, for example, the enterprise of logic itself, in which the thinker is not distinct from the thoughts that he or she thinks about – like the *Phenomenology*, the *Logic* concludes with a survey of the steps by which the conclusion was reached. Past logics (such as ARISTOTLE's (chapter 15) or Kant's) were 'finite': they failed to accommodate their *own* thoughts about the thoughts that they described. But Hegel's logic is 'infinite': the absolute idea contains all the thoughts required to think adequately about itself.

4 Nature and Spirit

The absolute idea also represents the relationship between the pure thoughts with which logic deals and the concrete worlds of nature and spirit. It is to these that Hegel turned in the second and third parts of his *Encyclopaedia* (1970, 1971). Nature, in Hegel's view, does not develop over time: its changes are cyclical and repetitive. It does, however, have a complex hierarchical structure, the successive phases of which embody successively higher categories: space, for example, with which the *Philosophy of Nature* (1970) begins, approximates closely to pure being, while the animal organism, with which it concludes, can only be explained in conceptual terms. Hegel did not attempt to deduce the details of nature from logic, but tried to supply from the natural sciences the empirical 'content' of the relatively abstract framework certified by logic. He was not loath, however, to criticize the theories of the day and distinctly preferred the more qualitative theories of Kepler and Goethe to Newtonianism and atomism.

The third main section of the *Encyclopaedia*, the *Philosophy of Mind* (1971), is, like the other sections, subdivided into three parts, dealing respectively with 'subjective spirit' – the INDIVIDUAL MIND (chapter 5), 'objective spirit' – the interpersonal SOCIAL STRUCTURES (chapter 11) that humans create, and 'absolute spirit' – ART (chapter 7), RELIGION (chapter 14) and philosophy. The *Philosophy of Right* (1991b) gives a fuller account of objective spirit or 'right'. Right has three main phases: 'abstract right', in which we become persons in virtue of owning PROPERTY (pp. 265–9) and are governed by LAWS (chapter 12) protecting our persons and property and sanctioned by PUNISHMENT (p. 628) (which is justified not by deterrent or UTILITARIAN (chapter 25) considerations, but solely by the occurrence of an infringement of right); 'MORALITY' (chapter 6), primarily the individual (Kantian) morality of conscience, according to which, for example, one is responsible only for the intended consequences of one's acts; and 'ethics' or 'SOCIAL MORALITY' (chapter 8) (*Sittlichkeit*), the institutions and norms that confer objective rights and duties on us and mould us into fully fledged human beings. Ethics in turn involves three phases: the family, whose members are united by love; 'civil society', the field of economic competition between individuals, whose acquisitive drives are nevertheless moderated by laws, policing and 'estates' (classes) and 'corporations' (trade guilds); and the STATE (pp. 265–9), which restores humans to unity on a higher level and makes them citizens rather than simply economic agents.

Spirit and the State

Hegel's state is a fairly liberal (but not very democratic) constitutional monarchy, designed to reconcile the rights secured by the French Revolution with social stability. It accords its citizens *both* 'objective' freedom, which involves a conformity between the rationality of the social order and the rationality that constitutes the deepest level of their selfhood, and a degree of 'subjective' freedom, which involves the freedom to make personal and moral choices, and which was unknown in the Greek city-state. A state is essentially one of a system of states and it must engage in warfare to maintain its unity by drawing the citizens together out of their private INTERESTS (p. 629). States which fail to do this fall into decay. A people or nation forming a state has a 'spirit' of its own, a way of thinking and acting that pervades its social and political life. The successive rise and fall of states constitutes 'world history', a history that is not haphazard, but rational, each national spirit being intelligibly related to its predecessors. Hegel marks this by viewing history as the work of a single spirit, the 'world-spirit', which circuitously realizes its final goal, the freedom and self-consciousness of humanity, by exploiting the passions of human agents who are only dimly aware of the purposes they serve. The spirit of a people informs not only its historic deeds, but also its art, religion and philosophy, though at higher levels these tend to become less marked by national peculiarities. They are the main ways by which a person gains insight into the world and into himself or herself; in art a person does so in a sensory form, in religion in the form of imagination or *Vorstellung*, and in philosophy by pure thought.

---

5 Dialectic and System

Hegel's system is knit together by dialectic, and dialectic also operates in the natural and spiritual realms in virtue of the thoughts embodied in them. 'Dialectic' derives from the Greek for the 'art of conversation, dialogue'. Hegel's dialectic does not, however, involve a dialogue between philosophers or between the philosopher and his or her subject matter. The dialectical 'movement' is intrinsic to the subject matter, such as forms of consciousness or categories, and the philosopher simply watches their development. Often, if not invariably, this involves the resolution of two opposites in a higher unity: for example, the simple unity of the family proves to be inadequate (or 'contradictory') on its own and thus gives rise to its opposite or 'negation', civil society, which is characterized by the individualism that enables its members to develop their own personalities and interests; but this in turn proves defective, and requires for its completion the higher unity of the state, the 'negation of the negation' which 'sublates', or at once destroys, preserves and elevates, the two opposites. Historical processes also exemplify this dialectic: for example, the unified city-state of antiquity gives way to the individualism of modernity, but Hegel's proposed state reconciles the two, giving free play to individualism while containing it within the differentiated unity of the state.

Another feature of dialectic is that Spirit essentially reflects on itself: for instance, logic is thinking about thoughts, the philosopher reflects on past philosophies and the historian reflects on historical events. But in reflecting on itself, spirit changes itself: to think about a thought we need more complex thoughts; in thinking about other philosophies, we develop a new philosophy; historical writing raises humans to a new level of awareness and thus changes the patterns of their thought and conduct. Thus spirit advances by continually reflecting on itself. This way of proceeding is often combined with the resolution of oppositions: for example, Hegel, in reflecting on apparently opposed philosophies (such as SPINOZA's monism (chapter 17) and LEIBNIZ's pluralism (chapter 17)), attempts to sublate them in an overarching unity.

This feature of Hegel's thought raises a difficulty. Do reflection and the resolution of oppositions come to an end or proceed to infinity? For example, are his logic and his philosophy complete in the sense that further reflection on them will generate no new categories not already contained in them, and that logic and philosophy are thus at an end? Has history come to an end in his own time or is there more to come (perhaps, as he occasionally suggests, in Russia or America), even if we cannot predict what it will be? On such questions as these Hegel was ineradicably ambiguous.

Human beings think not only about themselves and their thoughts, but about what is, initially at least, other than thought, namely, 'nature'. Thoughts are implicit in nature, but only gradually do humans make them explicit by their theoretical and practical activities, domesticating nature and coming to see it as a projection or extension of themselves. This is why Hegel regarded himself as an idealist: he believed not only that mind (or minds) exist, but, firstly, that the thoughts that constitute the core of the human mind are also implicitly embedded in things, and, secondly, that nature is progressively sublated or 'idealized' by the spiritual activities of human beings. We thereby achieve freedom, since freedom consists in self-determination, in not being determined by an 'other', and nature is now seen as being no longer starkly other than ourselves. Freedom is also enhanced by a person's self-understanding, which advances along with his or her understanding of nature. The workings of history and of the societies we inhabit, as well as the logical structures that underlie them, become increasingly perspicuous to us. Thus the growth of our self-consciousness accompanies that of our freedom.

Hegel held that his philosophical system expresses in the form of thought the essential 'content' of Trinitarian Christianity. In religious imagery, God the Father 'alienates' or externalizes himself by producing a natural world (the 'son') as the object of his 'consciousness', and becomes self-conscious in the spiritual reclamation that people make of nature and of themselves (the 'holy spirit'). In conceptual terms, the 'logical idea', the system of concepts studied by logic, 'freely releases itself' into nature which is then spiritualized by human beings. The question whether this amounts to atheism or not is another of those ambiguities (along with his attitudes to the political *status quo* and to the future course of history) that are intrinsic to his thought. Not surprisingly his followers divided into 'right', 'left' and 'centre' Hegelians, according to whether they were conservatives, radicals or moderate reformers in religious and political matters. Hegel's immense influence – in Germany, (on D. F. Strauss, Feuerbach and Marx), Britain (on Bradley, Bosanquet and McTaggart), Italy (on Gentile and Croce) and in France (on Kojève, Sartre and Derrida) – depends in large measure on the comprehensive richness of his thought and its accompanying ambiguity.

Further Reading

For a reliable and interesting account of Hegel's life and works, W. Kaufmann, *Hegel: Reinterpretation, Texts and Commentary* (1965) is still unsurpassed. The best brief general studies of Hegel's thought are G. R. G. Mure, *The Philosophy of Hegel* (1965) and I. Soll, *An Introduction to Hegel's Metaphysics* (1969). The philosophical background to his thought is lucidly presented by F. Copleston, *A History of Philosophy* Vol. VII, Part I: *Fichte to Hegel* (1965), and the essays in S. Priest (ed.) *Hegel's Critique of Kant* (1987) explore in more detail his relationship to Kant. The complexities of Hegel's terminology are unravelled in M. Inwood, *A Hegel Dictionary* (1992). Longer general studies include J. N. Findlay, *Hegel: A Re-examination* (1958), C. Taylor, *Hegel* (1975), and M. Inwood, *Hegel* (1983). On particular aspects of Hegel's thought, G. D. O'Brien, *Hegel on Reason and History* (1975), A. W. Wood, *Hegel's Ethical Thought* (1990), and M. Forster, *Hegel's Idea of a Phenomenology of Spirit* (1993) are to be recommended. Essays on various aspects of his thought and its influence are to be found in M. Inwood (ed.), *Hegel* (1985), F. Beiser (ed.), *The Cambridge Companion to Hegel* (1993), and R. Stern (ed.), *G. W. F. Hegel: Critical Assessments* (1993).

References

Hegel

Hegel, G. W. F. 1948 [1793–1800]: *Early Theological Writings* (translated by T. M. Knox). Chicago: University of Chicago Press.
—— 1977a [1801]: *Difference Between Fichte's and Schelling's System of Philosophy* (translated by H. S. Harris and W. Cert). New York: SUNY.
—— 1986 [1804–5]: *The Jena System 1804–5: Logic and Metaphysics* (translated by J. S. Burbidge and G. di Giovanni). Montreal and Kingston: McGill-Queen's University Press.

—— 1983 [1805–6]: *Hegel and the Human Spirit: A Translation of the Jena Lectures on the Philosophy of Spirit (1805–6) with Commentary* (translated by L. Rauch). Detroit: Wayne State University Press.

—— 1977b [1807]: *Phenomenology of Spirit* (translated by A. V. Miller). Oxford: Clarendon Press.

—— 1969 [1812–16]: *Science of Logic* (revised edn 1832) (translated by A. V. Miller). London: Allen and Unwin.

—— 1991a [1817]: *The Encyclopaedia Logic* (Pt. 1 of the *Encyclopaedia of the Philosophical Sciences*) (revised edns 1827, 1830, with posthumous edns 1840–5) (translated by T. F. Geraets, H. S. Harris and W. A. Suchting). Indianapolis: Hackett. Also translated by W. Wallace as *Hegel's Logic*, Oxford: Clarendon Press, 1975.

—— 1970 [1817]: *Philosophy of Nature* (Pt. 2 of the *Encyclopaedia*), (translated by A. V. Miller). Oxford: Clarendon Press. Also translated by M. J. Petry, 3 vols. London: Allen and Unwin.

—— 1971 [1817]: *Philosophy of Mind* (Pt. 3 of the *Encyclopaedia*) (1830 edn translated by W. Wallace and A. V. Miller). Oxford: Clarendon Press.

—— 1991b [1821]: *The Philosophy of Right* (translated by H. B. Nisbet, edited by A. W. Wood). Cambridge: Cambridge University Press. Also translated by T. M. Knox, Oxford: Clarendon Press, 1942.

—— 1975a [1835]: *Aesthetics: Lectures on Fine Art* (revised edn 1842), 2 vols, (translated by T. M. Knox). Oxford: Clarendon Press. Also translated by B. Bosanquet, edited by M. Inwood, as *Introductory Lectures on Aesthetics*, Harmondsworth: Penguin, 1993.

—— 1975b [1837, 1840]: *Lectures on the Philosophy of World History: Introduction: Reason in History* (translated by H. B. Nisbet). Cambridge: Cambridge University Press. Also translated by L. Rauch from a less recently edited text, as *Introduction to the Philosophy of History*, Indianapolis: Hackett, 1988.

—— 1984–6 [1832, 1840]: *Lectures on the Philosophy of Religion* (translated by P. Hodgson, R. F. Brown and J. M. Stewart). Berkeley: University of California Press. Also translated by E. B. Speirs and J. B. Sanderson, 3 vols, from a less recently edited text, London: Kegan Paul, 1895.

—— 1892–6: *Lectures on the History of Philosophy*, 3 vols (translated by E. S. Haldane and F. H. Simson). London: Kegan Paul. Also translated by T. M. Knox and A. V. Miller, *Introduction to the Lectures on the History of Philosophy*, Oxford: Clarendon Press, 1985.

Other writers

Beiser, F. (ed.) 1993: *The Cambridge Companion to Hegel*. Cambridge: Cambridge University Press.

Copleston, F. 1965: *A History of Philosophy*, vol. VII, Part I: *Fichte to Hegel*. New York: Doubleday.

Findlay, J. N. 1958: *Hegel: A Re-examination*. London: Allen and Unwin.

Forster, M. 1993: *Hegel's Idea of a Phenomenology of Spirit*. Cambridge, MA: Harvard University Press.

Inwood, M. 1983: *Hegel*. London: Routledge and Kegan Paul.

—— (ed.) 1985: *Hegel*. Oxford: Oxford University Press.

—— 1992: *A Hegel Dictionary*. Oxford: Blackwell.

Kaufmann, W. 1965: *Hegel: Reinterpretation, Texts and Commentary*. London: Weidenfeld and Nicolson.

Mure, G. R. G. 1965: *The Philosophy of Hegel*. London: Oxford University Press.

O'Brien, G. D. 1975: *Hegel on Reason and History*. Chicago: University of Chicago Press.

Priest, S. (ed.) 1987: *Hegel's Critique of Kant*. Oxford: Clarendon Press.

Soll, I. 1969: *An Introduction to Hegel's Metaphysics*. Chicago: University of Chicago Press.

Stern, R. (ed.) 1993: *G. W. F. Hegel: Critical Assessments*. London: Routledge.

Taylor, C. 1975: *Hegel*. Cambridge: Cambridge University Press.

Wood, A. W. 1990: *Hegel's Ethical Thought*. Cambridge: Cambridge University Press.

Discussion Questions

1 Does Hegel refute Kant's view that things-in-themselves are unknowable?

2 In what sense, if any, is Hegel an idealist?

3 Does the *Phenomenology of Spirit* have a coherent plan?

4 Can we have self-consciousness without conflict?

5 What is dialectic?

6 Is Hegel's 'logic' really logic?

7 Does Hegel have any good reason for believing that philosophy must be systematic?

8 Can Hegel give a coherent account of the transition from logic to nature?

9 What use does Hegel make of the notion of infinity?

10 What is spirit?

11 Do we need objective freedom as well as subjective freedom?

12 Is history rational?

13 Is Hegel committed to the view that history has come to an end?

14 Was Hegel an atheist?

15 Is it plausible to suppose that art, religion and philosophy have the same 'content'?

24

Marx

Richard Norman

The writings of Karl Marx span many disciplines besides philosophy, such as history, economics, and political and social theory. This chapter reviews recent work on the philosophical aspects of his theory of history, and on his view of ethics, in order to suggest that the connections between those two themes are essential to an understanding of Marx's philosophical significance.

1 Introduction

For a period of about 20 years after the 1939–45 war, Marx's ideas were given little serious academic attention. There were exceptions, such as Popper's influential book *The Open Society and its Enemies* (1945), but on the whole Marx was ignored by philosophy as he was by other intellectual disciplines. Since then, there has been a veritable explosion of serious interest in him, beginning in the late 1960s with the period of political radicalism in the universities of western Europe and North America. A huge amount has been written on all aspects of his thought – far more than I can do justice to in this chapter. I shall concentrate on just two themes which have been prominent in recent philosophical discussions of Marx: his theory of HISTORY (chapter 13), and his view of ETHICS (chapter 6).

The revival of serious interest in Marx's philosophy initially took a form which threw new light on his ethics. This was the discovery of his early writings, unpublished in his lifetime and for many years thereafter. In particular his *Economic and Philosophical Manuscripts*, written in 1844, first published in 1932 and first translated into English in 1959, reveal a whole new dimension of his thought. A key concept here is that of 'alienation', a term which Marx took over from HEGEL (chapter 23) and used to describe the relation of workers to their product and to their productive activity within a capitalist system of production. The workers' own labour, and the products of that labour, come to dominate and enslave them. Because their work is imposed on them by others and its products are appropriated by others, work lacks all meaning for the workers themselves. Instead of being a source of fulfilment through the employment of mental and physical energy, it 'mortifies his body and ruins his mind'. It thereby alienates the worker from his or her very humanity.

Marx's theory of alienation confirms the view that, at least in his early writings, Marx condemns capitalism not just for its historical obsolescence but because of its effects on the lives of those who live and work within such a system. The concept of 'alienation' also serves as a moral tool with which to criticize more than just the workings of a capitalist economy. Economic alienation is only one aspect of alienation. Other forms of it are religious alienation, which involves a human being's self-abasement before beings that are the product of his or her own imagination, and political alienation, which involves the domination of human beings by the state which is created and sustained through their own activity. One obvious reason why Marx's early writings received so much attention when they were discovered is that they showed very clearly the moral distance between Marx's own ideas and the character of self-proclaimed 'Marxist' regimes such as that in the Soviet Union.

The philosophical interest of the early writings was also that they revealed a distinctive and positive ethical theory lying behind the concept of 'alienation'. It is a theory in the same tradition as ARISTOTLE's (chapter 15) account of eudaimonia and MILL's (chapter 25) account of the 'higher pleasures': the view that the good life for human beings consists in the full actualization of their distinctively human capacities. For Marx, however, these capacities are not just intellectual and theoretical; they are, above all, practical – the capacity for free creative work which transforms the external world and gives it a human significance. A human being 'duplicates himself not only intellectually, in his mind, but also actively in reality and thus can look at his image in a world he has created' (Marx, 1977, p. 82). Alienated labour thwarts these capacities for self-objectification and self-realization. It de-humanizes human beings and the world they have created.

The discovery of these early writings generated controversy about their relation to Marx's later work. Some commentators saw an essential continuity. They could point to the passages in *Capital* (1867) and other economic writings where Marx describes how, 'within the capitalist system . . . all means for the development of production transform themselves into means of domination over, and exploitation of, the producers', and 'mutilate the labourer into a fragment of a man' (Marx, 1977, p. 482). Other commentators, however, regarded the theory of alienation and Marx's later theory of history as incompatible. The foremost advocate of this view was the French philosopher Louis ALTHUSSER (p. 714), whose 'structuralist Marxism' posited a decisive 'epistemological break' between Marx's early 'humanism' and the later 'scientific' writings. Althusserian Marxism was for a time the height of intellectual fashion. I do not intend to discuss it here, and do not find much of value in it, but it did serve as a reminder that the core of Marx's work is to be found in his mature social and historical theory, and that any philosophical engagement with Marx must come to terms with that work.

2 Marx and Analytical Marxism

A landmark in the study of Marx's mature work was the publication in 1978 of Cohen's book *Karl Marx's Theory of History: a Defence*. Cohen drew explicitly on the techniques and style of analytical philosophy in the attempt to introduce a new clarity and rigour into the exposition and defence of Marx's theory. The three main achievements of Cohen's book are: firstly, the provision of a clear and precise conceptual apparatus for Marx's theory; secondly, a general exposition and defence of the thesis of 'the primacy of productive forces'; and thirdly, the claim that the kind of explanation employed in Marxian theory is 'functional explanation'.

Cohen takes as a definitive text Marx's 1859 Preface to his *Critique of Political Economy*. The theory sketched there identifies three levels of social life: (1) the 'productive forces' (tools and materials, skills and techniques), to which there correspond (2) 'relations of production' which constitute the 'economic structure' and which give rise to (3) 'a legal and political superstructure' and 'forms of social consciousness'. Earlier critics of Marx, such as Acton and Plamenatz, had argued that the theory was incoherent because these three levels were not in fact distinct. Cohen therefore provides clear definitions of these concepts in order to show that the three levels can in fact be distinguished and that it is possible for Marx to make precise and definite claims about the explanatory relations between them. The essential claims are that the character of non-economic institutions is largely explained by the nature of the economic structure, and that the nature of the economic structure (that is, the set of relations of production) is largely explained by the level of development of the productive forces. Cohen refers to the second claim as 'the primacy of the productive forces', and, after providing textual evidence that Marx made this claim, he proceeds to offer his own general defence of it.

The first stage is the defence of a preliminary claim which Cohen calls 'the Development Thesis': that the productive forces tend to develop throughout history. He then suggests that the stronger Primacy Thesis can be defended on the basis of the Development Thesis together with a further fact: that a given level of productive power is compatible only with certain types of economic structure. For example, a society based on computer technology could not be a slave society. Therefore, though productive forces can develop within a given set of production relations, that development is liable to reach a point at which it is no longer compatible with those production relations. When this happens, it is to be expected that the incompatibility will be resolved by the alteration of the production relations, since otherwise further development of the productive forces would be impossible, and this is denied by the Development Thesis.

Cohen does not offer any similar general argument for the claim that the economic structure in turn largely explains the character of non-economic institutions, and I shall come back later to this omission, but I turn now to his third important contribution: his account of the kind of explanation employed by Marx's theory.

Marx and Functional Explanation

Marx's explanations, Cohen argues, are functional explanations. These are explanations of the form 'F occurs because it brings about E'. Such explanations appear to be employed in other fields, for example in biology, in statements such as 'Birds have hollow bones because hollow bones facilitate flight'. Such statements have a complex structure. The initial explanatory claim is that F brings about E, but the wider explanatory claim is then that F itself occurs *because* it brings about E. Attributing to Marx the use of functional explanations has the attraction of removing a puzzle in Marxian theory. Marx is clearly committed to the claims that production relations facilitate the growth of productive forces, and similarly that superstructural institutions help to sustain the economic structure. This seems to suggest that the relations explain the forces, and that superstructures explain economic structures, which seems to run directly counter to the central claims of the theory. Those claims are, however, that the relations of production obtain *because* they facilitate the growth of productive forces, and that the superstructural institutions have the particular character that they have *because* they thereby help to sustain the economic structure.

The use of functional explanations is, however, contentious, and their value is strongly contested by Elster, another philosopher associated with ANALYTICAL MARXISM (pp. 273–5). The mere fact that something has beneficial consequences is not, according to Elster (1985), sufficient to explain it. Consider as an example the crude explanations offered by some Marxists for the existence of racism: it divides the working class, and thereby serves the interests of the ruling class. Elster would say of this example that, though it may be true that racism serves the interests of the ruling class, this does not in itself provide any grounds for asserting that that is *why* racism exists. No explanation has been given unless we can cite a *mechanism*, an account of *how* racism is explained by its tendency to promote the interests of the ruling class. Such a mechanism might be identified by, for instance, a 'conspiracy theory' which claimed that racism was deliberately fostered by members of the ruling class in order to promote their interests. But evidence for this would have to be cited, and in the absence of such evidence no explanation has been given. Elster does not think that the misuse of functional explanation is confined to crude versions of Marxism. Marx's own work, he suggests, is flawed by the reliance on unsupported functional explanations. Marx offers no account of *how* the need to promote the development of productive forces explains the emergence of new production relations. The mechanism is supposed to be found in the operation of class conflict, but Marx would have to explain how the existing constraints on the growth of productive forces motivate the members of a class to change the relations of production, and this he fails to do. More seriously still, Marx's theory of history relies not just on unsupported functional explanations that invoke beneficial consequences for groups of human beings, but also on vague speculative explanations of social change and social institutions that promote the goals of supposed impersonal agents such as 'History' or 'Capital'.

Cohen would agree with Elster on the desirability of specifying a mechanism in order to back up a functional explanation. The real disagreement between them is that Elster thinks that functional explanations are worthless without such backing, whereas Cohen thinks that even if we cannot specify a mechanism, functional explanations may still explain, though they would explain more fully if they could be elaborated. What Cohen does recognize is that, though functional explanations may lack an elaboration, they do, like ordinary causal explanations, have to be backed by a *generalization*. The mere fact that F has a functional effect E in a particular case does not constitute an explanation of F; but it becomes a relevant explanation if it can be backed by a generalization of the form 'Whenever F would bring about a functional effect E, F occurs'.

3 Explaining Superstructure and Ideology

I think it is fair to say that Cohen does not specify in any detail the kinds of generalization that would back the functional explanations in Marx's theory of history, and that Cohen's own defence of that theory does not appeal to such generalizations. That defence, as outlined above, concentrates primarily on the role of productive forces in explaining the relations of production, but I want now to look briefly at the second level of Marxian explanation, the role of the economic structure in explaining legal and political institutions (the 'super-structure') and forms of consciousness ('ideology'). It is here that the question of what kind of generalization we are looking for intersects with another important problem: the question of the *scope* of Marx's 'economic deter-minism'.

Marx sometimes appears to claim that *all* legal and political institutions and *all* forms of consciousness can be explained by reference to the economic structure. This claim is wildly implausible. I shall not argue the point here, I shall simply assume that the claim has to be qualified in some way. The problem is then that the theory is in danger of becoming vague or vacuous. From Engels onwards, Marxists have taken refuge in such phrases as that the economic structure is determinant 'ultimately' or 'in the last instance', and it is notoriously difficult to pin down what such claims mean or how they could be assessed. Cohen has tackled the problem in his more recent writing, and has distinguished between 'inclusive' and 'restricted' construals of historical materialism. Whatever the appropriate general formulation, I take it that the explanatory power of historical materialism must be looked for in its capacity to explain *specific* superstructural and ideological phenomena: this particular institution, this particular theory or belief, are as they are because they help to sustain a particular structure of relations of production.

This now returns us to the question of the kind of generalization that could back such a claim. The claim would be, for instance, that liberal-democratic political institutions, or liberal-individualist theories of political freedom, prevail because they help to legitimate and support market economies, and this would be backed by the generalization that such institutions, or such theories, emerge and become dominant precisely when they can help to sustain market economies. There is a certain plausibility in this. In the case of my two examples, it may well be possible to show that liberal-democratic institutions and liberal theories of freedom are particularly well suited to market economies, and it is then a striking general fact that those institutions and theories come to the fore in just those historical circumstances where they can serve that function. This, however, does not settle the question of explanatory primacy. An alternative 'idealist' account would be that these institutions or these theories have been adopted because human beings have good *reasons* for adopting them, because they are in some appropriate sense 'good' institutions or theories; if they also happen to support certain kinds of economic structures, it is not surprising that they have done so, but that is not why they have been adopted. To support the functional explanation, then, something more than the generalization is needed. We have to be able to claim that the institution or the theory would not have been adopted *unless* it served to sustain the economic structure. The problem of how we can support counterfactual historical statements of this form is a notoriously difficult one, but I want to suggest that in such a context a plausible candidate to support it would be some kind of *normative* judgement: the institution or theory can be shown to be flawed or defective in some way, and *that* is why we are inclined to say that it would not have been adopted unless it served this function in relation to the economic structure.

4 Marxist Ethics

It is in the light of this suggestion that I want to return finally to the question of Marx's view of ethics, a topic that has been the subject of voluminous debate in the past 20 years. Marx regularly spoke of morality as a typical example of ideology, implying that all moral beliefs are by their very nature a product of class interests and class standpoints, that they are relative to particular social and historical conditions and that they can have no independent rational validity. However, Marx himself also seemed to be committed to his own moral judgements about the oppressive and exploitative character of class societies, and in particular about the degrading and dehumanizing conditions of work in the capitalist societies of his own day. As Lukes puts it, we then seem driven to the conclusion that 'Marxism's attitude to morality is paradoxical' (Lukes, 1985, p. 1).

The most promising way of attempting to resolve the paradox is to distinguish between different forms of morality. Lukes proposes a distinction between the morality of *Recht*, that is of JUSTICE AND RIGHTS (chapter 8) and the morality of *emancipation*, and suggests that 'the paradox in marxism's attitude to morality is resolved once we see that it is the morality of *Recht* that it condemns as ideological and anachronistic, and the morality of emancipation that it adopts as its own' (p. 29). This distinction, however, has to be qualified in various ways. On the one side, it is not clear that Marx would regard his own use of the language of 'emancipation' as an appeal to *morality*. Not all condemnation of aspects of human life counts as 'moral' condemnation, and Marx may have been quite consistent in maintaining that moral forms of condemnation are intrinsically ideological whilst other forms of condemnation are not. What is obviously needed here is some more precise account of the difference between 'the moral point of view' and other forms of evaluation.

The other qualification needed to Lukes' distinction is that, as he recognizes, Marx's attitude to the morality of *Recht* is not simple. Wood (1981) and others have argued that Marx did not regard capitalism as unjust. For Marx, the concept of justice is essentially a *juridical* concept. As such, it is a component in a set of rules by which a particular mode of production is regulated. Each historical mode of production has its own appropriate set of JURIDICAL INSTITUTIONS (chapter 12) and concepts. Therefore, from the standpoint of the juridical framework appropriate to the capitalist mode of production, particular acts may be unjust but capitalism itself cannot be. Other commentators, however, have pointed to passages in which Marx did appear to criticize injustice from a standpoint which transcends that of capitalism. Lukes suggests that 'Marx's view of capitalism's justice was both internally complex and hierarchically organized' (p. 58). Marx did identify a conception of justice which is internal to the capitalist mode of production, but he also criticized it from an external standpoint. This is the standpoint of 'the first phase of communist society', as Marx called it in his *Critique of the Gotha Programme* (1875). It is the standpoint defined by the principle that each individual should be rewarded in proportion to the labour he or she has contributed. That standpoint, however, will itself be transcended in the 'higher phase of communist society', embodying the principle, 'To each according to his needs'. The latter is not itself a principle of *justice*; it is the expression of a society of abundance in which juridical principles regulating the social allocation of goods are no longer necessary. Lukes goes on to criticize Marx's assumption that principles of justice can eventually be dispensed with. This assumption, he thinks, has diverted the Marxist tradition from the necessary search for an adequate account of justice and rights, and has left the way open for the appalling injustices and violations of human rights committed by 'Marxist' political movements and regimes.

Marx's ethical theory, then, is complex and contentious. I doubt whether it is possible to arrive at any definitive conclusion about it. His remarks on the subject are too brief, scattered, and contradictory for there to be such a thing as 'what Marx really thought' about ethics. My own concluding suggestion is simply a view about what is philosophically fruitful in Marx's approach to ethics, and it is a view which links it with my comments about his theory of history. That theory, I have indicated, is neither plausible nor helpful when formulated as a general theory which purports to explain *all* political and legal institutions and *all* forms of consciousness as products of an economic structure. I also suggested that, when interpreted as a more selective theory which explains *specific* institutions and forms of consciousness, it depends for its plausibility on being also a *critical* theory. Particular institutions, beliefs or theories are criticized as being flawed or defective in ways that can be explained when it is seen how they serve to sustain a particular economic structure and the power of a particular class. The same judgement now has to be made of Marx's ethical theory. Whatever Marx himself may have said, his theory is self-defeating if it is understood as the claim that *all* values are socially and historically relative and are the expression of specific class interests and positions. It is most fruitful when understood as a critical account of how particular values and ethical beliefs come to be distorted by reflecting a limited class standpoint and class interests. And there is of course a particular reason why Marx's ethical theory needs to be interpreted as being selective, not as all-inclusive; for if what Marx offers is a critical theory, it must itself appeal to values, and cannot therefore treat all values as the ideological by-products of economic structures. Marx's theory needs its own values.

Further Reading

No one work by Marx encapsulates his contributions to philosophy, and the use of an anthology is essential. A useful collection is the one edited by McLellan (Marx, 1977). A good brief general introduction to Marx's thought is that by Singer (1980). When completed, the best scholarly resource in English for advanced work will be Marx and Engels' *Collected Works* (1975–).

Popper's influential criticisms of Marx, and in particular of Marx's historicism, can be found in Volume 2 of his *The Open Society and its Enemies* (1945). Other important critical discussions of Marx's theory of history are those by Acton (1955) and Plamenatz (1954, 1963). Cohen's *Karl Marx's Theory of History* (1978) is strongly recommended. Some of Cohen's more recent work, both amplifying and modifying his earlier discussion, is collected in his *History, Labour, and Freedom* (1988). Elster's interpretation and assessment of Marx is set out at length in his *Making Sense of Marx* (1985), and much more briefly and readably in his *An Introduction to Karl Marx* (1986). There is good material on the theory of history in McMurtry (1978), Shaw (1978) and Wood (1981); Wood is also the most convenient general guide to Marx from a philosophical point of view. The best introduction to the debate on Marx and ethics is Lukes' *Marxism and Morality* (1985). Essays on the subject are collected in Cohen, Nagel and Scanlon (eds) (1980), in Nielsen and Patten (eds) (1981), and in Ware and Nielsen (eds) (1989). Nielsen's *Marxism and the Moral Point of View* is another useful guide. Wood's position is set out in an article in the collection by Cohen, Nagel and Scanlon (eds) (1980) and in his 1981 book. On Marx's concept of alienation, see Plamenatz (1975), Ollman (1971) and Meszaros (1972).

References

Acton, H. B. 1955: *The Illusion of the Epoch*. London: Cohen and West. Reprinted 1972, Routledge and Kegan Paul.
Cohen, G. A. 1978: *Karl Marx's Theory of History: a Defence*. Oxford: Oxford University Press.
—— 1988: *History, Labour, and Freedom*. Oxford: Oxford University Press.
Cohen, M., Nagel, T. and Scanlon, T. (eds) 1980: *Marx, Justice, and History*. Princeton: Princeton University Press.

Elster, J. 1985: *Making Sense of Marx*. Cambridge: Cambridge University Press.
—— 1986: *An Introduction to Karl Marx*. Cambridge: Cambridge University Press.
Lukes, S. 1985: *Marxism and Morality*. Oxford: Oxford University Press.
McMurtry, J. 1978: *The Structure of Marx's World-View*. Princeton: Princeton University Press.
Meszaros, I. 1970: *Marx's Theory of Alienation*. London: The Merlin Press.
Nielsen, K. 1988: *Marxism and the Moral Point of View*. Boulder: Westview Press.
Nielsen, K. and Patten, S. C. (eds) (1981): *Marx and Morality*. Canadian Journal of Philosophy, Supplementary Volume 7, Guelph: Canadian Association for Publishing in Philosophy.
Ollman, B. 1971: *Alienation*. New York and Cambridge: Cambridge University Press.
Plamenatz, J. 1954: *German Marxism and Russian Communism*. London: Longman.
—— 1963: *Man and Society*, vol. 2. London: Longman.
—— 1975: *Karl Marx's Philosophy of Man*. Oxford: Oxford University Press.
Popper, K. R. 1945: *The Open Society and its Enemies*, vol. 2. London: Routledge and Kegan Paul.
Shaw, W. 1978: *Marx's Theory of History*. Stanford: Stanford University Press.
Singer, P. 1980: *Marx*. Oxford: Oxford University Press.
Ware, R. and Nielsen, K. (eds) 1989: *Analyzing Marxism*. Canadian Journal of Philosophy, Supplementary Volume 15, Calgary: University of Calgary Press.
Wood, A. 1981: *Karl Marx*. London: Routledge and Kegan Paul.

Marx

Dates given in square brackets are dates of final composition, except for *Capital*, vol. 1, which was completed in 1865–6 and published in 1867.

Marx, K. 1977: *Selected Writings* (edited by D. McLellan). Oxford: Oxford University Press.
—— [1844]: *Economic and Philosophical Manuscripts*. In Marx (1977).
—— 1971 [1857–8]: *Grundrisse* (translated by M. Nicolaus). London: Penguin.
—— [1859]: Preface to *A Critique of Political Economy*. In Marx (1977).
—— [1864]: *Capital*, vol. 3 (translated by E. Untermann). London: Lawrence and Wishart.
—— [1867]: *Capital*, vol. 1 (translated by S. Moore and E. Aveling). London: Lawrence and Wishart.
—— [1875]: *Critique of the Gotha Programme*. In Marx (1977).
Marx, K. and Engels, F. (1975–): *Collected Works*, 58 vols. London: Lawrence and Wishart.

Discussion Questions

1   What is alienation? Does Marx's account succeed in explaining why people, in some societies at least, are alienated?

2   Are intellectual capacities or practical capacities more important for realizing the good life for human beings?

3   Can the style and techniques of analytical philosophy help us to understand and assess Marx's historical materialism?

4   Should we accept the primacy of productive forces in explaining social phenomena?

5 If there are levels of social life, how can we determine which aspects of society belong to each level?

6 How can we assess the claim that the economic structure is determinant 'in the last instance'?

7 If historical materialism cannot explain all the main features of society, can it explain any of them?

8 Can features of the legal and political superstructure and ideology of a society be explained by the nature of its economic structure? What other hypotheses are worth considering?

9 What are functional explanations? Can we interpret Marx's explanations as functional explanations?

10 Are functional explanations justified only for institutions or theories that are flawed or defective in some way?

11 Was Marx's attitude toward morality paradoxical? If so, can the paradox be overcome?

12 Can we eventually dispense with principles of justice and rights?

13 If Marx's theory needs its own values, can it treat all values as the ideological by-products of economic structures?

25

Bentham, Mill and Sidgwick ——————

Ross Harrison

Jeremy Bentham (1748–1832), John Stuart Mill (1806–73) and Henry Sidgwick (1838–1900) are the leading representative thinkers of the British utilitarian tradition. Bentham declared at the start of his first work, *A Fragment on Government* (1968–) (published in 1776) that the 'fundamental axiom' is that 'it is the greatest happiness of the greatest number that is the measure of right and wrong'. Happiness (or, as Bentham otherwise called it, utility) is hence taken as the unique measure of value.

Bentham was chiefly concerned with the applications of this fundamental principle. He was a practical thinker, centrally interested in making improvements in the real world. With J. S. Mill we get a more nuanced statement of the central principle aided by a more subtle surrounding psychology. His chief work in this area was his *Utilitarianism* (1963–) (which appeared as a sequence of articles in 1861 and as a book in 1863). Finally, Sidgwick in his *Methods of Ethics* (1874) criticized Mill but also added a more complete epistemological base for utilitarianism.

Recent work on these three has been much more on Bentham and Mill than on Sidgwick, and this balance will be followed here. In particular, in the last 30 years there has been a sustained revisionary interpretation of Mill, which has removed him from the criticisms of previous standard commentators. Since the central focus of attention in this chapter is with this recent work, the order of exposition will not follow chronological order. Instead, it moves between the original texts and recent commentators, and also back and forward between Bentham and Mill.

1 The Central Idea

It is simplest to take the central idea of utilitarianism from Bentham. In the first chapter of his major work *An Introduction to the Principles of Morals and Legislation* (1968–) Bentham says that 'by utility is meant that property in any object, whereby it tends to produce benefit, advantage, pleasure, good, or happiness (all this in the present case comes to the same thing) or (what comes again to the same thing) to prevent the happening of mischief, pain, evil, or unhappiness'. The key point is that there is a single source of VALUE (p. 199), which can be indifferently called utility, happiness, or pleasure. This is to be maximized.

Utilitarianism, Bentham's ethic, is a consequentialist ethic. Things are to be measured and evaluated by their actual and possible consequences. Right action is justified by future states of affairs rather than by past events. For example, Bentham's account of the justification of punishment is a deterrent account. PUNISHMENT (p. 611) is justified if it deters people from committing undesirable actions. It is justified, that is, by the prevention of future harms rather than by retribution for past wicked acts. More precisely, the proper aim of punishment for Bentham, as of anything else, is to produce pleasure and to prevent pain. Yet all punishment is in itself unpleasant, a pain. It can therefore only be justified for Bentham if this particular pain is the cause of a greater reduction in pain elsewhere. So if people are deterred by a punishment from doing things which would otherwise produce more pain (such as, for example, rape, theft or murder), then that punishment will be justified. If there are two alternative punishments, each of which would produce less pain than the actions they would deter, then the least painful option is the appropriate one. Reduction of pain, and success in deterring pain-causing behaviour, are all that count. No other questions about the appropriateness of a particular penalty are relevant.

Similarly, Bentham's account of the justification of obedience to the state looks to actual and possible future consequences rather than to past actions or events. An example of a contrasting justification which looks to the past is that of the original contract, which supposes that obedience is justified by an (actual or tacit) agreement to obey the state. Such a device was used by the leading contemporary defender of British law in Bentham's day, William Blackstone (1723–80). Bentham attacks Blackstone vehemently in his *Fragment on Government* (1968–) and ridicules this kind of justification. For Bentham, justification of obedience to government depends upon the calculation of consequences. As he puts it in the *Fragment*, it depends upon calculation of whether the 'probable mischiefs of obedience are less than the probable mischiefs of resistance'. Again, the justification is not based on a past act (a past promise) but on the avoidance of possible future harms.

These examples should suffice to give the central idea of utilitarianism, at least as it was expounded by Bentham. It can, of course, be criticized on many accounts; and there has been continuous criticism since Bentham's own day. Both J. S. Mill and Sidgwick, although they continued the utilitarian tradition, were also critics of Bentham. However, before Mill's criticism and extension of Benthamism is examined, more should be said about the use which Bentham himself makes of utilitarianism.

2 Bentham's Use of Utility

It is not accidental that the two examples given of utilitarianism in the previous section concerned the relations between an individual and the state. Bentham was uninterested in private ethics. Instead he was interested, as he puts it in the *Introduction*, in 'that system, the object of which is to rear the fabric of felicity by the hands of reason and of law'. The end is felicity (happiness); the utilitarian end. The means to be used, however, are reason and LAW (chapter 12): reason, because the method deployed will not be appeal to history, prejudice, or custom; and law, because the project is a POLITICAL (chapter 8) project. It is the project of designing a perfect system of law and government.

Such a project needs two kinds of fundamental assumptions: assumptions about what ought to be the case and assumptions about what is the case. The former set the evaluative ends, the latter describe the actual materials which have to be worked with in order to achieve these ends. The former is the VALUE THEORY (p. 209), and for Bentham this is clearly utilitarianism. The latter is a psychology, explaining how people actually act. Unless this is known, then it cannot be known what should be done to people to produce the desired end. The psychology which Bentham deploys is that people act in their own INTERESTS (p. 201). For Bentham, this is also understood in terms of pleasure and pain. People are taken to be seekers after pleasure and avoiders of pain.

It is of utmost importance in understanding Bentham that these two principles are not confused. The statement about what ought to happen (that the general happiness ought to be maximized) is quite separate from the statement about what people actually do (attempting to maximize their own happiness). They are clearly distinguished by Bentham and, indeed, no sense can be made of the overall project unless they are distinguished. For this depends upon taking people as they are (seekers after their own pleasure) and so constructing a system of law and government that they, acting in this way, will also do what they ought (promote the general pleasure).

One example of a Benthamite solution is the account of punishment given in the previous section. People moved by their own interest (the desire of avoiding the pain of punishment) are led to do what they ought by a correct system of threatened punishments. They are, that is, led by such SELF-INTEREST (p. 262) to consider also the interests of others and act in a manner which promotes the general happiness. The same principle can be applied to the design of institutions and was applied by Bentham to everything from the design of governments down to the designs of prisons. The key principle, in his words, was the 'duty and interest junction principle'. Things had to be cunningly arranged so that duty and interest coincided.

This is the kind of project for which J. S. Mill worked as a young man when he was an unreconstructed Benthamite. Later he became more detached. If we now move on to investigate this, and the criticism of Bentham that it supplies, we should remember that Benthamism was never intended to be anything other than a system of politics and government.

3 Traditional Interpretation: Mill

Although Mill took himself to be a utilitarian, he wanted to be a utilitarian with a difference. He himself was one of Bentham's critics, and in criticizing

Bentham it is arguable that he criticized the central core of utilitarianism itself. Such, at least, is part of the substance of the traditional interpretation of Mill; and it is this traditional interpretation which will be examined next, concentrating on *Utilitarianism* (1963–), which is the text that everybody reads and which Mill himself took to be a defence of the doctrine.

The first point of criticism concerns chapter two, which is entitled 'What Utilitarianism Is'. Mill here began by saying:

> The creed which accepts as the foundations of morals, Utility, or the Greatest Happiness Principle, holds that actions are right in proportion as they tend to promote happiness, wrong as they tend to produce the reverse of happiness. By happiness is intended pleasure, and the absence of pain; by unhappiness, pain, and the privation of pleasure.

This is exactly like Bentham's remarks quoted above: there is the same use of the word 'tend' and the same promiscuous movement between 'utility', 'happiness' and 'pleasure'.

However, Mill shortly afterwards claimed that 'it is quite compatible with the principle of utility to recognise the fact, that some *kinds* of pleasure are more desirable and more valuable than others'. Here, at least on the traditional interpretation, the trouble starts. For the central point of utilitarianism is its claim that there is a single source of value (which may be called by different names). If this is so, then it would seem that distinctions in this value can only be quantitative rather than qualitative. Yet Mill explicitly wants qualitative distinctions. He famously says that 'it is better to be a human being dissatisfied than a pig satisfied; better to be Socrates dissatisfied than a fool satisfied'. This may well be true; but the traditional objection holds that this is because Mill has introduced values in addition to satisfaction (or happiness or utility). The human being and Socrates, that is, are only better because they have more of these other values, compensating for their lesser satisfaction.

In 1859, just before Mill wrote *Utilitarianism*, he wrote a famous defence of political liberty, *On Liberty* (1963–). This contains a strong support of the value of such things as truth, individuality and autonomy. Its object is, as Mill says, 'to assert one very simple principle'; which is 'that the sole end for which mankind are warranted, individually or collectively, in interfering with the liberty of action of any of their number, is self-protection'. Mill holds, that is, that there should be a purely private area beyond the control of law or public opinion. He says specifically that someone's 'own good' is 'not a sufficient warrant for interference'. These may all be admirable sentiments, but the question is, again, whether Mill's assertion of them is compatible with utilitarianism.

Mill himself says that it is. Shortly after the assertion of his 'simple principle' he says that he regards 'utility as the ultimate appeal on all ethical questions'. However, the standard interpretations, starting with the nineteenth-century attack by J. F. Stephen (1829–94), again hold that Mill can only defend liberty by relying on other independent values; and so again by breaking with utilitarianism's single value. Conversely, if maximizing utility is the sole permitted goal, then paternalist interference with others would sometimes be permitted; for it would be permitted precisely on those occasions on which such interference increased their utility. Utilitarianism is concerned with maximizing the good, irrespective of whose good it is. Hence, contrary to what Mill asserts, someone's good would be a sufficient warrant for interference.

Here are two versions of the objection that, by trying to include more in the idea of happiness than Bentham does, Mill in fact breaks with the central spirit of utilitarianism.

The greatest negative energy of the commentators has been reserved not for chapter two but for chapter four of *Utilitarianism*. This short chapter, entitled 'Of What Sort of Proof the Principle of Utility is Susceptible', has produced an enormous amount of critical commentary. Most commentators since F. H. Bradley (1846–1924) and Sidgwick have held that Mill here made elementary and embarrassing errors; so that it has been suggested (Berger, 1984, p. 45) that Mill's current reputation would be very much higher if this short chapter had not been written.

It seems that the chapter intends to provide a proof of the utility principle. The supposed fallacies are hence fallacies of inference. The two most famous ones occur in the third paragraph. Here Mill starts by suggesting an analogy with proving that something is visible. 'The only proof capable of being given that an object is visible', he writes, 'is that people actually see it'. Similarly for something being audible: the proof is that people hear it. 'In a like manner', he continues, 'the sole evidence that it is possible to produce that anything is desirable, is that people do actually desire it'. The standard criticism of Mill is that he here derives the desirable (what ought to be the case) from the desired (what is the case). That is, he confuses ought and is; or in the terminology of G. E. MOORE (1873–1958) (chapter 28) he commits what Moore dubbed the naturalistic fallacy.

Nor is this the end of the infamous howlers that have been found in this short paragraph. For after showing, as he thought, that each person's happiness was 'a good to that person', Mill concluded that 'the general happiness' was 'therefore, a good to the aggregate of all persons'. Here by sleight of hand he seems to move from egoism to altruism; from the claim that everyone is interested in their own happiness to the claim that they are therefore interested in everyone else's happiness.

4 Re-interpretation 1: The Art of Life

This catalogue of apparent disasters might be thought to spell the end of Mill as a serious thinker; and so also the end of his revised version of utilitarianism. On the other hand, Mill's own criticisms of Bentham might be held to spell the end of the original utilitarian project. However, Mill has recently been subject to a sustained process of re-interpretation and defence. A 'new Mill' has emerged to whom it is harder to attach the traditional criticisms; and perhaps that re-interpretation can provide sustenance for a revised form of utilitarianism.

It was noted in section 3 that much of the criticism has been devoted to a single paragraph in a short chapter of a single one of Mill's works. One way that Mill has been re-interpreted is by getting a broader view. So, in *Utilitarianism* itself, consideration has been given to chapters not so far mentioned, particularly chapter five on JUSTICE (chapter 8). But it has also been noted that *Utilitarianism* is a relatively small part of Mill's total output. Mill's largest works – whether this is measured by bulk, by contemporary esteem, or by the amount of description he himself accords them in his *Autobiography* (1963–   ), which describes his intellectual development – are works of logic and metaphysics.

Mill made his name among his contemporaries with his *System of Logic* (1963–   ), which was published in 1843, and towards the end of his life he wrote his massive metaphysical work *An Examination of Sir William Hamilton's Philosophy* (1963–   ), which was published in 1865. It is therefore completely appropriate that John Skorupski's large study and re-interpretation of Mill (Skorupski, 1989) pays much more attention to the logic than anything else. This balance will not be followed in the present chapter since students read *Utilitarianism* and *On Liberty* much more than Mill's other books. However, it does suggest that a better view can be gained of these familiar texts if they are placed in the context of Mill's overall thought, and hence of the *Logic*.

The part of the *Logic* that is most relevant for the understanding of Mill's ethical and political thought is the last chapter, which is about 'morality and policy'. In it, Mill says that 'a proposition of which the predicate is expressed by the words *ought* or *should be*, is generically different from one which is expressed by *is* or *will be*'. In other words, Mill here very clearly distinguishes between is and ought. Furthermore, he says that every art has its leading principle. The leading principle of architecture, for example, is that it is desirable to have buildings. Standing above all these particular arts is the Art of Life itself. Its leading principle is that what is 'conducive to happiness' is desirable. Mill divides the art of life into 'three departments, Morality, Prudence or Policy, and Aesthetics; the Right, the Expedient, and the Beautiful or Noble'.

From this it can be extracted that Mill not only clearly distinguishes between is and ought, but that he also distinguishes between what is good and what it is right to do. Otherwise put, he only takes morality as part of what the principle of utility would promote. If, with this clue, we now return to *Utilitarianism*, but to the less familiar chapter on justice, we find there Mill saying that 'we do not call anything wrong, unless we mean to imply that a person ought to be punished in some way or other for doing it; if not by law, by the opinion of his fellow creatures; if not by opinion, by the reproaches of his own conscience'. So morality seems to concern only those parts of life in which there ought to be sanctions deterring specific kinds of conduct. For the rest of life, even though there may be principles of expediency, or matters of aesthetic taste, there is not in the same way obligations about what ought to be done.

The importance of this is that the root idea of utilitarianism as a personal ethic seemed to be that everyone ought all the time to be doing what produced the greatest utility; an impossibly strenuous obligation. In so far as Bentham avoids private ethics, he also avoids this problem of strenuousness. But Mill, unlike Bentham, is concerned with private ethics. Furthermore, the statements of the 'creed' quoted in section 3 above ('actions are right in proportion as they tend to promote happiness, wrong as they tend to produce the reverse of happiness', currently dubbed the 'proportionality criterion') does seem to advise such a strenuous performance. It says that, in proportion as utility can be increased, so something ought to be done. However, if we consider instead the statement just quoted from chapter five (currently dubbed 'the punishment criterion'), then this strenuousness can be avoided. Mill can be taken to hold that only certain very central human interests need protection by the imposition of such sanctions. Only these count as morality; and hence morality need not become over-strenuous.

Assuming that autonomy and security are among these vital human interests, we now see how we can get a coherent account of morality and law, as well as of Mill's proposals in *On Liberty*. For when such vital interests are concerned, they have to be protected either by law (using the threat of legal punishment) or else by morality (using the threat of public disapproval). Otherwise, in particular with the exercise of matters that are purely private, there should be no such sanctions.

The account here is like Bentham's theory of punishment. Certain kinds of conduct are subject to sanctions, either legal or moral. The reason people do not perform these actions (in the main) is because of their desire to avoid these sanctions. So, the connection between action and utility is indirect. Therefore, if Mill is still a utilitarian on this interpretation, it is of the indirect rather than the direct kind.

5 Re-interpretation 2: Happiness and Indirect Utilitarianism

The idea of a moral sanction did not originate with Mill. Bentham also talked of a 'moral' sanction. In chapter three of his *Introduction* he describes four sanctions: physical, political, moral and religious. He thinks that people can be deterred by the simple idea of pain (which might be caused physically, legally, socially or by God). Mill is also interested in how people can be made by sanctions to do desirable things. But what Mill adds to Bentham is a richer psychology, involving use of the association of ideas.

When Mill describes in his *Autobiography* his separation from the original utilitarian creed he says 'I never, indeed, wavered in the conviction that happiness is the test of all rules of conduct, and the end of life. But I now thought that this end was only to be attained by not making it the direct end.' As he puts it, 'the only chance is to treat, not happiness, but some end external to it, as the purpose of life'. This describes individual motivation. Yet the same points apply as with morality. In both cases, happiness is the ultimate end. But in both cases the approach is indirect. The immediate or apparent end of action may be not happiness but something else. And it is only this other thing that is explained or justified by happiness.

Mill's main concern in the infamous fourth chapter of *Utilitarianism* was not to show that happiness is an end of action (which he passes over quickly in the much-discussed paragraph) but, rather, to show that it is the only such end. For this he needs his fuller account of happiness in which the theory of the association of ideas is pressed into explanatory service. As he says there, something which becomes associated with something as a means to an end naturally 'comes to be desired for itself'. So, for example, virtue can start as a means to happiness, and then become an apparently self-sufficient end of action. The explanation of action by happiness is, again, indirect.

There is, therefore, considerable current support for the interpretation of Mill as an indirect utilitarian. This might seem to determine also an older interpretative issue, the question of whether Mill is a rule utilitarian. This was proposed by J. O. Urmson in 1953 (Schneewind (ed.), 1968, pp. 179–89). However, the main weight of the subsequent debate has run against this interpretation; and the more recent interpreters of Mill as an indirect utilitarian also do not usually think that this makes Mill a rule utilitarian.

Mill, Rules and Conduct

On any interpretation, Mill clearly gives a special position to rules. Morality is not only defined as 'the rules and precepts for human conduct'; Mill also emphasized the special position of 'secondary' principles. He thought that the past experience of humankind has shown us which kinds of action promote happiness and which do not. 'During all that time', he said, 'mankind have been learning by experience the tendencies of actions'.

All this is, however, compatible with Mill not meaning rules to apply in more than a shorthand manner. The rules, that is, can be held to be practical rules, giving knowledge about the tendencies of actions when no better information is available. Although it is practical to use such rules, this does not in itself mean that the action is only justified by the rule; and hence it is not rule utilitarianism in the narrow, or strict, sense. Furthermore, once the art of life conception is taken seriously, more is justified by utility than morality. Even if, that is, morality consists only of rules there are also the other parts of the art of life, such as prudence and aesthetics. They escape the analogy with law and punishment; and so escape whatever pressure this analogy may assert towards a rule utilitarian interpretation.

The proposed interpretation of Mill as an indirect utilitarian is sometimes made by contrast with Bentham. But Bentham can also be made out to be an indirect utilitarian. He was centrally concerned with the creation of the right system of law. Therefore, why someone acts in such a right system can also be interpreted as being indirectly connected with utility. They act directly because it is the law; or because they are afraid of the punishment. But the law is the right law because it promotes utility. Bentham also lays down secondary ends or goals, which are particularly prominent in his writings on civil law. The four secondary ends he lists in his *Civil Code* (1843b) are subsistence, abundance, equality and security. These are what a good system of law should promote. They again, as in Mill, stand in the position of being intermediate principles of justification. Again, as in Mill, they can be justified by reference to the past, or to the general, experience of humankind because they are ends that promote the fundamental principle of maximizing utility.

6 Mill's Metaphysics and Logic

It was noted above that recent work on Mill has stressed the breadth of his project and has revealed that its centre of gravity is more in the writings on logic than in the more familiar ethics and politics. No proper consideration can be given here of the logic and metaphysics; but it will be useful to have a glance at Mill's overall project before returning finally to his supposed proof of utility.

In both morals and metaphysics Mill can be seen as working in the central tradition of Bentham. They both thought that there are basically two kinds of philosophical position, which can be distinguished by the methods they use. On the one hand is the method of relying on INTUITIVE (pp. 590–8) or *a priori* knowledge. On the other is the empiricist method of relying on experience. Mill aligns himself with the latter. This method holds that moral and metaphysical conclusions, and hence political ends, are not to be established by some innate intuitive faculty, or moral sense; they are to be established according to the effects of varying courses of possible action on demonstrable and unmysterious experience, namely the happiness they produce.

This distinction not only explains Mill's position in moral and political philosophy but also his wider intellectual project. It gives the central purpose of his *Logic* as well as his *Examination* of Hamilton. The chief object of the *Logic* is to show how there can be right reasoning and discovery of truth when no basis is used except for experience. Mill here attempts to show that all candidates for truths known intuitively and independent of experience (such as MATHEMATICAL TRUTHS (chapter 10) or the belief that every event has a cause) are in fact founded on experience. The *Logic* also deals with MEANING (chapter 3) and with DEDUCTIVE ARGUMENT (p. 291) (where he holds that the real inference in a syllogism is the establishment of the major premise and is therefore inductive). However, its central focus is to produce an empiricist PHILOSOPHY OF SCIENCE (chapter 9), showing how knowledge may be acquired from experience.

Mill's experiential treatment of logic and mathematics is in stark opposition to the prevailing tone of this century's philosophy of logic. However, as recent work has brought out, it has similarities with the work of QUINE (b. 1908) (chapter 4). Neither Mill nor Quine ultimately hold logic or mathematics to be special. In the end, they too are subject to the tribunal of experience. So Mill's can also be seen as a naturalizing project; giving natural explanation rather than *a priori* justification. Things thought to be necessary are explained as the product of the natural effects of the environment on the mind. This applies for logic and mathematics with their supposed intuitive, or necessary, truths. It also applies for morality, analogously supposed by many to be intuitive or necessary.

Both Skorupski (1989) and Scarre (1989), who bring out this analogy with Quine, find a tension between this naturalism and Mill's own metaphysics (which is chiefly found in his long *Examination* of Hamilton). In the *Examination*, Mill presents an account of reality in which all items are constructed from the basic atoms of experience. Such constructions are a person's own MIND (chapter 5), OTHER MINDS (p. 680), as well as OBJECTS IN THE EXTERNAL WORLD (pp. 590–8) (which are famously classified as 'permanent possibilities of sensation').

The *Examination* is currently not much read or studied, but one interest of it is that it contains (in chapter twelve) the first appearance of the argument by analogy for the nature of other people's minds, the attack on which has done so much to shape current, post-Wittgensteinian, philosophy of mind. The basis of Skorupski and Scarre's attack is that the philosophy of science demands a realist attitude to the world, which is undercut by the PHENOMENALISM (pp. 55–6) of the METAPHYSICS (chapter 2).

7 Proof of the Principle of Utility

It has been noted that Mill's defence of the use of experience against the use of *a priori* intuition extends also to his writings in ethics. The chief object of *Utilitarianism* is to demonstrate that ethical principles do not need to rest on *sui generis* ethical intuitions. Hence the point of the long chapter on justice. Justice is shown not to be a separate intuition, but to be founded on the observable utility of the actions that justice recommends.

Hence also the point of the so-called proof. It is not intended as a deductive proof of utility. It is not intended to show that utility is an intuitive or *a priori* principle. Rather, it is intended to reveal its empirical support; to show how the principle connects with observations of what actually happens. It appeals not to moral sense, or moral intuitions, but, rather, to actual, observable, desires.

It is quite clear from the text itself that Mill never intended it as a deduction. Earlier in the work (in chapter one) he says that 'questions of ultimate ends are not amenable to direct proof'; the infamous chapter itself is entitled 'Of what sort of proof . . .'; and it starts with Mill repeating his claim that 'questions of ultimate ends do not admit of proof'. So instead of proof we have suggestions; not a deduction, but experience.

Something exactly similar had happened previously in Bentham, who also claims that the first principle, being a first principle, cannot be proved by something more ultimate. So Bentham provides, instead of a proof, something which may lead the reader to 'relish' the principle. Mill, similarly, provides something which may lead the reader to look on the principle more favourably.

As an empirical task, the claim is that, to see what might best serve as an ultimate end of conduct, some control can be got by seeing what, as a matter of fact, people actually do treat as ends. The desirable is not taken to be the same in meaning as what is desired. Rather, by observing what people actually desire, we get some kind of empirical control, or test, about what it is possible to desire. And, by seeing what it is possible to desire, we get an analogous empirical control, or test, on what should be desired. It is a necessary condition, not a sufficient one: there is no point in an ethics that proposes something as desirable when, as a matter of empirical fact, it is not possible to desire it.

What Mill is trying to show is that, as a matter of fact, happiness is the only thing that is actually desired (as an end); hence that it is reasonable to suppose that it is the only thing that it is possible to desire (as an end); hence that it is the only proper object of morality, prudence and life. The initial empirical observation here may be held to be highly dubious; although it is obviously helped by Mill's enlarged sense of happiness, which was discussed above. Following from this enlarged sense, it will not be a refutation that people take themselves to be aiming at something quite other than happiness (as long, that is, as happiness has to enter the explanation of this).

8 Bentham on Clarification

It has been seen how Mill wished to connect significant thought with experience. Bentham also took experience as a guide, but was more prepared than Mill to talk about this giving meaning. Without the principle of utility, he said, we have 'sounds instead of sense'; and his constant aim is to extirpate nonsense. The connection of both the central evaluative principle and the central psychological principle with pains and pleasures – that is, with the raw data of experience – endows both these central principles with meaning.

Bentham's practical project of producing the perfect system of law led him into an investigation of the nature of law. Law, he thought, had to be clarified and understood (so that, once understood, it could be reformed). Understanding the law means understanding rights and duties. Understanding is gained by placing things in contact with experience. Yet, since rights and duties seem to be neither observable entities, nor complexes of observable entities, this would not seem to be possible. However, Bentham solved this problem by inventing a technique he called 'paraphrasis', which anticipates twentieth-century techniques of analysis.

The idea is not to understand problematic words in isolation but, rather, 'some whole sentence of which it forms a part is translated into another sentence'. So in the analysis of what Bentham called 'fictional entities' (such as right, duty, property, obligation, immunity and privilege: the whole language of the law), he uses his technique of paraphrasis to place these terms in sentences for which he then gives substitute sentences not containing the offending term. For example, sentences about rights are explained by Bentham in terms of sentences about duties. A particular right is for him the benefit that is conferred on someone by the imposition of duties on others. With duties we still, of course, have fictional entities. But these, in turn, can be placed in sentences that are translated into sentences about the threat of punishment. Punishment is, for Bentham, the threat of the imposition of pain. So here, at last, we reach what Bentham calls real entities; that is, things that can be directly understood by perception. We reach pain and pleasure, which are the ultimate clarifiers both of how the law is and also of how the law ought to be.

Natural Rights and Nonsense

Bentham was opposed to the existence of natural rights. They formed part of the opposing rhetoric to utility and were thought by him to be nonsense. At first sight it might be thought that they could be saved by the same technique. However, comparing a natural right with a legal right exposes the difference. Both can be analysed in terms of corresponding duties. Yet, as we saw above, Bentham analyses a legal duty in terms of the law (or threat of punishment) which creates it. There is no corresponding law, he holds, with respect to supposed natural duties. Hence he holds that natural rights are just imaginary rights.

Bentham's most famous slogan expressing this view is that talk of natural rights is 'nonsense on stilts'. This comes in a work normally called *Anarchical Fallacies* (1843a), which is a critical analysis of the French *Declaration of Rights*, which was issued in 1791. Bentham thinks that the French are not really declaring existing rights but, rather, giving reasons why there ought to be rights. Yet, as he puts it, 'a reason for wishing that a certain right were established, is not that right; want is not supply; hunger is not bread'. So to suppose that such rights actually exist is nonsense. Furthermore, to suppose that they are unalterable – that is, to suppose in advance of experiment, that they are right for all time – is even worse than normal nonsense. It is nonsense on stilts.

---

9 Sidgwick

Finally, a coda on Sidgwick. Bentham's *Civil Code* was one of Sidgwick's favourite books and he started his intellectual life as a follower of Mill. However, just like Mill, be broke with, and criticized, his mentors. He was still prepared to say that he was a utilitarian, but, again, the utilitarianism is worn with a difference. Sidgwick produces so fundamentally different a base for utilitarianism that, again, it might be thought that he removes its central point.

It has been seen how both Bentham and Mill took themselves to be opposing schools of thought (or political movements) that relied upon direct intuition of the right answer. Against this they both posed observation and experience. Yet although Sidgwick argued for utilitarianism, he did so precisely on an intuitionist base. He saw himself as healing the split in the previous generation: the war between the utilitarians and the intuitionists. Sidgwick was both.

Healing splits, or understanding different points of view, was very much Sidgwick's personal and philosophical temperament. His central work is called the *Methods of Ethics*. This is, as the title says, a study not just of one but of several methods. Intuitionism, utilitarianism, common sense and egoism are all examined. The history of the subject is fully deployed. The problem is how, being completely impartial in the face of all this material, to find the rational basis for action.

The *Methods* is hence a study of good reasons. The maxims of common-sense morality, he thinks, do not meet the criteria he lays down for something being an intuitively good reason for action. However, these criteria are met by certain 'absolute practical principles' of a more abstract nature, such as that future good is as important as present good. Another such principle is that, as Sidgwick puts it, 'the good of any one individual is of no more importance, from the point of view (if I may say so) of the Universe, than the good of any other'. This involves utilitarianism; hence Sidgwick provided utilitarianism with an intuitionist foundation.

However, Sidgwick thinks that egoism is also an intuitive principle of action. So we are caught, he thinks, in a 'dualism of practical reason' with two independent principles that are both rationally compelling: an egoistic principle telling me to mind my own happiness and an altruistic principle telling me to mind the general happiness. This split was threatened in Mill and Bentham, but eluded (for Bentham, by making the egoistic principle a psychological principle rather than an evaluative one; for Mill, by allowing them both to be evaluative but giving them different spheres). For Sidgwick, however, the problem of collision is harsh. It would only be avoided, he thinks, if God (working as a sort of divine Benthamite legislator) kept the two in step. However, Sidgwick, who had considerable religious doubts, was reluctant to introduce God for this purpose. The famous last words of the first edition of the *Methods* state that 'the prolonged effort of the human intellect to frame a perfect ideal of rational conduct is seen to have been foredoomed to inevitable failure'. (Sidgwick himself said that he wanted to write a book in which the first word was 'ethics' and the last word 'failure'; in this, at least, he succeeded.)

Mill waged war on contemporary Cambridge professors, like Whewell, who used intuition. Mill, like Bentham, fought from outside the academy. They both proposed a secular ethic, in competition with the church-supported English universities and establishment. Sidgwick, by contrast, was a Cambridge professor. Like his predecessor, Whewell, he uses intuition, albeit with different results. He tries to dispense with God; but this gives him problems. However, writing as a professor, he succeeds in giving a thoroughly professional treatment of the subject, recognizable as such in this century. After all, it was Sidgwick who produced the critique that G. E. Moore (a later Cambridge professor) used to the effect that Mill confused the desired with the desirable and so confused is and ought. From this critique, much twentieth-century ethical thought follows.

Further Reading

Readers might reasonably begin with Bentham, *A Fragment on Government* and *An Introduction to the Principles of Morals and Legislation*; with Mill, *Utilitarianism* and *On Liberty*; and with Sidgwick, *The Methods of Ethics*, before turning to secondary sources.

Dinwiddy (1989) provides a good brief introduction to Bentham, with a more comprehensive examination in Harrison (1983). Hart (1982) offers engaging essays which have set the tone of contemporary Bentham studies. Bentham's theories of justice, government, law and democracy are considered by Kelly (1990), Lyons (1991), Postema (1986) and Rosen (1983).

Ryan (1974) gives an excellent and clear introduction to Mill, but some readers will want to move quickly to the more demanding recent studies by Scarre (1989) and Skorupski (1989). Schneewind (ed.) (1968) and Thomas (1985) are also valuable. Gray (1983) and Ten (1980) provide different perspectives on Mill's account of liberty. Robson (1968) explores Mill's social and political thought, while aspects of his ethical and political thinking are discussed by Berger (1984) and Semmel (1984).

Schneewind (1977) places Sidgwick in historical context, and Schultz (1992) reflects a recent renewal of interest in Sidgwick's philosophy.

References

Bentham

Bentham, J. 1776: *A Fragment on Government*. In Bentham (1968–).
—— 1789: *An Introduction to the Principles of Morals and Legislation*. In Bentham (1968–).
—— 1843a: *Anarchical Fallacies*. In Bentham (1962), vol. 2.
—— 1843b: *Principles of the Civil Code*. In Bentham (1962), vol. 2.
—— 1962 [1838–43]: *The Works of Jeremy Bentham* (11 vols) (edited by Sir J. Bowring). New York: Russell and Russell.
—— 1968– : *Collected Works* (edited by J. H. Burns). London: Athlone Press.

Writers on Bentham

Dinwiddy, J. 1989: *Bentham*. Oxford: Oxford University Press.
Harrison, R. 1983: *Bentham*. London: Routledge.
Hart, H. L. A. 1982: *Essays on Bentham*. Oxford: Oxford University Press.
Kelly, P. J. 1990: *Utilitarianism and Distributive Justice*. Oxford: Oxford University Press.
Lyons, D. 1991: *In the Interest of the Governed*. Oxford: Oxford University Press.
Postema, G. J. 1986: *Bentham and the Common Law Tradition*. Oxford: Oxford University Press.
Rosen, F. 1983: *Jeremy Bentham and Representative Democracy*. Oxford: Oxford University Press.

Mill

Mill, J. S. 1843: *A System of Logic*. In Mill (1963–), vols VII–VIII.
—— 1859: *On Liberty*. In Mill (1963–), vol. XVIII.
—— 1863: *Utilitarianism*. In Mill (1963–), vol. X.
—— 1865: *An Examination of Sir William Hamilton's Philosophy*. In Mill (1963–), vol. IX.
—— 1873: *Autobiography*. In Mill (1963–), vol. I.
—— 1963: *Collected Works*, 33 vols (general editor J. M. Robson). London: University of Toronto Press and Routledge and Kegan Paul.

Writers on Mill

Berger, F. R. 1984: *Happiness, Justice and Freedom*. Berkeley, CA: University of California Press.
Gray, J. 1983: *Mill on Liberty: a Defence*. London: Routledge.
Robson, J. M. 1968: *The Improvement of Mankind: the Social and Political Thought of John Stuart Mill*. Toronto: Toronto University Press.
Ryan, A. 1974: *J. S. Mill*. London: Routledge.
Scarre, G. 1989: *Logic and Reality in the Philosophy of John Stuart Mill*. Dordrecht: Kluwer.
Schneewind, J. B. (ed.) 1968: *Mill*. London: Macmillan.
Semmel, B. 1984: *John Stuart Mill and the Pursuit of Virtue*. New Haven, CT: Yale University Press.
Skorupski, J. 1989: *John Stuart Mill*. London: Routledge.
Stephen, J. F. 1967: *Liberty, Equality, Fraternity* (new edition, edited by R. J. White). Cambridge: Cambridge University Press.
Ten, C. L. 1980: *Mill on Liberty*. Oxford: Oxford University Press.
Thomas, W. 1985: *Mill*. Oxford: Oxford University Press.

Sidgwick

Sidgwick, H. 1874: *The Methods of Ethics*. London: Macmillan.

Writers on Sidgwick

Schneewind, J. B. 1977: *Sidgwick's Ethics and Victorian Moral Philosophy*. Oxford: Oxford University Press.
Schultz, B. 1992: *Essays on Henry Sidgwick*. Cambridge: Cambridge University Press.

Discussion Questions

1   Are there good reasons to believe that happiness is the unique measure of value?

2   Could the utilitarian principle be accepted even if people did not act to maximize their own utility?

3   Should we equate utility, pleasure and happiness?

4   Should our actions and institutions be evaluated by their actual and possible consequences? What other way might we have of assessing them?

5 What justifies punishment?

6 Is utilitarianism equally suited to designing public institutions and to guiding private ethics?

7 Was Bentham justified in rejecting a role for history, prejudice and custom in his design of a system of law and government?

8 Is it reasonable to attempt to design a *perfect* system of public institutions?

9 Can institutions be arranged to reconcile duty and interest?

10 Does utilitarianism fail if some *kinds* of pleasure are 'more desirable and more valuable than others'?

11 On what grounds are we justified in interfering with the liberty of another person?

12 Does Bentham or Mill provide a more acceptable account of happiness?

13 What sort of proof, if any, can be given for the utility principle?

14 Should we accept Mill's claim 'that the sole evidence that it is possible to produce that anything is desirable, is that people do actually desire it'?

15 Does 'the punishment criterion' protect utilitarianism from making impossible demands on our actions?

16 Is it more helpful to consider Mill as a rule utilitarian or as an indirect utilitarian? Was Bentham an indirect utilitarian?

17 What follows from the claim that the art of life includes prudence and aesthetics as well as morality?

18 Should we seek a natural explanation wherever an *a priori* justification is offered?

19 In what sense, if any, might one's own mind, the minds of other people, and objects in the external world be said to be *constructed*?

20 Is Mill's phenomenalism compatible with the requirements of the philosophy of science?

21 Is the fact that people often take themselves to be aiming at something other than happiness an empirical refutation of the claim that happiness is the only thing that is actually desired?

22 How successful was Bentham in showing us how to recognize and avoid nonsense?

23 If rights and duties are fictional entities, how can they be understood?

24 Are 'natural rights' imaginary?

25 How should we assess Sidgwick's project of providing an intuitionist base for utilitarianism?

26 If there are absolute practical principles, how can we determine what they are?

26

Pragmatism ———————————————

Susan Haack

Pragmatism, a style of philosophy initiated by Charles Sanders Peirce and William James, is best characterized by the method expressed in the pragmatic maxim, according to which the meaning of a concept is determined by the experiential or practical consequences of its application. Peirce's aspiration to a reformed, scientific philosophy free of metaphysical excesses is sustained by the realist elements of his view of perception and of natural laws; muted by nominalist leanings in James and Hegelian leanings in Dewey, pragmatism is transformed by Schiller into a revolutionary relativism – and, in our own time, by Richard Rorty into a conception of philosophy as, not a form of inquiry, but only 'carrying on the conversation' of Western culture.

1 Introduction: From Reformist to Revolutionary Pragmatism

'It has probably never happened', Peirce wrote in 1905, 'that a philosopher has attempted to give a general name to his own doctrine without that name's soon acquiring in common philosophical usage, a signification much broader than was originally intended'. His 'pragmatism', he continued, had by then acquired a signification so much broader than his original intention that it was 'time to kiss his child good-by' and 'to announce the birth of the word "pragmaticism," which is ugly enough to be safe from kidnappers' (Peirce, *Collected Papers*, 5.412).

Not unexpectedly, therefore, it is scarcely possible to give an accurate brief statement of the philosophical tendencies characteristic of pragmatism. The need to acknowledge, for instance, the significance for his conception of pragmatism of Peirce's shift from early nominalist sympathies to his mature realism, or of the influence on James' conception of pragmatism of his doctrine of the Will to Believe, makes it hard enough to specify what important philosophical ideas were shared by Peirce and James, the founders of pragmatism. And it is harder yet to find a characterization that would also comfortably accommodate Dewey, Schiller and Mead, let alone to extend it to include more recent pragmatists, neo-pragmatists and sympathizers as diverse as Ramsey, Lewis, Sellars, Quine, Putnam, Rescher, Rorty, and so on.

Schiller's observation that there are as many pragmatisms as pragmatists, shrewd as it is, suggests at worst only a formidable diversity; but the fact is that there are not merely different, but radically opposed, pragmatisms. The scientific philosophy envisaged by Peirce's pragmatism calls for 'inquiry into the truth for truth's sake,' and maintains that 'in order to reason well it is absolutely necessary to possess . . . a real love of truth', and that the truth 'is SO, whether you or I or anybody thinks it is so or not' (Peirce, 1.44, 2.82, 2.135). The literary post-philosophy envisaged by Rorty's pragmatism, in starkest contrast, aspires only to 'carrying on the conversation', and declares that 'true' means nothing more than 'what you can defend against all comers', and 'rationality' nothing more than 'respect for the opinions of those around one' (Rorty, 1979, pp. 377–8; 1991a, pp. 32, 37).

As a preliminary to understanding how pragmatism came to be so startlingly transmuted, it will be useful to distinguish two broad styles: the reformist and the revolutionary (a distinction adapted from Migotti, 1988). These have in common the aspiration to free philosophy of metaphysical excesses and, more specifically, of the artificial confines of the CARTESIAN THEORY OF KNOWLEDGE (chapter 17). Relinquishing the requirement of absolute certainty in knowledge, more inclined to NATURALISM (p. 635) than to apriorism, emphasizing the social aspects of inquiry, pragmatism of a reformist stripe acknowledges the legitimacy of traditional questions about the truth-relatedness of our cognitive practices, and sustains a conception of truth objective enough to give those questions bite. Pragmatism of a revolutionary stripe, by contrast, relinquishing the objectivity and denying the value of truth, can acknowledge no legitimate epistemological questions not strictly internal to the cognitive practices of this or that community. And, since it is a tautology that inquiry aims at the truth, the very possibility of bona fide inquiry, and *a fortiori* the conception of philosophy as a kind of inquiry, is thereby undermined.

That this distinction of reformist versus revolutionary does not map perfectly on to the list of pragmatists, neo-pragmatists and sympathizers, so far from detracting from its usefulness, precisely fits it to serve as a framework for understanding the transformation – or, one might better say, the vulgarization – of pragmatism. The diagnosis will be that the delicate balance of objectivity and fallibilism attempted in Peirce's reformist pragmatism, somewhat disturbed by James' nominalistic tendencies and by revolutionary, or revolutionary-sounding, Hegelisms in Dewey, is destroyed when Schiller (mis)interprets James as relativizing truth, and Rorty (mis)interprets Dewey as repudiating the theory of knowledge and as aspiring, not to the reconstruction, but the deconstruction, of philosophy.

2 C. S. Peirce (1839–1914)

At the heart of Peirce's pragmatism lies the pragmatic maxim: 'if one can define accurately all the conceivable experimental phenomena which the affirmation or denial of a concept could imply, one will have a complete definition of the concept, and there is *absolutely nothing more* in it' (Peirce, 5.412). Meaning is a matter of the conceivable experimental, experiential consequences of a concept's applying; *pragmatisch*, in the Kantian sense. The pragmatic meaning of 'x is F' is given by a list of conditionals; as the mature Peirce overcame youthful nominalist leanings, he insisted on the subjunctive formulation: 'if you were to do A_1, experiential consequence E_1 would result', 'if you were to do A_2, experiential consequence E_2 would result', and so on. Thus, a diamond really *is* hard if it *would* scratch other substances if it *were* rubbed against them – even if it never is rubbed. And Peirce stresses that the list of meaning-specifying conditionals is open-ended; meaning grows, as he puts it, as our knowledge grows.

Pragmaticism is, as Peirce acknowledges, a kind of positivism; one role of the pragmatic maxim is to reveal that 'almost every proposition of ontological metaphysics . . . is gibberish' (Peirce, 5.423). But the maxim is not intended to rule out METAPHYSICS (chapter 2) altogether, but rather to discriminate the illegitimate, the pragmatically meaningless, from 'scientific' metaphysics, which uses the method of science, observation and reasoning, and which is undertaken with the scientific attitude, that is, from the desire to find out how things really are – and not, as happens when philosophy is in the hands of theologians, from the desire to make a case for some doctrine which is already immovably believed. Scientific philosophy, as Peirce conceives it, is an observational science, differing from the other sciences not in its method but in its reliance on aspects of experience so familiar, so ubiquitous, that the difficulty is to become distinctly aware of them. (So it would be a misunderstanding to think of Peirce's aspiration to make philosophy scientific as in any way scientistic; Peirce expressly denies that philosophical issues could be resolved within, and certainly never suggests that philosophy ought to be replaced by, the natural sciences.)

It is as scientific metaphysics that Peirce presents his own metaphysical theories. For example, Peirce offers a theory of categories – firstness, potentiality; secondness, particular existence, reaction; and thirdness, generality, connection, law – based both phenomenologically and, like Kant's categories, on logic, but on Peirce's more adequate logic, capable, unlike Aristotle's, of expressing relations. Among his other important contributions to metaphysics are his tychism (there is chance, objective indeterminacy, as well as law, in the universe); his synechism (the ubiquity of continuity); agapism (the gradual evolution of the world from chaos towards order, 'concrete reasonableness'); and his scholastic realism (the reality of 'generals', natural kinds and laws).

But Peirce's conception of a reformed, scientific philosophy is perhaps most directly seen in his thoroughgoing critique of Cartesian epistemology, and in the more naturalistic theory of inquiry with which he proposes to replace it.

With Descartes, philosophy 'put off childish things, and began to be a conceited young man' (Peirce, 4.71). Descartes' method, according to Peirce, is a sham, a matter of feigned, 'paper' doubts which inevitably led to the eventual reinstatement of the beliefs supposedly doubted. There is no such faculty as the intuition on which Descartes' criterion of clearness and distinctness relies, and no such intuitive self-consciousness as his reliance on the *cogito* as the indubitable starting-point for the reconstruction of knowledge requires. Descartes' aspiration to certainty is misplaced, his subjective criterion of truth viciously individualistic.

Unlike Descartes, and in strikingly Darwinian spirit, Peirce sees human belief as continuous with animal expectation, human inquiry as continuous with animals' explorations of their environment. Following Alexander Bain, Peirce conceives of belief as a habit of action, a disposition to behave, and of doubt as the unsettled state resulting from the interruption of a belief-habit by recalcitrance on the part of experience. Real doubt – unlike Descartes' paper doubt – is thus involuntary and unpleasant. The primitive basis of the most sophisticated human cognitive activity, scientific inquiry, is a homeo-static process by which the organism strives to return to equilibrium, a process halted when a new habit, a revised belief, is reached.

This homeostatic process is its primitive basis, but it is not yet scientific inquiry. The beliefs thus 'settled' are likely only temporarily fixed; so the most sophisticated inquirers, realizing that, unless a belief is true, though it may be temporarily settled, it cannot be permanently so, and aspiring to indefeasibly settled belief, will always be motivated to further inquiry, never fully satisfied with what they presently incline to think. The primitive homeostatic process is thus transmuted into scientific inquiry.

Among possible methods for the 'fixation of belief', the SCIENTIFIC METHOD (chapter 9), Peirce holds, is distinguished by its appropriateness to the end of inquiry. Unlike the *a priori* method traditionally favoured by metaphysics, the scientific method, if it were sufficiently persisted in, would enable inquiry to come to rest with beliefs which are indefeasibly stable, permanently safe from recalcitrance. The scientific method, according to Peirce, is the method of OBSERVATION (pp. 300–5) and reasoning: more precisely, it is the method of accommodating the perceptual judgements forced upon one by experience into an explanatory framework, by means of reasoning of three types: abduction, the postulation of hypotheses to explain some puzzling phenom-enon; deduction of consequences from such abductive hypotheses; and the inductive testing of such hypotheses. As Peirce puts it, we wish our beliefs to conform to hard facts; and it is in the brute compulsiveness of experience that the hardness of fact consists.

Even MATHEMATICS (chapter 10), according to Peirce, is an observational science. Though mathematical truths are necessary, mathematical knowledge depends on experience, but on inner experience, the construction, manipula-tion and observation of imagined 'icons' or diagrams.

The desire to learn the truth requires an acknowledgement that one does not satisfactorily know already. The scientific inquirer is therefore a 'contrite fallibilist' who is ready to 'drop the whole cartload of his beliefs, the moment experience is against them' (Peirce, 1.14, 1.55). In the critical common-sensism of Peirce's mature philosophy – an attempted synthesis, as the phrase suggests, of KANT's (chapter 22) and Reid's responses to HUME (chapter 21) – the scientific inquirer is seen as submitting the instinctive beliefs of common sense to criticism, refinement and revision. A scientific doubt, as Peirce puts it, 'can never get completely set to rest until, at last, the very truth about that question gets established' (Peirce, 7.77).

It could with some justice be protested that the critical common-sensist's policy of deliberate critical scrutiny and attempted falsification of the beliefs with which he initially finds himself bears a more than passing resemblance to Descartes' method of doubt. And in any case Peirce's objections to the critical phase of Descartes' project seem largely to miss their mark. However, his critique of Descartes' assumption that any knowledge worthy of the name must be absolutely certain, of the subjectivity of his criterion of truth, and of his first-person, strictly individualistic approach, is more sustainable – and not only compatible, but intimately connected, with the key themes of Peirce's own theory of inquiry.

That theory is fallibilistic and, in a sense, thoroughly social: in the sense that Peirce thinks of the scientific inquirer as just one contributor to a vast enterprise extending both within and across generations. Scientific inquiry may be undertaken by individuals; but the individual inquirer will make his work freely available to others and, even if he fails, his will be one of the carcasses over which future generations of inquirers climb as they finally storm the fortress of knowledge. Fallible and imperfect as scientific inquiry is, if it were to continue long enough – Peirce is aware that there is no guarantee that it will – eventually a final, indefeasible 'ultimate opinion' would be agreed.

What supports Peirce's confidence that, if inquiry continued long enough, eventually consensus would be reached? The idea that evolutionary adaptation has given human beings an instinct for guessing right which enables them to come up with successful abductions, and the thesis that induction tends to be self-corrective, both play obvious roles here. Less obvious, but no less important, is the role of the unusual combination of the direct and the interpretative in Peirce's theory of perception; and, less obvious again, the role of the metaphysical doctrine Peirce sometimes calls 'extreme scholastic realism'.

Peirce distinguishes the percept, the perceptual event or presentation, from the perceptual judgement, the belief prompted by the experience. The perceptual judgement, he maintains, is thoroughly interpretative – indeed, but for its compulsive character, it is analogous to the conclusion of an abduction – and hence, though incorrigible, thoroughly fallible. But Peirce's acknowledgement of the interpretativeness of the perceptual judgement is combined with an insistence that the percept is not a REPRESENTATION (p. 597) but a presentation, and that we directly perceive, not images or mental representations, but real, external objects. Hallucinations and illusions may be indistinguishable phenomenologically from genuine perception; they may share its quality of insistency, of bruteness; they may even be experienced by more than one individual; but they are distinguishable by the fact that the behaviour of the real, external objects of genuine perception is predictable on the basis of our knowledge of the LAWS OF NATURE (pp. 310–11).

Peirce's 'extreme scholastic realism' is the thesis that there are real generals; that is, that there are natural kinds and laws which are independent of how we think them to be. (Peirce distinguishes his scholastic realism not only from nominalism, which maintains that generals are not real but figments, but also from PLATONISM (chapter 15) – which he dubs 'nominalistic platonism' because it maintains that generals exist; existence being for Peirce the characteristic mode of being of seconds, not thirds. And he distinguishes it from Scotistic realism, its closest ancestor, because, unlike Scotus, he holds that *which* generals are real, *which* general terms represent real kinds, is a matter for scientific inquiry to discover.) Scholastic realism is intended by Peirce as a hypothesis of scientific metaphysics. If there were no real generals, he argues, scientific inquiry would be impossible; for the very possibility of PREDICTION (pp. 293–4), induction and explanation depends on the reality of kinds and laws. There is a pattern of generals, of natural kinds and laws, underlying the particular objects and events we perceive, which is 'independent of how you or I or any number of men think'. And so it can be expected that the 'arbitrary, accidental element' in inquiry introduced by the peculiar circumstances and idiosyncracies of individual inquirers would eventually to be overcome as inquiry proceeds, and consensus eventually reached (Peirce, 8.13).

Peirce contrasts scholastic realism not only with nominalism and nominalistic platonism, but also with what one might call 'noumenalism', the idea that the really real is in principle inaccessible to human cognition. This is a characteristically pragmatist attitude, for the pragmatic maxim disqualifies as meaningless any hypothesis devoid of all possible experiential consequences, any question which would resist settlement no matter how long scientific inquiry were to continue.

The thesis that the goal of inquiry is permanently settled belief, and the thesis that the scientific attitude is a disinterested desire for truth, are united by Peirce's definition of 'true'. He does not think it false to say that truth is correspondence to reality, but shallow – a merely nominal definition, giving no insight into the concept. His pragmatic definition identifies the truth with the hypothetical ideal theory which would be the final upshot of scientific inquiry were it to continue indefinitely. 'Truth is that concordance of . . . [a] statement with the ideal limit towards which endless investigation would tend to bring scientific beliefs'; 'any truth more perfect than this destined conclusion, any reality more absolute than what is thought in it, is a fiction of metaphysics' (Peirce, 5.565, 8.13). These quotations reveal something both of the subtlety, and of the potential for tension, within Peirce's philosophy. His account of reality aims at a delicate compromise between the undesirable extremes of transcendentalism and idealism, his account of truth at a delicate compromise between the twin desiderata of objectivity and (in-principle) accessibility.

3 William James (1842–1910)

'There can *be* no difference anywhere that doesn't *make* a difference elsewhere' (James, 1907, p. 30): his version of the pragmatic maxim lies at the heart of James' pragmatism too. Unlike Peirce, however, James thought that philosophy would do well to go round Kant, rather than through him; and this is reflected in his interpretation of the maxim, which stresses *praxis*, the practical consequences of a concept's applying. The point is not that Peirce does not, like James, hold that meaning is purposive, that the meaning of a concept lies in its application; it is rather that the mature, realist Peirce, unlike James, regards this kind of formulation as unfortunate if it encourages 'subordinat[ing] the *conception* to the *act*, knowing to doing' (Peirce, 1900, p. 332). This difference of emphasis is magnified by James' readiness to construe 'the consequences of a belief' in a way that includes not only the consequences of the *truth of the proposition believed*, but also the consequences of *the person's believing it*.

It is not surprising, in view of this, that readers of James, and even James himself, sometimes have difficulty disentangling his pragmatism from his doctrine of the Will to Believe, his 'defence of our right to adopt a believing attitude in religious matters, in spite of the fact that our merely logical intellect may not have been coerced' (James, 1897, pp. 1–2). When a hypothesis by its nature cannot be decided on the basis of evidence; when it is live for us, that is, it appeals to us as a real possibility; when the choice between believing it and disbelieving it is forced, that is, unavoidable, and momentous for our lives – then '*our passional nature . . . lawfully may . . . decide*' (James, 1897, p. 11). RELIGIOUS BELIEFS (chapter 14) which in principle cannot be verified or falsified may be legitimated by their salutary effect on the believer's life.

Peirce – to whom *The Will to Believe* is dedicated – the following year is found describing the scientific attitude as the 'Will to Learn', and observing that, for himself, he 'would not adopt a hypothesis, and would not even take it on probation, simply because the idea was pleasing' to him; that to do so would be 'a crime against the integrity of the reason that God has lent' him (Peirce, 5.583, 5.598). He puts it, one might think, if anything too mildly; for by the standards of the pragmatic maxim as he interprets it, any hypothesis which is in principle incapable of settlement by observation and reasoning, would be no genuine hypothesis at all.

Also associated with James' pragmatism is his mature 'radical empiricism', by means of which he hopes to escape the dualism of Cartesian metaphysics and the subjectivity of Cartesian epistemology. What James calls 'pure experience' is, he holds, of itself neither mental nor physical; the separation into conciousness and content, knower and OBJECT (p. 666) known, is a matter of relations among different bits of 'pure experience'. (How can one and the same thing be both in space and in the mind? James answers, as one and the same point may be on two lines, if situated at their intersection.) The knowing relation, James suggests, is 'successful leading'; one counts as knowing a thing if one's idea of it enables one to act successfully towards it.

One might reasonably feel that the 'cash value' of radical empiricism scarcely matches that of Peirce's reconciliation of the direct and the interpretative elements in perception, and that James' talk of 'leading' is at best a promissory note. Its importance for the present argument lies, however, in its clear connection with James' account of the true as 'the satisfactory in the way of belief'.

Radical empiricism is monistic; it was, indeed, influential in the development of RUSSELL's (chapter 27) neutral monism. Nevertheless, it is compatible with the ideas of James' Hibbert lectures, entitled 'A Pluralistic Universe'. For radical empiricism, as James puts it, 'lays the explanatory stress upon the part, the element, the individual'; it is a 'mosaic' philosophy (James, 1912, p. 24). There is only one kind of stuff, but many portions or individual bits of it. This reveals James' marked predilection for the particular, the concrete.

Like Peirce, James thinks it not exactly false but inadequate to say that truth is correspondence with reality. Again much like Peirce, he characterizes 'truth absolute' as 'an ideal set of formulations towards which all opinions may be expected in the long run to converge' (James, 1909, p. 143). The difference between true beliefs and false ones is that they are verifiable, they lead us successfully. The true, James says, is the satisfactory, the useful, the expedient in the way of belief. True beliefs *work*. Critics like Moore and Russell were scandalized by what they saw as a crass identification of truth and utility – a criticism James describes as a 'slander' (James, 1909, p. 147); for, though indeed he had written that '*the true . . . is only the expedient in the way of belief*', he had gone on to explain, 'expedient in the long run and on the whole of course; for what meets expediently all the experience in sight won't necessarily meet all further experience equally satisfactorily. Experience . . . has ways of *boiling over*, and making us correct our present formulas' (James, 1907, p. 106).

Distinguishing his 'radical' empiricism from earlier variants, James disassociates himself from the disconnectedness of earlier empiricisms; and, specifically, from the theses that similars have nothing really in common, and that the causal tie is nothing but habitual conjunction. But, unlike Peirce, he does not appeal to the reality of kinds and laws to explain why, in the long run of experience, opinions can be expected to converge. Rather, his predilection for the particular leads him to a preoccupation with specific truths rather than truth as such. He manifests some discomfort with the notion of verifi*ability*, preferring to concentrate on particular truths actually verifi*ed*. This leads to apparent inconsistencies, as James seems sometimes to allow that beliefs which are verified are thereby shown to have been true all along, sometimes to suggest that beliefs become true when they are verified. Consistency can be restored by means of a distinction James sometimes makes, but does not always mark, between 'abstract' or 'absolute' Truth and 'concrete' or 'relative' truths, identifying abstract Truth with the verifiable, and concrete truths with the verified. Of course, what James calls 'concrete truths' are not really *truths* at all; his distinction is really between a belief's being true and its being shown to be true – or, more accurately, since he allows that what is at one time 'verified' may later turn out to be false, between a belief's being true and its being confirmed. James' stress on the particular – which the mature Peirce would no doubt have felt betrays nominalist leanings – manifests itself in his tendency to downplay abstract Truth and to emphasise concrete truths. And his use of 'concrete truth' for 'proposition now confirmed' encourages the idea that *truth* (and not merely 'concrete truths') is made by us, and changes over time.

4 John Dewey (1859–1952)

Dewey describes one of Peirce's best-known characterizations – '[t]he opinion which is fated to be agreed by all who investigate' (Peirce, 5.407) – as 'the best definition of truth' (Dewey, 1938, p. 345n.). Like James, however, he tends to stress the concrete over the abstract, actual verification over potential verifiability, truths over Truth. In much of what he writes one hears a certain ambivalence about just how radical he means to be. The intellectualist's horror of acknowledging that verification is, as etymology suggests, a matter of *making* a belief true, he declares, is 'largely sentimental'; but he goes on to explain that to make an idea true 'is to modify and transform it' (that is, presumably, to change the proposition concerned) until it is able to survive testing (Dewey, 1910, p. 139). A belief that is verified, he says, is thereby shown to have been true all along, but he goes on to explain that this means only that it was going to be verified (Dewey, 1910, pp. 142–4). The pragmatist does not deny, Dewey insists, that truth is correspondence of thought to existence, though he does deny that it is correspondence of thought to unknowable things-in-themselves; but he goes on to explain that this correspondence means *co-respondence*, a matter of 'interadjustment' of our ideas to problematic situations (Dewey, 1910, pp. 158–9).

Not surprisingly, perhaps – given that concrete truth is not really truth at all – Dewey is also drawn to the idea that it might be as well to stop using the word 'true', and to work instead with the concept of warranted assertibility.

Like Peirce and James, Dewey repudiates the 'quest for certainty'. Unlike them, he goes on to offer a psycho-sociological diagnosis of the motivation for that quest: it arose, he suggests, from the sharp dichotomy of theory versus practice, and the distaste for the practical, the changeable, the uncertain, embodied in the slave-owning culture of ancient Greece. The most HEGELIAN (chapter 23) of the pragmatists, Dewey is suspicious of traditional philosophical dualisms; and this is reflected in his epistemological writings, which are critical of the whole tradition from Plato through Descartes to his own contemporaries, because of its reliance on the dichotomies of object–subject, fact–value, mind–body, theory–practice. 'Special theories of knowledge differ enormously from one another. Their quarrels . . . fill the air. The din thus created makes us deaf to the way in which they all say one thing in common. . . . They all hold that the operation of inquiry excludes any element of practical activity that enters into the construction of the object known' (Dewey, 1929, p. 22).

Dewey, by contrast, insists that knowing is not isolated from practice, but is itself a kind of practice – to be judged, like other practices, by its purposive success rather than by some supposed standard of accuracy of reflection of its objects. The object of knowledge is not an immutable, independent reality, but is changed, and is in part constituted by, our cognitive interactions with it; for inquiry transforms a problematic, indeterminate situation into a determinate one.

Like Peirce, Dewey conceives of logic broadly. It is the theory of inquiry, of which FORMAL DEDUCTIVE LOGIC (chapter 4) – logic in the usual modern sense – is only a part. Peirce was an important contributor to the development of modern formal logic, discovering quantifiers and the logic of relations independently of FREGE (chapter 27), anticipating *Principia Mathematica*'s definition of number by more than 30 years, and devising truth-tables and venturing into three-valued logic more than a decade before Post and Łukasiewicz. Dewey's logical work is not formal, but this is not why Peirce is critical of it; Peirce's objection is that it is too purely descriptive, amounting only to a 'natural history' of inquiry, not a normative methodology. But by the time of *Logic, the Theory of Inquiry*, at any rate, Dewey is clearly acknowledging that logic is normative – stressing, however, that its recommendations about how inquiry should proceed can only be based on scientific study of what procedures have proven themselves to work.

The cumulative effect of the shifts of emphasis from Peirce through James to Dewey is, it might be fair to say, from an essentially reformist attitude to the philosophical tradition to a potentially revolutionary one. Peirce's theory of inquiry is behaviouristic, naturalistic and fallibilist; it is thoroughly anti-Cartesian, but clearly reformist in its approach. So too is James', but his stress on the so-far-satisfactory in the way of belief, especially given the misleading terminology of 'concrete truths', hints at something more revolutionary. Dewey is perhaps least misleadingly described as half-straddling the reformist–revolutionary distinction. For side by side with reformist elements – his distinction of state and content senses of 'belief', his insistence on a conception of experience much richer than the old sensationalist one, and, especially, his aspiration to transcend the old dichotomy of rationalism versus empiricism and to acknowledge the interlocking of experience and reason – are revolutionary, or at least revolutionary-sounding, suggestions about the making of truth, the modification of the objects of knowledge through inquiry, and the replacement of the traditional theory of knowledge by a critical scrutiny, internal to science, of the methods of inquiry science employs.

5 F. C. S. Schiller (1864–1937)

Schiller is uncompromisingly revolutionary. In his writings one finds a straightforward identification of truth with verification, and an unequivocal commitment to the making, and the mutability, of truth. James acknowledges that his account of concrete truths could not stand alone: 'to admit, as we pragmatists do, that we are liable to correction . . . involves the use on our part of an ideal standard' (James, 1909, p. 142). But Schiller offers a theory of concrete truths *as a complete theory of truth*. He denies outright that truth is correspondence with reality, an idea which he describes as not only worthless as a criterion but absurd in itself. Truth is practical working. 'True', he says, means 'valued by us'. A proposition is true if it 'forwards our ends'. Truth is mutable, since propositions become true only when successfully applied; 'a truth which will not . . . submit to verification, is not yet a truth at all' (Schiller, 1907, p. 8). Reality is also mutable, growing as truth grows. Truth is dependent on us, relative to our purposes. And so is reality; facts are not discovered but selected, even made, by us. In a spirit, no doubt, of deliberate provocation, Schiller likens his views to those of PROTAGORAS (chapter 15). Certainly his revolutionary, relativistic humanism could scarcely be further removed from Peirce's realistic pragmaticism.

'The apostle of Humanism', Peirce wrote of Schiller in 1905, 'says that professional philosophists "have rendered philosophy like unto themselves, abstruse, arid, abstract and abhorrent." But I conceive that some branches of sciences are not in a healthy state if they are not abstruse, arid and abstract'; and in 1908: '[i]t seems to me a pity that [Mr Schiller and the pragmatists of today] should allow a philosophy so instinct with life to become infected with the seeds of death in such notions as . . . the mutability of truth' (Peirce, 5.537, 6.485).

These observations are not only poignant but prophetic. Peirce's warnings of the dangers of Schiller's humanistic pragmatism bring to mind Russell's dismissal of pragmatism as an 'engineers' philosophy', bound to lead to cosmic impiety, or at least to fascism; Schiller's disdain for the mummified pedantry of the philosophical tradition brings to mind Rorty's unkind words about the logic-chopping of analytic philosophy.

6 Recent and Contemporary Pragmatisms

Rorty, most radical of contemporary self-styled neo-pragmatists, and the closest to Schiller, uses 'pragmatist' as the contrast to 'realist'. He tells us that truth is not the kind of thing one should expect to have a philosophically interesting theory about, that to call a proposition true is just to give it a rhetorical pat on the back (Rorty, 1982, pp. xxi, xiii). He transmutes inquiry into 'carrying on the conversation' of Western culture (Rorty, 1979, pp. 377–8) and experiential falsification into 'conversational objections' (Rorty, 1982, pp. 165–6); and refers to those who describe themselves as seeking the truth as 'old-fashioned prigs' (Rorty, 1991b, p. 86).

The affinity of Rorty's and Schiller's conceptions of pragmatism, it should be said, is not the result of Schiller's influence on Rorty; perhaps it is, in part, the result rather of Rorty's (mis)reading James much as Schiller did. Neither, it should also be said, is Rorty prepared, as Schiller is, to admit to relativism.

Indeed, it is not quite unambiguously clear that Rorty *is* properly construed as a relativist; but only because he seems to shift, as occasion demands, between a contextualist, and hence relativist, conception of epistemic justification (A is justified-relative-to-community-C in believing that p just in case he can defend the belief that p against the objections of members of C), and a tribalist one (A is justified in believing that p just in case he can defend the belief that p against the objections of *our* community). But, either way, Rorty's position is thoroughly anti-epistemological; for he is unambiguously committed to the thesis that criteria of evidence are not objectively grounded in their relation to the truth, but entirely a matter of conventional, conversational constraints. Indeed, as Rorty cheerfully acknowledges, this is not only thoroughly anti-epistemological, but anti-philosophical, undermining the traditional conception of philosophy as a form of inquiry. Still, he thinks there is a future for the ex-philosopher, but it is to be 'hermeneutic' rather than epistemological, 'edifying' rather than systematic, literary rather than scientific, a matter of 'carrying on the conversation of Western culture' rather than of inquiring into how things are.

Rorty appeals to Dewey's repudiation of the epistemological tradition. But the appeal is strained, for Dewey looks to the 'naturalization of intelligence', to a scientific approach to replace the 'spectator theory of knowledge' (Dewey, 1929, pp. 195, 196), while Rorty declares that epistemology needs no successor-subject, and, far from welcoming a shift towards science, anticipates the future of post-philosophy as a genre of literature or of literary criticism. True, James writes of the affinity of some moral philosophy with 'novels and dramas of the deeper sort' (James, 1987, p. 210). This is best construed, however, not as denying that moral philosophy is a form of inquiry, but as suggesting the role that imaginative empathy might play in such inquiry; and, so construed, need not conflict with Dewey's vision of a normative ethics in which scientific inquiry into the nature of true human flourishing would play an important role.

Peirce writes, with characteristic verve, of the need 'to rescue the good ship Philosophy for the service of Science from the hands of the lawless rovers of the sea of literature'; '[a]s for that phrase, "studying in a literary spirit",' he remarks, 'it is impossible to express how nauseating it is to any scientific man' (Peirce, 5.449, 1.33). Perhaps it is no wonder, then, that Rorty refers so dismissively to Peirce's 'undeserved apotheosis', and tells us that Peirce's only contribution to pragmatism was to give it a name (Rorty, 1982, pp. 160–1). But it would be a mistake to read Peirce's harsh remarks about literary philosophy as scientistic, or as hostile to literature; they express, rather, his insistence that philosophy, like science, is a form of inquiry, of truth-seeking, and that, in this pursuit, testability is paramount, and clarity and precision of language must take priority over euphony or elegance of style.

This point is doubly important because the revolutionary wing of contemporary pragmatism also shelters, besides Rorty and other admirers of literary philosophy, others of a notably scientistic stripe. Paul Churchland argues, from the non-propositional workings of the ganglia of the sea-slug and the successes of connectionist artificial intelligence in training up a computer to distinguish a mine from a rock on the ocean floor, that cognitive processing is not propositional, and truth not the goal of inquiry. Another contemporary proponent of vulgar pragmatism, Stich, maintains that the goal of inquiry is, not truth, but beliefs that conduce to whatever it is the subject values; ironically enough, he rests his case in part on a denial that truth is instrumentally valuable – and cites, as justification for calling this 'pragmatism', a passage in which James is arguing the utility of true beliefs.

Other contemporaries have sought habitable ground *between* the reformist and the revolutionary wings of the pragmatist tradition. An important theme here is the hope of some kind of *rapprochement* of the 'analytic' and 'CONTINENTAL' (chapter 30) camps. The hope is reasonable enough: the pragmatist tradition, after all, antedates the split; both Peirce and James make significant contributions to phenomenology (or, as Peirce sometimes calls it, 'phaneroscopy'); and Dewey's stress on the historical, the social, and on *praxis* have led some to see him as America's (thoroughly democratic) answer to Marx. Margolis, for example, believes it possible to develop a 'pragmatism without foundations' in which the plausible elements of realism can be reconciled with the plausible elements of relativism. Bernstein wants, instead, to move beyond the supposed opposition of realism and relativism by overcoming what he calls the 'Cartesian Anxiety', the quest for fixed constraints.

Pragmatists of a plainer reformist stripe would respond – perhaps after protesting the implication that their philosophy is driven by the neurotic need suggested by the term 'anxiety' – that it is not necessary to move beyond objectivity, or to reconcile it with relativism, provided it is tempered by a sufficiently thoroughgoing fallibilism. And it is to my mind within the tradition of reformist pragmatism that the most enduring contributions are to be found: Mead's theory of the social construction of the self, inspired by Peirce's critique of the intuitive self-consciousness assumed by Descartes; Lewis' pragmatic account of the *a priori*, itself an inspiration for Quine's call for 'a more thorough pragmatism'; Ramsey's BEHAVIOURISTIC (pp. 68–70) approach to belief, and Quine's, also, to meaning (Quine cites Dewey: 'meaning is . . . a property of behavior'); Quine's association of natural kinds, induction and evolutionary epistemology; Reichenbach's 'pragmatic vindication' of induction; Hanson's defence of the idea of an abductive logic of scientific discovery, Sellar's appeal to the notion of explanatory coherence, and

Harman's to inference to the best explanation; Putnam's explorations of conceptions of truth intermediate between metaphysical realism and relativism, Apel's of the need for an account of the pragmatic dimensions to supplement Tarski's semantic theory of truth; Rescher's investigations of criteria of success and improvement of cognitive methods, Jardine's of scientific progress; and many more. In my own work, such key ideas as explanatory integration (central to the articulated quasi-holism of my account of evidential support), the distinction of the state and the content senses of 'belief', and the combination of direct and interpretative elements in perception (both central elements of my account of the role of experience in justification), were mined, as I can testify, from the same vein.

This list illustrates the formidable diversity as well as the richness of the reformist tradition in pragmatism. This diversity is unified by what one might call the ongoing project of reformist pragmatism: the aspiration to find a middle ground between dogmatism and skepticism; a conception of truth as accessible enough to be realistically aspired to, yet objective enough to be worthy of the name; an articulation of the interplay between the world's contribution to knowledge, and ours. This is the essential spirit of reformist pragmatism, succinctly summed up by James: 'Please observe . . . that when . . . we give up the doctrine of objective certitude, we do not thereby give up the quest or hope of truth itself' (James, 1897, p. 17). So conceived, the tradition of reformist pragmatism still flourishes; and, though very far as yet for the 'catholic consent' Peirce saw (Peirce, 8.13) as the end of inquiry, it is, indeed, 'instinct with life'.

References to Material Cited in the Text

Apel, K.-O. 1983: C. S. Peirce and Post-Tarskian Truth. In *The Relevance of Charles Peirce*, ed. E. Freeman. La Salle, IL: The Hegeler Institute, Monist Library of Philosophy, 189–223.
Bernstein, R. J. 1983: *Beyond Objectivity and Relativism*. Philadelphia, PA: University of Pennsylvania Press.
Churchland, P. M. 1989: *A Neurocomputational Perspective: The Nature of Mind and the Structure of Science.* Cambridge, MA, and London: Bradford Books, MIT Press.
Dewey, J. 1910: *The Influence of Darwin on Philosophy.* New York, NY: Henry Holt.
—— 1925: *Experience and Nature.* La Salle, IL: Open Court, 1958.
—— 1929: *The Quest for Certainty.* New York, NY: Putnam, 1960.
—— 1938: *Logic, the Theory of Inquiry.* New York, NY: Henry Holt.
Haack, S. 1993: *Evidence and Inquiry: Towards Reconstruction in Epistemology.* Oxford: Blackwell.
Hanson, N. R. 1958: *Patterns of Discovery.* Cambridge: Cambridge University Press.
Harman, G. 1965: The Inference to the Best Explanation. *Philosophical Review*, 71, 86–95.
Jardine, B. 1986: *The Fortunes of Inquiry.* Oxford: Clarendon Press.
James, W. 1897: *The Will to Believe and Other Essays in Popular Philosophy.* New York, NY: Dover, 1956

—— 1907: *Pragmatism*, eds F. Burkhardt, and F. Bowers Cambridge, MA, and London: Harvard University Press 1975.

—— 1909: *The Meaning of Truth*, eds F. Burkhardt and F. Bowers Cambridge, MA, and London: Harvard University Press, 1975.

——1912 and 1909: *Essays in Radical Empiricism* (1912) and *A Pluralistic Universe* (1909), ed. R. J. Bernstein. New York, NY: Dutton, 1971.

Lewis, C. I. 1923: A Pragmatic Conception of the A Priori, *Journal of Philosophy*, xx, 169–77; reprinted in Thayer, H. S., *Pragmatism: The Classic Writings*, New York, NY: Mentor, 1970, and Indianapolis, IN: Hackett, 1983, 367–74.

Margolis, J. 1986: *Pragmatism Without Foundations*. Oxford: Blackwell.

Mead, G. H. 1934: *Mind, Self and Society*, ed. C. W. Morris. Chicago, IL: University of Chicago Press.

Migotti, M. 1988: Recent Work in Pragmatism: Revolution or Reform in the Theory of Knowledge?. *Philosophical Books*, XXIX, 65–73.

Peirce, C. S., *Collected Papers*, eds C. Hartshorne, P. Weiss and A. Burks. Cambridge, MA: Harvard University Press, 1931–58 (references by volume and paragraph number).

—— 1900: Review of *Clark University, 1889–1899: Decennial Celebration. Science*, 620–2; reprinted in Wiener, P. P. (ed.), *Charles S. Peirce: Selected Writings*, New York, NY: Doubleday, 1958, Dover, 1966.

Putnam, H. 1978: *Meaning and the Moral Sciences*. London: Routledge and Kegen Paul.

Quine, W. V. 1953: Two Dogmas of Empiricism. In *From a Logical Point of View*. Cambridge, MA: Harper Torchbooks, 20–46.

—— 1969: *Ontological Relativity and Other Essays*. New York, NY: Columbia University Press.

Ramsey, F. P. 1931: Belief and Propositions. In *The Foundations of Mathematics*, ed. R. B. Braithwaite. London: Routledge and Kegan Paul.

Reichenbach, H. 1951: *The Rise of Scientific Philosophy*. Berkeley and Los Angeles, CA: University of California Press.

Rescher, N. 1977: *Methodological Pragmatism*. Oxford: Blackwell.

Rorty, R. 1979: *Philosophy and the Mirror of Nature*. Princeton, NJ: Princeton University Press.

—— 1982: *Consequences of Pragmatism*. Brighton: Harvester Press.

—— 1991a: *Objectivity, Relativism and Truth*. Cambridge: Cambridge University Press.

—— 1991b: *Essays on Heidegger and Others*. Cambridge: Cambridge University Press.

Russell, B. 1910: Pragmatism; *and* William James's Conception of Truth. In *Philosophical Essays*. New York, NY: Longman's, Green and Co., 79–111 and 112–30.

Schiller, F. C. S. 1907: *Studies in Humanism*. London and New York, NY: MacMillan.

Sellars, W. 1973: Giveness and Explanatory Coherence. *Journal of Philosophy*, 61.

—— 1979: More on Giveness and Explanatory Coherence. In *Justification and Knowledge*, ed. G. Pappas. Dordrecht: Reidel, 169–81.

Stich, S. P. 1990: *The Fragmentation of Reason: Preface to a Pragmatic Theory of Cognitive Evaluation*. Cambridge, MA, and London: Bradford Books, MIT Press.

Further Readings Not Cited in the Text

Dewey writes on 'The Development of American Pragmatism' in his *Philosophy and Civilization*, New York, NY: Minton, Balch, 1931. Useful selections of the writings of the classical pragmatists are Thayer, H. S. (ed.), *Pragmatism:*

The Classic Writings (details under Lewis in 'References', above), and Rorty, A. (ed.), *Pragmatic Philosophy*, Garden City, NJ: Doubleday Anchor, 1966 (the former includes an interview with William James published in the *New York Times* in 1907, entitled, 'Pragmatism – What It Is'; the latter includes excerpts from criticisms of pragmatism by contemporaries such as Russell and Moore, and Reichenbach's 'pragmatic vindication of induction'). Thayer also has a fine article on Pragmatism in the *Encyclopedia of Philosophy*, ed. P. Edwards, New York, NY and London: Macmillan, 1967; see also his *Meaning and Action: A Critical History of Pragmatism*, Indianapolis, IN and New York, NY: Bobbs-Merrill, 1968. Scheffler, I., *Four Pragmatists*, London: Routledge and Kegan Paul and New York, NY: Humanities Press, 1974, is a clear introduction to Peirce, James, Mead and Dewey. Ayer, A. J., *The Origins of Pragmatism*, San Francisco, CA: Freeman, Cooper, 1968, is illuminating on the relation of pragmatism and Ayer's own, logical positivist, approach. The *Transactions of the Charles S. Peirce Society* is a quarterly journal of American philosophy, which carries articles on every aspect of pragmatism as well as reviews of significant books in the area.

Goudge, T., *The Thought of C. S. Peirce*, Toronto: Toronto University Press, 1950, and New York, NY: Dover, 1966, and Hookway, C., *Peirce*, London: Routledge and Kegan Paul, 1985, are useful introductions to Peirce's work. Murphey, M., *The Development of Peirce's Philosophy*, Cambridge, MA: Harvard University Press, 1961, and Indianapolis, IN: Hackett, 1993, has become a classic. Two collections of papers that have stood the test of time are *Studies in the Philosophy of Charles Sanders Peirce*, first series, eds Weiner, P. and Young, F. P., and second series, eds Moore, E. C. and Robin, R. S.; Amherst, MA: University of Massachusetts Press, 1952 and 1964. On Peirce's logic, Putnam, 'Peirce the Logician', *Historia Mathematica*, 9 (1982), 290–301, is a good starting point. See Ketner, K. L., *A Comprehensive Bibliography of the Published Works of Charles Sanders Peirce with a Bibliography of Secondary Sources*, Bowling Green, OH: Philosophy Documentation Center, 1986, for a bibliography of work on Peirce up to that date. A new, chronological edition of (selected) works of Peirce is being published by Indiana University Press, under the editorship of Max Fisch et al., the first five volumes (up to 1886) being available by 1995. There are several smaller volumes of selected papers, including Weiner, P. P. (ed.), *C. S. Peirce: Selected Writings*, New York: Doubleday, 1958, and *The Essential Peirce* (vol. I, 1867–1893), eds Kloesel, C. and Houser, N., Bloomington and Indianapolis, IN: Indiana University Press, 1992.

James's *Works* are published by Harvard University Press under the editorship of Burkhardt, F. and Bowers, F., Ralph Barton Perry (ed.), *The Thought and Character of William James*, two volumes, Boston: Little, Brown and Co., 1936, and (abridged, one volume) Cambridge, MA: Harvard University Press, 1948, is unparalleled as an intellectual portrait of the man and his work. See also Myers, G., *William James, His Life and Thought*, New Haven, CT: Yale University Press, 1986, and his bibliography. Corti, W. R. (ed.),

The Philosophy of William James, Hamburg: Felix Meiner, 1976, is a useful collection of articles on James's work.

Hook, S., *John Dewey: an Intellectual Portrait*, New York, NY: John Day, 1939, is a fine brief introduction. Tiles, J., *Dewey*, New York, NY and London: Routledge and Kegan Paul, 1988, will also be found useful. *John Dewey: The Man and his Philosophy*, Cambridge, MA: Harvard University Press, 1930, includes an essay by G. H. Mead. There is a volume in the Library of Living Philosophers devoted to Dewey's work (*The Philosophy of John Dewey*, ed. Schilpp, P. A., Evanston and Chicago, IL: Northwestern University Press, 1939); this includes a bibliography of Dewey's writings. Sleeper, R. W., *The Necessity of Pragmatism*, New Haven, CT: Yale University Press, 1986, a study of Dewey's logic, also includes critical bibliographies. See Boydston, J. and Poolos, K. (eds), *A Guide to the Works of John Dewey*, Carbondale, IL: Southern Illinois University Press, 1970, and *Checklist of Writings About John Dewey, 1887–1977*, Carbondale, IL: Southern Illinois University Press, 1978, for further references. Dewey's complete works are being published by Southern Illinois University Press under the editorship of Jo Ann Boydston; writings up to 1953 are available at the time of this writing.

On Schiller, see Abel, R., *Humanistic Pragmatism*, New York, NY: Free Press, and London: Collier-Macmillan, 1966, and *The Pragmatic Humanism of F. C. S. Schiller*, New York, NY: King's Cross Press, Columbia University Press, 1955.

On Mead, see Reck, A. J. (ed.), *Selected Writings*, Indianapolis, IN and New York, NY: Bobbs-Merrill, 1964, and Corti, W. R. (ed.), *The Philosophy of George Herbert Mead*, Winterthur, Switzerland: Amriswiler Bucherei, 1973, both of which include bibliographies of Mead's writings.

There is a volume in the Library of Living Philosophers on the work of C. I. Lewis (*The Philosophy of C. I. Lewis*, ed.Schilpp, P. A., La Salle, IL: Open Court, 1968); this includes a bibliography of Lewis's writings. See also Rosenthal, S., *The Pragmatic A Priori*, St Louis, MO: Warren H. Green inc., 1976.

The relation of Rorty's philosophy to Dewey's is debated in a symposium of McDermott, J., Sleeper, R. W. and Edel, A., in *Transactions of the C. S. Peirce Society*, XXI (1985), 1–38, with a reply by Rorty. That Rorty seriously misinterprets Peirce is argued in Haack, 'Philosophy/philosophy, an Untenable Dualism', *Transactions of the C. S. Peirce Society*, XXIX (summer 1993). *Rorty and Pragmatism*, ed. Herman J. Saatkamp, Jr, Nashville, TN: Vanderbilt University Press, 1995, includes papers by Rorty's critics, and replies by Rorty.

Discussion Questions

1 Explain Peirce's version of the Pragmatic Maxim, and the role it plays in his attitude to metaphysics.

2   What does Peirce mean by saying that 'pragmaticism could hardly have
    entered a head that was not already convinced there were real generals'
    (Peirce, 5.503)? Was he right about this?

3   Explain Peirce's definition of truth as the 'Ultimate Opinion'. Do you
    think it is a defensible account of the concept of truth?

4   What does Peirce mean by saying that philosophy should be undertaken
    with 'the scientific attitude'?

5   'Our passional nature . . . lawfully may . . . decide an option be-
    tween propositions, whenever it is a genuine option that cannot by its
    nature be decided on intellectual grounds' (James, 1897, p. 11). Do you
    agree?

6   What are the main themes of James' 'radical empiricism'? How does it
    differ from the empiricism of Locke or Hume?

7   ' "[T]he true" . . . is only the expedient in the way of belief '. What did
    James mean by this? Is it plausible?

8   Critically compare James' observation that 'books upon ethics, . . . so far as
    they truly touch the moral life, must more and more ally themselves with
    . . . novels and dramas of the deeper sort' (James, 1897, p. 210), with
    Dewey's that '[e]xperimental empiricism in the field of ideas of good and
    bad is demanded' (Dewey, 1929, p. 258).

9   Critically discuss Dewey's attitude to the idea that, when we verify a
    proposition, we discover it to have been true all along.

10 Explain and discuss the merits of Dewey's critique of 'the Spectator
    Theory of Knowledge'.

11 What does Schiller mean by saying that truth is relative to our purposes?
    Is he right?

12 Critically discuss Mead's theory of the 'social construction of the self'.

13 Explain Lewis' doctrine of the pragmatic *a priori*; is it a plausible
    approach to the question of alternative logics?

14 'Pragmatists think that the history of attempts to isolate the True, or the
    Good, or to define the word "true" or "good," supports their suspicion
    that there is no interesting work to be done in this area' (Rorty, 1982,
    p. xiv). *Is* that what pragmatists think?

15 'According to the pragmatists, to say "it is true that other people exist" *means* "it is useful to believe that other people exist" ... Now if pragmatists only affirmed that utility is a *criterion* of truth, there would be much less to be said against their view' (Russell, 1910, pp. 119–20). Is this a fair comment on James' account of truth?

27

Frege and Russell ——————————

R. M. Sainsbury

Gottlob Frege (1848–1925) and Bertrand Russell (1872–1970) both came to philosophy through mathematics. They both contributed to a doctrine known as logicism, according to which mathematics is a part of logic, and so is as unquestionable as logic. In pursuit of this aim, each developed the basis of what we now think of as modern logic. Each regarded his logical language as better able to represent thought than ordinary language. This view generated the notion of 'logical form', which has been crucial in the development of philosophy in this century. Each was led into fundamental discussions about meaning. In the areas in which their work overlapped, they agreed about which problems were central, but disagreed in many cases about how to solve them. All current work in logic, the philosophy of mathematics and the philosophy of language either takes for granted something owed to one or both of them, or else takes their views as the most important ones to defend or attack. This chapter will focus on the notion of meaning as it occurs in the works of these two philosophers and will expound two central ideas from each: Frege's notion of a concept, and his distinction between sense (*Sinn*) and reference (*Bedeutung*); and Russell's account of names and his theory of descriptions. In both cases, and especially Russell's, whose work ranged more widely than Frege's, this is a very small proportion of the ideas for which they are famous.

1 Introduction

Frege was born in 1848, and spent most of his adult life in the mathematics department of the University of Jena. His first major work, the *Begriffsschrift* or 'concept-script', in which he set out his formal language, was published in 1879, when Russell was a child of seven. In his *Grundlagen* (Groundwork of Arithmetic) of 1884 he gave an informal exposition of his logicist position, defining numbers in terms of extensions of concepts, which he took to be a purely logical notion. The two works were brought together in his *Grundgesetze* (Basic Laws of Arithmetic, 1893), in which the formal devices of the *Begriffsschrift* were applied to the logicist programme set out in the *Grundlagen*. Close to this time, he wrote the two articles upon which this chapter focuses: 'Function und Begriff' of 1891 ('Function and Concept', 1984), and '*Uber Sinn und Bedeutung*' ('On Sense and Meaning', 1892).

Russell's first exposition of logicism, and one of his earliest works, was in his *Principles of Mathematics* (1903). At a late stage in its preparation, he discovered that apparently true assumptions led to a contradiction concerning classes, a discovery known as Russell's paradox. He wrote to Frege in 1903, showing that Frege's logical system in the *Grundgesetze* permitted a proof of the contradiction. The blow had a paralysing effect upon Frege. An appendix to volume 2 of the *Grundgesetze* (which was added in 1903) suggested a weakening of the axiom (Basic Law V) which he regarded as the root of the trouble, but he came to see that this would prevent derivations which were needed for the logicist programme, and Dummett has suggested that it is likely that, by 1906, Frege had despaired of carrying through his logicism (Dummett, 1981, pp. 21–2).

Russell's own final response to the contradiction, taking the form of a theory of types, was published in 1908, and the full statement of his logicism, incorporating type theory, is his monumental *Principia Mathematica* (1910–13), written jointly with A. N. Whitehead.

The first decade or so of the century was a very fruitful period for Russell, and the two articles I shall mainly focus on date from then. They are 'On Denoting' (1905) and 'On Knowledge by Acquaintance and Knowledge by Description', which was published in 1911 and which is reprinted almost unchanged in his *Problems of Philosophy* (1912). This represents only a fragment of Russell's philosophy, omitting not only his work in the PHILOSOPHY OF MATHEMATICS (chapter 10), but also his logical atomism (see especially Russell, 1918–19), his theories of mind (see especially Russell, 1921) and his late works (which include *Inquiry into Meaning and Truth*, 1941, and *Human Knowledge*, 1956).

In addition to work in philosophy, Russell had wide-ranging interests, and never held an established university post. He wrote a number of popular books (for example, *Marriage and Morals*, 1929), won the Nobel Prize for literature in 1950, was a civil rights activist in the 1950s and 1960s, and became a well-known public figure, especially as a member of the Campaign for Nuclear Disarmament (he was arrested for participating in one of their protest demonstrations). His *Autobiography* caused a stir by its selective frankness, and by the rather unattractive picture it conveyed of the great man's tardy yet intense emotional development. He died in 1970, outliving Frege by 45 years.

2 Frege on Function, Concept and Object

Many sentences say something true or false about the world. What makes this possible? Perhaps, as Russell thought, a crucial point is that the words of the sentence stand for parts or features of the world. Perhaps, in 'London is beautiful', 'London' stands for London, and 'beautiful' for beauty. Even if this is the right start, it cannot be the end of the story, for nothing has been said to distinguish the sentence from the mere list 'London, beauty': the words in the list also stand for parts or features of the world. As Russell put it, the process of analysis, itemizing what the parts of a sentence stand for, seems to dissolve the *unity of the proposition*: the features that make a proposition, unlike a mere list, something that represents the world as being thus-and-so, and something that can be affirmed or denied.

Russell himself never gave any detailed solution to this problem. However, one of the cornerstones of Frege's approach, set out in detail in his 'Function and Concept' (Frege, 1891), suggests a way of approaching it.

In standard arithmetical notation, an expression like 'x^2' is said to stand for a function. If we replace 'x' by '3' we have an expression which stands for 9. The function for which 'x^2' stands yields 9 as its *value* when 3 is its *argument*; in general, this function yields as value the square of the argument. An expression like '$x^2 = 9$' is in some ways similar, in having the undetermined part 'x'. Can we view such an expression as also standing for a function? If we replace 'x' by '3' we get a sentence which is true; if we replace it by an expression for any other positive number, we get a sentence which is false. Frege suggested that this reveals how we can think of '$x^2 = 9$' as standing for a function: it stands for a function which yields the value *true* for the argument 3, and the value *false* for any other positive number as argument. This involves supposing that there are abstract objects, the True and the False, and equating being true with being appropriately related to the True, and similarly for being false.

A function is incomplete. Just as an expression for a function contains an undetermined part, say 'x', calling for completion by a determinate expression, say '3', so this feature is mirrored in the nature of the function itself. It needs an object as argument to yield a value.

A concept is a function of a special kind: one whose value, for every argument, is a truth value. If a concept-word is completed by inserting a word for an object, which Frege calls a proper name, into the blank space, the result is a sentence. The concept expressed by '( ) is beautiful' has an incompleteness which mirrors that of the expression: there is an undetermined part, here marked by '( )'. If we insert a proper name, say 'London', into the space, the result is the sentence 'London is beautiful'. Although he did stress the predicative nature of concepts (see, for example, Frege, 1892a, p. 187), Frege himself did not explicitly use this account to address the problem of the unity of the proposition. However, one can see in the account at least the beginning of a solution. It is one thing to devise a list, listing say an object and a concept; it is another to insert the object into the slot which constitutes the incompleteness of the concept. Frege thus has room for the difference with which Russell was concerned. Frege's immediate use of the analysis of sentences in terms of concepts and objects was to introduce his theory of generality in terms of quantifier and variable. 'All men are mortal' is to be understood as in effect claiming that the value of the function 'if x is a man then x is mortal' is the True whatever object is argument. His theory of quantification is one of his greatest achievements, and, while it has been refined, and alternatives developed, it is in no danger of being supplanted. Russell produced a similar theory (Russell, 1905). He claimed that, although he had read Frege's *Begriffsschrift* in the 1890s, he had not understood it. The poor quality of

Russell's first presentation compared to Frege's supports his claim to have rediscovered the theory for himself (Russell, 1967–9, p. 68). Russell's later accounts of the theory (particularly Russell, 1908, 1910–13 and 1918–19) though so much later than Frege's account, were probably more widely read and influential.

3 *Sinn* (Sense) and *Bedeutung* (Reference)

Compare a truth of the form '*a* is (identical to) *b*' with one of the form '*a* is (identical to) *a*'. We are to imagine '*a*' and '*b*' replaced by proper names, for example by 'Hesperus' and 'Phosphorus' respectively. These were names supposedly given by the ancients to Venus: 'Hesperus' was used for a planet which was first to be seen in the evening at certain times of the year; 'Phosphorus' was used for a planet which was last to fade in the morning at certain other times of the year. They did not realize that both appearances were of the same heavenly body. Each proper name stands for (*bedeutet*) Venus; Venus is the 'Bedeutung' of both names. In ordinary contexts 'Bedeutung' is best translated as 'meaning'. However, it has been common to mark Frege's somewhat technical use of the word by a different translation, most popularly 'reference', and I shall follow this precedent. That *a* is *b* can be a valuable extension of our knowledge: under appropriate circumstances, coming to know this has 'cognitive value'. However, that *a* is *a* seems trivial and uninformative, and of little or no cognitive value. This contrast, which it is natural to treat as involving two distinct items of knowledge, cannot be explained in terms of reference, since the two sentences coincide point-by-point in reference.

Frege correctly inferred that a complete account of a name must allude to other properties than its reference. For all that has been said, these further properties could be idiosyncratic (varying from person to person), or could be SYNTACTIC (pp. 151–3) (for example, residing merely in the fact that in the one case two different names are involved). However, Frege's hypothesis was that the difference is one of sense (*Sinn*), where this is connected with what must be grasped in coming to learn how to use a name, and with how something is presented or thought of. Sense is thus neither idiosyncratic, since it is implicated in coming to learn the proper public use of a word, nor merely syntactic, since it is implicated in how things are thought of. The sense of an expression is an abstract object, not a mere idea, and is in principle available to anyone. Whether a sentence expresses something of cognitive value to us will, on this theory, depend not only upon the reference of each of its names but also upon their sense. If we think that coming to know that *a* is *b* can extend our knowledge in a way that coming to know that *a* is *a* cannot (supposing we can so much as make sense of 'coming' to know the latter), then we are counting the things we know, objects of knowledge, as objects individuated by sense.

Whereas a brief, and in my view decisive, argument leads to the conclusion that there is more to a name than its reference, we should not think of Frege as offering any direct argument for the conclusion that this something is sense, regarded as public and semantic; rather, the merit of the view is supposed to emerge as it is elaborated, extended to expressions other than names, and applied to various problems.

The distinction between sense and reference was first introduced for proper names like 'Hesperus'. Do these notions also apply to whole sentences? Frege affirmed that an assertoric sentence expresses a thought, and argues that this should be taken as the sentence's sense and not as its reference. He held it to be obvious that, for example, 'Hesperus is Hesperus' expresses a different thought from 'Hesperus is Phosphorus'. Since names in the sentences agree in their reference, it would seem that we cannot identify the thoughts the sentences themselves express with their reference. So, if the thought a sentence expresses is either its sense or its reference, it must be its sense. This does not give Frege what he needs unless the antecedent of the conditional can be established. Given that sense was originally introduced to explain a difference between names which affects what is known, and to individuate OBJECTS OF KNOWLEDGE (pp. 652), and given that thoughts are possible objects of knowledge, it is at least plausible to stipulate that the sense of a sentence is the thought it expresses.

Can an assetoric sentence as a whole be credited with a reference? Reference was introduced in terms of the seemingly transparent relation holding between a name and its bearer. If we think of reference as wholly determined by this relation, then it would seem that the reference of a complete sentence like 'Hesperus is a planet' would simply be Hesperus. However, Frege invited us to consider another feature of the reference of 'Hesperus': it exhausts the word's contribution to the determination of the truth or falsehood of typical sentences in which the word occurs. In 'Hesperus is a planet', all that 'Hesperus' contributes to whether the sentence expresses something true or something false is to introduce Hesperus as its reference. So far as truth and falsity go (as opposed to cognitive value) only reference seems to matter.

To establish this connection between the reference of the parts of a sentence, and whether the whole sentence is true or false, Frege invited us to think of a special case: fiction. In the sentence 'Odysseus was put ashore at Ithaca while sound asleep' we have a sentence containing a proper name, 'Odysseus', which lacks reference (Frege, 1892b, p. 162). The sentence as a whole is neither true nor false. So it looks as if when a part lacks reference, the whole sentence lacks the property of being true and the property of being false.

Frege's suggestion was that we should see whole non-fictional sentences as having one or other of the truth values as their reference. We saw that almost this view was suggested to him by his treatment of concepts as kinds of functions. If the concept expressed by 'is a planet' takes the value True for argument Hesperus, then the sentence 'Hesperus is a planet' must be related in some special way to this value. Having the value as its reference seems just the right relation. The application of the notions of sense and reference to parts of speech other than proper names was guided by compositionality principles. Frege in effect stipulated that the sense and reference of a sentence are determined by the sense and reference of its parts in at least the following sense: substitutions of parts which agree in sense reference leave the sense reference of the whole unchanged. Given this, that the proper names 'Hesperus' and 'Phosphorus' differ in sense but are alike in reference establishes that the sentences 'Hesperus is Hesperus' and 'Hesperus is Phosphorus' differ in sense (express different thoughts) but are alike in reference (have the same truth value).

4 Identity Statements and Bearerless Names: Russell's View of Names as Associated with Descriptions

Frege's first characterization of sense is 'the mode of presentation of the thing designated'. The idea is that the same object can be presented in more than one way (as Venus is presented in one way in connection with uses of 'Hesperus' and another in connection with uses of 'Phosphorus'). Sense 'determines' reference in that expressions that agree in sense agree also in reference. However, Frege seemed to allow that sense without reference is possible: 'The expression 'the least rapidly convergent series' has a sense but demonstrably nothing is its reference' (Frege 1892b, p. 159). Though this is the orthodox interpretation of Frege, it has been challenged by Gareth Evans (1982), who points out that Frege very often used the case of fiction when discussing the possibility of sense without reference. His remarks about fiction, Evans suggests, could be interpreted as claiming that in fiction we pretend that there is a sense (and also that there is a reference). One does not have to suppose that there really is a sense. Evans' view receives support from such remarks of Frege's as: 'A sentence containing a proper name lacking reference is neither true nor false; if it expresses a thought at all, then that thought belongs to fiction' (Frege, 1979, p. 194). In other words, if a sentence contains a name without reference, then it lacks sense (except for the pretend thoughts of fiction); which can only be explained by the fact that a name lacking reference lacks sense. Not all the evidence supports Evans' view, as the sentence quoted above makes plain. If we return to the orthodox interpretation, we should not hold that, for Frege, sense 'determines' reference, if this is understood to entail that each sense is associated with a reference.

Frege says that an expression expresses its sense and designates its reference (we should presumably add 'if any'). Russell, using 'meaning' for sense and 'denoting' for reference, argued that a theory of this kind leads to 'an inextricable tangle' (Russell, 1905, p. 50). The exegesis of Russell's argument is no easy matter, and commentators disagree both on how it should be understood and on whether it is of any significance for Frege's views (see Hochberg, 1976, Blackburn and Code, 1978, and Pakuluk, 1993). What cannot be disputed is that Russell's own account of the workings of thought and language used a single notion, which he usually calls meaning, in place of Frege's two notions of sense and reference. According to this single notion, simple expressions like 'this' have meaning by standing for something. Complex expressions are capable of being understood so long as they are composed of simple expressions having meaning. To remind us of the distinction between how the account treats simple and complex expressions, Russell said of the latter that they have no meaning on their own account. One way to form a conception of the adequacy of Frege's two-notion theory is to compare it with Russell's contrasting single-notion one.

How could Russell have allowed that it is one thing to believe that Hesperus is Hesperus, and another to believe that Hesperus is Phosphorus, without allowing something like Frege's distinction between sense and reference? The answer, according to Russell, was that names like 'Hesperus' and 'Phosphorus' cannot be used to give the best account of what is going on in a thinker. Rather, 'the thought in the mind of a person using a proper name correctly can generally only be expressed explicitly if we replace the proper name by a description' (Russell, 1967, p. 29). By 'description', in this context, Russell means a definite description, that is, a phrase of the form 'the so-and-so'. Perhaps someone associates 'Hesperus' with 'the Evening Star' and 'Phosphorus' with 'the Morning Star'. Does not the original problem arise again? Since 'the Evening Star' and 'the Morning Star' stand for the same thing – or, in Frege's terminology, have the same reference – yet 'the Morning Star is the Morning Star' differs in cognitive value from 'the Morning Star is the Evening Star', must one not recognize something over and above what expressions stand for? Russell's answer is that one need not, for in such cases, where the phrase is complex, one can explain the difference in terms of the different parts of the complexes. One can explain the differences between 'the Evening Star' and 'the Morning Star' in terms of the fact that one phrase contains a word which stands for the morning and not the evening, and the other contains a word which stands for the evening and not the morning. There is no need to appeal to anything corresponding to Fregean sense. (For more details on how Russell developed this view, see section 6 below.)

Some names have no bearers, and yet have a systematic role in language (such as 'Santa Claus' or 'Vulcan' – the planet postulated, needlessly as it turned out, to explain the orbit of Mercury). On the conventional interpretation of Frege adopted here, he can account for this simply as a case of sense without reference. How could a single-notion theory like Russell's cope with such cases? Russell again appealed to the link between names (of the kind in question) and descriptions. We associate 'Santa Claus' with, for example, 'the bearded man from Lapland who brings Christmas presents', and 'Vulcan' with 'the planet lying between Mercury and the Sun'. Each component of these descriptions can, on Russell's single-notion view, be regarded as having meaning by standing for something; and this accounts, at one remove, for the intelligibility of the names without their having to stand for anything. Such names and their associated descriptions have no meaning on their own account, unlike genuinely simple expressions.

5 Names and Communication

How should we compare these theories? One way is to ask to what extent each provides the resources for a correct account of the working of language.

Frege's notion of sense is firmly connected to language: 'the sense of a proper name is grasped by everybody who is sufficiently familiar with the language' (Frege, 1892b, p. 158). He stressed that we must not confuse the sense of an expression, which is objective and in principle available to all, with the ideas in the minds of people when they use it, which, being psychological, are subjective and confined to a single person. He held that, unlike the public sense of an expression, 'every idea has only one owner; no two men have the same idea' (Frege, 1918, p. 361). One intuition is that Frege's insistence is correct: languages like English or German, or the formal languages which were Frege's main concern, are indeed public, and a correct account must be in public terms like sense, rather than idiosyncratic ones like ideas. We communicate in a public language, and the straightforward Fregean account of this is that we do so by sharing thoughts: for a speaker to succeed in communicating is for him to arouse in the mind of the hearer the thought that he or she expresses.

Russell's account as so far described, applies to names like 'Hesperus', is based on possibly idiosyncratic features of various speakers. We are to find the descriptions in the mind of someone who uses such a name, and Russell was explicit that 'the description required to express the thought will vary for different people, or for the same person at different times' (Russell, 1967, p. 29). On the face of it, this seems ill-adapted to provide a good account of the functioning of a public language.

Before investigating this, it is important to stress that Russell's theory connecting names and descriptions was not advanced primarily as a theory of a public language, but rather as an account of thought or JUDGEMENT (pp. 590–4). It was thus not advanced under the constraint of publicity which Frege took upon himself. However, in a brief passage, Russell showed how his ideas could be developed to provide an account of communication in a public language. The account is of interest because it moves away from the Fregean model of communication as thought-sharing.

Let us consider the two philosophers' reactions to a problem about names. When trying to say what the sense of a name like 'Aristotle' or 'Dr Lauben' is, Frege found it natural to produce a definite description. However, he observed that

> in the case of an actual proper name such as 'Aristotle' opinions as to the sense may differ. It might, for instance, be taken to be the following: the pupil of Plato and teacher of Alexander the Great. Anybody who does this will attach another sense to the sentence 'Aristotle was born in Stagira' than will a man who takes as the sense of the name: the teacher of Alexander the Great who was born in Stagira. (Frege, 1892b, p. 158)

Frege put this variability down to imperfections of ordinary language, and claimed that it ought not to occur in a perfect language. This is, in effect, an admission that sense, though appropriate to an account of a public language in virtue of the general feature of being public, fits uneasily with the fact that names are associated with definite descriptions in a variable, and to that extent non-public, way. The variability of associated descriptions, the apparently unequivocal character of our use of names, and the supposition that descriptions are often constitutive of sense, should have led Frege to deny that proper names in ordinary language have sense; but this would have undermined the explanation of the cognitive value of 'Hesperus is Phosphorus'.

Russell steered through this difficulty by saying that the feature of a name like 'Hesperus' that matters in communication, and the feature that fixes the name's contribution to whether what is said is true or false, is not the description associated with it by this or that user, but rather what the name stands for, where this is determined by the various associated descriptions. Suppose a speaker, S, utters the words 'Bismarck was astute'. In so doing, he will, on Russell's theory, think a thought more explicitly expressible as, perhaps, 'The first Chancellor of Germany was astute'. S communicates successfully with his interlocutor, H, just on condition that, for some description, perhaps 'the ugliest man in Europe', which also denotes Bismarck, H realizes that S has said something about the ugliest man in Europe which is true if and only if he is astute. It is not necessary that S and H should share a thought. All that is required is that the possibly various descriptions they associate with the name 'Bismarck' should stand for the same thing; for this is what it means to say that the name 'Bismarck' has a (public) reference in the language community to which S and H belong (Sainsbury, 1993).

The upshot is that if an account of names is to be couched in terms of definite descriptions, one does better to view the relationship in Russell's way than to view the descriptions as specifications of Fregean sense. Although Frege offered definite descriptions as examples of a name's sense, he was not committed to the view that the sense of a proper name can typically be given by a description, and a Fregean does best to deny this (see McDowell, 1977, Kripke, 1972).

6 Russell's Theory of Descriptions

We have seen that Russell provided an account of the intelligibility of definite descriptions without supposing they had to stand for anything; it is enough that their parts be intelligible, which is typically a matter of the parts standing for something. The notion of 'standing for', or as Russell often says 'meaning', is thus the single notion which is supposed to give a better account than Frege's twin notions of sense and reference.

In more detail, Russell thought genuinely simple singular and general terms had meaning by standing for something: a particular in the case of singular terms like 'this', a universal in the case of general terms like 'red'. Understanding such expressions involves acquaintance with what they stand for. There is just one other source of meaning, and that derives from the logical constants, like 'and', 'not', 'is identical to' and 'all'. Russell never gave a satisfactory account of how such expressions had meaning, but it is obvious that they contribute to the intelligibility of complex expressions.

Russell admitted a very narrow class of 'logically proper names', singular terms which a logician, as opposed to an ordinary person or a grammarian, should count as proper names. These are genuinely SIMPLE (pp. 687–93) singular terms, and understanding them involves acquaintance with what they stand for. Russell supposed that if two such terms, say 'a' and 'b', stood for the same thing, anyone who understood both would be aware of the truth of 'a is b'. Since most of what we ordinarily call proper names, such as 'Hesperus' and 'Aristotle', do not satisfy this requirement, he excluded them from the category of logically proper names, and explained their functioning in terms of associated descriptions, in the fashion already described. The only logically proper names in ordinary English, according to Russell, are 'this' and 'that'.

Definite Descriptions

Russell is famous for his theory of definite descriptions. He said that a phrase of the form 'the moon' is a quantifier phrase, like 'no moons' and 'all moons', and should not be likened to a logically proper name like 'this'. In particular, 'the' is the uniqueness quantifier, so 'the moon is cold' is true if, and only if, there is exactly one moon and it is cold, and 'the moon exists' is true if, and only if, there is exactly one moon. This enabled Russell to explain how a sentence like 'the golden mountain does not exist' can be true: it is true if, and only if, either nothing or more than one thing is both golden and a mountain. If the intelligibility of the phrase 'the golden mountain' required that it stand for something then, unless there are things which do not exist, the sentence 'the golden mountain does not exist' could not be true: if 'the golden mountain' stood for something, the sentence would be false, and if 'the golden mountain' did not stand for anything, the sentence would be unintelligible. Russell explained the intelligibility of the phrase in terms of the intelligibility of its parts: 'the' is in effect a logical constant like 'all' (since it is defined in terms of such expressions) and so has meaning in whatever way logical constants do; 'golden' and 'mountain' can have meaning by standing for the universals of goldenness and mountainhood.

Frege thought that even though there is certainly a concept corresponding to an expression like 'square root of −1', one should not without care permit oneself to use the expression 'the square root of −1': one would need to assure oneself that the expression had a reference before admitting it into a perfect language. If by any chance one does find oneself with expressions without reference, one can introduce the special stipulation that the unruly expression is to have the number 0 as its reference. As Russell said, this is an 'artificial' and unsatisfactory suggestion, and one out of keeping with other Fregean theses. To provide a reference by *ad hoc* stipulation is to forget that, for Frege, an expression's sense determines its reference (if any), and the sense of an expression is determined by that of its parts. Frege's view on this matter is not easy to understand, since it is very hard to see how a perfect language adequate for mathematics could fail to have the resources to permit such phrases as 'the prime number between 5 and 7'. Frege does indeed explain how the sentence 'there is no such thing as the prime number between 5 and 7' can be true, without attributing a reference to 'the prime number between 5 and 7'. Similarly to Russell, he would have us regard the sentence as saying that no object uniquely falls under the concept of being a prime number between 5 and 7. What is hard to see is how Frege could suppose that the syntax for a language could properly discriminate between concept-words which may, and those which may not, be prefixed by 'the'.

7 Indirect Discourse

Frege's doctrine of sense and reference has a complication we have not yet mentioned. He thought it obvious that in indirect speech, for example when we say that the ancient astronomers did not realize that Hesperus was Phosphorus, 'it is quite clear that in this way of speaking words do not have their customary reference but designate what is usually their sense' (Frege, 1892b, p. 159). In short, in indirect speech, words have an 'indirect' reference: it is their customary sense.

Rather than taking this as obvious, Frege could have used his compositional principles to prove it. If we replace one occurrence of 'Hesperus' by 'Phosphorus' in

The ancients believed that Hesperus is Hesperus

we turn truth into falsehood. Since, by compositionality, replacing a part by an expression with the same reference cannot affect the reference of the whole sentence, that is, its truth value, this shows that 'Hesperus', as it occurs in the displayed sentence, does not have Hesperus (that is, Phosphorus) as its reference.

The hypothesis that, in an indirect context, 'Hesperus' has as its reference the sense it has in ordinary contexts is suggested by the fact that, in an indirect context, we are trying to identify someone's thought, and a thought is a sense. It would be confirmed if we found that exchanging expressions in such contexts by ones having the same customary sense was guaranteed to leave the reference of the whole sentence unchanged. It would be refuted if we could find expressions with the same sense, and a sentence whose truth value was changed just by replacing one of them by the other. Perhaps 'pail' and 'bucket' have the same sense, yet replacing one by the other in 'John said that a pail is a bucket' alters the truth value (Wiggins, 1976). This observation might instead be used to show that on Frege's technical conception of sense, 'pail' and 'bucket' differ in sense. This puts pressure upon us to examine Frege's conception more carefully.

The indirect reference of a name is its customary sense; but what is its indirect sense? Frege himself said that 'we distinguish . . . customary sense from . . . indirect sense'. But he makes no more of the point, and Dummett has argued, convincingly in my view, that he would have done better to identify customary and indirect sense. In other words, he would have done better to deny any distinction between sense and reference in indirect contexts. This conclusion would follow from Frege's compositionality principles, if we could take as a premise that the conditions that govern SUBSTITUTIVITY *SALVA VERITATE* (p. 95) in the displayed sentence above coincide with the conditions governing it in a sentence like:

> Some philosophers dispute that the ancients did not realize that Hesperus is Phosphorus.

Frege's distinction between sense and reference arguably helps us understand indirect speech. The shift in reference as between ordinary and indirect contexts mirrors the fact that in ordinary contexts, truth is a matter of how things are, whereas in indirect contexts truth is typically affected by how things are thought to be. Given that Russell made no distinction like that between sense and reference, how can he deal with such contexts?

Russell's theory does not explicitly deal with the different substitutivity principles required by indirect contexts. His goal is to give an account of sentences like

> Othello believes that Desdemona loves Cassio

which does not require any single entity corresponding to a Fregean thought. Russell held that, although one might allow that there are such things as truths, one could not allow that there are such things as falsehoods; hence one could not analyse a sentence like the one just displayed as a relation between Othello and some single object (Russell, 1967, p. 72). To understand why he held this, one needs to appreciate what one might call his 'non-conceptualism' (Sainsbury, 1986). On pain of idealism, he believed that the mind had to stand in direct relations to the world, not relations mediated by ideas or other representations. A true proposition could be thought of as a fact; but a false proposition would be some kind of false representation, and, for Russell, there are no such things as representations. It is a pity that Russell never considered Frege's view of representations (thoughts) as abstract rather than mental.

Russell's analysis of the sentence 'Othello believes that Desdemona loves Cassio' is that it expresses a four-term relation of belief holding between Othello, Desdemona, love and Cassio. Using the standard conventions of first-order logic, we might write this as

> Believes(Othello, Desdemona, love, Cassio).

Suppose 'N' is some other name for Cassio; suppose Othello has encountered the use of this name, but wrongly believes that it designates someone else. Then we could not infer that Othello believes that Desdemona loves N. Yet on Russell's account, it would follow that such an inference is valid. In other words, Russell's theory fails to do justice to the substitution principles appropriate to indirect contexts.

Russell would accept this consequence, provided that the names in question are logically proper. For these, he held, unqualified substitution *salva veritate* is permissible. What makes us find the substitutions unacceptable is that we are thinking of these names not as logically proper ones, but as ones for which a correct account is of the kind, already sketched in section 6 above, that involves associated descriptions. Perhaps Othello associates 'Cassio' with one description, say 'the F' and 'N' with another, say 'the G'. The analysis of sentences ascribing belief would have to be complicated to deal with this, and Russell gives no hint about how to proceed in this direction. However, there is no question of problems for substitution principles, for these require for their premises identity statements. According to Russell, expressions of the form 'the F is the G' are not identity statements, for the expressions flanking the identity sign are not really referring expressions. The logical form of such a sentence is simply: something is uniquely F and is uniquely G. This does not even look as if it would licence substitution *salva veritate*.

8 Conclusion

How should we compare Frege's and Russell's contributions? Frege has sole claim to the theory that concepts are functions, and to the use of this in explaining quantifiers and variables. He was also the first to introduce the sense–reference distinction. Russell attacked him for this, and invented distinctive theories of names, communication and definite descriptions to explain phenomena which Frege explained in terms of sense and reference.

Suppose one added Russell's theory of descriptions to Frege's view. One could then imagine Frege insisting that every simple expression has a sense which consists in the mode of presentation of an object, where this could be understood in such a way as to ensure the existence of the object presented. The sense and reference of the simple expressions would then determine the sense, and reference if any, of the complexes they compose, and there would be nothing imperfect about sense without reference. The question would then remain: do we need sense as well as reference to explain the working of the simple expressions? It is essential to anything like Frege's view that the answer should be affirmative, and to anything like Russell's view that it should be negative.

Further Reading

The first thing is to read Russell and Frege. I suggest the following four articles to begin with: Frege, 1891, 1892b and Russell, 1905 (or perhaps better, in the first instance, the later and clearer discussion in ch. 16 of Russell, 1919), and Russell, 1967, esp. ch. 4.

A good commentary involving both philosophers is Salmon, 1986. He criticizes Frege's distinction between sense and reference from a Russellian perspective. On Frege, the best starting point is Kenny (1995). For further study, Dummett's writings are essential: Dummett, 1973, supplemented by his

1981. For an indication of the current state of thought about Frege on sense and reference, see the Frege issue of *Mind*, vol. 101, 1992. On Russell, you might try Sainsbury, 1979. Recent collections include Wade Savage, 1989 and Irvine and Wedekind (eds), 1993.

References

Frege and Russell

Frege, G. 1972 [1879]: *Begriffsschrift*. Translated by T. W. Bynum, *Conceptual Notation and Related Articles*. Oxford: Clarendon Press, 1972.
—— 1884: *Die Grundlagen der Arithmetik*. Breslau: W. Koebner. Translated by J. L. Austin, *The Foundations of Arithmetic*. Oxford: Blackwell and Mott, 1950.
—— 1891: Function and Concept. In B. McGuinness (ed.), *Collected Papers on Mathematics, Logic and Philosophy*, Oxford: Blackwell, 1984, 137–56.
—— 1892a: On Concept and Object. *Vierteljahrsschrift für wissenschaftliche Philosophie* 16, 192-205. Translation in B. McGuinness (ed.), *Collected Papers on Mathematics, Logic and Philosophy*, Oxford: Blackwell, 1984, 182–94.
—— 1892b: On Sense and Meaning. *Zeitschrift für Philosophie und philosophische Kritik*. Translation in Brian McGuinness (ed.), *Collected Papers on Mathematics, Logic and Philosophy*, Oxford: Blackwell, 1984, 157–77.
—— 1893: *Grundgesetze der Arithmetik, begriffsschriftlich abgeleitet*. Band I, Jena: Hermann Pohle. Parts translated by M. Furth, *The Basic Laws of Arithmetic: Exposition of the System*, Los Angeles: University of California Press.
—— 1918: Logical Investigations: Thoughts (translated by P. Geach and R. H. Stoothoff). In Brian McGuinness (ed.), *Collected Papers on Mathematics, Logic and Philosophy*, Oxford: Blackwell, 1984, 351–72.
—— 1979: *Posthumous Writings*. Oxford: Blackwell.
Russell, B. (1903): *The Principles of Mathematics*. Cambridge: Cambridge University Press.
—— 1905: On Denoting. *Mind* 14, 479–93. Reprinted in R. C. Marsh (ed.), *Logic and Knowledge*, London: Routledge and Kegan Paul, 41–56.
—— 1908: Mathematical Logic as Based on the Theory of Types. *American Journal of Mathematics* 30, 222–62. Reprinted in R. C. Marsh (ed.), *Logic and Knowledge*, London: Routledge and Kegan Paul, 59–102.
—— and Whitehead, A. N. 1910–13: *Principia Mathematica*. Cambridge: Cambridge University Press.
—— 1912: *Problems of Philosophy*. Oxford: Oxford University Press.
—— 1918–19: Lectures on the Philosophy of Logical Atomism. *Monist*, 28, 29. Reprinted in R. C. Marsh (ed.), *Logic and Knowledge*, London: Routledge and Kegan Paul, 177–281.
—— 1919: *Introduction to Mathematical Philosophy*. London: George Allen and Unwin.
—— 1921: *The Analysis of Mind*. London: George Allen and Unwin.
—— 1929: *Marriage and Morals*. London: George Allen and Unwin.
—— 1940: *Inquiry into Meaning and Truth*. London: George Allen and Unwin.
—— 1948: *Human Knowledge*. London: George Allen and Unwin.
—— 1967–69: *Autobiography*. London: George Allen and Unwin.

Other writers

Blackburn, S. and Code, A. 1978: The Power of Russell's Criticism of Frege: 'On Denoting'. *Analysis*, 38, 65–77.

Dummett, M. 1973: *Frege: Philosophy of Language*. London: Duckworth.
—— 1981: *The Interpretation of Frege's Philosophy*. London: Duckworth.
Evans, G. 1982: *The Varieties of Reference*. Oxford: Clarendon Press.
Hochberg, H. 1976: Russell's Attack on Frege's Theory of Meaning. *Philosophica* 18, 2. Reprinted in his *Logic, Ontology and Language*, München: Philosophia Verlag, 60–85.
Irvine, A. and Wedekind, Gary (eds) 1993: *Russell and Analytic Philosophy*. Vancouver: University of British Columbia Press.
Kenny, A. 1995: *Frege*. London: Penguin.
Kripke, S. 1972: *Naming and Necessity*. Oxford: Blackwell.
McDowell, J. 1977: On the Sense and Reference of a Proper Name. *Mind*, 86, 159–85.
Pakuluk, M. 1993: The Interpretation of Russell's Gray's Elegy Argument. In Irvine and Wedekind (1993), 37–65.
Sainsbury, R. M. 1979: *Russell*. London: Routledge and Kegan Paul.
—— 1986: Russell on Acquaintance. In G. Vesey (ed.), *Philosophers Ancient and Modern*, Cambridge: Cambridge University Press, 219–44.
—— 1993: Russell on Names and Communication. In Irvine and Wedekind (1993).
Salmon, N. 1986: *Frege's Puzzle*. Cambridge, MA: MIT Press.
Wade Savage, C. and Anderson, A. (eds) 1989: *Rereading Russell: Essays in Bertrand Russell's Metaphysics and Epistemology*. Minnesota Studies in the Philosophy of Science. Minneapolis: University of Minnesota Press.
Wiggins, D. 1976: Frege's Problem of the Morning Star and the Evening Star. In M. Schirn (ed.), *Studies on Frege*, Stuttgart and Bad Canstatt: Freidrich Frommann Verlag, 221–55.

Discussion Questions

1   What features make a proposition something other than a mere list?

2   Discuss the following objection to the claim that Frege's notion of a concept can be used to explain the unity of the proposition:

> There is no account of incompleteness except in terms of the unity of the proposition: incompleteness is just what generates the unity. So it cannot explain the unity.

3   Can expressions other than names have sense and reference?

4   Why does sense matter for cognitive value and reference matter for truth and falsity?

5   If a part of a sentence lacks reference, does the whole sentence lack truth and falsity?

6   Frege held that fictional sentences were neither true nor false. Russell, by contrast, held that fictional sentences were false. A third view is that some fictional sentences are true (like 'Hamlet was a prince') and others false (like 'Hamlet was decisive'). What reasons are there to choose between these views?

7   How do we explain why there is point to saying 'Hesperus is Phosphorus', but no point in saying 'Hesperus is Hesperus'?

8   Show that Frege's compositionality principle for reference entails a version of Leibniz's law of the indiscernibility of identicals (if $x = y$, anything true of x is true of y).

9 Discuss the following argument: Frege's theory uses two basic notions (sense and reference), Russell's only one (standing for); so Russell's theory should be preferred.

10 According to Russell, ordinary names are intelligible through their association with descriptions. This view involves regarding an expression like 'Vulcan' as not genuinely simple, because it is associated with a description, which is complex. So you cannot tell by looking whether an expression is simple or not. What test for genuine simplicity can Russell use?

11 Are there any logically proper names? Would it matter if there were none?

12 Discuss the following objection to the argument that Frege should deny that proper names in ordinary language have sense because they are associated with variable and, hence, non-public definite descriptions:

> To be public is one thing, to be invariant across a whole community is another. Frege could well hold that sense varies from person to person, without prejudice to the publicity of sense, provided he holds that such an idiosyncratic sense is public in the sense of being in principle graspable by anyone (even all those other people who in fact do not grasp it). By contrast, an idea of mine is private in that it cannot even in principle be had by you.

13 Can we distinguish between thoughts that are objective logical entities and ideas that are subjective psychological entities?

14 What are the philosophical consequences of adopting Russell's theory of definite descriptions?

15 How do logical constants have meaning?

16 What can be substituted *salva veritate* in indirect contexts? What are the philosophical implications of your answer?

17 Can Frege respond adequately to the objection that on his theory, one who reports a belief refers to things other than those that the belief itself refers to? (You need first to amplify the objection.)

28

Moore ———————————————————————

Thomas Baldwin

G. E. Moore (1873–1958) was one of the most influential British philosophers of the twentieth century. At an early stage in his career he established his reputation by his critical rejection of the idealist philosophy that was dominant in Britain at the end of the nineteenth century. He also rejected the empiricist philosophy that appeared to be the alternative to idealism, maintaining that its application in ethics leads to a fallacy – the 'naturalistic fallacy'. In place of both idealism and empiricism Moore advanced an extreme form of realism which centred on the hypothesis of a domain of 'propositions' as both objects of thought and possible states of affairs. In his later years Moore refined his techniques of 'philosophical analysis', combining them with a sustained defence of 'the common sense view of the world' against the assaults of sceptical and critical philosophers. He spent most of his career in Cambridge, where he was a friend and colleague of Russell (chapter 27) and Wittgenstein (chapter 29).

1 Ethical theory

Moore's first writings concerned the foundations of Ethics (chapter 6), in particular, Kant's (chapter 22) ethical theory. Moore argued that Kant (1724–1804) was wrong to suppose that the fundamental principles of ethics have any special connection with human reason or the Will (p. 599). Instead, they concern questions of value which are as objective and mind-independent as any ordinary matter of fact. Generalizing from this rejection of an idealist foundation for ethics, Moore is equally critical of empiricist theories which suggest that questions of value can be resolved by reference to 'nature', including Human nature (chapter 25). In opposition to both idealism and empiricism, therefore, Moore proposed in his famous ethical treatise *Principia Ethica* (Moore, 1903) that the fundamental truths of ethics have a status comparable to the truths of arithmetic: they are abstract necessary truths concerning the intrinsic value of states of affairs. In support of this thesis, he maintained that there is a fallacy, the 'naturalistic fallacy', in all theories which seek to resolve questions of value by defining values in terms of further facts, such as facts concerning human nature. His main argument for this charge was that any supposed definition of goodness, which he took to be the fundamental value, can be seen to be incorrect when we see that it incorporates a substantive ethical thesis. For example, suppose one were to *define* goodness as that which we desire to desire: then, Moore argues, we would have to accept that whatever one desires to desire is *ipso facto* good. Yet we cannot but observe that it is a substantial question whether this is the case, and thus that the proposed definition is incorrect.

This argument is in many ways problematic. Moore appears to assume that definitions must be obvious, if true; yet this is not itself obvious, as Moore recognized in his later writings. Furthermore, because Moore's argument is only an appeal to the way in which we think about questions of value, it is vulnerable to sceptics who offer an alternative set of ethical concepts without claiming that their new concepts capture the whole content of our ordinary ones. For they can argue that even if our ordinary concepts involve some purely abstract conception of value, then so much the worse for them; we would be better off without them. Hence Moore's position needs to be embedded in a broader METAPHYSICS (chapter 2) which elucidates ethical concepts and explains why they are indefinable. Moore himself offers a PLATONIST (chapter 15) metaphysics of goodness as a simple, non-natural, property whose *a priori* relationships to the natural properties of things we are able to discern through reflective intuitions. But this has little persuasive power for those not antecedently favourable to it, and many of those who accepted his claim that values are not definable in non-evaluative terms sought to justify it by arguing that the distinctive content of ethical statements arises from the fact that these statements have a special role as expressions of emotion, or as recommendations and prescriptions. From this latter perspective, Moore seemed right in thinking that ethical concepts are not definable in terms of non-ethical ones, but mistaken in concluding that ethical values constitute a *sui generis* domain of being.

This 'linguistic' reformulation of Moore's critique of ethical naturalism no longer finds much favour, because the implied conception of ethical thought as just a special type of non-descriptive discourse appears rather shallow. At the same time, versions of ethical naturalism which link human values to human nature have returned to favour. Such positions conflict with Moore's theory, but because Moore does not consider the hypothesis that goodness is both indefinable and natural, his discussion does not apply to naturalistic theories that do not offer a reductive definition of value. Since theories of this kind imply that ethical values have an irreducible role within human psychology as reasons for action, the debate about Moore's treatment of ethical naturalism connects with debates in current PHILOSOPHY OF MIND (chapter 5) concerning reductionism and naturalism in psychology.

Moore's ethical theory is now studied primarily because of his discussion of naturalism; but it is also famous as a version of ideal utilitarianism, according to which the ideal end of action is the maximization, not of pleasure, but of goodness – where goodness, though indefinable, is said to be found especially in the enjoyment of Art and Love. Moore's straightforward commendation of these values, which are celebrated without any of the weighty metaphysical hypotheses concerning their significance that are characteristic of Romantic thought, found a ready audience among his younger friends. In particular, the members of the 'Bloomsbury Group' (J. Maynard Keynes, Leonard Woolf, Clive Bell, Lytton Strachey and others) acknowledged their intellectual debt to Moore, taking from him the thesis that it is only certain refined states of consciousness that have positive intrinsic value.

2 The Rejection of Idealism

Just as Moore developed his ethical value in the light of his criticisms of idealist theory, in other early papers he developed his conception of a 'proposition', as the object of thought, in the course of his criticisms of idealist metaphysics. To begin with, Moore argues against BERKELEY (chapter 20) that it is a mistake to treat the 'object' of perception as if it were merely a subjective 'content' of 'idea'; instead, he argues, experience is essentially awareness of things whose existence is independent of us. He then generalizes this point to apply to thought as well as perception, arguing that even the truth of *a priori* propositions depends upon us no more than does the existence of the objects of experience. Since he takes it that true propositions coincide with the states of affairs that obtain just where a proposition is true, he takes it that propositions, the objects of thought, are structures of objects and properties whose existence is independent both of their truth and of our thought of them. The resulting THEORY OF JUDGEMENT (p. 669) is manifestly incompatible with idealist metaphysics; and, just like Moore's ethical theory, it is equally incompatible with an empiricist theory of judgement. Yet fairly soon he came to feel that this extreme realist theory was simply not credible. In his writings from 1911 onwards, he abandoned belief in the existence of propositions because he could no longer accept that reality included false propositions as well as true ones. He likewise abandoned his unquestioning realism concerning the objects of experience, and inclined towards the view that the objects of sense experience, which he called 'sense data', are non-physical representations of the physical world. Finally, in the light of this last point, he acknowledged that it is a good deal more difficult to find fault with traditional sceptical arguments concerning knowledge of the external world than he had earlier supposed.

3 Defending Common Sense

These problems largely set the agenda of Moore's later writings. In order to handle SCEPTICAL ARGUMENTS (pp. 46–8) Moore introduced his appeal to common sense. This appeal concerns the status of philosophical arguments. Moore maintained that the general principles which philosophers employ are answerable to our common sense judgements concerning particular matters of fact. Hence sceptical philosophers undermine the reasons one might have for accepting their general principles if they dispute our common-sense judgements. We are more certain that we know such things as that 'This is a pencil' than we can be of the premises of any sceptical argument that casts doubt on such knowledge. Moore's critics may well want to urge that this is too simple, in that sceptical arguments typically exploit tensions already inherent in our ordinary cognitive practices and Moore himself came to recognize that more had to be said. In his famous lecture of 1939, 'Proof of an External World' (Moore, 1959), he argued that, contrary to idealist claims, one could prove the existence of an external world simply by demonstrating the existence of one's hands. But Moore at this time explicitly denied that one could similarly prove the existence of *knowledge* of an external world; in order to effect such a proof, he maintained, one had to refute sceptical arguments, which one could not accomplish by waving one's hands at them. Moore then attempted this task of refutation, but had to acknowledge by the end of it that he was unsuccessful. One reason for this, I think, is that he lacked the confidence to rethink the full implications for EPISTEMOLOGY (chapter 1) of his appeal to common sense. It was therefore left to WITTGENSTEIN (chapter 29) to take over this task, where Moore had left off, in his notes *On Certainty* (Wittgenstein, 1969) which arose out of reflections prompted by Moore's writings.

4 Philosophical Analysis

Moore's discussions of his problems concerning the objects of thought (propositions) and the objects of experience (sense data) make essential use of his other characteristic philosophical method – philosophical analysis. As we saw, Moore's early theory of judgement involved the hypothesis of propositions as complex structures involving objects and properties which coincide with actual state of affairs when a proposition is true. Since the philosophical analysis of a proposition was supposed to reveal the structure of its constituent objects and properties, it followed that philosophical analysis had an important METAPHYSICAL (chapter 2) role. This role was, however, greatly enhanced as Moore appreciated the significance of RUSSELL's (chapter 27) work in LOGICAL THEORY (chapter 4). For he saw that Russell's conception of a logical fiction enables one to talk as if there were entities of a certain type, while presenting an analysis of the meaning of what is thereby said in which there is no reference to such entities. Moore used this idea in his discussions of propositions. For although he standardly represented himself as concerned with the truth of 'propositions', he did not want this talk to be taken as carrying with it a commitment to the existence of propositions as genuine entities to which reference is made in the analysis of what is meant by sentences in which we attribute thoughts to each other. Whether his position on this matter was altogether consistent can be doubted.

Moore's Paradox

There is something very odd about the sentence 'It is raining, but I do not believe that it is.' There is no explicit contradiction here; and indeed, when uttered in a suitable context, the sentence might well be true. Yet if we imagine ourselves hearing someone utter it, we would immediately feel that their utterance was absurd. The same situation arises for any sentence of the form '*p but I do not believe that p*' and it is characteristic of Moore's analytic acumen that he should have identified this puzzle, which Wittgenstein called 'Moore's Paradox'.

Moore proposed that the sense of absurdity here arises from a conflict between what speakers *assert* by their utterance, and what they *imply* by it. When Jones utters 'It is raining' he asserts that it is raining and thereby implies that he believes that it is raining; when he then goes on to say 'but I do not believe that it is' he asserts that he does not believe that it is raining. So what he implies by the first part of his utterance contradicts what he asserts in the second part. The truth or falsity of his utterance depends only on what he asserts; so his utterance might be true. But the conflict between what he implies and what he asserts none the less renders the utterance absurd.

Moore's explanation appears largely correct, although it remains disputed just what account should be given of the *implications* of the utterance. Wittgenstein's discussions of Moore's Paradox, which occur in his later writings, derived from his sensitivity there to wide-ranging differences between first-person and third-person discourse and thought, and connect with his earlier views about the METAPHYSICAL SUBJECT (p. 691).

Moore also applied his conception of philosophical analysis to his discussions of perception and its objects: he held that although we all know for certain such propositions as 'This is a hand', their *analysis* is deeply puzzling. He took it that the demonstrative 'This' refers here to a sense datum, typically an object of visual experience, and that the really difficult question concerns the relationship between such a sense datum and one's hand. Moore discussed several alternatives here, though in the end, I think, it was a PHENOMENALIST (pp. 55–6) position that he was most inclined to favour. Indeed one can best appreciate the role of analysis in Moore's philosophy from the fact that he favoured a phenomenalist analysis of propositions such as 'This is a hand' at the very time that he was advancing his proof of an external world by demonstrating the existence of his hands to his audience. For this shows that the appeal to common sense does not tell us much about the propositions of whose truth it assures us; we also require an analysis of these propositions, and this analysis can be as disconcerting as one likes, as long as the truth-values of our common-sense judgements are respected. Thus Moore's use of analysis undermines the apparent conservatism of his defence of common sense.

Moore is today regarded as a paradigm of an 'analytic philosopher'. Indeed, his early theory of judgement played a crucial part in the development of analytic philosophy, since it implied that the analysis of propositions is of direct philosophical significance. But because Moore remained detached from the all-encompassing doctrines of logical atomism and logical positivism, his use of philosophical analysis was always piecemeal and idiosyncratic. None the less, particularly because his work combines sophisticated techniques of logical analysis with the defence of common sense, it provides a classic example of 'analytic philosophy'.

Further Reading

Moore (1993) is a selection of writings drawn from all stages of Moore's philosophical career. Schilpp (1942) is a classic collection of papers concerned with Moore's philosophy, which also contains Moore's autobiography and his reply to his critics. Regan (1986) attempts to set the development of Moore's ethical theory in the context of the Bloomsbury Group. Baldwin (1990) is a critical study of all aspects of Moore's philosophy.

References

Works by G. E. Moore

G. E. Moore 1903: *Principia Ethica*. Cambridge: Cambridge University Press. Revised edition edited by T. R. Baldwin, Cambridge: Cambridge University Press, 1993.
—— 1912: *Ethics*. London: Williams and Norgate. Revised edition, London: Oxford University Press, 1966.
—— 1922: *Philosophical Studies*. London: Routledge.
—— 1953: *Some Main Problems of Philosophy*. London: George Allen and Unwin.
—— 1959: *Philosophical Papers*. London: George Allen and Unwin.
—— 1986: *Early Papers* (edited by T. Regan). Philadelphia: Temple University Press. (This volume contains Moore's papers from the period 1898–1903.)
—— 1993: *Selected Writings* (edited by T. R. Baldwin). London: Routledge. (This volume contains some of Moore's early papers, selections from Moore, 1922, Moore, 1953, Moore, 1959 and further late writings.)

Other writers

Baldwin, T. R. 1990: *G. E. Moore*. London: Routledge.
Keynes, J. M. 1949. My early beliefs. In his *Two Memoirs*. London: Hart-Davies. Reprinted in J. M. Keynes, *Collected Papers*, X, London: Macmillan.
Regan, T. 1968: *Bloomsbury's Prophet*. Philadelphia: Temple University Press.
Schilpp, P. A. (ed.) 1942: *The Philosophy of G. E. Moore*. Evanston: Northwestern University Press, 3rd edn, 1968, La Salle: Open Court.
Wittgenstein, L. 1969: *On Certainty*. Oxford: Blackwell.

Discussion Questions

1 Should the definition of a familiar word appear to us as obvious if it is correct?

2 Is it a mistake in principle to suppose that ethical values can be defined – for example, by reference to religious beliefs?

3 Must 'ethical naturalism' include a commitment to the thesis that ethical values can be defined?

4 Can one refute idealism by demonstrating the existence of a pair of hands?

5 Can one refute scepticism by demonstrating the existence of a pair of hands?

6 What could you do to vindicate your knowledge that you have two hands in the face of sceptical doubt to the contrary?

7 Is thought a relationship with a special kind of object – a 'proposition'? If so, what are false propositions? If not, what account should one give of the contents of thought?

8 When Macbeth has a vision as of a dagger, does he see anything? If so, what?

9 Does the term 'sense datum' have any worthwhile use in philosophy?

10 Is analysis the method of philosophy?

29

Wittgenstein —————————————————

David Pears

Wittgenstein has been a dominant figure in twentieth-century philosophy, his thought altering the terms of philosophical debate and challenging traditional conceptions of philosophy. His early work, culminating in the *Tractatus Logico–Philosophicus*, dealt with questions raised by FREGE AND RUSSELL (chapter 27) but also pursued his own distinctive agenda concerning logic, language and their implications for philosophy. A transition period began with dissatisfaction over the *Tractatus* and led to his second major work, the posthumous *Philosophical Investigations*. Both *Tractatus* and *Investigations* have fascinated readers by their unusual, but differing styles as well as by their philosophical content. This chapter concentrates on Wittgenstein's early discussions of logical necessity and factual propositions, his transitional accounts of meaning and the self, and his later examinations of the the possibility of a private language, the nature of rules and the foundations of mathematics. It also considers the development of his views on philosophical method. Readers might wish to read chapters on PHILOSOPHY OF LOGIC (chapter 4), PHILOSOPHY OF LANGUAGE (chapter 3), PHILOSOPHY OF MATHEMATICS (chapter 10), DESCARTES, SPINOZA AND LEIBNIZ (chapter 17), KANT (chapter 22), FREGE AND RUSSELL (chapter 27) and MOORE (chapter 28).

1 Life

Ludwig Wittgenstein was born in Vienna in 1889 and died in Cambridge in 1951. He studied engineering, first in Berlin and then in Manchester, and he soon began to ask himself philosophical questions about the foundations of mathematics. What are numbers? What sort of truth does a mathematical equation possess? What is the force of proof in pure mathematics? In order to find the answers to such questions, he went to Cambridge in 1911 to work with RUSSELL (chapter 27), who had just produced in collaboration with A. N. Whitehead (1861–1947) *Principia Mathematica* (1910–13), a monumental treatise which bases mathematics on logic. But on what is logic based? Wittgenstein's attempt to answer this question convinced Russell that he was a genius. During the 1914–18 war he served in the Austrian army and in spare moments continued the work on the foundations of logic which he had begun in 1912. His war-time journal, *Notebooks 1914–16* (1961), reveals the development of his ideas more clearly that the final version, *Tractatus Logico–Philosophicus*, which he published in the early 1920s.

He then abandoned philosophy for a life of a very different kind. He taught in a village school in Austria and after that worked in the garden of a monastery. He returned to philosophy in the late 1920s, drawn back into it by discussions with some of the members of the Vienna Circle and with the Cambridge philosopher Frank Ramsey (1903–30). They wanted him to explain the *Tractatus*, but their request for elucidations soon produced second thoughts. When he returned to Cambridge, he developed a different philosophy which made its first public appearance in 1953 in his posthumous book, *Philosophical Investigations*. Before its publication, direct acquaintance with his new ideas had been confined to those who attended his lectures and seminars in Cambridge.

In the second period of his philosophy, as in the first, his notes are the key to his published work. Written continuously from 1929 until his death, they would occupy many metres of shelves if they were all edited and published as books. Philosophers usually intend what they write to be read by others, but these notes are a kind of thinking on paper. It is true that some of the sets are evidently being steered towards publication, but in most of them Wittgenstein is facing problems alone. Since his death many books have been extracted from this material.

2 The General Character of Wittgenstein's Philosophy

Wittgenstein's philosophy is difficult to place in the history of ideas largely because it is anti-theoretical. It is true that in his early work he did produce a theory of LOGIC (chapter 4) and LANGUAGE (chapter 5), but it was a theory which demonstrated its own meaninglessness. That was a paradox which he presented, appropriately enough, in a metaphor borrowed from the Greek sceptic, Sextus Empiricus (*c.*150–*c.*225): 'Anyone who understands me eventually recognizes [my propositions] as nonsensical, when he has used them – as steps – to climb up beyond them. (He must, so to speak, throw away the ladder after he has climbed up it)' (Wittgenstein, 1922, 6.54). After 1929 he completely avoided theorizing. The task of philosophy, as he now saw it, was never to explain but only to describe. Since western philosophy had mainly been conceived as a search for explanations at a very high level of generality, his work stood to one side of the tradition.

Wittgenstein was not a SCEPTIC (pp. 46–58). The reason why he rejected philosophical theorizing was not that he thought it too risky and liable to error, but because he believed that it was the wrong way for philosophers to work. Philosophy could not, and should not try, to emulate science. That is a point of affinity with KANT (chapter 22), but while Kant's critique resulted in a system in which each of the many forms of human experience found a place, Wittgenstein attempted no such thing. His method was to lead any philosophical theory back to the point where it originated, which might be some very simple routine, observable even in the life of animals but rendered unintelligible by the demand for an intellectual justification. Or it might start from the 'crossing of two pictures' – for example, we construe SENSATIONS (pp. 180–2) as objects that are not essentially dependent on their links with the physical world, and so we attribute to them a basic independence modelled on the basic independence of physical objects. His aim was to cure this kind of illusion by a therapy that would gradually lead the sufferer to recognize, and almost to recreate its origin, and so to escape from its domination.

Philosophers are expected to be able to abstract the general from the particular, but Wittgenstein's gift was the opposite – a rare ability to see the particular in the general. He could demolish a theory with a few appropriate counter-examples. His method was to describe an everyday situation which brings a philosophical speculation down to earth. When he used imagery, it was carefully chosen to reveal the structure of the problem under examination. All this helps to explain why his later philosophical writings have been read and appreciated by people with very little philosophical training. However, the explanation of the wide appeal of his later work is not just stylistic. He is evidently taking apart a philosophical tradition that goes back to antiquity. That is a way of treating the past which can be found in many other disciplines today, and even when the scene that he is dismantling has not been precisely identified he can still be read with sympathy and with intuitive understanding.

3 Wittgenstein's Early Philosophy

In spite of the wider appeal of his later work, Wittgenstein was without a doubt a philosopher's philosopher. In the *Tractatus* he developed a theory of language that was designed to explain something that Russell had left unexplained in *Principia Mathematica*, the nature of logical necessity. The marginal status of theories in his early philosophy did not deflect this theory from its main goal, which was to show that logically necessary propositions are a kind of by-product of the ordinary use of propositions to state facts. A factual proposition, according to Wittgenstein, is true or false with no third alternative. For he agreed with Russell's theory of definite descriptions: failure of a complex reference simply makes a proposition false. So if two propositions are combined to form a third, compound, proposition, its truth of falsity will simply depend on the truth or falsity of its two components. Now suppose that we want to find out if it really is a contingent, factual proposition, like its two components. What we have to do is to take the two components and run through all their combinations of truth and falsity, and we will find that there are three possible outcomes to this test. The compound proposition may be true for some combinations of the truth-values of its components but false for others, in which case it is a contingent factual proposition. Or it may come out false for all combinations, in which case it is a contradiction. Or, finally, it may be a tautology, true for all combinations.

Contradictions and tautologies say nothing. However, they achieve this distinction in two opposite ways, the former by excluding, and the latter by allowing, every state of affairs. So propositions whose truth or falsity are guaranteed by logical necessity are limiting cases, extreme developments of the essential nature of factual propositions.

This explanation of logical necessity answered a question that the axiomatization of logic by Frege and Russell had left unanswered: why should we accept the axioms and rules of inference with which such calculi start? In fact, if every proposition can be tested independently for logical necessity, there does not seem to be any need to promote some of them as axioms and to deduce the others from them. Schopenhauer (1788–1860) had taken the same view of the axiomatization of geometry, which seemed to him to be rendered superfluous by spatial intuition.

Wittgenstein's early account of the foundations of logic relies on semantic insight. If a formula is logically necessary, we can see that it is. There is no need to prove its status from axioms, because a truth-functional analysis will reveal it. If one factual proposition follows from another, we can see that it does, and there is no need to demonstrate that it does by a proof that starts from a logically necessary formula. The two propositions will simply show that their senses are connected in a way that validates our inference. This treatment of logic leaves proof without any obvious utility – a problem that Wittgenstein took up later in his philosophy of mathematics.

Propositions as Pictures

Wittgenstein's early theory of language was also developed in another direction. If it threw light on the foundations of logic, it ought also to throw light on the structure of ordinary factual discourse. In order to understand this development, we have to go back one step and ask why he thought that factual propositions must be true or false with no third alternative. His reason was that he took them to be a kind of picture. If the points on the canvas of a landscape-painter were not correlated with points in space, no picture that he painted would succeed in saying anything. Similarly, if the words in a factual proposition were not correlated with things, no sentence constructed out of them would say anything. In both cases alike the constructions would lack sense. But, given the necessary correlations, the painting and the proposition have sense and what they say can only be true or false.

Now this runs up against an obvious objection. Many words designate complex things, which do not have to exist in order that the propositions containing them should make sense, and this casts doubt on the analogy between points on a canvas and words. The obvious response would be to claim that such words are complex and that the simpler words out of which they are compounded do have to designate things. Wittgenstein went further and argued that it must be possible to continue this kind of analysis to a point at which no more subdivision would be possible. His argument for this extreme version of logical atomism had nothing to do with empiricism. What he argued was that, if analysis stopped short of that terminus, the sense of a proposition containing a word which designated something complex would depend on the truth of a further

> proposition. This further proposition would say that things had been combined to form the complex but it would not be part of the sense of the original proposition. That, he argued, was an unacceptable result both for pictures and propositions. Their senses must be complete, self-contained and independent of one another.

The pictorial character of propositions is a theme with many developments in the *Tractatus*. Not only is it used to explain the foundations of logic and the internal structure of factual language; it also has implications for SCIENTIFIC THEORIES (chapter 9), it yields a treatment of the self which carries the ideas of HUME (chapter 21), Kant and Schopenhauer one stage further, and it allows Wittgenstein to demonstrate that factual language has definite limits.

Wittgenstein believed that ETHICAL (chapter 6), AESTHETIC (chapter 7) and RELIGIOUS (chapter 14) discourse lie beyond those limits. This has started a long-running controversy about the implications of his placing of the 'softer' kinds of discourse. Was he a positivist, as the philosophers of the Vienna Circle later assume? Or could the opposite conclusion be drawn from what he said about the *Tractatus* in a letter to L. Ficker: 'The book's point is an ethical one . . . My work consists of two parts: the one presented here plus all that I have *not* written. And it is precisely this second part that is the important one. My book draws limits to the sphere of the ethical from the inside, as it were' – that is, from inside factual language. If this epigram is taken literally, it appears to put a low value on his solutions to the problems of language and logic. However, nearly all his later work is concerned with the same problems, and there is really no need to subject the *Tractatus* to such a simple dilemma. Its point is Kantian: ethics (and the whole softer side of discourse, including philosophy itself) must not be assimilated to science.

4 Transition

The first modification of the system of the *Tractatus* appeared in 1929 in Wittgenstein's article, 'Some Remarks on Logical Form' (the only other piece of work that he published – everything else is posthumous). He no longer believed in the extreme version of logical atomism for which he had argued in 1922. The requirement, that elementary propositions be logically independent of one another, now struck him as excessive. The reason for his change of mind was simple: singular factual propositions always contain predicates belonging to ranges of contraries. So colour-predicates are incompatible with one another and there is no hope of analysing them into simpler predicates that would not be incompatible with one another. Position, length, velocity, and, in general, all measurable properties, show the same recalcitrance to the analysis required by the *Tractatus*. He therefore dropped the requirement.

There are two things that make this change of mind important. Firstly, though the *Tractatus* contains an atomistic theory of language, there are passages that reveal an underlying holism. For example, he says: 'A proposition can determine only one place in logical space: nevertheless the whole of logical space must already be given with it' (1922, 3.42). But the new view of elementary propositions is an open move towards holism. What is now said to be 'laid against reality like a ruler' (1922, 2.1512) is not a single, independent, elementary proposition, but, rather, a set of logically incompatible elementary propositions. For when one predicate in a group of contraries is ascribed to a thing, the others are necessarily withheld. It is plausible to regard this holism as the natural tendency of Wittgenstein's mind, and the atomism as something that he took over from Russell and eventually repudiated.

The change of mind also has a more general importance. The atomism of the *Tractatus* was offered not as a theory that was supposed to fit the observable surface of factual language, but as a theoretical deduction about its deep structure. Indeed, Wittgenstein was so confident of the validity of the deduction that he was not worried by his inability to produce a single example of a logically independent elementary proposition. This dogmatism evaporated when it occurred to him that the logical structure of language might be visible on its surface and might actually be gathered from the ordinary uses that we make of words in ordinary situations. This was the point of departure of his later philosophy.

5 His Later Philosophy: *The Blue Book*

The most accessible exposition of the leading ideas of Wittgenstein's later philosophy is to be found in the *Blue Book* (1958), a set of lecture-notes that he dictated to his Cambridge pupils in 1933–4. What he then did was so far out of line with the tradition that we may at first feel inclined to question whether it really is philosophy. His answer was that it might be called 'one of the heirs of the subject which used to be called "philosophy".' The conspicuous novelty is the absolute refusal to force all the multifarious variety of thought and language into the mould of a single theory. He criticized the 'contempt for the particular case' that any such attempt would involve, and he systematically repressed the craving for generality that has characterized western philosophy since Socrates first instigated the search for the essences of things. We may, of course, ask such questions as 'What is knowledge?', but we must not expect to find the answer wrapped up in the neat package of a definition. There will be many different cases, and though they will show a family resemblance to one another, they will not be linked by the possession of a single set of common properties. Socrates asked for a conjunction of properties, but we must be content with a disjunction.

That is an accurate placing of Wittgenstein's new philosophy in the history of ideas, but it leaves an important question unanswered. Why should a catalogue of examples be regarded as a solution to a philosophical problem? Is it not just a collection of the kind of material that poses the problem? The point of these questions is that 'the heir to philosophy' needs to be something more than well-documented negative advice not to theorize: it ought to teach us to see philosophical problems from the inside and to find a more positive way of laying them to rest.

There are, in fact, two discussions in the *Blue Book* that demonstrate that Wittgenstein's later work was a positive continuation of the philosophy of the past. One is the long investigation of MEANING (chapter 3) and the other is the treatment of the SELF (pp. 597-8). Both are very illuminating.

The discussion of meaning is a development of a point made in the *Tractatus*: 'In order to recognize a symbol by its sign, we must observe how it is used with a sense' (1922, 3.326). This remark consorts uneasily with the picture theory of propositions, which derives meaning from the original act of correlating name with object. The theory implies that meaning is rigid, because it is based on a single, self-contained connection which, once made, remains authoritative, without any need for interpretation or any possibility of revision. The remark points the way to a more flexible account of meaning which will accommodate all the different uses that we make of words and leaves room for plasticity. This is the difference between treating language as a fossil and treating it as a living organism.

The discussion of meaning in the *Blue Book* develops the isolated remark in the *Tractatus* and criticizes the rigidity of the theory offered elsewhere in the book. Ostensive definition, which was supposed to attach a word to its object, is shown up as a very inscrutable performance, compatible with many different interpretations of a word's meaning: the underlying assimilation of all descriptive words to names designating objects is rejected; and so too is the assumption that the meaning of a word is something that belongs to it intrinsically, and, therefore, independently of its use. This last point proved to be important. For if meaning never belongs to a word intrinsically, it will never be possible to explain the regularity of a person's use of a word by citing the rule that he or she is following. For the meanings of the words in which the rule is expressed will themselves need to be interpreted. This line of thought is developed in *Philosophical Investigations* (1953).

The treatment of the self in the *Blue Book* is very clear and strongly argued. As in the *Notebooks* and the *Tractatus*, it is presented as part of an examination of solipsism, but it is much easier to discern the structure of the later version of the argument. The central point is that the solipsist's claim, 'Only what I see exists', is not what it seems to be. The solipsist seems to be referring to himself as a person, but really he or she is using the pronoun 'I' to refer to something entirely abstract which is introduced merely as 'the subject which is living this mental life' or 'the subject which is having these visual impressions'. But if the subject is not given any independent criterion of identity, there is no point from which the reference to 'these impressions' can be made. The solipsist constructs something which looks like a clock, except that he pins the hand to the dial, so that they both go round together. Saying what exists, like telling the time, must be a discriminating performance. The idea that the subject is a vanishing point, which was developed by Hume, Kant and Schopenhauer, is here put to a new use.

6 *Philosophical Investigations*: the Private Language Argument

The so-called 'private language argument' of *Philosophical Investigations* is closely related to the rejection of a solipsism which is based on an ego without a criterion of identity. What the two critiques have in common is a requirement which was later expressed very concisely by W. V. O. Quine, 'No entity without identity'. The solipsist's ego lacks any criterion of personal identity, and similarly, if the quality of a sensory experience were completely disconnected from everything in the physical world – not only from any stimulus but also from any response – it would lack any criterion of TYPE IDENTITY (p. 173). The parallelism of the two critiques is very close in the lecture-notes in which Wittgenstein first developed the so-called 'private language argument'. Against the solipsist who says, 'But I *am* in a favoured position. I am the centre of the world', he objects, 'suppose I saw myself in a mirror saying this and pointing to myself, would it still be all right?' (Notes for Lectures on 'Private Experience' and 'Sense-data', 1968, p. 299). Against the PHENOMENALIST (pp. 55–6) who argues for detached sensation-types and says, 'But it seems as if you are neglecting something', he objects, 'What more can I do than *distinguish* the case of saying "I have tooth-ache" when I really have toothache, and the case of saying the words without having tooth-ache? I am also (further) ready to talk of any *x* behind my words so long as it keeps its identity' (1968, p. 297).

The interpretation of this important line of thought in his later work is difficult. The parallelism between the two critiques is always a helpful clue, a thread which we must never relinquish in the labyrinth of confusing indications.

One source of confusion is hardly Wittgenstein's fault. He himself never used the phrase 'private language argument'. It is his commentators who use it and, by doing so, they have created the illusion that a single, formal argument ought to be extractable from the text of *Philosophical Investigations*. But that is not the structure of his critique. He argued dialectically, and when his adversary tries to introduce the 'neglected *x*' behind the words reporting a sensation, he always tries to show his adversary that, if this *x* is not covered by ordinary criteria of identity based on the physical world, it will not have any criterion of identity at all.

At this point it is a good idea to ask who his adversary is. Evidently, his adversary is a philosopher who supports some kind of sense datum theory. But what kind? One suggestion that has been made is that it is the sense-datum theory which he himself adopted in the *Tractatus* (not very openly). Since he extended his critique to include other mental entities besides sensations, this suggestion has been generalized, and he has been taken to be criticizing the 'mentalistic theory of meaning of the *Tractatus*' (Malcolm, 1986, ch. 4). But a brief review of the development of his philosophy of mind will show that these suggestions are mistaken.

Anyone who compares what Wittgenstein said about simple objects in the *Notebooks* and in the *Tractatus* will see immediately that he was uncertain of their category in the former and in the latter was convinced that his uncertainty did not endanger his logical atomism. Maybe they were material particles or perhaps they were Russellian sense data. He did not care, because his argument for their existence did not depend on their category and he did not think that it needed verification by the actual discovery of examples. However, the possibility that they were sense data was worth exploring, especially after his abandonment in 1929 of the extreme version of logical atomism. So when he returned to these problems after the long interval that followed the publication of the *Tractatus*, he worked out the consequences of identifying them with sense data. This fitted in very well with the programme of the Vienna Circle philosophers. They were interested in the philosophy of science and predisposed to accept a simple stratification of language, with the phenomenal vocabulary on the basic level and the physical vocabulary on the upper level and complete inter-translatability between the two levels.

It is notorious that this kind of phenomenalism looks impregnable until we examine the route that led us into it. That is what Wittgenstein did, and he found an obstacle which seemed to him to make the route impassable. The original position from which it started was supposed to be one in which people spoke a phenomenal language with a vocabulary completely disconnected from the physical world. It is obvious that such a language would be necessarily unteachable, and since Wittgenstein used the word 'private' to mean 'necessarily unteachable', it would be a private language. What is not so obvious is how he thought that he could show that such a language would be impossible.

The primary target of his critique of private language is the sense-datum language that phenomalists claimed that each of us could set up independently of anything in the physical world and, therefore, in isolation from one another. But the scope of his attack is much wider, because it would show that no mental entity of any kind could ever be reported in such a language. However, neither in its narrow nor in its wide scope is it directed against anything in the *Tractatus*. For just as there was no commitment to phenomenalism in the early work, so too there was no commitment to the thesis that the meaning of a sentence is derived from the meaning of the thought behind it. If the critique of private language is related to anything in the *Tractatus*, it is to the critique of ego-based solipsism, but positively, as a further application of the same general demand for a criterion of identity.

It is necessary to distinguish two moves that Wittgenstein made in his dialectical critique of a necessarily unteachable sensation-language. The phenomenalist believes that we can set up this language and use it to report our sense data in complete independence from anything in the physical world. Against this, Wittgenstein's first move was the one that has already been described: he asked for the criterion of identity of the supposedly independent sensation-types. That is a purely destructive demand. His second move was to point out that a report of a sensation will usually contain an *expression* of the sensory type and seldom a *description* of it. This move was the beginning of a reconstruction of the situation, designed to lead to a better account of sensation-language.

The destructive move is made most perspicuously in *Philosophical Investigations*. Suppose that a word for a sensation-type had no links with anything in the physical world and, therefore, no criteria that would allow me to teach anyone else its meaning. Even so, I might think that, when I applied it to one of my own sensations, I would know that I was using it correctly. But, according to Wittgenstein, that would be an illusion, because in such an isolated situation I would have no way of distinguishing between knowing that my use of the word was correct and merely thinking that I knew that it was correct. Notice that he did not say that my claim would be wrong: his point is more radical – there would be no right or wrong in this case (Wittgenstein, 1953, § 258).

The common objection to this criticism is that it simply fails to allow for the ability to recognize recurring types of things. This, it is said, is a purely intellectual ability on which we all rely in the physical world. So what is there to stop a single person relying on it in the inner world of his mind? Perhaps Carnap was right when he chose 'remembered similarity' as the foundation of his *Logical Structure of the World* (1967).

Here Wittgenstein's second move is needed. If the ability to recognize types really were purely intellectual, it might be used in the way in which Carnap and others have used it, and it might be possible to dismiss Wittgenstein's objection by saying, 'We have to stop somewhere and we have to treat something as fundamental – so why not our ability to recognize sensation-types?' But against this Wittgenstein argues that what looks like a purely intellectual ability is really based on natural sequences of predicament, behaviour and achievement in the physical world. Pain may seem to be a clear example of a sensation-type which is independently recognizable, but the word is really only a substitute for the cry which is a natural expression of the sensation (1953, §§ 244–6). Or, to take another example, our ability to recognize locations in our visual fields is connected with the success of our movements in physical space. Our discriminations in the inner world of the mind are, and must be, answerable to the exigencies of the physical world.

At this point we might begin to regret Wittgenstein's refusal to theorize. If he had offered a more systematic account of the dependence of our sensory language on the physical world, the so-called 'private language argument' might have carried more conviction. In fact, many philosophers have been convinced by it, but there is a large opposition, containing few doubters and consisting almost entirely of philosophers who feel sure that the argument is invalid. The dialectical character of Wittgenstein's argument has contributed to this result.

7 *Philosophical Investigations*: Meaning and Rules

Another, similar-sounding, but in fact very different, question is discussed in *Philosophical Investigations*. Could a person speak a language that was never used for communication with anyone else? Such a language would be private in the ordinary sense of that word, because it would be unshared; but it would not be necessarily unteachable, because it would be a language for describing the physical world, and so it would not be private in Wittgenstein's sense. The question is important, but we have to go back to the theory of meaning of the *Tractatus* in order to see why it is important.

A rough, but useful, distinction can be drawn between two kinds of theory of meaning, the rigid and the plastic. The theory offered in the *Tractatus* is rigid. Once names have been attached to objects everything proceeds on fixed lines. The application of the names is settled once and for all, and propositions and truth-functional combinations of propositions, including the two limiting cases, namely tautology and contradiction, all unfold without any more help from us. The theory does not actually treat the meaning of a name as something intrinsic to it, because we do have to correlate the name with an object. If we want an example of a theory that does take the further step and treats meaning as an intrinsic feature of a symbol, there is the theory that a mental image automatically stands for things that it resembles. That illustrates the extreme degree of rigidity: we would have no options.

A plastic theory of meaning would reject the analogy between a descriptive word and a name, and it would deny that the meaning of a descriptive word can be fixed once and for all by ostensive definition. Both these moves are made in *Philosophical Investigations*. It is, of course, not denied that our use of a descriptive word will exhibit a regularity: what is denied is that it is a regularity that is answerable to an independent authority. We do have options. We may say, if we like, that we are following a rule, but that will not be an *explanation* of the regularity of our practice, because it is our practice that shows how we are interpreting the words in which the rule is expressed. Are there, then, no constraints? Is the use of descriptive language pure improvization? Evidently, there must be some limit to plasticity, and one obvious possibility is that it is imposed by the need to keep in step with other people. That is how the question, 'Does language require exchanges between members of a community of speakers?' comes to be important in *Philosophical Investigations*. When we trace the line of development from Wittgenstein's early to his late theory of meaning, we need to know how far he moved in the direction of plasticity.

His first two steps were taken soon after his return to philosophy in 1929. The meaning of a symbol can never be one of its intrinsic features, and even an ostensive definition cannot saddle it with a single, definite meaning, because an ostensive definition is always compatible with many different sequels. Meaning, then, must depend on what we do next with a word – on our use of it.

The Authority of Rules

Wittgenstein's next step in the development of his theory of meaning was to argue by *reductio ad absurdum*. Given that the meaning of a word is never contained in the word itself, either intrinsically or after an ostensive definition, it must be a mistake to hold that someone who follows a linguistic rule is obeying an independent, external authority. For any basis that we might propose for the so-called 'authority' will always leave it open what the speaker should do next, and, what is more, open between many different alternatives. If we try to remedy this situation by offering a more explicit statement of the rule that he is supposed to be following, he will still be able to interpret that statement in many different ways. So when we try to fix the right use of a word purely by precept and past applications, we fail, because we end by abolishing the distinction between right and wrong. We feel that the distinction requires a rigid external authority and so we eliminate all plasticity, but, when we do that, we find we have lost the distinction.

It would be absurd to suggest that the meaning of a *particular* instruction is determined by what a person does when he tries to obey it. If the instruction did not already stand there complete with its meaning, there would be no question of obedience. But when the same suggestion is made about a *general* instruction, or rule, it is not absurd but only paradoxical. In order to understand Wittgenstein's argument, we have to elucidate the paradox.

It shocks us, because in daily life there is no doubt about what counts as obeying the instruction, 'Always take the next left turn'. However, there is an important grain of truth in the paradox. For the reason why there is never any doubt about what counts as obeying this instruction is that in the ordinary course of our lives nobody ever does take it to mean anything bizarre, like, 'Always take the opposite turn to the one you took last'. But if someone did understand it in this eccentric way, a verbal explanation of what it really meant might well fail to put him right. For he might give our verbal explanation an equally eccentric interpretation. Now because this sort of thing never happens in real life, we find Wittgenstein's argument paradoxical. It simply does not fit our picture of the independent authority of a rule. However, his point is that it *could* happen, and that indicates something important. It indicates that our use of language to give general instructions and state rules depends on our shared tendency to find the same responses natural. We have to agree in our practice *before* rules can have any independent authority. The independent authority is limited by the require-ment that makes it possible. Wittgenstein's argument is not concerned with the real possibility of linguistic crankiness but with the logical structure of the situation.

It appears, then, that the intellectual performance of following a linguistic rule is based on something outside the realm of the intellect. Its basis is the fact that we, like other animals, find it natural to divide and classify things in the same way as other members of our species. This line of thought runs parallel to the line that Wittgenstein took about sensation-language. For there too the intellectual achievement of reporting sensations was based on pre-established natural responses and behaviour of a more primitive kind.

What limit to plasticity did Wittgenstein recognize? Did he treat agreement with the responses of other people as an absolute constraint? And did he recognize any other absolute constraints? It is difficult to extract definite answers to these questions from his later writings. Both in *Philosophical Investigations* and in *Remarks on the Foundations of Mathematics* (1978) he says that agreement in judgements is required if people are going to communicate with one another. But that does not rule out the possibility that a wolf-child might develop a language solely for his own use. It would, of course, be a language of written signs with which he would communicate with himself across intervals of time. But it would not require the co-operation of other people. So it looks as if Wittgenstein went no further than maintaining that, if there are other people around and if the language-user is going to communicate with them, the plasticity of his language will be limited by the exigencies of agreement with them. This squares with the fact that in several of his texts dating from the 1930s he allows that a person might set up a system of signs solely for his own use. However, though Wittgenstein does not deny this in *Philosophical Investigations* or in *Remarks on the Foundations of Mathematics*, he does not re-assert it either. There seems to be some ambivalence.

In any case, there is another, more important, constraint on plasticity which really is absolute. If we are going to discover regularities in nature, our language must exercise a certain self-discipline: it must follow routines which allow us to collect evidence, to make predictions and, later, to understand them. Sheer improvisation will not put us in a position to do these things. This obvious constraint is overlooked by those who attribute to Wittgenstein a 'community theory of language'. It is hardly likely that he overlooked it.

8 Wittgenstein's Philosophy of Mathematics

Wittgenstein's PHILOSOPHY OF MATHEMATICS (chapter 10) is another development of the same general idea. For here too our most elaborate intellectual constructions are said to be founded on basic routines that cannot be justified intellectually. When we count, we feel that we are using footholds already carved for us in a rock-like reality. 'But counting . . . is a technique that is employed daily in the most various operations of our lives. And that is why we learn to count as we do with endless practice, and merciless exactitude. . . . "But is this counting only a *use*, then? Isn't there also some truth corresponding to this sequence?" . . . it can't be said of the series of natural numbers – that it is true, but that it is useful, and, above all, it is *used*' (Wittgenstein, 1978, I, 4).

The application of this idea to the philosophy of mathematics has proved less fruitful than its application to the philosophy of language. The reason for this may only be the greater distance between the superstructure and the proposed basis in this case. Or some would argue that mathematics is really not amenable to this treatment. It is, for example, questionable whether it can yield a convincing account of proof in mathematics.

9 Conclusion

Inevitably people ask what message can be extracted from Wittgenstein's philosophy. If a message is a theory, then, as we have seen, the message is that there is no message. Like any other philosopher, he pushed the quest for understanding beyond the point at which the ordinary criteria for understanding are satisfied. However, unlike others, he believed that philosophical understanding is more like the experience of a journey than the attainment of a destination. He regarded philosophy as an activity that is like Freudian therapy. You relive all the temptations to misunderstand and your cure recapitulates the stages by which it was achieved.

So it is not the restoration of a state of unreflective health. In fact, rather than aiming to reestablish any kind of state, philosophy is concerned with the process.

If there is a single structure discernible in his philosophy, it is his rejection of all illusory, independent support for our modes of thought. Rigid theories of meaning treat linguistic rules as independent authorities to which we who follow them are supposed to be wholly subservient. But he argues that this is an illusion, because the system of instruction and obedience involves a contribution from each individual and presupposes a basic like-mindedness. Similarly, the necessity of mathematics is something which we project from our practice and then mistakenly hail as the foundation of our practice. Evidently, he was rejecting realism, but his treatment of rules shows that he was not recommending conventionalism in its place. Certainly, his investigations have a structure, but it is not the structure of traditional philosophy.

Further Reading

There are several ways in which Wittgenstein's writings may be approached for the first time. Someone unfamiliar with philosophy might read *Culture and Value*. This is a collection of remarks that are not direct contributions to philosophy; they are about art, religion, Wittgenstein's own life and especially about what it is like to be a philosopher.

A closer approach would be to read his *Cambridge Lectures 1930–1932* or *The Blue Book* (1958), which was written 1933–4. In the former he explains the leading ideas of the *Tractatus* to an audience of Cambridge students; the latter deals with the nature of his later philosophy and with two specific philosophical problems: meaning and the self. Both are easier to follow than his other works, because they are written in the continuous, consequential way in which treaties are usually written, unlike the major part of his *oeuvre* which consists of independent remarks, which are carefully, but not always perspicuously, arranged.

In the Preface to *Philosophical Investigations* he compares his remarks to sketches made by an artist on many different journeys, crossing and re-crossing the same terrain. This work can be appreciated only by someone who travels on the same routes, following in his footsteps – that is, only by someone who can read his remarks as contributions of the philosophical problems with which they are concerned. Reading a book of this kind is not like ordinary reading. It is, of course, partly a matter of taking in what he writes, but it is also much more than that. You have to stop and think after reading a remark, and sometimes you have to follow up a long train of thought before going on to his next remark. But how can you get into a position to read Wittgenstein's texts in this way? That is the problem.

One solution is to use *A Wittgenstein Workbook* (compiled by Coope, Geach, Potts and White; Oxford: Blackwell, 1970). This helpful companion takes 18 topics of central importance in Wittgenstein's thought, and for each of them gives references to his writings and to related discussions by other philosophers, and a list of questions to which the reader can work out answers.

Another solution is to use one of the many books about Wittgenstein's philosophy in a similar way. Instead of reading it through from beginning to end, take a chapter dealing with a particular topic, read it and then look up all the references to Wittgenstein's work in the footnotes. The chapter will help you to understand Wittgenstein's remarks and, in the reverse direction, the remarks will serve as a check on the accuracy of the interpretation offered in the chapter.

In general, his earlier philosophy is more difficult to penetrate than his later philosophy, because it is directly and immediately related to the work of Frege and Russell. But though it is easier to find points of entry into the dialectical discussions of *Philosophical Investigations*, a full understanding of them requires familiarity with the theories under criticism, whether they are those of other philosophers or of Wittgenstein's earlier persona.

References

Wittgenstein: General

Wittgenstein, L. 1977: *Culture and Value* (edited by G. H. von Wright and H. Nyman, translated by P. Winch). Oxford: Blackwell.

Wittgenstein's early period

—— 1961: *Notebooks 1914–1916* (edited by G. H. von Wright and G. E. M. Anscombe, translated by G. E. M. Anscombe). Oxford: Blackwell.
—— 1922: *Tractatus Logico–Philosophicus* (translated by C. K. Ogden). London: Routledge. Also translated by D. F. Pears and B. McGuinness, London: Routledge, 1961.

Wittgenstein's transitional period

1966: Some Remarks on Logical Form. *Proceedings of the Aristotelian Society*, supplementary vol. 9. Reprinted in *Essays on Wittgenstein's Tractatus*, R. Beard and I. Copi (eds), London: Routledge and Kegan Paul, 1966.
—— 1980: *Wittgenstein's Lectures, Cambridge, 1930–1932* (edited by D. Lee). Oxford: Blackwell.
—— 1979: *Ludwig Wittgenstein and the Vienna Circle: Conversations Recorded by Friedrich Waismann* (edited by B. McGuinness, translated by J. Schulte and B. McGuinness). London: Blackwell.
—— 1975a: *Philosophical Remarks* (edited by R. Rhees, translated by R. Hargreaves and R. White). Oxford: Blackwell.

Wittgenstein's later period

—— 1958: *The Blue and Brown Books* (edited by R. Rhees). Oxford: Blackwell.

—— 1968: Notes for Lectures on 'Private Experience' and 'Sense-data'. *Philosophical Review*, 77. [The notes taken on these lectures by R. Rhees are published in the journal *Philosophical Investigations*, 7, Jan. 1984.]

—— 1953: *Philosophical Investigations* (translated by G. E. M. Anscombe). Oxford: Blackwell, 1953.

—— 1978: *Remarks on the Foundations of Mathematics* (edited by G. H. von Wright, R. Rhees and G. E. M. Anscombe, translated by G. E. M. Anscombe). Oxford: Blackwell.

—— 1975b: *Wittgenstein's Lectures on the Foundations of Mathematics* (edited by C. Diamond). Hassocks: Harvester Press.

—— 1969: *On Certainty* (edited by G. E. M. Anscombe and G. H. von Wright, translated by D. Paul and G. E. M. Anscombe). Oxford: Blackwell.

—— 1967: *Zettel* (edited by G. E. M. Anscombe and G. H. von Wright, translated by G. E. M. Anscombe). Oxford: Blackwell.

Other writers

Baker, G. and Hacker, P. M. S. 1984: *Scepticism, Rules and Meaning*. Oxford: Blackwell.

Bolton, D. E. 1979: *An Approach to Wittgenstein's Philosophy*. London: Macmillan.

Budd, M. 1989: *Wittgenstein's Philosophy of Mind*. London: Routledge.

Carnap, R. 1967 [1928]: *Logical Structure of the World* (translated by R. A. George). London: Routledge.

Coope, C., Geach, P., Potts, T. and White, R. 1970: *A Wittgenstein Workbook*. Oxford: Blackwell.

Kenny, A. 1973: *Wittgenstein*. Harmondsworth: Penguin.

Kripke, S. A. 1982: *Wittgenstein on Rules and Private Language: An Elementary Exposition*. Oxford: Blackwell.

McGuinness, B. 1988: *Wittgenstein: A Life: Young Ludwig 1889–1921*. London: Duckworth.

Malcolm, N. 1986: *Nothing is Hidden*. Oxford: Blackwell.

Monk, R. 1990: *Lugwig Wittgenstein: The Duty of Genius*. London: Jonathan Cape.

Pears, D. F. 1987–8: *The False Prison: A Study of the Development of Wittgenstein's Philosophy* (vol. 1, 1987, vol. 2, 1988). Oxford: Clarendon Press.

Wright, C. 1980: *Wittgenstein on the Foundations of Mathematics*. London: Duckworth.

Discussion Questions

1 Does logic have a basis?

2 What kind of theory is philosophical theory? Is theorizing the wrong way for philosophers to work?

3 How can 'crossing two pictures' lead to philosophical illusions?

4 Can we accept a therapeutic method of dealing with philosophical problems?

5 What is the nature of logical necessity? How are logically necessary propositions related to factual propositions?

6   Must a proposition be a kind of picture in order to have sense? What kind of picture is in question?

7   Must elementary propositions be complete, self-contained and independent of one another? Can there be such propositions?

8   Is Wittgenstein's logical atomism compatible with an empiricist interpretation? Are other interpretations available?

9   What are the implications of placing ethical, aesthetic and religious discourse beyond the limits of factual language?

10 How does Wittgenstein's thought display holism? Discuss in relation to at least two stages of his development?

11 Should the logical structure of language be a deep structure or visible on the surface?

12 Is Wittgenstein's thought a continuation of philosophy or its heir?

13 Why should a catalogue of examples linked by family resemblance be regarded as a solution to a philosophical problem?

14 How is ostensive definition possible? What does your answer indicate about the nature of language?

15 How is the meaning of a word related to its use?

16 Is there anything wrong with the solipsist's use of 'I'? What are the implications of your answer for our account of the self?

17 What constraints does the need for a criterion of identity place on our account of sensory experience? What sort of identity is involved?

18 What are the consequences if there is no way of distinguishing between knowing that my use of a word is correct and merely thinking that I knew that it was correct?

19 If we must treat something as fundamental, why not treat our ability to recognize sensation-types as fundamental?

20 Are what look like purely intellectual abilities really based on natural involvements in the physical world?

21 Does the 'private language argument' succeed?

22 Is the meaning of a word contained in the word itself?

23 Can the meaning of a descriptive word be understood on analogy with the meaning of a name?

24 Is following a linguistic rule obeying an independent, external authority?

25 How can the authority of a linguistic rule depend on agreement in the practice of obeying it?

26 Can Wittgenstein's approach to mathematics account for proof?

30

Modern European Philosophy ———

David E. Cooper

Like Hegel and Marx, but unlike most contemporary analytical philosophers, twentieth-century continental philosophy responds to a sense of
crisis in modern culture. It looks back to Nietzsche's radical examination of
meaning, truth, rationality and the self, and to Husserl's development of
phenomenology, with its central focus on intentionality, which is the
feature by which mental states are about things and have contents or
objects. It explores attempts to replace the Enlightenment ideal of universal
objective truth available to all rational autonomous subjects, and seeks to
overcome a metaphysical tradition embracing this ideal. The chapter uses
the theme of anti-scientism to explore the thought and method of major
individual figures, from Nietzsche, Husserl and Heidegger to Foucault and
Derrida, who constitute the continental tradition.

1 Introduction

The purpose of this chapter is to outline the main developments, during the
twentieth century, of what is usually referred to, in the English-speaking
world, as 'continental philosophy'. This statement immediately invites two
questions. What is covered by the term 'continental philosophy'? And why the
twentieth century rather than some longer or shorter period?

  'Continental' should not be understood in strictly geographical terms, for
there are, for instance, French, German or Spanish philosophers who do not
count as 'continental', and British or American ones who *do*. A student signing
up a course called 'Continental Philosophy' would encounter only some of the
movements and authors that have flourished in mainland Europe in recent
times. The list would certainly include such movements as phenomenology,
existentialism, hermeneutics, critical theory, structuralism and deconstruction, and would just as certainly exclude Polish logic and the logical
positivism of the Vienna Circle. Our student would be disappointed not to
hear about Husserl, Heidegger, Sartre, Foucault, Derrida and Habermas, and
surprised to study FREGE (chapter 27), POPPER (pp. 291–4), or TARSKI (pp. 104–6)
instead. These three are Europeans, but not 'continentals'. There are, to be
sure, important figures whose status is more ambiguous – most notably
WITTGENSTEIN (chapter 29), some aspects of whose later work are as congenial to

admirers of 'continental philosophy' as other aspects are to its detractors. But enough has been said to establish that 'continental philosophy' must be delineated, not in geographical terms, but in ones of characteristic concerns and trends.

Before I turn to these, a brief word on the time-span selected. There are crucial nineteenth-century thinkers – Marx, Kierkegaard, and above all Nietzsche – with which a course called 'Continental Philosophy' would likely deal. But at the turn of the century, discussion of Marx was still confined to radical clubs and cafés, Nietzsche was soon to die in obscurity despite the proselytizing by some enthusiasts, and Kierkegaard's name was known only to a few avant-garde theologians. On the whole, in fact, philosophy as pursued in the universities of France and Germany during the latter half of the nineteenth century was thoroughly *un*continental in the sense I shall be trying to identify.

It is often suggested that the nineteenth century did not truly end until 1918. Politically, socially and economically, that may be so, but in philosophy – as in literature and painting – several of the figures who were to lend European culture its modern shape were already producing influential work before 1914. Indeed, the coincidence between new directions in philosophy and the arts is not merely temporal. It was no accident, for example, that late nineteenth-century enthusiasm for science should have inspired the 'realist' novel; nor, therefore, a coincidence that, at the turn of the century, the aesthetic revolt against 'realism' should have had its counterpart in philosophical criticisms of the ambitions of science.

2 The attack on Scientism

Those last remarks introduce us, in fact, to the salient mood of the movements in European philosophy which concern us: a mood of hostility, if not towards science itself, then towards some large claims made on behalf of it. These claims constitute what is sometimes called 'scientism' or, in an earlier parlance, 'positivism'. 'Scientism' refers to something like the following set of claims: it is in the practices of the natural sciences that the goals of European Enlightenment – the overcoming of superstition, of obfuscating religion, of metaphysical waffle – are to be realized, thereby heralding the intellectual maturity of human beings to establish OBJECTIVE KNOWLEDGE (chapter 1) of the universe, themselves included; and it is in the acquisition of such knowledge through the methods, both deductive and empirical, which are epitomized in the NATURAL SCIENCES (chapter 9) that there resides the goal of human reason, or even of human existence itself. (Human beings are the creatures who desire to *know*, as ARISTOTLE (chapter 15) put it.)

Histories of European philosophy that pass quickly from the heyday of German idealism (which includes HEGEL (chapter 23) and Schelling), via Kierkegaard and Nietzsche, to Husserl and Heidegger in our own century, also pass over the fact that during the final decades of the nineteenth-century professional philosophy in France and Germany was dominated by the proponents of 'scientism' or positivism and its relatives. The greatest influence on French thought of the time was Auguste Comte (1789–1857), the 'inventor' of positivism. According to his doctrine of 'the three stages', human progress has consisted in the replacement, firstly, of religion by metaphysical philosophy, and then of metaphysics by the empirical sciences (crowned, in his view, by sociology). In contemporary Germany, there flourished not only such fully-fledged positivists as Ernst Mach, but the many so-called Neo-Kantians who were keen to remove the more metaphysical elements, such as the unknowable 'thing-in-itself', from their master's theories, and to revise what remained in order to accommodate recent advances in scientific thought.

There is a nice contrast, certainly, between the 'continental' reaction to the dominance of 'scientism' and an almost reverse movement in Britain at the turn of the century, when the prevailing orthodoxy was a brand of Hegelianism soon to be savaged by RUSSELL (chapter 27) and MOORE (chapter 28). Both reactions indelibly stamped subsequent developments. Anglo-American (or 'analytic') philosophy has tended, over the last 90 years, to be much more 'science-friendly' than European philosophy. Where the sciences promise to take over traditional concerns of philosophy, there has generally been sanguine acceptance of a much-reduced, 'analytic' role for philosophy – as the clarification of troublesome concepts, say, or 'the logic of scientific discovery'. One thinks, too, of the efforts devoted to showing that phenomena which at first glance resist a scientific account of reality do not in fact do so: for example, there have been many attempts to show that MORAL JUDGEMENTS (chapter 6) do not state special, 'non-natural' facts, but are instead expressions of feeling, devices for persuasion, or other such perfectly 'natural' phenomena.

'Continental' philosophy, conversely, has exhibited no such willingness to accommodate either itself or the problematic objects of philosophical enquiry to a scientific world-view. Those, like Heidegger, who speak of having 'gone beyond' philosophy do so, not because – like Comte – they have turned to science instead, but because philosophy, as they see it, has become too embroiled in the 'scientism' they reject.

A popular philosophical reaction against 'scientism' in Europe at the turn of the century took the form of direct frontal assaults on the claims of science to establish truths even in those areas – like the studies of TIME (pp. 336–8), SPACE (pp. 336–8) and causality – which might seem to be its exclusive domain. The 'truths' of science are at best partial or relative, and for a more 'absolute' knowledge we must deploy a non-rational faculty, such as intuition or feeling.

One representative of this approach was the most famous philosopher of pre-war Europe, Henri Bergson (1859–1941), at whose impassioned public lectures, it is said, the fashionable ladies of Paris would swoon. According to Bergson, we have an inveterate tendency – useful enough for practical purposes, admittedly – to analyse phenomena, like time, into constituent elements definable by clear-cut concepts. True philosophy, however, must 'invert' this tendency and replace analysis by 'intuition', a 'kind of *intellectual sympathy* by which one places oneself within an object in order to coincide with what is unique in it and consequently inexpressible' (Bergson, 1950, p. 23). There is, he claimed, nothing 'mysterious' about 'intuition', since we all employ it in *self-knowledge*. When so employed, it reveals that there is a self which endures, but not in time as conceived of by physics (as a succession of temporal points), but rather in (or, better, *as*) an indivisible flow (*durée*) wherein the past somehow continues to be contained within a present experience. In general, it is impossible to 'grasp' time, space, self or material objects as we experience them in terms of the constituents postulated by scientific analysis. Just as I do not experience myself as a cause-and-effect mechanism, but as an indivisible force, so we should view the evolution of matter and life not as the product of mechanical causes, but as the expression of an indescribable 'vital impetus' (*élan vital*) (Bergson, 1928). It is only to certain religious mystics that this view has been fully revealed. Finally, the errors of 'scientism' and 'mechanism' are not of a merely intellectual kind. For the very habits of thought which engender mechanistic accounts of the world and of mind are also responsible for producing 'closed' societies, in which human beings are expected to conform and behave in well-drilled mechanical ways. We should instead aim at creating 'open' societies in which people are inspired by a sense of the flow and vitality of life. One can appreciate, perhaps, why Bergson appealed to the racier elements of Parisian high society.

Another fashionable figure of this era to have launched a 'frontal assault' on 'scientism' was the Spanish novelist and philosopher, Miguel de Unamuno (1864–1936), whose *Tragic Sense of Life* appeared in 1912. The reason life is 'tragic' and 'consciousness a disease' is the impossibility of reconciling 'intellectual necessities with the necessities of the heart and the will'. Science and reason may convince us that our lives are determined and must one day end, but 'feeling' convinces us that we are free and immortal. It would be mere prejudice to prefer the testimony of 'the brain' to that of 'the soul, the blood, [and] the heart'. Indeed, it is a prejudice of science and reason even to attempt to eliminate the contradictions. Rather, we should affirm 'Contradiction! Of course! . . . we only live in and by contradictions' (Unamuno, 1954, pp. 13–15).

Neither Bergson nor Unamuno are much discussed today, for their brand of anti-scientism, with its appeal to some non-rational faculty of understanding, was not to predominate. This is not to deny the echoes of such an approach in some later writers, especially those on the more religious wing of the existentialist movement, like Karl Jaspers (1883–1969) and Gabriel Marcel (1889–1973). Nor is it to deny that, at certain points, Bergson and Unamuno were prescient of later, mainstream developments. For example, Bergson offers a PRAGMATIST (chapter 26) interpretation of science as furnishing us, not with truths about reality, but with intellectual tools essential to the conduct of our lives. Such 'anti-realist' interpretations of science were to play an important role in later critiques of 'scientism'. And here is a passage from Unamuno which states a theme that, 60 years on, had become something of an *idée fixe*:

the logical starting-point of all philosophical speculation is not the I, . . . [nor]
representation, nor the world as it presents itself immediately to the senses; but
it is *mediate or historical representation, humanly elaborated . . . in the language
by means of which we know the world.* (Unamuno, 1954, p. 310. My
emphasis.)

3 The Legacy of Nietzsche: Three Themes

The predominant ways in which 'scientism' has been attacked by 'continental'
philosophers have been more oblique than the direct assaults just sketched. It
is possible to organize the forms of attack into three critical themes, each
displaying several variations. We might dub the three themes 'the critique of
scientific culture', 'the critique of scientific self-understanding', and 'the
critique of the rational subject'. To put it in the broadest terms, the main
charges against 'scientism' have been: (1) the dominance of 'scientism' in
modern times has had a devastating cultural and moral impact, (2) 'scientism'
rests on a false understanding of the nature and conditions of scientific
enquiry, and (3) 'scientism' presupposes an incoherent notion of a rational self
or subject capable of achieving objective knowledge about reality.

For most of the writers whom we shall be discussing, these three themes are
related. For example, Martin Heidegger (1889–1976) – almost certainly the
most influential of these writers – argued that the very reasons which compel
us to reject the 'Cartesian' notion of the Self (pp. 515–17) also force us to
recognize that scientific understanding of the world is of a secondary,
derivative kind. Moreover, it is precisely that notion of the self that has
encouraged people to regard nature as a mere 'object' for investigation and
exploitation, thereby bearing responsibility for the environmental destruction,
with its attendant impact upon human life, of technological modernity.
(Heidegger, 1978, ch. VII.)

Just as important as the three themes themselves is what one might call –
extending the musical metaphor – the single key in which, for the most part,
they have been developed. The crucial notion has been that of *meaning* or
significance, in a broad sense – or perhaps several senses – of these elastic
terms. This notion has played two rather different roles, sometimes combined,
in the rejection of 'scientism'. In the first place, it is held that meaning or
significance plays an ineliminable role in explanations and descriptions of the
world and of one another. But it is a notion, too, that is resistant to any
scientific world-view. (There can, no doubt, be a scientific account, in causal
terms, of what it is for spots to mean (or to be a symptom of) measles, but not
of what it is for a society's traditions to mean something for its members – or
so it has been argued.) Secondly, it is above all through reflection on meaning
or significance that the three critical themes can be supported. For instance,
according to Heidegger and Wittgenstein, among others, it is the inability of
any Cartesian account of mind to explain a person's understanding of his or
her language which is a main reason for rejecting it. A person who
understands his or her words is *necessarily* a participant in public, linguistic
practices in a way that a Cartesian subject is not.

In what follows, I shall consider how each of the themes has been developed, and how, so to speak, these developments have been organized by the key notion of meaning. Before that, however – and by way of illustrating these themes in action, so to speak – it is worth remarking on the special importance assumed in our century by a rather earlier figure, Friedrich Nietzsche (1844–1900). This importance is due, quite simply, to his having been the first to sound all the themes, loud and clear, and in just the dominant key referred to above. Most of Nietzsche's distinctive doctrines are rooted in a certain view of meaning which he developed in his early writings.

Nietzsche on Meaning

According to Nietzsche, nearly all our words are in a sense 'metaphors'. Nouns, for example, do not refer to classes of objects which, in nature, are the same; rather, they reflect *our* determination to impose an order upon the chaotic flux of 'the world of becoming', by forcing dissimilar items of experience into manageable linguistic categories. Hence our statements are not representations of how reality actually is; instead, our alleged 'truths are illusions of which one has forgotten that this is what they are – metaphors that have become worn out', and are no longer recognized *as* metaphors (Nietzsche, 1979, p. 314).

Metaphysicians, religious believers and scientists are all guilty of misunderstanding the nature of language when they take their claims about substance, God, gravity or whatever, as stating how things objectively are. For example, Nietzsche said, 'we are not free of God, because we still believe in grammar' – we still believe, that is, in the objective reference of our words (Nietzsche, 1960, ch. 3 sec. 5). Even the propositions of logic and mathematics are not 'truths', but only extremely useful tools for coping with life. Behind metaphysics, religion and science there is, moreover a 'hidden agenda' – the goal of *power*. Since scientists, like the rest of us, are necessarily motivated by a 'will to power' (over the world, other people, and themselves), it is disingenuous if they regard themselves as detached, rational spectators who are capable of neutral, objective judgement.

Nietzsche's account of meaning is not the only reason why, for him, the 'Cartesian' notion of the self as a rational subject must be rejected. For a self which persists through the changes in a person's life is itself a 'fiction', encouraged by our inveterate tendency to postulate some entity as the reference of a noun (in this case, the pronoun 'I'). This tendency is reinforced by, and in turn reinforces, the *moral* urge, for purposes of praise, blame and punishment, to insist that someone can be the very same person as one who earlier committed a certain deed. So the misunderstanding of our language, which is responsible for, *inter alia*, scientific objectivism, is not without its moral implications. Nor, indeed, is objectivism itself. The Nietzschean ideal is the 'overman' (*Übermensch*), who has the strength to recognize that there are 'no facts, only perspectives', and who in the 'Dionysian' spirit of the artist strives to forge his own authentic 'perspective' on the world. 'Scientism' stands in the way of this ideal, for a culture in which it prevails is too 'demotic' or popular, imbued as it is with the idea that there are fundamental truths about the world to be *discovered*, and to which all rational humans are bound to assent.

In Nietzsche, then, we find just that pattern of critique (of a scientific culture, of the rational subject, of scientific self-understanding), informed by reflections on meaning, which will recur, in various shapes, during the following century. So let me turn to how these critical themes have been developed, beginning with that of cultural critique.

4 Critique of Scientific Culture

With relatively rare exceptions – such as Spengler, who hailed the technologist as the new 'Faustian man', and the leader of the 'futurists', Marinetti, who urged people to 'hymn the man at the steering-wheel' – the major European intellectuals of the century have been hostile to technological modernity, and to the 'scientism' which they regard as its prevailing ideology. To begin with, there have been those who have continued, if by somewhat different means, the Nietzschean motif of a contrast between the scientist, who would straitjacket our perception of the world and our place in it, and the emancipated artist, who appreciates the creative, 'perspectival' character of understanding. We find this contrast, for example, in Theodor Adorno (1903–69), a luminary of the Frankfurt school of critical theory. For this school, whose main inspiration was MARX (chapter 24), 'scientism' is hand-in-glove with industrial capitalism, both of them products of the European Enlightenment. By dismissing as 'myth' or 'sentimentality' any human purposes beyond those of objective knowledge and the maximization of utility, 'scientism' provides the warrant for capitalism's transformation of traditional societies into giant industrial concerns. Since, according to Adorno, intellectual activity has become thoroughly dominated by this outlook, the antidote is to be sought among those avant-garde artists who have managed to resist the capitalist transformation of the arts into a tranquilizing entertainment industry. Art produces illusions, but honest ones, unlike those of science and technology, with their pretence of objectivity and moral neutrality. 'In illusion', therefore, 'there is a promise of freedom from illusion' (quoted in Bubner, 1981, p. 182).

More emphatically Nietzschean is the approach of Michel Foucault (1926–84) – usually, to his annoyance, labelled a 'structuralist' or 'post-structuralist'. Like Nietzsche, Foucault is a nominalist: the linguistic categories into which people or things are sorted do not reflect any natural, objective order in reality. And for both philosophers, such categories are to be explained in terms of the powers they confer. Thus, Foucault argues, 'the mad' do not constitute a natural category, but comprise various kinds of people whom an increasingly centralized and monochrome society deems it necessary to exclude from having a serious voice in the conduct of affairs. In so excluding them, moreover, the predominant, 'instrumental' conception of reason is immunized against effective criticism, since the critics have been reduced to the ranks of 'the mad'. In his early work, at least, Foucault displays a romantic nostalgia for these 'other', excluded voices – especially when they are heard in works of art. In what might have been one of Nietzsche's more 'Dionysian' passages, Foucault writes:

> The madness in which the work of art is engulfed is the space of our enterprise, . . . the endless path to fulfilment . . . Madness is contemporary with the work of art since it inaugurates the time of its truth . . . The world that thought to measure . . . madness . . . must justify itself before madness. (Foucault, 1967, pp. 288–9)

This romanticism may have paled in Foucault's later writings, but even here the thought remains that we silence the voices of the 'mad', 'delinquents', 'rebels' and 'dissolutes' at our peril. There is a 'sense in listening to them', for they may speak truths; and anyway, 'it is due to such voices' that human life has had the form of a *history*, not that of a mere evolution (Foucault 1981, p. 8).

More persistent, however, have been those forms of cultural critique that have invoked the related notions of 'objectification' and 'alienation'. The relevant sense of 'object', here, owes much to the etymology of the word (one which is more apparent in the German word '*Gegenstand*'). An 'object' is that which 'stands over against' the subjects who experience or encounter it. Objectification, therefore, is the practice of regarding things that are not independent of human subjects, or that do not 'stand over against' them, as if they did. Alienation, correspondingly, is the feeling or sense of being 'distanced' or 'separated' from things from which, in truth, one is not.

Talk of objectification and alienation belongs, of course, in the Hegelian and Marxist lexicons, but it is the role these notions have played in a different tradition – that of phenomenology – on which I shall focus.

Phenomenology and Alienation

The central claim common to the various schools of phenomenology is that human existence is, first and foremost, 'intentional' or 'semantic'. That is, our fundamental relationship to the world which we experience and engage in is through structures of meaning or significance. (The 'phenomena' which phenomenology examines are not, as in an earlier use, sensory appearances, but 'meanings', 'essences' or 'senses'.) Experiences, wrote the 'father' of phenomenology, Edmund Husserl (1859–1938), are 'related to . . . things through their . . . posited meanings' (1952, p. 89). Or, as the French phenomenologist Maurice Merleau-Ponty (1907–61) put it, 'we are condemned to meaning' (1962, p. xix).

Unfortunately, however, we tend, both in everyday life and scientific enquiry, to neglect the structures of meaning which enable us to experience things, and imagine we are encountering them as they are 'in themselves'. For Husserl, the antidote to this 'natural' attitude is to 'bracket' or 'put out of play' the physical world, so as to concentrate on the meanings through which we are related to it. So-called 'existential phenomenologists', like Heidegger and Merleau-Ponty, argued that our existence is too practically engaged with this world for such an abstraction to be possible. They did, however, agree with Husserl that we should 'bracket' the scientific picture of the world so as to reveal the significance for us of things in the everyday 'life-world', engagement with which necessarily precedes the 'objectifying' stance of science. Unless we do this, then, as Husserl put it, we create a dualistic picture of 'nature . . . alien to spirit' (Husserl, 1970, p. 390). Not only does this destroy any sense of intimacy with the world, but since the 'nature' of the scientists is devoid of meaning, *values* (which are a species of meaning) are relegated to the realm of 'mere appearances' or 'subjective taste'. Therein, for Husserl, resides the incapacity of science rationally to challenge the forces of a new political and moral 'barbarism', and an attendant 'crisis of European man'.

Heidegger, too, argued that science offers secondary, derivative accounts of the world. In our basic engagement with the world, things are encountered and identified as 'ready-to-hand', as things which are what they are in virtue of the place they occupy within human purposes – as bridges, say, or hammers. Only when, so to speak, we just stop and stare, and dissect things, do we view them, in the scientist's manner, as objects which are merely 'present-at-hand'. They are then abstracted from that 'relational totality' of 'significance' which constitutes the world of engagement (Heidegger, 1962, pp. 114ff). There is nothing mistaken in viewing things as 'present-at-hand': the danger resides, rather, in this taking over from all other legitimate ways of 'revealing' the world. And this is only too liable to happen, given the intimate connection between the 'objectifying' view and the seemingly unstoppable momentum of technology. Once the river's historical associations and the role it plays in joining communities are overlooked in favour of an 'objective' conception – as a moving mass of H_2O, producing such-and-such energy – the way is open to 'put it on tap', as a resource to be exploited for technological ends. Void of all internal significance, things are simply there for us to use, and destroy, as we will. It is the hegemony of the scientific-technological way of 'revealing' that, for Heidegger, makes ours an 'age of distress'.

If the 'objectification' of things brings 'distress', then so, even more, does the 'objectification' of human beings. Common to phenomenologists of all persuasions is the conviction that human existence is fundamentally different in kind from that of anything else, a claim emphatically expressed by Heidegger's term *Dasein* for the being of human beings. Humans, after all, are the unique sources of meaning: it is through their conscious acts, or their practical activities, that meaning comes into the world. Hence it is a mistake, fraught with moral implications, to pretend that human beings are 'natural' objects, whose behaviour is explicable in the causal terms employed by natural science. The most vivid critique of this pretence is to be found in the writings of the existentialist philosopher and man of letters, Jean-Paul Sartre (1905–80).

The existentialists formed a loosely-knit movement, and many of those to whom the name was attached, like Heidegger, rejected it. Existentialism is best understood as combining the primary conviction of phenomenology, concerning the 'intentional' character of human existence, with an insistence on individual authenticity and resoluteness of choice, inherited from the nineteenth-century Danish thinker, Søren Kierkegaard. Precisely because human beings are 'meaning-giving', authentic persons shape their lives through a set of values and interpretations which they have forged for themselves, in the teeth, if need be, of the conventional ways of the 'herd' or the 'public'.

Existentialism

In Sartre's well-known slogan, existentialism teaches that '[human] existence precedes essence' (Sartre, 1966, p. 26). His point is that human behaviour cannot be explained like that of an artefact, in terms of some set function, nor like that of an animal or stone, in terms of a fixed constitution or nature. One's character, for example, is not a constant inner force which causes actions, but simply the pattern formed by one's actions. Explanation of these actions makes essential reference to a person's purposes, which in turn issue from an 'original choice' whereby a person assigns a scheme of values and significance to his world.

Because it can induce 'anxiety' to face up to the ever-present possibility of reshaping one's values, or oneself indeed, people have an understandable tendency not to do so. They are then in 'bad faith'. The person of 'bad faith' 'objectifies' himself or herself, regarding his or her behaviour as, for example, the expression of some fixed nature, and is too ready to accept other people's pigeon-holing classifications of him or her. Thus a character in one of Sartre's novels proclaims, 'I am myself for all eternity paederast, villain, coward . . . I need no longer bear the responsibility of my . . . self: he who sees me causes me to be. I am as he sees me' (Sartre, 1986, pp. 116, 345). As that remark suggests, what is wrong with 'bad faith' is not only that it is a form of self-deception, but a ploy for abdicating moral responsibility.

Sartre's complaint against 'scientism' is that it aids and abets indulgence in 'bad faith'. Not only does the general approach of science encourage a view of everything, ourselves included, as explicable in natural, causal terms, but particular sciences, like sociology and psychoanalysis, regard us as playthings of hidden forces. What is threatened, here, is not only a sense of individual responsibility, for the 'fall towards objectivity' which 'scientism' encourages is also a 'fall [into] *alienation*', or 'self-estrangement' (Sartre, 1957, pp. 274–5). This is because regarding oneself as 'a subject for science' requires, as it were, the adoption of a third-person perspective that is disjointed from the experience of oneself during everyday, engaged existence (see Sartre, 1983).

5 Hermeneutics and the Possibility of Objectivity

I called our second theme 'the critique of scientific self-understanding'. We have already encountered aspects of this – for example, in Heidegger's insistence that the things that scientists investigate owe their primary identity to their place in a humanly significant 'relational totality', so that these investigations do not 'uncover' the things in their most fundamental nature. In this section, however, I focus on some of the attacks made against the claims, attributed to 'scientism', that the methodology of the natural sciences is, firstly, universal in scope, secondly, a display of objectivity and neutrality, and, thirdly, our best guarantor of progress towards truth.

The earliest attack, in our century, on the first of these claims was launched by Wilhelm DILTHEY (1833–1911) (p. 368), who resurrected the old term 'hermeneutics' for the study of 'the method of interpretation'. Dilthey's interest was in HISTORICAL AND CULTURAL UNDERSTANDING (chapter 13) which, he believed, was not to be obtained through the methods of the natural sciences. 'The methodology of the human studies is, from its starting-point onwards, different from that of the physical sciences' (Dilthey, 1986, p. 177). This is because the understanding that, say, an historian seeks is not 'inference from an effect to a cause', but grasp of the relationship of an 'expression to what is expressed' (1986, pp. 220–1). Ultimately this is a matter of grasping the relation between, for example, the documents or customs of an era and the underlying 'Life' which they manifest. This procedure will, of course, require an understanding of the language used in the era in question, and indeed the understanding sought is closely related to linguistic understanding. A word has the meaning it does in virtue of its place within a whole language: similarly, the meanings which the historian seeks are those that customs and so on have only through 'belonging to a whole' form of life.

The procedure is, however, a difficult one, not least because the enquirer, like the people he is studying, is 'determined by [a] horizon' of thought and feeling that is peculiar to an age. Nevertheless, the structures of language and of 'Life' are sufficiently universal for understanding to be possible 'on the basis of [an] empathy', whereby the enquirer succeeds in entering into, in 'recreating or reliving', the mental life of a past or alien culture, and thus grasps why the 'expressions' of that culture should have been as they were (Dilthey, 1986, p. 226). Empathy, which reveals 'the relation between expressions and the inner states expressed in them', has 'no analogy in the methods of science'. For one thing, it is only 'subjective certainty', the feeling that one has 'got it right', that validates hermeneutic understanding (1986, p. 230).

For a later leading proponent of hermeneutics, Hans-Georg Gadamer (b. 1900), Dilthey's trust in the empathetic method contradicts his insight into the determination of enquiry by a 'horizon'. If the historian is an historically situated 'child of his times', he or she cannot step outside the horizon these set so as fully to enter into the mental life of another culture. Gadamer's concern, however, is not to replace scientific or empathetic methods in human studies by something more suitable, but to attack the very possibility of neutrality and objectivity in methodological enquiry. In any field of enquiry, the use of a method – statistics, for instance – rests on selecting some 'possibilities for questioning' to the exclusion of others, and only certain features of our relation to the world as worth examining. Enquiry, therefore, relies on 'pre-under-standing' and 'pre-judices', 'biases of our openness to the world . . . conditions whereby we experience something' (Gadamer, 1977, p. 9).

The point is, in part, an historical one. Human consciousness is not atemporal in its forms, but indelibly 'affected by history', which necessarily structures the enquirer's 'possibilities of knowing' (Gadamer, 1977, p. 13). But there is a larger point, which Gadamer inherits from his teacher, Heidegger.

According to the latter's brand of phenomenology, phenomenology *is* hermeneutics, and this for the dual reasons that description of any experiences is itself interpretation, and that the experiences themselves are interpretations of the world as it is encountered. Interpretation, one might say, goes all the way down. There is no level of 'brute facts' or 'raw data' which would impress themselves upon the consciousness of a detached, objective observer. Confident references to 'the facts' merely reflect our forgetfulness of the interpretation which their description embodies. The reason, for Gadamer, why interpretation 'goes all the way down', why hermeneutics is 'universal' in scope, is that 'being that can be understood is language' or 'linguistically constituted' (Gadamer, 1979, p. xxii). This does not mean, as it apparently does for some of Derrida's wilder followers, that there exists nothing but language: rather that, not only does all understanding take place through the 'medium' of the enquirer's own language, but that this understanding is itself akin to linguistic translation. For one never encounters one's data 'raw', but always as 'mediated', to recall Unamuno's term, through that 'generative power' of language which shapes the inherited 'pre-understanding' which no enquiry can fully transcend. We are apt to forget this if we focus on the specialist, professional vocabularies of the sciences: but we should recall that, if these are to be finally intelligible to us, they must be 'reconnected' with background, ordinary languages through which the world is first 'open' to us.

It is not only adepts of phenomenology and hermeneutics who have challenged the possibility of objectivity by drawing attention to the limiting background or conditions of enquiry. Like Gadamer, Simone Weil (1909–43) – who is not assignable to any particular school – stressed the 'linguistic constitution' of the world, inviting us to ponder the 'paradox' that 'an order of things ... that appears as objective' has been 'constructed' through the deployment of language, and so 'depends entirely on ourselves' (Weil, 1978, p. 70). Rather differently, there have of course been plenty of authors – from card-carrying Communists, like Althusser, to the less orthodox Marxists of the Frankfurt school – who have variously continued Marx's programme of 'unmasking' the predominantly economic interests that shape allegedly objective enquiry. One thinks, for example, of Jürgen Habermas' (b. 1929) elaborate analysis of the 'knowledge-constitutive interests' which condition the different kinds of science – 'technical control', for instance, in the case of the 'empirical-analytical sciences' (Habermas, 1972).

The Nature of Truth

It will come as no surprise that philosophers thus keen to emphasize the historical 'situatedness' of enquiry, its 'pre-judices' or hidden interests, have no sympathy with the 'scientistic' understanding of the sciences as progressing towards truth, in the traditional sense of correspondence with reality as it is 'in itself'. There can be no reason to suppose, given their necessary lack of objectivity, that the sciences have arrived at truth in that sense: and unless there is good reason – which there is not – for discerning the sciences as progressive, truth of this kind is not even a viable 'regulative' goal. If, then we are to continue to speak of 'truth' in connection with such enquiries – and not simply 'bracket' it as an idle or irrelevant notion – this must be in some radically re-defined sense, which makes of truth something quite different from its 'scientistic' conception. Maybe it would be more honest, for example, if scientists candidly admitted an equation between truth and 'efficiency of results' – as Heidegger urged (1978, p. 376f). Or perhaps, as Habermas (1980) suggests, we should 'measure' truth in terms of a consensus on beliefs and values which responsible interlocutors *would* reach in 'ideal speech situations', freed from the factors which normally serve to 'distort' our deliberations.

Or maybe we should follow Foucault's practice of no longer using 'truth' as a term of appraisal, applied to those statements which succeed in stating how things really are. Instead, we should talk of 'regimes of truth', where 'truth' is something 'produced', not discovered, through the 'mechanisms' whereby 'types of discourse' determine which statements are 'sanctioned' (the 'true' ones) and which not (the 'false' ones) (Foucault, 1980, p. 131). We will, no doubt, be encouraged in this practice if we accept two further ingredients in Foucault's account. Firstly, the history of at least the human sciences is one of 'discontinuity' and relative 'incommensurability' between the succeeding 'discourses' or 'epistemes' which organize fields of enquiry and the criteria for acceptable statements. Secondly, 'we are subjected to the production of truth through power' (Foucault, 1980, p. 93): the idea being the rather Nietzschean one that our theories, especially about human beings, are not the products of idle intellectual curiousity, but – as with psychiatry, criminology, and the study of sexuality – elements in the exercise of 'bio-power', an intrusive vigilance towards, and control over, the human body.

Perhaps the most radical pronouncements on truth by a philosopher who comes within our brief are those of the self-confessed 'postmodernist', Jean-François Lyotard (b. 1925). In a much-quoted line, he defines 'postmodernism' as an attitude of 'incredulity towards metanarratives', by which are meant the grand attempts, from the Enlightenment until very recently, to 'legitimate' various 'discourses', both scientific and moral – for example, that of the progressive 'emancipation of the rational . . . subject' (Lyotard, 1984, pp. xxiiif). With these 'metanarratives' apparently now having become 'incredible', we must recognize that the sciences are merely 'games', governed by more-or-less arbitrary 'rules . . . specific to each particular kind'. True statements are simply those it is 'good' to make, these being the ones that 'conform to the relevant criterion . . . accepted in the social circle of the 'knower's' interlocutors' (1984, p. 19). Here is a reductive account of truth with which, one suspects, earlier critics of 'scientism', like Gadamer, would lack sympathy. Though at what point, exactly, they could halt the slide from their positions to that of Lyotard is unclear.

6 The Status of the Self

A recent history of European philosophy since 1750 is sub-titled 'The rise and fall of the self' (Solomon, 1988). In this century, the story has been of the 'fall', and provides us with our third and final theme. With a few exceptions who prove the rule, 'continental' philosophers have displayed a marked animus, if not against the very notion of the self, then certainly against what they take to be standard, traditional conceptions of it. In recent years, especially in Paris, there has been a veritable crescendo of obituaries on this and related notions

– 'the demise of the subject', 'the death of the author', 'the end of man', and so on.

These attacks on the self are, in fact, directed against a variety of targets, unfortunately not always distinguished by those who launch them. The animus of these attacks is partly explained by the belief that these targets are variously implicated in the programme of 'scientism'. One such target, so-called 'methodological individualism', is often held responsible for the 'positivist', 'atomistic' approach of social scientists who misguidedly emulate the methodology of the natural sciences. This is the idea, attributed to Comte and J. S. MILL (chapter 25), that the basic elements in the explanation of historical and social processes are individual human beings. Against this, the Marxist Louis Althusser (1918–90) proclaims that 'the human subject . . . is not the "centre" of history . . . [but] constituted by a structure which has no "centre" either, except in the imaginary misrecognition of the "ego"' (Althusser, 1977, p. 201). Far from individual subjects playing a fundamental role in explaining social processes, they are in some sense 'invented' by such processes – apparently in order that people should enjoy the delusion that they 'freely accept [their] *subjection*' to 'ideological state apparatuses'. (The similar thought that history is not 'made' by individual subjects, but is, in large part, 'a history of the different modes by which . . . human beings are made subjects', is familiar from Foucault's later writings (Foucault, 1982, p. 208).)

A very different target, reckoned to be embroiled in 'scientism' through encouraging the image of the 'detached spectator' confronting a world of independent objects, is what might be called 'the self-enclosed mind'. The classic example is Descartes' subject, whose direct knowledge is confined to the contents (ideas, images, and so on) of its own 'inner' realm, and which therefore faces an 'egocentric predicament' in arriving at any knowledge of a world and other minds outside this realm. A twentieth-century descendant of the Cartesian subject is Husserl's 'pure' or 'transcendental' ego. Descartes established the separateness of the subject by subjecting to doubt the very existence of an external world, while finding it impossible to doubt his own existence. Husserl does the same for the 'pure' ego by 'bracketing' or 'putting out of play' the empirical world. Since what is 'bracketed' includes the so-called 'natural' or 'worldly' ego (the self as studied by psychology, replete with character, motives, and so on), what remains after the 'bracketing' is simply a 'disinterested spectator of [the] worldly ego and its life', independent of the world (if such there be), and confined in its dealings to 'meanings' or 'essences' internal to consciousness (Husserl, 1975, pp. 10ff).

In retaining a broadly Cartesian notion of the self, Husserl was an exception that proves the rule, for he was soon to become the whipping-boy, on this account, for most succeeding phenomenologists. Heidegger speaks for many of them in condemning as 'absurd' the 'idea of a subject which has intentional experiences . . . encapsulated within itself' (Heidegger, 1982, p. 64). We noted in section 4 the insistence, *contra* Husserl, that intentionality or meaning owes its existence, not to the mental acts performed by a detached consciousness, but to the engagement by embodied persons in an 'unbracketable' public world. Cartesian and Husserlian conceptions of self must, therefore, be rejected. Thus, for Sartre, the self is not the seat of consciousness, but 'out there' in the world, a 'sum of actions' whose unity is due to their being actions assignable to a particular body. For Merleau-Ponty, too, if the self is understood as a source of meaning, then it cannot be regarded as something separate from body, since 'my body is [the] meaningful core', the indispensable instrument for lending order and significance to the world through which I move (Merleau-Ponty, 1962, p. 147). Moreover, if the self is the source of meaning then, as Heidegger argues, the 'self' of everyday life is not that of the individual person, the 'I', but the 'They-self' – for it is the anonymous 'Them', people-at-large, who are responsible for the structures of meaning into which the individual is 'always already' immersed (see Heidegger, 1962, pp. 149ff). The individual self should then be seen as something of an *achievement*, performed by the 'authentic' person who manages, within limits, to rise above 'Their' conventional ways of interpreting the world.

In the view of some more recent French thinkers, however, these existentialist repudiations of 'the self-enclosed mind' still smack too much of the 'humanism' with which western conceptions of the self have, allegedly, been imbued. By this is meant the idea that human beings – even when construed as social and embodied beings, rather than solitary 'pure' egos – enjoy a relative autonomy as the sources of meaning and intelligibility. 'Humanism', in this sense, is a third distinguishable target of those who proclaim the demise of the self or subject. And since they regard 'humanism' as the basis for Enlightenment optimism about the emergence of rational, autonomous persons with the capacity to delineate the objective order of things, then the errors of 'humanism' are also those of 'scientism'.

The rejection of 'humanism' was a stated aim of most of those loosely related anthropologists, semioticists, and psychologists labelled 'structuralists'. Claude Lévi-Strauss (b. 1908), for example, has argued that the autonomous sources of meanings are not human beings, either individually or in groups, but the structured 'codes' – like those governing the production of myths – through which alone the particular utterances or actions of people have the significance they do (see Lévi-Strauss, 1968). He does, however, assume that the formal features of these 'codes' – most notably, the 'binary oppositions' (like 'raw' versus 'cooked') which they display – have their foundation in the universal constitution of the human brain. For Jacques Derrida (b. 1931), at least, this is still 'humanism', for it respects the 'dream' of 'man' to secure a 'reassuring foundation' for the 'play' of language and thought (Derrida, 1978, p. 292).

Derrida has been the most influential living European philosopher during the last quarter of the century, alternatively deemed a messiah of the only philosophy possible in a 'postmodern' era that has 'exploded' the pretensions of metaphysics, and an obfuscating clown who has disgraced his calling. His critique of the self or subject, at any rate, is an interesting, if hardly perspicuous, one that is indebted to both structuralism and the gnomic pronouncements of Heidegger in the later years of his life.

According to Derrida, the notion of self or subject is inextricably tied to those of consciousness and presence: for a self is self-conscious, and self-consciousness is 'the perception of self in presence', or 'self-presence' (Derrida, 1982, p. 16). Now since 'we think only in signs', there could be no thinking, self-conscious creatures other than language-users. But reflection on signs and language soon reveals that presence – of which self-presence is but one instance – is a chimera. Here Derrida appeals to the work of the structuralist linguist, Saussure, who established, he thinks, that the sense of a sign is determined by its relations to and differences from other signs in the network of a language. It is not, then objects, ideas, concepts or whatever else might be deemed present in or to the mind of the speaker which gives his words the senses they have, but something 'absent' or permanently 'deferred' – a whole network of signs, whose use stretches backwards and forwards in time, within which those words 'circulate'. Put more dramatically, signs always signify other signs, and 'there is nothing outside of the text' functioning to fix their meanings independently of their unstable and unsurveyable 'dissemination' within a language as a whole (Derrida, 1976, pp. 7, 158).

The self or subject, then, turns out to be one of those many concepts of 'Western metaphysics', like 'substance' and 'idea', which in Derrida's view presuppose such untenable dichotomies as those between presence and absence, and signs and what they signify, and for that reason are to be 'deconstructed'. An understandable response is that, while the notions of self and self-consciousness are indeed linked, it is peculiar to construe the latter in terms of the presence to consciousness of some entity, the self – in which case Derrida is 'deconstructing' a straw-man. If so, the force of his argument turns on his insistence that subjects or speakers do not possess the degree of control over the senses of their words and thoughts which, arguably, 'humanist' conceptions of the self have assumed. This is why he is keen to establish that the subject is a 'function' of language, that (as Heidegger put it) 'language speaks man', and that 'there is no subject who is agent, author, and master' of language (Derrida, 1981, p. 28). Rather, a language is a particular network of signs and their 'différance' (a word coined from the French terms for difference and deferral).

Différance, 'the production of differences', 'the formation of forms', is not an easy notion to grasp: indeed, it is said to be 'unnameable' and 'unconceptualiz-able'. On one interpretation, Derrida is invoking a kind of hidden power or 'event', akin perhaps to the 'Being' spoken of by the later Heidegger, which in some mysterious way 'destines' any given way of articulating the world. On another, the term draws our attention, in a somewhat misleading way, to the sheer groundless contingency of any particular scheme of articulation which happens to obtain. On any tolerable interpretation, however, Derrida's account appears to mark the zenith or nadir (according to taste) of that anti-'humanist' animus against the rational, autonomous subject, which has been a major theme in the wider 'continental' critique of 'scientism'. It is a fitting point, therefore, at which to close this survey of a critique which, I have suggested, confers on 'continental' philosophy of this century its most characteristic features.

Further Reading

Some readers will turn immediately to one or more of the major figures discussed in this chapter, but others will seek further background reading before exploring the demanding texts. Lichtheim (1974) provides a general appreciation of the historical circumstances in which the philosophical works were produced. Solomon (1988) discusses features of recent European philosophy, with an historical perspective going back to figures such as Kant and Hegel. Passmore (1968) offers an attractive account of philosophy over the past century, although he mainly explores the development of Anglo-American philosophy. His work can be supplemented by Bubner (1981) on German philosophy, Descombes (1980) on French philosophy, or Kearney (1986) on trends in European philosophy. A tighter focus is provided by Bleicher's (1980) collection on hermeneutics; by Hammond, Howarth and Keat (1991) on phenomenology; by Cooper (1990) on existentialism; by Sturrock (ed.) (1979) on structuralism and post-structuralism; and by Culler (1982) on deconstruction.

If we turn to primary works, we can note that a classic reader, Kaufmann (1960), has led many students to develop an interest in existentialism and European philosophy. Nietzsche (1960) has had a similar effect. Early in the century Bergson (1950) established an agenda of concerns, although his own work has fallen out of fashion. Students can approach phenomenology through Husserl (1965), possibly with the assistance of Kockelmans (ed.) (1967). Heidegger (1962) is a classic text, needed to understand his own later work and many other developments. Sartre (1966) explores themes discussed in his literary and philosophical works. Adorno and Horkheimer (1979) is a major Frankfurt school text. Hermeneutic philosophy is examined in Gadamer (1976). Foucault (1984) provides a broad sample of the author's work. Habermas (1987) explores contemporary issues concerning modernism and postmodernism. Derrida (1973) offers an introduction to exciting, yet controversial views. Rorty (1991) expresses the response of an American philosopher deeply influenced by Heidegger and other recent European philosophers.

References

Adorno, T. and Horkheimer, M. 1979 [1944]: *Dialectic of Enlightenment* (translated by J. Cumming). London: Verso.

Althusser, L. 1977 [1969]: *Lenin and Philosophy and Other Essays* (translated by B. Brewster). London: New Left Books.

Bergson, H. 1928 [1907]: *Creative Evolution* (translated by A. Mitchell). London: Macmillan.

—— 1950 [1903] *An Introduction to Metaphysics* (translated by T. E. Hulme). New York: Liberal Arts.

Bleicher, J. 1980: *Contemporary Hermeneutics: Hermeneutics as Method, Philosophy and Critique.* London: Routledge and Kegan Paul.

Bubner, R. 1981: *Modern German Philosophy* (translated by E. Matthews). Cambridge: Cambridge University Press.

Cooper, D. 1990: *Existentialism: A Reconstruction*. Oxford: Blackwell.

Culler, J. 1982: *On Deconstruction: Theory and Criticism after Structuralism*. Ithaca: Cornell University Press.

Derrida, J. 1973 [1967]: *Speech and Phenomena: And Other Essays on Husserl's Theory of Signs* (translated by D. Allison). Evanston: Northwestern University Press.

—— 1976 [1967]: *Of Grammatology* (translated by G. Spivak). Baltimore: Johns Hopkins University Press.

—— 1978 [1967]: *Writing and Difference* (translated by A. Bass). London: Routledge and Kegan Paul.

—— 1981 [1972]: *Positions* (translated by A. Bass). Chicago: University of Chicago Press.

—— 1982 [1972]: *Margins of Philosophy* (translated by A. Bass). Chicago: University of Chicago Press.

Descombes, V. 1980 [1979]: *Modern French Philosophy* (translated by L. Scott-Fox and J. Harding). Cambridge: Cambridge University Press.

Dilthey, W. 1986: *Selected Writings* (translated by H. P. Rickman). Cambridge: Cambridge University Press.

Foucault, M. 1967 [1961]: *Madness and Civilization: A History of Insanity in the Age of Reason* (translated by R. Howard). London: Tavistock.

—— 1980: *Power/Knowledge: Selected Interviews and Other Writings 1972–77* (translated by G. Gordon). New York: Pantheon.

—— 1981: Is it Useless to Revolt? *Philosophy and Social Criticism*, 8.

—— 1982: The Subject and Power. In H. L. Dreyfus and P. Rabinow (eds), *Michel Foucault: Beyond Structuralism and Hermeneutics*, Brighton: Harvester, 208–26.

—— 1984: *The Foucault Reader* (edited by P. Rabinow). Harmondsworth: Penguin.

Gadamer, H.-G. 1976: *Philosophical Hermeneutics* (translated by D. E. Linge). Berkeley: University of California Press.

—— 1979 [1960]: *Truth and Method* (translated by W. Glen-Doeppel). London: Sheed and Ward.

Habermas, J. 1972 [1968]: *Knowledge and Human Interest* (translated by J. Shapiro). Boston: Beacon.

—— 1980 [1971]: The Hermeneutic Claim to Universality (translated by J. Bleicher). In J. Bleicher (1980).

—— 1987 [1985]: *The Philosophical Discourses of Modernity: Twelve Lectures* (translated by F. Lawrence). Cambridge: Polity Press.

Hammond, M., Howarth, J. and Keat, R. 1991: *Understanding Phenomenology*. Oxford: Blackwell.

Heidegger, M. 1962 [1927]: *Being and Time* (translated by J. MacQuarrie and E. Robinson). Oxford: Blackwell.

—— 1978: *Basic Writings* (translated by D. F. Krell). London: Routledge and Kegan Paul.

—— 1982 [1975]: *The Basic Problems of Phenomenology* (translated by A. Hofstadter). Bloomington: Indiana University Press.

Husserl, E. 1952: *Ideen zu einer reinen Phanomenologie und phanomenologischen Philosophie, Drittes Buch* (Ideas towards a Pure Phenomenology and Phenomenological Philosophy, 3rd book), The Hague: Nijhoff.

—— 1965 [1911, 1936]: *Phenomenology and the Crisis of Philosophy* (translation by Q. Lauer). New York: Harper and Row.

—— 1970 [1936]: *The Crisis of European Sciences and Transcendental Philosophy* (translated by D. Carr). Evanston: Northwestern University Press.

—— 1975 [1950]: *The Paris Lectures* (translated by P. Koestenbaum). The Hague: Nijhoff.

Kaufmann, W. (ed.) 1960: *Existentialism from Dostoyevsky to Sartre*. New York: Anchor.

Kearney, R. 1986: *Modern Movements in European Philosophy*. Manchester: Manchester University Press.

Kockelmans, J. (ed.) 1967: *Phenomenology: The Philosophy of Edmund Husserl and its Interpretations*. New York: Anchor.

Levi-Strauss, C. 1968 [1958]: *Structural Anthropology*, vol. 1 (translated by C. Jacobsen and C. Grundfest). London: Allen Lane.

Lichtheim, G. 1974: *Europe in the 20th Century*. London: Cardinal.

Lyotard, J.-F. 1984 [1979]: *The Postmodern Condition: A Report on Knowledge* (translated by G. Bennington and B. Massumi). Manchester: Manchester University Press.

Merleau-Ponty, M. 1962 [1945]: *Phenomenology of Perception* (translated by C. Morris). London: Routledge and Kegan Paul.

Nietzsche, F. 1960: *The Portable Nietzsche* (translated by W. Kaufmann). New York: Viking.

—— 1979: *Werke. Band III*. Munich: Ullstein.

Passmore, J. 1968: *A Hundred Years of Philosophy*. Harmondsworth: Penguin.

Rorty, R. 1991: *Essays on Heidegger and Others: Philosophical Papers, vol. 2*. Cambridge: Cambridge University Press.

Sartre, J.-P. 1957 [1943]: *Being and Nothingness: An Essay on Phenomenological Ontology* (translated by H. Barnes). London: Methuen.

—— 1966 [1946]: *Existentialism and Humanism* (translated by P. Mairet). London: Methuen.

—— 1986 [1943]: *The Reprieve* (translated by G. Hopkins). Harmondsworth: Penguin.

Solomon, R. 1988: *Continental Philosophy Since 1750: The Rise and Fall of the Self*. Oxford: Oxford University Press.

Sturrock, J. (ed.) 1979: *Structuralism and Since*. Oxford: Oxford University Press.

Unamuno, M. de 1954 [1912]: *Tragic Sense of Life* (translated by J. Crawford Flitch). New York: Dover.

Weil, S. 1978 [1959]: *Lectures on Philosophy* (translated by H. Price). Cambridge: Cambridge University Press.

Discussion Questions

1   What are the consequences for philosophy of rejecting the Enlightenment goal of rational subjects gaining universal objective knowledge?

2   Do we have access to truths that are not scientific truths?

3   What problems arise for the claim that we live 'in and by contradiction'?

4   To rid ourselves of scientism, should we reject or re-interpret science?

5   How can we assess the claim that everything given in philosophy is mediated by language and is therefore placed in history?

6   What, if anything, should replace the Cartesian subject?

7   Are nearly all of our words in a sense metaphors? What rival accounts of meaning should be considered?

8   Must metaphysics, science and religion be explained in terms of a 'will to power' rather than by detached, rational objectivity?

9   If there are no facts, how can there be perspectives?

10   How can we determine whether linguistic categories reflect a natural objective order in reality?

11   Must the world justify itself before madness?

12   Do the concepts of alienation and objectification help us in assessing culture and society?

13   What does phenomenology examine?

14   Does Heidegger's distinction between things 'ready-to-hand' and things as 'present-to-hand' help to overcome a crucially limited account of the world?

15   What is the effect of modern technology on the way we perceive ourselves and the world?

16   Are human beings natural objects explicable in terms of science?

17   Does the distinction between authenticity and bad faith have any bearing on how we ought to live?

18   What is the philosophical significance of the claim that human consciousness is historical in character?

19   Is truth produced through sanctioned regimes of discourse rather than discovered?

20   What is the place of the body in our accounts of selves?

21   Does rejecting presence and self-presence help to deal with the problem of the subject?

22   Are all ways of articulating the world matters of groundless contingency?

31

Applied Ethics ——————————————

John Haldane

Recent philosophy has returned to a traditional concern with providing
critical assessment of conduct and institutions. Under the term 'applied
ethics' areas as diverse as health care, warfare, business and the environment have been subject to close scrutiny in terms of rival ethical theories or
within the scope of a specific ethical theory. The chapter examines the rise
of applied ethics against the background of twentieth-century developments in ethics and political philosophy and suggests that there are dangers
in its current popularity. It considers a precedent for applied ethics and
examines its possible future development.

1 What is Applied Ethics?

In trying to understand what applied ethics is, and how it has developed
within English-speaking philosophy over the last 20 to 30 years, it is useful to
begin by making a threefold or three-level distinction, between MORALITY
(chapter 6), MORAL THEORY (pp. 209–11), and META-ETHICS (pp. 222–5). The first
of these consists of individual claims about what is of moral value, such as
honesty and loyalty, and about what ought to be done or avoided in general
and on particular occasions: for instance, always help those in great need, or
never inflict unnecessary pain. Sometimes claims of these sorts come in
groups and constitute a moral outlook or system. When this is so it becomes
possible to speak of a *morality* or an *ethic* – such as a Christian morality or an
ecological ethic. A morality in this sense is a body of moral claims usually
expressing a certain kind of concern or commitment.

It is likely, but not logically required, that a morality will be accompanied by
one or more PRINCIPLES (pp. 599–601) by reference to which particular claims
are justified. This brings us to the second of the three levels, for the
articulation of such principles within a systematic structure is what constitutes a *moral theory*. Here it is important to note two points: first, that one
can make moral claims, and more generally possess a morality, without having
a moral theory; and, second, that the same moral claims, and even the same
moralities or ethics, are compatible with different moral theories. Thus, for
example, one may hold that lying is wrong without having a systematic
account of what makes it wrong, and moreover this moral claim might be

justified by quite distinct theories such as those of consequentialism, deontology or Divine law (pp. 221–2). The immorality of lying might, for example, be taken to derive from its tendency to cause unhappiness, its intrinsic wrongness or its being at variance with a divine commandment.

The third level is different from the other two inasmuch as it is not concerned with what is right or wrong, good or bad, and with why things are so, but rather concerns the logical status of moral claims and moral theories. *Meta-ethics* is the most philosophical and abstract form of thinking about morality. It addresses such Metaphysical (chapter 2) and Epistemological (chapter 1) questions as whether values are objective, and what that might mean and whether thoughts about them can constitute genuine knowledge.

While a number of things now go by the description of 'applied ethics' the central aspect of this consists in the more or less systematic application of moral theory to particular moral problems (in terms of the threefold division, the application of second level to first level thinking). In its earlier stages these were principally life and death issues, such as those of abortion, euthanasia, suicide or warfare. More recently, however, there has been a considerable increase of interest among college and university students, professional philosophers and those outside higher education in the examination of moral issues, and this interest has led to an extension of *medical ethics* from questions of abortion and euthanasia and to the development of new fields of applied ethics such as *business ethics, computer ethics, environmental ethics, gender ethics, journalism ethics, reproductive ethics* and so on. Indeed, the point has now been reached at which there are very few if any areas of human activity that are not the subject of some named branch of applied ethics. Whether this is a good thing is itself an interesting and important question.

2 The Rise of Applied Ethics

The rise and expansion of this area of philosophy is due to a number of causes some more creditable to its practitioners than others. To begin with there is the fact that for the first half of the twentieth century English-speaking moral philosophy consisted almost exclusively of meta-ethics. The main concerns of this were, and remain, whether values and requirements are features of the world or merely products of human preference and commitment, and whether the language of morality is descriptive, expressive or prescriptive. Discussions of these questions became ever more distant from actual moral thinking, in part because by their nature they were abstracted from particular moral outlooks, but also because the language in which they were presented was a technical philosophical one owing nothing to familiar ethical vocabularies. Although during this period the study of meta-ethics produced some very good analytical philosophy, moral problems were left entirely unaddressed and the intermediary level of moral theory was also neglected.

This can now seem very odd because throughout the same period there had been two world wars, the rise of ideological totalitarianism, widespread attempts at genocide, and the development and use of weapons of mass destruction. But however it was that philosophers judged it none of their professional business to discuss these matters, the pressure increased for systematic moral thinking about fundamental values and the basis of conduct. By the mid-1960s a change in attitudes and practice was becoming apparent. The experience of students and academics in the United States was perhaps the most important social factor in the rise of applied ethics. Questions of civil rights, of sexual ethics, of the morality of warfare and of bioethics became prominent themes of public debate and the society began to divide between conservatives and radicals, absolutists and relativists. Setting aside the question of particular viewpoints, what became clear and was felt to be something of a scandal was that professional moral philosophy appeared to have nothing to say about these important moral issues.

In earlier times, a professional response might have been that a philosopher has no more business saying how one should act than a chemist has saying whether there should be more or fewer synthesized compounds in the world – in each case the professional duty is to understand the nature of reality, not to change it. But this sort of reply came to seem unacceptable. First, from its earliest days, philosophy has been concerned with both theoretical and practical reasoning. As well as asking what one should believe about the world – that is, what is true? – it has addressed the question about how one should act in it – that is, what is it good to do? Second, developments in meta-ethics themselves steadily weakened the case for non-involvement. One widely held reason for thinking that moral philosophy could not provide a guide to action was the belief that to the extent that systematic reflection showed anything about morality it revealed it to be a matter of subjective attitudes or commitments about which there could be no rational argument. One might perhaps show that someone was acting irrationally given the moral values and outlook he or she possessed (for instance, by being inconsistent), but one could not demonstrate that it was contrary to reason to have those values and outlook, for they were simply matters of subjective preference. By the late 1960s, however, meta-ethical subjectivism had begun to lose ground to more objectivist views. In the United Kingdom, there was a revival of ethical naturalism in the form of the thesis, advanced by writers such as Elizabeth Anscombe, Philippa Foot and Peter Geach, that moral claims relate to human well-being and are assessable as true or false, reasonable and unreasonable, by reference to this objective norm. In the United States, meanwhile, other earlier traditions were being revived, in particular certain forms of ethical rationalism which argue that questions of conduct can be answered by reference to standards of what are universally reasonable rules of action.

Some of the most interesting developments in North America which influenced the course of applied ethics there and elsewhere emerged out of POLITICAL PHILOSOPHY (chapter 8) and in turn are traceable to certain strands in modern epistemology. Clear and historically important examples of this are to be found in John Rawls' book *A Theory of Justice* (1971). There he is concerned to articulate principles of JUSTICE (pp. 259–65) that might underlie the political institutions and practices of a liberal state. In order to arrive at these, he employs a version of social contract theory inviting us to consider what principles we would rationally choose to have regulate our lives if we were not to know in advance what our social circumstances would be. This procedure thereby gives a form of rational justification for such principles. However, in thinking at a theoretical level about what principles do or would guide our conduct, it soon becomes apparent that such rationales may not entirely square with our moral inclinations and pre-reflective judgements. Here we face a problem of whether to revise the principles or abandon the moral intuitions. Rawls' discussion of this issue involves the idea of reflective equilibrium. The general principles implicit in our attitudes to real or imagined situations may need to be amended in the face of contrary judgements of further, often borderline, specific cases. By the same token where a principle itself is shown to be well-attested in other circumstances we may then need to revise our intuitive judgement of the troublesome case. The point here is that we should seek to maximize coherence in our moral and social outlook, and such 'equilibrium' is plausibly a rational requirement of reflection on questions of value and conduct.

Whatever the rights and wrongs of this sort of moral epistemology, it, and the revival of other broadly objectivist ethical theories, provided both an example and an impetus to applied ethics. In general one finds two methods being employed: firstly, that just described – that is, the derivation of principles from pre-theoretical moral judgements and their extension to other cases, constrained by demands of consistency and coherence; and, secondly, the direct application of well-established moral theories, such as UTILITARIANISM (chapter 25), to determine general policies and to resolve particular problems. Since the 1970s the employment of these methods, by writers such as Richard Hare, Anthony Kenny, Thomas Nagel, Peter Singer, Mary Warnock and Bernard Williams, has produced some interesting work on ethical and social questions which will survive just as well as contemporary research in more theoretical areas of philosophy.

Earlier, however, I suggested that not all features of the growth in applied ethics are to be welcomed. What I had in mind was the unseemly rush of some philosophers and those on the fringes of the subject to become part of what has proven to be a rapidly expanding and institutionally successful area of academic practice. It is not just that opportunism is undignified. The point is rather that through poor-quality products the very activity risks falling into disrepute, and thereby an opportunity for practical philosophy to re-establish itself as a major aspect of serious study may be lost as other philosophers turn against what they perceive to be intellectually shallow work, and the public patrons of applied ethics come to feel dissatisfied with it.

The Moral Danger of Applied Ethics

This latter prospect also raises a *moral* concern akin to that which partly motivated Socrates in his attack on the Sophists, the purveyors or moral and political wisdom in the Greek city-states of the fifth century BC. Although it is often supposed otherwise, even by those who should know better, moral philosophy is no easier to practise than any other area of the subject. Unlike philosophy of language, say, its initial starting points are usually commonplaces of reflective experience: for example, the question of truth-telling often involves dilemmas, but the attempt to structure satisfactory arguments about such matters involves deep and difficult problems, with the consequence that error and confusion are all too common. The suggestion of the Sophists and of some contemporary applied ethicists – that there are skills the more or less mechanical employment of which will yield answers to moral questions – is both a disservice to philosophy and a corrupting influence on the consciences of those whom it claims to be assisting. Moreover, as SOCRATES (chapter 15) saw, there is a danger that when sophistry is exposed, people's reaction is not to seek better counsel but to conclude that there can be no sound reasoning about questions of value and conduct, supposing instead that these are just matters of personal preferences. It would be a terrible irony if the recent rise of applied ethics led in due course to the spread of moral irrationalism.

---

3 A neglected precedent

Although the *term* is a recent one, there is in fact nothing new in the general *idea* of applied ethics. While it is true that there have been periods, such as the earlier half of this century, when philosophers were almost exclusively concerned with speculative questions, I noted earlier that from antiquity the importance of practical as well as theoretical philosophy has been recognized. It is worth observing, therefore, that there was (and to some extent remains) a very long and well-developed tradition of thinking about practical problems in the light of general principles, namely that of *moral casuistry*.

It should be said immediately that the term 'casuistry' is now most often used perjoratively to condemn some piece of thinking as attempting a specious justification or as involving equivocation or hypocrisy. Interestingly, this critical usage arose from perceived or imagined abuses of practical reasoning similar to those attributed to the Sophists. In this connection see, for example, the ridiculing of Jesuit casuistry by PASCAL (1623–62) (pp. 475–6) in his *Provincial Letters* (1967). However, the authentic tradition derives from the sincere effort to apply rigorous standards of critical argument to the resolution of questions of conduct. Historically, it developed through moral theology as Christians tried to work out the detailed implications of scriptural texts and the teachings of the early Church Fathers. In the Middle Ages, writers such as Thomas AQUINAS (1225–74) (p. 505) advanced quite complex theories of moral reasoning in which various elements of ethical judgement (*synderesis* and *conscientia*) were connected with an account of right reasoning (*recta ratio*). This tradition survived the Reformation and was further developed by both

Catholic and Protestant authors, such as Francisco Suarez (1548–1617) and Hugo Grotius (1583–1645), and later still, in increasingly secular versions, by Immanuel KANT (1724–1804) (chapter 22) and Jeremy BENTHAM (1748–1832) (chapter 25).

As well as being concerned with the *forms* of moral reasoning, the SCHOLASTIC (pp. 503–6) casuists were interested in resolving major dilemmas in particular fields of human activity, such as in sexual matters, economic affairs and the conduct of warfare. Their writings on the form and substance of morality contain many insights that are still worth recovering. One aspect of these writings relevant to the assessment of applied ethics as it is now practised is the way in which the casuists related moral problems and moral theory. The present-day expressions 'applied ethics' and 'applied philosophy' suggest a two-stage process. Firstly, one works out some general philosophical principles, then one applies them to a given issue. On this account there need be nothing philosophical about the second stage; rather it should be an algorithmic or mechanical process. For the medieval and modern casuists, by contrast, the treatment of particular cases is itself an exercise of moral reasoning no less than is the working out of general principles. Indeed, there need not be *two* distinct tasks involved. Rather, the determination of the general and the particular may be aspects of a single complex procedure similar in some respects to the establishment in Rawlsian methodology of a state of 'reflective equilibrium'.

A further mark of the difference between casuistry or practical moral philosophy and applied ethics is revealed in the fact that whereas contemporary writers usually suppose that there are no topic-specific moral values but only topic-indifferent general principles, the medievals and moderns tended to develop accounts of virtues and values specific to the different departments of life. Thus, for example, chastity was thought of as a distinctly sexual virtue and not an instance of, for example, prudence. Similarly, the medieval prohibition on usury derived from reflections on the values implicit in distinctive forms of social relationships. Perhaps the most important area of casuistical thought, however, was in relation to large-scale violence, concerning which it developed the doctrine of *just war* with its various topic-specific moral values, such as that of *non-combatant immunity*.

4 The Future of the Subject

Contemporary moral philosophers concerned with practice might therefore do better to adopt something of the approach of casuistry and practical philosophy rather than to think, as at present, in the somewhat limiting terms suggested by the phrase 'applied ethics'. There is certainly need and considerable scope for the philosophical study of the practice of thinking about practice – that is to say, there is a requirement for a 'meta-philosophical' account of moral reasoning.

If such an enquiry were to lead to a reconception of the subject of normative ethics along the lines suggested in connection with earlier styles of thought, that would certainly have implications for its future development. As it is, there can be little doubt but that the growth of publications, college and university courses, in-service professional training sessions, and other forms of activity concerned with the philosophical treatment of moral and social questions will continue at more or less its present rate until at least the end of the century.

It is impossible to be confident about developments beyond that point, but it seems likely that applied ethicists will look for new fields of operation. For the most part, that will involve seeking out existing areas of life that have not yet been made the subject of academic moral enquiry; but it will also lead to greater novelty as technology extends the limits of the possible and thereby changes patterns of behaviour, and as other factors bear upon the structure of personal and social relationships. We have seen how the development of electronic data-gathering and data-recording has given rise to increased concerns about privacy, and how reproductive technology has prompted worries about the proper limits of control over the creation of life. Doubtless at this very moment someone is writing a book on the ethics of 'virtual reality' technology, and before the decade is complete there will be other writings on the moral dimensions of technologies not as yet generally known of, nor even, perhaps, yet invented.

As these interests develop so will the publishing and other services that cater for them. Thirty years ago there were no academic philosophy journals concerned primarily or even largely with normative, first-order moral and social questions. Today, such journals abound and more are created every year. The present range includes the following: *Agriculture and Human Values, Bioethics, Business Ethics, Business and Professional Ethics Journal, Criminal Justice Ethics, Environmental Ethics, Environmental Values, Ethics and Animals, Ethics and Medicine, International Journal of Applied Philosophy, International Journal of Moral and Social Studies, International Review of Economics and Ethics, Journal of Agricultural Ethics, Journal of Applied Philosophy, Journal of Business Ethics, Journal of Environmental Ethics, Journal of Medical Ethics, Journal of Medicine and Philosophy, Journal of Religious Ethics, Journal of Social Philosophy, Philosophy and Public Affairs, Philosophy and Technology, Public Affairs Quarterly, Social Philosophy and Policy* and *Social Theory and Practice*. However the subject develops, there will be no shortage of journals – such, for good and ill, is academic professionalism.

Further Reading

Hare (1981) offers an advanced but clearly presented account of the author's 'prescriptivist' theory of morality developed in relation to different levels of thinking about moral problems. Kenny (1985) provides a series of clearly argued and well-balanced essays, the core of which concern the ethics of war and nuclear deterrence. Nagel (1979) has written a collection of subtly argued essays many of which develop deontological ways of thinking in connection with various moral problems. Singer (1979) is a clear and direct account of utilitarian theory and of its application to a range of life-and-death issues. It is very useful for seeing the attractions and the problems of consequentialism. Warnock (1992) presents a selection of writings by a philosopher who is prominent in public life in the United Kingdom, which explore the possibilities and limitations of philosophy in relation to practical problems. Williams (1981) offers a collection of influential essays by another prominent public philosopher developing the idea of the importance of personal character in relation to morality.

References

Most of the following books are collections of essays by one or more authors. However, Rachels (ed.) 1979, Singer (ed.) 1986 and Velasquez and Rostankowski (eds) 1985 are anthologies containing, in whole or in part, some of the most influential papers in various fields of applied ethics published in the last 20 to 30 years.

General works in applied ethics

DeMarco, J. P. and Fox, R. M. (eds) 1986: *New Directions in Ethics: The Challenge of Applied Ethics*. London: Routledge and Kegan Paul.
Evans, J. D. G. (ed.) 1987: *Moral Philosophy and Contemporary Problems*. Cambridge: Cambridge University Press.
Griffiths, A. P. (ed.) 1985: *Philosophy and Practice*. Cambridge: Cambridge University Press.
Hare, R. M. 1981: *Moral Thinking*. Oxford: Clarendon Press.
—— 1989: *Essays in Ethical Theory*. Oxford: Clarendon Press.
Kenny, A. 1985: *The Ivory Tower: Essays in Philosophy and Public Policy*. Oxford: Blackwell.
Louden, R. B. 1992: *Morality and Moral Theory*. Oxford: Oxford University Press.
Nagel, T. 1979: *Moral Questions*. Cambridge: Cambridge University Press.
Nuttall, J. 1993: *Moral Questions*. Cambridge: Polity Press.
Pascal, B. 1967 [1656]: *Provincial Letters* (translated by A. J. Krailsheimer). Harmondsworth: Penguin.
Phillips, D. Z. 1992: *Interventions in Ethics*. London: Macmillan.
Rachels, J. (ed.) 1979: *Moral Problems*. New York: Harper and Row.
Singer, P. 1979: *Practical Ethics*. Cambridge: Cambridge University Press.
—— (ed.) 1986: *Applied Ethics*. Oxford: Oxford University Press.
—— (ed.) 1991: *A Companion to Ethics*. Oxford: Blackwell.
Spaemann, R. 1989 [1982]: *Basic Moral Concepts* (translated by T. J. Armstrong). London: Routledge.
Velasquez, M. and Rostankowski, C. (eds) 1985: *Ethics: Theory and Practice*. Englewood Cliffs, NJ: Prentice-Hall.
Warnock, M. 1992: *The Uses of Philosophy*. Oxford: Blackwell.

Williams, B. 1981: *Moral Luck*. Cambridge: Cambridge University Press.
Winkler, E. and Coombs, J. (eds) 1993: *Applied Ethics: A Reader*. Oxford: Blackwell.

Animal Rights

Regan, T. 1983: *The Case for Animal Rights*. Berkeley, CA: University of California Press.
Frey, R. 1983: *Rights, Killing and Suffering*. Oxford: Blackwell.

Business Ethics

Beauchamp, T. and Bowie, N. 1979: *Ethical Theory and Business*. Englewood Cliffs, NJ: Prentice-Hall.
Velasquez, M. 1982: *Business Ethics*. Englewood Cliffs, NJ: Prentice-Hall.

Environmental Ethics

Attfield, R. 1991: *The Ethics of Environmental Concern* (2nd edn). Athens, GA: University of Georgia Press.
Rolston III, H. 1988: *Environmental Ethics: Duties to and Values in the Natural World*. Philadelphia: Temple University Press.

Gender Issues

Gilligan, C. 1982: *In a Different Voice: Psychological Theory and Women's Development*. Cambridge, MA: Harvard University Press.
Jaggar, A. 1983: *Feminist Politics and Human Nature*. Totowa, NJ: Rowman and Littlefield.

Medical Ethics

Harris, J. 1985: *The Value of Life: An Introduction to Medical Ethics*. London: Routledge and Kegan Paul.
Sommerville, A. *et al.* 1993: *Medical Ethics Today*. London: British Medical Association.

Punishment

Honderich, T. 1984: *Punishment: The Supposed Justifications*. Harmondsworth: Penguin.
Primoratz, I. 1989: *Justifying Legal Punishment*. Atlantic Highlands, NJ: Humanities Press.

Sex

Scruton, R. 1986: *Sexual Desire*. London: Methuen.
Soble, A. (ed.) 1980: *Philosophy of Sex*. Totowa, NJ: Rowman and Littlefield.

War

Teichman, J. 1986: *Pacifism and the Just War*. Oxford: Blackwell.
Walzer, M. 1977: *Just and Unjust Wars*. Harmondsworth: Penguin.
Glover, J. 1987: *Causing Death and Saving Lives*. Harmondsworth: Penguin.

Discussion Questions

Questions about Applied Ethics

1 Should all areas of human activity be subject to a branch of applied ethics?

2 How close should the main philosophical problems of ethics be to actual moral thinking and familiar ethical vocabularies?

3 How can we judge whether it is the professional business of moral philosophers to discuss matters such as totalitarianism, genocide, warfare, civil rights and sexual ethics?

4 Does either a conception of human well-being or a notion of universally reasonable rules of action provide a satisfactory basis for the objective assessment of conduct and institutions?

5 How can we determine whether there are right methods in applied ethics?

6 Are debates in applied ethics more likely to entrench or to challenge well-established moral theories, like utilitarianism or Kantian ethics?

7 Does applied ethics corrupt our consciences? How can this danger be avoided?

8 How should practical philosophy relate thought about general principles and thought about particular cases? What are the consequences of your answer for the possibility of applied ethics?

9 Are there different values and different virtues specific to different departments of life? How should we understand applied ethics in the light of your answer?

10 How might a meta-philosophical account of moral reasoning help us to choose between 'applied ethics' and 'casuistry' as the main form of moral philosophy about practice?

11 In what new fields might applied ethics find a field of operation?

Questions within Applied Ethics

12 What distinguishes just wars from unjust wars?

13 Is destroying a culture a wrong in addition to killing the people who are the bearers of that culture?

14 Is there any moral difference between abortion and infanticide?

15 Can we respect the autonomy of mental patients?

16 Do animals have rights?

17 Does the fact that humans live in an environment give rise to moral constraints on how we should treat that environment?

18 Does the market answer all questions of business ethics?

19 Should pornography be banned?

32

Feminism and Philosophy ————————

Jean Grimshaw

Recent decades have seen intense debates among feminists, especially in France and the United States, about the exclusion of women from philosophy, the representation of women in philosophical works, varying reasons the subject itself might be considered 'masculine', and different proposals for a feminist philosophy. Discussions have ranged from areas such as ethics and political philosophy, to areas in which questions of gender arise less spontaneously, like epistemology, metaphysics and philosophy of science. This chapter examines some main features of contemporary feminist philosophy and considers proposals for the future.

1 Introduction

For women who have been in any way sensitized to the issues concerning gender and the situation of women, which have been central to contemporary feminism, to be a woman studying philosophy is to be faced with a set of problems about one's own location within the discipline. Above all other academic disciplines, perhaps, philosophy, in its historical aspect, appears as a history of 'Great Men of Ideas', and in the roll call of 'great' philosophers from the past, women seem to be singularly absent. Women philosophers whose names are known to us have tended, as Michèle Le Doeuff (1991) points out, to be restricted to the role of disciple of, or correspondent with, the 'master'; as in the case of DESCARTES (chapter 17) and Princess Elizabeth of Bohemia (1618–80).

The formal barriers to the independent study of philosophy that existed in the past for women have now largely gone. Quite a lot of women study philosophy; many come to think of it as their 'intellectual home'. Yet relatively few of them 'make it' into academic posts, and those for whom philosophy continues to be central to their lives may also feel that there are ways in which philosophy can be alien and inhospitable to women. Being a woman and a philosopher, as Le Doeuff notes, is *always* something that is problematic, that has to be negotiated.

In the majority of mainstream courses in philosophy, issues concerning philosophy and gender continue to be largely invisible. This was often the case for those women philosophers who are now trying to theorize the relationship between feminism and philosophy. For them, the initial recognition that male philosophers *had* written a great deal about women, and that much of what they had written was riddled with sexism and misogyny, came as a shock. How was it possible that one could have studied philosophy for a long time, yet failed to notice this? How, for example, could one be required to study Rousseau (1712–78) without one's attention being drawn at any point to what he wrote about Sophie and the subordination of women? How could one possibly have studied Nietzsche (1844–1900) (chapter 30) without noting the crucial, if problematic, role that the concept of 'woman' plays in his thought? Along with the shock there frequently came a sense of dislocation. This arose from the recognition that whereas the study of philosophy had seemed to be something to which one's gender was irrelevant, much of philosophy in fact assumed and was addressed to a *male* subject.

The first (and essential) stage in thinking about philosophy and gender consisted in highlighting the endemic misogyny of many male philosophers; in noting the ways in which philosophy commonly assumed the exclusion of women (as citizens, as rational subjects, or as Moral agents (chapter 6), for example), and in charting the ways in which women were devalued or seen as inferior. This history of sexism and misogyny has largely been invisible to the academic philosophical mainstream. If noted, it has been dismissed as unimportant, a kind of local 'accident' whose recognition need not otherwise affect philosophical discussion and theorizing. And indeed, the mere exposure of sexism, however important, is 'negative' in the sense that, by itself, it does not theorize the ways in which such sexism might affect the substance of philosophical theories, what relationship feminism and philosophy might continue to have, or how women might relocate themselves within philosophy.

One strategy adopted by those who were concerned about this exclusion of women has been to attempt to include women in philosophical theories. A paradigm of such attempts at inclusion can be found in the writings of the eighteenth-century feminist, Mary Wollstonecraft (1759–97). In *A Vindication of the Rights of Woman* (1975), Wollstonecraft insisted that the possibility of realizing ideals of rationality and virtue, of which it was commonly thought that only men were capable, should be extended to include women. She noted that Rousseau regarded women as incapable of reason. Not so, she argued; to the extent that women were unable to reason adequately, it was because they had been prevented from so doing by a pernicious system of female education. Rousseau argued that the 'virtue' of a man was entirely different from the 'virtue' of a woman. Wollstonecraft replied that virtue should be the same regardless of sex.

But however important it has been to insist that women are not 'inferior' to men, and are no less capable of reason or virtue, the strategy of simply including women in philosophical theories soon breaks down. Firstly, it is frequently the case that one cannot simply 'include' women whilst leaving the rest of a theory intact. Rousseau is a case in point. His theory of the state and the education of the citizen was wholly premised on a private, patriarchal and rural family life, in which women were to be completely subordinated to men. Secondly, the attempted inclusion of women fails to ask questions about that from which they are excluded; is there a sense, for example, in which some ideals of reason and virtue might themselves be seen as 'masculine'? Much feminist philosophical work has been devoted to asking whether there are deeper senses in which the content of philosophical theories might be seen as 'masculine'. Can philosophy sometimes at least be seen as 'gendered' even in cases where such things as the nature of women and men is not apparently under discussion? Does the enterprise of philosophy itself have some kind of 'deep structure' that might also be seen in this way. The analysis of this kind of 'masculinity' reaches far deeper than merely detecting or analysing overt instances of misogyny or sexism, and it has been approached in more than one sort of way.

2 Philosophy and Masculinity

The first essential premise, on which the analysis of masculinity in philosophy is predicated, is as follows. Perhaps above all other disciplines, philosophy has historically liked to think of itself as based on reason; but a reason which is assumed to be universal and objective. The philosophical subject has often been assumed to be capable of a 'God's eye view', a 'view from nowhere'; a 'rational mind' that has no class, gender, race, social and historical location, perhaps even, in some philosophical theories, no body. Discussion of the social location of those who practise philosophy has been seen in contemporary terms (often dismissively) as a form of sociology of knowledge which has no relevance to questions about the truth or adequacy of philosophical theories themselves. But from a feminist perspective, questions about the social location of knowers, or those who claim to know, are not extrinsic to philosophy. Rather, they should be at its very heart, since the gendering of philosophy, and its frequent exclusion of women, are based on the denial of this location, on the assumption of a 'universality' which is in fact a concealed partiality. The 'human' subject in philosophy has often turned out to be a male subject.

The process of attempting to theorize the kinds of social location that are of relevance to the study of philosophy has, however, produced some differing views of the ways in which philosophy might be seen as 'masculine'. In her book *Speculum of the Other Woman* (1985), the French feminist philosopher, Luce Irigaray, who is also a practising psychoanalyst, offered a reading of the myth of the cavern in Plato's *Republic*. She argued that the myth rested on a profound denial and repression of the mother, the womb, and the fact of male dependence on women, and she interpreted this denial by offering a re-interpretation of the Freudian theory of the death drives. A psychoanalytic approach has been used by other philosophers as well. In an important article published in 1983, Jane Flax argued that philosophical theories arose out of typically *male* social experience, interests, fears and concerns. Drawing on the work of the feminist psychoanalytic writer, Nancy Chodorow (1978), who used an approach derived not from orthodox Freudianism but from object-relations theory, she argued that there are typical differences in 'gender personality' between women and men, arising from the fact that it is women who perform the main work of child-rearing. Men, Flax suggested, typically feel a need to distance themselves from the 'world of women', to devalue it, to associate with the world of masculinity 'outside' the home, and to stress a defensive autonomy and separateness against the fear of being engulfed by women. Flax noted features in the philosophy of PLATO (chapter 15), HOBBES (chapter 18), Descartes and Rousseau which, she argued, could be interpreted in the light of these typical masculine psychic structures. Such features included individualism, fear of the body and senses, a denial of human interdependence and interconnectedness, and a stress on the radical isolation of the human knower and the human self.

There are, however, considerable problems in this kind of analysis of 'masculinity' in the writings of philosophers. Male philosophers have said very different things; they have certainly not all espoused the kinds of atomistic or individualistic theories that Flax sees as paradigmatically masculine. In addition, there are great problems in trying to give such a general or ahistorical account of male social experience or of the male psyche. These kinds of problems might seem to suggest that trying to look for any very general features of philosophy that might be seen as 'masculine' is something of a hopeless quest, given the importance of historical variability and difference. Even though the majority of male philosophers have expressed derogatory views about women in one way or another, these ways have varied greatly. It is commonly the case that whatever is valued in a philosophical theory can be found to be associated with an ideal of masculinity; nevertheless, these ideals vary historically a great deal.

However, despite this difference, one is faced with the fact that misogyny and the exclusion of women seem to be endemic in philosophy, even if they may at times take very different forms. Is it possible to give any sort of general account of the features of philosophy that seem to underpin this constant and dreary history of the devaluation of women, which does not run quite this risk of historical over-generalization? Other approaches that women working in philosophy have adopted in attempting to answer this question depend not so much on looking at the more particular or specific features of individual theories, or on psychoanalytic speculation about the male psyche, but on trying to trace some of the structures of representation and ideology through which phallocentrism and the exclusion and devaluation of women get written into philosophy.

3 Dichotomies: Derrida and Feminism

Feminist writers have noted the constant tendency in philosophical theories towards forms of binarism, to thinking in terms of dichotomies. These are legion in the history of philosophy; they include man–woman, culture–nature, reason–emotion, mind–body, public–private and production–reproduction. They do not always take the same forms, and none of them is universal, but there are nevertheless important historical continuities. Within each dichotomy or binarism there is a hierarchy, a privileged term, and this privileged term is associated with men rather than with women.

The recognition of the importance of such binarisms has not been unique to the work of feminist philosophers. It has characterized much 'postmodern' philosophy as well. Jacques DERRIDA (pp. 716–17), for example, argues that most of western metaphysics has been constructed on a system of differences or binarisms in which one term is privileged at the expense of the other. It has been 'phallogocentric', based not only on the assumed logocentric authority and primacy of speech and 'presence' over writing, but also on the assumed phallocentric primacy of the transcendental male subject. Derrida's project of deconstruction aims to destabilize; to privilege the subordinate term in such metaphysical binarisms, and to show how the privileged term is in fact dependent on the subordinate term. Derrida aims, by complex strategies of textual analysis and argument, to prevent the original binarism from reasserting itself.

Derrida is one of the relatively few contemporary philosophers in whose work the concept of 'woman' plays a central role. 'Woman', in Derrida's work, becomes a figure for that which is undecidable, that which can evade the illusory fixity of traditional metaphysical structures of meaning. But feminist reactions to Derrida's work highlight some of the most interesting tensions and difficulties in the project of feminist philosophy. Derrida has been notoriously critical of feminism (and rarely in his own work refers to feminist writings). The reason seems to be as follows. The project of 'deconstruction' aims to subvert and undermine dualisms and dichotomies and to create a space for multiplicity and difference, including sexual difference. But, according to most interpretations of Derrida, he argues that if the feminist project includes any kind of assertion of female specificity – of women's right to the subjectivity that men have been able to assume as theirs – then it simply repeats the old dichotomies. Women, in fact, come to 'speak like men'. Derrida's own desire to 'speak like a woman', then, seems to amount to a desire to perform a vertiginous and elusive textual dance at the margins or in the interstices of traditional philosophical texts. It seems very different from the feminist project of finding a 'voice' for women in philosophy, of allowing women to speak in their own right. Some critics of Derrida have argued that his valorization of 'speaking like a woman' effects yet another erasure of *women*. To 'speak *like* a woman' is not the same as 'speaking *as* a woman'.

Irigaray and Women's Voice in Philosophy

Of course there are dangers, evident in some feminist writing, of simply recapitulating old and oppressive dichotomies. Simply to propose that 'the feminine' should be valued, if it involves no critique of the ways in which 'the feminine' is constructed as the shadow or inversion of the masculine, may reinstate that from which much feminist theory has tried to escape. The problem is to see how women can speak within philosophy, assume the status of philosophical SUBJECTS (pp. 515–17), without this reification of older categories. Luce Irigaray writes that it is the object of her work to 'jam the theoretical machinery'; a great deal of recent feminist philosophical writing has explored ways in which old philosophical dichotomies might be deconstructed so that they are no longer seen as polarized, as exclusive of each other; rather, they are re-defined as mutually interdependent. Nevertheless, Irigaray is also concerned that women should find a voice within philosophy. In her work, it is not a question of finding an 'essence' of woman, or of theorizing about women's 'nature'. She does not assume that we could know in advance what women might say, were they to speak 'in their own voice'.

4 Feminism and Philosophy

But how might we suppose that philosophy would change if the insights of feminist philosophical writing were taken seriously? At the present time, whilst there is a great deal of feminist philosophical writing being published, it has seemingly made little impact in many places on the traditional academic teaching of philosophy, or on 'mainstream' publication. 'Feminism' or 'feminism and philosophy' are often at best an 'option' on the margins, a 'special interest', in which it is usually implicitly assumed that only women will take a real interest. This is reflected in such things as the ways in which books are classified in libraries and in bookshops. Philosophical books by women are frequently not included in the shelves labelled 'philosophy'; they are placed under 'gender' or 'women's studies'. The long-term question about the relationship between feminism and philosophy concerns what might be called 'the nature of the hyphen', the 'and' which appears in the title of this chapter itself.

As I suggested earlier, the crucial premise of feminist philosophical writing is that questions about the social and historical location of philosophers are intrinsic to understanding the discipline, and they cannot be dismissed as extraneous or irrelevant. There is a need to recognize that philosophical theories arise from and speak to the concerns of particular social groups at particular periods in history. This view should not be equated with crude kinds of reductionism – the kind, for example, which assumes that discussion of philosophical theories can be reduced to discussion of the psyches of the philosophers who hold them. But it does imply that understanding philosophical theories will necessitate understanding something about the social interests and concerns which gave rise to them – and the power relations by which they may have been shaped.

Feminist philosophers have argued that this is as true of the less apparently 'gendered' areas of philosophy, such as EPISTEMOLOGY (chapter 1), METAPHYSICS (chapter 2) and the PHILOSOPHY OF SCIENCE (chapter 9), as it is of those where issues of gender have a more obvious place, such as ETHICS (chapter 6) or POLITICAL PHILOSOPHY (chapter 8, especially pp. 271–3). Philosophical enquiry should reject the 'false universalism' of supposing that philosophers can speak from nowhere, or construct theories that are universally applicable. The recognition of this has the consequence that the parameters of philosophical enquiry will inevitably change. Boundaries between what is and is not 'philosophy' will shift; one consequence of developing a feminist perspective on philosophy is that one becomes far less worried by the challenge, 'But is this *philosophy*?' – a challenge that has often been used to try to dismiss feminist questioning at the outset. But the critique of 'false universalism' also implies that feminist enquiry itself should recognize its own locatedness, and take into account the fact that the differences of social location, experience and perspective amongst women themselves may be as important as those between women and men.

But if the most important claim of a feminist approach to philosophy is that philosophical theories are socially located, and have tended to answer to the interests, concerns and experiences of men rather than of women, this still leaves open the important question of what the future of philosophy might be like were feminist perspectives on themselves to become part of the mainstream, rather than a 'special interest' on the sidelines. Women philosophers such as Irigaray have been concerned that women should be able, in philosophy, to assume the position of subjects and speak in their own voice. But the question remains whether the insistence on this voice should be seen as a strategic necessity born of circumstances in which women have often been excluded and silenced, or whether the concerns of women and men are likely to remain irreducibly different in ways that will imply a continuing need for philosophy written for, and mainly by, women themselves.

Approaches to this question vary. Those who believe that women's experiences and concerns will always diverge in some respects from those of men are more likely to continue to insist on the need for 'women's philosophy'. On the other hand, there are those such as Michèle Le Doeuff who believe that the project of feminist philosophy, in the long term, should be a new kind of universalism, different from the older kind of universalism which assumed the possibility of a 'God's eye view'. Le Doeuff argues that whereas it is commonly assumed that philosophy itself is 'universal' and feminist enquiry merely partial – a form of 'special interest' – it would be more appropriate to say that *philosophy* has been 'partial' in the sense that it has commonly excluded women both from the possibility of the production of philosophical theories or from being capable of exemplifying the ideals to which philosophical theories have been committed. Le Doeuff sees it as essential to the enterprise of philosophy that it posits 'objects' of thought which are assumed to be of interest to an audience not differentiated by extra-intellectual criteria such as gender. In other words 'feminist philosophy' should not be seen, in the end, as a 'special interest'. It is something that aims to change and inform the mainstream of philosophy, such that questions that now tend to be marginal or invisible will become normal, visible and part of the repertoire of all of those who study philosophy.

But if the production of philosophy arises from social interests and concerns, so also does its reception, and Le Doeuff's conception of an audience undifferentiated by any extra-intellectual criterion may seem to be a form of idealism which is too close to older philosophical ideals of 'universality'.

Nevertheless, it highlights what is perhaps the most interesting question about the future of feminist philosophical enquiry. There is an ongoing need to bring the many differing perspectives of women into philosophy, and to continue to address questions about the invisibility and marginalization of these. But feminist enquiry also addresses issues of general human interest and relevance; it is not an orthodoxy committed to a narrow or blinkered set of preconceptions about what should be seen as 'women's issues'. The tension between the project of creating frameworks within which women can speak and think as women, and the project of changing the face of philosophy so that women's perspectives are no longer 'marked' as marginal to the mainstream is both an essential one in current circumstances, and one whose resolution is perhaps the major task facing feminist philosophy at the moment.

Further Reading

Braidotti (1991) is not an easy book to read, but it is very useful in particular for its discussion of French philosophy as well as Anglo-American feminist writing, and for its perspectives on the relationship between feminism and postmodernism. Coole (1993) provides a general survey of issues concerning gender in political philosophy. Gatens (1991) is a recent and wide-ranging discussion of philosophical texts from a feminist point of view, and of feminist perspectives in philosophy. Griffiths and Whitford (eds) (1988) offers a collection of essays on feminism and philosophy covering a wide range of topics. Grimshaw (1986) is an accessible introduction to questions concerning women and philosophy, with a particular focus on ethics. Grosz (1990) surveys feminist approaches to philosophy, and offers a very useful account of what it might mean to say that philosophy is 'masculine'. Harding and Hintikka (1983) present a ground-breaking collection of essays which laid the foundations for a great deal of subsequent feminist enquiry into philosophy. Irigaray (1985) established the terms of debate for much current French feminist thought and has also been influential in the United Kingdom and the USA. The further reading collected in Larrabee (ed.) (1993) provides excellent background to the issue of whether women speak with a 'different voice' in ethics and the problems surrounding the idea of an 'ethic' of care. Le Doeuff (1991) is written in the form of a series of 'notebooks', and it includes an excellent discussion of Jean-Paul Sartre and Simone de Beauvoir, as well as raising broad issues about the location of women in philosophy and the objectives of feminist philosophy. Lennon and Whitford (eds) (1994) offer a useful collection from a feminist perspective addressing both traditional epistemology and postmodern views. Lloyd (1993) is a 'classic' discussion of ways in which conceptions of 'reason' in Western philosophy have been aligned with notions of 'masculinity'. Nicholson (ed.) (1990) is an invaluable collection of feminist essays, aiming to show why feminism has both an affinity with and yet also a deep ambivalence about many of the central themes of postmodernism. Nye (1988) surveys misogyny in a wide range of philosophical theories and offers an analysis of possible feminist responses. Pateman and Grosz (eds) (1986) contains a lively and interesting collection of essays both on general issues concerning the place of women in philosophy, and on more specific social and political questions. Scheman (1993) offers a wide-ranging, accessible and engaging collection of essays on feminism and philosophy providing an excellent introduction to some central issues. Spelman (1988) discusses how some feminist thinking has excluded many women in ways that are not unlike the exclusion of women in much of the philosophy that is written by men. Tronto (1993) defends an 'ethic of care', but argues that it should not be contrasted sharply with an ethic based on notions of 'rights' or 'justice'.

References

Alcoff, L. and Potter, E. 1993: *Feminist Epistemologies*. London: Routledge.

Braidotti, R. 1991: *Patterns of Dissonance*. London: Routledge.

Chodorow, N. 1978: *The Reproduction of Mothering*. Berkeley: University of California Press.

Coole, D. 1993: *Women in Political Theory* (2nd edition). Brighton: Wheatsheaf.

Derrida, J. 1976: *Of Grammatology*. Baltimore: Johns Hopkins University Press.

Flax, J. 1983: Political Philosophy and the Patriarchal Unconscious. In Harding and Hintikka (eds) (1983).

Garry, A. and Pearsall, M. 1989: *Women, Knowledge and Reality: Explorations in Feminist Philosophy*. London: Unwin Hyman.

Gatens, M. 1991: *Feminism and Philosophy*. Cambridge: Polity.

Griffiths, M. and Whitford, M. (eds) 1988: *Feminist Perspectives in Philosophy*. London: Macmillan.

Grimshaw, J. 1986: *Feminist Philosophers*. Brighton: Wheatsheaf.

Grosz, E. 1990: Philosophy. In S. Gunew (ed.), *Feminist Knowledge, Critique and Construct*. London: Routledge.

Harding, S. 1991: *Whose Science, Whose Knowledge?*. Buckingham: Open University Press.

Harding, S. and Hintikka, M. (eds) 1983: *Discovering Reality: Feminist Perspectives on Epistemology, Metaphysics, and the Philosophy of Science*. London: D. Reidel.

Irigaray, L. 1985: *Speculum of the Other Woman*. Ithaca: Cornell University Press.

Larrabee, M. J. (ed.) 1993: *An Ethic of Care*. London: Routledge.

Le Doeuff, M. 1991: *Hipparchia's Choice: An Essay Concerning Women, Philosophy etc.* Oxford: Blackwell.

Lennon, K. and Whitford, M. (eds) 1994: *Knowing the Difference: Feminist Perspectives in Epistemology*. London: Routledge.

Lloyd, G. 1993: *The Man of Reason: Male and Female in Western Philosophy* (2nd edn). London: Methuen.

Nicholson, L. (ed.) 1990: *Feminism/Postmodernism*. London: Routledge.

Nye, A. 1988: *Feminist Theory and the Philosophies of Man*. Croom Helm.

Pateman, C. and Grosz, E. (eds) 1986: *Feminist Challenges: Social and Political Theory*. London: Allen and Unwin.

Scheman, N. 1993: *Engenderings*. London: Routledge.

Spelman, E. 1988: *Inessential Woman: Problems of Exclusion in Feminist Thought*. Boston: Beacon Press.

Tronto, J. 1993: *Moral Boundaries*. London: Routledge.

Wollstonecraft, M. 1975 [1792]: *A Vindication of the Rights of Woman*. London: Penguin.

Discussion Questions

1 Why should being a woman and a philosopher always be 'something that is problematic, that has to be negotiated'?

2 Should women seek to be accepted as citizens, rational subjects and moral agents just like men or should they seek to alter our conceptions of citizenship, rationality and agency?

3 Are class, gender and ethnic origin of equal importance as social and historical locations in shaping our forms of rationality?

4 Does historical variability undermine the possibility of there being any general 'masculine' features in philosophy?

5 Does the feminist project, in asserting female specificity, repeat rather than undermine existing dichotomies?

6 What is the importance of distinguishing 'speaking like a woman' and 'speaking as a woman'?

7 Can women speak within philosophy without reifying the categories they seek to escape?

8 Why might feminists seek to 'jam the theoretical machinery'?

9 How might philosophy change if the weight of feminist philosophical writings were taken seriously?

10 Must feminist philosophers accept the claim that knowing the social and historical location of philosophers is crucial to understanding the discipline?

11 Compare the role of feminist philosophy in a less gendered area, such as epistemology, metaphysics, or philosophy of science, and in an area where questions of gender have a more obvious place, such as ethics or political philosophy.

12 Is universalism in philosophy necessarily 'false universalism'? What are the implications of your answer for the role of feminism in philosophy?

13 Are differences among women as important as differences between women and men for feminist enquiry?

Glossary

a priori–a posteriori **distinction**   an epistemological distinction. *A priori* propositions, unlike *a posteriori* propositions, do not require experience to establish their truth. We derive or justify *a priori* concepts, unlike *a posteriori* concepts, independent of experience.

abstract ideas   Locke's attempt, rejected by Berkeley, to explain how an idea can stand for individuals of a given kind, even though the individuals vary in their properties. Locke held that abstraction from the different properties would produce a general idea covering the right individuals.

abstract objects   objects, such as numbers or universals, that do not exist as spatio–temporal particulars. Philosophers disagree about whether there can be such objects or, if they do exist, how they are related to concrete physical objects.

ad hominem **argument**   a fallacious argument attacking the holder of a view rather than the position itself *or* a sound argument showing an inconsistency between a view held by a person and a consequence of that view. The person pointing out the inconsistency need not hold the initial view.

alienation/estrangement   Hegelian concept, also used by Marx and later European philosophers, to stand for a state of being cut off from something of importance, such as oneself, others, nature or the product of one's labour. The analysis and interpretation of alienation varies according to the philosopher.

altruism   the view that the well-being of others should have as much importance for us as the well-being of ourselves. Some argue that altruism, even if it is desirable, is not possible, and that our ethics must be based on egoism.

analysis   the central method of analytical philosophy, shaped by the development of modern logic and found in the work of Frege, Russell, Moore and Wittgenstein, according to which philosophical problems can be overcome through replacing the apparent structure of statements by their real logical structure. Many philosophers, while still considering themselves analytical philosophers, have altered or even abandoned this programme.

analytic–synthetic distinction   according to Kant's formulation of the distinction, in an analytic proposition the concept of the predicate is contained in the concept of the subject, and we can tell that the proposition is true by analysis. In a synthetic proposition, the concept of the predicate adds something new to the concept of the subject, and the truth or falsity of the proposition cannot be determined by analysis. There has been much dispute over the adequacy of this account, but there is general agreement that synthetic propositions tell us something about the world. Together with the metaphysical distinction between necessary and contingent propositions and the epistemological distinction between *a priori* and *a posteriori* propositions, this logical distinction sets the framework for much modern philosophy. Kant famously argued that some *a priori* necessary propositions are synthetic. Contemporary discussion has developed from Quine's criticism of the distinction as a dogma of empiricism.

aporia   a puzzle or perplexity. In the early Platonic dialogues, Socrates raised problems without offering solutions to them and showed that those he questioned could not offer an acceptable solution either. This aporetic method led to the development of the dialectical method, by which Socrates elicited truth through questioning. The term *aporia* (no way through) was introduced by Aristotle for puzzles concerning incompatibilities that arise among views we hold without prompting or among reputable beliefs adopted commonly or by the wise. His approach was to seek the minimal adjustments needed to reconcile these conflicting views.

argument from design   the argument for the existence of God, disputed by Hume, according to which the complex and intricate order of the world can only be explained (or can best be explained) by positing an intelligent and powerful creator.

artificial intelligence (AI)   the use of programs to enable machines to perform tasks which humans perform using their intelligence. Early AI avoided human psychological models, but this orientation has been altered by the development of connectionism, which is based on theories of how the brain works. In connectionism, complex functions, including learning, involve the transmission of information along pathways formed among large arrays of simple elements. AI raises questions about the conditions, if any, in which we would be justified in ascribing mental attributes to purely physical systems.

association of ideas   a view, especially important in Hume, explaining the patterned occurrence of our ideas according to laws of association. Philosophers today generally seek to maintain what is important in Hume while rejecting this mechanism.

autonomy   an autonomous being is one that has the power of self-direction, possessing the ability to act as it decides, independent of the will of others and of other internal or external factors.

axioms   propositions selected as the foundations of a field – classically geometry – which, together with methods of proof, allow other propositions to be proved in an ordered way. The axiomatic method has powerfully influenced philosophy, although each feature of the method has been criticized as inappropriate for philosophy.

Categorical Imperative   the fundamental formal demand (or set of demands) which Kant placed on our choice of principles on which to act. It is contrasted with hypothetical imperatives, which have force only if we have certain desires or inclinations. Formulations of the categorical imperative seem to be radically different from one another, and some critics argue that the categorical imperative produces an empty formalism. Sympathetic commentators believe that both of these problems can be overcome. The formulations test the principles on which we act according to whether they can be universal laws or laws of nature, whether we treat humanity in ourselves and others never simply as means but also as ends, whether we treat every rational being as a will making universal law, and whether we treat our shared moral life as taking place within a kingdom of ends. None of the principal notions used in expressing the Categorical Imperative is easy to understand.

categories   the basic general concepts of thought, language or reality, sometimes claimed to have an origin or justification differing from those of ordinary concepts. Aristotle and Kant provide the classical discussions of categories, although categories play different roles in their thought.

category mistake   an ascription of something to one category when it belongs to another. For Ryle, who introduced the term, discriminations among categories were not confined to the grand Aristotelian or Kantian categories, but worked their way with great subtlety through the whole of our language. The interesting mistakes are those with philosophical consequences.

causal theory of reference   the view of Kripke and others that names, and perhaps some other terms, gain meaning from an initial act of naming and then preserve meaning through suitable causal links.

causation   in causal relations between events, if an event of the first kind occurs, an event of the second kind will or must occur, and the first event will explain the occurrence of the second event. Possibly items other than events can enter into causal relations. Since Hume, we have been puzzled about whether causal relations are real or are just matters of our imposing our habits upon the world and over the nature of causal necessity.

certainty   Descartes sought to build knowledge on the basis of certainty, with no room for doubt. Although the project as a whole, as well as its detail, has been contested, certainty remains an ideal for many philosophers.

chaos theory   the theory of non-linear functions, such that small differences in the input of the function can result in large and unpredictable differences in the output.

class   a collection of entities satisfying a condition for membership in the class. To avoid problems arising if classes get too large, or belong to other classes, or are not completed, set theory distinguishes classes from sets.

clearness and distinctness   Descartes' criteria of indubitable truth derived from his reflection on the impossibility of doubting his own existence (see *cogito ergo sum*). Clear perceptions are 'present and accessible'. Distinct perceptions are 'sharply separated' from other perceptions and contain only what is clear. We can hope to specify clearness and distinctness in an illuminating way, but this might involve replacing perceptual characterizations by conceptual ones.

cogito ergo sum   Descartes' crucial claim 'I think therefore I am' provides a standard of certainty for the rest of his philosophy and leads on to the claim that what he is is a thinking thing.

concept   'concept' can be taken psychologically or logically for what we grasp in understanding an expression, but since Frege the logical side has had primary importance. For Frege, there was a crucial distinction between objects (referred to by names or subjects) and concepts (referred to by predicates). Different accounts of logical form might challenge this claim. If concepts are thought of as components of propositions, scepticism about propositions can produce scepticism about concepts as well.

consciousness   a philosophical explanation of what consciousness is or how it might be explained eludes us. If we stick to what it is like to be a conscious human being, we have no explanation; if we try to explain consciousness in terms of what goes on in our brains, the sheer feel of consciousness itself is left aside.

consent   from Locke, the liberal theory of government has required the consent of the governed for political rule to be legitimate. Because explicit consent is not always available, Locke introduced a notion of tacit consent, but it is not always easy to distinguish tacit consent from non-consent to determine whether tacit consent is consent.

consequentialism   the view that the value of an action is determined by the value of its consequences rather than by the principle on which the action is performed or the virtue it expresses. Utilitarianism is a consequentialist theory, where the relevant value is individual happiness or well-being.

conservative   in politics, a loosely defined term indicating adherence to one or more of a family of attitudes, including respect for tradition and authority and resistance to wholesale or sudden changes.

consistency   propositions are consistent if they can all be true. A system of propositions can be shown to be inconsistent if it contains a contradiction (a proposition and its negation). Consistency and completeness are two key concerns of modern logic.

constructivism   in the philosophy of mathematics, a broad position (encompassing both intuitionism and formalism but also going beyond them) which holds that mathematical entities exist only if they can be constructed and that proof and truth in mathematics are co-extensive. Constructivists oppose the realist (or Platonist) view that mathematical objects or truth exist independently of human procedures. This has the consequence that certain classical results whose proof rely on Platonic assumptions are not constructively valid.

contents of consciousness   mental states, like statements and other linguistic items, have contents, but it is a philosophical problem how this can be so.

Furthermore, there are disputes over the extent to which internal factors and external environmental factors respectively contribute to determining the contents of mental states.

contingent–necessary distinction   contingent propositions happen to be true or false but could be otherwise. Necessary propositions must be true. It is not clear that there are any necessary propositions or, if there are, that they are restricted to analytic propositions or other propositions true because of their logical form. A contingent event is one that does not necessarily take place. If there are necessary events, natural rather than logical necessity is involved.

continuum   a collection of points, such that between any two points there are distinct points. Classical examples of a continuum are a line, plane or space.

continuum hypothesis   the claim that there are only two classes into which any thinkable collection of infinitely many distinct real numbers may fall.

contradiction   a conjunction of a proposition and its negation, which, according to the principle of non-contradiction, cannot be true. Aristotle pointed out the dangers of accepting contradictions. Except in some specially designed logics, anything can follow from a contradiction.

conventionalism   the view that human conventions rather than independent realities or necessities shape our basic concepts of the world, scientific theories, ethical principles and the like. On this view, we could have chosen other conventions, which would have been as satisfactory as the conventions entrenched in our actual account of the world or morality. Some conventionalist positions allow for a contribution by reality as well as by conventions, but it is difficult to distinguish these contributions.

counterfactual conditional   a conditional (if p, then q) in which the 'if clause' is contrary to fact; for example, 'if the water had been boiling, you would have been scalded'. There is no generally satisfactory analysis of counterfactual conditionals, although some philosophers believe that we need them to deal with many important philosophical problems.

criterion   a test or standard by which truth, existence, identity or meaning can be determined. Questions arise over the choice of criteria and over the relation between criteria and that for which they are criteria.

critique   Kant introduced the term for the critical examination of reason by itself. Later European philosophers have pursued a method of critique, but some have relinquished Kant's commitment to reason as the key element of their reflective method.

Dasein   in Heidegger's pursuit of what he considered to be the central question in philosophy – that is, the question of the meaning of Being – he spoke of our Being as human beings as *Dasein* (being there). In talking of ourselves in this way, he meant *Dasein* to break with the whole history of ontology, including the inherited Cartesian conception of the self, and to replace it with a new orientation.

deconstruction Derrida's method aiming to overcome crucial metaphysical dichotomies. By showing that one term of an opposition is unjustifiably privileged with respect to the other, deconstruction allows us to use the pair of terms freed from metaphysical distortion. His approach to deconstruction employs sophisticated and surprising responses to language, culture and society derived from Freud and others.

defeasible the standard criteria for the correct application of a defeasible concept allow for that application to be retracted in the light of further evidence. Verification of claims using defeasible concepts is never conclusive, in principle being always open to revision. For example, in epistemology, a defeasible knowledge claim is one made confidently, but in recognition of the possibility (no matter how apparently unlikely) that further evidence could give reason for the claim to be withdrawn.

definite description a description picking out something as the sole individual having a certain property. Russell's theory of definite descriptions analyses sentences containing definite descriptions to remove the burden of finding objects to which these expressions seem to refer.

deontology an ethics based on acting according to duty or doing what is right, rather than on achieving virtue or on bringing about good consequences. It is too crude to make sharp divisions or to deny a place for more than one approach to ethics. Kant is the most important deontological theorist.

dialectic the Socratic method of discovering truth through questioning and debate, altered and developed by his Greek successors, and still a model of overwhelming importance in philosophy. Kantian dialectic expressed reason's capacity to reach contradictory conclusions from apparently sound premises. Hegel's dialectic drove the necessary unfolding and development of concepts in history. Marx's dialectic explained the historical development of society through class conflict and the relations between the forces and relations of production and the base and superstructure.

didactic offered with an intention of instructing or teaching.

dualism the view that each person is two entities, a mind with mental attributes and a body with physical attributes, instead of a single entity with attributes of both sorts.

egoism the view that we are always motivated by self-interest or that we always should be so motivated. Contemporary rational choice theorists attempt to understand how actual social institutions can be based on the choices of individuals acting according to egoist principles. The prisoner's dilemma and other problem cases show difficulties with this approach.

eliminative materialism the view that our mental concepts, such as belief and desire, are inappropriate for a serious scientific account of human beings and should, or will be, eliminated.

empiricism the claim that all knowledge or all meaningful discourse about the world is related to sensory experience or observation. Logical empiricism (or logical positivism) combined modern logical analysis with the demands of empiricism and was most famous for its verificationist theory of meaning.

Enlightenment   broad intellectual movement in eighteenth-century Europe, particularly Britain, France and Germany, characterized by a rejection of superstition and mystery and an optimism concerning the power of human reasoning and scientific endeavour (hence its alternative name: The Age of Reason).

entailment   the intuitive notion of strict logical implication, such that *necessarily* if p, then q (that is, it is impossible that p and not q).

essence   for Aristotle, that which remains the nature of a thing throughout its change from potentiality to actuality. More generally, the necessary defining characteristic of a thing, such that without that characteristic the thing would not be the thing it is.

ethical intuition   the immediate awareness of an ethical property or an ethical truth, but for Rawls intuitionism is the claim that there is an irreducible body of first principles which cannot be ordered in terms of priority.

ethical naturalism   the view, criticized by G. E. Moore, that ethical properties like goodness can be defined in terms of the natural properties that justify their use. Moore's alternative account in terms of non-natural intuition of goodness has seemed implausible, but new ways of conceiving relations among properties have also been important in the revival of ethical naturalism.

eudaimonia   flourishing or well-being, the central aim of Aristotelian ethics, the realization of which is a complete and self-sufficient combination of virtue and its rewards in happiness. It is important to realize the complexity of the notion and not to reduce it to one of its components.

event   we can think of events as changes in objects or in relations among objects, so that the basic entities in our account of the world are objects and relations rather than events. However, some philosophers see advantages in recognizing events as basic, although events might have to take on some of the character of objects for this to be acceptable.

evolutionary epistemology   an approach to the development of human knowledge in evolutionary terms, either as an integral part of natural selection or as an independent process modelled on biological natural selection. Evolutionary epistemology is part of a broader programme of naturalized epistemology. Rather than seeking to secure our knowledge claims against sceptical doubts, naturalized epistemology tries to explain major features of our knowledge as necessary or inevitable features of ourselves as natural beings.

expert system   computer with 'built-in' expertise, which, used by a non-expert in a particular subject area, can evaluate or make other decisions concerning that subject.

explanation   an account characteristically telling us why something exists or happens, or must exist or happen. The covering law model of explanation proposed by Hempel has been widely influential, but has many critics. There are controversies over the nature of functional or teleological explanation, over the legitimacy of inferring to the best explanation, and over Dilthey's contrast between scientific explanation and historical understanding.

fallibilism   Peirce's view that none of our beliefs, even the apparently most fundamental, is certain and that any of our beliefs can be revised. Peirce believed that, rightly understood, relinquishing certainty does not open the way to sceptical doubt.

family resemblance   Wittgenstein's term in his later philosophy for the way in which expressions apply to things or kinds of things not sharing a common defining property, but instead sharing some of an interwoven complex of likenesses, as in the facial features of family members. He made the same point regarding the overlapping features of games.

fictional entities   not all expressions pick out things which exist. Non-existing or fictional entities can play havoc with our account of language and reality. If they do not exist, we are tempted to enrich our ontology with an existence-like status to allow reference to them. Analysis, in one form or another, might avoid such temptations by showing that we can mean what we need to mean without committing ourselves to odd ontological items. Problems remain for real as opposed to notional fictions. We can say what is true or false about Anna Karenina or Sherlock Holmes, yet we cannot be certain how to understand our ability to do so.

first philosophy   in Aristotle, the study of the general characteristics of all types of existence or the principles of being. More generally, especially since Descartes, the position that there is an essential role for philosophy, prior to any science. Such a claim is challenged by scientistic views, which reverse the priority.

form of life   what Wittgenstein takes to be fundamental in his later account of understanding language as variously embedded in shared human activity. The crucial notion of 'form' shifts from logical form in his early writing to form of life. What is fundamental in understanding the possibility of language shifts from objects to language games and forms of life.

formal   in general, formal considerations have to do with the abstract structure, or pattern, of a subject, rather than with its content. Hence formal logic, for example, is concerned not with the content of particular sentences in an argument, but only with their structure of truth values.

foundationalism   the view that knowledge is possible only if some items serve as a certain foundation for the rest. Special attention is drawn to the alleged certainty of the proposed foundations and to the relation between the foundations and the rest of knowledge.

free will and determinism   there are threats to freedom involving the apparent determination of human action independent of our will. These include divine foreknowledge and in modern philosophy the possibility that our actions are determined by causal laws. One way out would be to argue that freedom and a particular form of determinism are compatible by showing that determinism has weaker implications than at first seems the case. One could also argue that what one values in freedom is not risked by determinism and is not aided by indeterminism. Nevertheless, some philosophers still claim that, on a proper understanding of freedom and foreknowledge or freedom and causal laws, we cannot have both.

function   a function is a relation between the value of variables and the value of the function as a whole. Giving a definite value to the variables yields a definite value to the whole function.

functional explanation   also teleological explanation, in which an item is explained by the role or function it has in producing something which promotes or preserves the entity or kind of entity of which it is a part. Functional explanation is prominent in biology and in some of the social sciences. There is disagreement whether functional explanation is a rival to causal explanation or a form of causal explanation.

good   many approaches to ethics are centred on achieving what is good, although others are based on doing what is right. Priority to one goal need not exclude the other, but might shape the contents or limit how we pursue the other. We can ask about the relationship between human goodness and the goodness of other things, such as a knife that cuts well. On some views, goodness is reduced to one quality, like happiness or pleasure or satisfying desire, but others think of goodness as inherently complex. In either case, goodness has a place in moral psychology, motivating our actions and explaining our emotions.

happiness   according to different ethical views, happiness might be one goal in life, the only possible goal, or a fortunate by-product of the pursuit of other goals. Happiness might concern one's aggregate of pleasure or require a complex balance involving virtue, pleasure, achievement and good fortune.

hedonism   the belief that pleasure is the greatest good and highest aspiration of mankind. In early utilitarian thinking, this belief provided the interpretation of 'utility' or 'good'.

hermeneutics   a method of interpretation, initially of biblical texts but later extended to other texts and with Dilthey to whole cultures. Characteristically, the method improves our understanding of what is obscure, corrupt, or incomplete by placing it in the context of a whole. The hermeneutic circle is a problem which classically arises because the understanding of an item in a text depends on our understanding of the whole text, while the understanding of the whole text depends on our understanding of that and other items. This interdependence of interpretation, however, need not be vicious, although it might call for modesty rather than dogmatism in advancing any interpretation.

historicism   the view that concepts, beliefs, truths and even standards of truth can be understood only in relation to the whole moral, intellectual, religious and aesthetic cultures of the historical periods in which they arise or flourish.

This position is linked to demands for a hermeneutic method to achieve appropriate understanding. The term is also used by Popper for the view that history is governed by necessary laws of development.

holism   the view that wholes have some priority over the elements, members, individuals or parts composing them. Social holism claims that individuals can be understood only in terms of the practices or institutions in which they take part and is a rival to some aspects of individualism. Methodological holism and methodological individualism propose different methodological constraints on the study of phenomena without pronouncing on their real constitution, while metaphysical holism claims that wholes are distinct entities, whose existence cannot be reduced to that of the items composing them. Holistic views in the philosophy of science and the philosophy of language propose that the meaning and truth of our claims cannot be assessed one by one, but must be assessed as part of theories, bodies of theory, or all we believe about the world.

iconographic   derived from the Greek word for 'image': hence, an artefact of some kind (such as a painting) that visually resembles the object it represents.

idealism   the view that the existence of objects depends wholly or in part on the minds of those perceiving them or that reality is composed of minds and their states. There are many varieties of idealism, ranging from Plato's doctrine of independently existing ideas or forms to Berkeley's subjective idealism and Hegel's absolute idealism. Kant attempted to combine empirical realism with transcendental idealism.

ideas   for Plato, the unchanging independently existing bases of the perceived world and thought about the world, and in seventeenth- and eighteenth-century philosophy, the vehicles of sensory representation of external objects and of thought. Locke and Leibniz initiated disputes whether ideas could be innate, in us independent of sensory experience. Berkeley rejected Locke's distinction between the ideas of primary qualities (which resemble the qualities that produce them) and the ideas of secondary qualities (which are produced by qualities that they do not resemble). Hume argued that ideas originated in impressions, but still retained sensory and intellectual functions for ideas. Kant separated these functions (and used the term 'idea' for other purposes).

identity   in order to use a concept we must be able to individuate different entities falling under that concept and to identify these individual entities over time. It is unclear whether or not individuating and identifying entities must refer to the kind concepts under which they fall. A special case of identity, discussed by Locke, Hume and many contemporary philosophers, is personal identity. Both the memory and bodily criteria for personal identity have encountered difficulties, leading Parfit to question the importance of personal identity. The identity theory of mind, according to which mental states are identical with states of the central nervous system led to much discussion, although other forms of materialism have supplanted it in current controversy. Kripke's rejection of the notion of contingent identity in favour of necessary identity helped to renew discussion of the nature of the identity relation itself.

illocutionary act in J. L. Austin's theory of speech acts, what one does in uttering what one utters. A perlocutionary act is what one does by uttering what one utters.

imagination the ability to represent objects or states of affairs which cannot exist, which do not exist or which do not exist here and now. Imagination is both condemned for its link with falsity and prized for its role in artistic creativity and human understanding. In Kant's account, imagination performs indispensable roles in perception as an intermediary between our sensibility and understanding which allows us to have knowledge of a unified world.

immaterial substance Berkeley argued that the notion of material substance could not be sustained, but that immaterial substances, human minds and God, were crucial to our account of reality.

immutable literally, not able to change.

individualism an approach to ethics, social science and political and social philosophy which emphasizes the importance of human individuals in contrast to the social wholes, such as families, classes or societies, to which they belong. In different contexts, individualism is contrasted to holism and collectivism. Metaphysical individualism claims that social objects like societies can be reduced to individuals. Methodological individualism does not make metaphysical claims, but rather constrains the ways we explain social action.

induction a process of reasoning contrasted with deduction in which conclusions are drawn that all individuals of a kind have a certain character on the basis that some individuals of the kind have that character.

inference the process of reasoning whereby one statement (the conclusion) is derived from one or more other statements (the premises).

infinite regress an infinite regress in a series of propositions arises if the truth of proposition P_1 requires the support of proposition P_2, and for any proposition in the series P_n, the truth of P_n requires the support of the truth of P_{n+1}. There would never be adequate support for P_1, because the infinite series needed to provide such support could not be completed.

intensionality a feature characterizing sentences about mental states, according to which the truth value of the sentence may be altered by replacing expressions in the sentence by other expressions referring to the same objects. In extensional contexts, unlike intensional contexts, such substitutions do not affect the truth value of the sentence.

intentionality a characteristic feature of mental and linguistic states according to which they have an object or content and are thus about something.

irreducible to reduce Xs to Ys would be to show how Xs were, in reality, only Ys or in a linguistic guise to show that X-talk could be systematically eliminated in favour of Y-talk in a way involving no loss of content. Properties are said to be irreducible then, if they resist such reductions.

Leibniz's Law if A = B, for any true statement about A there will be a corresponding true statement about B, and vice versa. There are disputes over the way to deal with statements for which this law does not seem to hold.

logical atomism the view held for a time by Russell and Wittgenstein that for language to have meaning it must be analysable into mutually independent propositions, the atomic elements of which correspond to elements in states of affairs. For Wittgenstein at this stage, propositions had meaning by logically picturing possible states of affairs. Russell's logical atomism, unlike Wittgenstein's, was tied to an empirical interpretation.

logical positivism a general philosophical position, also called logical empiricism, developed by members of the Vienna Circle on the basis of traditional empirical thought and the development of modern logic. Logical positivism confined knowledge to science and used verificationism to reject metaphysics not as false but as meaningless. The importance of science led leading logical positivists to study scientific method and to explore the logic of confirmation theory.

logomachy a controversy of no real substance, depending on a merely verbal dispute.

material biconditional the biconditional if and only if ('iff') is a relation between two statements p and q, such that p implies q and q implies p. The biconditional is material if the implications are contingent and strict if the implications are necessary.

materialism the doctrine that all items in the world are composed of matter. Because not all physical entities are material, the related doctrine of physicalism, claiming that all items in the world are physical entities, has tended to replace materialism.

maxim a statement expressing a general truth or rule of conduct.

method philosophical methods are combinations of rules, procedures and examples determining the scope and limits of philosophy and establishing acceptable ways of working within those limits. The question of philosophical method is itself a matter for philosophy and constitutes a major feature of philosophy's reflective nature. Philosophers disagree about what is an appropriate philosophical method and about the relationship between philosophical method and the methods of other disciplines, especially scientific method.

methodological concerning the study of method, particularly scientific method. Questions asked in contemporary methodology concern not only the characterization of scientific method, but also whether a single such characterization is necessary, or can do justice to the multitude of approaches and devices actually used.

model in science, a representation such that knowledge concerning the model offers insight about the entity modelled. Whether models are heuristic devices or essential features of scientific explanation is a matter of debate. Mathematical models are interpretations of a formal system assigning truth values to the formulae of the system, thus testing the system for consistency.

modern for philosophical purposes, the period of philosophy and general intellectual life following Descartes and his contemporaries. The broad characteristics of the period are often taken to include an emphasis on individualism, the intellect, the universality of judgement, and the consequence of adopting these features as starting points.

modus ponens and modus tollens *modus ponens*, or affirming the antecedent (the if clause in an if-then proposition), is an argument of the valid form, 'If p, then q; p; therefore q'. *Modus tollens*, or denying the consequent (the then clause in an if-then proposition), is an argument of the valid form, 'If p, then q; not q; therefore not p.'

natural selection central thesis of the biologist Charles Darwin which suggests that within every population of living organisms there are random variations which have different survival value. Those which aid survival (or enhance reproductive capacity) are 'selected' by being genetically transmitted to succeeding generations.

necessary see *contingent–necessary distinction*

neutral monism a position according to which the difference between minds and bodies derives from different arrangements of the same neutral entities. The entities are neutral because they themselves are neither mental nor physical. This position proposed a solution to the mind–body problem, but there are difficulties with the neutral status of that which constitutes minds and bodies and with how arrangements of what is neutral can issue in minds and bodies. If experiences are proposed as the neutral entities, it is not clear whether neutral monism clarifies or obscures the nature of experience.

nominalism the view that the only feature that particulars falling under the same general term have in common is that they are covered by the same term. Nominalism is opposed to realism, for which universals are required to explain how general terms apply to different particulars. For nominalism, language, rather than independent reality, underlies perceived likeness. Many philosophers are attracted to the ontological austerity of nominalism, but problems remain concerning how language, especially predication, works on nominalist principles.

non-Euclidean geometry Euclids's Fifth 'Parallels' Postulate (or Axiom XI) is rendered informally as: 'through a given point P not on a line L, there is one and only one line in the plane of P and L that does not meet L'. Non-Euclidean geometries explore systems in which two different denials of this postulate are used: Lobachevskyan geometry contains an infinite number of parallels through P; Reimannian geometry contains no parallels through P. Reimannian geometry has played a crucial role in the development of the general theory of relativity.

non-monotonic logics   in logic, deductive validity is cumulative, or *mono-tonic*, in that no matter what further premises are added to an originally valid argument, the argument remains valid. Non-monotonic logics, used in artifi-cial-intelligence research, explore logical systems in which monotonicity does not hold.

Ockham's Razor   the principle enunciated by the medieval nominalist William of Ockham that entities are not to be multiplied beyond necessity. Applied to systems of ontology or bodies of scientific theory, the principle encourages us to ask whether any proposed kind of entity is necessary. This principle of metaphysical economy retains influence in contemporary philoso-phy, although in judging rival systems it is not always clear which best meets the requirements of Ockham's Razor.

omnipotence and omniscience   attributes of being all powerful and all knowing, traditionally ascribed to God. The two combined with divine goodness give rise to the problems of explaining how there can be evil in the world. Puzzles about omnipotence have led to explanations that it is constrained by logical and metaphysical possibility. Divine omniscience, including foreknowledge, has been seen as a threat to human free will, and other philosophers have been concerned about what an omniscient being without a body in space and time could know.

ontology   the study of the broadest categories of existence, which also asks questions about the existence of particular kinds of objects, such as numbers or moral facts.

operator   an expression which alters the logical properties of other expres-sions to which it is applied. A sentential operator can be applied to sentences to yield new sentences.

paradox   an argument which seems to justify a self-contradictory conclusion by using valid deductions from acceptable premises.

perception   our awareness of the world and its contents through sensory experience. The analysis of perception and the attempt to deal with skeptical arguments about perceptual knowledge are central philosophical topics. Perception involves both our capacity to be sensorily affected by external objects and our ability to bring these objects under concepts, although other capacities might also have a role to play. What we perceive and how these objects of perception are related to us and to physical objects are matters of continuing concern.

phenomenology   for Hegel, the study of the dialectical development of Spirit through stages towards rational, self-conscious freedom; for Husserl, a philo-sophical method based on the reflective and descriptive study of conscious-ness focused on the intentionality of mental states. The structure of consciousness revealed, which includes an ego that exists absolutely, aimed to provide a sure foundation for knowledge. In response to Frege's early criticism, Husserl attempted to draw a sharp boundary between phenomenol-ogy and psychology. In his later writing, Husserl altered many features of his notion of phenomenology, and other writers, especially Heidegger, used the term in radically different ways.

picture theory of meaning Wittgenstein's view in the *Tractatus Logico–Philosophicus* that a proposition has meaning in virtue of sharing a form with an actual or possible state of affairs. The proposition provides a logical picture of the state of affairs, and is true if its elements stand in the same relation as the objects in the state of affairs. Philosophers disagree over the extent to which Wittgenstein moved away from this theory in his later writings.

pluralism in metaphysics, the belief that there is more than one kind of fundamental reality or of fundamental existents. Hence, pluralism stands in contrast to monism (one kind of fundamental reality or existent) and dualism (two kinds of fundamental reality or existent). In ethics, the belief that there is more than one kind of fundamental good or supreme ethical value.

polis the Greek term for city-state, from which the term 'politics' is derived. The character of the polis was examined in ancient times, and many later thinkers yearned for its re-establishment as an ideal of political life.

possible world the analysis of statements in terms of 'possible worlds' comes from the semantic treatment of modal logic – the logic of possibility and necessity. A possible world is a way the world might have been. A necessary statement is one that is true in all possible worlds; a contingent statement is one that is true in at least one possible world.

postmodernism if Descartes is seen as the father of modernism, then postmodernism is a variety of cultural positions which reject major features of Cartesian (or allegedly Cartesian) modern thought. Hence, views which, for example, stress the priority of the social to the individual; which reject the universalizing tendencies of philosophy; which prize irony over knowledge; and which give the irrational equal footing with the rational in our decision procedures all fall under the postmodern umbrella.

prescriptive statement a statement, for example in ethics, which says how things should be, as opposed to a descriptive statement, which says how things are.

presupposition a generally implicit assumption (though it can be made explicit) underlying a claim or a process of inference.

primary and secondary qualities seventeenth-century scientists and philosophers attempted to distinguish qualities like size and shape, which produce in us ideas (ideas of primary qualities) that resemble the qualities themselves, from qualities that produce in us ideas (ideas of secondary qualities), like colour and taste, which do not resemble the qualities themselves. The former ideas, unlike the latter, offered something that could be measured, and were thus considered a suitable basis for scientific explanation. Berkeley argued against the distinction.

principle of non-contradiction the logical principle rejecting the possibility that propositions of the form 'p and not p' are true, that a subject can be and not be, or that we can ascribe and deny the same attribute to the same subject.

proposition   that which is characteristically stated by a declarative sentence and can be true or false. Understanding the nature and structure of propositions is often seen as the central task of the philosophical examination of logic. Philosophers consider the apparently different functions of components of propositions (names, predicates and logical constants) and how they are unified into something capable of having a truth value. They ask about how the form, meaning and use of propositions are related and how different propositions have logical relations. They ask how linguistic or psychological states can have propositional contents. The existence of propositions, as opposed to sentences, is challenged by those suspicious of their abstract nature.

quantifier   modern predicate logic uses quantifier expressions some ($\exists$) and all ($\forall$) in sentences with variables (x, y, . . .), predicates (F, G, . . .), relations (R, . . .), identity and logical constants (and, or, not, if-then). ($\exists$x) ($\exists$y) (if Fx and Gy, then x = y) reads 'For some x and for some y, if x is F and y is G, then x is identical with y'. The individual or multiple use of the universal quantifier 'all' and the existential quantifier 'there exists' to bind variables in sentences has been seen as the key to the development of a powerful and flexible system of modern predicate logic.

quantum mechanics   a modern physical theory (much developed and refined since Neils Bohr's ground-breaking work in 1913) which deals with the structure and behaviour of subatomic particles. It has given rise to philosophical problems of its own (some quantum phenomena seem to require a non-classical logic) and has also been used by both sides in the philosophical dispute between realist and instrumentalist construals of scientific theories.

rational numbers   any number of the form x/y, where x can be any positive or negative integer or 0, and y is a positive integer. An irrational number is any real number which is not rational.

real number   a real number is any number which can be represented as a non-terminating decimal.

realism   a variety of doctrines in different areas of philosophy holding that entities or facts of contested sorts exist. There are, of course, different arguments concerning the reality of numbers in mathematics, the reality of moral facts in ethics, and the reality of time in physics or metaphysics. The kind of reality ascribed to universals differs from the kind of reality seen as belonging to common-sense material objects or to theoretical entities in science. Various realisms are hence opposed by nominalism, idealism, instrumentalism, reductionism, eliminativism, conventionalism, constructivism, relativism and anti-realism. Kant argued for both empirical realism and transcendental idealism. In recent years, many philosophers have discussed Michael Dummett's argument for anti-realism, in which he rejects the claim that every proposition must be either true or false and argues that realism must be false because it implies this claim.

reason   an ability to move from the truth of some beliefs to the truth of others. Some philosophers have seen this capacity as more or less sufficient to determine one correct systematic account of reality, while others have argued that such an account, if possible at all, must be based primarily upon experience. Kant, following Aristotle, saw reason divided between theoretical and practical reason, the latter issuing in actions rather than beliefs, but held that at a deep level the two capacities were the same. Hegel saw reason and much else altering at different stages of historical development. Hume restricted practical reason to finding means to obtain ends set out by the passions, others have rejected the means–ends account. Reason enters the account of institutions through models of the interaction of the choices of individuals and through the direct assessment of practices and societies.

recursive function   a function for which the value of the function for any argument X_{n+1} is a function of the value of the function for the argument X_n.

reflective equilibrium   a term used by Nelson Goodman and John Rawls for a two-way reconciliation between judgements and principles. Judgements about individual cases are guided by principles, but principles can be modified in light of judgements. Equilibrium is reached when principles and judgements fit one another without further alteration. An equilibrium is always liable to be upset by new cases, but that is also true, although less transparently so, if one tries to determine principles by other procedures.

relativity (theory of)   the special theory of relativity is a modern physical theory due to Einstein, giving an account in which neither space nor time has an independent absolute value or existence but is each relative to the other. Thus the classical view of space and time is replaced with one in which the two are aspects of the same underlying reality: Space-time. The general theory of relativity extended the special (from considering frameworks in uniform relative motion to considering frameworks in arbitrary relative motion to one another) and is the currently accepted basis for our theory of gravitation.

rights   legal or moral capacities, often correlated with duties, which may be exercised without interference by others, including the state, or in some cases with the assistance of others. Rights can regard such matters as belief, actions, relationships, property, or the safety and integrity of oneself. Some rights involve limiting the rights of others or the creation of duties. Rights can be considered one by one or from the standpoint of a system of rights and duties. Philosophers discuss the status of rights in morality, in particular whether rights can provide the basis of moral or political philosophy or must be understood within the context of other notions, such as principles, virtues, utility, or a social contract, from which their legitimacy might derive. Philosophers have discussed the claim that rights 'trump' other considerations, the claim that there are collective as well as individual rights, and the claim that animals have rights. Exploring this last question can help to see what one must be like in order to hold rights. Philosophers have also considered the relationship between legal and moral rights and, in the face of

Bentham's attack on natural rights, have examined the notion of natural, universal or human rights.

rigid designator a subject term designating the same object in all different possible situations (or possible worlds) in which the object exists, so long as the meaning of the term is held constant. A non-rigid designator with constant meaning can designate different objects in different possible situations (or possible worlds).

Rorschach test a personality test, bearing the name of its Swiss inventor, in which a set of ink-blots is shown to a patient, who has to describe what they resemble or suggest.

rule a principle guiding action. For Kant, concepts are rules, the understanding is the faculty of rules, and our use of rules is central to our account of objectivity. Much of Wittgenstein's discussion of following a rule runs parallel to the Kantian insight that rules do not determine their own application. The question of what gives a rule authority and holds it and its application in place led to the rejection of the possibility of a private language and Wittgenstein's emphasis on practices and forms of life. Interrelations among rules, roles and practices are central concerns in the philosophy of social science. Discussions of what constitutes a legal rule and how such rules have normative force are main features of the philosophy of law.

rule utilitarianism a version of utilitarianism in which general rules rather than acts are assessed for utility, thus shifting concern from individuals to practices and institutions. Acts are endorsed not in their own right, but because they accord with practices or institutions which meet the test of maximizing utility.

Russell's paradox a paradox based on the notion of class membership discovered by Bertrand Russell and undermining the crucial notion of class or set in Frege's foundations of mathematics. The paradox led to important changes in set theory and in the notion of a set, in part also to prevent further paradoxes from arising. The paradox arises from asking whether the class of all classes that are not members of themselves is a member of itself.

sanctions negative and positive sanctions are punishments or rewards for behaviour that transgresses or is in accord with a rule.

scope in logic, the shortest propositional function in which a logical operator occurs. Scope ambiguities are common in ordinary language but are eliminable during formalization.

semantics in the study of language, semantics is concerned with the meaning of words, expressions and sentences, often in relation to reference and truth. Semantics is contrasted with syntax (the study of logical or grammatical form) and pragmatics (the study of the contribution of contextual factors to the meaning of what language users say). Meta-semantic theories study key semantic notions such as meaning and truth and how these notions are related.

sense data in empiricist theories of perception, which were popular earlier this century, that which is given by the senses. Questions arise concerning whether anything is purely given in perception, what might be given, and how what is given might be related to the external objects of common sense.

set a set is a collection of definite distinguishable entities. Set theory, however, allows for the null set: the set that has no members.

social contract an actual or hypothetical contract providing the legitimate basis of sovereignty and civil society and of the rights and duties constituting the role of citizen. The contract can be agreed between people and a proposed sovereign or among the people themselves.

solipsism the view confining reality to oneself and one's experiences.

subjective–objective distinction the subject contributes what is subjective to such things as perceptual, moral and aesthetic judgement and experience; the objects of such judgements and experience contribute what is objective. The subjective seems prone to variation among subjects, while the objective appears to provide a basis for universal agreement. There is disagreement over the contribution of the subject and the object to such judgements. Different notions of objectivity might be suitable in different domains. Historical judgements, for example, might be objective if the historian making them is unbiased rather than through having a favoured relation to relevant objects.

sublation a change which both cancels and preserves an entity or concept by raising it to a higher level. The full complex meaning of this term (*aufheben* in German) was established by Hegel.

substance something which can exist by itself, is the substrate underlying the existence of other things, and is the subject of which other things are predicated. In his *Metaphysics* Aristotle considered what can be substance: matter, form, or a combination of matter and form. According to various criteria he used, different answers seemed plausible, although he finally preferred form. Seventeenth-century philosophers, including Descartes, Spinoza and Leibniz, came to strikingly different solutions to the problem of what qualifies as being substance. Locke's account seems to suggest an unknowable substratum which falls out of any account of knowledge, but it can also be seen to offer a corpuscular substrate linked to his doctrine of primary qualities and their explanatory role in science.

sui generis literally, of its own kind, or unique.

supervenience a property F supervenes on a property G, firstly, if anything which has property F has it in virtue of having property G and, secondly, if something has property F in virtue of having property G, then anything else having property G would also have to possess property F. Supervenience is intended to allow for non-reductive relations among hierarchies of properties.

syllogism an argument according to Aristotle's logical theory involving a major premise, a minor premise, and a conclusion.

things-in-themselves Kant distinguished appearances (phenomena) from things-in-themselves (noumena). Things-in-themselves are meant to exist independently of how we experience them, in particular independently of space, time and the categories.

thought for Frege, a thought is the sense of a sentence which can be used to make an assertion or to ask a question that is answerable by either 'Yes' or 'No'. The contents of thoughts can be true or false. Thoughts in this sense are logical or conceptual rather than a matter of individual psychology. Different individuals may share the same thought, although they cannot share the same act of thinking.

thought experiment an attempt to conceive the consequences of an intervention in the world without actually intervening. In some cases, an actual experiment would be preferable but is impossible in practice or perhaps even in theory.

three-valued logic classical logic allows 'true' and 'false' as the only values for propositions, as expressed by the law of excluded middle (which states that every proposition is either true or false). Three-valued logic can reject this law by adding an additional value like 'indeterminate' or can replace the two initial values with three other values like 'necessarily true', 'necessarily false', and 'contingent'.

transcendental for Kant, 'transcendental' is contrasted with 'transcendent'. Something transcendent goes beyond the limits of experience, while something transcendental relates to the conditions of the possibility of experience.

truth propositions, statements, sentences, assertions and beliefs have been offered as appropriate bearers of truth or falsity. Understanding truth is filled with difficulty. Philosophers have explored the possibility that truth is: a correspondence between what we say and how things are; a matter of coherence between statements and a background of settled beliefs; an ideal limit which enquiry will approach; a feature of assertions which function well in enquiry or in life more generally; a matter of giving a truth definition for a language; a redundancy, because 'It is true that p' is equivalent to 'p'; or disclosedness of being. Some of these theories are compatible and might be integrated in a more comprehensive theory. On some accounts, each proposition is true or false on its own, while others adopt a holistic view. The relation between meaning and truth is of central philosophical concern.

truth function the truth value of a combination of propositions which depends only on the truth values of the constituent propositions and the logical constants (and, if-then, or, not) by which they are combined. Truth functions can be set out in truth tables:

p	q	p or q
T	T	T
T	F	T
F	T	T
F	F	F

Not all propositions are truth functions of their constituents. For example, the truth value of 'I believe that it will rain' is not determined by the truth value of 'It will rain'.

understanding   the capacity to use concepts and to bring individuals under them. Kant distinguished sensibility, understanding and reason as fundamental to our capacity for experience and knowledge. He understood concepts as rules and saw the understanding as the faculty of rules, including both empirical concepts and the categories as pure concepts of the understanding. In the social sciences and history, Dilthey and Weber have contrasted understanding (*verstehen*) and explanation, with explanation providing the causal accounts of science and understanding offering insight into such things as human lives, culture and historical periods. Hermeneutics has been proposed as the method appropriate to understanding. Philosophers have disagreed over the claimed difference between explanation and understanding, about the character of understanding, and about the methodological implications of recognizing understanding as a distinctive mode of knowledge.

universals   abstract objects intended to explain how general terms have meaning and how they apply to individuals. There were medieval disputes over universals involving realism, which accepted their existence, and nominalism, which denied it. Some philosophers see problems in embracing any abstract object, especially in this case because their relation to individuals seems opaque, yet it is also difficult to see how an account of how names have meaning and refer to individuals will explain the contribution of predicates and relations to the meaning and truth or falsity of sentences or propositions. Explaining these roles might not require classic universals, derived from independently existing Platonic forms, but there are other possibilities short of nominalism.

verification principle   a central doctrine of logical positivism according to which the meaning of a proposition is its method of verification. Claims without a method of verification, such as those of religion and metaphysics, are meaningless. Verificationism thus offered a criterion of meaningfulness.

verisimilitude   literally and as used in aesthetic criticism, the appearance of being true or real. In philosophy, a surrogate for the truth of scientific theories offered by Karl Popper as part of his vision of the nature of scientific progress.

vicious regress   an attempt to solve a problem which re-introduced the same problem in the proposed solution. If one continues along the same lines, the initial problem will recur infinitely and will never be solved. Not all regresses, however, are vicious.

Vienna Circle an intellectual (mostly philosophical) group, led by Moritz Schlick, which met from 1924–36, though its influence continued for much longer. Their general position, pro-science and hostile to speculative meta-physics, gave rise to the doctrines of logical positivism.

virtue an excellence of moral or intellectual character. Plato, Aristotle and many subsequent philosophers explored the nature of the virtues, their relations among themselves and to non-virtuous states, their place in our psychology and their role in achieving happiness. Virtues offer a basis for ethical life rivalling those provided by Kantian principles or a utilitarian calculation of happiness, although an account of ethics might reasonably include principles, consequences and virtues. A recent revival of virtue ethics has been motivated in part by dissatisfaction with the abstract universal nature of the main alternative views. The emphasis on cultivating virtues in concrete human individuals could correct this, but it is not clear that a perfectionist concern for individual excellence is satisfactory to ground ethics.

Index

Abelard, P., 'moderate realism' 504
absolute, the, metaphysics 68
absolute idea, Hegelian logic 611
absolute knowledge, Hegel's phenomenology of spirit 609
absolute monarchy 550, 551
absolute presuppositions, metaphysics 70–1
abstract ideas, Berkeley 555, 557–62, 564
abstract objects
  Frege 664, 665
  Hobbes' denial of 536
  omnipotence of God and 455
  philosophy of mathematics 326, 344–5, 350
Ackerman, B., distribution and production 280
action
  concern of ethics with 199; autonomy 216–17; utilitarianism 209–10
  philosophy of, theory of speech acts and 8
action theory 22
Acton, H. B., on Marx's political economy 619
actual language relation 105
Adams, R. M.
  best possible worlds 474
  theistic voluntarism 460
admiration, ethics of 200–3, 220
Adorno, T., anti-scientism 708
adverbs, semantic theories 113, 114
aesthetics 229–56
  aesthetic experience and judgement 230–5, 580–1; aesthetic attitude 234–5; aesthetic objectivism and subjectivism 231–4; concept of beauty 235; Hume and Kant 230–5, 580–1; Mill 632, 634

art 229–30, 235–52; criticism 580–1; definitions of 235–7; expression 243–7; Hume 230–4, 246–7, 251–2, 580–1; institutional theory 236; meaning 247–50; point of 250–2; representation 241–3; seeing in 243; theories of 237–41
discussion questions 255–6
ethics and 199, 202–3
further reading 252–3
afterlife, evil and 475
agnosticism 447
  God and ineffability and 453–4
AI see artificial intelligence
Albert the Great, Aristotelian revival 505
Albo, J., ineffability of God 454
alienation
  anti-scientism 709–10, 711
  Marx's theory of 617–18
Alston, W., theism 543
Althusser, L.
  anti-scientism, status of self 715
  structuralist Marxism of 618
altruism, utilitarianism and 631, 639
analytic behaviourism 169
analytic empiricism, logic and set theory and 338–45
analytic geometry, the infinite 333–8
analytic Marxism 273–5, 277, 619–21
analytic philosophy 1–23, 25–37
  action theory 22
  analysis as method for metaphysics 72–9
  analytic–synthetic distinction 3–4, 6, 7–9
  Austin's theory of speech acts 8–9
  causal theory of reference 15–16, 23
  cognitive science 13–15

continental philosophy and 655, 704
evaluative–descriptive distinction 4–6, 8–9, 10
foundationalism 5, 6, 9–10
history of 2
intentionalistic theories of meaning 17–18
labels and stereotypes attaching to 25–6
Moore 681–3
philosophical priorities, philosophy of language 97–8, 100, 115
post-positivist philosophy of science 11–12
principal concerns of moral philosophy 27–37; ethical theory 32–4; meta-ethics 28–32; political philosophy and 34–7
Quine's criticism of analytic–synthetic distinction 7–8
Rawls' theory of justice 10–11, 34–5
science and 26, 27
theory of speech acts 8–9
truth-conditional theories of meaning 18–20
virtues of 26–7
Wittgenstein: philosophical psychology 20–1; philosophical scepticism 21–2; rejection of foundationalism 9–10, 58; rule following 21
anarchy, Nozick's view of the state and 265–9
ancient Greek philosophy see Greek philosophy
Anglo–American philosophy see analytic philosophy
anomalous monism, instrumentalism compared 187

Anscombe, E., ethical
    naturalism 724
Anselm, Saint
    'extreme realism' 504
    God and ineffability 453
    omniscience 457
anti-realism
    constructionist thesis of
        historical fact 417
    historical narratives 433–6
    omnipotence of God and 455
    philosophy of logic 159–60
anti-scientism 703–17
    critique of scientific
        culture 708–11
    hermeneutics and possibility of
        objectivity 711–14
    Nietzsche's legacy 706–8
    status of self 714–17
antimonies of pure reason,
    Kant 594
Apel, K.-O., pragmatism 655–6
aporia, Aristotelian
    investigation 490
applied ethics 722–31
    description of 722–3
    discussion questions 731
    further reading 728–9
    meta-philosophical account of
        moral reasoning 727–8
    moral casuistry 726–7
    moral danger of 726
    rise and expansion of 723–6
Aquinas, Saint Thomas
    Aristotelianism 505
    casuistry 726
    God's existence 448
    God's ownership of the
        cosmos 461
    goodness of God 460
    omniscience 457
Archard, D., political and social
    philosophy 257–89
argument from design 578
Aristotelian theory
    Hobbes' opposition to 536–7
    Locke's opposition to 546–7
    philosophy of
        mathematics 331–3, 334, 336
    revival of in logic and
        metaphysics 503–6
Aristotle 483, 489–92
    influence on Hellenistic
        philosophy 493
    mathematical proofs 333
    omniscience 457
    theories of art, *mimesis* 237
    virtue theory 29–30
Armstrong, D. M.
    identity theory of mind 171–2
    laws and generalizations 311
art
    aesthetics of *see* aesthetics
    anti-scientism and 708, 709
    goodness to be found in,
        Moore 679
    history of, value judgements
        and objectivity 430, 431

artificial intelligence
    computer model of mind 13–
        15, 174–6
    connectionism 176, 189, 655
    parallel distributed
        processing 188–9
    refutation of 15
assertives, illocutionary acts 9
assertoric sentences 666
atheism 447, 451
    Berkeley 556
    burden of proof 463–5
    Hegel 614
    ideal-observer theory 461
atomism 7
    corpuscularianism and 545–7
    Descartes 514
    of social scientists,
        methodological individualism
        and 715
    Wittgenstein: holism
        replaces 689–90;
        propositions as pictures 688–
        9
attribute of extension,
    Spinoza 518
attribute of thought, Spinoza 518,
    519
Augustinian philosophy 500–2
    eternal or everlasting God 458–
        9
    faith and reason 502, 503
    omniscience 457
    theodicy 474
Austin, J., theory of law 397, 398,
    402
Austin, J. L., theory of speech
    acts 8–9
authority, arguments from 501–2
autonomy
    Kant, moral law and 216–17,
        222, 598–601
    law and politics 392–3
    liberalism and 281–3
    see also free will
Averroes of Cordoba (Ibn Rushd),
    Aristotelian revival 504, 505
Avicenna of Baghdad (Ibn Sina),
    Aristotelian revival 504
axiomatization of geometry 346–8
    Schopenhauer's view 688
axioms
    of infinity and reducibility 343–
        4, 688
    semantic theories of
        meaning 19, 92–6, 100–2,
        110
Ayer, A. J.
    Cartesian perspective 53
    religious beliefs 444, 445

Baldwin, T., Moore 678–84
Barnes, J., theism and
    dualism 453
Barth, K., fideism 464
Bayesianism 295–8
    Bayes' theorem 297–8
    Bayesian updating 298
    Dutch book argument 297, 314

Beardsley, M. C., intentionalism,
    interpreting art 247–8, 249
bearerless names, Russell 667–8
beauty, concept of 235
Bedeutung see sense reference
    distinction
behaviourism 5, 168–70, 177
    accommodating the familiar and
        exotic 73
    cognitive science and 13–14
    consciousness and qualia
        problems 181
    instrumentalism and 186
    Turing test 169–70, 182
Being, metaphysics as science
    of 65
belief, knowledge as, justified 38–
    46, 58–9
Bell, C., value of art 251
Bell, D., the end of ideology 257–
    8
Bell, D., Kant 589–606
ben Maimon, Moishe, Aristotelian
    revival 504
Bentham, J., utilitarianism 627–9
    casuistry 727
    as a consequentalist ethic 628
    discussion questions 641–2
    empiricist method 637
    fictional entities 637–8
    further reading 640
    happiness and pain 627–8, 629,
        637–8
    indirect form 634–5
    Mill's ideas 629–31, 633, 634–5,
        636
    natural rights and nonsense 638
    obedience 628
    paraphrasis 637–8
    punishment 628, 629
    rationality and games
        theory 375–6
    Sidgwick's ideas 639
    theory of law 401–2, 411–12,
        628, 629, 634–5, 637–8
Berger, F. R., on Mill 631
Bergson, H., anti-scientism 704–5
Berkeley, G. 555–70
    abstract ideas, relative ideas and
        immaterialism 555, 557–62,
        564
    British Empiricism 543
    common sense and the 'new
        philosophy' 556–7
    conceivability, perceivability
        and intrinsic properties 564–
        6
    discussion questions 570
    esse est percipi 556
    further reading 568
    God: belief in 448; perception
        of 55, 56; from
        phenomenalism to
        theism 566–8
    Moore's criticism of 680
    qualities, ideas and
        sensations 50, 562–4

representation of the infinite
and infinity 336
revisionary metaphysics 64
scepticism: idealism 55–6, 556,
567–8; perceptual
relativities 50
Berlin, I.
individuality 423
liberalist themes 258–9, 283
Bernstein, R. J., pragmatism 655
best explanation, coherence,
justified beliefs 43
binarisms, philosophical
feminism and 735–7
self or subject and 717
biology
Descartes' view of nature 511,
512; mind-body dualism 516
logic of natural selection 318–
19
reductionism 319–20
teleological explanations 177–
80, 317–18
black-letter rules, philosophy of
law 396, 409
Blackburn, S., metaphysics 64–89
Blackstone, W., natural law theory
Bentham's criticism 401–2, 628
context 409
blame, ethics of 200–4, 212–13,
220
Block, N. J., case against
functionalism 181
Bloomsbury Group, influence of
Moore on 680
Bloor, D., foundationalism 349
Boethian philosophy 503
omnipotent and omniscient
God 457
Boethius 503
Bonaventure, Saint, view of
Aristotle 505
Boyd, R., explaining
phenomena 299
Boyle, R., Locke and 541, 546
Bradley, F. H., on Mill 631
Brentano, F., philosophy of
mind 179, 182
British Empiricism 543
Brouwer, L. E. J.
intuitionism 345–6
reflexivity 351
Brunschwig, J., Hellenistic
philosophy 494
Buchanan, A., cultural
membership 282
Burnyeat, M., logic of self-
refutation 488

Calvin, J., reformed
epistemology 463
Cambridge change, God's
immanence 462
Cantor, G., numbers 338–9, 341,
348
capitalism, Marx
analytical Marxism 273–5,
619–22
ethics 622–4

theory of alienation 617–18
Carnap, R.
behaviourism 168–9
remembered similarity 694
Cartesian dualism 13–14, 168–9,
170, 171, 516–17, 518–19
Cartesianism
notions of self, anti-
scientism 706, 707, 715–16
pragmatism and 644, 655;
Dewey 651–2; James' radical
empiricism 649–50; Peirce's
criticism 252, 645–6, 647
see also Descartes
Cartwright, N., unifying scientific
theories 299–300
casuistry, applied ethics 726–7
categorical imperative 29, 34,
214–19, 599–601
categories 65
Hegel 608, 610
Kant 594, 608
Peirce's theory of 645
study of Being and 65
Cauchy, A. L., the infinite 338
causa sui, omnipotence of
God 455–6
causal theory of reference 15–16,
23
theistic voluntarism 460
causation
computer functionalism 14–15
explanation and understanding:
covering-law model 309–10,
364–5, 421; rational
reconstruction 424; social
science 359–68, 374–82
Hume 573–5; Berkeley's theism
and 567–8; constant
conjunction account of 308–
9, 310–11, 583; direction
of 311–12; disputes
about 584; implications
of 575–6; miracles and
religion 578–9
instrumentalism 186–7
James' pragmatism 650
knowledge as justified belief 44,
45
metaphysics of science 308–10;
covering-law model of
explanation 309–10;
direction of causation 311–
12; probabilistic
causation 312–14
Mill's empiricist method 635
philosophy of history: covering-
law model of
explanation 421; dispositions
contrasted 422–3
certainty
Descartes: methodological
scepticism 52, 53, 517;
pragmatism 644, 646, 651–2;
Moore's common sense
arguments 681
Chalcidius 503

Champaux, William of, 'extreme
realism' 504
chaos theory, idealizations 327–8
character, moral freedom 203–5
characterization, historical
phenomena 430–2
charity, principle of, philosophy
of language 103, 115–16
Chisholm, R. M., objections to
representational theory 184–
5
Chodorow, N., masculinity in
philosophy 734
Chomsky, N.
language of cognitivism 174
tacit knowledge, grammars 111,
123
Christian theology
casuistry 726–7
evil 472–3
goodness of God 459
mathematical knowledge 330,
335
relation with medieval
philosophy: reason 502–5;
Saint Augustine 500–1
theism 446
Churchland, P. M.
eliminativism and
neurophilosophy 188
objections to representational
theory 185
pragmatism 655
Churchland, P. S.
neurophilosophy 188
objections to representational
theory 185
Church's theorem 146–7
Cicero, influence on Hume 572,
583
civil war, Hobbes' theories
on 531–6
Clarke, T., scepticism 21–2
class societies, Marxist
morality 622–4
classes
choices in metaphysics 66–7,
69
logic, set theory and
empiricism 338–45
Russell's paradox 342, 663
CLS (Critical Legal Studies)
movement 410–11
coercion, injustice of
capitalism 274
cogito ergo sum 516, 517
cognitive science 13–15, 174
artificial intelligence and
computer models of
mind 13–15, 174–6
cognitive systems, social systems
and 380
cognitivism, value
judgements 428
Cohen, G. A., analytical
Marxism 273, 274, 275,
619–21
Cohen, J., foundationalism 276

coherence, justified beliefs 42–3
collective agency, analytical Marxism 275
colligatory concepts, historical narratives 435–6, 437
Collingwood, R. G.
  absolute presuppositions 70–1
  expression theory of art 239
  historical explanation 423; rational reconstruction 424, 426
colour
  Berkeley's idealism 557–8
  not a property, Descartes 512
commissives, illocutionary acts 9
common sense
  and analysis as method for metaphysics 74–5
  Descartes' world 513, 518
  identity theory of mind and 171
  inner-cause thesis: eliminativism 188; instrumentalism 186–7; 'language of thought' hypothesis 183–6, 187
  Moore defends 678, 680–1, 682
  'new philosophy', Berkeley 556–7
  Peirce's pragmatism 646–7
  see also folk psychology
communitarianism 35–6, 269–71, 283, 381
community theory of language, Wittgenstein 697
compatibilism, free will and determinism 458
computer models
  artificial intelligence 13–15, 174–6, 188–9, 655
  computer (Turing machine) functionalism 15
Comte, A.
  atomism 715
  Hume's influence on 584
  influence of 704
conceivability, Berkeley 564–6
concepts
  Berkeley's argument 557–8, 564–6
  function and object, Frege 662, 663–5
  Hegel: doctrine of concept 610; logical idea 614
conceptual analysis 258
  as aim of philosophy 5–6, 12–13
  role in mathematics 350–1
conceptual knowledge, Locke's notion 544–5
conceptual polarities, scepticism 51–2
conceptual understanding, Hegel's disfavour for 608
conceptualism
  Kant 336–8, 591–8
  philosophy of mathematics 331–3, 334, 336, 337–8, 350–2

Condorcet, M. de, natural sciences 360, 361
configurational understanding, historical narratives 435, 436–7
connectionist artificial intelligence 176, 189, 655
conscience, Hegel 611
consciousness 66, 70
  anti-scientism 705, 712–13, 715–16, 717
  grammars, tacit knowledge 111, 123
  Hegel 609, 613–14
  Hume 596
  Kant 597–8
  Leibniz 525
  Locke 549
  Marx's theory of ethics and history 623–4
  Moore's thesis 680
  qualia, philosophy of mind 180–2
  radical empiricism in James' pragmatism 649–50
consent, Lockean political authority 551
consequentialist criterion, philosophy of history 430
consequentialist ethic 33, 34, 628, 723
conservative holism, utilitarianism 210–11
conservativism 276, 277–8
consistency
  coherence 43
  intuitionism, formalism and open questions 347–8
constatives, theory of speech acts 8
constructionism, knowledge of historical fact 417–18
content, radical empiricism in James' pragmatism 649–50
contextual effects and implications, pragmatics 129–30
continental philosophy 25–6, 702–18
  analytic philosophy 655, 704
  anti-scientism 703–6; critique of scientific culture 708–11; hermeneutics and possibility of objectivity 711–14; Nietzsche's legacy 706–8; status of self 714–17
  definition 702–3
  discussion questions 720–1
  further reading 718
contingent cosmos, existence of God 468–9
contractualism
  categorical imperative and 34, 216–19, 601
  moral categoricity 220
  Rawls' theory of justice 34, 261, 262–3, 264

convention T, truth-conditional theories of meaning 18–19, 106
conventional regularity, meta-semantic theory 115, 117, 120–2, 132–3
conventionalism 5
  theory of law 407, 408–9
  Wittgenstein 698
conversational implicature 124–7
  irony 127
  maxims of conversation 17, 126–7, 128–9
  metaphor 127–8
  relevance theory 129–30
Cooper, D. E., modern European philosophy 702–18
cooperative principle
  conversational implicature 126–7; metaphor 127–8
coordination game, utility theory 376–7
Copernican revolution, Kant 591–2
corpuscularianism 545–7
correctness, semantic theories 105–7
correspondence theory of truth
  meta-ethics 224, 225
  philosophy of language 91
cosmic impiety, pragmatism to lead to 653
cosmos
  existence of God 467–72
  philosophy of mathematics: analytic geometry and the infinite 333–8; Aristotelian conceptualism 331–3; Platonic realism 329–31
covering-law model of explanation
  deterministic assumptions 424–5
  metaphysics of science 309–10, 313, 317
  philosophy of history 421–7
  social science 364–5
Craig, W., existence of God 468
Critical Legal Studies (CLS) movement 410–11
critical philosophy, Kant 590–601
critical theory, Marx 623–4
criticism, of art 580–1
  see also aesthetics
critique
  function of 277
  of scientific culture 708–11
Croce, B., expression theory of art 239
cultural membership, liberalism and 282
Cummins, R., functionalism 177–8, 179

Danto, A.
  historical narratives 432
  knowledge of historical fact 416
  narrative sentences 427–8

Darwin, C., natural selection 318–19
Dasein 710
Davidson, D.
  anomalous monism and instrumentalism compared 187
  philosophical priorities 98, 115–16
  truth-conditional theory of meaning 18–20, 102–14; adverbs and events 113, 114; correctness 105–7; epistemology 109–11; format 102–4; Frege argument 103–4; mental states 19–20, 107–9; metaphysics 112–14; utterance interpretation 131–3
Davies, B.
  God as Being 462
  goodness of God 459, 472
  via negativa philosophy of God 453
Davies, M., philosophy of language 90–139
death, afterlife and evil 475
decision procedure, theories of justice 263
deconstruction
  literary interpretation 250
  metaphysical binarisms 736
Dedekind, J. W. R., definition of real numbers 341
deductive argument, Mill 635
deductive inferences
  mathematics 328
  science 291
deductive-nomological theory *see* covering-law model of explanation
definite descriptions, Russell's theory of 671, 687
deity *see* God
delusion, scepticism and 48, 49
democracy, politics and 278
Democritus, atomism 545
demonstrative knowledge, Locke 544
Dennett, D. C.
  homuncular functionalism 177–8
  instrumentalism 186–7
  morality, mental health 177
  objections to representational theory 185
deontological theories 33, 34, 723
Derrida, J.
  critique of self or subject 716–17
  dichotomies in philosophy: feminism 736; self or subject 717
Descartes, R. 509–17
  abstract objects 536
  anti-scientism, status of self 715–16
  cogito ergo sum 516, 517

discussion questions 527–9
dreams 49, 516
dualism 13–14, 168–9, 516–17, 518–19; behaviourism 170; identity theory 171; objections to 168
  as father of modern philosophy 510
  further reading 525–6
  God 513–15, 516; material substance 514; mathematical knowledge 330; methodological scepticism 52, 53–4; omnipotence of 455
  Hobbes' materialism 536
  humanity 515–17
  illusion 516
  Locke's ideas on consciousness 549
  masculinity in philosophy 735
  nature 510–13
  revisionary metaphysics 64
  scepticism 47, 52–4, 517; anti-Cartesianism 57–8; dreams 49; philosophy of religion 463
  Wittgenstein's private language argument 20–1, 57
  see also Cartesianism
descriptions
  causal theory of reference 15–16
  theory of: analytic techniques 73; Russell 670–2; Wittgenstein's agreement with 687
  Wittgenstein's rigid and plastic meaning 695–7
descriptive metaphysics 64–5
descriptive utterances 4–6, 8–9, 10
desire, ethics 201–3
determinate meaning, literary interpretation 249
determinism
  free will and 204, 361, 362–4; Hume 575, 583; omniscience of God 457–8
  Hellenistic philosophy 493
deterministic assumptions, covering-law model of explanation 424–5
development thesis, Cohen's analytic Marxism 619
Dewey, J.
  Cartesian model, scepticism 57
  practice and theorizing 449
  pragmatism 644, 651–2, 654, 655
dialectic method
  Aristotle 490–2
  Hegel 612–14
  Hellenistic philosophy 493–5
  Kant 594
  Socrates 483–8
  Wittgenstein 692–4
dichotomies, philosophical

feminism 735–7
  self or subject 717
Dickie, G., definition of art 236
difference principle
  Nozick's recommendation for 268
  Rawls 208, 261, 263, 267, 270, 283, 284
Dilthey, W.
  anti-scientism 712
  meaning 368
  relativism 381
directives, illocutionary acts 9
dispositions, causal laws contrasted, philosophy of history 422–3
distribution-production economics and politics of 279–80
  equality 284
Divine being *see* God
divine law 723
divine right of kings 550, 551
dogmatism, literary interpretation 250
Donagan, A., philosophy of history 421, 422
Donnellan, K., causal theory of reference 16
Dray, W. H.
  historical narratives 435
  rational reconstruction 424
  value judgements 428, 429, 430
dreams
  Descartes 49, 516
  scepticism 49
Dretske, F., mental states 179
Dreyfus, H. L., computer model of mind 176
dualism
  Cartesian 13–14, 167–8, 516–17, 518–19; behaviourism 170; identity theory 171; objections to 168
  intersection with philosophy of religion 453
Duhem–Quine thesis 7
  scientific theory 302–3, 304–5
Dummett, M.
  anti-realism 159
  case for analysis 76–9
  implicit knowledge 111
  language: indirect discourse 672–3; philosophical priorities 98, 99–100
  mathematics: intuitionism 346; logicism 345, 663
Durkheim, E., social explanation 367
Dutch book argument, Bayesianism 297, 314
duty
  Hobbes 533–5
  legal positivism and reductionism 390–1
  Locke 550

utilitarianism 629, 632–3,
637–8
Dworkin, R.
liberal equality 284
rights and social good 281
theory of law: borderline and
pivotal disputes 399; law
and adjudication 396, 408,
409; law as integrity 407–9;
theory as interpretation 404–
6, 408

economics
in analysis of law 412
Hegel 612
Hume's politics 582–3, 584
Marx: analytic Marxism 619–20;
ethics 622–4; superstructure
and ideology 621–2; theory
of alienation 617–18
politics of 279–80
social theory 372; rationality
and games theory 375–9
Edgeworth, F. Y., social
action 375–6
egalitarianism *see* equality
ego, anti-scientism and status of
self 715
ego-based solipsism,
Wittgenstein's private
language argument 692, 693
egoism, utilitarianism and
Mill 631
Sidgwick 639
Einstein, A.
mathematical knowledge, nature
of 330, 339
theory of relativity, induction
problem 294
elenchos, Socratic 484–7
eliminative behaviourism 169
eliminativism
and analysis as method for
metaphysics 74–5
classes, metaphysics 67
folk psychology 188, 189–91
intersection with religion 453
neurophilosophy and 187–8
Elster, J., analytic Marxism 273,
620
functional explanations 620
emotions
anti-scientism 704, 705
ethics 200–2, 212–13, 220–1
evaluative–descriptive
utterances 4
expression theory of art 237,
238–40, 243–7
intentionality 183
emotivism
aesthetic subjectivism 232
meta-ethics 29, 30
empathy, identifying
intentions 369–70
empiricism 39
of Bentham 637
falsificationism 11
Hume 543, 567–8, 574, 576,
577–9, 583

Kantian metaphysics of
experience 54–5, 590–8, 601
Locke's ideas on 543, 545
Mill 543, 635–6
Moore rejects 678, 680
natural explanations, social
science 361, 362–3, 364, 365,
367
naturalized epistemology of
science 307–8
philosophy of mathematics 326;
logic and set theory 338–45
post-positivist philosophy of
science 11–12
radical, James' pragmatism 649–
50
religious belief 444–5
religious experiences and
secular explanations 462–5,
577–9
scepticism 48–50
sensationalist, Dewey's
pragmatism 652
theism, Hume and
Berkeley 567–8
employment, politics 280
endoxa, Aristotelian
investigation 490, 493
Enlightenment
Hume 579
Locke's influence on 541–2
metaphysics 67–8
natural sciences 360
reason 379–81
scientism 703
entitlement principle, Nozick 266,
267, 268
Epicureans 494
Epicurus, atomism 545
epistemology 38–63
applied ethics 725
discussion questions 61–3
knowledge as justified
belief 38–46; causality 44,
45; coherence 42–3; defining
knowledge 38–40, 46, 58;
foundationalism 41–2;
further reading 59;
internalism and
externalism 43–5; realist
assumptions 45;
reliabilism 44, 45; truth-
tracking 45
philosophical priorities;
language and mind 97–8,
115; religion 462–5
scepticism 21–2, 46–60; anti-
Cartesianism 57–8;
delusion 48, 49; dreams 49;
error 48, 49, 51; further
reading 59–60; Hellenistic
philosophy 493, 495–6;
history of 47; idealism and
phenomenalism 55–6, 680;
Locke's response to 54,
542–3; methodological and
problematic 51–3, 517;
Moore's common sense

argument 680–1;
perception 49–50, 53–4,
55–6; perceptual
relativities 50; responses
to 53–4; transcendental
arguments 54–5
of science 290–308;
Bayesianism 295–8;
induction problem
stated 290–1;
instrumentalism versus
realism 298–300; naturalized
approach 307–8; pessimistic
meta-induction 305–7,
319–20; Popper's
falsificationism 291–4,
303–4; theory, observation
and incommensurability
300–2; underdetermination of
theory by evidence 302–5
semantic theories 109–11
equality 283–4
analytic Marxism 274–5
the family 279
law as expression of 406, 408
Nozick's view of 266, 267–8,
284
Rawls 208, 261, 267, 283, 284
separation from liberalism,
Berlin 258–9
Erigena, J. S. 503
error, scepticism 48, 49, 51
essentialism
liberalism's rejection of, legal
philosophy 410
semantic theories and, rigid
designators 112–13
estrangement *see* alienation
eternal God 458–9
ethics (moral philosophy) 22–37,
198–228
admiration 200–3, 220
analytic and political
philosophy 34–7
applied 722–31;
description 722–3;
discussion questions 731;
further reading 728–9; meta-
philosophical account of
moral reasoning 727–8;
moral casuistry 726–7; moral
danger of 726; rise and
expansion of 723–6
blame 200–4, 212–13, 220
desire 201–3
discussion questions 227–8
ethical naturalism 724;
Moore 678–9
ethical rationalism 724
ethical theory 32–4, 205–7;
applied ethics 723–4, 727;
features of 722–3; Hellenistic
philosophy 494; Marx 618,
622–4; Moore 678–80;
plurality of value 211–13;
Rawls' theory of justice 208;
roles for 209–11; *see also*
utilitarianism

features of morality 722
further reading 225–6
Hegel 611–12
Hume 579–80, 599
ideal observer theory 461
Kant's categorical imperative
  and contractualism 29, 34,
  210, 214–19, 598–601, 678
Locke 545, 548
meta-ethics 28–32, 222–5, 722,
  723
moral education and
  justice 264–5, 279
moral freedom 203–5
moral intuitions 33, 219–21
moral judgements: ideal
  observer theory 461;
  philosophy of law 397–9,
  400–1, 402–4, 407–10;
  theistic voluntarism 460
philosophy of mind 177
practical reason 213–16, 599,
  724, 726
principle of moral
  categoricity 212–13, 220, 221
Rawls' theory of justice 10–11,
  34–5, 208
religion and: belief 445;
  reason 219–22
scope of 198–200;
  aesthetics 199, 202–3;
  concern with action 199;
  logic compared 199
supervenience 85–6, 205
utilitarianism 205–7;
  contractualism
  compared 210, 218–19; as
  general theory of ethical
  value 209–11;
  impartiality 207–9
Wittengstein propositions as
  pictures 689
Euclidean geometry 328
  axiomatization of 346–8;
  Schopenhauer's view 688
  principles of inference 328
Europe, applied ethics 724
European philosophy
  (modern) 702–18
  anti-scientism 703–6; critique of
  scientific culture 708–11;
  hermeneutics and possibility
  of objectivity 711–14;
  Nietzsche's legacy 706–8;
  status of self 714–17
  'continental' philosophy
  defined 702–3
  discussion questions 720–1
  further reading 718
evaluative utterances 4–6, 8–9, 10
Evans, G., on Frege's sense and
  reference 667
events, metaphysics, semantic
  theories 114
everlasting God 458–9
evil, God's existence and 456–7,
  472–5
  greater good defence 473–4, 524

evolutionary theory, logic of
  natural selection 317,
  318–19, 344–5
excluded middle, principle of 346
existential phenomenologists,
  alienation 709–10
existentialism, anti-scientism
  in 705, 710–11, 716
experience see empiricism
explanation
  best explanation, justified
  beliefs 43
  covering-law model of 309–10,
  313, 317, 364–5, 421–7
  functional: Marxism 620–2;
  philosophy of science 317–
  18; social science 367
  machine functionalism 177–8
  Peirce's pragmatism 648
  and understanding: philosophy
  of history 421–7; philosophy
  of social science 359–68,
  374–84
exploitation, analytical
  Marxism 274
expression theory of art 237,
  238–40, 243–7, 248
expressives, illocutionary acts 9
expressivist-instrumental
  politics 278
externalism, knowledge as
  justified belief 44–5

faith
  Kant's critique of pure
  reason 601
  in medieval philosophy:
  reason 502–3; Saint
  Augustine 500–1
  philosophy of mathematics 334,
  335
  see also theism
fallibilism
  conflict with interpretation
  theory 420
  defining knowledge 40–1
  pragmatism 647, 655
false universalism, feminism and
  philosophy 737–8
falsificationism 11, 291–3
  failings of 293–4
  metaphysics 69
  underdetermination of
  evidence 303–4
falsity see truth
familiar classes, choice in
  metaphysics 66–7
family, the
  communitarianism 269–70
  feminism 272
  Hegel's ideas on 612
  Locke's state of nature 550
  private–public distinctions 278–
  9
Farrell, B. A., consciousness 181
fascism, pragmatism to lead
  to 653
feminism 271–3

criticisms of liberalism 271–3,
  277, 283
critique 277
critique of arrogance of
  reason 487
democratic theory and
  practice 278
equality 283–4
law and equality 406
in philosophy 732–41;
  Derrida 736;
  dichotomies 735–7;
  discussion questions 741;
  further reading 739–40;
  impact on philosophy of
  feminist philosophical
  writings 737–9; masculinity
  in philosophy 734–5; overt
  sexism and misogyny 733–4;
  women's voice 736–7
public–private distinction 272,
  279
rational authority and
  relativism 381
Ferguson, A., influence of Hume
  on 583
Feyerabend, P.
  folk psychology,
  eliminativism 188
  history of science 11, 12
  incommensurability 301–2
Fichte, J. G.
  Hegel's work 607, 608
  idealism and religious world-
  view 68
fideism 464
  medieval philosophy 502–3,
  504–5
Filmer, R., political authority 550,
  551
Finnis, J.
  natural law 403–4
  striking a balance in law 411
first philosophy 66
Firth, R., ideal observer theory,
  goodness of God 461
Fishkin, J. S., equality of
  opportunity 279
Flax, J., masculinity in
  philosophy 734–5
Flew, A.
  atheism and theism, burden of
  proof 463
  religious claims 444
Fodor, J.
  machine functionalism 172–3,
  177–8, 179, 183
  methodological solipsism, folk
  psychology 189–90
  psycho- and
  teleosemantics 185, 186
folk psychology 189–91
  eliminativism 188, 189–91
  identity theory of mind 171
  neuroscience 188
Fontenelle, B. de, scientific
  revolution 361
Foot, P.

ethical naturalism 724
moral categoricity 213
foresight, hindsight and,
    Hume 581
formalism
    artistic form 237, 238, 239, 240,
        248; music 245
    law and adjudication 395, 396,
        410–11
    philosophy of mathematics 325;
        intuitionism and open
        questions 345–9
forms of life, religious 446–50
Foucault, M., anti-scientism 708–
    9, 714, 715
foundationalism 5
    justice theories 275–6
    justified beliefs 41–2
    philosophy of
        mathematics 349–51
    rejection of 6, 75;
        Wittgenstein 9–10, 58,
        349–50
    transcendental arguments 54–5
Francks, R., Descartes, Spinoza
    and Leibniz 509–26
free agents, paradigmatic
    metaphysical problems 65
free will
    Descartes 517
    evil 474
    God and: omnipotence 455;
        omniscience 457–8
    Hegel 613
    Hobbes 536
    Hume 575, 583
    Leibniz 525
    limits of ontology 84
    moral freedom 203–4
    social science philosophy 362,
        363–4, 373
    Spinoza 520, 521
    see also autonomy
freedom (liberty)
    equality 283
    equality of, Rawls 261
    freedom and determinism,
        Marx 362
    Hayek on justice as individual
        freedom 258
    law and, Hume 581–2
    moral 203–5
    political, Mill 630–1
Frege, G. 662, 663–5
    abstract objects 73
    analysis as method for
        metaphysics 73, 75
    biography 662
    contribution to analytic
        philosophy 2, 15–16
    discussion questions 676–7
    Frege argument 103–4
    function, concept and
        object 662, 663–5
    further reading 674–5
    indirect discourse 672–3
    logic, set theory and
        empiricism 2, 339–42, 662;

Russell's paradox 342, 663;
    Wittgenstein's ideas on 688
names and communication;
    Russell's account
    compared 155–8, 668–70;
    Sinn (sense) and Bedeutung
    (reference) 16, 154–6, 157–8,
    662, 665–7, 669–70, 671–4
philosophical priorities 99, 100
reflexivity 351
Strawson's view on subject-
    predicate duality 99
frequency theory of
    probability 314
Friedman, M., unifying scientific
    theories 299
Fuller, L., theory of law 409–10
function
    concept and object, Frege 663–5
    mathematical concept of 334
functional explanation
    Marxism 620–2
    philosophy of science 317–18
    social science 367
functionalism 14
    computer/Turing machine
        type 14–15
    emotions 183
    homuncular 177–80
    identity theory and
        eliminativism 188
    instrumentalism 186
    intentionality 179, 182–3
    levels of description 173–4
    machine type 172–4, 176,
        177–9
    morality 177
    problems with consciousness
        and qualia 180–2

Gadamer, H.-G., anti-
    scientism 712–13
Galileo
    the Galilean world-view 68
    laws of, Descartes' view of
        nature 510–11
Gallie, W. B., historical
    narratives 432
games, social theory 370–1, 375–9
Gardner, S., aesthetics 229–56
Gauss, K. F., imaginary
    numbers 339
Geach, P., ethical naturalism 724
gender, effects in philosophy see
    feminism, in philosophy
geometry
    analytic, the infinite 333–8
    Euclidean: axiomatization
        of 346–8, 688; principles of
        inference 328
    Hobbes 536
    Locke 543–4, 547–8; Berkeley's
        argument with 557–8
    proofs and idealizations 327–8
Geras, N., analytical Marxism 274
Gettier examples, fallibilism (Rolls
    Royce example) 40, 41, 46
Gilligan, C., moral
    development 272

Glymour, C., underdetermination
    of evidence 305
God
    attributes of 450–62; eternal or
        everlasting 458–9; evil 456–
        7; goodness 52, 53–4, 221,
        456, 459–61, 472;
        immanence 462;
        ineffability 453–4;
        omnipotence 454–7;
        omniscience 451–2, 457–8;
        transcendence, God as
        individual being or
        Being 461–2
    Berkeley's theories 55, 56, 448,
        566–8
    classification of terms applied
        to 451; thought
        experiments 451–2
    Descartes' theories 52, 53–4,
        513–15, 516
    existence of: Berkeley 55, 56,
        448, 566–8; cosmological
        arguments 467–70; evil 472–
        5, 524; garden analogy 444;
        Hegel 613–14; Hume 567–8,
        583; Kant's critique of pure
        reason 601; miracles 475,
        577–9; ontological
        arguments 466–7; religious
        experiences and secular
        explanations 462–5;
        teleological arguments 470–2
    grammar and, Nietzsche 707
    Leibniz's theories 523–5
    Locke's views 448, 461, 542–3,
        548–9, 550
    medieval philosophy:
        Aristotelian revival 504–5;
        reason and faith 502–3; Saint
        Augustine 500–1, 504, 505
    Platonic realism, philosophy of
        mathematics 329–30, 335
    reason and morality 221–2
    religious beliefs and forms of
        life 446–50
    Spinoza's radical theology 519–
        20
Gödel, K.
    incompleteness theorems 325
    intuitionism, formalism and
        open questions 347–8
gold, Locke's corpuscular
    theory 545–7
Goldman, A., causality, knowledge
    as justified belief 44
Goldstein, L. J.,
    constructionism 417
Gombrich, E. H., pictorial
    representation 242–3
Goodman, N.
    inductive logic 161–2
    musical expression 245
    resemblance theory of art 242
    semiotic theory of art 240, 242
goodness and the good
    autonomy 221–2
    categorical imperative 217

communitarianism 270, 271
God 52, 53–4, 221, 456,
  459–61, 472, 475; evil and
  the greater good
  defence 473–4, 524
Hobbes 533
Mill 632
Moore's ethical theory 678–80
Rawls' theory of justice 35, 261,
  262, 271, 280–1
reason, morality and
  religion 221–2
rights 281
value pluralism 280–1
Gorman, J. L., knowledge of
  historical fact 416, 418
grammar, God and, Nietzsche 707
grammars, consciousness and,
  tacit knowledge 111, 123
gravitational theory
  Cartesian ideas on 512
  mathematical realism 335
Grayling, A. C., epistemology 38–
  63
Greek philosophy 482–99
  Aristotle 489–92
  discussion questions 498–9
  ethics 198–9
  further reading 496
  Hellenistic methodology 492–6
  Plato 47, 488–9
  scepticism 47
  Socrates, dialectical
    method 483–8
Grice, H. P.
  conversational implicature 124–
    7; irony 127; maxims of
    conversation 17, 126–7,
    128–9; metaphor 127–8;
    relevance theory 129–30
  on meaning 17–18, 115–24;
    conventional regularity 115,
    117, 120–2, 132–3;
    expression meaning and
    language structure 122–4;
    logical possibility 154–5;
    speaker's meaning 17, 115,
    118–20
  philosophical priorities 98,
    115–16
Grimshaw, J., feminism and
  philosophy 732–41
Grosseteste, R., Aristotelian
  revival 505
Grotius, H., casuistry 727
Gunderson, K., consciousness 181
Gutting, G., religious
  experiences 464, 465

Haack, S., pragmatism 643–61
Habermas, J., anti-scientism 713,
  714
Haldane, J., applied ethics 722–31
Hamilton, A., influence of Hume
  on 583
Hamilton, W. R., quaternions 339
Hanslick, E., musical
  formalism 245, 246
Hanson, N.

abductive logic of scientific
  discovery 655
observability in science 300
happiness
  Hobbes' view on war 532, 533,
    535
  Hume's moral philosophy 579
  Mill's empiricist method 635
  naturalism and identity 83
  utilitarianism 202, 207, 627,
    629, 630, 631, 633–4, 637,
    639
Hare, R.
  applied ethics 725
  ideal observer theory, goodness
    of God 461
Harman, G., inference to the best
  explanation 655
Harrison, R., Bentham, Mill and
  Sidgwick 627–40
Hart, H. L. A.
  conception of legal theory 399,
    402–4
  formalism and rule-
    scepticism 395
  legal positivism 391–2, 394,
    397–400
  primary and secondary
    rules 398
Harvey, W., Descartes'
  disagreement with 512
Hasker, W., evil 475
Hayek, F. A. von, justice as
  individual freedom 258
Hegel, G. W. F. H. 607–16
  art: informed by spirit of a
    people 612; superiority
    of 235
  biography 607–8
  dialectic and system 612–14
  discussion questions 616
  further reading 614
  hindsight and philosophical
    reflection 70–1
  Kant's mistrust of,
    transcendence 68
  logic 610–11, 613–14
  nature and spirit 611–12
  phenomenology of spirit 609
  response to Kant 608
Heidegger, M.
  anti-scientism 704, 706, 711,
    715–16; Dasein 710;
    phenomenology 710, 713
  coping/activity versus
    reflection 449
Hellenistic methodology 492–6
Hempel, C., covering-law model
  of explanation 309–10, 313,
    317, 421–7
henotheism 446
hermeneutic circle, social
  theory 369, 381–2
hermeneutics, possibility of
  objectivity 381–2, 711–14
Heyting, A., intuitionism,
  mathematics 346
Hick, J.

Irenaean approach to evil 474
philosophical priorities 463,
  464
Hilbert, D.
  axiomatization of Euclidean
    geometry 346–7
  conventionalist and
    instrumentalist approach 346
  Gödel's First Incompleteness
    Theorem 347–8
  reflexivity 351
hindsight, philosophy of
  history 427–8, 433–4, 581
Hinduism
  experience of God 465
  goodness of God 459
history, philosophy of 415–42
  discussion questions 441–2
  explanation and
    understanding 373–4, 383–4,
    421–7
  further reading 439
  Hegel 612, 613
  historical materialism 273, 621
  historical reductionism 319–20
  historicism: medieval
    philosophy 501–2; rational
    reconstruction 425–6
  Hume 575, 581–2
  knowledge of historical
    fact 415–20
  Marx 617, 618, 619–22, 623–4
  narrative and realism 432–8
  objectivity and value 427–32,
    438
history of philosophy
  absolute presuppositions 71
  revived interest in 22
Hobbes, T. 530–40
  discussion questions 539–40
  further reading 537
  masculinity in philosophy 735
  materialist metaphysics 530,
    536–7
  naturalism: rationale for the
    state 533–4; social
    science 362, 364
  optics, theories of 530, 536–7
  politics of 530, 531; human
    state and war 378, 530,
    531–3; relation to his other
    philosophy 536–7; strengths
    and weaknesses 535–6;
    subjects' obligations and
    sovereigns' rights 531, 533–5
  social contract 378, 530, 536
holism 7
  social science 359–60, 382–3;
    interpretative
    understanding 370–3; natural
    explanation 360–8;
    rationality and games
    theory 375–9; rationality and
    relativism 379–84
  underlying philosophy of
    language 689–90
  utilitarianism 210–11

Hollis, M., philosophy of social
science 358–87
homuncular functionalism,
philosophy of mind 177–80
Hubbard, B. A. F., on Plato 489
Hugh of St Victor 503
humanism, anti-scientism 716–17
humanistic pragmatism,
Schiller 653
humanity
Descartes 515–17
Hegel: nature and spirit 611–12;
phenomenology of spirit 609
Hume, history and
politics 581–3
Leibniz 525
Locke's views 542–3
Moore's ethical theory 678–9
principle of, philosophy of
language 107, 115–16
Spinoza 520–1
state of war and, Hobbes 530,
531–6
Hume, D. 571–88
attack on metaphysics of
theism 448
on Berkeley's rejection of
abstract ideas 557
biography 571–2
causation 573–5; Berkeley's
theism 567–8; constant
conjunction account of 308–
9, 310–11, 583; disputes
about 584; implications
of 575–6; miracles 578–9
consciousness 596
discussion questions 587–8
economics 582–3, 584
empiricism 543, 567–8, 574,
576, 583
external objects 576
free will and determinism 575
further reading 585
history 575, 581–2
hostility to metaphysics 67, 68,
69; absolute
presuppositions 71
ideal observer theory, goodness
of God 461
influence of and disputed
questions 583–5
justice 260, 579–80
liberty and law 581–2, 584
miracles 475, 577–9
moral philosophy 579–80, 599;
normative propositions 223–
4
personal identity 576–7
politics 575, 581–3
scepticism 57, 576, 583;
Berkeley's ideas 566, 567–8;
influence on Kant 54–5
social science: naturalism 363,
364; social action and
passion 376, 579
taste and aesthetic
judgement 230–4, 251–2,
580–1; projection 246–7

toleration 582
Husserl, E.
phenomenology and
alienation 709–10
status of self 715–16
Hutcheson, F., inspiration for
Hume 579
Huxley, T. H., Hume's influence
on 584

Ibn Rushd (Averroes of Cordoba),
Aristotelian revival 504, 505
Ibn Sina (Avicenna of Baghdad),
Aristotelian revival 504
ideal observer theory, goodness of
God 461
ideal utilitarianism, Moore's
ethical theory as version
of 679–80
idealism
Berkeley 55–6, 555, 556–7;
abstract and relative ideas
and immaterialism 557–62,
564; esse est percipi 556;
Moore's criticism 680;
qualities and sensations 562–
4; theism 566–8
debate with realists 71–2
expression theory of art 239
Hegel 613
Hume 574
Kant 591–8; Moore's
rejection 678; 'subjective
idealism' 608
knowledge of historical
fact 417–18
Lockean 542–8; Berkeley's
argument with 557–62
mind–matter distinction 68–9
Moore rejects 678, 680
Peirce's pragmatism 648
scepticism 55–6, 556, 680
identity
naturalism and,
metaphysics 79–84
personal: Hume 576–7;
interpretative
understanding 372–3;
Locke 549; solipsism and
Wittgenstein's private
language argument 692
identity statements, Russell 667–
8, 674
identity theory 14, 171–2
functionalism and
eliminativism 186, 188
problems with consciousness
and qualia 181
ideology
the end of 257–8
explanation of 621–2
illocutionary acts, theory of
speech acts 8–9
illusion
in art, anti-scientism 708
Descartes 516
illusion theory of art 242–3
Müller–Lyer illusion 300, 301

Peirce's theory of
perception 647–8
imagism, Berkeley 558–62, 564
immanence
of God 462
Kant's transcendental
metaphysics 596
immaterialism
Berkeley 557–62, 564, 566–8
Descartes, behaviourism 170
Hobbes' rejection of 536
Locke 549
impartiality, utilitarianism 207–9
implicit knowledge 111
incommensurability, epistemology
of science 300–2
indirect discourse, Frege and
Russell 672–4
indirect speech acts, intentionalist
theories of meaning 17–18
indirect utilitarianism, Mill 633–5
individualism
Hegel's dialectic 613
Locke's influence on 541–2
masculinity in philosophy 735
methodological 273, 415
philosophy of history 422–3
social science 359–60, 382–3;
interpretative
understanding 370–3; natural
explanation 360–8;
rationality and games
theory 375–9; rationality and
relativism 379–84
individuation of objects,
Descartes 514
induction
Peirce's pragmatism 648
philosophy of logic,
possibility 161–2
induction problem
Bayesianism 295–8
falsificationism 291–5, 303–4
pessimistic meta-
induction 305–7, 319–20
statement of 290–1
underdetermination of
evidence 303–5
inductive reasoning, Hume 574,
578
ineffability, of God 453–4
inferences
Hume, miracles and
religion 578
logic: truth–falsity
dichotomy 140, 141–63;
Wittgenstein 688
in mathematics 328–9
metaphysics: naturalism and
identity 82–3; semantic
theories 114
in science 290–1
infinite, the
analytic geometry 333–8
Hegel's absolute idea 611
intuitionism, formalism and
open questions 345–9

logic, set theory and analytic
    empiricism 338–45, 688
Infinity, Axiom of, philosophy of
    mathematics 343
innate ideas
    Aristotelian conceptualism 332
    Hellenistic philosophy 494
    Hume 574, 583
    Locke's rejection of 542–3
institutional theory of art 236
institutions
    analytic Marxism 619, 621–2
    Marx's approach to ethics 623–
        4
    theory of justice 10, 260;
        applied ethics 725;
        communitarian
        criticism 269–70
    utilitarianism 629
instrumental good, political
    association as 270
instrumental-expressivist
    politics 278
instrumentalism 186–7
    ethics and: morality 218;
        practical reason 214–15
    functionalism and
        eliminativism 188
    versus realism, epistemology of
        science 298–302, 305–7, 345
integrity, law as 407–10
intentional action
    rational reconstruction 424
    theory of speech acts 8–9
intentionalism, works of art 247–
    9
intentionality
    anti-scientism 709–10, 715–16
    Berkeley 565
    of God 470
    identification of 369–70
    musical formalism 245
    philosophy of language 96,
        97–8
    philosophy of mind 179, 182–3;
        folk psychology 190;
        'language of thought'
        hypothesis 183–6
    of speakers 17–18; see also
        conversational implicature
internalism, knowledge as
    justified belief 43–4
interpretation
    Hume 575, 581
    knowledge of historical
        fact 419–20
    semantic theories 106–7,
        115–16, 132–3
    theory of law as 404–6, 408
    of works of art 247–50, 581
interpretative understanding,
    social science 367–74
intrinsic properties, Berkeley,
    conceivability and
    perceivability 564–6
intuition
    aesthetic objectivism 231
    anti-scientism 704–5

Kant 593, 594, 596–7
Locke's intuitive knowledge 544
Mill's empiricist method 635–6
philosophy of mathematics 325;
    Dummett's meaning-theory
    influenced by 76–7, 79;
    formalism and open
    questions 345–9
Rawls' theory of justice as
    alternative to 261–2, 263,
    725
Sidgwick's utilitarianism 638–9
Inwood, M., Hegel 607–16
Irenaean approach, evil 474
Irigaray, L.
    myth of the cavern in Plato's
        Republic 734
    women's voice 736–7
irony, conversational
    implicature 127
Irwin, T. H., on Aristotelian
    dialectic 491
Islam
    Aristotelian revival 504–5
    evil 472–3
    theism 446

Jackson, F., problems with
    consciousness and
    qualia 181
James, W.
    Hume's influence on 584
    language games 70
    personal identity 373
    phenomenology 655
    pragmatism 70, 643, 649–51,
        652, 653, 654, 656
Jaspers, K., anti-scientism 705
Jones, P., Hume 571–88
Judaism
    evil 472–3
    theism 446
jurisprudence see law, philosophy
    of
justice, theories of
    conflict and pluralism 276–7
    conservatism 277–8
    critique 277
    economics and politics 279–80
    equality 283–4
    foundations for 275–6
    Hobbes 530
    Hume 260, 579–80
    Marxism 622, 623;
        analytical 273–5
    Nozick 265–9, 276; critique of
        Rawls' theory of justice 265,
        267; difference principle 268;
        entitlement principle 266,
        267, 268; equality 266,
        267–8, 284; ownership 265,
        266, 267–9, 274; rights 265–
        6, 268
    Rawls 10–11, 34–5, 259–65,
        276–7; as alternative to
        utilitarianism 261–2, 263–4;
        applied ethics 725; choice
        in 262–3; communitarian
        criticisms 269–71;

contractualism 34, 261,
    262–3, 264; contribution to
    liberalism 259, 264;
    difference principle 208, 261,
    263, 267, 270, 283, 284;
    feminist criticisms 272–3;
    foundationalism 276; as
    heuristic device 262; moral
    education 264–5; Nozick's
    critique of 265, 267; value
    pluralism 280
justified true belief, knowledge
    as 38–46, 58–9
    see also scepticism

Kant, I. 589–606
    aesthetics 230–5
    arguments against
        scepticism 54–5
    biography 589–90
    casuistry 727
    categorical imperative and
        contractualism 29, 34,
        214–19, 599–601; Moore's
        criticism 678
    discussion questions 605–6
    further reading 602–3
    Hegel's response to 608
    Hume's influence on 54–5, 584
    idealism and religious world-
        view 68
    intuitionism, mathematics 345–
        6
    metaphysics of experience 590–
        8, 601; Copernican
        revolution 591–2;
        maxims 599–601; sensibility
        and understanding 593–4;
        synthetic knowledge a
        priori 592–3;
        transcendence 594–8
    natural law 390
    opposition to metaphysical
        arguments in religious
        traditions 448–50
    on space and time 336–8,
        592–3
Kantian reading, Aristotelian
    dialectic 491, 492
Karnofsky, E. S., on Plato 489
Kelsen, H., legal positivism and
    reductionism 391, 401
Kenny, A.
    applied ethics 725
    theism and dualism 453
Kepler, J.
    laws of, Descartes' view of
        nature 510–11
    Platonic realism 329–30
Kierkegaard, S.
    influence on existentialism 710
    Socratic influences 483
Kitcher, P., naturalized
    epistemology of science 307
Kivy, P., expression in
    music 245–6
knowledge
    acquisition of 39; empiricist
        school 39, 543, 573–5, 576;

rationalist school 39, 510, 516–17, 520–1, 525
as justified belief 38–46; causality 44, 45; coherence 42–3; defining knowledge 38–40, 46, 58; foundationalism 41–2; further reading 59; internalism and externalism 43–5; realist assumptions 45; reliabilism 44, 45; truth-tracking 45
see also scepticism
Körner, S., philosophy of mathematics 325
Kretzmann, N., Divine simplicity 462
Kripke, S.
  identity theory, modal distinctions 181
  metaphysics, naturalism and identity 81
  reality and language, causal theory of reference 16, 185
  on rule following 21
Kuhn, T.
  history of science 11–12
  incommensurability 301–2
  reason and paradigms 379–80
Kvanvic, J., omniscience 457
Kymlicka, W., cultural membership 282

labour, Marx's theory of alienation 617–18
labour theory of property, Locke 550
labour theory of value, analytical Marxism 273, 274
Langer, S., musical works as symbols 246
language, philosophy of 90–139
  analytic philosophy 3–12, 15–16
  anti-scientism and: hermeneutics 712–14; Nietzsche's legacy 706–8; status of self 714–17
  causal theory of reference 15–16, 23; theistic voluntarism 460
  discussion questions 138–9
  Frege and Russell's theories 16, 154–8, 339–44, 662, 663–74
  further reading 133–4
  language games 9–10, 70
  metaphysics 70, 96–100; semantic theories 75, 112–14
  mind 8, 22–3, 96–100
  philosophy of mathematics 339–43, 349–51
  pragmatics 124–33; contribution to explicit content 131–3; conversational implicature 124–7
  questions of meaning 91–2
  semantics 91, 92, 100–14; Dummett's meaning-

theory 78; logical possibility 149–51; meta-semantics 92, 96, 115–24, 132–3; metaphysics 75, 112–14; moral judgements 29–30; semantic theories 18–20, 102–14; tacit knowledge 111, 123; *see also main entry for* semantics
  theories of meaning 92–6; axioms and theorems 92–6, 100–2; Davidson 18–20, 102–14; Dummett 76–9; Grice 17–18, 115–24, 132–3, 154–5; intentionalistic 17–18; subject and predicate terms 93–4
  Wittgenstein: language games 9–10; logical necessity 687–8; meaning and rules 694–7; private language argument 20–1, 57, 692–4; propositions as pictures 688–9
'language of thought' hypothesis 183–6, 187
Laslett, P., political philosophy 257
law, philosophy of 388–414
  Bentham 401–2, 411–12, 628, 629, 634–5, 637–8
  criteria of validity and legal positivism 394
  discussion questions 413–14
  enterprise of legal theory 396–401
  further reading 412–13
  Hobbes's views on 532, 533–6
  Hume 581–2, 584
  law and adjudication 394–6, 408, 409, 410–11
  law and force 389–90
  law as integrity 407–10
  law and politics 392–3
  Mill's utilitarianism 633
  natural law 401–4
  philosophical reconstruction of legal doctrine 411–12
  reductionism and positivism 390–2, 397, 398, 401–4
  theory as interpretation 404–6, 408
  Unger and Critical Legal Studies movement 410–11
laws, scientific, accidental generalizations 310–11
Le Doeuff, M., feminist philosophy 732, 738
Leavis, F. R.
  intentionalism 248
  value of art 251
Leftow, B., eternal God 458
legal positivism 390
  black-letter rules 396, 409
  criteria of validity 394
  Hart's development of 397–400
  natural law 390, 401–4

reductionism 390–2, 397, 398
  theory as interpretation 406
Leibniz, G. W. 521–5
  discussion questions 527–9
  further reading 525–6
  God 523–5
  humanity 525
  Leibniz's Law 95, 181
  monads 523, 524
  nature 522–3
  system of universal harmony 523–4
Lévi-Strauss, C., rejection of humanism 716
Levin, M., materialism and morality 177
Levine, J., functionalism 182
Lewis, C. I., pragmatic *a priori* 655
Lewis, David
  asymmetry of causation 312
  identity theory of mind 171–2
  laws and generalizations 311
liberalism
  autonomy 281
  communitarian criticisms of 269–71, 283
  economics 279–80
  equality 283–4
  the family 279
  feminist criticisms of 271–3, 277, 283
  Marx, role of economic structure 621–2
  moral status of individual within 281–2
  politics 278; legal philosophy 393, 410–11
  private–public distinction 279
  Rawls' theory of justice 259–65, 280–1
  role of ethical theory in 35, 36
  themes anticipated by Berlin 258–9
  understanding of the individual 281, 282–3
  value pluralism 280–1
libertarianism
  Nozick's views 265–9
  omniscience of God 458
  politics 278
  rational authority and relativism 381
  Rawl's theory of justice 35
liberty *see* freedom
life
  art of, Mill 632, 634
  forms of, religious 446–50
linguistic meaning *see* language, philosophy of
linguistics, philosophy of 91
Linville, M., omniscience of God 457
literary interpretation 247–50
literary theory, semiotic theory of art 240
literature
  pragmatism 654–5

Socratic influences 483
Loar, B., on Chomsky, tacit
    knowledge 123
Locke, J. 541–54
    corpuscularianism 545–7
    discussion questions 553–4
    empiricism of 543
    *Essay Concerning Human
        Understanding* 541–9
    ethics (moral philosophy) 545,
        548
    further reading 551–2
    God 542–3; belief in 448;
        ownership of the
        cosmos 461; political
        authority and
        ownership 550; reason 548–9
    idealism 542–8; Berkeley's
        argument with 557–62
    knowledge and scepticism 54,
        542–9
    personal identity 549
    political philosophy, *Treatises
        of Government* 549–51
    reason 543
    rights and ownership 550–1;
        Nozick's views 266, 268
logic 140–66
    analysis as method for
        metaphysics 72–9
    Aristotelian revival 503–6
    Dewey 652
    discussion questions 165–6
    further reading 163–4
    Hegel 610–11, 613–14
    Leibniz's Law 95
    Mill 632, 635–6
    omnipotence of God 455
    Peirce 652
    reducibility of mathematics to:
        first order predicate
        calculus 349; set theory and
        analytic empiricism 338–45,
        662, 663, 688
    truth–falsity dichotomy of
        propositions 140, 141–63;
        function, concept and
        object 663–5; indirect
        discourse 672–4; Nietzsche's
        anti-scientism 707;
        possibility 144–58, 160–3;
        rigid and plastic
        meaning 695; sense and
        reference 16, 153–8, 662,
        665–70; theory of
        descriptions 670–2, 687;
        unity of the proposition
        problem stated 664
logical empiricism *see* positivism
logical positivism *see* positivism
logicism 5, 325, 338–45, 662
    accommodating the familiar and
        exotic 73
    Russell's paradox 342, 663
logico-linguistic categories,
    semiotic theory of art 240
Long, A. A., Hellenistic
    philosophy 492, 493

love, goodness to be found in,
    Moore 679
Lovejoy, A. O., value of studying
    history 427
Lukes, S., on Marxist
    morality 622, 623
Lycan, W. G.
    on Grice's analysis of
        meaning 124
    philosophy of mind 167–97
Lyotard, J.-F., truth 714

Macdonald Ross, G., Descartes,
    Spinoza and Leibniz 509–26
Mach, E.
    influence of 704
    underdetermination of
        evidence 305
machine functionalism,
    philosophy of mind 172–4,
    176, 177–9
MacIntyre, A.
    communitarianism 269, 270
    historical narratives 434
    liberal pluralism 35
MacKenzie, D., VIPER computer
    chip 351
Mackie, J., existence of God 471
Madison, J., influence of Hume
    on 583
madness, anti-scientism 708–9
Malcolm, N., religious beliefs and
    forms of life 448, 450
Malebranche, N.
    God and harmony 524
    influence on Hume 572
Mandelbaum, M., Marxism 438
manifold of intuitions, Kant 596–
    7
Marcel, G., anti-scientism 705
Margolis, J., pragmatism 655
Marinetti, F. T., scientism 708
Martin, C. F. J., medieval
    philosophy 500–8
Martin, M.
    existence of God 471
    non-cognitivism 449
    rational reconstruction 424
    verificationism 444
Marx, K. 617–26
    analytic Marxism 273–4,
        619–21
    critique 277
    discussion questions 625–6
    distribution and
        production 280, 619, 620
    ethics 618, 622–4
    freedom and determinism 362
    further reading 624
    theory of alienation 617–18
    theory of history 617, 618,
        619–21; ethics 623–4;
        functional explanation 620–
        2; productive forces and
        relations 619, 620;
        superstructure and
        ideology 621–2
Marxism
    analytic 273–5, 277, 619–21

falsifiability 292–3, 304
functional explanation 367
historical narratives 437–8
law and equality 406
masculinity, in philosophy 734–5
materialism *see* physicalism
mathematics, philosophy of 325–
    57
    analytic geometry and the
        infinite 333–8
    applicability of 326–9, 351–2
    Aristotelian conceptualism 331–
        3, 334, 336
    discussion questions 355–7
    foundationalism 349–51
    further reading 352–3
    intuitionism, formalism and
        open questions 325, 345–9
    logic, set theory and analytic
        empiricism 325, 338–45, 662,
        663, 688
    Platonic realism 329–31, 334
    Wittgenstein 345, 685, 697;
        axiomatization of logic
        and 688; non-
        reductionism 349–50
mechanics
    Descartes' view of nature 511–
        13, 515–16
    Newtonian 335, 336–7
medieval philosophy 500–8
    Augustinian 500–2
    Boethian 503
    discussion questions 507–8
    faith and reason 502–3
    further reading 506
    logic and metaphysics,
        Aristotelian revival 503–6
    metaphysics 67–8
    use of analytic techniques 73
men, effects of gender in
    philosophy *see* feminism, in
    philosophy
mental states 14, 22
    semantic theories 19–20, 107–9
    see also mind, philosophy of
mentalism, materialism 13–14, 15
Menzel, C.
    Menzel–Morris machine 456
    omnipotence of God 455, 456
Merleau-Ponty, M., anti-
    scientism 709, 716
meta-ethics 28–32, 222–5, 722,
    723
meta-induction, epistemology of
    science 305–7, 319–20
metaphor
    conversational implicature 17–
        18, 127–8
    Nietzsche 707
metaphysics 64–89
    absolute presuppositions 70–1
    analysis and logic as method
        for 72–9
    analytical behaviourism 169
    Aristotelian revival 503–6
    binarisms: feminism 735–7; self
        or subject 717

classes 66–7, 69
consciousness 66, 70
discussion questions 88–9
of experience, Kant 590–8
further reading 86–7
Hobbes 536–7
hostility to 67–8; Hume 67, 68, 69; logical positivists 69–71; pragmatism 70; realism to pluralism 71–2
Kantian metaphysics of experience 590–8, 601
materialist, Hobbes 536–7
Mill 632, 635–6
mind and 66–70, 96–100
motivations for study of 65
philosophy of language 96–100; semantic theories 112–14
philosophy of religion: divine attributes 450–62; philosophical priorities 462–5; religious beliefs and forms of life 446–50
physicalism (materialism) 68–9
point of art 252
revisionary/descriptive distinction 64–5
of science 66–7, 308–20; causation 308–10; covering-law model of explanation 309–10; direction of causation 311–12; laws and accidents 310–11; limits of ontology 83–4; logic of natural selection 317, 318–19; naturalism and identity 79–84; pragmatism 645, 646–7, 649; probabilistic causation 312–14; quantum mechanics 316–17; supervenience 84–6; teleology 317–18; theoretical reduction 319–20
as science of Being 65
meta-semantics 92
meta-semantic theory 96, 115–24, 132–3
methodological individualism 273, 715
methodological solipsism, folk psychology 189–90
Mill, J. S. 627
atomism 715
empiricism 543, 635
God and evil 472
Hume's influence on 584
metaphysics and logic 632, 635–6
naturalism, social science 363–4
self-regarding private activity 279
utilitarianism 629–33; art of life 632, 634; conservative holism 210; discussion questions 641–2; egoism and altruism 632; fallacies of

inference 631; further reading 640; happiness 202, 207, 630, 631, 633–4, 637; indirect form of 633–5; justice 632–3; political freedom 630–1; proof of principle of utility 636–7; proportionality criterion 630, 633; punishment criterion 632, 633; Sidgwick's ideas 639; value 630
Millikan, R. G., mental states 179
mimetic theory of art 237–8, 239, 240, 241, 248
mind, philosophy of 167–97
artificial intelligence and computer models 13–15, 174–6, 188–9
behaviourism 168–70, 177, 182
cognitive psychology 174
discussion questions 195–7
eliminativism 187–8, 189–91
emotions 183
folk psychology 171, 188, 189–91
further reading 191–2
Hobbes's view 536
homuncular functionalism 177–80
identity theory 171–2, 181
instrumentalism 186–7
intentionality 179, 182–6
intersection with philosophy of religion 453
'language of thought' hypothesis 183–6, 187
machine functionalism 172–4, 176, 177–9
metaphysics 66–70; philosophy of language 96–100
Mill's account of reality 636
mind-body dualism 167–8, 170, 171, 516–17, 518–19
morality 177
neurophilosophy 188–9
philosophy of language 8, 22–3, 96–100
qualia and consciousness, problems with 180–2
Spinoza 518–19
teleological theories 177–80
Wittgenstein's private language argument 692–4
mind-independence, Berkeley 555–68
Mink, L. O., historical narratives 433, 435
miracles 475, 577–9
Mises, R. von, frequency theory of probability 314
misogyny, in philosophical works 733
see also feminism, in philosophy
modal distinctions, identity theory 181
modernism

Descartes' reputation as father of 510
Spinoza's work 517–18
modernity, Rawls' theory of justice 259
Moerbeke, William of, Aristotelian revival 505
monads, Leibniz 523, 524
monism
anomalous, instrumentalism compared 187
literary interpretation 249, 250
neutral, Russell 650
of radical empiricism 650
Spinoza 518–20
monotheism 446
Montaigne, M. E. de, Socratic influences 483
Moore, A. W., philosophy of logic 140–66
Moore, G. E. 2, 678–84
analysis as method for metaphysics 73
common sense defended 680–1, 682
discussion questions 683–4
empiricism 678
ethical theory 678–80
further reading 683
idealism rejected 678, 680
Moore's paradox 682
the naturalistic fallacy 631, 639, 678–9
philosophical analysis 681–3
realism 678
moral philosophy see ethics
Morris, T. V., omnipotence of God 455, 456–7
Menzel–Morris machine 456
Müller–Lyer illusion 300, 301
music
expression theory of art 243–7
Platonic realism 329–30

Nagel, T.
applied ethics 725
egalitarianism 284
problems with consciousness and qualia 181
names 15–16
bearerless 667–8
function, concept and object 664
sense and reference 16, 154–8, 662, 665–70; indirect discourse 672–4; theory of descriptions 670–2
Wittgenstein's rigid and plastic meaning 695
narratives, philosophy of history 432–8
narrative sentences 427–8
natural law 389
limits of ontology 83–4
positivism 390, 401–4
social sciences 361
see also naturalism
natural rights, Bentham opposed to 638

natural selection
  logic of 317, 318–19
  mathematics 344–5
naturalism
  aesthetic objectivism 231
  Descartes' view of 510–13, 515
  ethical 678–9, 724
  Hegel, spirit 611–12
  Hellenistic philosophy 494,
    495–6
  Hobbes 530, 531–3; rationale
    for state 533–4; social
    science 362, 364
  identity and, metaphysics 79–
    84
  Leibniz 522–3
  Mill and Quine 635–6
  Moore 678–9
  Peirce's pragmatism 648
  social sciences 360–8
  Spinoza 518–20
naturalistic fallacy, Moore 631,
    639, 678–9
naturalistic theory of art 241,
    251–2
naturalized epistemology,
    scientific knowledge 307–8,
    344–5
necessity
  Dummett's meaning-theory 78
  existence of God 468–9
  Hume, causation 573–4
  limits of ontology 83–4
  Mill's empiricist method 635–6
  semantic theories, rigid
    designators 112
  social science 361, 362–3
  supervenience 85
Neo-Kantians, influence of 704
Neo-Platonists 333–4
  mathematical knowledge 330
  Pseudo-Dionysius the
    Areopagite 503
Nerlich, G., space and time 337
neurophilosophy 188–9
neutral monism, Russell 650
'new philosophy', common sense
    and, Berkeley 556–7
Newton, I. 330, 335, 336–7
Nielsen, K., verificationism 444
Nietzsche, F.
  anti-scientism 706–8
  aspirations of art 252
  concept of woman 733
  nominalism of 708
  Socratic influences 483
no-class theory, philosophy of
    mathematics 343–4
nominalism, anti-scientism 708–9
non-cognitivism, religious
    belief 448–50
non-contradiction, principle of,
    Aristotelian dialectic 491
Norman, R., Marx 617–26
noumenalism, scholastic realism
    contrasted 648
Nowell-Smith, P.,
    constructionism 417

Nozick, R. 265–9
  critique of Rawls' theory of
    justice 265, 267
  difference principle 268
  entitlement principle 266, 267,
    268
  equality 266, 267–8, 284
  ownership 265, 266, 267–9, 274
  rights 265–6, 268, 281
  truth-tracking 45

Oakeshott, M.
  conservatism 277–8
  history 422
obedience, Bentham's justification
    of 628
obiter dicta, law and
    adjudication 395, 396
object
  function and concept,
    Frege 663–5
  radical empiricism in James'
    pragmatism 649–50
  subject and: Hegelian logic 611;
    Kantian metaphysics 591–8
  see also perception; properties
    of objects
objectification, anti-
    scientism 709–10, 711
objective knowledge
  Frege's realism 340
  scientism 703
  see also knowledge, as justified
    belief
objective spirit, Hegel 611
objectivity
  aesthetic objectivism 231–2
  anti-scientism 707
  of ethics 28–34;
    judgements 223–5; meta-
    ethics 723, 725
  Hegelian logic 610–11
  Hume, miracles and
    religion 578
  Peirce's pragmatism 644, 648
  possibility of,
    hermeneutics 381–2, 711–14
  value and, philosophy of
    history 427–32, 438
obligations
  legal positivism and
    reductionism 390–1
  of subjects 533–5, 550
  utilitarianism 629, 632–3,
    637–8
observable-unobservable
  distinctions, epistemology of
    science 298–9, 300–7
Ockham, William of
  logic and theology 505
  Ockham's razor: atheism and
    theism 463;
    underdetermination of
    evidence 303, 305
Okin, S. M., liberal
    patriarchalism 272
omnipotence 454–7
omniscience 451–2, 457–8
ontology

existence of God 466–7
  limits of, metaphysics 83–4
  philosophical priorities 97–8,
    115
open questions, intuitionism and
    formalism 345–9
operators, semantic theories 101
Oppenheim, P., covering-law
    model of explanation 309–10
optics, theories of
  Descartes' view of nature 511
  Hobbes 530, 536–7
  Newton 330
original contract, Bentham's
    justification of obedience 628
Owen, H. P., theistic
    voluntarism 460
ownership
  analytical Marxism 274
  equality 283–4
  God's ownership of the
    cosmos 461
  Locke 266, 268, 550
  Nozick's arguments 265, 266,
    267–9
  see also justice, theories of

panentheism 447
pantheism 447
  Spinoza 519–20
Papineau, D., philosophy of
    science 290–324
paradoxes, metaphysics 65
parallel distributed processing,
    artificial intelligence 188–9
paralogism of pure reason,
    Kant 594
paraphrasis, Bentham 637–8
partial consideration, doctrine
    of 559
particularism, Berkeley's argument
    with 557–8
Pascal, B.
  Jesuit casuistry 726
  practical reason 214, 475–6
passion, social action and,
    Hume 376, 579
Passmore, J., point of art 250
Pateman, C., politics 278, 279
patriarchalism 272, 284, 733
PDP see parallel distributed
    processing
peace, Hobbes' theories on
    war 531–6
Pears, D., Wittgenstein 685–701
Peirce, C. S.
  logic 652
  phenomenology 655
  pragmatism 643, 644–8;
    comparisons and comments
    on 649, 650, 652, 653, 654–5
perception
  in art see aesthetics
  Berkeley 55–6, 555, 556–7;
    abstract ideas, relative ideas
    and immaterialism 556–62;
    conceivability and intrinsic
    properties 564–6; esse est
    percipi 556; Moore's

criticism 680; qualities, ideas
and sensations 50, 562–4
Descartes' world 512, 513
Hegel's phenomenology of
spirit 609
Hume 573, 576–7
Locke 543–4
Moore's theories 680, 682
Peirce's theory of,
pragmatism 647–8
scepticism and 49–50, 53–4;
idealism and
phenomenalism 55–6, 556;
perceptual relativities 50;
transcendental arguments 55
sensations and concepts and,
Kant's metaphysics of
experience 590–8, 601
sense-data theory of:
conversational
implicature 127;
mathematical
reductionism 342;
Moore 680; scepticism 56,
680; Wittgenstein's private
language argument 692–3
perceptual supervenience 85
perfectionism 280–1
performatives, theory of speech
acts 8
personal identity
Hume 576–7
interpretative
understanding 372–3
Locke 549
solipsism and Wittgenstein's
private language
argument 692
pessimistic meta-induction,
epistemology of science 305–
7, 319–20
phainomena, Aristotelian
investigation 490
phaneroscopy, Peirce 655
phenomenal feels, consciousness
and qualia problems 181
phenomenalism 5
Berkeley 56, 563–6;
theism 566–8
flight from analysis 75
Hume 566, 567–8
Moore 682
scepticism 56, 556
Wittgenstein's private language
argument 692, 693
phenomenology
of aesthetic experience 235
alienation 709–10
Peirce and James 655
of spirit, Hegel 609
Phillips, D. Z., religious beliefs
and forms of life 448, 449
physicalism (materialism)
alliance with eliminativism 188
Berkeley's idealism 556,
557–62, 564, 566–8
cognitive science 13–15
Descartes 512, 514, 515, 518

Hobbes 530, 536–7
identity theory of mind 171–2
Leibniz 522, 523
machine functionalism 172–3
materialist identity thesis 14
mentalism 15
metaphysics 68–9
mind-body dualism 167–8, 170
morality 177
qualia and consciousness
problems 181, 182
Spinoza 518, 519
picture theory of meaning,
Wittgenstein's attack on 448,
449
Place, U. T.
behaviourism 170
identity theory 171
Plamenatz, J., on Marx's political
economy 619
Plantinga, A.
ineffability of God 454
omnipotence of God 455
philosophical priorities 463,
464
Plato 488–9
God's ownership of the
cosmos 461
masculinity in philosophy 735
moral freedom 204
myth of the cavern in
Republic 734
nature of knowledge 38
Platonic dialogues 488–9;
Schiller's pragmatism likened
to Protagoras 653;
Socrates 483–8
point of art 250
polytheism 459
revisionary metaphysics 64
scepticism 47
Platonic realism, philosophy of
mathematics 329–31, 334
Platonism, nominalistic, Peirce's
pragmatism 648
pleasure, aesthetic judgement 231
see also happiness
pluralism
Leibniz 521–5
liberal 35, 276–7
literary interpretation 249–50
metaphysics 72
politics and law 392–3
Rawls' theory of justice 34–5
see also value pluralism
Poincaré, H., underdetermination
of evidence 305
polar concept argument,
scepticism 51–2
political freedom, Mill 630
political and social
philosophy 257–89
applied ethics 724–5
communitarianism 35–6,
269–71
discussion questions 288–9
equality 283–4
feminism 271–3, 732–41

further reading 285–6
Hobbes 530, 531, 532–7
Hume's views on 581–3
liberalism *see* liberalism
Locke 549–51
Marx: analytical Marxism 273–
5, 619–20; political
alienation 618; role of
economic structure 621–2
moral rights 34–6
Nozick 265–9
perceptions of and scope
for 275–8
politics 278–80
principal concerns of 27–8,
34–6
Rawls' theory of justice 10–11,
34–5, 208, 259–65, 725
value pluralism 280–1
politics
history of,
characterizations 430–1, 432
interactions with political
philosophy 278–80
relationship with law 392–3,
410–11
polytheism 446, 459
Pompa, L., philosophy of
history 415–42
Popper, K.
falsificationism 11, 291–3;
failings of 293–4;
underdetermination of
evidence 303–4
on historicism 373–4
on Marx 617
the 'open society' 258
propensity theory of
probability 315
science as conjectures and
refutation 365
positive ideas, Berkeley 560–2
positivism
analytic–synthetic
distinction 3–4, 11, 12
challenge to Cartesian
dualism 168
Dummett's meaning-theory 78
empiricism of 444–5
in European philosophy 704
evaluative–descriptive
utterances 4–6
hostility to metaphysics 69–70;
absolute presuppositions 70–
1
legal 390; black-letter rules 396,
409; criteria of validity 394;
Hart's development of 397–
400; natural law 390, 401–4;
reductionism 390–2, 397,
398; theory as
interpretation 406
pragmatism a kind of 645
Rawls' theory of justice 10–11
religious belief 444–5
verification principle 4, 11, 12
Wittgenstein's propositions as
pictures 689

see also scientism
possibility
  Dummett's meaning-theory 78
  philosophy of logic 144–58,
    160–3; semantic
    approach 149–51; sense and
    reference 153–8; syntactic
    approach 151–3
possible worlds
  evil 474
  omnipotence of God 455
post-empiricism, naturalism,
    social sciences 365
post-modernism
  binarisms, feminism 736
  Derrida's critique of self or
    subject 716–17
  Lyotard 714
post-positivist philosophy of
    science, place in analytic
    philosophy 11–12
post-structuralism, semiotic theory
    of art 240
practical reason
  ethics 213–16, 599, 724, 726
  religious belief 475–6
  social science 372
pragmatics, philosophy of
    language 124–33
  contribution to explicit
    content 131–3
  conversational implicature 124–
    8
pragmatism 643–61
  Bergson 705
  Bernstein 655
  Churchland 655
  Dewey 644, 651–2, 654, 655
  diversity of pragmatisms 643–4,
    652, 655–6
  idealism and pluralism 72
  James 70, 643, 649–51, 652,
    653, 654, 656
  Margolis 655
  Peirce 643, 644–8; comparisons
    and comments on 649, 650,
    652, 653, 654–5
  reformist tradition in 655–6
  religious beliefs and forms of
    life 449
  Rorty 644, 653–5
  Schiller 644, 653, 654
  Stich 655
  theory of law 407
preconception, doctrine of,
    Hellenistic philosophy 494–5
predicate terms see subject–
    predicate terms
prediction
  covering-law model of
    explanation 310, 364–5, 421
  Peirce's pragmatism 648
primacy thesis, analytic
    Marxism 619, 622
prisoner's dilemma, utility
    theory 377–8
private language argument,
    Wittgenstein 20–1, 57, 692–4

private–public distinctions
  political philosophy 272, 278–9
  politics and law 392–3
probability
  epistemology of science,
    Bayesianism 295–8, 314
  metaphysics of science:
    asymmetry of causation 312;
    frequency theory 314–15;
    interpreting quantum
    mechanics 316–17;
    philosophy of
    probability 314–17;
    probabilistic causation 310,
    312–14; propensity
    theory 315; subjective
    theory 314
  scepticism 47
production, economics and
    politics of 279–80
  analytic Marxism 619–20
professional ethics 199
  see also applied ethics
projection, expression in
    music 246–7
proletarian activism, analytical
    Marxism 275
propensity theory, probability 315
properties of objects
  Berkeley's perception-
    relativity 555, 556–7
  Descartes 512, 515
  Kant's metaphysics of
    experience 590–8, 601
  Locke 545–7
  Spinoza 518, 519
property, ownership of see
    ownership
propositional attitudes see mind,
    philosophy of
propositional knowledge 40
propositions
  meaning of sentences as 91
  Moore's conception of 678, 680,
    681–2
  Nietzsche's anti-scientism 707
  omniscience 457
  place in analytic philosophy 3–
    5, 7–9, 11
  truth–falsity dichotomy 140,
    141–63; analytic–synthetic
    distinction 3–4, 7–8;
    concepts, function and
    object 663–5; indirect
    discourse 672–4;
    possibility 144–58, 160–3;
    rigid and plastic
    meaning 695; sense and
    reference 16, 153–8, 662,
    665–70; sentence-types and
    tokens 140, 141–4, 150–1,
    156–7; theory of
    descriptions 670–2, 687
  unity of the proposition 663–5
  Wittgenstein: holism 689–90;
    logical necessity 687–8;
    propositions as pictures 688–
    9

Przeworski, A., scientific method
    in social science 364–8
Pseudo-Dionysius the
    Areopagite 503
psychoanalysis
  falsifiability 292–3, 304
  masculinity in philosophy 734–
    5
psychology
  philosophical: private language
    argument 20–1, 57, 692–4;
    Wittgenstein's language
    arguments 9, 20–1, 57, 692–4
  philosophy of mind:
    behaviourism 169;
    cognitivism 174; homuncular
    functionalism 177–80;
    identity theory 171–2;
    machine functionalism 172–
    4, 177–9
  reductionism 319–20
  utilitarianism 629
psychosemantics, 'language of
    thought' hypothesis 183–6
public language, Frege and
    Russell's accounts
    compared 669–70
public–private distinctions
  political philosophy 272, 278–9
  politics and law 392–3
public safety, Hobbes 535–6
punishment, utilitarianism 628,
    629, 632, 633
Putnam, H.
  machine functionalism 172–3,
    182
  naturalism and identity 81
  realism and relativism 655
  reality and language, causal
    theory of reference 16, 185
Pyrrhonians, scepticism 47
Pythagoreans, harmony 329

qualia, and consciousness,
    problems with 180–2
qualities, Berkeley 50, 562–4
quantification, truth-conditional
    semantic theory 113–14
quantification theory, Frege and
    Russell 342, 664–5
quantificational terms, Dummett's
    meaning-theory 78
quantifiers, Peirce 652
quantum mechanics,
    probability 315–17
Quine, W. V. O.
  attack on analytic–synthetic
    distinction 7–8
  Duhem–Quine thesis 7, 302–3,
    304–5
  flight from analysis 75
  logical propositions: as
    messages of linguistic
    medium 143–4, 149, 150;
    sense and reference 154–5,
    156, 157–8; sentence-types
    and tokens 150–1
  Mill's work compared 635–6
  naturalistic self-image 80

pragmatism 655
reducibility of mathematics to
logic 344; naturalized
epistemology 344–5
solipsism and Wittgenstein's
private language
argument 692

Rabelais, F., Socratic
influences 483
racism, analytic Marxism,
functional explanations 620
radical empiricism, James'
pragmatism 649–50
radical interpretation, semantic
theories 106–7, 132–3
Ramsey, F. P., pragmatism 655;
laws and generalizations 311
ratio decidendi, law and
adjudication 395, 396
rational choice Marxism *see*
analytic Marxism
rational reconstruction
historical explanation 424–7
semantics 111
social science 370
voluntarist assumptions 424–5
rationalism 39
Descartes 516–17
ethical 724
faith in medieval
philosophy 502, 503, 504–5
Leibniz 525
Locke's influence on 541–2,
543, 548–9
natural laws 361
scepticism 48–9
Spinoza 520–1
see also reason
rationality
challenges to liberalism 282–3
social theory: games 375–9,
382–3; relativism 379–82
Rawls, J., theory of justice 10–11,
34–5, 259–65, 276–7
as alternative to
utilitarianism 261–2, 263–4
applied ethics 725
choice in 262–3
communitarian criticisms 269–
71
contractualism 34, 261, 262–3,
264
contribution to liberalism 259,
264
difference principle 208, 261,
263, 267, 270, 283, 284
economics and politics 279
feminist criticisms 272–3
foundational sense 276
foundationalism 276
as heuristic device 262
moral education 264–5
Nozick's critique of 265, 267
reflective equilibrium 725
value pluralism 280
Raz, J., liberalism 281
group rights 282

realism
anti-realism and, philosophy of
logic 159–60
Aristotelian dialectic 491
debates about, metaphysics 71–
2, 77, 78–9
Frege's logicism 340
knowledge as justified belief 45
Kuhn's apparent denial of 11–
12
language and reality: causal
theory of reference 15–16;
evaluative–descriptive
utterances 4–5
Margolis' pragmatism 655
Mill's empiricist method 636
Moore 678, 680
naturalism, social sciences 365,
367
objectivity and truth, meta-
ethics 30–1
philosophy of history:
knowledge of historical
fact 415–20; narratives 432–8
philosophy of
mathematics 329–31, 334,
335; Frege 340; Quine 344–
5; Russell 342–4
scholastic, Peirce's
pragmatism 647–8
versus instrumentalism,
epistemology of science 298–
302, 305–7, 344–5
Wittgenstein rejects 698
reason
anti-scientism 706
arrogance of reason, Socratic
elenchos 487
ethics: categorical imperative
and contractualism 29,
214–19, 599; morality and
religion 219–22; practical
reason 213–16, 599, 724, 726
faith, in medieval
philosophy 502–5
feminism in philosophy 733–4
Hobbes' view of human
nature 532–3
Kant, Moore's criticism of his
ethical theory 678
Kant's critique of 590–8, 601
pragmatism 646
religious belief 475–6
role in aesthetic judgement 234
social science 372
see also rationalism
Recht, morality of 622, 623
reducibility
axiom of, philosophy of
mathematics 343–4
Cartesian 512
reductionism 5, 6
accommodating the familiar and
exotic 73
flight from analysis 75
legal positivism 390–2, 397,
398
metaphysics of science 319–20

philosophy of
mathematics 338–45, 349–50
rejection by Wittgenstein 9,
345, 349–50
reductive behaviourism 169
redundancy theories, truth 30
reference
causal theory of 15–16, 23, 460
sense and *see* sense reference
distinction
reflection
Hegel's dialectic 70–1, 613
Heidegger's coping/activity
versus 449
reflective equilibrium 725
reflexivity, philosophy of
mathematics 350–1
reformed epistemology 463
Reichenbach, B., good and
evil 474
Reichenbach, H., pragmatism 655
Reid, T., influence of Hume
on 583
relations, logic of, Peirce 652
relative ideas, Berkeley 560–2
relativism 270, 276
communitarianism 270, 381
a form of scepticism 58
pragmatism 654, 655; Schiller's
humanistic version 653
rationality: philosophy of
history 425, 438; social
theory 379–82
of scientific theories 301–2
relativity, theory of
induction problem 294
nature of mathematical
knowledge 330, 339
relevance theory, conversational
implicature 129–30
reliabilism, knowledge as justified
belief 44, 45
religion
definitional issues 447
history of, value judgements
and objectivity 430, 431
from morality to 221–2
religious alienation 618
religion, philosophy of 443–81
cosmological arguments for
existence of God 467–70
discussion questions 479–81
divine attributes 450–62
evil and the existence of
God 472–5
further reading 476–7
Hume 577–9
metaphysics 67–8
miracles 475, 577–9
motivation for religious
belief 475–6
motivations for study of 443–4
ontological arguments for
existence of God 466–7
possible philosophical
models 445–6
pragmatism 649

religious beliefs and forms of
life 446–50
religious experiences and
secular explanations 462–5,
577–9
teleological arguments for
existence of God 470–2
verificationism questioned 444–
5
see also God
religions, categorization
issues 447–8
Renaissance, Socratic
influences 483
representation
in art 241–3; mimetic
theory 237–8, 241; seeing
in 243
communication, Grice 17
indirect discourse 673
representational theory of
thinking 184–5
connectionism 189
folk psychology 189–90
resemblance theory, of art 241–2
retrospectivity (hindsight),
philosophy of history 427–8,
433–4, 581
revelation
medieval philosophy 501
superiority of knowledge over,
Locke 548–9
revisionary metaphysics 64
revolutionary change
analytical Marxism 275
Hume 582
right
Hegel's phases of 611
Mill 632
Rawls' theory of justice 261
rights
Bentham 637–8
Hegel's spirit and the state 612
Hobbes' identification of 531,
533, 534–5
legal: politics 392–3; positivism
and reductionism 390–1
Locke 266, 268, 550–1
moral: consequential/
deontological theories 33, 34;
political philosophy 34–6
natural 402
Nozick's arguments 265–6, 268,
281
rights-based liberalism, moral
status of the individual 281–
2
rigid designators, semantic
theories and
metaphysics 112–13
Robinson, H., Berkeley 555–70
Roemer, J., analytical
Marxism 274
role theory
philosophy of history 423
social science 372
romanticism, of Foucault 709

Romantics, expression theory of
art 239
Rorty, R.
communitarianism 269
conflict and pluralism 277
local quality of philosophy of
mind 79
pragmatism 644, 653–5
Roscelin, 'extreme realism' 504
Rousseau, J. J.
attitude to women 733
masculinity in philosophy 735
Rowe, W., evil 474–5
rule-scepticism, law and
adjudication 395, 396
rulers
absolute monarchy 550, 551
divine right of kings 550, 551
Hobbes on rights of 531, 533–5
the law 397
Lockean political
authority 550–1
rules
ethical rationalism 724
morality of 397–401, 402–4,
407–10
rule utilitarianism 634
Wittgenstein 21, 694–7
Russell, B. 2, 662
analysis as method for
metaphysics 73–4, 75
biography 663
Cartesian perspective 53
descriptions, theory of 670–2,
687
discussion questions 676–7
dismissal of pragmatism 653
further reading 674–5
on Hume, past and future 574
identity statements 667–8, 674
indirect discourse 673–4
knowledge of historical
fact 415–17
logic, set theory and
empiricism 342–4, 662, 663;
no-class theory 343–4;
Russell's paradox 342, 663;
Wittgenstein's ideas 688
Moore's appreciation of his
work on logical theory 681
names and
communication 155–8;
bearerless names 667–8;
Frege's account
contrasted 155–6, 669–70;
Strawson on 156–7
neutral monism 650
reflexivity 351
unity of the proposition 663–5
Ryle, G.
behaviourism 168–9
connectionism 189
scepticism 51–2

safety, public, Hobbes 535–6
Sainsbury, R. M., Frege and
Russell 662–75
Salmon, W., probabilistic
causation 313

Sandbach, F. H., Hellenistic
philosophy 493
Sandel, M.,
communitarianism 269–70
Sartre, J.-P., anti-scientism 710–
11, 716
Saussure, F. de, influence on
Derrida's notions of self 717
Scanlon, T., Kantian
contractualism 218
Scarre, G., Quine and Mill 636
scepticism 39, 46–60
anti-Cartesianism 57–8
delusion 48, 49
Descartes 52–3, 517
dreams 49
error 48, 49, 51
further reading 59–60
Hellenistic philosophy 493;
epistemic naturalism 495–6
history of 47
Hume 54–5, 57, 566, 567–8,
576, 583
idealism and
phenomenalism 55–6, 680
Kant's transcendental
arguments 54–5
Locke's response to 54, 542–3
methodological and
problematic 51–3, 517
Moore's common sense
argument 680–1
perception 49–50, 53–4, 55–6
perceptual relativities 50
responses to 53–4
Wittgenstein 21–2, 681
Schelling, F. W. J. von, Hegel's
work 607, 608
Schiffer, S.
folk psychology and
eliminativism 190
on Grice's analysis of
meaning 124
Schiller, F., goal of art 251
Schiller, F.C.S., pragmatism 644,
653, 654
Schlesinger, G.
existence of God 471
omnipotence of God 456–7
scholastic realism, Peirce's
pragmatism 647, 648
scholastics
casuistry 727
Hobbes' antagonism
towards 536
occult powers of 512
Schrödinger's equation 316
science, philosophy of 290–324
discussion questions 323–4
epistemology of science 290–
308; Bayesianism 295–8, 314;
incommensurability 301–2;
induction problem
stated 290–1;
instrumentalism versus
realism 298–302; naturalized
approach 307–8; pessimistic
meta-induction 305–7,

319–20; Popper's falsificationism 291–4, 303–4; underdetermination of theory by evidence 302–5
further reading 320–1
metaphysics of science 308–20; causation 308–10; covering-law model of explanation 309–10, 313, 317; direction of causation 311–12; laws and accidents 310–11; logic of natural selection 317, 318–19; pragmatism 645, 646–7, 649; probabilistic causation 312–14; probability 314–17; teleology 317–18; theoretical reduction 319–20
post-positivist, place in analytic philosophy 11–12
scientism 703–6
critique of scientific culture 708–11
hermeneutics and possibility of objectivity 711–14
Nietzsche's legacy 706–8
status of self 714–17
Scotistic realism, Peirce's pragmatism distinguished from 648
Scotus, D., human mind 505
Scotus Erigena, J. 503
Scruton, R., conservatism 277–8
Searle, J. R.
opposition to computer model of mind 15, 176
US contemporary philosophy 1–23
Sedley, D. N.
Hellenistic philosophy 492, 493
teleology of Aristotelian dialectic 491
seeing in, representation 243
selective attention, doctrine of 559
self
anti-scientism 706, 707, 714–17
isolation of, masculinity in philosophy 735
Wittgenstein 691
self-consciousness
anti-scientism, Derrida 717
Hegel 609, 613–14
Kant's metaphysics 597–8
self-enclosed mind, anti-scientism 715–16
self-interest, utilitarianism 629, 631
self-knowledge, intuition 705
self-refutation, logic of 488
Sellars, W.
explanatory coherence 655
intentionality 183–4
phenomenal feels, consciousness and qualia problems 181

semantical properties, intentional states 183–4
semantics 91, 92
Dummett's meaning-theory 78
law and adjudication 394–5
meta-semantics 92; Grice's meta-semantic theory 96, 115–24, 132–3
metaphysics: flight from analysis 75; semantic theories 112–14
moral judgements, meta-ethics 29–30
philosophy of logic, possibility 149–51
semantic theories 100–14; Davidson's truth-conditional theory of meaning 18–20, 102–14; semantic questions 92–6; tacit knowledge 111, 123
semiotic theory of art 240–1, 242
sensations
Berkeley: ideas and qualities 562–4; perceptual relativities 50
perceptual experiences, Kant 590–8, 601
qualia and consciousness problems 180–2
sensationalist experience, Dewey 652
Wittgenstein 687; sensation-types 692, 693–4
sense certainty, Hegel's phenomenology of spirit 609
sense-data theory of perception
conversational implicature 127
mathematical reductionism 342
Moore 680
scepticism 56, 680
Wittgenstein's private language argument 692–3
sense reference distinction (Sinn and Bedeutung) 16, 153–8, 662, 665–70
indirect discourse 672–4
theory of descriptions 670–2, 687
sensibility, Kant 593–4
sensitive knowledge, Locke 544
sensory states, Hume, Kant's manifold of intuitions 596
sentence analysis
function, concept and object 339–44, 663–5
indirect discourse 672–4
sense and reference 16, 153–8, 662, 665–70
sentence-types and tokens 140, 141–4, 150–1, 156–7
sentences as propositions 91
theory of descriptions 670–2
truth-conditional semantic theory of meaning 18–20, 102–14
unity of the proposition problem stated 663–4

Wittgenstein's private language argument 693
set theory, logic and analytic empiricism 338–45, 348, 688
sexism, in philosophical works 733
see also feminism, in philosophy
Sidgwick, H.
ideal observer theory, goodness of God 461
on Mill 631
utilitarianism 206, 627, 638–9; conservative holism 210; discussion questions 642; further reading 640
Siger of Brabant, Aristotelian revival 505
Simmonds, N. E., philosophy of law 388–414
Singer, P., applied ethics 725
Sinn see sense–reference notion
skepticism see scepticism
Skorupski, J.
ethics 198–228
on Mill 202, 207, 210, 632, 636
Smart, J. J. C.
identity theory 171
making predictions 299
materialism and morality 177
Smith, A.
ideal observer theory, goodness of God 461
influence of Hume on 583
social choices, democracy 278
social contract
game theory 377
Hobbes 378, 530, 531–6
Rawls' theory of justice 10, 34, 725
social philosophy see political and social philosophy
social science, philosophy of 358–87
discussion questions 386–7
further reading 384
interpretative understanding 367–74
naturalism 360–8
rationality and games theory 375–9, 382–3
rationality and relativism 379–82
reasons and paradigms 379–80
roles 372
social wholes, Plato's metaphysics 64–5
socialism
democratic theory and practice 278, 280
employment 280
equality of freedom 283
exploitation 274
sociobiology, logic of natural selection 319
sociology
of knowledge, feminism in philosophy 734

philosophy distinguished 406
Socrates
    analytic techniques 73
    attack on Sophists 726
    dialectical method 483–8;
        elenchos 484–7
    Wittgenstein rejects search for
        generality 690
solipsism
    Berkeley's idealism
        contrasted 56, 564–5
    methodological, folk
        psychology 189–90
    Wittgenstein: private language
        argument 692, 693; self 691
Sophists, moral danger of applied
    ethics 726
Sorell, T., Hobbes 530–40
Sorensen, R. A., philosophical
    theology 452
soul
    in harmony with universe 330
    monads and, Leibniz 523, 524
sovereigns
    absolute monarchy 550, 551
    divine right of kings 550, 551
    the law 397
    political authority, Locke 550
    rights of, Hobbes 531, 533–5
space-time structure
    anti-scientism 704–5
    Einstein's use of non-Euclidean
        geometry 339
    Kantian framework for 336–8,
        592–3
spectator theory of knowledge,
    Dewey 654
speech acts
    Austin's theory of 8–9
    Grice's intentionalist theories of
        meaning 17–18
    see also conversational
        implicature
Spengler, O., scientism 708
Sperber, D., pragmatic
    theory 128–30, 131
Spinoza, B. 517–21
    discussion questions 527–9
    further reading 525–6
    God 519–20
    humanity 520–1
    nature 518–19, 520
spirit
    absolute idealism 68–9
    Berkeley's notion of 566–7
    Hegel's ideas on: dialectical
        method 613–14; nature 611–
        12; phenomenology 609
state
    Bentham's utilitarianism 628–9;
        justification of obedience 628
    existence and scope of,
        Nozick 265, 266–7, 268–9
    Hegel 612–13
    Hobbes' views on role of 530,
        533–6
    political alienation 618
Stephen, J. F., on Mill 630

Stich, S.
    criticism of
        instrumentalism 187
    folk psychology and
        eliminitavism 190, 191
    pragmatism 655
Stoics 493, 494–5
Strawson, P. F.
    on logic 140
    material bodies 114
    revisionary and descriptive
        metaphysics 64
    scepticism 55, 57
    sense and reference 156–8
    subject–predicate terms 98–9
    transcendental deduction 598
Stroud, B., scepticism 21–2, 57
structuralism
    anti-scientism 716–17
    semiotic theory of art 240
Stump, E., Divine simplicity 462
Suarez, F., casuistry 727
subject, object and
    Hegelian logic 611
    Kantian metaphysics 591–8
subjective theory of
    probability 314
subjectivism, aesthetic 231–4
subject–predicate terms
    Locke 546
    philosophical priorities 98–9
    theories of meaning 93–4,
        100–2, 112–13
substance
    Berkeley's idealism 55
    Locke: corpuscularianism 545–
        7; immaterialism 549
    Spinoza 519–20
supervenience 84–6, 205
surplus value, analytical
    Marxism 274
Swinburne, R.
    existence of God 469, 471; good
        and evil 474
    how God knows 452
    omniscience 457
    theism and dualism 453
    via positiva philosophy of
        God 453
symbols
    mathematical 336, 345–9
    musical works as 246
    Wittgenstein 691
syntactic approach, logical
    possibility 151–3
synthesis, of intuitions, Kant 596–
    7
synthetic knowledge *a priori* 336–
    7, 592–3
synthetic philosophy, analytic–
    synthetic distinction 3–4
    Quine's attack on 7–8
system, dialectic and, Hegel 612–
    14

T-sentences, truth-conditional
    theories of meaning 18–20,
    106

tacit consent, Lockean political
    authority 551
tacit knowledge, semantic
    theories 111, 123
Taliaferro, C., philosophy of
    religion 443–81
Tarski, A., semantic definition of
    truth 18–19, 104, 106, 110,
    656
taste, aesthetic judgement, Hume
    and Kant 230, 232–3, 580–1
Taylor, C.
    communitarianism 269
    cultural membership 282
Taylor, R., cosmological arguments
    for existence of God 468
teleology
    of Aristotelian dialectic 491–2
    existence of God 470–2
    metaphysics of science 317–18
    teleological functionalism 177–
        80
teleosemantics 186
Tennant, good and evil 474
Teune, H., scientific method in
    social science 364–8
theism 446–7, 450–1
    arguments for existence of God:
        cosmological 467–70;
        evil 472–5; garden
        analogy 444; miracles 475;
        ontological 466–7; religious
        experiences and secular
        explanations 462–5;
        teleological 470–2
    dualism 453
    ideal-observer theory 461
    phenomenalism from,
        Berkeley 566–8
    Spinoza's radical theology 519
    see also faith
theistic voluntarism 460–1
theodicy, evil 473, 474
theology
    casuistry 726–7
    Descartes 513–15, 516
    Dummett's meaning-theory in
        metaphysics 78
    Leibniz 523–5
    philosophy of mathematics 334
    prior to Enlightenment 67–8
    relation with medieval
        philosophy: reason 502–5;
        Saint Augustine 500–1
    Spinoza 519–20
    supervenience 84–5
    see also religion, philosophy of
theorems, philosophy of language,
    theories of meaning 92–6
theories, scientific
    incommensurability 301–2
    induction problem 290–8
    instrumentalism versus
        realism 298–302
    underdetermination of 302–5
theory theory 189, 191
Theravada Buddhism 447

thought, Spinoza's attribute of 518, 519
thought experiments, classification of terms applied to God 451–2
three-valued logic, Peirce 652
Tiles, M., philosophy of mathematics 325–57
Tilghman, B. R., religious beliefs and forms of life 448, 449
time
  paradigmatic metaphysical problems 65
  space-time structure: anti-scientism 704–5; Einstein's use of non-Euclidean geometry 339; Kantian framework for 336–8, 592–3
token identity 14
  metaphysical reductionism 320
toleration, Hume 582
Tolstoy, L., theory of art 251
transcendental metaphysics 54–5
  God as individual being or Being 461–2
  Irwin's Aristotelian dialectic 491
  Kant 54–5, 596; Copernican revolution 591–2; idealism and religious world-view 68; transcendental aesthetic 594; transcendental analytic 594, 596–8; transcendental deduction 597, 598; transcendental dialectic 594; transcendental logic 594; transcendental unity of apperception 598
  Peirce's pragmatism 648
Trigg, R., non-cognitivism, religion 449
tritheism 446
truth
  Aristotelian dialectic 490–1
  correspondence theory of: meta-ethics 224, 225; questions of meaning 91
  Dummett's meaning-theory to resolve controversies over 76
  hermeneutics and possibility of objectivity 713–14
  mimetic theory of art 237–8
  objectivity and, meta-ethics 29–32
  philosophy of history: narratives 432–8; value judgements and objectivity 427–8
  picture theory of meaning 448
  pragmatism: Dewey 651; James 649, 650–1, 656; Peirce 644, 646–7, 648, 651; Rorty 644, 653–4; Schiller 653; spirit of reformist pragmatism 656
  redundancy theories 30
  Socratic *elenchos* 485–6

Tarski's semantic definition of 18–19, 104, 106, 110, 656
truth-conditional theories of meaning 18–20, 102–14
  mathematics, Russell 342–3
truth–falsity dichotomy
  Moore's extreme realism 680
  Moore's paradox 682
  propositions 140, 141–63; analytic–synthetic distinction 3–4, 7–8; concepts, function and object 663–5; Nietzsche's anti-scientism 707; possibility 144–58, 160–3; rigid and plastic meaning 695; sense and reference 16, 153–8, 662, 665–70, 672–4; sentence-types and tokens 140, 141–4, 150–1, 156–7; statement of problem 663–4; theory of descriptions 670–2, 687
truth-functions, philosophy of mathematics 342–3
truth-tables, Peirce 652
truth-telling, moral danger of applied ethics 726
truth-tracking, knowledge as justified belief 45
Turing machine (computer) functionalism 15
Turing test 169–70, 182
twin earths example, Putnam 16, 182
type-type identity theory 14

Unamuno, M. de, anti-scientism 705–6
underdetermination of theory (UTD) 302–5
understanding
  conceptual, Hegel's disfavour for 608
  explanation and, philosophy of history 421–7
  Kant 593–4
  Locke's view on 543
  social science: explanation 359–60, 374–84; interpretative understanding 367–74
Unger, P., knowledge as justified belief 45–6
Unger, R. M.
  communitarianism 269
  Critical Legal Studies movement 410–11
unity of the proposition, Frege and Russell 663–5
universal harmony, system of, Leibniz 523–4
universalism, feminism and philosophy 737–8
universality, philosophy of law 404–6
universals
  Berkeley's argument 557–8
  conceptions of understanding in metaphysics 77

moral standards, relativism 270, 276
Urmson, J. O., rule utilitarianism 634
USA, contemporary philosophy in 1–23, 25
  applied ethics 724–5
UTD *see* underdetermination of theory
utilitarianism 205–7, 627–42
  categorical imperative and contractualism compared 210, 218–19
  as a consequentalist ethic 628
  as general theory of ethical value 209–11
  happiness and pain 202, 207, 627, 629, 630, 633–4, 637, 639
  ideal, Moore's ethical theory as version of 679–80
  impartiality 207–9
  indirect form of 633–5
  justice 632–3
  Mill's proof of principle of utility 636–7
  moral categoricity 220
  obedience 628
  practical reason 215
  proportionality criterion 630, 633
  punishment 628, 629, 632, 633
  rationality and games theory 375–6
  Rawls' theory of justice as alternative to 261–2, 263–4
  reinterpretation of Mill 631–5
  self-interest and duty 629
  Sidgwick's intuitionist thought 638–9
  state and individual 628–9
  theory of law 401–2, 411–12, 628, 637–8
  value 205–8, 209–10, 627, 629, 630
utility theory, games theory and rationality 376–9
utopia, Nozick's view of the state 265–9

vacuum, Descartes' denial of possibility of 514
validity, criteria of, legal positivism 394
value
  ethical: casuistry and applied ethics 727; meta-ethics 28, 723; Moore's theory 678–9; moral danger of applied ethics 726; utilitarianism 205–8, 209–10, 627, 629, 630
  flight from analysis, metaphysics and semantics 75
value judgements, objectivity and, philosophy of history 427–32, 438
value pluralism

ethics 211–13
political and social
philosophy 280–1
Rawls' theory of justice 259,
260
value theory, utilitarianism 629
Van Gulick, R., mental states 179
vanishing point, Wittgenstein's
treatment of self 691
verification
constructionist thesis of
historical fact 418
Dewey's pragmatism 651
falsificationism 11
James' pragmatism 650–1
metaphysics 69
philosophy of mind:
behaviourism 169–70;
challenge to Cartesian
dualism 168
principle of 4, 12
religious beliefs 444–5
Schiller's pragmatism 653
via imaginativa, positiva,
negativa, philosophy of
God 452–3
vices, and freedom 203–5
Vienna Circle
hostility to metaphysics 69
religious belief 444
Wittgenstein: propositions as
pictures 689; sense-data
theory 693
see also positivism
virtue
feminism in philosophy 733–4
as means to happiness,
Mill 634
naturalistic explanation and,
social sciences 360
virtues
acquisition of, liberalism 281
ethics and: casuistry 727; virtue
theory 29–30, 33–4
freedom and 203–5
Hume: liberty 582; moral
philosophy 579–80
see also goodness
vitalism, Leibniz's views 523
Vlastos, G., Socratic
elenchos 485–6, 487
voluntarist assumptions, rational
reconstruction 424–5

wager argument, religious
belief 475–6
Walsh, W. H., historical narratives
colligatory concepts 435

evaluative presuppositions 437
Walzer, M.
communitarianism 269, 270,
271
equality 284
foundationalism 276
Wang, H., philosophy of
mathematics 325–6
war
Hegel's spirit and the state 612
Hobbes' theories on 531–6
the just war, casuistry 747
Wardy, R., ancient Greek
philosophy 482–99
Warnock, M., applied ethics 725
warranted assertibility,
Dewey 651
Weber, M., social science
explanation and
understanding 374
social action 369–70, 372
Zweckrationalitat and
Wertrationalitat 372
Weierstrass, the infinite 338
Weil, S., anti-scientism 713
Weldon, T. D., political
philosophy 258
welfare society, coercion and
injustice of capitalism 274
well-being, ethical value of 205–7
see also utilitarianism
Whig historians, historical
narratives 437–8
White, H., historical
narratives 432, 433
White, M., philosophy of
history 422, 432
Wiggins, D., principle of
humanity 107
Williams, B.
applied ethics 725
contemporary philosophy 25–37
moral categoricity 213
Wilson, D., pragmatic theory 128–
30, 131
Wimsatt, W.
functionalist theories of
mind 179
intentionalism, interpreting
art 247–8, 249
Wittgenstein, L. 2, 685–701
aesthetics: aesthetic
judgements 234; essence of
art 236
attack on picture theory of
meaning 448, 449
axiomatization of logic 688

on the basic routines in
philosophy of
mathematics 697
biography 685–6
discussion questions 700–1
early philosophy 687–9
further reading 698–9
'games' of social life 370–1
general character of his
philosophy 686–7
holism underlying language and
logic 689–90
influence on positivists and
their hostility to
metaphysics 69, 70
later philosophy 390–1
logical necessity 687–8
logicist reduction 345, 349–50
meaning and rules 691, 694–7
Moore's paradox 682
possibility 148, 162–3
private language argument 20–
1, 57, 692–4
propositions as pictures 688–9
rejection of foundationalism 9–
10, 58, 349–50
rule following 21, 695–7
scepticism, position on 21–2,
57–8, 686
self 691
transitional philosophy 689–90
Wollheim, R.
expression in works of art 246
intentionalism 248
naturalistic theory of art 252
representation and seeing
in 243
Wollstonecraft, M., rationality and
virtue 733
Wolterstorff, N., God
everlasting 458
women
effects of gender in philosophy
see feminism, in philosophy
patriarchialism 272, 284, 733
Wright, C., rational
reconstruction 111
Wykstra, S., evil 475

Yandell, K., religious
experiences 464
Young, G. M., philosophy of
history 429, 433

Zeno of Elea, paradoxes of
motion 65, 334
Zermelo–Fraenkel axiom 348